TeamSAP

PRESENTS

The World of Professional Golf 1999

Mark H. McCormack

An IMG PUBLISHING Book

An IMG PUBLISHING Book

First published 1999

Designed and produced by Davis Design

ISBN 1-878843-24-9

Printed and bound in the United States of America.

Contents

1 The World Ranking 1
2 The Year In Retrospect 12

MAJOR CHAMPIONSHIPS
3 Masters Tournament 27
4 U.S. Open Championship 39
5 British Open Championship 51
6 PGA Championship 63

OTHER SIGNIFICANT EVENTS
7 The Players Championship 73
8 Alfred Dunhill Cup 78
9 Cisco World Match Play 83

WORLDWIDE TOURS
10 American Tours 89
11 European Tours 135
12 Asia/Japan Tours 156
13 Australasian Tour 190
14 African Tours 199
15 Senior Tours 212
16 Women's Tours 260

APPENDIXES
The World Ranking 312
World's Winners of 1998 316
Multiple Winners of 1998 324
World Money List 325
World Money List Leaders 333
Career World Money List 334
Senior World Money List 335
Women's World Money List 337
U.S. PGA Tour 340

Special Events	404
Nike Tour	414
Canadian Tour	435
South American Tour	448
PGA European Tour	454
Challenge Tour	499
Asian Tour	522
Japan PGA Tour	526
Omega Tour	552
Australasian Tour	567
African Tours	577
U.S. Senior PGA Tour	596
European Seniors Tour	630
Japan Senior Tour	643
South Africa Senior Tour	648
U.S. LPGA Tour	654
European LPGA Tour	679
Japan LPGA Tour	687
Women's Australasian Tours	713
Women's African Tour	718

1. The World Ranking

The Official World Golf Ranking is issued every Monday following the completion of the previous week's tournaments from around the world. It is endorsed by the four major championships — Masters Tournament, U.S. Open Championship, British Open Championship and U.S. PGA Championship — and by the five professional tours which make up the PGA Tours International Federation. These are the PGA Tour in the United States, PGA European Tour, Japan PGA Tour, PGA Tour of Australasia and Southern Africa Tour.

The concept of a world ranking for men's professional golf was first expressed in this annual for the year 1968, and that was the exclusive source until 1986 when the Sony Ranking, based upon my original guidelines, was launched during the week of the Masters with the sanction of the Championship Committee of the Royal and Ancient Golf Club, organizers of the British Open. Over the next decade, the Sony Ranking came to be endorsed (or informally utilized in making player invitations) by the major championships and professional tours.

Then, on July 15, 1997, an unprecedented meeting occurred at the Turnberry Hotel in Scotland. Never before had representatives of all the world's major golf organizations gathered together as they did to endorse the Official World Golf Ranking. As founder of the system, I was and remain the chairman of this group.

Other members of the Governing Board are Tim Finchem (Commissioner, U.S. PGA Tour), Ken Schofield (Executive Director, PGA European Tour), Arthur Sanderson (Chief Executive, PGA Tour of Australasia), Arnold Metz (Commissioner, Southern Africa Tour), Kosaku Shimada (Executive Director, Japan PGA Tour), Will Nicholson (Chairman, Competition Committee, Augusta National Golf Club), Colin Maclaine (Past Captain, R&A), Pat Rielly (Past President, PGA of America), Jim Awtrey (Chief Executive Officer, PGA of America) and Dr. Trey Holland (Vice President, U.S. Golf Association).

Briefly, the Official World Golf Ranking consists of events from the tours of the PGA Tours International Federation. Points are awarded according to the players' finishing positions, and the points are related to the number and ranking of the top-100 ranked players and the top-30 "home tour" players in the tournament field. The four major championships are rated separately to reflect the higher quality of the events. In addition, The Players Championship in the United States, Volvo PGA Championship in Europe, and the Australian, Japan and South African Open Championships are allocated higher minimum points levels to reflect their status.

The Official World Golf Ranking points for each player are accumulated over a two-year "rolling" period, and the points awarded in the most recent 52-week period are doubled. Each player is then ranked according to his average points per tournament, which is determined by dividing his total number of points by the number of tournaments he has played over that two-year period. There is a minimum requirement of 20 tournaments for each 52-week period.

The winners of the four major championships are awarded 50 points, and there are 30 points for second place, 20 points for third place, 15 points for fourth place, and down to one point for a player completing the final round. The winner of The Players Championship is awarded 40 points, and points are awarded down to 50th place. The Volvo PGA Championship has a minimum of 32 points for the winner, and points are awarded down to 40th place.

Minimum points levels for official tour events have been set at six points for winners in Southern Africa (other points are awarded down to ninth place), eight points for winners in Australasia and Japan (other points down to 12th place), and 12 points for Europe and the United States (other points down to 16th place). The Australian, South African and Japan Opens have minimums of 16 points for winners (other points down to 21st place).

Greg Norman was No. 1 in the world at the start of 1998, but yielded that position after one week to Tiger Woods, who held the top position for all but eight weeks, when Ernie Els took over twice for four-week spans, and Woods finished the year as No. 1 for the 29th consecutive week.

Before 1986 the ranking was only published annually, and Jack Nicklaus was ranked No. 1 for the first 10 years. Then Tom Watson led for five years and Seve Ballesteros, for three years. Norman has been dominant since then, in the era of weekly updates, holding No. 1 for 331 of the 663 weeks. This included a record of 96 consecutive weeks from June, 1995 to April, 1997. He was the only player never to have been out of the top 10 since 1986 until he underwent shoulder surgery in April, 1998, and did not compete again until November. As a result, Norman was No. 18 in the final ranking of 1998.

When the Sony Ranking was introduced, Bernhard Langer was No. 1 for the first three weeks. These are the other top-ranked players and their time spans from then through 1998: Ballesteros (60 weeks), Nick Faldo (97 weeks), Ian Woosnam (50 weeks), Fred Couples (16 weeks), Nick Price (43 weeks), Tom Lehman (one week), Els (nine weeks) and Woods (53 weeks).

Woods, who became a professional at the end of August, 1996, broke all records in his rise from amateur status. He took just six weeks to reach the top 100 and eight weeks to reach the top 50, whereas the previous best was 31 weeks for both by Robert Gamez. Woods ended 1996 with the No. 33 ranking. He reached the top 10 in his 33rd week and the previous best was 177 weeks by Jose Maria Olazabal. On June 15, 1997, Woods became the youngest-ever No. 1 player at the age of 21 years, 24 weeks. The previous youngest player to be No. 1 was Langer at 29 years, 31 weeks.

Whereas non-Americans dominated the leading positions for most of the decade before the emergence of Woods, in 1998 the tide was resoundingly turned with Americans holding the top four positions in the final ranking of the year. Following Woods were Masters and British Open champion Mark O'Meara, David Duval and Davis Love III. Next on the list were Els (South Africa), Price (Zimbabwe), Colin Montgomerie (Scotland), Lee Westwood (England) and Vijay Singh (Fiji), with America's Phil Mickelson completing the top 10.

Westwood, with seven international victories, had the highest net gain in points during 1998 as he rose from No. 23 to No. 8. O'Meara earned the most points in 1998, a total of 408 points in 26 events (15.69 average) as he advanced to No. 2 from No. 10. Duval had the best average, 15.76, with

394 points in 25 events while climbing to No. 3 from No. 12. Woods was second in average, 15.75, with 378 points in 24 events. A total of eight players earned more than 300 points for the year and 18 players earned more than 200 points.

As a by-product, the Official World Golf Ranking system is able to identify the strongest tournaments in the world. Following were the highest-rated tournaments in the world for 1998:

	Event	No. of World Ranked Players Participating					World Rating Points
		Top 5	Top 15	Top 30	Top 50	Top 100	
1	PGA Championship	5	14	26	43	85	736
2	The Players Championship	4	14	28	45	76	700
3	British Open Championship	5	13	27	45	71	693
4	Masters Tournament	5	15	29	43	60	661
5	U.S. Open Championship	4	14	29	38	61	632
6	Bay Hill Invitational	4	12	24	36	65	581
7	Memorial Tournament	3	9	19	27	54	481
8	Sprint International	4	9	14	23	50	427
9	NEC World Series of Golf	5	10	17	24	35	426
10	GTE Byron Nelson Classic	2	8	15	24	49	425
11	Tour Championship	4	10	20	27	30	424
12	MCI Classic	3	9	16	24	46	413
13	Doral-Ryder Open	4	9	17	23	39	411
14	Mercedes Championships	5	12	18	22	27	398
15	National Car Rental Classic	4	6	12	24	43	390
16	AT&T Pebble Beach Pro-Am	2	10	15	22	40	380
17	MasterCard Colonial	–	6	15	24	52	376
18	Motorola Western Open	1	6	12	19	43	338
19	Buick Challenge	2	5	11	23	45	331
20	Phoenix Open	2	6	14	21	44	331
21	Buick Invitational	2	7	10	18	39	324
22	Buick Classic	2	5	17	21	31	320
23	Tucson Chrysler Classic	–	4	12	19	43	294
24	Honda Classic	2	4	11	18	40	288
25	Nissan Open	1	4	10	17	35	285
26	Bob Hope Chrysler Classic	–	2	10	18	39	260
27	Las Vegas Invitational	1	4	9	18	41	260
28	Nedbank Million Dollar Ch.	4	10	12	12	12	260
29	BellSouth Classic	2	4	6	15	36	258
30	Michelob Championship	1	2	8	17	38	248

Age Groups of Top 100 World Ranked Players

Under 25	25-27	28-30	31-33	34-36	37-39	40-42	43-45	Over 45
			Parnevik					
			Watts					
			Olazabal					
			Stricker					
			Jobe	Love				
			Franco	Montgomerie				
			Mayfair	Singh	Couples	O'Meara		
		Els	Day	Elkington	Calcavecchia	Price		
		Mickelson	B.Estes	Janzen	Lehman	Stewart		
	Duval	Furyk	Parry	Maggert	Huston	Langer		
	Westwood	Clarke	Bradley	Magee	Tway	Cook		
	Leonard	Maruyama	Johansson	Verplank	Faxon	Sutton		
	Appleby	Leaney	O'Malley	Jimenez	Glasson	S.Jones	Norman	
	Bjorn	Hart	Toms	Turner	Minoza	Woosnam	Hoch	
	Cink	R.Karlsson	Flesch	Andrade	Nobilo	Sluman	Roberts	
	Sjoland	Coltart	McCarron	Chamblee	Azinger	Funk	Romero	
	Chalmers	Stankowski	Tolles	Triplett	S.Pate	N.Ozaki	Stadler	
	Tanaka	Goosen	Baker	Ames	Dodds	Faldo	Haas	M.Ozaki
	Allenby	Herron	Herrera	Durant	C.Perry	Rocca	McNulty	T.Watson
Woods	Miyamoto	Geiberger	Lonard	Kendall	Frost	Mize	Torrance	Kite

Although players in their 20s (Woods, Duval, Westwood) and in their 40s (O'Meara) attracted most of the attention in 1998, professional golf remained a game for 30-somethings, as the graph above illustrates. Of the top 100 golfers in the world, exactly half were ages 31 through 39, with the largest group being the 20 players at ages 31-33. Add the 13 players at ages 28-30 and the 14 players at ages 40-42, and over three-quarters of the top 100 were from ages 28 to 42. There also were more players over age 45 (three) than under age 25 (one).

The top 200 players in the Official World Golf Ranking as of December 31, 1998 are to be found on pages 6 and 7, and in greater detail in the Appendixes. The opposite page makes note of the trends which occurred during the year.

The greatest upward movements within the top 50 — to no one's surprise — were made by Westwood, Duval, O'Meara, Singh and Woods, while Norman understandably had the greatest decline, followed by Tom Lehman, Brad Faxon and Steve Jones. Of those moving into the top 50, John Huston was the most outstanding as he advanced from No. 140 to No. 29. Other significant upward movements were made by Hal Sutton, Scott Verplank, Glen Day and Billy Mayfair. Those falling out of the top 50 were led by Faldo, who dropped from No. 17 to No. 57. Also slipping were Frank Nobilo, Tommy Tolles and Paul Stankowski.

Other movements below the top 50 included the advance of Steve Flesch from No. 388 to No. 74, and the fall of 1996 PGA champion Mark Brooks from No. 62 to No. 255. Patrik Sjoland, Steve Pate and Trevor Dodds were among those on the rise, and David Ogrin, Costantino Rocca and David Frost joined Brooks with their declines.

1998 World Ranking Review

Major Movements Within Top 50

Upward

Name	Net Points Gained	Position 1997	Position 1998
Lee Westwood	194	23	8
David Duval	168	12	3
Mark O'Meara	149	10	2
Vijay Singh	136	15	9
Tiger Woods	114	2	1
Darren Clarke	107	36	17
Jose Maria Olazabal	99	42	25
Jim Furyk	86	22	12
Bob Tway	73	49	33
Fred Couples	71	20	11
Brian Watts	69	37	19
Lee Janzen	64	34	23

Downward

Name	Net Points Lost	Position 1997	Position 1998
Greg Norman	274	1	18
Tom Lehman	161	9	22
Brad Faxon	135	14	40
Steve Jones	113	24	35
Loren Roberts	96	27	47
Ian Woosnam	96	25	37
Scott Hoch	90	13	20

Major Movements Into Top 50

Name	Net Points Gained	Position 1997	Position 1998
John Huston	182	140	29
Hal Sutton	141	96	34
Scott Verplank	134	346	50
Glen Day	115	148	44
Billy Mayfair	115	119	42
Bob Estes	97	130	45
Brandt Jobe	58	66	36
Andrew Magee	51	72	48
Stewart Cink	47	55	46
Thomas Bjorn	43	73	41
Carlos Franco	37	59	39
Jeff Sluman	35	56	38

Major Movements Out of Top 50

Name	Net Points Lost	Position 1997	Position 1998
Nick Faldo	158	17	57
Frank Nobilo	125	26	60
Tommy Tolles	113	32	96
Paul Stankowski	107	31	77
Mark McNulty	78	30	73
Tom Kite	73	38	87
Craig Parry	62	40	53
Scott McCarron	62	44	75
Robert Allenby	49	50	85
Craig Stadler	46	39	65
Per-Ulrik Johansson	36	48	64
Naomichi (Joe) Ozaki	28	46	56

Other Major Movements

Upward

Name	Net Points Gained	Position 1997	Position 1998
Steve Flesch	96	388	74
Patrik Sjoland	92	133	51
Steve Pate	81	221	76
Trevor Dodds	80	388	90
Stephen Leaney	80	137	58
Miguel Angel Jimenez	76	125	54
Skip Kendall	74	210	89
Katsumasa Miyamoto	74	320	95
Hidemichi Tanaka	73	193	80
Joe Durant	72	266	86
Greg Chalmers	65	171	68
Harrison Frazar	60	–	135
Frank Lickliter	60	270	112

Downward

Name	Net Points Lost	Position 1997	Position 1998
Mark Brooks	130	62	255
David Ogrin	84	61	141
Costantino Rocca	73	52	92
David Frost	67	51	95
Yoshinori Kaneko	65	92	243
Corey Pavin	65	76	234
Wayne Westner	63	108	323
Duffy Waldorf	60	58	130
Hisayuki Sasaki	58	120	253
Paul Goydos	53	75	132
Larry Nelson	52	93	286

The World Ranking

(As of December 31, 1998)

POS.	NAME, COUNTRY	POINTS AVERAGE
1	Tiger Woods, USA	12.30
2	Mark O'Meara, USA	10.43
3	David Duval, USA	9.67
4	Davis Love III, USA	9.43
5	Ernie Els, South Africa	9.18
6	Nick Price, Zimbabwe	8.98
7	Colin Montgomerie, Scotland	8.91
8	Lee Westwood, England	8.65
9	Vijay Singh, Fiji	8.51
10	Phil Mickelson, USA	7.76
11	Fred Couples, USA	7.65
12	Jim Furyk, USA	7.23
13	Masashi Ozaki, Japan	6.77
14	Jesper Parnevik, Sweden	6.47
15	Justin Leonard, USA	6.42
16	Steve Elkington, Australia	6.18
17	Darren Clarke, N. Ireland	5.72
18	Greg Norman, Australia	5.65
19	Brian Watts, USA	5.23
20	Scott Hoch, USA	5.22
21	Mark Calcavecchia, USA	5.19
22	Tom Lehman, USA	5.08
23	Lee Janzen, USA	5.02
24	Tom Watson, USA	4.75
25	Jose Maria Olazabal, Spain	4.62
26	Steve Stricker, USA	4.60
27	Payne Stewart, USA	4.49
28	Bernhard Langer, Germany	4.45
29	John Huston, USA	4.40
30	Stuart Appleby, Australia	4.29
31	Jeff Maggert, USA	4.25
32	John Cook, USA	4.25
33	Bob Tway, USA	4.09
34	Hal Sutton, USA	4.00
35	Steve Jones, USA	3.61
36	Brandt Jobe, USA	3.60
37	Ian Woosnam, Wales	3.44
38	Jeff Sluman, USA	3.38
39	Carlos Franco, Paraguay	3.36
40	Brad Faxon, USA	3.36
41	Thomas Bjorn, Denmark	3.33
42	Billy Mayfair, USA	3.30
43	Shigeki Maruyama, Japan	3.27
44	Glen Day, USA	3.25
45	Bob Estes, USA	3.16
46	Stewart Cink, USA	3.10
47	Loren Roberts, USA	3.08
48	Andrew Magee, USA	3.05
49	Bill Glasson, USA	3.05
50	Scott Verplank, USA	3.00
51	Patrik Sjoland, Sweden	2.89
52	Frankie Minoza, Philippines	2.83
53	Craig Parry, Australia	2.80
54	Miguel Angel Jimenez, Spain	2.75
55	Fred Funk, USA	2.74
56	Naomichi Ozaki, Japan	2.74
57	Nick Faldo, England	2.70
58	Stephen Leaney, Australia	2.67
59	Dudley Hart, USA	2.62
60	Frank Nobilo, New Zealand	2.57
61	Eduardo Romero, Argentina	2.56
62	Paul Azinger, USA	2.52
63	Michael Bradley, USA	2.51
64	Per-Ulrik Johansson, Sweden	2.50
65	Craig Stadler, USA	2.44
66	Peter O'Malley, Australia	2.41
67	Robert Karlsson, Sweden	2.38
68	Greg Chalmers, Australia	2.38
69	Andrew Coltart, Scotland	2.36
70	Greg Turner, New Zealand	2.34
71	David Toms, USA	2.30
72	Jay Haas, USA	2.29
73	Mark McNulty, Zimbabwe	2.28
74	Steve Flesch, USA	2.22
75	Scott McCarron, USA	2.22
76	Steve Pate, USA	2.16
77	Paul Stankowski, USA	2.14
78	Billy Andrade, USA	2.12
79	Brandel Chamblee, USA	2.08
80	Hidemichi Tanaka, Japan	2.06
81	Kirk Triplett, USA	2.04
82	Stephen Ames, T&T	2.02
83	Retief Goosen, South Africa	2.00
84	Tim Herron, USA	1.98
85	Robert Allenby, Australia	1.92
86	Joe Durant, USA	1.89
87T	Tom Kite, USA	1.89
87T	Sam Torrance, Scotland	1.89
89	Skip Kendall, USA	1.89
90	Trevor Dodds, Nambia	1.86
91T	Costantino Rocca, Italy	1.86
91T	Brent Geiberger, USA	1.86
93	Chris Perry, USA	1.84
94	David Frost, South Africa	1.84
95	Katsumasa Miyamoto, Japan	1.81
96	Tommy Tolles, USA	1.80
97	Peter Baker, England	1.79
98	Larry Mize, USA	1.79
99	Eduardo Herrera, Colombia	1.78
100	Peter Lonard, Australia	1.75

POS.	NAME, COUNTRY	POINTS AVERAGE
101	Hajime Meshiai, Japan	1.69
102	Olin Browne, USA	1.68
103	Steve Lowery, USA	1.64
104	Tateo Ozaki, Japan	1.62
105	Jay Don Blake, USA	1.62
106	Padraig Harrington, Ireland	1.62
107	Toshimitsu Izawa, Japan	1.61
108	Stephen Allan, Australia	1.57
109	Russell Claydon, England	1.56
110	Phillip Price, Wales	1.56
111	Kenny Perry, USA	1.55
112	Frank Lickliter, USA	1.55
113	Jarmo Sandelin, Sweden	1.55
114	Mathias Gronberg, Sweden	1.54
115	Kevin Sutherland, USA	1.52
116	Rocco Mediate, USA	1.48
117	Keiichiro Fukabori, Japan	1.45
118	Bradley Hughes, Australia	1.43
119	Dan Forsman, USA	1.42
120	David Carter, England	1.42
121	John Daly, USA	1.40
122	Peter Senior, Australia	1.40
123	Phil Blackmar, USA	1.38
124	J.P. Hayes, USA	1.37
125	Alex Cejka, Germany	1.37
126	Sven Struver, Germany	1.36
127	Ignacio Garrido, Spain	1.36
128	Toru Suzuki, Japan	1.34
129	Robert Damron, USA	1.34
130	Shingo Katayama, Japan	1.33
131	Duffy Waldorf, USA	1.32
132	Mark James, England	1.31
133	Paul Goydos, USA	1.31
134	Tommy Armour III, USA	1.31
135	Harrison Frazar, USA	1.30
136	Joey Sindelar, USA	1.29
137	Kazuhiko Hosokawa, Japan	1.29
138	Nobuhito Sato, Japan	1.26
139	Kaname Yokoo, Japan	1.26
140	David Gilford, England	1.25
141T	David Ogrin, USA	1.24
141T	Tom Byrum, USA	1.24
143	Rick Fehr, USA	1.23
144T	Willie Wood, USA	1.22
144T	Toru Taniguchi, Japan	1.22
146	Nolan Henke, USA	1.22
147	Paul McGinley, Ireland	1.20
148	Russ Cochran, USA	1.20
149	Joakim Haeggman, Sweden	1.19
150	Scott Simpson, USA	1.17

POS.	NAME, COUNTRY	POINTS AVERAGE
151	Mark Wiebe, USA	1.16
152	Miguel Angel Martin, Spain	1.15
153	Clark Dennis, USA	1.15
154	Jim Carter, USA	1.15
155T	Angel Cabrera, Argentina	1.14
155T	Peter Jacobsen, USA	1.14
157	Gary Orr, Scotland	1.13
158	Raymond Russell, Scotland	1.13
159	Gordon Brand Jr., Scotland	1.13
160T	Doug Martin, USA	1.13
160T	Hiroyuki Fujita, Japan	1.13
162	David Howell, England	1.12
163	Phil Tataurangi, New Zealand	1.11
164	Tony Johnstone, Zimbabwe	1.11
165	Todd Hamilton, USA	1.11
166	Paul Broadhurst, England	1.11
167	Bruce Lietzke, USA	1.10
168T	Peter Mitchell, England	1.10
168T	Bob Friend, USA	1.10
170	Mathew Goggin, Australia	1.10
171	Jean Van de Velde, France	1.09
172	Steve Webster, England	1.09
173	Ted Tryba, USA	1.07
174	Mike Reid, USA	1.06
175	Tom Pernice Jr., USA	1.05
176	Fuzzy Zoeller, USA	1.05
177	Len Mattiace, USA	1.05
178	Mamoru Osanai, Japan	1.02
179	Katsunori Kuwabara, Japan	1.02
180	Brad Fabel, USA	0.98
181	Santiago Luna, Spain	0.98
182	Jamie Spence, England	0.98
183T	Mike Brisky, USA	0.97
183T	Yoshinori Mizumaki, Japan	0.97
185	Jose Coceres, Argentina	0.95
186	Mike Hulbert, USA	0.94
187	Nobumitsu Yuhara, Japan	0.93
188	Michael Long, New Zealand	0.93
189	Fulton Allem, South Africa	0.91
190	Mitsutaka Kusakabe, Japan	0.89
191	Tsukasa Watanabe, Japan	0.88
192	Jerry Kelly, USA	0.88
193	Bradley King, Australia	0.88
194	Satoshi Higashi, Japan	0.87
195	Kim Jong-duck, Korea	0.86
196	David Ishii, USA	0.86
197	Brian Henninger, USA	0.85
198	Craig Hainline, USA	0.85
199	Lee Rinker, USA	0.84
200	Rick Gibson, Canada	0.84

Detailed Structure For Allocation of World Ranking Points

TOTAL RATING POINTS Pos.	0-50 Sthn.Africa Minimum	51-60	61-70 Austr & Japan Minimum	71-80	81-90	91-100	101-110 Eur & USA Minimum	111-120	121-130	131-140	141-150 Austr, Japan &SAf Opens Min.	151-160	161-170	171-180	181-190	191-210	211-230	231-250	251-280	281-310	311-340	341-370	371-400	401-430	431-460	461-490	491-520 Volvo PGA Champ. Minimum	521-560	561-600	601-650	651-700	701-750	751-800	801-850	851-900 Players Champ.	MAJOR CHAMPIONSHIPS
1st	6	7	8	9	10	11	12	13	14	15	16	17	18	19	20	21	22	23	24	25	26	27	28	29	30	31	32	33	34	35	36	37	38	39	40	50
2nd	4	4	5	5	6	7	7	8	8	9	10	10	11	11	12	13	13	14	14	15	16	16	17	17	18	19	19	20	20	21	22	22	23	23	24	30
3rd	2	3	3	4	4	4	5	5	6	6	6	7	7	8	8	8	9	9	10	10	10	11	11	12	12	12	13	13	14	14	14	15	15	16	16	20
4th	2	2	2	3	3	3	4	4	4	5	5	5	5	6	6	6	7	7	7	8	8	8	8	9	9	9	10	10	10	11	11	11	11	12	12	15
5th	2	2	2	2	3	3	3	3	3	4	4	4	4	5	5	5	5	6	6	6	6	7	7	7	7	8	8	8	8	9	9	9	9	9	10	12
6th	1	2	2	2	2	2	2	3	3	3	3	3	4	4	4	4	4	5	5	5	5	5	6	6	6	6	6	7	7	7	7	7	8	8	8	10
7th	1	1	2	2	2	2	2	2	3	3	3	3	3	3	4	4	4	4	4	4	5	5	5	5	5	6	6	6	6	6	7	7	7	7	7	9
8th	1	1	1	2	2	2	2	2	2	2	3	3	3	3	3	3	4	4	4	4	4	4	4	5	5	5	5	5	6	6	6	6	6	6	6	8
9th	1	1	1	1	2	2	2	2	2	2	2	3	3	3	3	3	3	3	4	4	4	4	4	4	4	5	5	5	5	5	5	6	6	6	6	7
10th		1	1	1	1	2	2	2	2	2	2	2	2	3	3	3	3	3	3	3	4	4	4	4	4	4	4	4	5	5	5	5	5	5	5	7
11th			1	1	1	1	2	2	2	2	2	2	2	2	3	3	3	3	3	3	3	3	3	4	4	4	4	4	4	4	4	5	5	5	5	6
12th				1	1	1	1	2	2	2	2	2	2	2	2	2	3	3	3	3	3	3	3	3	3	4	4	4	4	4	4	4	4	5	5	6
13th					1	1	1	1	2	2	2	2	2	2	2	2	2	2	3	3	3	3	3	3	3	3	3	4	4	4	4	4	4	4	4	5
14th					1	1	1	1	1	2	2	2	2	2	2	2	2	2	2	3	3	3	3	3	3	3	3	3	3	3	4	4	4	4	4	5
15th						1	1	1	1	1	2	2	2	2	2	2	2	2	2	2	2	3	3	3	3	3	3	3	3	3	3	3	4	4	4	5
16th							1	1	1	1	1	1	2	2	2	2	2	2	2	2	2	2	2	3	3	3	3	3	3	3	3	3	3	3	4	4
17th								1	1	1	1	1	1	2	2	2	2	2	2	2	2	2	2	2	3	3	3	3	3	3	3	3	3	3	3	4
18th									1	1	1	1	1	1	2	2	2	2	2	2	2	2	2	2	2	2	3	3	3	3	3	3	3	3	3	4
19th									1	1	1	1	1	1	1	2	2	2	2	2	2	2	2	2	2	2	2	2	3	3	3	3	3	3	3	4

20th	1	1	1	1	1	1	1	2	2	2	2	2	2	2	2	2	2	2	2	2	3	3	3	3	3	3	4
21st		1	1	1	1	1	1	1	1	2	2	2	2	2	2	2	2	2	2	2	2	2	3	3	3	3	3
22nd			1	1	1	1	1	1	1	1	2	2	2	2	2	2	2	2	2	2	2	2	2	2	3	3	3
23rd				1	1	1	1	1	1	1	1	2	2	2	2	2	2	2	2	2	2	2	2	2	2	3	3
24th					1	1	1	1	1	1	1	1	2	2	2	2	2	2	2	2	2	2	2	2	2	2	3
25th					1	1	1	1	1	1	1	1	1	1	2	2	2	2	2	2	2	2	2	2	2	2	3
26th						1	1	1	1	1	1	1	1	1	1	2	2	2	2	2	2	2	2	2	2	2	3
27th							1	1	1	1	1	1	1	1	1	1	2	2	2	2	2	2	2	2	2	2	3
28th								1	1	1	1	1	1	1	1	1	2	2	2	2	2	2	2	2	2	2	2
29th									1	1	1	1	1	1	1	1	1	1	2	2	2	2	2	2	2	2	2
30th										1	1	1	1	1	1	1	1	1	1	1	2	2	2	2	2	2	2
31st										1	1	1	1	1	1	1	1	1	1	1	1	2	2	2	2	2	2
32nd											1	1	1	1	1	1	1	1	1	1	1	1	2	2	2	2	2
33rd												1	1	1	1	1	1	1	1	1	1	1	1	2	2	2	2
34th													1	1	1	1	1	1	1	1	1	1	1	1	1	2	2
35th														1	1	1	1	1	1	1	1	1	1	1	1	1	2
36th															1	1	1	1	1	1	1	1	1	1	1	1	2
37th															1	1	1	1	1	1	1	1	1	1	1	1	2
38th																1	1	1	1	1	1	1	1	1	1	1	2
39th																	1	1	1	1	1	1	1	1	1	1	2
40th																		1	1	1	1	1	1	1	1	1	2
41st																			1	1	1	1	1	1	1	1	2
42nd																				1	1	1	1	1	1	1	2
43rd																				1	1	1	1	1	1	1	1
44th																					1	1	1	1	1	1	1
45th																						1	1	1	1	1	1
46th																							1	1	1	1	1
47th																								1	1	1	1
48th																									1	1	1
49th																									1	1	1
50th																										1	1
51st plus all completing final round in major championships																											1

WORLD
Event Rating Points

Current Rank of Player	Rating Points
1st	50
2nd	34
3rd	30
4th	27
5th	24
6th	21
7th	20
8th	19
9th	18
10th	17
11th	16
12th	15
13th	14
14th	13
15th	12
16th to 30th	11
31st to 34th	10
35th to 38th	9
39th to 43rd	8
44th to 50th	7
51st to 55th	6
56th to 60th	5
61st to 70th	4
71st to 80th	3
81st to 100th	2
(5x165)	—
Total Available	825

HOME TOUR
Event Rating Points

Year Ending Rank of Player	Rating Points
1st	8
2nd	7
3rd	6
4th	5
5th	4
6th to 15th	3
16th to 30th	1
Total Available	75

World Golf Rankings 1968-1998

Year	No. 1	No. 2	No. 3	No. 4	No. 5	No. 6	No. 7	No. 8	No. 9	No. 10
1968	Nicklaus	Palmer	Casper	Player	Charles	Boros	Coles	Thomson	Beard	Nagle
1969	Nicklaus	Player	Casper	Palmer	Charles	Beard	Archer	Trevino	Barber	Sikes
1970	Nicklaus	Player	Casper	Trevino	Charles	Devlin	Coles	Jacklin	Beard	Huggett
1971	Nicklaus	Trevino	Player	Palmer	Casper	Barber	Crampton	Charles	Devlin	Weiskopf
1972	Nicklaus	Player	Trevino	Crampton	Palmer	Jacklin	Weiskopf	Oosterhuis	Heard	Devlin
1973	Nicklaus	Weiskopf	Trevino	Player	Crampton	Miller	Oosterhuis	Wadkins	Heard	Brewer
1974	Nicklaus	Miller	Player	Weiskopf	Trevino	M. Ozaki	Crampton	Irwin	Green	Heard
1975	Nicklaus	Miller	Weiskopf	Irwin	Player	Green	Trevino	Casper	Crampton	Watson
1976	Nicklaus	Irwin	Miller	Player	Green	Watson	Weiskopf	Marsh	Crenshaw	Geiberger
1977	Nicklaus	Watson	Green	Irwin	Crenshaw	Marsh	Player	Weiskopf	Floyd	Ballesteros
1978	Watson	Nicklaus	Irwin	Green	Player	Crenshaw	Marsh	Ballesteros	Trevino	Aoki
1979	Watson	Nicklaus	Irwin	Trevino	Player	Aoki	Green	Crenshaw	Ballesteros	Wadkins
1980	Watson	Trevino	Aoki	Crenshaw	Nicklaus	Pate	Ballesteros	Bean	Irwin	Player
1981	Watson	Rogers	Aoki	Pate	Trevino	Ballesteros	Graham	Crenshaw	Floyd	Lietzke
1982	Watson	Floyd	Ballesteros	Kite	Stadler	Pate	Nicklaus	Rogers	Aoki	Strange
1983	Ballesteros	Watson	Floyd	Norman	Kite	Nicklaus	Nakajima	Stadler	Aoki	Wadkins
1984	Ballesteros	Watson	Norman	Wadkins	Langer	Faldo	Nakajima	Stadler	Kite	Peete
1985	Ballesteros	Langer	Norman	Watson	Nakajima	Wadkins	O'Meara	Strange	Pavin	Sutton
1986	Norman	Langer	Ballesteros	Nakajima	Bean	Tway	Sutton	Strange	Stewart	O'Meara
1987	Norman	Ballesteros	Langer	Lyle	Strange	Woosnam	Stewart	Wadkins	McNulty	Crenshaw
1988	Ballesteros	Norman	Lyle	Faldo	Strange	Crenshaw	Woosnam	Frost	Azinger	Calcavecchia
1989	Norman	Faldo	Ballesteros	Strange	Stewart	Kite	Olazabal	Calcavecchia	Woosnam	Azinger
1990	Norman	Faldo	Olazabal	Woosnam	Stewart	Azinger	Ballesteros	Kite	McNulty	Calcavecchia
1991	Woosnam	Faldo	Olazabal	Ballesteros	Norman	Couples	Langer	Stewart	Azinger	Davis
1992	Faldo	Couples	Woosnam	Olazabal	Norman	Langer	Cook	Price	Azinger	Love
1993	Faldo	Norman	Langer	Price	Couples	Azinger	Woosnam	Kite	Love	Pavin
1994	Price	Norman	Faldo	Langer	Olazabal	Els	Couples	Montgomerie	M. Ozaki	Pavin
1995	Norman	Price	Langer	Els	Montgomerie	Pavin	Faldo	Couples	M. Ozaki	Elkington
1996	Norman	Lehman	Montgomerie	Els	Couples	Faldo	Mickelson	M. Ozaki	Love	O'Meara
1997	Norman	Woods	Price	Els	Love	Mickelson	Montgomerie	M. Ozaki	Lehman	O'Meara
1998	Woods	O'Meara	Duval	Love	Els	Price	Montgomerie	Westwood	Singh	Mickelson

(*The World of Professional Golf* 1968-1985; World Ranking 1986-1998)

World Ranking of Leading Players 1986-1998

	1986			1987		1988		1989		1990		1991		1992		1993		1994		1995		1996		1997		1998	
	1st Ranking	August 31	December 28	August 30	December 27	August 28	December 25	August 27	December 31	August 26	December 30	August 25	December 29	August 30	December 27	August 29	December 26	August 28	December 25	August 27	1st 2-Year Ranking	September 1	December 31	August 31	December 31	August 30	December 31
Woods																							33	1	2	1	1
O'Meara	5	5	10	26	26	30	29	27	27	30	22	15	14	13	12	19	28	82	83	61	41	10	10	9	10	3	2
Duval																				40	33	20	19	28	12	2	3
Love			147	60	60	82	91	62	65	59	44	25	23	12	10	11	9	18	25	17	20	14	9	10	5	4	4
Els														80	40	27	20	7	6	5	3	2	4	3	4	5	5
Price	52	40	54	46	47	33	41	43	38	47	38	41	24	10	8	4	4	1	1	2	2	11	13	4	3	6	8
Montgomerie									162	107	81	36	36	24	20	16	14	9	8	6	6	6	3	5	7	7	6
Westwood																						104	64	31	23	10	7
Singh								130	87	64	76	56	77	37	38	20	16	19	15	13	16	17	20	18	15	8	9
Mickelson														163	145	68	47	22	22	25	24	9	7	7	6	11	10
Couples	42	62	73	53	46	27	19	16	15	11	11	9	6	2	2	6	5	5	7	8	7	7	5	13	20	9	11
Furyk																				152	78	39	49	20	22	14	12
M. Ozaki	96	35	23	19	18	18	11	13	12	12	17	22	30	20	15	13	12	12	9	10	10	5	8	8	8	13	13
Parnevik													161	175	196	88	72	33	39	43	37	59	39	17	18	15	14
Leonard																				91	54	28	29	11	11	17	15
Elkington						175	163	143	142	80	62	46	44	27	18	18	19	40	43	11	9	13	14	14	16	24	16
Clarke															146	114	58	49	74	66	88	98	62	30	36	25	18
Norman	6	2	1	1	1	1	2	1	1	1	1	4	5	7	5	2	2	2	2	1	1	1	1	2	1	12	17
Watts																	171	105	61	45	54	47	50	45	37	22	19
Hoch	37	36	33	24	27	26	41	24	24	39	39	42	41	101	116	87	88	36	30	26	19	18	15	12	13	16	20

2. The Year in Retrospect

As the 1998 year in golf began and everyone got a lesson in meteorology from El Niño, no one could have anticipated the events that would transpire over the next 12 months, and that a 41-year-old father of two who coaches little league baseball would end up as the story of the year.

When Phil Mickelson started by winning the rain-soaked Mercedes Championships, most of golf's pundits predicted another year where youth would dominate. Tiger Woods certainly had the track record. As the No. 1 player in 1997, Woods dominated in wins (five, including one major championship) and official PGA Tour earnings ($2,066,833). He also elevated golf to unprecedented levels in terms of worldwide exposure and economic impact. Surely, Tiger would be a key factor in 1998.

Then there was David Duval, who capped off 1997 with three consecutive victories including the Tour Championship. Duval had momentum on his side entering 1998, and no predictions would have been complete without including the 26-year-old from Jacksonville Beach. A 25-year-old, Justin Leonard, winner of the 1997 Kemper Open and British Open, made everyone's short list of contenders, as well. So did 27-year-old Phil Mickelson, 28-year-old U.S. Open champion Ernie Els and 33-year-old PGA champion Davis Love III. Who among them would be the dominant golfer of 1998?

The answer would be none of the above.

Mark O'Meara, who finished 1997 ranked 10th in the world and who entered 1998 with 21 worldwide victories, didn't appear on anyone's short list. By the year's end, O'Meara would be honored as Player of the Year by the U.S. PGA Tour, the PGA of America and the Golf Writers Association of America. He would win the Masters and British Open and would defeat Woods in the final of the Cisco World Match Play. He would jump to No. 2 in the World Ranking and his worldwide earnings for the year would reach $2,677,788, pushing his career earnings to $13,672,515.

Even though he had become the "King of the West Coast Swing" for his eight PGA Tour victories in California and Hawaii, O'Meara entered 1998 as one of the players who, along with Mickelson and Colin Montgomerie, inherited the title, "Best Player Never to Win a Major Championship" after Love's 1997 PGA Championship victory. The title didn't bother O'Meara, however. "It's a compliment," he said. "You have to be a good player to even be considered for the title."

O'Meara didn't consider himself a great player, or at least he was self-deprecating in his public statements about his golf. "I'm a nice player," he said of himself. With dramatic victories in two major championships, along with eight other top-five finishes, O'Meara set the tone for what would be a monumental year. When he fired a final-round 64 to tie his good friend and neighbor Woods for second place in the season-opening Mercedes Championships, O'Meara offered a glimpse of the drama and surprises that lay ahead.

Unfortunately, early in the year golf suffered from a backlash of negative publicity. Just three short months after U.S. PGA Tour Commissioner Tim Finchem announced record-setting television contracts which would push purses above the $2 million-per-event mark beginning in 1999, two independent forces combined to put a damper on the American tour. The first was a force of nature, a mammoth warming of the Pacific waters north of Australia called El Niño.

A cyclical event, the 1998 weather system dumped more rain on coastal California in the first two months of the year than the state normally sees in an 18-month period. Pebble Beach, host site of the AT&T Pebble Beach National Pro-Am, came dangerously close to losing holes to erosion as crashing waves and torrential downpours forced the evacuation of thousands of coastal residents.

Five out of eight tournaments in the first two months of the PGA Tour season were hampered by the effects of soggy weather, with the AT&T Pebble Beach event starting in January and finishing in August as a result of uncooperative weather. This not only threw cold water on what should have been the fastest start in the history of the PGA Tour, it put the entire golf industry into a lethargy that took months to overcome.

While the rain dampened play in the opening weeks of 1998, a court battle in Eugene, Oregon, moved the PGA Tour out of the sports pages and onto the networks' news broadcasts. Casey Martin filed a lawsuit under the Americans With Disabilities Act (ADA). In his suit Martin claimed that by not allowing him to ride in a golf cart during competition the PGA Tour had discriminated against him. Martin suffered from Klippel-Trenaunary-Weber Syndrome, a rare congenital disorder, which damaged the vascular system of his right leg.

According to the PGA Tour, the rights of professional sports organizations to make their own rules were being challenged. "If the court finds that the Americans With Disabilities Act limits the Tour's rules-making ability, the authority of the Tour and of all professional sports to determine the rules of their games will be seriously eroded," Gary Crist, former general counsel for the PGA Tour and PGA of America, said of the case.

On February 11, U.S. Magistrate Thomas Coffin ruled in favor of Martin, granting a permanent injunction. Of his ruling, Coffin said, "I've heard evidence from some of the witnesses ... who said that this would be the end of PGA Tour golf as it is known. That's clearly not the case. Granting a cart to Mr. Martin does not mean, in any way, shape or form, that anyone else out there has some right to ride a cart. Any perception that he has an unfair advantage by riding a cart, as I've said, is simply wrong."

The decision sparked an appeal from the PGA Tour, and polarized reactions from players. "This opens up a whole new can of worms," Tour Policy Board member Tom Lehman said, "If someone doesn't get a cart now and wants one, what are we going to do?"

The public sided with Martin, who was seen as a champion of the disabled while the Tour was cast as mean-spirited. Columnists called the Tour everything from "wrong" to "stupid" for fighting Martin on the cart issue, and as the court battle and El Niño dragged on, *Golf World* dubbed the early months of the season, "The PGA Tour's Winter of Discontent."

Thank goodness spring wasn't far behind. One of the players who sided with Martin, saying, "they should let him ride," was Greg Norman, who would find himself in the midst of a medical problem in 1998, despite starting the year with a victory in his own event, the Greg Norman Holden International in Australia. After rounds of 76 and 78 to miss the cut at the

Masters, golf's all-time leading money winner visited Dr. Richard Hawkins of the Steadman Hawkins Sports Medicine Foundation in Vail, Colorado. Hawkins discovered chronic injuries including bone spurs and inflammation in the rotator cuff of Norman's right shoulder. Arthroscopic surgery was performed shortly after that.

Norman, who had not been out of the top 10 in the World Ranking since its inception in 1986, was sidelined for six and a half months, returning to competitive play at the Franklin Templeton Shark Shootout in November — another event he hosts in California — and he and partner Steve Elkington won on the third extra hole of a playoff with John Cook and Peter Jacobsen.

With Norman out for most of the year, the stage was set for a shift in the World Ranking and for new forces to emerge in professional golf. That shift began in early spring and culminated in November with the naming of O'Meara as Player of the Year. My picks for the top six players of 1998 begin there.

MARK O'MEARA

Event	Position
Mercedes Championships	T-2
Bob Hope Chrysler Classic	T-6
AT&T Pebble Beach National Pro-Am	WD
Buick Invitational	T-57
Ericsson Australian Masters	6
Honda Classic	T-22
Bay Hill Invitational	MC
The Players Championship	T-42
Masters Tournament	1
MCI Classic	T-24
Greater Greensboro Chrysler Classic	MC
GTE Byron Nelson Classic	T-15
Deutsche Bank-SAP Open TPC of Europe	3
Kemper Open	T-3
U.S. Open Championship	T-32
Motorola Western Open	MC
British Open Championship	1
PGA Championship	T-4
Fred Meyer Challenge	10
NEC World Series of Golf	T-7
Trophee Lancome	T-2
Alfred Dunhill Cup	T-3
Cisco World Match Play	1
National Car Rental Classic	T-64
Tour Championship	T-13
Sumitomo Visa Taiheiyo Masters	T-38
PGA Grand Slam	4
Nedbank Million Dollar Challenge	T-4

It wasn't just the fact that he won two major championships in the same year, becoming at age 41 the oldest man to accomplish that feat, it was the dramatic, charging fashion in which he won that vaulted O'Meara to the top of the list in 1998. Even though he traveled to Augusta with three top-10 finishes under his belt for the year, at the Masters O'Meara was a good player thought of more for his friendship with Woods than as a serious Masters contender. On Sunday afternoon, however, it was O'Meara who startled the galleries and made history by birdieing three of the last four holes to win the year's first major by one stroke over David Duval and Fred Couples. When his 18-foot birdie putt on the 18th hole found the cup and he thrust his fists skyward in victory, O'Meara became the first man since Arnold Palmer in 1960 to birdie the last two holes to win the Masters.

The high drama wasn't over, though. After finishing tied for 32nd in the U.S. Open, O'Meara came from seven strokes back after the opening round and two back with 18 holes to play in the British Open to shoot a final round of 68 and tie Brian Watts at even-par 280. In the ensuing four-hole playoff, O'Meara won his second major of the year with a total score of 17 to Watts' 19. In doing so, O'Meara became the first since Nick Price in 1994 to win two majors in a single season, and he edged Jack Nicklaus by a year in the age category for that record (Nicklaus was 40 when he won the U.S. Open and PGA Championship in 1980). O'Meara also vaulted from 10th in the World Ranking to second behind Woods.

As if two majors was not enough, O'Meara traveled back to Britain in October for the Cisco World Match Play at the Wentworth Club near London. In three days of 36-hole matches, O'Meara defeated Montgomerie, Vijay Singh and Woods to win the title. The second match turned into a blowout, as O'Meara defeated Singh in tournament-record 11-and-10 fashion. Then, in a gruelling 36-hole final, O'Meara came from four down after 16 holes to tie the match at the 35th green. On the 36th hole, O'Meara sank a 15-foot birdie putt from the front fringe to defeat Woods and solidify himself as the top player of 1998.

Hot on O'Meara's trail, however, was my second pick of the year:

DAVID DUVAL

Event	Position
Mercedes Championships	T-6
Bob Hope Chrysler Classic	T-4
Phoenix Open	T-27
AT&T Pebble Beach National Pro-Am	WD
Buick Invitational	MC
Tucson Chrysler Classic	1
Doral-Ryder Open	T-23
The Players Championship	T-18
Masters Tournament	T-2
Shell Houston Open	1
BellSouth Classic	T-14
MasterCard Colonial	T-14
Memorial Tournament	3
U.S. Open Championship	T-7
Canon Greater Hartford Open	T-7
British Open Championship	T-11
PGA Championship	MC

Sprint International	MC
Fred Meyer Challenge	1
NEC World Series of Golf	1
Trophee Lancome	T-2
Buick Challenge	T-6
Michelob Championship	1
National Car Rental Classic	T-43
Tour Championship	T-8
Nedbank Million Dollar Challenge	T-10

Any other year and David Duval would have been a shoo-in for Player of the Year honors. In fact, Commissioner Tim Finchem admitted that many PGA Tour members called him and voiced their indecision given the stellar records both Duval and O'Meara amassed over 1998. Duval turned out to be the runner-up to O'Meara in the balloting, just as he was runner-up in the Masters Tournament. By April in Augusta, however, Duval was already in the midst of an impressive stretch. For the 12-month period from his first win at the 1997 Michelob Championship through the 1998 Michelob Championship, Duval won seven times and had 15 top-10 finishes not including his win in the Fred Meyer Challenge with partner Jim Furyk.

Coming off three straight wins in 1997 (Michelob Championship, Walt Disney World/Oldsmobile Classic and Tour Championship), Duval picked up 1998 victories in the Tucson Chrysler Classic, Shell Houston Open, NEC World Series of Golf and a repeat victory in the Michelob Championship. Officially Duval earned a record $2,591,031 on the PGA Tour, and his worldwide earnings were $2,855,489.

Perhaps most important to Duval, however, was his capturing the Vardon Trophy for the lowest stroke average on the PGA Tour. Needing to play well in the Tour Championship to beat Tiger Woods for the title, Duval followed an uninspiring opening round of 75 with rounds of 69, 69 and 68 to end the year with a 69.13 stroke average, the lowest since 1993 when Nick Price averaged 69.11 for the year.

After the final putt fell at the Tour Championship and the Vardon Trophy was clinched, Duval conceded that he probably would not win Player of the Year honors. "You win two major championships in a year and you're probably going to be chosen as Player of the Year, deservedly so," Duval said. "This feels great for me because I've won the things I can control. The money title and scoring title were things I knew I could control, and I got them. The other stuff is out of my hands." Asked how he would celebrate, Duval said, "All I know is I'm buying tonight, and my friends like the expensive stuff."

Player of the Year honors seem certain for Duval at some point in his future, but for 1998 at least he was content to walk away with the No. 3 ranking in the world behind Woods and O'Meara. In the future, however, Duval will have to look both inside and outside the U.S. PGA Tour for his challengers. My third pick of the year heralded from the PGA European Tour, but also captured one U.S. PGA Tour victory. He was:

LEE WESTWOOD

Event	Position
Johnnie Walker Classic	T-4
Ericsson Australian Masters	T-13
Dubai Desert Classic	T-6
Qatar Masters	T-21
Bay Hill Invitational	T-13
The Players Championship	T-5
Freeport-McDermott Classic	1
Masters Tournament	44
Italian Open	T-6
Benson and Hedges International Open	T-66
Volvo PGA Championship	T-16
Deutsche Bank–SAP Open TPC of Europe	1
National Car Rental English Open	1
Buick Classic	T-47
U.S. Open Championship	T-7
Murphy's Irish Open	15
Standard Life Loch Lomond	1
British Open Championship	T-64
TNT Dutch Open	T-3
PGA Championship	MC
Smurfit European Open	WD
Canon European Masters	T-12
One 2 One British Masters	T-12
Trophee Lancome	T-72
Linde German Masters	T-6
Belgacom Open	1
Cisco World Match Play	T-3
Volvo Masters	T-12
Sumitomo Visa Taiheiyo Masters	1
Dunlop Phoenix Tournament	1
Nedbank Million Dollar Challenge	T-4

With seven wins on three different continents, 25-year-old Lee Westwood, a happy-go-lucky native of the village of Worksop near Nottingham, England, staked his claim as the up-and-coming European force in professional golf. In the process Westwood earned $599,586 in only eight appearances on the U.S. PGA Tour, which included a victory at the Freeport-McDermott Classic, a tie for fifth place at The Players Championship and a tie for seventh in the U.S. Open, prompting *Golf World* to print that "Westwood deserves to be (the PGA Tour) Rookie of the Year." Of course, Westwood wasn't eligible for the honor since he wasn't an official PGA Tour member, but if he had chosen to change his status, he certainly would have walked away with the title.

Given the fact that four of Westwood's other victories came on European soil, he was probably glad he stayed put. Those PGA European Tour wins included back-to-back wins at the Deutsche Bank - SAP Open TPC of Europe and the National Car Rental English Open where, in that two-week stretch, the young Englishman put together eight consecutive rounds in the 60s.

By the time Westwood fired an eight-under-par 276 to win the Standard Life Loch Lomond, his third European Tour title of the year, many were predicting that Westwood would dislodge Montgomerie as Europe's premier player. Had his U.S. and Asian victories been taken into account, Westwood would have certainly passed Montgomerie in earnings and stroke average.

As the PGA European Tour season ended, Westwood finished third on the Order of Merit with £814,386 in 19 starts. His 69.85 scoring average also placed third behind Montgomerie and Darren Clarke, even though Westwood's four European victories edged Monty by one and Clarke by two.

When he capped off his season by traveling to Japan, it would have been hard for Westwood to predict another streak of back-to-back victories, but that's exactly what happened. Westwood picked up late-season wins at the Sumitomo Visa Taiheiyo Masters and the Dunlop Phoenix Tournament before traveling to South Africa where he finished tied for fourth place in the Nedbank Million Dollar Challenge.

His final worldwide total was $2,814,153, as he also climbed 15 positions to No. 8 on the World Ranking. "All the best players have a proven record in different countries, and that's what I've wanted," Westwood said.

Hard work paid off for Westwood in 1998, but no one in golf worked harder throughout the year and throughout his entire career than my fourth pick:

VIJAY SINGH

Event	Position
Mercedes Championships	T-13
Phoenix Open	T-22
South African Open	T-9
AT&T Pebble Beach National Pro-Am	WD
Doral-Ryder Open	T-4
Honda Classic	2
Bay Hill Invitational	T-22
The Players Championship	T-54
Masters Tournament	MC
MCI Classic	T-24
Macau Open	T-2
MasterCard Colonial	MC
Memorial Tournament	T-68
Kemper Open	T-42
Buick Classic	T-24
U.S. Open Championship	T-25
Motorola Western Open	2
Canon Greater Hartford Open	T-12
British Open Championship	T-19
Buick Open	T-8
PGA Championship	1
Sprint International	1
NEC World Series of Golf	T-14
Greater Milwaukee Open	T-42

Bell Canadian Open	T-22
Buick Challenge	T-58
Linde German Masters	T-2
Cisco World Match Play	T-3
National Car Rental Classic	T-12
Tour Championship	2
Johnnie Walker Super Tour	1
PGA Grand Slam	2

Long recognized as the hardest-working man in golf, Vijay Singh finally reached the one goal that had eluded him throughout his career: wining a major championship. On a tree-lined golf course near Seattle, Washington, Singh fired a course-record-tying 66 at Sahalee Country Club in the second round to take the lead. While he would share that lead throughout much of the weekend with Steve Stricker, Singh played great golf over the final two rounds, shooting 67 and 68 for a 271 total and a two-stroke victory. The PGA Championship was Singh's 25th career victory, but it was the one the man from Fiji wanted the most. "This is a dream come true," he said.

That dream continued into the next week as Singh ventured to Castle Rock, Colorado, for the PGA Tour's only modified-Stableford competition of the year, the Sprint International. He led the event wire-to-wire, finishing with 47 points, six more than Phil Mickelson and Willie Wood, his nearest competitors. Wood said of Singh's back-to-back wins, "I guess the hard work is finally paying off. It's such a fine line between playing good and playing great that it's hard to pinpoint."

Singh summed up his August eruption when he said, "Knowing you can rely on how you're hitting the ball, that you have it coming down the stretch, that's where all the hard work comes in." The hard work continued to pay off as Singh won the Johnnie Walker Super Tour, and added his fifth second-place finish at the Tour Championship. The other seconds were at the Honda Classic, Macau Open (tie), Motorola Western Open and Linde German Masters (tie), all of which combined for worldwide earnings of $2,848,612. The $2,238,998 he won on the PGA Tour was good enough for second place on the money list behind Duval, the highest finish in Singh's career. He rose from No. 15 to No. 9 on the World Ranking.

He also played a key role in the upset victory by the International Team over the United States squad in the Presidents Cup. Singh finished with a 3-1-1 record in the rout at Royal Melbourne.

One of the players Singh, along with teammate Stuart Appleby, defeated in Australia was none other than my fifth pick of the year:

TIGER WOODS

Event	**Position**
Mercedes Championships	T-2
Johnnie Walker Classic	1
AT&T Pebble Beach National Pro-Am	WD
Buick Invitational	T-3
Nissan Open	2
Doral-Ryder Open	T-9

Bay Hill Invitational	T-13
The Players Championship	T-35
Masters Tournament	T-8
BellSouth Classic	1
GTE Byron Nelson Classic	T-12
Memorial Tournament	T-51
U.S. Open Championship	T-18
Motorola Western Open	T-9
British Open Championship	3
Buick Open	T-4
PGA Championship	T-10
Sprint International	4
NEC World Series of Golf	T-5
Alfred Dunhill Cup	T-3
Cisco World Match Play	2
National Car Rental Classic	T-7
Tour Championship	20
PGA Grand Slam	1
Casio World Open	T-15
Nedbank Million Dollar Challenge	2

Only one player could finish the season with one U.S. PGA Tour victory, one PGA European Tour victory, one match-play victory, four second-place finishes, 18 top-10 finishes in 26 starts, and a secure spot atop the World Ranking and have it written that he was in the midst of a slump. But Tiger Woods' past performances were such that anything shy of perfection had to be deemed by many as a slump. Still, Woods started the season with a tie for second in the Mercedes Championships, a win in the Johnnie Walker Classic in his mother's homeland of Thailand, a tie for third place at the Buick Invitational, and a playoff loss to Billy Mayfair in the Nissan Open.

After a closing-round 64 to jump to a tie for second place in the Mercedes Championships, Woods fired a stunning 65 in the final round of the Johnnie Walker Classic to make up an eight-stroke deficit and catch Ernie Els. He would go on to win the event on the second playoff hole. In the Nissan Open he closed with 66, but was unable to convert a birdie putt during the playoff with Mayfair. He admirably defended his record-setting Masters title, finishing in a tie for eighth, then in his next start, he won the BellSouth Classic in Atlanta with rounds of 69, 67, 63 and 72.

Woods fired a final round of 66 in the British Open at Royal Birkdale. Unfortunately for him, his 281 total was one stroke short of Mark O'Meara and Brian Watts, so Woods had to settle for a third-place finish. Four top-five finishes later, Woods shot 12 under par in the 36-hole final of the Cisco World Match Play only to lose to O'Meara on the final hole. It was the lowest score ever by a losing finalist in the event.

Later in the autumn, Woods received an invitation to the PGA Grand Slam, a match-play event that pits the winners of the four major championships head-to-head. Because O'Meara won two majors, Woods, who had the best major championship record of any non-winner, accepted a spot in the four-man field and proceeded to beat Lee Janzen and Singh to win the event.

To close out his "slump-ridden" year, Woods fired a final-round 66 in the

Nedbank Million Dollar Challenge to tie Nick Price at the end of regulation play. Price birdied the fifth playoff hole to win the event, but Woods' second-place finish solidified his position atop the World Ranking and he had worldwide earnings of $2,927,946 to lead the World Money List by a narrow margin over Duval, Singh and Westwood, all of whom topped $2.8 million.

Another player who found himself criticized in the press, but whose record-setting performance is unmatched in PGA European Tour history is my sixth pick of the year:

COLIN MONTGOMERIE

Event	Position
Dubai Desert Classic	T-10
Doral-Ryder Open	MC
Honda Classic	3
Bay Hill Invitational	T-8
The Players Championship	MC
Masters Tournament	T-8
Benson and Hedges International Open	T-5
Volvo PGA Championship	1
Deutsche Bank–SAP Open TPC of Europe	T-10
National Car Rental English Open	4
U.S. Open Championship	T-18
Peugeot Open de France	T-23
Murphy's Irish Open	2
Standard Life Loch Lomond	T-7
British Open Championship	MC
Volvo Scandinavian Masters	T-16
PGA Championship	T-44
Smurfit European Open	MC
BMW International Open	MC
Canon European Masters	T-12
One 2 One British Masters	1
Trophee Lancome	T-11
Linde German Masters	1
Cisco World Match Play	T-5
Volvo Masters	3
Nedbank Million Dollar Challenge	T-10

Defeating Davis Love III for the Andersen Consulting World Championship of Golf title (as reported in the 1998 edition of this annual) should have been the kickstart to a wonderful run by Colin Montgomerie, but putting woes plagued the man from Troon, Scotland, for much of the year. "Pathetic," is how Montgomerie described his putting. "Unfortunately, it isn't the instrument. It's me."

Still, Montgomerie was able to capture three top-10 finishes on the U.S. PGA Tour, including a tie for eighth place at the Masters, before returning to Europe, where he tied for fifth at the Benson and Hedges International.

He then fired a 14-under-par 274 total at the Wentworth Club to win the Volvo PGA Championship by one stroke over Els, Patrik Sjoland and Gary

Orr. That was one of three victories Montgomerie picked up in Europe. The other two, the One 2 One British Masters and Linde German Masters, came late in the season, just in time for Montgomerie to wrestle the money title away from Westwood and Clarke.

With three wins and 14 top-25 finishes out of 17 starts in Europe, Montgomerie captured an unprecedented sixth straight money title with £993,077 in official earnings. It was a record Montgomerie was proud to receive, but admitted was hard to come by. "They'll have to wait at least one more year, but it's getting tougher," Montgomerie said of his triumph.

Although Montgomerie remained No. 7 on the World Ranking, he had another disappointing year in the major championships, including a missed cut in the British Open. His best finish in the majors was a tie for eighth at the Masters.

Somewhat lost in the battle between Montgomerie and Westwood was the man who had a chance in the last week to dislodge both of them and assume the role of Europe's leading player: Northern Ireland's Darren Clarke. Beginning the year ranked 36th in the world, Clarke played well enough in the Masters to tie Montgomerie, Woods and Justin Leonard for eighth place.

Clarke then broke out in Europe with a win at the Benson and Hedges International and three second-place finishes from the first of May through the first of August. By the time he shot a closing-round 63 to win the season-ending Volvo Masters, Clarke led the PGA European Tour in scoring (69.45) and was second to Montgomerie on the money list with £902,867. By the end of the year, Clarke jumped to 17th in the World Ranking ahead of U.S. Open champion Lee Janzen, among others.

Janzen only had two top-10 finishes all year in the United States, along with four missed cuts and a disqualification. After a tie for fourth at the Shell Houston Open, Janzen got the one victory that mattered most to him, the U.S. Open. Even par, the same score Janzen shot to miss the cut at the Tucson Chrysler Classic, proved good enough to win the championship. Janzen did little else throughout the year, however. He missed the cut at the PGA Championship and shot 11 over par to finish tied for 24th in the British Open. He did have two top-10 finishes late in the year in Japan.

While Montgomerie, Westwood and Clarke were battling for supremacy, the rest of the PGA European Tour was evolving. The old guard, players like Nick Faldo, Seve Ballesteros, Bernhard Langer and Ian Woosnam, had no European wins between them, although Sam Torrance proved to be an exception by winning the Peugeot Open de France at age 44. Jose Maria Olazabal, 32, also demonstrated his endurance by winning the Dubai Desert Classic.

Instead, players like Thomas Bjorn, Stephen Leaney and Miguel Angel Jimenez broke through with two wins each. Leaney also won the Australasian Players Championship, while Jimenez had six top-10 finishes to move himself into fourth place on the final money list. Bjorn finished sixth with £470,798. Patrik Sjoland, who won the Italian Open, also exerted himself with eight top-10 finishes including five in the top three. Sjoland edged out Bjorn for the fifth spot on the money list by less than £30,000.

Jesper Parnevik, another member of the U.S. PGA Tour who made some brief appearances in Europe, picked up a win at the Scandinavian Open. He also won in the United States, capturing the Phoenix Open.

There was plenty of triumph and tragedy throughout the 1998 professional golf year, but no event stunned us more than the untimely death of Renay Appleby, wife of Australian player Stuart Appleby. Traveling together on a long-awaited vacation after the British Open, Renay was accidentally pinned between two automobiles outside a London train station. Her death sent shock waves throughout the golf community as the Applebys were one of the most liked couples. Three weeks after the accident, Appleby returned to competitive golf at the PGA Championship wearing a necklace that bore Renay's name. "Hopefully it will be a good luck charm," Appleby said through tears at a news conference. He also thanked everyone for supporting him, but acknowledged that his life would never be the same. "I'll keep moving forward," he said. "But it's not normal. Things are different. It's not going to be easy."

Fans expressed their sympathy throughout the rest of the year as Appleby endured. It wasn't until the International Team trounced the Americans in the Presidents Cup in early December that Appleby felt at peace on the golf course. Appleby said, "Renay wanted me to make this team so badly. We talked about it all the time. I know she's happy for me now, but now it's almost Christmas. This golf ... this was wonderful. But soon it will be Christmas. Christmas without Renay."

Appleby was the crowd favorite at the Holden Australian Open, but that event went to Greg Chalmers. Two weeks later, however, Appleby broke through at the Schweppes Coolum Classic by shooting a record 17-under-par 271. It was Appleby's first professional victory on Australian soil — his second of the year, including the Kemper Open — and it came in front of his and Renay's family, ironically enough, five days before Christmas.

Masashi (Jumbo) Ozaki, No. 13 on the World Ranking, was again the top money winner on the Japan Tour and won three events, the Yonex Open Hiroshima, KBC Augusta and Philip Morris Championship. There were plenty of other stories on the Japanese front, including Shigeki Maruyama, who won the PGA Philanthropy and became a hero during the Presidents Cup with a 5-0-0 record. Maruyama's performance elevated him into the top 50 in the World Ranking (he finished the year at No. 43) and showed that he could remain a dominant force on the world stage.

Oklahoma native Brian Watts, a regular on the Japan Tour, also made headlines in 1998 with his runner-up finish in the British Open, along with victories in the Yomiuri Open and Casio World Open. By virtue of his British Open performance, Watts earned a spot on the U.S. PGA Tour where he was planning to compete in 1999.

Other multiple winners on the Japan Tour included American Brandt Jobe, who won back-to-back weeks in the Japan PGA Championship and Ube Kosan Open, then followed it up five weeks later with a victory in the Mizuno Open. Hidemichi Tanaka also had three victories, at the Japan Open, Aiful Cup and Okinawa Open. Westwood carded back-to-back victories when he followed his win at the Sumitomo Visa Taiheiyo Masters with another at the Dunlop Phoenix Tournament, while Katsumasa Miyamoto also had two wins at the Tsuruya Open and the Japan Series.

On the Asian Tour, Frankie Minoza won three of six events, capturing the Ericsson Philippine Masters, Rolex Masters and Ericsson Philippine Open.

In addition, he won the Kirin Open, an official event on both the Asian and Japan Tour schedules. Edward Fryatt, a journeyman who has played the U.S. PGA Tour and the Nike Tour in his career, captured the Benson and Hedges Malaysian Open, while Scott Rowe won the Maekyung LG Fashion Open. Singh capped off the Asian Tour season with a resounding win in the Johnnie Walker Super Tour.

Fryatt also won on Asia's Omega Tour in the Volvo China Open. Chris Williams and Kang Wook-soon each had two Omega triumphs. Williams won the Volvo Masters of Malaysia and FedEx PGA Championship; Kang's victories were back-to-back in the Perrier Hong Kong Open and Omega PGA Championship.

Nick Price continued to prove that he is one of greatest players in the world by winning on the U.S. PGA Tour at the FedEx St. Jude Classic and three times in Africa at the Dimension Data Pro-Am and back-to-back at the Zimbabwe Open and Nedbank Million Dollar Challenge.

Multiple winners were not confined to Europe, Asia, Africa and Australia, however. In the United States, in addition to Duval and Singh, Phil Mickelson, Fred Couples, Billy Mayfair, John Huston and Hal Sutton all picked up multiple victories. Couples won the Bob Hope Chrysler Classic and the Memorial Tournament, while Mickelson added to his season-opening Mercedes Championships win with an August victory in the delayed AT&T Pebble Beach National Pro-Am.

Mayfair defeated Woods in a playoff for the Nissan Open, then added to his victory total in the summer with a win at the Buick Open. Huston set a PGA Tour scoring record in his win at the United Airlines Hawaiian Open, then waited until the autumn to add his second victory at the National Car Rental Classic.

Singh was the only player to put together back-to-back wins, but Hal Sutton, who only had one previous win in 12 years (the 1995 B.C. Open), came through with a late-season surge that produced victory at the Westin Texas Open and a dramatic playoff win over Singh in the Tour Championship. By virtue of his victories, Sutton came from No. 96 to finish the year ranked No. 34 in the world. Mickelson finished the season in the No. 10 spot on the World Ranking, while Huston and Mayfair finished No. 29 and No. 42 respectively.

Jim Furyk only had one official victory at the Las Vegas Invitational, but his good play throughout the year, including seven top-10 finishes, for a third-place position on the U.S. money list moved him to No. 12 in the World Ranking. He and partner Duval also earned a victory in the unofficial Fred Meyer Challenge.

On another U.S. tour, Hale Irwin was once again proving his dominance on the Senior PGA Tour with eight victories and official earnings of $2,861,945, the most money ever won by any player on any single tour. His Senior World Money List total was a record $3,155,189. In what could only be described as a phenomenal year, Irwin finished out of the top five only two times in 22 official events through the season, and he set a record scoring average of 68.59 for the year, winning his third consecutive Byron Nelson Award in the process.

During the first few weeks it looked as though Irwin's chief rival, Gil

Morgan, would be setting the pace for the Senior Tour. Morgan won three events in the first six weeks, the MasterCard Championship, LG Championship and Senior Slam. But then Irwin took charge, winning three of his next six events and becoming the first player since World War II to win three consecutive PGA Seniors' Championships.

Morgan continued to win throughout the year as well, capturing four more titles before year's end, but even seven victories could not match the dominance Irwin showed throughout the year. As part of his run, Irwin came back from an opening-round 77 to win the U.S. Senior Open, establishing a mark for the highest first-round score ever shot by the eventual winner. He also became one of only seven players ever to win both the U.S. Open and U.S. Senior Open. With a late-season win at the Energizer Senior Tour Championship, Irwin picked up his 20th Senior Tour title and locked up the Jack Nicklaus Award as the Senior PGA Tour's Player of the Year.

Tommy Horton was again the leader on the European Seniors Tour with three victories in the El Bosque Seniors Open, De Vere Hotels Seniors Classic and The Belfry PGA Seniors Championship. Brian Huggett had consecutive victories in the Schroder Senior Masters and Senior British Open, while Bobby Verwey won back-to-back in the Lawrence Batley Seniors and Credit Suisse Private Banking Seniors Open.

Elsewhere, Toru Nakayama was a double winner in Japan in the TPC Starts and Old Man Par Senior Open, but Australian Graham Marsh swept in to win the Japan Senior Open. Tertius Claassens and Allan Henning each won twice in South Africa. Claassens won back-to-back in the Wild Coast and Mmabatho events on the Vodacom Senior Series. Henning won the Vodacom's Welkom event and the John Bland Invitational. Bland himself became the Franklin Templeton Senior South African Open champion.

Meanwhile, another competitive rivalry was being established in the women's game, one that would bring renewed and international interest to the U.S. LPGA Tour. By the time she arrived on the LPGA Tour, 20-year-old Korean Se Ri Pak was already generating quite a buzz, particularly in her hero-starved homeland. Whenever Pak played, throngs of Korean media followed her every shot. They weren't disappointed.

At the McDonald's LPGA Championship, Pak captured her first major title and her first professional title all in one week. It wasn't even close. With an opening-round 65, followed by 68, 72 and 68, Pak either held or shared the lead from the first hole through the last. Her three-stroke victory over Lisa Hackney and Donna Andrews began what *Golf World* magazine called, "The Pak Attack," an assault on the women's game unlike any since Pak's hero and mentor, Nancy Lopez, arrived in 1978.

Pak continued to set impressive standards with her second victory, a stunning performance in one of the most exciting U.S. Women's Opens in history. After 72 holes on the difficult Black Wolf Run course in Kohler, Wisconsin, Pak was tied with amateur Jenny Chuasiriporn. The Monday playoff was a kind of nip-and-tuck drama and in the end, it came down to a birdie putt on the 20th green of the day. When Pak's putt found the hole she jumped into her father's arms, and let the tears stream down her face. America was mesmerized, but Korea fell into a frenzy.

"The first time I won, at the McDonald's, a major, I was very happy, but some people said I was lucky to win," Pak said. "After I won the U.S. Open, I think people realized I knew how to play golf. I'm extremely happy."

She would become even happier. One week after capturing the imaginations of millions, Pak exerted her dominance by firing an LPGA record of 61 in the Jamie Farr Kroger Classic. She went on to shoot a four-round total of 261, another record, for a 23-under-par total, a third record, to win the event by nine strokes. Pak became not just a golf story, but a national phenomenon, igniting more interest in the women's game than the LPGA had seen in two decades.

Two weeks later, Pak would do it again, winning the Giant Eagle Classic for her fourth win of the year. It seemed that Pak owned women's golf in 1998.

But then there was a determined young Swede, Annika Sorenstam, the most dominant player on the LPGA Tour over the previous two years, who had carded two victories of her own before Pak's dramatic U.S. Women's Open victory.

Sandwiched between Pak's wins at the Jamie Farr Kroger Classic and Giant Eagle Classic, Sorenstam picked up her third win of the year in New York at the JAL Big Apple Classic. With the money title and Player of the Year honors still up in the air, Sorenstam continued her steady play, picking up another win at the Safeco Classic late in the season.

Sorenstam's consistency proved to be enough. Not only did she capture the money title and Player of the Year honors, she became the first female professional to average under 70 strokes per round for an entire year, capturing the Vare Trophy with a 69.99 average.

Later that month, The Associated Press named Se Ri Pak the Female Athlete of the Year. When asked how the Female Athlete of the Year could be overlooked as the Player of the Year in her own sport, LPGA Commissioner Jim Ritts said, "I don't know, but I think it's great. The fact that we have two players creating such a buzz can mean nothing but good things for the LPGA."

Sorenstam also won in Europe, as did Helen Alfredsson of Sweden, who had two American victories. Other double winners in the United States were Sweden's Liselotte Neumann (who also won in Japan), Danielle Ammaccapane and Kelly Robbins. Australia's Karrie Webb won at home and on the LPGA Tour, while England's Laura Davies won in Europe and the season-ending PageNet Tour Championship.

In Europe, Sophie Gustafson led with three victories, one in an unofficial event, and Sherri Steinhauer came over from the LPGA Tour to win the Weetabix Women's British Open. On other international circuits, Michiko Hattori dominated the Japan LPGA Tour with five victories, while Kaori Higo, Kaori Harada, Akiko Fukushima and Young-Me Lee won twice each. Hiromi Kobayashi had victories in Japan and the United States. Marnie McGuire won the AAMI Women's Australian Open, following Webb's victory in the Australian Ladies Masters.

3. Masters Tournament

Just before packing his bags and heading north for the green vestiges of Augusta, Georgia, 41-year-old Mark O'Meara broke out the buckets, sponges and liquid soap and lathered up his Toyota 4-Runner in the driveway of his suburban Orlando, Florida, home. The year's first major championship awaited him, but rather than going into self-induced exile or beating balls or changing his routine, O'Meara continued to wash his cars, take his family out to eat at a local restaurant and coach his eight-year-old son's little league baseball team.

"I can't say my career is a failure because I haven't won a professional major," O'Meara said before putting the rags and brushes away and pulling out his clubs for the Masters Tournament. "The expectations for me weren't the same as they were for Phil Mickelson or Tiger Woods or some of the other talented players who have come along. All that matters is how I feel about what I've achieved."

And before the 1998 Masters, O'Meara felt great about his accomplishments both on and off the golf course. Having started on the PGA Tour in 1981 with $4,000 and a used Volkswagen, O'Meara was blessed with a wonderful wife and two children, a fine home, a good life and 20 worldwide victories to his credit. He finished 1997 ranked 10th in the World Ranking, and his worldwide career earnings exceeded $11 million, but that never changed the grounded, down-to-earth O'Meara. When asked about having never won the Masters, he smiled and said, "I've won the Australian Masters." The Open? "Hey, I've won the Canadian Open."

But when asked about being labeled "The Best Player Never To Have Won A Major," O'Meara quickly pointed out that he had a U.S. Amateur to his credit. "Bobby Jones counted his U.S. Amateurs (as majors)," he said. "Jack Nicklaus counted his U.S. Amateurs. Why is it okay for those guys to count the U.S. Amateur and not Mark O'Meara?"

A good point, but not one a man like O'Meara would ever press. "I'm a very good golfer, and I've achieved a lot more than I ever thought I would," he said. "People around me put more emphasis on winning a major than I do. You don't hear me saying I'm gearing up for the Masters. I can't tell you my game is going to be right on the second week of April every year. Sure, I think I have the heart to win a major championship. There's no way I would have won the tournaments I've won, the way I won, if I didn't have the heart. But would I trade all I've got for a major? Are you kidding? I'd have a hard time saying, 'If I won a major championship, my career would be complete.' I think my career is complete.

"Have I been disappointed in the fact that I haven't won a major championship to this point? Yes, a little bit. But I can't put myself down over the great things that have happened to me in the game of golf. I think I've had a wonderful career. I'm a good player, but I wouldn't classify myself as a great player. Jack Nicklaus and Ben Hogan and Gene Sarazen are great players. You can go down the line. Players who have dominated the major championships and played for a long time … those are the great players. Me? I'm a nice player."

As a nice player, O'Meara had plenty of victories and many close calls in major championships. In the 1995 PGA Championship at Riviera, O'Meara led after 36 holes, but a final-round 73 dropped him into a tie for sixth. Other than that, however, his best finishes in major championships were ties for third place in the 1988 U.S. Open and the 1985 and 1991 British Opens.

Perhaps the emphasis on O'Meara's zero-for-56 record in professional majors was heightened by his relationship with Woods, the 1997 Masters champion. Upon entering the professional ranks, Tiger purchased a condominium near O'Meara's house, and the two became fast friends. They fished and played golf together, even teaming up for a 1-and-2 record in the 1997 Ryder Cup at Valderrama. Woods called O'Meara "a big brother," while O'Meara said of the relationship, "There are things I can learn from Tiger, especially his tremendous drive. Being around him has rekindled my juices."

In fact, O'Meara became a footnote in Woods' historic 1997 Masters victory when, days before leaving for Augusta, Woods hustled O'Meara out of $65 by shooting what O'Meara would later call "a pretty easy 59" at the Isleworth club in Orlando. "It could have easily been a 57." A week later, Woods set 18 tournament records while winning the Masters by 12 strokes. If that match was a sign of things to come, the April 1998 re-match, where O'Meara took $100 from Woods at Isleworth a week prior to heading up to Augusta should have given a clue to the week ahead. But no one, not even O'Meara, could have predicted the events of the coming week. After all, O'Meara was 41 years old and zero for 13 in the Masters with his best showing being a tie for fourth in 1992. Was winning the coveted green jacket out of the question?

A week later, with Woods watching on television from the nearby Butler Cabin, not only did O'Meara win the Masters, he did so by birdieing the 71st and 72nd holes, making him the first since Arnold Palmer in 1960 to birdie the last two holes at Augusta National to win. His 105 putts beat the rest of the field by three. When the last one — a sidehill 18-footer — fell, O'Meara shed his major championship shackles.

The week began with a nostalgic look backward as six-time Masters winner Jack Nicklaus was honored on Tuesday in a touching ceremony on the east driving range, outside the stately white clubhouse. Augusta National chairman Jackson Stephens heaped accolades on the great champion before unveiling a plaque honoring Nicklaus' many accomplishments over his 40 years at the Masters. The plaque, which was mounted in the stone drinking fountain between the 16th green and the 17th tee, detailed Nicklaus' six Masters victories, his scoring records and his benchmark as the youngest at the time (age 23 in 1963) and the oldest (age 46 in 1986) Masters champion. Stephens then hedged a little when he said of the monument, "We have taken the precaution of leaving a little extra space at the bottom of the plaque — just in case."

Nicklaus graciously accepted the tribute, then, with his wife Barbara and five children in attendance, the normally stone-faced Nicklaus lost his composure and choked on his words as he brushed tears from his eyes. "Barbara has been with me at every Masters but one," Nicklaus said. Then, unable to complete the next few sentences, Nicklaus said, "I'm having a horrible time talking. I didn't realize I was so sentimental." It would be a week of many firsts, even for the 58-year-old Nicklaus.

Another Masters legend, three-time winner and 86-year-old honorary starter Sam Snead received some early but unwanted attention when, after displaying stroke-like symptoms during the ride from Ft. Pierce, Florida to Augusta, Snead was rushed and subsequently admitted to an area hospital. Snead's son Jackie was driving his father north toward Augusta when the 1949, 1952 and 1954 Masters winner became nauseous and began slurring his speech. As it turned out, Snead was simply suffering the effects of oxygen depravation to the brain from a circulatory problem related to fatigue. "If a 21-year-old kid went at it like I've been, he'd be begging to go into the woods and relax for a while," Snead quipped in his biting West Virginia drawl after receiving the diagnosis. Feisty as ever, "the Slammer" was back on the tee Thursday morning along with 86-year-old two-time champion Byron Nelson and 96-year-old Gene Sarazen. High-stepping and dismissing his earlier problems with a wave, Snead said, "I've just been run ragged, that's all." His 230-yard opening tee shot proved that point.

Even so, Snead was happy that he didn't have to brave the elements for an entire round on Thursday. A storm front that suspended the par-three contest and pushed back Thursday starting times one hour finally blew out on Thursday, but in its wake, winds that sometimes exceeded 40 miles an hour whipped through the Georgia pines drying out already fast greens and reeking havoc on many competitors' game plans. "Par was a great accomplishment," Woods said after scoring one under par in his opening bid to repeat as champion.

Former champion Jose Maria Olazabal, who bested Woods by one and tied Paul Stankowski and Scott Hoch at two-under-par 70, shook his head after the round and said, "The intensity of the wind was unbelievable. Anything under par was a good score today. It was very difficult to guess where the wind was coming from."

Stankowski agreed that the wind was tough, but he thought the conditions might have helped his concentration. "We guessed (on club selection) pretty well out there," he said. "I've always liked playing in the wind. You don't expect to hit perfect shots and that forces you to focus more."

A little greater focus and a little of the magic that he found in 1992 helped propel Fred Couples into the first-round lead with a three-under-par 69. Couples birdied the first three holes of the round, a start that Couples said "gave me an unbelievable boost." He made pars throughout the remainder of the first nine before making his first bogey at the 11th hole. Then the second miracle of Couples' Masters career occurred on the treacherous par-three 12th. Swirling winds knocked Couples' eight-iron shot down, but for the second time in six years, his ball seemingly defied gravity by remaining perched on the edge of the steep bank above Rae's Creek.

"The bank's not shaved as much as when I did that before," Couples said. "But, it was basically the same thing."

This time around Couples had to take off his right shoe and stand in the water in order to play his pitch, and, unlike 1992 when he got up-and-down for par on the 12th and went on to win, he missed the six-foot putt for par and had to settle for a bogey four. Couples was still happy with the day and with his lead. "I don't feel I'm quite the player I once was, but I think at any given time I'm capable of playing well, and today was one of those days. I didn't struggle. You're not going to play this course in 30-mile-an-hour winds and shoot 69 too many times."

After his bogeys at the 11th and 12th, Couples birdied the 13th and 17th to get back to three under par for the day, but not without some scary moments due to the wind. "I went to mark a putt at 14 and it probably moved a foot sideways," Couples said. On the 17th his ball also wobbled as he was reaching to mark it, which was cause for concern. Earlier, John Daly had taken a penalty stroke at the 17th after his ball moved during address.

Fortunately, Couples escaped any penalties. He did, however, have a few anxious moments after checking the scoreboard. Earlier in the day, before the wind reached its peak, 66-year-old Gay Brewer, the 1967 Masters winner who hadn't made the 36-hole cut at Augusta National since 1983, electrified the crowds with a opening-round 72, a number that caught Couples' attention. "We were talking about his round all day long," Couples said. "My caddie kept saying, 'Look, just hang in there because you need to play better to beat this guy.' His 72 was a lot better than my 69. It's definitely the story of the day."

Just like Couples, the most memorable shot in Brewer's unlikely round came at the par-three 12th. Paired with Doug Ford in the first group of the day, Brewer didn't have to contend with the gusting winds until the second nine, at which time he hit an eight iron into Rae's Creek on No. 12. "But then I holed the wedge for a par and it felt like an ace," Brewer said. "That kind of pumped me up. Then I hit it stiff on 16 and 17 and birdied both of them." Brewer became the oldest contestant ever to shoot par or better in the Masters, besting his old mark of 70 at age 63 in 1995. "My goal every year is to make the cut," a smiling Brewer said afterward. "I've been here enough times to know where to hit the ball. The problem is doing it."

Other stories of the day included U.S. Amateur champion Matt Kuchar who, despite the pressure of playing with Woods, tied Brewer at even par. "This is a dream come true," the ever-smiling Kuchar said. "The fans were great to me and so was Tiger. I couldn't have asked for anything more."

Nicklaus would have had trouble asking for more as well. Two days after being honored, Nicklaus shot one-over-par 73. Under mild conditions, Nicklaus' scores might not have created a stir, but with players like Greg Norman shooting 76, Tom Watson with 78, Tom Lehman with 80, and 1995 champion Ben Crenshaw with 83, no one, not even O'Meara, who opened with an uninspiring 74, seemed out of it.

As for O'Meara, the windy conditions might not have suited his game but, according to his coach, Hank Haney, the wind helped O'Meara's chances. On Tuesday night Haney openly predicted that Woods would successfully defend his title. "The field can't spot a guy 60 yards off the tee on this golf course, and that's how much farther Tiger hits the ball than everybody else out here," Haney said. Then on Thursday, as winds gusted so strongly that the tall, thin Haney was almost blown over while standing next to the putting green, he recanted his earlier prediction. "These conditions change everything," he said. "This brings the field closer together. It gives guys like Mark a chance."

As the sun set in Augusta, with 10 players yet to complete their rounds because of the late start, Haney had no idea how prophetic his comments would become. Nor did he realize the drama that lay ahead. The leaderboard at the 62nd Masters looked like this:

Fred Couples	69	Phil Blackmar	71
Paul Stankowski	70	David Duval	71
Jose Maria Olazabal	70	Colin Montgomerie	71
Scott Hoch	70	Tiger Woods	71
Paul Azinger	71	Fuzzy Zoeller	71

If rain and wind slowed play on Thursday, winds and threesomes ground things to a snail's pace on Friday. Late Thursday night Augusta officials made the decision to send players out in threes on Friday, a departure from traditional twosomes that have been a part of the Masters format since the tournament's inception. While the format did allow every player to complete both rounds by sunset on Friday, five-and-a-half-hour rounds were the norm on the second day.

"You're used to playing in a flow," Woods said after shooting a second-round 72. "You just couldn't get into a flow out there today." Woods' pairing with Colin Montgomerie (71-75) and Fuzzy Zoeller (71-74) attracted a great deal of attention because of the uproar after Zoeller's 1997 comments that were deemed to be racially insensitive. For the players it was no big deal. In fact, during dinner Thursday evening, it dawned on Montgomerie that, depending on how David Duval (who had to finish his opening round on Friday morning) played, Montgomerie would either be playing with Gay Brewer or Fuzzy and Tiger. "Looks like it's going to be an interesting day either way," Montgomerie joked. The only thing interesting turned out to be the fact that the threesome took five hours and 15 minutes to play. "This was just another pairing," Woods said afterward.

Scores continued to rise. The golf course that was called by some "too easy" after Woods' record-setting performance in 1997 bared its teeth again as winds from the north and west continued to gust. Six over par made the cut, the highest 36-hole advancing total since 1989, and the field averaged 75.3 strokes for the day. Nick Faldo, Tom Watson and Nick Price missed the weekend with scores of 151, and Norman packed his bags after shooting 154.

Norman looked distant, rushing shots en route to a second-round 78. Afterward he said, "It's disappointing, but I'm not worried about it. I probably should have spent 15 days on the disabled list instead of five." As it turned out, Norman was suffering from a degenerated rotator cuff in his shoulder that would require surgery only a few weeks later. That Friday afternoon, however, unaware of the severity of his injury, Norman hugged his wife, Laura, and said, "Let's go home and hide some Easter eggs."

Brewer, three strokes off the lead after the first round, fell back to earth with an 86 to miss the cut, while Lehman didn't stick around for the weekend after shooting 156. Vijay Singh, who came into the Masters with the longest string of consecutive cuts made (53), saw that streak end when he shot 76-80.

Still, there was magic in the pines during the second round as 62-year-old Gary Player became the oldest competitor to make the cut at the Masters. After following his opening 77 with a stellar 72 (one of only 26 rounds of par or better), Player said, "I've always enjoyed the wind. I've won a lot of golf tournaments under similar conditions. But, to shoot 72 at age 62 is really a thrill."

Another thrilling even-par round came from Nicklaus, who shot 72 with three birdies, including a downhill 18-footer at the 18th. The amateur Kuchar, who shot a second-round 76 to make the cut at four over par, said, "Sometimes I have to pinch myself. I mean, I'm playing in the same golf tournament as Jack Nicklaus." At the halfway mark, Nicklaus led Kuchar by three, 145 to 148. The 58-year-old champion entered the weekend just six shots off the lead.

That lead was still held by Couples who followed his opening 69 with an impressive round of 70. After turning in 35 with two birdies and one bogey, Couples missed two short par putts on the 10th and 11th, but came right back with birdies at the 12th and 13th. Another birdie at the par-three 16th capped the round and left Couples feeling comfortable about his chances. "I'm looking forward to the next two rounds because I'm playing good and I love this place," Couples said.

Despite the attention he received, Couples didn't hold the halfway lead alone. David Duval, who broke out of his winless slump with three consecutive victories at the end of 1997, shared the low round of the day with a 68 that included birdies on the 13th, 14th, 16th and 17th holes. Only two other players had rounds in the 60s: Craig Stadler, who tied Duval for the day's low at 68 that, coupled with his opening 79, allowed the 1982 champion to play the weekend, and Mickelson, who shot a 69 after opening with a 74. Mickelson stood four strokes back at the halfway mark, tied with Azinger (71-72), Woods (71-72), Jay Haas (72-71) and Olazabal (70-73), and one shot ahead of O'Meara.

O'Meara followed his 74 with a two-under-par round of 70 that included eight one-putts and one chip-in. On greens Player called "incredible" for their severity and speed, O'Meara took only 27 putts, and only 12 during his bogey-free second nine. A chip-in on the par-three 12th was one of four birdies O'Meara carded in the second round, and it set the tone for what would be a short-game display of historic proportions.

At the end of the second round, the leaderboard looked like this:

Fred Couples	70 - 139	Jay Haas	71 - 143
David Duval	68 - 139	Jose Maria Olazabal	73 - 143
Scott Hoch	71 - 141	Phil Mickelson	69 - 143
Paul Azinger	72 - 143	Mark O'Meara	70 - 144
Tiger Woods	72 - 143	Scott McCarron	71 - 144

The third round saw a crowd of players congregating at the top. With the winds calming and the temperatures rising, the average score on Saturday was 71.4, fully four shots lower than the average for the first two days. Twelve players broke 70 as opposed to three who made it to the 60s on Friday, and the field was 26 under par as compared to the first two days when the field was 235 over par.

In contrast to 1997, when Woods ran away and hid from the rest of the field on Saturday, 19 players finished the day within six strokes of the lead, including Woods and the other three winners of 1997 major championships — Davis Love III, Ernie Els and Justin Leonard. Fifteen of the 19 had played on at least one of the previous two Ryder Cup or Presidents Cup teams, a testament to the star quality of this Masters.

The low score of the day was 67, shot by Love, Per-Ulrik Johansson, Darren Clarke and Jim Furyk. Of those, Furyk made the best recovery, rebounding from an opening 76 to play the 18 holes from the second nine on Friday through the turn on Saturday in nine under par. Furyk's round left him tied with Duval (who could only manage 74) at 213, three off the lead.

The lead was still held by Couples, who was even par for his round when, at the par-five 13th, he hit a 205-yard three iron for his second shot and immediately said, "Oh baby." The shot ended up 18 inches from the hole. He tapped in for eagle, and despite bogeys on the 14th and 18th holes, Couples shot 71 and carried a two-stroke lead over Mickelson, Azinger and O'Meara into the final round.

Mickelson would have shared the lead except for bogeys on the 17th and 18th holes. On the 17th, his approach flew over the green, and on the 18th, his second shot fell short. Usually deft with his short game, Mickelson failed to save par on either occasion, and even though he finished with a three-under-par 69, the bogeys took away some of his momentum. Azinger, on the other hand, parred the last hole to shoot 69, putting him into final-round contention for the first time since winning the 1993 PGA Championship and subsequently taking a year off to battle cancer.

Meanwhile, O'Meara shot 68 with 22 putts, including 12 one-putts and another chip-in. His four-birdie, no-bogey round was O'Meara's best third round in a Masters, but despite being two shots out with 18 holes to play, O'Meara still had to field questions about having never won a major. With son Shaun accompanying him in the interview room after his round, O'Meara said, "I've got a great wife and great kids, and I sleep at home pretty well at night. If someone wants to classify me as a failure for never winning a major championship, that's their right."

The reporters nodded, thanked O'Meara, then sent him on his way. There were other stories on Saturday that required their attention, most notably the performance of Nicklaus, who found the magic of old to rally to a two-under-par 70 and a 54-hole total of 215, five shots out of the lead. "I thought I was snake bit," Nicklaus said after missing seven putts inside 13 feet on the first nine. On the second nine, however, Nicklaus birdied the 11th when his approach shot landed three feet from the flag, bogeyed the 12th, then birdied the 15th and 16th before sinking a downhill 15-footer for par on the 18th.

By the time the putt on the 16th found the cup, the crowd had picked up on the rumblings of Nicklaus, and the gallery was out in mass. No one has ever owned the 16th at Augusta like Nicklaus. In 1963, Nicklaus made a 16-foot birdie putt on the 16th to take the final-round lead in what would be the first of his Masters victories. Again in 1975, Nicklaus needed something spectacular to happen at the 16th, and a 40-foot birdie that gave Nicklaus the lead over Tom Weiskopf and Johnny Miller proved just the right shot at the right moment. During the 1986 Masters, at the age of 46, he followed his eagle at the 15th with a five-iron shot for near ace at the 16th. The subsequent birdie, followed by another at the 17th, propelled Nicklaus to an unprecedented sixth green jacket. When the 15-footer for birdie found the hole at the 16th again on that Saturday afternoon in 1998, everyone wondered if another miracle was in the making.

Afterwards, Nicklaus said, "The competitor in me says, 'Jack, I don't care what age you are and I don't care who's out in front of me. I'm a competitor who can still play and still win.' That may not be realistic, but it's the way I have to think or else there's no sense being here."

"Wow, that's amazing," said Woods, who shot 72 and also finished 54 holes at 215, of Nicklaus' performance. When he turned attention back to his own game, Woods said, "Considering the conditions, the way I struck the ball, the places I put myself, I'm proud of how I hung in there. I haven't lost anything yet. I'm right there. I'm still in contention."

Also in contention was the amateur, Kuchar, who galvanized galleries with his 68 which included 32 on the first nine. With a smile that captured the hearts of golf fans, Kuchar said, "I could picture my grandfather and see the smile on his face when my name came up on the leaderboard." It was the kind of moment that marked this as one of the most dramatic Saturdays in Masters history.

Woods stated the obvious. "Anything can happen on Sunday," he said. He had no idea how right he would be. With 18 holes to play, Couples remained on top of a leaderboard that looked like this:

Fred Couples	71 - 210	Scott Hoch	73 - 214
Phil Mickelson	69 - 212	Jose Maria Olazabal	71 - 214
Paul Azinger	69 - 212	Tiger Woods	72 - 215
Mark O'Meara	68 - 212	Colin Montgomerie	69 - 215
Jim Furyk	67 - 213	Jack Nicklaus	70 - 215
David Duval	74 - 213	Ernie Els	70 - 215
Jay Haas	71 - 214		

The mild conditions continued on Sunday as the wind that had dominated the first two rounds quieted, leaving the door open for a birdie shootout that wouldn't end until the top half of the field had shot an aggregate 50 under par. Among the early starters, David Toms, a first-time Masters participant and stranger to the leaderboard, started the day nine strokes back before birdieing seven of the last nine holes for a second-nine record 29 and an eight-under-par 64. Posting a four-day total of 283, five under par, Toms was the leader in the clubhouse before the actual leaders had a chance to get going.

Toms was one of 21 players to birdie the 555-yard par-five second, but when he bogeyed the par-three fourth from the greenside bunker, then birdied the 360-yard par-four seventh to turn at one under for the day, no one paid any attention. Then Toms came to life. He hit a seven iron to within 15 feet on the difficult, downhill 485-yard par-four 10th. When that putt went in for birdie, Toms stood two under for the day, and after making par at the 11th, even he didn't consider himself a contender. His seven iron, played safely to the center of the par-three 12th, netted another birdie from 12 feet. Then, after a booming drive, Toms hit four iron to the fringe of the par-five 13th, but his first putt trickled six feet beyond the hole. He made the putt coming back for birdie and Toms was on a roll. He made a six-foot birdie putt on the 14th after hitting eight iron from the fairway, and after driving the ball perfectly on the par-five 15th, Toms hit a five wood over the green, chipped to within four feet and made another birdie, his fourth in a row, and his fifth in six holes. That wouldn't be all, however. Toms hit a five iron to within eight feet on the par-three 16th, and made what he termed, "my best putt all day," for another birdie. On the 17th it appeared the streak would come to an end after Toms hit a lackluster sand-wedge approach to 25 feet. But when the putt went in, Toms had equaled a six-birdie-in-a-row record set by Johnny Miller in 1975 and matched by Mark Calcavecchia in 1992. When he parred the 18th from the right side of the green, Toms also tied Calcavecchia's second-nine course-record 29.

"I had no idea the birdie streak was coming," Toms said. "My goal was to finish in the top 24. I had no idea I'd made six birdies in a row until I checked my card. It's probably the highlight of my career."

A couple of hours later, the Augusta crowds were electrified when Nicklaus birdied the second, third, sixth and seventh holes, with a bogey on the fourth to turn at four under par for the tournament, two strokes off the lead. "People were saying, 'You better look out for Jack,' and it wasn't even funny," Couples said. The buzz became distracting as Nicklaus continued his good play on the second nine. According to Montgomerie, who played behind Nicklaus, "It was difficult. The galleries were applauding Jack for breathing, which slowed things up a bit. Still, the man is amazing."

Not amazing enough, however. Nicklaus followed a bogey on the 12th with another birdie on the par-five 13th, then another birdie on the 15th put him at five under par for the tournament with the leaderboard changing by the minute. But Jack could manage no better than pars on the final three holes for a valiant 68, five under par for the tournament and, eventually, a tie for sixth with Toms at 283.

"I've said for many years that if there's ever going to be a golf course where I have a chance to compete in a major championship it will be this golf course," Nicklaus said. "I said I needed to shoot 64, and as I walked down the 15th I said to Steve (Nicklaus' son and caddie for the week), 'If I can get an eagle and a couple of birdies, I have a chance.' I got one birdie, so that's about right. That's what I needed, about three shots lower. Experience means an awful lot out here. Nobody can take a run at every putt, so a little experience and patience pays off out here. If I ever had a chance to make a run at these guys this was the place."

He made a gallant run, but in the end Nicklaus was right: 64 was what he needed to shoot for a seventh green jacket. His final-round 68, though miraculous, was four shots shy. When asked whether finishing as strongly as he did at age 58 was as rewarding as winning the Masters at age 46, Nicklaus cut his patented cold stare at the questioner and said, "Absolutely not. There's no greater accomplishment than winning. There is nothing as emotional as coming down the stretch and winning. That's what I'm here for. That's enough to go practice this silly game so we can win, you know. That's why we do it."

An hour and a half behind Nicklaus, the leaders were embroiled in a battle that wouldn't be decided until the last putt fell.

Couples, paired with O'Meara in the final twosome, made an inauspicious start with a bogey on the first hole, but rallied quickly with birdies at the second, fourth, seventh and eighth, while O'Meara continued his barrage of one putts by birdieing the second, third and fourth with one putts on five of the first nine greens for 33. Still, Couples held a two-stroke lead at nine under par going to the ninth hole.

After driving the ball perfectly on the ninth, Couples and his caddie debated between a pitching wedge and a sand wedge for the 105-yard approach shot to the green. After several minutes of indecision, Couples put the sand wedge away and chose the pitching wedge, which he proceeded to hit too tenuously. The shot spun off the front edge of the green and Couples made bogey. Meantime, O'Meara, who drove his ball in the left trees, scrambled for yet another one-putt par, and Couples headed to the 10th tee with his lead dwindled to one.

"Number nine was a huge blunder," Couples said afterward. "You should be able to hit it up top 100 times in a row from there. I laid it up just short of the hill while Mark is in the brush. He gets it up and down and I make bogey from there. You know, at that time I'm killing myself. If you can't get it up the hill from 105 yards, you shouldn't be out there. That just killed me."

Couples' analogy of getting it up top 100 times in a row would be true under normal circumstances, but with all the pressure of the Masters title on the line, anything could happen. The old adage that has become a part of Masters lore is that the tournament doesn't start until the back nine on Sunday. With nine holes to play, a dozen players remained within striking distance, and Couples, who was trying to become only the fifth player ever to lead after all four rounds, began to feel a little shaky on the back nine. "I feel like I lost a little something out there," he said afterward.

That loss wasn't immediately evident as Couples made pars on the 10th, 11th and always-difficult 12th. But then on the dogleg-left 13th, a hole where Couples' length and natural draw should have worked to his advantage, things seemingly slipped away. Couples hit an enormous hook off the tee into an area television commentator Ken Venturi called "never, never land." His ball flew so far left that it ended up on a maintenance road no one expected would ever come into play.

"My thought process on the tee was that I had hit three perfect drives (on 13), but there was a little bit of wind ... just enough to play with you," Couples said. "I tried to hit it a little harder and over-lobbed it. It hit a branch and went way left."

Couples wedged his errant ball over the trees and back into the fairway for what seemed like the miracle shot of the tournament.

Then, in another moment of indecision, Couples debated over whether to hit a six or seven iron into the green. For the second time in five holes he went with the longer club, and for the second time, he never fully committed. The ball flew right off the clubface, and Couples lowered his head in disgust as his ball bounced off the bank and splashed into Rae's Creek. Couples took a double-bogey seven. For the first time in four days, he had relinquished the lead.

Playing ahead of Couples and O'Meara, Duval was on a roll. After becoming one of the unlucky 13 to bogey the first hole (from the greenside bunker), Duval pitched to within eight feet and made the putt for birdie on the second hole. He then followed it up with a sand wedge to one foot for a tap-in birdie at the par-four seventh, and a nine-iron approach to within 18 inches for another birdie at the ninth to turn in 34. Duval continued his good play by pitching in from 40 feet for birdie at the 10th. On the 11th the consistently long-driving Duval hit a booming tee shot to within sand-wedge range of the green on the 455-yard par-four. Although his approach ended up 12 feet away, Duval calmly stroked the putt right into the hole for his third consecutive birdie, and his fourth in five holes. After a solid par at the 12th, Duval easily reached the par-five 13th in two shots and two-putted for birdie from the left side of the green. When he also reached the 500-yard par-five 15th in two shots with a solid three iron, then two-putted for yet another birdie, Duval had come from three shots back at the start of the day to snatch the lead away from Couples.

Also in pursuit was Furyk, who, until hitting the ball over the 15th green, stood a good chance at capturing his first green jacket. Furyk opened the tournament with an unimpressive 76, but rallied on Friday and Saturday with rounds of 70 and 67 to enter the final day three under par and three shots off of Couples' lead. He would pull to within one on the second nine, but when birdie efforts slid by on the 17th and 18th holes, Furyk fell to his knees in anguish. His final-round 68 was good enough for sole possession of fourth place at 281, but two strokes short of his ultimate goal of winning a major title.

O'Meara crept even with Couples after the 13th, but, after Duval birdied the par-five 15th, both men were three shots out of the lead. Although O'Meara birdied the 15th as well, he gained no ground on Duval and lost ground to Couples, whose second shot almost went in the hole and stopped only inches away. The tap-in eagle put Couples one ahead of O'Meara. Then Duval three-putted from 40 feet for bogey on the 16th, and he and Couples were tied.

Both Couples and O'Meara parred the difficult par-three 16th, while Duval missed a 17-foot birdie opportunity on the 17th that would have given him the lead alone. While Duval was in the process of missing another birdie putt of 22 feet on the 18th, Couples was missing a 10-foot birdie chance on the 17th.

That's when O'Meara took over. Having needed only 25 putts so far in the round, a calm, collected O'Meara hit his approach shot to within six feet on the 17th. As he was walking up the sloping fairway toward the 17th green, O'Meara gazed out at the lengthening shadows and gathering crowds as the sun began its slow descent behind the pines. "This is what it's all about," O'Meara said to his caddie, Jerry Higgenbotham. Higgenbotham nodded, and O'Meara rammed in the birdie putt on the 17th to gain a share of the lead with Couples and Duval.

On the 18th, O'Meara drove the ball perfectly, but Couples pulled his tee shot into the steep, left fairway bunker. From where Couples stood he couldn't see the flag, nor did he have much of a chance to get the ball close. His shot flew right, and landed in the greenside bunker. O'Meara hit his approach shot onto the green, pin high, 20 feet to the right. Couples blasted out of the bunker to within four feet, and everyone assumed that a two- or three-way playoff was inevitable. But Venturi, whom Arnold Palmer defeated in 1960 by birdieing the final two holes, said, "I think he's going to make this," as O'Meara stepped up to his putt.

"I was a little nervous," O'Meara said. "I wanted to make it so there wouldn't be a playoff. I squeaked it in there the way I wanted, just hoping it would go in. And it did."

When it did, the crowd erupted, but O'Meara, ever the gentleman, called for quiet as a visibly disappointed Couples made his four-footer to finish tied for second with Duval. O'Meara then embraced his wife and kids, and wished them a happy Easter. Later, he donned his green jacket after removing the yoke labeled "Best Player Never To Have Won A Major."

O'Meara's closing 67 gave him a 269 total, while Couples and Duval tied at 280, with Couples shooting 70 and Duval, 67. Furyk was fourth at 281, one stroke ahead of Azinger and two in front of Nicklaus and Toms. Woods tied for eighth place, six strokes behind, along with Clarke, Leonard and Montgomerie.

"Mark played great down the stretch. He did what he had to do to win and I congratulate him," Duval said. "This completes his legacy as a true champion. On 18 I had a chance to win the golf tournament, and that's all you can ask for. It didn't surprise me (when O'Meara made the birdie putt at 18). I've played enough with Mark to know what he can do. He was my partner in the Presidents Cup, and that's just how he putts. He's the best putter out here, and he makes an awful lot of them."

As far as O'Meara was concerned, his legacy would have been complete with or without a Masters title, but at least, as he says, he doesn't have to answer "those" questions any more.

"I think that this is something any young individual growing up wants," O'Meara said. "If they love competition, and if they're going to put any major on top of their list, they would have to put Augusta National on the top. The history and drama over the years has set this tournament apart. I made some great putts out there, and around this golf course I think that's a necessity. You have to putt well to win this championship; and, fortunately for me, that's what I did. Obviously, this is a great day for Mark O'Meara and my family."

4. U.S. Open Championship

Before the first tee shot was struck in the 98th United States Open Championship at The Olympic Club in San Francisco, some were predicting another upset by the bay, recalling past championships played at this scenic venue. Jim Murray, the *Los Angeles Times* columnist who died later in the year, said, "I'm convinced the Open will be won by Mark Wiebe or Glen Day." When told Wiebe had failed to qualify and wouldn't be playing, Murray responded, "It doesn't matter. He'll win it anyway. Or maybe Kevin Sutherland will win. It will be anybody but the favorites. The Olympic Club doesn't allow those people to win. The Open at Olympic is always barnacled with unknowns."

Murray might not have been a great prognosticator, but, as a golf historian, he had cause to predict victory by an obscure upstart — any obscure upstart. After all, The Olympic Club had hosted the Open three times in the past, and on each of those occasions an unheralded player rose to defeat one of the favorites.

In 1955 Ben Hogan, the greatest golfer of his day, was supposed to win at Olympic. Hogan felt so confident he had won after shooting 287 for the week that he accepted congratulations from Gene Sarazen, Tommy Bolt and others in the locker room before putting his golf clubs in the trunk of his car. In the background Hogan heard that Jack Fleck had made a birdie on the 71st hole and needed another on the 72nd to tie. Then, moments later, Hogan heard that Fleck had reached the 18th in two. "I wish he would make either a two or a four," Hogan said. Fleck did neither. He made a three to tie, and won the 18-hole playoff the following day in one of the biggest upsets in Open history.

That upset paled by comparison to 1966, however, when Arnold Palmer carried a seven-stroke lead into the final nine holes. Palmer's closest competitor, Billy Casper, was no Glen Day, but he was no Arnold Palmer either. He was cautious, conservative and constantly battling the bulge around his midsection. Everyone expected Arnie to win, so when it didn't happen, the 1966 Open became the one that Palmer gave away instead of the one that Casper won. Even Casper knew it. As they walked off the final green of the Monday playoff, Casper put his arm around Palmer and said, "I'm sorry Arnold." Palmer graciously accepted Casper's words, and congratulated him on his win, but the effects of that Open were monumental. Palmer never won another major title, while Casper went on to win the 1970 Masters. History would record that it was at The Olympic Club where Palmer's glory days ended.

Then, in 1987, Scott Simpson won instead of third-round leader and crowd favorite Tom Watson. While Simpson's victory lacked the miraculous stature of Fleck's win over Hogan or the heartbreak of Palmer's collapse to Casper, the Lake Course at The Olympic Club remained three-for-three in victimizing golf's idols while forging heroes from the depths of an Open field. According to Olympic Club golf professional Jim Lucius, "The guys who won the Open here almost had to apologize because of who finished second."

So, with history as his barometer, Murray predicted that it wouldn't be Tiger Woods or Colin Montgomerie or Ernie Els or Davis Love III or even reigning Masters champion Mark O'Meara who would walk away from The Olympic Club with the most coveted title in American golf. But, it wouldn't be Glen Day (although Day would finish in a respectable tie for 23rd, ahead of Els, Love, O'Meara and Justin Leonard), Kevin Sutherland, Mark Carnevale or Mark Wiebe either. The victor, in one of the greatest comebacks in history, was 1993 U.S. Open champion Lee Janzen, who made up seven strokes in the final 15 holes and shot 68 for an even-par 280 total to defeat Payne Stewart by one.

With his win, Janzen became only the 18th player to win the U.S. Open a second time, and his comeback was the largest since Johnny Miller made up six strokes to win in 1973. While his 280 total didn't set any scoring records, Janzen led the tournament in consistency by hitting 40 fairways and 50 greens in regulation, and his gritty performance down the stretch, coming back by patiently taking on the rough, the trees, the hard greens and the history of Opens past, gave Lee McLeod Janzen, father of Conner, the greatest Father's Day present any dad could ever receive.

"I'm extremely lucky to have the opportunity to play golf for a living," Janzen said. "To play as good as I played this week and to win the trophy that I wanted to win more than any other trophy, for the second time, was just — it's too much. To win the U.S. Open twice, you can't do anything better than that as far as I'm concerned."

He didn't know he had won when he finished. He assumed until the last moment that he would be headed for a Monday playoff with Stewart. When Stewart's birdie putt on the 72nd slid just below the hole, the emotions of a second U.S. Open victory overwhelmed Janzen. He tearfully embraced his wife Beverly before going to the 18th green to accept the trophy.

It was a fitting end to a week filled with Open drama, and tenacious Janzen was a fitting champion for Olympic.

The Open started as it normally did, with many of golf's greatest players embarrassed by 18-inch-high rough and hard, dry, fast greens that seemed to reject even the soundest of putting strokes. Watson, no stranger to Open conditions said, "This rough is the most difficult rough that I have seen in a U.S. Open, ever. Around the greens is the worst. Even though it isn't as long as it was at Oakmont in 1982, it is clingy rough. You just don't know what the ball is going to do when you hit a shot out of it around the green."

Tom Lehman said, "You just don't want to hit it in the rough, period. But it is difficult because of the slope in the fairways. It is hard to keep the ball from running into the rough, so I don't care who you are, you're going to be playing out of the rough at some point in time throughout the week. When it happens, you just have to swallow the pill, knock it back in the fairway, and try to make a four or a five the hard way."

In the opening round, Woods had little trouble finding the narrow fairways or the small greens — much to the surprise of critics who predicted Tiger's demise on the narrow, penal Olympic course — but the young champion required 32 putts in his opening-round 74 including two three putts and a shocking four putt on the ninth green. "I left a lot of shots out there today," Woods said. "I only missed three fairways."

David Duval, another pre-tournament favorite said it was "tough" after opening with 75. As he was being escorted down a flight of stairs into an area of the clubhouse where players checked their scorecards, Duval jokingly asked, "Are they taking us down here to execute us?"

The USGA definitely had serious penalties in mind when they prepared the golf course. Trying to hit a 70-yard shot on the fourth hole, Frank Lickliter thrashed through the hay-thick primary rough and bent the shaft of his sand wedge. Fortunately, since the rough and not an ill-tempered display by Lickliter bent the club, he was able to have it reshafted during the round, and he went on to shoot a respectable 73.

Not everyone had trouble early, however. Several of Murray's "barnacled unknowns" showed up on the first-round leaderboard. Among them was 21-year-old Ted Oh, a former University of Nevada-Las Vegas player in his first full year as a professional. Although Oh made a name for himself when he qualified for the 1993 Open at Baltusrol at age 16, he failed to gain his PGA Tour card at the 1997 qualifying tournament and, before qualifying for a spot in the field at Olympic, he had struggled through some mediocre performances in various Florida mini-tours.

For a while in San Francisco, however, Oh was the man of the hour. With birdies at the first, fourth and eighth holes, Oh found himself temporarily atop the leaderboard with a first-nine 32. The treacherous second nine, and the realization that he was leading the U.S. Open, jumped out in front of Oh. He made an early double bogey on the 11th, a bogey on the 12th and then another bogey on the 609-yard par-five 16th. Another double bogey on the 17th and a bogey on the 18th pushed Oh to 42 on the second nine.

"I was playing my game, attacking every hole, being aggressive, then all of a sudden, I switched to a different strategy," Oh said. "Instead of trying to make birdies, I started trying not to make bogeys. I guess it's experience. I just need more." Oh's opening 74 tied him with Woods, Jim Furyk, Darren Clarke and Casey Martin, who received more attention for the golf cart he rode than for the scores he shot.

Martin, who won a court battle to ride in PGA Tour events because of a crippling disability, got a special exemption from the USGA to ride a golf cart in the Open. Martin had troubles with the second nine, bogeying the 17th and 18th for his 74.

While a bogey on the 347-yard 18th was considered a serious mistake in the opening round, a bogey at the 17th was considered by many to be a good score. The 468-yard uphill par-four is normally played as a par-five for the Olympic members, but the USGA transformed it into a par-four for the championship. The hole proved to be one of the toughest of the week, with the field averaging 4.718 strokes compared to 4.741 strokes on the 533-yard par-five second.

According to Nick Price, "If that hole is 468 yards, I want to buy some real estate from the USGA." A disgruntled Jack Nicklaus said, "The 17th is just a way to get from the 16th green to the 18th tee." Only 61.5 percent of the tee shots found the 17th fairway, and even fewer found the green in two. O'Meara, who managed to make par on the 17th during his even-par 70, said, "Seventeen is a par-five. The USGA might put four on the card, but it's designed as a par-five, and it plays like a par-five." The hole played tough even by par-five standards. On Thursday, there were only five birdies,

60 pars, 70 bogeys, 18 double bogeys and two "others," or scores higher than bogeys.

One of those birdies came from Stewart, who, for the fifth time in the last nine years found himself atop the leaderboard after the first round of the U.S. Open. Stewart got off to a fast start when he hit three wood to the left side of the green on the 533-yard par-five first hole, then chipped to 15 feet, and made the putt for birdie. He gave the stroke back, however, when an errant four-iron approach to the fourth green left Stewart with little chance. He was able to chip his ball to within 11 feet, but missed the par putt. On the 457-yard par-four fifth hole, Stewart caught the first of what he would call "several good breaks" when his tee shot flew through the fairway and into the rough. His lie was such that he could advance the ball, but he pushed his approach into Watson's "clingy" greenside rough. Fortunately, Stewart caught another good lie and was able to get up-and-down for what he termed, "the best save of the day."

Pumped up from the save at the fifth, Stewart hit a sand-wedge shot to the par-four seventh that almost went in the hole for eagle. The ball stopped three inches from the cup, and he tapped in for another birdie. After the seventh, Stewart settled into a rhythm of hitting fairways, greens, and two-putting for pars. That trend continued until the par-five 16th where he hit a nine-iron approach shot to within eight inches of the hole, and tapped in for his third birdie of the day. He went on to birdie the 17th and the 18th to shoot an impressive four-under-par 66, good enough to lead Mark Carnevale by one stroke.

"I'm hitting the ball the way I want to and it feels good to have my game in that kind of shape coming into the Open," Stewart said. "You know what to expect before you get here. You know the rough is going to be penal. The greens are going to be hard and fast. You know coming in here that par is going to be a great score." When asked what he thought about his 66 if par was a great score, Stewart said, "It's really, really, really good. I enjoyed it."

Not surprisingly, Stewart pointed to his birdie at the 17th as the best of the day. Uphill, with a fairway that tended to kick balls down and to the right all week, the 17th realistically played over 500 yards with a green designed to accept short-iron third shots, not 200-plus-yard approaches. Stewart said of the hole, "I approach this golf course as a par 71 because I really feel that is a par-five hole. When you're standing back there and hit a great drive, as I did yesterday in a practice round, and you've got three wood to the green, it is a par-five. So today I made an eagle. It was a birdie on the scorecard, but in my mind it was an eagle. My drive was in the short right-hand rough, and I said to my caddie, 'Let's just try to chase a two iron up the gap. If it gets up there, fine. If it doesn't, we'll try to get it up-and-down.' So I chased a two iron up there and made a 45-foot birdie putt. Then I hit the worst shot of the day on the 18th tee. I almost shanked a two iron into the right rough, but I was fortunate to catch a lie where I didn't have to chip out. I was able to hit it onto the green about 12 feet. The putt was very, very quick, but I just bled it down there and it went in. Viola! 66!"

That kept Stewart alone atop the leaderboard despite an impressive three-under-par 67 by the 38-year-old Carnevale. The epitome of a "barnacled unknown," Carnevale worked as a stockbroker and a bartender while playing state opens and mini-tour events, trying to break through as a professional golfer. He finally qualified for the PGA Tour in 1992, and with a victory at the Chattanooga Classic, earned Rookie of the Year honors that year.

Unfortunately, Carnevale quickly found himself back on the Nike Tour where he finished second on the money list in 1997 to make his return to the PGA Tour. He earned a place in the Open after going through local and regional qualifying. Carnevale made birdie on the 17th in the opening round. Afterward he said, "You work so hard to get to this point, and all of a sudden you notice that this is it. This is where all the attention of the golf world is. All of a sudden you realize I'm here."

Another player who came to that realization after playing his way into contention was 34-year-old Joe Durant, who as recently as 1992 found himself working in a discount off-course golf shop in Ft. Walton Beach, Florida. His career took a turn when he won the Nike Mississippi Gulf Coast Classic in 1996, and earned a spot on the PGA Tour for 1997. Durant retained his playing privileges with three top-10 finishes in 1997, but his opening 68 in his first U.S. Open was the highlight of his career to that point.

"Everyone dreams of winning a U.S. Open," Durant said. "I can't think that far ahead. I couldn't even begin to describe it."

There were a few players on the leaderboard who had been there before and who could describe it. Lehman, who finished second to Els in the 1996 Open at Congressional, also started with 68. Lehman put it into perspective when he said, "It's only the first round. This is a very, very hard golf course. Of the last four Opens where I've played well I think this may be the most difficult course. I am not saying that I can't play well here, obviously, but it means that this course requires my best golf."

Those sentiments were echoed by Jose Maria Olazabal, who along with Bob Tway, tied Lehman and Durant with opening 68s. "This golf course is very difficult and we are going to find ourselves in a very difficult situation sometimes," Olazabal said. The only blemish on Olazabal's three-birdie scorecard came at the 17th, where he missed the green with a three iron, chipped to within six feet, and missed the putt.

Jesper Parnevik finished in red figures with three birdies and two bogeys in a one-under-par performance. That left Parnevik tied with John Daly and Jeff Maggert as the last players under par after the first day.

Six players congregated at even par after the opening round. Among them was Masters champion O'Meara and perennial U.S. Open favorite Montgomerie who came over from Britain two weeks early to prepare for Olympic. After his round Montgomerie said, "I'm very happy with level par. I couldn't see them putting the pins in some of those positions. It's scary. That's why the scores are so high. It's incredible the way the USGA can limit scoring. There was not one pin that was a gift. From the first hole on, it was very difficult."

Andrew Magee, Tom Kite and David Ogrin also shot opening-round 70s. But the biggest surprise of the opening round came from U.S. Amateur champion Matt Kuchar, who ignited galleries with an impressive even-par performance.

Janzen bogeyed the ninth, 12th and 17th holes en route to a 73, which tied him with Nicklaus, Lickliter, Vijay Singh, Olin Browne, Stewart Cink, Brad Faxon, John Huston and, ironically, Glen Day at three over par.

When the sun finally set behind the mangled cypress trees that O.B. Keeler once described as looking like "they had been designed by a man who had gotten drunk on gin and tried to sober up on absinthe," the leaderboard at Olympic looked like this:

Payne Stewart	66	Jeff Maggert	69
Mark Carnevale	67	Andrew Magee	70
Tom Lehman	68	Colin Montgomerie	70
Joe Durant	68	Tom Kite	70
Jose Maria Olazabal	68	David Ogrin	70
Bob Tway	68	Mark O'Meara	70
Jesper Parnevik	69	*Matt Kuchar	70
John Daly	69		

The second round began with a number of notable players on the bubble, and it ended with the USGA having to defend itself for turning the 18th green into a putt-putt hole. Exactly 60 players shot 147 or better, giving the Open the smallest post-cut field in 21 years. Among those who didn't fall into that low 60 were Nick Faldo, who blamed his putting for his 77 and 72 scores; Love (78-75), who entered the week with back problems and never felt comfortable with his swing; Oh (74-81), who played the first nine holes in three under par and the last 27 holes in 18 over par, and Watson, who finished second at Olympic in 1987, but hit only 14 of 36 greens in his 73-75 effort.

While Love had no chance to make the cut, his experience on the 18th green set the tone for what would become an admonishment of the USGA's idea of a test of championship golf. Left with a downhill four-footer, Love tapped his putt then watched as it came to a stop less than an inch from the hole, then started rolling again, gaining speed as it headed down to the front of the green. As Love stared at the ball, a member of the gallery, who had been watching similar putts do similar things all day, shouted, "It's not fair Davis."

That sentiment was mild compared to what some had to say about the back-left pin placement the USGA chose. Throughout the day, balls rolled up the hill to the hole, stopped, then retreated back down the hill. The only thing missing was a dragon and a windmill. "The decision (to use the back-left pin location) didn't turn out the way we had hoped," said USGA executive director, David Fay. "You can't even get a Stimpmeter reading on that green."

The reason the USGA chose a back placement was the fear that a front placement all four days would leave the green too worn for Sunday's final round. "We certainly didn't want to use that (back) location on Sunday," said USGA director of competitions Tom Meeks, who was the man responsible for selecting the hole placement. "If a player has an eight-foot putt to win the U.S. Open, he ought to have a fair chance to make it. I just hope no one thinks that hole was picked intentionally to see those balls do that. I was embarrassed. I thought it might work because of some different preparation we made, but the bottom line was, it didn't."

Daly, who parred the hole, let the USGA have it, saying, "Thank God our tour doesn't do that. It was absolutely stupid. We work too hard out there, and people watching on TV have got to think, 'These guys are idiots.'"

Kirk Triplett, who was on his way to missing the cut with rounds of 73 and 79, caused a stir on the 18th when, after his ball rolled up to the hole and started back down, he incurred a two-shot penalty when he stopped the ball with his putter. "I think he was trying to make a statement," Fay said. "That was a little frustration showing."

By Sunday, many of the players and most of the spectators had put aside thoughts of the Friday hole location, but in hindsight, when searching for shots that could have turned the tournament in another direction, the 18th green during the second round stood as a glaring example. Stewart, who capped his three-birdie finish on Thursday with a three-birdie start on Friday before making bogey at the fourth and sixth, another birdie at the seventh, and bogeys on the 14th and 17th, hit a great wedge shot inside 10 feet on the last hole. He almost made the first putt, leaving the ball inches from the hole. Then the ball picked up speed and Stewart was left with a 25-foot second putt. He missed, three-putted, and made bogey. Instead of an even-par 70, Stewart had to settle for 71. His lead was whittled to one stroke over Maggert and Tway.

"Whenever you start seeing balls roll up to the hole and then roll back away from the hole, that borders on ridiculous," Stewart said. "I don't think I was the only player who spoke to my USGA walking marshal or official about that pin today."

Lehman, who would also be looking for a few extra shots at the end of Sunday, "blew a gasket" in front of a USGA official. The normally reserved Lehman took double bogey on the 18th, and while he later apologized for his outburst, the last hole on Friday would definitely come back to haunt him.

Despite his play on the 18th, Stewart felt good about his lead. "I would be more pleased if my scores were 71-66 (instead of 66-71) because then I wouldn't have that ill taste in my mouth from the 18th," Stewart said. Then, in a passing statement, Stewart looked up at the scoreboard and said, "Lee (Janzen) is playing pretty good. There are some good scores out there."

Another of those good scores was the 69 by Kuchar. The young amateur started slowly, with routine pars on the first six holes before hitting a sand wedge to three feet on the seventh and making the putt for birdie. He then hit an eight iron to within eight feet on the par-three eighth hole and made that putt for another birdie. With the crowd firmly behind him, Kuchar parred the 10th and 11th holes before thrilling the gallery with another birdie from 20 feet at the par-four 12th. At that point, Kuchar was not only playing well, he was making a serious run at the lead. Then at the 422-yard par-four 14th, Kuchar had what he termed, "a disaster. I was debating between a seven-iron and a six-iron approach and I hit the seven iron. It was the wrong club and I came up short in the bunker. It was a fairly easy bunker shot, but I was a little uncomfortable and tried to get too cute with it. I left it in the rough, and it's tough getting up-and-down out of this rough. So, I made double bogey."

Kuchar came right back, though. After missing the green at the par-three 15th, he chipped in for another birdie from 30 feet. "It looked like the wheels were coming off when I missed the green at 15," he said. "Then the chip went in and, all of a sudden, the momentum came right back." When asked how he felt to be close to the lead after two rounds of the national championship, Kuchar said, "I'm just trying to take it one shot at a time. I'm having a lot of fun."

Also having a lot of fun was Janzen, who followed his opening 73 with a second-day low score of 66, leaving him tied at one under par with Kuchar and Lee Porter who followed his 72 with a second-round 67. Janzen started the day off with a two-putt birdie on the first hole, then hit a five iron to within three inches on the par-three third. "I almost had an expensive bar tab there," he said of the near-ace. After a three-putt bogey at the par-four sixth, Janzen birdied the eighth, ninth and 11th holes with putts of 15, 35 and eight feet respectively. A 30-foot birdie putt at the 15th followed by a 12-foot birdie at the 16th put Janzen at six under par for the day, three under for the tournament, and in a tie for the lead with Stewart. Then at the 17th, Janzen pushed his second shot into a tree and, after leaving his third shot short, walked away with a double bogey. Still, while he trailed Stewart by two, Janzen had hit four more fairways and one more green in regulation than the leader. His 26 out of 36 greens in regulation was second only to Price who hit 28 greens but took 65 putts to finish.

"I figured that no matter who wins the U.S. Open this week, someone's going to shoot one, two or three over par during one round," Janzen said. When asked about the fairness of the pin placements, particularly on the 18th, Janzen said, "I come to the U.S. Open expecting nothing to be fair. I expect that if you hit it in the rough you can't hit it out. Put it above the hole, you can't two-putt. If you hit it in a bunker, you don't have a shot. If you don't hit good shots, you don't make the cut. So it becomes a test of wills. We come here to find out who overcomes adversity the best and who has the most patience."

That attitude would serve him well as the weekend approached. At the end of two rounds, the leaderboard looked like this:

Payne Stewart	71 - 137	Mark Carnevale	73 - 140
Jeff Maggert	69 - 138	Joe Durant	73 - 141
Bob Tway	70 - 138	Nick Price	68 - 141
*Matt Kuchar	69 - 139	Brad Faxon	68 - 141
Lee Porter	67 - 139	Stewart Cink	68 - 141
Lee Janzen	66 - 139		

As if it hadn't shown its teeth during the first two days, Olympic bared fangs for the weekend. Hard, dry greens got harder and dryer, and fairways that provided a lot of roll in the first two days, became springboards on Saturday and Sunday. Anything remotely off line was destined for the deep rough from which bogey was a much coveted score. As it had been throughout the week, the 17th was the toughest hole, yielding one birdie and 19 pars for the day. Only 15 percent of the field hit the green in regulation, the lowest percentage of any hole since the USGA began keeping statistics in 1980, and, for the day, the field averaged 4.833 at the 17th, making it, by far, the hardest hole of the day.

Lehman, who, for the third year in a row, posted the low round on Saturday at the U.S. Open, made one of the 19 pars on the 17th. As a testament to how difficult the course played, Lehman's 68 was the highest score to be the best in a U.S. Open round in the 1990s. It was, Lehman said, "extremely difficult. The sun baked the fairways and the wind made them fast. The ball kept on rolling. It was difficult to keep the ball in the fairway, much more difficult than the other two days."

Lehman hit eight fairways on Saturday compared to the 11 he hit while shooting 68 on Thursday. He birdied the first three holes, then bogeyed the next three. Fortunately for Lehman, he only took 28 putts on Saturday, his lowest putting total of the week. "The greens were slower than I expected," Lehman said. "I knew that if I maintained my composure I could get back into the tournament. I really thought even par would be a good score."

Janzen certainly would have taken it. For the second straight day, Janzen double-bogeyed the 17th, only on Friday he was six under par when he came to the 17th tee, and on Saturday, he was one under. "I hit what I thought was a good three iron from 205 yards," Janzen said. "It landed in the middle of the green and rolled over. From there I left it in the semi-rough, then I chipped on and two-putted for double bogey." He finished with 73.

As easily as that, Janzen went from one under par to one over. "You can't fall asleep out there," he said. "A slight miscue, and you can end up with a shot you can't recover from. Six times today I hit good shots and the ball rolled out of the fairway. Three times it cost me a bogey, and on the 17th I hit all good shots and made double bogey. That's what it's like at the U.S. Open."

Although he managed three birdies in a one-over-par Saturday effort, Price agreed with Janzen's assessment. "Experience told me it was going to be a very difficult day," Price said. "I didn't really look at the scores on the computer before I went out, but basically the way the first four holes played, I knew that par was going to be an exceptionally good score today. This is the first time we saw the sun come out for five or six hours. There were a couple of fairways that were faster than some of the greens we putt on tour. It doesn't matter if you're teeing off with a one iron, a three wood or a driver, it's all the same. You're still threading a needle. Fortunately, with the exception of three or four holes where I drove the ball in the rough, I played very solidly today." Solidly enough, in fact, that Price found himself five shots off the lead and tied with Janzen going into the final round.

Not so fortunate, but still playing respectably under the circumstances, was Kuchar, who shot 76 on Saturday to enter the final round tied with Porter. "The winds were swirling, and it was just a tough day," Kuchar said. Still, the young Georgia Tech player remained the crowd favorite. "They're rooting for me," he said, "so, I'm doing the same. I think I learned that from Arnold Palmer. He'd give people a wink and they'd respond to him."

Despite the swirling winds and narrowing fairways, Daly chose Saturday as the first day of the week in which to bring the driver out of his car trunk. On the sixth hole Daly ripped a drive 368 yards. Then on the seventh, Daly drove the green from 288 yards. "People don't come out here to watch us hit two irons all day," Daly said. It might have pleased the crowds, but the driver did little for Daly's game. He shot his second straight 75 and entered the final day at nine over par, 12 strokes off the lead.

That lead continued to be held by Stewart. With an eagle at the first, a birdie on the eighth, bogeys on the third, ninth and 15th, and 12 pars, including one on the 17th, Stewart widened his lead to four strokes over Lehman and Tway with an even-par 70 for a 207 total. "There's no reason to think

I'm not going to come out and play good golf tomorrow," Stewart said. "If I come out and let the situation intimidate me, then that's my own fault."

With three rounds in the books, his prospects were good:

Payne Stewart	70 - 207	Jeff Maggert	75 - 213
Tom Lehman	68 - 211	Stewart Cink	73 - 214
Bob Tway	73 - 211	Mark Carnevale	74 - 214
Nick Price	71 - 212	Jim Furyk	68 - 215
Lee Janzen	73 - 212	Lee Porter	76 - 215
Steve Stricker	69 - 213	*Matt Kuchar	76 - 215

The victims came early and often in the final round. Els, who battled an ailing back all week, also had trouble with the greens. With a closing 76, Els finished tied for 48th out of 60 players who made the cut. "It was amateur stuff, the type of play you would expect of a five-handicapper," Els said.

Equally disenchanted were Leonard, whose 71-75-77-71 performance left him tied for 40th; Woods, who finished 10 over par and tied for 18th, and Duval, who, after closing with 69 to finish seven over par and tied for seventh place, said, "The course was hard yesterday, hard the day before that, hard the first day, and hard today."

Kuchar found the conditions hard as well, but he said he "couldn't think of a better place to spend my birthday." In fact, before teeing off, the gallery serenaded the new 20-year-old with an off-key rendition of "Happy Birthday to You." That didn't seem to help Kuchar's play, however. After birdieing the first hole, Kuchar bogeyed the third, fourth, fifth, 13th and 16th to finish four over par on the day, and nine over for the championship.

But it was hard for Kuchar to find anything bleak about his U.S. Open experience. "This has been the most memorable birthday I've ever had," Kuchar said. "Everything has been great. It's an honor to play in the national championship. It's an honor to play with Ernie (Els) and Justin (Leonard) and those guys. My focus and concentration goes up when I play with them. The greatest thing, though, is that after my finish I'm coming back (to the 1999 U.S. Open at Pinehurst) as a fully exempt player. That's fantastic."

Another who found the conditions difficult was Montgomerie, who historically had played well in his U.S. Open appearances. He had to shoot 69 on the final day to finish at 10 over par. "I found out what I was doing wrong on the practice ground this morning, which was a bit late unfortunately," Montgomerie said. "My alignment was wrong, and I struggled from day two onward."

Montgomerie also struggled with the behavior of a few hecklers. They cheered his missed fairways and poor putts, with one beer-clutching fan calling Monty a "prima donna," and another admonishing Europe's No. 1 player to "shut up and play." Montgomerie responded politely, saying, "It's all to do with the Ryder Cup, you see.

"I seem to be blamed for winning the Ryder Cup, but I had 11 very strong individuals with me as well. It doesn't take an individual to win a Ryder Cup, but I seem to be the cause right now. It's always the minority who are more vocal than the majority, unfortunately. I've always enjoyed this tournament and I always will. It's a mental battle. You get rewarded for good shots and you definitely get penalized for bad ones. I'm a great fan of that and always will be."

As those words were being spoken, one man who is also a fan of that kind of test was discovering that he had a chance to win another U.S. Open, while another was slowly seeing his future slip away.

After bogeying the second and third holes, Janzen was seven strokes down with 15 holes to play, then a very lucky break got Janzen's juices flowing. After pushing his four-wood tee shot on the fifth hole, Janzen found his ball stuck in a tree, a fate that had befallen Tommy Nakajima in 1987 at Olympic. Nakajima had put things into perspective by saying, "That's golf." Janzen was thinking the same thing as, while walking back to the tee, he was informed that a gust of wind had dislodged the ball and it had fallen out of the tree. A rejuvenated Janzen punched the ball back into play, then hit a six-iron shot to the back fringe, from where he chipped in for par. "I went from being lucky to make double bogey to walking away from that hole with a par," Janzen said. "I didn't count myself out after that."

According to Steve Stricker, who was playing with Janzen, "You could tell he was on a mission all of a sudden. He started striding down the fairways with purpose."

He strode to one more birdie at the seventh hole and an even-par 35 on the first nine. After hitting driver, six iron to within eight feet and making another birdie at the 11th, Janzen began to be noticed by the one person that mattered: Stewart, the leader. "The first time I noticed him was when I went to the 10th green and saw that he was one under par for the day through 11," Stewart said. "At that stage, you could kind of feel who was playing good and who wasn't."

Stewart was in the latter category. "It was the worst ball-striking day of the week for me," he said. Stewart made bogeys on the fifth and seventh holes and turned at two over par for the day, one under for the tournament. Lehman and Tway, Stewart's closest challengers at four strokes back when the day began, had also played the first nine in two over par. Stewart looked to the scoreboards to see who might be closing the gap. Price, who entered the day five strokes back, shot one over par on the first nine and was tied with Lehman and Tway. Anything could happen.

Anything did on the par-four 12th hole. Stewart split the middle of the fairway with an iron, but found his ball in a sand-filled divot. From there he pushed his second shot into the greenside bunker from which he did not save par. "I felt it was ground under repair," Stewart said of the divot, but the USGA disagreed. Not only that, but USGA official Tom Meeks informed Stewart at the 12th green that the group was being timed for slow play, and that he needed to improve the pace. "It wasn't the best time for that," Stewart said.

At the same time Stewart was making bogey on the 12th, Janzen was hitting a five iron to within five feet and making the putt for birdie on the 13th. For the first time since Thursday morning, Stewart had relinquished the lead. Stewart and Janzen were tied, then Stewart bogeyed the 13th to fall behind.

From the 14th through the 18th, Janzen and Stewart played a nip-and-tuck game of who would make the fewest mistakes. Janzen got the upper hand when he parred in for an impressive 68 and 280 total, but Stewart added another birdie at the 14th to draw even, hitting a three wood and a nine iron to within 15 feet and making the putt. On the par-five 16th, however, Stewart missed the fairway and took a devastating bogey. "I got a little quick with a seven iron and came up in the bunker," Stewart said of the 16th. "From there I didn't get up and down."

A par on the 17th left Stewart with a last chance to match his 1991 performance and join Nicklaus as the only players to lead two U.S. Opens wire-to-wire. His drive on the 18th found the fairway, but his wedge shot flew off-line to the right, and Stewart was left with a right-to-left breaking 20-footer to tie Janzen and force a Monday playoff. As the putt rolled toward the hole, Janzen, watching on television from the clubhouse, said, "He's made it." But the putt lost speed and slid below the hole and an emotional Janzen had his second U.S. Open title. Stewart finished one stroke behind with 74 for a 281 total.

"I guess it didn't really dawn on me that I could actually win the golf tournament until that moment. I really thought that the best I could do was a playoff," Janzen said. "There have been times I've said to myself, 'You're not that good. You were lucky.' But to win the U.S. Open twice, I know I've put myself in a special place."

Stewart, who also finished second when Janzen won in 1993, said, "Hey, I was beaten by a great round of golf. Congratulations to Lee. You've got to give him all the credit. He was in the third-to-the-last group and went out and shot 68. There was nobody in contention in the golf tournament that shot under par except for Lee Janzen, so he deserves to be the champion today. I hit six fairways in regulation today, and Lee hit 12. I hit nine greens in regulation, and Lee hit 14. Bingo. That's why he won the golf tournament, and I didn't. But I also think The Olympic Club won. There was one person who shot even par for the tournament. This golf course stood up to the test of an Open Championship."

He wasn't in contention, but Paul Azinger had the best round of the day, finding eight birdies in the brutal conditions to shoot 65 and elevate himself into a tie for 14th with Furyk, Kuchar and Parnevik. Jeff Sluman also edged under par for the day, equaling Janzen's two-under-par performance. Sluman finished tied for 10th with Cink, Mickelson and Stuart Appleby. With 10 straight pars coming in, Duval also nipped par by one shot, finishing tied for seventh with Maggert and Lee Westwood. "It felt good to be under par today," Duval said, "but I'm still trying to grasp it and learn so that I'll know how to approach the Open next year."

Tway, who finished third with a final-round 73 for a 284 total, said, "It was more of a struggle than the other days. If I'd gotten off to a good start and been in the golf tournament, I might have been more disappointed than I am, but I was just trying to hang on today."

Lehman shot a final-round 75 to finish tied for fifth at 286 with Stricker, who shot a final-round 73. But it was Nick Price, who also hung on to shoot a final-round 73 and finish alone in fourth at 285, who gave the day's most prophetic comment. "I kept hitting some good shots and I had some opportunities, but as we were playing No. 11, I turned to my caddie Jimmy and said, 'Even par is going to be the number.'"

Price was exactly right. Lee Janzen, The Olympic Club and even par won the 1998 U.S. Open.

5. British Open Championship

Late in the year, Curtis Strange remarked that if Mark O'Meara had never won any of the four major championships, he would still think of him as a wonderful golfer. Strange was right, O'Meara was indeed a marvelous ball-striker and steady player. But that wasn't the point. The world looks not for wonderful golfers, it looks for champion golfers, those who raise their games to higher levels when they compete for major titles.

Strange's comment followed O'Meara's extraordinary season. After years of winning week-to-week tournaments, O'Meara abruptly blossomed into one of the game's dangerous players, one who played his best when it mattered most. In April he won the Masters Tournament with a blazing finish, and in July he won the British Open at rugged Royal Birkdale. He was the fourth consecutive American winner of the British title.

In weather that was often foul, O'Meara shot 72-68-72-68–280, even par, tied Brian Watts, another American, and won a four-hole playoff determined on total score, 17 to 19. If there were such a title, certainly O'Meara would have become the champion golfer of 1998.

His was a dramatic turnaround. Through a career in the four major championships that began in 1980, when he was still an amateur, through 1997, Mark had never been at his best on the big occasions. He had played in 57 of the game's four most significant tournaments and hadn't won one. Nor had he so much as challenged the leaders more than a time or two, most recently in the 1991 British Open, also at Birkdale. Tied with Ian Baker-Finch after 54 holes, O'Meara closed with 69 and placed third, three strokes behind Baker-Finch, who had 66.

He had placed third at Sandwich in 1985, the year of his first British Open, by shooting 72 in the last round. He might have won with 69. Sandy Lyle, who did win, beat him by two strokes in the closing round, and Payne Stewart, who took second, beat him by four.

O'Meara had played a series of indifferent final rounds. He had closed with scores in the 60s in only three of 13 British Opens, one of 16 U.S. Opens, two of 15 PGA Championships, and not one of 13 Masters Tournaments.

Suddenly, in 1998, O'Meara turned into a strong finisher. He closed with 67 and won the Masters, 69 in the U.S. Open, good for no better than a tie for 32nd place, and 68 at Royal Birkdale, winning the British Open.

Where he had played dull golf in the past, now he made critical birdies. In those three final rounds of 1998 he birdied 17 holes, averaging a fraction under six in each, and he shot five of those 12 rounds in the 60s.

He had won at Augusta by birdieing three of the last four holes, and he claimed the British Open with one birdie on the 17th and another on the first playoff hole, where he beat the surprising Watts, who had never contended for anything outside Asia and Japan. The third-round leader, Watts held on through the regulation 72 holes, but he missed makeable putts on the first two holes of the four-hole playoff and couldn't recover.

By winning both the Masters and British Open, O'Meara joined a select band of the game's elite. It had taken him a long time. At the age of 41, he was the oldest man to have won two major championships in the same year. Ben Hogan had been the oldest, winning the 1953 Masters and U.S. Open two months before his 41st birthday (he also won the British Open), and Jack Nicklaus the second oldest, winning the 1980 U.S. Open and PGA Championship eight months after turning 40.

O'Meara won the British Open at a course he obviously liked. He had played the last three rounds of the 1991 British Open in 68-67-69–204, and also at Birkdale had won the 1987 Lawrence Batley Invitational, a PGA European Tour event.

Royal Birkdale sits in the resort town of Southport, a few miles north of Liverpool, western England's main seaport. Bordering the Irish Sea, the west coast's wildly rolling, tumbling dunesland abounds with marvelous links courses. It is home to another British Open club — Royal Lytham and St. Annes, just a few miles north of Southport, where Tom Lehman won in 1996.

Set on more rugged ground, Birkdale is the more formidable of the two. Like slender ribbons, its fairways weave through valleys between high dunes covered with tawny rough that in places reaches to the knees, so unyielding the grass occasionally rips the club from a player's hands.

Laid out originally by George Low in 1897, Birkdale was rebuilt in 1931 by the architectural team of F.G. Hawtree and the great English golfer J.H. Taylor. It had been modified twice, most recently in time for the 1998 Open. It is a long course that had been played at 6,892 yards in 1971 and 6,940 yards in 1991. Keeping up with the increased distance modern players hit the ball, the club stretched it to 7,018 yards for 1998.

Although the added length may have strengthened it, Birkdale didn't need much help; it had always been a rigorous examination. As it was configured for the Open, it tested the golfers to the fullest. Four of its longest par-fours ranged from 450 to 498 yards, its two par-fives measured 544 and 547 yards, and its four par-threes reached from 177 to 203 yards. Only the fifth, at 344 yards, played shorter than 400 yards.

For most of the field, though, length wasn't the prime objective. The fairways were so narrow and the punishment for missing them so severe, the players often drove with irons to keep the ball in play. When they missed, they were often left with no option except a pitch back to playable ground.

The sixth measured 480 yards, well within range of second shots for players of this caliber, but it played into a prevailing wind to an elevated green set among high dunes covered in scrub growth. It was an intimidating hole that asked more than many players could give. In four rounds it yielded only 16 birdies, an average of four each day, but on Saturday it gave up none. This was the day the second shot was most commonly played with a driver.

As the championship approached, no one knew quite what to expect, except those who had played in previous Birkdale Opens felt sure that it would play differently from 1991. Every one of its greens had been rebuilt, some holes lengthened, and tees re-positioned on others.

When the early starters arrived the first morning they found the weather had changed considerably. Where it had been foul during practice days, it had turned warm and pleasant for the opening round. A bright sun warmed the air, and a faint breath of air ruffled the tall and wispy rough.

Birkdale seemed altogether harmless. Every green was in easy reach, and drives on the dreaded sixth left 180- to 200-yard seconds. Indeed, the course played so much gentler than anyone expected, 27 men shot in the 60s, 24 others matched par 70, and 88 of the 156 starters shot 72 or less. It would never play so easy again. Over the next three days Birkdale surrendered only 16 more sub-70 scores, although none on the Saturday of the third round, when the weather was at its worst.

The field took advantage the first day's reprieve, averaging 72.06 strokes. Both Tiger Woods and John Huston drove the average down by shooting 65s. Nick Price and Fred Couples, old British Open hands, shot 66s, along with Loren Roberts, who lost a playoff for the 1994 U.S. Open to Ernie Els. Five others shot 67, 10 more 68, and seven men shot 69. Davis Love III, the 1997 PGA champion, was among those at 67; Jesper Parnevik, the Swede who had come so close at Turnberry in 1994 and at Royal Troon in 1997, shot 68, the same score as Watts, the American who played most of his golf in Japan.

Meantime, a year after making up five strokes in the last round and snatching the title from Parnevik and Darren Clarke, Justin Leonard stumbled around in 73. So did Seve Ballesteros, John Daly, Jose Maria Olazabal, Tom Watson and Colin Montgomerie, whose British Open curse continued. A first-class golfer, Montgomerie had said a year ago that he always saved his worst golf for the Open.

For the first time in some years, Americans dominated the leaderboard, holding six of the first 10 places. The other four places were held by Price, Robert Allenby, Fredrik Jacobson and Vijay Singh. Except for Jacobson, a 23-year-old Swede playing his first British Open, and Allenby, the other eight played the PGA Tour.

The first round asserted once again that Woods is capable of shooting any score at all. There is little question he is the most dangerous player in the game, supremely confident and bold, although occasionally too impetuous.

By the time Woods teed off, at 9:55 a.m., Huston had been out for an hour and 20 minutes, running off a series of pars. Off to a ragged start at the first, where he holed from 25 feet to save his par four, he righted his game, parred the next eight holes, and turned for home in 34, even par.

Huston's 34 wasn't bad, but he would need something better coming in, because by then Woods stood two under par. Suddenly Huston's game caught fire. He birdied four holes on the homeward nine, bogeyed one, eagled another, came back in 31 and jumped to the top of the leaderboard.

His iron play had been inspiring. He rifled approaches to 10 feet on the 10th, to 12 feet on the 11th, dropped his tee shot within eight feet on the 12th, played a 217-yard seven iron from the rough to four feet on the 18th and birdied them all. Playing the 17th downwind, Huston reached the green with a three wood and six iron and holed from 40 feet for the eagle three, one of seven this hole surrendered that day.

After his introduction to Birkdale, Huston had speculated that 290 might win, but now he wondered.

He had good reason, because once Woods recovered from his stumbling start, he streaked out in 30, four under par, which delighted his huge gallery. He missed the first green but holed from eight feet for his par, then drove into an ugly lie in deep rough on the second.

"It was a terrible place," Woods said. "One of those lies that might mean you can move the ball only four feet."

Nothing, though, seemed beyond this young man. Now he played one of the unforgettable shots of the week. With his ball deep down in thick grass, Tiger lashed into the shot. The ball jumped out, soared over a bunker, and carried 120 yards to the green. Another par was saved.

Then he made his move. After driving with a five iron on the third, a 407-yard hole, Woods pitched to 10 feet, played a two iron and nine iron to 12 feet on the fifth and played a five iron to the back edge of the seventh, a par-three, and holed all three putts. After a routine par four on the eighth, Woods stepped onto the ninth tee, a 411-yard par-four with a fairway that bends left-to-right around a high dune that masks a hidden bunker. Tiger had gone for the green in his practice rounds but had promised not to try during the championship proper because of the risks. Now, though, with sun beaming down and the barest hint of a breeze, Woods went for it.

Without throwing everything he had into the shot, Woods cleared the dune easily. His ball carried to the spectators' crosswalk, which, mercifully, was empty, and ran within 20 yards of the green. The gallery roared; this is what they had come to see. With only a sand wedge left, Woods pitched to six feet and putted into the cup.

Out in four under par, he slacked off coming in, playing the second nine in 36, even par. He lost a stroke at the 12th but birdied the 13th, at 498 yards the longest of the par-fours, the 15th, a par-five playing into the wind, and the 17th, a downwind par-five. Six under now, a par on the 18th and he would shoot 64. After a glorious drive, Woods played an eight iron that skipped off the back of the green, and he bogeyed.

These were the first-round leaders:

John Huston	65	Fredrik Jacobson	67
Tiger Woods	65	Brad Faxon	67
Nick Price	66	Davis Love III	67
Fred Couples	66	Vijay Singh	67
Loren Roberts	66	Robert Allenby	67

When Huston had stepped off the final green early Thursday afternoon, he said he planned to do nothing more than enjoy the day because, he said, "Who knows what the weather will be like tomorrow?"

He found out soon enough. While Thursday had been a pleasant day, Friday began with rain and ended with powerful winds that tested not only patience but grit as well.

A light drizzle began about 7 o'clock, 15 minutes before the first group teed off, but by 7:30 rain poured heavily, slackened off for a while, then struck hard again at about 10:30. It finally eased off around noon, the clouds broke up, the sunshine poured through, and the wind swept in from the Irish Sea. It blew steadily at 25 miles an hour and gusted above 30.

Although water had begun collecting on the tees during the morning downpour, the Royal and Ancient Golf Club, organizers of the championship, had not even considered interrupting play, but with lightning reported close by and a late afternoon gale rising, Hugh Campbell, chairman of the R and A's Championship Committee, suspended the round.

Fierce winds swept across the open dunes at forces calculated at 50 miles an hour, buffeting the golfers, bending the flagsticks, and moving balls at rest on the greens. Campbell stopped the round at 5:27 and resumed play at 6:05, after the storm had passed.

The scoring reflected the punishing conditions. Where 27 men had broken 70 in the opening round, only seven shot in the 60s on Friday, and seven others matched par 70. Where the field had averaged 72.1 in the first round, it averaged 74.8 in the second round, nearly three strokes more.

Some of the scores were disheartening. After opening with 65, Huston shot 77 and Woods shot 73. Roberts went from 66 to 76, Couples from 66 to 74, and Price from 66 to 72. After opening with 67s, Love slipped to 73, Singh and Brad Faxon to 74, Allenby to 76, and Jacobson to 78.

Nevertheless, on a day made for avoiding risks, others gained ground. Watts shot 69 and moved into first place, at 137, three under par. O'Meara shot 68 and moved into a tie for sixth place, at 140, and recent U.S. Open champion Lee Janzen, Tom Kite, Scott Dunlap and Des Smyth moved up by shooting 69s.

While these men had shot exceptional scores under extraordinary conditions, all of them had been outplayed by Justin Rose, a 17-year-old English amateur. Rose shot 66, two strokes better than O'Meara, whose 68 was the best of the professionals. With his 138, Rose leaped into a tie for second with Woods and Price, just one stroke behind Watts.

Thomas Bjorn, from Sweden, followed his opening 68 with 71, yet still climbed from 11th place into a tie for fifth, at 139, followed by Love, O'Meara, Couples, Parnevik, Stephen Ames and Jim Furyk, all at 140, level par.

While it is always surprising for one as young as Rose to play such extraordinary golf in so important a championship, he had signaled he was no ordinary young golfer three years earlier. At 14 he had nearly qualified for the 1995 British Open, and in August of 1997, shortly after turning 17, he had become the youngest golfer ever to play in the Walker Cup.

Admittedly Rose played through the best of the weather. He teed off at 11:30, shortly before the clouds broke up and the wind reached its full strength. He seemed nervous at the start, three-putting the third from no more than six feet, but he recovered quickly with birdies on the fourth and fifth, and even though he bogeyed two of them, he played the remaining 13 holes in three under par.

Rose lost a stroke at the sixth, which was about par for that day, since the field averaged 4.79 strokes, but he wrung an extraordinary birdie from the ninth, where he holed a ridiculous putt of 50 or 60 feet.

Out in 33, Rose sailed through the next four holes in even par, then struck again on the 14th by drilling a three iron to 15 feet and holing. Two under par, he bunkered his approach to the 16th and missed from five feet.

With the wind at his back now, Rose put aside his driver on the 17th, threaded a three wood down the middle of the narrow fairway, and laid a sweet seven iron no more than 10 feet from the cup. He holed it for an eagle three, and birdied the 18th from 20 feet.

Four under par, his 66 had matched the lowest score an amateur had ever shot in the Open. Frank Stranahan, an American, had shot 66 in the last round at Troon in 1950, and Woods had matched it at Royal Lytham and St. Annes in 1996.

Watts had stuttered at the start as well. Teeing off in the rain at 8:25, he bogeyed the first, but he picked up two quick birdies with pitches to 15 feet on the second and 10 feet on the third. Quickly, he lost both strokes, one on the fourth, where he drove into the rough and three-putted from the green's collar, and the other on the severe sixth, where he pulled his drive into the left rough, took two more to reach the green and two-putted from 25 feet.

With the sky clearing and the wind just beginning to freshen, Watts played nearly flawless golf from then on. He holed from 30 feet and birdied the seventh, ripped a stunning four iron to five feet on the 12th, and finished off with a two-putt birdie on the 17th. Back in 34, two under par, Watts had begun a surprising move that would last until the very end.

Asked about the weather, Watts said, "You want to enjoy it, but I won't lie to you, it's really tough out there. I can't say I enjoyed playing in it, but I deal with it as it comes."

Finishing just ahead of Watts, O'Meara made a giant leap from from a tie for 62nd into a contending position, just three strokes behind Watts. Mark said he played much better than he had in the opening round, that he drove better and kept his ball in play.

"I hit a lot of fairways and a lot of greens," he said. "I didn't knock down the flags, but I had a lot of chances."

Playing through the worst of the weather and putting erratically, Woods saved himself with another of his strong finishes. Five over for the day after the 16th, he birdied the two closing holes, saving his four on the 17th by pitching to six feet from a greenside bunker, then pitched to 12 feet and holed on the last.

Huston sprayed shots from one side to the other, went out in 37 with a double bogey on the fifth, blundered home in 40, and played no further role in the championship.

The second-round leaders:

Brian Watts	69 - 137	Mark O'Meara	68 - 140
Justin Rose	66 - 138	Fred Couples	74 - 140
Tiger Woods	73 - 138	Stephen Ames	72 - 140
Nick Price	72 - 138	Jim Furyk	70 - 140
Thomas Bjorn	71 - 139	Jesper Parnevik	72 - 140
Davis Love III	73 - 140		

While Friday's had been a trying round, worse was coming. Foul on Friday, the weather turned ugly on Saturday. Five men had entered the round under par, but at day's end not one was left. Instead, only Watts, with 73, held at level-par 210 for 54 holes, while Parnevik, Furyk and O'Meara, all with 72s, stood two strokes behind, at 212.

The wonder was that they had scored so well. The day was cold and overcast, and winds stronger than Friday's battered the players and turned a round at Royal Birkdale into torture. Balls couldn't be controlled and some holes simply couldn't be played. To reach the sixth, which once again played through a crosswind, the best players in the game hit drivers from the fairway. The first and second holes were almost as tough. The first gave up only two birdies all day and the second just one. No one birdied either the sixth, which was understandable, or the 11th, a simple par-four of 408 yards that played through the same crosswind as the sixth.

Of the 24 second-round leaders, only 10 parred the first, at 449 yards a vicious starting hole, and only 13 parred the second, which might have been tougher. More than one man couldn't drive the ball far enough to reach the fairway. O'Meara, Couples and Janzen made sixes on the first, Janzen followed with another on the second, and Peter Baker made seven on the second after bogeying the first.

Those two holes ruined Lee Westwood, the winner at Loch Lomond the previous week. The PGA European Tour's hottest player, Westwood had begun the Open with two rounds of 71, but he opened the third with a six on the first hole, a seven on the second and a five on the third. Six strokes gone after three holes, Westwood shot 78, his championship over.

As flags atop the grandstands snapped in the winds, the field averaged 77.5 strokes. Of the 81 men who had survived the cut, 23 shot in the 80s and only 13 shot under 75. Birkdale that day embarrassed some great players. Janzen shot 80, both Price and Leonard shot 82, and Phil Mickelson shot 85. Both Price and Mickelson played the second nine in 45. Mickelson played the last seven holes in nine over par.

There were some bright spots, though. That Costantino Rocca and Katsuyoshi Tomori shot 70s approached wizardry, and that young Rose held his composure and shot 75 suggested sorcery.

While some halfway leaders lost their positions, others gained ground with scores that would have cost them on other days. With their 72s, Furyk, Parnevik and O'Meara climbed into a tie for second. Rocca and Tomori gained the most ground. Barely surviving the cut, with 146s, they climbed over 52 players, from a tie for 65th to a tie for 10th, along with David Duval and Raymond Russell.

Ever the optimist, Rocca looked ahead and said, "If I have another round like this, I think I will make top 10."

Even though Watts had not only held onto first place but lengthened his lead to two strokes, Rose won the gallery's hearts. He earned it. After bogeying the first two holes, three-putting the first and one-putting the second for his five, he ran off seven consecutive pars and made the turn in 36. Coming back he lost three strokes quickly, but he played a superb pitch to three feet and birdied the long 15th, which played into the wind, and had a chance to save par at the home hole. He missed from five feet.

As his final putt fell, the gallery went wild, raising thundering cheers that rocked the countryside, as this young man turned in an 18-hole score beaten by just 13 professionals. More importantly, only four men posted better 54-hole scores.

Rose had actually led the championship after Watts bogeyed both the 11th and 12th. Justin stood one over par for 48 holes then, but his lead didn't last through the 13th, the longest of the par-fours. Rose bogeyed and Watts birdied with a six-iron approach that bounced onto the green, curled right, and ghosted within two feet of the cup. A swing of two strokes.

Putting erratically early in the day, Watts showed he could score while he played less than his best. He had missed from seven feet and bogeyed the first, missed another seven-footer on the sixth, three-putted the seventh, and missed from five feet on both the 11th and 12th. It changed with the 13th, which he called the turning point. The birdie steadied him enough to par the next three holes and birdie the 17th. Back to level par for 53 holes, he parred the 18th and remained at the top of the leaderboard.

While Watts had done supremely well, O'Meara's had been the day's most critical move. With 212, he had climbed within reach of Watts, an untested player at this level of competition. It hadn't been easy. When he double-bogeyed the first hole, Mark fell five strokes behind Watts, who hadn't played a shot, and then nearly lost at least two more at the sixth, where he became involved with a *Rules of Golf* problem that confused everyone, including the officials.

The sixth green sits among high dunes covered with all sorts of underbrush and knee-high grass. With the wind blowing right-to-left, O'Meara drove nicely, but he still had 230 yards to the green. Using his driver, the club of choice that day, Mark started his ball right of the green, expecting the wind to bring it back. It didn't. It cleared the crest of the dune and disappeared in undergrowth so dense he would be lucky to find it.

What happened next stemmed from ambiguous wording in the definition of a lost ball. The relevant clause states that a ball is lost if, "it is not found or identified by the player within five minutes after the player's side or his or their caddies have begun to search for it."

By the time Mark and his caddie reached the dune, 30 or so spectators were thrashing through the undergrowth searching for the ball. As O'Meara recalled, he guessed three minutes had passed when he said to his caddie, "Jerry, this isn't looking too good. Give me a ball and I'll walk back."

He had walked perhaps 30 yards when he heard spectators shouting they had found the ball. But since no one waved him back, he went on to the point where he had played the shot.

Now officials huddled over interpretations of the rule. After a short time they signaled O'Meara to come back. Next they evidently determined that the five minutes had passed before the spectators found the ball and it was indeed lost. One official put O'Meara in a golf cart and drove him back out to play another shot. Another huddle and they changed their minds, decided the ball had been found within the allotted five minutes, and he should play from the undergrowth, lying two.

Now there was a further complication. When O'Meara had begun his first trip back down the fairway, one man assumed Mark had abandoned the ball and picked it up. Fortunately, the spectator hadn't moved, and when the matter had been settled, Mark could drop the ball on the proper spot. When after each of two drops his ball rolled more than two club-lengths from the spot where it hit the ground, O'Meara was allowed to place his ball. This was a great break. He played a nice pitch and made five. Had he been forced to play another shot from 230 yards out, it would have been his fourth, and he might have scored anything.

From then on he made no mistakes, played the remaining 12 holes in two under par, and salvaged what had begun as a grim day.

The leaders after the third round:

Brian Watts	73 - 210	John Huston	73 - 215
Jesper Parnevik	72 - 212	Brad Faxon	74 - 215
Jim Furyk	72 - 212	Thomas Bjorn	76 - 215
Mark O'Meara	72 - 212	Tiger Woods	77 - 216
Justin Rose	75 - 213		

Obscure players like Watts are supposed to lead the first round, then disappear into the mist of also-ran, their weaknesses exposed by strong courses and better players. Not this time, for if anyone wanted to win this championship he would have to deal with Watts. Only now did the fans begin to learn just who he was.

Since golf had begun expanding after the Second World War, the British Open had attracted the game's most cosmopolitan field. Watts expanded the meaning. The son of an English father and a German mother, he had been born in Montreal, raised in Dallas, lived in Oklahoma, and made his living playing golf in Japan. A former NCAA champion from Oklahoma State University, Watts played the U.S. PGA Tour for a while, but lost his eligibility, and in 1993 headed for Asia and Japan.

He did very well. He won five tournaments in 1994, and had total winnings of $1.4 million, which helped pay for his frequent commutes to Edmond, Oklahoma, to visit with his wife, Debbye, and their son, Jason.

At Birkdale he played with a smooth, rhythmic swing that depended on exquisite timing, the kind that had often failed under pressure. So far, though, it had produced one fine shot after another, and now he had a chance to win the biggest prize of his career.

Paired with Parnevik, who was playing in the last group for the third consecutive year, he went off immediately behind O'Meara and Furyk. Young Rose and Huston played ahead of them, and Woods teed off 40 minutes earlier.

On their way to the Open, O'Meara and Woods had stopped off in Ireland, where they played some of the better courses. Battling blustery weather at Waterville, on Ireland's west coast, Woods blindly tried to overpower the wind while O'Meara played a controlled game, hitting to spots that would set up opportunities for pars.

Their different approaches had shown in the first three rounds of the Open. In the pleasant, mild weather of the first round, Woods shot 65 and O'Meara 72. When the wind kicked up on Friday, Woods shot 73 and O'Meara 68. The next day, in stronger winds, Woods shot 77 and O'Meara 72. His scoring on the two bad days indicated that Woods had yet to learn patience and take what the golf course allows rather than relying so much on his power.

Reeling after his third-round 77, Woods looked everyone in the eye and said, "I'm in pretty good shape. Right now I'm only five strokes back. I have to post a good round and see what happens."

Reflecting on the weather, he added, "If the conditions tomorrow are like today, or more difficult, it would be best for the guys behind, because knowing you can gut it out and shoot even par, or one or two under if you're really playing well, you have a great chance of winning. If it's calm, you'd have to shoot 63 or 64." Bravado perhaps, but Tiger had it just about right.

While the wind slackened off and swung around to a different heading, a dull, gray overcast hid the sky, periodic rains fell, and the spectators caught just an occasional glimpse of sunlight.

In the more forgiving atmosphere, Woods raced around Birkdale in 66 and set the target score at 281 while the leaders still had holes to play. It was a marvelous round, but Woods had calculated correctly. He needed 63 to win.

Even in the milder weather, Birkdale remained largely unforgiving. Only nine men shot in the 60s, and just seven others shot 70. Along with Woods, Russell, a 25-year-old Scot, shot 66, rising six places into a tie for fourth, O'Meara shot 68, and Watts a par 70.

Meantime, the last round opened with serious questions about Rose, Woods, Watts and O'Meara.

Every one of the four played a role in the final round on a day when eight men could have won — O'Meara, Watts, Woods, Rose, Russell, Furyk, Parnevik and Faxon. Each of them had to make something happen, but only O'Meara did enough. Beginning five strokes behind, like Woods, Faxon lost three further strokes by the eighth and dropped back, and Parnevik played steady golf but needed more. After 13 holes Furyk had pulled into a tie for the lead, but then he bogeyed the 15th and failed to birdie the 17th, both par-fives, ending his bid. Meantime, the irrepressible Rose smiled and giggled his way to 69 and 282, tying Parnevik, Furyk and Russell for fourth place.

Still holding his composure with holes running out, Rose remained in the hunt until the end, but with two holes to play, he needed two birdies for 281 or an eagle and a birdie for 280. Instead he finished par-birdie.

Russell caused at least as much surprise as Rose. A 25-year-old Scot who battled hepatitis all year, Russell had missed 12 cuts in 14 events on the PGA European Tour, and yet in the Open he was beaten by only three men.

It is interesting to speculate what might have happened had Wood birdied three of the *first* four holes instead of three of the *last* four. Had he started with a rush he might have upset some swing tempos.

Even though it wasn't good enough to win for him, Woods' finish was spectacular. He began his finishing kick by playing a tremendous 270-yard three wood from gnarled rough to the edge of the 15th green and birdied, overshot the 17th green with his second but then holed a little pitch, and followed up by holing a 40-foot birdie putt on the 18th. With 281, he could only wait and see if his inspired finish had any effect.

Evidently it hadn't bothered Watts or O'Meara, who, meantime, fought it out between them. Neither man faltered. As for Tiger's effect on Rose, it seems entirely unlikely anything could unnerve that precocious young man.

Justin finished with a flourish. After failing to eagle the 17th, which he had to do, he left his approach in heavy grass short of the 18th, then pitched over a bunker and into the hole for a final birdie.

The gallery's roar upset the peace of all of western England. Rose had come back in 33 and finished higher than any English amateur since 1921, when amateur Roger Wethered tied Jock Hutchison at St. Andrews (Hutchison won the playoff). Rose had shot two rounds in the 60s, eagled the 17th during his second-round 66, birdied 12 holes, parred 43, and bogeyed 14. He never lost more than one stroke on any hole. It was astonishing for one so young.

Meantime, as the gallery gloried in their new hero, O'Meara and Watts decided the championship.

Playing as steadily as ever, Watts ran off three straight pars before dropping a stroke at the fourth, where he three-putted from 30 feet, but he holed from 35 feet and birdied the fifth. When four more pars took him through the ninth in 34, even par, he still led O'Meara by two strokes.

Playing ahead of Brian, Mark had found trouble on the sixth once again, where his approach hit a slope at the edge of the green and kicked sharply into the same sort of knee-high grass as his second shot the previous day. One hack and a good chip saved a bogey.

Even par for the day, he slipped to one over by overshooting the short seventh, but then a misdirected shot to the eighth set up a miracle birdie. Played from an awkward lie in the left rough, with the ball well below his feet, O'Meara's approach missed the green badly, but it scooted up a mound, ran through heavy stuff at the top, curled left, caught a closely cropped downslope, and trickled onto the green, hole high.

Still two strokes behind, O'Meara slipped into the lead when he birdied both the 11th and 12th, holing solid putts from 15 and 20 feet, just before Watts bogeyed the short 12th. Brian was lucky to lose only one stroke. A wild tee shot dived into impossibly high grass behind a mound. Now O'Meara stood at even par and Watts and Furyk, still in the hunt, one over par.

At about the time Watts was bogeying the 12th, O'Meara bunkered his approach to the 13th and bogeyed as well. Now all three were tied at one over par.

O'Meara jumped ahead once again by ripping a four iron hole-high about four feet right of the 14th and birdieing again. Meantime, Watts continued grinding out the pars.

Furyk finally fell back by driving into the rough and bogeying the 15th — his putt went into the hole and spun out — and O'Meara dropped another stroke on the 16th by pulling his approach and misreading the par-saving putt.

Now Woods came into play. Before O'Meara completed the 16th and Watts the 15th, Woods holed his birdie on the 18th. Now he, O'Meara and Watts were tied at one over par. Both Brian and Mark had an advantage over Woods, though — they had the 17th ahead of them, a hole that had given up 16 birdies by the time O'Meara stepped onto the tee.

It looked questionable that Mark would birdie as well when he pulled his drive into the tangled rough, but he hacked it out with a nine iron, followed with another nine iron to 20 feet, and holed the putt. He was even par, one stroke ahead.

Moments later Watts matched O'Meara with a birdie of his own, and after O'Meara parred the home hole, Watts saved himself with a remarkable bunker shot.

His second shot, played from the left rough, had fallen short, but it had squirted from the grass loaded with overspin, ran for a distance, and with its last gasp tumbled into an awkward position in the left greenside bunker.

His chances looked hopeless. He must make the par to force a playoff, but he faced as difficult a shot as anyone could imagine, especially for a man who had never played under such tension. With his ball lying on a downslope so close to the bunker's rear wall he could only place one foot in the sand, he would have to pitch over the bunker's arching front face and pray the ball would run to the hole.

He played it perfectly. When he chopped down, the ball shot up, cleared the bunker face, hit the green running, and died no more than eight inches from the cup. For one heart-stopping moment it looked as if it might fall.

The shot stands among the finest bunker shots anyone could remember at a critical moment of a championship of such stature. It rivaled Bobby Jones' recovery on the 17th at Hoylake in the 1930 British Open, Bob Tway's pitch into the final hole at Inverness when he snatched the 1986 PGA Championship from Greg Norman, and Sandy Lyle's astonishing recovery from a fairway bunker to Augusta's 18th green that set up the winning birdie in the 1987 Masters. Watching Watts play his shot, even O'Meara applauded.

The par had earned Brian a 70 for the day, but O'Meara had shot 68 and picked up the strokes he needed. Now they moved to the 15th to begin the four-hole playoff.

Watts played the better shots into the first two greens, but twice he missed the putts. O'Meara holed his birdie on the 15th, and with three more pars, he won the championship.

Watts had played wonderfully, never losing control of his game until a few loose drives on the playoff holes, but he had been up against a man who had finally learned how to win.

Mark had won by fighting off the tension and letting others make the mistakes. He played the last 11 holes in three under par and holed a critical putt on the 17th after nearly giving the championship away. He had persisted through one of the Open's more gripping finishes, ending as the gallery at the 18th cheered themselves hoarse watching a series of dramatic finishes — Woods' final birdie that earned him that great 66, Rose's unlikely pitch into the cup that brought him within a stroke of Woods, and then Watts' stirring bunker shot.

The victory was especially fulfilling for O'Meara. He had been close at times, but it seemed he hadn't a game big enough to win a major championship. Now, though, with two major victories in the same year, O'Meara stood at the top of the game.

6. PGA Championship

From the first moment the PGA of America announced that its annual championship would be played at Sahalee Country Club in the Seattle suburb of Redmond, Washington, golf historians fondly looked back a half-century to 1946 and recounted the last time the PGA visited the Pacific Northwest. It was in Portland, Oregon, during a time when Americans were welcoming their boys home from the battle fronts and embarking on such things as the Marshall Plan, that a small, smiling Texan with steely gray eyes and a work ethic unseen by anyone in golf walked away with the PGA Championship. The 1946 PGA Championship, Ben Hogan's first major title, came at a pre-software time when the Northwest was as rugged and exacting as Hogan himself, and the PGA Championship was back after World War II to its full-fielded glory with Byron Nelson, Sam Snead, Jimmy Demaret and Lloyd Mangrum all vying for the coveted Rodman Wanamaker Trophy. In the end Hogan cruised to victory in the match play event, defeating Ed Oliver, 6 and 4 in the final.

That was the second PGA Championship in the region in three years, the 1944 event having been played in Spokane, Washington. In 1998 golf's final major was played north of San Francisco for the first time since Hogan's win, and many wondered if Sahalee would crown an equally historic champion. Although the culture of the region had certainly evolved in a half-century, the unyielding nature of the Northwest — typified by the towering, timeless Douglas firs that line the fairways of Sahalee — remained unchanged. Seattle native Fred Couples summed up the challenge when he said, "I hit more trees in one round at Sahalee than I would in a month of playing anywhere else. I'm not sure I've ever broken 80 there." With that as the benchmark, the winner of this championship would have to be the same kind of rugged workhorse that Hogan had been. It seemed that a grinder might win the 80th PGA Championship.

So, it was with no sense of irony that on Sunday, August 16, PGA of America president Ken Lindsay handed the Wanamaker Trophy to the hardest working man in modern golf, a practice-tee legend who lived by Hogan's edict that "there aren't enough hours in the day to practice all the shots you need." Vijay Singh, a native of Lautoka, Fiji, who, as recently as 1985 worked in a Malaysian golf shop for $250 a month, and who subsequently awed his peers with his relentless passion for practice, steered his game around the unforgiving terrain in 271 shots, two better than his nearest competitor.

Like Hogan, Singh is a man of few words who lets his clubs do the talking. And, like Hogan, Singh is a man who has set new standards for practice, spending more hours on the tee, week in and week out, than any of his fellow professionals. The fact that both Singh and Hogan captured their first major championships in the Northwest only added to the comparisons, but, for Singh, the win at Sahalee was nothing more than a culmination of years of hard work, and some last minute advice from his wife. "I never expected this to happen this way," Singh said. "I've practiced so hard for this. It's a dream come true."

The dream of a two-stroke victory over Steve Stricker on one of the most challenging tests of golf ever chosen by the PGA of America couldn't have been more rewarding because Singh's wife, Ardena, played such a key role. Singh had missed the cut at the Masters, tied for an uninspiring 25th at the U.S. Open, and finished 10 strokes back of Mark O'Meara in the British Open, all because of continued struggles with his putter. Finally, at Ardena's urging and at the suggestion of short-game guru Dave Pelz, Singh decided to return to a cross-handed putting style, a grip he had used as a child. The results were three consecutive rounds in the 60s at Sahalee, with the closing 68 providing the winning margin over Stricker who finished with a final round of even-par 70.

"It's been a struggle with the putter all year until the Western Open," Singh said. "Ardena said, 'You might as well try cross-handed.' It was a suggestion I didn't think about until I got to the Western Open, and it was just one of those things that, when you try it and it works, you go ahead with it. I'm surprised I hadn't tried it a few years ago."

If he had tried it earlier, Singh might have earned more than the five career PGA Tour victories that he brought into this championship, but then, the timing for Singh could not have been better. "I practiced so hard all my life, and I want to win golf tournaments. Every time I tee it up, I want to go out and win. This year I turned things around. I started putting well and started feeling like I could go out there and win again. Who knows what's going to happen from here onward."

Before looking onward, Singh had a few smiling moments to reflect on the most memorable week of his career.

The week started on a heart-wrenching note for everyone when, on Tuesday, Stuart Appleby returned to competitive golf after the tragic and untimely death of his wife, Renay, in London two weeks earlier. In a press conference, a tearful Appleby said of his wife, who was killed in an automobile accident at Waterloo Station, "I feel like she was the first prize in the raffle of life. I was lucky enough to win her." There were no dry eyes in the room as Appleby explained how he was coping with such a loss. "You've got to talk about the person like they're still there. You never have a fear to mention their name. You laugh at things and the jokes that you might have told. You just feel as though that person is still there. Physically, yes, she's never going to be there. Mentally, she'll always be there. It's a very unusual circumstance, so I guess I have to assure everyone that I'm okay. We're all in this big group of people together in this world, and there are no preferences dealt out when someone disappears from us like that. Everyone just needed to see how I am once I got back out here. I wish I could direct myself a little easier and have a plan as to where I need to go, but mainly I'm taking life one day at a time and just trying to get a rhythm. At my best I feel good, and at my worst I feel terrible. It's a feeling I wouldn't wish on anyone."

Physically and emotionally, Appleby had the support of every spectator, every player and every member of the press as he teed off with Singh at 1:16 p.m. on Thursday. Although he shot 77-73 and missed the cut, Appleby found a little perspective, and, with the help and support of a legion of sympathetic fans, he rediscovered that golf is just a game.

One of the players who spoke to Appleby and who provided some empathetic wisdom was defending PGA champion Davis Love III. Having lost his father in a plane crash, Love counseled Appleby on the grief he was experiencing, and offered his support. "Stuart is going to be asked about (Renay) every time he goes to a new city," Love said. "Until he goes through the whole tour and speaks to every one of his friends and every tournament director and every marshal at every tournament it's not going to be over for him. That's the hardest part. Stuart and Renay were very popular on the tour, and my father was very well-known and very popular in his business. That makes it tough. Everywhere you go for a year people want to say their piece, and it's very difficult."

Love also had some comments about Sahalee, and what the players could expect. "The course is great," he said. "In most majors, your accuracy off the tee is a premium, but this one is going to be different. The difficulty here is going to be staying patient enough to hit a lot of good iron shots. It's hard to keep your patience when you don't get to a hole where you can just bomb a driver and have an easy shot to take a breather. There aren't any breather holes out here." When asked if the golf course suited a particular player's game, Love invoked a name that was on everybody's mind. "Mark (O'Meara) is a patient, scrambling, hardworking golfer who is just getting his due now," Love said. He is one of the greatest players of all time."

O'Meara, the Masters and British Open champion, arrived at Sahalee vying to become the first since Hogan in 1953 to win three of golf's modern major titles in the same year. "If you'd told me at the beginning of the year that I would have the opportunity to win two of the majors, I would have jumped and prayed for the chance. The odds are against me, I know that. But it doesn't stop me from going out and trying to give it my best," O'Meara said. "If I have a chance on Sunday afternoon, hopefully I can dwell on what I've learned from the Masters and the British Open, and use it to my advantage.

"Now that I've won two majors in one year, it's a wonderful accomplishment and it's great, but you've got to move forward. That's in the past. Now is the present. We've got the PGA Championship in which we have a great field on a very neat, very different type of golf course. It's a beautiful course in a beautiful setting, and the golf course looks like it's going to be a very good test and a very good challenge for all the players."

With 20 of the 150 players who teed off on Thursday breaking par, O'Meara's one-under-par 69 certainly put him in the thick of things. O'Meara's Orlando neighbor, Tiger Woods, tamed Sahalee by firing a course-record 66 to the delight of thousands of fans. The round started out a little bumpy, however, as Woods hit a two iron off the first tee directly into the right rough. From there he pushed an eight-iron approach to the right of the green and proceeded to make a five. On the second hole, Woods hit the shot that "probably made the round." After driving the ball into the middle of the fairway with a three wood, he hit a three-iron approach from 220 yards. "I got ahead of it a little and I thought for sure the ball was in the water," Woods said. "But it carried the water probably two or three feet and rolled onto the green. I made birdie and sneaked away with one there."

The most important club in Woods' bag was the putter he borrowed from O'Meara a few weeks before. Of the seven birdies, three bogeys and eight pars, Woods made no fewer than five putts from outside 15 feet, including a 35-footer for birdie on the 215-yard, par-three 17th. He also found the fairways more often than even he expected, in part because he never pulled the driver out of his bag. "It's a more mature Tiger than you saw last year at this time," Woods said. "I've got more shots now."

He also had length that puts him ahead of the field even if he didn't hit driver. "My length is definitely a huge advantage on this golf course, because I'm able to hit two irons and three woods where guys are sometimes having to hit drivers," Woods said. He demonstrated that on the 18th, when he hit a 305-yard three wood into the middle of the fairway, out-distancing his fellow competitors Nick Price and Jeff Sluman by over 50 yards. Woods parred the 18th, but the point was already made. Although he never took the head cover off his driver, Woods averaged 271 yards off the tee, hit 13 of 18 greens in regulation, and took 27 putts to complete his record-setting round.

O'Meara wasn't surprised at all by Woods' efforts. "I saw on the leaderboard that Tiger shot four under, but I expected him to play well," O'Meara said. "He was swinging well in the practice rounds and this is a good golf course for him."

It was also a good golf course for Glen Day, who, except for a double bogey on the 15th, would have matched Tiger's record-setting pace. With birdies on the first four holes and another on the 11th, Day held the early lead before making a bogey on the 13th, a birdie on the 14th, then double bogey on the 15th and another bogey on the 18th. Still, Day finished the day only two strokes back, tied with Bob Estes, Frank Lickliter, Paul Azinger, Bill Glasson, Shigeki Maruyama, Billy Andrade and Scott Gump at two under par.

"I got kind of greedy on the last few holes," Day said. "The only real mistake was a three-putt from four feet on 15. I hit the kind of putt I wanted, but on the next putt, I completely lost my mind and it showed." Then, in a moment of reflection, Day said, "Golf is a weird game, and there are three more days to go, so we'll see what happens. They don't pay you for leading on Thursday."

Nor do they pay you for bombing tee shots on a golf course that demands finesse. John Daly started the week by vowing to "grip it and rip it" on the narrow Sahalee course, and that's exactly what he did. Blasting a tee shot with the driver on the first hole (a shot the rest of the field chose to play with an iron), Daly proceeded to thrill his fans with mammoth drives, some of which found the fairways and others that were so far off line he needed a guide to get back into play. At least six Daly drives exceeded 300 yards, with one on the par-four fourth traveling 322 yards. Daly's go-for-broke approach cost him any chance to repeat his 1991 PGA victory. He opened with a 10-over-par 80, including a triple-bogey seven on the 18th after hitting his drive underneath a television truck.

"You can get away with hitting driver for a while, but it's going to get you in the end," said David Duval, who also took a triple bogey en route to shooting 76.

One player who was able to control his driver, and as a result post one of his best major championship rounds since battling cancer, was Azinger, one of the eight players who shot two-under-par 68. "This is the best I've played since coming back," Azinger said. "I'm flighting the ball better, and my putting has finally come around."

The same could not be said for U.S. Open champion Lee Janzen who said that, with the exception of the one week of the Open, "I haven't putted well all year." Payne Stewart, who finished second to Janzen at the Open, also shot an opening 76, while hometown favorite Couples, who opened with 74, said, "It's a demanding enough golf course from the fairways. When you're in the rough you can't really get it to the greens. I had a few good pars, but overall it was pretty mediocre stuff."

Better than mediocre, but certainly not on anyone's scope after day one was Vijay Singh, who shot even-par 70 before heading to the practice tee for his daily workout. By the time he left on Thursday evening, the leaderboard looked like this:

Tiger Woods	66	Bill Glasson	68
Bob Estes	68	Shigeki Maruyama	68
Glen Day	68	Billy Andrade	68
Frank Lickliter	68	Scott Gump	68
Paul Azinger	68		

The second round started with unusually dry, warm conditions hardening an already narrow golf course, and bringing many players back into contention. The first was Colin Montgomerie, who followed his even-par opening round with a three-under 67. After a routine par at the first, Monty reached the 507-yard par-five second in two shots. Although his eagle effort from 50 feet came up short, a two-putt birdie got things rolling. On the fourth hole, he hit a two iron off the tee, then flew a wedge 10 feet beyond the hole and made that putt for birdie as well. A three-putt bogey at the third from 50 feet provided Montgomerie's only blemish until the 18th, where, after adding three more birdies on the 12th, 14th and 16th, he missed the fairway with his drive and missed the green with his approach. The 35-foot par effort nipped the edge of the hole. Although admitting to "not hitting the ball very well," Montgomerie made more than his share of putts, including two from outside 20 feet and one chip-in from 35 feet. "I played conservatively," he said. "It's a course I knew in practice would suit me. If I can putt the same way on the weekend, I obviously have a chance. I haven't come over here to finish second. I'm in good position now."

Another player in good position was O'Meara, who shot 70 on Friday to go into the weekend at one under par. O'Meara ignited the crowd with a chip-in birdie from 50 yards on the sixth, one of only 17 birdies on the 480-yard par-four on Friday. Then he drained a 25-foot eagle putt on the par-five 11th. "I'm pleased and proud of the fact that after two rounds I've played as well as I have and I've at least given myself a chance going into the weekend," O'Meara said.

Quite a few players had no chance to even play on Saturday and Sunday. Among them Janzen, who shot 76-72, and Daly, who followed his 80 with a more subdued 72. Other notables to miss the cut included Jesper Parnevik (70-76), Jim Furyk (72-74), Justin Leonard (70-77), Tom Watson (72-76), Lee Westwood (74-76), Payne Stewart (76-74) and Duval (76-78).

Azinger could not hold the momentum he had gained on Thursday, either, closing with a three-over 73 to enter the weekend one over par for the championship. Creeping up the leaderboard, Love carded a two-under 68 on

Friday to go with his even-par opening round, which placed him among only 14 players under par at the halfway mark.

Couples rebounded from a disappointing 74 to shoot 71 and slip in under the cut. He advanced to the weekend with a five-over-par total, tying a disappointed Andrade, who started the day two shots off the lead, but could manage no better than 77.

Woods had his share of problems as well. After making seven birdies on Thursday, Woods could only squeeze in one birdie in his two-over-par effort. "It was just one of those rounds where I didn't hit the ball particularly well, and I didn't give myself a lot of chances to make birdies," Woods said. "But I hung in there and my short game was great. I'm very pleased to shoot 72 given the way I hit the ball all day."

Far from out of it, Tiger found himself tied for fifth place with Love, Brad Faxon, Andrew Magee and a resurgent and healthy Steve Elkington, all of whom reached two-under-par 138. Day followed his opening 68 with 71 to enter the weekend tied with O'Meara, Lickliter, John Cook and David Frost at one under.

As the day wore on and the leaderboard became more crowded, a few unfamiliar names crept towards the top. Scott Gump, a former Nike Tour player who finished no higher than tied for 13th in 1997 and barely kept his playing privileges, was on top of the leaderboard at five under par through the 14th, but two consecutive bogeys dropped Gump to three-under 137, where he finished tied with Montgomerie and Stricker. "I haven't been in this position too many times, so I'm having fun," Gump said.

Stricker, a two-time winner who struggled through most of 1997, also had fun reaching five under late in the round before heading to the 215-yard par-three 17th armed with a five iron. He hit what he thought was a perfect shot, but a wind gust blew the ball into the water short of the green, and a befuddled Stricker had to settle for a double-bogey five. "I had no idea where the wind was coming from," Stricker's caddie later confessed. "I had him too confused."

Confused or not, Stricker entered the weekend two shots out of the lead in a major championship, his best position in two years. The leader he and the others were chasing turned out to be Singh, who followed his even-par 70 with a course-record-tying 66 that included birdies at the first, second, fourth, seventh, ninth and 13th holes, and bogeys at the 11th and 17th. With iron play that gave him five birdie opportunities from inside 10 feet, Singh capitalized on what he termed "improved ball striking."

"I hit a lot of greens and lot of fairways and I putted well," Singh said, leaving many to wonder what shots Singh hit poorly. "If you're on the correct side of the pins you have a good chance to make birdies and that's what I did today. I just want to go out tomorrow and the day after that and do what I did today."

While two more 66s were not in the cards for Singh, he did have a memorable weekend ahead. With two rounds completed at the 80th PGA Championship, the leaderboard shaped up like this:

Vijay Singh	66 - 136	Tiger Woods	72 - 138
Colin Montgomerie	67 - 137	Davis Love III	68 - 138
Scott Gump	69 - 137	Frank Lickliter	71 - 139
Steve Stricker	68 - 137	David Frost	69 - 139
Steve Elkington	69 - 138	John Cook	68 - 139
Andrew Magee	68 - 138	Mark O'Meara	70 - 139
Brad Faxon	68 - 138	Glen Day	71 - 139

There was not a lot of early moving in the third round, but there were some gritty performances that stood out. Woods struggled with his accuracy for the second day in a row, but no one could tell from his scorecard. Woods' two-birdie, two-bogey, even-par round appeared to be the model of consistency until you examined the various misadventures Tiger suffered off the tee. Hitting only five fairways, Woods called it "a long, long day. It could have been a lot worse. I didn't hit the ball particularly well, and I had to do a lot of scrambling. Basically, I just hung in there and stayed patient, and I made some pretty solid up-and-downs."

Woods spent the better part of the Saturday morning on the practice range with his coach Butch Harmon. "I was trying to find my golf swing," Woods admitted. "It wasn't too far off, and on the back nine I hit a lot of good shots." Those shots boosted Woods' optimism going into the final round. "If I go out and hit the ball (on Sunday) really well and give myself some chances, I know I'm going to knock down the putts because I'm putting really well right now. I'm making a lot of par putts, birdie putts when I have the chance, and it's just a matter of giving myself 18 chances tomorrow to make some putts. I'd like to post something in the mid-60s, post it early, and see what happens," he said. "Fourteen and 18, those are the magic numbers ... 14 fairways and 18 greens. If I do that, I like my chances."

Even though Woods felt he had played as well as he could given his errant tee shots, he wasn't the low man from Orlando. O'Meara continued his quest toward golf immortality by posting 69 to enter the final round at two under par, well within reach of the leaders.

Those leaders turned out to be Stricker and Singh.

Not to be outdone, Stricker, who had never led a major, tied Woods' and Singh's course record on Saturday by firing a bogey-free 66 of his own. Stricker's round included birdies on the second and third holes, a brilliant recovery from the rough for par on the par-four sixth, and a birdie at the eighth. "I got off to a good start and stayed aggressive throughout the whole day," Stricker said. "This was one of the best rounds I've ever played. Under the circumstances and under the pressure, it gives me a lot of confidence." Stricker's final birdie came after hitting a 165-yard shot from a fairway bunker to within eight feet of the flag on the par-four 16th. After pushing his tee shot on the par-four 18th, Stricker hit a 50-yard wedge shot that spun to within eight feet of the hole. "I was able to spin it off of that lie a little," he said. After converting his par putt, Stricker summed up the hole and the round by saying, "Something like that just keeps me going. It put the finishing touches on a good round."

Singh had the finish of all finishes on Saturday, playing the last nine holes in four under par, which, coupled with his three-bogey, two-birdie first nine, gave Singh a third-round 67 and left him tied with Stricker going into the final day. "It was really an up-and-down round," Singh said. "I felt a little nervous on the first tee, and I mis-hit a few shots, especially in the first few holes. Then I got my thoughts together on the back side and put a lot of good shots together and made some good putts."

Singh's up-and-down round started out on the down side as he drove his ball into a poor lie in the right rough of the second hole. After chipping out and watching the ball roll through the fairway on the other side, Singh hit sand wedge onto the green at the 507-yard par-five, but into a spot where, in his words, "I had no chance to two-putt." Three putts later Singh had bogeyed one of the few true birdie holes on the first nine. Four holes later he drove the ball into the middle of the fairway at the 480-yard par-four sixth. A seven-iron approach to 20 feet netted a birdie, but Singh gave that shot back quickly when his two-iron tee shot at the seventh hit a tree. After a three-wood approach fell just short of the green, Singh chipped up to within six feet, but missed his par effort. One hole later, Singh made another birdie when he hit his six-iron approach to within 15 feet and sank the putt on the 444-yard par-four eighth hole. But a bogey at the 213-yard par-three ninth dropped Singh to one over for the day at the turn.

At the turn, Singh knew he was striking the ball better than his score indicated, so he said to his caddie, "Let's not change any game plan. We'll keep doing what we've been doing. It worked for two days, and I don't know why it shouldn't work for the rest of the day." A birdie at the 546-yard par-five 11th boosted Singh's confidence, but then at the 12th, after driving the ball in the bunker, Singh hit what he deemed the shot of the day. "After hitting my tee shot in the bunker I was just trying to play anywhere in front of the green," Singh said. "The ball came out really well. That got me fired up for the rest of the day." After a par at the 12th, Singh went on to birdie the 13th when his eight-iron approach stopped five feet from the hole. Then at the 374-yard par-four 14th, he hit a nine iron to within three feet for another birdie, and at the 15th a sand-wedge approach to eight feet gave Singh his third birdie in a row. Three pars finished off the round with a two-putt from 35 feet on the 18th that Singh said was "one of the best putts I hit all week."

Of his position going into the final round, Singh said, "After all the practice for all those years, you have to feel that your time will come soon. I just hope it's going to be tomorrow. I have a chance to do what I've always dreamed of doing: win a major championship."

While six players including Woods, O'Meara, Love and Billy Mayfair were within five shots of Singh and Stricker going into the final round, the two leaders shared a four-stroke advantage over their nearest competitors with 18 holes to play. It was the first time either of the leaders had played in the final pairing of a major championship, and neither was taking anything for granted. Singh said, "Anybody within five or six shots of the lead has a chance of winning this tournament. Obviously, there will be a little more pressure on myself and Steve, but hopefully I will go out there and do what I did today. We'll have to wait and see what happens on the front side tomorrow."

Stricker, was equally cautious when he said, "It may be difficult. I haven't been in this situation before, so I'm going to have to worry about my own game, and try to get myself going in a nice positive direction, feeling good about what I'm doing and not really paying attention to what Vijay or anybody else is doing."

While seemingly calm, the pressure was palpable as the two leaders went through their post-round routines and tried to prepare themselves for a Sunday afternoon round to determine whose name would be enshrined on the Wanamaker Trophy. With 18 holes to play, the leaderboard looked like this:

Vijay Singh	67 - 203	Skip Kendall	68 - 208
Steve Stricker	66 - 203	Frank Lickliter	69 - 208
Steve Elkington	69 - 207	Mark O'Meara	69 - 208
Davis Love III	69 - 207	Tiger Woods	70 - 208
Billy Mayfair	67 - 207		

Before the leaders teed off on Sunday, all eyes turned to O'Meara, the man attempting to make history. Saturday night, with O'Meara five shots back, instructor Hank Haney said, "Mark is just a hang-in-there kind of guy. That's just his deal. But hanging around might work here."

In both the Masters and the British Open, O'Meara had "hung around" while others folded. But in this historic quest, O'Meara didn't hole the putts that he needed early in the round, shot 68 and tied for fourth place at 276, five strokes behind. "I realized that if I got off to a quick start on Sunday, I had as good a chance as anyone else," O'Meara said. "Unfortunately, the bogeys at six, seven and eight kind of took the wind out of my sails. It would have been a tremendous honor to go alongside Ben Hogan's name, but it wasn't meant to be. It's not easy winning out here on tour, especially in a major."

Couples made a strong showing for the hometown crowd, finishing the weekend with rounds of 67 and 68 to shoot 280 and move into a tie for 13th with John Huston, Bill Glasson, Paul Azinger, Robert Allenby, Steve Flesch, Bob Tway and Faxon.

One of the players watching O'Meara's performance was Nick Price. "We were on the ninth green when Mark posted his five under, and I said to Jimmy, my caddie, 'He wants it. He wants this championship.'"

Price also wanted the championship, even though he began the day at one over par, seemingly out of contention. Although he had been striking the ball well all week, Price's putter didn't come around until Sunday when he had what he termed "my best putting round in a year." It started when he two-putted for birdie from 25 feet on the par-five second, and continued with a scrambling eight-foot par putt on the third, and a 14-foot par save at the sixth. Birdie putts from three and six feet on the ninth and 10th holes moved Price onto the leaderboard. When his 25-foot eagle putt at the 11th fell into the cup, he actually started thinking he had a chance to win. "I felt like if I could post seven under that I would have a chance. But that's a tall order with those last six holes."

He made good runs at the 16th and 17th but neither birdie putt would fall. When Price tapped in for par at the 18th he had shot a course-record 65 and finished the PGA Championship at four-under-par 276, tied with O'Meara and Lickliter for fourth place. That score was three shots short of what Price thought he needed. As it turned out, seven under wouldn't have been enough. Elkington posted a 67 to take third place at 274, while Mayfair and Love finished tied for seventh at 277. Cook took ninth at 278, while tied for 10th at 279 were Woods, Perry and Skip Kendall.

By the afternoon, as the leaders reached the fifth hole, the tournament had boiled down to a battle between Singh and Stricker, with both players being more nervous than their demeanors showed.

Singh had trouble sleeping Saturday night, at one point looking at the clock and seeing that it was 2:00 a.m. "I was lying in bed thinking, what's going to happen tomorrow?" Singh said. "Then my wife says, 'Aren't you asleep?' and I said, 'Oh, yeah, I'm asleep.'" That nervousness carried over to the locker room on Sunday when Singh asked Price for some advice on how to approach his final round. Price told him to "go out there and play your own game. You know what to do. You've played it enough."

Singh took Price's advice, even though the butterflies were still churning in his stomach as he and Stricker approached the first tee.

Both parred the first, but when Stricker bogeyed the par-five second, Singh breathed a little easier. His relief was short-lived, however. Stricker birdied the third and followed it up with another birdie at the fourth to take a one-stroke lead, while Singh parred four holes in a row. On the fifth, Singh hit what he called, "a pretty good six iron" to within four feet. He made the putt and reclaimed a share of the lead.

Stricker had trouble finding the fairway and bogeyed the sixth and ninth. At the turn, Singh held a two-shot lead. Then, on the 11th, Singh got the break of the tournament when his three-wood second shot sailed left toward the towering Douglas firs. According to Singh, "I was kind of fortunate there. The ball hit the tree and came back on the green, and I two-putted (for birdie) from about 25 feet."

Stricker made birdie as well, then pulled to within one when Singh made bogey at the 12th. On the 15th, Stricker appeared poised to regain a share of the lead when his approach shot stopped four feet from the hole. In what would be described as one of the finest shots of the tournament, Singh hit his approach just outside Stricker's. When Singh made his birdie, the pressure turned back to Stricker who answered with a birdie of his own. "Fifteen is when I really started thinking that it was just between Vijay and me," Stricker said. "I felt like we had enough of a cushion that it was just going to be between the two of us. I tried to put a little pressure on him at 16 with my approach but he hit it right up there after I hit my shot."

Both made pars on the 16th. Then on the 17th, with Stricker once again trying to apply the pressure, things backfired. Both found the left-greenside bunker on the par-three hole, and both played admirable recovery shots to within 15 feet of the hole. When Singh putted first and made his par, and Stricker let his putt slip below the hole, Singh had a two-shot lead with one hole to play.

A routine par on the 18th, a hug from his wife and another from his son Qass, and the PGA had a new champion. "I never expected it to happen like this," a jubilant Singh said afterward. "It's a dream come true. I set my mind to go out and win every tournament, but you only have four chances a year to win a major championship, and the best players in the world are playing in major events. To win this event and know that so many great players have won it ... It's unbelievable."

7. The Players Championship

One year after Steve Elkington ran away from the rest of the field at The Players Championship, the TPC at Sawgrass reclaimed its stature as one of the more demanding tests in professional golf, and 25-year-old Justin Leonard reaffirmed his position as one of the up-and-coming stars on the PGA Tour. Leonard won The Players Championship by two strokes with a Sunday charge, the type of finish that had distinguished him in the previous year.

Eight months before arriving in Ponte Vedra Beach, Florida, for The Players Championship, Leonard elevated himself to new heights by winning the British Open. Trailing by five strokes going into the final round, a methodical and gritty Leonard charged home with 11 one-putt greens and birdies on the 70th and 71st holes to catch and then pass Jesper Parnevik and Darren Clarke at Royal Troon. Then Leonard put on another charge that fell one stroke short of champion Davis Love III at Winged Foot in the 1997 PGA Championship, thwarting Leonard's bid to become the first player since Nick Price in 1994 to win two consecutive major titles and the ninth since the inception of the Masters in 1934.

Leonard's 1997 performance reminded everyone that major champions don't always have the flashiest games, but they have the determination to get the job done when it counts. His driving statistics were not great — tied for 135th on the PGA Tour, and his average of hitting 63.3 percent of greens in regulation placed him in an unimpressive tie for 133rd. Still, Leonard finished the year ninth in scoring.

In his first three years on the PGA Tour, Leonard had three victories and 25 top-10 finishes in 102 starts. He also became known as a "comeback kid," because in both his 1997 victories (British Open and Kemper Open) Leonard came from five strokes back after 54 holes to win. Then, in the final round of The Players Championship, Leonard did it again, winning from five strokes behind in one of the biggest non-major tournaments of the year. "Last year, with the British Open and the PGA and then the Ryder Cup (where Leonard had a 1-3 record at Valderrama), I took home a lot of information that I needed to digest in the off-season," he said. "I think this week revealed some of that. A couple of years ago, I thought maybe I was at the steeper end of the learning curve. Now I'm beginning to realize that I'm nowhere near it."

The other professionals who teed off in the warm, breezy conditions on the TPC at Sawgrass probably disagreed with Leonard's self-deprecating analysis. While 24 players broke par for the week, no one approached Steve Elkington's 1997 16-under-par mark, and Greg Norman's 24-under-par tournament record was safe from the start. Hard, dry ground and extra long rough coupled with gusting breezes off the nearby Atlantic allowed the ever-feisty TPC course to feed on wayward tee shots. Although there were 15 opening scores in the 60s, the field averaged 74.2 shots in the first two rounds, and, as the pressure increased on the weekend, 51 players were over par for the final two days.

Elkington was not among those trying to tame the TPC beast. After battling infections for much of 1997 and the first part of 1998, the defending champion finally had to undergo nasal surgery the week before The Players Championship. Despite his best efforts to recover in time to play, after-effects from the surgery forced Elkington to withdraw. It was the first time in Players Championship history that the defending champion did not return.

That didn't dampen the drama however. The opening round saw the emergence of a few familiar names amidst a crowd of fresh faces. While Leonard bogeyed the first two holes but scrambled back for an opening even-par 72, Fred Couples, a winner earlier in the year at the Bob Hope Chrysler Classic, set the early mark with 67. Couples soon found himself tied with affable 35-year-old Rocco Mediate, a 12-year veteran whose last victory came at the 1993 Kmart Greater Greensboro Open. By the time the sun set on Thursday, however, the tournament had as the leader a winless four-year veteran with a checkered playing history.

Glen Day, a native of Poplarville, Mississippi, whose slow play was so legendary that he was nicknamed "All" Day, took little time in shooting 66 to jump ahead of Couples and Mediate by one stroke. Although he had four top-10 finishes in 1997, Day had never won in the United States, never won in Europe where he played between 1991 and 1993, and had one win in Asia (1990 Malaysian Open) despite two years of playing there. Still, his good play and mild demeanor made him a favorite and, despite the nickname, Day had learned to pick up the pace of his play. "I was a little faster than a snail but slower than a turtle," Day said. "I think I've got it down now so I don't make anybody mad any more."

He might have been faster but before teeing off at The Players Championship, Day had yet to regain the kind of game that made him the third highest rookie on the money list (behind Ernie Els and Mike Heinen) in 1994. That changed after his 66. "My granddaddy, God rest his soul, used to say, 'The harder you try, the behinder you get,'" Day said in his Southern drawl. "Corny old saying, but it's the truth. Now I laugh at the mistakes and stay calm when I'm playing well. That's why I'm playing better."

He continued to play better than in previous years, but Day slipped a little bit, shooting one-over-par 73 in the second round to put him in a tie with Jerry Kelly and infrequent competitor Bruce Lietzke, who played in The Players Championship because, "I owed it to the Tour. I owe the Tour a lot, and I ended up coming here even though the fishing forecast for Texas was fantastic this week."

The fishing wasn't bad in Ponte Vedra, as Lietzke, Kelly and Day entered the weekend only two strokes behind the mid-point leaders. They were the 1995 Players Championship winner, Lee Janzen — who followed his first-round 70 with 67 — and Japan's Naomichi (Joe) Ozaki, brother of Jumbo, who opened with rounds of 69 and 68.

Tom Kite, coming off laser eye surgery that enabled him to remove the glasses he had worn for his entire career, shot the second day's low round, following his even-par 72 with 66 to move to within one of Janzen and Ozaki, while a hometown favorite, Len Mattiace, a winless journeyman in his fifth year on the PGA Tour, shot 69-71 to linger alone three strokes back.

Leonard hit only nine greens in regulation on his way to 69 that put him just four shots off the 36-hole lead. Tied with Leonard at three under par was John Daly, who was happy just to be playing golf again. It was during the 1997 Players Championship that Daly's alcoholism almost cost him his career.

After a night of drinking and driving, Daly did substantial damage to his room and had to be taken away by ambulance. Months later, a clean, sober and humble Daly returned to the PGA Tour under the watchful eye of officials. The anniversary of the 1997 incident only heightened the scrutiny around the PGA Tour's longest hitter, but that didn't seem to phase Daly, who remained in contention until late Saturday when a 76 dropped him out of sight.

Leonard, on the other hand, showed his grit on Saturday by scrambling for what his father, Larry, called, "maybe the best 70 I've ever seen." Struggling with his iron play for the third day in a row, Leonard required only 24 putts in his two-under-par effort and five-under 211 total for 54 holes.

Other moves were made on Saturday as well. England's Lee Westwood rallied from an opening-round 74 with 71 on Friday, and an impressive early 68 on Saturday to temporarily move him within four of Janzen and Ozaki. Then Nick Faldo and Mark Calcavecchia mounted charges, Faldo's ending with a third-round 70 to move him to two under par, while Calcavecchia managed 68 to finish at four under for the three days.

None of those early efforts mattered, however, and by the end of play on Saturday, Leonard was the only early competitor within five strokes of the lead. By late afternoon all eyes had turned to two of the players playing in the final two groups: Janzen and Day. Kite had ballooned to 78, while Ozaki found trouble early, finishing with 76. Janzen, playing with Ozaki in the final group behind Day and Kite, quickly widened his lead with a 10-foot birdie putt on the ninth hole, and another birdie of similar length on the 14th.

Day made a charge of his own, tying Janzen at eight under par before falling back with two bogeys. Then, Day made a testy 15-foot birdie putt on the tricky par-five 16th to pull back within two, but Janzen topped him with a birdie of his own at the 16th. When the smoke cleared, it appeared to be a two-man race with Janzen, the 1993 U.S. Open champion and seven-time PGA Tour winner, shooting 69 for a 206 total, 10 under par, and holding a three-shot lead over Day, who shot 70, going into the final round.

Janzen felt good about his chances. "I think my game is better now than when I won the Open," he said.

Day was a little less optimistic. "Seems like a lot of the tournaments when I play really good somebody shoots zero," he said. When asked about his chances on the tough TPC course, however, Day quipped, "You start out holding on, and you hope you're still holding on at the end."

Holding on and undaunted, Justin Leonard hit his quota of balls late that afternoon, then went to dinner with his caddie, Bob Riefke. "We talked about it," Riefke said. "We knew that if he could get off to a good start, anything could happen."

Anything and everything did.

It started with Daly, rejuvenated and long as ever, rallying with a closing 69 after his disappointing Saturday performance. His performance electrified the gallery early in the day, setting the tone for what was to come. Then Payne Stewart who had posted lackluster scores of 72, 71 and 75, began rolling in putts from everywhere. His 65 turned out to be the low round of the tournament, good enough for a tie for eighth place. Westwood and

Calcavecchia made their presence known with a couple of 69s to go with their Saturday 68s, while Tom Lehman made a run by capping two rounds of 70 and one 72 with a closing score of 68, good enough, it would turn out, for a second-place tie with Day, who shot 71, two strokes behind Leonard.

No one paid much attention to Leonard, even though he was seen wandering through the champions' room in the clubhouse before the beginning of the round. Janzen, who saw Leonard, jokingly said, "we need to get better security in here."

Leonard got off to a grand start, roping a one-iron shot 245 yards to within 15 feet on the second hole and making the putt for eagle, then hitting that same one iron to within tap-in range on the 215-yard, par-three eighth. Behind him in the final group, Janzen almost whiffed his first drive of the day. "I'm lucky I made contact, my thumb slipped so badly," he said. The shot flew right and Janzen made bogey, thus setting the tone for what would be a struggling 78, the worst collapse of his career. "Nothing good was happening, and I ran out of holes to do anything about it," he said.

Day, playing in the final pairing with Janzen, shot 33 on the first nine and opened a two-stroke lead over Len Mattiace, a local favorite and former Florida High School Player of the Year. Surging with the best performance of his career, Mattiace ignited the fans with birdies at the 10th and 11th holes. Then on the 12th he made another birdie to move to 10 under par while Day was making two bogeys. Suddenly, Mattiace was leading the tournament.

Meanwhile, Leonard reeled off one of the most impressive series of one-putts in Players Championship history. He made a 20-foot birdie putt on the 10th, a 10-foot birdie putt on the 11th, a five-foot par putt on the 12th, then back-to-back 30-foot birdie putts on the 13th and 14th. By the time he reached the 16th tee, Leonard was 11 under par, one stroke ahead of Mattiace and four ahead of Day.

Larry Leonard, who did not make the trip to Royal Troon to see his son's first major victory but watched every shot and every putt here, said, "He was out there having a lot of fun, really enjoying himself like there's nothing to it."

Leonard made par on the difficult 17th, then three-putted the 72nd hole, for a five-under-par 67 and 278 total, but by that time it didn't matter. Mattiace, who plays the TPC at Sawgrass no fewer than 40 times a year, flew the island green with his tee shot on the par-three 17th. His third shot found the small, greenside bunker. From an awkward lie, Mattiace hit another shot into the water. Mattiace walked away with a quadruple-bogey eight. His wife, Kristen, watching in the gallery with the couple's infant daughter Gracee and Mattiace's wheelchair-bound mother Joyce, said, "I just covered my face and said, 'He doesn't deserve this.'"

Despite the empathy of a legion of fans, Mattiace put the incident into perspective. "I walked off 17 and saw my mother in a wheelchair, and I thought, I just made an eight, but I'm out here playing. It's just a game." With a smile and the attitude of a champion, Mattiace birdied the 18th for 70 and a 282 total to finish in a tie for fifth place.

Meanwhile, Leonard, who still sends his golf shirts home to be laundered, methodically retrieved his belongings, gave his mom a hug, and smiled at the crystal trophy and $750,000 first-place check that awaited him. Asked about his status as a "comeback kid," Leonard said, "I thought about it a little bit. It's fun to be able to make up ground like that, to shoot a really good score on Sunday when the trophy is right there on the 18th green waiting for somebody to come get it.

"I've never given up. Not that other guys give up, but if they get three or four over, they might try to do something they wouldn't ordinarily try, like to make a 40-footer. I've learned to be patient."

That patience paid off throughout The Players Championship. After Friday's round, Tom Lehman said, "(Justin and I) played together, and I saw how he was playing those first two days. I mean, Justin was in one of those 'get me off the course before I hurt myself' modes. He wasn't hitting it very well. But, he managed to get out at three under, even when he obviously wasn't playing his best golf."

No one questioned Leonard's ability to come back from all kinds of adversity after the final putt fell on Sunday. Even Janzen, who had seen a three-shot lead slip away, couldn't help but pay deference to Leonard's performance. As Leonard was giving his acceptance remarks, Janzen slipped in behind him and poked the new champion in the ribs. When Leonard barely flinched, Janzen smiled and said, "Amazing. He's not even ticklish."

Maybe not. But on this sunny Sunday in Florida, Leonard definitely got the last laugh.

8. Alfred Dunhill Cup

With everything else going on in St. Andrews, Scotland, notably the presence of what could be described as a "dream team" from the United States, it was easy to overlook that South Africa would be hard to beat in the defense of its title. South Africa proved not to be unbeatable — losing to Germany on the second day — but Retief Goosen certainly was.

The 29-year-old from Johannesburg provided the eighth instance, since the group stages were introduced in 1992, of a player going through the competition winning each of his five matches. Since Goosen had also achieved the feat in 1997, his run of 10 successive wins was the major factor in South Africa winning the Alfred Dunhill Cup for the second year running.

Not since Australia won the first two stagings of the tournament in 1985 and 1986 had a team managed to retain its title and Goosen was left one short of Greg Norman's record of winning 11 successive matches over the Old Course.

Others, especially Tiger Woods on his debut in the event, may have scored lower but Goosen always brought home the points. Even in his team's defeat by Germany, Goosen's one-stroke win (76-77) over Alexander Cejka had a crucial bearing on the standings in their group. His win over Stuart Appleby of Australia in the semi-finals secured South Africa's place in the final, where he led the way at the top of the order, beating Santiago Luna, the man who had tamed Tiger, as Spain was defeated 3-0 in the final.

"Retief was our trump card," said Ernie Els. "He deserves a medal for the way he has performed these last two years. I mean, 10 wins out of 10 is incredible around here. He has been the player we've relied on all the time. I can't praise his contribution highly enough."

The closing ceremony was a re-run of the previous year as David Frost, the captain, collected the trophy with his teammates, the threesome wrapped up against the cold wind which had been gusting up to 50 miles an hour over the Eden Estuary. "Back home, when the weather is bad we don't play golf," Els said. "We stay inside." Their rivals for the title will not be fooled again another year. When the going gets tough, as they say.

"To have two players as strong as Ernie and Retief is great," said Frost, a veteran of South Africa's defeat in the 1991 final to Sweden. "It doesn't matter how strong the wind blows, because no one is stronger than these two guys. I'm just here in case something goes wrong."

Although the defending champions, under a seeding system which took into account the world ranking of the leading two players from each country, South Africa was seeded sixth and drawn in Group Four with Zimbabwe, their neighbors and friendly rivals. The two teams had never met in the Alfred Dunhill Cup and would do so on the Saturday to decide the group winner. First South Africa enjoyed a 3-0 opening victory over France and Zimbabwe won by a similar score over Germany.

The attention at the start of the week was all on the Americans, the No. 1 seeds and hot favorites with the bookmakers. Their lineup was one of the strongest ever to be assembled for the competition, featuring as it did Woods, the world's No. 1 ranked player; Mark O'Meara, ranked No. 4 and the reigning Masters and British Open champion, and John Daly, whose recent playing record may have suffered along with his personal traumas, but who happened to win the 1995 Open at St. Andrews.

It was playing in the Alfred Dunhill Cup in 1993, when the United States won the second of three titles, that Daly fell in love with the Old Course and found the inspiration for the second of his major championship victories. He had won four of his five matches and his return to the event was even more special for the fact that he thinks he may never qualify or be selected for that little USA-Europe shindig every couple of years.

"This is my Ryder Cup," Daly said. "I am never going to be on the American Ryder Cup team, so this means a lot to me."

The venue makes that doubly so. "There is something so special about St. Andrews," Daly added, "not just because I won the Open here but because of the way the golf course is. I can hit my driver pretty much on all the holes and that makes it fun for me."

England was the unlucky team to be drawn against the United States in Group One on the opening day. The task was summed up by Lee Westwood, who was not particularly bothered who he was drawn with to play since "whoever it is, they are going to be half-decent, aren't they? It is either going to be the world No. 1, the world No. 4 or the man who won the Open the last time it was here." Westwood got the last of the three, Daly, but trailed by one playing the 17th hole.

In practice Daly had required no more than a sand iron for his second shot at the famous 461-yard 17th hole, the mere fact of which may have intimidated Westwood as he tried to cut off too much of the dogleg and found himself out of bounds in the garden of the hotel. "I was trying to draw the ball off the television tower with a fade," Westwood said. A double bogey from the young Englishman gave Daly a three-stroke win, 70-73.

A clean sweep was completed when O'Meara beat Peter Baker 67-74 and Woods defeated David Carter by eight strokes. Taking advantage of the tranquil conditions, Woods' 66 was effortlessly compiled. For the same reason that Daly prospers on the Old Course, Woods can utilize his length and imagination around the greens to maximum advantage. There was nothing outrageous about his performance and observers who walked all 18 holes made the comparison with Bobby Jones' 66 at Sunningdale in 1930. "More than anything, I had extra motivation seeing John out there doing really well," Woods said.

Sweden also won in Group One, 3-0 against Japan, but elsewhere the Asian challenger was stronger, particularly in Group Three where Korea beat New Zealand 2-1. Korea's only previous victory at St. Andrews came in a preliminary round against Colombia in 1989, but now Shin Yong-jin beat Michael Long 75-76 and Kang Wook-soon beat Frank Nobilo by four with a 71. With Appleby matching Woods' 66, Australia swept Argentina 3-0 in Group Three, but there was another potential upset in Group Two.

While Spain sneaked past Ireland 2-1 thanks to Luna's extra holes win over Darren Clarke, Scotland only defeated China by the same score. Colin Montgomerie, having had his problems with a Paraguayan and an Indian in the past, lost to China's leading player, Zhang Lian-wei 72-73. Andrew Coltart had a comfortable five-shot win over Cheng Jun with a 73, and Gary Orr's par at the last hole — after three bogeys in a row — was good enough for a one-stroke win (75-76) when his opponent, Wu Xiang-bing, three-putted from the back of the green.

"The Far Eastern countries have improved dramatically over the last 10 years," said Montgomerie. "They can compete as well as anyone and proved that again today." Monty had faced the wrath of the Scottish tabloid newspapers before, so he was probably not surprised to see the headline "The Great Wally of China" in one of them the following day. He also had to face the gentle rib-tickling of his teammates. "So the ploy worked, with Colin taking care of their dangerman," Coltart chided his captain. "Just pretend it is the Volvo Masters you are playing in, Colin."

The Scottish captain fared better the following day, a miserable one for the most part, cold with wind and rain and the odd ray of sunshine. Montgomerie beat Paul McGinley as Scotland defeated Ireland 2-1. Upsets were again in the air, but China, despite again pushing hard, lost 2-1 to Spain, while a 3-0 defeat for Korea against Australia was not a true reflection of the majority of the contest. New Zealand recovered to beat Argentina.

There was a double shock in Group Four. Zimbabwe's Nick Price scored a 70 which was not equalled until conditions eased slightly later in the day, but Jean Van de Velde's 71 beat Mark McNulty by 10 strokes and Thomas Levet edged Tony Johnstone by two to give France a 2-1 win. Germany's win over South Africa was by the same score but in reality was even closer.

It took playoff wins for both Thomas Gogele over Frost and Sven Struver over Els to secure the win, but what only became apparent later was that the Germans needed a clean sweep — denied them by Goosen beating Cejka 76-77 — to retain a chance of progressing in the competition. "I didn't realize at the time I needed to win, too," said Cejka, whose six-footer at the last to take the match in extra holes came up an inch short.

The mathematics of the situation in Group Four meant that despite France and Germany scoring impressive wins, neither could win the group and progress to the semi-finals. The winner of the Zimbabwe-South Africa contest was guaranteed to progress. "It is disappointing, but we must think of the good thing, that we managed to beat the defending champions," Struver said.

The Americans continued on their merry way with another 3-0 victory, this time over Japan, with Woods and O'Meara shooting 70s to win comfortably and Daly beating Nobuo Serizawa by three despite a 77.

With Sweden also beating England 3-0 — its worst-ever start in the competition — the deciding match in Group One on Saturday was a shootout between the Swedes and the United States. With Sjoland in front against O'Meara in the bottom match and Woods always in control against Mathias Gronberg — he would win the match by seven strokes with another 66 — the vital match became the encounter between Daly and Per-Ulrik Johansson.

Both went to the turn in level par and then the Swede bogeyed the 11th. Despite a birdie at the next, Johansson dropped further behind. Daly drove onto the front of the green at the 316-yard hole but, finding a bank between his ball and the cup, he elected to chip and the ball disappeared for an eagle.

By the 17th the match was once more even. Johansson took the safe route with his approach, finding the front right of the green. Daly's massive drive had left him only 90 yards to the pin but his wedge shot came up short.

Daly now faced a difficult chip shot, but not as difficult as the one he would face moments later. The chip-and-run was "two or three inches," according to Daly, short of pace and the contours of the terrain took the ball perilously close to the Road bunker. One of the game's most frightening hazards now lurked between Daly's ball and the green, with a road, a wall and out of bounds awaiting on the other side.

The "flop shot" that Daly produced, from a tight lie on hardpan ground, was sheer brilliance, leaving him three feet away. With Johansson three-putting, the hole was halved. "What he is trying to tell you," Woods interjected as Daly described the shot later, "is that it was a hell of a shot."

O'Meara, who saw the stroke from down the fairway, told a particularly persistent questioner, "We don't have that shot. You can't play that shot. You would have been over the road and over the wall, and so would I."

Daly was just short of the green at the last hole with his drive but Johansson pitched to four feet before the American got the chance to putt two feet past. Johansson had to hole the putt to take the match into extra holes and, with Woods also clearly ahead of Gronberg, Sweden's hopes of an upset disappeared when Johansson's putt did not. Sjoland and O'Meara eventually tied with 68s and decided not to play off with the result of the group already decided. "We don't blame Per," said Sjoland. "This is a team game and we win and lose as a team."

"Once again our strategy of letting our big man go first worked out to our advantage," O'Meara said. "I knew his match would be pivotal because Tiger was playing well and was going to win his match and I was behind for most of the day." Daly said, "It was just awesome. My three matches have come down to the wire and I've pulled through, which makes me feel proud. It has been nice to get the butterflies in my stomach again."

While Sweden was unlucky in coming up against the No. 1 seeds and though the Americans had by far the lowest stroke total for the first three days — Woods himself was 14 under par — Sweden had the second best total and England the fourth best, better than group winners South Africa and Spain.

Friends as well as rivals from growing up together, Zimbabwe's match with South Africa had the feel of local competition. Els always held a commanding lead against Johnstone, Price got the better of Frost, and McNulty succumbed on the second nine to Goosen. "It is never easy playing your friends, but we played well and this was a good time to get our games back together," said Frost, the South African captain. "You don't want to peak too early and hopefully we are doing it at the right time."

Australia just had to win one game against New Zealand to go through and, thanks to Craig Parry's 70-71 win over Long, that's all they managed. For Spain and Scotland, however, nothing less than victory would do. With Jose Maria Olazabal beating Orr by three and Coltart hitting a pitch to a foot at the last to edge Luna by one, the outcome came down to the playoff between Montgomerie and Miguel Angel Jimenez.

Montgomerie found his drive in a seeded divot, could not get close with his second shot, and then had to watch as Jimenez caught his sand wedge heavy. The effect was for the ball to run out to within tap-in range of the cup. As the etiquette of the game demands, the Spaniard apologized to his opponent but it did not make it any easier for the Scottish captain to bear.

"I didn't hit it very well," Jimenez admitted. He had similarly mis-hit his approach to the 18th and only the fact that his four-foot putt lipped out had kept the match alive. "It is the new shot of golf," Jimenez added with a smile. "Hit it fat and let it run to the hole."

The following morning, Spain had to face the Americans and Olazabal's 72 was good enough to beat O'Meara by four. Daly beat Jimenez by two with a 73 to extend his record in the competition to eight wins in nine matches. He was the only member of his team to remain unbeaten this time despite the fact that Woods was level with Luna playing the 17th.

Woods made the green, but was 45 feet from the pin on the front right. He left his approach putt six feet short and then saw Luna play a delicate chip over the infamous bunker to two feet. "It was impressive," Woods said. While Luna made his par, Woods missed his to fall one stroke behind. Both drove into the Valley of Sin, Woods having slightly skied his tee shot. The American putted up to four feet past the pin, then Luna, in trying to leave his putt just short of the hole, saw his effort roll back off the green.

"I wanted to get my ball just over the hill, so it would run to the hole," Luna said. "I did not want to hit it too hard and see it run past but I did not get the right speed and it rolled back. My caddie said, 'Relax, and take two putts,' and I did. This time I got the speed right and I knew I would take four."

So Woods had to hole his putt for a birdie to take the match into extra holes. By now it had long been known that this would be the pivotal match, but Woods missed the putt on the left. "I pulled a couple of short putts at the last two holes," Woods said. "I just didn't hit them the way I would have liked and it wasn't good enough to take the matches into extra holes. I have to hand it to Santiago."

"I think it was more difficult for him today," said Luna, ranked No. 190 in the world. "He is the No. 1 and is meant to beat me."

"Santiago's win was a great scalp for him," said Olazabal. "He is a player who I believe if he believed in himself more would do better."

Although Steve Elkington defeated Els by one, Frost and Goosen were both well ahead in their matches and Australia went down 2-1. If the South Africans were expecting to face the Americans in the afternoon, they could not afford to take the Spaniards lightly. Goosen was trailing by two at the turn but came home in 34. Luna holed from 18 feet for a par at the 17th to take the match to the last hole level and the Spaniard then drove through the green at the 354-yard 18th.

Luna was unlikely to keep his chip from the thick rough on the green and, in the Valley of Sin for the second time in the day, he had to get down in two for a par. He did so, but Goosen, having found the green from the tee, two-putted for a birdie. Goosen was the only player to match par in the afternoon. Frost won by two against Jimenez despite a 76, while Els' 75 brought him home two in front of Olazabal.

"Retief is going to be promoted next year," Frost said. "Ernie has had enough of playing at the back so Retief is going to move down from the front."

"Definitely, everything about this week brings out the best in me," Goosen said. "I'm looking forward to coming back next year and trying to break Greg Norman's record."

9. Cisco World Match Play

There is a room in Mark O'Meara's home called the Media Room where the busy golf professional and father can get away from it all. "It's the guys' room," O'Meara said. "The kids have their own room and this is mine. I can take a nap, watch a movie, or the Golf Channel or tennis or football. I don't spend a lot of time watching golf at home but the European golf comes on early in the morning and I watch a lot of that."

One of the things O'Meara likes to watch on the Golf Channel are the reruns of past World Match Play tournaments, and you can be sure the 1998 final will get a lot of air time in the future. In beating Tiger Woods, the world's No. 1 player and his youthful friend, O'Meara got to add another trophy to his den, alongside the Masters Tournament trophy and the British Open Championship's claret jug.

"There is no way I can honestly say that I could have dreamed at the start of the year that I would be here as the Masters champion, the Open champion and now the World Match Play champion," he said. "I don't think I take enough time, nobody does, to cherish the moment. But believe me, I know how special those events are and how wonderful it is at this stage of my life to accomplish these things."

At age 41, O'Meara, already the oldest man to win two major titles in the same season, also became the oldest winner of the World Match Play Championship. He did it in style, too, the sort of high-class effort we saw at Augusta and Royal Birkdale. O'Meara had to come from behind to beat Colin Montgomerie, then defeated Vijay Singh, the defending champion, by a record score of 11 and 10, before his classic encounter with Woods.

It went all the way to the 36th hole and contained a dazzling array of shots and, when it really mattered, two crucial putts from the winner. "I am very happy for Mark," Woods said. "Until now Mark has not been getting enough credit for as good a player as he really is. He's a great player and he's won two majors and now the World Match Play. It's amazing, he's had a great year and now he's getting his just dues and it's about time."

The final, played out against the backdrop of a perfect autumnal day on the West Course at the Wentworth Club in Virginia Water, England, only capped what was a highly successful 35th playing of the event. With a new sponsor in Cisco Systems and presenting sponsor in Diners Club International came one of the best fields for the tournament in recent years. Woods, playing in the London area for the first time, brought a palpable air of excitement to the proceedings. He was seeded No. 2, behind Singh, who had recently added the PGA Championship to his win at Wentworth of the year before. Ernie Els, a three-time winner, was seeded third and O'Meara was the fourth to receive a bye in the first round.

Singh, who beat Els in the final in 1997, was one of the few players to take the title after playing all four rounds and with the course playing soft after a full summer of rain, the classic 36-hole format would again prove testing on stamina as well as ability. The first day match-ups offered the home crowd four British players to follow and the fascination of who would qualify for what were sure to be some thrilling quarter-finals.

The pairing who knew the winner would be facing Woods the following day was Ian Woosnam against Darren Clarke. Woosnam had been a late addition to the field after a double withdrawal. Stewart Cink, the young American player, was the first to pull out of the event as he sought to boost his status on the American money list and earn a place in the top 30 for the Tour Championship. Bernhard Langer was Cink's replacement but was forced to step down on the eve of the tournament with a recurrence of neck and back problems.

Woosnam's slightly lackluster season had been plagued by a lack of inspiration with his putting, never meeting the high standard of his iron play. He found difficulties in reading the greens but seemed to be immediately at home on a course where he has won two World Match Plays and two Volvo PGA Championships. Woosnam won the first two holes against Clarke, who bogeyed both, and the tone was set for the day. Three up after 15, the Welshman went to lunch two ahead. Although Clarke birdied the second in the afternoon to narrow the gap to one, a run of three holes in a row to Woosnam from the fifth brought him what was ultimately a 4-and-3 win.

"Neither of us played very well but I holed a few more putts," said Woosnam. "One of the best things that has happened to me for a long time was the way I putted today. I am fortunate to be here and I've got nothing to lose, but I know I'll have to raise my game tomorrow."

The same did not have to be said by or about Lee Westwood. The 25-year-old Englishman enjoyed a dream debut in the tournament, in keeping with the rest of his year. The World Match Play had long been one of his favorite events and he admitted to once missing school to watch Woosnam on television. The occasion was the final in 1987 which was held over to the Monday due to a storm earlier in the week. Westwood said, "I was ill and even though I probably could have gone to school, the World Match Play final was on the television."

Westwood also said, "It is great being out on the course and looking back down the fairway and seeing a match coming up towards you. It's just like watching it on television." Westwood provided some fine entertainment as he beat Stuart Appleby 8 and 7.

He is not the sort of character to worry about things unnecessarily and it was not until Westwood was walking down the first fairway that he turned to his caddie, Mick Doran, and asked what tactics they were going to employ. Doran, whose knowledge of Wentworth goes back further than his boss and included caddieing for Costantino Rocca when the Italian won the Volvo PGA in 1996, replied, "Try not to make any bogeys and make as many birdies as you can."

Westwood obeyed the instructions so well that Appleby, the young Australian whose life had been thrown into turmoil when his wife Renay was killed in an accident at Waterloo Station in July, never had a chance to get into the match.

By the time the pair walked off the 12th green, Westwood had just made five birdies in a row, seven in the last nine holes, and was six up. The reply from Appleby said much about the young man's strength of character. The Australian won three of the remaining holes before lunch and his 67 deserved more than to be three down. On the other hand, as Westwood reflected, his estimated 64 probably deserved a larger lead.

Five more birdies in the afternoon, making a total of 13 for the day with just one bogey, meant Westwood cantered to his victory and a quarter-final match against Els. "I will have to treat Ernie as I treated Stuart, with respect," Westwood said. "Everybody here is capable of beating anyone else and you just have to accept that if you want to win this event, you've got to beat people like Ernie and Tiger. But I was glad I was playing today and not sitting around, and 12 under does no harm to your confidence."

Montgomerie made it through to his date with O'Meara but not quite as comfortably as the 4-and-3 win over Thomas Bjorn might suggest. The Dane led three times in the match and only wilted as his back injury worsened. Bjorn had not played since the Trophee Lancome three weeks before and had been told by doctors to stop playing for the remainder of the year. While he was not doing any further damage, Bjorn decided the dates at Wentworth and the Volvo Masters were too good to miss and, until Montgomerie won four holes in a row from the fifth to take the lead decisively, it was an intriguing contest.

"I managed to birdie the sixth, seventh and eighth this afternoon and that was the crucial time," said Montgomerie, who had been struggling with his long game at the time. "I changed my backswing, my swing, my whole set-up. It seemed to work."

An incident at the seventh in the morning did not have lasting consequences, despite Montgomerie going one down because of it, dropping another hole at the ninth and not seeming to recover his humor until winning the 12th. The seventh is the only blind driving hole on the course, the landing area being down in a valley. "It's the only hole where the players can't see where their drives end and the spotters can't see who hit first," Montgomerie explained.

The two drives ended side by side and Montgomerie went straight to the one beside which his spotter was standing with a board with his name on it. He marked the ball with a tee peg, picked it up and then discovered it was Bjorn's ball. That meant a one-shot penalty but the Scot was relieved that it was not an immediate loss of hole.

"I just fancied his ball, it was nearer," Montgomerie said in jocular fashion afterwards. He added, "I wasn't trying to improve my lie, or to gain any advantage, but you shouldn't go around picking up other people's balls."

The best match of the first round was the encounter between Patrik Sjoland and Steve Stricker. The American, Stricker, runner-up in the PGA Championship, took the lead three times in the morning but found himself tied at lunch. The Swede was twice ahead before falling behind again at the ninth in the afternoon, but the 10th proved a perfect illustration of how dangerous a match player he is.

Sjoland's forte is his fabulous short game and although Stricker was much more at home on a course playing so long, an ability to get the ball in the hole can never be underestimated. The 10th is a par-three of 186 yards and Stricker struck a seven iron to five feet. Sjoland missed the green, had an awkward chip that he could get no closer than 16 feet, but holed the putt for a three. Stricker duly missed his birdie and the hole was halved.

The American then bogeyed the 11th and, once the 16th and 17th were traded, they went to the 18th hole tied. A three wood and a four wood put Stricker just short of the green, while Sjoland drove poorly and his second shot stopped in the right rough 130 yards from the pin. A brilliant nine iron to a foot gave him a four and Stricker left his chip 14 feet short and then missed the putt. "I was lucky," Sjoland admitted. "I was fortunate that the ball ran all the way to the hole after pitching on the green."

Sjoland did not last long the next day against Singh, although he did win four holes in a row to prevent a record defeat before losing 7 and 6. If Singh had known what was about to happen to him the next day, he might have been more perturbed but, as it was, his performance was outstanding. His morning round of 62 left him nine up, one outside the record, but his outward 29 tied the mark of Tony Jacklin in 1972 and Bernhard Langer in 1990 and his seven-up lead at that stage was a record.

Singh birdied the first, holing from 20 feet, won the third with a par, eagled the fourth, with a four iron to two feet, birdied the next two, won the seventh with a par and birdied the eighth. "Everything was on song," said Singh, who, just for good measure, chipped in at the third in the afternoon to go 11 up. "It was Seve who once told me that if you get a big lead, you just keep going. You can't feel sorry for your opponent. He played well at the end but I didn't think he could win all 11 holes. Impossible. There was no way he was going to win."

Getting a bye for the first time, Singh said he was "pretty eager to get going," but O'Meara had to come from behind against Montgomerie. The Scot won the first with a par and was in front for the entire morning, but significantly O'Meara won the 17th and 18th, with a birdie and an eagle — he holed from 50 feet at the last — to cut the deficit to one at the interval.

A pulled drive at the third seemed to drain the confidence from Montgomerie and a bogey there set O'Meara on a run of seven holes out of eight. Seeking an opportunity, O'Meara birdied five of the next seven holes before winning 5 and 4. "I gave him the upper hand and he relaxed and played like the Masters and Open champion he is," Montgomerie said.

While O'Meara was joking that he might need "two shots a side" against Singh in their semi-final and that if "Vijay shoots a 62 in the morning again I'll caddie for him in the afternoon," the identity of the other semi-final players was taking time to resolve itself.

Westwood and Els halved the first 10 holes before Westwood established a three-up lead by lunch. Els was credited with a 68, Westwood a 65. The South African, albeit not playing as well as on previous visits, has come to love both the tournament and the venue. The start he made in the afternoon might have seen off lesser champions than Westwood.

Els won the first four holes and by the seventh was two up, but it was not to be good enough. He bogeyed the 11th, then saw Westwood hit a three wood to two feet for an eagle at the 12th and then birdie the 13th to regain the lead. Another birdie came at the 16th as Westwood won 2 and 1. This was the first time in his five appearances that Els had gone home before the final. "Lee is the player to beat now," he said.

Westwood replied, "I am delighted to beat Ernie. No matter what tournament I would be pleased, but especially around Wentworth and in a tournament he has made his own. The shot at the 12th was one of my best for a long time. It was bang on line and I thought it was going in until it stopped dead."

Woosnam and Woods went further, all the way to the 37th, but it was the

Welshman who rued his chances. Three up after eight holes, Woosnam could have gone further ahead on a course he knows so well and which the American, as well as trying to shake off the flu, was learning for the first time.

With the quality of the line-up, and especially Woods' presence, a record crowd of over 17, 000 had been drawn to this leafy corner of Surrey. Woods got back to one down after the first round, and was two up after eight in the afternoon, but Woosnam birdied the 15th to be two up with three to play.

The end was ugly for the Welshman. He three-putted the 16th, missing from three feet, holed from 15 feet to remain one up playing the last, but again three-putted at the last, missing from four and a half feet this time.

"The putt he made on 17 showed what a big champion he is, but he gave me a couple of breaks," Woods said. "It was definitely a lucky escape at the last." With Woosnam in trouble off the tee at the first, a par was good enough to take Woods through. "Lee is 21 under par, that's not bad. I'm going to have my work cut out tomorrow."

Woods has given golf a youthful image the world over, but in a way Westwood is at the forefront of the new generation in Europe. The Englishman was three up after seven but Woods squared the match at the 16th and won the last to sneak a lead at the interval.

As fine a ball-striker as Woods is, Westwood lost nothing in comparison from tee to green, and it was only just as Westwood, after a heavy run of tournaments, was beginning to feel the strain of his exertions that Woods suddenly found inspiration on the greens. When the match ended on the 14th green with a 5-and-4 victory for the American, Woods had single-putted seven of the last eight greens.

Woods birdied the seventh, eighth, 10th and 12th in the run. "I putted awful all day and you can't expect to do that and beat someone like Tiger putting as he was," Westwood said.

The day's play had been held up for two and a half hours by overnight rain, but O'Meara made sure he was still finished in good time with a blistering display against Singh. The Fijian, having dished it out the day before, just had to take it. O'Meara was six up after seven and went to the turn in 31.

Being 10 up after 18 matched the record. In the afternoon O'Meara won the second and third and lost the fourth, but a half on the eighth was enough for another record. No match had ever finished on that green before. Tom Watson's 11-and-9 win over Dale Hayes in 1978 was the previous best.

"It was one of those rounds this morning where I was in the zone," O'Meara said of his estimated 63. "It was different in the afternoon because you have to change your mindset. You're thinking, 'God Almighty, if I lose 11 holes in a row it could be the biggest turnaround in golf. It's nice to have the record, but Vijay probably doesn't want to be included in it."

So it was on to the all-American dream final. It was the first final for 23 years to feature two Americans, but one that had been played out many times at Isleworth, the Orlando, Florida, club where they both live. "He took 30 bucks off me that last time we played," O'Meara said. "I know he wants to be beat and I want to beat him," Woods said. "But I'll be happy if he wins and he'll be happy if I win."

When Woods refused to concede a putt early on, O'Meara knew this was no friendly match. The 22-year-old won the first three holes, chipping in at the second and holing from 35 feet at the third. He went four up at the sixth, but O'Meara's nine iron to two feet at the 11th got one back. Woods birdied the 16th, but then put his second shot at the 17th into the trees on the right and, finding it unplayable, conceded the hole.

Woods went to lunch three up, and O'Meara noticed a screen in the clubhouse saying it was a big lead. "I was thinking, that's not a big lead. I can make some birdies and turn the tide," O'Meara said.

The one at the first, with a three iron to 11 feet, was important and the match was square by the sixth. There O'Meara holed from outside Woods and he won the next by hitting a seven iron to two feet. The golf now was breathtaking. Woods' six iron to a foot at the ninth levelled the match again and he birdied the next to go one up.

Walking off the 12th tee, Woods told his opponent that whoever won, it had been a great match. It would get better. O'Meara's two iron into the green hit the flagstick and finished two feet away. They were all square. O'Meara birdied from nine feet at the 14th and Woods missed from inside again, but a wild drive from O'Meara at the next hole squared the match again.

O'Meara again drove poorly at the 16th. He could only find a greenside bunker with his second shot and came out to 15 feet. He holed the putt for a par. "It was a must-make putt," he said. Woods admitted he knew his opponent was going to hole that putt but he got too aggressive with his nine-footer for birdie. "I pushed it and then pushed the one back," he said. The result was three putts, a huge mistake. O'Meara, from nowhere it seemed, was now one up.

Woods skied his drive at the par-five 17th, kicked out at the ground in anger, but hit a brilliant banana-bender around the dogleg for his second shot and kept alive the chance of a birdie which he duly took to keep the match alive.

Both found bunkers at the last hole, laid up and then Woods, from the rough, hit his third shot to eight feet pin high. O'Meara, from the fairway, saw his wedge spin back off the green to 18 feet but with another outrageous putt, he ended the match there and then. Woods could do nothing, defeated by one hole. "It was an incredible way to end the tournament," O'Meara said. "I knew he was going to hole his."

"The ebb and flow in match play is a beautiful thing," Woods said. "In an 18-hole match there is usually only one swing, but over 36 holes it can happen and there must have been four or five swings which shows what a great format it is. He made some great putts down the stretch which won the match."

In giving so much to each other as friends, the pair together have given much more to the golfing world. Said O'Meara, "I could never hit a golf ball like Tiger. He's got a lot more power and sometimes more imagination. What I might have is a bit more wisdom and a bit more patience. I enjoy the fact that you are nervous out there and that there is uncertainty at the end. To keep coming through when you have is something that makes me proud of myself."

10. American Tours

As 1998 got underway, some of the biggest question marks concerned David Duval. Did Duval just happen to hit the right biorhythm in the last part of 1997? Or was he a great player in waiting? It didn't take long to answer those questions. At the season-opening Mercedes Championships, Duval had a chance to win four tournaments in a row, going back to the 1997 Michelob Championship. He was only one stroke back after the third round, but it was not to be. Phil Mickelson won in dramatic fashion, holding off charges by Tiger Woods and Mark O'Meara while Duval fell back with 73.

That would be one of the few times that Duval would fade. He came roaring back, capturing the Tucson Chrysler Classic by four strokes for his fourth victory in eight starts. Then in April, he was two Mark O'Meara putts away from donning a green jacket in Augusta at the Masters Tournament, proving that Duval was not only capable of winning PGA Tour events, but contending in the biggest tournaments in the world.

When the last putt dropped for birdie and a final round of 64 at the Shell Houston Open, Duval had his fifth victory in 12 starts and recognition as America's best player midway through the year. He would win again at the NEC World Series of Golf, making him one of only nine players since 1960 to win three PGA Tour events in two consecutive years. "When you hear the list of players you've joined and the first two names are Nicklaus and Palmer, that's pretty amazing stuff," Duval said. He would elevate himself into an even more elite category in October when he successfully defended his Michelob Championship title for his fourth victory of the year. He also won the unofficial Fred Meyer Challenge with partner Jim Furyk.

As wonderful as Duval's play was, it wasn't enough to earn Player of the Year honors. Those went to Mark O'Meara in voting by members of the PGA Tour and Golf Writers Association of America, and the points system of the PGA of America. O'Meara, at age 41, shed the title of best player never to win a major championship in a huge way in 1998, capturing the Masters by one stroke over Duval and Fred Couples and the British Open in a playoff with Brian Watts. O'Meara also had a victory over Tiger Woods in the Cisco World Match Play. As Jim Furyk said, "You win two majors, you're Player of the Year, period." A majority of players obviously agreed.

Duval and O'Meara weren't the only multiple winners. Couples added two more trophies to his mantle, picking up wins at the Bob Hope Chrysler Classic and Memorial Tournament. Billy Mayfair had victories at the Nissan Open and Buick Open, while Vijay Singh, long recognized as the hardest working man in golf, hit the jackpot with back-to-back wins at the PGA Championship and Sprint International. Phil Mickelson added to his season-opening Mercedes Championships with a win in the storm-delayed AT&T Pebble Beach National Pro-Am, and John Huston added to his Hawaiian victory late in the year with a win at the National Car Rental Classic.

Perhaps the most compelling multiple-winner story came late in the year when 40-year-old Hal Sutton, who only had one victory since 1986, picked up a win at the Westin Texas Open, then followed it with a dramatic playoff victory over Singh in the season-ending Tour Championship. Sutton could not contain himself when speaking about what it meant to be back in the game he loves. "There was a time when I was embarrassed to hit balls on the range with these guys," he said. "All this does is make me want to practice tomorrow because I know how quickly this can leave you."

The year of 1998 provided many other memories, including Tom Watson's unlikely return to the winner's circle at age 48, and Steve Elkington's return to the game after numerous health problems, as well as Stuart Appleby's win at the Kemper Open, followed by the tragic loss of his wife Renay in an automobile accident in London. Tiger Woods won once in the United States, in Atlanta, but ended up with the best major championship record of any player who didn't win. Greg Norman underwent reconstructive surgery on his left shoulder in April and was out of action for most of the year.

Duval narrowly edged Woods for the Vardon Trophy, the award for the lowest scoring average. His 69.13 average beat Woods by less than a tenth of a stroke, while his $2,591,031 in official earnings was the largest in PGA Tour history. "I've done all I can do, and I'm really happy," Duval said. "I controlled the things that were in my control. That's what's important."

U.S. PGA Tour

Mercedes Championships—$1,700,000

Winner: Phil Mickelson

At one point it looked as though 1998 would begin just like 1997 left off. Notable winners Tiger Woods, David Duval, Ernie Els, Phil Mickelson and Mark O'Meara all appeared on the leaderboard at the season-opening Mercedes Championships, but in the end it was Mickelson, the 27-year-old lefthander, who staved off late-round charges by Woods and the King of the California Swing, O'Meara, to come away as the year's first champion.

"I'm looking at 1998 as a really big proving ground," Mickelson said after finishing 1997 without coming close in a major championship. "At the end of your career, the only thing people remember is the number of major championships you've won."

It wasn't a major, but the Mercedes Championships provided some major moments under some memorable weather conditions. An El Niño-driven storm soaked Carlsbad and the rest of the California coast, causing play to be suspended on numerous occasions and forcing the PGA Tour to impose the lift, clean and place rule for the final three rounds. Fortunately, Thursday's conditions were ideal. Forty-year-old John Cook, who makes his home in nearby Rancho Mirage, led after the first round with a seven-under-par 65. At four under par, three shots back, Mickelson found himself tied with the man everyone was watching: David Duval. He had won the last three events of 1997. If he could make it four in a row, he would be the first player since Ben Hogan in 1953 to win four consecutive starts.

Mickelson put an end to those plans, however. During a rain-soaked, stop-

and-start second round that had to be finished on Saturday, Mickelson shot 67 to tie Cook for the lead at 135, nine under par. By sunset on Saturday, Mickelson found himself alone atop the leaderboard with 68 and a 203 total, 13 under par, with Duval lurking one shot back. It was a lead the lefthander would never relinquish, as Mickelson shot 68 again in the final round for a 271 total.

Not that there weren't a fair number of scary moments. On Sunday, Woods mounted one of the charges for which he's become known, blazing the 7,002-yard La Costa Resort and Spa course in 64 strokes for a 272 total. That score not only turned out to be one shot shy of the winner, but Tiger didn't even beat one member of his own group. Tiger's playing companion on Sunday, his friend and neighbor O'Meara, also shot 64 to finish tied with Woods for second at 16 under par, one behind the champion Mickelson.

"Mark and I knew 18 under was going to be the number," Tiger said. He was wrong. Seventeen was good enough.

Bob Hope Chrysler Classic—$2,300,000

Winner: Fred Couples

Golfers with bad backs aren't supposed to win five-round tournaments, but don't tell that to Fred Couples. After a dismal 1997, which included persistent back problems, only 15 tournament starts, his first non-top-30 money finish in 11 years and the tragic loss of his father to leukemia, Couples proved he was back on track by winning the Bob Hope Chrysler Classic in grand fashion.

After firing two straight rounds of 65, the taciturn Bruce Lietzke took a one-shot lead into the final three days of play. Perhaps the only man in golf more easy-going than Couples, the 46-year-old Lietzke said, "I only entered nine tournaments last year, but this year I'm going for 10." He came very close to starting that marathon with a victory. A third-round 71 dropped him off the pace, but a fourth-round 62 put Lietzke three shots ahead of Couples going into the fifth and final round. Couples had scores of 64, 70, 66 and 66.

On Sunday Couples made a typical Couples move. He birdied the ninth after bouncing his tee shot off of an NBC golf cart. He birdied No. 14 from the lawn of a nearby resident, then reached the green on the par-five 18th and two-putted to catch Lietzke with his third consecutive 66 and a 332 total, 28 under par. Lietzke finished with 69.

Throughout the drama, however, there was no doubt that this was a very different Fred Couples. "Nothing can replace my dad," Couples said. "It's the oldest cliche in the book: There are more important things than golf. I realize that now more than ever. I hated to see him suffer, and it's better that he's not suffering anymore."

It was Tom Couples who convinced his son to accept captain Tom Kite's appointment to the Ryder Cup team, even though Fred's back continued to be questionable through most of the 1997 season. Then Tom watched as his son attained one of America's only winning records in Spain. It would be the last time he saw Fred compete. On Thanksgiving, with Fred scheduled to participate in the weekend Skins Game, Tom passed away. "It never hits you until it's final," Fred says. "So, in terms of last year, no, it wasn't a good one. But, you've got to move on."

Fred did move on. In front of a gracious Palm Springs crowd which included former president Gerald Ford and 90-year-old host Bob Hope, Couples birdied the 18th hole a second time to win a playoff, and put 1997 behind him. "Next year I get to play with Mr. Hope," the ever-optimistic Couples said. "That will be fun."

Phoenix Open—$2,500,000

Winner: Jesper Parnevik

When Tiger Woods aced the par-three 16th (a regular watering hole for Arizona State students) during the 1997 Phoenix Open, the resulting ballyhoo rivaled the Super Bowl in both decibels and enthusiasm. While the 1998 event was no less uproarious, it was another young player who found kinship among the sun worshippers.

Swedish sensation Jesper Parnevik came into the Phoenix Open with a reputation as a man who marched to his own drummer. With the trademark upturned bill of his SAP America cap and a less-than-traditional taste in clothing, Parnevik not only fit in with the Phoenix party crowd, he set the tone for the players as well. Opening with two consecutive three-under-par 68s, Parnevik fired 66 on Saturday to move to the top of the leaderboard along with 1997 qualifying tournament medalist Scott Verplank.

On Sunday, dressed in black and carrying a Montecristo victory cigar in his golf bag, Parnevik set out to gain his first victory on the U.S. PGA Tour. On the second nine, however, there was trouble. Parnevik was spraying his tee shots, and when he let an easy birdie opportunity slip away on the 13th hole, he temporarily lost the lead to Tommy Armour III and Steve Pate.

Determined not to fall victim to the fate he had suffered at the 1997 British Open, where he let a lead slip away on the final nine, Parnevik birdied the 14th and 15th holes to gain a lead he would never relinquish. He finished with 67 for a 269 total, 15 under par, for a three-stroke margin over Armour, Pate, Tom Watson and Brent Geiberger. His par on the tempestuous 16th might have lacked the drama of Tiger's 1997 ace, but with victory in his grasp, Parnevik was no less excited.

When he lit the victory cigar on the 18th tee, the crowd was no less enthusiastic either.

AT&T Pebble Beach National Pro-Am—$2,500,000

Winner: Phil Mickelson

Although the players only finished 54 holes, the 1998 AT&T Pebble Beach National Pro-Am made history as the longest tournament in PGA Tour history. In fact, it took six months and 20 days to crown Phil Mickelson with his 13th career PGA Tour victory, his eighth on the West Coast. The reason for the delay was the El Niño weather pattern that washed away portions of the California coast in the early part of the year. Portions of the historic Pebble Beach links were almost lost because of the torrential rains, wind and flooding produced by El Niño in January and February. Fortunately, by August, things were back to normal and the most unusual event of the year was completed in record-breaking style.

The first nine holes were completed on January 29, with rain postponing the second nine until January 30. At that point the tournament was shortened to 54 holes. While the second round was completed, as scheduled, on January 31, the third round was a total washout. Not wanting to cancel the event, as they were forced to do in 1996, Tour officials came up with the idea of pushing the final round back six months, finishing the tournament on the Monday after the PGA Championship.

One hundred and thirty-three of the original 168 participants appeared for the final round, despite the travel inconveniences and other scheduling conflicts. The Tour even chartered a jet to transport players from Seattle after the PGA Championship, to Monterey, California. Pebble Beach officials quickly cleaned up after an antique car show that graced the grounds over the weekend, and by the time the first ball was airborne on August 17, the courses (the final round had to be played on three courses — Pebble Beach, Spyglass Hill and Poppy Hills) were dry, hard and hot.

In order to replicate conditions from earlier in the year, officials had to invoke the lift-clean-and-place rule, even though conditions in August were ideal. That allowed Mickelson, who was one stroke out of the lead when play was suspended back in January, to fire a final-round 67 at Pebble Beach for a 54-hole total of 14-under-par 202, the lowest score in tournament history. Tom Pernice, Jr. also shot 67 and finished second, one stroke behind. Paul Azinger, Jim Furyk and J.P. Hayes tied for third at 204.

While the weather didn't claim any victims in the August version, the shift in playing conditions and momentum from the layoff certainly did. In January, Tom Watson and Tim Herron were leading the tournament at 10 under par after 36 holes. Watson played his best from January through May. He didn't make the cut at the PGA Championship, and, despite his fine play earlier, he didn't enter the final round here with much enthusiasm or confidence. Watson shot 72 at Poppy Hills and finished tied for eighth. Herron, who made the cut at the PGA Championship but finished dead last with closing rounds of 79 and 76, could manage no better than 74 at Spyglass Hill. He finished tied for 19th.

Other momentum victims included Jay Haas, who was one stroke back in January and who played great through April, but who had also struggled through the summer. Haas, however, had a fine weekend at the PGA Championship, finishing with strong rounds of 73 and 69, but he couldn't carry it over through Monday. His final-round 70 left Haas tied with Fuzzy Zoeller and Steve Elkington at 205, three strokes off Mickelson's winning pace.

Tom Lehman, who also stood one back when play was suspended, shot 71 and finished tied for ninth with Watson, Chris Smith and Bob Gilder. "The best thing would have been to say, 'Sorry, Mother Nature won. I'm going home,'" Lehman said.

Mickelson couldn't have disagreed more. "It's weird to have a one-round tournament, but after what happened in 1996, I was awfully glad they made the decision they did," he said. With a $450,000 first-place check, plus another $100,000 bonus from Bank of America for finishing as the leading money winner on the West Coast swing, Mickelson might hope for more weather-related decisions in the future.

Buick Invitational—$2,100,000

Winner: Scott Simpson

As was the case for all of the West Coast swing, El Niño-driven weather continued to be the big story at the Buick Invitational. While Torrey Pines and La Jolla, California, held up better than Pebble Beach a week earlier, torrential rains forced PGA Tour officials to shorten the event to 54 holes. It took 55 holes, but it was worth it for 42-year-old San Diego native Scott Simpson. Always a hometown favorite at Torrey Pines, Simpson, who had Chargers quarterback Stan Humphries as his caddie, came from eight strokes behind and eventually defeated Skip Kendall on the first playoff hole. Steve Pate was the leader after 36 holes with scores of 67 and 65 for a 132 total. Kendall was at 134 after a second-round 63, and Simpson was in 20th place at 140 on scores of 69 and 71.

It was the first victory in over four years for the 1987 U.S. Open champion, who fell out of the top 125 money winners in 1997 for the first time in his career. Shooting eight-under-par 64 in the final round for his 204 total, Simpson watched from the clubhouse as some of the game's young guns, including Tiger Woods, Davis Love III and Kevin Sutherland fell one short of his 12-under-par benchmark. Of those, Love seemed to stand the best chance of catching Simpson on the second nine of the final day. But, instead of making birdies, Love bogeyed two of the last five holes and came to the 18th needing an eagle to tie Simpson and join the playoff. Love's eagle attempt died one roll short. In the end it was Kendall, a winless professional in his third year on the PGA Tour, who sank a 10-footer on the 54th hole for his 70 and 204 total to tie Simpson and force a playoff.

On the first extra hole, with rain clouds looming over the Pacific and nervous PGA Tour officials hoping to finish, Simpson made one of the day's best up-and-downs from the right greenside rough. Kendall three-putted, lipping out a tenuous four-footer to seal Simpson's victory.

The three-putt aside, the Buick Invitational was Kendall's best finish to date. It was also a rebirth for Simpson, a wily veteran who plans to be around for a while.

United Airlines Hawaiian Open—$1,800,000

Winner: John Huston

When he holed out a five-iron shot from the pines at Augusta National to eagle the 18th and take the first-round lead in 1997, John Huston prompted the most anticipated cliche of the tournament: "Huston, the eagle has landed." When Tiger Woods ran away with that event, breaking every record Augusta could throw his way, Huston seemed destined to become a name only golf fanatics would remember. After the closing ceremonies at the United Airlines Hawaiian Open, however, Huston was in the record books. His 28-under-par victory broke the scoring record of 27 under par held by Ben Hogan (1945 Portland Invitational) and Mike Souchak (1955 Texas Open).

The calm conditions left Waialae Country Club at the mercy of players who had been battling the weather all winter. Huston took advantage of the benign layout, making 31 birdies en route to 260 total and a seven-stroke victory over rejuvenated veteran Tom Watson, who finished 21 under par. Huston's scores were 63, 65, 66 and 66.

Huston led wire to wire, sharing the lead with David Ogrin on Thursday before pulling away from the field. It couldn't have come at a more appropriate time. Huston had fallen to 141st on the money list in 1997, his worst finish in his nine years on the PGA Tour. Shoulder problems left him almost paralyzed. "It was all I could do to crawl out of bed," he said of the problems. After working with weights and strengthening his muscles, Huston used a one-time exemption as a top-50 career money winner to retain his card and play this year. Now, with a victory and a place in the record book, all those problems are behind him.

When it was over, 70-year-old Mike Souchak called Huston to congratulate him. "I'm delighted with what he did today," Souchak said. "It's terrific."

Tucson Chrysler Classic—$2,000,000

Winner: David Duval

For the Tucson Conquistadores, organizers of the Tucson Chrysler Classic, the 1998 tournament was an exciting but bittersweet event. Beginning in 1999, the 53-year-old Arizona tournament will be played opposite the Andersen Consulting Match Play, one of the new World Golf Championship events. The top 64 players in the World Ranking will be eligible for the Match Play, and that will no doubt weaken the Tucson field.

This year, however, the Conquistadores had many of the world's best, including the hottest player on the PGA Tour, David Duval. Early in 1997, Duval was dubbed the best player without a Tour win. When he made a 40-foot birdie putt on the 72nd hole to lock up a four-stroke Tucson victory, he captured his fourth win in eight starts, an impressive accomplishment for any golfer of any era.

Duval's win wasn't a cake-walk, however, despite a course-record 62 in the second round and a seemingly insurmountable seven-stroke lead going into the final 18 holes. With six holes to play, Duval hooked his tee shot out of bounds on the Omni Tucson National Resort's relatively easy par-four 13th hole. "I'll hit fewer than 10 hooks for the year," Duval said. "It's not a shot I think about."

He had to think about it on Sunday. The errant tee shot resulted in a triple bogey. Suddenly, the insurmountable lead was cut to one stroke over clutch charger and reigning British Open champion Justin Leonard. In early 1997, everyone would have expected Duval to wilt into obscurity. This was a new David Duval, a man who had proven he could win. Splitting the middle of the water-lined 18th fairway (the toughest driving hole on the course) Duval easily reached the green and, while three putts would have still meant victory, he ran in the 40-footer, giving the Conquistadores and Tucson fans an ending to remember.

Duval's final-round 73 gave him a 269 total, 19 under par, following his earlier scores of 66, 62 and 68. Leonard, the opening-round leader with 65, had other scores of 70, 68 and 70 to finish at 273, tied for second place with David Toms, who had a closing pair of 68s.

Nissan Open—$2,100,000

Winner: Billy Mayfair

While every California event suffered from the devastating effects of El Niño, weather had nothing to do with the Nissan Open moving from its traditional site at Riviera Country Club to nearby Valencia. Riviera was also to host the 1998 U.S. Senior Open, and the members didn't want their course closed twice in the same season, so the PGA Tour obligingly moved its annual Los Angeles event.

A lot of players, including Orange County native Tiger Woods, were happy with the move. Woods, who once played a U.S. Open qualifier at Valencia, felt his local knowledge gave him a leg up on many of his fellow competitors. Others thought the move to Valencia ought to be permanent. "I don't think any of us like that drive down Sunset Boulevard, only to get to Riviera and not have a place to park," John Daly said.

Payne Stewart joined Daly by saying, "(Valencia) is very convenient for the pros. It's just a lot less hassle." Opening rounds of 70 and 67 bolstered Stewart's opinion of the new site. Going into the weekend, he was one shot in back of leader Billy Mayfair who "got (his) stroke back," en route to shooting an opening-round 65.

Mayfair, the 1987 U.S. Amateur champion, hadn't won a PGA Tour event since the 1995 Tour Championship. His best finish in two years was a tie for second at the Las Vegas Invitational, but his most lingering memory was the collapse he suffered in the final round of the 1995 NEC World Series of Golf. In that event, Mayfair had a four-stroke lead with four holes to play, but that lead evaporated when he missed a short tap-in on the 72nd hole and eventually lost a playoff to Greg Norman. "It was very painful for me," said Mayfair, who has refused to watch video of that tournament.

Since then Mayfair's putting stroke has undergone intense scrutiny by players and analysts who accuse Billy of "slicing" his putts. Soon, Mayfair's confidence was shaken, but the Las Vegas finish in 1997 "gave me the urge to win again," he said. Still, it seemed that the putting stroke might be his downfall in Los Angeles. On Saturday, he missed numerous putts inside 10 feet, while showing deadly accuracy with his long putts in shooting 69. "I had putting flaws," he admitted, but a late-afternoon workout on the putting green gave him the confidence he needed going into Sunday's final round.

Mayfair would need more than confidence, however. On Saturday Woods, in typical Tiger fashion, began attacking the golf course, intimidating the field, and whipping the hometown crowd into a frenzy with his spectacular play. A third-round 65 moved Woods to within two strokes of then-leader Tommy Armour III, and one shot behind Mayfair. On Sunday, Armour shot 73 and dropped to a tie for sixth place. Tiger, playing in the group ahead of Mayfair, fired a final-round 66 and took the lead with a 272 total, 16 under par.

On the 18th hole the final day, Tiger made a 15-foot birdie putt from the fringe to take the lead outright for the first time in the tournament, a putt that prompted the now-famous upper-cut with his right fist. The crowd went berserk. Mayfair, standing on the 18th tee, said, "I heard the roar, and I knew he'd probably made birdie."

Mayfair wasn't ready to concede. After driving the ball in the middle of the fairway on the par-five 18th, he confounded many spectators by hitting his second shot into a deep greenside bunker. He would later admit that he "intended to hit it (in the bunker)." Mayfair is among the tour's top 10 in sand saves, a statistic that became well known among Los Angeles faithful after he hit his sand shot to within six feet and made the putt for birdie and 67 to tie Woods at 272.

Of course, few gave Mayfair a chance in the playoff. After all no one had proven himself better in playoff competition than Woods. However, Tiger blocked his tee shot into the right trees on the 18th (the first playoff hole) and thus eliminated any advantage his tremendous length might provide. Mayfair, as he had done so many times throughout the week, played within himself, splitting the middle of the fairway with a drive, laying up with his second shot, then hitting a wedge shot from 85 yards that looked for a moment as if it might go in for an eagle three. The ball spun back and stopped eight feet from the hole. When Tiger missed his 15-foot birdie attempt, Mayfair, with his "slicing" stroke, birdied the hole for a second straight time to capture his first victory in three years.

"I'm rejuvenated," an exuberant Mayfair said after his win. "The biggest thing is I know I can win again."

Doral-Ryder Open—$2,000,000

Winner: Michael Bradley

Every golfer has done it, and even for those who haven't had it happen in years, there is the constant, nagging dread that comes with knowing it could surface at any moment. It's not a snap hook, or a shank, although those aberrations do raise their ugly heads on occasion. It's the missed one-foot putt, the short one, the tap-in, the gimme, that darts into one side of the hole only to spin out in mock defiance that drives all golfers nuts. No one laughs when it happens, because everyone knows he could be next. For most golfers it is a round-breaker, the kind of deflating incident from which there is no recovery. In a 72-hole event, or in an 18-hole round it is still only one shot, but too often the missed putt destroys a player's confidence and, in many cases, breaks the golfer's will.

With only one win in his six years on the PGA Tour (1996 Buick Challenge) and coming into the Doral-Ryder Open ranked 107th on the money list, no one gave Michael Bradley much of a chance. On Sunday, with West Coast winners Billy Mayfair and John Huston in chase, and Tiger Woods mounting yet another charge up the leaderboard, Bradley had it happen to him on the 11th green at Doral's famous Blue Monster course: an eight-inch putt, a tap-in, a gimme, disappeared into the left side of the hole then came spitting out the other side. "I don't know what happened," Bradley would later say. "I went through my normal routine and everything. After that putt, I didn't know what was going to happen."

Most assumed that the putt would do to Bradley what it would do to most mortals, send him into a downward spiral. After all, Bradley had a reputation as a player with enormous talent, a great golf swing and a confidence problem. "I told him when he started believing in himself, he would see results," noted teaching professional Peter Kostis said of Bradley. With eight holes to play on Sunday in a brutal South Florida wind with the greatest names in golf lurking close behind, who would have thought that Doral would be the place for Bradley to start believing?

"The mental side has always held me back," Bradley said. "I've always known I have the physical talent to play." Unfortunately, if the missed putt weren't enough of a distraction, Bradley also had to question his physical ability. Before venturing to Miami, Florida, for the first East Coast event of the year, Bradley learned that he had an aggravated sciatic nerve. That kind of injury is as devastating to a golfer as a torn Achilles tendon. "Sometimes my back just kind of quits," he said.

It didn't quit at Doral, and neither did Bradley. After a spectacular second-round 66, Bradley found himself teeing off as a third-round leader for the first time. A solid 70 on Saturday kept him in the lead through 54 holes, something the 31-year-old had also never experienced. On Sunday, however, with winds whipping upwards of 30 miles per hour and Huston, Mayfair and Woods threatening to go low while Bradley missed his short putt, it looked as though the tide might turn. When Mayfair birdied the 13th and 15th holes to go one stroke ahead, it looked as though the hero of Valencia might become the first player since J.C. Snead in 1971 to win two consecutive events on the West Coast and East Coast.

But Bradley had some game left, and after birdieing the 16th while Mayfair was three-putting the 17th, Bradley found himself atop the leaderboard again. He would stay there. While the challenging 18th hole at Doral has provided many memorable and often dismal moments over the years, few have been as redemptive as Bradley's spectacular up-and-down from the right fringe. After safely finding the fairway, Bradley took the water out of play, but pushed his second shot off the right edge, leaving himself a delicate chip that he later admitted, "could have very easily gone in the water." After making what CBS commentators called "a wonderful chip," Bradley stood over a six-foot putt (a distance nine times longer than the putt he had missed on No. 11). This time, however, there was never a doubt. When the putt went in the center of the cup, Bradley held up his arms and looked toward the sky. The relief was obvious. He finished with 71 for a 278 total, one stroke better than Huston and Mayfair.

"If I'd (missed that putt) five years ago, I don't think I would have won the golf tournament," Bradley said of his hiccup on the 11th hole. "I would have lost it mentally. Now, I realize, it's not life or death anymore."

Honda Classic—$1,800,000

Winner: Mark Calcavecchia

It's less than an hour's drive from Palm Beach to Ft. Lauderdale, Florida, but for Mark Calcavecchia, the journey has taken 11 years. It was 1987 when Calcavecchia commuted from his Palm Beach home and won the Honda Classic. In 1998 he still commuted from home (although the golf course that hosts the event changed in that span), and he still brought his aggressive style of play. It worked in 1987, and it worked again in 1998.

With a style of play that has become fashionable among the PGA Tour's young guns, Calcavecchia is considered the old man (age 37) of the new generation of hit-it-at-the-pin players dominating the Tour. That torpedoes-be-damned style paid off as Calcavecchia birdied five of the last seven holes en route to a three-stroke victory over Vijay Singh and a five-stroke margin over Colin Montgomerie. "There wasn't a pin I didn't aim at," Calcavecchia would later say of the round. It paid off. In the final nine holes of his closing-round 65, Calcavecchia didn't have a putt longer than 15 feet. His earlier scores were 70, 67 and 68 for a 270 total.

As great as Calcavecchia played, there was no room for error. Singh one-putted the first six greens on Sunday and, at one point, tied Calcavecchia for the lead on the second nine. He finished with 67 for a 273 total. Montgomerie also hit it close all day, but he had what he described as "a pathetic putting round." Still, Monty's final-round score of 66 was good enough for a lone third-place spot at 275. Fourth place at 276, along with Stuart Appleby and Jeff Maggert, and a new course record of 64 went to John Daly, who but for a second-round 76 might have come away with his first victory in over two years.

As it was, Calcavecchia picked up his first American victory since the 1995 BellSouth Classic. "Winning takes care of everything," he said after the victory. "It takes care of Ryder Cup points, Presidents Cup points, money, and all the goals that I have. Winning motivates me."

Bay Hill Invitational—$2,000,000

Winner: Ernie Els

It was fitting that the final threesome on the final day of Arnold Palmer's Bay Hill Invitational would consist of three of last year's major champions. Arnold couldn't have been more pleased. Tiger Woods, who shot an opening-round 64, joined U.S. Open champion Ernie Els and PGA champion Davis Love III for the 36-hole Sunday finish.

Rain hampered the opening rounds, but Woods, who finished his first round on Friday afternoon, looked comfortable going into the weekend. By the end of the day Saturday, however, the battle was joined. Love fired an impressive second-round 66 to share the lead at 134 with Tiger going into the 36-hole Sunday wrap-up. Of the marathon final day, Love, the oldest member of the final triumvirate (at age 33) said, "Some weeks it's not possible, but as long as we're trying to get in 72 holes, I think that's good."

Els also thought it was good. Two shots off the pace set by Woods and Love going into the final day, Els felt that his new conditioning regime, which had sculpted his 215-pound frame into that of a football player, would help him overtake the leaders.

He was right. Sixteen holes into the final day, Els assumed a lead that he would never relinquish. "Ernie played great," Woods said. "He made all the putts he needed to make." Those putts led to a third-round 65 for Els which he followed with a 73 and a 274 total, good enough for a four-stroke victory over Jeff Maggert, who fired closing rounds of 69 and 68, and Bob Estes, who closed with rounds of 67 and 71. Bernhard Langer also proved that he was ready for the Masters by following up his opening 69 and 71 with two rounds of 69 to tie Mark Calcavecchia for fourth place at 279.

Woods and Love didn't fare as well. Woods shot a third-round 73, then errant iron play cost him on the last 18 holes. He closed the day with 77 and dropped into a tie for 13th place at 284. Love was distracted early by a heckler, but he said, "It had nothing to do with how I played." He opened Sunday with an uninspiring 75 and followed it up with an equally lackluster 76 for a 285 total.

"I knew I had to get out early," Els said. "Tiger and Davis can turn it on at times. The 65 came at the right time." So did Els' first American victory of the year. He had already won the South African Open, lost a playoff to Woods in the Johnnie Walker Classic in Thailand, finished second in the South African PGA, and tied for third at both the Heineken Classic in Australia and the Dubai Desert Classic. Of those finishes, the loss to Woods in Thailand hurt Els the most. Tying his shoes in the parking lot before Sunday's final round at Bay Hill, Els said, "(Tiger) didn't so much win it as I lost it." After trouncing Woods in the final 36 holes, the easy-going Els said he hadn't forgotten about Thailand, "But out there today I was not thinking about revenge."

The Players Championship—$4,000,000

Winner: Justin Leonard

See Chapter 7.

Freeport-McDermott Classic—$1,700,000

Winner: Lee Westwood

It was only fitting that the first American victory for 24-year-old Lee Westwood would come at a TPC course called English Turn in a wind that often approached 30 knots. That was nothing new for a golfer who grew up in Worksop, near Nottingham, England. New Orleans is a far cry from the English Midlands, but Westwood, who proved himself to his U.S. counterparts at the 1997 Ryder Cup, felt right at home.

After rounds of 69 and 68, Westwood went into the weekend three strokes behind lefthander Steve Flesch, who was also new to the PGA Tour leaderboards, having earned his 1998 Tour card as the winner of the 1997 Nike Tour Championship. On Saturday, however, Westwood carded an impressive 67 despite wind gusts that made it difficult to stand. Flesch hung in with a round of 71, but found himself one stroke behind the young Englishman going into the final round.

Wind conditions did not improve on Sunday, but Westwood's game remained steady. "He was fearless," Flesch said of Westwood's performance. Carrying a three-shot lead into the final nine, Westwood attacked with birdies at Nos. 10 and 11. He then made a crucial 10-foot putt for bogey on No. 13 after double-hitting a putt from the high fringe and receiving a one-stroke penalty. From there, with a four-shot lead, he ignored the pleas of his caddie to play conservatively, and hit his best drive of the tournament on the narrow par-five 15th hole. Westwood easily reached the green in two and two-putted for another birdie. He finished with 69 for a 273 total, 15 under par, to win by three strokes over Flesch, who shot 71 for his 276 total.

"You look at all the great players and they've all traveled well and won everywhere around the world," Westwood said. "That's what I want to do. Hopefully not just win one time over here, but many."

Masters Tournament—$2,700,000

Winner: Mark O'Meara

See Chapter 3.

MCI Classic—$1,900,000

Winner: Davis Love III

It's a two-hour drive, an 18-minute flight and a three-hour boat ride from Davis Love's house on Sea Island, Georgia, to Hilton Head Island, South Carolina, but as far as Love is concerned, Harbour Town Golf Links might as well be his newly adopted home. "It's great to play well near your home," Love said. "I had a lot of friends in the gallery, saw a lot of familiar faces, which makes it nice. I'm comfortable with this golf course. I've been putting these greens, this overseeded Bermuda, since I was 13 years old, so it really helps."

Love slipped into the ultimate comfort zone at the MCI Classic, hitting all but two fairways on the weekend, and hitting 29 of 36 greens in the last two days. Of the seven birdie putts he made on Sunday, none were longer than eight feet. His scores were 67, 68, 66 and 65 for a 266 total, 18 under par. His seven-shot margin of victory tied John Huston's Hawaii performance as the biggest shellacking of the year so far. "This was one of the best rounds I've ever played," Love admitted. "I drove the ball as good as you can, and made a lot of putts."

"My hat's off to him," said second-place finisher Glen Day whose final-round 67 gave him a 273 total and his third top-three finish in as many starts. "I played as good as I could today, but Davis played great."

In fact, Love proved he's capable of almost flawless golf. His first-nine 31 on Sunday included two birdie putts of less than two feet, and three of five feet or less. The fewest number of greens he hit was 13 on Friday when he shot 68. After another solid ball-striking performance on Saturday, Love carried a two-stroke lead over Phil Mickelson into the final day.

It should have been great drama with two of the game's young guns going head-to-head. The last time Love and Mickelson paired off together was in the U.S. finals of the Andersen Consulting World Championship held also on Love's home turf in Georgia. Love won that match on the second extra hole. One year later in Love's new backyard, things were never that close. "Phil and I are good friends," Love said. "I wanted to beat him, but when I got way ahead I wanted him to play better."

It was nip and tuck between the friendly rivals for the first couple of holes. Then on the third, Mickelson hit an approach shot to within six feet, and Love capped it with an eight-iron approach that stopped two feet from the hole. Mickelson missed, Love made, and it was all but over. Love got the lead up to eight shots at one time before making bogey on No. 17. "I knew

I wasn't going to get to 20 (under par), so I was just trying to cruise home," he said.

Love couldn't have been happier after slipping into his fourth 42-long tartan plaid jacket (given to the winners of the MCI Classic). "We have to make something out of these (jackets.) Maybe we'll start covering chairs with them," he said. After a laugh, a more serious Love said, "This is the end of five weeks of hard work. I don't want that to get lost. I've been working hard. I've been close. I've had some good rounds; I just haven't had four good rounds. I finally got four, and it's a really good feeling."

Greater Greensboro Chrysler Classic—$2,200,000

Winner: Trevor Dodds

A year before teeing off in the opening round of the 1998 Greater Greensboro Chrysler Classic in North Carolina, Trevor Dodds was on the couch at his home in St. Louis battling the nausea and fatigue that come with radiation and chemotherapy treatments. In 1997 the 38-year-old native of Namibia was diagnosed with testicular cancer. "When you're lying on your back feeling miserable and your little girl is standing over you it puts things into perspective," Dodds said. "The cancer changed a lot in my approach to life. I now put golf in the proper place."

The proper place for Dodds is now the winner's circle. After opening rounds of 68 and 69 put him five strokes behind Bob Estes going into the weekend, Dodds shot a third-round 70, and entered the final day three shots off Estes' pace. On Sunday, the otherwise benign Forest Oaks Country Club bared its teeth as the winds picked up, the greens dried out, and the scores went skyward. Estes shot a final-round 73 that dropped him into third place, while Scott Verplank, who also was attempting to make a comeback from elbow surgery, managed an even-par 72 by holing a 30-foot birdie on the 18th hole.

While Dodds' final-round 69 wasn't the best round of the day (Jim Estes shot 68 and finished tied for 16th), his 276 total was one shot better than Bob Estes and good enough to force a playoff with Verplank. Dodds' routine par won the playoff after Verplank hit an errant tee shot into the right rough and was unable to recover. "I fell asleep out there," Verplank said of his playoff collapse. "I should have taken a deep breath and thought about what I was doing."

Dodds earned his PGA Tour card by finishing fifth on the 1997 Nike Tour money list, but his six previous victories on the Canadian Tour prepared him for the pressures of the playoff. "It prepared me so that when I got a chance to win I wouldn't be overwhelmed."

Shell Houston Open—$2,000,000

Winner: David Duval

Late last year Paul Stankowski predicted that once David Duval started winning he might not stop. At the time many predicted that Duval would eventually break his winless streak and take home a victory or two, but no one could have foreseen the display Duval would put on after his first win. In 12 starts from the last three events in 1997 through the Shell Houston Open, which he won with a final-round 64, the 24-year-old Duval won five times and was two birdies away from donning his first green jacket at the Masters (where Duval and Fred Couples finished tied for second place).

The Houston win proved that Duval is capable of making a come-from-behind charge when needed, something he hadn't had to do in his previous four victories. After a third-round 73, admittedly his worst round of the year, Duval knew that "it would take a 63 or 64" if he were to have any chance of catching Jeff Maggert and Dan Forsman, who were tied at 10 under par. Duval opened Sunday's round with a seven-foot birdie putt on the first hole and proceeded to go out in 32 on the first nine, a good start, but one Duval knew he would at least have to equal on the second nine. Two eagles at the two par-fives and a three-foot birdie putt on the par-three 16th propelled Duval into a tie with Lee Janzen at 12 under par. Janzen's tee shot on the 17th hole found the water, and he made double bogey.

Meanwhile on the 18th, Duval raised his putter as a downhill 20-footer for par crept into the side of the hole for the closing 64 and a 276 total, 12 under par, one shot higher than he thought he needed, but one shot better than the rest of the field. Maggert made a charge with birdies at Nos. 13 and 15, but his 25-foot birdie putt on the 18th, which would have forced a playoff, came up short.

"I just go out there and play and do my best to just stay out of my own way, and let what will be, be. Lately, it's been awfully nice," Duval said.

BellSouth Classic—$1,800,000

Winner: Tiger Woods

It was the perfect Mother's Day present for Tida Woods, even though she wasn't in Atlanta to watch her son win his seventh PGA Tour title in 37 starts. "She heard this was a tough course to walk," Tiger said of his mother's absence, but according to Tiger, "She watched at home." After Sunday's final round, as he hoisted the BellSouth Classic trophy, Tiger Woods admitted that his mother's decision to skip walking the rain-soaked Greg Norman-designed TPC at Sugarloaf and stay home on Mother's Day was a good one. "After four days of sinking with every step, I'm whipped," Tiger said.

Not so whipped that he couldn't shoot a course-record 63 in the third round after two days of on-again, off-again rain delays. And not so whipped that he couldn't quiet some critics who, despite his resounding victory over Ernie Els at the Johnnie Walker Classic in Thailand in January, cried that the 22-year-old Woods was in the worst slump of his illustrious professional career.

In addition to the Thailand win, an official PGA European Tour title, Tiger's 10-month record between winning in the United States in the 1997 Motorola Western Open and the 1998 BellSouth Classic included two second-place finishes and one third among seven top-10 finishes. Even so, Tiger's "slump" could have continued in Atlanta had it not been for some good breaks and some miraculous shotmaking.

With dangerous funnel clouds looming nearby, and after a deluge that dumped over two inches of rain in an hour on Thursday, Woods finished his delayed opening round with an uninspiring 69 and found himself four strokes behind Mark Calcavecchia. But that's when things got interesting.

Many had forgotten that Woods took four weeks off after the Masters in 1997 and came back to win the GTE Byron Nelson Classic. Many more forgot that he took a two-week hiatus before his last PGA Tour victory, the Motorola Western Open. His layoff between the 1998 Masters and the BellSouth Classic was three weeks, and it was soon apparent that a rested, rejuvenated and dangerous Tiger had shown up in Atlanta as well. After finishing nine holes of his second round on Saturday morning, Woods found himself one shot off the lead heading into the afternoon. By nightfall, he had a three-stroke lead and the TPC at Sugarloaf had a new course record.

Sunday, Woods admittedly didn't bring his "A" game, but he had the shots when he needed them. On the par-five fourth hole, for example, Woods struck a tree with his tee shot and the ball landed a mere 100 yards from the tee. His second shot was no better, a pulled three iron that ended up in a creek bordering the left side of the fairway. Then, from 238 yards, Woods crushed a four iron to within 10 feet of the flag, and although his par putt slid by the hole and he had to settle for bogey, he could have, by his own admission, "made eight there."

He also could have lost it on No. 11, a par-three where Woods pulled an eight-iron shot into wet, knee-high grass left of the green. After much deliberation, Woods flopped a wedge to within 10 feet and salvaged a par.

Fortunately for Woods, his closest competitor, Jay Don Blake, had no miracles in his bag on Sunday. While 11 of the top-15 finishers fired final rounds in the 60s, Blake, the only man with a reasonable chance to catch Woods, could only manage a two-under-par 70, and his 18-foot birdie putt on the last hole, which would have put him into a playoff, slid by on the low side.

"What I did today, Jack Nicklaus made a pretty good living doing," said Woods, finishing with a 72 and 271 total for a one-stroke margin over Blake, after he turned to a nearby camera and wished Tida a happy Mother's Day. "(Jack) won a few times when he wasn't at his best, didn't he?"

GTE Byron Nelson Classic—$2,500,000

Winner: John Cook

At the end of 1995, a dispirited John Cook considered giving up the game. He was 95th on the money list, almost 40 years old, and a father of teenagers. Then in 1996 a rejuvenated Cook won two times on the PGA Tour and finished 19th on the money list. He won again in 1997. Then in 1998, on a windy Dallas afternoon, Cook won again, capturing his 10th PGA Tour victory at the GTE Byron Nelson Classic with a final-round 65 for a 265 total, 15 under par, to win by three strokes over the trio of Fred Couples, Hal Sutton and Harrison Frazar.

The win was a surprise to everyone, including Cook, who thought he was playing for second place. Couples, who finished with a disappointing 72, carried a two-stroke lead into the final 18 holes and, after making two birdies on the front nine on Sunday, Couples seemed well on his way to his second victory of the year. Then disaster struck. Couples couldn't find the fairway on the second nine. He bogeyed No. 12 after an errant drive nestled under the lip of a bunker, and on the benign par-five 15th, he pulled his drive into the deep rough and had to settle for par.

It was on No. 17, however, that the tournament turned. Couples struck a six iron on the 170-yard, par-three hole that he would later say, "was close to perfect," or so he thought. A stiff wind from the left pushed the ball out onto the rocks that fronted the green, and after bouncing around for a moment, Couples' ball bounded back into the water. He took triple bogey, thus clinching the victory for Cook.

Not that Cook backed into the victory. His weekend scores of 66 and 65 tied Davis Love III, who won the MCI Classic, for the lowest final 36-hole score for a tournament winner so far in 1998.

MasterCard Colonial—$2,300,000

Winner: Tom Watson

At age 48, Tom Watson wasn't sure he would ever win on the PGA Tour again. Despite dominating the game, winning 33 titles between 1974 and 1986 plus five British Opens, Watson hadn't won an American event since the 1996 Memorial Tournament. "I didn't feel old today," Watson said after firing a final-round 66 for a 265 total, 15 under par, on the hard, dry Colonial Country Club in Fort Worth, Texas, to capture the tournament Ben Hogan made famous in the first year it was held after Hogan's death. "There is a great satisfaction in winning," Watson said.

Watson's win by two strokes over Jim Furyk was no fluke. He entered the week with two second-place finishes so far in the year, and when he teed off at the MasterCard Colonial he still led the rain-delayed AT&T Pebble Beach National Pro-Am. Still, few expected Watson, who suffered from a decade of putting woes, to put together the kind of tournament he did. Tied after three rounds with Furyk and Harrison Frazar, Watson birdied the third hole on Sunday to take charge. Frazar had to scramble to shoot 71, which dropped him from contention, but Furyk, who shot 68, caught Watson and shared the lead going into the ninth hole.

According to Watson, the shot that turned the tournament in his favor was the approach shot at the ninth. After hitting his tee shot into a fairway bunker where the ball rested well below his feet, Watson neatly clipped an eight iron to within 10 feet of the hole. "The whole tournament boiled down to that one shot," Watson said. "I was just trying to make contact and not hit it fat. Fortunately, I caught it flush."

With his nerves intact and his putter working again, a rejuvenated Watson never looked back as he finished with the 66 and made the MasterCard Colonial his 43rd career victory worldwide.

Memorial Tournament—$2,200,000

Winner: Fred Couples

Any time he plays three weeks in a row, Fred Couples' back problems can become an issue. In recent weeks, Couples' ability to close on a lead had also been questioned. After losing leads with poor iron play during final rounds at the Masters and the GTE Byron Nelson Classic, some wondered if the winner of this year's Bob Hope Chrysler Classic had lost his ability to finish strongly when needed. Couples put those questions to rest at the Memorial Tournament in Dublin, Ohio, with a resounding four-stroke victory.

As if the margin of his win was not enough, Couples completed his final-round 69 for a 271 total in stop-and-start conditions that would have disrupted the healthiest of players. Lightening caused two delays, pushing Couples' finish closer to dusk than he or tournament organizers would have liked. After rounds of 68, 67, 67 and the closing 69, Couples couldn't have been happier. "I'm playing about as well as I can play, better than I have in a long time," Couples said while sitting with tournament host Jack Nicklaus.

Because of his back, Couples decided to only play the remaining three major championships, the Tour Championship and the Las Vegas event before the Presidents Cup matches in December. "I figured Jack Nicklaus would be here," Couples joked, when asked about his chances of making the Presidents Cup team.

Couples' victory moved him to fourth place in the Presidents Cup standings behind David Duval, Tiger Woods and Justin Leonard. Andrew Magee, who finished second to Couples with rounds of 67, 71, 68 and 69, didn't worry about his future on the Presidents Cup or Ryder Cup teams. "Freddie's my nemesis," Magee said. "I can't catch him."

Despite some great final-round efforts, no one could catch Couples. Duval followed his opening-round 74 with rounds of 66, 67 and 69 to finish alone in third place, five behind Couples, while Jim Furyk finished fourth. Davis Love III, who started the final round three back of Couples, closed with 73 to finish tied with Brandel Chamblee for fifth.

Kemper Open—$2,000,000

Winner: Stuart Appleby

For 54 holes it looked as though hometown favorite Fred Funk would please his friends and family in Potomac, Maryland, by winning his first Kemper Open at the TPC at Avenel. Having led since the first hole on the first day, and with hard-charging players such as Tiger Woods, Fred Couples, Ernie Els and David Duval taking the week off to prepare themselves for the U.S. Open in San Francisco, Funk appeared ready to stick it out and win his first PGA Tour event since the 1996 B.C. Open.

Then, on an unseasonably cool June Sunday, Funk had the kind of unmemorable round reserved for nightmares and bad jokes. On the first five holes Funk made bogey, par, bogey, triple bogey and bogey. "On the card it looks terrible, but I could have shot 90 today," Funk said of his closing-round 77 to finish in a five-way tie for third place at 278, four strokes behind. "I just wanted it too much. I felt badly for the fans, and I feel bad for me, too. It would have been a great story. This would have been a lot easier if it had been anywhere else. At home like this, it really hurts."

Funk's collapse opened the door for 27-year-old Australian Stuart Appleby, whose only previous PGA Tour victory was the 1997 Honda Classic. Having never been more than three strokes off the pace, and lurking most of the week one or two behind Funk, Appleby was able to sneak in with a one-over-par 72 for a 274 total to win by one stroke over Scott Hoch. He secured the victory with a spectacular three-iron approach from an awkward lie to the last hole. "I don't know how often I could hit that shot again," Appleby said. Hoch, who started the final round four strokes behind Funk, couldn't convert on numerous birdie chances and shot 71.

After accepting the Kemper Open trophy on the 18th green, Appleby took a philosophic view of his win. "I suppose this can be a kickstart," he said. "Justin (Leonard) used it as a kickstart (in 1997), and he felt like he was a little fortunate to win. There are a few times when a tournament pans out in your favor. When it happens, you have to take it."

Buick Classic—$1,800,000

Winner: J.P. Hayes

With rain dampening every round of the Buick Classic, a whopping 30 players withdrew and headed to San Francisco for the U.S. Open. For J.P. Hayes, a journeyman whose best career finish was a tie for sixth at the 1992 Anheuser-Busch Classic, the U.S. Open wasn't a factor. He hadn't qualified and, with just $16,712 in earnings in 1998, Hayes was more concerned about keeping his PGA Tour card than contending in any major championships.

After the sun came out, and the dust settled at the Westchester Country Club in Harrison, New York, Hayes not only had a victory, he had secured a two-year exemption, an invitation to the 1999 Masters, and cashed the biggest paycheck ($324,000) of his career. "I was calm," Hayes said. "I really surprised myself. I thought in this situation I'd be throwing up all over myself."

The situation was a playoff with Jim Furyk, one of the hottest winless players of 1998. After being tied at seven under par following the rain-delayed completion of the second round, Furyk and Hayes both knew that the soft greens and lift-clean-and-place conditions were perfect for low scoring in the third and final round. In that regard, Furyk had the upper hand. His second-round 63 held up as the tournament low score. But Hayes, who opened with rounds of 66 and 67, was the model of consistency throughout the week.

Both players had up-and-down final rounds, but as the final droplets of rain came down on No. 18, it all came down to one hole. Hayes, who came to the 18th with a one-stroke lead, assumed a birdie on the par-five finishing hole would lock up the victory. He was wrong. After a beautiful save from the greenside bunker for his birdie, Hayes watched as Furyk hit a monstrous 240-yard three-wood shot to within 12 feet of the hole. Furyk made an eagle, both players shot 68 for 201 totals, and a playoff was underway.

Coming off the eagle on the last, and with six previous top-10 finishes in 1997, momentum clearly seemed in Furyk's favor. Before arriving at Westchester, Hayes had broken 70 only twice all year, but Hayes converted an eight-foot birdie putt on the first playoff hole for the victory.

"It's an incredible feeling of satisfaction to play this well under the circumstances," Hayes said.

For Furyk, who moved to fifth place on the money list with his finish, another week in second place was more bitter than sweet. "I'm disappointed," he said. "About 50 people have already congratulated me for a great week, but when you lose in a playoff, finish second when you have a chance to win, second just isn't good enough."

U.S. Open Championship—$3,000,000

Winner: Lee Janzen

See Chapter 4.

Motorola Western Open—$2,200,000

Winner: Joe Durant

Although he hung around the leaderboard all four days, even holding a one-shot advantage after Friday's second round, few prognosticators gave journeyman professional Joe Durant, winless in almost a decade of on-again, off-again tour performances, much of a chance. But, with stellar play that included a closing round of 66 while playing with the new U.S. Open champion, Lee Janzen, Durant erased the doubters and put his name on the impressive list of Motorola Western Open winners. In so doing, Durant overcame oppressively hot Chicago weather conditions to shoot a 17-under-par 271 total at Cog Hill to win by two strokes over Vijay Singh.

"I never thought I could do it," Durant said of his performance. "I would have bet on the other guys instead of me. To be honest, when it got close to the end I started thinking about Augusta." Before he could even consider teeing off in the 1999 Masters, however, Durant had to beat a hot-putting Singh as well as Greg Kraft and Janzen.

Kraft, who held the opening-round lead with 67, five under par, followed it up with rounds of 70 and 66 to go into the final round two shots ahead of Durant, but two shots behind the leader, Singh, who followed his opening consecutive 68s with a third-round 65. Durant teed off four shots off the pace and only one ahead of Janzen, who had strung together rounds of 68, 69 and 69 to put himself five strokes back.

During the final round Singh faltered, missing the first, fourth and seventh greens to begin what would end up being an lackluster even-par day. Meanwhile, Durant was doing what he had done all week, hitting greens in regulation and making putts when needed. In total, Durant hit 65 of 72 greens in regulation, and despite flubbing a chip and making bogey on the last, his final-round 66 was good enough to overtake Singh. "I hit an almost perfect seven iron for a tap-in birdie at 17," Durant said. "That's when it sank in that maybe I could win this thing."

Janzen, who said he was "pulling hard for Joe, trying to help him get that first one," shot 71 to finish tied for third at 277 with a hard-charging Dudley Hart, who shot a course-record-tying 63 on Sunday. Kraft shot a disappointing 75 to finish at 278, tied for fifth with Steve Stricker.

As for Durant and his dreams of Augusta, he said, "I had a couple of chances to play (Augusta National) with friends, but I kept saying, 'I'm never going to play there until I qualify for the Masters.' Well, I'm in, finally."

Canon Greater Hartford Open—$2,000,000

Winner: Olin Browne

The only person more surprised than Larry Mize by Olin Browne's victory at the Canon Greater Hartford Open was Olin Browne. After his final round, Browne, happy with his good showing, had all but conceded the tournament to Mize, who held a four-stroke lead with four holes to play. To pass the time "just in case," Browne, who led the tournament earlier in the day before making double bogey at the 10th, enjoyed a putting contest on the practice green with his son (Olin, Jr., age 10) and his daughter (Alexandra, age seven).

Then the unthinkable occurred. Mize, who had entered the day at 13 under par and tied for the lead with Scott Hoch and Grant Waite, and who had patiently and methodically stretched his lead to four shots with birdies on the 11th, 12th, 13th and 14th holes, made double bogey at the short par-four 15th after hitting a wayward five iron off the tee into an unplayable lie. His lead was still two strokes, however, and after hitting his tee shot to within 12 feet on the par-three 16th, things seemed to be back in order. But Mize three-putted, missing a par putt of one foot. His lead was then one.

Hoch, who also held the lead early in the round and was playing with Mize, couldn't capitalize on the opportunities Mize kept presenting. Hoch missed short par putts on the 10th, 17th and 18th holes to finish with an uninspiring, one-over-par round of 71, two shy of what he needed. "I had the tournament," Hoch said. "I just didn't make the shots I needed to make."

All Mize needed was a par at the last hole to shoot 68 and take home his fourth PGA Tour victory. A bad club selection from the fairway caused Mize to fly his approach shot over the green and into the rough from which he was unable to recover. "I made a stupid mistake," Mize said. "You're pumped up. I know to take the lesser club. I think that's what aggravated me the most. You know all the other stuff just happens, but to make that mistake on 18, that's really the killer."

Mize shot 67 to finish at 266 along with Stewart Cink, who wedged a Friday 65 between three rounds of 67, and, much to his own surprise, Browne, who shot rounds of 67, 66, 66 and 67.

A three-way playoff commenced on the 18th, the hole Mize had just bogeyed to lose the tournament in regulation. Perhaps with that in mind, Mize found the right fairway bunker with his tee shot, which made hitting the green all but impossible. Browne also missed the green to the left, which gave Cink, who hit his approach to within 15 feet, a decided advantage.

Browne took that advantage away, holing his chip from 50 feet. The crowd roared, Mize conceded, and when Cink missed his 15-footer, it was over. Browne, whose only victories have come on the Nike Tour (where he won four times before earning his 1998 Tour card), had the victory. "It was a magical moment," Browne said. "The game teaches you resilience and it teaches you to accept defeat, which is a hard thing for an athlete to do. I'm feeling very fortunate at the moment."

Quad City Classic—$1,550,000

Winner: Steve Jones

While Steve Jones was never more than three strokes out of the lead at the Quad City Classic, he never held the outright lead until he drained a 25-foot eagle putt on the par-five sixth on Sunday. That putt put Jones one stroke ahead of third-round leader David Toms and two ahead of Kenny Perry and Scott Gump.

An additional birdie at the 11th, coupled with consistent pars on the remaining seven holes was enough to propel Jones to his eighth career title, by one over Gump and two over Perry, and his first victory since the 1997 Canadian Open. "I knew the back side at Oakwood on Sunday is tough," Jones said. "You think you need to shoot four under par, but that's not true. You need to make pars."

That wisdom and veteran experience proved true. Toms, the defending Quad City champion who started Sunday's round at 15 under par, one ahead of Gump and two ahead of Jones, slid from contention with a double bogey on the 16th. Kenny Perry, who began the day tied with Jones at 13 under, was in the midst of late-round charge when a bogey at No. 16 derailed his chances. Gump, who led after the second round and, like Jones, was never more than three shots off the pace, bogeyed the 15th and was unable to recover, although his birdie at No. 18 moved him into second place at 16 under par, one shot ahead of Perry.

Jones had his best four days of golf in over two years with rounds of 64, 65, 68 and 66 for his 263 total. Afterward he said, "I was just trying to have fun today."

Deposit Guaranty Golf Classic—$1,200,000

Winner: Fred Funk

While the world's top players were battling the winds at the British Open, 42-year-old Fred Funk braved the heat and humidity of Madison, Mississippi, and managed to shoot four rounds in the 60s to capture his fifth career PGA Tour victory. Granted, the Deposit Guaranty Golf Classic is not a major, or in some people's minds even a minor, but for Funk, who shot 69, 64, 69 and 68 for a 270 total to win by two strokes, it was a victory to savor.

"My goal is not to be number one or even in the top 10," Funk said after the victory. "I feel I'm the kind of player who can get into the top 30 or even the top 15. That's the zone I'm in now."

The players he faced, including Franklin Langham and Tim Loustalot who tied for second with Paul Goydos at 272, were short on wins and long on hope. Going into Sunday's final round, five of them had shot 12 under par or better. Funk began the day tied with Mike Brisky at minus 14, but when Brisky had trouble early and ended the day with a 74, it opened the door for Funk, who cruised home with a closing round of 68, four under par.

"There are guys out here I can't beat," Funk said afterward. "I can beat them on a given day or week, but not for a year." Those players were in England while Funk was winning in Mississippi. But everyone would agree that 18 under par would win a fair number of full-field events on any tour.

CVS Charity Classic—$1,500,000

Winner: Steve Pate

With a 15-under-par score of 269, Steve Pate proudly joined the ranks of Tony Lema, Arnold Palmer, Billy Casper and Raymond Floyd as a winner of the PGA Tour event at the Pleasant Valley Country Club in Sutton, Massachusetts. Sadly, Jones will always carry the distinction of being the tournament's final winner. This was the last year for Pleasant Valley and the CVS Charity Classic, as the PGA Tour bumped the event to make room for the World Golf Championships in 1999.

"I've killed every tournament I've ever won," Pate said jokingly. In 1987, after Pate won the Southwest Classic in Abilene, Texas, the Tour cancelled that event. After he won the Honda Classic at the TPC at Eagle Trace, the Tour moved the event to another course. "It's either the tournament or the venue," Pate said.

After going winless since the 1992 Buick Invitational, and questioning his ability to come back after breaking his wrist in an auto accident, Pate will take a victory any way he can get it. This time, it came with a closing-round 67 to edge out Scott Hoch and Bradley Hughes by one stroke. Pate never led until late on Sunday when third-round co-leader Dave Stockton, Jr. struggled with an even-par 71 and the other co-leader, Willie Wood, shot 70. Hoch shot a final-round 65 and Hughes shot 66, but neither could catch Pate who cruised home with his second consecutive 67.

Happy with the win, Pate was melancholy about being unable to defend his Pleasant Valley win. "It's very disappointing that we're not coming back," he said. "It's small and intimate enough, you get to know these people as friends."

FedEx St. Jude Classic—$1,800,000

Winner: Nick Price

It took two extra holes, but after a year of near misses, Nick Price finally returned to the PGA Tour winner's circle by capturing his 37th worldwide victory at the FedEx St. Jude Classic in Memphis, Tennessee. Even though Price shared the lead with Bob Estes at the end of play on Saturday, it wasn't until the second nine on Sunday that Price looked like the same man who won three major championships between 1992 and 1994. With three holes to play, Price made eagle on the par-five 16th to tie Jeff Sluman for the lead. Price then had a chance to win the tournament in regulation with a seven-foot birdie putt on No. 18. When it rolled over the right edge of the cup a stunned Price felt like he might have let the tournament slip away. "I didn't want to go to extra time," he said. "My nerves weren't too good at that point."

Tied at 268, after Sluman finished with 65 and Price, 66, both Sluman and Price made pars on the first extra hole. Then on the par-four 12th, the second hole of the playoff, Sluman pushed his tee shot into the water, but recovered by hitting his third shot 12 feet from the hole. He never got the chance to try his par putt, however. Price, who won the St. Jude Classic in Memphis in 1993, split the middle of the fairway but pulled his approach 20 feet left of the hole. "I had a feeling (Jeff) was going to make that putt," Price said. With that in mind, Price rolled in his birdie putt and walked away with his first PGA Tour victory of the year.

"I have played pretty solid all year," he said. "I won a tournament in South Africa in February, and I had a couple of close shaves at the U.S. Open and then in Holland last week, but it has been a frustrating year for me. Nothing has happened. It has just been a big void." That void was filled with a $324,000 first-place check, enough for Price to jump from 42nd to 18th on the money list.

Sluman, a two-time PGA Tour winner, took the loss in stride. "Anytime you're one off the lead and shoot 65 (on Sunday) that's usually enough to win," he said. "Nick shot a great round. I did all I could. I didn't make a bogey and had six birdies. What can you do?"

Glen Day matched Sluman's Sunday 65, but Day finished at 270, two shots out of the playoff, but one ahead of Bob Estes, who shot 69 to finish alone in fourth place.

Buick Open—$1,800,000

Winner: Billy Mayfair

After defeating Tiger Woods with a spectacular birdie on the first playoff hole at the Nissan Open in March, Billy Mayfair all but disappeared into a summer of obscurity. Between that victory and the opening round of the Buick Open in Grand Blanc, Michigan, Mayfair missed four cuts and finished no higher than 31st in 11 starts. Then Mayfair found lightening in a bottle for a second time, finishing the week with a 17-under-par 271 total to win the Buick Open by two strokes over a charging Scott Verplank.

"I didn't come here with a lot of expectations," Mayfair said. "I was in bed with the flu on Tuesday. I barely got out of bed for the pro-am on Wednesday, so basically, I didn't have much confidence. I can't really explain it."

There weren't any miraculous shots that needed explaining in the first two days. Still recovering from flu-like symptoms, Mayfair opened with inauspicious rounds of 70 and 69 to enter the weekend six shots back of Brandel Chamblee, who shot 65 and 68. Then on Saturday, Mayfair's much-criticized putting stroke came through. He posted a 65, the low round of the day and good enough to gain a share of the lead with Steve Stricker.

Going into Sunday's final round, a dozen players lurked within three shots of the lead, including Verplank, Tiger Woods and defending champion Vijay Singh. It was Mayfair, however, who got things rolling on the last day. After missing the first fairway, Mayfair sank a 30-foot putt for birdie, then pitched a wedge shot into the hole from 40 yards on the second hole for another birdie. With soggy fairways prompting officials to invoke the lift-clean-and-place rule, a crowd of players posted low numbers ahead of the leaders. Before Mayfair reached the heart of the second nine, Joey Sindelar and Andrew Magee both shot 64s. Then Verplank made a charge with a tap-in eagle at the 13th and a birdie at 17 to finish with a 64 of his own and a 15-under-par total, which temporarily tied Mayfair.

Mayfair broke the tie with a birdie on No. 12 and another on No. 14. With storm clouds gathering in the distance, Mayfair held his two-stroke lead through the remaining holes, finished with a 67 and picked up his second win of the year. The threatening weather prompted PGA Tour official Mark Russell to say, "It's a miracle we got it in." While not necessarily referring to the weather, Mayfair would certainly agree that it was a miracle.

PGA Championship—$3,000,000

Winner: Vijay Singh

See Chapter 6.

Sprint International—$2,000,000

Winner: Vijay Singh

If Vijay Singh's courageous win at the PGA Championship in Seattle was the break he had been working for 15 years to get, his follow-up victory at the Sprint International in Castle Rock, Colorado, was proof-positive that the man whose name means "victory" had hit the big time. With a renewed confidence and a putter that had come out of dormancy after its owner went back to a cross-handed grip, Singh romped through the Rockies in grand style only one week after hoisting his career to a new level.

Singh led or tied for the lead in the modified Stableford competition every day, opening with 15 points on Thursday, 12 on Friday, six on Saturday, and capping his victory with a 14-point day on Sunday, for a total of 47 points, six points more than runners-up Phil Mickelson and Willie Wood. Eight points were awarded for double eagles, five for eagles, two for birdies, none for pars, and players were docked one point for a bogey and three points for anything higher. Winning at Castle Pines meant making lots of birdies, and the format was better suited for someone such as Tiger Woods than Vijay Singh.

Woods, who finished fourth with 38 points, took advantage of the format with some grand shots that included two eagles on Thursday, followed by his third hole-in-one as a professional on Saturday. Double bogeys on Friday and a seven-point day on Sunday, however, kept Woods out of serious contention.

The man who always appears ahead of Tiger on the alphabetical listing did make a charge, however. Willie Wood, 5-foot-7 and shorter off the tee than some amateurs, made the most serious run at Singh in the final round. Playing in the same pairing with Vijay, Wood was forced to stand witness to a first-nine eruption. Singh made five birdies and no bogeys in the first nine holes, opening a seven-point lead at the turn. A 40-foot birdie putt on the 12th, however, pulled Wood to within two points of Singh (42-40), but a critical three-putt on the 14th dashed Wood's chances. Even though he climbed back to within one point after the 16th, Singh slammed the door on the par-five 17th with an eagle putt that never wavered as it found the cup.

"This is where all the hard work comes in," Singh said afterward. "Knowing you can rely on how you're hitting the ball is what you've got to have coming down the stretch."

Singh certainly had it in Colorado, and, if the judgment of his peers is any indication, he could have it for some time to come. "I've always thought he had the best swing out here," Brad Faxon said of Singh. "He hits a big, high cut and takes the left side of the golf course out of play. He can turn the ball over when he wants to, and I've seen him play some excellent shots around the greens. And he's making some putts!"

With a work ethic that is second to none of the PGA Tour and a two week earning spree of $900,000, Singh definitely elevated himself from "great ball striker" to "champion" in a 12-day time span in August. He's not through however. "I'll probably be in the top 10 (in the World Ranking) after this," he said. "Being No. 1 in the world doesn't happen in two weeks. You have to play well for a long time to get there."

NEC World Series of Golf—$2,250,000

Winner: David Duval

From October 1997 through May 1998, David Duval was golf's hottest player, but then a summer dry spell ensued. After shooting 76 and 78 to miss the cut in the PGA Championship, Duval took the next week off and watched Vijay Singh leap over him into the top spot on the money list. Then, on a hot Sunday afternoon in Akron, Ohio, Duval reminded everyone why he owned that leading money position for most of the year. His final-round 68, 269 total and two-stroke victory in the NEC World Series of Golf elevated Duval to become only the second player in history to win $2 million in a single season.

"It's Sunday night and I'm the best golfer this week," Duval said. "On Thursday morning, and until I sank that last putt, Vijay Singh was the best golfer. For the entire year, who's done more than Mark O'Meara? You've got to have a lot of arrogance to say you're better than Tiger Woods or Phil Mickelson or Jim Furyk or Justin Leonard. I just don't have enough arrogance to do that. I believe in what I do, but we all have our weeks."

Duval led after every round but the first, when he shot 69 and Mickelson posted four-under-par 66. After 66 of his own on Friday, Duval never looked back. Saturday, Duval shot another 66 and opened a one-stroke lead over John Cook, who shot 62 that had everyone, including Cook, thinking 59. Mickelson posted another 66 to frame his one-off round of 71, and entered the final round two back, with O'Meara lurking only three back.

On the 497-yard second hole, Duval set the standard by hitting a mere five-iron approach shot to within 12 feet and draining the putt for eagle. He then proceeded to split narrow fairways with huge drives, and go around the 7,139-yard Firestone South course almost as if it were a pitch-and-putt. After his one miscue, when he pulled a five-iron approach on the 15th into the high rough, Duval showed his wedge mastery by pitching to within inches for his par. Then on the 18th, a 464-yard par-four, Duval hit a pitching-wedge second shot and began the victory march up the final fairway for his 11-under-par total.

While he lacked Duval's mammoth length, Mickelson matched him shot-for-shot and finished alone in second place, with 68 and a 271 total, two strokes back.

Duval's third victory of the year made him one of only nine players since 1960 to win three PGA Tour events in two consecutive years. The others were Jack Nicklaus, Arnold Palmer, Billy Casper, Raymond Floyd, Tom Watson, Lee Trevino, Johnny Miller and Nick Price. Not bad company.

As for the money, Duval could afford to be philosophical. "I don't know how significant the money is," he said. "It's a possibility that I could reach $3 million with the number of events I'm going to play and if I won the Tour Championship, but I probably won't be the only one to break $2 million this year. It's not that important until the end. Come the Tour Championship on Sunday afternoon, if I'm still on top of the money list, that would be a big accomplishment. I'd be proud of that."

Greater Vancouver Open—$2,200,000

Winner: Brandel Chamblee

If you won in 1997 you weren't playing in the Greater Vancouver Open because the NEC World Series of Golf attracted all of the previous year's champions. That didn't mean the field was weak, as U.S. Open champion Lee Janzen, Open runner-up Payne Stewart, Sprint International runner-up Willie Wood, Paul Stankowski and John Daly all came north of the border to the Northview Golf and Country Club in Surrey, British Columbia.

Of all those names, Stewart looked to be the favorite, especially after he opened the tournament with a seven-under-par 64. Alas, Stewart's other scores of 69, 65 and 70 fell three strokes short of Brandel Chamblee, a 36-year-old winless professional who finally broke through in Vancouver, capping his victory with a 36-foot birdie putt on the 72nd hole.

"Even if you come close, other than the money, when you finish second it's a pretty empty feeling," Chamblee said. That empty feeling was filled for Chamblee when he fired four rounds in the 60s for a 265 total and his first PGA Tour victory in a decade of trying. "I've been playing so well this week and hitting it so well, if I just stayed out of my own way I knew everything was going to be fine," he said. "I kept telling myself to enjoy it. You work your whole life to get into the situation where you can trust your golf swing and golf game."

That trust came through on Sunday when Chamblee quickly caught and then passed Stewart who entered the final round with a one-stroke lead. By the time he reached the second nine, Chamblee's game was on auto-pilot towards a 66 and the victory was his. Chamblee's earlier scores were 67, 64 and 68.

For Stewart, whose closing 70 was his worst round of the week, another second-place finish was disappointing, but it was something to take in stride. "Whenever you're leading a golf tournament and have a chance to win, sure it's disappointing," he said. "I'm not going to lose sleep over it. Life will go on."

Greater Milwaukee Open—$1,800,000

Winner: Jeff Sluman

It took Jeff Sluman 10 years to follow up his 1987 PGA Championship victory with another (the 1997 Tucson Open), but with his win in the 1998 Greater Milwaukee Open, Sluman seemingly decided to make winning an annual habit. Or it could be that age and guile have finally won out over youth and athleticism. "I'll be 41 in a few days and I think I'm probably a better player than I've ever been," Sluman said after four rounds that never exceeded 68. "That's the nice thing about golf. I used to get ahead of myself. If I was leading on the 15th hole Sunday, I would be thinking about an acceptance speech. Can't do that. Not out here, with all these great players."

Sluman never really considered himself among all those great players, but he did think he was better than his two career wins. After shooting 68, 66, 63 and 68 for a 265 total to win by one over a charging Steve Stricker, he certainly moved closer to his own expectations. Still, there were plenty of great players posting some great numbers at the Brown Deer Park Golf Club over the Labor Day weekend. Sluman's 63 on Saturday was not even the low round of the tournament. Both Nolan Henke and Chris Perry (who finished tied for third at 268, along with Mark Calcavecchia) shot tournament-record 62s on Friday, second-place finisher Stricker fired 63 on Friday, and 64s were common, while 68s were as high as you could go if you wanted to stay in contention.

That's exactly what Sluman did on Sunday, 68, although for a while it looked like he might lap the field. On the fifth hole, he chipped in from 45 feet for birdie to assume the outright lead, and he chipped in again for eagle at the sixth to build his lead to three. The late-round bogeys at the 11th and 18th were anticlimactic, as Stricker, the only player with a chance to catch Sluman, had run out of holes despite birdieing the last four of the tournament.

Bell Canadian Open—$2,200,000

Winner: Billy Andrade

Going into the final round of the Bell Canadian Open in Oakville, Ontario, the tournament seemed to boil down to two players: Bob Friend, who had never won on the PGA Tour, and Billy Andrade, who hadn't won an event in seven years. It was Andrade, the Rhode Island native who had back-to-back victories in 1991, who came through in a playoff for his third career victory, but not before a fight.

Friend led the tournament at the end of the second and third rounds on scores of 69, 67 and 68, but his two-stroke lead going into Sunday was tenuous. On Saturday, Andrade caught and passed Friend, but then Andrade chunked a nine iron into the water on the par-five 18th hole. He made a double-bogey seven. His scores so far were 68, 69 and 69.

On Sunday, things got more interesting. Throughout the first nine Friend hit some of the most misguided shots of the week, but made up for them with a short game display that would have made Seve Ballesteros jealous. He hit only four greens in regulation on the first nine holes, but managed to play the side in one under par. He temporarily lost his lead when he bogeyed the eighth while Andrade was making birdie. On the ninth, it looked as though Friend's touch had worn off and Andrade would take the lead, but then Friend holed a 40-foot bunker shot to go ahead again.

The erratic and unpredictable play didn't stop there. On the final six holes, Friend went birdie, bogey, birdie, bogey, par and finally birdie. His lone par came after his second shot landed on the 17th green some 100 feet away from the hole and obscured by an encroaching bunker. Friend solved that problem by hitting a wedge shot off the putting surface to within four feet and making the subsequent putt for par. "That was one of the greatest chip shots I've ever hit," Friend said. "If you practice something like that at your club, you're asked to leave. It's like 'Mr. Friend, replace your divot, we're going to give you your money back.'"

Andrade's play had been slightly more consistent and a couple of shots better than Friend's. As they approached the 508-yard par-five 18th, Andrade held a one-stroke lead. Friend knew he had to play aggressively, so he tried to hit his second shot onto the well-guarded green. Although it appeared the shot was destined for the water, Friend caught a break and the ball finished in the greenside bunker, a spot where he felt nothing if not at home. Andrade, however, chose the 72nd hole to let things get interesting. For the second day in a row, Andrade hit the ball in the water, only this time it was his second shot that found the hazard. After a mediocre approach shot, Andrade stood over a 35-foot par putt, while (to no one's surprise) Friend had played a brilliant bunker shot to within six feet.

"The whole day I kept thinking 'I'm going to win the golf tournament,'" Andrade said. "When you don't win for a while you don't think you'll ever win. I knew I could do it, but I hadn't done it in so long I didn't know when it was going to come."

If he needed more of a sign that this might be it, sinking the 35-footer did it for him. Andrade recalled some of his high school basketball skills as he leapt into the air after the putt fell. When Friend made his six-footer, he and Andrade were tied at 13-under-par 275, and they both walked back to 18th tee for the playoff. Andrade shot 69 and Friend, 71, in the final round.

It could have been bad vibrations or a feeling that luck wasn't likely to shine on them twice in a row, but both players hit overly conservative second shots well right of the water on the 18th. This time, however, Friend over-played his third shot and, despite his short-game wizardry throughout much of the day, he flew the ball over the green and into the water. Then, faced with a tenuous third shot of his own, Andrade purposefully hit the ball into the same greenside bunker that Friend had found earlier.

Both players got up-and-down, Friend for bogey and Andrade for par, but not before Andrade had to be reminded to replace the ball mark he had moved out of Friend's line. "My mind was racing," he said. "I think that last hole aged me 10 years."

Long-awaited victories will do that.

B.C. Open—$1,500,000

Winner: Chris Perry

Chris Perry's father, Jim, won 215 Major League Baseball games and the much-coveted Cy Young Award for his pitching, while his uncle Gaylord won 314 games and his own Cy Young Award. But Chris, who was runner-up to Jay Sigel in the 1983 U.S. Amateur, traveled to Endicott, New York, in September, still winless in 14 years as a professional golfer. With such rich baseball family history, it was only fitting that Perry should end his winless streak during the last week of the 1998 baseball season. At the B.C. Open, Perry confirmed his decision to forego baseball in pursuit of a dream on the PGA Tour.

"I could have played baseball, but I just liked the individuality of golf," Perry said after collecting his $270,000 winner's check. "I love baseball, but if you make a mistake in golf it's because you did it."

Perry didn't make many mistakes during his week at the refurbished En-Joie Golf Club. He was never more than two strokes out of the lead, and his opening three rounds of 67, 70 and 69 left him two behind Bruce Fleisher with 18 holes to play. Fleisher, at age 49, patiently awaiting the Senior PGA Tour and who admits that he has "no desire to continue out here (on the PGA Tour)," made three bogeys on the first nine and shot a final-round 76 after earlier scores of 69, 72 and 63.

Meanwhile, Perry was battling for the lead with Nolan Henke and Peter Jacobsen. Things were nip-and-tuck until the second nine, where Perry pulled away with three consecutive birdies to finish with a 67 and a total of 273, 15 under par. Jacobsen also shot 67 to go with his earlier rounds of 68, 70 and 71 for a 276 total, three more than Perry, but one less than Henke.

It was a finish Perry had been waiting years to enjoy. "The first win is pretty tough," he said. "I've been in position, but just haven't played my best on Sundays. I drew on all those experiences. It was time for me to win. I never really lost faith in myself. You've just got to believe you can do it."

Then, recalling fond memories of his childhood and the lessons he learned from a family full of athletes, Perry said, "My dad pitched for 17 years. He went to spring training early, and he threw in the off-season. I always saw how hard he worked and I've always been a real hard worker. Now, I feel like I've won the Cy Young Award."

Westin Texas Open—$1,700,000

Winner: Hal Sutton

Even though Hal Sutton led by one stroke with 18 holes to play and was never more than two strokes out of the lead, few people gave Sutton much of a chance in a final-round showdown with favorite Justin Leonard at the Westin Texas Open in San Antonio. After all, Leonard had rallied from five strokes behind on three different occasions to win the 1997 British Open and Kemper Open and the 1998 Players Championship. Sutton had only one win in 12 years, and that had come at the 1995 B.C. Open, where he finished with a final-round 61. Two-and-a-half seasons later, few took Sutton seriously, and Sutton even told reporters after the third round that he was simply "leading during a break in the action."

As predicted, Leonard jumped out early in the final round with an eagle at the fifth hole, pulling him into a tie for the lead with Sutton and Jay Haas. From that point on the tournament was a race, with Sutton pulling two ahead with birdies at Nos. 11 and 12, then Leonard started a birdie charge with a 10-footer at the 14th, and another birdie putt of similar length at the 15th. Haas, although never able to go ahead, continued to hold his own, sharing the lead three times in the final 12 holes.

When Leonard's sand wedge at the 16th stopped three feet from the hole, and the ever-steady putter rammed home another birdie to take a two-shot lead, the end seemed in sight. Leonard was about to do it again. Then the unthinkable happened. Leonard "came out of a five iron" on the par-three 17th, missing the green to the right. His chip wasn't much better, and he was left with a 12-foot putt for par. He missed, while Sutton was making an eight-foot birdie putt on the 16th, and the two were tied again.

On the 18th, Leonard's tee shot took a bad hop and finished under the lip of a fairway bunker. Leonard recovered and left himself a seemingly easy five-footer for par and a playoff with Sutton. Everyone, including Sutton, was stunned when Leonard's putt didn't go in. "Yes, I'm disappointed," said Leonard, who closed with a 68 for a 271 total to tie for second place with Haas, one stroke behind Sutton. "I'm disappointed to give myself that good a chance and not be able to pull it through."

With a final-round 68 Sutton had a 270 total, 18 under par. His earlier scores were 67, 68 and 67. Sutton, who had two putts from eight feet over what he described as "the worst spike marks I've seen all year," for the victory, felt Leonard's pain. "I've been in that saddle," he said. "It's difficult to win once, twice, nine times or 29 times. It is a special thing. I took it for granted once, and I'd never take it for granted again. Just when you think it's easy and you've got the world by the tail, it jumps up and bites you."

Jay Haas, whose last victory came in the 1993 Texas Open, certainly felt like he had been bitten. Like Sutton and Leonard, Haas shot a final-round 68, but finished one shot behind Sutton's 270 mark. Loren Roberts, Steve Lowery, Andrew Magee and Mike Reid finished tied for fourth at 273.

Buick Challenge—$1,500,000

Winner: Steve Elkington

Located 80 miles south of Atlanta in the gently rolling Georgia countryside President Franklin Roosevelt found so appealing that he built his Little White House there, Callaway Gardens, a quiet little resort full of flowers, butterflies, cottages and golf seemed an unlikely venue for a dramatic career comeback, but that's exactly what happened at the Buick Challenge. Steve Elkington, who was plagued throughout most of the year with sinus problems and a second bout of viral meningitis, fired a final-round 65 to come from four strokes behind and tie Fred Funk with a tournament-record 267 total, 21 under par. On the first playoff hole, a two-putt par gave Elkington the victory.

"The last 27 holes is about as good as I can play," said Elkington, who went from the 45th through the 72nd hole in 13 under par. The 73rd hole wasn't bad either. After driving into the rough on the right side of the fairway, Elkington called on his textbook swing and hit an eight iron into the center of the green. Funk, who added a final-round 69 to his earlier rounds of 63 and 67 and 68, pushed his drive into the right bunker. When his second shot caught the lip, and his third shot ended up in the high rough surrounding the green, making a chip-in next to impossible, Funk knew that despite setting a 54-hole tournament record at 18 under par, the 1996 Buick Challenge champion had let his best chance slip away.

"It's disappointing to lose because I led the tournament all week and my bread and butter is hitting fairways," Funk said. "I just ran into a buzzsaw with Elkie making all those birdies. I didn't hold up my end of the bargain to finish it off."

Another disappointed player was Bill Glasson, although Glasson was lucky to be playing at all. Elbow surgery kept him from reaching his maximum swing speed, but that didn't stop Glasson from shooting two consecutive 65s after an opening 69. On Sunday, Glasson got off to an early charge, catching Funk on the first nine. It was his putter, not his elbow, that gave Glasson problems down the stretch. Two three-putts in the final nine holes cost him a chance to win outright, and a missed 15-footer on the 72nd hole kept him out of the playoff with Funk and Elkington. "I didn't play well enough to deserve to win," said Glasson, who finished with 69. "I just didn't hit the shots when I needed to."

J.L. Lewis finished off the foursome of players who played all four rounds in the 60s. His 66-69-66-68–269 total was good for fourth place. David Duval kept his lead on the money list by finishing at 273 to tie for sixth with Steve Flesch.

As for Elkington, whose 1994 Buick Challenge victory launched his best 12 months as a professional, including the 1995 PGA Championship, the beauty of the countryside helped him through the week. "It's a relaxing week for most of us who come down here," he said. "It's a nice fall event and probably one of the best conditioned golf courses we play all year. Fortunately, I got a little better each day. This tournament is what springboarded me into the best year I've ever had in 1995. It couldn't have been better timing to win a tournament."

Michelob Championship—$1,800,000

Winner: David Duval

Less than a year before teeing off in Williamsburg, Virginia, at the 1998 Michelob Championship, David Duval had carried the unwanted yoke of being perhaps the best player never to have won a PGA Tour event. He had created new ways to finish second in his three years. That ended in 1997 at Kingsmill Golf Club, where he got the first of three consecutive victories. Three more wins in 1998 had elevated Duval into the highest company.

The streak continued when Duval successfully defended his title, and added a fourth 1998 victory to his record with a three-shot margin over Phil Tataurangi. It was not really that close. Duval led by six strokes with five holes to play. His 65-67-68-68–268 performance earned him another $342,000, and pushed his career earnings over $6 million, and his winnings since teeing off at Kingsmill in 1997 well over the $3 million mark.

Barry Cheesman, a year removed from the Nike Tour, finished third with 272, and Bradley Hughes tied for fourth with Payne Stewart at 273.

Having won three events in 1997 and four so far in 1998, Duval joined an elite group of professionals — a group that gives Duval reason to pause. "When they tell you, 'Hey, Tom Watson was the last guy to do this,' it's almost unsettling," he said. "Or when you read a list of players you've joined and the first two names are Palmer and Nicklaus, it's a funny feeling."

In addition to his four 1998 wins, Duval left Williamsburg with 11 top-10 finishes and a tour record $2.46 million in earnings. According to Scott Hoch, who won the Michelob event in 1996, "Nobody out here, nobody I've ever seen, makes this game look easier than he does. He has got that extra gear, like Nicklaus. When he wants to go long, he can go long. You put him on a course like Kingsmill where he can reach every par-five and he's very, very tough."

Las Vegas Invitational—$2,000,000

Winner: Jim Furyk

For those who knew Jim Furyk, it didn't seem like two and a half years since he had won a golf tournament. That was probably because Furyk had 23 top-10 finishes, near-misses in the Masters and U.S. Open, and a heroic performance in the Ryder Cup. Despite having no victories, Furyk entered the Las Vegas Invitational ranked seventh on the money list, ahead of two-time winner Billy Mayfair, Justin Leonard and Davis Love III. In 1997 he finished fourth on the money list.

In the five-round marathon where the scores are always low, Furyk was one of only two players (Scott Verplank was the other) who didn't have a single round in the 70s. A first-round 67 left him two strokes behind leaders Mark Calcavecchia and Robert Damron. Furyk shot 68 in the second round, which kept him in the same spot, two shots out of the lead. While the names atop the leaderboard changed on the third day, Furyk's 69 kept him within two shots. Bob Tway moved ahead Friday with a 69 to enter the weekend at 14 under par. Furyk stood at 12 under, while Calcavecchia was at 11 under.

Then Furyk made his move. A fourth-round 63, the low score of the tournament, moved Furyk to the top of the leaderboard, two ahead of Calcavecchia and three in front of Verplank. For his part, Calcavecchia knew what he was facing with Furyk in the lead. "I played with Jim on a real tough day at Westchester this year, and it really surprised me how conservatively he played," Calcavecchia said. "I was impressed. It was the way Jack Nicklaus would have played. He uses his mind well."

Furyk called on all his skills on Sunday as he birdied four of the first seven holes and surged into a five-stroke lead over Verplank and a six-shot margin over Calcavecchia. Just when it looked as if Furyk would win in a cakewalk, with Furyk up by five with five holes left, Calcavecchia birdied the last three holes, and five of the last eight. Furyk's run of birdies stopped on the second nine and, after making bogey on the 17th and hitting his approach into the greenside bunker at the 18th, Furyk had to save par from the sand if he was to hold on to what had once seemed an insurmountable lead. It was a frustrating situation that Furyk knew all too well.

"The near-misses got frustrating," he said. "I wouldn't say there was any self-doubt because I always had confidence I was good enough to win. But every time you come close and it doesn't happen, it makes it harder to get over the hill. I've been saying for two years that I'm not putting any pressure on myself, but, yes, it gets to you. Still, I thought it was just a matter of time. When I'm playing well, I'm as good as anyone in the world. I wouldn't be worth a nickel if I didn't think like that."

Furyk hit his bunker shot on the last hole to within eight feet. As Furyk struck the putt, he knew he had made it, but he almost reacted to the victory too soon. Calcavecchia said, "He was giving it the fist when it was still a foot from the hole." The ball did find the right side of the hole, and, early celebration or not, Furyk had his third career victory with a 68 and 335 total and his second in Las Vegas.

National Car Rental Classic—$2,000,000

Winner: John Huston

After 54 holes of the National Car Rental Classic at Walt Disney World, it looked as though Davis Love III would cruise home with another victory, a $360,000 first-place check and a top-five place on the PGA Tour money list going into the Tour Championship. Love never counted on John Huston closing with a six-under-par 66, and Love didn't expect to play the par-five holes in one over par on the last day. Love also did not expect to hit poor short-iron approaches into the 71st and 72nd holes. "That is just inexcusable," Love said afterward.

Still, Love finished alone in second place with a closing 71 for a 273 total, one stroke behind Huston, his best finish since winning the MCI Classic in April before injuring his back and going through a summer of struggles. "I'm just trying to improve every week, and hopefully next week will be better," Love said.

The week couldn't have been much better for Huston, who shared the lead at seven under par after 36 holes with Love, Tom Purtzer, Doug Martin, Rocco Mediate and Glen Day before Love shot a 65 on Saturday and seemingly pulled away from the rest of the field. Poised four shots behind with 18 holes to play, Huston, who overcame serious shoulder injuries this year and broke the PGA Tour's 72-hole scoring record with a 28-under-par, seven-shot victory in the United Airlines Hawaiian Open in February, played his best golf of the last half of the year. He made four birdies on the second nine to finish at 272, leapfrogging past Love and capturing his second title of the year.

Huston's 66 wasn't the only story of the day. Blaine McCallister, who came into the tournament "on the bubble" in terms of keeping his PGA Tour card in 1999, also fired a 66 to move into a tie for 44th place, good enough for the final spot in the top 125 money earners for the year.

The tournament-within-a-tournament proved just as exciting as the battle between Huston and Love, as McCallister edged out P.H. Horgan III for the last exemption for 1999. Horgan, who came into the week in 127th place after playing in 33 events, birdied the 14th, 15th and 16th holes, and seemed poised to cruise in. But on the 17th, Horgan's tee shot landed under a tree root and he made a double bogey. McCallister edged him out by $4,204, but the blow to Horgan was far more expensive.

In a moment of disappointment after the round Horgan made a waving motion in reference to the top 30 money winners who were headed to the Tour Championship. "I'd like to have those guys come down here to the 125th spot and see how it feels. Playing down here, you're playing for your career," he said.

Tour Championship—$4,000,000

Winner: Hal Sutton

As the top 30 money winners arrived in Atlanta for the Tour Championship, held for the first time at historic East Lake Golf Club (the course where Bobby Jones played his first and last rounds of golf), the PGA Tour's money title, the Vardon Trophy for the lowest stroke average and Player of the Year honors were still up in the air. Throw in the fact that the newly refurbished East Lake course was, according to Jim Furyk, "as difficult as any major championship course we play," and the stage was set.

As early as Tuesday afternoon, two days before the first tee shot, players such as Tiger Woods and Mark O'Meara were predicting that any score under par had a chance to win.

Vijay Singh, the PGA champion and two-time 1998 winner, had no problems in the first round, however. Singh defied all predictions by firing a seven-under-par 63 to open up a three-stroke lead over two-time 1998 winner Billy Mayfair, and a four-shot margin over Furyk and Tom Lehman. "A 63 on this golf course is a great score," Furyk said. No one predicted that kind of scoring every day, and they were correct.

Singh stumbled in the second round, carding a triple bogey on the 440-yard par-four fourth hole. He clawed his way back, making five birdies and never relinquishing the lead as he finished with 70, one of the more dramatic even-par rounds of the tournament. Going into the weekend, only three players were under par, with Singh holding on to a two-stroke lead over Furyk. Sutton, who followed his opening-round 69 with a 67, was the third player under par after Friday. "It feels good, but there's a long way to go," Sutton said. He couldn't have been more correct.

While the weather conditions remained unseasonably warm, dry and calm, none of the 30-member field burned up the golf course. Woods, who had a horrendous start, shooting 75-76 in the first two days, entertained the crowd on Saturday by donning a huge "Afro" wig for his walk to the first tee and up the 18th fairway. "It's Halloween," Woods said. "I just wanted to have fun with it. When you're dead last in the tournament you have to do something."

Woods improved his standing from last place on Saturday by shooting a one-under-par 69, one better than Singh had that day. Still, Singh retained the lead by shooting his second straight even-par round, but his margin over Furyk and Sutton narrowed to one stroke. Furyk shot a 69, while Sutton shot a 68, and, although neither had led the tournament, they were the only two players to finish under par each of the three days.

Singh only held his lead through the first six holes on Sunday. With iron play that lacked its usual precision, Singh bogeyed the first, sixth and seventh holes of the final round, while Furyk bogeyed the second and sixth. Meanwhile, Sutton bogeyed the first, then reeled off six straight pars before birdieing the par-four eighth. Furyk then made an eagle three on the ninth to break the logjam. With nine holes to play, Furyk held a one-stroke lead over Sutton and Singh and a two-shot advantage over Jesper Parnevik.

On the final nine, Singh, Furyk and Sutton all slipped in and out of the top spot, with Furyk carding two more birdies, but following each birdie with a bogey. Singh made birdies at the 10th and 13th, while Sutton bogeyed the 13th, but followed up with a birdie at the 14th. Parnevik, playing ahead of Furyk, Sutton and Singh, made three more birdies, but a bogey on the 16th destroyed his chances. Even though the mercurial Swede made pars on the 17th and 18th, it wasn't enough to catch the leaders. With two holes to play, Singh had regained a one-stroke advantage.

All three players parred the difficult par-four 17th, so it all came down to the 18th, a 232-yard, uphill, par-three hole. Furyk, playing ahead of Sutton and Singh, hit his tee shot slightly left and through the green, leaving a difficult sidehill chip. When his pitch came up short, Furyk needed to make a 10-footer to have any chance at a playoff. He missed, and his tap-in bogey gave Furyk a 71, his first over-par round of the week and a 275 total.

Sutton hit first on the 18th, and his four-wood shot came up short in the bunker. Then Singh, who hit what he described as "a good three iron," watched as his ball ran through the green and stopped in the four-inch-high Bermuda rough behind the green. Sutton blasted out to within three feet, but Singh's chip rolled down the hill and stopped 25 feet away.

Singh hit his first putt poorly, leaving himself a four-footer for bogey, which he slipped into the left side of the hole. Sutton then made his par, and the two players finished regulation play tied at 274, Singh having shot 71 and Sutton, 70.

In the playoff, Sutton hit his four wood again, but made a better swing and the ball ended up four feet from the pin. Singh also chose his three iron again, but this time, rather than rolling through the green, the ball rolled to the crest of the hill, stopped, and rolled back away from the hole, leaving him with another 25-footer, this time for birdie. Although he hit a good putt, Singh did not make the birdie. Sutton's putt never wavered and when it hit the bottom of the hole, an overwhelmed Sutton pumped his fist, and hugged his caddie.

David Duval followed an opening-round 75 with rounds of 69, 69 and 68 that featured an impressive 31 on the second nine to finish tied for eighth place. His $120,533 gave Duval a total of $2,591,031 in official PGA Tour earnings for the year, good enough for the money title. His strong finish jumped him ahead of Woods in scoring (69.10 to 69.14) for the Vardon Trophy.

Special Events

Panama Open Panasonic—$175,000
Winner: Bob Friend

After matching each other almost shot-for-shot in the final two days of the Panama Open Panasonic, American Bob Friend and Rick Todd had to go one extra hole before Friend won at the Coronado golf course. Friend followed his opening-round 68 with scores of 74, 69 and 70 for a 281 total to tie Todd, who also shot 69-70 on the weekend after a 71-71 start. With a closing-round 75, Roger Rowland slipped into a tie for third with Esteban Toledo at 282. Brian Kontak shot closing rounds of 72-72 to finish alone in fifth.

Fred Meyer Challenge—$925,000
Winners: David Duval and Jim Furyk

Greg Norman, the defending champion with partner Brad Faxon in the Fred Meyer Challenge, was still recuperating from shoulder surgery when the 12 two-man teams ventured to Aloha, Oregon, for the two-day invitational. It seemed only fitting that with Norman out of action, the hottest player would walk away with the victory. David Duval added to his 1998 record by rallying from two strokes behind to shoot 61 along with partner Jim Furyk.

With their first-day 65, Duval and Furyk's 18-under-par 126 total bettered first-round leaders Steve Elkington and Craig Stadler by four strokes. Elkington and Stadler followed their opening 63 with 67 to drop into a tie for second place with Scott McCarron and Paul Stankowski, who followed up their 66 with 64 in the second round.

Subaru Sarazen World Open—$2,000,000
Winner: Dudley Hart

Whether or not he defends his title, or whether or not there is a title for him to defend since the event was not picked as part of the PGA Tour's World Golf Championship package for 1999, Dudley Hart has the satisfaction of knowing that he not only beat a talented field from around the world in suburban Atlanta to capture the Subaru Sarazen World Open, he did so with a stretch of stellar golf that was the best he'd ever had as a professional. From his 17th hole on Friday through the 11th on Saturday, Hart, whose only other victory came in the 1996 Canadian Open, jumped ahead of the open winners from around the world by playing 13 holes in 12 under par. His front-side 28 on Saturday broke that nine's record by two, and his third-round 62 tied the 18-hole course record set by Calcavecchia during the 1997 Sarazen World Open.

"I birdied two of the first three holes and was playing pretty good (on

Saturday), but when I looked up on the board I was behind," said Bob Tway. "Dudley obviously played a fantastic round of golf."

Tway played pretty well himself. A six-under-par 66 in the opening round gave Tway a one-shot lead over Edward Fryatt (who qualified for the event by winning the 1997 Indian Open and the 1998 China Open). Fryatt would briefly capture the lead on Friday after shooting his second straight round of 67, but that lead quickly faded on Saturday as Fryatt ballooned to a third-round 83.

Under normal circumstances, Tway's third-round 66 would have been good enough to put him well ahead of any contender, but Hart's 62 left him only one behind Tway with 18 holes left.

While not as good as Saturday's round, Hart played well enough on Sunday to jump to a four-shot lead after nine holes. His only blemish of the day, and the only time he let his legendary temper flair, came at the par-five 10th where Hart pulled his tee shot into the trees, nicked a limb on his recovery, and had to settle for a bogey. A birdie on the 13th erased all bad memories from his mind, however, and Hart cruised home for the win.

Armed with a $360,000 winner's check, Hart flew back to Ft. Lauderdale where he and his wife Suzanne immediately departed for a belated honeymoon in Cabo San Lucas. No doubt, the World Golf Championships and the future of the Sarazen World Open were the last things on his mind.

Franklin Templeton Shark Shootout—$1,100,000

Winners: Steve Elkington and Greg Norman

After missing the cut at the Masters, Greg Norman decided to undergo an examination for problems he was having with his shoulder. Bone spurs had begun to aggravate and inflame the rotator cuff in his left shoulder, and surgery was immediately scheduled. Until the second week in November, Norman did not play a single competitive round of golf. In fact, he did not strike a golf ball with a full swing until October. "I enjoyed getting my life back," he said. "I did not miss the game one bit. I think this was the best thing that could have happened to me."

An even better ending to the injury saga came at Sherwood Country Club in Thousand Oaks, California, when Norman holed four consecutive birdie putts, the last three in a playoff, to win his own tournament, the Franklin Templeton Shark Shootout, along with his partner, Steve Elkington. After a closing round of 58 in a scramble format, the Norman-Elkington team stood tied with Peter Jacobsen and John Cook, who shot a final-round 55 to reach 27-under-par 189 in the 54-hole competition. Then the Shark of old came to life with birdie putts on the first and second par-four playoff holes to keep the match alive. After the fourth birdie putt found the hole, Norman proved he had a clean bill of health and another win — his first in the event that bears his nickname.

"My challenge is not to get back to being No. 1 in the world," Norman said. "My challenge is getting back to a level of golf I know I can play and whatever that dishes out that's okay. If I do as well at the game as I've done in the past, I'll be happy. If don't, I'll still be happy."

PGA Grand Slam—$1,000,000

Winner: Tiger Woods

The PGA Grand Slam is normally played between the winners of the year's four major championships, but because Mark O'Meara won both the Masters and the British Open in 1998, his Orlando neighbor and friend Tiger Woods received an invitation to the November event for having had the best major championship record outside the three winners. Woods proceeded to defeat U.S. Open champion Lee Janzen 3 and 2 in the first round, while PGA Championship winner Vijay Singh eliminated O'Meara 2 up.

In a hotly contested final, Woods joined Greg Norman as the second alternate player to win the Grand Slam title. Norman did it in 1994, the year Nick Price won both the British Open and PGA Championship. Woods did it with a 2-up victory over Singh on a windy day at the Poipu Bay Resort in Kauai, Hawaii.

Singh led for most of the match and, after Woods conceded the 12th hole, took a 2-up advantage into the home stretch. Then Singh reeled off three consecutive bogeys. When Woods birdied the 15th, the lead changed in his favor. Woods gave up his advantage when he bogeyed the 16th. The match was tied with two holes to play.

At the par-three 17th, both players hit the green and Singh, with a 25-foot birdie effort, was the first to play. His putt hung on the lip but failed to drop. Woods then ignited the crowd by making a 12-foot birdie putt.

With the wind howling, Singh was forced to attack the pin with his second shot on the 18th, but instead his ball found the ocean. When Woods hit his second shot on the green, the match was conceded.

Woods collected $400,000 while Singh made $250,000. Janzen defeated O'Meara 1 up for third place. Janzen collected $200,000 while O'Meara made $150,000.

World Cup of Golf—$1,500,000

Winners: England/Scott Verplank

When Nick Faldo teed off at the Gulf Harbor Country Club in Whangaparaoa, New Zealand, with partner David Carter, it had been 18 months since the three-time Masters and British Open champion last collected a winner's check at the Nissan Open. In the months leading up to the World Cup of Golf, Faldo changed equipment companies and teachers, but still he was struggling with his game. But Faldo had made a promise to help rectify what he viewed as an untenable situation. England had never captured a World Cup title in the event's 44-year history. With that in mind, Faldo and Carter ground out four solid rounds to beat the Italian team of Costantino Rocca and Massimo Florioli by two strokes, and edge out the hard-charging American team of Scott Verplank and John Daly by three shots. Argentina and Scotland tied the United States for third place.

Faldo looked like the Faldo-of-old throughout most of the week. His consistent tee-to-green play resulted in opening rounds of 68 and 70, which, coupled with Carter's 73-71 start, gave England a 282 total and a three-stroke lead over the Scottish team of Colin Montgomerie (72-69) and Andrew Coltart

(70-74). Padraig Harrington (72-72) and Paul McGinley (67-76) kept Ireland in the hunt at 287, tied for third with Argentina, five back of England's lead with two rounds to play.

On Saturday the scores headed upward as none of the 64 contestants broke 70, and the field averaged 78.76 for the day. By those standards, Faldo's 73 and Carter's 76 were not bad scores. Still, at the end of the day, England had lost its lead to the Argentines, thanks to rounds of 71 by Angel Cabrera and 72 by Ricardo Gonzalez. With one round to play, Argentina stood at 430, with England at 431. Harrington and McGinley also made a move with rounds of 72 and 73 respectively to move Ireland into a tie for third place with Italy at 432. Costantino Rocca added 71 to his previous rounds of 65 and 74 to give Italy a chance at the title and give himself the individual lead by one over Faldo and Cabrera.

In the final round, England rallied around Faldo's consistency and the resurgent putting of Carter. Although Carter had to undergo shoulder massages before each round, he came through with a closing 68, birdieing the last hole to insure the victory for England.

Afterward, Faldo, who shot a final-round 69 to give the team a 568 total, jokingly said, "I carried Carter all week, and now he's the bloody hero. Isn't that great?" Then, in a more serious tone, Faldo said, "If I could have putted, it would have been a stroll."

It was anything but a stroll for England, as the American team launched a charge in the final round. Verplank's final-round 63 matched the course record, and the U.S. led by one stroke through the 16th hole. Then Daly, who had shot 70, 77 and 77 the three previous days, but who was six under par through the 16th on Sunday, dropped two shots on the last two holes and left the door open for Faldo and Carter. Daly's 68 gave the Americans a third-place tie, and Verplank's heroics earned him the individual title with 279, one better than Faldo and Rocca.

For his newly found game, Faldo, as usual, credited hard work. "The workload I've given myself in the last three months to get my game back has finally paid off," he said. "Now, I want to get back into the world's top 10 again."

Callaway Golf Pebble Beach Invitational—$300,000

Winner: Tom Lehman

As Tom Lehman, winless since the 1996 Tour Championship and still recovering from a shoulder injury that plagued him throughout most of 1998, admitted after collecting his $60,000 winner's check at the Callaway Golf Pebble Beach Invitational, "This is not the biggest tournament around, but I can build on it." Lehman's solid play certainly boosted his confidence. An opening-round 66 gave him a two-stroke lead, and while his second-round 70 allowed players like Rocco Mediate and Kirk Triplett to inch closer, Lehman was never in danger of losing his lead.

On Saturday, however, Lehman's 69 was not enough to retain the lead. Mediate played brilliantly, firing a third-round 66 to take a one-stroke lead over Lehman and a three-shot lead over Jim Carter going into the final round. Not to be denied, Lehman charged home with a closing-round 68 and

273 total, while Mediate could manage no better than a final-round 71, good enough for a second-place tie with Triplett, who closed the weekend with rounds of 68-67 for a 275 total.

No one knows if Lehman's total would have won the rain soaked and long-delayed AT&T Pebble Beach National Pro Am (shortened to 54 holes and won by Phil Mickelson with a score of 202), but for Lehman, who said of the AT&T fiasco, "Sorry, Mother Nature won," the Pebble Beach victory was the first leg on a journey back to the winner's circle. As he put it afterward, "This is a stepping stone."

JCPenney Classic—$1,750,000

Winners: Meg Mallon and Steve Pate

In 1993, Meg Mallon and Steve Pate decided that they would make a good team in the JCPenney Classic mixed-team event, because, in Mallon's words, "We got each other's jokes." Six years later, they laughed their way to victory with a bogey-free 62, the lowest final round in tournament history. Their 29-under-par 255 total not only overtook third-round leaders Rachel Hetherington and Rocco Mediate, it broke the previous tournament record of 27 under par set by Beth Daniel and Davis Love III in 1995.

"I thought a 62 was possible, yes. But was it likely? No," Pate said. "It's a tough format to get on a roll," he said of the modified alternate-shot format on Sunday. "But Meg got to putt a lot in stretches and that helped. I putted a few from three feet and I made them."

Hetherington and Mediate shot 69 in the final round. They led by two with nine holes to play but, while Hetherington and Mediate parred in, Mallon and Pate birdied five of the last eight holes.

"Steve hit it great, and, fortunately, I had the putter working," Mallon said. "You want to reward good shots your partner makes. We thought winning would eventually be inevitable. Whether or not it would actually happen, we weren't sure, but this is the best I've played for four rounds with him. We just didn't make any mistakes."

Office Depot Father-Son Challenge—$860,000

Winners: Bob Charles and David Charles

Sixty-two-year-old Bob Charles shot his age in the final round of the Office Depot Father-Son Challenge with help from his 30-year-old son and partner David. The Charles team led after the first round when they shot 57, and they held on to win by four strokes over Craig and Kevin Stadler, despite the Stadlers' shooting 60 in the final round.

"David is maybe 40 yards longer off the tee than I am, and playing the game from where he hits his drives is totally different that what I'm used to," Bob Charles said. "I wish I had his length off the tee on the Senior Tour, but I never have, even when I was younger."

Even though his length was an advantage, the younger Charles, who is a tournament director for the PGA of America, deferred to his father when it came to iron play and reading putts.

Presidents Cup

Winner: International

The International team, which had suffered defeats in the two previous Presidents Cup events, stunned the Jack Nicklaus-captained United States squad 20½-11½ at Royal Melbourne Golf Club. By Saturday evening, the International group from Australia, New Zealand, Africa, Asia and South America had built such a commanding lead over such American players as Tiger Woods, David Duval, Mark O'Meara and Fred Couples that the outcome seemed a foregone conclusion.

Barring an 11-1 rout by the Americans in the singles matches, the Presidents Cup was going to the Internationals. When Duval conceded a tap-in putt on the 17th hole to Nick Price in the second match on Sunday, giving the Internationals a 2-and-1 victory, the celebration broke out in earnest.

The American team, which was stocked with five of the world's top 10 players, stood in silence as Shigeki Maruyama of Japan, who had defeated the likes of Woods, Couples, Duval, Mark Calcavecchia, Lee Janzen, Scott Hoch, Phil Mickelson and John Huston to finish 5-0 for the matches, accepted the congratulations of his teammates.

"It never dawned on me that we would lose," Calcavecchia said. "We all played okay, but I don't think anybody did their best out there for the team. Did the International team want it more? Maybe they did. The amazing thing was that it wasn't even close. That's probably the worst part. Losing by a point or two would have been different, but they all just played well. I'm not sure that one guy on our team played outstanding."

A gracious Peter Thomson, captain of the International team, suggested that his squad took full advantage of local knowledge. "We played on virtual home soil," he said referring to Royal Melbourne, a course that Greg Norman and Steve Elkington knew well. "Until we beat that team in the United States I don't think we can crow too much."

Couples and Woods provided the only outright win for the Americans on Friday morning, when they defeated Ernie Els and Vijay Singh, 5 and 4 in a foursomes match. Davis Love III and Justin Leonard halved their match with Price and Stuart Appleby, but the Americans entered the lunch break down 3½-1½. It was a deficit they would never make up.

By Friday night, the Internationals had taken a commanding 7-3 lead. On Saturday the International team's lead grew to 14½-5½, which meant that Thomson's team only needed two wins or four halves in the 12 singles matches to win. They closed it out early when Craig Parry defeated Leonard 5 and 3 in the first match, and Price won over Duval in the second.

With the event decided, the remaining players battled for pride. The Americans earned six points in the singles, including Woods over Greg Norman, 1 up, in the match that attracted the most attention.

Despite the drumming, Nicklaus had nothing but praise for the International team. "These guys played great," he said. "To have these guys from all over the world come together as a group ... It is easy for us. We all come from one place. But to take a squad like Peter had and put them together, to fight for each other and root for each other and win is really special. I'm sure Peter is very, very proud."

Lexus Challenge—$1,000,000

Winners: Jim Colbert and Kevin Costner

It was not the U.S. Open and he didn't run out of golf balls trying to reach an unreachable par-five, but *Tin Cup* star Kevin Costner did manage to sink a few putts to help his partner, Jim Colbert, in the Lexus Challenge. The Colbert-Costner team shot a 24-under-par 120 total to win by one stroke over Hubert Green and Matt Lauer.

Costner, who learned to play golf in order to portray a journeyman golfer in the movie, has had two second-place finishes in this event, so the victory was especially sweet. "I really wanted to win this tournament. I was sure hoping I wasn't going to come in second again," Costner said. After the pair opened with a 58, Costner said, "I learned that I can play better when I focus."

They needed it during the second round. Green and Lauer went on a birdie barrage en route to a tournament-record 56, but Colbert and Costner answered with a 62. "It was a great relief when Jim (Colbert) made a birdie or a par," Costner said. "When he started to make some birdies it really took the pressure off of my shoulders."

Larry Nelson and Sean Connery finished third at 126, while defending champions Raymond Floyd and William Devane were fourth at 127.

Nike Tour

Throughout its nine-year history, the Nike Tour has been considered an incentive-based stepping stone for those who want to play the PGA Tour. From its inception in 1990 through the 1998 season, 30 Nike Tour graduates accumulated 53 victories on the PGA Tour, and the alumni list included Tom Lehman, John Daly, David Duval, Jim Furyk, Jeff Maggert, Stuart Appleby, Stewart Cink and Steve Flesch. Like every current Nike Tour player, the goal of those professionals was promotion to the "Big Tour." It was never anyone's expectation for the Nike Tour to make international news, and for most of its history, it didn't.

The 1998 Nike Tour season began at the center of a controversy that riveted, and in some cases polarized, the golf community. Networks led their evening news broadcasts and cable talk shows filled up hours of air time debating the plight of an affable young golfer who qualified for a 1998 exemption on the Nike Tour. Casey Martin, a former teammate of Tiger Woods at Stanford University, earned his right to play the Nike Tour at the PGA Tour's qualifying tournament, but it took a favorable ruling from a U.S. District Court for Martin to compete.

Because of a rare degenerative disorder, Martin's right leg could not fully support his weight for an extended period of time, which made walking a golf course nearly impossible. Since its inception, the PGA Tour has had a rule prohibiting competitors from riding golf carts. Senior PGA Tour players are allowed to ride, but the rules state that others must walk. Due to his disability, Martin believed that he should be allowed to ride as well, and he sued the PGA Tour under the 1992 Americans With Disabilities Act for that right.

While awaiting his day in court, Martin was awarded a temporary restraining order allowing him to use a golf cart in competition until his case was heard. With more national media in attendance than at any point in Nike Tour history, Martin made his debut at the Nike Lakeland Classic in Florida. The 25-year-old Martin politely answered all the questions then drove himself and the Nike Tour onto the front pages of the world's newspapers by shooting 19-under-par 269 for 72 holes, good enough for a one-stroke victory. His closing 69, capped by a two-putt par from 15 feet on the 72nd hole, edged out second-place finisher Steve Lamontagne, but with the pressure and controversy of his debut, Martin's win provided a storybook caption to the larger legal battle.

"A total weight has been lifted," Martin said. "All the stuff about the court and all the talk about me playing in a cart, it weighs on you emotionally. Just to win is an amazing relief. I really tried not to think about winning, but you can't help it. I was trying to just focus on each shot."

Martin would remain on center stage throughout the year, even though the Nike Lakeland Classic would be his only win, and he would not be among the 15 leaders who earned PGA Tour cards in 1998. Martin added marquee value, as evidenced by the increased galleries when he played, and despite the differing views on the issue of his golf cart, Martin conducted himself courageously and professionally, and as a result, won the battle of public opinion.

Martin wasn't the only story of the year. In mid-May, another former Stanford golfer entered the record books on the Nike Tour. Notah Begay III became only the third player to shoot 59 in a PGA Tour-sanctioned competitive round. Begay's record-tying number came in the second round of the Nike Dominion Classic in Glen Allen, Virginia. With birdies on the 17th and 18th holes, Begay, in his words, "guaranteed myself a piece of immortality." He wasn't guaranteed a victory, however. Two closing 74s dropped Begay out of the lead, and Bob Burns rallied to win by one stroke.

Two weeks later, Doug Dunakey stood over a two-foot putt for a 58 at the Heatherwood Golf Club in Springboro, Ohio. Dunakey, who had 10 birdies and an eagle on his card at that point, missed the two-footer, settled for par, and joined Begay, Chip Beck and Al Geiberger as the only four players in PGA Tour history to shoot 59. He also joined Begay and Beck when he didn't win the Nike Miami Valley Open. Craig Bowden shot a closing 67 for a two-stroke victory over Dunakey and Ryan Howison.

"My bad shots didn't end up any good and my good shots didn't end up any good either," Dunakey said of his post-59 play. "I think I was a little out of sync, and I had some trouble with my distance control, but overall, it was quite a week." One week later, Dunakey picked up his first victory at the Nike Cleveland Open in Concord, Ohio.

In the end, they looked like graduating cadets — 15 men who had endured a grueling year of basic training to finally earn their commissions. Burns won the Nike Tour Championship in Mobile, Alabama and, in addition to capturing the money title with $178,664 in official earnings, was named the Nike Tour Player of the Year.

There were five two-tournament winners: Burns, Joe Ogilvie, Robin Freeman, Matt Gogel and Charles Raulerson. All but Gogel qualified for the PGA Tour. Other qualifiers were Begay, Dunakey, Eric Booker, John Maginnes, Dennis Paulson, Woody Austin, Mike Sposa, Jimmy Green, Sean Murphy, Emlyn Aubrey and Tom Scherrer.

Canadian Tour

The 1998 Canadian Tour took on a southern flair as eight of the tour's events were won by American players, two by a South African and one each by a Zimbabwean, a New Zealander and an Australian. Canada did manage a team victory at the Dundee Realty International Team Matches in Saskatoon, Saskatchewan, where Ashley Chinner won three straight matches to propel the victory. "I played in two of the previous competitions and Canada got waxed on the final day," Chinner said. "It's been a fun two days, but at the end it's always nice to get the win." That was one of the few bright spots for Canadian players.

The year opened with American Jay Hobby sinking a six-foot eagle putt in a playoff to snatch the Payless Open away from Ontario's Ian Leggatt. In the Telus Edmonton Open, Brian Kontak of Tempe, Arizona, defeated Bryan DeCorso of Guelph, Ontario, in a playoff. "When I had the lead, I didn't focus enough," DeCorso said. "I'm disappointed with my performance." That would become the mantra of many Canadian players throughout the year.

Meanwhile, Kontak was ecstatic over his first victory. "This is a breakthrough win for me," he said. "A win on this tour is great preparation for the next level." Kontak repeated one week later when he fired a seven-under-par 63 in the final round of the Henry Singer Alberta Open to beat David Morland of Aurora, Ontario, by three shots. "I ran into a buzzsaw today," Morland said.

That buzzsaw took on many different forms throughout the year, but the story remained the same. In May, Ian Hutchings of Zimbabwe birdied the final three holes to pass three Americans and win the BC Tel Open. DeCorso, who tied for 11th, was the highest finishing Canadian. Then Scott Wearne of Australia shot a 68 to win the Telus Calgary Open by three strokes. In that event Vancouver's Philip Jonas finished tied for third.

American Perry Parker won Winnipeg's MTS Classic, while Alberta's Keith Whitecotton finished tied for fourth. Then Kontak did it again, winning his third Canadian Tour event by birdieing the first playoff hole of the Infiniti Championship to beat Ian Leggatt of Cambridge, Ontario. "Ian played great and made it close," Kontak said. "That's the way it should be."

In the Canadian Masters, Mike Grob of Billings, Montana, parlayed an early hole-in-one into a runaway five-shot victory, while Leggatt, the highest finishing Canadian, could manage no better than a tie for seventh, eight strokes out of the lead.

Perry Parker picked up his second win of the season at Ottawa's Eagle Creek Classic, edging Winnipeg's Todd Fanning by one stroke. Then New Zealander Paul Devenport and South African Tim Clark took over the month of August. Devenport made four birdies and a double eagle in the first 10 holes to defeat Calgary's Wes Martin in the final match of the American Express - Shell Cup, and many had to wonder how good a native would have to play to finally win. The answer was better than 43 under par, since that's what Clark shot in a two-week stretch in August. His 27-under-par 261 won the New Brunswick Open by one shot over Australia's David McKenzie, while it took a 16-under-par total and one playoff hole for Clark to win the Samsung Canadian PGA Championship over Chris Tidland of Stillwater, Oklahoma.

In the season-ending Bayer Championship, it looked as though a native Canadian would finally earn a win. Keith Whitecotton began the final round with a one-stroke lead, while Chinner and Todd Fanning were within two shots. Then Tidland shot a 65 to pull away and earn a three-stroke victory over Chinner, Fanning, Grob and Ken Duke of Little Rock, Arkansas. "It still hasn't hit me, but I'm going to savor this win for a while," Tidland said. For the Canadian players, the entire season will linger for a while as well.

South American Tour

The biggest news from the 1998 South American Tour dealt with the 1999 season. At the year's first event, the TPG Open in Venezuela, officials announced a deal with Latin American Golf Partners. Twelve events in 1999 will feature purses of at least $200,000, which officials hope will attract greater interest from international players for the October-through-January circuit.

Some international names enjoyed success in 1998 even without the advantage of increased prize money. Globe-trotting American Scott Dunlap broke through with a win in early November at the Peru Open, after opening with 64. Dunlap's 275 total at Los Incas Country Club edged Paraguay's Angel Franco by two strokes. Argentina's Mauricio Molina finished third at 281.

Dunlap wasn't the only American to leave his mark in South America. At the Litoral Open in Rosario, Argentina, Tim Hegna held on to shoot 71 and defeat Armando Saavedra by one stroke. In late November, Jeffrey Schmidt won the JPGA Argentina event in a playoff with Argentina's Ricardo Montenegro.

South Americans showed their stuff when Alfred Dunhill Cup hero Raul Fretes of Paraguay captured the Argentina Masters. Fretes, who gained prominence when he defeated Colin Montgomerie at St. Andrews, finished with 67 to fend off such players as Argentina's Eduardo Romero, America's Blaine McCallister and Germany's Bernhard Langer. Fretes concluded the year by winning the Argentina Open by five strokes.

11. European Tours

Colin Montgomerie's reign on the PGA European Tour continued for another year in 1998, although not by a comfortable margin. With a third-place finish in the season-ending Volvo Masters, Montgomerie held off Darren Clarke and Lee Westwood to win the European money title for an unprecedented sixth consecutive year. "Their time will come, and pretty soon. Lee and Darren are both world-class players," Montgomerie said. He finished with £993,077 in Europe and Clarke, who won the Volvo Masters, was second with £902,867. Westwood was third with £814,386, almost £300,000 more than the next finisher, Miguel Angel Jimenez.

"It's getting closer," Montgomerie said. "It didn't come down to the last putt like it did against Sam Torrance in 1995, but at the same time the standard is improving. As I have said many times before, I have had to improve along with it. Although I've had a slight hiccup during the year, I feel that I am improving. My course management is improving and I am mentally tougher than ever before."

Unlike the past two years, when Montgomerie led the World Money List with over $3 million each time, the 35-year-old Scot was not Europe's best international performer. He won the Volvo PGA Championship, but then only two late-season events, the One 2 One British Masters and Linde German Masters, while going another year without achieving his great ambition of winning a major championship. His best in the majors was a tie for eighth place in the Masters and his worst, a missed 36-hole cut in the British Open, as he finished eighth on the World Money List with $2.2 million.

In Montgomerie's place was Westwood, an Englishman who was 10 years younger. Westwood doubled his worldwide career victory total in 1998 with seven triumphs — the most by anyone in the world not on the senior tours, winning once in the United States, four times in Europe and twice in Japan. His worldwide earnings were $2.8 million for fourth place, but little more than $100,000 out of the top position. He charged from No. 23 on the World Ranking into the top 10 at No. 8, one position behind Montgomerie.

Westwood won the Freeport-McDermott Classic on the week before the Masters. Two months later, he won back-to-back in Europe, beating Clarke by one stroke in the Deutsche Bank-SAP Open TPC of Europe, then taking the National Car Rental English Open. In the summer Westwood added titles in the Standard Life Loch Lomond and, in a playoff, the Belgacom Open. A trip to Japan yielded victories in the Sumitomo Visa Taiheiyo Masters and Dunlop Phoenix Tournament.

Clarke, age 30, from Northern Ireland had two victories, but both were impressive, the Volvo Masters and the Benson and Hedges International, where he held off Montgomerie in the final round. Other multiple winners in Europe, with two wins each, were Thomas Bjorn of Denmark, Stephen Leaney of Australia and Miguel Angel Jimenez of Spain. Jesper Parnevik, who also won in the United States, came home to take the Volvo Scandinavian Masters.

Americans Mark O'Meara and Tiger Woods made the most of their brief appearances on the PGA European Tour. Woods led off the 1998 schedule with a victory in the Johnnie Walker Classic in Thailand. O'Meara claimed the British Open then came back for the Cisco World Match Play title, winning over Woods in the final.

It was not a good year for the old guard. Bernhard Langer, who finished second on the European money list in 1997, did not have a victory and fell to 18th place. Ian Woosnam was also winless and dropped to 20th place. Seve Ballesteros and Sandy Lyle showed no signs of returning to prominence, but Jose Maria Olazabal won the Dubai Desert Classic and 45-year-old Sam Torrance won for the first time since 1995.

Nick Faldo's troubles continued and he dropped his long-time coach, David Leadbetter. Faldo did not win an individual tournament but salvaged England's first World Cup victory in 46 years, with David Carter as his partner. Faldo shot 280 and Carter, 288, but it was Carter's 18-foot birdie putt that sealed the two-stroke triumph over Italy. "Isn't that just typical," Faldo joked at the presentation. "I carried him for four days and today he turns into the bloody hero."

PGA European Tour

Johnnie Walker Classic—£800,000

Winner: Tiger Woods

See Australasian Tour chapter.

Heineken Classic—A$1,400,000

Winner: Thomas Bjorn

See Australasian Tour chapter.

South African Open—R3,710,855

Winner: Ernie Els

See African Tours chapter.

Alfred Dunhill South African PGA—R3,327,705

Winner: Tony Johnstone

See African Tours chapter.

Dubai Desert Classic—£770,000

Winner: Jose Maria Olazabal

Playing through illness has been nothing new for Jose Maria Olazabal. For two and a half years, he struggled through what he believed was a case of rheumatoid arthritis that made it impossible for him to walk, much less play golf. So when he woke up in the middle of the night and realized he had a temperature of 102 degrees caused by a case of acute pharyngitis, it was nothing for the 32-year-old Spaniard.

Despite doctors advising him to stay in bed, Olazabal played in the Dubai Desert Classic in the United Arab Emirates, and he was the only player to have four consecutive rounds in the 60s. His final round of 68 elevated him to a 269 total and a three-shot victory over Stephen Allan and a four-shot margin over Ernie Els and Robert Karlsson. Olazabal's earlier scores were 69, 67 and 65.

"All I was trying to do was finish 18 holes," Olazabal said. "If anyone had told me that I would win the golf tournament I would have slapped his cheeks and told him he was mad."

It wasn't an automatic victory for the Spaniard, however. Karlsson led the tournament for 65 of the 72 holes until, at the 13th on Sunday, Olazabal holed a 77-yard pitch shot for an eagle. "Until then I didn't care about the others," Olazabal said. "I was just trying to keep my score going. I certainly wasn't thinking about winning."

With the lead in hand after No. 13, Olazabal started thinking about winning. The thoughts were short-lived, however. After a three-putt bogey at the 16th, Olazabal was tied with Allan, a 24-year-old Australian. At the 18th, however, Allan, unaware that Olazabal had three-putted behind him, went for the green from a questionable lie in the left rough and instead found the water. "I figured I needed birdie to tie," Allan said. "I never really contemplated not going for it. It was my first chance to win, so hopefully it can be a learning experience for me."

It was certainly a learning experience for Olazabal who contemplated retirement after his foot problems were misdiagnosed almost two years prior. A German doctor discovered that Olazabal's problems stemmed from his lower back, not arthritis as originally thought, and as he hoisted the trophy in front of the crowd in Dubai, Olazabal thanked the man who made it all possible. "I feel like a lucky man," he said. "If it hadn't been for my German doctor I wouldn't be here today."

Qatar Masters—£606,060

Winner: Andrew Coltart

As the touring pro from the Old Course Hotel in St. Andrews, Scotland, and the reigning winner of the Australasian Tour money list, one might think that a PGA European Tour victory by Andrew Coltart would be a natural, logical extension to a blossoming career. Maybe, but Coltart's first victory in Europe wasn't without a great deal of anxiety. "I didn't stop worrying until I reached the final green," Coltart said after the Qatar Masters. "You start wondering when it's going to happen, and it's sickening when it doesn't happen."

After a final-round 67 and a two-stroke victory over Patrik Sjoland and Andrew Sherborne with a 270 total at the Doha Golf Club, Coltart needn't worry any more. "I tried not to put any expectations on myself and just do the best I could," Coltart said. "I'm exhausted."

Prior to the Qatar Masters, Coltart had three second-place finishes — at the 1995 Catalonia Open, 1996 Johnnie Walker Classic and 1996 Scottish Open. He also won the Australian PGA title just five months prior to teeing off in Doha, but that didn't help his confidence. Because of the added pressures he had placed on himself to win in Europe, Coltart slipped from seventh on the money list in 1996 to 46th in 1997. But his sports psychologist and fiancee have helped the young Scot put things into perspective. "I am trying to be much more relaxed about things," he said.

Sherborne, who led Sjoland by two and Coltart by three strokes with 18 holes to play, wasn't relaxed after his Sunday performance. "I played like a pig," Sherborne said of his one-under-par 71. "I didn't deserve to win."

Moroccan Open—£350,000

Winner: Stephen Leaney

With four solid rounds in the 60s, 29-year-old Australian Stephen Leaney not only captured his first PGA European Tour victory, thus insuring his player's card through another season, he ran away from the field with a Moroccan Open record of 17-under-par 271 and an eight-shot margin of victory over Robert Karlsson. "This is as good as I've played in my life," said the PGA European Tour rookie, who had scores of 68, 67, 69 and 67.

It could have been better, however. With a 10-stroke lead going into the par-five 15th hole, Leaney lost his tee shot out of bounds. "I lost my concentration," he said, but he didn't loose his edge. Leaney's closest competitor was Karlsson, who had impressive rounds of 70, 71, 67 and 71. Mathias Gronberg finished third at six under par, while Spain's Miguel Angel Martin made up for a second-round 78 by shooting 68 and 69 on the weekend to finish four under par for the tournament and tied with Mark Davis for fourth place.

As for Leaney, this was the perfect ending to a week that began with a celebration of his 29th birthday, a trip from Australia to London to Morocco (passing through 10 time zones), and breaking in a new putter in his record-setting win. "It was the longest birthday I've ever had," Leaney said. It was certainly one he will long remember.

Portuguese Open—£350,000

Winner: Peter Mitchell

Not many people can take their families on an extended vacation to Lisbon, play a few rounds of golf, and come back home with an extra £58,330 along with a PGA European Tour title. "We rented a villa and it was a bit of a holiday," said Englishman Peter Mitchell of his stay during the Portuguese Open. "I was nice and relaxed."

So relaxed was Mitchell that he found himself leading the tournament by one stroke after three rounds. His 67-70-67 start gave Mitchell the advantage over Sweden's Jarmo Sandelin, who fired a tournament-low round of 64 on Saturday. On Sunday, with his wife and three daughters watching, Mitchell shot a three-under-par 70 for a 274 total to win by one over Sandelin and England's David Gilford.

While Mitchell's play down the stretch was steady, Sandelin seemed destined for at least a playoff. With a flurry of birdies, he caught Mitchell on the 13th hole, but a bogey at No. 15 and a three-putt bogey on No. 18 thwarted his chances.

Mitchell's putting was outstanding, prompting him to give thanks to a lesson he received two weeks prior. "Bill Furgeson gave me a lesson in Qatar, basically telling me to stop my right knee from wandering about." It paid off. "I putted great all week," Mitchell said.

His wife and daughters had a wonderful time as well. "I'd take the girls out every week with me if I could," Mitchell said of the family outing. If they bring him the sort of good fortune he received in Lisbon, that might not be a bad idea.

Cannes Open—£300,000

Winner: Thomas Levet

It was not without a few anxious moments, but after hitting a sand shot on the 72nd hole that, in his words, "might fall on my head or in my pocket," Frenchman Thomas Levet was able to make a 10-foot putt for bogey which locked up his first PGA European Tour victory in the Cannes Open. It was the first time a Frenchman had won the event, which made the victory even sweeter. The Cannes win also earned Levet, who was a seven-time winner on the French circuit, his PGA European Tour card, something that eluded him at last year's qualifying tournament.

"This was incredible," Levet said. "I proved that dreams can come true." After shooting rounds of 69, 71 and 65, Levet took a four-shot lead into the final day, but his dreams were almost dashed on two occasions before he won with 73 and a 278 total, six under par. An up-and-down first nine on Sunday cost Levet his lead to a trio of charging competitors. Phillip Price, who started the day seven shots back, closed with an impressive 67 to finish at five under par, along with Greg Turner, who shot 69, and Sven Struver, who also finished with 69. In the end, Levet had to make a slippery 10-footer for bogey, after leaving one shot in the greenside bunker at No. 18. "I had no idea where the ball was," Levet said of the errant bunker shot. "I was so surprised I almost burst out laughing."

He certainly burst into a grand smile after the putt for bogey and the victory slipped into the cup.

Peugeot Open de Espana—£550,000

Winner: Thomas Bjorn

Whether it's the weather or the great food, Thomas Bjorn plays well in Spain and, he says, he owes a lot of his current success to his experiences there. "I'm much stronger mentally than I was last year, because of my Ryder Cup experience," Bjorn said of his last visit to Spain. In his next trip, the 27-year-old Dane fired an impressive 21-under-par 267 total in Barcelona, which propelled Bjorn to a one-shot victory over Greg Chalmers and Jose Maria Olazabal in the Peugeot Open de Espana.

"After winning the Heineken Classic in Australia at the end of January, I had high expectations," Bjorn said. "When I missed a couple of cuts I decided to go home and do some thinking about my attitude."

That attitude adjustment period obviously paid off. After five weeks of rest, Bjorn shot 68 and 67 and closed with two rounds of 66 to win. "I didn't expect to win so soon after taking five weeks off," he said. "But I never hit the ball better."

He also raised his game to a new level. On Sunday, with Olazabal and Chalmers matching him shot for shot through the first nine, Bjorn made three consecutive birdies on the second nine, starting at the 14th, where he made a difficult 15-footer. At No. 15, he made a slippery six-footer, and at the par-three 16th, he chipped in from 25 feet. "It's things like that which go your way if you're going to win," Olazabal said of Bjorn's performance.

While enjoying his victory, Bjorn was already looking ahead to greater challenges. "I've beaten the best players in the world to win three times on the European Tour," he said. "Now I feel I can take on the majors."

Italian Open—£491,139

Winner: Patrik Sjoland

It is highly unusual for a player to have a 68 and two consecutive rounds of 65 in a 54-hole event and lose by three shots, but that's exactly what happened to Jose Maria Olazabal at the Italian Open. Olazabal tied for second place with Joakim Haeggman and their performances were bested by Sweden's Patrik Sjoland who played a tournament he described as "an 11 on a scale of one to 10."

After an opening 64, the 26-year-old Sjoland, who arrived in Milan winless on the PGA European Tour, and who has struggled for six years to come back from a life-threatening car accident where he was thrown through the sunroof of his vehicle, put on one of the most impressive ball striking displays of the year. His second-round 65 opened up a three-shot lead over Thomas Bjorn and a four-shot margin over Olazabal.

Sjoland's final-round 66 for a 195 total was much the same. He drove the ball perfectly, and he hit every green in regulation. By the 15th hole, where the young Swede made his sixth birdie of the day to move to 21 under par, it was over.

An elated Sjoland said of the victory, "This is definitely the best I have hit the ball in my life. I knew I had to make some birdies because Olazabal got off to a good start, too." Despite the flawless ball striking, Sjoland didn't rank his closing 66 as highly as the previous two days. "It was a nine on a scale of 10," he said. Still, it was enough for the win, and a rejuvenated Sjoland set his sights on higher goals.

"My ambition is to win again, and get a chance to play in the U.S. Open," Sjoland said.

Turespana Masters Open Baleares—£350,000

Winner: Miguel Angel Jimenez

The lead changed 10 times during the final round, but in the end it was Miguel Angel Jimenez, a man who battled through the pain of kidney stones and celebrated the joy of learning that his wife was expecting their second child, who birdied the 71st hole and won his third career title in the Turespana Masters Open Baleares. "To get the good news about the baby and then win my first tournament in four years was fantastic, especially because of all the pain I went through due to my kidney stones," Jimenez said after finishing with scores of 69, 68, 70 and 72 for a 279 total, nine under par at Santa Ponsa.

Jimenez wasn't the only contender in pain, however. Miguel Angel Martin, who held the first-round lead and was never more than two shots off the pace, also battled through kidney stones, missing the pro-am because of the pain. Like Jimenez, Martin played through the pain. In fact, after making an eagle at the par-five sixth on Sunday, Martin took the lead and held it through the 14th. Martin was still in contention until he received a warning for slow play and immediately dropped two stokes to Jimenez on the last two holes. "It made me mad, and I lost my concentration," Martin said of the slow-play warning. The final two holes pushed Martin back to even par for the day and seven under for the tournament, two shots off Jimenez's winning score.

Paul McGinley also shared the lead at one time, but, like Martin, McGinley failed to produce on the final two holes, taking bogeys on Nos. 16 and 18 in the final round. "It's bitterly disappointing," McGinley said.

Despite the pain, Jimenez was anything but disappointed. "This was a magical victory," he said.

Benson and Hedges International—£750,000

Winner: Darren Clarke

Nine months before they went head-to-head in the first PGA European Tour event of the year on British soil, Colin Montgomerie and Darren Clarke played together in Spain as leaders of the victorious European Ryder Cup team. In the final round of the Benson and Hedges International in Thames, England, they were paired again, only this time they were competitors, tied at 10 under par with Italy's Massimo Florioli, and battling it out for the £125,000 first-place check.

As the No. 5 player in the world, Montgomerie was the clear favorite. But Clarke, who admittedly had to overcome an attitude problem, fired his second straight 67 for a 273 total to capture the title by three strokes over Santiago Luna. Montgomerie shot a final-round 72 and tied for fifth place, five strokes behind.

"My attitude holds me back," Clarke said. "I was guilty of trying to force things rather than just let it happen. The problem is that I have a thick head, but I've learned a lot about patience."

His attitude, patience and confidence were perfect when he birdied five holes on the first nine and played the second nine in a conservative, patient and winning even-par way. Montgomerie, who had been experiencing problems with his putter throughout most of the year, continued his putting woes.

"That is the worst I've ever putted in a final round when I've been in contention, and I've been in contention a lot over the last 10 years," Montgomerie said of his 34-putt final round. Then, in deference to his Ryder Cup partner's victory, Monty said, "As my confidence on the greens went, so Darren's grew."

Volvo PGA Championship—£1,200,000

Winner: Colin Montgomerie

One week after an abysmal putting round that cost him the Benson and Hedges International, Colin Montgomerie, still struggling on the greens, sank two 10-footers on the last two holes to capture his first Volvo PGA Championship. In doing so, Montgomerie beat the No. 1-ranked player in the world, Ernie Els, Sweden's Patrik Sjoland and Scotland's Gary Orr by one stroke.

The victory was no cakewalk for the man who has dominated Europe's money list for five years running. Through 33 holes, Montgomerie was even par and contemplating the trip back home to his wife and newborn daughter if he missed the cut (which was projected and fell at one under par). Then, in one of the most impressive, mid-round recoveries since Tiger Woods shot 40, 30 to open the 1997 Masters, Montgomerie played the next 18 holes (from the 16th on Friday through the 15th on Saturday) in 11 under par. "That run was what won me the tournament," Montgomerie said.

Orr and former Scottish Amateur champion Dean Robertson made significant charges. Orr was four under par on the first nine on Sunday, putting him temporarily in the lead. He could only manage an even-par second nine, however, which was one less than Orr needed to catch Montgomerie. Robertson also held the lead at one point, but after hitting his tee shot left on the 16th, a double bogey cost him any chance. Robertson finished two shots back and tied for fifth place.

With Montgomerie and Els in the one-two spots, the Volvo PGA Championship lived up to its billing as the top PGA European Tour event outside the British Open, and it wasn't too early for Ryder Cup discussions to begin. Sweden proved that it has the depth to have several players on the 1999 team. In addition to Sjoland's 13-under-par performance, Thomas Bjorn framed two rounds of 69 with a 70 and a 68 to finish two strokes off the pace, tied with fellow Swede Mats Hallberg.

Italy's Costantino Rocca made a good showing, finishing five off Montgomerie's winning pace, and Lee Westwood, who came into the Volvo PGA Championship with one victory on the U.S. PGA Tour, finished six strokes back. Also at six back was Sam Torrance, who let it be known that he would rather play on the Ryder Cup team than be captain. Another Swede and Ryder Cup favorite, Per-Ulrik Johansson, finished seven under par, seven shots out of the lead.

Deutsche Bank–SAP Open TPC of Europe—£1,100,000

Winner: Lee Westwood

Almost two months to the day after winning his first tournament on American soil at the Freeport-McDermott Classic in New Orleans, Lee Westwood found himself in the winner's circle for the second time of the year in Alveslohe, Germany. Westwood's final-round 66 gave him a 265 total and a one-shot win over Darren Clarke and a four-shot margin over Masters champion Mark O'Meara at the Deutsche Bank–SAP Open TPC of Europe.

Westwood began the final round one stroke behind Clarke and Paul Broadhurst. Although Broadhurst faltered with a final-round 76 to finish tied for 13th place, Clarke made up for a lackluster first nine by making four birdies in his last five holes for 68 to pull within one stroke of Westwood. After Westwood bogeyed the 16th hole, a playoff looked likely. But on No. 18, Westwood, who set the course record at Gut Kaden Golf Club the day before with a stellar round of 61, stroked a 20-foot birdie putt straight into the hole for the victory.

"I finally closed the door, so it's the biggest birdie of the week," Westwood said after making the putt at No. 18. "It's difficult when a player like Clarke is chasing you."

Westwood bettered Clarke by two strokes on the final day, leaving Clarke to say of his Ryder Cup teammate, "I tried to make it tough for Lee. I don't like being beaten, but I'm pleased that I managed to stick in there. I holed a few near the end, but Lee's fantastic three on the last killed me off."

National Car Rental English Open—£650,000

Winner: Lee Westwood

While the goal of the USGA in the U.S. Open is to "identify" the greatest player in the world, the hottest European player in the game heading over to San Francisco was clearly Lee Westwood, whose 17-under-par 271 total won the National Car Rental English Open by two strokes over Olle Karlsson and Greg Chalmers. It was Westwood's second victory in two weeks, and with rounds of 68, 68, 67 and 68, he proved that, in addition to talent, he is a model of consistency on the PGA European Tour.

"The only thing I haven't got is a major title," Westwood said after accepting the trophy and the £108,330 check. "That has to be my next goal. I'm certainly playing well enough to do it."

His play couldn't have been much better down the stretch. After Colin Montgomerie faded from contention after putting woes continued to plague his game, Westwood found himself in a match-play situation with Chalmers, who shot a record 61 on Saturday then began Sunday's round with three consecutive birdies.

By the time they reached the 16th, a 185-yard par-three hole, Westwood and Chalmers were tied at 17 under par. Westwood made what he described as a "bad error" on the 16th, when he pulled his six-iron shot into the high grass well left of the green, but Chalmers couldn't capitalize. His shot landed in the bunker, short of the hole. When Westwood thrashed a wedge out of the grass and onto the green some 30 feet from the hole, the advantage shifted to Chalmers, who blasted out of the bunker to within 10 feet. Westwood turned the match around when he made the 30-footer. Chalmers missed, and it was over.

"That was the entire golf tournament right there," Westwood said. "I didn't expect (Chalmers) to hole once I made mine, but he would surely have made his putt had I missed. I was lucky to get away with that."

Almost unnoticed in the head-to-head match between Westwood and Chalmers was Karlsson, whose final-round 66 gave him a share of second place with Chalmers at 15 under par. Montgomerie, who admitted to leaving "dozens and dozens of shots out on the course," finished fourth, three strokes off Westwood's winning pace.

Madeira Island Open—£300,000

Winner: Mats Lanner

With Europe's top players at the U.S. Open, Sweden's Mats Lanner, who had lost his playing rights 18 months earlier, regained his winning ways by capturing the Madeira Island Open in Mochico, Portugal. Lanner's one-stroke victory over New Zealand's Stephen Scahill was his second at the Santo de Serra Golf Club. The Alfred Dunhill Cup veteran also won in 1994, but his play since that victory had been so poor that he was forced to rely on sponsors exemptions just to compete. "This feels like getting my job back," Lanner said after it was over.

For a while it looked as though Lanner would have to wait for another exemption to get his chance. After opening with rounds of 70 and 66, Lanner trailed Scahill by three strokes as the young New Zealander followed an even-par 72 with a course-record 61. Scahill remained in the lead at 14 under par on Saturday after shooting 69, but Lanner's 68 moved him to within two. Andrew Beal, who opened with rounds of 71, 68 and 67, lurked four shots back going into the final 18.

Normally a final-round 73 would have meant dropping back in the field, but with Scahill only able to manage a final-round 76, Lanner's 277 total, 11 under par, enabled him to become the Madeira Island Open's only repeat winner. It also gave him a two-year exemption.

Still, on the final hole, leading by one, Lanner thought he had given the tournament away when his approach shot plugged in the top of a bunker guarding the front of the green. He blasted the bunker shot to within two feet, and tapped in for the win. "I will remember that bunker shot for the rest of my life," Lanner said.

Beal, who matched Lanner's consistent final round with a 73 of his own, finished alone in third place at 279, three shots off the pace, while Thomas Gogele and Francisco Cea, both of whom closed with final-round 73s, tied for fourth at 282. First-round leader David Tapping, who opened with 66, shot 73, 73 and 77 to finish at 289, 12 shots off Lanner's pace.

Peugeot Open de France—£500,000

Winner: Sam Torrance

In early summer, when Sam Torrance's name was bounced around as a possible European captain for the 1999 Ryder Cup, a bemused Torrance let it be known that he had no time for the captaincy since he intended to be playing on the European team. At Golf National in Paris, Torrance gave credence to that prediction with a near wire-to-wire victory at the Peugeot Open de France. It was Torrance's 21st European title, but his first since 1995. At age 44, Torrance was the second oldest man in the field, which sweetened the victory even more.

"I never felt like the second oldest player," Torrance admitted. "I'm fit and strong and young at heart, and I feel I have a few more victories left in me before I'm 50."

Torrance proved his fitness by opening on Thursday with a tournament-low score of 64 to take a two-stroke lead over Pedro Linhart and Eduardo Romero. The next two days Torrance recorded scores of 70 and 72, which kept him atop the leaderboard at 10 under par, but opened the door for a flurry of players who were within three shots of the lead.

That lead was briefly relinquished on Sunday when Italy's Massimo Florioli, who started the day at five under par, shot a first-nine 31. Moments later, Torrance birdied the 10th hole to regain the lead which he held to the finish. A bogey by Torrance at the 15th briefly opened the door again for a charging Bernhard Langer, who started the final round three shots off the pace at seven under par, but then the German missed birdie attempts at Nos. 16 and 17 while Torrance hit approach shots on Nos. 17 and 18 to within one foot. "I knew I required a birdie," Torrance said. "I made two."

Olivier Edmond also made a charge, but his final-round 67 fell two shots shy of Torrance's 12-under-par 276 total. Edmond shared second place with Langer, Florioli, who followed his first-nine 31 with an even-par 36, and Mathew Goggin, who started and ended the day two off the lead. Michael Campbell, who reached 10 under par on Saturday and briefly shared the lead with Torrance, fell back into a tie for 11th after finishing with a three-over-par 75.

Ecstatic about his victory, Torrance left no doubt as to his ultimate goals. "I did it to get back on the Ryder Cup team," he said.

Murphy's Irish Open—£1,000,000

Winner: David Carter

It was easy for 27-year-old David Carter to put his victory at the Murphy's Irish Open into perspective even after defeating Europe's No. 1 player, Colin Montgomerie, in a playoff. "When you almost die, to come out and play golf, and to win, is an unbelievable feeling," Carter said.

Fourteen months before teeing off at Druids Glen Golf Club, Carter came dangerously close to dying. In fact, according to Carter, "The doctor said he thought I had only three or four hours left when I was found."

He was found in his hotel room in Dubai, unconscious because of a build-up of fluid on his brain. Emergency surgery relieved the pressure and saved

Carter's life, but for months his golf remained in question. "The pressure was building up, and I would have been left paralyzed, which would have led to death if I had not been discovered," Carter recounted.

Memories of that incident were fresh in Carter's mind as he rode a cart back to the par-four 18th for the playoff. Even though he had led the tournament by five shots with eight holes to play, then taken double bogey on No. 13, bogey at No. 16 and bogey at No. 18 to finish tied with Montgomerie, Carter still felt comfortable that the tournament was his. "I felt it was meant to be," he said. "Everything that I had been through, I thought it was just meant to be."

Montgomerie, the two-time defending champion, felt differently. After opening with six-under-par 65, Montgomerie slipped to three under by shooting 74 on Friday. He remained at three under, three strokes behind, until late in Sunday's round. Flawless golf down the stretch, however, culminated in a final-round 68 and a tie with Carter at 278, six under par. Carter's closing round was 71.

In the playoff, Montgomerie's typical precision driving abandoned him, and he drove the ball into the high rough. His second shot found the water in front of the green, and when Carter reached the green in regulation, Montgomerie conceded. It was Carter's first PGA European Tour win, and, regardless of his perspective, one he will certainly never forget.

Standard Life Loch Lomond—£850,000

Winner: Lee Westwood

It isn't often that a player will three-putt a green and have the tournament turn in his favor, but that's exactly to happened to Lee Westwood at the par-four 14th hole during the final round of the Standard Life Loch Lomond event. An aggressive contender, Westwood was frustrated by four consecutive missed putts from inside 10 feet. Although he was tied for the lead at the time, Westwood took a gamble on the 14th, launching a drive that carried 280 yards onto the well-guarded green, and leaving himself a 20-foot putt for eagle.

Sweden's Dennis Edlund, the co-leader coming into the 14th, was so shaken by Westwood's drive that he missed the green and made bogey. Even though Westwood three-putted for par, the gamble paid off, and he led by one stroke.

On the 15th, still unnerved by Westwood's heroics, Edlund hooked his drive into an unplayable lie and proceeded to make a triple bogey. He would go on to shoot 74 and finish tied for second, four strokes behind Westwood, with Ian Woosnam, Robert Allenby, Eduardo Romero and David Howell.

Westwood cruised in with a final-round 70 for a 276 total, following scores of 69, 69 and 68. It was Westwood's eighth worldwide victory in nine months. "I play better when I focus only on playing, and I play better when I'm aggressive," Westwood said. "That's why I play — to get the adrenaline going."

British Open Championship—£1,750,000

Winner: Mark O'Meara

See Chapter 5.

TNT Dutch Open—£800,000

Winner: Stephen Leaney

Holding off late Sunday charges by some of Europe's most dominant players, Stephen Leaney shot a final-round 67 to cap an 18-under-par 266 total in the TNT Dutch Open for his second victory of the year. "I was desperate to win because the field wasn't so strong at the Moroccan Open (which Leaney won in March). I wanted to prove I could beat the big boys," he said.

Those big boys included Darren Clarke, who shot 63 on Sunday but finished at 267, one stroke behind Leaney, and Lee Westwood and Nick Price, who finished tied for third, two strokes off the pace. "I knew I had to be aggressive with so many big players charging up from behind," Leaney said.

His aggressive play paid off, despite a major distraction. After Thursday's opening round, Leaney and the rest of the field learned that Renay Appleby, the wife of Stuart Appleby, had been killed in a traffic accident in London. Leaney, a fellow Australian and good friend of the Applebys, took the news very hard. "I could hardly sleep Thursday night or the next night," he said. "Suddenly what I shot and whether I won or lost was no big deal. It puts things into perspective. I was thinking about Stuart throughout the tournament."

Volvo Scandinavian Masters—£800,000

Winner: Jesper Parnevik

It's rare that a golfer gains an advantage by playing in front of a hometown crowd, but according to Jesper Parnevik, were it not for the throng of cheering spectators at the Kungsangen Golf Club in his native Stockholm, he would have never had a chance to win his second Volvo Scandinavian Masters. "I just had to win for the people," Parnevik said. "It was hard going out leading when I was putting bad, but the fans want you to win — they expect you to win — especially when you're in the lead."

Parnevik carried a two-stroke lead from the end of the second round through the final putt on Sunday despite a final-round 70 that included two three-putts on the first nine and 37 putts overall. "My putting put a strain on my whole game," Parnevik said, even though his 11-under-par 273 total was good for a three-stroke victory. "It's a worry going into the PGA Championship."

Parnevik had no worries on his home turf as he cruised to his second title of the year. Second-place finisher Darren Clarke, who followed rounds of 67, 70 and 68 with a closing 71, never made a charge, which was understandable given the distractions he faced. Clarke rushed home to Belfast after the final putt fell to be with his wife who was expecting their first child. "I would have withdrawn had anything happened. Your wife and baby are far more important than your golf," Clarke said.

Even Parnevik, the darling of millions of gleeful Scandinavian fans, wholeheartedly agreed with Clarke's priorities.

German Open—£700,000

Winner: Stephen Allan

Although he never led the German Open until the final round, and he stood six strokes behind the leaders after the second day, 24-year-old Australian Stephen Allan turned out to be the man to beat at the Sporting Club Berlin. Allan, who started with an even-par 72 then followed it with 71, made a charge on Saturday when he fired 68. Still, Allan trailed Ignacio Garrido by four strokes going into the final day with five other players between Allan and the lead.

On Sunday, Allan played the first 12 holes in four under par. With Garrido dropping to seven under par with a closing 74, a window was opened for Allan. It apparently shut on No. 13 when Allan made a triple bogey, but birdies at Nos. 15 and 16 and two closing pars for a 69 left Allan alone at eight-under-par 280, one stroke ahead of Garrido, Padraig Harrington (73-69-70-69), Steve Webster (69-73-69-70) and Mark Roe (71-70-69-71).

First-round leader Paul Lawrie followed his opening 67 with rounds of 73, 72 and 72, while second-round leader Michael Campbell had a rough weekend, shooting 73-74 on Saturday and Sunday to fall into a tie for seventh, four strokes behind Allan.

"I knew my game was good enough to win," Allan said. "It's just a case of getting it all together. The more experience you get, the more comfortable you become."

Smurfit European Open—£1,250,000

Winner: Mathias Gronberg

With a field that included the likes of Colin Montgomerie, Darren Clarke, Bernhard Langer, Lee Westwood and Payne Stewart, and a purse that was second only to the British Open on the PGA European Tour, no one expected 28-year-old Swede Mathias Gronberg, winless since the 1995 European Masters, to win the Smurfit European Open at The K Club in Dublin, Ireland. Not only did Gronberg win, he ran away from the field, marching home with rounds of 68, 71, 67 and a final 69 for a 275 total, 13 under par, to win by 10 strokes over Miguel Angel Jimenez and Phillip Price.

"My strategy was simple: keep mistakes to a minimum," Gronberg said.

He succeeded. The only hiccup in the week was a 30-minute rain delay on Sunday, but that didn't stop Gronberg. He was the only player to post three rounds in the 60s and his final-round 69 was only topped by Angel Cabrera, who closed with 67 but finished 12 strokes back.

Gronberg led every day except Friday when Langer fired 65 to tie Jose Rivero at six under par. Rivero shot 75-76 on the weekend, and Langer shot 75-75, which allowed Gronberg to take his victory virtually unopposed. His 10-shot margin was the largest this year.

As for Europe's elite, Montgomerie missed the cut and Westwood withdrew six holes into his final round, citing hip problems. Clarke faired better, finishing alone in fourth, although he was 11 shots off Gronberg's winning pace. With The K Club vying to host the 2005 Ryder Cup, Gronberg would love to keep his winning ways going for a few more years.

BMW International Open—£850,000

Winner: Russell Claydon

After a nine-year career that included seven runner-up finishes but no victories, Russell Claydon was satisfied, but he wondered if he was destined to go winless forever. "It never really bothered me about finishing second because I've always tried my hardest," he said. Still the nagging question of when the first win would come haunted the 32-year-old all the way through the final round of the BMW International Open in Munich, Germany. Then, with one-putts on eight of his last 11 holes, and a miraculous par save to start his second nine on Sunday, Claydon put away his bridesmaid garb and stepped into the winner's circle for the first time.

"I'm really pleased," he said after shooting 66, 72, 64 and 68 for a 270 total, 18 under par, to edge out Jamie Spence by one stroke. "I think I got the right breaks at the right time and I was able to capitalize on them."

After trailing Thomas Bjorn in the first two rounds, Claydon fired a tournament-low 64 to move atop the leaderboard alongside crowd favorite Bernhard Langer who shot 68, 67 and 67. Langer faltered on Sunday with 71, which left the door open for Spence (68-71-66-66) and Thomas Gogele (65-71-67-69), who placed third at 272.

Any of those players could have caught Claydon were it not for a break on the 10th and some of the best putting this year. On the 10th, Claydon made a poor swing and when his ball dove left, he thought he might have lost it. After a frantic search, Claydon found his ball with moments to spare, and scrambled to make a 12-footer for par. That break gave him the surge he needed. Claydon went on to birdie the 11th, 12th, 15th and 17th holes, one-putting each time.

"My putting obviously did it for me," he said. "That used to be the weakest part of my game." It certainly wasn't weak on Sunday, but despite his propensity for finishing second, Claydon said he didn't feel any pressure coming down the stretch. "The pressure was on Bernhard (Langer) to win in front of his supporters," he said. "That took the pressure off of me."

Canon European Masters—£800,000

Winner: Sven Struver

Going into the final round of the Canon European Masters in Crans-sur-Sierre, Switzerland, Sven Struver didn't think he had a chance. After all, Patrik Sjoland had a four-stroke lead over Struver, Darren Clarke stood five strokes back, and, according to Struver, "Someone always shoots low on Sunday here."

Low, it would turn out, was Struver's 66, which included a testing sidehill four-footer for birdie on the 18th. Sjoland, who followed his opening rounds of 65 and 66 with a tournament-low 62 on Saturday, couldn't find the magic on Sunday, as he groped his way in with 70. "I never thought at the start of the day that 66 would be good enough," Struver said.

Struver's round left him tied at 263 with Sjoland at the end of regulation and the two marched back out to the 18th tee for a playoff. With momentum and experience on his side, Struver made the identical putt for birdie in the playoff that he had made moments earlier to finish his round. When Sjoland missed his effort, Struver had his first victory of the year. "I've never won in sudden death, so this was great experience," Struver said.

He hopes that experience will carry him through until 1999 when the Ryder Cup will be contested in Brookline, Massachusetts. "There are still another 35 tournaments to go, but it's a good start for me," Struver said. "It's been a good season as well. We'll just have to wait and see."

Darren Clarke, who started the day alone in third place, finished in the same position after closing with a final-round 67 for a 265 total, two behind Struver and Sjoland.

One 2 One British Masters—£750,000

Winner: Colin Montgomerie

After lackluster performances for the better part of two months, Colin Montgomerie went back to the practice tee and found two old friends: his long-time coach Bill Ferguson and his left-to-right fade. "I've worked hard and it has paid off," Montgomerie said after closing with a three-under-par 69 for a 281 total to win the One 2 One British Masters by one stroke over Pierre Fulke and Eduardo Romero. "The game was becoming a bit of a struggle. I hadn't performed decently in two months. Calling Bill when I did was the right thing to do."

It looked for a while as though Montgomerie's effort wouldn't be enough, especially with Darren Clarke on top of his game. But Clarke lamented the failure of his putting on the weekend. "My putting was awful," Clarke said. "I missed at least 15 putts from inside 12 feet on the weekend alone." Clarke followed his opening rounds of 67 and 71 with scores of 74 and 75 to finish six strokes behind.

Equally upset was Ignacio Garrido, although the Spaniard's regret had different roots. Garrido had fewer swings than any golfer other than Montgomerie during the week. Because his caddie inadvertently left an extra five iron in his bag on the second day, Garrido incurred two penalty strokes. He finished two behind Montgomerie.

Even so, Montgomerie, who had finished first, second, second and second in his previous four appearances at the Marriott Forest of Arden Country Club in Coventry, England, stood on the first tee on Sunday one stroke behind Paolo Quirici. Blustery conditions played into Montgomerie's hands. The Scot took 69 shots on Sunday while Quirici could only manage an even-par 72.

Fulke and Romero made the only serious charges at Montgomerie, shooting 67 and 68, respectively, for 282 totals.

Trophee Lancome—£800,000

Winner: Miguel Angel Jimenez

If all the leaders had made par on the par-three 18th, it would have been quite a different result in the Trophee Lancome in Paris, with David Duval picking up his second victory in four weeks. As it turned out, Duval, who led by one over Mark O'Meara and Miguel Angel Jimenez with one to play, dunked his tee shot into the water and proceeded to take a double bogey. Duval finished with 67 and fell into a tie with Greg Turner and Jarmo Sandelin at 275.

O'Meara and Jimenez appeared destined for similar fates at the last hole when their tee shots landed left of the green near the grandstands. O'Meara, the first to play, made bogey to shoot 69 and 275, tied with Duval and the others. Just when it appeared that a five-way playoff was eminent, Jimenez, who received a free drop from the stands, chipped in for a birdie and an amazing two-stroke victory with his 69 and 273 total.

"When the ball bounced on the green I knew it was in," Jimenez said. "This has to be the most dramatic victory of my career."

The normally calm Jimenez showed his first emotions of the week when the ball went into the cup. After a series of hugs from his wife and caddie, he pocketed the £133,330 first-place check.

Linde German Masters—£1,000,000

Winner: Colin Montgomerie

After relentlessly practicing under the watchful eye of Bill Ferguson and proving, in his words, that he had "the new swing more or less under control," Colin Montgomerie took one more step toward his sixth consecutive PGA European Tour money title by winning the Linde German Masters at Gut Larchenhof Golf Club in Cologne.

If not for a second-round spurt by U.S. PGA champion Vijay Singh, Montgomerie would have led the event wire to wire. As it was, his 65-68-66-67–266 total, 22 under par, edged Singh and Robert Karlsson by one shot, and gave Montgomerie his third European title of the season and the 17th of his career. The £166,660 first-place check also widened the gap between Montgomerie and his nearest challengers, Lee Westwood and Darren Clarke. With only two events remaining, Montgomerie liked his chances of winning a record sixth money title, but remained cautiously reserved.

"Winning the money title a sixth time would be great because there are so many good players in Europe," he said. "But it wouldn't be as sweet as the first five times."

Westwood, Montgomerie's nearest contender for the money title, shot 66-67-72-66–271 to finish tied for sixth place, five strokes off Montgomerie's pace. Steve Webster and Per-Ulrik Johansson joined Montgomerie, Singh and Karlsson as the only players with four rounds in the 60s — Webster shooting 68-65-68-67 to finish alone in fourth at 268, and Johansson shooting 68-67-67-67 for 269 and sole possession of fifth.

Belgacom Open—£400,000

Winner: Lee Westwood

Although Lee Westwood never led until the last putt fell, from the first drive on Thursday until the final 25-footer on the first playoff hole, all eyes in the Belgacom Open were on Westwood. All year on the PGA European Tour, Westwood was involved in a battle with Colin Montgomerie, the five-time leading money winner, and Darren Clarke for the 1998 money title. After Montgomerie won two out of four tournaments in September, the Scot seemed to be in command.

Not so fast, said Westwood. "I came into this tournament with the thought that if I could win, then the Volvo Masters (the last tournament of the European season) would be in my hands. It won't matter what Monty does if I win there."

Despite trailing by three strokes after the first round to Robert Karlsson, Greg Turner and Van Phillips, Westwood felt confident that things would eventually go his way. Even after Friday's second round, when Westwood added a 68 to his opening 67 and trailed by three to Fredrik Jacobson, he didn't panic. The weekend awaited, and Westwood was striking the ball as well as he had all year.

Turner and Jacobson put forth gallant efforts on the weekend with Turner adding 67 and 69 to his 64-70 opening rounds, and Jacobson keeping things going with 67 on Saturday and 69 on Sunday. The two shared the lead at 12 under par with 18 holes to play, but Westwood, who had his second 67 of the week, entered the final round one shot off the pace.

On Sunday, Westwood got off to a fast start and never slowed down. With an eagle and six birdies on the 6,900-yard Royal Zoute Golf Club, Westwood's final-round 66 caught Jacobson. Then his 25-foot birdie putt to defeat the Swede in a playoff almost caught Montgomerie, who chose not to play in Belgium. With his win, Westwood moved to within £45,266 of Monty's money lead.

"The money title wasn't a consideration at the beginning of the year," Westwood said. "But now I've got a chance to win it, so I'll give it my all."

Alfred Dunhill Cup—£1,000,000

Winner: South Africa

See Chapter 8.

Cisco World Match Play—£640,000

Winner: Mark O'Meara

See Chapter 9.

Open Novotel Perrier—£350,000

Winners: Jarmo Sandelin and Olle Karlsson

Although they carried a three-stroke lead into the final round of the Open Novotel Perrier in Medoc, France, the team of Jarmo Sandelin and Olle Karlsson quickly saw their lead disappear. In the singles round, where both players' scores were added together, the teams of Seve Ballesteros and Miguel Angel Jimenez and of Richard Boxall and Derrick Cooper tied Sandelin and Karlsson with eight holes to play. The hottest of the three teams seemed to be Boxall and Cooper. The Englishmen had closed a six-stroke deficit, capping it off when Boxall made a 45-foot eagle putt at the par-five 10th hole.

Sandelin and Karlsson would not be denied. Two birdies on the par-five 14th and two more on the 18th for rounds of 70 and 66 respectively, while Boxall and Cooper were making bogeys on the 11th and 12th, sealed the victory for the Swedes. Their 26-under-par 329 total edged the English pair by three strokes.

"On the 14th we decided to play up short where we were more comfortable and we both made birdies," Sandelin said. "That was the key hole for us." Karlsson said, "We knew we had to play well on the 18th, as we only had a one-shot lead. It's easy to make a bogey if you're not concentrating, but we both hit perfect drives and felt comfortable."

Volvo Masters—£1,000,000

Winner: Darren Clarke

Almost lost in the battle for the money title between Colin Montgomerie and Lee Westwood was the fact that Darren Clarke was not only having a tremendous 1998 season, but the Northern Irishman could conceivably slip into the running for the money title by winning the Volvo Masters in Jerez, Spain. That's exactly what Clarke had in mind when he arrived at the Montecastillo Golf Club.

"My goal coming in was to win the event," Clarke said. "The Order of Merit was out of my hands. Monty is such a hard man to dislodge."

Indeed, it would have taken quite a few unlikely elements falling into place for Clarke, who was third on the money list going into the Volvo Masters, to jump past Montgomerie and Westwood. But, as the week progressed, those stars seemed to be lining up perfectly, with one noted exception, Montgomerie.

In order for Clarke to have a chance, he would need to win the Volvo Masters, Westwood would need to finish worse than third, and Montgomerie worse than eighth. After the third day that scenario looked to be out of the question. Westwood was tied for the lead at 11 under par after three rounds, and Montgomerie was alone in third place. Clarke entered the final round in fifth place, three strokes off the pace and seemingly out of contention for the money title.

Then on Sunday, disaster struck Westwood as he hit four tee shots on the 172-yard par-three 14th before finding a ball in play. A quadruple-bogey seven sunk any chances the Englishman had, and he went on to finish with an uninspiring 75 for a 280 total, tied for 12th place.

Meanwhile, Clarke not only made up the three strokes he needed to catch the leaders, he shot a course-record-tying 63, good enough to propel him past Montgomerie and Andrew Coltart. Clarke's 271 total won the event by two shots over Coltart, so two of the three pieces to the puzzle were in place.

Montgomerie refused to be the third. He matched Clarke's first-nine 30 on Sunday, and refused to go away, even after the Irishman captured the lead. Montgomerie's five-birdie, one-bogey 68 was good enough for sole possession of third place, and good enough for a record-setting sixth consecutive Order of Merit title.

"They'll have to wait at least one more year, but it's getting tougher," Monty said. "The standards on the European Tour are improving all the time, and I've had to match that. My course management is better, and I feel mentally tougher. I'm proud of the way I finished. I did all the right things, really."

So did Coltart, who shot a final-round 66 to nudge Montgomerie out of second place by one stroke. Even that score wasn't good enough to catch Clarke. And even though he had to settle for the second spot on the money list, Clarke couldn't have been happier with his season-ending win. "I'm delighted to have won one of our premier events," he said.

Challenge Tour

One player dominated the European Challenge Tour. Warren Bennett won five times — once more than Thomas Bjorn did in 1995 — to top the money list with £81,052. The next man on the list was Sweden's Per Nyman with £37,196. Bennett was denied a sixth win in the AXA Grand Final at Belas in Portugal when the 26-year-old Englishman was beaten in a playoff by Argentine Jorge Berendt.

"Warren is a sensational player," Berendt said. "He doesn't miss anything and beating him is a big boost for me. I watched his game all day and he plays so easily. Whether it's a bogey or a birdie it makes no difference. He knew I desperately wanted to win but he didn't make it easy for me."

Without holing a 20-foot birdie putt at the fourth extra hole, Berendt would not have made the top 15 who qualified for the PGA European Tour in 1999. He finished 12th on the money list and will be joined on the main tour by Massimo Scarpa, Roger Winchester, Ricardo Gonzalez, John Bickerton, John Mellor, Fredrik Lindgren, John Senden, Soren Hansen, Max Anglert, Christopher Hanell, Stephen Gallacher and Daren Lee.

But Bennett was the star performer with victories in the Challenge de France, BTC Slovenian Open, Open des Volcans, Challenge Tour Championship and the Russian Open.

Bennett had won the silver medal as the leading amateur in the 1994

British Open at Turnberry, but his professional career was hampered by a neck injury. Though he got through the qualifying tournament in 1996, he only managed to play a handful of tournaments on the regular circuit the following year.

When he returns to the big stage, Bennett is convinced he will be better prepared. "I think I'm a better player technically, but the biggest difference from the last two years has been my health," he said. "My neck is okay now and I have been able to play three weeks in a row for the first time since 1995.

"Obviously, I'm more mature now. When I turned pro I was a bit naive, but now I feel ready to get back on the main tour. Having said that, my great run took me by surprise. I was playing well but to win four times and finish second once in a five-week run was unexpected. That sequence was a bit special and when you are in contention you know you can win."

12. Asia/Japan Tours

Lee Westwood knew from the commotion elsewhere on the course that someone was making a run at him down the stretch in the Sumitomo Visa Taiheiyo Masters. Since he couldn't read the Japanese on the scoreboards, he didn't know for sure who it was, but figured it had to be Masashi (Jumbo) Ozaki on the prowl again.

Ozaki didn't catch the new British star, but the second-place finish contributed nicely to another sparkling Japan PGA Tour season for the wondrously ageless golfer. It fit in among three victories and five other runner-up showings as the 51-year-old Ozaki breezed to his 12th seasonal money-winning championship. With earnings of ¥179,627,400, Ozaki finished a distant ¥47 million ahead of American Brian Watts, who placed second in the standings for the second and likely last time. Watts, who forced Mark O'Meara into a playoff before losing at the British Open, was to be playing the PGA Tour in America in 1999 after six fine seasons in Japan.

Ozaki's three victories — in the Yonex Open Hiroshima, the KBC Augusta and the Philip Morris — pushed his total to 109 victories, 90 in official tournaments on the Japan PGA Tour. He played in 24 of the year's 36 tournaments, was either first or second in eight, and had a scoring average of 69.2 as he took the money crown for the fifth year in a row and ninth time since 1988. The other players in Japan must be asking, "How long can this keep going on?" They probably would like to convince him that he ought to try the Senior PGA Tour in America before he gets too old.

Two other players — Hidemichi Tanaka, who finished third on the money list with ¥103,941,437, and American Brandt Jobe, who was fourth with ¥97,566,406 — each collected three victories in 1998, while Watts, Carlos Franco of Paraguay, Katsumasa Miyamoto and Westwood notched a pair each, with Westwood scoring back-to-back victories in the Taiheiyo Masters and the Dunlop Phoenix, two of the richest events of the Japanese season, at the end of his outstanding international season.

Although 14 of the year's titles went to non-Japanese players, all except three were taken by foreign regulars on the Japanese circuit, the two by Westwood and the early-season Chunichi Crowns by Davis Love III. He and six others — Fiji's Dinesh Chand, Toru Taniguchi, Shingo Katayama, Mamoru Osanai, Kaname Yokoo and Miyamoto — won for the first time on the Japan PGA Tour.

The bubbly Shigeki Maruyama, the 1997 money runner-up, had only one victory in 1998, but charmed the galleries as one of the leaders in the International team's impressive triumph in the Presidents Cup in December in Australia. Franco, who like Watts was switching to the U.S. tour in 1999, and Naomichi (Joe) Ozaki also played for the Internationals. Naomichi Ozaki was chosen by Captain Peter Thomson to replace brother Masashi, an automatic qualifier who declined his berth. The Presidents Cup experience offered some balm for Naomichi Ozaki, who blew two victory chances and went winless in Japan in 1998, as did Tsuneyuki (Tommy) Nakajima, a star on the tour for many years. Nakajima, who has 45 victories on his stellar record, hasn't won since early in the 1995 season.

Elsewhere in Asia, Frankie Minoza of the Philippines — who also won on the Japan PGA Tour — posted three victories on the old Asian Tour for a total of four wins for the year. Edward Fryatt of England won on the Asian Tour and again on the Omega Tour, while Chris Williams of England and Kang Wook-soon of Korea each won twice on the Omega Tour. Kang's victories were in two important late-season tournaments, the Perrier Hong Kong Open and Omega PGA Championship.

Asian Tour

Ericsson Philippine Masters—US$100,000

Winner: Frankie Minoza

Frankie Minoza, the popular and much-traveled Filipino, also has a lot of homeboy in him as he showed in the Ericsson Philippine Masters in mid-February at Villamor Golf Club near Manila. He opened the tournament with 69, one stroke behind three fellow Filipinos bunched at 68 — Rodrigo Cuello, Felix Casas and Robert Pactolerin. The group thinned itself out in a hurry. Casas shot 74 in the second round but settled down with a pair of 72s to tie for sixth place. Pactolerin self-destructed, going from 75 in the second round to a 76-75 close to tie for 34th.

The tournament remained a battle between Minoza and Cuello. Minoza took the halfway lead with 67. Cuello, with 69, and America's Brad Wilson (67) tied for second at 137. Then Minoza and Cuello turned it into a runaway. Minoza shot 70 in the third round, and Cuello posted 69 and tied him at a comfortable 206 — six strokes ahead of Wilson (75) and the Philippines' Mars Pucay (68). Minoza wrapped it up with a closing 71 in gusting winds for a 277 total and a one-stroke win over Cuello (72).

Benson and Hedges Malaysian Open—US$300,000

Winner: Edward Fryatt

If England's Lee Westwood is the future king of the PGA European Tour, what does it say for the man who beats him? That was the pleasant question for Edward Fryatt. The lanky Fryatt is also an Englishman — sort of. He has lived in Las Vegas since the age of four. He came face-to-face with Westwood in the Benson and Hedges Malaysian Open at Saujana Golf and Country Club in February, and had the uncomfortable feeling of being caught from behind, shooting 70-69-70-69 to Westwood's 70-72-67-69 for the tie at 278. Then Fryatt had the thrill of beating him in a playoff.

But first, this was as wild a free-for-all as the Asian Tour had ever seen. Neither man seemed to be in serious contention when the tournament opened. Korea's Choi Sang-ho owned the first round with 65 and led by two over India's Vivek Bhandari. Choi disappeared with 75 in the second round, but the battle was just heating up. The ever-present Frankie Minoza of the

Philippines, winner of the Philippine Masters the week before, barged into a share of the halfway lead with 66, tying Canada's Philip Jonas (69) at 137. They led by one over Bhandari (71) and Paraguay's Raul Fretes (69).

The tournament shook down into a three-way tie through the third round, when three new faces surfaced. Fryatt shot 70, Westwood 67, and American Tom Kalinowski 71 to deadlock at 209. Kalinowski fell out with a closing 75, while Fryatt and Westwood each shot 69 for 278.

Rolex Masters—US$300,000

Winner: Frankie Minoza

It was another one of those mad scrambles, and when no one was looking, up popped Frankie Minoza again to take the Rolex Masters, his second victory in three weeks, after the Philippine Masters. Even though he shot four rounds in the 60s at the Singapore Island Country Club's Bukit Course — 68-69-67-69 — Minoza did not lead any round until the final. His 273 total gave him a one-stroke victory over Canadian Jim Rutledge, who closed with a tournament-low 64 to make up five of the six strokes by which he trailed Minoza at the start of the round.

Canadian Scott Rowe, a rookie, and American Eric Epperson shared the first-round lead with 66s, and Minoza was two behind. Minoza trailed by five in the second round, when Rowe took the lead alone with another 66 for a 132. Epperson faded with 74, and Myanmar's Kyi Hla Han took second on 66–133. Then a surprise leader came to the fore — American Rob Moss. He trailed by one after the first round, five after the second, and he shot 66 in the third and edged into the lead by one stroke over Minoza and Korea's Park Nam-sin (67). But the craft and patience of the tested veteran served Minoza well in the final round. He posted his 69 for the 273 and the win. But, apart from the late-charging Rutledge, Minoza had no real threat. Of the other leaders through the rounds, none shot lower than 72 in the final round.

Ericsson Philippine Open—US$250,000

Winner: Frankie Minoza

You couldn't say that Frankie Minoza was overstaying his welcome. He was home. But he must have been wearing on the nerves on his fellow golfers on the Asian Tour. Minoza took the Ericsson Philippine Open, this time slipping out of the lead then coming from behind in the final round. Here's what was testing his friends' patience: This was his second win in a row (after the Rolex Masters in Singapore), his third victory in four straight outings, and another big helping of home cooking. He started the rampage by taking the Ericsson Philippine Masters in mid-February.

This one may have been his sweetest. He had made numerous tries at the Philippine Open, but just couldn't bring it in. And it looked like more of the same frustration at the par-72 Riviera Golf and Country Club. Minoza, after an opening 66, found himself in a battle at the halfway point. He shot a second-round 69, and found himself tied by Taiwan's Chang Tse-peng (67) at 135. Christian Chernock, with a 67–205 in the third round, led him by three going into the finale. Then Minoza got the break he needed. Chernock ran into trouble and closed with 75. Minoza's par 72 was good enough for a 10-under total and a two-stroke win.

Maekyung LG Fashion Open—US$254,360

Winner: Scott Rowe

Scott Rowe, a Hong Kong-based Canadian, was having a good rookie season on the Asian Tour. Then he came to the Maekyung LG Fashion Open in Seoul and turned it into an outright success. Rowe, who flirted with victory earlier in the season, got the full taste of it with a three-round, four-stroke runaway at Lake Side Country Club early in May.

Rowe shared the first-round lead with Paraguay's Raul Fretes on a five-under-par 67, and he was on his own from there. A 68 in the second round gave him a 135 total and a three-stroke lead over Korea's Kwon Young-suk (68) and Park Nam-sin (69). Heavy rains and strong winds wiped out the third round Saturday, and Rowe came back and wrapped it up with 69 for a 12-under-par 204 total. Kwon closed with 70 and was a distant second at 208. The win capped a busy two and a half months for Rowe. He started with the Philippine Masters, then was 26th in the Benson and Hedges Malaysian Open, 13th in the Rolex Masters, and 12th in the Philippine Open.

Johnnie Walker Super Tour—US$350,000

Winner: Vijay Singh

Despite traveling for six days through Malaysia, Thailand, Taiwan and China, Vijay Singh shot a course-record 62 on the Mission Hills course in Southern China in the final round to win by two strokes in the nine-player Johnnie Walker Super Tour. Singh led after a second-round 66, but then shot 71 and dropped behind defending champion Jesper Parnevik when the Swede shot 67 at Ta Shee Golf and Country Club in Taipei to go with his earlier rounds of 68 at Palm Resort in Johor and 70 at the Thai Country Club in Bangkok.

When the tournament moved to China, Singh jumped ahead. Birdies on the first four holes allowed Singh to reclaim the lead. Then he hit a four-iron approach shot to within 18 feet of the par-five sixth. When the eagle putt hit the hole, Singh was in the lead to stay. Four more birdies widened Singh's lead, and he had a chance to shoot 61 when a 12-foot birdie putt on the 72nd hole slid past the hole, and he settled for 62.

"It was an incredible round," Singh said after shooting 19-under-par 269 to claim the $100,000 first-place check by two strokes.

Parnevik shot 66 in the final round and finished alone in second place, while Ernie Els finished third at 278. "I had hoped to challenge, but the way Vijay was playing there was not very much I could do," Els said. Laura Davies, the only woman in the field, shot a final-round 78 to finish at 308, 20 over par for the week. Davies said, "Although I have not played particularly well, I've thoroughly enjoyed the experience. I've learned a lot and had great fun. Everyone has been very encouraging."

Japan PGA Tour

Token Corporation Cup—¥110,000,000

Winner: Hajime Meshiai

Hajime Meshiai conjured up some of his old magic and came from well off the pace in the final round to capture the season-opening Token Corporation Cup, his first victory in almost two years. In bringing back memories of his brilliant play of the early 1990s, the 44-year-old Meshiai frustrated the bid of Masashi (Jumbo) Ozaki to successfully defend the title at Kedoin Golf Club in southwestern Japan just when he had positioned himself to do so. Ozaki had to settle for second place.

Meshiai muddled along with a 70-71 start as Hidemichi Tanaka opened the tournament eagle-birdie and went on to a 65. Tanaka led Hideyuki Sato by one and Ozaki by two, but couldn't follow it up Friday, giving way to Frankie Minoza, the Philippines' top player. Minoza fired a bogey-free 66 for 134, three shots in front of runner-up Koki Idoki. Eight players were at 138 and Ozaki shared the 139 slot with five others.

Ozaki, still disdaining senior golf though 51 years old, rebounded Saturday with a blazing 65 and stormed into a one-stroke lead over Minoza, Idoki, Todd Hamilton and Shoichi Kuwabara with his 204. Meshiai, who won the Token Cup event at the start of his great 1993 season, began his move that day, shooting 67 for 203. He carried that momentum into the final round and was virtually flawless Sunday. He ran off eight birdies without dropping a stroke and the 64 put him in the clubhouse in front at 16-under-par 272. Then he watched as Ozaki missed a tying birdie putt on the 18th green, his quest for his 107th victory in Japan futile.

Daido Drinko Shizuoka Open—¥75,000,000

Winner: Eduardo Herrera

Eduardo Herrera, who has made his mark in Japan, half a world away from his home in Colombia, scored his fourth victory in 11 years with a come-from-behind effort in the weather-shortened Daido Drinko Shizuoka Open. Violent winds forced a rare cancellation of the Friday round and a one-quarter reduction in the prize money.

The victim of Herrera's charge at Shizuoka Country Club in Ogasa was Kaname Yokoo, who was seeking his first win in his three seasons on the Japan PGA Tour. Yokoo had taken the lead when play resumed Saturday, shooting 68 for a 133 total and a two-stroke lead over Herrera (66-69), David Smail, Tsuyoshi Yoneyama and Nobuo Serizawa. Peter McWhinney, the Australian who led the first day with 64, slipped back to 137 Saturday.

Key to Herrera's triumph was the 593-yard, par-five fifth hole, which he eagled in each of the last two rounds. Yokoo had two birdies and a bogey on the front nine, his lead cut to one stroke. The Colombian caught up with a birdie at the 12th, took a one-stroke lead with another at the 13th and matched Yokoo par-for-par coming in. His 68 gave him a 13-under-par 203 total. Yokoo shot 71 for 204 and American Brian Watts closed with 69 for 205.

Just System KSB Open—¥100,000,000

Winner: Carlos Franco

The Cinderella year of Carlos Franco began at the Ayutaki Country Club at Kagawagun, Kagawa Prefecture. Franco's victory in the Just System KSB Open sparked him to such a fine season that he earned one of the coveted berths on the International team for the Presidents Cup in Australia in December. The Paraguay native was the first South American to make a Presidents Cup team.

Franco, who had three earlier victories on the Japan PGA Tour since first earning playing privileges as the champion of the 1994 Asian Tour, won the KSB event in style, carrying the lead through the final 54 holes and finishing with a flourish to post a four-stroke victory with his 17-under-par total. He chipped in for an eagle at the par-five 18th for a closing 65 on the par-71 Ayutaki course.

The 32-year-old Franco emerged to take the lead on a foul-weather Friday — fog, rain and three interruptions of play — with a extraordinary 65. He had opened the tournament with 70, one of 14 players at that score, a stroke behind an eight-man logjam in first place. Strung out behind Franco at the halfway point were Shinichi Yokota at 136, Brian Watts at 137 and Frankie Minoza at 138. Franco widened his margin to three strokes with a 67 Saturday. Minoza, in second place at 205, was the only player within five of Franco entering the final round and Minoza had to shoot 66 Sunday just to stay close with Franco polishing off the victory with the 65.

Descente Classic Munsingwear Cup—¥100,000,000

Winner: Dinesh Chand

Move over, Vijay Singh, you have company from your homeland in international golf. Dinesh Chand, a 26-year-old newcomer from Fiji on the Japan PGA Tour, took little time making his mark, winning the Descente Classic Munsingwear Cup tournament just six months after joining the circuit in October, 1997. Outplaying two veterans through most of the final round at Taiheiyo Country Club, Chand survived bogeys on the last two holes to post a two-stroke victory with his 17-under-par 271 total.

Chand, who had faded after having a share of the first-round lead the previous week, came at it from the other direction in the Descente event. He was inconspicuous, five off the lead, after Thursday's first round as Chen Tze-chung grabbed a piece of the first-round lead for the second week in a row. The well-known T.C., who has a U.S. title (1987 Los Angeles Open) on his six-victory record, opened with 66, joining Hidemichi Tanaka at the top. Tanaka hadn't won in two years, Chen since 1993 in Japan.

Chen took sole possession of the lead when he followed with a four-birdie

68, his 134 total giving him a two-shot edge over Ryoken Kawagishi (70-66), three over Tanaka (71), Taichi Teshima (72-65), Hideki Kase (70-67) and Chand (71-66). It was Kase's turn in front Saturday. The 16-season veteran whipped up a 65 for a 202 total, just a stroke better than Chand, who shot his second straight 66. Chen, with a double bogey and two bogeys on the first nine, dropped three shots off the pace with 71. Chand maintained his momentum Sunday, getting an early boost from a chip-in birdie at the second hole and a cushion for the shaky finish from another chip-in for an eagle at the 13th. He had a 68 for the 271 total. With 67, Carlos Franco tied for second at 273 with Tanaka, who shot 66.

Tsuruya Open—¥100,000,000

Winner: Katsumasa Miyamoto

The Tsuruya Open seems to have become a haven for deprived victory seekers. Katsumasa Miyamoto became the third consecutive player to score his initial Japan PGA Tour win in the tournament when he registered a one-stroke triumph at Sports Shinko Country Club. The runner-up, Australian Peter McWhinney, had scored his first win in Japan two years earlier in the Tsuruya event.

The two battled down the stretch on Sports Shinko's Yamanohara course, Miyamoto gaining his one-stroke margin when he eagled the par-five 17th hole to climax a wild-and-wooly round of 68 that included seven birdies, three bogeys and a double bogey. It was the fourth straight round in the 60s for the 25-year-old Miyamoto and gave him a 17-under-par 271 total. McWhinney, a third-round co-leader, also took a double bogey en route to his 70–272 finish.

Kaname Yokoo was the first-round leader with 66. Zaw Moe of Myanmar shot 67, and six others, including McWhinney and Chen Tze-chung, again an early contender, had 68s. Miyamoto fired a bogey-free 65 Friday and moved into a share of the lead with Taichi Teshima at 134, then slipped a stroke off the pace with a second 69 Saturday. McWhinney, Moe and veteran Saburo Fujiki led with 202 totals. Moe finished third behind Miyamoto and McWhinney in the final standings with a 71.

Kirin Open—¥100,000,000

Winner: Frankie Minoza

In 1990, Frankie Minoza opened the door to the success that he would enjoy in later seasons by winning the crossroads Dunlop Open and with it the Asian Tour title and its two-year exemption to play the much longer and richer Japan PGA Tour. Eight years later, the talented player from the Philippines reprised that achievement with victory in the Kirin Open (same tournament, different name) and again it clinched the Asian Tour championship, the Japan Tour exemption and a coveted spot in the British Open later in the year.

In the two months prior to the Kirin Open, a fixture on the Japan PGA Tour that doubles as the only Asian Tour stop in Japan, Minoza, now 38, played on both circuits and had three wins on the Asian Tour. After collecting the Kirin check, he couldn't be caught in the money race on that circuit with just one tournament in Korea left on the schedule.

Minoza, who now has five Japan Tour titles but hadn't won since the 1995 Daikyo Open, made his big move the second day at the Ibaraki Golf Club in Ina, Ibaraki Prefecture. After opening with a 71, three strokes behind leader Cheng Tse-peng on a blustery day, Minoza fired a 66 Friday and advanced into a three-way tie for the lead with Shigeki Maruyama (71-66) and Carlos Franco (70-67). Minoza got his third round off to a rousing start when he made a hole-in-one at the second and inched into the lead Saturday with his 69–206 total. He didn't handle Sunday's chilly weather well, going three over par on the first 12 holes, but his lone birdie at the 16th and two closing pars gave him a one-stroke victory over Brian Watts, Hidemichi Tanaka and Tsukasa Watanabe. He shot 73 and finished five under par with 279.

Chunichi Crowns—¥120,000,000

Winner: Davis Love III

Davis Love III, whose only accomplishments of note on the international scene have been in the major team events, took on the best of the Japan PGA Tour in the Chunichi Crowns, and showed why he ranks as one of the best players in the world. Love led all the way as he acquired his first title abroad by an eight-stroke margin on the Wago course of Nagoya Golf Club. In the process, Davis dethroned Masashi (Jumbo) Ozaki, who had won the Chunichi Crowns the previous three years and five times in all. Ozaki got off to a poor start with 73 and never seriously threatened, even though shooting 65 in the third round.

The 34-year-old American star initiated his title run with a six-under-par 64. He produced an eagle and five birdies to take a two-stroke lead over Canadian Rick Gibson and three over Seiki Okuda, Yoshinori Kaneko and faded star Tsuneyuki (Tommy) Nakajima, who made history the next day when he holed his tee shot on the 341-yard, par-four first hole for the rarest of aces. Nakajima, who owns 45 victories but hadn't won in three years, failed to capitalize on his good fortune. His 73 left him five shots behind Love, who struggled with winds that "made things really tough out there" but maintained a one-stroke lead over Gibson with a 71–135.

The weather was even worse Saturday, but Love virtually locked up the victory by carving out a 67 in the wind and rain. The 202 total gave him a five-stroke margin over Ozaki and fellow American Brian Watts. Recurring rainstorms forced a two-hour rain delay Sunday, but it and the presence of Ozaki and Watts in his grouping didn't faze the 1997 PGA champion. He pulled away to the 19th victory of his career with another 67 and a final, 11-under-par 269. Watts, Gibson and Masanobu Kimura finished at 277, Ozaki and Nakajima at 278.

Fuji Sankei Classic—¥120,000,000

Winner: Carlos Franco

Carlos Franco of Paraguay became the first multiple winner on the 1998 Japan PGA Tour when he took the Fuji Sankei Classic title in early May at the Kawana Hotel golf course. Franco put together a steady, unspectacular 69 in the final round for a one-stroke victory over Chen Tze-chung of Taiwan with his nine-under-par 275 total. It was the fifth win in Japan for Franco, who took the Just System KSB Open in March, and the sixth triumph by a foreign player in the first eight tournaments of the year.

Mitsutaka Kusakabe fired a seven-under-par 64 in the opening round to take a three-stroke lead over Tsuyoshi Yoneyama and Shinichi Yokota, but none of them were around at the finish. Kusakabe, a three-time winner on the tour, couldn't stand prosperity this time. He shot 76 Friday and yielded first place to Yoshinori Kaneko (68-69), who promptly lost the lead as well — to Franco. Kaneko, Japan's No. 2 money winner in 1996, shot 71 Saturday and slipped two strokes behind Franco, who added a 67 to his opening 69-70. Todd Hamilton joined Kaneko at 208 with a 68.

Franco didn't make a birdie until after the turn Sunday, but the two he made on the second nine were all he needed to edge Chen, who came up just short again in his almost weekly challenges. Aussie newcomer Steve Conran placed third at 277, and Brandt Jobe, eight strokes back starting the round, shot 64 to tie Frankie Minoza for fourth place.

Japan PGA Championship—¥120,000,000

Winner: Brandt Jobe

American Brandt Jobe extended the title frustrations of Masashi (Jumbo) Ozaki in the Japan PGA Championship. Ozaki, a six-time winner of the PGA but stuck on his awesome 106-victory mark since late 1997, made his most serious bid at Grandage, but Jobe was up to the challenge of a head-to-head confrontation, winning the season's first playoff on the first extra hole for his fourth title in four years on the Japanese circuit.

Neither of them was far away, but neither led the PGA during the first three rounds. The first day it was Toshiaki Odate. He shot 65 and led Yukihiro Yamamoto by one stroke. Taiwan's Yeh Chang-ting shared third place at 67 with Brian Watts, who was fined ¥200,000 for hitting two balls into the sea at the Fuji Sankei and denied a spot in the upcoming Japan Open. Yeh took over first place Friday with five birdies and four bogeys for 71 and 138, a shot better than Seiki Okuda and Odate, who had a 74. Jobe and Ozaki were among six players at 140.

Keiichiro Fukabori, another of the 140 shooters, seized the lead Saturday and needed only a 70 to do it. The 210 total gave Fukabori a two-stroke advantage over Jobe (72), Ozaki (72), Yeh (74), Odate (73) and David Smail of New Zealand (71). Closing 68s Sunday brought about the Jobe-Ozaki tie, Jobe nailing a birdie at the par-three 17th to forge the deadlock. In the playoff, the American parred the replayed, par-five 18th and Ozaki missed a six-foot par putt to take the defeat. Jobe was the first foreign winner of the PGA Championship since David Ishii took the title in 1987.

Ube Kosan Open—¥100,000,000

Winner: Brandt Jobe

The secret came out after Brandt Jobe became the first back-to-back winner of the year with a two-stroke victory in the Ube Kosan Open at Ajisu. Brandt's wife, Jennifer, had joined him in Japan the previous week before he won the PGA Championship and, of course, was on hand as he registered his two-stroke triumph over Shigeki Maruyama on the Mannenike East course of Ube Country Club. "I would say that she is officially my good luck charm," said Jobe who became the leading money winner with the ¥18 million check. Two of Jobe's five victories in Japan that came in 1997 also were scored in successive weeks. Brandt's win was the eighth by a foreign player in the season's first 10 events.

The 32-year-old Oklahoma native, who was a collegiate All-American at UCLA and has played much of his professional golf in Asia, took charge quickly in the Ube Kosan. After starting three strokes behind leaders Kazuhiko Hosokawa and Kazuhiro Fukunaga who had 65s on Thursday, the American spurted in front Friday with a bogey-free, eight-under-par 64. He had an eagle and six birdies. With 133, Jobe led Yeh Chang-ting by a shot. Two back were Hosokawa (69) and veteran Nobuo Serizawa, who shot a course-record 62 with an eagle, nine birdies and a bogey.

Jobe then distanced the field Saturday, starting the round with three consecutive birdies and an eagle. He stuttered a bit later on with four bogeys and two more birdies, but his 65–201 total, 15 under par, opened his lead to five strokes. On Sunday, he precluded any serious challenges with four birdies on the first nine, but a few missteps on the back nine resulted in just a 70 and a two-shot victory with 271. Maruyama, like Masashi Ozaki a 1997 headliner still winless in 1998, closed with 66–273.

Mitsubishi Galant—¥120,000,000

Winner: Toru Taniguchi

When all was said and done, Toru Taniguchi was the winner of the Mitsubishi Galant tournament and it was his first victory in six years on the Japan PGA Tour. But the most interesting story of the week at Tosa Country Club at Kami, Kochi Prefecture, centered around 44-year-old Noboru Fujiike, who had never won anything other than a regional event in 1983. Out of the blue, Fujiike shot the first 60 ever in Japan and led the first round by six strokes. What's more, he started the day with a bogey. Ten birdies and an eagle followed. "I just can't tell you how much fun I had out there today," grinned Fujiike. "Even in practice rounds, the best I ever shot was a 62." Sad to report, he eventually shot a 77 Sunday to finish in a 16th-place tie. Fujiike's 60 was 11 under par, the best ever on a par-71 course, but five players have been 11 under on par-72 courses.

Fujiike shot 71 in the rain-delayed second round and kept the lead — by two over Shigeki Maruyama, who shot 64 for 133. Then on Saturday, Fujiike yielded first place at 201 to Taniguchi, who put a pair of 65s behind his opening 71; Kazuhiko Hosokawa (69-65-67) and Katsunori Kuwabara (66-68-67). The decision Sunday came down to the final hole and a two-stroke swing as Taniguchi birdied for 67 a 268 total while Hosokawa bogeyed for 68 and 269. Masashi Ozaki finished third at 272.

JCB Classic Sendai—¥100,000,000

Winner: Yoshinori Mizumaki

Yoshinori Mizumaki spent a fruitless spell in America earlier in the decade, but the experience he gained served him well in the JCB Classic Sendai, when he found himself in a confrontation with Shigeki Maruyama, who had done everything but win in the preceding weeks. Mizumaki clung to a one-stroke lead through the final holes to win his sixth career title.

Ryoken (Ricky) Kawagishi shared the first-round lead with Nobuo Serizawa and Tatsuo Takasaki with five-under-par 66s on the hilly course at Shibata in Northern Japan. Then Mizumaki came to the fore. He shot 66 Friday and moved into a one-stroke lead at 134. Tied at 135 were Koki Idoki, Takaaki Fukuzawa, Mamoru Osanai and Tetsu Nishikawa, who birdied six of the first seven holes, had nine birdies in all and shot 64. Mizumaki widened his margin to three strokes Saturday, shooting 68 for 11-under-par 202 total. Maruyama moved into contention with 66, taking over second place with 205 and setting up the final-day duel.

The 39-year-old Mizumaki birdied four of the first six holes to extend his lead to five strokes over Maruyama. However, his putting stroke became a bit balky on the second nine and by the time the two reached the final hole Mizumaki's margin was down to one, primarily because of three of Maruyama's five birdies in his bogey-free 66, the last coming at the 17th. Neither got it close at the home hole and had to settle for pars. The winner shot another 68 for a 270 total.

Sapporo Tokyu Open—¥100,000,000

Winner: Toru Suzuki

It was touch and go until the last two holes of the Sapporo Tokyu Open in Hokkaido at the Sapporo Kokusai Country Club. Then Toru Suzuki went birdie-birdie and made off with the victory, his first in two years and fourth of his career. With the three-under-par 69 and 272 total, Suzuki scored a two-stroke victory over David Ishii.

Carlos Franco shared the first-round lead of seven-under-par 65 with Suzuki and Tsuyoshi Yoneyama, one shot in front of Frankie Minoza, Kaname Yokoo and Akihito Yokoyama. Suzuki slipped a shot behind Friday, shooting 69 while Franco and Yoneyama were carding 68s to lead with 133. Suzuki regained first place Saturday, trading places with Franco and Yoneyama. He shot 69 for 203 while the other two took 72s for 205. Ishii, whose best previous finish in 1998 had been 21st place, was at 206 after rounds of 70-66-70 and he made a good run at Suzuki Sunday before settling into second place with 68–274. Franco finished third at 70-275, while Yoneyama tied for sixth with 72–277.

Yomiuri Open—¥50,000,000

Winner: Brian Watts

Bad weather shortened a Japan PGA Tour event for the second time in 1998. This time the Yomiuri Open was reduced to 36 holes as rain pummelled the Yomiuri Country Club course at Nishinomiya and fog set in. Although his prize money for victory was cut in half to ¥9 million, American Brian Watts accepted the title with pleasure. "While I'm very happy to win, it feels kind of strange to claim a title after only 36 holes," Watts remarked. "I guess I'm a bit lucky."

One round was played before the rains came. Toru Suzuki, carrying over the momentum he achieved the previous weekend in winning the Sapporo Tokyu Open, opened with a 65 to lead Watts and Kaname Yokoo by one, and Frankie Minoza, Yoshinori Mizumaki, Shigeki Maruyama and Kazuhiko Hosokawa by three.

After steady downpours washed out the Friday round, Watts claimed the lead — and, as it turned out, the victory — Saturday with a 68–134 total, one stroke in front of Yokoo (66-69) and two ahead of Maruyama (68-68), Satoshi Higashi (70-66) and Katsumasa Miyamoto (69-67). Suzuki shot 72 and slipped to sixth place at 137. They tried to play Sunday despite the rain and fog, but the event was called off with the leaders on the 11th hole. Watts and Yokoo were both one over par at that point. It was Watts' 11th Japanese victory in his sixth season

Mizuno Open—¥100,000,000

Winner: Brandt Jobe

Brandt Jobe became the first player of 1998 to collect three victories in Japan when he captured the Mizuno Open at the end of June, regaining the top spot on the money list. The Oklahoman took advantage of the final-round collapse of fellow American Brian Watts, winning by four strokes with a three-under-par 69 even though starting the day one shot off the lead. He finished with a 13-under-par 275 total as he put the win alongside earlier victories in the Japan PGA Championship and the Ube Kosan Open. It was his sixth triumph in three seasons in Japan.

A flash of the past highlighted the opening round as 51-year-old Hisao Inoue, who has played for 23 years, surprised with an eight-under-par 64 at Setonaikai Golf Club at Kasaoka, Okayama Prefecture, yet only led by one stroke over Tsukasa Watanabe, no youngster himself at 41. Things took a more expectable turn Friday as Jobe shot 65–132 and went three shots ahead of two other recent winners — Toru Suzuki (Sapporo Tokyu) and Yoshinori Mizumaki (JCB Sendai).

Watts, winner of the previous week's rain-shortened Yomiuri Open and the Mizuno Open three of the previous four years, came from five back Saturday to edge into a one-stroke lead, shooting 68 to Jobe's 74, which dropped him to 206 with Watanabe and Keiichiro Fukabori. But Watts came apart Sunday with a 76, enabling Jobe to convert his 69 into the victory, two ahead of Suzuki (70) and Mizumaki (69).

PGA Philanthropy—¥100,000,000

Winner: Shigeki Maruyama

Shigeki Maruyama found out what had been missing as time and again he came up short in his bid for his first win of 1998 — a hot putter in very hot weather. Maruyama, a four-time winner in 1997 when he was second on the money list, put on a dazzling display on the sun-drenched greens of Shiromizu Golf Club in the third round of the PGA Philanthropy tournament that just gave him enough of a cushion to take a one-stroke victory.

Non-winners had their days the first two rounds before Maruyama took over. Taiwan's Hsieh Chin-sheng, 35, was the first-round leader with 64, one shot ahead of Maruyama, compatriot Chen Tze-chung and six others. The next day, one of those six, Yukihiro Yamamoto, without a victory in his 13 seasons, took the lead with 65–130. Maruyama was right on his heels at 131 and blazed into the lead Saturday, riding his putter to a seven-under-par 64 and a three-stroke lead with his 195 total. Maruyama one-putted each of the first nine greens, three of them for birdies — "the first time in my life I ever did that" — and polished off the 64 with four more birdies on the second nine. Toru Suzuki, winner of the Sapporo Tokyu Open three weeks earlier, also shot 64 to climb into second place.

Suzuki and Maruyama, college teammates at Nihon University, went head-to-head in the final round. After making four birdies and taking two bogeys on the first 15 holes, Maruyama made a wonderful save at the 16th after putting his tee shot in the water and Suzuki missed a chance to close the gap when he failed to birdie the hole. Maruyama completed the round with 69 for 264, just enough, as Satoshi Higashi closed with 64 for 265 and took second place when Suzuki bogeyed the 18th for 68–266. It was Maruyama's eighth win.

Yonex Open Hiroshima—¥100,000,000

Winner: Masashi Ozaki

It was almost a foregone conclusion that Masashi (Jumbo) Ozaki would end his victory drought when he elected to play in the Yonex Open Hiroshima after being off for a month. He had won the tournament at Hiroshima Country Club eight times since 1971, most recently in 1994 and 1995. It took a little doing in Sunday's final round, but Ozaki, now 51 years old, finally put the 107th victory of his career into the books, shooting a 66 that gave him a one-stroke win over Australian Peter McWhinney. It was his 86th official victory in Japan and his first of 1998.

McWhinney, who had an earlier runner-up finish in the Tsuruya Open in April, took the setback in stride, rationalizing, "I think I had a solid round (68) today, but it's just a challenging job to beat Jumbo."

Young players held sway the first two days. Shingo Katayama shot 66 Thursday to lead Toru Suzuki, Takao Nogami, Akihito Yokoyama and Satoshi Ogawa by one stroke. He then gave way to rookie Takao Nogami, who added a 66 to his first-round 67 for 133, one stroke better than McWhinney, who shot 65, and three ahead of Katayama, Suzuki and Shinichi Yokota.

McWhinney followed with a 69 Saturday and that propelled him into first place with his 13-under-par 203, but just a stroke ahead of the charging Ozaki, who worked up a 66–204. Ozaki doubled the 66 Sunday with seven birdies and a bogey for the winning 270 and pronounced, "I'm nearly back in form. I'm okay now, mentally, too."

Aiful Cup—¥100,000,000

Winner: Hidemichi Tanaka

Discouraged by his winless 1997 and plunge from 16th to 44th on the money list, Hidemichi Tanaka spent the off-season in Hawaii working on his game. It finally paid off in late July with victory in the Aiful Cup, a new tournament at Aomori Country Club in Kyodo Prefecture. "I'm still not sure what to say about the win today," said the 27-year-old Hiroshima native after posting the third victory of his seven-year career and first since the 1996 Pepsi Ube Kosan.

Tanaka never led until the final holes. Steve Conran of Australia was a strong contender from the start, taking the lead with a seven-under-par 65. Conran shot 71 Friday but still led, along with Kosaku Hirano, at 136, one in front of Kinpachi Yoshimura, Nobumitsu Yuhara and Zaw Moe. Conran had a 63 and a new co-leader Saturday. Toshimitsu Izawa banged out a 66 to join him at the top at 204.

Tanaka, three strokes behind after rounds of 68-70-69, birdied the first two holes Sunday, added four more on the second nine, put a 66 on the board and watched as his 273 total held up for the victory. Tatsuo Takasaki also shot 66 and tied Izawa for second place at 274, while Conran faded to 10th place with a closing 73–277.

NST Niigata Open—¥60,000,000

Winner: Masayuki Kawamura

Masayuki Kawamura turned the NST Niigata Open into a rout — all in one day. One stroke out of the lead going into the final round at the Forest Golf Club at Toyoura, Niigata Prefecture, the 31-year-old Kawamura blitzed the field with a course-record 63 and waltzed to an eight-stroke victory. That margin matched that of Davis Love III at the Chunichi Crowns as the biggest of the season.

Kawamura's victory overshadowed the first-day theatrics of rookie Takeshi Saito. Playing in his first tournament on the Japan PGA Tour, Saito aced the fourth hole, made another eagle, four birdies, took two bogeys, shot 66 and shared the lead with Canadian Rick Gibson.

This came after a two-hour rain delay and before play was suspended with 24 golfers still on the course. Nobuo Serizawa, just one stroke off the lead Thursday, took over Friday with 69–136 as Gibson shot 71 and Saito 76 en route to a tie-for-66th finish.

Daisuke Serizawa, 11 years on the tour without a victory, supplanted Nobuo Serizawa at the top with a 66–204 total, placing a stroke in front of Kawamura (69-69-67) and three ahead of Nobuo Serizawa (71) and Kiyoshi Murota (64). That set the stage for Kawamura. He racked up 10 birdies and absorbed a single bogey for the 63–268 total, 20 under par. It was a second victory to go with his triumph in the 1995 Tokai Classic. He credited a new putter that he had been using this season. It was like someone else was putting for me, he said afterward.

Sanko Grand Summer—¥100,000,000

Winner: Shingo Katayama

Shingo Katayama became the fourth first-time winner in Japan in the Sanko Grand Summer Championship, but he had to do it the hard way — in a playoff — after frittering away a four-stroke lead in the final round. What's more, Katayama considered himself "fortunate just to be here," reflecting on the three months he missed earlier in the year while recuperating from herniated disk surgery in March.

The 25-year-old Katayama dropped a three-foot par putt on the third extra hole to defeat Kazuhiko Hosokawa.

Katayama started with 67, trailing leader Nobumitsu Yuhara by three strokes. Yuhara had an eagle and six birdies en route to his 64. Katayama advanced into a tie for the lead with Masakazu Noritake, another non-winner, on Friday. He had a 66 while Noritake was adding a 68 to his opening 65 for his 133 total. Although it was his highest of three scores, Katayama shot his first no-bogey round of the season to take his four-stroke lead over Hosokawa Saturday. He eagled the par-five first hole and tacked on two birdies for 68–201, while Hosokawa was climbing into second place with a 67 for the 205.

Katayama shot 73 Sunday, opening the door for Hosokawa when he took two of his four bogeys on the last two holes. Hosokawa eagled the fifth hole and made three birdies as he shot 69 to force the playoff. The two matched pars on the first two extra holes before Hosokawa suffered the fatal bogey at the third.

KBC Augusta—¥100,000,000

Winner: Masashi Ozaki

Masashi (Jumbo) Ozaki shifted into high gear when action resumed after the usual two-week hiatus in mid-August as Ozaki headed toward yet another money-winning championship. Just as he had done to get things started with his victory in the Yonex at Hiroshima, Ozaki won the KBC Augusta tournament which he had mastered in the past. Three times, in fact. The two previous seasons, in fact.

Ozaki, age 51, had a relatively easy time of it at the Keya Golf Club course, coasting to a four-stroke victory with an even-par 72 in the final round after leading most of the week. Just back after a disappointing showing in the PGA Championship in America, where he missed the cut, Ozaki birdied the last four holes for 66 and the first-round lead. Toru Taniguchi, the Mitsubishi Galant winner, and Keiji Teshima trailed by one stroke.

Ozaki yielded the lead to Katsunori Kuwabara Friday. Kuwabara shot 67 for 136, Chen Tze-chung matched that for 137 and Ozaki, with 72, finished at 138 with Ikuo Shirahama, Nobuo Serizawa and Teshima. On the third day,

Ozaki rose to a three-shot lead over Kuwabara when he accumulated eight birdies and carded a 65. Kuwabara took a 70 for his 206. Kuwabara couldn't muster a challenge Sunday, shooting 73 but holding the runner-up spot, four behind Ozaki's 13-under-par 275 total. The second 1998 victory increased his overall career total to 108, 89 on the tour.

Japan Match Play—¥100,000,000

Winner: Katsunori Kuwabara

As so often happens in such competitions, the Japan Match Play Championship wound up with two unlikely finalists battling for the title the first week of September at the Nidom Classic course at Tomakomai in Hokkaido. Katsunori Kuwabara and Shinichi Yokota, with just two victories between them, squared off for the title and it turned out to be an exciting match, going 38 holes before Kuwabara took the victory when Yokota missed a 12-foot par putt.

Neither player had a breather in the earlier rounds. Kuwabara, whose only previous victory in seven seasons was in the 1995 Acom International, scored 2 and 1 over Hiroyuki Fujita and Brian Watts, then 3-and-2 wins over Eduardo Herrera and Zaw Moe. Yokota, who won his first title the previous year in the ANA Open, had a somewhat easier time. He defeated Hajime Meshiai, 3 and 2, in the first round; Peter McWhinney, 5 and 4, in the second round, and Frankie Minoza, 2 and 1, in the quarter-finals before taking out the defending champion, Shigeki Maruyama, 3 and 2, in the semi-finals.

Kuwabara had a five-hole lead at one point in the 36-hole final, but Yokota made up that ground to force the overtime work, only to lose on the 38th.

Suntory Open—¥100,000,000

Winner: Mamoru Osanai

Two players who missed the Japan Match Play Championship the previous week — one by underperformance and the other by choice — had the best shots at the title in the Suntory Open at Sobu Country Club at Inzai, Chiba Prefecture. The one who won was Mamoru Osanai, who became the fifth first-time winner. Osanai gamely shrugged off the stretch-run threat by Masashi (Jumbo) Ozaki and opened a three-stroke victory margin.

Neither was in the picture the first day at Sobu as Saburo Fujiki shot 67 and led Mitsunori Harakawa by one and 10 players, including U.S. Open champion Lee Janzen, by two. Two of those 69 shooters — Norio Hosoya and Hideki Kase — assumed the lead Friday with two more 69s for 138 as both Osanai and Ozaki moved within a stroke, Osanai with 68 and Ozaki with 69. Hosoya, a winless 12-year player, gained entry through qualifying and made the cut for the first time in the season.

Osanai went in front to stay Saturday, shooting 66 for a 205 total and taking a two-stroke lead over veteran Kase, the 1990 Japan PGA champion. Janzen was then in a massive 10th-place tie at 211. But it was Ozaki, from 210, who ran at Osanai Sunday. After two early birdies, Osanai went into a tailspin and bogeyed four holes in a row starting at the fourth and, when

Ozaki made his fifth birdie at the 13th, he caught the 28-year-old, third-year man. Undaunted, Osanai birdied the 14th, 16th and 17th to bring home a 69 for 274 and the three-stroke victory over Ozaki. Janzen closed with 63 and tied for sixth.

ANA Open—¥100,000,000

Winner: Keiichiro Fukabori

It was a little different this time. When Keiichiro Fukabori won his first tournament, the Just System KSB Open, in 1997, he muddled to a 74 and finished in first place as the other contenders collapsed around him. In picking up his second win, the 29-year-old Fukabori assembled a steady, three-under-par 69 at Sapporo Golf Club in Hokkaido and came from one stroke off the pace to capture the ANA Open by two, in the process fending off the bids of Masashi Ozaki and American star Lee Janzen.

Another visitor, Stuart Appleby of Australia, shared the first-round lead with Ozaki and little-known Yuji Igarashi with 69s as Sapporo proved a stern test for the field. At 70 were Carlos Franco, Peter McWhinney, Chen Tze-chung and Kenichi Kuboya. Katsumasa Miyamoto, who won his first tournament — the Tsuruya Open — earlier in the year, took aim on another when he shot 67 on a rainy Friday and advanced into a one-stroke lead with his 138. Appleby had a 70 for 139 and Janzen moved into a tie for third with Hajime Meshiai, winner of the season-opening Token Cup, at 140. Ozaki fell back with 73–142.

Fukabori made his first move Saturday. He registered a four-birdie 68, the best round of the day, to climb within one stroke of Miyamoto, who shot 71 for 209. Par rounds put Appleby at 211, Janzen at 212 and Ozaki at 214 going into the final day. Janzen made a solid bid Sunday, shooting 69, but had to settle for a second-place tie with Miyamoto (72) at 281. Too late, too, with 68 was Ozaki, who finished fourth, but that check strengthened his hold on the No. 1 spot on the money list.

Gene Sarazen Jun Classic—¥110,000,000

Winner: Todd Hamilton

Little had been heard during the season from Todd Hamilton, the first of the young American players to make a mark on the Japan PGA Tour in the early 1990s. Hamilton, who first qualified to play in Japan when he was the Asian Tour champion in 1992, had collected six victories in the ensuing years but none since the PGA Philanthropy in 1996. The 31-year-old Illinois native ended the dry spell in the Gene Sarazen Jun Classic, scoring a come-from-behind, two-stroke victory on the Rope Club course in late September.

Hamilton's triumph capped a week in which one or another foreign player topped the standings at the end of every round. First, it was Colombia's Eduardo Herrera, the defending champion and early-season winner at Shizuoka, who shot 66 on a damp Thursday to lead Hajime Meshiai and Satoshi Higashi by one stroke. Herrera fired a 70 Friday and Australia's Craig Parry tied him with a 68 for his 138 as Hamilton moved into the picture with a torrid 66 for 139. He was joined there by Carlos Franco (68).

Paraguay's Franco, already a two-time 1998 victor, surged to the fore with a dazzling 65 for his 14-under-par 202 total, banking an eagle, seven birdies and two bogeys to go two shots ahead of Parry (68), three ahead of Hamilton (68) and four in front of Herrera (70). Franco's game short-circuited Sunday and Hamilton and Parry in particular were quick to take advantage. Hamilton opened with two of his seven birdies on the first two holes, but didn't overtake Parry, who had four birdies in a five-hole stretch midway through the round, until he birdied the par-five 15th and 16th holes. He finished with 65 and an 18-under-par 270 total, two strokes ahead of Parry (68–272). Franco struggled to a 73–275.

Japan Open—¥120,000,000

Winner: Hidemichi Tanaka

Naomichi (Joe) Ozaki was on the verge of a salvage operation in the Japan Open championship. After suffering through seven winless months, during which he was rarely in contention, the youngest Ozaki (42) was perched in front by three strokes with just one round remaining. He couldn't finish it off, and Hidemichi Tanaka was there to gather up the spoils. Tanaka, who had his game back on track and already had a victory on his 1998 record, came from three strokes behind at the Oarai Golf Club in Ibaraki Prefecture to land the title, its ¥24 million check and 10-year exemption. He shot 69 for a 283 total, nipping Ozaki by a shot.

The two had passed the lead back and forth throughout the tournament. Ozaki had it first, in tandem with Koki Idoki, when the two opened with 71s on a rain-plagued Thursday, though giving it up the next morning when Kazuhiro Takami, Yuichi Tabo and Hideki Haraguchi, three of 27 players who failed to complete their rounds before dark, posted 70s when they finished. Tanaka was in a group of par-shooters and he took a one-stroke lead with a 70–142 later in the day. Ozaki (72), Toshimitsu Izawa (70) and Hsieh Chin-sheng were at 143.

Back came Ozaki with 68 Saturday to establish his three-stroke lead at 211 over Tanaka (72), Toru Taniguchi and Hiroyuki Fujita. Then, on Sunday, the 27-year-old Tanaka surged ahead when he made his third consecutive birdie at the eighth. The advantage went to three when he followed an Ozaki bogey at the 13th with the last of his five birdies at the 14th. Then Tanaka restored Ozaki's chances when he bogeyed the 16th and drove into the woods at the 18th. He hit a tree with his next shot, but found an opening with a splendid shot onto the green. His two-putt bogey gave him his fourth career win in eight seasons when Ozaki failed to get a tying birdie.

Tokai Classic—¥110,000,000

Winner: Toshimitsu Izawa

The 79 he shot in the final round of the Japan Open surely left a bad taste in the mouth of Toshimitsu Izawa, but he didn't let it bother him a few days later when he teed it up in the Tokai Classic. By week's end, he had that title in his pocket, quashing the skepticism that had grown around his 1996 victory in the Open. Until the Tokai triumph, that had been his only win in his 10 seasons. Izawa overcame a one-stroke deficit going into the final round on Miyoshi Country Club's West Course and rolled to a three-shot victory at 11 under par with a 277 total.

Izawa's key round was the second when he fired 66 to jump from 18th place after a 73 into a tie for the lead at 139 with Yasuharu Imano, Tsuyoshi Yoneyama and Kaname Yokoo. "I'm hitting it close and putting relatively well this week," said Izawa after his seven-birdie, one-bogey round. Winless Imano inched a shot ahead of Izawa with 69–208 Saturday, Izawa shooting 70. Threatening then just two shots back were American Mark Calcavecchia, Nobuhito Sato and Yoneyama, and Italian Costantino Rocca was at 211.

None of them made any noise Sunday and Imano crashed to a 76 and a seventh-place tie at 284. Veteran Nobumitsu Yuhara grabbed the runner-up slot with 68–280, the only player to finish within six strokes of Izawa.

Nikkei Cup—¥110,000,000

Winner: Mitsutaka Kusakabe

It happens to the best of them. Masashi (Jumbo) Ozaki, even at age 51 the dominant player in Japan, was well on track toward his third victory of the year in the Nikkei Cup being played for the first time in mid-October after 13 years as a July fixture. Then, on the second nine Sunday, his game came unglued, giving Mitsutaka Kusakabe the opportunity to acquire the victory. With 69 and 280 on a typhoon-generated windy day, Kusakabe beat Ozaki by one stroke.

Ozaki never trailed until the disaster struck on Sunday. He opened with a rousing, seven-under-par 65 — all birdies — and led Todd Hamilton and Katsunori Kuwabara, two earlier winners in 1990, by three strokes. On Friday, he shot a mere 70 but still widened his margin to four strokes, then over Hamilton, Kuwabara, Katsumasa Miyamoto and Toshimitsu Izawa.

Because of a weather-delayed start, the leaders finished their final holes Sunday morning. Ozaki parred the last two holes for 72, retaining first place at nine under par by a shot over Yasuharu Imano, who shot 68. Kusakabe also had a second straight 68, but trailed by four because of his opening-round 75. The decisive shot for Kusakabe that afternoon came on the second nine when he chipped in for an eagle at the par-five 14th amid Ozaki's missteps — three bogeys and a double bogey over the final eight holes for 74 and 281. Brian Watts finished third at 282.

Bridgestone Open—¥120,000,000

Winner: Nobuhito Sato

The final-round woes of the Ozaki family visited the third brother in the Bridgestone Open in late October. Just as had happened to Naomichi in the Japan Open and Masashi in the previous week's Nikkei Cup, Tateo (Jet) Ozaki failed to hold a 54-hole lead on the last day and wound up losing a playoff to Nobuhito Sato at Sodegaura Country Club in Chiba. It was a tough blow for the least successful of the talented Ozakis, with "only" 12 victories. Jet, 44, had not won since early 1993. On the other hand, the younger Sato, 28, had scored his only earlier victory in the JCB Classic Sendai the previous season.

Tsuneyuki (Tommy) Nakajima had a flash of his old form, opening the Bridgestone with a six-under-par 66, one better than Ozaki, who had two eagles in his 67. Lee Janzen, the U.S. Open champion, playing in his third Japanese tournament in seven weeks, shared the 68 slot with Toru Suzuki. Nakajima reverted to his troubled game Friday, shot 76 and yielded the lead to Ozaki, who moved two strokes in front with his 69–136. Shigeki Maruyama scored 67 and joined 69-shooters Brandt Jobe, Shingo Katayama and Sato at 138. Ozaki held onto the two-shot margin with a 67–203 Saturday, Sato seizing sole possession of the runner-up spot with a matching 67. Steve Conran was third at a distant 208.

It was a two-man battle Sunday, Sato catching Ozaki and forcing the playoff with a 10-foot birdie putt at the 72nd hole. The two replayed that par-five 18th to start the overtime and Sato again birdied from 10 feet to win the tournament.

Philip Morris Championship—¥200,000,000

Winner: Masashi Ozaki

The Ozaki name remained in the forefront for the third week in a row, but on a decidedly positive rather than a negative note this time. Two weeks after he blew the Nikkei Cup on the final holes and a week after brother Tateo lost the lead and a playoff in the Bridgestone Open, Masashi (Jumbo) Ozaki stormed from eight strokes off the pace with a sparkling, eight-under-par 64 to win the Philip Morris Championship, the first of the bigger-money events on the autumn schedule.

The lead changed hands in each of the first three rounds at the ABC Golf Club at Tojo, Hyogo Prefecture. The first to hold it was Toru Suzuki, the June winner in the Sapporo Tokyu Open, who had been in a slump since playing in the British Open. "I think I'm back on track," said Suzuki after opening with a six-under-par 66, one better than seven other close pursuers. One of the 67-shooters — Kaname Yokoo — repeated Friday and the Tokyo native took the lead by a stroke over Tateo (Jet) Ozaki, by two over Mamoru Osanai, the Suntory winner, and unheralded Shusaku Sugimoto.

In turn, Sugimoto, likewise a non-winner, grabbed first place Saturday, shooting 67, the day's best round, for 203 and a two-stroke lead over Carlos Franco.

The Ozaki typhoon struck Sunday. Masashi, who had fought back from a 75 start with a pair of 68s, made just about every putt he looked at, racking up an eagle and eight birdies to offset just enough his two bogeys. With the 64 and 275 total, he edged Franco (71) and Mitsuo Harada (70) by one shot, as he scored the 109th victory of his career.

Acom International—¥120,000,000

Winner: Kaname Yokoo

Kaname Yokoo, who had been close to victory often during 1998, his third year on the Japan PGA Tour, broke through with a vengeance in the Acom International in early November. Achieving what only American star Davis Love III had also done during the season, the 26-year-old Yokoo led the Acom from start to finish to score his first victory, the sixth player (aside from Love) to do so in 1998.

The Acom, until 1998 played in August, is scored with points rather than strokes and Kaname had 17 in the first round at the Seve Ballesteros Golf Club at Iwaki, Fukushima Prefecture. That gave him a four-point lead over Toshimitsu Izawa, seven over third-place Toru Suzuki. Yokoo's big boost was a five-point eagle at the third hole. He picked up 14 more with seven birdies and gave two back with a pair of bogeys.

He only managed five points Friday, but remained four in front of Izawa and Shusaku Sugimoto, rebounding from his final-round fold-up in the Philip Morris event. Pointless Thursday, Sugimoto ran up nine two-point birdies without a bogey for his 18 points Friday. Yokoo made another eagle Saturday and built his lead to seven with 14 more points and a 36-point total. Katsumasa Miyamoto moved into second place at 29 with a 12-point day and gave Yokoo a run for his ¥21.6 million money. Yokoo's six-birdie, two-bogey performance yielded 10 final points and his 46-point total gave him the title by three over Miyamoto, who finished at 43.

Sumitomo Visa Taiheiyo Masters—¥150,000,000

Winner: Lee Westwood

"I look forward to coming back next year and the year after that and the year after that," promised a delighted Lee Westwood. Little wonder. The newest British phenom had just won the Sumitomo Visa Taiheiyo Masters, one of the richest events in Japan, for the third year in a row, putting an exclamation point on a wonderful season during which he also won in America and finished third on the PGA European Tour on the strength of four victories.

No one had ever taken the Taiheiyo Masters title three consecutive times in the tournament's 26-year history and it didn't appear that Westwood would either after the first round. He shot par 72 on the Taiheiyo Club's Gotemba course and trailed Eduardo Herrera by seven strokes. The 33-year-old Herrera, a four-time winner in his decade of play in Japan, made eight birdies and a bogey on the fastest putting surfaces he had faced, for the two-shot lead on Ryoken Kawagishi and Nobuo Serizawa.

Friday was a day for the local fans as Serizawa, who lives just 10 minutes away from the course, took a three-stroke lead with a four-under-par 68 for 135. Tateo (Jet) Ozaki and Frankie Minoza, with 70s, were at 138. Westwood, after a practice session with his coach, Peter Cowen, shot 67, the best round on the breezy day, and moved closer at 139 with Herrera (74) and Kawagishi (72). Frankie Minoza took his turn on top Saturday. His 67–205 gave him a one-stroke lead on Westwood, who matched the 67 for 206.

Things did not begin well for Westwood on Sunday. He bogeyed the first two holes, "but I kept my composure." He made six birdies and took one more bogey after that. Toward the end, he faced a challenge from the ever-dangerous Masashi (Jumbo) Ozaki. Ozaki, a two-time winner at Gotemba in recent years, who had begun the day four behind Westwood, birdied the 18th for 67–277, cutting Westwood's margin to a single shot with two holes to play. But the Englishman calmly holed a seven-foot par putt at the 17th and birdied the 18th for 69, a 275 total and a two-stroke victory, the 12th of his career.

Dunlop Phoenix Tournament—¥250,000,000

Winner: Lee Westwood

The biggest purse of the year lured the best field to the Dunlop Phoenix as usual, but those who just arrived that week might just as well have stayed at home. Coming off his strong victory the previous Sunday, Lee Westwood made his Japan visit two-for-two with a triumph in the ¥250 million event, one of the originals on the Japan PGA Tour. Westwood led the last three days and held off the bid of Northern Ireland's Darren Clarke in the final round, putting a three-stroke victory on the board, the seventh of his outstanding year.

Ryoken (Ricky) Kawagishi, again an early-rounds contender, jumped in front Thursday with a 66 at Phoenix Country Club. He led Yoshinori Kaneko by one shot, Westwood and South Africa's Ernie Els by two. Then Westwood took charge. He shot 67 Friday with three birdies on the last six holes and moved two strokes into the lead. Clarke also finished strongly with four birdies from the 13th. With 67–137, he shared second place with Kawagishi (71) and Kaname Yokoo (69).

Little changed Saturday. Westwood and Clarke, both on top of their games, fired 66s to remain one-two in the standings. Naomichi (Joe) Ozaki shot the best score of the tournament, 64, and advanced into a third-place tie with American Fred Funk at 204, three behind the leader. Although he never trailed in his duel with Clarke in the final round, Westwood got a helping hand from Lady Luck.

Westwood regained a two-stroke lead with a birdie at the ninth. Then he pulled a four-iron shot at the 10th, but it bounced off a tree onto the green and he holed a 50-footer for another birdie. "That was really the turning point," Westwood said. "As soon as something like that happens, you think it's going to be your day." Of course, it was. He went on to a 70 for a 271 total and the three-stroke victory, making only one bogey over the final 48 holes. Clarke shot 71–274 and Naomichi Ozaki placed third with 72-276.

Casio World Open—¥150,000,000

Winner: Brian Watts

Brian Watts made his next-to-last appearance as a regular on the Japan PGA Tour a memorable and lucrative one when he captured the Casio World Open, an 18-year-old tournament that now has been won 11 times by American pros. Watts, who has enjoyed great success in his six seasons in Japan, scored his 12th victory when he defeated Toshimitsu Izawa on the second hole of a playoff.

The American, who gained international recognition when he lost in another playoff — to Mark O'Meara in the British Open — became eligible to play on the PGA Tour in America on the strength of his winnings for that runner-up finish and planned to do so in 1999, eight seasons after he lost his card and began to play in Asia.

The efforts of Watts and the rest of the field were overshadowed much of the time by the first tournament appearance in Japan of Tiger Woods, the No. 1-ranked player in the world. After a good opening round of 69, though, Woods faded from contention and eventually finished 10 strokes off the pace in a tie for 15th.

It was a disappointing week for Naomichi (Joe) Ozaki, too. Once again, he couldn't hold a 54-hole lead and failed in another bid for a 1998 victory. Ozaki opened the tournament at the Ibusuki Golf Club in Western Japan with a five-under-par 67 and the lead, one shot in front of Japan Open champion Hidemichi Tanaka, Mamoru Osanai and American Paul Stankowski. Woods, who hit a spectator in the face with his first tee shot, was bunched with Watts and four others at 69.

Tanaka shot 69–137 and took a one-stroke lead over Ozaki and Toshimitsu Izawa at the halfway point as Woods absorbed a string of four consecutive bogeys and took a 74. Ozaki regained first place with a bogey-free 67 for 205. Watts (67) and Izawa (68) settled at 208. Woods had classy company at 214 — Masashi (Jumbo) Ozaki, who had locked up his phenomenal 12th seasonal money title weeks before.

When Naomichi Ozaki could muster only a 71 Sunday, he slipped to third place, missing the Watts-Izawa playoff by two strokes as those two shot 68s for 274. After both men birdied the first extra hole, Izawa, the Tokai Classic winner, missed a 10-foot birdie putt before Watts converted his from six to annex the victory. The ¥27 million winner's check boosted Watts into the No. 2 spot on the money list.

Japan Series—¥100,000,000

Winner: Katsumasa Miyamoto

Katsumasa Miyamoto didn't take very long to prove that his initial victory early in 1998 might well be the beginning of a bright career. Before the year was out, Miyamoto put a second win on his record, this one the elite Japan Series for the Hitachi Cup at the expense of No. 1 Masashi (Jumbo) Ozaki. The 25-year-old Miyamoto defeated the remarkable man who is twice his age in a four-hole playoff at Tokyo's Yomiuri Country Club the first week of December.

Miyamoto got a huge jump on the field Thursday when he started the 26-player tournament — winners and money leaders only — with a six-under-par 64, bagging an eagle and six birdies to go with two bogeys to lead by four over three-time-winner Ozaki and Nobuhito Sato. He increased his edge to five strokes Friday when he followed with 67 for 131. Sato, the Bridgestone champion, shot another 68 for 136, five players were at 137 and Ozaki, with 70, slipped to 138.

Although he lost his touch in the rain Saturday and stumbled to a 75, Miyamoto clung to a share of the lead at 206 with Brian Watts, winner of the previous week's Casio World Open. Watts shot 69. Masashi Ozaki moved back within a stroke of the leaders with 70. Sunday's finish was reminiscent of a couple of others that kept Ozaki from having another truly spectacular season. Despite some erratic play, Ozaki seemed to have victory in hand until Miyamoto eagled the 17th hole and Ozaki took a fourth bogey at the 18th. In the playoff, the two men matched strokes through three holes before Miyamoto dropped a five-foot birdie putt at the fourth to end it.

Okinawa Open—¥80,000,000

Winner: Hidemichi Tanaka

Hidemichi Tanaka became the third and last player on the 1998 Japan PGA Tour to add three victories to his record when he won the season-ending Okinawa Open the second week of December at Daikyo Country Club. Masashi Ozaki and Brandt Jobe were the other triple winners. Tanaka, who took the Japan Open Championship and the Aiful Cup earlier in the year, came from two strokes off the pace to claim the title with a 67 finish and an 11-under-par 273 total. The ¥14.4 million prize placed Tanaka third on the final money list.

Tanaka lingered just off the pace through the first three rounds after opening with a 70. A sixsome — David Ishii, Stewart Ginn, Masayuki Kawamura, Tatsuo Takasaki, Masahiro Kuramoto and Yoshimitsu Fukuzawa — shared the first-round lead with 67s.

Ishii, the Hawaiian who has had slim pickings on the circuit in recent years after winning 13 times up to 1994, remained on top Friday with 68–135, joined there by Takashi Kanemoto (70-65). Ishii slipped to 72 Saturday, Kanemoto took a 73 and Akihito Yokoyama moved into a two-stroke lead with 68–204. Tanaka shot 69 for 206, then brushed aside Yokoyama and all other competition with the 67 Sunday for his fifth career victory. Yokoyama managed a 72 despite three bogeys and a double bogey and took second place.

Omega Tour

London Myanmar Open—US$225,000

Winner: Taimur Hussain

Taimur Hussain didn't know it at the time, but that was a huge promise he had made in 1995, by winning two tournaments — the Nomura Cup, the Asia-Pacific region's top amateur tournament, then the Pakistan Open, still as an amateur. He kept that promise three years later, at age 24, by becoming the first Pakistani not only to win on the Omega Tour but to win an international tournament when he took the first event on the 1998 Omega Tour, the London Myanmar Open, at the Bagan Golf Resort.

"The key was my eagle on the ninth, which allowed me to take the lead for the first time," Hussain said. He pitched in from 30 feet for a three. That gave him a grip on the final round, and he tightened it with birdies from 15 feet at the 12th and eight feet at the 13th. "Even when I missed from four feet at No. 15, I knew what I had to do to win, and I was confident I could par the last three holes." Which he did. Hussain, with scores of 70, 73, 68 and 69 for a 280 total, eight under par, scored a one-stroke victory over China's Zhang Lian-wei, who had taken the early lead with birdies at the second and third holes.

Hussain turned professional after winning the 1995 Pakistan Open, and tried to qualify for the Japan PGA Tour. He didn't make it, but observers felt it was only a question of time until he broke through. It happened here, but for a while, he didn't seem to have a chance. American Robert Huxtable was on track for his first professional victory. He shared the lead through the first two rounds and held it alone through the third round. Meanwhile, Hussain was working his way out of the pack, from as much as eight strokes behind after 36 holes, and two after 54 holes. Then Huxtable blew to an 83 in the final round, leaving the stage to Hussain and Zhang.

Classic Indian Open—US$300,000

Winner: Firoz Ali

"Ali played a superb round today, and if he plays the same tomorrow, it's going to take a 63 or 64 to catch him," American Dean Wilson was saying after the third round. Wilson was right. But a par 72 was the best Wilson could do. Firoz Ali, the 26-year-old Indian, who started the final round with a three-stroke lead, shot a workman-like 70 to take the Classic Indian Open at Royal Calcutta by five strokes over Wilson on rounds of 69, 68, 67 and 70 for a 14-under-par 279 total. His home fans responded by carrying him on their shoulders from the 18th green.

"I was very nervous at the start of the day," Ali said. "But on the back nine I felt very relaxed, and when I made a birdie on the 14th to go four up, I knew I was going to win." Wilson cut Ali's lead to one stroke after two birdies and a bogey going out, but coming in, he could manage only 36 to Ali's 33.

It was the end of a weather-troubled tournament. American Mike Cunning led the first round with 66, but the most compelling story came from Australian Leith Wastle, who opened with 80 and came back with 66 to make the cut. In the third round, Ali turned a bogey into a birdie by chipping in from 40 feet. He added a birdie at the 12th, and another at the 15th before bogeying the 17th. In the final round, there were two key moments — when he saved par at No. 6 and birdied No. 9. "After playing those holes well," Ali said, "I felt confident I could win."

Orient Masters—US$200,000

Winner: Chawalit Plaphol

Boonchu Ruangkit, 41, the star of Thai golf, had become something of big brother and mentor of young countryman Chawalit Plaphol, 24. Sometimes, however, friends must part, and that time came in the Orient Masters at Xiamen early in April. "Boonchu has been teaching me to be more patient and not chase so many birdies," Chawalit said after the third round. "And even though I know Boonchu will be chasing me tomorrow, I will not be too nervous. I'm feeling very confident."

In the final round, Chawalit — whether he remembered that advice or not — birdied three of the last four holes to score a five-stroke victory over Boonchu. "When most people play alongside Boonchu they get scared," Chawalit said. "He is a very intimidating opponent, but I felt comfortable playing with him today."

Boonchu saluted his young friend. "He still has a lot to learn," Boonchu said, "but I think this will be just the first of many wins for him." Korea's Park No-seok and American Brian Quinn led through the first two rounds, with Chawalit nipping at their heels. Then he bolted to a three-stroke lead in the third with a five-under-par 67. In the final round, Chawalit was two ahead of Boonchu with four holes to play, then he made his clinching move. He canned an 18-foot putt at the 18th for a birdie. Boonchu answered with a birdie at the 16th, then Chawalit clinched it with birdies at the last two holes. That wrapped up a total of 278 on scores of 71, 71, 67 and 69.

Volvo China Open—US$400,000

Winner: Edward Fryatt

Golfers talk a lot about confidence and where you find it. For Edward Fryatt — an Englishman who carries a British passport but has lived in the United States since age four — it came from a playoff victory over English star Lee Westwood in the Malaysian Open a month earlier. Still riding the crest in mid-April, Fryatt shot scores of 69, 65, 69 and 66 for a 269 total, 19 under par, for a two-stroke victory over Japan's Takeshi Ohyama in the Volvo China Open at Shanghai Sunisland International. "It's nice to be on a bit of a roll," Fryatt said. "Beating Westwood did a lot for my confidence."

The tournament opened with a six-man tie for the lead at 66, with Fryatt three strokes back. Fryatt jumped into a share of the halfway lead with a course-record 65. But it wouldn't be that easy. American Aaron Meeks, who was challenging along with his twin brother Eric, took the third-round lead with 67 wrapped up by a dazzling birdie. Meeks fired a three-wood second shot 227 yards across water to 20 feet at the 530-yard hole. Two putts later he was one up on Fryatt, who bogeyed the 17th, and South Africa's Nico van Rensburg, who lowered the course record by a stroke with 64.

Fryatt started the final round one stroke behind Aaron Meeks, but by the turn he was tied with Ohyama at 15 under par. Then Fryatt ran off four straight birdies from the 10th, but he bogeyed the 17th, and Meeks was then two behind with one hole to play. Meeks, trying to reach the 18th again, failed and bogeyed, and Ohyama birdied it to leapfrog into second place. Meeks finished third, and brother Eric tied for sixth.

Macau Open—US$200,000

Winner: Satoshi Oide

First it was Taimur Hussain, at the London Myanmar Open, becoming the first Pakistani to win on the Omega Tour, and then came Satoshi Oide, the first Japanese. Oide, after sharing the lead in the first round, shot a four-under-par 67 in the final round to win the Macau Open. He won by two strokes over Venezuela's Gilberto Morales and Fiji's Vijay Singh.

This almost wasn't the tournament Oide won but the one in which Nick Faldo finally tied for 13th. Faldo was in such dire straits with his putter that in the final round, he putted with his nine iron on six greens. He even made three birdies with it. "I played better and had more fun today," Faldo said. Still, with a closing 71, he had gone seven straight rounds without breaking par.

Oide (69-75-72-67–283), after joining a four-way tie for the lead in the first round, slipped back into the pack and trailed by four strokes going into the final round. "The important hole was definitely the 13th," Oide said. He had run off three straight birdies from No. 7, and at the par-five 13th, he chipped in from 94 yards for an eagle. Morales' chances died when he triple-bogeyed the 13th and bogeyed the next two holes, shooting 73. Singh matched Oide with a closing 67. "I didn't make any bogeys, and that was the key for me today," Singh said. But that was his only round under 72.

Guam Open—US$200,000

Winner: Jerry Smith

American Jerry Smith said his strategy in the final round was to stick to his own game and not even check the leaderboards. Good thing. He was going for his first victory in a four-round event, but he might have fallen asleep, his position was so comfortable. Smith, who had four top-10 finishes in 1997, claimed his first Omega Tour victory with ease, winning by six strokes over India's Arjun Atwal and South Africa's Chris Williams. Smith had scores of 69, 67, 66 and 70 for a 16-under-par total of 272 at the Leo Palace Resort.

"I'm not as young as some of the other players on this tour," said Smith, 34, "and I would dearly love to use this victory as a springboard to the Nike or PGA Tour." After trailing Japan's Katsumune Imai by three strokes in the first round, Smith took a share of a two-stroke lead in the second round, tying Taiwan's Lin Chien-bing, both with 67s for 136 totals. Lin then blew to a pair of 79s. Smith maintained his two-stroke margin through the third round with 66, holding off Williams, who shot a personal-best 64, a course record.

"With the way the scores are going this week, I won't be able to let up tomorrow," said Smith, whose third round included a three-birdie finish from the 16th hole, on putts of 20, 15 and three feet. The scoring cooled off in the final round, but Smith didn't. He carded five birdies and three bogeys for 70, the second-lowest round of the day. "When I saw I was five ahead, I was pretty confident of winning," Smith said, "although my wife Jennifer (his caddie) said she was the most nervous when we were standing on the 18th green."

Fila Open—US$150,000

Winner: Robert Huxtable

The Ghost of Myanmar seemed to be stalking America's Robert Huxtable again. The entire Omega Tour would remember that just seven months earlier, in the London Myanmar Open, Huxtable led going into the final round and blew to 83. Now, at the Fila Open at Tae Young Country Club in Seoul, South Korea, Huxtable was in a four-way tie for the lead going into the final round, and he started out with a scare. "Those first two bogeys made me a bit concerned after my debacle in Myanmar," Huxtable said. He pulled himself together, tied South Korea's Park Nam-sin, and won with a six-foot birdie putt on the second hole of a playoff. It was his first win on the Omega Tour.

Huxtable, playing Tae Young in rounds of 69, 70, 66 and 71 for a 276 total, 12 under par, moved into the lead in the third round, tied with Venezuelan Gilberto Morales and Koreans Choi Kyung-ju and Kim Wan-tae. The three failed to keep pace in the fourth round, Choi shooting 72, Morales 73, and Kim 75. Park, two behind at the turn, birdied the 12th, 13th and 14th holes. Huxtable was tied with him and had a 20-foot birdie putt at the 18th for the win. He missed. They went back to the 18th for the playoff, and Huxtable again missed a 20-footer for the win. But he wrapped it up with the six-footer at the second hole. "I've always said that when I get my first win in Asia," Huxtable said, "it will help me to win more tournaments."

Sabah Masters—US$150,000

Winner: Simon Yates

Simon Yates had some uncertain moments down the homestretch, but he held on long enough to join the parade of first-time winners on the Omega Tour. "I wasn't nervous at all today," Yates insisted. "I was annoyed more than anything else because I played so poorly." What brought on this discomfort was a pair of bogeys at the closing holes, but he had built enough of a cushion that he still could come away with a one-stroke victory in the Sabah Masters over South African Des Terblanche, the defending champion.

Yates, a Scot based in Thailand, started the final day leading Terblanche by one stroke. He rolled in a 25-foot putt at the 11th hole to go up by two, and when Terblanche bogeyed the 15th, he was three ahead with three holes to play. Then the trouble started. At the par-four 17th, Yates hit his second shot over the green and into a dry lateral hazard. "I had 163 yards to the pin," Yates said, "and hit a nine iron 185 yards. I guess I was just a bit pumped up." Then he bogeyed the 18th. Memories of the 1997 Volvo Masters of Malaysia began to rise, when he sank to a tie for fourth after leading in the final round. But when Terblanche missed a 30-foot birdie try at the 18th, Yates had his first win. He did it with a 10-under 278 total on scores of 67, 71, 67 and 73 at the Shan-Shui Club.

A strange episode set the stage. Australian Adrian Percey took the first-round lead with 66, but he was disqualified later for riding in a cart from the No. 5 green to No. 6 tee. That left Yates and Taiwan's Lu Chien-soon tied for the lead at 67. Terblanche took the second-round lead with 66, and Yates leapfrogged him in the third round with 67.

Volvo Masters of Malaysia—US$200,000

Winner: Chris Williams

If there was one man more surprised than Chris Williams, it was Zaw Moe. Williams, South Africa-based Englishman, was stunned at winning the Volvo Masters of Malaysia, his first victory in two years on the Omega Tour. "Never at one stage during the round did I think I could win," Williams said. Myanmar's Moe was equally stunned because he gave the tournament away. Moe had run off three 67s in the rain-plagued event and was leading Taiwan's Wang Ter-chang by six strokes, Australia's Adrian Percey by seven and Williams by nine. Then Moe exploded to 78 and Williams, boosted by a hole-in-one at the 14th, shot 69 to tie him and Percey, who shot 71. Percey was ousted from the playoff on the first extra hole, and Williams beat Moe on the fourth, holing a 20-foot birdie putt.

"It's been five years since my last victory, and I'm totally overwhelmed," Williams said. He had no real expectations in this tournament, though his scores were hardly something to be ashamed of — 71-68-71-69–279, nine under par. It wasn't strong enough until Moe started unraveling. Moe completed his third-round 67 in the morning and actually was leading by seven with a birdie on the first hole of the final round. Then he started to come apart. He went out in 39, and after a birdie at No. 10, he continued his slide to 78. A problem that troubled him in the first round hadn't been corrected after all. "I couldn't stop pushing my shots," Moe said.

Ericsson Singapore Open—US$500,000

Winner: Shaun Micheel

In one of the more interesting scrambles on the Omega Tour, a Korean shot his all-time low, a Taiwanese gambled and lost, a South African shook off the rust, and an unknown American broke through. It was Shaun Micheel, who made only two bogeys all week, winning the Ericsson Singapore Open by two strokes, but not before the others had their say.

Korea's Lee Ju-il took the first-round lead with his career low, a seven-under-par 65. He would crash to a 77-78 finish and tie for 68th in a field of 73. Taiwan's Lu Chien-soon took the halfway lead with 134, but temptation cost him a better fate. Finding himself within reach of the course record of 64, he went for the 18th green in two. But his three-wood second shot from 240 yards came down short in the water, and he took a bogey six. He tied for fourth, five strokes behind.

And the battle between Micheel and South Africa's Hendrik Buhrmann was on. "Before last week's event, I had barely picked up a club in over four months," said Buhrmann. "So I'm very pleased with the way I'm playing." In the third round, both birdied the first three holes on their way to sharing a three-stroke lead. In the fourth round, Micheel leaped ahead at the par-three No. 6, holing a 40-foot putt for a birdie to Buhrmann's bogey. "I relaxed a little after that and managed to get into a good rhythm just before the turn," Micheel said. That was a comfort. On scores of 67, 69, 67 and 69 for a 16-under-par 272 total, he was 15 under on the first nine and only one under on the second nine. He was five ahead at the turn after birdies at No. 7 and No. 9, and with a solid par coming in held off Buhrmann's three-birdie charge.

Kolon Sports Korean Open—US$300,000

Winner: Kim Dae-sub

Name a sensational young Korean golfer and it is almost certain to be Se Ri Pak, anywhere golf is played. Not this time. Try Kim Dae-sub. It might be up there with Se Ri's some day. All Kim did in the Kolon Sports Korean Open in Seoul was overcome a four-stroke deficit in the final round and race off with a five-stroke victory. Think of this: Kim was 16 years old, a schoolboy and an amateur.

"I didn't feel any pressure," Kim said, "because at the start of the day I didn't think that I was good enough to win against the professionals. I just concentrated on playing my own game and tried not to think about winning. I was hitting it well off the tee all day, and when I got it close, I managed to hole most of my birdie chances."

He made six birdies and an eagle, and only one bogey in a final-round 65 for a 10-under-par total of 278, beating fellow Korean Choi Sang-ho and American Fran Quinn. Kim, who shot 76, 70 and 67 in his first three rounds, got rolling in the fourth round with a birdie from eight feet at No. 2, then birdied No. 5 from two feet to go to two under par. He dropped a 16-footer at No. 7, then birdied No. 9 to get to seven under for a share of the lead.

Next in his remarkable performance, Kim took the lead outright at nine under with birdies at the 11th and 12th. He all but wrapped up the tournament when he chipped in from 40 yards for an eagle at the 15th. His future looked clear enough, but he had reservations. "I'd like to turn pro as soon as possible," he said, "but I think it's important for me to finish school and get my degree first."

Kuala Lumpur Open—US$200,000

Winner: Nico van Rensburg

It was a long time coming, and even then it seemed tantalizingly out of reach for South African Nico van Rensburg. He had to go five extra holes — the longest playoff in Omega Tour history — before beating American Jerry Smith to take the Kuala Lumpur Open at The Mines Resort in Malaysia in mid-October.

"I am so relieved — it's been three years since my last win," said van Rensburg, age 32. "I was very tired out there, but I kept thinking that I had to keep going and be patient." Van Rensburg last won in the 1995 Merlion Masters on the Omega Tour. He took this victory by sinking a six-foot birdie putt at the 18th, after they paired it on the first four playoff holes.

Smith was five under par and leading by two strokes with nine holes remaining. Van Rensburg broke from the pack with birdies on the 13th, 14th and 17th holes. He earned the tie with rounds of 70, 70, 69 and 69 for a 278 total, matching Smith's 69-73-66-70 scores, while third-round leader Chawalit Plaphol, the China Orient Masters champion, ballooned to 79 and tied for 12th place. In the playoff van Rensburg stayed alive with a sand save on the second trip to the 18th and got up and down on the third, then didn't waste his big chance on his fifth try.

FedEx PGA Championship—US$150,000

Winner: Chris Williams

It was a thrill England's Chris Williams could do without. Just two months earlier, he had won the Volvo Masters of Malaysia by coming from behind. This time, at the FedEx PGA Championship, he led by five strokes going into the final round, and had to survive a scary finish for a one-stroke victory.

"When you start dropping shots, it's almost impossible to stop the trend," said Williams. After shooting 70, 66 and 69 in the first three rounds, he held himself together for a closing par 72 at the Raffles Country Club in Singapore for an 11-under-par 277 total and a one-stroke victory over American Ted Purdy. "I was finding it so hard to control my adrenaline at the end there," Williams said. "I could barely feel the putter in my hands, and I was very relieved to have that three-shot lead going into the final hole."

Williams began that late-October Sunday leading by five over India's Jeev Milkha Singh, and by seven over Purdy. Then he rode to a wild finish. He birdied three straight holes from No. 3, then took his first bogey at No. 8. He bogeyed the 10th, then dropped a 20-foot birdie putt at the 11th. Then he three-putted the 14th for a bogey that reduced his lead to three. He birdied the 16th, then got up and down at the par-three 17th about the time Purdy had birdied the 18th up ahead to cut his lead to three. Williams needed it. At the 18th, he put his second shot into the water, took his penalty drop, and chipped to within 10 feet and sank the putt.

Ericsson Classic—US$200,000

Winner: Lu Wen-teh

It was a wire-to-wire victory for Taiwan's Lu Wen-teh, it just took a little longer than usual — two extra holes, in fact, and then with a stroke of good luck. Lu ended up deadlocked after 72 holes with Felix Casas of the Philippines and Carlos Espinosa of Mexico at eight-under-par 280 — six strokes ahead of the field — at Formosa First Golf Club.

On the first playoff hole, Casas' birdie chip shot lipped out, leaving all three alive. On the second playoff hole, the par-four 18th, Casas knocked himself out of the playoff with a wild tee shot into the water. Espinosa put his approach to 20 feet, but just missed on his birdie try. Lu's sand wedge approach from 90 yards was on its way into possible trouble, but it hit the flagstick and dropped to within six feet of the hole. "I hit a very lucky shot," Lu said. "It was downwind, and the only chance I had of stopping the ball was by hitting the flag. I didn't even hit the shot very well. It was a bit thin. But luck was on my side." He holed the putt for the birdie and the win.

Lu, who shot rounds of 66, 72, 72 and 70, led for the first three rounds, but he seemed doomed when he hit his tee shot into the water at the par-three 15th and double-bogeyed. Casas and Espinosa led Lu by one stroke with three holes to play. At the 16th, Lu birdied and tied Espinosa at seven under, but Casas also birdied and took the lead at eight under. Then at the 18th, Casas parred, and Lu and Espinosa birdied from about 20 feet to tie him and force the playoff.

Hero Honda Masters—US$200,000

Winner: Jyoti Randhawa

"At last I've got a victory on the Omega Tour," said India's Jyoti Randhawa, and with nearly the same breath, he credited the main reason: "I'd been hitting my irons close all week, but coming up short with too many of my putts. Today, my caddie told me to give it a good hit, and it definitely worked." And it worked in a hurry, giving him his first Omega Tour win, the Hero Honda Masters at Delhi Golf Club early in November.

Randhawa, age 26, who was four strokes off the lead in the first round, shot 69-67-73-66–275 and started the final round two strokes behind. He got busy immediately, dropping a four-foot birdie putt on No. 1. Then he pulled away from a pack of struggling leaders on the front nine. He birdied No. 2 from six feet to take the lead, and moved another stroke up with a birdie out of the sand at No. 8. At the same time, he got a big boost from India's Jeev Milkha Singh, who bogeyed Nos. 5, 7 and 9.

Liking the taste of the lead, he spiced it with a birdie from 20 feet at No. 10 to pull four strokes clear. A threat appeared briefly when Singh made a charge on the second nine. Randhawa kept his four-stroke edge with birdies at the 14th and 15th. He suffered his only bogey of the day when he missed a three-footer for a par at the 17th, but he got the stroke back at the 18th, holing out from 20 feet for a birdie. Singh locked up second place with birdies at the 13th and 14th, finishing two ahead of American Gerry Norquist.

Thailand Open—US$200,000

Winner: James Kingston

It was an old question in the Thailand Open — doesn't anybody here want to win this thing?

South Africa's James Kingston could have won in regulation, but he missed a three-foot putt on the final hole. India's Jeev Milkha Singh tied him with 66, six under par at Thana City Golf and Country Club at Bangkok. South African Craig Kamps missed a three-way playoff when he bogeyed the last hole. And to complicate matters, Kingston missed a four-foot putt on the first playoff hole, but won anyway when Singh was wide with a three-footer that would have tied him.

"When I missed from four feet in the playoff, I was all ready to go back to the tee again," said Kingston, who shot 69-64-69-70–272, 18 under par. "I thought there was no way Jeev was going to miss his putt."

Kingston took a one-stroke lead going into the final hole of regulation when he birdied the par-three 17th with a 12-foot putt, but fell back into a tie with Singh by three-putting the 18th for a bogey. Kingston had led by one stroke starting the final round, and stretched his lead to three with a first-nine 34. Singh, in the group ahead, cut into his lead with birdies at the 10th and 11th, and caught him with a birdie at the par-five 16th. Kingston went up by a stroke with a 12-foot birdie at the 17th, then gave it away with the three-putt at the 18th, and the playoff was on. Singh settled for his third top-three finish in three weeks.

Perrier Hong Kong Open—US$300,000

Winner: Kang Wook-soon

Korea's Kang Wook-soon had just spent two months off with a back injury, so he wasn't wasting any time when he turned out for the Perrier Hong Kong Open late in November. He posted a card of 69-70-66-67–272, 12 under par, for a two-stroke win over Edward Fryatt, and he attributed it all to a sense of comfort at Hong Kong Golf Club "It's like a Korean course," Kang said. "I think that's why I always seem to play well here." He was runner-up twice there, in the 1997 Hong Kong Open and the 1996 Alfred Dunhill Masters.

His strategy was simple for the final round: Get off to a fast start and keep his nose ahead. "I knew at the start of the day there were a lot of people at the top of the leaderboard close together," he said, "so I had to play aggressively." He started the round two strokes behind third-round leader Hsieh Chin-sheng of Taiwan, who slipped steadily away and tied for sixth with a 73. Kang opened with a birdie at No. 1, after firing his approach to two feet. He logged four more birdies, and only a bogey at the 18th marred his round. Fryatt, who began the day three strokes off the lead, mounted a serious challenge, racking up six birdies, but a double bogey at the 16th did him in.

Omega PGA Championship—US$500,000

Winner: Kang Wook-soon

He said there was pressure, and he could feel it, but it looked like a walk in the park for Korea's Kang Wook-soon as he made history in the Omega PGA Championship. Kang, who won the Perrier Hong Kong Open the previous week, took the Omega PGA by three strokes over Taiwan's Hsieh Chin-sheng, shooting rounds of 66, 65, 66 and 66, for a 17-under-par total of 263 at Clearwater Bay Golf and Country Club. Kang thus became the first player to win back-to-back events on the Omega Tour, and the first to lead the Omega money list twice (the first was in 1996). And he was only the second player to win four times on the Omega Tour, joining Thailand's Boonchu Ruangkit.

Kang started the final round with a four-stroke lead and a case of nerves. "When I was on the practice green before my round, I suddenly felt the pressure," Kang said. "It was the first time I felt nervous all week, and I found it very difficult to settle down on the course." It didn't show. His lead never sank beneath three, and he kept his pursuers frustrated at every turn. He shot 33 on the front and to keep his lead at three over China's Zhang Lian-wei and four over Hsieh. If they got a glimmer of hope, he snuffed it out with birdies at the 17th and 18th. Zhang double-bogeyed the 18th and cost himself a share of third place with American Eric Rustand, who tied the course record with a blistering eight-under 62.

Volvo Asian Match Play—US$265,000

Winner: Gerry Norquist

Gerry Norquist surprised even himself in the season-ending Volvo Asian Match Play Championship. "At no time this week did I expect to win," he said. "When I came here, I thought I would have no chance." He expected Mission Hills Golf Club, at Shenzhen, China, to be a big-hitters' course, which would put him at a disadvantage. Then he found himself only the third player to win four tournaments on the Omega Tour with a 2-and-1 win over fellow American Eric Meeks in the 36-hole final. The victory was his only one of the year, but it capped off a strong season in which he didn't miss a cut in 25 starts.

Norquist was never down in the final, and went up by three when he birdied the first and second holes in the afternoon. He also birdied No. 3, for three in a row, but Meeks matched him with a birdie of his own. "The only time I thought I could win was on the 71st hole," Norquist said, and little wonder. He had to survive playoffs in the first, second and quarter-final rounds.

In the final of the Hugo Boss Foursomes, Canada's Jim Rutledge and Thailand's Chawalit Plaphol teamed to beat England's Edward Fryatt and American Jerry Smith on the 22nd hole.

13. Australasian Tour

No one has ever questioned the fact that Australia and New Zealand have produced many top-flight golfers throughout the years, with Greg Norman and Steve Elkington most recently topping the list. Players such as Craig Parry and Greg Turner were not as well known outside the region, but their roles in the International victory over the United States in the Presidents Cup in December at Royal Melbourne may have improved their reputations around the world.

Certainly, the Presidents Cup added a new element of respectability to the Australasian Tour. After the Presidents Cup, people in the United States looked back and took greater notice of players such as Bradley King, who won the Victorian Open in early January, and Bradley Hughes, winner of the Ericsson Australian Masters. Neither King nor Hughes were members of the 1998 Presidents Cup team, but with players like Parry and Turner winning on the Australasian Tour in 1997 and becoming Presidents Cup heroes in 1998, observers may decide that it's never too early to take a look Down Under.

For his first victory in nine seasons, King saw a seven-stroke lead in the Victorian Open diminish to a single shot when Sweden's Daniel Chopra birdied seven out of 14 holes in the final round. King hung on to win by an impressive five-stroke margin.

The next week Tiger Woods battled from eight strokes back at the beginning of the final round to tie Ernie Els at the end of regulation play of the Johnnie Walker Classic. Woods birdied the second playoff hole to win the title in Phuket, Thailand. He pumped his fist in victory, and later said, "My reaction said it all. I've never done anything like this before as a pro, coming from so far behind."

Thomas Bjorn added his name to the winners at the Heineken Classic, despite a final-round 74 at The Vines Resort in Perth. After trailing Ian Woosnam by one stroke going into the final round, Bjorn and the rest fought brutal winds that sent scores skyrocketing. Woosnam fired a closing 76 to finish second, but it was Bjorn, who had not received an invitation for the Masters, who gained the most. "By winning today, perhaps I sent my own message to Augusta National," he said.

The next week, Norman finally won the tournament that bears his name when he posted the lowest 72-hole score in the history of the Greg Norman Holden International at the Australian Golf Club in Sydney. Norman's 272 total bested Jose Maria Olazabal by two strokes.

Afterward, the PGA European Tour and U.S. PGA Tour players returned home, but the quality of the golf continued to thrive in Australia.

In the Ericsson Australian Masters, Mathew Goggin equalled Norman's tournament-record 27 under par only to lose to Hughes by five strokes. In addition to shattering the tournament record, Hughes established a course record of 63 (beating Bernhard Langer's record by one stroke) at the Huntingdale Golf Club in Melbourne. "I might have only hit one bad shot," Hughes said.

Peter O'Malley captured his first victory in his home country in the Canon

Challenge at Terrey Hills Golf and Country Club in Sydney by shooting a tournament-record 271 and running away from the field. Then Goggin captured his first win at the Australasian Tour Championship by birdieing the first playoff hole at the Royal Canberra Golf Club to defeat King.

When play resumed in October Stuart Bouvier won the Ford Open Championship, and in November David Howell picked up the MasterCard PGA Championship title. Stephen Leaney added his name to the winner's list when he took the Australasian Players Championship title, and Greg Chalmers edged out Stuart Appleby in the Holden Australian Open.

That might not have been Appleby's week, but on the last week of the year, when he played before his and late wife Renay's family, Appleby thrilled the crowds with a win in the Schweppes Coolum Classic, his first since losing Renay in an automobile accident in July.

Victorian Open—A$200,000

Winner: Bradley King

Despite winning the 1988 Nedlands Masters, 1989 Joondalup PGA Classic and 1990 Audi Open on the European Challenge Tour, Bradley King almost gave up competitive golf for fear of going broke. "I was very close to quitting, because I had no more money to play," King said. That was before the Victorian Open. After a record-setting, 16-under-par 272 total, and an even-par 72 final round that kept at bay a charging Daniel Chopra (who shot 67 to tie for second at 277), King walked away with a victory and a check for $37,894, his biggest pay day as a professional.

"You just don't know how good this win is, and how badly I needed it," King said. "It was bloody hard out there and close to nerve-racking. It's a tough feeling but it's a good feeling too when you can come through it. This gives me confidence to go out and play."

That confidence came in no small measure because of the way the tournament finished. King led by seven strokes after firing rounds of 68, 65 and 67. That was no guarantee. In 1996, he led by four going into the final round of the Canon Challenge in Sydney. The lead evaporated and King finished tied for third.

Destiny seemed ready to repeat itself in Melbourne, not because of any swing problems King was having, but because Chopra birdied seven out of the first 14 holes, whittling King's lead down to one with four holes to play. King kept his composure, while Chopra bogeyed the 16th and 18th holes to drop back into a share of second place with Terry Price, who eagled the last hole, and Greg Chalmers.

Johnnie Walker Classic—£800,000

Winner: Tiger Woods

Facing an eight-shot deficit to defending champion Ernie Els with 18 holes to play, Tiger Woods mounted the most impressive charge of his professional career, firing a seven-under-par 65 to close the gap and tie Els at 279 in the Johnnie Walker Classic in Phuket, Thailand. Then in the playoff, Woods sank a 14-foot birdie putt on the second hole to win.

An enormously popular player in his mother's homeland, Woods prompted a stampede of over 100 fans onto the 18th green. "My reaction said it all," Woods said of the moment. "Pure adrenaline and excitement. I thought I needed to shoot 62. I figured 11 under would do it."

As it turned out, nine under par was enough. Peter O'Malley, who began the final round three strokes back, reached 11 under and assumed the lead on the final nine, but he made a double bogey on the 17th and bogey on the 18th to fall to seven under, tied for fourth place, two behind Woods and Els.

Els also had a chance to put away the victory on the final nine, but a three-putt bogey at the 16th and another bogey at the 17th forced Els to make birdie at No. 18 in order to catch Woods and force the playoff.

Woods, who had to wait and watch 10 groups before knowing his fate, channeled his energies on the tee when the playoff finally commenced. He outdrove Els by 40 yards on the first playoff hole, but both men settled for par. On the second hole, Els missed the green to the left, but chipped up for a tap-in par. It was too little, too late, as Woods drained his birdie putt.

"It's amazing what Tiger did," Els said. "But I never should have found myself in a playoff."

Heineken Classic—A$1,400,000

Winner: Thomas Bjorn

While he never slipped more than four shots off the pace, and for most of the 72 holes of the Heineken Classic he hovered one or two shots back, no one expected Thomas Bjorn to outduel the likes of Ian Woosnam and Jose Maria Olazabal to win, but that's exactly what happened. After opening rounds of 70 and 68 left him three back of Woosnam and Bernhard Langer, Bjorn shot another 68 on Saturday that put him one off Woosnam's mark and one ahead of Olazabal going into the final round.

Afternoon scores skyrocketed as the "Freemantle Doctor," a gale force wind that whips inland every afternoon off the Indian Ocean at The Vines Resort in Perth, Australia, toughened the course by at least four shots. For Bjorn, it was a six-shot wind. His Sunday score of 74 was his worst of the week, but his 280 total bested Woosnam by one. The Wee Welshman could do no better than a struggling 76, which left him at seven under par for the tournament, one ahead of Olazabal, Ernie Els, Peter Baker and Padraig Harrington, but one behind a jubilant Bjorn.

In his awards speech, Bjorn had nothing but praise for Woosnam. The two had played together at the 1997 Ryder Cup. According to Bjorn it was that experience that led him to his victory. "Ian is more responsible than anyone for me being in this position today," he said.

Greg Norman Holden International—A$1,000,000

Winner: Greg Norman

It's always nice to win your own golf tournament, but in 11 previous attempts, Greg Norman had been a gracious host of the Holden International tournament that bears his name, but he had always shaken someone else's hand at the awards ceremony. This year was different. After falling behind Jose Maria Olazabal by seven strokes at the halfway mark, Norman fired a course-record 64 at the 7,087-yard Australian Golf Club in Sydney. Norman still trailed Olazabal by one going into the final round. That deficit lasted through 11 holes, but when Norman's birdie putt at the 12th found the cup, the tide turned in his favor.

Olazabal made one last effort to catch Norman on the par-five 18th by hitting a 231-yard three wood out of the rough and onto the green, but Norman followed by hitting a three iron from the same distance onto the putting surface. When both players two-putted for birdies, Norman had a final-round 67 and a two-stroke victory with a 272 total, 16 under par.

"I loved playing with Greg," Olazabal said. "I enjoyed being in that situation with a chance to win knowing that the opponent I was playing with is a great player."

For Norman, the victory couldn't have been sweeter, as he said, "The satisfaction I really reaped out of this win is the fact that I flicked the switch on concentration and focus, and I wasn't going to let anything get in. It's been a hard week, and I am very pleased and very relieved to have won."

Ericsson Australian Masters—A$750,000

Winner: Bradley Hughes

After celebrating his 31st birthday the Tuesday of tournament week, Bradley Hughes marched around the Huntington Golf Club in Melbourne in record-setting fashion, winning the Ericsson Australian Masters by five strokes. His one eagle and eight-birdie, 10-under-par 63 in the first round set a course record and opened a lead that no one would catch. Hughes followed with scores of 72 and 66, and by the time his final putt fell for 67 on Sunday, Hughes had shot 24-under-par 268 and broken Greg Norman's Australian Masters scoring record by four strokes. He won by five over Mathew Goggin.

"Everything came together this week, right from the first day when I only missed one green in regulation, and that was only by six inches," Hughes said. "Obviously, this performance shows that I can play well and it's now a matter of trying to do it every week. Norman does. He's atop the leaderboard all the time. That's what you aim for. You don't want to be a flash in the pan with one win here and one win there. You want to be in contention all the time, because the more you are up there, the more you are going to win."

Goggin, a former Australian Amateur champion from Tasmania, came through with a closing round of 71 to finish alone in second at 273. Frank Nobilo finished with a six-under-par 67 to tie for third at 275 with Canadian Rick Gibson. Nobilo's performance was especially gritty because of a near-altercation he had with a small band of intoxicated spectators on the third hole. Fortunately, the anxious moments quickly passed, and he proceeded to play great golf.

Stuart Appleby and Mark O'Meara both closed with 71s, but Appleby edged O'Meara out of fifth place by one, while Robert Allenby, Andrew Coltart and Mark Brooks finished tied for seventh at 280.

Hughes collected $142,102.50 in prize money, and picked up another $2,500 from a $100 bet he placed on himself before the opening round. The odds on him winning were 25-1.

Canon Challenge—A$500,000

Winner: Peter O'Malley

Having never won in his own country, Peter O'Malley might have shown some sign of nerves when he teed off at Terry Hills Golf and Country Club in Sydney for the Canon Challenge. But O'Malley had long ago decided that the question of when he would win at home would be answered in due time. All he could do was play the best golf he could, and winning would take care of itself. Little could O'Malley have known that four days later he would hold a course record after an opening round of 63, and be nine strokes ahead of his nearest competitor when Sunday's final putt fell.

"It's hard to lead any tournament from beginning to end, but I did not feel a lot of pressure out there," said O'Malley, who shot 17-under-par 271. "I knew I had it won if I didn't do anything silly."

On the first nine Sunday, O'Malley hit his tee shot toward the pin on the 160-yard par-three fourth. The pin was only two yards short of a slope but, somehow, O'Malley stopped his ball six feet from the hole, while his competitors, Paul Gow and American Todd Demsey, both watched their shots trickle down the slope and off the green. Gow made a bogey. Demsey made a double bogey, and when O'Malley's birdie putt fell, the victory trot began.

"I tried to put pressure on him in the first couple of holes, but I couldn't do it," said Gow, who finished second. "He is a world-class performer. That's why he won."

"It's been a long time coming," said O'Malley, whose other rounds were 73, 64 and 71. "It is nice to win again. I haven't done that since the end of 1995 (in the Benson and Hedges International). As for it being a weight off my shoulders, everyone else has made a bigger deal about me not winning at home than I have, but I guess I don't have to think about that now. It is nice to finally win at home."

Australasian Tour Championship—A$500,000

Winner: Mathew Goggin

Through the first nine holes of the final round at the Australasian Tour Championship, it looked as though Bradley King, who rescued his career with a victory in the Victorian Open, would make it two victories in little more than two months. After starting tied for the lead with Mathew Goggin, King birdied three of the first four holes to take a four-stroke lead into the turn. Then King took 10 putts on three holes and handed the title to Goggin.

"The last 12 greens were like landing strips," King said. His four-putt at the 10th sent shudders through the crowd and opened the door for Goggin. "I thought I hit a pretty good first putt, but a gust of wind slowed it and stopped it four feet short of the hole. The wind also pushed the second putt off line, but I don't know what happened after that. I was pretty mad."

King recovered with a birdie at the 11th, and he continued to hold a two-stroke lead as he and Goggin approached the 18th green. Then King's putter abandoned him again, and he three-putted the 18th while Goggin made a birdie. The two finished regulation play with 73s and 278 totals.

On Royal Canberra Golf Club's 562-yard 18th hole in the playoff, King reached the green in three shots, but left himself 30 feet for birdie. Goggin hit his second shot beyond the green, then chipped to within six feet. After King three-putted again for bogey, Goggin made his birdie putt and walked away with the victory.

"I'm pretty amazed at the way things turned out," he said. "I did not play well, but I hung in there. Brad was playing steadily and not making mistakes until that four-putt. That let everyone back in the tournament. I just got over the last hurtle. My initial reaction is shock, but I now have a feeling of relief. I have been playing well for some time. If you put yourself up there week in and week out, you are going to win. Today was my day."

Ford Open Championship—A$500,000

Winner: Stuart Bouvier

Although it took longer than he had anticipated, and he had to come from three strokes behind with one round to play, former Australian Amateur champion Stuart Bouvier finally broke through with his first professional victory at the Ford Open Championship at the Kooyonga Golf Club in Adelaide. The 29-year-old Bouvier held on to shoot a final-round 70 for a 282 total to edge out Craig Parry and Stephen Allan by two strokes.

Parry, who was favored because of his experience, held the lead through 14 holes, but made a double bogey at the 15th. Bouvier made a birdie at the 16th, turning the tide in his favor. Parry's double bogey was unfortunate, not only because of its crucial timing, but because of how it happened. He missed the green on the 165-yard par-three, but his ball wound up in a good lie in a bunker. Just as he was starting his downswing, a spectator took a photograph and the flash caused Parry to flinch.

"It caught me right on the downswing, and it was very disappointing," said Parry, who finished with 75. "It makes me angry, but there is no point in complaining. The main thing was that I did not hole enough putts. It all boils down to that."

Bouvier, known for his short game, did hole the putts he needed, even though his iron play continued to be inconsistent. He missed seven consecutive greens in the final round, but still managed to hold on for the victory. "If my technique had been sound when I was young, I would not have gone through all this trouble," Bouvier said. "I did not want to win this way, but a win is a win. It has done a lot for my confidence. All I want now is some consistency in my game. It would not worry me if I never had another win if I could find that consistency."

MasterCard PGA Championship—A$600,000

Winner: David Howell

Holding a seven-stroke lead over Stephen Ames and Terry Price with three holes to play in the MasterCard PGA Championship, England's David Howell could not have lost the tournament unless his heart had stopped beating. So it was with some trepidation that the gallery watched as Howell's caddie placed his hand on Howell's chest and began timing his heart rate while they were standing on the 16th tee.

"I have a condition where my heart races and he was just checking it," Howell said. "It does not seem to have anything to do with excitement. It doesn't worry me and it usually stops when I bend down to mark my ball on the green. I'll have it checked again when I get home, and I think they plan to put a heartbeat monitor on me."

Howell took the lead with an opening-round 69, then extended it with 66 on Friday and an even-par 72 in gale-force winds on Saturday. Even though Price birdied the par-five fifth to get to within five strokes, that was as close to Howell as anyone would get. With nine holes to play, the lead was seven, and it remained there through the end. As he stood over a short par putt on the 18th to shoot 68 and 13-under-par 275, Howell said to himself, "Well, if I miss it, I have another three or four or five putts to get down."

Ames and Price held on to finish tied for second at 282.

"I am over the moon at winning my first professional tournament," the 23-year-old Howell said. "It was great to be able to move forward and increase the lead. All through the back nine I was in control. I was confident of carrying it off although there was always the nagging doubt at the back of my mind that someone might make four birdies in a row. But no one made a move, and that made it much easier for me."

Australasian Players Championship—A$800,000

Winner: Stephen Leaney

When former U.S. Open champion Corey Pavin took a three-shot lead into the final six holes of the Australasian Players Championship, everyone thought that victory was easily in the American's grasp.

Then 29-year-old West Australian Stephen Leaney started making putts. He made putts from 10, three, 15, 12, 25, 20 and 40 feet, one-putting seven consecutive greens en route to shooting a second-nine 32. His birdies at the 11th, 13th, 14th and 16th holes, followed by a four-iron shot to within eagle range on the par-five 17th gave Leaney a 68 for a 17-under-par 275 total, good enough to catch Pavin and force a playoff. Leaney's final putt came on the first playoff hole when he drilled an eight-foot birdie putt to seal the victory and collect the A$144,000 first-place check.

"Stephen just made everything," said Pavin, who shot 69. "I can't think of a putt he missed today. His back was to the wall coming down the stretch and he performed admirably."

Peter O'Malley, David McKenzie and Richard Backwell finished tied for third at 279, 13 under par, four short of Leaney and Pavin.

"I wish I had won today," said Pavin, whose last victory came in the 1996

Colonial Invitational. "But it was an acceptable way not to win. If you go out and throw it away, then you've got a reason to be very upset. I'm not upset. I'm certainly disappointed, but my hat's off to Stephen. He beat me, and that's the best I've played in a long time."

Holden Australian Open—A$1,000,000

Winner: Greg Chalmers

With Stuart Appleby, who lost his wife in an automobile accident following the British Open, leading the Holden Australian Open at Royal Adelaide with one round to play, almost everyone was pulling for Appleby. When Greg Chalmers fired a final-round 70 to defeat Appleby, even Chalmers found the victory bittersweet. He said he felt like a "villain" for winning, and, in a tearful acceptance speech, Chalmers said to Appleby, "The whole country is behind you."

Appleby said Chalmers didn't need to worry. "I would try to beat him too," he said. "That's our job. I felt the support of the crowd. They were nice, very generous. I enjoyed being in contention again today, but I always do. I'm striking the ball pretty solidly and I'm putting well."

Appleby missed a 15-footer on the last hole which would have forced a playoff with Chalmers, but it wasn't that close for most of the day. Chalmers went ahead early and remained four strokes in the lead throughout most of the round. He bogeyed the 15th and 18th to give Appleby and Peter Senior a chance. Chalmers finished with an even-par 288 total, one ahead of Appleby (72) and Senior (70).

"I played with Chalmers for the past two days, and he set up the victory on Saturday," Senior said. "He shot three under on the back nine in a really strong wind. That gave him the momentum to come out with his sights set a little higher today than they normally would have been. He made a good start and you could see the confidence oozing out of him. He made a couple of mistakes towards the end, but held on and did what he had to. All credit to him."

New Zealand Open—NZ500,000

Winner: Matthew Lane

Matthew Lane had to borrow money from his father to fly from Los Angeles to his home for the New Zealand Open. Lane, who had lost his American PGA Tour card, was considering giving up the game. Then in a dramatic final round, Lane fired an eight-under-par 64 to win the tournament, earn a place on the Australasian Tour, and make enough to pay back his father.

"I was wondering whether I should get a job or something for a few months, but this gives me a chance to come back here," a tearful Lane said after the victory.

Trailing by three strokes going into the final round, Lane made five early birdies, then picked up an eagle before the turn. When he birdied the 18th with a 21-foot putt for a 279 total, nine under par, the victory was complete. Rodney Pampling, who closed with 69, finished second, three strokes behind. "Hopefully this will be a stepping stone for him," Pampling said.

Lane couldn't have been more thankful that his father had paid for him to come. "I told him that if I made the cut I would pay him back, and he said not to worry," Lane said. "He just wanted to see me play well this week."

Schweppes Coolum Classic—A$300,000

Winner: Stuart Appleby

As if a four-stroke victory in the Schweppes Coolum Classic on the heels of the International team's Presidents Cup triumph wasn't enough, Stuart Appleby sweetened the victory by equaling the tournament record with a 17-under-par 271 total. It was the 27-year-old native Australian's first professional victory on his home soil, and Appleby credited his late wife, Renay, with inspiring him. "I was a little worried it was going to be an emotional week for me," said Appleby, who had members of his and Renay's family in his gallery. "Renay just loved this place, and it was her dream holiday at the end of the year."

Renay certainly would have loved her husband's outstanding performance over the 6,660-yard Hyatt Coolum Resort in Queensland. After opening with rounds of 69 and 70 to trail Craig Spence by seven strokes at the halfway mark, Appleby surged ahead by firing a course-record 63. His final-round 69 widened the lead to four strokes when Spence closed with a 72. Tony Carolan moved into a tie for third at 278 with defending champion Craig Parry after shooting a final-round 65.

Appleby, who finished second in the Holden Australian Open two weeks earlier, said his confidence was at an all-time high and, responding to a suggestion that he stood a good chance to win a major title in 1999, said, "I believe I can. I had my first top 10 in the U.S. Open this past year."

14. African Tours

Nick Price's putting woes turned around just at the right time for those who hoped the Zimbabwean would successfully defend his homeland title and his 1997 victory in the Nedbank Million Dollar Challenge. They weren't disappointed. Price carried the tide into late November when he captured the Zimbabwe Open and, one week later, Price out-dueled Tiger Woods in a playoff for the million dollars. It was Price's fourth victory of the year — three in Africa and the FedEx St. Jude Classic on the U.S. PGA Tour.

It also was Price's second win of the year in Sun City at the Gary Player Golf Club. In late February, Price successfully defended his Dimension Data Pro-Am title at the same club. "I play well on the Gary Player course," Price said. He also played well in the Presidents Cup in Australia, defeating David Duval 2 and 1 in the singles matches to clinch the title for the International team.

Price wasn't the only homegrown story on the Southern African Tour in 1998. Ernie Els, who later won the Bay Hill Invitational, ignited the home-country crowd with his early season win at the South African Open, while players like Sammy Daniels, Ashley Roestoff and Justin Hobday made names for themselves with multiple victories in the Vodacom Series.

The season opened in dramatic fashion, with Brazilian-born Zimbabwean Adilson da Silva capturing the Nashua Wild Coast Sun Challenge by shooting a final-round 66. Still, it looked as though third-round leader, South Africa's Clinton Whitelaw, would wrap up a wire-to-wire victory. With two double bogeys in the final three holes, Whitelaw, the Moroccan Open champion, handed da Silva the victory, prompting the winner to say, "It just goes to show that even a blind rabbit can find the hole sometimes."

No one handed over the South African Open, however. Els simply won it. After running neck-and-neck with David Frost for much of the first three rounds, Els turned his play up on the second nine of the final round. His three-birdie, one-bogey 34 for a 15-under-par 273 total gave Els his third South African Open title.

Els almost made it two in a row, but as if the Southern African Tour had not exceeded its drama quotient the first two weeks of the year, the third event, the Alfred Dunhill South African PGA Championship, saw Zimbabwe's Tony Johnstone, winless in four years and contemplating other employment, shoot a final-round 72 to hang onto a two-stroke victory over Els. Afterward Johnstone said, "This is what I live for. I had almost forgotten that feeling, and the day someone tells me that I can't have that feeling anymore, then I'll pack it in."

There were plenty of others who got that feeling during 1998, including a few who experienced it for the first time. Phalaborwa's Brenden Pappas captured his first professional win after five seasons at the Vodacom Series: Gauteng, played at the Royal Johannesburg Golf Club. Gary Matthews, a 24-year-old rookie who played golf in America at the University of Arizona, captured his first win at the Vodacom Series: Free State, while 27-year-old Keith Horne also earned his first professional victory by holding a wire-to-wire lead in the Vodacom Series: Kwazulu-Natal. Then in July at the Vodacom

Series: Mpumalanga at the White River Country Club, the tour welcomed another first-time winner when Callie Swart sank a six-foot birdie putt on the last hole for the victory. With beers in both hands afterward, Swart said, "Man, I'm not used to this."

Others on the tour were used to it, including Andrew McLardy, who picked up a win at the Kalahari Classic, and Mark McNulty who won the Vodacom Players Championship. For the 44-year-old McNulty, a native of Zimbabwe, the victory was particularly sweet. Not only was it the second time he had won the championship, it vaulted McNulty to the top of the money list for a record seventh time.

Spain's Alfred Dunhill Cup hero Santiago Luna burst through with a dramatic victory in the Hassan II Trophy in Morocco, while players like Wayne Bradley and Bobby Lincoln also picked up wins at the Bearing Man Highveld Classic and the Platinum Classic respectively. Marc Cayeux won the Zambia Open, but by year's end, the story, once again, was Price. His dramatic and successful defense of back-to-back titles proved that in 1998, he was a cut above the rest.

Nashua Wild Coast Sun Challenge—R500,000

Winner: Adilson da Silva

Port Edward's Wild Coast Country Club certainly seemed appropriately named on the first day of February as the South African Tour's first event ended in a wild and unexpectedly dramatic fashion. After leading from the first hole on Thursday through the 15th hole on Sunday, it seemed as though South African Clinton Whitelaw had the Nashua Wild Coast Sun Challenge sewn up. Even after Brazilian Adilson da Silva birdied the final hole to shoot 66 and finish at six-under-par 274, one behind Whitelaw, few took notice. Whitelaw had been the model of consistency throughout the week, following his opening-round 65 with two rounds of 69 and he was even par through 15 holes in his final round.

Then, on the par-five 16th, mere moments after da Silva's birdie at the 18th, Whitelaw — a former South African Open winner and the reigning Moroccan Open champion — chunked his third shot into the water that guards the front of the green. A double bogey ensued, and suddenly da Silva had taken the lead while watching a television monitor in the clubhouse. Whitelaw's troubles continued on the 18th where, needing birdie to tie da Silva and force a playoff, Whitelaw took another double bogey and dropped into a tie for sixth place.

The last challenge to da Silva came from American Scott Dunlap who, after a tournament-low score of 63 on Saturday, needed a birdie at the last hole to force a playoff. Instead, Dunlap made bogey and fell into a tie for second place at four under par with Chris Davison, Hennie Walters and Marco Gortana.

"After I made birdie at the 12th I said to my caddie, 'We're in with a chance,'" da Silva recalled. "Walking up the 17th I told him not to tell me the leaderboard because I didn't want to know at that stage. After every birdie I just kept telling myself, 'Just one more birdie.'"

His last birdie proved to be just enough, and afterward, da Silva felt fortunate to come away with the victory. "It's just great," he said. "It goes to show that even a blind rabbit can find the hole sometimes."

South African Open—R3,710,855

Winner: Ernie Els

After losing in a playoff to Tiger Woods at the Johnnie Walker Classic, Ernie Els felt his putting was the weakest part of his game. Two weeks later at the South African Open, an event Els had won twice before, there was a new putter and a new confidence in the bag of the defending U.S. Open champion. "The putter worked well this week," Els said after an 18-under-par performance for a 273 total that was three strokes better than second-place finisher David Frost. "It's a nice feeling to make some putts under pressure. I made some really good putts, especially in the final round."

The Durban Country Club had been toughened significantly, with fairways narrowed and rough grown to U.S. Open length. Still, Els managed eight birdies en route to an opening-round 64. After an even-par second round that left him two strokes behind Frost, Els put together a 68 and 69 weekend, which no one in the field could match. Finishing with consecutive 71s, Frost had his best tournament finish in over a year.

Afterward, Els spoke with great emotion about the importance of winning his third South African Open. "It's very important to me," he said. "When you look at the trophy, there are so many great names on it." Els mentioned Gary Player, who won the event 13 times, and Bobby Locke, who won it nine times, then he added, "This event is really high on my list."

Alfred Dunhill South African PGA—R3,327,705

Winner: Tony Johnstone

No one expected Tony Johnstone to outgun Ernie Els in South Africa, not even Johnstone. "I've seriously considered different types of work," Johnstone said of his earlier putting woes. Now those considerations are a distant memory, and after four winless seasons, the Alfred Dunhill South African PGA trophy is on his mantle. "It's the best golf I've played in years," Johnstone said. "I'm hoping now that I'm back in business."

Johnstone shot rounds of 68, 64, 67 and 72 for a 271 total, 17 under par at Houghton Golf Club in Johannesburg, to win by two strokes over Els, whose scores were 69, 69, 66 and 69.

Johnstone's putter was certainly back in business during the final round. Els, coming off a win at the South African Open, made a lengthy birdie putt on No. 14 to tie Johnstone for the lead, but a bogey at No. 15 by Els put Johnstone back on top. Then Els birdied the 16th and regained a share of the lead, but Johnstone quickly took it away with a six-foot birdie putt on No. 17. When both players hit their approach shots at the 18th into the greenside bunker, it became a battle of short games, a battle that clearly favored Els.

"Everything in this game revolves around the putter," Johnstone said. "I tried a lot of them. The broomhandle putter, the left-handed putter ... You name it, I tried it, and nothing seemed to work."

Fortunately for Johnstone, his putting stroke was not tested at the 18th. His sand shot stopped 18 inches from the hole, and the tap-in par clinched his victory by one stroke.

Dimension Data Pro-Am—R2,000,000

Winner: Nick Price

When Nick Price stood on the 18th green at the Gary Player Country Club in Sun City and said, "I seem to manage my game really well over this course," it seemed an understatement of epic proportions. Price won the Nedbank Million Dollar Challenge there in 1993 and 1997, and this would be his second consecutive victory in the Dimension Data Pro-Am. He retained the title by shooting a 12-under-par 276 total to beat Mark McNulty by five strokes.

"Obviously, I'm very happy," Price said after posting a closing 72. His earlier scores were 69, 67 and 68. "The golf course was playing very difficult, and the rough was brutal. If you missed the fairway, you had to accept bogey. This week is easily the longest I've ever seen the Gary Player course play. I was out there playing defensively. Mark was being aggressive, and he came unstuck with some loose irons, but to be fair, it was a hard day to put pressure on. He needed a 67 out there today to win, and on this course that was a tall order."

McNulty did manage to pull within three strokes of Price with a birdie at the par-five second, but that was as close as he could come. A 73 to go along with his earlier rounds of 73, 66 and 69 left McNulty alone in second place, one stroke ahead of South African Tjaart van der Walt, who shared the first-round lead with Price.

"I think both Mark and I would have liked to have played a little better (on Sunday)," Price said. "When you're putting for par, it's not exactly exciting for the gallery. I think I did what I had to do, and that was to play conservatively and keep an eye on Mark. It's important for me to get this win under my belt early in the year. I've been getting better every week, and hopefully this will be a good year for me."

Stenham Royal Swazi Sun Open—R500,000

Winner: Paul Friedlander

Usually when you start the final round one stroke off the lead, birdie the first four holes, then pick up two more birdies and an eagle, your chances of winning are pretty good. That's exactly what Paul Friedlander thought when he carded a five-under-par 67 in the Stenham Royal Swazi Sun Open. Friedlander started one back of American Bruce Vaughan. Another American, Scott Dunlap, made an impressive charge, birdieing the second through sixth holes and picking up more birdies at the 12th and the 15th. When Dunlap's birdie putt at the 17th fell in, he and Friedlander were tied.

"I knew playing the 16th that Scott was 14 under at that stage," Friedlander said. "I figured he would definitely make a birdie at the 17th, so I knew I had to birdie one of the last two holes to win."

Friedlander's strategy was correct. He hit a pitching wedge from 142 yards to within 11 feet at the 17th, and sank that putt for a birdie to take a one-stroke lead into the final hole. That's where the trouble began. He pulled his tee shot into the left rough, where it plugged in its own pitch mark. After taking his drop, Friedlander chipped to within four feet, and it looked as though the victory was his.

"Both my caddie and I got the line wrong on that putt at 18," Friedlander said after missing the four-footer and ending regulation play tied with Dunlap at 201, 15 under par. "I did all that work on 17 and then was just stupid on 18. You'd think after 20 years of playing this course I'd be able to read the greens properly."

He would get two more chances to read the 18th green properly, however. The first time Friedlander and Dunlap played the 18th in the playoff, both made pars, and they marched back to try it again. The second time, Dunlap bogeyed, while Friedlander hit his tee shot safely onto the green and two-putted for par and the victory.

Vodacom Players Championship—R1,000,000

Winner: Mark McNulty

Although he carried a five-stroke lead into the final round of the Vodacom Players Championship, Mark McNulty thought if he had been forced to play a few more holes he might have lost the tournament. "I think I gave my heart surgeon a real palpitation as well," McNulty said. "My nerves are not good. Actually, I think it's more a case of frustration. All week I have been struggling to find that part of my swing which makes the ball go straight, but, after 64 holes, my caddie and I seemed to work it out."

That revelation came just in time. Scott Dunlap, who started the day six strokes behind McNulty, narrowed the gap to one through the first eight holes. Then McNulty helped Dunlap's cause by making a bogey on the eighth. The seemingly insurmountable lead had evaporated. McNulty also bogeyed the ninth and the 10th, and Dunlap held a two-stroke lead.

Then McNulty and his caddie figured out what was wrong with his swing. "I just wasn't moving onto my right side properly," he said. "I played horrendously on the front nine. I had to constantly think of mending the situation and Scott really made it difficult for me, especially when I was dropping shots."

McNulty hit his approach shot to within six feet on the 12th and made birdie while Dunlap bogeyed the same hole. Tied for the lead, McNulty birdied the par-five 15th, while Dunlap had to settle for par. Dunlap bogeyed the 16th and McNulty had the lead for good. His birdie putt on the 18th widened his margin to three strokes. McNulty had a 275 total on rounds of 67, 69, 68 and 71, while Dunlap tied Warren Abery for second at 278.

Vodacom Series: Western Cape—R165,000

Winner: Alan McLean

After a rain delay forced officials to begin the final round of the Vodacom Series: Western Cape on the first and second nines, it seemed that the damp conditions had cooled the hot play of Alan McLean, who led by six strokes.

The 27-year-old McLean bogeyed the first two holes, then reasserted himself with birdies on four of the next six. An out-of-bounds tee shot cost McLean a double bogey at the 11th. None of his challengers could make a move, however, and McLean finished with an impressive five-stroke margin over James Loughnane and Sean Ludgater. McLean had rounds of 63, 67 and 71 for a 201 total, 15 under par.

"Rondebosch never used to my favorite course but it is now," McLean said. "I think the secret to my round today was that my putter never let me down as it has a couple of times in the past. Apart from a few bad shots, I was pretty solid today. I think the win will do a lot for my confidence when I go to the Canadian Tour in May."

Kalahari Classic—R75,000

Winner: Andrew McLardy

With a five-stroke lead going into the final round of the Kalahari Classic, Andrew McLardy could afford to play conservatively in the windy conditions. That's exactly what he did, carding a 73 for a 205 total and a three-stroke margin over Ryan Dreyer. Callie Swart finished third at 209, while Des Terblanche was fourth at 210.

"I was watching the leaderboard throughout the day and I could see that no one was making a real run at me," said McLardy, whose earlier scores were a pair of 66s. "Generally, I played a lot safer. It was pretty tough out there. There was a two or three club wind on some holes, and the pins were really tucked away. I don't think they wanted me to fire a third 66."

The victory boosted McLardy's confidence. "I'm happy with the win, and I think this will take the pressure off of me," he said. "It might even make future wins easier. I played well on the recent Vodacom summer tour without really converting my chances. Hopefully, this victory will help me handle similar situations a lot better."

Pietersburg Classic—R100,000

Winner: Desvonde Botes

At age 23, Desvonde Botes not only added a sixth title to his record when he won the Pietersburg Classic by five strokes, he also finished with a 197 total, 19 under par — his lowest 54-hole mark as a professional. A first-round 62 gave Botes a lead that he would never yield. He enlarged his margin to four with a 67, then a 68 clinched the victory over Sammy Daniels, who also shot a closing 68. Sean Farrell finished alone in third at 203.

"There's always a danger of losing such a big lead," Botes said. "I played very solidly, and I kept myself in there all the time."

Vodacom Series: Eastern Cape—R165,000

Winner: Sammy Daniels

Thirty-six-year-old Sammy Daniels only had one win, the 1992 Uitenhage Classic, before arriving at the Humewood Country Club in Port Elizabeth for the Vodacom Series: Eastern Cape event. Three days later, Daniels had outdueled five competitors over the final nine holes of play, endured a grueling three-hole playoff against Ian Palmer, and walked away with his second career victory.

After opening scores of 70 and 68, Daniels shot a six-birdie, three-bogey round of 69 to finish the regulation 54 holes at 207, nine under par. With five holes to play Daniels, Palmer, Darren Fichardt, Richard Kaplan and defending champion Des Terblanche were all tied. Daniels moved ahead with birdies at the 15th and 16th, but Palmer caught him with a birdie of his own at the 17th. Palmer also finished with 69.

In the playoff, Daniels and Palmer both birdied the first hole, the par-four 18th. The second time through, both parred the 18th. For the third playoff hole, the two moved to the par-five 17th, where Daniels' length worked to his advantage. After hitting his second shot pin high in the left rough, Daniels chipped to within 15 feet and made the putt for a birdie.

Vodacom Series: Kwazulu-Natal—R165,000

Winner: Keith Horne

Keith Horne won his first professional championship on his home course of Prince's Grant in Durban in the Vodacom Series: Kwazulu-Natal event by shooting three rounds of 68 for a 12-under-par 204 total. While Horne's victory was wire-to-wire, there were a few anxious moments. Chris Williams started the final round three strokes behind, closed the gap to one but fell back and finished in second place, three strokes off Horne's pace. "I played well," Williams said. "I wasn't making any mistakes, but Keith was playing a lot better than me."

For Horne, age 27, who was an assistant professional at Prince's Grant under Hugh Baiocchi, the win was particularly satisfying. "It's very special for me to win in front of my home crowd," he said. "The guys at Prince's Grant have been very supportive. If it weren't for them, I'd be an industrial relations manager somewhere in Durban. They've given me a lot of confidence in my ability."

Vodacom Series: Mpumalanga—R165,000

Winner: Callie Swart

Callie Swart had to fight off a strong challenge to capture his first professional victory at the Vodacom Series: Mpumalanga at the White River Country Club. Swart battled back and forth with Brenden Pappas and Ashley Roestoff throughout the round. Then on the final hole, Pappas had a four-foot putt to take the lead away from Swart, who was faced with a six-footer for birdie. Pappas missed, but not before Roestoff turned up the heat by making a 25-

footer to tie Swart at 10 under par. Swart then made his six-footer for the victory at 11-under-par 202. Roestoff was second at 203 and Pappas, third at 204.

"I aged about five years during that round," said Swart, who shot rounds of 66, 67 and 69. "I'm not used to this. Both Ashley and Brenden made me very tired out there today."

Fish River Sun Pro-Am—R200,000

Winner: Ashley Roestoff

Starting the final round two strokes out of the lead held by Colin Sorour, Ashley Roestoff ended a two-year drought by shooting 68 to win the Fish River Sun Pro-Am. Roestoff's three-under-par 213 total was four strokes better than second-place finisher Sorour, who shot 74 in the closing round. Andre Cruse, Hennie Otto and Stephen Wilson finished tied for third at 219.

Roestoff started the last round with a birdie on the second hole, and it soon became apparent that, despite scrambling saves on the first nine, Sorour was struggling with his swing. At the seventh, Sorour's short par putt lipped out, and Roestoff tied him for the lead — a lead Roestoff assumed alone at the 12th after another birdie. Another birdie at the 14th extended Roestoff's margin, and Sorour's bogey at the 18th sealed the victory.

"It feels great to win again," Roestoff said. "I've been playing well now for six months and it's about time I made it count. You wonder if you've lost that winning feeling, but it's nice to know I've got it back."

Royal Swazi Sun Classic—R150,000

Winner: Justin Hobday

Despite threats from Grant Muller, Bradley Davison and a late charge from Titch Moore, Justin Hobday was able to shoot a final-round 69 to finish at nine-under-par 207 for the 54 holes, good enough for a three-stroke victory in the Royal Swazi Sun Classic. It wasn't that easy, however. Moore posted 66 to claw his way to second place. Muller made four birdies on the first nine, and caught Hobday with another birdie at the 10th. They both birdied the 11th, then Muller collapsed with bogeys at the 13th and 16th and a double bogey at the 14th, allowing Hobday to cruise in with the victory. Muller and Davison tied for third place at 211.

"I've been ready for this win for some time now and I just played really solidly today," said Hobday, whose earlier scores were 70 and 68. "I got off to a great start, and then I played solidly the whole round. I just never got into trouble the entire day."

ABSA Corporate Bank Challenge—R150,000

Winner: Warren Abery

After two rounds of 67 to open a one-stroke lead, Warren Abery played Johannesburg's 7,228-yard Roodepoort Country Club in even-par 72 in the final round for a 54-hole total of 206 for a three-stroke victory in the ABSA Corporate Bank Challenge. The biggest challenge to Abery came from Pelop Panagopoulos of Greece, who, after shooting 67 and 73 in the first two rounds, closed strongly with 69.

Panagopoulos shared second place with Brett Liddle and Bryan Prytz. One shot back at the start of the final round, Chris Williams closed with 75 to finish tied for fifth at 210 with Wallie Coetsee, Ashley Roestoff and Wayne Bradley.

Bearing Man Highveld Classic—R100,000

Winner: Wayne Bradley

It turned out to be a battle of birdies down the stretch, and in the end it was Wayne Bradley, who entered the final round of the Bearing Man Highveld Classic at Witbank Golf Club tied for the lead with Richard Fulford, dropping a 15-footer for birdie at the 18th hole to edge a charging Sammy Daniels by two strokes. The final round was marred by some of the coldest weather of the year.

"I thought I had more breathing space than I really did at the end," Bradley said. "Standing on the last green I was surprised that I needed a two-putt to win. Fortunately, the first one went in."

Bradley finished with a 14-under-par 202 total on scores of 68, 67 and 67. Daniels also closed with 67 for a 204 total, and nine players were tied for third place at 207.

Vodacom Series Free State—R165,000

Winner: Gary Matthews

After playing collegiate golf at the University of Arizona and a competitive stint on the Nike Tour, 24-year-old South African rookie Gary Matthews certainly felt ready for a victory. Even though Matthews was the only man in the field at the Vodacom Series: Free State who could boast of having played Tiger Woods six times and beaten him twice while the two were in college, the final round at the Schoeman Park Golf Club wasn't easy.

Matthews went into the final round tied with Alan Mitchell and Wallie Coetsee, and none of the three made an early move. Matthews birdied the sixth, seventh, ninth and 13th holes before suffering a bogey at the 16th, staying close to the lead.

Justin Hobday, playing ahead of the final group, finished with 70 for a 206 total. Matthews parred the 17th and, when he hit his approach shot to within three feet on the 18th, he felt sure the tournament was his. He made that for 70 and a 205 total, 11 under par, to win by one stroke. Mitchell shot 71 to tie Hobday for second place, and Coetsee shared fourth at 207 with Dean van Staden.

FNB Botswana Open—R150,000

Winner: Justin Hobday

Four weeks after winning the Royal Swazi Sun Classic, Justin Hobday became the first to win two 1998 Vodacom Series events when he captured the FNB Botswana Open over Richard Kaplan with a birdie on the first playoff hole.

After opening with rounds of 66 and 67, Hobday was tied for the lead with Kaplan, who followed his opening 71 with a course-record 62, and Keith Horne (68-65). Horne collapsed with three consecutive bogeys beginning at the 13th, while Kaplan birdied the 14th and 15th to pull ahead of Hobday by one. Hobday sank a birdie putt on the 18th to tie Kaplan at 12-under-par 201, as both finished with 68s. Hobday played the 18th, the first playoff hole, almost identically, dropping a birdie putt while Kaplan pushed his 10-foot birdie effort past the hole.

Phalaborwa Mafunyane Trophy—R150,000

Winner: Sammy Daniels

Even though he entered the final round of the Phalaborwa Mafunyane Trophy at Hans Merensky Country Club with a two-stroke lead, that wasn't good enough for Sammy Daniels. He followed his first two rounds of 67 with a tournament-low 65 and 199 total, 17 under par, good enough for a five-shot victory over Hendrik Buhrmann (67-69-68). Des Terblanche finished well with a 66 to elevate himself into third place at 206. Wayne Bradley, Chris Davison, Michiel Bothma and Bobby Lincoln tied for fourth at 208.

Vodacom Series: Gauteng—R165,000

Winner: Brenden Pappas

After a see-saw final round, the Vodacom Series: Gauteng came down to a two-foot putt on the 54th hole. If John Dickson made it, he would regain a share of the lead and force a playoff with Brenden Pappas. Dickson missed, giving Pappas a one-stroke victory. "You never like to see that happen to anybody," Pappas said. "But in the past I've often finished second to good players and I've been really patient. I've worked on my game and finally the dice has rolled my way."

After opening with 67 and 66, Pappas started the final day two strokes behind Dickson, who carded a second-round 62 to go with his first-round 69. Pappas finished with 69 for a 202 total, 11 under par, while Dickson had 72 and a 211 total.

FNB Namibia Open—R150,000

Winner: Ashley Roestoff

Early in the year, Ashley Roestoff had set a goal of winning two tournaments before December. A good final round in the FNB Namibia Open at the Windhoek Country Club, and he could complete that goal with a month to spare. Roestoff hit his first approach shot to within three feet and made a birdie. From that point on, he was out in front. Another birdie from 20 feet at the fourth, another at the seventh, and Roestoff found himself in command.

The only serious challenges to Roestoff came from Sammy Daniels and Bobby Lincoln, who tied for second place, two strokes behind. Roestoff had a 203 total, 10 under par, with scores of 69, 68 and 66. Daniels and Lincoln both finished with 68s and 206 totals.

Hassan II Trophy—US$415,000

Winner: Santiago Luna

With eight players within three strokes of the lead in the Hassan II Trophy at Royal Dar-es-Salam in Morocco, Spain's Santiago Luna had his work cut out for him in the final round. Several players, including former U.S. Open champion Steve Jones and American Tom Pernice slipped in and out of the lead throughout the final round. Pernice finished first with 67 and a 277 total, 15 under par.

Jones and Stephen Ames had chances down the stretch, but both missed short birdie putts on the 18th which would have tied Pernice and forced a playoff. It came down to Luna, who had taken advantage of his exceptional length throughout the week. He finished with a par and 69 to tie Pernice at 277.

In the playoff on the long par-four 16th, Luna took charge, blowing his tee shot well past the bunkered shot of Pernice. A nine-iron approach and two putts were all Luna needed to capture the title. "I concentrated out there today," Luna said. "I didn't know what anyone else was doing until the 16th. I was so focused, I just tried to shoot a good score."

Platinum Classic—R250,000

Winner: Bobby Lincoln

Bobby Lincoln shot a final-round 66 in the Platinum Classic at the Mooinooi Golf Club for a 14-under-par 202 total and a three-stroke victory over Ashley Roestoff. It was Lincoln's first win since beating Ernie Els in the 1992 Trustbank Tournament of Champions. "I made some good putts for birdies when I started feeling unsettled on the back nine," Lincoln said. "That made the difference."

Lincoln started with two 68s and shared the lead with Andre Cruse and Marc Cayeux at eight under par. Birdies at the first, second and eighth holes put Lincoln ahead by two strokes with nine holes to play. Unfortunately, the Mooinooi is a nine-hole course, and Lincoln had to wait almost 40 minutes before making the turn — enough time for doubt to creep into his mind.

"That delay was really unsettling because I had a good rhythm going," Lincoln said. He made bogeys at the 10th and 11th, allowing Roestoff to close to within one, but regained his rhythm and reeled off birdies at the 12th, 13th, 14th and 16th. Roestoff birdied the 14th and 16th as well, then made an eagle on the 17th to pull within one. Lincoln birdied the 17th, and when Roestoff three-putted the 18th for bogey, Lincoln breathed a sigh of relief.

Zambia Open—R300,000

Winner: Marc Cayeux

Despite being plagued by a charging Chris Davison, stomach troubles, nerves and a chirping cellular telephone on the final hole, 20-year-old Marc Cayeux of Zimbabwe held on to shoot a final-round 68 for a 273 total to capture the Zambia Open by one stroke. "I haven't felt well all week, and I didn't think I would even shoot level par, never mind finishing under par," said Cayeux, whose earlier scores were 68, 70 and 67.

Starting the day one stroke off the 54-hole lead held by Hennie Otto, Cayeux birdied the first, second and eighth holes at the Lusaka Golf Club to open a one-stroke lead. On the 10th, Otto bogeyed from a bunker while Cayeux made a 20-foot birdie putt. His lead was three going into the home stretch.

Davison mounted a late charge, closing with 65 to move to 10-under-par 274. Otto recovered for 70 and finished at 10 under par as well. That left Cayeux, who stood over a two-foot putt for par at the last hole to finish at 11 under for the tournament. "I was pretty nervous on that last putt, especially when the cell phone went off," Cayeux said. "In fact, I was nervous from the start of the day. I managed to relax a bit after nine holes."

After backing away and composing himself, Cayeux sank the two-footer for the win, and tearfully embraced his older brother Glenn. "I owe this one to my family for all their support," he said.

Zimbabwe Open—R450,000

Winner: Nick Price

It is always satisfying to win your country's open championship, but for Nick Price, who became the first to successfully defend the Zimbabwe Open title, the victory was especially pleasing. Price, who helped re-design the Royal Harare Golf Club, demolished the course record by shooting a final-round 63 for a 17-under-par total of 271, five strokes ahead of his nearest competitor, South African Tjaart van der Walt.

"In the final round of the PGA Championship I putted well, but it still wasn't as good as today," Price said. "I could have won two majors this year if I had putted like this."

Putting was particularly crucial for Price because his iron play wasn't up to his normally precise standards. "The wind was difficult this week, and it made a one or two club difference," he said. "It was difficult to get the distances right with my irons, and as a result there was apprehension in my iron play because you don't want to miss these greens."

Price didn't miss many greens in the final round, and said later, "I holed a good birdie from 25 feet at the first, and then had good putts at three, four and five, so all the time it felt like it was coming. When I lined up the putt at six (a 45-footer for eagle), it was perfect and I knew it was going in just as I hit it. That really got me going."

Birdies at the eighth, ninth, 10th, 11th and 14th capped off the victory. "When I putt well I always know I'm capable of scoring low," Price said. "I've been looking for a bit of fire in my putting. You don't win tournaments by putting badly, but my putting has been far too sporadic for my liking. Today, I had a good line and length."

Nedbank Million Dollar Challenge—US$2,460,000

Winner: Nick Price

A large crowd assembled for the final round of the Nedbank Million Dollar Challenge in Sun City, South Africa, certainly got its money's worth as Nick Price won his third Million Dollar title in the most dramatic fashion yet — in a five-hole playoff against Tiger Woods.

Price carded six consecutive birdies from the ninth through the 14th holes, but Woods matched Price almost shot for shot throughout the day. On the 17th, Woods made an 18-foot birdie putt to pull within one and the crowd erupted. Then on the 18th, needing a birdie to force the playoff, Woods chose to chip with a wedge from the fringe, 25 feet from the hole.

"I had to make that chip," Woods said. "I had no choice. I knew when I hit it was on line, but I didn't know if it had enough pace or not."

It did, and when the chip found the hole, Tiger ignited the crowd with his uppercut fist-pump. Woods and Price both finished regulation play with 66s and were tied at 15-under-par 273, one shot ahead of Justin Leonard, who barely missed joining the playoff when his birdie effort at the 18th slid by the hole.

Price showed no surprise at Woods' heroics at the 18th. In fact, he expected it. "His birdies at 17 and 18 just show what kind of player he is," Price said. "Even when he mis-hits his drives, they go 30 yards past mine, and that's a tall order on this course. Tiger is still learning to manage his game, and when he reaches his 30s he's going to be an awesome golfer." Price jokingly added, "I'm just glad I'll be on the Senior Tour by then."

Woods had a chance to win on the third playoff hole when he hit his approach to within 12 feet while Price missed the green. Price pitched to within a foot for par, and Woods pulled his birdie effort. Two holes later, Price hit his approach shot to within six feet. Woods, two feet outside Price, missed his birdie putt, and Price made his.

"What a day! I couldn't have scripted it any better," Price said. "To beat someone like Tiger makes this win even more special. He's a phenomenon."

15. Senior Tours

Although there were plenty of colorful distractions, including the first victory on any tour by long-hitting, cigar-chewing John Jacobs, and wins by the pipe-puffing, kilt-wearing Brian Barnes, Lee Trevino, Jim Colbert, 62-year-old Gary Player and the ever-talkative Joe Inman, the 1998 United States Senior PGA Tour was dominated by one man: Hale Irwin. The man who finished 1997 with 10 victories and more money than anyone had ever earned on any tour dominated again in 1998, winning seven official events, one unofficial event, and shattering his year-old money record by earning a staggering $2,861,945. His worldwide total was $3,155,189. In addition, Irwin finished in the top five in 20 out of 22 events and picked up two senior major titles, his third consecutive PGA Seniors' Championship and his first U.S. Senior Open.

In two years, Irwin won 16 out of 45 official events, dominating like no senior before him. The only player who has come close to that sort of domination was Lee Trevino, who won 10 tournaments in 56 starts in 1990 and 1991, but even that seems paltry compared to what the 53-year-old Irwin did in 1997 and 1998. As Joe Inman put it, "In another two or three years there might be another dominant player, but right now, Hale is the man."

While Irwin's dominance was unmatched, it did take him a little time to get warmed up. He didn't win an event until March, when he captured the Toshiba Senior Classic in Newport Beach, California. After that, he repeated his back-to-back wins at the PGA Seniors' and the Las Vegas Senior Classic. He took back-to-back wins again at the Ameritech Senior Open and, in dramatic fashion, at the U.S. Senior Open. Five weeks later, Irwin won again at the BankBoston Classic. He capped his season off with victories at the Energizer Senior Tour Championship and the unofficial Senior Match Play Challenge.

The only senior who even remotely made a run at Irwin was Gil Morgan, the Oklahoma native who found new life and new game on the Senior PGA Tour. Morgan started the year as the tour's most dominant player, winning three official and one unofficial event in the first seven weeks of the season before falling victim to Irwin's record-setting performance at the PGA Seniors' Championship. Morgan would win three more times throughout the year, pushing his victory total to seven.

While Irwin and Morgan dominated the headlines, there were other stories on the Senior PGA Tour in 1998. Jim Colbert made a comeback from prostate cancer to win The Transamerica. He broke into tears at the awards ceremony when he dedicated his trophy to Arnold Palmer, also a prostate cancer survivor.

Larry Nelson made a bit of noise early in the year, winning the American Express Invitational and Pittsburgh Senior Classic, but health problems kept the former U.S. Open and PGA champion from providing the type of challenge to Irwin and Morgan that some had expected. Nelson was able to pick up another late-season victory at the Boone Valley Classic, making him the third winningest senior of 1998.

Inman, the Rookie of the Year, also picked up a late-season victory at the

Pacific Bell Senior Classic. After catching his breath, Inman summed up the Senior PGA Tour when he said, "Two years ago I didn't have a job and I didn't know what I was going to do. This is like a second chance. It's really a dream come true."

In addition to the 38 official events in the United States, there were 19 tournaments on the European Seniors Tour, and seven each in Japan and South Africa. The biggest overseas prize, the Senior British Open, was won by Brian Huggett in a playoff over Eddie Polland at Royal Portrush in Northern Ireland. Tommy Horton led the European Seniors Tour for the third consecutive year, winning three tournaments for a total of 13 victories over that span. Horton led the money list with £127,656.

Toru Nakayama won two senior events in Japan, but the Japan Senior Open title was taken by Australian Graham Marsh, who continued his career-long success in that country. John Bland was the winner of the Franklin Templeton Senior South African Open, and Tertius Claassens and Allan Henning each won twice in South Africa.

U.S. Senior PGA Tour

MasterCard Championship—$1,000,000

Winner: Gil Morgan

It seems silly to win three events in a row and be asked about being second best. For Gil Morgan, it's a standard question. After winning six official events in 1997 (including the last two of the year), Morgan found himself second in every respect (money, wins and Player of the Year votes) to record-setter Hale Irwin who won nine official events and became the first senior golfer to win $2 million in a single season. In Kailua-Kona, Hawaii, however, it was Morgan who set the pace for 1998, winning the MasterCard Championship by six strokes over Irwin and Gibby Gilbert.

In beautiful Hawaiian conditions, 19 players (all Senior PGA Tour winners from 1997) ripped up the 7,053-yard Hualalai Golf Club and showed the world that the old guys have plenty of game left. After opening with a seven-under-par 65, Morgan was tied with Gilbert, but after another stellar round of 66 on Saturday, Morgan was alone atop the leaderboard, two ahead of Gilbert and three in front of Dave Stockton. Irwin, having flown to Hawaii just two days after his daughter's wedding, stood six strokes back going into the final round.

Last year's record-setter would not be denied, however. Irwin came out Sunday and fired a course-record 64 for a 201 total. He stood alone with that record for less than an hour, however. Morgan also shot 64 on Sunday to finish at 195 and capture the event, and the $200,000 first-place check, in grand fashion.

"Gil has picked up right where he left off last year," Irwin said of his rival's victory. "He's put the early bull's-eye on his back."

Royal Caribbean Classic—$850,000

Winner: David Graham

Whoever said the over-50 crowd didn't have the stamina of the younger, better-conditioned athletes obviously didn't visit Key Biscayne, Florida, during the Royal Caribbean Classic, the Senior PGA Tour's first full-field event of 1998. In a grueling and record-setting 10-hole playoff, Dave Stockton and David Graham battled like young warriors until just before sunset, when Graham came within six inches of holing a 129-yard approach shot on the 18th hole to finally capture the title.

Neither player backed down or slouched his way around. Graham sandwiched a 68 between two rounds of 67, which he capped off with three consecutive birdies on Sunday for a 202 total to force the playoff. Stockton opened the tournament with a 64, which he followed up with rounds of 67 and 71.

While Stockton wasn't pleased with his performance on Sunday, each player had opportunities thwarted by the other during the playoff. On the third extra hole, Graham hit his approach to within two feet, and Stockton missed the green. But Graham knew things weren't over yet. "I told my caddie that he could hole it," Graham said. That's exactly what Stockton did. Seven holes later, however, with an orange sunset settling over a dwindling crowd, Graham hit it stiff again, and Stockton couldn't match him a second time.

LG Championship—$1,200,000

Winner: Gil Morgan

"Sometimes things just go your way," Gil Morgan said as he received the $180,000 first-place check from the LG Championship in Key Biscayne, Florida. For Morgan, a lot of things went his way. First, he recovered from four double bogeys in 54 holes to shoot six-under-par 210 for three days. Second, he chipped in from 40 yards out for an eagle after hitting a four iron well short of the par-five 18th green. Third, he needed just 11 putts on his second nine on Sunday, and fourth and finally, the tournament leader after two days, Jim Albus, ballooned to 77 on Sunday, thus opening the door for a scrambling Morgan to slip in and win.

"He had blown himself out of this tournament twice this week," Jim Colbert, who tied for fourth, said of Morgan's performance. Morgan couldn't have agreed more. "I felt like I had too many foul balls this week," he said. "I was very fortunate."

Not as fortunate were Dale Douglass, who was bidding to be the second oldest winner on the Senior PGA Tour, and Raymond Floyd, who hadn't won in 18 months. When Albus collapsed, Floyd held the lead until he made consecutive bogeys at Nos. 12 and 13. Then Floyd, Douglass and Morgan were tied, and it looked as though it would be a two- or three-way playoff. Morgan ended that thinking with his pitch-in on the last hole. Floyd and Douglass tied for second place, two strokes behind.

Afterward, a joking Douglass shouted, "I was robbed." Although he wasn't asked, Morgan would no doubt plead guilty to the crime.

GTE Classic—$1,100,000

Winner: Jim Albus

In 1997, while lying at home with his leg in a cast one year after recovering from neck surgery, Jim Albus wondered if the career that had begun on his 50th birthday was finally fading into twilight. One year later, fast approaching his 58th birthday, and looking back on two years' worth of injuries, Albus couldn't have been happier when a one-under-par final round of 71 bounced him to first place with a 207 total at the GTE Classic in Tampa, Florida.

"I try to de-emphasize the importance of golf," Albus, a former New York club pro said, "but it's hard not to enjoy this. After the way I struggled the last couple of years, this has to rank right up there in my mind."

Brian Barnes, who led after both the first and second rounds, shot a final-round 75 to finish three shots back, while Vicente Fernandez, who began the final round one shot in front of Albus, closed with 73 and finished two shots off the pace. On the back nine of the final round Jose Maria Canizares opened up a two-shot lead, but quickly let it slip away when he three-putted the 16th for bogey, then three-putted the 17th for double bogey. Meanwhile, Albus made up-and-down pars on two of the last three holes, and two-putted for par on the 18th to win by one stroke over Canizares, Simon Hobday and Kermit Zarley.

Because he was unaware of Canizares' troubles behind him, Albus didn't know his three-footer on No. 18 was for the win. "I'm glad nobody told me," he later said. "There's no way I could have made that putt."

American Express Invitational—$1,200,000

Winner: Larry Nelson

A lot of players take their transition to the Senior PGA Tour seriously, but few abandon their outside careers in their first senior seasons. Larry Nelson isn't one of them. After winning a U.S. Open and PGA Championship in the early 1980s, Nelson pared back his PGA Tour schedule and concentrated on his golf course design and development business. With a group of investors, Nelson amassed a healthy portfolio of golf courses and built a respectable design firm. Then, on his 50th birthday, Nelson appeared on the Senior PGA Tour, but not before divesting himself of all his outside interests. "You can't play well and concentrate on the other aspects of business," Nelson said. "You either have to play, or do other things."

Nelson decided to play, and after leading wire-to-wire in the American Express Invitational in Sarasota, Florida, he appeared to have made the right decision. With an opening round of 63, Nelson assumed a lead he would never relinquish. He followed it up with rounds of 69 and 71 on the weekend for a 203 total to win by four shots over Dave Stockton, who said of Nelson's game, "There were no weaknesses, but there were no gigantic strengths either."

That was the same thing people said when Nelson was winning three major championships in seven years on the PGA Tour. At least now, no one can accuse him of being distracted by outside interests.

Senior Slam—$600,000

Winner: Gil Morgan

It might only have been two rounds instead of three, with four players instead of a full field, in Mexico at the Cabo del Sol Ocean Course instead of a course somewhere stateside, but Gil Morgan, the most dominant player so far in 1998, still won. His 10-under-par 134 total on rounds of 66 and 68 lapped the other three contestants by six shots and earned Morgan a healthy $300,000 paycheck.

The event featured the winners of all four of 1997 major senior championships, which should have provided great theater and uplifting golf. There was a note of sadness before the event began, however. Larry Gilbert, winner of the 1997 Ford Senior Players Championship, died of cancer. Isao Aoki replaced Gilbert and earned $90,000 for his consecutive 73s. Graham Marsh, winner of the 1997 U.S. Senior Open, was 18 strokes behind Morgan after 36 holes but still earned $60,000 for shooting rounds of 80 and 72.

The man who should have given Morgan the biggest run for his money, Hale Irwin, who counted the PGA Seniors' Championship among his nine wins in 1997, couldn't get his putter working. He left no fewer than five birdie attempts short, and had to settle for a 140 total with scores of 71 and 69.

"I just tried to play conservatively," Morgan said. "I was pleased by how I played the last two days."

Toshiba Senior Classic—$1,100,000

Winner: Hale Irwin

It took a putting tip from his son, and one of the most spectacular rounds in Senior PGA Tour history, but Hale Irwin finally got his first victory of 1998 in the Toshiba Senior Classic in Newport Beach, California. Not that going winless into March would be any big deal, but when you're coming off a year like Irwin's with nine victories in 1997 and a record $2.3 million in official earnings, a two-and-a-half month winless draught can give the impression of a major slump.

Irwin answered those questions by firing a record-setting 62 in the final round at the Newport Beach Country Club for a 200 total, 13 under par, to win by one stroke over Hubert Green. In doing so he passed no fewer than 11 players including second-round leader Green and two-time 1998 winner Gil Morgan. "I owe a lot of this to my son, Steve," Irwin said. "He told me earlier that I was standing too close to the ball when I was putting. On the putting green this week I remembered what he said and made an adjustment." It worked. Irwin had 23 putts in breaking the course record. "I putted extremely well, and that tends to get the job done," Irwin said.

Green, who led Jim Albus by one going into the final day, started Sunday five shots ahead of Irwin, and said, "Great players get great breaks, then they make the most of them." Green shot 68 in the final round, but made a costly bogey on the 17th to put him one shot back of Irwin's pace.

When asked to put the round into perspective, Irwin said, "I don't think I've had a more memorable round on either tour. I don't know when I've passed that many people before."

Liberty Mutual Legends of Golf—$1,500,000

Winners: Charles Coody and Dale Douglass

It was the event that led to the formation of the Senior PGA Tour, so it seemed more than appropriate that two veterans, Charles Coody (age 60) and Dale Douglass (62), won the Liberty Mutual Legends of Golf by defeating youngsters David Graham and Hugh Baiocchi in a playoff. "Beating the kids out here makes this extra special," Coody said.

The team's play was extra special as well. After opening rounds of 62 and 66, Coody and Douglass started the final round in a tie with pre-tournament favorites Larry Nelson and Dave Stockton, but one stroke behind the leaders, Graham and Baiocchi. After a slow start on Sunday, Coody and Douglass came alive, making birdies on eight of the final 10 holes on the Summer Beach course at Amelia Island, Florida. The stunning run included two consecutive birdie putts of over 30 feet for a 64 and 192 total. "We're healthy, we feel good, and we don't know we're old," Douglass said.

Douglass certainly didn't act his age when, on the second extra hole, he made a downhill, left-to-right breaking birdie putt to clinch the victory. Coody and Douglass are no strangers to the winner's circle, however. They won this event in 1990 and 1994, but neither of them had a victory (individually or collectively) since 1996 when Douglass won the Bell Atlantic Classic and Coody won the du Maurier Champions.

In the press room after the victory Douglass' first words were, "Okay, everybody who's surprised, raise your hand." They weren't present, but Nelson and Stockton were definitely surprised. Despite a final-round 65, Nelson and Stockton could manage no better than a third-place finish, one shot behind.

Southwestern Bell Dominion—$1,000,000

Winner: Lee Trevino

He hadn't won since 1996, and many wondered if the merriment was all but gone from the once Merry Mex, Lee Trevino. But Trevino, age 58, wasn't quite through with his playing career, despite the repeated references he had made to spending more time with his family. While speaking of spending time with his wife and two children, Trevino was working on his conditioning, dropping weight, gaining strength and rekindling the old desire to be a champion. It all came together for him in San Antonio, Texas, in the Southwestern Bell Dominion.

After rounds of 70 and 68, Trevino found himself one stroke off the lead set by Bob Dickson. Dickson, whose last tournament victory was in 1973, felt the pressure, and after a triple bogey on the 10th hole, he dropped from contention with a final-round 76. Trevino, however, improved his scores every day, finishing the tournament with a final-round 67 and 205 total to take home the $150,000 first-place check by two strokes over Mike McCullough.

"I felt if kept working I could win again," Trevino said. "There was never a question that I wouldn't win again, but this gives me more confidence."

The Tradition—$1,400,000

Winner: Gil Morgan

Despite having never won a major title on the PGA Tour, Gil Morgan successfully defended his first Senior PGA Tour major championship, dominating The Tradition in an even more impressive fashion than he did when he shot 22 under par and won in 1997 by six shots. On top of his game in every respect, Morgan outplayed the field and the elements in the Scottsdale, Arizona, desert, prompting Hale Irwin to call Morgan "the best player out here. He's doing all the right things."

Morgan and Vicente Fernandez were the only two players under par in every round at the difficult Cochise course at Desert Mountain, while only 19 players broke par for the tournament. Just as the 1997 event was hampered by weather, the first round was delayed two and a half hours by an ice storm that left the golf course looking like a ski resort. That didn't seem to affect Morgan who shot 71, then came back with rounds of 66, 69 and 70 for a 276 total and two-stroke victory over Tom Wargo.

Despite Morgan's great play, Wargo held the lead after each of the first three rounds with scores of 68, 67 and 69, but Morgan was never more than three shots off the pace. Going into Sunday and playing with Morgan, Wargo had a two-shot lead, which vanished when he hit his tee shot over the green and into a pond at the par-three seventh hole. After making double bogey, Wargo found himself tied with Morgan. After he bogeyed No. 9, Wargo lost the lead for good and finished with 74. When Morgan sank a 10-foot par putt on the final hole, no one could catch him.

Despite defending his first major championship, Morgan played down the idea that he's the best player on the Senior PGA Tour. "I was pretty good this week, but I don't know about being the best player out here," he said.

Dave Stockton, who finished three strokes back and tied for sixth place, summed up the feelings of everyone else on the Senior PGA Tour when he said, "(Gil) was a nice guy on the regular tour, but it was like he was a nonentity. He's not a nonentity now."

PGA Seniors' Championship—$1,500,000

Winner: Hale Irwin

It's safe to say that when Pat Reilly trademarked the word "three-peat" he wasn't thinking about Hale Irwin or the Senior PGA Tour. At that time Reilly was coaching the Los Angeles Lakers and Irwin had one more U.S. Open win and a Ryder Cup victory left in him, and no one could have imagined a "three-peat" champion in a senior major golf championship. Nicklaus had never done it, so chances were it couldn't be done.

Not only did Irwin prove that theory wrong by winning his third straight PGA Seniors' Championship (becoming the first man since club professional Eddie Williams in the mid-1940s to win the oldest senior event three straight times), he proved that with nine victories in 1997 and a record $2.3 million in earnings in one year, no one was about to take his crown away. On the same PGA National course in Palm Beach Gardens, Florida, that hosted the 1989 PGA Championship, Irwin showed Nicklaus, Dave Stockton, Gil Morgan,

Dale Douglass and Larry Nelson who the best player was by firing a 13-under-par 275 total and running away with the championship by seven shots.

Morgan, who was also a repeat winner of a major title, capturing his second straight Tradition two weeks prior to the PGA Seniors', played a nine-hole practice round with Irwin and knew there was trouble ahead. "He said that it was his fourth practice round," Morgan said. "Right then I knew Hale meant business. I couldn't help thinking, 'Uh-oh.'"

Those thoughts were echoed by most of the participants after Irwin fired two consecutive rounds of 68 and took a four-shot lead into the weekend. "It was like two different golf tournaments going on," Nelson said. "One was seeing how well Hale would play, and the other was seeing who would finish second."

Irwin finished with rounds of 69 and 70 while Nelson won the battle for second, finishing with a six-under-par 282 total, one stroke ahead of Morgan. In most majors under most conditions, Nelson's scores would have placed him in the heat of contention. But, for the third year in a row, Irwin took the PGA Seniors' to a new level.

Las Vegas Senior Classic—$1,400,000

Winner: Hale Irwin

Despite desert winds that kicked up above 40 knots at times, and a final-round score that was 7.5 shots higher than his final-round average for the year, Hale Irwin was able to stumble home with yet another victory at the Las Vegas Senior Classic. It was Irwin's third win of the year (his second in a row) tying him in the victory category with Gil Morgan.

This one wasn't the cakewalk that Irwin's previous 1998 victories had been. After rounds of 69, 67 and 70 gave him a six-shot lead going into the final day, Irwin had what he termed, "a little slippage," in his game. A first-nine 40 on Sunday, amidst some of the strongest winds the players had seen all year, cut Irwin's lead down to one shot over Dale Douglass and Jose Maria Canizares. Between the ninth green and 10th tee Irwin had a meeting with himself, after which he shot 35 on the second nine and edged out Vicente Fernandez, who was en route to shooting a daily low of 68, by one stroke. Still, Irwin missed three straight birdie putts inside 15 feet on the final nine. Fernandez had one more opportunity on the 18th hole, but his 30-footer for birdie came up just short.

Irwin wasn't the only player affected by the rough winds. Twenty-two players shot 80 or higher on the final day and the scoring average for the day was 78.28, the highest so far of the year. Still, Irwin offered no excuses. "I've been on such a roll the last couple of months, the last couple of years, actually," he said. "You're not going to play every round perfectly. I know that. It's going to happen." For Irwin, who pocketed another $210,000 and pushed his yearly earnings to just under $1 million in just over four months, perfect play is a relative thing.

Bruno's Memorial Classic—$1,150,000

Winner: Hubert Green

There's nothing like winning in front of a hometown crowd, but when you capture your first victory in 12-and-a-half years on a golf course you co-designed, with family and friends watching you hit every shot, then the moment becomes sweeter than a glass of Birmingham iced tea. Hubert Green, whose last victory was the 1985 PGA Championship, thrilled the masses in his native Alabama by winning the Bruno's Memorial Classic in come-from-behind style, playing the last six holes six under par to finish one stroke ahead of Hale Irwin. "I really didn't think I had a chance going to the back side (on Sunday)," Green said. "When you're three shots back of Hale with nine to play, you're not in great shape. Heck, when you're two shots ahead of Hale with nine to play, you're still not in great shape."

Ten players were within three strokes of the lead with nine holes to play, but Green was at the bottom of the pack. Then, after an eagle, a par and four birdies on the last six holes, Birmingham's native son found himself at 13-under-par 203 and alone atop the leaderboard. "I can't ever remember having a stretch of holes like that," Green admitted. "I've only been six under on six holes one other time." That was at the Western Open back in the old Butler National days, but when asked about the year, Green could only say, "It was back in the dark ages."

Green's scores were 70, 69 and 64. He might not remember the last time he played this well, but he vividly recalls the last time he and Irwin tangled down to the wire. Six weeks prior to the Bruno's in Newport Beach, California, at the Toshiba Senior Classic, Green had a one-shot lead over Jim Albus going into the final day, but Irwin fired a final-round course-record 62 to lap the field.

"This is a little pay-back for Newport Beach," Green told his caddie after capping off his six-hole run. "It always means a lot to beat the best in the game, and Hale is that."

"You can't win every week," said Irwin, whose rounds were 69, 70 and 65. "Hubert played great, and I'm happy for him." When asked about Green's charge, Irwin said, "I was sort of surprised when I looked up and saw Hubert's name on the leaderboard. Terry (Dill) was the guy I thought we had to catch. We could tell from the crowd noise that something was going on, but I didn't know who or what it was."

Second-round leader Terry Dill, who started the week with a course-record 63, knew exactly what the noise meant. While waiting on the 17th tee Dill heard an eruption one hole ahead. He turned to Gil Morgan and said, "That local boy just made a putt."

Dill was right. Green made a 10-foot birdie putt on No. 18 to cap his terrific second nine and put the tournament out of reach. Afterward Dill (who finished tied for third) smiled and said, "You can't do much when a guy plays the last six holes six under." Dill then jokingly said, "I think Hubert got home and finally slowed his swing down where somebody could see it."

"It felt great to be home," Green said. And yes, he admitted, "I did slow my swing down."

Home Depot Invitational—$1,100,000

Winner: Jim Dent

On Saturday evening, May 9, Jim Dent heard the sweetest words a father can hear. "Daddy, please come home. Your birthday is here," Victoria Dent (age three) told her father over the phone from Augusta, Georgia. If Dent hadn't been the defending champion, and if he hadn't just shot a second-round 68 to share the lead going into the final day of Arnold Palmer's Home Depot Invitational, he might have heeded his daughter's wishes and driven up to his four-acre retreat to spend Mother's Day with the family. After all, the Dents had plenty to celebrate. In addition to Jim turning 59 the day before Mother's Day, his son James Dent, had just come home from winning the Division II Minority College Championship. As it was, Dent stayed in Charlotte, North Carolina, celebrating his birthday alone in his hotel room, savoring his position atop the leaderboard, and trying to overcome the strong feelings of deja vu.

"I thought about last year," Dent said late Sunday afternoon, once the $165,000 winner's check was securely in his back pocket. "But now I have a victory, an invitation to the Tournament of Champions and I'm playing good. Everything's beautiful."

In 1997 Dent found himself leading the Home Depot Invitational with eight holes to play, but a missed one-footer on the last hole of regulation sent him into a playoff with Lee Trevino and Larry Gilbert. Although Dent won that playoff, he couldn't help but think about his poor play on the 18th again in 1998. Dent had held the lead outright late Saturday afternoon, but after hitting his second shot in the water and making bogey on No. 18, he found himself in a tie with Britain's John Morgan.

"I should have just taken it home on that hole, but I made a mistake," Dent said. "If I'd hit it in the middle of the green and just made par, I would have had the lead."

Despite feeling as if he might have blown his best opportunity, Dent found himself atop the leaderboard again early in Sunday's round. But after ballooning to a 39 on the second nine, and weathering an hour-and-10-minute rain delay (the second delay of the tournament) Dent stood on the 18th needing to make another two-foot putt to remain tied for the lead and force another playoff, this time with 62-year-old Bob Charles. Dent made the putt for his 72 and 207 total, nine under par.

Charles, who began the final day five shots off the pace, didn't enter the tournament with any thoughts of winning. "This golf course is way too long for me at my age," he said. "I'm just out here playing for grocery money." Still, Charles shot 67 and missed a golden opportunity on the first playoff hole to become the second oldest champion in the history of the Senior PGA Tour. "I simply hit a bad putt," Charles said of the missed six-footer, which sent the playoff to a second extra hole.

Dent took care of business on the second extra hole, making another two-foot putt to become the only successful defending champion in the 18-year history of the Charlotte event. "It feels wonderful to win because of who I had to beat," Dent said. "Mr. Charles has been a champion all over the world. He is first class all the way."

Saint Luke's Classic—$1,000,000

Winner: Larry Ziegler

In the final moments it looked like no one wanted to win the $150,000 first-place check in the Saint Luke's Classic in Belton, Missouri. Even though he finished with three consecutive bogeys, Larry Ziegler was able to hold on to a one-shot lead and capture his first Senior PGA Tour victory in almost seven years. "It took guys collapsing at the end for me to win, and I'm very fortunate," said Ziegler, who had scores of 69, 67 and 72 for a 208 total, two under par.

Less fortunate was Tom Shaw who made a six-footer for par on the 71st hole to pull even with Ziegler. Then Shaw hit a poor drive on the last hole that found a hazard and led to a double-bogey finish and a final-round 70. Ziegler's bogey on the last won the hole and the tournament by one stroke.

Also collapsing in the final round were defending champion Walter Morgan, who tied Ziegler for the lead after 13 holes on Sunday then played the last four holes in five over par to shoot 71 and tie for third place at 211 with Isao Aoki and Hugh Baiocchi. Bruce Summerhays finished his final round with a double bogey on No. 17 and a triple bogey on No. 18. Had he parred in, Summerhays would have won by one stroke. As it was, he shot 74 and finished four strokes behind Ziegler.

"I've played a lot of golf, and it's not as much fun as it used to be," the 58-year-old Ziegler said. "A lot of people probably deserve (this win) more, but nobody appreciates it more."

Bell Atlantic Classic—$1,100,000

Winner: Jay Sigel

After an opening round of 74, local favorite Jay Sigel, who makes his home only 25 miles from the Hartefeld National course in Avondale, Pennsylvania, was six shots off the pace and far off his normal game. "I usually hit the ball high, but I haven't been hitting it high lately," Sigel said.

One of the advantages of playing close to home, however, is that your friends are close by. After receiving a tip from a friend and regular playing partner at his home club, Sigel put together one of the most impressive rounds in Senior PGA Tour history. His 10-under-par 62 on Saturday included a Senior PGA Tour-record 27 on the first nine. Sigel had one eagle and seven straight birdies in that nine-hole stretch, prompting his playing companion, John Paul Cain, to say, "That was the most perfect nine holes I've ever seen played."

Sigel jumped to a three-shot lead over Dale Douglass then stretched it five shots with nine holes to play. Jose Maria Canizares closed the gap with a final-round 65, while Sigel made double bogey on the 15th hole to shoot 69. They both finished with 11-under-par 205 totals and a playoff ensued. It wasn't Sigel's high ball, but his putter that seemed to abandon him in the playoff, as he missed putts from six and eight feet on the first two extra holes. "How many chances was I going to get?" Sigel asked himself.

One more chance was enough. On the third extra hole, Sigel drained a seven-foot birdie putt to win his fifth career Senior PGA Tour event.

Pittsburgh Senior Classic—$1,100,000

Winner: Larry Nelson

If there is a downside to equaling a course record in consecutive rounds, it's what you have to do for an encore. After two rounds of 65, Larry Nelson took an eight-shot lead into the final round of the Pittsburgh Senior Classic, but he found his focus drifting. "It's a little more difficult playing with an eight-shot lead than what I thought it was," Nelson said. "I wanted to win by more than my lead."

With wind that picked up and gusted to 35 knots on the final day, a repeat of Nelson's previous two days would have been tough for anyone, but still, a final-round 74 for a 204 total and a five-shot victory over Bob Duval wasn't exactly what Nelson had in mind. "The wind was difficult and it took the aggressiveness out of my game," Nelson said. "I guess I was just trying to get through without being embarrassed."

There was no embarrassment the first two rounds when, after an opening bogey on the first hole, Nelson went 40 straight holes without another bogey. His play was so far above the rest of the field that second-place finisher Duval, who shot 72-69-68 to edge out Jay Sigel by one stroke, said, "It was a pretty good tournament except for one person." In fact, 14 players including Al Geiberger, Hubert Green, Raymond Floyd, Gil Morgan and Gary Player finished within four shots of Duval's second-place score, but none could come close to catching Nelson.

Nationwide Championship—$1,350,000

Winner: John Jacobs

"It's pretty special to beat Hale Irwin and Gil Morgan when they're playing well," John Jacobs said after tapping in a par putt on the 72nd hole to win his first event on any American tour. "Those two have had a run."

That run came to an end in Alpharetta, Georgia, at the Nationwide Championship when Jacobs shot two consecutive 67s for a 206 total to outduel Irwin and Morgan at the Golf Club of Georgia. With birdies on four of the first six holes, Jacobs took the lead from Morgan early in Sunday's round, then he stretched it to two strokes at the turn before temporarily relinquishing it to a charging Irwin. After a back-and-forth battle in which all three players held or shared the lead on the final nine, Jacobs stood on the tee at the par-three 17th assuming the worst.

"I turned to my caddie and said, 'I have to make two birdies to win,'" Jacobs said. He then pointed to an area on the right side of the green and told his caddie, "If I can hit it on the right side, maybe I'll get lucky and it will roll down."

His six-iron shot from 199 yards did, indeed, get lucky and roll down to within 18 inches of the hole. "It was just one of those shots where you pick a spot and say, 'Please Lord, let me make one of the better swings of the day.' After I hit it, when I was walking up, I was thinking, 'I hope this is as close as it looks.'" It was. After tapping in, Jacobs took the lead for keeps.

In the fairway on the par-five 18th, Jacobs' caddie turned to him and asked, "Do you want to lay up?"

Jacobs replied, "I've made plenty of bogeys laying up, and I've made plenty of bogeys going for it. What do you think?"

The caddie nodded and said, "You're right. Hit your shot."

His shot turned out to be a 235-yard four iron that ran through the green and left Jacobs with a precarious little pitch. When he didn't make his par, he thought he might have lost.

"I knew I had a one-stroke lead over Hale, but I didn't know what Gil was doing," Jacobs said.

Meanwhile Morgan also birdied the 17th to pull within one, but when he tried to reach the 18th green in two shots from the left rough, the results were quite different. "I had a chance to win without any ties or anything by going for the green," Morgan said. "I really thought I needed to take that chance." Morgan's ball found the water, and for the first time this year, he did not win a tournament he had led going into the final round.

As for the winner, he was "Ecstatic. I'm happy as hell to win. I always figured I would win, but I didn't know how or when. I knew I was good enough. At least now there won't be any more doubt."

As for Irwin, who shot rounds of 70, 70 and 67 to finish alone in second place at 207, he shrugged and said, "Oh well, Avis again." Morgan and Leonard Thompson tied for third place at 208.

BellSouth Senior Classic—$1,300,000

Winner: Isao Aoki

Isao Aoki's two-stroke win was his second BellSouth Senior Classic victory in three years, and his fifth American victory as a senior. It was also a record-setting week in Nashville, Tennessee, for Aoki, who established a tournament record of 18-under-par 198, and who opened with rounds of 62 and 66 to set a 36-hole Senior PGA Tour record of 16 under par. With Aoki holding an eight-shot lead going into the weekend, the eight top money winners on the Senior PGA Tour, including the big three, Hale Irwin, Gil Morgan and Larry Nelson, didn't seem to have a chance.

Nelson had a gallant run, however. Six consecutive birdies pulled Nelson to within two strokes of Aoki on the final day, and his final-round 64 would normally have been enough to win. But Aoki's short game prevailed, and his final-round 70 was enough for a two-shot margin of victory.

"With a wedge and that kind of short stuff, he's a wizard," said Irwin, whose closing-round 65 left him three behind Aoki. "He's such an accomplished player and a great putter. I was actually surprised when he missed."

After the round and the victory, a smiling Aoki said, "I like the United States." With $5.5 million in earnings as a senior, Aoki will likely be on this side of the Pacific for a long time to come.

AT&T Canada Senior Open—$1,100,000

Winner: Brian Barnes

Brian Barnes is the only man in history to beat Jack Nicklaus in Ryder Cup competition twice in one day. Those matches, which Nicklaus says he has no desire to remember, occurred in 1975. In the more than 20 years that followed, Barnes maintained a colorful career that included 13 worldwide victories (none of which came on the PGA Tour) and a bout with alcoholism and depression that led him to the brink of suicide in 1993. Five years later, sober but still without a PGA Tour victory, Barnes broke through with a two-shot win over Dana Quigley, Bruce Summerhays and Tom Jenkins at the AT&T Canada Senior Open.

Even though he owns two Senior British Open titles, Barnes entered the tournament as a non-exempt player on the Senior PGA Tour, which meant he had been hoping to either qualify or gain sponsors exemptions for each event. For the first seven months of 1998, Barnes drove across the United States in a recreational vehicle that doubled as a residence for him and his wife. While he has no intention of giving up that lifestyle, his victory allows him to pick and chose where he will play for the next year. "This has done far more for me (than the Senior British Open titles)," Barnes said. "Now I'm in a position until this time next year to play in every event that I want to."

The victory wasn't easy, however. After a three-under-par 69 opening round, Barnes stood four strokes back of Summerhays and Tom Jenkins. On Friday, Barnes shot 67 to share the lead with Jenkins, who followed his first-round 65 with 71. Walter Hall, a winless Senior PGA Tour rookie, was one stroke back at the midway point after posting scores of 69 and 68.

Hall, who won the 1997 Belfry PGA Seniors Championship, continued his good play on Saturday with another round of 69, placing him at 10 under par and in the lead by three over Summerhays, Jenkins and Barnes, and five ahead of Quigley, who followed a pair of 71s with a third-round 69.

The tournament became a four-man race on the second nine on Sunday with Jenkins, Summerhays (both of whom shot 70 in the final round), Quigley, who shot 68, and ultimately Barnes, who also shot 68, all holding or sharing the lead on the final nine holes. The turning point came at the par-five 14th when Barnes, trailing Quigley by one shot, sank a 75-foot eagle putt while Quigley and Jenkins both bogeyed the hole. Barnes then followed up his heroics with a 12-foot birdie putt at No. 15, where he assumed the lead for good.

"That was the tournament right there," Quigley said of Barnes' eagle putt at No. 14. "I had him by a shot and he wound up having me by two." Hall shot a final-round 74 to finish at 280, three shots off Barnes' winning score, while Mike McCullough came through with a tournament-low 64 to finish at 282, tied for sixth with Hank Cooper.

For Barnes, the win brought back memories of victories past. "I found myself walking slower and taking more time with the shots," he said. "Whenever I've won tournaments, I've gotten into that kind of zone."

Cadillac NFL Classic—$1,100,000

Winner: Bob Dickson

Before the 1998 Cadillac NFL Classic, Bob Dickson hadn't won a golf tournament since Richard Nixon was president and Andy Williams still hosted the San Diego Open, but his name remained in the records books along with some elite company. Dickson is one of only a handful of players, including Bob Jones, ever to win the U.S. and British Amateur Championships in the same year. That year was 1967, and while Dickson had two victories in a lengthy career on the PGA Tour, he hadn't found himself atop the leaderboard in 25 long years.

During Sunday's final round in Upper Montclair, New Jersey, Dickson risked going down in the history books for a far more obtuse reason. Tied with Jim Colbert and Larry Nelson at nine under par on the last hole, Dickson needed to two putt from 50 feet in order to made the impending playoff. Unfortunately, after he stroked his first putt, he realized that neither he nor his caddie had taken the flagstick out of the hole. Fortunately, the putt came up six feet short. If Dickson had hit the pin with his putt, he would have incurred a two-shot penalty and dropped into a tie for ninth with Jim Dent, Tom Jenkins, Bruce Summerhays and Lee Trevino at 209.

As it was, Dickson made the second putt for 70 to finish at 207. He then went on to birdie the first playoff hole with a 20-foot birdie putt to win his first Senior PGA Tour title. His earlier scores were 68 and 69. "My caddie and I both fell asleep at that switch," Dickson said of leaving the pin in on the 72nd hole. "In 50 years of playing golf, I had never done that before, nor will I ever do it again."

Fortunately, the mental lapse didn't cost Dickson, who was embroiled in a battle on Sunday that could have gone any number of directions. After carrying a one-stroke lead at 10 under par into the final round, Mike McCullough shot 77 to drop to a tie for 15th place. McCullough's stumble opened the door, and with nine holes left, 11 players were within one shot of the lead. Among those who had a chance were Dana Quigley, who wedged a second-round 72 between two rounds of 68, Bruce Crampton, who shot 67, 70 and 71, and J.C. Snead, whose final-round 68 was one shy of Dickson, Nelson and Colbert.

Despite years on the tour, the Cadillac NFL Classic was Dickson's first playoff. There's nothing like being one-for-one.

State Farm Senior Classic—$1,250,000

Winner: Bruce Summerhays

Bruce Summerhays certainly wouldn't have needed any excuses, and no one would have thought less of him had he not come out on top at the inaugural State Farm Senior Classic in Columbia, Maryland. After all, Summerhays never led the event until the final nine, and even then as many as a dozen players were within striking distance. In fact, Summerhays started Sunday's round three strokes behind David Graham, and six players stood between the former club professional and the lead. One of those six, the man every player had their eyes on, was Hale Irwin.

Then on the 17th hole, after making seven birdies and four bogeys to get to three under par on the day, 10 under for the week and in the lead by one over Irwin, Summerhays drove the ball into a deep sand-filled divot, a tough break, but one Summerhays never fretted. "There was no reason to be scared, because I've hit these shots before," Summerhays said. Then, as if he had expected to drive the ball in the divot, Summerhays blasted the shot onto the green, where he two-putted for a routine par. On No. 18, he likewise converted an 18-foot birdie putt, and the tournament was his with rounds of 69, 68 and 69 for a 206 total.

Irwin, the model of consistency with three straight rounds of 69, finished tied for second at 207 along with Senior PGA Tour rookie Walter Hall who shot 68, 70 and 69. Seven players, including second-round leader Graham, Terry Dill and Hubert Green finished two back at 208. Graham followed rounds of 69 and 65 with a disappointing 74, but that wasn't the worst round recorded by a leader. Tom Jenkins, who entered Sunday's round tied with Graham, shot 79 and finished at 213.

Summerhays credited his experiences as a father of eight and a grandfather of 10, as well as his peak physical conditioning, for the victory. "The reason I'm in my prime now is that I'm in shape," he said. "If you're not in shape, this tour will wear you down." Then, reflecting on his steely nerves coming down the stretch, Summerhays said, "There's nothing you haven't seen when you have eight children. You learn to play in commotion. Being out there was like being home."

Ford Senior Players Championship—$2,000,000

Winner: Gil Morgan

The Senior PGA Tour rivalry between Hale Irwin and Gil Morgan took center stage in Dearborn, Michigan, at the Ford Senior Players Championship as both players teed off in the third of the four major championships. Earlier in the year Morgan won the Tradition and Irwin won the PGA Seniors' Championship. Irwin held a slight edge in money and Player of the Year points, but neither had won since April.

Neither took the rivalry too seriously. They engaged in a water-pistol duel on the first tee, an unusual display of clowning between these regular combatants. After dueling on the course for three rounds, however, the stage was set for a dramatic standoff. Irwin led Morgan by three strokes after the first round, 66 to 69, but Morgan rebounded with 64 to take a two-shot lead over Irwin, who had 69 on the second day. Morgan retained his lead on Saturday, but Irwin pulled to within one stroke by shooting 67 to Morgan's 68.

On Sunday, Morgan took command early by extending his lead to four strokes. No one could draw closer than two strokes the rest of the day. By day's end Morgan set a tournament record at 21 under par with his 66 and 267 total, three ahead of Irwin's 68 and 270. "My gosh, he played fabulously," Irwin said of Morgan's performance. "I don't think I have ever seen two rounds of golf where the putting was so good."

Although Irwin's second-place check allowed him to retain his edge on the money list, Morgan became the first man since Lee Trevino in 1992 to win two senior major championships in the same season. He also became the first since Trevino to show up on the first tee of a major championship with a toy prop. "(The water pistols) just showed up in our lockers," Morgan said. "I don't know how that happened."

"You guys are always wanting a rivalry," Irwin said. "Gil and I just thought we'd spice things up a bit." Water pistols notwithstanding, Morgan's tournament record certainly did that.

Ameritech Senior Open—$1,300,000

Winner: Hale Irwin

When a player opens with scores of 62 and 66 and enters the final round with an eight-stroke lead, it could be hard for that player to stay focused. When the nearest competitor continues to make birdies and recovers from seemingly disastrous breaks, holding that lead becomes even tougher. That was the situation facing Hale Irwin at the Ameritech Senior Open at Kemper Lakes Golf Club in Long Grove, Illinois, a suburb of Chicago.

Irwin entered Sunday's round with an impressive eight-shot lead over Larry Nelson and Bruce Summerhays. Summerhays faltered early in the final round, but Nelson continued to plug away. With Irwin making pars, Nelson tried a heroic three-wood shot to the well-guarded par-five 11th green, a risky shot that didn't pay off. Nelson hit it in the water and made bogey, his second in a row and the tournament seemed over. But Nelson came back with three consecutive birdies and he was right back in the hunt.

At the par-four 16th, Nelson attempted more heroics with a big tee shot that also found the water. It seemed to be over, again. But then on the 17th, Irwin made one of his few mistakes of the tournament, pulling a seven-iron shot into the water and taking double bogey. His lead was only two strokes with one hole to play.

That prompted Nelson to try one last do-or-die shot. On the dogleg-left par-four 18th, Nelson took out driver and aimed for the green. The ball sailed over the lake and the scoreboard, but came to rest in a greenside bunker. After failing to make his bunker shot, Nelson settled for par. Irwin, however, birdied the 18th after taking the conventional route with an iron off the tee. Afterward, a smiling Irwin said, "I'd like to thank Larry for winning today and losing for the week."

Irwin had a 201 total, 15 under par, on rounds of 62, 66 and 73. Nelson finished at 204, shooting 69, 67 and 68.

U.S. Senior Open—$1,500,000

Winner: Hale Irwin

Hale Irwin had flashbacks to 1990 as he walked onto the green at the 72nd hole of the U.S. Senior Open. It had been eight years since Irwin made a 40-foot putt to tie Mike Donald and force a 19-hole U.S. Open playoff. Irwin won that playoff for his third Open title. As he stared at a 15-foot birdie putt on the 18th green at Riviera Country Club, history and momentum were definitely on his side. "I couldn't see any break in the putt, and I wanted to see a break. You just can't believe greens around here have straight putts." But it was straight, and when it fell in, Irwin had a U.S. Senior Open title, his 14th victory in 18 months.

Irwin's one-over-par 285 total gave him a one-stroke win over Argentinean Vicente Fernandez, who closed with an impressive 68. Irwin shot 69, but more impressive than the final round or the final putt was Irwin's ability to come back from an opening-round 77. "You can dig your way out of a hole if you have belief and a plan for going about it," Irwin said. His next two rounds were 68 and 71.

His plan didn't include chipping in on the 18th on Saturday from 35 feet, but that is exactly what Irwin did to stay within three shots of Raymond Floyd, who led the first three rounds on scores of 70, 70 and 73. Playing in the final twosome with Floyd, Irwin finally caught the leader at the seventh, then passed him with a birdie at the 16th. Fernandez, playing two groups ahead, posted his 286 total, which left Irwin tied for the lead with two holes to play. When his birdie attempt on No. 17 slipped past the hole, Irwin fell to the ground in disbelief. When the birdie went in at No. 18, a jubilant Irwin thrust his fist skyward and accepted congratulations from Floyd, who shot 74 and was third at 287.

After stopping to watch several replays of the putt, Irwin reflected on his victory. "Coming back from where I was to win in the manner in which I did ... I am very proud," he said.

Utah Showdown—$1,000,000

Winner: Gil Morgan

The Utah Showdown turned out to be less of a showdown and more of a showcase for one of the Senior PGA Tour's more dominant players, but under the circumstances Gil Morgan happily accepted his sixth trophy of the year. Morgan, who entered the week in a two-man race with Hale Irwin for Player of the Year honors, strolled his way around the scenic Park Meadows Country Club in Park City, Utah, in 200 shots, 16 under par, capping his four-stroke victory with a second consecutive round of 67.

"I wasn't sure it was my type of golf course," Morgan said. "(Dave) Stockton kept telling me what a wonderful place Park City was. I looked at the temperature back home in Oklahoma and it was 107 degrees, so a little trip to the mountains with the family sounded pretty good. I'm glad I made the trip."

Organizers of the Utah Showdown, who had been given an ultimatum by the Senior PGA Tour to find a sponsor or relinquish the date, were equally glad Morgan decided to make the trip, citing his marquee value as one of the reasons the event might continue in future years. Less enthused by Morgan's presence were John Mahaffey and Isao Aoki who finished tied for second at 204. Hugh Baiocchi shot a closing 66 to finish alone in fourth place, while first-round co-leader Bob Duval followed his opening 66 with rounds of 71 and 70 to tie four others in fifth place, seven strokes back.

Coldwell Banker Burnet Classic—$1,500,000

Winner: Leonard Thompson

It might have been shortened by rain to 36 holes, and it took two extra holes, but Leonard Thompson couldn't have been happier with his first win on the Senior PGA Tour. "To win any time is nice, but the first one is always special," Thompson said after accepting the trophy at the Coldwell Banker Burnet Classic. Even more special was the fact that Thompson's victory came exactly nine years to the week after he won the Buick Open, his third and last victory on the PGA Tour. "I should make sure I play this week every year," Thompson said.

For two days, Coon Rapids, Minnesota, looked more like a rain forest than the American heartland. Heavy rain and lightening hampered play throughout the day on Friday, with tournament officials finally shortening the event to 36 holes. When the sun came out, Bunker Hill Golf Club became a steam bath with Hale Irwin, the Senior PGA Tour's most dominant player, opening with a round that was as hot as the weather. Irwin's 65 gave him a three-stroke lead over Thompson and a two-shot margin over Aoki. On Sunday, however, Irwin, the defending champion, bogeyed two of the last five holes to shoot 70, one more than he needed to tie Aoki (66-68) and Thompson (68-66).

When his second shot on the first playoff hole landed in a bunker, Thompson climbed in, nervously hit his shot, then shared a laugh with his caddie. "After I hit the bunker shot, Eddie (Thompson's caddie) handed me the rake instead of my putter. I said, 'Eddie, you nervous here? You handed me the rake.' I guess we were both nervous."

Nervous or not, Thompson parred the first hole to tie Aoki. Then, on the second playoff hole, Thompson hit a booming tee shot. Aoki's drive landed in the trees, forcing him to chip back to the fairway. When Aoki made bogey, Thompson had his first win as a senior. "It's taken longer than I expected, but it sure feels great," Thompson said.

First of America Classic—$1,000,000

Winner: George Archer

After seven major surgeries, including a hip replacement, George Archer, the 1969 Masters champion, thought it might be time to retire. "It's no fun being out here if you're not in the hunt," Archer said. "I want to be in it on the last nine. That's the fun of golf."

On a sunny Sunday afternoon at the First of America Classic in Ada, Michigan, Archer found that fun again when he shot a stunning 64 on the Egypt Valley Country Club course to win by five strokes, outgunning second-round leader Bruce Summerhays, who finished tied for third, and Jim Dent, who shot a final-round 68 to place second. "If you'd told me I would shoot 199 here I would have said you're a blinking idiot," Archer said. "If the odds in Vegas were 100 to 1, I wouldn't have put a dollar on myself."

He might not have placed any bets on himself, but Archer did cash in his biggest payday ever when he picked up the $150,000 first-place check. "I didn't think I would break 200 out here," Archer said. "This is a hard golf course."

Archer opened with 68 but trailed Dave Stockton and Jose Maria Canizares by one stroke. A second-round 67 allowed Archer to remain alone in second place, but Summerhays, who followed his opening 68 with 65, stood alone with a two-shot lead. Canizares and Dent were three strokes back.

Archer played with Dent and Summerhays in the final round and, after birdieing the second and third holes, Archer stood tied for the lead. An eight-foot birdie putt on the sixth gave Archer the outright lead. After two more birdies on the first nine and another on the 10th, Archer opened a three-shot lead with eight holes to play. With a renewed vigor, Archer pulled away from the field, opening the five-shot lead before he was through.

"George played great," Summerhays said. "He was hitting knuckleballs out there and they just kept going. He hardly missed a fairway and I missed a lot."

Northville Long Island Classic—$1,000,000

Winner: Gary Player

Back in the 1950s when Gary Player would adjourn from the golf course for a full-scale workout, his peers called him "nuts." Even Jack Nicklaus questioned his friend's devotion to a weight and fitness program that Nicklaus opined might hinder Player's flexibility and longevity as a golfer. Now, as Nicklaus considers hip-replacement surgery, the 62-year-old Player still does 1,000 sit-ups a day, and isn't above chastising reporters and spectators for their lack of fitness. He's also still winning golf tournaments with scores that would impress players 20 years his junior.

Three straight rounds of 68 for a 204 total were enough to propel Player to a one-stroke victory over J.C. Snead and Walter Hall at the Northville Long Island Classic in Jerico, New York. It was Player's age and fitness as much as his play that garnered the attention. "It's a big thrill because of all the hard work, the exercise I've put in over the years to keep myself fit," Player said.

Stamina and grit, coupled with fitness and a fiery competitive drive propelled Player to his 19th career victory as a senior. Trailing Hall and Tom Shaw by two strokes with 18 holes to play, Player birdied the third, seventh and 10th holes to draw even with the leaders. Then, on the 11th, his nine-iron approach shot almost found the hole, stopping inches away for another birdie. Still, he knew he had to finish strong if he was to have a chance. That opportunity came on the par-four 16th.

"For someone who has finished second something like 80 times, well, you want to win the golf tournament, so I shot it right over the bunker at the flag," he said. The aggressive strategy worked. Player's ball stopped six feet from the hole, and he made another birdie. Pars on the 17th and 18th, and Player stood atop the leaderboard.

Hall had three chances to catch Player on the final three holes, but he was unable to convert any of the birdie putts facing him from inside 10 feet. "I can't feel too bad about losing to Gary Player," said Hall, who shot 71. "I didn't embarrass myself and I was in the lead or close all day."

For Player, who became the second oldest winner of a Senior PGA Tour event behind Mike Fetchick, who won at 63, the joy of competing won't die anytime soon. "There was a survey that said the average professional athlete retires at age 32," he said. "I won at almost double that. This is a big thrill for me."

BankBoston Classic—$1,000,000

Winner: Hale Irwin

Hale Irwin won nine tournaments and $2.3 million in 1997. Irwin entered 1998 with greater expectations than anyone could have imagined, and he moved one step close to achieving those goals when he successfully defended his title at the BankBoston Classic in Concord, Massachusetts.

Irwin fired 69 in the first round and 64 in the second to tie Joe Inman for the lead at 11 under par. It wasn't Inman who Irwin would have to fend off on the final 18 holes. A charging Jay Sigel, who birdied six of the first eight holes, temporarily gained a two-shot advantage.

Irwin would have none of that. He birdied the sixth and the eighth to catch Sigel, then, just so there would be no question, Irwin birdied the 15th and closed with a final-round 68 to finish at 15-under-par 201, two ahead of Sigel (68-69-66), and three ahead of David Graham (68-68-68) and Inman (67-66-71). Allen Doyle made a good showing (70-66-69) to finish tied for fifth with Al Geiberger (67-67-71).

"I'm happy I can still win when I'm not playing my best," Irwin said. "I was nervous out there and I love that. If I were not nervous on the first tee, or on the 18th green, it might be time to quit." Quitting is not in Irwin's plans as he tries to break his own earning and victory records. "(Reaching the $3 million mark) will be a pretty hard chore," he said. "I'll have to keep up this level of play."

Emerald Coast Classic—$1,100,000

Winner: Dana Quigley

First Dana Quigley and the rest of the Senior PGA Tour field dodged a hurricane, then Quigley dodged a bullet en route to victory at the Emerald Coast Classic in Milton, Florida. Hurricane Earl blew through the Florida panhandle, leaving officials wondering if the event would take place.

For a while it looked like it would be a repeat of last year's tournament, where Isao Aoki defeated Gil Morgan on the second playoff hole. Aoki jumped out to a two-shot lead over Leonard Thompson after shooting 65 and 66. David Lundstrom and Hale Irwin were poised at three back while Quigley, who opened with 69 and 66, stood four back with 18 holes to play.

In the final round, Aoki faded, finishing the day with 70 and eventually tied for fourth, which left the door open for Irwin, Quigley and Jim Colbert.

"People would have thought I was an idiot out there talking to myself, but it kind of calms me down to do that," Quigley said. "It takes me out of feeling the pressure too much. I'm not like Hale. I don't have a lot of experience to dwell on." Quigley only had one other win as a professional, the 1997 Northville Long Island Classic, but the joy of that win was tarnished by the death of his father only hours before he accepted the trophy. "His dying will make me remember that day forever," Quigley said.

He'll always remember the September Sunday in Florida as well, although for very different reasons. While he didn't have a lot of experience to draw from, Quigley matched Colbert birdie-for-birdie on the final nine holes. Irwin joined them for a while, but his putter went into temporary retirement

Masters Tournament

Allsport/Andrew Redington

With neighbor Tiger Woods doing the honors, Mark O'Meara wore Augusta's green jacket with his first professional major title at the Masters Tournament.

Allsport/David Cannon

David Duval closed with 67, one too many.

Allsport/Andrew Redington

Fred Couples led through 54 holes.

Allsport/David Cannon

Tiger Woods tied for eighth in his defense.

Allsport/Andrew Redington

Jack Nicklaus, with wife Barbara, was honored by chairman Jackson Stephens.

Allsport/David Cannon

Jim Furyk took fourth with a 67-68 finish.

Allsport/David Cannon

Phil Mickelson faded in the final round.

U.S. Open

Fred Vuich

Lee Janzen shot a final-round 68 despite two bogeys in his first three holes.

Michael Cohen

It took a gritty performance — and some luck on the fifth hole — for Janzen to win his second U.S. Open title.

Michael Cohen

Payne Stewart led for three days.

Michael Cohen

Tom Lehman had another costly finish.

Michael Cohen

Bob Tway fell back early on the last day.

Michael Cohen

Nick Price was doomed by his putting.

Fred Vuich

Amateur Matt Kuchar was a star.

British Open

Fred Vuich

O'Meara needed a 68 and a playoff to win.

Michael Cohen

Mark O'Meara became the seventh golfer in history to win the Masters and British Open in the same year.

Michael Cohen

Brian Watts was an improbable contender.

Fred Vuich

Tiger Woods' bid came too late.

Michael Cohen

Jim Furyk slipped into a tie for fourth.

Michael Cohen

Young Justin Rose stole the galleries.

Michael Cohen

Jesper Parnevik made his usual threat.

Fred Vuich

Scot Raymond Russell finished with 66.

PGA Championship

Allsport/Harry How

A career ambition was realized when Vijay Singh won the PGA Championship.

Michael Cohen

Steve Stricker was second alone.

Michael Cohen

Mark O'Meara almost won a third major.

Allsport/Harry How

Steve Elkington fell short by three.

Michael Cohen

Nick Price took a share of fourth place.

Michael Cohen

Frank Lickliter had three scores in the 60s.

The Players Championship

Allsport/Craig Jones

Five strokes down entering the last round, Justin Leonard shot 67 and won by two in The Players Championship.

Allsport/Peter Taylor

Leonard's charge included this birdie on the 14th hole.

Allsport/David Cannon

Glen Day hung on to tie for second.

Allsport/Craig Jones

LeeJanzenstumbledonthelastday.

Allsport/Scott Halleran

Tom Lehman's final 68 wasn't enough.

Allsport/Craig Jones

Mark Calcavecchia finished in fourth place.

Alfred Dunhill Cup

Allsport/David Cannon

South Africa retained the title with a team of Retief Goosen, David Frost and Ernie Els.

Allsport/Paul Severn

Els won three of five matches.

Allsport/Andrew Redington

Frost was South Africa's winning captain.

Allsport/Andrew Redington

Goosen kept a perfect record at St. Andrews.

Allsport/Andrew Redington

John Daly won all four of his matches.

Allsport/Stephen Munday

Tiger Woods made his Alfred Dunhill debut.

Allsport/Andrew Redington

Mark O'Meara completed the USA's Dream Team.

Allsport/Andrew Redington

Santiago Luna defeated Woods.

Allsport/Stephen Munday

Colin Montgomerie lost to Zhang Lian-wei.

Cisco World Match Play

Allsport/Stephen Munday

Tiger Woods congratulated Mark O'Meara after the Cisco World Match Play.

Allsport/Harry How

Ernie Els fell in the quarters.

Allsport/David Cannon

Ian Woosnam was a late choice.

Allsport/Ezra O. Shaw

Vijay Singh went down by a record margin.

Allsport/David Cannon

Lee Westwood made an impressive debut.

Presidents Cup

Allsport/Craig Jones

Shigeki Maruyama had a perfect record.

Allsport/Craig Jones

Craig Parry's chip-in ignited the crowd.

Allsport/Jack Atley

Greg Norman lost to Tiger Woods in their historic first encounter in the singles.

late in the day, and he could manage no better than a one-under-par 69 to finish tied for fourth.

On the 18th, with Colbert looking at a makeable birdie putt, Quigley rammed a 35-foot birdie putt into the hole. Colbert then missed his birdie and Quigley had his second professional win on rounds of 69, 66 and 65 for a 200 total, one stroke ahead of Colbert, who finished with 66.

"Someone upstairs was pushing that baby in the hole the whole way," Quigley said of the birdie putt on the 18th. "It was just like it was magical. Honest to goodness, I can't explain it, and it certainly doesn't make any sense. The putter just moved and the ball just went on line."

Comfort Classic—$1,150,000

Winner: Hugh Baiocchi

The only scare Hugh Baiocchi got during his 20-under-par victory in the Comfort Classic at the Brickyard in Indianapolis was when he glanced at the leaderboard and saw a message that said "Sosa 61." A resident of South Africa and as unfamiliar with baseball as most Americans are with cricket, Baiocchi didn't realize the message meant that Sammy Sosa had just become the third man in baseball history to hit 61 home runs in a season. "I saw 'Sosa 61' and thought, 'Who the devil is Sosa? He must have come out of the pack.'"

No one had come out of the pack, even though the average score at the Brickyard Crossing Golf Club for the week was 70.5, the lowest of any full-field senior event in 1998. In fact, 15 under par (Baiocchi's score after the second round) would have normally meant a large lead. Baiocchi's lead was one stroke. Bruce Summerhays, the leader after the first round, lurked at 14 under par, and senior rookie John Mahaffey stood at 12 under, along with Simon Hobday.

None of those competitors could make a run at Baiocchi. Mahaffey fell back with a closing 73, and Summerhays finished with 68, his worst round of the week. Baiocchi also shot his highest score when he closed with a 67, but it was good enough for a two-stroke margin over Summerhays. Baiocchi had a 196 total with earlier scores of 66 and 63.

Finishing strong, and keeping his record of top-five finishes alive was Hale Irwin, who birdied five of the last six holes to shoot 68 on Sunday and move into a tie for fifth place with Terry Dill, Ed Dougherty, Chi Chi Rodriguez and Steve Veriato. "After the 10th hole, it didn't look good," Irwin said. "I just tried to get something good started."

Kroger Senior Classic—$1,100,000

Winner: Hugh Baiocchi

It wasn't the most conventional way to pick up a second consecutive victory, but Hugh Baiocchi will take it. "Today was virtually a lottery," Baiocchi said after the Kroger Senior Classic. "I'm glad I had the winning ticket. I didn't start out terribly well, so maybe I was a little lucky the way things transpired."

The way things transpired had more to do with the weather in Mason, Ohio, than anyone's play. After two pleasant days when Baiocchi shot 67 and 66, Baiocchi found himself tied for the lead with Bob Charles, Frank Conner, Larry Nelson and Bruce Summerhays at seven under par.

The leaderboard looked much different by early Sunday afternoon. Harold Henning, who started the day one shot off the lead, birdied three of the first four holes and was standing over a 15-foot birdie putt at the fifth that would have opened a two-shot lead over Baiocchi, who started off with two pars and a bogey. That's when the sky opened up, and play was suspended. An hour later, the final round was cancelled.

"I was really thinking I could win," Henning said. "Who knows what would have happened?"

What happened was that all five of the leaders hung around the locker room until the clouds finally moved out, and a playoff ensued. "It was pretty strange," Conner said. "We didn't have a chance to warm up that much. It was pretty evident nobody was ready."

The course wasn't ready either. Standing water precluded play on the 17th and 18th holes, so the players would play the 16th again and again until a winner could be determined. The first time around, everyone missed the green, but all made pars. The second trip through was a little better. Nelson was the only player who missed the green and he was in the fringe. Conner and Baiocchi had the best opportunities. After Nelson, Charles and Summerhays missed their birdie chances, Conner stood over a 17-footer he felt he needed to make. "I felt that if I made my putt, it would have put pressure on Hugh," Conner said. "I made a good putt. I just misread it a little bit."

Baiocchi made his 15-footer for birdie as the twilight sky slowly turned to black. "It was getting pretty dark," Baiocchi said after the win. "I don't know if we would have been able to go one more time."

Boone Valley Classic—$1,300,000

Winner: Larry Nelson

Eight weeks before teeing off in Augusta, Missouri, at the Boone Valley Classic, Larry Nelson thought his playing days might be over. A herniated disk in his neck sidelined Nelson for two months, but upon returning to competition the last week in September, Nelson showed that he still had plenty of game left as he fired a final-round 66 to win by two strokes over Graham Marsh. It was Nelson's second consecutive 65 that week, which, coupled with an opening round of 70, proved more than enough to win with a 200 total.

"I'm pretty pleased to be able to shoot 65-65 in the last two rounds," Nelson said. "This is the first time in 11 weeks that I've played five days in a row."

Things didn't look too promising for Nelson on his first day back. Not that his opening-round 70 was bad but Gary McCord, CBS commentator and Senior PGA Tour rookie, took the early lead with a 65 that sparked the galleries. McCord's magic was short-lived. A second-round 78 dropped him out of contention and, even though he rallied on Sunday with a closing 70 to finish tied for 13th with Hale Irwin, Jim Holtgrieve, Kurt Cox, Dan Wood and Mike Hill, McCord couldn't hide his disappointment.

"It was like I forgot what I was doing out there," McCord said. "I made a lot of mental mistakes and a lot of bad choices. I've got to get rid of those." In a moment of levity upon being asked about the challenges of the Senior Tour, McCord quipped, "It's like going to school and getting beaten up every time you go to recess."

The man who has usually done the beating on the Senior Tour also had a frustrating week. Irwin, the defending champion and a hometown favorite who still resides in a St. Louis suburb, shot 69-73-71–213 to finish in the tie for 13th, the first time in 19 starts that Irwin finished out of the top five.

"I'm very disappointed," Irwin said. "I sort of hit the wall this week. Unfortunately, it was here at home. I just didn't have what it took to play better this week. I haven't played well for about a month now."

Marsh, nicknamed "Swampy" by his peers, played well, but not well enough to overtake a charging Nelson. After a lethargic start on Sunday, Marsh, who led Nelson by one when play began, closed with two eagles in the last five holes to make it a close race, but he also had two bogeys in the last five, and his final-round 68 was two shots shy of what he needed.

"It seemed as if every time I did something good, I followed it up with a bogey," Marsh said. "I gave myself a chance at the end, but Larry was just a little better today."

Vantage Championship—$1,500,000

Winner: Gil Morgan

In what has become something of a broken record on the Senior PGA Tour, the final round at the Vantage Championship in Clemmons, North Carolina, came down to a duel between Hale Irwin and Gil Morgan, two players who, between them, had won 27 out of 71 events since January 1997. This time it was Morgan, needing only 84 putts in 54 holes, who came away victorious.

The opening rounds weren't scripted as planned, as Brian Barnes, Bud Allin and Raymond Floyd lit up the scoreboards with first-round 64s. Allin would go on to shoot 75 on Saturday, and finish tied for 18th. Barnes would also find trouble on Saturday, shooting 71-68 on the weekend to finish tied for 12th, while Floyd's fall from the top was a little slower. The former Masters and U.S. Open champion followed his 64 with a 69-70 weekend, also good enough for a tie for 12th with Barnes, Ed Dougherty, Allen Doyle, David Lundstrom and Larry Nelson.

Jerry McGee fired a seven-under-par 63 in the second round that, coupled with his opening 66, gave McGee a three-stroke lead over Irwin and Joe Inman and a four-shot margin over Morgan. McGee had problems, however. His driver was so inconsistent that the often hot-tempered player said, "I don't care what anybody thinks. I'm going to hit three wood (off the tees) tomorrow, and I don't care if I shoot 90."

He didn't shoot 90, but a closing 71 dropped McGee into a tie for third place with Tom Wargo at 200. That left the door open for Irwin and Morgan, and both seized the opportunity. It was nip and tuck throughout most of the round, with Irwin retaining the early lead. But Morgan's putter prevailed, and a birdie at the 16th gave him the lead for good. He shot 65 for a 198 total, one better than Irwin, who finished with 67.

At the par-five 18th, Irwin needed an eagle to force a playoff with Morgan, but, after realizing he had no chance of reaching the green with his second shot, he laid up and tried to hole his third shot from the fairway. "It was just too far," Irwin said. "I wanted it so badly, but even with a driver off of a tee I couldn't have hit that green."

Morgan's win was his sixth of the season, tying him with Irwin, and moving him just under the $2 million mark for the year. As for the record he and Irwin have amassed in 1997 and 1998, Morgan said, "I'm going to take advantage of this run while I can, because it's going to go away pretty soon. That's the nature of the animal. Everybody is replaced in five or 10 years."

The Transamerica—$1,000,000

Winner: Jim Colbert

With 18 senior victories under his belt, you might believe that winning had lost some of its luster for the Senior PGA Tour's career money leader. But as an emotional Jim Colbert accepted the $150,000 winner's check in The Transamerica and the California sun nestled below the rolling hills of the Napa Valley, Colbert couldn't have been happier.

"This was by far the most meaningful golf tournament I've ever won," Colbert said after his final-round 67 for a 205 total to edge David Lundstrom by one stroke. It was not the difficulty of the 6,632-yard Silverado Country Club that made this victory so special for Colbert, nor was it the fact that he came from one shot behind Jay Sigel, Hugh Baiocchi and Lundstrom to win in the final round. The reason for Colbert's emotional response was the fact that 15 months earlier Colbert underwent surgery for prostate cancer. The Transamerica was his first victory since returning to competition.

"I needed this one for me," he said. "But I was thinking about Arnold (Palmer, who missed the Transamerica to undergo follow-up radiation treatments in his own battle with prostate cancer). There never has been a greater fighter than him. He wanted to play this week even though he's taking radiation. I hope he shares in this win."

Colbert certainly won in a style that would have pleased Palmer. Draining a long birdie putt at the second hole to catch the leaders, Colbert bobbed in and out of the lead throughout most of Sunday's round. Colbert's competitive energy kicked in on the second nine and he shifted his game into a higher gear. "I put a premium on winning," he said. "I know there are more important things in the world, but it's real important to us. When I got close to the lead, I said to myself, 'We're going to get this done, somehow.'"

Colbert birdied four out of five holes on the last nine, but after making pars at the 17th and the par-five 18th, he was forced to wait while Sigel and Lundstrom finished. Sigel bogeyed the par-five 18th to fall into a tie for third at 207 with Jose Maria Canizares, Leonard Thompson and Bruce Summerhays, who shot a tournament-low 64 on Sunday. Lundstrom, a Senior Tour rookie, hit the green, but when his 20-foot birdie putt slid by the hole, Colbert had his 19th senior victory.

"This means a lot to people besides me," he said. "I know, because I can't go 100 yards now without someone mentioning how they had prostate cancer and beat it. That's okay. I know we've saved lives with the increased awareness." Then with a smile on his face, Colbert asked, "They got any champagne around this place?"

Raley's Gold Rush Classic—$1,000,000

Winner: Dana Quigley

It's the dream of every golf club professional in America: hone your game, make it on the Senior PGA Tour, and earn a million dollars. Most pros like the fantasy, but they realize it is just that. For Dana Quigley, the dream became a reality in El Dorado Hills, California, when the former Massachusetts club professional took only 23 putts in the final round while shooting a 64 for a 203 total, good enough for a three-stroke victory over John Morgan in the Raley's Gold Rush Classic.

Quigley picked up his third victory in 15 months and his second of 1998. With it, Quigley, who averaged $40,000 a year from lessons and other member services, picked up a $150,000 first-place check. That pushed Quigley's 1998 earnings over the $1 million mark.

"I've got so many thoughts," Quigley said afterward. "It's tough to start with one special one. Being able to do it in front of my two children and wife is more than I could bargain for."

Quigley was three strokes behind Morgan going into the final round, but when the birdies started falling, Quigley's confidence started rising. "Dana has got a terrific mental attitude," Morgan said. "When he makes a few putts, he gets on a high and thinks he can make everything."

Birdies on the sixth and seventh holes elevated Quigley's confidence, and when he made a four-foot birdie putt on the par-five 13th to tie Morgan, Quigley knew the tournament was his for the taking. At the 14th, another par-five, Quigley hit his second shot through the green and into a back bunker. He blasted out to within three feet and made another birdie putt. He had the lead to himself, and would not give it back.

Morgan had his chances, however. Serrano Country Club has three par-fives on the second nine, and Morgan failed to birdie any of them. Then he missed a five-footer on the par-three 15th. "You can't do that if you want to win tournaments," Morgan said.

EMC^2 Kaanapali Classic—$1,000,000

Winner: Jay Sigel

After compiling an impressive amateur record, Jay Sigel carried that consistency with him to the Senior PGA Tour and has found a great deal of success. Since venturing into the professional ranks in 1994, Sigel has earned more than $1 million each year, and, upon arriving in Hawaii for the EMC^2 Kaanapali Classic, he had two 1998 victories and stood in fourth place on the money list behind Hale Irwin, Gil Morgan and Larry Nelson.

"My consistency is a tribute to my attitude and fortitude or whatever you want to call it," Sigel said. "When I came out here, all I wanted to do was play like I had been playing."

For a while it looked as though that consistency would give Sigel another easy victory. After a first-round 61, the second lowest score in Senior Tour history, Sigel held a three-stroke lead over Hugh Baiocchi, Bob Eastwood and Walter Hall. A struggling and uncharacteristic round of 72 then crept into Sigel's mix, but it didn't do much damage. He still led by one over Terry Dill and Larry Laoretti.

"I had one of my worst putting rounds," Sigel admitted. "It was a real shocker." So much so that Sigel carried his putter with him into his hotel room to work on his stroke. "I didn't sleep with it, but I was thinking about it," he said. "I practiced a lot in my hotel room and I was up early putting on the green, trying to keep my rhythm."

Sigel putted much better on Sunday, opening a three-stroke lead with two holes to play. Then a poor club selection almost cost him. On the 155-yard par-three 17th, Sigel hit an eight iron over the green and into the water. "It was a nine-iron shot," he admitted. "I was trying to hit it middle-back of the green, not at the pin. A wind gust got it and threw it in the water." Sigel went on to make a double bogey.

Fortunately for Sigel, Dill bogeyed the same hole and his lead was still two. That turned out to be the winning margin after Sigel parred the 18th for a 68 and 201 total. Baiocchi and Laoretti finished second at 203, and Dill, who bogeyed the 18th, finished third at 204.

"I had a chance, but couldn't take advantage of it," Dill said. "Jay had a great week. He was tough to catch."

Pacific Bell Senior Classic—$1,100,000

Winner: Joe Inman

It had been a long struggle for Joe Inman. His last victory before arriving in Los Angeles for the Pacific Bell Senior Classic had come in the 1978 Kemper Open. From 1988 to 1997, Inman sold golf clubs before finally qualifying for the PGA Senior Tour, and a second chance. "When I won the Kemper, I didn't want it to be my only child," Inman said. "I wanted a big family."

On a Sunday afternoon in Los Angeles, at a golf tournament that Gil Morgan was poised to win, Inman shocked everyone with three consecutive birdies down the stretch and a par save at the 17th for what turned out to be a one-stroke victory over Lee Trevino, and a two-shot margin over Morgan and Brian Barnes.

"I've played in a lot of golf tournaments and I've had a lot of shaky Sundays," Inman said. "Today it was nice to finally stand up and come through."

Even though he had shot 66-68 for a share of the lead going into the final round, Inman thought he was the underdog to co-leader Morgan, who had matched Inman's scores. "I heard voices in my head saying, 'Look how good Doc (Morgan) is playing,'" Inman said. "We all have doubts. That's not abnormal. What you have to do is say, 'I hear you, but I don't believe you.'"

Morgan, the defending champion, quickly opened a two-stroke lead on Sunday with a birdie on the fifth hole, but then his birdies stopped, and he closed with a 70. Trevino stepped up, birdieing the 13th hole to temporarily take the lead. A bogey on the 17th, while Inman was capping his birdie barrage on the back nine, turned the lead over for good. Inman needed a two-putt for par on the 18th to seal the win. When he left his first putt four feet short, Inman thought he might have blown it. He said, "I'm thinking, 'Oh my god, Joe, you can't do anything easy, can you?'"

Even Trevino, whose final-round 65 was the lowest of the tournament, wanted to see Inman make it. "I was pulling for him to make that four-footer," he said.

When the putt hit the bottom of the hole for a 68 and 202 total, tears streamed down Inman's face. "The real crying will start when I get home tomorrow," he said. "I'm overwhelmed."

Energizer Senior Tour Championship—$2,000,000

Winner: Hale Irwin

When Hale Irwin won the season-ending Energizer Senior Tour Championship and collected his $347,000 first-place check, he became the first man to win as much as $2,861,945 in one season on a single professional tour. He had dominated the Senior PGA Tour with 20 top-five finishes in 22 events, two major championships and seven victories. At 53 years old, Irwin was awed by his accomplishments.

"Don't wake me up, because this is a heck of a dream," Irwin said after shooting a final-round 65 to run away from Gil Morgan and win the Senior PGA Tour's final official event by five strokes. He had earlier scores of 66, 73 and 70 for a 274 total, 14 under par. "I'm going down the road real nice right now. Somewhere along the line the streak will slow down a bit, but I don't feel as though it's going to happen right now."

It certainly didn't happen at the Dunes Golf and Beach Club in Myrtle Beach, South Carolina. Irwin led after the first day by hitting brilliant irons under cloudy and windy conditions, but he lost the lead to Raymond Floyd on Friday. Floyd, whose only 1998 victory had come early in the year in the Senior Skins Game (an unofficial event for the Senior PGA Tour), followed his opening 69 with a second-round 68 to take a two-shot lead over Irwin and Jim Albus. Morgan, Irwin's most consistent nemesis throughout his run, lurked three strokes back after shooting two rounds of 70.

It didn't take long for Morgan to improve his position. When the clouds moved out and the temperatures warmed on Saturday, Morgan's game heated up as well. A 68 gave him the lead by one stroke over Irwin and Floyd, who could manage only an even-par 72. As had been the case so many weeks in 1997 and 1998, the final round was a showdown of the Senior Tour's top two guns, Irwin and Morgan.

For Irwin, it was the perfect match-up for the perfect ending to a perfect season. "Some people may just be happy going out and playing golf and getting their money," he said. "That's not how I live my life."

That became evident when Irwin began firing irons at the flags and began sinking putts for birdies. While Morgan could only manage one birdie in his final-round bid, Irwin birdied four out of six holes in one stretch. By the time he reached the 11th tee, Irwin had the lead for good. He lengthened that margin to five strokes on the second nine.

Floyd, who played with Irwin and Morgan in the final group, struggled through some swing changes. A final-round 76 left Floyd tied for 11th place. "I never hit a good shot," he said. "I could have shot 85 out there today."

Irwin savored his victory and his year, and with a cautious eye looked ahead to 1999, when Tom Watson will be eligible for the Senior PGA Tour. "You talk about raising the bar," Irwin said. "There are a whole group of players about to come in who are absolutely going to raise the bar. It's all part of the sport's natural evolution."

Senior Match Play Challenge—$720,000

Winner: Hale Irwin

It only took 27 holes on the final day for Hale Irwin to win two matches and walk away with a victory in the inaugural Senior Match Play Challenge at Bighorn Golf Club in Palm Desert, California. Irwin defeated David Graham 6 and 4 in the morning semi-finals. Then in the afternoon, Irwin took only 13 holes to close out Gil Morgan 6 and 5 in the final. In the 27 holes, Irwin made 12 birdies, and twice he didn't have to finish a hole because his competitors conceded before reaching the green.

European Seniors Tour

El Bosque Seniors Open—£100,000

Winner: Tommy Horton

The 1998 European Seniors Tour started its seventh season as it had finished the last two years with Tommy Horton accepting the winner's plaudits after the first event. Just as he did a year earlier when he won the season opener after closing the previous year with a victory, Horton followed his three consecutive wins at the close of the 1997 campaign with a resounding victory in early May of 1998 in the inaugural El Bosque Seniors Open in Spain, the first of five new events.

The 57-year-old Englishman shattered one record and matched another as he rolled to a nine-stroke triumph at El Bosque Golf Club near Valencia. The fourth in a row set a new standard on the circuit and the margin he achieved over runner-up Noel Ratcliffe with his 15-under-par 201 total matched the mark he established in his victory in the 1997 Scottish Seniors Open. It was his 18th win on the European Seniors Tour (19th as a senior with his late 1997 triumph in South Africa) and 31st of his fine career.

Admitting afterward that "this week was far better than I had hoped for," Horton jumped off to a three-stroke lead Friday with a six-under-par 66 and nudged the margin to four with 67 Saturday. Ireland's David Jones was at 137, but was quickly out of the picture Sunday, eventually shooting 78. Horton's runaway Sunday began with a birdie at the first and a 30-foot eagle putt at the third. He added birdies at the sixth and 15th holes and had his lone bogey at the 18th for 68 and his 201 total, one stroke off the tour record. Ratcliffe took the runner-up spot with 71–210. Tied for third at 212 were Craig Defoy, American Bob Lendzion, Brian Huggett and 68-year-old Bernard Hunt.

Beko Classic—£150,000

Winner: Bob Lendzion

Bob Lendzion, a globe-trotting American playing in Europe for the first time, picked up the most impressive title of his career when he won the Beko Classic on the Gloria Golf Resort course at Antalya, Turkey.

Lendzion is a 50-year-old professional who has spent his off-season winters competing in mini-tour and PGA events in the United States and on circuits throughout the world. He became the sixth American to win on the European Seniors Tour when he dropped a four-foot birdie putt on the first hole of a playoff after he had tied for first at the end of regulation play with veterans Antonio Garrido of Spain and Bobby Verwey of South Africa. His only previous victories of consequence came in the 1986 U.S. Club Professionals Championship and the 1992 Chile Open.

Australia's Geoff Parslow held the Beko lead for two days. His 68 the first day was the only round under 70. His 71 for 139 Saturday put him two strokes in front of Verwey, the 1991 Senior British Open winner, and two ahead of Lendzion, who had a pair of 71s following his third-place finish in his first start the previous week, and three others. Garrido was at 143. Parslow remained in the picture until he triple-bogeyed the 14th.

The three playoff contenders and two others — John Garner, who shot 68, and Tommy Horton, the defending champion who was gunning for his fifth win in a row — were hot on his heels when Parslow faltered. Horton, who had shot 75 Saturday, was out in 31, but lost his putting touch on the back nine and matched Garner's 68, joining him, Jim Rhodes and David Jones in fourth place at 213, two off the winning score.

Garrido shot 68, Lendzion 69 and Verwey 70 for their 211s. Garrido trapped his approach and Verwey put his 15 feet from the cup on the first extra hole, the 18th. After the Spaniard made par from the bunker and the South African missed his birdie putt, Lendzion confidently ran in his four-footer for the victory.

AIB Irish Seniors Open—£87,305

Winner: Joe McDermott

Joe McDermott clearly had the luck of the Irish going for him. The Florida-based Irishman was in the field of the AIB Irish Seniors Open only because he had holed a five-wood shot for a double-eagle two when he needed such heroics to qualify for the 1998 circuit. Then, he ignited a closing rush in the final round at Woodbrook Golf Club near Dublin with a hole-in-one at the 13th hole, spurting on to a second-nine 30 and a 66 that brought him into a three-way tie with Australian veterans Noel Ratcliffe and Terry Gale. Five playoff holes later, the 57-year-old McDermott was the winner, like Bob Lendzion the week before, a first-time victor.

Lendzion, in fact, took a shot at two in a row in the AIB Irish Seniors. His opening 69 put him just a stroke off the leading pace of Ratcliffe, Brian Waites and Tony Jacklin, back in Europe for a spell from the U.S. Senior PGA Tour. Lendzion had moved to eight under par before driving out of bounds and taking a triple bogey at the 18th hole Saturday. Ratcliffe, runner-up in the El Bosque Open two weeks earlier, took over the lead that day with 69 for 137, one shot ahead of Waites (68-70) and Antonio Garrido (72-66) and two in front of Gale (71-68) and defending champion Tommy Horton. McDermott was at 70-72–142.

McDermott posted his 66–208 first, Gale joined him with 69, and Ratcliffe, with the opportunity to win outright with a par, hit a feeble wedge shot at the 18th and took a bogey to bring about the playoff. Ratcliffe went out on the first extra hole when he bogeyed after hooking his tee shot into trouble. The other two played the 18th four more times before McDermott dropped a 10-foot birdie putt and Gale missed from nine feet to end it.

Philips PFA Golf Classic—£100,000

Winner: Neil Coles

The most durable winner in European golf struck again, when 63-year-old Neil Coles scored his 42nd professional victory, 42 years after the first one of his distinguished career. It came at the end of May in the Philips PFA Golf Classic as Coles prevailed in the European Seniors Tour's third straight playoff. The Englishman's impressive record includes 11 victories as a senior, the last five since the formal circuit was founded in 1992 following four wins in the 1980s in the PGA Seniors and the 1987 Senior British Open.

The title battle in the tournament, in which members of Britain's Professional Footballers Association (PFA) compete for a separate crown, evolved into a duel between Coles and Northern Ireland's David Jones at Marriott Meon Valley Hotel and Country Club near Southampton. After England's Michael Slater had his day in the sun Friday with a leading 66, Jones moved into a one-stroke lead with 65 for 135 after Saturday's round. Coles was one back following his 67 and 69. Joe McDermott, winner of the last event, was at 137.

Playing together in the final group, Coles and Jones stayed close together all day Sunday and shrugged off all threats, reaching the 18th tied at 12 under par. With Jones just three feet from the cup, Coles, whose chipping and putting was superb all week, ran in a 20-footer, forcing the playoff when Jones dropped his short one. Coles had 67 and Jones 68 for their 203 totals, three ahead of their nearest challenger, American David Oakley, who closed with 66 to nose out McDermott by one stroke.

Coles and Jones replayed No. 18 in the playoff and Coles again dropped a 20-footer. The title was his when Jones left his try on the lip. "I feel for David, who played so well all day," Coles remarked, "But I won't get many more goes at winning." The way he plays, that remains to be seen.

Jersey Seniors Open—£70,000

Winner: Bob Shearer

He wasn't the youngest, but Bob Shearer wasted little time putting a victory on his senior golf record. The Australian, a prominent player in his homeland in his earlier career, won the Jersey Seniors Open just 11 days after his 50th birthday in his second start on the European Seniors Tour. Three years earlier, John Bland of South Africa won the London Masters two days after he turned 50.

"Never in my wildest dreams did I expect to win here," said Shearer, after recording his two-stroke victory at La Moye Golf Club on the Isle of Jersey. "I haven't played much competition over the past 10 years and thought it would take awhile to get into the swing of things."

In fact, Shearer was little noticed until the end. The winner of 23 titles in his regular tour days, mostly in Australia, he had finished 42nd the week before in his senior debut in the Philips PFA. When the final round began at windswept La Moye, he trailed the leader, Michael Slater, by eight strokes. Little-known Englishman Slater had posted rounds of 69-67 and had a three-shot lead over Brian Waites (68-71). Far back was Shearer (71-73), a stroke behind Tony Jacklin, who was to climb in the standings Sunday, too, challenge for the title and finish in second place at 213. Holland's Jan Dorrestein, the first-round leader with 67, plummeted with rounds of 79-78.

Shearer won the tournament with 32 on the final nine Sunday. Out in 35, he ran off three consecutive birdies starting home, faltered with a three-putt bogey at the 13th, but birdied the 16th and 18th for 67 and the winning 211 total. Jacklin made his move on the first nine with a birdie at the fifth and a chip-in eagle at the sixth, but two bogeys at the start of the second nine put a fatal crimp in his bid for a double at La Moye, where he won on the regular European Tour in 1981. Slater, who slumped to 78, and Waites, who shot 75, tied for third at 214. At 215, American Bob Menne was the only other man to finish under par.

De Vere Hotels Seniors Classic—£90,000

Winner: Tommy Horton

Tommy Horton does things big — big margins, big rallies. Horton, who set a European Seniors Tour record with a nine-stroke victory at the start of the season, picked up his second win in the De Vere Hotels Seniors Classic when he made up a seven-stroke deficit in the final round, that, too, was an unprecedented comeback. With the triumph, Horton's 19th on the circuit, he became the year's first multiple winner and moved into his familiar spot atop the money list.

Horton had put himself in the hole when he shot 76 in Saturday's second round. Ian Richardson, a local favorite with Grantham ties, took a two-stroke lead that day at Belton Woods Golf Club with 67 for a 137 total, wresting it away from Norman Wood, the first-round leader at 67. Richardson, winner of the Motor Seniors in his rookie year on the tour, seemed most seriously threatened by Northern Ireland's David Jones, a playoff loser to Neil Coles in the Philips PFA two weeks earlier, at 139, and Tony Jacklin, Denis O'Sullivan and Wood at 141. Horton trailed eight players with his 68-76–144.

Horton felt he benefited Sunday from a three-hour rain delay that soaked the Belton Woods course. "I like playing when the ball is holding so I can attack the flags," he noted after riding a 67 to his five-under-par 211 total and one-stroke victory over Richardson, who opened the door with a closing 75. Horton clipped off seven birdies, four with approaches inside two feet, the final birdie coming with a two-iron tee shot to eight feet on the par-three 17th. Still, Richardson had a chance to force a playoff with a birdie at the par-five 18th, but he wound up with a 30-foot putt that he failed to convert. Jones also shot 75 and Jacklin failed to challenge, posting 74 and tying O'Sullivan for fifth.

Ryder Seniors Classic—£100,000

Winner: Bill Hardwick

One spectacular finish followed another when Bill Hardwick blazed to victory in the Ryder Seniors Classic at Welcombe Hotel and Golf Club at Stratford upon Avon. A week after Tommy Horton staged an eight-stroke, final-round rally to win the De Vere Classic, Canadian Hardwick ripped off a seven-under-par 63 to capture his first European Seniors title. His eight-under-par 202 total on the short, par-70 Welcombe course gave him a two-stroke victory over Italy's Renato Campagnoli, who spiced his closing-round 68 with a hole-in-one, and England's David Creamer, who birdied the last two holes for 69. It was the fourth runner-up finish in six seasons for Creamer.

Hardwick lingered on the competitive fringe the first two days with so-so rounds of 70 and 69. Three of the tour's lesser lights — Creamer, Jim Rhodes and Bill Lockie — shared the first-round lead with 66s as 20 players broke Welcombe's par 70. Barry Sandry, another British club pro, joined Creamer and Rhodes (69s) at the top Saturday when he fired 63 for a 135 total, one stroke in front of Campagnoli and two ahead of the likes of Tony Jacklin, Maurice Bembridge and the Jersey victor, Bob Shearer.

It took Hardwick just a remarkable five holes to seize the lead Sunday. With an eagle from a fairway bunker at the par-five second and four birdies in that opening stretch, the Toronto-based pro, playing in Europe for the third season, went in front at seven under par. Although the battle remained close all afternoon, that was all he needed, it turned out, as runners-up Campagnoli and Creamer finished at six under. Hardwick had moved to eight under before the turn, but still had six chasers within two strokes. He played the second nine even to secure the victory. "I've never had a burst like that before," remarked the 57-year-old Hardwick. Three-time Ryder Seniors winner Neil Coles never threatened.

Swedish Seniors—£80,000

Winner: Maurice Bembridge

Victories had not been easy to come by for Maurice Bembridge in his four seasons and, when opportunity knocked in the Swedish Seniors, he nearly let it get away. "I gave everybody a chance to catch me," said Bembridge, who never trailed in the tournament at Fagelbro Golf Club, but needed an extra hole and a 12-foot birdie putt to land his second victory two years after the first in the 1996 Jersey Seniors Open.

Jittery on the greens, the 54-year-old former Ryder Cupper, who teaches in Switzerland when he is off the tour, lost a two-stroke lead he carried into Sunday's final round and eventually three-putted the 18th green to fall into a tie with English club pro Jim Rhodes. "I gave everybody a chance to catch me with some awful putting," observed the stocky little pro, who had jumped off in front Friday with Rhodes and Norman Wood at one-under-par 70 on the Fagelbro course near Stockholm and opened the two-shot gap with a 67 Saturday.

Rhodes was the man at 139 and he had his chances Sunday. Bembridge lost the lead on the first nine, but battled back and was in front by two again when he and Rhodes reached the 17th. Rhodes cut the margin in half when he holed a long birdie putt there before Bembridge's three-putt on the last hole. Bembridge made amends there a few minutes later in the playoff with the 12-footer after Rhodes missed from longer range. In the near-miss category Sunday were Alberto Croce of Italy, who shot 66–210 and missed the playoff by a stroke, and American J.R. Delich, who closed with 67 for 211. Noel Ratcliffe, the defender, had his shot with a run of five birdies and a eagle in one seven-hole stretch Sunday, but two second-nine bogeys did him in. He still shot 67 and finished at 212 with John Hudson.

Lawrence Batley Seniors—£90,000

Winner: Bobby Verwey

The playoff pattern continued when the players returned to Britain for the Lawrence Batley Seniors at Huddersfield Golf Club. Overtime was required for the fifth time in the circuit's ninth event the first week of July and the protagonists, uniquely, were the two playoff victims of Bob Lendzion in the season's second tournament in Turkey — Bobby Verwey of South Africa and Antonio Garrido of Spain, the defending champion. Verwey snatched the victory, his fourth on the European Seniors circuit, on the first extra hole.

Verwey, a winner of six tournaments in America, Germany and his native land during his regular tour career, opened with a potent 66 at Huddersfield Friday, taking a one-stroke lead over Brian Waites and T.R. Jones and two over Noel Ratcliffe, David Jones, Terry Gale and Jim Rhodes, who was coming off his playoff loss the week before to Maurice Bembridge. Garrido started poorly with 74. Verwey stumbled Saturday, shooting 75 for 141 and dropping three strokes off the leading pace of J.R. Delich (69-69) and Hugh Inggs (70-68). Garrido jumped back into contention with five-under-par 66 for 140.

That Verwey and Garrido wound up in the playoff Sunday was a bit unexpected until the final holes because Waites seemed to have victory in hand. Although he, like the other two, bogeyed the 12th and 13th holes, Waites had been three under for the round and rebounding birdies at the next two holes moved him three shots in the clear. However, Waites double-bogeyed the 16th and bogeyed the 17th, finishing at 211 in a tie for third with Inggs. Verwey also bounced back at the par-five 14th with an eagle and wound up shooting 69–210. Garrido birdied the 14th and 18th for his 70–210, setting up the overtime. It started at the par-three eighth. Both players missed the green on the 161-yard hole, but Verwey responded with a splendid bunker shot to 30 inches and won a playoff for the first time in eight career tries when Garrido chipped to eight feet and missed the putt.

Credit Suisse Private Banking Seniors Open—£100,000

Winner: Bobby Verwey

Bobby Verwey defied conventional wisdom when he put victories back to back with a two-stroke triumph in the Credit Suisse Private Banking Seniors Open. Nothing kills momentum, the sages say, more quickly than a layoff, and two open weeks on the schedule over the British Open period followed Verwey's playoff victory in the Lawrence Batley Seniors. Yet, the rich-voiced South African came out blazing when the seniors resumed action at the end of the month at Bad Ragaz Golf Club near Zurich, Switzerland. He shot 66, trailing leader Malcolm Gregson by one stroke, took over first place Saturday, and fought off several contenders to capture his fifth victory on the circuit.

His second consecutive 66 moved Verwey two shots in front of Italian Alberto Croce and American Bill Brask, who had a 65 Saturday for his 134. Gregson slipped to 70–135, the total also of Maurice Bembridge, the Swedish Seniors winner (67-68); Hugh Inggs of South Africa (70-65); Neil Coles (69-66) and Jim Rhodes (68-67).

Although Brask caught him with birdies on the first two holes Sunday, Verwey, 57, then birdied twice, turned in 33, two under at Bad Ragaz (par 70), and led by three strokes. However, Verwey bogeyed the next two holes, but survived an onslaught from Bembridge, Tommy Horton and Liam Higgins in the stretch. He birdied the 16th and finished with 68 and a 10-under-par 200. Bembridge, cheered on by partisans from nearby Ostchweizerscherge, where he is the resident professional, shot 67. Horton, the leading money winner and only other 1998 double victor at that point in the season, rang up a 64, tying for second place at 202. Although it only gave him a seventh-place finish, Irishman Higgins birdied the last six holes for a tournament-record-equalling 63.

"That was a hard day's work," said Verwey. "It's tough hanging on and I knew somebody like Tommy would make a late run at it."

Schroder Senior Masters—£150,000

Winner: Brian Huggett

A mini-Ryder Cup reunion of sorts produced the winner of the Schroder Senior Masters. Brian Huggett, winless since 1995, emerged from the season's sixth playoff as the victor over Neil Coles and Eddie Polland, with whom he played in the 1973 Ryder Cup at Muirfield. The triumph was the eighth as a senior and 30th overall in the fine career of the 61-year-old Welshman.

Polland, the youngest (51) of the overtime trio, had carried a two-stroke lead into the final round after supplanting Barry Sandry, also 51, the front-runner after the first 18 holes with 66. Polland shot 68 Saturday for 139, two better than Sandry (66-75) and Coles (73-68). Huggett was four off the pace after his 72-71 start.

Huggett set the target 209 score Sunday when he toured the par-72 Edinburgh course in 66, a new mallet putter helping him fashion it with an eagle — a four-iron second to nine feet at the 10th — and six birdies. "I've been putting like a 36-handicapper for the past two years," said Huggett about his long absence from the winner's circle. "I was owed a few."

When Coles finished with 68 and Polland 70, the three men went back to the 18th tee for the playoff. Huggett ended things quickly when he set up his winning three-foot birdie putt with a splendid six-iron approach on the home hole.

Sandry, the Broome Manor club professional who played in the final group with Coles and Polland, shot 71 and was in serious contention Sunday until absorbing three bogeys in the closing stretch. His 212 put him into a tie for fourth place with Tommy Horton, the leading money winner. Gary Player, just three strokes behind after 36 holes, faded to 12th with a 73–215, while brother-in-law Bob Verwey finished in a four-way deadlock for eighth place in his quest for a third-straight victory.

Senior British Open—£375,000

Winner: Brian Huggett

Take nothing away from Brian Huggett's victory in the Senior British Open. The Welshman laced together four solid rounds over Royal Portrush's testing 6,692 yards in early August, then victimized Eddie Polland in a playoff for the second time in eight days.

Huggett's march to victory at the ultimate expense of Polland in Eddie's home country of Northern Ireland also brushed aside Tommy Horton, the European Seniors Tour's No. 1 player, who has never won the Senior Open, and Brian Barnes, the victor in 1995 and 1996. The first-round leaders — club pro Jim Rhodes (68) and David Jones and Ian Clark (69s) — quickly fell out of contention as Australian Terry Gale (70-70) and Horton (72-68) moved in front Friday, a shot ahead of Huggett (71-70) and two atop Polland (71-71).

Horton, twice a runner-up in the tournament, inched two strokes ahead with 69 Saturday for a 209 total and Barnes jumped into contention with 68 for 211. Huggett and Polland stayed close with 71s. Huggett and Horton battled for the lead most of the round Sunday, then let Polland and Barnes back in the picture. The Welshman dropped three shots over four holes starting at the 13th and Horton killed his chances with a double bogey at the 16th. Polland holed long birdie putts at the 16th and 17th to overtake Huggett, while Barnes birdied the 15th and 17th and just missed a tying 20-footer at the 18th. Huggett shot 71 and Polland 70 for the deadlocking 283s.

Huggett then took the title with a solid par on the first extra hole as Polland missed the green and a nine-foot par putt.

West of Ireland Seniors Championship—£90,000

Winner: John Morgan

John Morgan made the most of his brief return to the scene of his earlier success. Morgan, who opted for the greater riches of the U.S. Senior PGA Tour after three fine seasons in Europe, came back for a three-tournament visit around the Senior British Open. The inaugural West of Ireland Seniors Championship was the Englishman's last stop before he returned to America, where he won some $350,000 but no titles in 1997, and he took a victory with him, holding on to edge new Irish professional Denis O'Sullivan by a stroke at East Clare Golf Club at Bodyke. It was the seventh seniors title for Morgan, who led the money list in 1994 and was runner-up the next two seasons.

Morgan never trailed at East Clare. He shared the first-round lead with Australian Terry Gale at 67, one shot ahead of Northern Ireland's David Jones and Americans Bill Brask and Chick Evans. Morgan shot a course-record 66 Saturday for a 133 total and Jones matched it to trail by one. Bill Hardwick at 136 and Gale and Brask at 137 remained in contention.

Jones, 51, winless in his second season, matched birdies and bogeys in the early going Sunday but found himself in the lead when the 54-year-old Morgan got off to a poor start. But Jones gave it back when he hit a tee shot into the water at the par-three eighth, took a double bogey and then bogeyed the 11th. Two over for the round after the 11th, Morgan regained form with a birdie at the 12th. Another followed at the 16th and he parred in for 72–205, 11 under par.

O'Sullivan, a former Irish Amateur champion in his first year as a professional, was already in at 206 after firing a second consecutive 67 sparked by an eagle at the par-five fifth hole. Gale, who had caught Morgan at the 11th hole, bogeyed the 15th and 17th and dropped into a fourth-place tie with Brask at 208, a stroke behind Jones, who three-putted the 17th for 73 after rallying with birdies at the 12th and 16th.

The Belfry PGA Seniors Championship—£175,000

Winner: Tommy Horton

Three weeks after the Senior British Open, Tommy Horton redeemed himself by securing The Belfry PGA Seniors and reclaiming the No. 1 spot on the money list. "I had something of a shock at the Senior British Open when I had a chance to win in the final round and well and truly blew it," observed Horton after posting his two-stroke victory on The Belfry's PGA National course at the end of August. "That hurt, so it was nice to get back into contention again and hold on to win."

In claiming his third win of the season and 20th on the European Seniors Tour, Horton seized the third-round lead with a six-under-par 66 for a 206 total and eased home with 71–277 in contrast to his Sunday performance at

Royal Portrush, where he also led after 54 holes, but collapsed with a closing 77. Horton faltered only once all week at PGA National. After being a part of a most unusual logjam of 10 leaders who all shot 69 in the opening round, he slipped four strokes behind with a 71 Friday. David Creamer shot into the lead with 66 for 136, a stroke ahead of the frequently contending David Jones of Northern Ireland.

Both men vanished Saturday as Horton's 66 gave him a two-stroke lead over Arnold O'Connor (67) and three over John Fourie (70). Horton, who won the PGA Seniors in 1992 and was runner-up the last two years, got off with a bang Sunday when he almost holed a wedge approach at the first hole. With two more birdies and a bogey, Horton turned in 34. He stumbled with bogeys at the 11th and 14th, but insured the victory with a final birdie at the 15th and pars the rest of the way. Italy's Renato Campagnoli, playing his final event before undergoing hernia surgery, and Jim Rhodes, the club pro at South Staffs having a excellent season, matched 69s as playing partners and tied for second at 279. They could have seriously challenged Horton, since they had 12 birdies between them.

Golden Charter PGA Scottish Seniors Open—£150,000

Winner: David Huish

David Huish's victory in the Golden Charter PGA Scottish Seniors Open was rewarding in several ways beyond the £25,000 paycheck. The playoff triumph over Northern Ireland's David Jones at Dalmahoy was witnessed by many friends of the Edinburgh-born Scot, the professional at nearby North Berwick for 31 years, and was surely dedicated to his wife Diane, whose severe heart attack had meant a nine-week absence from the European Seniors Tour for him. It was the second victory for the 54-year-old Huish, whose earlier claim to fame besides the 1996 win in the Collingtree Seniors was as the midway leader in the 1975 British Open at Carnoustie.

The playoff — the eighth in the first 15 tournaments — came after Huish and Jones had sparred in the same grouping all four rounds before winding up tied at 15-under-par 273. Jones, who lost an earlier playoff to Neil Coles in the Philips PFA Classic and now has three runner-up finishes in his brief seniors career, jumped off in front Thursday with 66. Only three others were in the 60s and Huish opened with four others at 70.

Huish came back, though, with 65 to move one stroke ahead of Jones (70–136) and both players held position with 70s Saturday. They and American David Oakley, the third man in the final grouping of Davids, played wonderful golf Sunday, making an eagle and 21 birdies among them. Jones, with 67, caught Huish, with 68, and Oakley missed the playoff by a stroke despite 66 when he bogeyed the 18th.

After matching pars on the first extra hole, Huish picked up the title with a routine par at the 18th after Jones drove into trouble, pitched out and skulled a third shot over the green en route to a bogey five. Christy O'Connor, Jr., playing in his second tournament since turning 50, closed with a sparkling 65 to tie Bill Brask at 276 and, referring to the excellent overall play of the field at Dalmahoy, remarked, "The scoring is incredible. It matches what you would expect on the main European Tour."

Efteling European Trophy—£100,000

Winner: Paul Leonard

It was a first for Holland and a first for Paul Leonard as well. The European Seniors Tour made its initial stop in the Netherlands for the Efteling European Trophy and Leonard, reviving a bizarre putting style, ended a career-long victory drought in a most decisive manner. The 53-year-old from Northern Ireland played the regular European circuit in the 1970s with limited success and remained winless through three seasons on the over-50 tour until romping to a seven-stroke victory at the Efteling Golf Park in mid-September. He was the fifth first-time winner of the 1998 season.

Desperate to solve his woes on the greens, the Belfast-born Leonard cut down a long-handled putter and dropped his right hand down the shaft just inches above the hosel when he played. "I had been playing well but my putting was a nightmare," Paul explained. "I had to do something drastic, so I returned to a style I used 20 years ago on the European Tour. It certainly worked."

Yes, it did, right from the start. Leonard never trailed, ringing up 14 birdies and taking just two bogeys over the 54 holes on the three-year-old course at a Dutch theme park. He shared the first-round lead with tour leader Tommy Horton, Noel Ratcliffe and Irish amateur Denis O'Sullivan at four-under-par 68, then surged six strokes ahead of Ratcliffe, Maurice Bembridge and John Fourie Saturday with a 66 for 134. Any doubts vanished early Sunday when Leonard holed a nine-foot birdie putt on the first hole and was eight in front after two. His closing 70 gave him a 12-under-par 204 total and four players — O'Sullivan (70), Bembridge (71), Neil Coles (69) and Liam Higgins (69) — wound up tied for second at 211.

"Whether it will last, I don't know," concluded Leonard. "But it was good for me this week."

Elf Seniors Open—£90,000

Winner: Brian Waites

It certainly was no pitch-and-putt, but at 5,804 yards with a par of 69, it is little wonder that the Pau Golf Club yielded the first-ever winning score under 200 on the European Seniors Tour.

Brian Waites was the achiever and he did it with a vengeance, amassing a mere 195 strokes in scoring a four-shot victory over the impressive first-year pro Denis O'Sullivan, who was a second-place finisher for the second consecutive week. It was the fourth senior victory for the 58-year-old Englishman since a near-career-ending automobile crash in 1991. He had won the PGA Seniors twice before the accident and, although a club professional all his adult life, scored seven victories in earlier years.

Not surprisingly, Bill Hardwick posted the best starting score of the season at Pau. The Canadian shot a five-under 64 to lead Waites and unheralded American Lloyd Monroe by two shots, Bobby Verwey and Jim Rhodes by three Friday. Waites repeated his 66 Saturday, O'Sullivan shot 64, and the two headed the field after 36 holes with their 132 totals. They were one stroke in front of Arnold O'Connor, who lost any chance Sunday when he triple-bogeyed the 15th hole. Hardwick shot himself out of it with 79 Saturday and the closing day's title action actually involved only Waites and O'Sullivan.

Waites closed brilliantly with 63. With birdies at the third, ninth and 11th, he opened a two-stroke lead over the Irishman, who closed well, thanks to his putter, but never seriously threatened to catch Waites. The former Ryder Cupper capped his record tournament performance with birdies on the last three holes for the 63–195 total. O'Sullivan had 67 for 199. South African John Fourie birdied five of his first seven holes Sunday, shot 65 and jumped into third place.

"I never looked like getting into trouble," said Waites of his winning performance. "I was playing very much within myself. I just stayed out of trouble."

Is Molas Seniors Open—£90,000

Winner: Malcolm Gregson

Malcolm Gregson, one of Britain's brightest stars in the 1960s and 1970s, had not fared as well as expected on the European Seniors Tour since his arrival at the tail-end of the 1993 season, acquiring just two titles to go with the seven he landed in his earlier career, and had not won since midway through the 1996 campaign. But Gregson showed some of his old style when the seniors visited a former stop on the PGA European Tour on the island of Sardinia for the final regular event of the season. He never trailed at the Is Molas Golf Club and withstood a charge from the ever-challenging Tommy Horton to score a two-stroke victory with his seven-under-par 209 total.

Gregson shared the first-round lead at 67 with club pro Jim Rhodes, who time and again through the season was among the early leaders and won more than £60,000 overall. Craig Defoy and Brian Waites, coming off his Elf Open victory, had 68s, while Horton muddled to a 75. Despite 73 Saturday, Gregson remained in the lead though tied at 140 with Spain's Jose Cabo and Michael Slater, as Horton went to work with 70.

On Sunday, Horton was red hot. Playing well ahead of the leaders, he nailed four birdie putts of some consequence on the front nine, bogeyed the 13th with a three-putt, then ran in sizeable putts at the 15th, 16th and 17th to finish with 66. At five-under 211, he had caught Gregson, still out on the course. Malcolm responded with a 10-foot birdie putt at the 16th, another from 20 feet at the 17th and parred the 18th for 69 and the 209.

"I'm pleased to have held off Tommy," he said afterward. "You are always looking over your shoulder for him. I've had a pretty disappointing season, but my putting came good this week. I feel more like 45 than 55."

The runner-up check clinched a third straight money title for Horton. David Jones, fourth on the money list even though winless, tied for third at 212 with Bill Brask and Slater.

Senior Tournament of Champions—£120,000

Winner: John Garner

It had been a very long time between victories — 26 years to be exact — when John Garner eked out a win in the rain-shortened Senior Tournament of Champions in late October that concluded the 1998 European Seniors Tour season. Winless in two seasons on the senior circuit, the 51-year-old Garner's lone victory during his career on the regular circuit came in the Benson & Hedges Match Play in 1972, which led to his qualification for the 1973 Ryder Cup team and the ignoble distinction of not playing a match because he was considered too far off form at the time. Garner was certainly on form at Buckinghamshire Golf Club for the Senior Tournament of Champions' third staging on the splendid parkland course designed by John Jacobs, even though the weather wasn't.

Bill Brask, who impressed in Europe with his 19th-place finish on the final money list, grabbed a one-stroke lead with a four-under-par 68 in Friday's opening round before the rains came. Garner positioned himself well as one of six 69 shooters. Eddie Polland, Liam Higgins, Alberto Croce, Christy O'Connor, Jr. and Craig Defoy were the others. The leading groups had barely started Saturday when heavy rain and gales halted play for the day, with the exclusive 36-player field to resume Sunday where each man had left off the day before.

Polland gained the upper hand as the round wore on Sunday. Birdies at the 10th, 15th and 16th gave him a two-stroke lead over Garner, Brask and Higgins and it appeared he would make up for his two playoff losses to Brian Huggett earlier in the season. However, a shanked chip from a tough lie at the 17th and a missed three-foot par putt at the 18th wiped out the lead. The short-hitting Garner gambled with his driver on a long carry over water at the 17th, cut the dogleg and reached the green on the 363-yard hole, picking up the deciding birdie after missing his eagle from eight feet. He made a tricky five-foot second putt at 18 to clinch it with his 70 for 139. Higgins parred there for 71 to tie Polland. Brask finished with 73–141.

Praia D'El Rey European Cup—£150,000

Winner: European Seniors Tour

See European LPGA Tour section.

Japan Senior Tour

Komatsu Nagoya TV Open—¥50,000,000

Winner: Hisao Inoue

The Japan Senior Tour launched its light 1998 schedule at the end of May by crowning a first-time winner in the Komatsu Nagoya TV Open at Hananoki Golf Club. Hisao Inoue never trailed in the opener. He shared the first-round lead with Ichiro Teramoto, the 1997 Japan Senior PGA champion, at five-under-par 67, one stroke in front of Haruo Yasuda and Fujio Kobayashi, two ahead of Hiroshi Ishii. Inoue broke it open Saturday, repeating his 67 and moving three strokes abreast of Yasuda. He reached his ultimate six-shot victory margin with a closing 69 for his 13-under-par 203 total. Yasuda managed just a par round, and Ishii with 70 and Tadao Nakamura overtook him for second place at 209, Seiji Ogawa's winning score in 1997. Inoue was the sixth different winner of the event.

TPC Starts—¥50,000,000

Winner: Toru Nakayama

Toru Nakayama almost let one get away in the TPC Starts tournament the following week at Narita Golf Club. He lost a three-stroke lead in the final round and had to go three extra holes against Seiichi Kanai before capturing his second career seniors victory.

Nakayama, the 1997 Castle Hill winner, started brilliantly with rounds of 67 and 68, but still had company at the top as Joji Yokoi shot those same scores in reverse for his nine-under-par 135. Nakayama established his three-shot margin Saturday even though shooting 73, as nobody did better than 71. Then, on Sunday, Nakamura opened the door with 74 for 282 and Kanai took advantage with 68, the day's best round by three strokes, to force the playoff.

Castle Hill Open—¥30,000,000

Winner: Koichi Uehara

Koichi Uehara converted a fast start into his first senior victory when the Japan Senior Tour concluded the opening segment of its 1998 season at Castle Hill Country Club. Uehara's opening eight-under-par 64 took on added significance when rain shortened the Castle Hill Open to 36 holes. His 71 in the following round was more than adequate as his 135 gave him a three-stroke victory over Akira Kawamata and Hisao Inoue, winner of the Komatsu Nagoya TV Open two weeks earlier.

The first-day 64 staked Uehara to a four-stroke lead over Toshiki Matsui and five over Inoue and Australian Terry Gale, the only other players to break 70 Friday before the rains came.

Old Man Par Senior Open—¥5,840,000

Winner: Toru Nakayama

Toru Nakayama became the Japan Senior Tour's only double winner of 1998 when the new Old Man Par Senior Open was played in late August. Nakayama, scoring his third senior victory, posted a seven-under-par 137 to win the scheduled 36-hole event at the Ohara Onjuku course, in the circuit's only action between mid-June and the second week of September.

Toshiki Matsui, the first-round runner-up in the last previous tournament, led the uniquely named Old Man Par with an opening 66, two in front of Hiroshi Kazami and Koji Nakajima, as Nakayama and three others began with 69s. Nakayama followed with 68 to grab the title as Matsui faltered with 77. Kazami shot 70 to take the runner-up spot with 138, three ahead of Nakajima, Seiji Ogawa, Mitoshi Tomita and Hisao Inoue.

HTB Senior Classic—¥8,000,000

Winner: Hsieh Min-nan

Hsieh Min-nan added a sixth victory to his impressive record on the Japan Senior Tour when he romped to a four-stroke win in the 36-hole HTB Senior Classic, the lone September event on the schedule. It was his second HTB triumph.

The 58-year-old Hsieh, who campaigned full time on the regular Japan Tour for many years, opened the tournament at Mitsui Kanko Iris Golf Club with a five-under-par 67, a stroke better than Fujio Kobayashi and two in front of four others — Koichi Uehara, Hisao Inoue, Fumio Tanaka and Masaru Amano. Nobody could mount much of a charge Sunday and Hsieh's 71 for 138 established the four-shot gap. Uehara (68) and Kobayashi (69) shared the runner-up slot.

Japan PGA Senior Championship—¥50,000,000

Winner: Seiichi Kanai

Appropriately, the most successful player on the Japan Senior Tour took the prestigious Japan PGA Senior Championship with the season drawing to a close. Seiichi Kanai, who won the Senior PGA first in 1990, scored his 11th victory on the circuit in early October at Shimoakima Country Club in Annaka. The 59-year-old Kanai came from three strokes off the pace to finish with a one-under-par 288 total and a one-stroke winning margin.

Kanai, who hadn't won since the start of the 1996 season, didn't have the look of a champion at Shimoakima after a first-round 74 left him four strokes off the pace of Teruo Sugihara, the 1995 winner. Akira Kawamata, a Thursday runner-up at 71 with Fujio Kobayashi, moved into first place with a 70

Friday, one shot up on Sugihara (72) and Haruo Yasuda (70). Kanai then trailed by five after a 72–146.

Koji Nakajima, the defending champion who had started 74-69, climbed into a share of the lead with Yasuda Saturday, shooting 70 for 213. Yasuda had 71 for his 213. Kanai mounted his threat with 70 for 216, which tied him for third with Kuo Chie-hsiung. Both Nakajima and Yasuda came apart Sunday, shooting 75 and 77 respectively, opening the door for Kanai, whose one-under 71 was all he needed to edge Nakajima. Sugihara, Kuo and Kikuo Arai finished at 289.

Japan Senior Open—¥50,000,000

Winner: Graham Marsh

Returning to the land where he enjoyed great success in his younger days, Graham Marsh finished his long international campaign on a high note. Winless in 1998 and out of the top 10 for the first time in four seasons in America, the 54-year-old Australian captured the Japan Senior Open Championship. In the process of registering a four-stroke victory, Marsh broke Isao Aoki's four-year stranglehold on that title.

Marsh, who had 25 wins in Japan during his splendid career on regular professional tours throughout the world, and Aoki, who has an even more gaudy international record and eight senior victories in the United States, got away stirringly with 65s the first day on the Ube Country Club course at Sadohara. Marsh had seven birdies and Aoki had five birdies and an eagle. Only two other players — Fumio Tanaka with 68 and Hsieh Min-nan with 69 — broke 70.

Marsh spurted four strokes in front with 70–135 Friday as Aoki slipped to 74 but retained second place. The Japanese great lost another shot Saturday as he had 70, the leader 69 for 204. Marsh, a five-time senior winner in America, wrapped it up Sunday with 70 and 14-under-par 284. Toru Nakayama, the circuit's only two-time winner in 1998, bounded into second place with 68–278. That nearly gave him the money title, but Seiichi Kanai, the tour's most successful player, won enough with his tie for eighth place to win it by a mere ¥110,000.

South Africa Senior Tour

Vodacom Senior Series: Pretoria—R100,000

Winner: Gabriel Putsoe

Normally, a final-round 73 dooms a tournament leader, unless he or she is nursing a big margin at the start of the day. It worked the other way around for Gabriel Putsoe in the Vodacom Senior Series: Pretoria, the opening event on the scatter-scheduled Franklin Templeton Senior Tour in South Africa. It shot Putsoe to a seven-stroke victory at Silver Lakes Country Club, much to the chagrin of the more experienced Allan Henning.

Putsoe and Henning had pulled well ahead of the rest of the field in the mid-July event after two rounds. Henning had followed his stout start, a seven-under-par 65, with 73 for a 138 total, while Putsoe, in second place in the first round with 68, matched the 138 with a 70 on Thursday. John Howie was six back in third place. When Henning faltered badly the last day and nobody else put up a serious challenge, Putsoe had an easy time of it en route to his 73–211 total. Henning wound up with an 80 and still finished second, one stroke in front of Howie and John Fourie.

Vodacom Senior Series: Wild Coast—R100,000

Winner: Tertius Claassens

Gabriel Putsoe and Allen Henning made late challenges again in the Vodacom Senior Series: Wild Coast tournament, but Tertius Claassens, a first-year senior who was a strong campaigner in South Africa in his younger days, held them off despite a closing 76 at Wild Coast Country Club.

Claassens had established enough of a cushion the first two days that the faulty final round didn't ruin him. Claassens began the tournament with 70 Wednesday, jumping three strokes into the lead over Joe Dlamini, Ranjith Singh and Peter Mkata. He widened the gap with 72, for a 142 total, four better than runner-up Dlamini, 73-73.

Mkata shot 74 for 147, one shot ahead of Muss Gammon and Henning. Putsoe had 71 in the final round, finishing in a second-place tie with Henning at 221 as Claassens staggered home the winner with the 76 for a 218 total, eight over par.

Vodacom Senior Series: Mmabatho—R100,000

Winner: Tertius Claassens

The six-week gap in the schedule before the third event — the Vodacom Senior Series: Mmabatho — had virtually no effect on the early stars of the season. The top of the final standings was a match for the last previous tournament as Tertius Claassens made it two wins in a row and Gabriel

Putsoe and Allan Henning again tied for second place.

The sequence was quite different, though. Claassens trailed by four strokes the first day when Henning started with 67. Putsoe shot 68, sharing second place with Shadrack Molefe. Claassens made his move Saturday with a 67 of his own, his 138 total thrusting him into a leader deadlock with Putsoe (68-70) as Henning slipped a bit with 72 for 139. Claassens finished strongly and was leading by five after 17 holes before hitting into the water at the final green and taking a double bogey. He still shot 70 for an eight-under-par 208 total and a three-stroke victory over Putsoe, who closed with 72, and Henning, who had a final-round 71 for his 210 total.

Vodacom Senior Series: Welkom—R100,000

Winner: Allan Henning

Persistence finally paid off for Allan Henning in the Vodacom Senior Series: Welkom tournament. In a run of eight tournaments spread over two seasons of senior golf in South Africa, Henning had finished either second or third every time. He shed the bridesmaid mantle at Oppenheimer Park Golf Club, squeezing out a one-stroke victory over the omnipresent challenger, Gabriel Putsoe.

Henning, long successful on his home circuit, never trailed at the Welkom tournament. He fired a five-under-par 67 in the first round, distancing himself from Solly Sepeng, his nearest competitor, by four strokes. Putsoe, Ian Smith and Peter Loeb had 72s. Tertius Claassens, winner of the previous two tournaments, withdrew. Although merely matching par the second day, Henning remained in front with his 139 total. Putsoe shot 69 to take over second place at 141, while Sepeng had a 72 for 143.

Putsoe seized the lead in the early going of the final round. But Henning hung tough, capping a four-stroke swing when he chipped in at the par-four 16th and finished with 70 for a 209 total, nipping Putsoe, who shot 69, by one stroke.

Franklin Templeton Senior South African Open—R200,000

Winner: John Bland

John Bland's victory in the Franklin Templeton Senior South African Open in mid-November was as heartwarming as it was efficiently crafted. The year had been a struggle for him on the U.S. Senior PGA Tour, but the illness and death in August of his wife Helen overwhelmed all else. He only played 18 times in America, where he had enjoyed great success during the previous 27 months. Back in action on the Kensington Golf Club course on which he had scored three victories earlier in his career, the 54-year-old Bland rolled to a six-stroke victory in a successful defense of the title.

Bland, who won the 1997 title at Houghton, was in the picture all the way at Kensington. He trailed first-round leader John Fourie by one stroke with his opening 69, sharing the runner-up spot with two-time 1998 winner Tertius Claassens. Following up with a 68 of his own, Bland seized a two-stroke lead over Fourie, who shot 68-71–139.

He fended off minor threats from Allan Henning and Simon Hobday in the last round with a fast start and steady golf the rest of the way. Bland birdied the second and fourth holes and just missed an eagle at the eighth to put considerable distance on the field. He needed that as things turned out. Both Henning and Hobday made their runs, Henning with consecutive birdies at Nos. 13, 14 and 15 and Hobday, who started the day nine strokes back, with an eight-under-par round going before bogeying the 17th. Bland, who had just two bogeys in 54 holes, birdied the 15th and finished with 68 for 205. Hobday (65), Henning (67) and Fourie (72) tied for second place at 211.

Vodacom Senior Classic—R450,000

Winner: Solly Sepeng

No less sentimental and noteworthy than John Bland's victory but for entirely different reasons was Solly Sepeng's triumph in the Vodacom Senior Classic the following week at Dainfern Country Club. Sepeng, a black golfer with a cross-handed swing grip who had labored in obscurity during his 26-year professional career, scored his first victory in South African PGA golf, winning by two strokes over the season's strongest field with his 15-under-par 201 total.

Denied access to the better courses during the apartheid days, Sepeng learned his golf on makeshift courses with sand greens and won his only tournaments on the all-black Tournament Professional Association. The winner's check of R70,650 was more than double his cumulative previous earnings since he turned professional in 1972. He also received R15,000 in bonus money and a plane ticket that would enable him to go to Europe to play on the European Seniors Tour. "I can't believe that something like this has happened to me after all these years," remarked the 58-year-old Sepeng.

Simon Hobday, the 1997 winner, launched his defense with a five-under-par 67 and shared the lead with John Fourie. Gary Player and Daddy Naidoo were at 68 and Sepeng shared the 69 spot with John Bland and John Howie. Then Sepeng seized first place Friday with a dazzling 64 for a 133 total, two strokes in front of Hobday (67-68) and Howie (69-66), and three ahead of Bland (69-67). Fourie shot 74 and fell out of contention.

Sepeng exhibited great poise Sunday, clicking off a birdie and eight pars on the incoming nine, holding off the challenge of Hobday. Hobday had three birdies on the second nine, but could only match Sepeng's 68 and place second at 203, one stroke ahead of Bland. Player shot 210, Lee Trevino, 220, and Harold Henning, for whom Sepeng once caddied, 216.

John Bland Invitational—R100,000

Winner: Allan Henning

Allan Henning made a double hit in the season-ending John Bland Invitational at Randpark Golf Club. Not only did he land his second title of the 1998 campaign but he jumped into the No. 1 spot on the Franklin Templeton Senior Tour's money list. The victory came in a playoff against John Fourie after the two men tied after 54 holes with 11-under-par 205 totals.

Fourie had entered the final round sharing first place with the tournament's namesake after shooting 65 for 135. He had trailed first-round leader Joe Dlamini by four strokes Friday. Bland had rounds of 68-67, while Henning remained close with 68-69–137, one shot ahead of Dlamini (66-72) and Simon Hobday (68-70).

Henning was rock solid Sunday, running off four birdies and 14 pars for a closing 68, while Fourie was scoring 70 and Bland 72 to finish third at 207. Key to the Henning-Fourie deadlock were their birdies at the difficult, par-three 17th. In the playoff, which began at the par-five 18th, Henning was on the green in two with a pair of splendid wood shots and two-putted for the winning birdie. Fourie, who drove into the rough and failed to reach the green with his second shot, missed his par putt.

16. Women's Tours

Women's professional golf had a showdown in 1998 that featured nail-biting excitement, healthy debate and some of the greatest golf in the history of the game. On one side of the showdown stood Sweden's Annika Sorenstam, the game's most dominant female player in 1997. She didn't disappoint. With four victories and a second straight money title, Sorenstam wrapped up Rolex Player of the Year honors again on the LPGA Tour in the United States. She became the first woman in LPGA history to average less than 70 strokes per round for the entire year. A closing 72 at the PageNet Tour Championship in Las Vegas gave Sorenstam an average of 69.99 and another addition to her already prominent place in golf's record books.

While she didn't win until early June, Sorenstam made up for lost time after winning the Michelob Light Classic in St. Louis. Three weeks later, she picked up her second victory at the ShopRite Classic, and two weeks after that, she won again at the JAL Big Apple Classic. Then in early September, Sorenstam won her fourth event at the Safeco Classic. She also had a victory in Europe at the Compaq Open. "I get goose bumps thinking about it," she said in Las Vegas. "It's a dream come true."

There were many dreams that came true in women's golf, but none more compelling than the story of Sorenstam's chief rival throughout 1998, a young girl from South Korea who came to America in search of a life in the game she loved. Before she struck her first shot as a professional, pundits predicted that 21-year-old Se Ri Pak would win early and often. She had talent, drive, work ethic and a measure of discipline that vastly exceeded her age. But no one could have imagined just what an impact the 1997 qualifying tournament medalist would have on the game and on her home country.

Pak's first victory came in the season's second major, the McDonald's LPGA Championship in Wilmington, Delaware. Her second occurred eight weeks later in Kohler, Wisconsin, at the U.S. Women's Open Championship. Not only did Pak win the Open, her second major of the year, she did so in a dramatic 20-hole playoff with amateur Jenny Chuasiriporn, 20, a Duke University student. The duel provided more excitement than any women's event in recent memory and, after the final birdie putt fell, Pak not only became a celebrity worthy of coverage in magazines such as *People* and *Newsweek*, she became a goddess in her home country. Parliament passed a unanimous resolution honoring Pak's achievements, and the South Korean president called her "a national hero."

As heady as all that attention and excitement seemed, it didn't distract Pak. Four days after dueling with Chuasiriporn, Pak fired a 10-under-par 61 to assume the lead in the Jamie Farr Kroger Classic. It was the lowest round ever in an LPGA event, and when Pak won, people began recalling the rookie season of another young phenom, Nancy Lopez in 1978. Pak won again two weeks later at the Giant Eagle Classic, putting her into contention for Player of the Year and every other award the LPGA had to offer.

But late-season fatigue, capped off by a collapse and brief hospitalization while visiting South Korea, caused Pak to lose most of the momentum she had gained. It also gave Sorenstam an opening to Player of the Year honors. Pak ran away with the Rookie of the Year award, but that didn't stop the debate. Even after the LPGA awards ceremony in New York, many were still arguing over which accomplishments deserved more credit.

In addition to Pak and Sorenstam, Sweden's Helen Alfredsson reasserted herself after a noticeably long absence. With no wins in America since 1994, Alfredsson overcame hip surgery and bad memories of past failings to win twice on the LPGA Tour and three times overall. Another Swede, former U.S. Women's Open champion Liselotte Neumann, gained two early-season wins. Between Neumann, Alfredsson and Sorenstam, Swedish golfers accounted for eight LPGA victories.

Overall, women's golf not only looked exciting in 1998, it looked more international. Four of the top five LPGA money winners were born outside the United States — two from Sweden, one from South Korea and one, Karrie Webb, from Australia — and less than half of the 38 regular season LPGA events were won by Americans. Donna Andrews was the top American, third on the LPGA Money List. It was only fitting that the season-ending Tour Championship would be won by England's Laura Davies, the LPGA Tour's longest hitter and, before Sorenstam, the most prolific international player.

It was perhaps a small consolation, but the United States did win the Solheim Cup over Europe.

With most of its top players in America, the struggling European LPGA Tour did not even announce a 1998 schedule until the spring and then it included only eight tournaments. Two more events were added later, and there was also an unofficial event in Morocco and a team event against the European Seniors Tour, as well as the Solheim Cup, which was contested on American soil in Dublin, Ohio.

"It has been tough, but we have come through it," said managing director John Mort. "The tour staff and players have worked very hard, and now there is light at the end of the tunnel. We are all looking forward to 1999."

Alfredsson was the leading European money winner with £125,975, followed by two other Swedes, Sophie Gustafson and Maria Hjorth, with Trish Johnson in fourth place, leading the British contingent. Gustafson won two tournaments, plus the unofficial Princess Lalla Meriem Cup in Morocco, and was the only player to win more than once in Europe. American Sherri Steinhauer took the Weetabix Women's British Open title.

The ever-healthy Japan LPGA Tour was led by Michiko Hattori with five victories and ¥81,570,823. Two victories each were recorded by Akiko Fukushima, Kaori Higo, Hiromi Kobayashi and Young-Me Lee, and Neumann claimed her third victory of the year in Japan, along with two in America.

There were seven tournaments in Australia, including victories by Webb in the Ladies Masters and Marnie McGuire in the Women's Open. In South Africa, Barbara Pestana won the Ladies Open and Laurette Maritz won the Ladies Masters.

U.S. LPGA Tour

HealthSouth Inaugural—$600,000

Winner: Kelly Robbins

Kelly Robbins started 1998 as she ended 1997, working hard and playing to win. After finishing third in money, scoring and Player of the Year points to Annika Sorenstam and Karrie Webb, Robbins continued to work, as she had for the last three years, on her putting stroke and her concentration. That paid off in Orlando, Florida, when Robbins followed a disappointing opening-round 76 with scores of 67 and 66 for a 209 total, seven under par, to win the HealthSouth Inaugural, finishing two strokes ahead of Meg Mallon and three ahead of Patty Sheehan.

"Kelly can shoot 66 and make it look easy," said Juli Inkster, who led after the second round, and shared the lead until she double-bogeyed No. 15 on Sunday for a 74 to finish four strokes back. Unfortunately for many in the field, double bogeys were common. Winds whipped through the Grand Cypress Resort, at times gusting up to 30 miles per hour. Forty players shot 80 or better, and the average score turned out to be 77.6.

In that context, Robbins' opening 76 doesn't seem that bad, except that Jenny Lidback fought off the winds to shoot an opening-round 69. By Saturday the winds had calmed, and so had many of the players' games. Inkster fired a 66 the second day to share what would turn out to be the low score of the tournament. It was Robbins, however, who was able to put back-to-back rounds together and propel herself into the lead.

Sorenstam and Webb chose to skip the season opener, but with newcomers like Se Ri Pak and Kelli Kuehne making their official debuts as LPGA regulars, the field was anything but weak. It was also a week when veterans tried to show the world that they still had the right stuff. Notables like Nancy Lopez (who finished tied for 13th) and Pat Bradley (who finished tied for 19th, 10 shots off Robbins' winning score) joined Inkster and Sheehan on the leaderboard.

But coming from seven shots back, it was Robbins who proved that with or without Annika and Karrie, she is still one of the best players in professional golf. After winning, she called her mother's answering machine and said, "Wow, here we go." Her season was off to a grand beginning.

Office Depot—$600,000

Winner: Helen Alfredsson

At the end of the 1996 season, Sweden's Helen Alfredsson didn't know if she would ever play golf again. The pain in her right side had become unbearable, and as a result, her golf swing had become unmemorable. In November of that year, she underwent surgery to correct a broken pelvis. Fourteen months later, in January of 1998, Alfredsson fought off stiff competition to win the Office Depot event in West Palm Beach, Florida, her first victory in four years.

It wasn't an easy comeback. In addition to physical therapy and reinventing a golf swing that, for the first 11 years of her professional life, had compensated for a physical handicap, Alfredsson had to overcome the memories of one of the most spectacular collapses in U.S. Women's Open history. In 1994, she set an 18-hole scoring record, firing 63 at the Indianwood (Illinois) Country Club and, at one point, accumulating a seven-stroke lead. Fourteen strokes over par later, Alfredsson finished tied for ninth, and spent the next four years explaining and reconciling what might have been.

All that ended at the Ibis Golf and Country Club in 1998 when a physically healthy and newly confident Alfredsson played four consecutive under-par rounds to finish at 11-under-par 277 and atop the leaderboard. Alfredsson's scores were 68, 71, 67 and 71 for a two-stroke victory over another Swede, Liselotte Neumann. While the LPGA's two premier stars — Annika Sorenstam and Karrie Webb — weren't in attendance, Alfredsson fought off some serious competition en route to her comeback. Kelly Robbins, coming off a season-opening victory at the HealthSouth Inaugural, had an opportunity to make it two in a row, but failed to convert two crucial pars on the second nine Sunday and placed third with a 67 and 282 total. Also in contention was Alfredsson's best friend on tour, Neumann, who missed an eight-foot eagle putt on the last hole that would have forced a playoff. She shot 68 for her 279 total. "The best people to beat are your best friends," Alfredsson said after firing a final-round 71 to do just that.

"I'm happy to feel good again," Alfredsson said. "I could be bitter, but I'm grateful that I actually got back. You learn lessons. Maybe this was mine."

Los Angeles Women's Championship—$650,000

Winner: Dale Eggeling

Once again, El Niño reeked havoc on professional golf, shortening the Los Angeles Women's Championship from 54 to 36 holes and drenching the Oakmont Country Club in Glendale, California. That didn't bother 43-year-old Dale Eggeling. In fact, Eggeling joked that people her age would "take them any way you can get them."

Eggeling got this victory by making up five shots in the final round, firing an impressive 69 for a three-under-par 141 total, then sinking a 15-foot birdie putt to defeat Japan's Hiromi Kobayashi in a playoff. "I never thought about winning," she later said. "I didn't think I had a chance."

But for some short game miscues by Kobayashi, Eggeling's assessment might have been correct. The young Japanese player opened the tournament with a stunning six-under-par 30, but her short game abandoned her and she played the final 27 holes three over par for scores of 67 and 74. Eggeling finished an hour and a half ahead of Kobayashi, but had to wait until Kobayashi birdied the final hole to force the playoff. On the first extra hole, the par-five 18th, Kobayashi took three to get down from the greenside bunker, while Eggeling hit a wedge to within 15 feet and rolled the putt into the hole.

"I cried when I made that putt," she said. She also hugged her caddie, her husband (Mike) and Kobayashi. "My son (Dustin) is 10," she says. "He's at an age now where he appreciates the sport, and I want my son and my husband to be proud of me."

Cup Noodles Hawaiian Ladies Open—$650,000

Winner: Wendy Ward

After charging to a lead with an opening-round 65, Wendy Ward wasn't able to relax until the last putt dropped in the Cup Noodles Hawaiian Ladies Open in Kapolei, Hawaii. Even then, it didn't seem like it was over. Ward followed her 65 with a 69, but found at the end of the second round she was two strokes behind Dana Dormann, who fired two consecutive rounds of 66 in pursuit of her first victory since 1993.

Annika Sorenstam, Brandie Burton and Meg Mallon were lurking only four shots back after two rounds, and with those players that close, no lead seemed safe. During the final round, Laura Davies made a run, firing 69 to tie Kristi Albers for the day's low score, but it wasn't enough. Ward shot 70 and Dormann shot 72, and they finished tied at 204, 12 under par, at the end of regulation play. "I've been working on a low-round-of-the-day focus," Ward said. She missed that low-round-of-the-day mark by one in the final round, but it was still enough to force the playoff.

On the first extra hole, Ward tapped in a par putt, and walked off the green assuming the playoff would continue. It would not. Dormann missed her four-footer for par, making Ward the champion. "This one kind of snuck up on me," Ward says. But she will take them any way they come.

Welch's/Circle K Championship—$500,000

Winner: Helen Alfredsson

For the second time in eight weeks, Helen Alfredsson proved that the pain is gone, the swing is back, and the winning edge is hers again. "Some people say Swedish people are calm and collected," Alfredsson said after capturing the Welch's/Circle K Championship in Tucson, Arizona. "I am not. My mother says I'm like a race car driver in rush-hour traffic." That high-gear style obviously paid off as Alfredsson put lingering questions about her recent hip surgery behind her, and became the year's first multiple LPGA winner with a 274 total, 14 under par, on scores of 68, 64, 70 and 72.

Oddly enough, Alfredsson's good friend and fellow Swede, Liselotte Neumann, who finished second to Alfredsson in her first victory at the Office Depot, finished second again, firing a final-round 68 to get to 13 under par and one shot off the pace. Dana Dormann, also a second-place finisher in 1998, finished tied with Neumann, but hers was a bitter second. Dormann missed a one-foot putt en route to shooting a final-round 69. Had it been 68, she would have forced a playoff with a struggling Alfredsson who three-putted the last green to shoot a final-round even par.

As it was, even par on the final day was enough for a win, a smile and another joke from one of the LPGA's more jocular entertainers. "This is ironic," Alfredsson said as she accepted the trophy, which features the likeness of a tree. "I was in the trees all day."

Standard Register Ping—$850,000

Winner: Liselotte Neumann

The first three months of the LPGA schedule could aptly have been entitled, "The Season of the Swedes." Surprisingly, however, the LPGA's most famous Swede, Annika Sorenstam, didn't win an event in the first quarter of the year. Granted Sorenstam only entered four tournaments, finishing in the top 10 in all four starts, but that wasn't good enough to keep up with Helen Alfredsson, who won twice in three months, and Liselotte Neumann, who finished second on two occasions and broke through with her first victory at the Standard Register Ping in Phoenix, Arizona.

Neumann's victory wasn't easy, however. After opening with a four-under-par 69, Neumann had her best Friday of the year when she fired a 67 to take a two-shot lead into the weekend. As good as it was, Neumann's 67 on Friday was overshadowed by Juli Inkster who followed up her first-round 74 with a course-record 64. But Inkster couldn't keep it going through the weekend. Her final rounds of 72 and 73 left her in a tie for ninth. Neumann, however, followed up her good play with a 69 on Saturday that gave her a four-shot lead going into Sunday's final round.

Still, she almost lost it. With bogeys on two of the last three holes, Neumann limped into the clubhouse with a final-round 74 for a 279 total, 13 under par, and in a tie with a charging Rosie Jones who closed out on Sunday with a three-under-par 70. Both players made pars on the first extra hole (the 17th), Jones with a two-putt and Neumann with a spectacular up-and-down from the greenside bunker. Both made routine pars on the second extra hole. But at the third extra hole (the 18th) Neumann redeemed herself by making birdie.

The first friend to congratulate Neumann was her toy poodle Pee Wee. Kelly Robbins, who finished nine shots back, unsuccessfully held the canine by the 18th green. Taking a victory lap around the green, Pee Wee jumped into Neumann's arms after the victory.

"I know there's going to come a day when I'm not playing that well," Neumann said afterward. "You ride the wave. If I get a little nervous, it's good because it means winning still means a lot to me."

Nabisco Dinah Shore—$1,000,000

Winner: Pat Hurst

Going into the first round of the Nabisco Dinah Shore, Californian Pat Hurst might have been the sentimental favorite in Rancho Mirage, California, but she didn't show up on the odds-makers' top-10 list of probable champions. After all, Hurst not only hadn't won a major, she only owned one career LPGA victory (the 1997 Oldsmobile Classic). Even going into Sunday's final round, after having led the tournament since the first hole on the first day, Hurst was the decided underdog to such notables as Liselotte Neumann, Helen Alfredsson, Laura Davies, Annika Sorenstam and Karrie Webb, all of whom lurked within three shots of the lead.

But the home course advantage and a renewed sense of commitment was enough to push Hurst over the top, propelling her to a one-shot, wire-to-wire victory over Helen Dobson and a two-shot margin over Alfredsson and Davies. She had scores of 68, 72, 70 and 71 for a 281 total, seven under par. "There was never a doubt," said Hurst's caddie, Gary Lukash. "(Pat) had nerves of steel, and she stayed in every shot, even with the best players in the world."

The best players in the world had nothing on Hurst, who consistently out-drove the long-hitting Webb all day on Sunday. On the 14th hole on Sunday, Hurst sank a 12-foot putt for birdie to widen her lead over Neumann. Then on No. 17, she saved par with a testy, downhill four-footer, and on No. 18, she rammed in a five-footer for par to shoot 71 and win her first major title. Alfredsson shot a final-round 70 to tie a charging Davies, who closed with 68. Neumann and Donna Andrews finished three strokes back, while Sorenstam and Webb were five back, tied for seventh.

"(Pat) feels really comfortable here," Hurst's husband, Jeff Heitt said. Given the fact that Hurst once worked as a teaching pro at La Quinta Country Club, less than 20 miles away from Rancho Mirage and Mission Hills Country Club, it was no wonder she felt right at home.

Her only uncomfortable moment came after winning when she was expected to take the traditional post-tournament swim in the lake that borders the 18th green. "I can't swim," Hurst said. Still, to keep tradition alive, the new champion waded up to her knees in the water then scurried back to the shore. "I wasn't going in over my head," she said.

Longs Drugs Challenge—$600,000

Winner: Donna Andrews

Carin Koch began the final day of the Longs Drugs Challenge tied for the lead with Donna Andrews and Barb Mucha. Playing well, hitting fairways and greens, and making a few putts, Koch thought she had a good chance to win her first professional tournament. Then, as a storm cloud gathered overhead, Andrews hit a nine iron from 106 yards at the same time that a loud clap of thunder shook the area. Andrews' ball took one hop and landed in the hole for an eagle, prompting an equally thunderous ovation from the Sacramento, California, gallery.

"I'm a little disappointed," said Koch, who maintained a two-shot lead with seven holes to go, but despite sound play, lost by one to Andrews. "When Donna makes it from the fairway for an eagle, you can't do much about it," Koch said.

"I got some good breaks," admitted Andrews. Still, one shot might have been the turning point, but it wasn't the entire golf tournament. Andrews played solidly all week, shooting 70, 69, 70 and 69 for a 10-under-par 278 total, one better than Koch, and four better than Annika Sorenstam. "You'd like to say it's all skill, but there is definitely some luck involved," Andrews said. "I got the good breaks, and that's what it takes to win a golf tournament."

Andrews' final break came at the 16th, where she pulled her six-iron approach shot, but a good kick and roll left her with a six-foot birdie putt which she promptly made to take the lead away from Koch for good. With a par on No. 18, Andrews held on to capture her sixth career victory.

City of Hope Myrtle Beach Classic—$600,000

Winner: Karrie Webb

Four rounds in the 60s, a little motivation from her housemates and a pending thunderstorm all combined to help Karrie Webb successfully defend her title at the City of Hope Myrtle Beach Classic in South Carolina. It was Webb's ninth career victory, and her second of the 1998 season. Webb's highest score for the tournament was 68 (in the first and third rounds) and her four-day total of 19-under-par 269 was good enough for a three-stroke margin of victory.

Friday was the only day Webb beat her four housemates, Liselotte Neumann, Meg Mallon, Kelly Robbins and Beth Daniel. It was the second time the fivesome had roomed together, the first being three weeks earlier at the Standard Register Ping, where Neumann was the winner. This time it was Webb who closed with 67 to win by three strokes over Meg Mallon, who battled flu-like symptoms all week.

Mallon started the week feeling lousy but playing great. Her opening-round 62 tied an LPGA record and gave her a three-shot lead over Cindy McCurdy and a six-shot margin over Webb. By Friday, however, the illness prevailed and Mallon's 73 put her one shot off Webb's two-day pace. Both Mallon and Webb shot 68 on Saturday, which set up a duel of the housemates on Sunday.

Mallon birdied the first three holes on the final day and took a temporary lead, but Webb slammed the door quickly. By the time they walked off the 16th green, Webb had a five-shot lead. It was trimmed to three before the finish, but there was never a doubt as to the outcome. "Karrie played perfect, excellent golf," Mallon said. "I didn't help my cause when I birdied the first three holes. I think it just fired her up." A smiling Webb simply said, "I'm happy with the way my year has started. I'm looking forward to the rest of the year."

Chick-fil-A Charity Championship—$700,000

Winner: Liselotte Neumann

After Thursday's pro-am at the Chick-fil-A Charity Championship, Liselotte Neumann decided to get in a couple of sets of tennis with her caddie. Unfortunately, the match was called early due to injury. "I was trying to reach a really strong serve and my foot got stuck to the ground," Neumann said. "I turned my ankle, and I didn't know if I was going to be able to play."

Not only was Neumann able to hobble through 54 holes at Eagles Landing Country Club in Stockbridge, Georgia, she dominated a field that sported the likes of Karrie Webb, Kelly Robbins, Helen Alfredsson and defending champion Nancy Lopez. With a taped ankle and iron play that was, in her words, "all over the flag," Neumann cruised to a 14-under-par 216 total and a three-shot victory over Lorie Kane and a resurgent Dottie Pepper. Her scores were 67, 65 and 70.

"Lotta's a great player. She gives herself a lot of chances and doesn't make a lot of mistakes," Kane said. What few mistakes Neumann did make turned in her favor. At the sixth hole on Sunday, Neumann hit a low pull-hook that seemed destined for the out-of-bounds markers. Somehow, the ball landed softly enough that she not only stayed in bounds, she had an open shot to the green. Neumann made easy par, and no one came close after that. "I got a great break there," she said. "I don't know if the ball hit something, but it could have gone out of bounds. It was a good break."

Another nice break came in the last minutes of Saturday's round, only this one was at the expense of another player. Pat Hurst, who held the first-round lead, came to the 18th tee tied with Neumann at 11 under par. Twenty minutes later, Neumann held a three-shot lead.

Hurst, who, by her own admission, "misses it right," when she makes a bad swing, pushed her tee shot into the right rough, then pushed a three wood into the trees. After ricocheting off a spruce pine and bouncing on the cart path, Hurst's ball landed next to a jungle gym in the backyard of a nearby resident. Neumann birdied the hole and Hurst made double bogey.

A three-shot lead was more than enough for Neumann, who cruised home with a closing round of 70, prompting her famously infectious smile. She also smiled when asked how that tennis match stood before she twisted her ankle. "I tell everybody I was leading, and my caddie came over, pushed me down and kicked me in the leg." Then she laughed and said, "That's my story."

Mercury Titleholders Championship—$1,000,000

Winner: Danielle Ammaccapane

Although she entered the 1998 season with five victories under her belt including the 1997 Edina Realty LPGA Classic, Danielle Ammaccapane wasn't entirely comfortable sharing the lead going into the final round of the Mercury Titleholders Championship in Daytona Beach, Florida. Her unease, like that of Carin Koch, who also shared a spot atop the leaderboard after three rounds, came from the fact that the third co-leader with 18 holes left to play was Annika Sorenstam.

"If I could pick anybody who I wouldn't want behind me, it would be Annika," Koch said. "You always know she's there."

But with a struggling 73 on Sunday, Sorenstam wasn't there, and neither was Koch who finished with a two-over-par 74. Ammaccapane, however, while not bringing her "A" game, had enough game left to shoot a final-round 71 for a 276 total and win by one shot over a charging Michelle Estill, who birdied the last hole to shoot her second straight round of 69.

Despite the lackluster finish, Sorenstam finished third, two shots off the pace, and Koch finished fourth, three shots behind Ammaccapane.

Sara Lee Classic—$750,000

Winner: Barb Mucha

After winning the Sara Lee Classic in Nashville, Tennessee, by defeating Donna Andrews, Jenny Lidback and Nancy Lopez in a four-way playoff, Barb Mucha needed lessons. Not golf lessons, but guitar lessons. In addition to pocketing $112,500 for her first victory since the 1996 Chick-fil-A Charity Championship, Mucha also took home a $30,000 Gibson Vince Gill guitar as a gift from the hospitable citizens of the country music capital. "I just won a new hobby," Mucha said while clutching the guitar. It was her old hobby of making putts, however, that allowed her to birdie two of the last three holes to shoot a final-round 69 for a 205 total, then close out three of the game's finest players with a 12-foot birdie putt on the second playoff hole.

While the playoff included one Hall of Fame legend, Lopez; a former Nabisco Dinah Shore champion, Andrews, and Lidback, who won the 1995 du Maurier, it was Mucha who came into the week with the hot game. In her two prior starts Mucha had two top-four finishes. She also managed to overcome three missed putts of five feet or less on the first nine and rallied with four birdies on the second nine. That proved to be the difference. Both Lopez and Andrews missed seven-foot birdie putts on the first playoff hole, while Lidback, who followed a course-record-tying 63 on Saturday with a two under 70 on Sunday, managed no better than par, par in the playoff.

"I'm two for two in playoffs," Mucha said, referring to her first playoff victory in the 1990 Boston Five Classic. "I like that record."

McDonald's LPGA Championship—$1,300,000

Winner: Se Ri Pak

Six years after first picking up a golf club and seven months after capturing medalist honors at the 1997 LPGA Tour qualifying tournament, 20-year-old Se Ri Pak of South Korea became the fifth youngest player since 1930 to win a major championship, and the youngest winner of the McDonald's LPGA Championship since Sandra Post captured the title at age 20 in 1968. Pak led wire-to-wire for a 273 total and edged out Tiger Woods by eight months in becoming the youngest major champion of the last three decades. Like Tiger, Pak's didn't show her youth on the golf course. In four days of play, Pak had only one round in the 70s (a third-round 72), prompting LPGA Hall-of-Famer JoAnne Carner, who played with Pak the first two rounds, to predict that, "(Se Ri) is not going to have any problem whatsoever out here."

She didn't have any problem being paired with Carner and Hall of Fame champion Nancy Lopez on Thursday and Friday, nor did she seem to mind the sea of Korean flags being waved by fans on every hole. Pak took charge, and the lead, early by firing rounds of 65 and 68 the first two days. After Saturday, Pak shared the lead with Lisa Hackney at eight under par. A winless rookie tied for the lead going into the final 18 holes of a major championship could have let the pressure take over, but Pak didn't. Lopez said of the young Korean's performance, "When you're young and everything is new, you don't fear failure. If she knocks her putts by, she just makes them coming back."

Pak didn't miss many, even after Hackney birdied the 11th hole on Sunday to gain a share of the lead with eight holes left. On No. 15, Pak drained a 20-foot putt for birdie, and on the par-five 16th, she reached the green in two, lagged her first putt to within inches, and tapped in for birdie. With pars on Nos. 17 and 18 for a 68, Pak held on to a three-shot lead and a place in the record books alongside Patty Berg (who won the Titleholders at age

19 and the LPGA Championship at age 20), Woods (who won the Masters at age 21) and Lopez (who was 21 when she won her first LPGA Championship).

Corning Classic—$700,000

Winner: Tammie Green

With four straight sub-par rounds and three rounds in the 60s, Tammie Green not only won the Corning Classic in Corning, New York, she ran away from the field and established a tournament record. "It was one of those dream tournaments," Green said. "I really felt like the folks of Corning wanted me to win this golf tournament."

They got their wish. Green started out the week with an impressive five-under-par round of 67 that put her atop the leaderboard with Penny Hammel. After a second-round 70 dropped her two shots off the pace set by Brandie Burton, who followed her opening 68 with a round of 66, Green took charge and never looked back. By the end of play on Saturday she had a 66 and a two-shot lead over Burton and a four-shot lead over Helen Alfredsson.

Sunday's round was a lesson in pinpoint accuracy. Hard, dry fairways and that fact that the 6,062-yard Corning Country Club is the shortest course on the LPGA circuit pushed the scores lower than at any time in tournament history. Emilee Klein shot a final-round 67 to finish 13 under par, which equaled the tournament record. Klein lost by seven shots, however, as Green went low on Sunday, finishing off the field with a round of 65 and a four-day, record-shattering total of 20-under-par 268.

"It was an awesome display of golf," Brandie Burton said of Green's performance. "I enjoyed watching her."

Wegmans Rochester International—$700,000

Winner: Rosie Jones

After a night of lightening, high winds and generally dangerous weather that suspended play and forced a Monday finish, Rosie Jones stood on the 10th tee at the Locust Hill Country Club in Pittsford, New York, bright and early on Monday with a 30-foot putt for birdie and a one-shot lead over the field. "I'm sure she was nervous," said Jones' playing companion, Hollis Stacy. Jones showed no signs of nerves, however, when she rammed the 30-footer into the cup, and went on to win the Wegmans Rochester International by two strokes over Juli Inkster.

"Bingo," Jones said. "The first putt I hit goes in the hole and that kind of freed me up a little bit. I didn't have a constrictive feeling."

"That was probably the key to her round," Stacy, who finished the day with a two-under-par 70, three strokes back of Jones, said of the putt. "When you start out like that you think, 'Wow, it's my day.' And it was her week."

The week didn't start out well for Jones. After an opening-round 74 put her seven strokes off the lead, her concern was making the 36-hole cut, not winning the golf tournament. A second-round 69 pulled her to within four of Inkster, who followed her opening-round 71 with 68. Saturday, the only day not hindered by weather, clearly belonged to Jones. Her round of 64 allowed her to leapfrog over eight players and take a four-stroke lead over Sherri Steinhauer into the final 18 holes.

Play was delayed three different times on Sunday before officials suspended the final round at 5:03 p.m. and announced that play would resume on Monday morning. That's when Jones made her putt, and cruised on to an even-par 72 round and a 279 total for a two-shot victory over Inkster. Meg Mallon made a valiant charge, posting 67, but it was too little, too late. Mallon finished tied for fourth, one behind Stacy and four behind Jones.

"I don't get to win as much as the really great players, so when it comes, you just have to enjoy it," Jones said. "I've won at least once in four straight years, and that just says something for my longevity and my consistency."

Michelob Light Classic—$600,000

Winner: Annika Sorenstam

Despite two major championships and a reputation as one of the greatest players in the game, Annika Sorenstam wasn't accustomed to charging from behind to win tournaments. "I don't know when I've come from behind on the last few holes," she said after doing just that in St. Louis, Missouri, at the Michelob Light Classic. "Normally when I win, I'm ahead coming down to the last few holes. It's a different feeling. It's a thrill."

Part of the thrill came from the fact that after shooting an impressive opening-round 67, then squandering the lead to Donna Andrews by shooting 73 in the second round, Sorenstam was able to recover with a third-round 68, making birdies at 17 and 18 to force a playoff at 208. Her wedge shot at No. 18 impressed even Andrews, who held a one-stroke lead at the time. "I thought it went in," Andrews said of Sorenstam's shot. "Annika hit a great shot. I'm just happy that I had a chance."

Andrews' chance came in the playoff on the 18th hole. After both players made par on the 522-yard par-five, they retreated to the tee to play it again, prompting Sorenstam to say to Andrews, "As consistent as you and I are, we could be here all day."

Twenty minutes later, Sorenstam held up her arms in jubilation as her four-foot birdie putt found the hole. "Every win is special," she said.

Despite her playoff loss, Andrews' second-place finish pushed her to the top of the money list for the year, prompting her to say, "I think if I finished second in every tournament, I would be happy."

Oldsmobile Classic—$650,000

Winner: Lisa Walters

Before Lisa Walters teed off in the final round of the Oldsmobile Classic in East Lansing, Michigan, Wendy Ward, who set the 72-hole LPGA scoring record of 23 under par in 1997, approached her in the locker room and said, "break the record." At that time Walters didn't know what the scoring record was, or who held it. After finishing with a final-round 66 for a 265 total to equal the 23-under-par mark and capture her first victory since 1993, Walters not only knew she held a place in history, she also knew that there was still a little life left in her career.

"My confidence level is the highest it has been in a long time," said Walters, who won by six strokes over Donna Andrews. "A few years ago I was whining and complaining. I thought I was a better athlete than the way I was playing."

Like many professional golfers, Walters has suffered from lower back problems that could require surgery in the future. There were no pains at Walnut Hills Country Club, however. After opening with consecutive rounds of 67, Walters found herself two shots behind Andrews, who opened the tournament with a career-low round of 64. On Saturday, however, Andrews could only manage an even-par 72, while Walters continued to improve, firing a 65 to open up a five-stroke lead.

"She wasn't going to come back to us," Andrews said of Walters' performance. "I knew I would have to shoot lights out to beat her."

Andrews did manage to finish with 67 to lock up second place, but even if she had equaled her earlier 64, she still would have been shy of Walters' pace. With another great round of 66, Walters widened her lead to six shots over Andrews and seven over Karrie Webb.

After it was over, Walters said, "I don't think I've ever finished double digits under par before. It's probably the best four rounds I've ever played in my life."

Friendly's Classic—$600,000

Winner: Amy Fruhwirth

Everyone on the LPGA Tour agrees that Amy Fruhwirth (pronounced Froo-worth) is one of the friendliest players in women's professional golf. In fact, her nickname on tour is "Giggles." So, there was no better tournament or venue than the Friendly's Classic at the Crestview Country Club, within sight of the Friendly's theme park in Agawam, Massachusetts, for Fruhwirth to capture her first LPGA title.

After enduring numerous rain delays, and a golf course so drenched from torrential downpours that the maintenance staff pumped water off the course for 20 hours prior to the opening round, Fruhwirth opened with an impressive 69, but trailed rookie Heather Daly-Donofrio by two strokes. The second round was delayed by weather until Saturday, and after being at the golf course for almost 14 hours, Fruhwirth birdied the last three holes and walked off the 18th green having shot 71 and 68 to hold a three-stroke lead over Daly-Donofrio (who shot 71 and 73), Kim Saiki and five other players, all tied at five under par. Going into the final 18 holes, 10 players were within four shots of Fruhwirth's eight-under-par lead.

No one could catch "Giggles" on Sunday. Despite being so nervous that her caddie wouldn't allow her to look at scoreboards throughout the round, Fruhwirth closed with an even-par 72 for a 280 total to win by two strokes over Saiki and a charging Charlotta Sorenstam who had rounds of 69, 70 and 73 before closing with 70. "My goal was four rounds under par," Sorenstam said. That goal would have been enough for at least a tie, but Saturday's one-over-par round cost Charlotta a chance at victory.

Saiki played well, but a closing 71 wasn't enough to overtake Fruhwirth. Pamela Kometani, one of the six players tied at five under par going into the final day, shot an even-par 72 to finish alone in fourth place with 283. Daly-Donofrio, who hovered around the lead until late, closed with another 73 to finish in a six-way tie for fifth at 284 with Nancy Scranton, Sherri Steinhauer, Maria Hjorth, Rosie Jones and Lisa Kiggens.

As for Fruhwirth, who could barely stop giggling long enough to accept the Friendly's trophy, she said of her day, "It's a relief that I was able to keep my game together and win because I really, really felt nervous." Nervous or not, Fruhwirth's victory elevated her from 70th to 29th on the money list, and put an even larger smile on the friendliest player on the LPGA Tour.

ShopRite Classic—$1,000,000

Winner: Annika Sorenstam

Priming herself for a run at her third U.S. Women's Open title, Annika Sorenstam honed her game in Galloway Township, New Jersey, by firing a 54-hole tournament-record 17-under-par 196 total in the ShopRite Classic, good enough for a four-stroke victory over Juli Inkster.

Although she had to share the opening-round lead with Caroline McMillan, Tina Barrett and Moira Dunn, Sorenstam never trailed the entire event. Despite good play by Inkster, who followed a four-under-par 67 with 66, Sorenstam bettered her opening-round 66 by tying the course record of 65 on Saturday. Her only bogey of the tournament came when she three-putted the 12th green on Saturday, but her play was still good enough to carry a two-shot lead into the final 18.

Inkster made a run early in the final round with birdies at the fourth, fifth and sixth holes that trimmed Annika's lead to one shot, but she could never draw any closer. Sorenstam hit 17 greens en route to shooting another 65. "She's grossly great," Inkster said of Sorenstam. "I feel like when I play good, I can play with the best of them, but when I play her, I have to play perfect golf."

While Sorenstam's efforts were described by many as perfect, there were other impressive efforts during the final round. Karrie Webb, who had struggled during the first two rounds, set a course record by firing 64 for a total of 207, 11 shots off the winning total. Lorie Kane also played well, following her opening-round 69 with two rounds of 67. Her 203 total secured sole possession of third place behind Inkster.

Helen Dobson had a closing round of 65 which moved her into fourth place at 204, one ahead of four contenders including Barrett, Kelly Robbins, Lisa Walters and Donna Andrews.

U.S. Women's Open—$1,500,000

Winner: Se Ri Pak

Even though no course records were set and no tournament scoring records broken, the 1998 U.S. Women's Open will certainly go down as one of the most unforgettable events in all of women's golf. As an older, wiser crowd of faltering veterans watched, two 20-year-olds dueled for 20 extra holes on the Blackwolf Run golf course in Kohler, Wisconsin, in front of the largest women's golf crowds ever assembled. In the end, it was Se Ri Pak, the South Korean phenom who finished first at the LPGA qualifying tournament in November, then won the first major championship she ever played in when she captured the McDonald's LPGA Championship, who prevailed by holing an 18-foot birdie putt on the second sudden-death hole to defeat Jenny Chuasiriporn, an amateur from Duke University. In winning, Pak became the youngest U.S. Women's Open champion in history.

In broken English, a joyful Pak said, "First time I win McDonald's a major, I'm really happy, but after some people thinking I'm lucky to win. Then I win U.S. Open. I know more how to play golf."

She proved that she knew how to play when she took a one-stroke lead over Liselotte Neumann into the weekend. While veteran favorites such as Nancy Lopez, Juli Inkster, Meg Mallon, Kelly Robbins and defending champion Alison Nicholas missed the 36-hole cut, Pak shot three under par (69 and 70) in the first two rounds, one of only two under-par performances. Neumann, at two under (70 and 70), posted the other.

The winds picked up on the weekend, however, and par became an elusive target. "It's a tough golf course," said Helen Alfredsson, whose 73 tied Scotland's Mhairi McKay for the low third round. "Until now, Oakmont with no wind was the toughest golf course I've ever played. Here, when the bleeding starts, it's hard to stop it."

The field averaged 77.87 stokes on Saturday, almost seven shots over the par 71 the USGA had in mind. First-round co-leader Laura Davies, who opened with a 68, followed with 75 and 78, then said, "You can be out of the Open before you're in the Open out here. These greens can make a fool out of you."

Pak's short phrases summed up the feelings of almost everyone. "Today really windy," she said. "More thinking. More smart play. More headache." After the hemorrhaging subsided, Pak, who shot 75 for a 214 total, one over par, retained a one-shot lead over Neumann and McKay. Chuasiriporn, one of five amateurs to make the cut, also shot 75 to be four strokes behind.

On Sunday, Chuasiriporn made her move. Her one-over-par 72 was the second lowest score of the day, capped off when she made a 45-foot birdie putt on the 72nd hole that NBC commentator Johnny Miller called, "One of the greatest putts ever in an Open championship." Certainly the crowd gathered around the 18th green agreed with Miller's assessment. As Chuasiriporn covered her mouth in disbelief, the gallery exploded when the putt disappeared.

"I wasn't really thinking about making it," the affable Chuasiriporn said. "I don't even know how long it was, 45 feet, maybe? I was just trying to get the speed and I left the break to Joey (her brother and caddie). Then, even after I made birdie, I didn't know how I stood."

She stood tied for the lead with Pak, who, seemingly oblivious to what had transpired ahead of her, drilled a tee shot into the middle of the 18th fairway, then hit an approach to within eight feet. With Neumann shooting 76 to finish at 291 and McKay posting 78 to close tied at 293 along with Stefania Croce, Tammie Green and Trish Johnson, the championship came down to two putts, the 45-footer Chuasiriporn made to shoot 290, and the one Pak had for birdie at the 72nd to shoot 289. When Pak's ball skirted on the high side of the hole, she had finished with 76 and regulation play ended without a winner. The championship would be decided by a Monday playoff.

Because of their ages, it was a foregone conclusion that regardless of the outcome of the playoff, the U.S. Women's Open would have its youngest champion in history. Not so readily known, however, was that with Chuasiriporn being the American-born daughter of first generation Thai immigrants, and Pak coming from Daejeon, South Korea, the 1998 Open was the first time two players of Asian descent ever squared off for the national championship.

Those who expected nervousness from two 20-year-olds battling for the No. 1 title in women's golf were surprised, but in no way disappointed on Monday. Chuasiriporn began the round as she left off on Sunday by chipping in for birdie on the first, then holing two more birdie putts to assume a four-shot lead through the first five holes. Just when it looked like a rout was in progress, Chuasiriporn made a critical error on the par-three sixth, hitting her ball into the greenside hazard and making triple-bogey six. Still, at the turn the amateur retained a two-shot advantage over Pak.

But, Pak, the intense rookie who has stated she wants to be "the best golfer in the world," would not be denied. With birdies on the 11th, 12th and 14th holes, along with a world-class scrambling bogey from the water hazard on the 18th, Pak made up for lost ground and tied Chuasiriporn, who failed to get up and down for par on the 18th. Both had 73s, two over par. As if enough history had not already been made, the U.S. Women's Open would, for the first time, be decided by a sudden-death playoff.

Back on the 10th hole, both Pak and Chuasiriporn made par, but on the 11th, the second extra hole, after missing a 20-foot birdie putt, Chuasiriporn had what she described as a "sixth sense," of what was to come. "We had both been reading the greens well, and it was just a matter of one good stroke. She got it first."

When Pak's nine-foot birdie putt disappeared for the win, she punched the sky and tearfully embraced her father who had flown over from Korea to watch his daughter compete. "First time I cry in my life," she said. "I'm really happy, really grateful. I didn't give up."

Jamie Farr Kroger Classic—$800,000

Winner: Se Ri Pak

Six days after grinding through a 92-hole marathon to become the youngest-ever U.S. Women's Open champion, Se Ri Pak, who ignored the pleas of her family to take the week off, made history again by breaking the LPGA 18-hole scoring record, and the four-round scoring record en route to victory at the Jamie Farr Kroger Classic in Sylvania, Ohio. "I told everyone I'm not tired. I'm 20 years old. I just want to play," Pak said.

Pak "just played" her way into the record books on Friday (after a ho-hum opening-round 71) by firing a bogey-free 32-29 for a 10-under-par 61, breaking the single-round LPGA scoring record by three strokes. She kept things going on Saturday with another impressive round of 63, which moved her to 18 under par, nine shots ahead of Karrie Webb and 10 shots better than first-round leader Dana Dormann.

Although she could have shot three over par on Sunday and still won the tournament, Pak shot a final-round 66 to break the LPGA 72-hole scoring record with a 261. Her 23-under-par total (Highland Meadows is a par-71 course) tied the all-time LPGA scoring record relative to par.

Almost lost in the record-setting runaway was a stellar performance by Lisa Hackney, who shot a closing-round 65 to edge Karrie Webb out of second place. Webb, the model of consistency, shot 67, 70, 67 and 67 to finish alone in third place.

JAL Big Apple Classic—$775,000

Winner: Annika Sorenstam

For Annika Sorenstam to arrive at a tournament and not be the center of attention was an unusual and welcome change for the 27-year-old Swede. It didn't bother Sorenstam that Se Ri Pak, the rising LPGA star who won the U.S. Open and then followed it up with a record-setting victory at the Jamie Farr Kroger Classic, was getting all the attention at the JAL Big Apple Classic in New Rochelle, New York. In fact, it was a welcome relief.

The peace and quiet didn't last long. In four rounds at Wykagyl Country Club, Sorenstam shattered the tournament record by shooting rounds of 67, 66, 65 and 67 for a 19-under-par total of 265 and an eight-shot victory over Joan Pitcock. It was Sorenstam's third victory of the year, elevating her to first place on the money list ahead of Pak. "Se Ri deserves all the attention, but I can play, too," Sorenstam said after it was over.

According to her fellow competitors, Sorenstam can do more than play. "She's playing another game," Pitcock said. Sorenstam led by one shot over Meg Mallon at the end of the second round, but by the time the sun set on Saturday, she had extended that lead to six over Michelle Estill, who shot a third-round 65 but couldn't make up any ground on Sorenstam. "Annika is such a good ball-striker, but most of all, she never gets ruffled," Estill said.

On Sunday, Sorenstam bogeyed two of the first four holes and the lead slipped to three, but she came back with three consecutive birdies and it was all over. Pitcock made a charge on Sunday, birdieing three of her last six holes to shoot 66 — good enough for second place, but not even close to Sorenstam. "She's afraid of nothing," Pitcock said.

This was Sorenstam's 15th career victory in just five years on the LPGA Tour, a record unmatched by anyone who is not already in the Hall of Fame.

Giant Eagle Classic—$800,000

Winner: Se Ri Pak

Se Ri Pak has always idolized Nancy Lopez, and at the Avalon Lakes Golf Club in Warren, Ohio, Pak came one step closer to matching Nancy's incomparable record. Closing with a 67 for a 15-under-par total of 201, Pak picked up her fourth victory as a rookie, including two major championships. That tied Karrie Webb for second most victories by a rookie. Lopez still holds the record with nine wins in her rookie year of 1978.

While Pak's play was stellar, the Giant Eagle Classic win came as a result of a costly mistake by second-round leader Dottie Pepper. Coming to No. 18, Pepper, who never looks at scoreboards, assumed a birdie would win the tournament and a par would tie Pak and force a playoff. "The only time I saw Pak was on 18," Pepper said. "I saw her miss that putt, and I assumed it was for birdie." Pak's putt had actually been for eagle, and her two-putt birdie at 18 gave her a one-shot advantage over Pepper.

Pepper reached the par-five 18th with a five wood, but she ran her 40-foot eagle putt well past the hole, then missed the birdie putt. Tapping in for par, Pepper assumed she was bound for a playoff with Pak until she saw her caddie, John Killeen taking off his bib. Pepper asked, "Why are you taking off your bib? We're going back to the tee, aren't we?"

Killeen said, "Well, no, we're not."

For a moment, Pak also assumed she was in a playoff until a tournament official congratulated her. "Someone told me I was in a playoff, then someone else said, 'you won,'" a very happy Pak recalled.

The victory moved Pak back atop the money list ahead of Annika Sorenstam, but Pak didn't consider herself worthy of Sorenstam's company. "She has won the big tournaments many times already," Pak said. "I am still like a baby. I don't want to push myself. I just want to play my game."

So far, her game has been the best in women's golf.

du Maurier Classic—$1,200,000

Winner: Brandie Burton

Going into the LPGA's fourth major championship the two biggest stories in women's golf were rookie Se Ri Pak — winner of the previous two majors — and Annika Sorenstam — who had three victories in seven weeks before heading to Windsor, Ontario, for the du Maurier Classic. Not only were no Americans favored in the season's final major, only three of the top 10 money winners were from the United States. Brandie Burton, a former du Maurier champion, wasn't on anyone's radar before the tournament began, but after stringing together rounds of 68, 64 and 66 and opening a three-shot lead with one round to play, Burton, a Californian, had everyone's attention.

"Two years ago I was calling this work," said Burton, who has been plagued by injury since 1993. "It took awhile, but I knew my heart was meant to be fluttering over eight-foot putts."

Burton's heart fluttered early in the final round when she missed a four-foot putt on the first, then bogeyed two of the next three holes. That opened the door for players including Sorenstam and Meg Mallon, who began the day three shots back. However, the Essex Golf and Country Club, a course that had relinquished more rounds in the 60s than any other in major championship history, reared its head the final day. Mallon could manage no better than a 75, while Betsy King, who started Sunday's round five shots back, shot an even-par 72, her worst round of the week. Sorenstam did post her fourth straight under-par round, but a final-round 70 fell one shot short.

Burton made a courageous birdie on 17, but almost gave it away on No. 18 when her second shot squirted right, then luckily bounced off a tree and came to rest 60 yards short of the green. She then chipped to within eight feet. When the putt fell for a 72 and 270 total, Burton had her second major title, her first victory in five years, a spot on the Solheim Cup team, and, in her words, "a tremendous weight off my shoulders."

Sorenstam, who finished one shot back and alone in second, said of Burton's victory, "She really showed style and finesse around the greens. It was looking good for me at a time, but I was beaten by somebody who played really well."

Star Bank Classic—$600,000

Winner: Meg Mallon

Just when it looked like Dottie Pepper would finally break through after a year of near misses, Meg Mallon birdied four out of five holes on the final nine to tie Pepper at the end of regulation play at the Star Bank Classic in Beavercreek, Ohio. Then, on the first playoff hole, Pepper missed a four-foot putt for par, the same length putt she missed two weeks before to lose to Se Ri Pak. "I got faked out by the speed and fell in love with the line," Pepper said afterward.

Even so, it was a disappointing loss for Pepper, who shot a closing 66 to go with her previous rounds of 63 and 70. After holding a one-shot lead over Mallon after the first day, Pepper fell two back in the second round but quickly made up ground on Sunday. Still, it looked like her efforts wouldn't be enough as Juli Inkster shot a first-nine 29 to briefly capture the lead. When Inkster hit her tee shot in the water on the 13th and made double bogey, the door was reopened for Pepper, Mallon and a charging Donna Andrews. Mallon took advantage with birdies on Nos. 11, 12, 13 and 15, then closing with three pars for a 68 and 199 total to tie Pepper. Andrews had a 20-foot birdie putt on the last, which would have put her in the playoff, but it slid below the hole, missing on the same line as Pepper's four-footer a few minutes later.

Patience was the key to Mallon's tournament-record 17-under-par victory. She played 55 bogey-free holes. After it was over, a relieved Mallon admitted, "They say play one shot at a time, but it's hard to do. I learned a lot today."

How to win is a nice lesson to learn.

Weetabix Women's British Open—£575,000

Winner: Sherri Steinhauer

See European LPGA Tour section.

Rainbow Foods Classic—$600,000

Winner: Hiromi Kobayashi

It was a grueling test of endurance through rain delays and one playoff hole, but as the sun set over Maple Grove, Minnesota, Hiromi Kobayashi prevailed as the champion of the Rainbow Foods Classic for the second time in four years. She had also finished second in the event on two occasions, including 1997, when she couldn't convert her par effort from the front bunker on the final hole, keeping her out of a playoff with eventual winner Danielle Ammaccapane.

After coming back from a rain delay to complete her second round before teeing off again on Sunday, Kobayashi stood on the 18th, her 29th hole of the day with the same shot that she had a year before, and, uncharacteristically, she hit it in the bunker again. "I said to myself, 'Why did you hit it in that bunker twice?'" she said. "The pin was in the same position as last year, and the situation was tough like last year. But this time I finished better."

This time she saved par from the bunker for 69 to go with her previous rounds of 69 and 68. Unlike last year, this time there would be a playoff. Tracy Hanson, who also had to finish her second round and play her third round on Sunday, came in strong with scores of 67, 70 and 69 for a 206 total.

Kobayashi and Hanson had played 29 and 32 holes respectively on Sunday, and darkness was approaching as the playoff ensued on the 530-yard par-five 18th hole. This time, Kobayashi didn't find the bunker, but her third shot onto the green was a bit anticlimactic. With 127 yards left to the hole, Hanson hit a nine-iron shot that flew over the flag, over the green, and found the water. "Nine iron was the perfect club for me from that distance," Hanson said. "I thought I'd hit it stiff, but I completely airmailed it."

For Kobayashi, Minnesota might become her newly adopted home. "I don't know why I play so well here," she said, "but it feels great."

State Farm Rail Classic—$700,000

Winner: Pearl Sinn

When Pearl Sinn, a South Korean native who grew up in the United States, first qualified for the LPGA Tour, she told her mother, "One of these days I'm going to win one of those Rolex watches (given to first-time winners) just for you." Nine years later, Sinn was able to follow through on that promise with a win at the State Farm Rail Classic in Springfield, Illinois.

It took a closing 65 for a 200 total, 16 under par, for Sinn to overtake Michele Redman, Tammie Green, Cindy McCurdy, Vickie Odegard and Martha Nause, all of whom shared the lead at 11 under par after the second round. Sinn started the final round two strokes back, but she birdied two holes on the first nine, then reeled off birdies on three of the first four holes on the final nine before it dawned on her that she might actually win. "I didn't think I was in it, then I birdied 12 and 13, and I thought I might have a chance," she said. "I tried to stay aggressive and go for the pins."

On the 15th, Sinn thought she might have blown her best chance when she missed a birdie putt, while, behind her, Redman and Green were both making birdies to take a one-shot lead. Redman pulled her tee shot into the water on the 15th and made bogey, and Green three-putted the 16th for bogey. Meanwhile, Sinn added another birdie with a 20-foot putt on the 17th.

"I thought I was still one shot behind going into the 18th," Sinn said. Actually, she had a one-shot lead. When her second shot landed in the fringe leaving her with a sidehill putt, all she was thinking about was getting down in two. "I still can't believe that putt went in on the 18th," she said after making the birdie. "I had everything going against me, but when it's your time, I guess it takes care of you."

Redmond made up one shot in the last two holes, but still finished one back of Sinn's closing effort, while Green finished two back.

Safeway Championship—$600,000

Winner: Danielle Ammaccapane

As if the name Ammaccapane isn't hard enough to pronounce and spell, imagine how hard it was for the scoreboard volunteers in suburban Portland, Oregon, when the Ammaccapane sisters, Danielle and Dina, finished first and third respectively in the Safeway Championship. Emilee Klein finished second, between the Ammaccapanes.

For Danielle, it was her second win of the year, and it couldn't have come on a better golf course. She held the course record at Columbia Edgewater Country Club, having shot 64 in 1990. In her opening round, she thought she might beat that record. "I was thinking about the record after I made the turn in 31," Danielle said. "I wanted to at least tie it, but I left a couple of putts hanging on the lip."

Her opening 65 was good enough for a three-shot lead over Klein, Pat Hurst, Dale Eggeling and Laurie Rinker-Graham. Meanwhile, Dina was well back, having opened with 71.

On Saturday, Danielle played more bogey-free golf en route to 67 and a three-shot edge over Klein. Danielle didn't feel secure with her lead going into the final round. "I thought I would have to shoot three or four under to win," she said. "The way Emilee had been playing, I expected her to go four or five under."

Going head-to-head in the final pairing, Klein was unable to make a charge, but Ammaccapane didn't bring her best game either. Cruising along at one under par for the day, Danielle watched as Klein drew to within two on the 16th after a 30-foot birdie putt found the edge of the hole. On the 18th, Ammaccapane left the door open by hitting her first errant tee shot of the day. She had to sink a three-foot putt for bogey to win with 72 and a 204 total.

"I was shaking," she admitted. "My insides were churning. I'd never been in that situation in any of my other wins."

Klein gave it her best effort, chipping just over the edge of the cup from 60 feet, but she had to settle for par, and a final round of 70, one less than she needed. Three back and at least as ecstatic as the winner, Dina had followed her opening 71 with 70, but on Sunday, she had her best round of the year, finishing with 66 to charge into third place. "I'll probably go to dinner tonight with my sister," Dina said, "and she's buying."

Safeco Classic—$600,000

Winner: Annika Sorenstam

One week before joining her European teammates for the Solheim Cup, Annika Sorenstam got the ultimate tune-up when she picked up her fourth victory of the year in Kent, Washington, at the Safeco Classic. "I worked hard on my backswing," Sorenstam said. "On Thursday, everything fell into place. It was important to play well this week to get our momentum going for the Solheim Cup."

Momentum was definitely on Sorenstam's side in Sunday's final round when she caught and passed third-round leader Patty Sheehan. For a while it looked like Sheehan's tournament all the way. A 30-foot birdie putt on the first hole and Sheehan assumed a three-shot lead. Her driver soon abandoned her, and she bogeyed the second, seventh, 14th and 16th holes. "I couldn't get the ball into play off the tee, and you can't win a golf tournament that way," Sheehan said. She finished with a final-round 74 and a tie for second place with Laura Davies.

Meanwhile, Sorenstam birdied the third, fifth, ninth and 11th holes en route to a bogey-free 68 to go with her earlier rounds of 68, 70 and 67 for a 273 total, five strokes better than Sheehan and Davies.

Solheim Cup

Winner: United States

In the end, grit and determination made the difference. Only two players had played for all five United States teams in the 10 years of the Solheim Cup. They were Betsy King, who finished 0-2-1 in the 1998 matches, and Dottie Pepper, who not only finished 4-0-0 at Muirfield Village Golf Club in Dublin, Ohio, she also provided emotional leadership and a fair amount of cheer-leading to the American team. It was Pepper, charging her teammates and angering her opponents, who propelled the U.S. to a 16-12 victory over the strongest European team ever assembled.

Led by captain Pia Nilsson, a Swede-heavy European team seemingly towered over the Americans going into the matches. Annika Sorenstam, Helen Alfredsson and Liselotte Neumann had captured eight 1998 LPGA victories. Two of those players, Alfredsson and Neumann, along with team-mates Laura Davies, Trish Johnson and Alison Nicholas, had never missed a Solheim Cup, so experience was clearly on the European side. Throw in the fact that Lisa Hackney, another member of the European squad, was the 1997 LPGA Rookie of the Year.

All advantages were put aside when the matches got underway. The European team fell behind early and never recovered.

In Friday morning's foursome matches, Pepper and partner Juli Inkster won four of the first five holes in their match with Davies and Trish Johnson. Although the Europeans made a strong showing on the second nine, it wasn't enough, and the Americans drew first blood, winning 3 and 1. That was followed by more victories. Meg Mallon and Brandie Burton defeated Alfredsson and Nicholas, 3 and 1. Kelly Robbins and Pat Hurst defeated Neumann and Lisa Hackney, 1 up, with Hurst's eight-iron approach to the 18th green hitting the flag. The only shining moment for the Europeans came when Sorenstam and Catriona Matthew won 3 and 2 over Donna Andrews and Tammie Green.

The Friday afternoon four-balls weren't much better for the Europeans. Davies and Charlotta Sorenstam did manage to halve with King and Chris Johnson to get things underway, but Hurst continued her good play, as did partner Rosie Jones, in a 7-and-5 blowout of Hackney and Sophie Gustafson. That was the largest margin of victory in Solheim Cup history, and the assault didn't stop there. After a narrow 2-and-1 victory by Alfredsson and Marie-Laure de Lorenzi over Robbins and Sherri Steinhauer, Pepper came through again with Burton. They defeated Sorenstam and Catrin Nilsmark, 2 up. The Americans led 5½-½ after the first day.

On Saturday morning, Sorenstam took another thumping as she and Matthew lost to Andrews and Steinhauer, 3 and 2. That boosted the Americans to a 5-3 margin on Saturday and a 10½-5½ lead with the singles matches remaining. The Pepper-Inkster team was part of that winning tradition on Saturday, as they defeated Alfredsson and de Lorenzi 1 up in the morning. Captain Judy Rankin gave Pepper the afternoon off, but that didn't stop Dottie from being out on the grounds, cheering on her teammates. Her exploits raised the ire of many of the Europeans, but as Robbins put it, "How many times do you have Dottie Pepper running out to high-five you and hug you?"

The gap closed slightly on Sunday morning, as the Europeans rallied with four early singles wins. Davies defeated Hurst, 1 up, followed by Alfredsson beating Inkster, 2 and 1. Shortly after that, Andrews missed an eight-iron approach shot into the 17th and lost to Sorenstam, 2 and 1. Europe seemed poised to rally when Neumann won her only point of the matches by defeating Burton, 1 up. What had seemed a commanding lead was suddenly down to a single point, and the momentum had clearly swung back to the Europeans. "It's enough to make you sick," Rankin said of the day at that point.

Rankin's sickness faded, however, as she got a good dose of Pepper. In the fifth match, Pepper took over and defeated Trish Johnson, 3 and 2. Pepper then retreated to spur her teammates on. Immediately behind Pepper, Robbins won a hard-fought 2-and-1 battle with Charlotta Sorenstam, but in the seventh match de Lorenzi parred the 18th hole to defeat Chris Johnson, 1 up.

When Jones and Green came through with wins, the outcome seemed inevitable. Immediately behind Green, Steinhauer clinched the match by birdieing the 15th and 16th to defeat Matthew, 3 and 2.

First Union Betsy King Classic—$650,000

Winner: Rachel Hetherington

Just winning her first LPGA event in her second season wasn't going to be exciting enough for Australia's Rachel Hetherington. To make things more interesting, Rachel birdied the 72nd hole to force a playoff with the defending champion and the world's No. 1 player, Annika Sorenstam. Then, in nerves-of-steel fashion, Hetherington birdied the first extra hole for the win.

"I really can't believe I won it," Hetherington, whose previous best was a tie for fifth place, said after the victory. Part of that disbelief could have stemmed from the fact that, despite leading the tournament by one stroke over Beth Daniel going into the final round, Hetherington refused to look at the scoreboard. "I knew I was up there somewhere," she said.

Also "up there" were the powerhouse of Daniel, Sorenstam, Laura Davies and Se Ri Pak, all of whom moved to within two strokes of the lead on the final nine holes. Daniel made consecutive birdies at the 13th and 14th holes to pull into a tie for the lead, but Hetherington didn't know it, because she didn't check out the scoreboards.

Davies and Pak, who both began the final round three shots off the lead, made charges, but both shot 71s to fall back into a tie for fourth with Meg Mallon. Again, Hetherington had no idea, because she didn't want to look.

Sorenstam started her charge, birdieing the 15th, 16th and 17th holes to pull into a tie with Hetherington. Playing directly ahead of Hetherington, Sorenstam made a dramatic birdie putt on the 18th to take the lead outright. For everyone watching the scores, it looked as though Sorenstam, who shot 66 (the low round of the tournament), would win her third consecutive Betsy King Classic. Fortunately, Hetherington wasn't watching the scores.

Standing on the fairway at the 18th when Sorenstam's final birdie putt fell, Hetherington had a sense for what had happened, but she wasn't sure. "I knew it was for birdie because everybody was screaming. Or maybe it was for eagle. I thought about asking my caddie, but then I thought, 'Do I really want to know?'"

Hetherington hit a five-wood second shot to the 475-yard par-five green that stopped 20 feet beyond the hole. If Sorenstam's putt had, in fact, been for eagle, she needed to make that 20-footer to tie. If Sorenstam had made birdie, making it meant a win. Hetherington made one of her best putts of the day, but the ball stopped one dimple short of falling in for an eagle three and the outright win. It was only then, after tapping in for birdie and a 69 for a 274 total, that Hetherington learned she was in a playoff.

Back on the 18th tee again, Hetherington knew she had played the hole perfectly only moments before. With those thoughts in mind, she hit her tee shot in almost exactly the same spot as before, and she again hit a five wood to almost exactly the same spot on the green. Meanwhile, Sorenstam flew her second shot over the green and chipped to within seven feet. Hetherington, who knew exactly how she stood at that point, calmly two-putted for a birdie. When Sorenstam missed, Hetherington had her first LPGA victory.

AFLAC Tournament of Champions—$750,000

Winner: Kelly Robbins

When she won the HealthSouth Inaugural in January, Kelly Robbins called her mother and said, "Here we go." Unfortunately, Robbins' game went in the wrong direction after that. Plagued by odd occurrences that led to a loss of confidence, Robbins had six top-10 finishes, but she also missed seven cuts. Her confidence received a boost when she went 3-1-0 during the Solheim Cup matches, but when the tour moved to Opelika, Alabama, for the AFLAC Tournament of Champions, Robbins was not among the names mentioned as favorites.

Among the invitation-only field, names like Sorenstam, Andrews, Inkster,

Pepper and Pak were considered better bets than Robbins. As the sun set on Thursday, and the crowds began to realize that Robbins had fired a tournament-low 66, attitudes began to change. Even after she briefly relinquished the lead to Se Ri Pak at the end of play on Friday, Robbins seemed in control of her game and her emotions.

On Saturday, Robbins had another great round, adding a 67 to her earlier scores of 66 and 73. Meanwhile Pak fell out of contention with a third-round 79, while Sherri Steinhauer continued to be the model of consistency, posting her third straight round of 70. Robbins had a four-shot lead over Steinhauer and a five-shot lead over Inkster and Alison Nicholas with 18 holes to play.

Six birdies and a final round of 70 later, Robbins had cruised to a 12-under-par 276 total and a four-shot victory over Inkster. Steinhauer shot 71 on Sunday to finish alone in third place at seven under, while Sorenstam followed a disappointing 74 on Saturday with a two-under-par 70 on Sunday to finish fourth.

Samsung World Championship—$550,000

Winner: Juli Inkster

With wind so strong that many players had to brace themselves as they walked down the fairways of the Tierra del Sol Golf Club at The Villages in Lady Lake, Florida, Juli Inkster proved that age and experience can win out over youth when the going gets tough. Inkster, 38, was the oldest contestant in the 16-player field at the Samsung World Championship of Women's Golf, and when the final putt fell, she stood alone as the best, but not before having a few tenuous moments chasing and then passing Annika Sorenstam.

"Annika has beaten me every time we've gone head to head," Inkster said. "I know I can play with her, but I had to prove it to myself."

She did just that during Sunday's final round. After opening with rounds of 70, 73 and 66, Inkster found herself one stroke off of Sorenstam's lead. Dottie Pepper, who led after the first two rounds, stood two strokes behind. For Inkster, it was a chance at redemption. Back in June Inkster had led the ShopRite Classic only to watch as Sorenstam birdied the last three holes to grab the victory. As the final round wore on, Inkster knew that someone was going to make a move, and this time, it might be her.

Four birdies on the first nine had allowed Inkster to open a one-stroke lead. A sand-wedge approach to eight feet on the 16th netted a birdie and a two-shot lead. On the 17th, a 165-yard par-three, Inkster hit a six iron to within 10 feet and made that putt for another birdie. When Sorenstam bogeyed the same hole after hitting her tee shot into the greenside bunker, Inkster held a four-stroke lead. It was trimmed to three after Sorenstam birdied the 18th, but by then the outcome was decided. Inkster had her victory with 70 for a 275 total to Sorenstam's 70 and 278 total.

Nichirei International—$702,000
Winner: United States

See Japan LPGA Tour section.

LPGA Japan Classic—¥95,440,000
Winner: Hiromi Kobayashi

See Japan LPGA Tour section.

PageNet LPGA Tour Championship—$1,000,000
Winner: Laura Davies

It had only been four months since her last win, the Chrysler Open in Europe, but when Laura Davies arrived at the Desert Inn Resort in Las Vegas, she wouldn't have bet two shillings on herself, even though Davies is known to be a gambler. "The spread on me was 25 to 1," Davies said. "Hopefully someone made some money."

Davies definitely made some money, although not from wagering on herself. She had opening rounds of 66 and 67, and a weekend where she followed a poor 75 on Saturday with 69 on Sunday to finish with a 277 total and win by four strokes. Davies picked up a cool $215,000 first-place check and her first official LPGA victory since the 1997 Standard Register Ping.

Davies called it, "The most uncomfortable four-shot win of my career," after she beat Brandie Burton, Karrie Webb and Pat Hurst. Most of the discomfort stemmed from putting woes that have plagued Davies all year. "My putting needs help," she said. "I've never holed a huge number of long birdie putts, but now I'm missing the shorter ones, which I never used to do. My mental approach is not exactly textbook, I suppose, but when you've done well, it's very difficult to accept mediocrity. Now, I'm scared to blow a lead; it's almost like trying to win for the first time."

Her putting was better in spurts, but Davies' third-round 75 included 38 putts. Fortunately, her length allowed her to hang on, even though Hurst closed to within one stroke on Sunday's first nine before falling back. In the first two days, Davies played the par-five holes in 11 under par. She played the rest in even par, and that was good enough to win.

Another winner in Las Vegas was Annika Sorenstam, who finished tied for 14th with an even-par 288 total. After an opening-round 74, followed by two rounds of 71, Sorenstam easily captured Player of the Year honors, the money title and the Vare Trophy after three rounds. On Sunday, she needed to shoot an even-par round of 72 to be the first player in LPGA history to average under 70 for the entire season. After a 218-yard seven-wood shot to the par-five 15th hole which landed 12 feet away and resulted in an eagle, Sorenstam closed with the 72 she needed to finish the season with a scoring average of 69.99 — the best in LPGA Tour history.

"It's a dream come true," Sorenstam said. "I get goose bumps just thinking about it."

European LPGA Tour

Evian Masters—£500,000

Winner: Helen Alfredsson

A name change to the European LPGA Tour could not disguise the fact that the women's circuit in Europe was once again short of tournaments and sponsors. While the bigger tournaments have thrived, the smaller events have not survived, making the Evian Masters in Evians-les-Bains, France, the only tournament on the schedule before the middle of July.

Played at the beginning of June, the Evian Masters boosted its prize fund to £500,000 to make sure many of the leading players who play full-time in America returned to the French spa resort. Helen Alfredsson, having won twice on the LPGA Tour on the other side of the Atlantic, continued her good play and won by four strokes with a brilliant final-round 65.

Alfredsson had an 11-under-par total of 277 to defeat Maria Hjorth, who finished one stroke ahead of Trish Johnson and Alison Nicholas. With nine holes to play, Alfredsson was joined in the lead by Catriona Matthew, who went to the turn in 31 with five birdies but stumbled home in 40 to finish 10th.

It was Alfredsson's fourth win since returning to the game following back surgery. "Now it is such a treat to be enjoying golf again," she said. "And it is so exciting to be back playing in Europe. I just wish there were more chances to play over here."

Ladies' Austrian Open—£80,000

Winner: Lynnette Brooky

Lynnette Brooky, a 30-year-old from New Zealand in her fourth year in Europe, fended off some of the leading names on the circuit to win her first title at the Austrian Open. Brooky, paired with Laura Davies in the final round, shot 69 to finish one stroke ahead of Trish Johnson with a 13-under-par 203 total. Davies finished one shot further behind in a four-way tie for third place.

Brooky made three birdies in a row from the 14th and could afford to miss a short putt at the last hole. This did not prove as crucial as it did at the German Open in 1997, when Brooky three-putted the last hole then saw Joanne Mills hole a full wedge shot in the playoff.

"I was really nervous coming down the last couple of holes," Brooky admitted. "But it is fantastic to win, especially when you have players such as Trish and Laura breathing down your neck."

Brooky had opened the three-round tournament with 64, equalling the course record set earlier in the day by Samantha Head, one of two identical twins from England.

Chrysler Open—£125,000

Winner: Laura Davies

After 10 months without a victory, Laura Davies was getting "totally frustrated." Being such a prolific winner in recent years, the former No. 1 player could not wait to raise another trophy, and she finally got her chance at the Chrysler Open in Frillesas, Sweden. Davies romped to a six-stroke victory over Trish Johnson and Spain's Raquel Carriedo, with Alison Nicholas one shot further back.

Davies finished with an eight-under-par total of 284 after rounds of 72, 71, 71 and 70, the closing effort coming in a blustery wind and matched only by Johnson, who was the runner-up for the second successive week.

"After 10 months since my last win, this is a huge relief," said Davies after her 28th European victory. "My form is slowly returning and I am looking forward to the rest of the season. I was very nervous when I set out at the start of the final round and, everything considered, this victory is very special."

Ladies' German Open—£100,000

Winner: Lora Fairclough

Lora Fairclough completed her fourth European LPGA Tour win, but her first since winning twice in 1995, at the Ladies' German Open in Hamburg. Fairclough was in command after a first-round 67. Despite slipping to her worst effort of the four days with a 74 in the last round, the 28-year-old from Lancashire won by three strokes over Joanne Morley and France's Stephanie Dallongeville with a 10-under-par score of 282.

The victory ended a miserable two years for Fairclough, whose playing opportunities had been limited by the lack of European events. A spirited performance in the 1994 Solheim Cup was followed by just missing out on an appearance two years later. Fairclough was in the automatic places on the points list for the entire qualifying period until the very last week.

"I let it all get to me and was missing drives by 80 yards. My game was awful," Fairclough said. "But I've learned so much from the last two years." Unfortunately, while the victory raised her to sixth on the current Solheim Cup points list, she dropped out of the top-seven automatic places when the team was selected three weeks later.

McDonald's WPGA Championship of Europe—£300,000

Winner: Catriona Matthew

Until Catriona Matthew won the McDonald's WPGA Championship of Europe, Scotland had not seen a home winner of a men's or women's tour event for 10 years. Scotland took the Alfred Dunhill Cup at St. Andrews in 1995, but in individual play, the last home winner was Cathy Panton at the Scottish Open at Cawder. In the men's game, it was Ken Brown at the Glasgow Open in 1984.

Panton now helps organize the McDonald's WPGA Championship and handed Matthew her check for £45,000. "It was amazing to have a Scottish winner," said Matthew, who learned her golf at North Berwick and went to Stirling University, just down the road from Gleneagles. Matthew had shared the lead from the opening day when her 71 was the best score in the wet and windy conditions. The 28-year-old, who won the 1996 Australian Open but had not won in Europe as a professional, added rounds of 69, 67 and 69 to secure a five-stroke margin over Laura Davies and Helen Alfredsson. "I am delighted to hang on against two such world-class players," Matthew said.

While the victory put Matthew in line for a Solheim Cup place, her main goal for the season was to finish in the top-30 of the U.S. LPGA Tour money list. She plays most of her golf in the States, accompanied by her husband Graeme as caddie. At the beginning of the week, the pair decided to split, although only on the golf course. Andy Dearden, who caddied for Alison Nicholas at her U.S. Women's Open win in 1997, took over Matthew's bag. "It was a joint decision but he would probably say he sacked me," Matthew said of Graeme. "We just thought it would be a good idea to try something different."

Weetabix Women's British Open—£575,000

Winner: Sherri Steinhauer

After an opening round of 81, Sherri Steinhauer was thinking about changing her airline ticket home to Friday evening. "I never thought I would become the champion," said Steinhauer. But the 35-year-old, who won the 1992 du Maurier Classic, made the cut with 72 in the second round, improved further with 70 on the third day and then matched the best of the week with 69 in the final round.

By the time all those who had started ahead of her on the leaderboard had completed 72 holes, Steinhauer had a one-stroke win over Sophie Gustafson and Brandie Burton. Steinhauer finished at four-over-par 292, while Janice Moodie was fourth and Karrie Webb fifth.

Generally, the favorites in what was the strongest field ever assembled for the event were found wanting by a difficult Royal Lytham layout which was battered by strong winds and occasional rain throughout the four days. Laura Davies, the winner at Royal Birkdale 12 years before, and Helen Alfredsson missed the cut. Se Ri Pak, on her first appearance in Europe after winning two major championships in her rookie season in America, finished 34th and Annika Sorenstam, the world's No. 1 player, was 11th.

Burton and Betsy King led after first-round 71s. Burton found herself out in front at one-over-par 145 after 36 holes, then Moodie, enjoying a fine rookie season, led going into the final round at three over par, by one stroke over King. The veteran American crashed to 77 and Moodie, 75, while the only players to come near Steinhauer's fine last-day effort were Gustafson, the big-hitting Swede with 70, and Burton with 71.

Steinhauer played the last eight holes in three under par and holed an eight-footer at the 18th to set the target. Burton then needed to hole from 30 feet at the 18th to join her but saw the putt barely miss the hole. Moodie, a former Curtis Cup player, missed from three feet at the 14th and from six feet at the 16th. Needing a birdie on one of the last three holes, she missed the green at the 16th to drop another stroke.

Compaq Open—£300,000

Winner: Annika Sorenstam

There was no question that Pia Nilsson would select her countrywoman, sometime pupil and the world's No. 1 player, Annika Sorenstam, among her five wild cards for the European Solheim Cup if she needed to do so. But Sorenstam helped out her old coach by winning the last qualifying event, the Compaq Open, and gained one of the seven automatic places.

With rounds of 70, 71, 71 and a closing 67, there was also little doubt that Sorenstam would retain the title, earn her fifth career win in Europe, and celebrate a victory on home soil for the third successive year. With a score of 279, nine under par, Sorenstam won by 10 strokes, the same margin as compatriot Mathias Gronberg achieved on the same weekend at the Smurfit European Open.

"That was one of my best rounds of golf for a long time," said Sorenstam after her fourth victory of the season. "It was great to get so far ahead, although I wasn't taking anything for granted."

Sharing second place were Catrin Nilsmark and Helen Alfredsson, two more of the six Swedes who were to make the Solheim Cup team, and England's Johanna Head. Sorenstam's win knocked Maria Hjorth out of the seven automatic Solheim places — completed by Alfredsson, Laura Davies, Trish Johnson, Alison Nicholas, Marie-Laure de Lorenzi and Catriona Matthew — and Hjorth also just missed out on Nilsson's wild cards, which went to Liselotte Neumann, Nilsmark, Charlotta Sorenstam, Sophie Gustafson and England's Lisa Hackney.

Donegal Irish Ladies' Open—£100,000

Winner: Sophie Gustafson

Sophie Gustafson needed to play only one hole on the final day to win the Donegal Irish Ladies' Open. A week after being named as a wild card for the European Solheim Cup team, Gustafson rewarded the faith placed in her by captain Pia Nilsson by beating Denmark's Iben Tinning in a playoff.

High winds of up to 60 miles an hour meant that balls were being blown across the greens at the Glashedy Links at Ballyliffin, and after only eight players had completed their final rounds — with none breaking 80 — the day's play was cancelled. That left Gustafson and Tinning tied at two under par for three rounds, but the Swede made a par at the 18th to Tinning's six to win at the first extra hole.

"It was a shame that play was abandoned," said Gustafson, who had not got to the first tee when the round was cancelled. "But it worked out perfectly for me." The 24-year-old led from the first round with a 68, a score she repeated on the third day after recovering from a 78 in the previous round.

Air France Madame Open—£63,000

Winner: Patricia Meunier Lebouc

With Patricia Meunier Lebouc playing on the European LPGA Tour and Antoine Lebouc making his way on the European Challenge Tour, the couple rarely got time together. But the first time Antoine got the chance to watch his wife play in a tournament, Patricia won the Air France Madame Open.

Meunier, just short of her 26th birthday, added to her previous wins in the national Opens of England and Ireland with a 208 total and a one-stroke victory over Sweden's Maria Hjorth at Deauville. Earlier rounds of 69 and 67 meant a closing 72 from the Frenchwoman was good enough despite the Swede's final round of 70. England's Diane Barnard was two shots further back and Nicola Moult was fourth.

"This was the first time that Antoine has seen me play in a tournament," said Meunier. "Usually, we go our separate ways and meet up only on Mondays. To win in front of the French fans makes it even more special."

She also credited sessions with her aunt, Nicole Ortis, who is a sports psychologist, after a poor start to the season. "I've worked hard with my aunt during the low period and I knew I could turn it around," she said. "Sometimes you have to take one step back to take two forward. This week I was very confident. I didn't hole too many putts but I reckon I hit 70 percent of my shots absolutely perfectly."

Marrakesh Palmeraie Open—£80,000

Winner: Sophie Gustafson

Sophie Gustafson ended the season in style by leading from start to finish to win the Marrakesh Palmeraie Open. It was her second win in two months and the third of her career and followed her runner-up finish in the Weetabix Women's British Open and her debut in the Solheim Cup.

Gustafson opened with a 66, a course record, and then added rounds of 67 and 68 for a 201 total and an eight-stroke win over Marie-Laure de Lorenzi, with England's Wendy Dicks one shot further back. Gustafson finished at 15 under par for the tournament with 17 birdies over three rounds.

The £12,000 winner's check gave Gustafson second place on the money list, but Helen Alfredsson, who was not playing in Morocco, had already clinched the No. 1 spot for the first time after finishing as runner-up five times.

Princess Lalla Meriem Cup—US$70,000

Winner: Sophie Gustafson

Sophie Gustafson capped off her season in fine style in the unofficial Princess Lalla Meriem Cup at Royal Dar-es-Salam in Rabat, Morocco. The event, run in conjunction with the men's Hassan II Trophy, provided Gustafson with her third win of the year and second in Morocco in a month.

Patricia Meunier Lebouc, also continuing her strong end to the season, briefly took the lead on the final day with a first nine of 31 with five birdies, but the Frenchwoman slipped away over the second nine as Gustafson came home with four birdies. The Swede's closing 69 gave her a 54-hole total of 206 and a five-stroke win over Lebouc with Federica Dassu one stroke further behind.

Praia D'El Rey European Cup—£150,000

Winner: European Seniors Tour

A terrific fight back in the singles brought the European LPGA Tour a 10-10 tie in the second Praia D'El Rey European Cup, but the result meant the European Seniors Tour retained the trophy.

Having won the foursomes 3-2 on the opening day, the LPGA slipped behind when they won only half a point out of the five fourball matches on Saturday. They were left needing to win seven of the 10 singles on the final day and only just came up short.

Sophie Gustafson, Trish Johnson, Catriona Matthew and Karen Lunn all won their matches at the top of the order for the women to go into the lead. But the way the rest of the matches were shaping up, the crucial encounter became that between Catrin Nilsmark and Brian Huggett. The match featured the woman who holed the winning putt in the 1992 Solheim Cup and a man just short of his 62nd birthday who was a part of the Great Britain and Ireland team which tied the 1969 Ryder Cup at Birkdale.

Huggett, the reigning British Seniors champion, might have gone 2 up at the 13th, but his approach shot hit the bottom of the flag and rebounded 25 yards off the green. Instead, Nilsmark squared the match and was 1 up playing the last. But while the Swede came up short of the green, the Welshman hit a four iron to eight feet and holed the putt for the half. "It was a great feeling," said Huggett. "To still be able to hole them when it matters is very, very satisfying."

The European LPGA's hopes of winning disappeared when Lora Fairclough lost 2 and 1 to David Jones, but in the anchor match Marie-Laure de Lorenzi had the pleasure of tying the contest by beating her fellow captain Tommy Horton, 3 and 2. "It feels as though we won," said de Lorenzi. "It was a great day for all the girls and I am so proud of them."

The match started as it finished the previous year, with arguments over the tee positions, but that was dismissed with the quality of the golf. Rookie senior Christy O'Connor, Jr. was nine under for 14 holes as he beat Mhairi McKay, 5 and 4, while Maria Hjorth made nine birdies, including seven in a row, while defeating Eddie Polland by the same score. "This year the story was the scoring and not the bickering," said Horton.

Japan LPGA Tour

Daikin Orchid Ladies—¥60,000,000

Winner: Ae-Sook Kim

An unusual pattern continued at the start of the 1998 Japan LPGA Tour. For the fourth year in a row, a foreign professional took the title away from the home-country contingent in the season-opening Daikin Orchid Ladies tournament in early March. This time Korea's Ae-Sook Kim earned the victory in a three-way playoff after tying with Mayumi Murai and Hisako Ohgane at 211, five under par, after 54 holes at Ryukyu Golf Club on Okinawa.

The victory was surprising in two respects. Kim had never before won in 13 seasons in Japan, though a frequent strong contender. More shocking, though, was the final-round flame-out of Ayako Okamoto. The 46-year-old Okamoto, who has 61 victories on her international record, led the tournament for the first two days, starting with a five-under-par 67 that gave her a one-stroke lead over Kim, Megumi Matsuo and Ayumi Sobue.

A 71 enabled Okamoto to retain that one-shot edge, then over Matsuo, with five players, including Kim, Murai and Ohgane, two back at 140. When Okamoto faltered Sunday with 76, those three tied with 71s. The 34-year-old golfer from Seoul nailed the title on the first playoff hole — the par-five 18th — when she lofted her third shot over a stand of trees to five feet and dropped the birdie putt. Murai missed a tying four-footer and Ohgane bogeyed.

Saishunkan Ladies—¥60,000,000

Winner: Michiko Hattori

Michiko Hattori signaled the outstanding season that would lie ahead when she won the Saishunkan Ladies tournament title in a three-hole playoff against South Korea's Ok-Hee Ku. The duel between two of Asia's leading women players came about when they posted matching 215s at Kumamoto Airport Country Club and they played the par-five 18th hole three times before Hattori won with a six-foot birdie putt. It was the eighth professional victory for the 29-year-old Hattori.

Hattori had opened the tournament with a four-under-par 68 and led by two over Chie Yoshida. Only two others broke par that day and one of them, Mieko Nomura, took the 36-hole lead with a 71–141 Friday. Hattori shot 75 and dropped into a tie for second with Yoshida (70-73). Ku was two strokes further back, but she made up all the ground Sunday in her bid for her 14th victory in Japan with 70, the day's best round. Hattori forced the playoff when she birdied the 18th for 72 and her 215. Yoshida finished third at 219 and Nomura plummeted to 79 and into a three-way tie at 220.

Yellow Hat Tokyo Ladies Open—¥50,000,000

Winner: Akemi Yamaoka

The veterans grabbed the headlines in the Yellow Hat Tokyo Ladies Open as 47-year-old Akemi Yamaoka broke from a first-place tie with 49-year-old Nayoko Yoshikawa after 36 holes and hung on for a one-stroke victory at the Wakasu Golf Links on the southern outskirts of Tokyo. It was Yamaoka's fourth win on the Japan LPGA Tour, coming more than a year after her last triumph in the Mitsukoshi Cup Ladies.

Yamaoka was never out of the lead at Wakasu. She opened with a three-under-par 69 and shared first place with Kaori Harada. Yoshikawa made up two strokes Saturday, shooting 67 as she overtook Yamaoka (69) at 138. Harada slipped two off the pace with 71–140. Both Yamaoka and Yoshikawa struggled on the second nine Sunday. Yamaoka fell a stroke behind with a bogey at the 13th, but Yoshikawa lost strokes at the 14th and 16th and Yamaoka saved her victory when she sank a 26-foot par putt at the 16th. She finished with a 74 for 212, edging Yoshikawa (75) and Harada (73) by the single stroke.

Kenshoen Ladies—¥50,000,000

Winner: Chihiro Furukawa

It was a long time between victories for Chihiro Furukawa. A 12-year veteran who hadn't won since 1988, Furukawa scored her second victory in mid-April in the Kenshoen Ladies tournament at the Dohgo Golf Club at Ehime. Furukawa shot 70 and won by one stroke with her nine-under-par 207 total.

Furukawa never led until the end. The first-round lead went to Yuka Shiroto, who broke the course record with 65 and led by three over Akane Ohshiro, Natsuko Noro and Furukawa. Noro had the hot hand Saturday, shooting a solid 67 (no bogeys) and taking a two-stroke advantage over Furukawa (69). Shiroto shot herself out of contention with 78. Furukawa's 70 did the trick Sunday as Noro slipped to 73 and Kaori Harada, the defending champion, fell a shot short as well as she matched Shiroto's record 65 for her 208.

Glory Queen's Cup—¥50,000,000

Winner: Kaori Harada

Kaori Harada's triumph in the Glory Queen's Cup tournament revolved around success and failure on the par-four 18th hole on the Shizu course of Shishido Golf Club. Harada just missed a closing birdie there, but par was all she needed to score her sixth career victory. Michiko Hattori, gunning for her second win of the season, had already missed a par putt there that would have matched Harada's one-under-par 215, and Yuko Motoyama, playing with Harada in the final group, muffed a tricky four-foot par putt at 18 to scotch her bid for her first victory.

Hattori was among five players leading the field after the first round with

70s as Harada opened with 73 and Motoyama with 74. Motoyama birdied three of her last four holes for 68 and a share of the halfway lead at 142 with Akemi Yamaoka. Hattori had a 73, Harada 70 and, with 143s, they lingered just a stroke off the pace. Harada went after the title Sunday, mustering a solid 72. She parred the last four holes in the clutch.

Nasu Ogawa Ladies—¥50,000,000

Winner: Michiko Hattori

This time, Michiko Hattori made a first-round lead stand up. Just as she had the previous week, Hattori opened on top in the Nasu Ogawa Ladies tournament at Tochigi. Unlike the last time, Hattori went on to score her second victory of 1998, although it was a matter of survival at the end. She staggered to a final-round 76 in the rain-plagued tournament to fall into a tie with Chieko Nishida, then won the playoff.

She now had nine victories on her professional record. Hattori handled the wet weather well the first two days. She took a one-stroke lead over Nishida and two over seven others, including defending champion Woo-Soon Ko, with her opening 69 and remained one shot in front after shooting 71 as rain fell again Saturday. Hiroe Tani was at 141 with Nishida and two others at 143. In what she termed "a lousy round" Sunday, Hattori managed just one birdie and wound up in the tie with Nishida when she bogeyed three of the last four holes for the 76. Nishida, who suffered a double bogey at the ninth hole, birdied the 18th from 12 feet to force the playoff. Hattori rolled in a seven-foot birdie putt on the first playoff hole.

Katokichi Queens—¥50,000,000

Winner: Tamayo Ueda

Tamayo Ueda, a non-exempt player in the field as a wild card entry, nosed out four others to capture the Katokichi Queens title at Sakaide Country Club in Kagawa. Ueda, winless in six years of campaigning, hampered much of that time by back troubles, nervously dropped a three-foot par putt on the last hole for 74 and an even-par 216 total to edge Hiromi Takamura, Mikino Kubo, Huang Yu-Chen and Mieko Nomura by one stroke.

Playing in her first tournament in 10 months, the 28-year-old Ueda opened with 71 in a four-way tie two strokes behind co-leaders Chihiro Furukawa, the Kenshoen Ladies winner, and 23-year-old Takayo Bandoh. Ueda surged in front Saturday, posting another 71 for 142 and a one-stroke lead over Takamura and Yoshiko Masuda. Battling windy conditions Sunday, Ueda fashioned three birdies and five bogeys into the 74 to eke out the victory as Takamura could only match that score and Masuda plunged to a 78–221. "It's been a long time," said the delighted winner. "I saved the winning ball for my parents."

Gunze Cup World Ladies—¥60,000,000

Winner: Liselotte Neumann

Three of the game's biggest guns came to Japan for the Gunze Cup World Ladies tournament and one of them — Sweden's Liselotte Neumann — made off with the title in the season's first four-round event.

It didn't appear that any of the three — Karrie Webb, Laura Davies or Neumann — would do that after the early rounds. None were in contention for two days as South Korea's Woo-Soon Ko, shooting for her sixth victory in Japan, commanded the field. She led by one stroke over countrywoman Young-Me Lee the first day and went four shots ahead of Huang Yu-Chen Friday with 70–137. Neumann was the closest of the international stars, bouncing back Friday from an opening 75 with a 70. She overtook the Korean professional with a sparkling 65, the low round over the first 54 holes at Tokyo's Yomiuri Country Club — an eight-stroke swing as Ko shot 73. Neumann recovered from a triple bogey at the 10th hole Sunday for 72, deadlocked at 282 with Ko, who also shot 72, and Young-Me Lee, who mustered a 69 finish.

That set the stage for a strange playoff on the 202-yard, par-three 18th. All three bogeyed it twice and Neumann picked up her fifth victory in Japan when she parred it the third time around. Webb finished at 287 and Davies at 294.

Yakult Ladies—¥60,000,000

Winner: Aiko Takasu

Overtime continued to be the norm at Kasugai Country Club in Aichi in the Yakult Ladies tournament. Two of the last three events had been decided with playoffs and four of the first eight tournaments of the season had gone extra holes. So, it was no surprise when the Yakult Ladies was unsettled at the end of regulation play. Aiko Takasu prevailed in that playoff, defeating Fumiko Muraguchi and Kayo Yamada in two extra holes. It was Takasu's 17th victory in her 25-year career.

The 45-year-old Japanese star brought about the playoff unintentionally. One stroke off the lead behind Hisako Takeda and her four-under-par 140 after 36 holes, Takasu seized first place early Sunday and was breezing when she encountered trouble on the way in. She bogeyed four of the last five holes, posted a 72 and found herself in the three-way tie at three-under 213 with Muraguchi and Yamada, both of whom closed with 69s to get into the playoff.

In the overtime competition, Yamada went out with a bogey on the first hole and Takasu nailed the victory with a 20-foot birdie putt after Muraguchi missed hers from 24 feet. It was Takasu's first victory of the season and her second Yakult win at Fukuoka International Country Club.

Chukyo TV Bridgestone Ladies—¥50,000,000
Winner: Ok-Hee Ku

Deprived of her 14th victory in Japan earlier in the season by a tough playoff loss to tour leader Michiko Hattori, Ok-Hee Ku did not let it happen again when she wound up in another tie in the Chukyo TV Bridgestone Ladies. The 41-year-old South Korean defeated Miyuki Shimabukuro with a tap-in par on the first extra hole at Kasugai Country Club in Aichi Prefecture.

Ku emerged from a large group of early contenders at Kasugai. American Kris Tschetter, Taiwan's Yu-Chuan Tai, Aki Takamura and Shimabukuro shared the first-round lead with 69s, with five others, including Ku, at 70. The two ultimate playoff adversaries finished the second round at the top with 138s, Ku after a 68 and Shimabukuro after a 69, and that's the way things finished after the players slogged over a rain-soaked course Sunday.

Both struggled to 75s, Ku starting with a double bogey and taking another later along with five birdies and four bogeys. They almost opened the door for five others — Nayoko Yoshikawa, Chieko Nishida, Fuki Kido, Ae-Sook Kim and Tschetter — who tied at 213, one behind them. In the playoff on the par-four 18th, though, Ku made the easy par for the win as Shimabukuro was chipping for hers unsuccessfully.

Toto Motors Ladies—¥50,000,000
Winner: Young-Me Lee

The South Korean contingent produced a second straight winner and third of the season in the Toto Motors Ladies as Young-Me Lee squeezed out a one-stroke victory at Toto Hanno Country Club. Lee, in her 12th year on the Japan circuit, registered a 69 Sunday for an eight-under-par 208 total as she broke from a three-way tie at the start of the final round and edged Kaori Harada by the single shot. Fusako Nagata, who had shared the second-round lead with Lee and Harada, had a 72 and placed third.

Kayo Fukumoto gave way to that threesome Saturday after leading the first day with 69. Harada was among four players with 70s on Friday, Lee began with 71 and Nagata started with 73. Fukumoto slipped a stroke off the pace at 140 with a 71 Saturday and finished with 74 in a tie for seventh.

Lee, a six-time winner in Japan but without a victory since 1996, had five birdies and two bogeys in her winning 69 Sunday. She joined Ae-Sook Kim (Daikin Orchid) and Ok-Hee Ku (Chukyo TV Bridgestone) as 1998 titlists from South Korea.

Resort Trust Ladies—¥50,000,000
Winner: Kaori Harada

Kaori Harada, intent on not "making a goof for the second straight week," got her second victory of the season in the Resort Trust Ladies in early June, joining Michiko Hattori as the year's only multiple winners. While a 70 would not normally be considered a blunder by most people, that score dropped Harada into second place the previous Sunday in the Toto Motors tournament. On the other hand, in the Resort Trust Harada used a 70 to score a two-stroke victory, frustrating the bid of Akiko Fukushima, 1997's leading money winner, for her first 1998 win.

The tournament's first-round leaders — Aki Nakano and Harumi Sakagami — disappeared from view after the opening 67s. Harada, who began with 69, and Fukushima, who started with 70, moved into joint leadership at 137 after 36 holes at the Maple Point Club at Kita in Yamanashi Prefecture. It was a battle until well into the second nine Sunday before the 31-year-old Harada pulled away to a companion victory for her earlier one in April's Glory Queen's Cup and career win No. 7. Three bogeys between the 12th and 16th holes shot down Fukushima. She slipped to 74 and tied for fifth, four strokes behind Harada's nine-under-par 207. Natsuko Noro finished second, shooting 70 for 209.

The victory pushed Harada past Hattori into the No. 1 slot on the money list.

Suntory Ladies Open—¥50,000,000

Winner: Marnie McGuire

A six-week respite from tournament golf back home in New Zealand obviously did Marnie McGuire a lot of good. "When I got here (to Arima Royal Golf Club in Kobe for the Suntory Ladies Open), I had no expectations on how I was going to do," she observed. What she did was lead the tournament alone for the first three days and complete things with a three-stroke victory Sunday. McGuire posted a five-under-par 283 total in recording her first win in two years on the Japan LPGA Tour and the fifth of her career.

The victory march of the 29-year-old New Zealander went like this: a 68 and a one-stroke lead over Nayoko Yoshikawa and Keiko Suzuki the first day ... a 71 and a two-stroke lead over Suzuki (69-72) and Hiromi Takamura (73-68) the second day ... a 72 and a four-stroke lead over Fuki Kido (76-69-70) and Aki Nakano (71-72-72) the third day ... and another 72 for the three-shot win over Yuri Kawanami (74-69-74-69). McGuire put together a steady round Sunday, rolling along one under par until taking her only bogey on the final hole.

Dunlop Ladies Open—¥50,000,000

Winner: Huang Yu-Chen

Another country was heard from in the Dunlop Ladies Open. Taiwan's Huang Yu-Chen, winless since joining the Japan LPGA Tour in 1995, broke that ice at the Cypress Golf Club in Hikami, winning by four strokes despite a closing, one-over-par 73 on a rainy Sunday afternoon in Hyogo Prefecture. Huang, 25, whose principal claim to fame was her victory in the 1994 Asian Games, had the only sub-par total — three-under-par 213.

Yuri Fudoh, seeking her first victory, too, had her moment the first day when 70 gave her the opening-round lead, one in front of Chieko Nishida, the only other player under par. Huang, who was among four players at even par Friday, moved into first place Saturday with a four-under-par 68 for 140, two ahead of Nishida. The Taiwanese player had eight birdies in her round. She only had three Sunday and they were evened out by a double bogey and a bogey on the wet day. Akiko Fukushima started too far back to seriously challenge, but her 69 Sunday was one of only two in the field and it jumped her into a four-way tie for second with Nishida (75), Mayumi Inoue (72) and Man-Soo Kim (73).

Japan Women's Open—¥70,000,000

Winner: Natsuko Noro

As happens more often than one would expect, one of the lesser-known players on the Japan LPGA Tour captured its most prestigious title when Natsuko Noro won the Japan Women's Open at Miyoshi Country Club at Nishikamogun. The 32-year-old Noro, a regular on the circuit for eight years, had only one victory — the 1995 Miyagi TV Cup — on her record before fashioning her two-stroke victory to the delight of a partisan gallery and her husband, who had replaced her regular caddie for the week and slipped away after the finish so that she could have the victory stage to herself that Sunday afternoon.

Noro had to contend primarily with Huang Yu-Chen and Marnie McGuire, winners of the previous two tournaments, virtually all the way. Fresh from her decisive victory in the Dunlop, Huang matched Noro's opening 68 at Miyoshi as 53-year-old Michiko Okada tied for third at 70 with Akemi Yamaoka and Mayumi Murai. Despite no birdies and a 74, Huang remained on top Friday, then with Shin Sora of South Korea, who had a pair of 71s for her 142. Noro endured a 75, slipping a stroke behind at 143 with McGuire (69) and Okada (73).

Noro bounced back with 71 Saturday, moving a stroke ahead of Huang (73) and McGuire (72). Akiko Fukushima surged into contention with 68 for 214. Noro's closing 72, the product of four birdies and four bogeys, gave her a two-under-par 286 and the important title, but it was touch-and-go until the 72nd hole, where Huang, tied with Natsuko, took a double bogey for 73 and dropped into second place at 288. McGuire fell back to 292 when she closed with 77.

Toyo Suisan Ladies—¥50,000,000

Winner: Michie Ohba

Many times, tournaments are won with the help of the misfortunes of others. That's what happened in the Toyo Suisan Ladies tournament as Michie Ohba, a local favorite at Kosaido Sapporo Country Club in northern Japan, won the first tournament of her four-year career.

Woo-Soon Ko seemed to have things well in hand in her bid for a sixth victory on the circuit. Inspired by the U.S. Women's Open victory of Se Ri Pak a few days earlier, Ko jumped off to a one-stroke lead at Kosaido Sapporo with a six-under-par 66 and widened the gap to three on a rainy Saturday with 70–136. It could have been more but for a missed birdie at the par-five 16th and a bogey at the 17th. Yuri Fudoh, Tomiko Ikebuchi and

Nayoko Yoshikawa were at 139, and virtually ignored eight strokes back after rounds of 69-75 was Ohba.

Even when Ohba stirred the local crowd with a solid, six-under-par 66 — six birdies, no bogeys — it still seemed to be Ko's victory. But, knowing that Ohba was in with 210, Ko fell apart on the closing holes. She bogeyed three of the last four for 75 and lost by a stroke.

Sumitomo Visa Taiheiyo Ladies—¥60,000,000

Winner: Aki Nakano

Circumstances virtually repeated themselves from one week to the next at the Sumitomo Visa Taiheiyo Ladies tournament. Aki Nakano won that event in much the same way as Michie Ohba captured the Toyo Suisan the previous Sunday, coming from well behind in the final round and getting unwilling assistance from the overnight leader. It was Nakano's sixth Japan LPGA Tour victory, but her first in more than two years.

American Pat Hurst, who has ties to the Asian country through her Japanese-American mother, took a commanding, three-stroke lead Saturday at the Taiheiyo Club's Gotemba West course. She added a 68 to her opening-round 70 that had put her in a five-way tie for the lead with Natsuko Noro, the Japan Women's Open champion, Toshimi Kimura, Kazue Sata and Nakano.

Nakano shot 71 Saturday and held second place as the other co-leaders fell back. The 35-year-old Nakano made up the deficit in the early going Sunday, catching the Nabisco Dinah Shore champion with a birdie at the 10th hole. She surged ahead with four more birdies the rest of the way for a five-under-par 67 and 208 total, while Hurst was suffering a pair of bogeys on her way to a 74 and a third-place finish at 212. Yuri Fudoh matched Nakano's 67 and vaulted into second place at 211.

Golf 5 Ladies—¥50,000,000

Winner: Akiko Fukushima

Perhaps being back on winning ground helped. Regardless, Akiko Fukushima, who won six times in 1997 on her way to the money-winning title, finally landed her first 1998 victory almost five months into the season in the Golf 5 Ladies, one of the six tournaments she won the previous year. She came from one stroke off the pace Sunday at Mizunami Country Club and won by one shot over South Korean veteran Ok-Hee Ku with her closing 69 and eight-under-par 206. It was Fukushima's 12th victory.

The 25-year-old Fukushima was never more than a shot out of the lead before taking over Sunday. She was among four players at 69 who trailed first-round leader Yukiko Ishiguro by a stroke Friday, and was one behind the frontrunner, New Zealand's Marnie McGuire, Saturday after shooting 70 for 139. McGuire, the Suntory winner six weeks earlier, had a pair of 69s.

Fukushima birdied the last two holes for the 70 and pointed back to them after she won as having been critical to the victory. She birdied the first two holes Sunday and added three other birdies later in the round along with two bogeys en route to the 69. "I wasn't hitting the ball close and well today.

So, the birdies on the final two holes yesterday were the key for this victory," Fukushima observed. Ok-Hee Ku also shot 69 Sunday and placed second. McGuire had a 72, finishing third at 210.

Mizuno Ladies—¥60,000,000

Winner: Fuki Kido

Fuki Kido took the worry factor out of the picture for herself and her mother in the gallery as she rolled to the most decisive victory in the first five months of the season in the Mizuno Ladies tournament at the Asahi International Country Club at Tojo. The 36-year-old Kido, who had gone three years without a victory, rolled to a six-stroke triumph with her seven-under-par 281.

Kido was three back with her opening 72, joined Aki Nakano, the Sumitomo Visa Taiheiyo winner, at the top with a 70 for 142 Friday and was never headed after that. A bogey-free 69 for 211 established a three-stroke lead Saturday over Nakano and Yuka Irie, who had shared first place Thursday with Kozue Azuma and Chikako Matsuzawa.

South Korea's Young-Me Lee made a bid on the first nine Sunday, moving within two strokes, but she absorbed a double bogey at the 11th and a bogey at the 12th and Kido ran away with birdies at the 13th and 15th. The 70–281 gave Kido the fourth victory of her 12-season career. Lee wound up with 71–287 and Irie tied her for second place with her 73.

NEC Karuizawa 72—¥60,000,000

Winner: Yuka Irie

For the second time in three weeks, a tournament on the Japan LPGA Tour had a repeat winner. In a foggy setting similar to the one when she took the NEC Karuizawa 72 tournament in 1997, Yuka Irie won again in 1998, this time by a much more comfortable margin of four strokes. The victory continued Irie's one-win-a-year pattern that began with the 1995 Chiyoda Ladies and followed with the 1996 Golf 5 and the 1997 NEC Karuizawa 72, which had so much trouble with fog that she wound up winning a 45-hole tournament by a stroke.

Just a shot behind the 66s of Kaori Harada and Kyoko Ono after the opening round on the North course of Karuizawa 72 Golf Club this year, Irie duplicated her opening-round 67 for 134. The seven-birdie, two-bogey round, played in a drizzle Saturday after a three-hour morning fog delay, jumped the 29-year-old Irie five strokes in front of Akiko Fukushima and six ahead of Harada and Michiko Hattori.

Irie struggled on the first nine Sunday, going two over par on the first eight holes and then leading by just a stroke over Hattori. But Irie righted the ship with a birdie at the ninth and added three more on the second nine for 70 and the four-stroke victory with her 12-under-par 204. Impressive, especially when you consider that probably the three best players on the Japan LPGA Tour — Hattori, Harada and Fukushima — tied for second at 208.

New Caterpillar Mitsubishi Ladies—¥60,000,000

Winner: Kyoko Ono

Kyoko Ono, who had a promising start the week before in the NEC Karuizawa 72 go badly, reversed the sequence in the New Caterpillar Mitsubishi Ladies tournament and parlayed it into the first victory of her three-year career. The 29-year-old Ono, the fifth first-time winner of the season, came from three strokes off the pace in the final round, winning with a three-under-par 216 total at the Daihakone Country Club in Kanagawa Prefecture in late August.

In sharp contrast to her fruitless 66 start at Karuizawa, Ono muddled to a 74 in the opening round of the New Caterpillar Mitsubishi, five strokes behind leader Chikayo Yamazaki, who had been struggling with her game all year. Ono made a move Saturday with a three-under-par 70 as Fuki Kido, who also shot 70, the day's best round, took the lead at 141 in her quest for a second victory in three weeks. She led Yamazaki (73) by one and Ono by three. Amid generally high scoring Sunday, Ono found her one-under-par 72 good enough to win by two strokes over Kido (77) and Yuri Fudoh (72).

Goyo Kensetsu Ladies—¥60,000,000

Winner: Harumi Sakagami

Harumi Sakagami scored her first victory in the Goyo Kensetsu Ladies in out-of-the-ordinary circumstances. The 24-year-old Sakagami outlasted the more experienced Atsuko Hikage and Kaori Higo to win the title in a four-hole playoff, the sixth player and second in a row to record a maiden victory on the 1998 circuit. What made things a bit odd was the fact that four players had tied for the lead at 138, yet none of them made the playoff. While Fusako Nagata and Aiko Hashimoto (72s) and Chie Yoshida and Mayumi Murai (73s) were descending, Sakagami and Higo (67s) and Hikage (68) were ascending into the playoff. Hashimoto had shared the first-round lead with Mitsuyo Hirata at 67.

Sakagami and Hikage birdied the second extra hole, ousting Higo, who managed only a two-putt par. Then Sakagami, in with her par, claimed the victory on the fourth when Hikage missed a three-foot par putt, ending the year's longest playoff.

Fuji Sankei Ladies Classic—¥60,000,000

Winner: Masako Ishihara

The run of first-time winners and extended finishes continued in the Fuji Sankei Ladies Classic. Masako Ishihara defeated Akiko Fukushima and South Korea's Shin Sora, Fukushima on the first extra hole and Sora on the second at Fujizakura Golf Club at Kawaguchiko.

The collapse of Taiwan's Hsiu-Feng Tseng Sunday gave them their title shots. Tseng had supplanted Chieko Nishida as the tournament leader Saturday. Her second-round 70 for 138 moved the Taiwanese pro two strokes in front of Nishida, who had begun play Friday with a four-under-par 67. Tseng was alone in the 68 slot. Going into the final round, Sora trailed by three, Ishihara by four and Fukushima by seven. Fukushima's huge rally was all for naught, however, as her two playoff adversaries scored eliminating birdies at the first extra hole. Ishihara then claimed her first victory with another birdie on the next hole.

Japan LPGA Championship—¥70,000,000

Winner: Michiko Hattori

Michiko Hattori added extra luster to her status as the current No. 1 player in Japan when she won the Japan LPGA Championship, her second major title, in trying conditions on the difficult Miho Golf Club course in Ibaraki Prefecture. Hattori, the 1994 Japan Women's Open champion, lost the battle with the tight fairways and windy conditions but won the war, capturing her third victory of the season by three strokes despite a final-round 76 and a two-over-par 290 total. It was her 10th victory in seven seasons.

Hattori did not reach the top until the third round. She trailed Kaori Higo and Yuko Moriguchi by two strokes with her opening-round 72. She was still two back after 36 holes, but was then alone in second place behind South Korea's Lee Oh-Soon. Her chances for doing it faded when she shot 77 Saturday. Hattori birdied the last two holes for 69 and bolted into a four-stroke lead over defending champion Akiko Fukushima and Yuri Fudoh with her 214.

In Sunday's shaky round, Hattori bogeyed five of the first 12 holes, but steadied and parred in for the 76 that produced the three-shot win over Yuri Kawanami. Interestingly, the low score of the rugged final round was a 69 by Higo, the first-round co-leader, who had crashed with 79-83 in the middle rounds.

Yukijirushi Ladies Tokai Classic—¥60,000,000

Winner: Kaori Higo

Kaori Higo, who had hinted that victory might be imminent with strong starting and finishing rounds in the Japan LPGA Championship, fulfilled that indication the following week. The 29-year-old Higo ended a 14-month victory drought, winning the Yukijirushi Ladies Tokai Classic with a similar scoring sequence, wrapping a pair of 67s around a 73 to put a sixth title on her career record. Her nine-under-par 207 total at Ryosen Golf Club in Inabe, Mie Prefecture, gave Kaori a four-stroke victory over Michiko Hattori and Yuri Kawanami.

Higo jumped off to a two-stroke lead over Ok-Hee Ku and Akane Ohshiro with the 67 start Friday, clung to first place despite a 73 Saturday and won easily Sunday with the day's best round. Key to the 67 Sunday was a run of three consecutive birdies on the second nine, beginning at the 11th. Hattori, seeking her fourth win of the season, and Akio Takasu, also a 1998 winner, started the final round just one shot off the pace, but Hattori shot 70 and Takasu 73.

Miyagi TV Cup Dunlop Ladies Open—¥60,000,000

Winner: Akiko Fukushima

Akiko Fukushima made a late-season drive toward a third consecutive money-winning title with a decisive victory in the Miyagi TV Cup Dunlop Ladies Open at Rainbow Hills Golf Club in Tomiya, Miyagi Prefecture. With the ¥10,800,000 first-place check, the 25-year-old Fukushima climbed into the No. 2 spot in the standings behind Michiko Hattori, who had a rare poor week and missed the cut.

Fukushima broke from a 36-hole tie with South Korean veteran Ok-Hee Ku and won by four strokes, even though shooting just a one-under-par 71 Sunday in a round that included four birdies and three bogeys. Ku, 42, had opened the Miyagi TV Cup with five birdies and a leading 68, a shot in front of Fukushima and four others, and followed with 69, overtaken at 137 by Fukushima. On Sunday, she slumped to a 75 and finished in a second-place tie with compatriot Hee-Won Han, who closed with a 69–212. Her 208 gave Fukushima her second win of the season and 13th of her career.

Kosaido Ladies Golf Cup—¥60,000,000

Winner: Mayumi Murai

Mayumi Murai had struggled through rather lean times with just one victory since 1993 and it appeared that another opportunity was going to escape her in the Kosaido Ladies Golf Cup the first week of October. The co-leader after two rounds at Chiba Kosaido Country Club in Ichihara, Chiba Prefecture, the 33-year-old Murai incurred three bogeys without a birdie on the first 10 holes Sunday. Then she turned things around on the home stretch, racking up birdies on each of the last four holes for a 71 and a one-stroke victory with her three-under-par 213 total.

It was another disappointing ending for Ok-Hee Ku. She entered the final round in a tie for the lead for the second week in a row after holing a 40-yard wedge shot for 72–142. Again she failed to capitalize, closing with 73 for 215, tied for third with Nayoko Yoshikawa a stroke behind Huang Yu-Chen, who was the clubhouse leader at 214 until Murai's blazing finish. The Dunlop winner had the day's best round — 69.

Murai's first victory since the Chukyo TV Bridgestone in 1996 was the sixth of her career.

TaKaRa World Invitational—¥80,000,000

Winner: Aki Takamura

As the rich TaKaRa World invitational neared its exciting end, the winner clearly would be Takamura — but which one? In a rare showdown between Aki and Hiromi Takamura, the two unrelated players had distanced the rest of the field, but not each other. Their duel went to the final hole, where 26-year-old Aki took the title and the ¥14,400,000 check with a par as 45-year-old Hiromi, winless since 1994, three-putted for a bogey. Aki finished with a 73 and an even-par 288 total, Hiromi with 74 for 289. Natsuko Noro, the

Open champion, was a distant third at 293. The winner, who joined the circuit in 1992 with Akiko Fukushima, the two-time money champion, now has seven titles on her record, most notably the 1996 Japan Women's Open.

The biggest surprise of the early going at Caledonian Golf Club at Sanbu was the exodus of three international stars, especially defending champion Liselotte Neumann, a two-time winner of the tournament. She, Laura Davies of Britain and Jane Geddes of the United States all missed the 36-hole cut as Hiromi Takamura was taking the lead from Toshimi Kimura, who had an eagle and three birdies en route to 69 Thursday. Hiromi's 72–144 gave her a one-shot lead ever Ok-Hee Ku, again on the prowl for her 15th Japanese victory, as nobody broke par on Caledonian's slick greens.

Aki Takamura shot 69 Saturday to join Hiromi Takamura in a one-shot lead over Nayoko Yoshikawa and Cheng Mei-Chi at 215. After 13 holes, the two leaders were six strokes ahead of the rest and they remained tied until the 18th did in Hiromi.

Fujitsu Ladies—¥60,000,000

Winner: Kaori Higo

When inexperienced Nahoko Hirao was unable to take her second-round lead in the Fujitsu Ladies tournament to victory, Kaori Higo was there to carry it. Higo rode the strong, gusty fringe winds of Typhoon Zeb to a 70, a five-under-par 211 total and a one-stroke win, her second in five weeks and seventh in 10 years.

Hirao, playing in just her second season in Japan, had taken a three-stroke lead after 36 holes at the Tokyu 700 Club in Chiba, adding a 70 to her first-round 67. The Friday leader, Toshimi Kimura, who opened with 66 in her quest for her sixth victory, blew to 78 on the rainy Saturday and out of contention. At 140, Miyuki Shimabukuro held the runner-up slot going into the final round, with Higo (69-72) another stroke back with Yuri Fudoh and Kumiko Hiyoshi. Despite the winds, Higo had three birdies and took a lone bogey as she sailed past Hirao, who wound up in third place at 213 after shooting 76 Sunday. Hiyoshi, who hadn't won since the 1994 Japan Women's Open, shot 71 to slip into second place at 212.

Hisako Higuchi Kibun Classic—¥70,000,000

Winner: Michiko Hattori

Michiko Hattori faltered only momentarily in midstream on the way to her fourth victory of the season, widening her lead in the race for the 1998 money-winning title to nearly ¥9,000,000. Hattori never trailed in the Hisako Higuchi Kibun Classic and won by two strokes with her four-under-par 212 total, shooting 71 in the closing round at the Greenbrier West Village course.

The 29-year-old Hattori opened with a solid, four-birdie 68, leading Huang Yu-Chen by a stroke, Chihiro Furukawa by two. The slip came the second day, when she shot 73 and dropped back into a tie with Hee-Won Han, a rookie who had just qualified for the tour in August; Man-Soo Kim and Furukawa. Han had rounds of 73-68 for her 141. Only Hattori, among that foursome, broke par Sunday, and Kaori Harada avoided losing more ground in the money competition with Hattori by shooting the day's best score — 67 — and spurting into a second-place tie with Han, who had a 73. The victory increased Hattori's career total to 11.

Nichirei International—US$702,000

Winner: United States

For one day, the top players on the Japan LPGA Tour entertained hopes of ending the string of defeats it has suffered in the Nichirei International at the hands of teams from the U.S. LPGA Tour which rarely have included all of the current stars. However, after trailing by just a point at the end of the Friday round of stroke-play better ball, the Japanese saw their chances sag badly in the second round of four ball and they wound up absorbing their 13th consecutive loss and their worst defeat since 1993, 24-12.

The U.S. team won the last two matches of the starting round at Tsukuba Country Club at Ina, Ibaraki Prefecture, to hold a bare 5-4 margin overnight, then opened up a five-point lead Saturday by capturing six of the nine matches and halving another. The Americans turned the competition into a rout Sunday, taking 12 of the 18 singles matches and halving a 13th.

U.S. Captain Pat Hurst, who has a Japanese heritage, led off each day's competition with a victory, teaming with Hiromi Kobayashi, a Japanese regular on the American circuit in decisive four-ball victories. They swamped Hiromi Takamura and Akio Takasu with a record 58-67 triumph Saturday. Four other American team members — Charlotta Sorenstam, Emilee Klein, Sherri Steinhauer and Rosie Jones — won three times, while Betsy King and Janice Moodie went 2-0-1. Akiko Fukushima, Japan's leading money winner in 1996 and 1997, and Taiwan's Huang Yu-Chen shone in defeat, teaming for two four-ball wins and taking their singles matches.

LPGA Japan Classic—¥95,440,000

Winner: Hiromi Kobayashi

Hiromi Kobayashi may have had mixed emotions as she contributed as a member of the U.S. Tour team to its defeat of the best players on her home circuit the previous week in the Nichirei International, but she had nothing but pride to display at Musashigaoka Golf Club on the second Sunday of November. She had just defeated a strong international field in the LPGA Japan Classic, an official stop on both the U.S. and Japan LPGA Tours, with friends and family watching her breathtaking finish and subsequent playoff victory. Kobayashi, a regular in America since 1990, had won the Rainbow Classic earlier in the year in America, her third on the U.S. Tour, to go with nine victories in Japan.

What was joy for Kobayashi was disappointment for Tina Barrett, who saw her bid for her first victory since 1989 go by the boards when it appeared certain it was in the bag. Barrett, who had begun the tournament with a seven-under-par 65, two shots in front of the field, then fell back with 74 Saturday, recovered beautifully with a 66 Sunday for 205, only to watch as

Kobayashi completed a run of three consecutive birdies on the 18th green of the Hanno course for 69 and a 205 total. Canadian Lone Kane, the second-round leader at 134 thanks to a course-record-tying 64, slipped to 73 and placed third, two behind Kobayashi and Barrett.

The two deadlocked players played the par-five 18th three times before Kobayashi tapped in an 18-inch birdie putt for the win as Barrett, who had holed a 35-footer for the 66 earlier, three-putted.

Itoen Ladies—¥60,000,000

Winner: Michiko Hattori

Michiko Hattori was simply awesome when the Japan PGA Tour resumed its normal run of three events to close out the season. In probably the most superlative performance of her eight-year career, the 30-year-old Hattori won the Itoen Ladies by a whopping 11 strokes and did it with a tour record score of 197, 19 under par at the Great Island Club at Chonan, Chiba Prefecture. The ¥10,800,000 check virtually clinched the money title as her 1998 earnings reached ¥78,680,823. Either Kaori Harada or Ok-Hee Ku would have had to win both of the last two tournaments to have a mathematical chance. The 197 total eclipsed by two the record of 199, shot by Laura Davies when she won the Itoen in 1996.

Hattori, fresh after a week off, came out blazing at Great Island Friday. She fired a seven-under-par, bogey-free 65 to take a two-stroke lead over Suzuko Maeda, the only player within four strokes of her. Hattori followed with a 66 Saturday and only Ok-Hee Ku prevented it from becoming a complete runaway. The South Korean veteran matched the all-time tour record with a 63, yet still trailed Hattori by three going into the final round. The next players were seven behind.

It quickly became no contest Sunday with Hattori on the way to another 66 and the 197 and Ku headed in the other direction to a 74 that put her in a second-place tie with Kaori Higo. The victory, Hattori's fifth of the season, was the 12th of her career.

Daio Seishi Elleair Ladies Open—¥65,000,000

Winner: Chikayo Yamazaki

The first-round leader was the eventual winner for the second week in a row on the Japan LPGA Tour. Chikayo Yamazaki jumped off with a five-under-par 67 and a one-stroke lead in the Daio Seishi Elleair Ladies Open and finished with a six-under-par 210 total and a two-stroke victory on the Matsuyama course of the Elleair Golf Club at Ehime in southwestern Japan. It was her third tour victory, the others coming on a one-a-year basis the previous two seasons, although the 1997 win came in the year's second tournament.

Yamazaki led Takayo Bandoh by a stroke and Aki Takamura and Nahoko Hirao by two after the opening round. She settled for a par 72 Saturday and Takamura moved within a stroke with 71 for 140. Yamazaki's 71 Sunday completed the job as she finished two shots ahead of Takamura, Jae-Sook

Won and Ok-Hee Ku, the defending champion who was a runner-up for the second week in a row. When neither she nor Kaori Harada won the tournament, the money race was over and Michiko Hattori, who tied for 12th with Harada and six others, was the year's No. 1.

JLPGA Meiji Nyugyo Cup—¥60,000,000

Winner: Young-Me Lee

Young-Me Lee completed her best of 12 seasons in Japan with a two-stroke victory in the important JLPGA Meiji Nyugyo Cup tournament, a limited-field event that concluded the long season on November 29. The South Korean veteran won the Toto Motors tournament in May, one of only five multiple winners for the year, and finished eighth on the circuit's money list with more than ¥42 million. Before the Toto Motors, she had five victories over the previous 11 seasons in Japan but hadn't won since 1996.

Lee's Meiji Nyugyo Cup triumph at Hibiscus Golf Club had elements of sameness to the Toto Motors finish. She and Kaori Harada again found themselves tied for the lead going into the final round. This time it was a fourth round and they began Sunday's play two strokes up on the field.

Harada, who slipped to third place on the money list the previous week, had shot a 65 in Friday's second round to take over from Hisako Takeda, the first-round leader with 67. Harada was at 134 and Lee moved into second place with 69-67–136. The Korean caught Harada Saturday, shooting 70 to her 72 for 206, and outshot her again Sunday by two strokes, 70 to 72, to record the seventh victory. Again finishing second to Lee, Harada nonetheless reclaimed the No. 2 spot on the money list with the ¥5.4 million runner-up check, running her year's total to ¥68,443,639, more than ¥2 million ahead of Ok-Hee Ku.

Women's Australasian Tours

Republic of China Open—US$112,170
Winner: Helen Wadsworth

Improving eight shots on her first round, Helen Wadsworth won the Republic of China Open with the only sub-par round of the tournament in difficult conditions at the Formosa County Club. The first round was cancelled because of inclement weather, then wind and rain made conditions hazardous over the weekend. An eagle and two birdies helped Wadsworth to a closing round of 70 for a four-over-par total of 148, two strokes ahead of American Laura Philo.

Toyota Philippine Open—US$98,001
Winner: Kristel Mourgue d'Algue

Kristel Mourgue d'Algue won her first professional title with a playoff victory over Korea's Il Mi Chung in the Toyota Philippine Open after they finished tied with 219 totals at Sta Elena Golf Club in Manila. Mourgue d'Algue turned professional after winning the NCAA title in 1995 following a illustrious amateur career in which the 24-year-old became the French, Spanish, Italian and Swedish champion. Like her mother, Cecilia, she was runner-up in the British amateur, while her father, Gaetan, was twice the French champion.

Thailand Open—US$89,541
Winner: Connie Wei

Korea's II Mi Chung finished runner-up the second week running when she was beaten by Taiwan amateur Connie Wei in the Thailand Open at Panya Park. Chung still took the professional prize of $13,500 but lost the initiative when she lost a ball at the 10th hole and took a seven. Chung closed with a 75, compared to the superb 70 from Wei which gave her a one-stroke victory at even-par 216. France's Valerie Michaud was three strokes behind and defending champion Sophie Gustafson was fourth after a closing 79.

Malaysian Open—US$84,997
Winner: Sandrine Mendiburu

France's Sandrine Mendiburu secured her second professional victory with a one-stroke win over Loraine Lambert in the Malaysian Open at Glenmarie Golf and Country Club in Subang. The Australian closed strongly with a 68 to make up six shots on Mendiburu but the 25-year-old, who was both the

French and American Junior champion, held on with a five-under-par total of 211. Il Mi Chung, after two second-place finishes, was a further stroke behind as she tied for third.

Indonesian Open—US$99,398

Winner: Tina Fischer

Tina Fischer proved she had recovered from the car accident that curtailed her 1997 season by winning the Indonesian Open at the Paitai Indah Kapuku course in Jakarta by seven strokes. Loraine Lambert was runner-up for the second consecutive time, but her 78 in the last round left Fischer well clear after scores of 68, 72 and 72 for a four-under total of 212.

Australian Ladies Masters—US$700,000

Winner: Karrie Webb

Banishing the memories of the year before, Karrie Webb finally completed her dream of winning in her home country at the Australian Ladies Masters. About 50 of Webb's family and friends journeyed to Royal Pines Resort on Queensland's Gold Coast from her hometown of Ayr, in the far north of the state, to see Webb win by five strokes over Annika Sorenstam and Korea's Hyun Soon Park.

The previous year, Webb let a five-stoke lead with nine holes to play slip away to Gail Graham, but she made no mistake this time after a third-round 64 put her five ahead of the field again. The 23-year-old closed with 70 for a 16-under-par total of 272. Sorenstam, Webb's closest challenger going into the final round, cut the lead to two strokes, but Webb birdied the 15th and the 16th holes to move clear again while Sorenstam doubled-bogeyed the 17th. Webb's younger sister, Katie, doused the new champion in champagne after the winning putt dropped.

"This is probably the happiest day of my life and I would definitely say this is my biggest win," Webb said. "This is something I always wanted to do, and to do it in front of my family and friends is really special. Now that I have this win under my belt, I think I can take a few easier breaths when I come back to Australia to play."

AAMI Women's Australian Open—A$350,000

Winner: Marnie McGuire

The rivalry between Australians and New Zealanders is always highly competitive. So when the diminutive Kiwi Marnie McGuire won the AAMI Women's Australian Open, the local media immediately reminded her that Peter Thomson won the New Zealand Open nine times. "Then I'll have to keep coming back here for another eight years," McGuire said.

McGuire, who plays her golf mainly in Japan, took the lead with two rounds of 72 in horrendous weather on the Yarra Yarra course in Melbourne. A 69 when conditions eased on the Saturday left her one ahead of Kelly

Robbins, who shot a course-record-equalling 65 in the third round.

Despite four birdies in the first six holes from McGuire, the American drew level after nine holes, but the gap was back to two when McGuire birdied the 12th and Robbins bogeyed the 13th. The winner finished in style with birdies at the 16th and 18th.

"I'm not surprised," said McGuire, who closed with a 67 for a 280 total. "I'm more excited. We went head-to-head all the way and we both played great golf. I was not worried when she caught me after nine holes. I knew there were some more birdie opportunities out there. But I did not think I had it won until I hit my approach to a foot at the last.

"I did not feel nervous until after I drove at 18 and was in the fairway three shots clear. Then I felt a lot of butterflies in my stomach. It is great to win and a boost to my career to have played the final round with an established star. I've played with Lotta (Neumann) and Laura (Davies) in Japan and I know what I have to do to beat them, but this gives me confidence going over to the U.S. tour to play next year.

"It is important for me to win outside Japan. This makes me an international winner. And, of course, it means a lot to me to be a Kiwi who has won in Australia." Defending champion Jane Crafter birdied the last four holes to finish third, seven behind the winner.

Women's African Tour

Vodacom Ladies South African Open—R125,000

Winner: Barbara Pestana

Barbara Pestana was the runaway winner of the Vodacom Ladies South African Open played at the Kensington Club in Johannesburg. The 34-year-old from Cape Town, who has played in Europe without winning, clinched her victory by eight strokes after rounds of 70, 71 and 68 for a 10-under-par total of 209. England's Nicola Moult was second, with Helen Wadsworth two strokes further back.

Vodacom South African Ladies Masters—R125,000

Winner: Laurette Maritz

Returning to Kensington later in the year for the Vodacom South African Ladies Masters, Barbara Pestana almost pulled off a notable double, but her final round of 66 was matched by Laurette Maritz. The two-time winner of the South African Open, and a three-time winner on the European circuit, Maritz had scored a 67 in the second round. She continued her impressive golf while under attack from Pestana on the final day and held on for a one-stroke win at a 12-under-par total of 207. Australian Joanne Mills was third at six under.

APPENDIXES

The World Ranking
(As of December 31, 1998)

Pos.		Player	Country	Points Average	Total Points	No. of Events	96/97 Total	96/97 Minus	1998 Plus
1	(2)	Tiger Woods	USA	12.30	566	46	452	-264	378
2	(10)	Mark O'Meara	USA	10.43	532	51	383	-259	408
3	(12)	David Duval	USA	9.67	532	55	364	-226	394
4	(5)	Davis Love III	USA	9.43	481	51	482	-309	308
5	(4)	Ernie Els	SAf	9.18	505	55	554	-357	308
6	(3)	Nick Price	Zim	8.98	458	51	437	-257	278
7	(7)	Colin Montgomerie	Sco	8.91	508	57	489	-329	348
8	(23)	Lee Westwood	Eng	8.65	536	62	342	-208	402
9	(15)	Vijay Singh	Fij	8.51	502	59	366	-230	366
10	(6)	Phil Mickelson	USA	7.76	396	51	419	-293	270
11	(20)	Fred Couples	USA	7.65	306	40	235	-179	250
12	(22)	Jim Furyk	USA	7.23	412	57	326	-198	284
13	(8)	Masashi Ozaki	Jpn	6.77	318	47	346	-230	202
14	(18)	Jesper Parnevik	Swe	6.47	330	51	285	-171	216
15	(11)	Justin Leonard	USA	6.42	385	60	413	-252	224
16	(16)	Steve Elkington	AUS	6.18	247	40	266	-159	140
17	(36)	Darren Clarke	NIr	5.72	326	57	219	-137	244
18	(1)	Greg Norman	Aus	5.65	243	43	517	-326	52
19	(37)	Brian Watts	USA	5.23	251	48	182	-119	188
20	(13)	Scott Hoch	USA	5.22	287	55	377	-246	156
21	(28)	Mark Calcavecchia	USA	5.19	301	58	265	-164	200
22	(9)	Tom Lehman	USA	5.08	264	52	425	-305	144
23	(34)	Lee Janzen	USA	5.02	276	55	212	-132	196
24	(19)	Tom Watson	USA	4.75	190	40	219	-151	122
25	(42)	Jose Maria Olazabal	Spn	4.62	245	53	146	-73	172
26	(43)	Steve Stricker	USA	4.60	198	43	145	-135	188
27	(47)	Payne Stewart	USA	4.49	220	49	167	-115	168
28	(21)	Bernhard Langer	Ger	4.45	227	51	264	-155	118
29	(140)	John Huston	USA	4.40	251	57	69	-58	240
30	(44T)	Stuart Appleby	Aus	4.29	253	59	207	-108	154
31	(29)	Jeff Maggert	USA	4.25	217	51	232	-157	142
32	(35)	John Cook	USA	4.25	238	56	207	-135	166
33	(49)	Bob Tway	USA	4.09	225	55	152	-105	178
34	(96)	Hal Sutton	USA	4.00	236	59	95	-55	196
35	(24)	Steve Jones	USA	3.61	184	51	297	-201	88
36	(66)	Brandt Jobe	USA	3.60	162	45	104	-64	122
37	(25)	Ian Woosnam	Wal	3.44	172	50	268	-186	90
38	(56)	Jeff Sluman	USA	3.38	213	63	178	-121	156
39	(59)	Carlos Franco	Par	3.36	148	44	111	-69	106
40	(14)	Brad Faxon	USA	3.36	178	53	313	-201	66
41	(73)	Thomas Bjorn	Den	3.33	163	49	120	-79	122
42	(119)	Billy Mayfair	USA	3.30	198	60	83	-59	174
43	(33)	Shigeki Maruyama	Jpn	3.27	196	60	237	-145	104
44	(148)	Glen Day	USA	3.25	185	57	70	-51	166
45	(130)	Bob Estes	USA	3.16	161	51	64	-39	136
46	(55)	Stewart Cink	USA	3.10	192	62	145	-79	126
47	(27)	Loren Roberts	USA	3.08	148	48	244	-158	62
48	(72)	Andrew Magee	USA	3.05	180	59	129	-79	130
49	(41)	Bill Glasson	USA	3.05	122	40	139	-73	56
50	(346T)	Scott Verplank	USA	3.00	150	50	16	-12	146

( ) : Figures in brackets indicate 96/97 positions

Pos.		Player	Country	Points Average	Total Points	No. of Events	96/97 Total	96/97 Minus	1998 Plus
51	(133)	Patrik Sjoland	Swe	2.89	159	55	67	-40	132
52	(69)	Frankie Minoza	Phi	2.83	133	47	107	-72	99
53	(40)	Craig Parry	Aus	2.80	165	59	227	-146	84
54	(125)	Miguel Angel Jimenez	Spn	2.75	151	55	75	-56	132
55	(68)	Fred Funk	USA	2.74	192	70	159	-113	146
56	(46)	Naomichi Ozaki	Jpn	2.74	178	65	206	-130	102
57	(17)	Nick Faldo	Eng	2.70	115	44	277	-200	42
58	(137)	Stephen Leaney	Aus	2.67	131	49	51	-30	110
59	(79)	Dudley Hart	USA	2.62	144	55	99	-65	110
60	(26)	Frank Nobilo	NZl	2.57	131	51	256	-169	44
61	(54)	Eduardo Romero	Arg	2.56	105	41	122	-75	58
62	(107)	Paul Azinger	USA	2.52	106	42	65	-43	84
63	(53)	Michael Bradley	USA	2.51	123	49	151	-112	84
64	(48)	Per-Ulrik Johansson	Swe	2.50	105	42	141	-88	52
65	(39)	Craig Stadler	USA	2.44	105	43	151	-98	52
66	(83)	Peter O'Malley	Aus	2.41	140	58	112	-68	96
67	(80)	Robert Karlsson	Swe	2.38	112	47	86	-46	72
68	(171T)	Greg Chalmers	Aug	2.38	119	50	54	-35	100
69	(84)	Andrew Coltart	Sco	2.36	151	64	118	-85	118
70	(77)	Greg Turner	NZl	2.34	110	47	100	-64	74
71	(101)	David Toms	USA	2.30	124	54	90	-52	86
72	(57)	Jay Haas	USA	2.29	112	49	136	-92	68
73	(30)	Mark McNulty	Zim	2.28	91	40	169	-126	48
74	(388T)	Steve Flesch	USA	2.22	109	49	13	-12	108
75	(44T)	Scott McCarron	USA	2.22	122	55	184	-112	50
76	(221)	Steve Pate	USA	2.16	119	55	38	-19	100
77	(31)	Paul Stankowski	USA	2.14	122	57	229	-151	44
78	(63)	Billy Andrade	USA	2.12	127	60	144	-91	74
79	(126)	Brandel Chamblee	USA	2.08	108	52	72	-48	84
80	(193)	Hidemichi Tanaka	Jpn	2.06	134	65	61	-47	120
81	(67)	Kirk Triplett	USA	2.04	106	52	118	-72	60
82	(81)	Stephen Ames	T&T	2.02	87	43	97	-70	60
83	(60)	Retief Goosen	SAf	2.00	126	63	174	-106	58
84	(70)	Tim Herron	USA	1.98	123	62	147	-96	72
85	(50)	Robert Allenby	Aus	1.92	117	61	166	-123	74
86	(266)	Joe Durant	USA	1.89	104	55	32	-16	88
87T	(38)	Tom Kite	USA	1.89	85	45	158	-97	24
87T	(117)	Sam Torrance	Sco	1.89	102	54	80	-56	78
89	(210)	Skip Kendall	USA	1.89	117	62	43	-22	96
90	(388T)	Trevor Dodds	Nam	1.86	93	50	13	-10	90
91T	(52)	Costantino Rocca	Ity	1.86	117	63	190	-137	64
91T	(136)	Brent Geiberger	USA	1.86	104	56	64	-32	72
93	(103)	Chris Perry	USA	1.84	116	63	82	-46	80
94	(51)	David Frost	SAf	1.84	103	56	170	-107	40
95	(320)	Katsumasa Miyamoto	Jpn	1.81	94	52	20	-10	84
96	(32)	Tommy Tolles	USA	1.80	101	56	214	-145	32
97	(186)	Peter Baker	Eng	1.79	95	53	56	-37	76
98	(99)	Larry Mize	USA	1.79	84	47	76	-54	60
99	(91)	Eduardo Herrera	Col	1.78	91	51	79	-50	62
100	(65)	Peter Lonard	Aus	1.75	103	59	114	-67	56

( ) : Figures in brackets indicate 96/97 positions

Pos.		Player	Country	Points Average	Total Points	No. of Events	96/97 Total	96/97 Minus	1998 Plus
101	(114)	Hajime Meshiai	Jpn	1.69	103	61	81	-56	78
102	(158)	Olin Browne	USA	1.68	99	59	70	-43	72
103	(94)	Steve Lowery	USA	1.64	97	59	105	-64	56
104	(71)	Tateo Ozaki	Jpn	1.62	99	61	109	-60	50
105	(97)	Jay Don Blake	USA	1.62	86	53	90	-58	54
106	(78)	Padraig Harrington	Ire	1.62	94	58	122	-82	54
107	(183)	Toshimitsu Izawa	Jpn	1.61	82	51	44	-28	66
108	(220)	Stephen Allan	Aus	1.57	83	53	34	-17	66
109	(178)	Russell Claydon	Eng	1.56	67	43	52	-35	50
110	(237)	Phillip Price	Wal	1.56	81	52	40	-25	66
111	(64)	Kenny Perry	USA	1.55	79	51	123	-102	58
112	(270)	Frank Lickliter	USA	1.55	96	62	36	-22	82
113	(138)	Jarmo Sandelin	Swe	1.55	82	53	71	-45	56
114	(322)	Mathias Gronberg	Swe	1.54	77	50	25	-20	72
115	(128)	Kevin Sutherland	USA	1.52	88	58	84	-46	50
116	(88)	Rocco Mediate	USA	1.48	71	48	81	-64	54
117	(147)	Keiichiro Fukabori	Jpn	1.45	90	62	66	-38	62
118	(200)	Bradley Hughes	Aus	1.43	86	60	47	-39	78
119	(87)	Dan Forsman	USA	1.42	71	50	89	-52	34
120	(179)	David Carter	Eng	1.42	78	55	58	-38	58
121	(227T)	John Daly	USA	1.40	63	45	39	-30	54
122	(95)	Peter Senior	AUS	1.40	74	53	93	-75	56
123	(74)	Phil Blackmar	USA	1.38	73	53	118	-67	22
124	(386)	J.P. Hayes	USA	1.37	70	51	16	-8	62
125	(202)	Alex Cejka	Ger	1.37	63	46	39	-28	52
126	(167T)	Sven Struver	Ger	1.36	79	58	60	-39	58
127	(82)	Ignacio Garrido	Spn	1.36	72	53	99	-59	32
128	(166)	Toru Suzuki	Jpn	1.34	90	67	70	-44	64
129	(123)	Robert Damron	USA	1.34	87	65	78	-39	48
130	(325T)	Shingo Katayama	Jpn	1.33	53	40	18	-9	44
131	(58)	Duffy Waldorf	USA	1.32	70	53	130	-92	32
132	(90)	Mark James	Ens	1.31	63	48	85	-46	24
133	(75)	Paul Goydos	USA	1.31	80	61	133	-93	40
134	(316T)	Tommy Armour III	USA	1.31	76	58	24	-14	66
135	(689T)	Harrison Frazar	USA	1.30	60	46	0	0	60
136	(190T)	Joey Sindelar	USA	1.29	75	58	55	-40	60
137	(159)	Kazuhiko Hosokawa	Jpn	1.29	94	73	79	-57	72
138	(217T)	Nobuhito Sato	Jpn	1.26	72	57	36	-18	54
139	(238)	Kaname Yokoo	Jpn	1.26	88	70	42	-30	76
140	(146)	David Gilford	Eng	1.25	55	44	59	-36	32
141T	(61)	David Ogrin	USA	1.24	72	58	156	-102	18
141T	(89)	Tom Byrum	USA	1.24	72	58	96	-52	28
143	(85)	Rick Fehr	USA	1.23	53	43	81	-52	24
144T	(214)	Willie Wood	USA	1.22	66	54	38	-26	54
144T	(271T)	Toru Taniguchi	Jpn	1.22	55	45	24	-15	46
146	(151)	Nolan Henke	USA	1.22	61	50	58	-43	46
147	(102)	Paul McGinley	Ire	1.20	65	54	96	-71	40
148	(100)	Russ Cochran	USA	1.20	71	59	100	-65	36
149	(112)	Joakim Haeggman	Swe	1.19	51	43	69	-42	24
150	(177)	Scott Simpson	USA	1.17	54	46	50	-42	46

( ) : Figures in brackets indicate 96/97 positions

Pos.		Player	Country	Points Average	Total Points	No. of Events	96/97 Total	96/97 Minus	1998 Plus
151	(113)	Mark Wiebe	USA	1.16	59	51	73	-46	32
152	(86)	Miguel Angel Martin	Spn	1.15	46	40	86	-60	20
153	(689T)	Clark Dennis	USA	1.15	54	47	0	0	54
154	(195)	Jim Carter	USA	1.15	70	61	55	-35	50
155T	(161)	Angel Cabrera	Arg	1.14	48	42	47	-29	30
155T	(127)	Peter Jacobsen	USA	1.14	56	49	65	-39	30
157	(260T)	Gary Orr	Sco	1.13	59	52	33	-26	52
158	(99)	Raymond Russell	Sco	1.13	68	60	94	-62	36
159	(246T)	Gordon Brand Jr.	Sco	1.13	53	47	36	-27	44
160T	(118)	Doug Martin	USA	1.13	72	64	85	-51	38
160T	(129)	Hiroyuki Fujita	Jpn	1.13	54	48	55	-29	28
162	(213)	David Howell	Eng	1.12	73	65	52	-37	58
163	(171T)	Phil Tataurangi	NZl	1.11	68	61	54	-34	48
164	(239T)	Tony Johnstone	Zim	1.11	50	45	32	-26	44
165	(132)	Todd Hamilton	USA	1.11	52	47	70	-54	36
166	(105)	Paul Broadhurst	Eng	1.11	63	57	96	-67	34
167	(367T)	Bruce Lietzke	USA	1.10	44	40	14	-12	42
168T	(139)	Peter Mitchell	Eng	1.10	56	51	73	-57	40
168T	(689T)	Bob Friend	USA	1.10	56	51	0	0	56
170	(518)	Mathew Goggin	Aus	1.10	57	52	7	-4	54
171	(163)	Jean Van de Velde	Frn	1.09	61	56	59	-48	50
172	(252T)	Steve Webster	Eng	1.09	50	46	32	-18	36
173	(211)	Ted Tryba	USA	1.07	72	67	59	-35	48
174	(144)	Mike Reid	USA	1.06	54	51	58	-34	30
175	(335)	Tom Pernice Jr.	USA	1.05	60	57	21	-11	50
176	(153)	Fuzzy Zoeller	USA	1.05	42	40	46	-36	32
177	(176)	Len Mattiace	USA	1.05	69	66	67	-42	44
178	(603T)	Mamoru Osanai	Jpn	1.02	43	42	2	-1	42
179	(194)	Katsunori Kuwabara	Jpn	1.02	66	65	59	-39	46
180	(134)	Brad Fabel	USA	0.98	60	61	75	-45	30
181	(360)	Santiago Luna	Spn	0.98	46	47	19	-15	42
182	(135)	Jamie Spence	Eng	0.98	45	46	62	-39	22
183T	(131)	Mike Brisky	USA	0.97	56	58	77	-51	30
183T	(197)	Yoshinori Mizumaki	Jpn	0.97	56	58	50	-32	38
185	(106)	Jose Coceres	Arg	0.95	41	43	76	-53	18
186	(145)	Mike Hulbert	USA	0.94	58	62	76	-48	30
187	(351)	Nobumitsu Yuhara	Jpn	0.93	57	61	23	-16	50
188	(110)	Michael Long	NZl	0.93	51	55	62	-41	30
189	(109)	Fulton Allem	SAf	0.91	41	45	65	-40	16
190	(170)	Mitsutaka Kusakabe	Jpn	0.89	49	55	46	-25	28
191	(164)	Tsukasa Watanabe	Jpn	0.88	58	66	68	-44	34
192	(173)	Jerry Kelly	USA	0.88	57	65	73	-54	38
193	(528T)	Bradley King	Aus	0.88	35	40	5	-4	34
194	(236)	Satoshi Higashi	Jpn	0.87	58	67	49	-31	40
195	(227T)	Kim Jong-duck	Kor	0.86	37	43	30	-15	22
196	(142)	David Ishii	USA	0.86	49	57	71	-52	30
197	(162)	Brian Henninger	USA	0.85	47	55	60	-33	20
198	(689T)	Craig Hainline	USA	0.85	34	40	0	0	34
199	(165)	Lee Rinker	USA	0.84	54	64	69	-41	26
200	(246T)	Rick Gibson	Can	0.84	46	55	36	-28	38

( ) : Figures in brackets indicate 96/97 positions

World's Winners of 1998

U.S. PGA TOUR

Mercedes Championships	Phil Mickelson
Bob Hope Chrysler Classic	Fred Couples
Phoenix Open	Jesper Parnevik
AT&T Pebble Beach National Pro-Am	Phil Mickelson (2)
Buick Invitational	Scott Simpson
United Airlines Hawaiian Open	John Huston
Tucson Chrysler Classic	David Duval
Nissan Open	Billy Mayfair
Doral-Ryder Open	Michael Bradley
Honda Classic	Mark Calcavecchia
Bay Hill Invitational	Ernie Els (2)
The Players Championship	Justin Leonard
Freeport-McDermott Classic	Lee Westwood
Masters Tournament	Mark O'Meara
MCI Classic	Davis Love III
Greater Greensboro Chrysler Classic	Trevor Dodds
Shell Houston Open	David Duval (2)
BellSouth Classic	Tiger Woods (2)
GTE Byron Nelson Classic	John Cook
MasterCard Colonial	Tom Watson
Memorial Tournament	Fred Couples (2)
Kemper Open	Stuart Appleby
Buick Classic	J.P. Hayes
U.S. Open Championship	Lee Janzen
Motorola Western Open	Joe Durant
Canon Greater Hartford Open	Olin Browne
Quad City Classic	Steve Jones
Deposit Guaranty Golf Classic	Fred Funk
CVS Charity Classic	Steve Pate
FedEx St. Jude Classic	Nick Price (2)
Buick Open	Billy Mayfair (2)
PGA Championship	Vijay Singh
Sprint International	Vijay Singh (2)
NEC World Series of Golf	David Duval (4)
Greater Vancouver Open	Brandel Chamblee
Greater Milwaukee Open	Jeff Sluman
Bell Canadian Open	Billy Andrade
B.C. Open	Chris Perry
Westin Texas Open	Hal Sutton
Buick Challenge	Steve Elkington
Michelob Championship	David Duval (5)
Las Vegas Invitational	Jim Furyk (2)
National Car Rental Classic	John Huston (2)
Tour Championship	Hal Sutton (2)

SPECIAL EVENTS

Panama Open Panasonic	Bob Friend
Fred Meyer Challenge	David Duval (3)/Jim Furyk
Subaru Sarazen World Open	Dudley Hart
General Motors Mexican Open	Eduardo Romero
Franklin Templeton Shark Shootout	Steve Elkington (2)/Greg Norman (2)
PGA Grand Slam	Tiger Woods (3)

World Cup of Golf	England/Scott Verplank
Callaway Golf Pebble Beach Invitational	Tom Lehman
JCPenney Classic	Meg Mallon (2)/Steve Pate (2)
Office Depot Father-Son Challenge	Bob Charles/David Charles
Presidents Cup	International
Lexus Challenge	Jim Colbert (2)/Kevin Costner

NIKE TOUR

Lakeland Classic	Casey Martin
South Florida Classic	Eric Johnson
Greater Austin Open	Michael Allen
Monterrey Open	Joe Ogilvie
Louisiana Open	John Wilson
Shreveport Open	Vance Veazey
Upstate Classic	Tom Scherrer
Huntsville Open	Dennis Paulson
South Carolina Classic	Gene Sauers
Carolina Classic	Brian Bateman
Dominion Open	Bob Burns
Knoxville Open	Robin Freeman
Miami Valley Open	Craig Bowden
Cleveland Open	Doug Dunakey
Lehigh Valley Open	Eric Booker
Greensboro Open	Joe Ogilvie (2)
Hershey Open	Michael Clark
St. Louis Golf Classic	Chris Starkjohann
Wichita Open	Emlyn Aubrey
Dakota Dunes Open	John Maginnes
Omaha Classic	Matt Gogel
Ozarks Open	Anthony Painter
Fort Smith Classic	Mark Hensby
Permian Basin Open	Stiles Mitchell
Tri-Cities Open	Matt Gogel (2)
Boise Open	Mike Sposa
Oregon Classic	Charles Raulerson
San Jose Open	Robin Freeman (2)
Inland Empire Open	Charles Raulerson (2)
Nike Tour Championship	Bob Burns (2)

CANADIAN TOUR

Payless Open	Jay Hobby
BC Tel Open	Ian Hutchings
Telus Calgary Open	Scott Wearne
Dundee Realty Int'l Team Matches	Canada
Telus Edmonton Open	Brian Kontak
Henry Singer Alberta Open	Brian Kontak (2)
MTS Classic	Perry Parker
Infiniti Championship	Brian Kontak (3)
Canadian Masters	Mike Grob
Eagle Creek Classic	Perry Parker (2)
American Express - Shell Cup	Paul Devenport
New Brunswick Open	Tim Clark
Samsung Canadian PGA Championship	Tim Clark (2)
NewTel Atlantic Cup Int'l Team Matches	International
Bell Bay International Team Matches	International
Bayer Championship	Chris Tidland

SOUTH AMERICAN TOUR

TPG Open	Claudio Muskus
Peru Open	Scott Dunlap
City of La Plata Open	Roberto Coceres
Litoral Open	Tim Hegna
Argentina Masters	Raul Fretes
JPGA Argentina	Jeffrey Schmidt
Las Delicias Open	Sebastian Fernandez
Argentina Open	Raul Fretes (2)

PGA EUROPEAN TOUR

Dubai Desert Classic	Jose Maria Olazabal
Qatar Masters	Andrew Coltart
Moroccan Open	Stephen Leaney
Portuguese Open	Peter Mitchell
Cannes Open	Thomas Levet
Peugeot Open de Espana	Thomas Bjorn (2)
Italian Open	Patrik Sjoland
Turespana Masters Open Baleares	Miguel Angel Jimenez
Benson and Hedges International	Darren Clarke
Volvo PGA Championship	Colin Montgomerie
Deutsche Bank–SAP Open TPC of Europe	Lee Westwood (2)
National Car Rental English Open	Lee Westwood (3)
Compaq European Grand Prix	Cancelled
Madeira Island Open	Mats Lanner
Peugeot Open de France	Sam Torrance
Murphy's Irish Open	David Carter
Standard Life Loch Lomond	Lee Westwood (4)
British Open Championship	Mark O'Meara (2)
TNT Dutch Open	Stephen Leaney (2)
Volvo Scandinavian Masters	Jesper Parnevik (2)
German Open	Stephen Allan
Smurfit European Open	Mathias Gronberg
BMW International Open	Russell Claydon
Canon European Masters	Sven Struver
One 2 One British Masters	Colin Montgomerie (2)
Trophee Lancome	Miguel Angel Jimenez (2)
Linde German Masters	Colin Montgomerie (3)
Belgacom Open	Lee Westwood (5)
Alfred Dunhill Cup	South Africa
Cisco World Match Play	Mark O'Meara (3)
Open Novotel Perrier	Jarmo Sandelin/Olle Karlsson
Volvo Masters	Darren Clarke (2)

CHALLENGE TOUR

Ivory Coast Open	John Mellor
Tusker Kenya Open	Ricardo Gonzalez
Is Molas Challenge	Magnus Persson
Rimini International Open	Massimo Scarpa
Albarella International Open	Fredrik Lindgren
Modena Classic	Marc Pendaries
Challenge de France	Warren Bennett
KB Golf Challenge	Stephen Gallacher
Diners Club Austrian Open	Kevin Carissimi
NCC Open	Johan Rystrom
Fontana Open	Uli Weinhandl
Lancia Golf Pokal	Alex Cejka
Championnat de France Professionnel	Jean Van de Velde

Omnium National Champ. Lloyd Italico	Massimo Scarpa (2)
Osmanli Bankasi Klassis Turkish Open	Thomas Nielsen
Open dei Tessali	Pehr Magnebrant
MasterCard Challenge	Robert Lee
Audi Quattro Trophy	Marcello Santi
BTC Slovenian Open	Warren Bennett (2)
Volvo Finnish Open	Christian Cevaer
Open des Volcans	Warren Bennett (3)
Rolex Trophy	David Park
Interlaken Open	John Senden
Challenge Tour Championship	Warren Bennett (4)
Finnish Masters	Massimo Scarpa (3)
Moscow Country Club Russian Open	Warren Bennett (5)
Denmark Closed Event	Ben Tinning
Netcom Norwegian Open	Gary Emerson
Navision Open	Soren Hansen
Ohrlings Swedish Match Play	Kevin Carissimi (2)
Open de Strasbourg - La Wantzenau	John Senden (2)
Warsaw Golf Open	Jose Manuel Lara
Eulen Open Galea	Alvaro Salto
Telia Grand Prix	Mats Lanner (2)
San Paolo Vita Open	Roger Winchester
AXA Grand Final	Jorge Berendt

ASIAN TOUR

Ericsson Philippine Masters	Frankie Minoza
Benson and Hedges Malaysian Open	Edward Fryatt
Rolex Masters	Frankie Minoza (2)
Ericsson Philippine Open	Frankie Minoza (3)
Maekyung LG Fashion Open	Scott Rowe
Johnnie Walker Super Tour	Vijay Singh (3)

JAPAN PGA TOUR

Token Corporation Cup	Hajime Meshiai
Daido Drinko Shizuoka Open	Eduardo Herrera
Just System KSB Open	Carlos Franco
Descente Classic Munsingwear Cup	Dinesh Chand
Tsuruya Open	Katsumasa Miyamoto
Kirin Open	Frankie Minoza (4)
Chunichi Crowns	Davis Love III (2)
Fuji Sankei Classic	Carlos Franco (2)
Japan PGA Championship	Brandt Jobe
Ube Kosan Open	Brandt Jobe (2)
Mitsubishi Galant	Toru Taniguchi
JCB Classic Sendai	Yoshinori Mizumaki
Sapporo Tokyu Open	Toru Suzuki
Yomiuri Open	Brian Watts
Mizuno Open	Brandt Jobe (3)
PGA Philanthropy	Shigeki Maruyama
Yonex Open Hiroshima	Masashi Ozaki
Aiful Cup	Hidemichi Tanaka
NST Niigata Open	Masayuki Kawamura
Sanko Grand Summer	Shingo Katayama
KBC Augusta	Masashi Ozaki (2)
Japan Match Play	Katsunori Kuwabara
Suntory Open	Mamoru Osanai
ANA Open	Keiichiro Fukabori
Gene Sarazen Jun Classic	Todd Hamilton

Japan Open	Hidemichi Tanaka (2)
Tokai Classic	Toshimitsu Izawa
Nikkei Cup	Mitsutaka Kusakabe
Bridgestone Open	Nobuhito Sato
Philip Morris Championship	Masashi Ozaki (3)
Acom International	Kaname Yokoo
Sumitomo Visa Taiheiyo Masters	Lee Westwood (6)
Dunlop Phoenix Tournament	Lee Westwood (7)
Casio World Open	Brian Watts (2)
Japan Series	Katsumasa Miyamoto (2)
Okinawa Open	Hidemichi Tanaka (3)

OMEGA TOUR

London Myanmar Open	Taimur Hussain
Classic Indian Open	Firoz Ali
Orient Masters	Chawalit Plaphol
Trans Strait Invitational	Lin Keng-chi
Volvo China Open	Edward Fryatt (2)
Macau Open	Satoshi Oide
Guam Open	Jerry Smith
Fila Open	Robert Huxtable
Sabah Masters	Simon Yates
Volvo Masters of Mayaysia	Chris Williams
Ericsson Singapore Open	Shaun Micheel
Kolon Sports Korean Open	*Kim Dae-sub
Kuala Lumpur Open	Nico van Rensburg
FedEx PGA Championship	Chris Williams (2)
Ericsson Classic	Lu Wen-teh
Hero Honda Masters	Jyoti Randhawa
Thailand Open	James Kingston
Perrier Hong Kong Open	Kang Wook-soon
Omega PGA Championship	Kang Wook-soon (2)
Volvo Asian Match Play	Gerry Norquist

AUSTRALASIAN TOUR

Victorian Open	Bradley King
Johnnie Walker Classic	Tiger Woods
Heineken Classic	Thomas Bjorn
Greg Norman Holden International	Greg Norman
Ericsson Australian Masters	Bradley Hughes
Canon Challenge	Peter O'Malley
Australasian Tour Championship	Mathew Goggin
Ford Open Championship	Stuart Bouvier
MasterCard PGA Championship	David Howell
Australasian Players Championship	Stephen Leaney (3)
Holden Australian Open	Greg Chalmers
New Zealand Open	Matthew Lane
Schweppes Coolum Classic	Stuart Appleby (2)

AFRICAN TOURS

Nashua Wild Coast Sun Challenge	Adilson da Silva
South African Open	Ernie Els
Alfred Dunhill South African PGA	Tony Johnstone
Dimension Data Pro-Am	Nick Price
Stenham Royal Swazi Sun Open	Paul Friedlander
Vodacom Players Championship	Mark McNulty
Vodacom Series: Western Cape	Alan McLean
Kalahari Classic	Andrew McLardy

Pietersburg Classic	Desvonde Botes
Vodacom Series: Eastern Cape	Sammy Daniels
Vodacom Series: Kwazulu-Natal	Keith Horne
Vodacom Series: Mpumalanga	Callie Swart
Fish River Sun Pro-Am	Ashley Roestoff
Royal Swazi Sun Classic	Justin Hobday
ABSA Corporate Bank Challenge	Warren Abery
Bearing Man Highveld Classic	Wayne Bradley
Vodacom Series: Free State	Gary Matthews
FNB Botswana Open	Justin Hobday (2)
Phalaborwa Mafunyane Trophy	Sammy Daniels (2)
Vodacom Series: Gauteng	Brenden Pappas
FNB Namibia Open	Ashley Roestoff (2)
Hassan II Trophy	Santiago Luna
Platinum Classic	Bobby Lincoln
Zambia Open	Marc Cayeux
Zimbabwe Open	Nick Price (3)
Nedbank Million Dollar Challenge	Nick Price (4)

U.S. SENIOR PGA TOUR

MasterCard Championship	Gil Morgan
Royal Caribbean Classic	David Graham
LG Championship	Gil Morgan (2)
GTE Classic	Jim Albus
American Express Invitational	Larry Nelson
Senior Slam	Gil Morgan (3)
Toshiba Senior Classic	Hale Irwin
Liberty Mutual Legends of Golf	Charles Coody/Dale Douglass
Southwestern Bell Dominion	Lee Trevino
The Tradition	Gil Morgan (4)
PGA Seniors' Championship	Hale Irwin (2)
Las Vegas Senior Classic	Hale Irwin (3)
Bruno's Memorial Classic	Hubert Green
Home Depot Invitational	Jim Dent
Saint Luke's Classic	Larry Ziegler
Bell Atlantic Classic	Jay Sigel
Pittsburgh Senior Classic	Larry Nelson (2)
Nationwide Championship	John Jacobs
BellSouth Senior Classic	Isao Aoki
AT&T Canada Senior Open	Brian Barnes
Cadillac NFL Classic	Bob Dickson
State Farm Senior Classic	Bruce Summerhays
Ford Senior Players Championship	Gil Morgan (5)
Ameritech Senior Open	Hale Irwin (4)
U.S. Senior Open	Hale Irwin (5)
Utah Showdown	Gil Morgan (6)
Coldwell Banker Burnet Classic	Leonard Thompson
First of America Classic	George Archer
Northville Long Island Classic	Gary Player
BankBoston Classic	Hale Irwin (6)
Emerald Coast Classic	Dana Quigley
Comfort Classic	Hugh Baiocchi
Kroger Senior Classic	Hugh Baiocchi (2)
Boone Valley Classic	Larry Nelson (3)
Vantage Championship	Gil Morgan (7)
The Transamerica	Jim Colbert
Raley's Gold Rush Classic	Dana Quigley (2)
EMC^2 Kaanapali Classic	Jay Sigel (2)

Pacific Bell Senior Classic	Joe Inman
Energizer Senior Tour Championship	Hale Irwin (7)
Senior Match Play Challenge	Hale Irwin (8)

EUROPEAN SENIORS TOUR

El Bosque Seniors Open	Tommy Horton
Beko Classic	Bob Lendzion
AIB Irish Seniors Open	Joe McDermott
Philips PFA Golf Classic	Neil Coles
Jersey Seniors Open	Bob Shearer
De Vere Hotels Seniors Classic	Tommy Horton (2)
Ryder Seniors Classic	Bill Hardwick
Swedish Seniors	Maurice Bembridge
Lawrence Batley Seniors	Bobby Verwey
Credit Suisse Private Banking Seniors Open	Bobby Verwey (2)
Schroder Senior Masters	Brian Huggett
Senior British Open	Brian Huggett (2)
West of Ireland Seniors Championship	John Morgan
The Belfry PGA Seniors Championship	Tommy Horton (3)
Golden Charter PGA Scottish Seniors Open	David Huish
Efteling European Trophy	Paul Leonard
Elf Seniors Open	Brian Waites
Is Molas Seniors Open	Malcolm Gregson
Senior Tournament of Champions	John Garner

JAPAN SENIOR TOUR

Komatsu Nagoya TV Open	Hisao Inoue
TPC Starts	Toru Nakayama
Castle Hill Open	Koichi Uehara
Old Man Par Senior Open	Toru Nakayama (2)
HTB Senior Classic	Hsieh Min-nan
Japan PGA Senior Championship	Seiichi Kanai
Japan Senior Open	Graham Marsh

SOUTH AFRICA SENIOR TOUR

Vodacom Senior Series: Pretoria	Gabriel Putsoe
Vodacom Senior Series: Wild Coast	Tertius Claassens
Vodacom Senior Series: Mmabatho	Tertius Claassens (2)
Vodacom Senior Series: Welkom	Allan Henning
Franklin Templeton Senior S.A. Open	John Bland
Vodacom Senior Classic	Solly Sepeng
John Bland Invitational	Allan Henning (2)

U.S. LPGA TOUR

HealthSouth Inaugural	Kelly Robbins
Office Depot	Helen Alfredsson
Los Angeles Women's Championship	Dale Eggeling
Cup Noodles Hawaiian Ladies Open	Wendy Ward
Welch's/Circle K Championship	Helen Alfredsson (2)
Standard Register Ping	Liselotte Neumann
Nabisco Dinah Shore	Pat Hurst
Longs Drugs Challenge	Donna Andrews
City of Hope Myrtle Beach Classic	Karrie Webb (2)
Chick-fil-A Charity Championship	Liselotte Neumann (2)
Mercury Titleholders Championship	Danielle Ammaccapane
Sara Lee Classic	Barb Mucha
McDonald's LPGA Championship	Se Ri Pak
Corning Classic	Tammie Green

Wegmans Rochester International	Rosie Jones
Michelob Light Classic	Annika Sorenstam
Oldsmobile Classic	Lisa Walters
Friendly's Classic	Amy Fruhwirth
ShopRite Classic	Annika Sorenstam (2)
U.S. Women's Open	Se Ri Pak (2)
Jamie Farr Kroger Classic	Se Ri Pak (3)
JAL Big Apple Classic	Annika Sorenstam (3)
Giant Eagle Classic	Se Ri Pak (4)
du Maurier Classic	Brandie Burton
Star Bank Classic	Meg Mallon
Rainbow Foods Classic	Hiromi Kobayashi
State Farm Rail Classic	Pearl Sinn
Safeway Championship	Danielle Ammaccapane (2)
Safeco Classic	Annika Sorenstam (5)
Solheim Cup	United States
First Union Betsy King Classic	Rachel Hetherington
AFLAC Tournament of Champions	Kelly Robbins (2)
Samsung World Championship	Juli Inkster
PageNet Tour Championship	Laura Davies (2)

EUROPEAN LPGA TOUR

Evian Masters	Helen Alfredsson (3)
Ladies' Austrian Open	Lynette Brooky
Chrysler Open	Laura Davies
Ladies' German Open	Lora Fairclough
McDonald's WPGA Champ. of Europe	Catriona Matthew
Weetabix Women's British Open	Sherri Steinhauer
Compaq Open	Annika Sorenstam (4)
Donegal Irish Ladies' Open	Sophie Gustafson
Air France Madame Open	Patricia Meunier Lebouc
Marrakesh Palmeraie Open	Sophie Gustafson (2)
Princess Lalla Meriem Cup	Sophie Gustafson (3)
Praia D'El Rey European Cup	European Seniors Tour

JAPAN LPGA TOUR

Daikin Orchid Ladies	Ae-Sook Kim
Saishunkan Ladies	Michiko Hattori
Yellow Hat Tokyo Ladies Open	Akemi Yamaoka
Kenshoen Ladies	Chihiro Furukawa
Glory Queen's Cup	Kaori Harada
Nasu Ogawa Ladies	Michiko Hattori (2)
Katokichi Queens	Tamayo Ueda
Gunze Cup World Ladies	Liselotte Neumann (3)
Yakult Ladies	Aiko Takasu
Chukyo TV Bridgestone Ladies	Ok-Hee Ku
Toto Motors Ladies	Young-Me Lee
Resort Trust Ladies	Kaori Harada (2)
Suntory Ladies Open	Marnie McGuire
Dunlop Ladies Open	Huang Yu-Chen
Japan Women's Open	Natsuko Noro
Toyo Suisan Ladies	Michie Ohba
Sumitomo Visa Taiheiyo Ladies	Aki Nakano
Golf 5 Ladies	Akiko Fukushima
Mizuno Ladies	Fuki Kido
NEC Karuizawa 72	Yuka Irie
New Caterpillar Mitsubishi Ladies	Kyoko Ono
Goyo Kensetsu Ladies	Harumi Sakagami

Fuji Sankei Ladies Classic	Masako Ishihara
Japan LPGA Championship	Michiko Hattori (3)
Yukijirushi Ladies Tokai Classic	Kaori Higo
Miyagi TV Cup Dunlop Ladies Open	Akiko Fukushima (2)
Kosaido Ladies Golf Cup	Mayumi Murai
TaKaRa World Invitational	Aki Takamura
Fujitsu Ladies	Kaori Higo (2)
Hisako Higuchi Kibun Classic	Michiko Hattori (4)
Nichirei International	United States
LPGA Japan Classic	Hiromi Kobayashi (2)
Itoen Ladies	Michiko Hattori (5)
Daio Seishi Elleair Ladies Open	Chikayo Yamazaki
JLPGA Meiji Nyugyo Cup	Young-Me Lee (2)

WOMEN'S AUSTRALASIAN TOURS

Republic of China Open	Helen Wadsworth
Toyota Philippine Open	Kristel Mourgue d'Algue
Thailand Open	*Connie Wei
Malaysian Open	Sandrine Mendiburu
Indonesian Open	Tina Fischer
Australian Ladies Masters	Karrie Webb
AAMI Women's Australian Open	Marnie McGuire (2)

WOMEN'S AFRICAN TOUR

Vodacom Ladies South African Open	Barbara Pestana
Vodacom South African Ladies Masters	Laurette Maritz

Multiple Winners of 1998

Hale Irwin	8	Hugh Baiocchi	2	Kang Wook-soon	2
Gil Morgan	7	Thomas Bjorn	2	Hiromi Kobayashi	2
Lee Westwood	7	Bob Burns	2	Mats Lanner	2
Warren Bennett	5	Kevin Carissimi	2	Young-Me Lee	2
David Duval	5	Tertius Claassens	2	Davis Love III	2
Michiko Hattori	5	Tim Clark	2	Meg Mallon	2
Annika Sorenstam	5	Darren Clarke	2	Billy Mayfair	2
Frankie Minoza	4	Jim Colbert	2	Marnie McGuire	2
Se Ri Pak	4	Fred Couples	2	Phil Mickelson	2
Nick Price	4	Sammy Daniels	2	Katsumasa Miyamoto	2
Helen Alfredsson	3	Laura Davies	2	Toru Nakayama	2
Sophie Gustafson	3	Steve Elkington	2	Greg Norman	2
Tommy Horton	3	Ernie Els	2	Joe Ogilvie	2
Brandt Jobe	3	Carlos Franco	2	Perry Parker	2
Brian Kontak	3	Robin Freeman	2	Jesper Parnevik	2
Stephen Leaney	3	Raul Fretes	2	Steve Pate	2
Colin Montgomerie	3	Edward Fryatt	2	Dana Quigley	2
Larry Nelson	3	Akiko Fukushima	2	Charles Raulerson	2
Liselotte Neumann	3	Jim Furyk	2	Kelly Robbins	2
Mark O'Meara	3	Matt Gogel	2	Ashley Roestoff	2
Masashi Ozaki	3	Kaori Harada	2	John Senden	2
Massimo Scarpa	3	Allan Henning	2	Jay Sigel	2
Vijay Singh	3	Kaori Higo	2	Hal Sutton	2
Hidemichi Tanaka	3	Justin Hobday	2	Bobby Verwey	2
Tiger Woods	3	Brian Huggett	2	Brian Watts	2
Danielle Ammaccapane	2	John Huston	2	Karrie Webb	2
Stuart Appleby	2	Miguel Angel Jimenez	2	Chris Williams	2

World Money List

This list of the 400 leading money winners in the world of professional golf in 1998 was compiled from the results of men's (excluding seniors) tournaments carried in the Appendixes of this edition. This list includes tournaments with a minimum of 36 holes and four contestants and does not include such competitions as skins games, pro-ams and shootouts.

In the 33 years during which World Money Lists have been compiled, the earnings of the player in the 200th position have risen from a total of $3,326 in 1966 to $256,174 in 1998. The top-200 players in 1966 earned a total of $4,680,287. In 1998, the comparable total was $138,872,490.

Because of fluctuating values of money throughout the world, it was necessary to determine an average value of non-American currency to U.S. money to prepare this listing. The conversion rates used for 1998 were: British pound = US$1.65; Japanese yen = US$0.00754; South African rand = US$0.19; Australian dollar = US$0.64; Canadian dollar = US$0.67.

POS.	PLAYER, COUNTRY	TOTAL MONEY
1	Tiger Woods, USA	$2,927,946
2	David Duval, USA	2,855,489
3	Vijay Singh, Fiji	2,848,612
4	Lee Westwood, England	2,814,153
5	Mark O'Meara, USA	2,677,788
6	Nick Price, Zimbabwe	2,272,421
7	Jim Furyk, USA	2,229,334
8	Colin Montgomerie, Scotland	2,206,532
9	Justin Leonard, USA	1,918,364
10	Hal Sutton, USA	1,871,240
11	Phil Mickelson, USA	1,870,246
12	Darren Clarke, N. Ireland	1,870,057
13	Ernie Els, South Africa	1,860,730
14	Davis Love III, USA	1,747,668
15	Fred Couples, USA	1,725,865
16	Jesper Parnevik, Sweden	1,685,543
17	John Huston, USA	1,646,657
18	Mark Calcavecchia, USA	1,482,695
19	Lee Janzen, USA	1,473,862
20	Masashi Ozaki, Japan	1,413,338
21	Scott Verplank, USA	1,385,269
22	Billy Mayfair, USA	1,364,239
23	Steve Stricker, USA	1,363,448
24	Glen Day, USA	1,345,122
25	John Cook, USA	1,303,084
26	Scott Hoch, USA	1,298,053
27	Bob Tway, USA	1,283,447
28	Jeff Sluman, USA	1,278,012
29	Fred Funk, USA	1,210,886
30	Payne Stewart, USA	1,203,746
31	Tom Lehman, USA	1,154,793
32	Jose Maria Olazabal, Spain	1,100,130

POS.	PLAYER, COUNTRY	TOTAL MONEY
33	Tom Watson, USA	1,084,360
34	Brian Watts, USA	1,075,802
35	Miguel Angel Jimenez, Spain	1,055,692
36	Andrew Magee, USA	1,007,759
37	Bob Estes, USA	1,001,332
38	Steve Pate, USA	1,001,254
39	Jeff Maggert, USA	992,964
40	Steve Elkington, Australia	990,847
41	Stuart Appleby, Australia	987,555
42	Patrik Sjoland, Sweden	941,821
43	Dudley Hart, USA	936,613
44	Stewart Cink, USA	914,189
45	Thomas Bjorn, Denmark	858,616
46	Andrew Coltart, Scotland	851,727
47	Brandt Jobe, USA	841,857
48	Steve Jones, USA	824,811
49	Billy Andrade, USA	823,351
50	Skip Kendall, USA	817,164
51	Steve Flesch, USA	815,736
52	Trevor Dodds, Nambia	815,340
53	Bernhard Langer, Germany	811,051
54	Chris Perry, USA	800,171
55	Hidemichi Tanaka, Japan	794,257
56	Brandel Chamblee, USA	755,936
57	Katsumasa Miyamoto, Japan	749,680
58	Carlos Franco, Paraguay	728,186
59	Shigeki Maruyama, Japan	710,950
60	Frankie Minoza, Philippines	708,708
61	David Carter, England	673,831
62	Stephen Leaney, Australia	669,457
63	Naomichi Ozaki, Japan	668,141
64	Joe Durant, USA	657,553
65	David Toms, USA	643,823
66	Mathias Gronberg, Sweden	637,109
67	Frank Lickliter, USA	607,047
68	Olin Browne, USA	590,240
69	John Daly, USA	586,636
70	Kaname Yokoo, Japan	586,429
71	Michael Bradley, USA	583,001
72	Costantino Rocca, Italy	581,730
73	Jay Haas, USA	579,954
74	Bob Friend, USA	579,039
75	Tom Pernice, Jr., USA	576,450
76	Ian Woosnam, Wales	574,680
77	Tommy Armour III, USA	573,263
78	Brent Geiberger, USA	573,098
79	Paul Azinger, USA	568,233
80	Craig Stadler, USA	564,375
81	J.P. Hayes, USA	563,772
82	Peter O'Malley, Australia	542,465
83	Brad Faxon, USA	538,990
84	Nick Faldo, England	537,637
85	Retief Goosen, South Africa	536,953
86	Sven Struver, Germany	535,565

POS.	PLAYER, COUNTRY	TOTAL MONEY
87	Peter Baker, England	535,285
88	Craig Parry, Australia	534,530
89	Santiago Luna, Spain	533,780
90	Tim Herron, USA	531,073
91	Greg Chalmers, Australia	524,706
92	Scott McCarron, USA	516,847
93	Rocco Mediate, USA	514,446
94	Toshimitsu Izawa, Japan	506,509
95	Kirk Triplett, USA	496,595
96	Greg Turner, New Zealand	491,389
97	Stephen Allan, Australia	491,085
98	Bradley Hughes, Australia	488,367
99	Kenny Perry, USA	487,551
100	Phillip Price, Wales	475,341
101	Sam Torrance, Scotland	475,036
102	Loren Roberts, USA	473,535
103	Robert Allenby, Australia	473,493
104	Toru Suzuki, Japan	473,126
105	Katsunori Kuwabara, Japan	472,732
106	Joey Sindelar, USA	466,797
107	Larry Mize, USA	464,294
108	Harrison Frazar, USA	462,106
109	David Frost, South Africa	461,041
110	Eduardo Romero, Argentina	460,662
111	Robert Karlsson, Sweden	457,792
112	Stephen Ames, Trinidad & Tobago	452,482
113	Scott Simpson, USA	449,777
114	Kevin Sutherland, USA	449,329
115	Peter Jacobsen, USA	447,586
116	Nolan Henke, USA	444,561
117	Jarmo Sandelin, Sweden	443,559
118	Kazuhiro Hosokawa, Japan	442,809
119	Padraig Harrington, Ireland	442,171
120	Hajime Meshiai, Japan	437,571
121	Clark Dennis, USA	436,195
122	Paul Stankowski, USA	434,263
123	Keiichiro Fukabori, Japan	431,576
124	Steve Lowery, USA	430,540
125	Jim Carter, USA	428,384
126	Fuzzy Zoeller, USA	428,375
127	Ted Tryba, USA	426,286
128	Len Mattiace, USA	422,516
129	David Howell, England	415,437
130	Bruce Lietzke, USA	412,938
131	Scott Gump, USA	408,592
132	Jay Don Blake, USA	405,305
133	Paul McGinley, Ireland	404,166
134	Willie Wood, USA	401,410
135	Russell Claydon, England	389,287
136	Jean Van de Velde, France	385,363
137	Nobuhito Sato, Japan	385,265
138	Eduardo Herrera, Colombia	384,321
139	Robert Damron, USA	378,817
140	Per-Ulrik Johansson, Sweden	377,837

POS.	PLAYER, COUNTRY	TOTAL MONEY
141	Gary Orr, Scotland	372,207
142	Toru Taniguchi, Japan	369,834
143	Paul Goydos, USA	368,413
144	Phil Tataurangi, New Zealand	365,714
145	Esteban Toledo, Mexico	359,444
146	Frank Nobilo, New Zealand	358,404
147	Bill Glasson, USA	357,722
148	Greg Norman, Australia	354,479
149	Angel Cabrera, Argentina	353,848
150	Nobumitsu Yuhara, Japan	347,309
151	Neal Lancaster, USA	346,563
152	Mike Hulbert, USA	342,004
153	Jerry Kelly, USA	340,144
154	Russ Cochran, USA	339,389
155	Yoshinori Mizumaki, Japan	334,882
156	Alexander Cejka, Germany	331,746
157	Greg Kraft, USA	330,518
158	Tateo Ozaki, Japan	329,443
159	Shingo Katayama, Japan	328,233
160	Massimo Florioli, Italy	325,593
161	Lee Porter, USA	325,415
162	Dan Forsman, USA	324,528
163	Peter Mitchell, England	323,243
164	J.L. Lewis, USA	319,572
165	John Maginnes, USA	317,375
166	Satoshi Higashi, Japan	313,584
167	Paul Broadhurst, England	312,714
168	Mamoru Osanai, Japan	311,748
169	Barry Cheesman, USA	310,535
170	Katsuyoshi Tomori, Japan	310,333
171	Doug Martin, USA	308,218
172	Peter Senior, Australia	304,278
173	Tsuyoshi Yoneyama, Japan	299,994
174	Steve Webster, England	295,425
175	Peter Lonard, Australia	294,253
176	Mitsutaka Kusakabe, Japan	293,540
177	Brian Henninger, USA	291,764
178	Duffy Waldorf, USA	290,092
179	Omar Uresti, USA	289,847
180	Brad Fabel, USA	285,474
181	Mark Wiebe, USA	284,411
182	Todd Hamilton, USA	283,035
183	Ignacio Garrido, Spain	280,765
184	Shinichi Yokota, Japan	280,020
185	Doug Barron, USA	279,552
186	Thomas Gogele, Germany	278,778
187	David Ishii, USA	276,247
188	Yasuharu Imano, Japan	274,691
189	Craig Hainline, USA	273,321
190	Pierre Fulke, Sweden	272,617
191	Jamie Spence, England	271,555
192	Ben Bates, USA	266,535
193	Chen Tze-chung, Taiwan	264,186
194	Lee Rinker, USA	264,164

POS.	PLAYER, COUNTRY	TOTAL MONEY
195	Edward Fryatt, England	262,949
196	Mathew Goggin, Australia	260,822
197	Jeff Gallagher, USA	260,737
198	Chris DiMarco, USA	260,334
199	Olle Karlsson, Sweden	259,875
200	Mark Brooks, USA	257,839
201	Tsukasa Watanabe, Japan	257,724
202	Kevin Wentworth, USA	256,174
203	Grant Waite, New Zealand	255,884
204	Tommy Tolles, USA	255,053
205	Hideki Kase, Japan	253,155
206	Tom Byrum, USA	252,832
207	David Gilford, England	252,233
208	Zaw Moe, Myanmar	251,377
209	Franklin Langham, USA	251,272
210	Peter McWhinney, Australia	248,281
211	Eric Booker, USA	246,314
212	Ryoken Kawagishi, Japan	245,752
213	Hiroyuki Fujita, Japan	245,394
214	P.H. Horgan III, USA	242,600
215	Blaine McCallister, USA	241,904
216	Saburo Fujiki, Japan	241,697
217	Mike Reid, USA	241,105
218	Larry Rinker, USA	240,743
219	Mark McNulty, Zimbabwe	240,169
220	David Sutherland, USA	239,330
221	Masayuki Kawamura, Japan	236,972
222	Tony Johnstone, Zimbabwe	236,042
223	Mike Springer, USA	230,795
224	Gordon Brand, Jr., Scotland	230,259
225	Mitsuo Harada, Japan	229,976
226	Seiki Okuda, Japan	229,723
227	Corey Pavin, USA	228,820
228	Vanslow Phillips, England	228,376
229	Dave Stockton, Jr., USA	226,160
230	Mike Weir, Canada	225,017
231	Ian Garbutt, England	224,512
232	David Ogrin, USA	224,423
233	Brett Quigley, USA	224,076
234	Mike Brisky, USA	223,798
235	Dinesh Chand, Japan	223,542
236	Mark Roe, England	221,756
237	Kazuhiro Takami, Japan	221,477
238	Shusaku Sugimoto, Japan	220,029
239	Michael Long, New Zealand	218,966
240	Bob Gilder, USA	218,663
241	Tsuneyuki Nakajima, Japan	216,147
242	Roger Wessels, South Africa	212,914
243	Paolo Quirici, Switzerland	211,472
244	Doug Tewell, USA	211,435
245	Raymond Russell, Scotland	210,389
246	Bruce Fleisher, USA	210,086
247	Tatsuo Takasaki, Japan	209,493
248	David Smail, New Zealand	207,104

POS.	PLAYER, COUNTRY	TOTAL MONEY
249	Tom Kite, USA	205,962
250	Hsieh Chin-sheng, Taiwan	205,192
251	Robin Freeman, USA	202,349
252	Rick Gibson, Canada	201,661
253	Mark James, England	201,254
254	Sandy Lyle, Scotland	200,763
255	Phil Blackmar, USA	200,219
256	R.W. Eaks, USA	199,499
257	Steven Conran, Australia	199,081
258	Spike McRoy, USA	198,270
259	Mats Lanner, Sweden	198,208
260	Kelly Gibson, USA	197,134
261	Woody Austin, USA	196,983
262	Rick Fehr, USA	196,745
263	Taichi Teshimi, Japan	196,724
264	Clarence Rose, USA	195,793
265	Kang Wook-soon, Korea	195,620
266	Mike Standly, USA	191,976
267	Scott Dunlap, USA	190,104
268	Derrick Cooper, England	189,686
269	Pete Jordan, USA	187,807
270	Shoichi Kuwabara, Japan	185,923
271	Kim Jong-duk, Korea	185,587
272	Chris Smith, USA	185,323
273	Koki Idoki, Japan	183,101
274	Thomas Levet, France	182,953
275	Bob May, USA	181,746
276	Mats Hallberg, Sweden	181,425
277	Tim Loustalot, USA	179,967
278	Yeh Chang-ting, Taiwan	179,763
279	Paul Lawrie, Scotland	178,810
280	Bob Burns, USA	178,664
281	Jose Coceres, Argentina	176,396
282	Gary Hallberg, USA	175,540
283	D.A. Weibring, USA	174,504
284	Mark Carnevale, USA	174,470
285	Richard Coughlan, Ireland	174,035
286	Bobby Wadkins, USA	173,717
287	Ricardo Gonzalez, Argentina	172,345
288	Joe Ogilvie, USA	171,812
289	Shigemasa Higaki, Japan	171,474
290	Jim Payne, England	171,282
291	Yoshinori Kaneko, Japan	168,874
292	Gabriel Hjertstedt, Sweden	167,072
293	Philip Walton, Ireland	166,966
294	Brian Claar, USA	166,493
295	Doug Dunakey, USA	164,816
296	Kiyoshi Maita, Japan	163,934
297	Zhang Lian-wei, China	163,905
298	Hirofumi Miyase, Japan	163,560
299	Toshiaki Odate, Japan	161,929
300	Nobuo Serizawa, Japan	161,728
301	Michael Jonzon, Sweden	158,910
302	Stewart Ginn, Australia	158,660

POS.	PLAYER, COUNTRY	TOTAL MONEY
303	Scott Henderson, Scotland	157,705
304	Dennis Edlund, Sweden	156,769
305	Jay Delsing, USA	155,994
306	Tim Conley, USA	155,918
307	Joakim Haeggman, Sweden	155,897
308	Jeev Milkha Singh, India	155,781
309	Jose Rivero, Spain	155,501
310	Jim Gallagher, Jr., USA	153,992
311	Dennis Paulson, USA	153,822
312	Fredrik Jacobson, Sweden	153,274
313	Gene Sauers, USA	152,638
314	Michael Campbell, New Zealand	152,069
315	John Riegger, USA	150,874
316	Masanobu Kimura, Japan	150,698
317	Miguel Angel Martin, Spain	149,219
318	Chris Williams, England	148,238
319	Glen Hnatiuk, Canada	148,098
320	Dean Robertson, Scotland	147,770
321	Andrew Sherborne, England	147,696
322	Jonathan Lomas, England	147,306
323	Kiyoshi Murota, Japan	146,421
324	Hugh Royer III, USA	146,314
325	Takao Nogami, Japan	145,850
326	Anthony Wall, England	145,500
327	Shaun Micheel, USA	145,421
328	Mark Mouland, Wales	145,375
329	Raphael Jacquelin, France	144,705
330	Charles Raulerson, USA	142,976
331	Donnie Hammond, USA	141,843
332	Olivier Edmond, France	140,917
333	Mike Sposa, USA	140,139
334	Katsunari Takahashi, Japan	139,774
335	Ronnie Black, USA	139,631
336	Rodger Davis, Australia	139,455
337	Brian Davis, England	139,425
338	Masahiro Kuramoto, Japan	139,197
339	Marc Farry, France	138,577
340	Bradley King, Australia	137,408
341	Jerry Smith, USA	136,578
342	Notah Begay III, USA	136,289
343	Daniel Chopra, Sweden	135,712
344	Emlyn Aubrey, USA	134,867
345	Gerry Norquist, USA	134,703
346	Raul Fretes, Paraguay	134,627
347	Marco Gortana, Italy	134,488
348	Warren Bennett, England	133,737
349	Kent Jones, USA	133,339
350	Jimmy Green, USA	131,942
351	Stephen Scahill, New Zealand	131,267
352	Jim Rutledge, Canada	130,830
353	Sean Murphy, USA	130,030
354	Tom Scherrer, USA	129,134
355	Andrew Beal, England	128,718
356	Andrew Oldcorn, Scotland	125,546

POS.	PLAYER, COUNTRY	TOTAL MONEY
357	Eiji Mizoguchi, Japan	123,677
358	Seve Ballesteros, Spain	123,518
359	Greg Owen, England	122,770
360	Richard Boxall, England	122,650
361	Lin Keng-chi, Taiwan	122,012
362	Akihito Yokoyama, Japan	121,436
363	Matt Gogel, USA	121,390
364	Mike Small, USA	120,211
365	Steen Tinning, Denmark	119,477
366	Casey Martin, USA	119,158
367	Fulton Allem, South Africa	118,714
368	John Wilson, USA	117,460
369	Fabrice Tarnaud, France	117,289
370	Hideyuki Sato, Japan	117,279
371	John Bickerton, England	117,238
372	Anthony Gilligan, Australia	117,029
373	Ikuo Shirahama, Japan	116,415
374	Roger Chapman, England	116,115
375	Rodney Pampling, Australia	115,565
376	Sonny Skinner, USA	113,918
377	Gary Evans, England	112,064
378	Kenichi Kuboya, Japan	111,841
379	Nico van Rensburg, South Africa	111,594
380	Per Haugsrud, Norway	111,065
381	Jay Williamson, USA	110,921
382	Daisuke Serizawa, Japan	110,530
383	Peter Teravainen, USA	110,229
384	John Senden, Australia	109,156
385	Paul Eales, England	108,852
386	Chris Zambri, USA	108,511
387	Keith Fergus, USA	108,423
388	Ian Leggatt, Canada	108,337
389	Brian Bateman, USA	107,590
390	Tom Purtzer, USA	107,439
391	Jim McGovern, USA	106,726
392	Curt Byrum, USA	106,047
393	Clinton Whitelaw, South Africa	105,800
394	Mark Davis, England	105,456
395	Kinpachi Yoshimura, Japan	105,002
396	Deane Pappas, South Africa	104,828
397	Rolf Muntz Holland	104,663
398	Ryan Howison, USA	104,473
399	Brian Kamm, USA	104,430
400	Eamonn Darcy, Ireland	103,485

World Money List Leaders

YEAR	PLAYER, COUNTRY	TOTAL MONEY
1966	Jack Nicklaus, USA	$168,088
1967	Jack Nicklaus, USA	276,166
1968	Billy Casper, USA	222,436
1969	Frank Beard, USA	186,993
1970	Jack Nicklaus, USA	222,583
1971	Jack Nicklaus, USA	285,897
1972	Jack Nicklaus, USA	341,792
1973	Tom Weiskopf, USA	349,645
1974	Johnny Miller, USA	400,255
1975	Jack Nicklaus, USA	332,610
1976	Jack Nicklaus, USA	316,086
1977	Tom Watson, USA	358,034
1978	Tom Watson, USA	384,388
1979	Tom Watson, USA	506,912
1980	Tom Watson, USA	651,921
1981	Johnny Miller, USA	704,204
1982	Raymond Floyd, USA	738,699
1983	Seve Ballesteros, Spain	686,088
1984	Seve Ballesteros, Spain	688,047
1985	Bernhard Langer, Germany	860,262
1986	Greg Norman, Australia	1,146,584
1987	Ian Woosnam, Wales	1,793,268
1988	Seve Ballesteros, Spain	1,261,275
1989	David Frost, South Africa	1,650,230
1990	Jose Maria Olazabal, Spain	1,633,640
1991	Bernhard Langer, Germany	2,186,700
1992	Nick Faldo, England	2,748,248
1993	Nick Faldo, England	2,825,280
1994	Ernie Els, South Africa	2,862,854
1995	Corey Pavin, USA	2,746,340
1996	Colin Montgomerie, Scotland	3,071,442
1997	Colin Montgomerie, Scotland	3,366,900
1998	Tiger Woods, USA	2,927,946

Career World Money List

The following is a listing of the 50 leading money winners for their careers through the 1998 season. It includes players active on both the regular and senior tours of the world. The World Money List from this and the 32 previous editions of this annual and a table prepared for a companion book, *The Wonderful World of Professional Golf* (Atheneum, 1973), form the basis for this compilation. Additional figures were taken from official records of major golf associations, although the shortcomings in records-keeping in professional golf outside the United States in the 1950s and 1960s and exclusions from U.S. records in a few cases during those years prevent these figures from being completely accurate. Conversions of foreign currency figures to U.S. dollars are based on average values during the particular years involved.

POS.	PLAYER, COUNTRY	TOTAL MONEY
1	Greg Norman, Australia	$20,975,766
2	Masashi Ozaki, Japan	18,478,253
3	Fred Couples, USA	17,912,228
4	Nick Price, Zimbabwe	17,731,694
5	Bernhard Langer, Germany	17,309,786
6	Nick Faldo, England	16,371,845
7	Colin Montgomerie, Scotland	16,328,570
8	Hale Irwin, USA	16,057,323
9	Raymond Floyd, USA	15,367,175
10	Lee Trevino, USA	14,572,554
11	Davis Love III, USA	14,380,832
12	Isao Aoki, Japan	14,034,166
13	Mark O'Meara, USA	13,672,515
14	David Frost, South Africa	13,453,641
15	Ian Woosnam, Wales	13,430,111
16	Ernie Els, South Africa	13,408,331
17	Tom Kite, USA	13,350,907
18	Payne Stewart, USA	12,528,869
19	Scott Hoch, USA	12,472,147
20	Mark Calcavecchia, USA	12,330,203
21	Corey Pavin, USA	11,663,906
22	Seve Ballesteros, Spain	11,610,151
23	Vijay Singh, Fiji	11,517,622
24	Tom Watson, USA	11,376,904
25	Jim Colbert, USA	11,253,389
26	Gil Morgan, USA	10,758,281
27	Jose Maria Olazabal, Spain	10,704,245
28	Bob Murphy, USA	10,645,698
29	Bob Charles, New Zealand	10,568,936
30	Naomichi Ozaki, Japan	10,564,913
31	Tsuneyuki Nakajima, Japan	10,564,849
32	Dave Stockton, USA	10,293,691
33	Jack Nicklaus, USA	10,103,762
34	Steve Elkington, Australia	9,971,928
35	Curtis Strange, USA	9,967,289
36	Paul Azinger, USA	9,790,422
37	Tom Lehman, USA	9,784,149
38	Graham Marsh, Australia	9,764,602

POS.	PLAYER, COUNTRY	TOTAL MONEY
39	Craig Stadler, USA	9,696,618
40	Gary Player, South Africa	9,613,147
41	George Archer, USA	9,337,298
42	Ben Crenshaw, USA	9,323,055
43	John Cook, USA	9,002,661
44	Chi Chi Rodriguez, Puerto Rico	8,558,571
45	Phil Mickelson, USA	8,539,110
46	Lanny Wadkins, USA	8,180,548
47	Mike Hill, USA	8,177,559
48	Lee Janzen, USA	8,149,139
49	Jay Haas, USA	8,083,481
50	Brad Faxon, USA	8,027,480

These 50 players have won $599,760,320 in their careers as professional golfers.

Senior World Money List

This list includes official earnings on the U.S. PGA Tour, U.S. Senior PGA Tour, European Seniors Tour, Japan Senior Tour and South Africa Senior Tour, along with other winnings in established unofficial events when reliable figures could be obtained.

POS.	PLAYER, COUNTRY	TOTAL MONEY
1	Hale Irwin, USA	$3,155,189
2	Gil Morgan, USA	2,494,047
3	Larry Nelson, USA	1,667,709
4	Jay Sigel, USA	1,483,192
5	Jim Colbert, USA	1,322,643
6	Hugh Baiocchi, South Africa	1,268,959
7	Dave Stockton, USA	1,207,357
8	Isao Aoki, Japan	1,160,897
9	Dana Quigley, USA	1,103,882
10	Bruce Summerhays, USA	1,098,942
11	David Graham, Australia	1,071,300
12	Jose Maria Canizares, Spain	1,025,425
13	Vicente Fernandez, Argentina	996,338
14	Leonard Thompson, USA	927,753
15	Raymond Floyd, USA	877,305
16	Hubert Green, USA	854,303
17	Lee Trevino, USA	837,742
18	Graham Marsh, Australia	815,925
19	John Jacobs, USA	799,654
20	Bob Duval, USA	767,073
21	Mike McCullough, USA	741,735
22	Dale Douglass, USA	725,893
23	Terry Dill, USA	705,923
24	George Archer, USA	705,076

POS.	PLAYER, COUNTRY	TOTAL MONEY
25	Tom Wargo, USA	693,079
26	Bob Murphy, USA	673,748
27	Walter Hall, USA	668,700
28	Joe Inman, USA	653,902
29	Jim Albus, USA	651,880
30	Jim Dent, USA	627,729
31	J.C. Snead, USA	622,307
32	Brian Barnes, Scotland	571,890
33	Bob Charles, New Zealand	570,567
34	Gary Player, South Africa	534,797
35	Bob Dickson, USA	513,815
36	Walter Morgan, USA	500,713
37	Frank Conner, USA	495,434
38	Bob Eastwood, USA	472,663
39	John Morgan, England	470,139
40	Tom Jenkins, USA	455,212
41	David Lundstrom	451,979
42	Simon Hobday, South Africa	429,524
43	Gibby Gilbert, USA	426,584
44	Bobby Stroble, USA	426,574
45	Dave Eichelberger, USA	418,893
46	Ed Dougherty, USA	412,697
47	Bud Allin, USA	403,964
48	Tom Shaw, USA	385,421
49	John Mahaffey, USA	373,012
50	John Bland, South Africa	361,078
51	Kermit Zarley, USA	357,978
52	Jerry McGee, USA	351,605
53	Al Geiberger, USA	344,680
54	Jack Nicklaus, USA	337,974
55	Charles Coody, USA	326,758
56	Larry Laoretti, USA	306,450
57	John Schroeder, USA	305,196
58	Mike Hill, USA	287,859
59	Fred Gibson, USA	276,436
60	Larry Ziegler, USA	274,986
61	Buzz Thomas, USA	269,515
62	Bruce Crampton, Australia	251,506
63	Tommy Horton, England	223,007
64	Allen Doyle, USA	214,853
65	Dan Wood, USA	199,202
66	Kurt Cox, USA	194,376
67	Jimmy Powell, USA	186,068
68	DeWitt Weaver, USA	184,968
69	Brian Huggett, Wales	181,307
70	Rocky Thompson, USA	181,301
71	Butch Baird, USA	169,917
72	Eddie Polland, N. Ireland	164,414
73	Harold Henning, South Africa	161,219
74	Billy King, USA	153,044
75	Arnold Palmer, USA	138,954
76	David Jones, N. Ireland	134,696
77	Chi Chi Rodriguez, Puerto Rico	132,684
78	Jim Rhodes, England	120,810

POS.	PLAYER, COUNTRY	TOTAL MONEY
79	Noel Ratcliffe, Australia	119,634
80	Bobby Verwey, South Africa	118,330
81	Tommy Aaron, USA	116,029
82	Seiichi Kanai, Japan	113,355
83	Johnny Miller, USA	112,183
84	Gary McCord, USA	112,173
85	Toru Nakayama, Japan	110,325
86	Neil Coles, England	109,169
87	Jack Kiefer, USA	108,774
88	Terry Gale, Australia	108,179
89	Walter Zembriski, USA	106,979
90	Steven Veriato, USA	104,630
91	Denis O'Sullivan, Ireland	103,109
92	Brian Waites, England	102,325
93	Bob E. Smith, USA	97,211
94	Tony Jacklin, England	95,129
95	Bruce Lehnhard, USA	93,658
96	Hisao Inoue, Japan	93,288
97	Haruo Yasuda, Japan	92,392
98	Miller Barber, USA	91,594
99	Antonio Garrido, Spain	90,403
100	Bob Lendzion, USA	89,374

Women's World Money List

This list includes official earnings on the U.S. LPGA Tour, European LPGA Tour, Japan LPGA Tour and Women's Australasian Tours, along with other winnings in established unofficial events when reliable figures could be obtained.

POS.	PLAYER, COUNTRY	TOTAL MONEY
1	Annika Sorenstam, Sweden	$1,170,898
2	Se Ri Pak, Korea	882,770
3	Meg Mallon, USA	812,208
4	Liselotte Neumann, Sweden	769,936
5	Karrie Webb, Australia	737,780
6	Helen Alfredsson, Sweden	731,253
7	Donna Andrews, USA	721,478
8	Pat Hurst, USA	689,597
9	Juli Inkster, USA	661,462
10	Laura Davies, England	654,107
11	Brandie Burton, USA	652,084
12	Michiko Hattori, Japan	629,044
13	Dottie Pepper, USA	582,792
14	Lorie Kane, Canada	539,299
15	Hiromi Kobayashi, Japan	539,216
16	Kaori Harada, Japan	530,065
17	Ok-Hee Ku, Korea	512,569
18	Danielle Ammaccapane, USA	507,564

POS.	PLAYER, COUNTRY	TOTAL MONEY
19	Sherri Steinhauer, USA	477,282
20	Kelly Robbins, USA	475,826
21	Kaori Higo, Japan	475,153
22	Akiko Fukushima, Japan	445,477
23	Rosie Jones, USA	427,491
24	Chris Johnson, USA	411,310
25	Lisa Hackney, England	383,923
26	Natsuko Noro, Japan	380,966
27	Wendy Ward, USA	372,395
28	Huang Yu-Chen, Taiwan	367,690
29	Michelle Estill, USA	365,387
30	Emilee Klein, USA	357,225
31	Dale Eggeling, USA	345,217
32	Tammie Green, USA	338,884
33	Young-Me Lee, Korea	334,266
34	Lisa Walters, Canada	333,933
35	Barb Mucha, USA	332,644
36	Betsy King, USA	332,069
37	Fuki Kido, Japan	329,152
38	Charlotta Sorenstam, Sweden	319,526
39	Yuri Fudoh, Japan	315,807
40	Dana Dormann, USA	310,878
41	Rachel Hetherington, Australia	302,986
42	Tina Barrett, USA	289,489
43	Catrin Nilsmark, Sweden	287,138
44	Aki Takamura, Japan	274,257
45	Maria Hjorth, Sweden	270,873
46	Nayoko Yoshikawa, Japan	262,418
47	Ae-Sook Kim, Korea	259,656
48	Helen Dobson, England	254,664
49	Mayumi Murai, Japan	254,114
50	Yuri Kawanami, Japan	253,613
51	Aki Nakano, Japan	249,487
52	Janice Moodie, Scotland	247,334
53	Hiromi Takamura, Japan	246,051
54	Catriona Matthew, Scotland	239,716
55	Cindy Figg-Currier, USA	238,800
56	Carin Koch, Sweden	237,238
57	Aiko Takasu, Japan	236,270
58	Marnie McGuire, New Zealand	234,298
59	Woo-Soon Ko, Korea	228,376
60	Jenny Lidback, Peru	220,330
61	Pearl Sinn, Korea	210,488
62	Sophie Gustafson, Sweden	208,623
63	Man-Soo Kim, Korea	204,145
64	Dawn Coe-Jones, Canada	203,335
65	Trish Johnson, England	200,886
66	Fumiko Muraguchi, Japan	200,198
67	Penny Hammel, USA	191,291
68	Akemi Yamaoka, Japan	191,169
69	Kyoko Ono, Japan	190,043
70	Michie Ohba, Japan	184,128
71	Kim Saiki, USA	179,073
72	Michele Redman, USA	177,550

POS.	PLAYER, COUNTRY	TOTAL MONEY
73	Chieko Nishida, Japan	177,044
74	Cindy McCurdy, USA	174,267
75	Hsiu-Feng Tseng, Taiwan	173,858
76	Chikayo Yamazaki, Japan	173,038
77	Harumi Sakagami, Japan	166,142
78	Alison Nicholas, England	164,383
79	Amy Fruhwirth, USA	161,515
80	Vickie Odegard, USA	160,754
81	Michelle McGann, USA	156,380
82	Hollis Stacy, USA	155,320
83	Joan Pitcock, USA	155,240
84	Chihiro Furukawa, Japan	151,777
85	Nancy Lopez, USA	151,169
86	Dina Ammaccapane, USA	150,942
87	Kris Tschetter, USA	150,914
88	Hee-Won Han, Korea	150,116
89	Tracy Hanson, USA	150,027
90	Cathy Johnston-Forbes, USA	145,320
91	Patty Sheehan, USA	143,771
92	Gail Graham, Canada	141,623
93	Lee Oh-Soon, Korea	141,270
94	Yuka Irie, Japan	139,677
95	Yuko Motoyama, Japan	138,500
96	Kristi Albers, USA	137,234
97	Kumiko Hiyoshi, Japan	137,040
98	Akane Ohshiro, Japan	136,766
99	Masako Ishihara, Japan	134,218
100	Kayo Yamada, Japan	133,165
101	Shin Sora, Korea	132,470
102	Mikino Kubo, Japan	131,927
103	Miyuki Shimabukuro, Japan	131,691
104	Beth Daniel, USA	131,353
105	Stefania Croce, Italy	130,222
106	Takayo Bandoh, Japan	129,033
107	Jackie Gallagher-Smith, USA	127,325
108	Alicia Dibos, Peru	127,256
109	Megumi Matsuo, Japan	127,094
110	Mhairi McKay, Scotland	126,974
111	Hisako Ohgane, Japan	126,263
112	Yoko Inoue, Japan	125,736
113	Deb Richard, USA	122,764
114	Nancy Scranton, USA	122,432
115	Mayumi Hirase, Japan	121,340
116	Tomiko Ikebuchi, Japan	118,375
117	Mieko Nomura, Japan	115,557
118	Huang Yueh-Chyn, Taiwan	111,258
119	Jane Geddes, USA	111,049
120	Hisako Takeda, Japan	106,787
121	Susie Redman, USA	106,202
122	Jae-Sook Won, Korea	105,542
123	Anna Acker-Macosko, USA	103,593
124	Luciana Bemvenuti, Brazil	103,365
125	Jane Crafter, Australia	103,227

American Tours

Mercedes Championships

La Costa Resort & Spa, Carlsbad, California — January 8-11
Par 36-36–72; 7,022 yards — purse, $1,700,000

	SCORES				TOTAL	MONEY
Phil Mickelson	68	67	68	68	271	$306,000
Mark O'Meara	71	70	67	64	272	149,600
Tiger Woods	72	67	69	64	272	149,600
John Cook	65	70	70	70	275	74,800
Nick Price	66	70	69	70	275	74,800
Mark Calcavecchia	70	74	66	67	277	55,462.50
Stewart Cink	71	67	71	68	277	55,462.50
David Duval	68	70	66	73	277	55,462.50
Gabriel Hjertstedt	69	68	69	71	277	55,462.50
Ernie Els	67	71	71	69	278	46,537.50
Frank Nobilo	67	69	70	72	278	46,537.50
Scott McCarron	70	71	70	68	279	43,775
Steve Jones	69	71	72	68	280	38,675
Davis Love III	70	72	67	71	280	38,675
Loren Roberts	70	72	68	70	280	38,675
Vijay Singh	75	72	67	66	280	38,675
Paul Stankowski	69	72	69	70	280	38,675
David Frost	74	72	68	68	282	34,000
Steve Elkington	72	73	71	68	284	31,450
Scott Hoch	70	70	69	75	284	31,450
Jeff Sluman	70	75	71	68	284	31,450
Nick Faldo	71	75	70	69	285	28,475
Brad Faxon	72	72	70	71	285	28,475
David Toms	73	75	70	67	285	28,475
Phil Blackmar	73	69	73	71	286	26,562.50
Justin Leonard	73	73	69	71	286	26,562.50
Greg Norman	73	72	73	70	288	25,925
Billy Ray Brown	69	74	71	75	289	25,585
Tim Herron	74	75	68	73	290	25,245
Stuart Appleby	77	72	73	72	294	24,905

Bob Hope Chrysler Classic

Bermuda Dunes, California — January 14-18
Bermuda Dunes CC: Par 36-36–72; 6,927 yards — purse, $2,300,000
Indian Wells CC: Par 36-36–72; 6,478 yards
PGA West, Palmer Course: Par 36-36–72; 6,931 yards
La Quinta CC: Par 36-36–72; 6,901 yards

	SCORES					TOTAL	MONEY
Fred Couples	64	70	66	66	66	332	$414,000
Bruce Lietzke	65	65	71	62	69	332	248,400
(Couples defeated Lietzke on first extra hole.)							
Andrew Magee	63	68	64	68	70	333	156,400
David Duval	65	67	68	67	68	335	101,200
Steve Jones	66	70	65	65	69	335	101,200
Stewart Cink	65	67	67	68	69	336	79,925

	SCORES					TOTAL	MONEY
Mark O'Meara	67	67	65	68	69	336	79,925
Skip Kendall	69	66	69	68	67	339	69,000
Fuzzy Zoeller	66	69	68	66	70	339	69,000
Kirk Triplett	71	67	69	66	67	340	50,983
Paul Stankowski	69	69	65	70	67	340	50,983
John Huston	67	70	67	68	68	340	50,983
Brad Fabel	64	70	66	69	71	340	50,983
Mark Wiebe	73	65	66	66	70	340	50,983
Bob Tway	65	68	67	69	71	340	50,983
Rick Fehr	71	66	68	69	67	341	36,800
Pete Jordan	65	72	72	64	68	341	36,800
Chris Perry	69	70	70	64	68	341	36,800
Blaine McCallister	66	67	73	69	67	342	27,876
Loren Roberts	70	68	66	68	70	342	27,876
Bob Estes	68	68	67	67	72	342	27,876
David Toms	66	71	66	67	72	342	27,876
Mark Calcavecchia	69	67	70	65	71	342	27,876
Steve Lowery	64	71	70	70	68	343	19,090
Paul Azinger	69	69	67	70	68	343	19,090
Omar Uresti	73	65	66	71	68	343	19,090
Glen Day	68	67	67	71	70	343	19,090
Paul Goydos	68	67	72	63	73	343	19,090
Dave Stockton, Jr.	67	70	71	67	69	344	14,624
Steve Stricker	69	70	68	67	70	344	14,624
Neal Lancaster	66	71	68	70	69	344	14,624
Jay Don Blake	70	71	68	67	68	344	14,624
Stuart Appleby	70	70	69	67	68	344	14,624
Larry Mize	69	69	69	70	67	344	14,624
Scott Verplank	73	68	70	64	70	345	10,623
Robert Damron	68	73	68	65	71	345	10,623
Craig Stadler	73	64	70	67	71	345	10,623
Barry Cheesman	72	68	64	69	72	345	10,623
Jerry Kelly	70	68	70	64	73	345	10,623
Ted Tryba	67	70	70	71	67	345	10,623
Steve Flesch	67	69	70	72	67	345	10,623
Naomichi Ozaki	67	69	70	73	66	345	10,623
Scott Gump	66	68	70	71	71	346	7,375
Larry Rinker	70	71	67	68	70	346	7,375
Fred Funk	71	74	65	66	70	346	7,375
Doug Martin	69	67	69	69	72	346	7,375
Corey Pavin	70	71	68	69	68	346	7,375
Russ Cochran	73	67	69	69	68	346	7,375
P.H. Horgan III	68	65	69	73	72	347	5,811
Michael Christie	69	69	67	71	71	347	5,811
Dan Forsman	67	74	67	69	70	347	5,811
Hal Sutton	68	66	71	71	72	348	5,310
Chris Smith	67	71	70	68	72	348	5,310
Lee Janzen	69	67	71	69	72	348	5,310
Jay Haas	66	71	71	70	70	348	5,310
Larry Nelson	71	71	69	67	70	348	5,310
Donnie Hammond	70	70	68	70	70	348	5,310
Steve Pate	70	69	69	70	70	348	5,310
Lee Porter	68	69	68	71	73	349	5,014
Jeff Sluman	72	65	71	69	72	349	5,014
Franklin Langham	66	70	69	72	72	349	5,014
Len Mattiace	69	67	73	69	71	349	5,014
Lee Rinker	72	73	67	67	70	349	5,014
Brent Geiberger	69	71	70	69	71	350	4,876
Tommy Tolles	67	72	65	67	80	351	4,807
Bob Gilder	72	68	69	70	72	351	4,807

	SCORES					TOTAL	MONEY
Frank Lickliter	69	69	69	71	74	352	4,715
Brian Kamm	69	74	69	67	73	352	4,715
Jesper Parnevik	71	70	68	68	76	353	4,623
Chris DiMarco	72	70	70	67	74	353	4,623

Phoenix Open

TPC of Scottsdale, Scottsdale, Arizona — January 22-25
Par 35-36–71; 6,992 yards — purse, $2,500,000

	SCORES				TOTAL	MONEY
Jesper Parnevik	68	68	66	67	269	$450,000
Tommy Armour III	68	70	70	64	272	165,000
Brent Geiberger	64	70	72	66	272	165,000
Steve Pate	69	69	70	64	272	165,000
Tom Watson	68	70	68	66	272	165,000
Billy Andrade	69	67	71	67	274	86,875
Glen Day	68	70	69	67	274	86,875
Dudley Hart	70	68	69	68	275	70,000
John Huston	73	67	68	67	275	70,000
Frank Lickliter	72	67	66	70	275	70,000
Scott McCarron	67	70	70	68	275	70,000
John Daly	70	70	66	71	277	55,000
Paul Stankowski	70	67	67	73	277	55,000
Nolan Henke	69	71	69	69	278	38,750
Mike Hulbert	63	72	73	70	278	38,750
Lee Janzen	71	68	67	72	278	38,750
Skip Kendall	73	67	67	71	278	38,750
Tom Lehman	71	68	72	67	278	38,750
Frank Nobilo	69	69	71	69	278	38,750
Larry Rinker	65	72	71	70	278	38,750
Scott Verplank	73	63	66	76	278	38,750
Olin Browne	70	68	73	68	279	24,000
Nick Price	67	72	68	72	279	24,000
Vijay Singh	69	65	71	74	279	24,000
Steve Stricker	64	71	73	71	279	24,000
David Sutherland	72	68	70	69	279	24,000
Jay Don Blake	70	69	70	71	280	17,000
Robert Damron	71	71	71	67	280	17,000
David Duval	65	70	72	73	280	17,000
Kelly Gibson	67	66	76	71	280	17,000
Paul Goydos	71	71	70	68	280	17,000
Justin Leonard	67	71	70	72	280	17,000
Kenny Perry	70	70	72	68	280	17,000
Rick Fehr	67	71	74	69	281	12,357
David Toms	72	67	69	73	281	12,357
Fred Funk	72	70	68	71	281	12,357
Steve Jones	65	69	71	76	281	12,357
Larry Mize	69	68	69	75	281	12,357
Chris Perry	69	72	72	68	281	12,357
Chris Smith	72	69	68	72	281	12,357
Mark Carnevale	69	70	72	71	282	9,000
Russ Cochran	72	70	70	70	282	9,000
Jim Furyk	72	68	71	71	282	9,000
Jonathan Kaye	72	67	73	70	282	9,000
Billy Mayfair	72	68	72	70	282	9,000
Duffy Waldorf	68	70	69	75	282	9,000

	SCORES				TOTAL	MONEY
Mark Brooks	71	70	69	73	283	6,725
Tom Byrum	71	71	69	72	283	6,725
Chris DiMarco	72	69	72	70	283	6,725
Rocco Mediate	70	72	69	72	283	6,725
Bob Estes	73	69	72	70	284	5,962
Dan Forsman	68	73	72	71	284	5,962
Scott Simpson	70	70	74	70	284	5,962
Kevin Sutherland	71	67	74	72	284	5,962
Jeff Maggert	69	71	71	74	285	5,700
Doug Martin	72	68	74	71	285	5,700
Len Mattiace	70	71	73	71	285	5,700
Doug Barron	67	70	76	73	286	5,475
Phil Blackmar	71	69	72	74	286	5,475
Brandel Chamblee	69	72	70	75	286	5,475
Donnie Hammond	72	70	74	70	286	5,475
Andrew Magee	70	71	75	70	286	5,475
Phil Mickelson	68	71	72	75	286	5,475
David Edwards	68	73	73	73	287	5,275
Mike Springer	69	73	69	76	287	5,275
Don Pooley	68	71	72	77	288	5,200
Steve Flesch	68	73	77	71	289	5,125
David Ogrin	70	72	72	75	289	5,125
Stuart Appleby	73	69	75	73	290	5,025
Lee Rinker	69	73	74	74	290	5,025
Ted Tryba	71	69	75	77	292	4,950
Wayne Levi	74	68	77	75	294	4,900

AT&T Pebble Beach National Pro-Am

Pebble Beach, California — January 29-February 1
Pebble Beach GL: Par 36-36–72; 6,799 yards — August 17
Spyglass Hill GC: Par 36-36–72; 6,861 yards — purse, $2,500,000
Poppy Hills GC: Par 36-36–72; 6,855 yards

	SCORES			TOTAL	MONEY
Phil Mickelson	65	70	67	202	$450,000
Tom Pernice, Jr.	67	69	67	203	270,000
Paul Azinger	67	69	68	204	130,000
Jim Furyk	69	67	68	204	130,000
J.P. Hayes	70	67	67	204	130,000
Steve Elkington	70	68	67	205	83,750
Jay Haas	68	67	70	205	83,750
Fuzzy Zoeller	70	70	65	205	83,750
Bob Gilder	68	70	68	206	65,000
Tom Lehman	64	71	71	206	65,000
Chris Smith	69	67	70	206	65,000
Tom Watson	67	67	72	206	65,000
Trevor Dodds	69	69	69	207	44,166.67
Pete Jordan	70	69	68	207	44,166.67
Spike McRoy	71	69	67	207	44,166.67
David Toms	67	71	69	207	44,166.67
Jeff Gallagher	68	71	68	207	44,166.66
Kirk Triplett	70	68	69	207	44,166.66
Tim Herron	68	66	74	208	32,500
Jesper Parnevik	67	72	69	208	32,500
Payne Stewart	71	70	67	208	32,500
Mark Brooks	68	72	69	209	26,000

	SCORES			TOTAL	MONEY
Glen Day	70	71	68	209	26,000
Davis Love III	68	68	73	209	26,000
Stewart Cink	70	69	71	210	16,791.67
Harrison Frazar	71	67	72	210	16,791.67
Scott Gump	73	70	67	210	16,791.67
Rocco Mediate	70	68	72	210	16,791.67
Naomichi Ozaki	71	69	70	210	16,791.67
Sonny Skinner	70	71	69	210	16,791.67
Jeff Sluman	71	70	69	210	16,791.67
Tommy Tolles	73	71	66	210	16,791.67
Clark Dennis	76	71	63	210	16,791.66
Doug Martin	72	68	70	210	16,791.66
Sam Randolph	72	72	66	210	16,791.66
Craig Stadler	70	68	72	210	16,791.66
Ben Bates	70	71	70	211	10,500
Bob Friend	69	73	69	211	10,500
Franklin Langham	73	70	68	211	10,500
Tim Loustalot	73	69	69	211	10,500
Len Mattiace	72	68	71	211	10,500
Lee Porter	70	68	73	211	10,500
Tom Purtzer	71	70	70	211	10,500
Clarence Rose	75	70	66	211	10,500
Fulton Allem	67	73	72	212	6,590.91
Gary Hallberg	68	71	73	212	6,590.91
Donnie Hammond	72	70	70	212	6,590.91
P.H. Horgan III	68	76	68	212	6,590.91
Peter Jacobsen	68	70	74	212	6,590.91
Kent Jones	73	68	71	212	6,590.91
Justin Leonard	68	73	71	212	6,590.91
Corey Pavin	71	70	71	212	6,590.91
John Riegger	72	69	71	212	6,590.91
Mike Small	74	70	68	212	6,590.91
Billy Ray Brown	72	70	70	212	6,590.90
Mike Brisky	72	69	72	213	5,350
Jim Carter	69	72	72	213	5,350
John Cook	71	71	71	213	5,350
Richard Coughlan	70	70	73	213	5,350
Jim Estes	71	73	69	213	5,350
Brad Faxon	72	68	73	213	5,350
Steve Flesch	73	68	72	213	5,350
Dudley Hart	71	68	74	213	5,350
John Johnson	71	70	72	213	5,350
Brian Kamm	70	72	71	213	5,350
Neal Lancaster	71	70	72	213	5,350
Jim McGovern	72	71	70	213	5,350
Lee Rinker	74	69	70	213	5,350
David Sutherland	70	74	69	213	5,350
Kevin Sutherland	72	69	72	213	5,350

Buick Invitational

Torrey Pines Golf Course, San Diego, California
South Course: Par 36-36–72; 7,022 yards
North Course: Par 36-36–72; 6,592 yards
(Fourth round cancelled — rain.)

February 5-8
purse, $2,100,000

	SCORES			TOTAL	MONEY
Scott Simpson	69	71	64	204	$378,000
Skip Kendall	71	63	70	204	226,800
(Simpson defeated Kendall on first extra hole.)					
Davis Love III	62	73	70	205	109,200
Kevin Sutherland	68	67	70	205	109,200
Tiger Woods	71	66	68	205	109,200
Tommy Armour III	67	73	66	206	61,350
Russ Cochran	67	70	69	206	61,350
Brent Geiberger	67	72	67	206	61,350
Steve Jurgensen	63	73	70	206	61,350
J.L. Lewis	70	67	69	206	61,350
Spike McRoy	70	66	70	206	61,350
Steve Pate	67	65	74	206	61,350
Stewart Cink	65	72	70	207	40,600
Bob Gilder	72	67	68	207	40,600
Craig Stadler	69	70	68	207	40,600
John Daly	70	70	68	208	30,450
Robert Damron	68	67	73	208	30,450
Doug Martin	65	71	72	208	30,450
Jeff Sandy	63	72	73	208	30,450
Jeff Sluman	67	69	72	208	30,450
Bob Tway	63	72	73	208	30,450
Trevor Dodds	66	72	71	209	20,160
Kelly Gibson	72	65	72	209	20,160
Lee Janzen	70	71	68	209	20,160
Tom Kite	65	70	74	209	20,160
Payne Stewart	66	72	71	209	20,160
R.W. Eaks	65	75	70	210	13,978.13
Bob Estes	66	73	71	210	13,978.13
Paul Goydos	67	73	70	210	13,978.13
Tom Pernice, Jr.	71	69	70	210	13,978.13
Jay Don Blake	70	71	69	210	13,978.12
Blaine McCallister	73	69	68	210	13,978.12
Sonny Skinner	69	73	68	210	13,978.12
Mike Standly	70	71	69	210	13,978.12
Lennie Clements	66	73	72	211	8,428.50
Rick Fehr	69	71	71	211	8,428.50
Steve Flesch	72	67	72	211	8,428.50
Brian Henninger	73	66	72	211	8,428.50
Jerry Kelly	67	73	71	211	8,428.50
Neal Lancaster	67	71	73	211	8,428.50
Billy Mayfair	76	66	69	211	8,428.50
Scott McCarron	68	69	74	211	8,428.50
Lee Porter	69	70	72	211	8,428.50
Steve Stricker	70	66	75	211	8,428.50
Omar Uresti	68	71	72	211	8,428.50
Bobby Wadkins	65	73	73	211	8,428.50
Duffy Waldorf	71	71	69	211	8,428.50
D.A. Weibring	67	73	71	211	8,428.50
Glen Day	70	68	74	212	5,050.50
Joe Durant	68	70	74	212	5,050.50
Scott Gump	69	70	73	212	5,050.50

	SCORES			TOTAL	MONEY
Sandy Lyle	69	71	72	212	5,050.50
Andrew Magee	68	74	70	212	5,050.50
Phil Mickelson	70	69	73	212	5,050.50
David Ogrin	68	70	74	212	5,050.50
Larry Rinker	71	68	73	212	5,050.50
Paul Azinger	66	72	75	213	4,557
Mark Calcavecchia	69	72	72	213	4,557
Dan Forsman	71	71	71	213	4,557
Jeff Gallagher	71	69	73	213	4,557
Peter Jacobsen	69	73	71	213	4,557
Rocco Mediate	68	74	71	213	4,557
Mark O'Meara	71	70	72	213	4,557
Mike Springer	68	73	72	213	4,557
Greg Twiggs	67	74	72	213	4,557
Fuzzy Zoeller	63	75	75	213	4,557
John Adams	71	71	72	214	4,242
Michael Bradley	69	71	74	214	4,242
Jim McGovern	74	68	72	214	4,242
Dave Stockton, Jr.	73	69	72	214	4,242
Vance Veazey	71	71	72	214	4,242
Len Mattiace	71	71	73	215	4,053
Chris Perry	65	75	75	215	4,053
John Riegger	69	71	75	215	4,053
Kirk Triplett	71	70	74	215	4,053
Dave Barr	71	71	74	216	3,885
Jay Haas	70	72	74	216	3,885
Frank Lickliter	69	72	75	216	3,885
Esteban Toledo	68	72	76	216	3,885
Ben Bates	71	71	75	217	3,780
David Edwards	75	67	78	220	3,738

United Airlines Hawaiian Open

Waialae Country Club, Honolulu, Hawaii — February 12-15
Par 36-36–72; 7,012 yards — purse, $1,800,000

	SCORES				TOTAL	MONEY
John Huston	63	65	66	66	260	$324,000
Tom Watson	67	64	70	66	267	194,400
Trevor Dodds	65	70	65	68	268	122,400
Greg Kraft	69	67	63	70	269	74,400
Brett Quigley	68	68	67	66	269	74,400
Mike Reid	65	68	69	67	269	74,400
Olin Browne	67	66	66	71	270	54,225
R.W. Eaks	72	63	70	65	270	54,225
Frank Lickliter	68	64	66	72	270	54,225
Steve Stricker	66	67	68	69	270	54,225
Brandel Chamblee	68	67	66	70	271	38,160
Peter Jacobsen	69	68	67	67	271	38,160
Steve Jones	68	70	67	66	271	38,160
Larry Mize	71	66	66	68	271	38,160
Duffy Waldorf	68	66	67	70	271	38,160
Jay Don Blake	70	67	65	70	272	27,000
Russ Cochran	70	67	67	68	272	27,000
Robert Gamez	68	67	65	72	272	27,000
Skip Kendall	67	63	70	72	272	27,000
Kenny Perry	67	67	68	70	272	27,000

	SCORES				TOTAL	MONEY
Tommy Armour III	67	67	71	68	273	18,000
Keoke Cotner	70	67	67	69	273	18,000
Jim Furyk	69	68	67	69	273	18,000
Brent Geiberger	68	70	66	69	273	18,000
Craig Stadler	69	65	69	70	273	18,000
Mike Weir	68	71	68	66	273	18,000
Tom Byrum	64	68	69	73	274	11,981.25
Brian Henninger	67	67	70	70	274	11,981.25
P.H. Horgan III	67	68	68	71	274	11,981.25
Jeff Maggert	65	69	69	71	274	11,981.25
David Ogrin	63	69	73	69	274	11,981.25
Hugh Royer III	67	65	72	70	274	11,981.25
Esteban Toledo	69	68	67	70	274	11,981.25
Curtis Strange	65	67	71	71	274	11,981.25
Fred Couples	70	69	65	71	275	8,874
Tim Herron	66	71	68	70	275	8,874
Billy Mayfair	69	67	68	71	275	8,874
Howard Twitty	70	69	70	66	275	8,874
Vance Veazey	70	69	66	70	275	8,874
Keith Clearwater	67	65	73	71	276	6,308
Brad Fabel	71	68	66	71	276	6,308
Kelly Gibson	68	68	65	75	276	6,308
Paul Goydos	66	68	69	73	276	6,308
Jim McGovern	67	70	67	72	276	6,308
Don Pooley	70	65	69	72	276	6,308
Loren Roberts	68	69	71	68	276	6,308
Iain Steel	71	68	67	70	276	6,308
Omar Uresti	68	67	69	72	276	6,308
Woody Austin	65	72	67	73	277	4,329
Richard Coughlan	72	65	71	69	277	4,329
Clark Dennis	67	70	72	68	277	4,329
Jeff Gallagher	67	70	72	68	277	4,329
Len Mattiace	70	67	70	70	277	4,329
Naomichi Ozaki	71	68	66	72	277	4,329
Tim Simpson	70	68	64	75	277	4,329
Dave Stockton, Jr.	70	67	69	71	277	4,329
Billy Ray Brown	69	65	72	72	278	3,960
Jimmy Johnston	72	67	71	68	278	3,960
Kent Jones	69	69	68	72	278	3,960
Blaine McCallister	69	69	70	70	278	3,960
Sonny Skinner	69	67	72	70	278	3,960
Taylor Smith	71	68	66	73	278	3,960
Paul Stankowski	67	71	69	71	278	3,960
Doug Barron	69	70	71	69	279	3,780
Jim Carter	70	69	71	69	279	3,780
Corey Pavin	71	67	69	72	279	3,780
Craig Barlow	67	70	73	70	280	3,690
Jay Delsing	68	70	74	68	280	3,690
Fulton Allem	66	68	76	71	281	3,528
Mark Carnevale	68	70	67	76	281	3,528
Steve Flesch	68	69	71	73	281	3,528
Tom Lehman	71	68	72	70	281	3,528
John Morse	70	68	70	73	281	3,528
Gene Sauers	68	70	70	73	281	3,528
Mike Springer	69	70	71	71	281	3,528
Gary Hallberg	68	71	71	72	282	3,384
Glen Hnatiuk	71	64	71	77	283	3,330
David Ishii	65	69	74	75	283	3,330
Spike McRoy	68	71	70	75	284	3,276

Tucson Chrysler Classic

Omni Tucson National Resort, Tucson, Arizona — February 19-22
Par 36-36–72; 7,148 yards — purse, $2,000,000

	SCORES				TOTAL	MONEY
David Duval	66	62	68	73	269	$360,000
Justin Leonard	65	70	68	70	273	176,000
David Toms	70	67	68	68	273	176,000
Tim Herron	69	70	67	69	275	88,000
Steve Lowery	68	70	68	69	275	88,000
Tom Lehman	66	71	69	70	276	67,000
Andrew Magee	69	68	72	67	276	67,000
Bob Tway	70	68	71	67	276	67,000
Scott Hoch	69	66	71	71	277	50,000
Steve Pate	70	66	72	69	277	50,000
Joey Sindelar	72	70	66	69	277	50,000
Tommy Tolles	69	70	68	70	277	50,000
Jim Furyk	69	70	68	70	277	50,000
Robert Damron	69	72	68	69	278	35,000
Glen Hnatiuk	68	74	67	69	278	35,000
Sandy Lyle	69	69	70	70	278	35,000
Mike Standly	70	67	72	69	278	35,000
John Daly	70	70	69	70	279	27,000
Jerry Kelly	72	69	70	68	279	27,000
Mike Reid	71	71	72	65	279	27,000
Payne Stewart	69	70	70	70	279	27,000
Russ Cochran	69	71	70	70	280	20,800
Rocco Mediate	73	67	67	73	280	20,800
Steve Stricker	73	68	68	71	280	20,800
Bob Estes	72	70	70	69	281	15,266.67
Doug Martin	70	72	69	70	281	15,266.67
Billy Mayfair	71	69	69	72	281	15,266.67
David Sutherland	67	72	73	69	281	15,266.67
John Huston	72	66	71	72	281	15,266.66
David Ogrin	70	69	67	75	281	15,266.66
Fulton Allem	71	71	72	68	282	10,200
Jay Don Blake	69	72	69	72	282	10,200
Michael Bradley	70	73	70	69	282	10,200
Mark Calcavecchia	68	71	70	73	282	10,200
Trevor Dodds	68	72	74	68	282	10,200
Paul Goydos	71	72	65	74	282	10,200
Dudley Hart	72	70	71	69	282	10,200
Nolan Henke	69	70	73	70	282	10,200
Kenny Perry	71	69	72	70	282	10,200
Curtis Strange	70	71	69	72	282	10,200
Ted Tryba	70	69	72	71	282	10,200
Grant Waite	71	69	72	70	282	10,200
*Jeff Kern	68	72	70	72	282	
Mike Brisky	72	69	73	69	283	6,800
P.H. Horgan III	72	71	71	69	283	6,800
Len Mattiace	72	69	72	70	283	6,800
Scott Verplank	73	70	67	73	283	6,800
Ronnie Black	73	69	70	72	284	5,206.67
Mark Brooks	71	68	69	76	284	5,206.67
Christoffer Hanell	69	72	71	72	284	5,206.67
Jonathan Kaye	67	74	69	74	284	5,206.67
Mike Hulbert	70	73	70	71	284	5,206.66
Lee Rinker	74	69	68	73	284	5,206.66
John Adams	71	69	74	71	285	4,608

	SCORES				TOTAL	MONEY
Yoshinori Mizumaki	72	71	70	72	285	4,608
Dave Rummells	69	72	71	73	285	4,608
Kevin Sutherland	72	70	71	72	285	4,608
Willie Wood	73	68	73	71	285	4,608
Billy Andrade	69	74	71	72	286	4,380
Barry Cheesman	72	71	71	72	286	4,380
Richard Coughlan	73	69	72	72	286	4,380
David Edwards	70	73	70	73	286	4,380
Steve Jones	68	71	76	71	286	4,380
Jeff Sluman	73	70	70	73	286	4,380
Nick Faldo	70	73	72	72	287	4,180
Dan Forsman	73	68	74	72	287	4,180
Jim Gallagher, Jr.	70	71	72	74	287	4,180
Keith Nolan	69	70	77	71	287	4,180
Brent Geiberger	69	70	75	74	288	4,060
J.L. Lewis	72	71	75	70	288	4,060
Jim McGovern	68	74	71	76	289	3,980
Loren Roberts	70	73	73	73	289	3,980
John Cook	70	73	75	72	290	3,900
Bruce Lietzke	69	74	73	74	290	3,900
Jay Delsing	67	72	74	78	291	3,820
Omar Uresti	71	72	73	75	291	3,820
Kirk Triplett	72	70	72	79	293	3,760

Nissan Open

Valencia Country Club, Valencia, California
Par 36-36–72; 6,977 yards

February 26-March 1
purse, $2,100,000

	SCORES				TOTAL	MONEY
Billy Mayfair	65	71	69	67	272	$378,000
Tiger Woods	68	73	65	66	272	226,800
(Mayfair defeated Woods on first extra hole.)						
Stephen Ames	66	71	70	68	275	142,800
John Daly	73	71	66	66	276	92,400
Payne Stewart	70	67	69	70	276	92,400
Tommy Armour III	69	68	67	73	277	67,987.50
Bob Estes	69	70	67	71	277	67,987.50
Jeff Gallagher	69	71	68	69	277	67,987.50
Scott Hoch	67	71	68	71	277	67,987.50
Barry Cheesman	72	73	67	66	278	52,500
Jay Haas	73	70	67	68	278	52,500
Scott Verplank	68	72	70	68	278	52,500
Skip Kendall	69	73	64	73	279	42,000
Hal Sutton	72	69	66	72	279	42,000
Fred Funk	71	70	70	69	280	33,600
Loren Roberts	68	73	72	67	280	33,600
Kevin Sutherland	70	73	67	70	280	33,600
Kirk Triplett	74	69	68	69	280	33,600
Bobby Wadkins	69	72	70	69	280	33,600
Jim Carter	71	68	71	72	282	24,465
Brandel Chamblee	73	70	70	69	282	24,465
Jerry Kelly	68	71	71	72	282	24,465
Frank Lickliter	71	71	70	70	282	24,465
Michael Bradley	71	71	70	71	283	17,430
Rick Fehr	71	67	70	75	283	17,430
Guy Hill	71	74	67	71	283	17,430

	SCORES				TOTAL	MONEY
Tom Pernice, Jr.	71	74	70	68	283	17,430
Brett Quigley	69	70	69	75	283	17,430
Dan Forsman	71	74	71	68	284	13,650
Tom Kite	68	75	69	72	284	13,650
Scott Simpson	70	73	70	71	284	13,650
Mike Springer	70	73	70	71	284	13,650
Mark Wiebe	68	72	69	75	284	13,650
Doug Barron	75	71	68	71	285	11,602.50
Omar Uresti	73	73	69	70	285	11,602.50
John Cook	70	71	72	73	286	9,465
Steve Jones	71	72	74	69	286	9,465
Jonathan Kaye	74	68	75	69	286	9,465
Neal Lancaster	72	71	78	65	286	9,465
Tom Lehman	73	71	68	74	286	9,465
Lee Rinker	70	73	71	72	286	9,465
Clarence Rose	71	75	70	70	286	9,465
Richard Coughlan	71	72	73	71	287	6,258
Chris DiMarco	69	72	76	70	287	6,258
Nick Faldo	73	70	73	71	287	6,258
Harrison Frazar	73	71	72	71	287	6,258
Bob Friend	71	74	71	71	287	6,258
P.H. Horgan III	68	78	72	69	287	6,258
Larry Rinker	69	75	68	75	287	6,258
Mike Standly	67	73	73	74	287	6,258
Willie Wood	71	75	72	69	287	6,258
Niclas Fasth	73	70	75	70	288	4,924.50
Keiichiro Fukabori	67	74	75	72	288	4,924.50
Andrew Magee	69	75	71	73	288	4,924.50
Phil Mickelson	67	76	74	71	288	4,924.50
Joe Daley	69	72	75	73	289	4,746
Robert Gamez	72	72	70	75	289	4,746
D.A. Weibring	73	73	72	71	289	4,746
Brad Fabel	74	72	72	72	290	4,557
Kent Jones	75	68	75	72	290	4,557
Shigeki Maruyama	67	79	75	69	290	4,557
Dennis Paulson	75	71	71	73	290	4,557
Iain Steel	72	72	73	73	290	4,557
Fuzzy Zoeller	72	74	73	71	290	4,557
Fred Couples	70	73	74	74	291	4,389
Sonny Skinner	71	72	73	75	291	4,389
Craig Barlow	73	73	72	74	292	4,284
Ben Bates	69	75	71	77	292	4,284
Brent Geiberger	70	71	74	77	292	4,284
Kelly Gibson	74	71	71	77	293	4,137
Lee Porter	75	71	75	72	293	4,137
Ted Schulz	73	72	75	73	293	4,137
Duffy Waldorf	72	73	76	72	293	4,137
Glen Day	72	74	79	69	294	3,990
Blaine McCallister	72	72	72	78	294	3,990
Mike Reid	70	74	76	74	294	3,990
Kevin Wentworth	72	72	74	77	295	3,906
Ken Conant	74	72	74	82	302	3,864

Doral-Ryder Open

Doral Resort & Spa, Blue Course, Miami, Florida — March 5-8
Par 36-36–72; 6,939 yards — purse, $2,000,000

	SCORES				TOTAL	MONEY
Michael Bradley	71	66	70	71	278	$360,000
John Huston	70	69	73	67	279	176,000
Billy Mayfair	72	70	68	69	279	176,000
Vijay Singh	71	68	72	70	281	82,667
Mike Brisky	68	71	71	71	281	82,667
Stewart Cink	70	68	71	72	281	82,667
Davis Love III	73	72	70	67	282	64,500
Scott Hoch	72	66	74	70	282	64,500
Tim Herron	70	67	76	70	283	48,000
Jim Furyk	77	62	73	71	283	48,000
Len Mattiace	73	67	72	71	283	48,000
John Cook	71	66	74	72	283	48,000
Bob Tway	68	71	72	72	283	48,000
Tiger Woods	70	69	71	73	283	48,000
Dudley Hart	71	70	73	71	285	31,000
Ted Tryba	71	70	73	71	285	31,000
Lee Rinker	71	72	71	71	285	31,000
Paul Azinger	73	71	69	72	285	31,000
Raymond Floyd	71	68	73	73	285	31,000
P.H. Horgan III	71	70	70	74	285	31,000
Ronnie Black	68	71	74	73	286	23,200
Bernhard Langer	70	70	73	73	286	23,200
Olin Browne	73	70	75	69	287	16,857
Neal Lancaster	70	71	76	70	287	16,857
Fred Funk	72	73	71	71	287	16,857
David Duval	70	72	73	72	287	16,857
Tommy Tolles	69	72	72	74	287	16,857
Joey Sindelar	71	69	72	75	287	16,857
Rocco Mediate	71	67	73	76	287	16,857
Doug Martin	69	71	77	71	288	12,150
Mark Calcavecchia	68	75	73	72	288	12,150
Stuart Appleby	70	74	72	72	288	12,150
Blaine McCallister	74	70	72	72	288	12,150
Bob Friend	72	71	71	74	288	12,150
Jesper Parnevik	75	69	70	74	288	12,150
Nick Price	71	70	77	71	289	9,420
Hal Sutton	69	74	74	72	289	9,420
Jeff Sluman	76	68	73	72	289	9,420
Bobby Wadkins	75	70	70	74	289	9,420
Jay Haas	72	68	73	76	289	9,420
Michael Christie	71	71	75	73	290	7,400
Nolan Henke	72	70	75	73	290	7,400
Lee Porter	69	71	76	74	290	7,400
Andy Bean	70	74	71	75	290	7,400
Curtis Strange	68	71	75	76	290	7,400
Kenny Perry	70	71	77	73	291	5,349
Larry Rinker	73	70	75	73	291	5,349
Chris DiMarco	73	71	74	73	291	5,349
Mike Weir	71	69	77	74	291	5,349
Jim Carter	69	72	76	74	291	5,349
Clarence Rose	73	71	73	74	291	5,349
Harrison Frazar	71	72	73	75	291	5,349
R.W. Eaks	73	71	77	71	292	4,608
Jeff Gallagher	74	67	79	72	292	4,608

	SCORES				TOTAL	MONEY
Chris Perry	72	69	77	74	292	4,608
Scott Gump	73	72	72	75	292	4,608
Sonny Skinner	71	72	73	76	292	4,608
John Morse	70	71	76	76	293	4,420
Bob Gilder	70	73	74	76	293	4,420
Nick Faldo	72	70	74	77	293	4,420
Jack Nicklaus	70	74	72	77	293	4,420
Kelly Gibson	76	67	78	73	294	4,260
Grant Waite	76	69	75	74	294	4,260
Richard Coughlan	74	68	77	75	294	4,260
Bruce Lietzke	71	74	73	76	294	4,260
Kent Jones	72	70	78	75	295	4,160
Wayne Grady	73	71	77	75	296	4,080
David Sutherland	76	66	78	76	296	4,080
Ed Fiori	74	70	76	76	296	4,080
Sandy Lyle	71	74	74	78	297	4,000
Guy Hill	74	71	76	77	298	3,920
Steve Stricker	77	68	75	78	298	3,920
Chris Smith	74	70	74	80	298	3,920
Mike San Filippo	71	72	76	80	299	3,840
Frank Lickliter	76	69	79	79	303	3,800

Honda Classic

TPC at Heron Bay, Coral Springs, Florida — March 12-15
Par 36-36–72; 7,268 yards — purse, $1,800,000

	SCORES				TOTAL	MONEY
Mark Calcavecchia	70	67	68	65	270	$324,000
Vijay Singh	70	68	68	67	273	194,400
Colin Montgomerie	69	69	71	66	275	122,400
John Daly	68	76	68	64	276	74,400
Jeff Maggert	67	68	76	65	276	74,400
Stuart Appleby	70	67	72	67	276	74,400
Craig Stadler	73	66	71	68	278	52,380
Bob Friend	70	70	70	68	278	52,380
Brent Geiberger	70	68	71	69	278	52,380
Bob Estes	70	69	70	69	278	52,380
Kevin Sutherland	70	68	70	70	278	52,380
Stewart Cink	68	70	74	67	279	37,800
R.W. Eaks	73	68	70	68	279	37,800
Jim Furyk	72	70	69	68	279	37,800
Larry Mize	74	69	71	66	280	27,000
Steve Flesch	72	71	70	67	280	27,000
Grant Waite	71	70	71	68	280	27,000
Barry Cheesman	70	68	74	68	280	27,000
Brian Henninger	73	69	69	69	280	27,000
Lee Janzen	70	66	73	71	280	27,000
Steve Pate	69	70	70	71	280	27,000
Andrew Magee	73	70	72	66	281	15,795
David Sutherland	71	72	71	67	281	15,795
Russ Cochran	76	67	71	67	281	15,795
Chris DiMarco	72	69	71	69	281	15,795
Mark O'Meara	75	66	69	71	281	15,795
Jerry Kelly	70	68	71	72	281	15,795
Bernhard Langer	70	69	70	72	281	15,795
Tommy Tolles	70	73	65	73	281	15,795

	SCORES				TOTAL	MONEY
Doug Martin	73	69	73	67	282	10,240
Paul Goydos	75	68	71	68	282	10,240
Chris Perry	72	70	71	69	282	10,240
Dudley Hart	73	71	69	69	282	10,240
Harrison Frazar	71	71	70	70	282	10,240
Bobby Wadkins	75	69	68	70	282	10,240
John Huston	73	71	68	70	282	10,240
Esteban Toledo	75	68	68	71	282	10,240
Tom Watson	70	73	67	72	282	10,240
Len Mattiace	70	72	73	68	283	6,840
Mike Springer	73	69	73	68	283	6,840
Ben Bates	73	70	72	68	283	6,840
Jim McGovern	74	69	72	68	283	6,840
Donnie Hammond	70	70	74	69	283	6,840
David Ogrin	75	69	68	71	283	6,840
Rocco Mediate	73	69	69	72	283	6,840
Olin Browne	72	72	67	72	283	6,840
Joey Sindelar	71	71	75	67	284	4,759
Clarence Rose	73	71	71	69	284	4,759
Fuzzy Zoeller	71	69	73	71	284	4,759
Tim Herron	73	71	69	71	284	4,759
Ted Tryba	75	68	69	72	284	4,759
Jim Gallagher, Jr.	71	73	74	67	285	4,198
Paul Stankowski	74	70	72	69	285	4,198
Joe Durant	75	69	71	70	285	4,198
Payne Stewart	76	66	71	72	285	4,198
Gene Sauers	76	66	71	72	285	4,198
Dave Rummells	74	67	76	69	286	3,996
Stephen Ames	72	71	73	70	286	3,996
Spike McRoy	75	67	73	71	286	3,996
Pete Jordan	74	70	71	71	286	3,996
Ryan Howison	70	71	71	74	286	3,996
Steve Jurgensen	73	71	75	68	287	3,816
Keith Nolan	72	72	73	70	287	3,816
Nolan Henke	71	72	73	71	287	3,816
John Morse	74	70	72	71	287	3,816
Phil Blackmar	71	71	68	77	287	3,816
Brian Kamm	71	72	75	70	288	3,708
Guy Hill	71	73	73	72	289	3,672
Kent Jones	73	68	76	73	290	3,600
Hugh Royer	74	69	74	73	290	3,600
Jeff Gallagher	73	71	71	75	290	3,600

Bay Hill Invitational

Bay Hill Club & Lodge, Orlando, Florida — March 19-22
Par 36-36–72; 7,207 yards — purse, $2,000,000

	SCORES				TOTAL	MONEY
Ernie Els	67	69	65	73	274	$360,000
Jeff Maggert	70	71	69	68	278	176,000
Bob Estes	69	71	67	71	278	176,000
Bernhard Langer	68	73	69	69	279	88,000
Mark Calcavecchia	70	69	69	71	279	88,000
Craig Parry	70	71	70	69	280	69,500
Steve Stricker	67	72	68	73	280	69,500
Jim Furyk	70	72	69	70	281	60,000

	SCORES				TOTAL	MONEY
Colin Montgomerie	71	68	73	69	281	60,000
Craig Stadler	70	73	70	70	283	50,000
Andrew Magee	69	74	70	70	283	50,000
Stephen Ames	69	74	73	67	283	50,000
Grant Waite	71	70	74	69	284	37,500
Greg Kraft	71	70	70	73	284	37,500
Lee Westwood	70	69	69	76	284	37,500
Tiger Woods	64	70	73	77	284	37,500
David Toms	70	72	69	74	285	28,000
Russ Cochran	70	74	67	74	285	28,000
Jay Don Blake	69	75	71	70	285	28,000
Doug Martin	71	73	70	71	285	28,000
Davis Love III	68	66	75	76	285	28,000
Steve Lowery	69	74	70	73	286	20,000
Tom Lehman	70	71	71	74	286	20,000
Kevin Sutherland	69	72	72	73	286	20,000
Vijay Singh	68	72	71	75	286	20,000
Lee Rinker	73	70	69	75	287	15,400
Tom Kite	75	69	70	73	287	15,400
Steve Pate	69	75	71	72	287	15,400
Tom Watson	71	72	70	75	288	12,443
Olin Browne	71	73	71	73	288	12,443
Dan Forsman	71	73	73	71	288	12,443
Fred Couples	70	74	71	73	288	12,443
Fuzzy Zoeller	73	71	70	74	288	12,443
Robert Damron	65	74	74	75	288	12,443
Scott Hoch	72	67	73	76	288	12,443
Mike Reid	72	71	71	75	289	9,217
Joey Sindelar	74	69	69	77	289	9,217
Skip Kendall	72	70	72	75	289	9,217
Paul Goydos	69	74	74	72	289	9,217
Brad Faxon	70	72	71	76	289	9,217
Stewart Cink	72	68	74	75	289	9,217
Justin Leonard	73	70	76	71	290	7,400
Jay Haas	68	74	75	73	290	7,400
Brett Quigley	70	74	71	75	290	7,400
Kirk Triplett	70	74	74	73	291	6,020
Jay Delsing	69	71	75	76	291	6,020
Rick Fehr	68	72	75	76	291	6,020
Scott Verplank	71	73	72	75	291	6,020
Scott McCarron	70	73	75	74	292	5,200
Padraig Harrington	71	73	76	75	295	4,980
Rocco Mediate	69	75	73	78	295	4,980
Robert Gamez	74	69	78	76	297	4,800
John Daly	68	75	70	85	298	4,720
Mike Brisky	74	69	79	78	300	4,640
Frank Lickliter	72	72	78	83	305	4,600
Michael Bradley	69	75	76	WD		

The Players Championship

TPC at Sawgrass, Stadium Course, Ponte Vedra Beach, Florida — March 26-29
Par 36-36–72; 6,896 yards — purse, $4,000,000

	SCORES				TOTAL	MONEY
Justin Leonard	72	69	70	67	278	$720,000
Glen Day	66	73	70	71	280	352,000

	SCORES				TOTAL	MONEY
Tom Lehman	72	70	70	68	280	352,000
Mark Calcavecchia	69	75	68	69	281	192,000
Len Mattiace	69	71	72	70	282	146,000
Scott Hoch	73	69	70	70	282	146,000
Lee Westwood	74	71	68	69	282	146,000
Payne Stewart	72	71	75	65	283	116,000
Phil Mickelson	69	73	70	71	283	116,000
Nick Price	71	72	70	70	283	116,000
Scott Verplank	71	71	72	70	284	96,000
Ernie Els	71	72	70	71	284	96,000
Lee Janzen	70	67	69	79	285	77,333.33
Bruce Lietzke	69	70	74	72	285	77,333.33
John Cook	71	73	71	70	285	77,333.33
John Daly	71	70	76	69	286	66,000
David Sutherland	72	73	69	72	286	66,000
Omar Uresti	72	71	70	74	287	48,685.71
Doug Barron	71	72	74	70	287	48,685.71
Hal Sutton	74	69	74	70	287	48,685.71
Naomichi Ozaki	69	68	76	74	287	48,685.71
David Duval	69	77	70	71	287	48,685.71
Bob Tway	72	71	75	69	287	48,685.71
Nick Faldo	75	69	70	73	287	48,685.71
Dudley Hart	74	70	71	73	288	30,533.33
Jose Maria Olazabal	72	74	70	72	288	30,533.33
Steve Jones	71	71	73	73	288	30,533.33
Lee Rinker	72	73	72	71	288	30,533.33
Tom Kite	72	66	78	72	288	30,533.33
Jesper Parnevik	72	72	72	72	288	30,533.33
Craig Stadler	71	70	72	76	289	24,250
Jerry Kelly	68	71	77	73	289	24,250
Larry Mize	73	73	73	70	289	24,250
Tommy Armour III	71	75	71	72	289	24,250
Brad Faxon	71	73	72	74	290	18,885.71
Tom Watson	71	74	71	74	290	18,885.71
Scott McCarron	72	72	71	75	290	18,885.71
Billy Andrade	70	74	75	71	290	18,885.71
Jim Furyk	70	75	73	72	290	18,885.71
Kirk Triplett	71	71	73	75	290	18,885.71
Tiger Woods	72	73	73	72	290	18,885.71
Steve Pate	71	71	74	75	291	12,560
David Frost	69	71	73	78	291	12,560
Mark O'Meara	70	75	72	74	291	12,560
Kevin Sutherland	72	70	73	76	291	12,560
Billy Mayfair	69	75	69	78	291	12,560
Stewart Cink	71	73	74	73	291	12,560
Bob Estes	72	70	74	75	291	12,560
Fred Couples	67	73	73	78	291	12,560
Brandel Chamblee	72	73	76	70	291	12,560
Steve Stricker	74	72	70	76	292	9,626.66
Jeff Maggert	69	71	76	76	292	9,626.66
Michael Bradley	74	72	76	70	292	9,626.66
Vijay Singh	72	71	75	75	293	9,200
Scott Gump	72	68	76	77	293	9,200
Per-Ulrik Johansson	69	74	78	72	293	9,200
Rocco Mediate	67	73	77	77	294	8,920
Nolan Henke	69	73	77	75	294	8,920
Paul Goydos	72	70	80	72	294	8,920
Davis Love III	73	72	69	80	294	8,920
Ted Tryba	70	74	72	79	295	8,680

	SCORES				TOTAL	MONEY
Joey Sindelar	73	69	81	72	295	8,680
Frank Nobilo	72	72	75	77	296	8,480
Robert Gamez	74	72	77	73	296	8,480
Grant Waite	76	70	75	75	296	8,480
Brian Henninger	73	72	73	79	297	8,280
Phil Blackmar	72	74	76	75	297	8,280
Skip Kendall	74	72	73	79	298	8,160
Donnie Hammond	71	75	72	81	299	8,040
Fred Funk	73	73	75	78	299	8,040
Larry Rinker	78	67	81	74	300	7,880
Mark Wiebe	76	69	76	79	300	7,880

Freeport-McDermott Classic

English Turn Golf & Country Club, New Orleans, Louisiana — April 2-5
Par 36-36–72; 7,116 yards — purse, $1,700,000

	SCORES				TOTAL	MONEY
Lee Westwood	69	68	67	69	273	$306,000
Steve Flesch	66	68	71	71	276	183,600
Jim Carter	68	69	71	71	279	81,600
Glen Day	64	75	69	71	279	81,600
Steve Lowery	72	66	70	71	279	81,600
Mark Wiebe	69	68	71	71	279	81,600
Duffy Waldorf	67	69	70	74	280	56,950
Trevor Dodds	67	72	71	72	282	47,600
Bob Estes	70	71	72	69	282	47,600
Lee Rinker	71	70	73	68	282	47,600
Ian Woosnam	70	70	71	71	282	47,600
P.H. Horgan III	70	68	76	69	283	31,329
Robert Damron	73	71	68	71	283	31,329
Jeff Gallagher	68	69	73	73	283	31,329
Scott Hoch	74	69	70	70	283	31,329
Naomichi Ozaki	69	67	72	75	283	31,329
Jesper Parnevik	71	71	69	72	283	31,329
Phil Tataurangi	71	67	70	75	283	31,329
Paul Azinger	69	74	68	73	284	18,488
Ronnie Black	72	67	70	75	284	18,488
Mark Brooks	73	70	71	70	284	18,488
Franklin Langham	73	70	69	72	284	18,488
Len Mattiace	71	67	76	70	284	18,488
Jose Maria Olazabal	72	69	73	70	284	18,488
Esteban Toledo	72	72	68	72	284	18,488
Mike Weir	72	71	73	68	284	18,488
Davis Love III	72	72	66	75	285	12,580
Blaine McCallister	67	73	71	74	285	12,580
Chris Perry	72	70	71	72	285	12,580
Doug Barron	73	68	74	71	286	10,328
Phil Blackmar	70	72	71	73	286	10,328
Niclas Fasth	67	75	72	72	286	10,328
Bob Friend	71	70	72	73	286	10,328
Neal Lancaster	68	72	72	74	286	10,328
D.A. Weibring	67	74	75	70	286	10,328
Billy Ray Brown	72	72	73	71	288	7,834
R.W. Eaks	71	69	75	73	288	7,834
Dan Forsman	72	68	76	72	288	7,834
Kelly Gibson	67	75	72	74	288	7,834

	SCORES				TOTAL	MONEY
Omar Uresti	71	72	70	75	288	7,834
Mark Wurtz	69	75	74	70	288	7,834
Jay Delsing	66	73	78	72	289	5,338
Harrison Frazar	70	69	76	74	289	5,338
Brian Henninger	68	73	73	75	289	5,338
Jimmy Johnston	71	69	80	69	289	5,338
Pete Jordan	71	69	78	71	289	5,338
Steve Jurgensen	70	72	76	71	289	5,338
David Toms	70	70	80	69	289	5,338
Bobby Wadkins	71	69	74	75	289	5,338
Willie Wood	72	71	73	73	289	5,338
Scott Gump	68	73	73	76	290	4,026
J.P. Hayes	70	70	75	75	290	4,026
Frank Lickliter	67	74	75	74	290	4,026
Tom Pernice, Jr.	70	73	73	74	290	4,026
Bob Tway	69	74	72	75	290	4,026
Tommy Armour III	67	74	75	75	291	3,842
Mike Heinen	70	72	78	71	291	3,842
Costantino Rocca	73	71	74	73	291	3,842
Ben Bates	72	71	73	76	292	3,706
Donnie Hammond	69	75	74	74	292	3,706
Greg Kraft	70	74	75	73	292	3,706
Spike McRoy	70	70	80	72	292	3,706
Lee Porter	71	73	73	75	292	3,706
John Adams	73	68	77	75	293	3,536
Clark Dennis	69	70	75	79	293	3,536
Brad Faxon	72	72	76	73	293	3,536
Bruce Fleisher	76	68	74	75	293	3,536
Ted Tryba	71	71	74	77	293	3,536
Fulton Allem	74	69	80	71	294	3,366
Russ Cochran	68	72	76	78	294	3,366
Tim Conley	73	70	75	76	294	3,366
Steve Elkington	71	70	79	74	294	3,366
Tommy Tolles	68	74	72	80	294	3,366
Scott Verplank	70	71	80	74	295	3,264
Brad Fabel	75	69	77	75	296	3,196
Kent Jones	74	70	76	76	296	3,196
Sonny Skinner	71	71	74	80	296	3,196
Craig Barlow	72	70	80	75	297	3,094
John Riegger	70	73	76	78	297	3,094
Tim Simpson	73	71	74	79	297	3,094

Masters Tournament

Augusta National Golf Club, Augusta, Georgia — April 9-12
Par 36-36–72; 6,925 yards — purse, $2,700,000

	SCORES				TOTAL	MONEY
Mark O'Meara	74	70	68	67	279	$576,000
Fred Couples	69	70	71	70	280	281,600
David Duval	71	68	74	67	280	281,600
Jim Furyk	76	70	67	68	281	153,600
Paul Azinger	71	72	69	70	282	128,000
Jack Nicklaus	73	72	70	68	283	111,200
David Toms	75	72	72	64	283	111,200
Darren Clarke	76	73	67	69	285	89,600
Justin Leonard	74	73	69	69	285	89,600

	SCORES				TOTAL	MONEY
Colin Montgomerie	71	75	69	70	285	89,600
Tiger Woods	71	72	72	70	285	89,600
Jay Haas	72	71	71	72	286	64,800
Per-Ulrik Johansson	74	75	67	70	286	64,800
Phil Mickelson	74	69	69	74	286	64,800
Jose Maria Olazabal	70	73	71	72	286	64,800
Mark Calcavecchia	74	74	69	70	287	48,000
Ernie Els	75	70	70	72	287	48,000
Scott Hoch	70	71	73	73	287	48,000
Scott McCarron	73	71	72	71	287	48,000
Ian Woosnam	74	71	72	70	287	48,000
Willie Wood	74	74	70	70	288	38,400
*Matt Kuchar	72	76	68	72	288	
Stewart Cink	74	76	69	70	289	33,280
John Huston	77	71	70	71	289	33,280
Jeff Maggert	72	73	72	72	289	33,280
Brad Faxon	73	74	71	72	290	26,133
David Frost	72	73	74	71	290	26,133
Steve Jones	75	70	75	70	290	26,133
Michael Bradley	73	74	72	72	291	23,680
Steve Elkington	75	75	71	71	292	22,720
Andrew Magee	74	72	74	73	293	21,280
Jesper Parnevik	75	73	73	72	293	21,280
Phil Blackmar	71	78	75	70	294	18,112
John Daly	77	71	71	75	294	18,112
Lee Janzen	76	74	72	72	294	18,112
Davis Love III	74	75	67	78	294	18,112
Fuzzy Zoeller	71	74	75	74	294	18,112
Tom Kite	73	74	74	74	295	15,680
Bernhard Langer	75	73	74	74	296	14,720
Paul Stankowski	70	80	72	74	296	14,720
Corey Pavin	73	77	72	75	297	13,440
Craig Stadler	79	68	73	77	297	13,440
John Cook	75	73	74	76	298	12,480
Lee Westwood	74	76	72	78	300	11,840
*Joel Kribel	74	76	76	75	301	
Gary Player	77	72	78	75	302	11,200

Out of Final 36 Holes

			TOTAL
Billy Ray Brown	76	75	151
Nick Faldo	72	79	151
Raymond Floyd	74	77	151
Retief Goosen	74	77	151
Tim Herron	76	75	151
Sandy Lyle	74	77	151
Billy Mayfair	76	75	151
Nick Price	75	76	151
Tommy Tolles	75	76	151
Tom Watson	78	73	151
Olin Browne	72	80	152
Larry Mize	73	79	152
Masashi Ozaki	75	77	152
Bob Tway	74	78	152
Billy Andrade	75	78	153
Bradley Hughes	75	78	153
Frank Nobilo	77	76	153
Costantino Rocca	81	72	153
Stuart Appleby	77	77	154
Shigeki Maruyama	74	80	154

	SCORES		TOTAL
Greg Norman	76	78	154
Jeff Sluman	78	76	154
Ben Crenshaw	83	72	155
David Ogrin	77	78	155
Mark Brooks	80	76	156
Tom Lehman	80	76	156
Vijay Singh	76	80	156
Seve Ballesteros	78	79	157
Fred Funk	79	78	157
Gabriel Hjerstedt	79	78	157
Ignacio Garrido	85	72	157
Scott Simpson	79	78	157
*Craig Watson	79	78	157
Gay Brewer	72	86	158
*Tim Clark	80	78	158
Tommy Aaron	81	79	160
*Ken Bakst	82	78	160
Bill Glasson	82	79	161
Charles Coody	79	85	164
Arnold Palmer	79	87	166
Billy Casper	81	86	167
Doug Ford	86		WD

(Professionals who did not complete 72 holes received $5,000.)

MCI Classic

Harbour Town Golf Links, Hilton Head Island, South Carolina — April 16-19
Par 36-35–71; 6,915 yards — purse, $1,900,000

	SCORES				TOTAL	MONEY
Davis Love III	67	68	66	65	266	$342,000
Glen Day	67	67	72	67	273	205,200
Phil Mickelson	67	71	65	73	276	110,200
Payne Stewart	69	71	64	72	276	110,200
Fulton Allem	68	71	68	70	277	76,000
Frank Lickliter	67	66	75	70	278	61,512.50
Nick Price	67	69	70	72	278	61,512.50
Joey Sindelar	69	67	70	72	278	61,512.50
Doug Tewell	66	73	67	72	278	61,512.50
Ernie Els	73	68	70	68	279	45,600
John Huston	66	73	67	73	279	45,600
Larry Mize	69	70	70	70	279	45,600
Kenny Perry	74	68	66	71	279	45,600
Bob Estes	68	68	71	73	280	33,250
Brad Faxon	70	71	69	70	280	33,250
Tom Lehman	70	73	69	68	280	33,250
Rocco Mediate	68	69	70	73	280	33,250
Mike Brisky	70	71	67	73	281	23,940
Rick Fehr	69	73	72	67	281	23,940
Lee Janzen	71	66	72	72	281	23,940
Len Mattiace	69	67	69	76	281	23,940
Jesper Parnevik	68	71	73	69	281	23,940
Bob Tway	69	73	69	70	281	23,940
Neal Lancaster	68	72	71	71	282	15,037.15
Mark O'Meara	70	73	69	70	282	15,037.15
Tommy Armour III	74	70	67	71	282	15,037.14

	SCORES				TOTAL	MONEY
R.W. Eaks	68	69	72	73	282	15,037.14
Fred Funk	73	70	67	72	282	15,037.14
Jay Haas	66	66	76	74	282	15,037.14
Vijay Singh	68	72	68	74	282	15,037.14
Scott Gump	72	72	66	73	283	11,780
Scott Hoch	69	70	76	68	283	11,780
Don Pooley	73	70	69	71	283	11,780
Steve Lowery	69	72	72	71	284	9,804
Doug Martin	72	71	68	73	284	9,804
Steve Pate	69	70	69	76	284	9,804
Jeff Sluman	72	71	69	72	284	9,804
Tom Watson	71	71	72	70	284	9,804
Brent Geiberger	72	72	68	73	285	7,600
Jerry Kelly	70	70	70	75	285	7,600
Billy Mayfair	73	71	67	74	285	7,600
Blaine McCallister	73	69	70	73	285	7,600
Bobby Wadkins	71	70	69	75	285	7,600
Fuzzy Zoeller	71	73	67	74	285	7,600
Billy Andrade	72	71	71	72	286	5,563.20
Michael Bradley	73	68	72	73	286	5,563.20
Mark Brooks	72	72	71	71	286	5,563.20
Darren Clarke	72	71	72	71	286	5,563.20
Skip Kendall	71	72	71	72	286	5,563.20
Robert Damron	72	71	72	72	287	4,547.34
David Ogrin	70	72	74	71	287	4,547.34
David Frost	69	71	74	73	287	4,547.33
Pete Jordan	72	72	69	74	287	4,547.33
Mike Standly	70	72	71	74	287	4,547.33
Curtis Strange	70	74	71	72	287	4,547.33
Jim Carter	72	71	73	72	288	4,237
Brad Fabel	70	73	74	71	288	4,237
Tim Herron	71	69	70	78	288	4,237
Justin Leonard	71	72	69	76	288	4,237
Frank Nobilo	68	68	74	78	288	4,237
Clarence Rose	72	72	70	74	288	4,237
John Cook	68	72	74	75	289	3,952
David Edwards	70	71	73	75	289	3,952
Dudley Hart	72	72	68	77	289	3,952
Brian Henninger	69	75	70	75	289	3,952
P.H. Horgan III	69	71	73	76	289	3,952
Per-Ulrik Johansson	71	71	71	76	289	3,952
Spike McRoy	71	71	74	73	289	3,952
Omar Uresti	70	74	72	73	289	3,952
D.A. Weibring	72	70	71	76	289	3,952
Billy Ray Brown	72	71	72	75	290	3,724
Kelly Gibson	67	72	74	77	290	3,724
Hal Sutton	72	67	77	74	290	3,724
Lennie Clements	73	71	72	75	291	3,572
Russ Cochran	72	70	76	73	291	3,572
Hugh Royer III	71	71	72	77	291	3,572
Gene Sauers	70	70	73	78	291	3,572
Ted Tryba	72	72	76	71	291	3,572
Jim Furyk	73	71	76	72	292	3,439
John Mahaffey	70	73	77	72	292	3,439
Doug Barron	71	73	74	75	293	3,382
Bob Friend	69	74	75	76	294	3,344
Nolan Henke	72	70	75	78	295	3,306
Nick Faldo	70	74	73	83	300	3,268

Greater Greensboro Chrysler Classic

Forest Oaks Country Club, Greensboro, North Carolina — April 23-26
Par 36-36–72; 7,062 yards — purse, $2,200,000

	SCORES				TOTAL	MONEY
Trevor Dodds	68	69	70	69	276	$396,000
Scott Verplank	67	71	66	72	276	237,600
(Dodds defeated Verplank on first extra hole.)						
Bob Estes	67	65	72	73	277	149,600
Neal Lancaster	70	67	70	71	278	105,600
Frank Nobilo	71	65	71	72	279	88,000
Fred Funk	72	69	67	72	280	76,450
Phil Mickelson	74	65	71	70	280	76,450
Michael Bradley	69	71	72	69	281	63,800
Lennie Clements	68	68	72	73	281	63,800
Hal Sutton	65	67	74	75	281	63,800
Jim Furyk	70	67	73	72	282	46,640
Dudley Hart	68	68	74	72	282	46,640
Jerry Kelly	70	68	68	76	282	46,640
Skip Kendall	68	73	63	78	282	46,640
Ted Tryba	71	67	67	77	282	46,640
Clark Dennis	69	70	73	71	283	30,862.86
Jim Estes	70	70	75	68	283	30,862.86
Harrison Frazar	71	71	71	70	283	30,862.86
Mike Hulbert	69	73	72	69	283	30,862.86
Jeff Maggert	71	69	71	72	283	30,862.86
Tim Herron	71	69	71	72	283	30,862.85
John Maginnes	68	72	70	73	283	30,862.85
Stuart Appleby	70	69	70	75	284	18,542.86
Ben Bates	71	72	71	70	284	18,542.86
Steve Flesch	71	70	71	72	284	18,542.86
David Toms	70	70	73	71	284	18,542.86
Fuzzy Zoeller	67	73	69	75	284	18,542.86
Brad Faxon	67	70	71	76	284	18,542.85
Donnie Hammond	69	70	69	76	284	18,542.85
Stephen Ames	71	70	66	78	285	12,787.50
Ronnie Black	71	69	73	72	285	12,787.50
David Edwards	69	69	72	75	285	12,787.50
Steve Elkington	71	71	67	76	285	12,787.50
David Frost	66	75	68	76	285	12,787.50
Guy Hill	71	71	69	74	285	12,787.50
Mike Standly	69	71	75	70	285	12,787.50
Bobby Wadkins	68	71	74	72	285	12,787.50
Billy Andrade	73	69	71	73	286	9,680
Rocco Mediate	68	72	74	72	286	9,680
Chris Perry	66	75	68	77	286	9,680
Lee Rinker	70	69	72	75	286	9,680
Kelly Gibson	70	69	73	75	287	7,480
J.P. Hayes	71	72	69	75	287	7,480
Jimmy Johnston	69	69	74	75	287	7,480
Len Mattiace	71	71	70	75	287	7,480
John Riegger	72	70	76	69	287	7,480
Clarence Rose	73	70	69	75	287	7,480
Joe Durant	72	71	75	70	288	5,468.58
Gabriel Hjertstedt	70	70	71	77	288	5,468.57
Glen Hnatiuk	69	73	72	74	288	5,468.57
Greg Kraft	69	71	74	74	288	5,468.57
Steve Lowery	75	68	72	73	288	5,468.57
Dave Stockton, Jr.	70	71	72	75	288	5,468.57

	SCORES				TOTAL	MONEY
Doug Tewell	71	71	72	74	288	5,468.57
John Adams	71	71	74	73	289	4,928
Fulton Allem	69	74	69	77	289	4,928
Richard Coughlan	74	68	73	74	289	4,928
Tim Loustalot	70	73	73	73	289	4,928
Brett Quigley	69	69	76	75	289	4,928
Sonny Skinner	72	69	73	75	289	4,928
Mark Wurtz	70	70	73	76	289	4,928
Barry Cheesman	70	71	74	75	290	4,664
Jeff Gallagher	74	69	73	74	290	4,664
Robert Gamez	71	72	71	76	290	4,664
Peter O'Malley	70	72	73	75	290	4,664
Kevin Wentworth	69	71	74	76	290	4,664
Tom Byrum	70	70	76	75	291	4,444
Jim Carter	71	70	73	77	291	4,444
Jonathan Kaye	69	74	73	75	291	4,444
Tom Kite	70	69	76	76	291	4,444
Billy Mayfair	70	69	75	77	291	4,444
Joe Daley	73	69	75	75	292	4,290
Robert Damron	70	73	75	74	292	4,290
Guy Boros	73	70	73	77	293	4,202
Brian Henninger	76	67	75	75	293	4,202
John Daly	72	70	76	79	297	4,136
Steve Stricker	72	71	74	81	298	4,092

Shell Houston Open

TPC at The Woodlands, The Woodlands, Texas — April 30-May 3
Par 36-36–72; 7,042 yards — purse, $2,000,000

	SCORES				TOTAL	MONEY
David Duval	69	70	73	64	276	$360,000
Jeff Maggert	71	71	64	71	277	216,000
Fred Couples	72	68	70	68	278	136,000
Dudley Hart	70	72	70	67	279	88,000
Lee Janzen	69	69	71	70	279	88,000
Dan Forsman	68	70	68	74	280	64,750
Jerry Kelly	71	71	70	68	280	64,750
Dave Stockton, Jr.	74	71	67	68	280	64,750
Hal Sutton	70	73	69	68	280	64,750
Stephen Ames	72	68	71	70	281	54,000
Skip Kendall	73	72	70	67	282	50,000
Joe Durant	70	72	71	70	283	39,200
Steve Flesch	75	71	69	68	283	39,200
Scott Hoch	66	76	73	68	283	39,200
John Huston	71	69	73	70	283	39,200
Franklin Langham	66	74	71	72	283	39,200
Olin Browne	69	77	68	70	284	28,000
Jim Gallagher, Jr.	74	72	68	70	284	28,000
Mike Hulbert	67	73	71	73	284	28,000
Bruce Lietzke	67	76	72	69	284	28,000
Grant Waite	73	72	69	70	284	28,000
Ben Bates	71	71	73	70	285	17,550
Guy Boros	67	76	72	70	285	17,550
Bobby Gage	71	73	74	67	285	17,550
Donnie Hammond	68	76	69	72	285	17,550
Clarence Rose	76	70	70	69	285	17,550

	SCORES				TOTAL	MONEY
Mike Sullivan	70	72	74	69	285	17,550
David Sutherland	73	69	74	69	285	17,550
Phil Tataurangi	70	73	74	68	285	17,550
Kelly Gibson	72	71	71	72	286	12,150
Pete Jordan	73	71	70	72	286	12,150
Phil Mickelson	71	75	72	68	286	12,150
Chris Perry	76	69	72	69	286	12,150
Omar Uresti	74	72	69	71	286	12,150
Willie Wood	70	75	72	69	286	12,150
Brandel Chamblee	74	72	70	71	287	8,812.50
Bob Gilder	72	72	74	69	287	8,812.50
Tom Kite	69	75	69	74	287	8,812.50
Peter O'Malley	70	70	74	73	287	8,812.50
Kenny Perry	71	71	75	70	287	8,812.50
Doug Tewell	68	75	75	69	287	8,812.50
Esteban Toledo	74	69	72	72	287	8,812.50
D.A. Weibring	75	69	71	72	287	8,812.50
Dave Barr	72	73	72	71	288	6,600
Peter Jacobsen	75	70	72	71	288	6,600
Sonny Skinner	74	71	71	72	288	6,600
Doug Barron	75	70	72	72	289	5,206.67
J.P. Hayes	70	75	74	70	289	5,206.67
Keith Nolan	70	76	72	71	289	5,206.67
Paul Stankowski	70	75	74	70	289	5,206.67
Blaine McCallister	71	71	74	73	289	5,206.66
John Morse	69	76	72	72	289	5,206.66
Richard Coughlan	72	73	73	72	290	4,586.67
Greg Kraft	70	75	73	72	290	4,586.67
Jim McGovern	73	73	71	73	290	4,586.67
Payne Stewart	71	74	74	71	290	4,586.67
Rick Fehr	71	70	71	78	290	4,586.66
Robert Thompson	73	72	72	73	290	4,586.66
Jim Carter	74	71	73	73	291	4,340
Joe Daley	72	74	73	72	291	4,340
John Mahaffey	73	73	76	69	291	4,340
Brett Quigley	74	70	75	72	291	4,340
Lee Rinker	69	76	72	74	291	4,340
Joey Sindelar	73	72	73	73	291	4,340
Doug Martin	72	74	72	74	292	4,180
Craig Parry	72	72	75	73	292	4,180
Jay Delsing	67	73	78	75	293	4,080
Gabriel Hjertstedt	72	73	71	77	293	4,080
Mike Standly	72	74	75	72	293	4,080
Fred Funk	72	74	73	75	294	3,980
Lanny Wadkins	68	76	76	74	294	3,980
Bradley Hughes	70	76	73	77	296	3,920
Zoran Zorkic	72	74	74	77	297	3,880

BellSouth Classic

TPC at Sugarloaf, Duluth, Georgia — May 7-10
Par 36-36–72; 7,259 yards — purse, $1,800,000

	SCORES				TOTAL	MONEY
Tiger Woods	69	67	63	72	271	$324,000
Jay Don Blake	67	68	67	70	272	194,400
Steve Flesch	66	71	68	69	274	104,400

	SCORES				TOTAL	MONEY
Esteban Toledo	66	75	66	67	274	104,400
Stewart Cink	67	71	65	72	275	61,020
Bill Glasson	68	73	68	66	275	61,020
John Huston	68	68	71	68	275	61,020
Bob Tway	73	69	66	67	275	61,020
Scott Verplank	67	74	69	65	275	61,020
Clark Dennis	72	65	71	68	276	46,800
Trevor Dodds	71	67	72	66	276	46,800
Clarence Rose	70	70	69	68	277	39,600
Grant Waite	68	70	72	67	277	39,600
David Duval	67	73	73	65	278	31,500
Lee Janzen	71	69	68	70	278	31,500
Jerry Kelly	68	71	69	70	278	31,500
Craig Parry	69	66	72	71	278	31,500
Glen Hnatiuk	67	69	70	73	279	27,000
Stephen Ames	70	69	70	71	280	21,816
Bob Estes	69	74	66	71	280	21,816
Scott Gump	70	70	68	72	280	21,816
Spike McRoy	68	68	72	72	280	21,816
Bobby Wadkins	70	72	69	69	280	21,816
Jim Gallagher, Jr.	74	70	68	69	281	15,840
Greg Kraft	71	71	69	70	281	15,840
Hal Sutton	67	72	70	72	281	15,840
Joe Daley	68	74	69	71	282	13,320
Larry Mize	70	72	69	71	282	13,320
Dicky Pride	71	73	67	71	282	13,320
Glen Day	72	72	68	71	283	10,935
Paul Goydos	71	70	67	75	283	10,935
Tim Herron	68	69	77	69	283	10,935
Franklin Langham	71	69	70	73	283	10,935
Steve Pate	72	68	74	69	283	10,935
Nick Price	73	70	69	71	283	10,935
Robert Gamez	74	68	68	74	284	7,569
Brian Henninger	71	72	68	73	284	7,569
Guy Hill	71	69	69	75	284	7,569
Mike Hulbert	73	70	68	73	284	7,569
Jimmy Johnston	70	69	74	71	284	7,569
Tom Lehman	72	72	70	70	284	7,569
Frank Lickliter	67	76	71	70	284	7,569
Scott McCarron	71	73	69	71	284	7,569
Tom Pernice, Jr.	69	71	73	71	284	7,569
Kenny Perry	71	71	71	71	284	7,569
*Matt Kuchar	70	69	71	74	284	
Russ Cochran	73	71	71	70	285	5,244
Bob Friend	74	70	69	72	285	5,244
Hale Irwin	72	70	74	69	285	5,244
Craig Barlow	70	69	71	76	286	4,361.15
Dan Forsman	70	69	76	71	286	4,361.15
Barry Cheesman	70	74	73	69	286	4,361.14
Jeff Gallagher	72	67	67	80	286	4,361.14
Jay Haas	71	71	74	70	286	4,361.14
J.L. Lewis	69	73	74	70	286	4,361.14
Steve Stricker	70	73	66	77	286	4,361.14
Andrew Magee	73	68	73	73	287	4,086
Jeff Sluman	71	70	74	72	287	4,086
Mark Calcavecchia	65	75	76	73	289	3,978
Bobby Gage	73	69	71	76	289	3,978
Gene Sauers	71	72	67	79	289	3,978
Paul Stankowski	71	73	74	71	289	3,978
Brad Faxon	72	70	75	73	290	3,870

	SCORES				TOTAL	MONEY
Rocco Mediate	72	72	73	73	290	3,870
Billy Andrade	70	74	72	75	291	3,780
Brandel Chamblee	73	69	75	74	291	3,780
Kent Jones	70	72	73	76	291	3,780
Robin Freeman	69	72	73	79	293	3,690
Gary Hallberg	73	71	76	73	293	3,690
Steve Jurgensen	70	72	74	78	294	3,636
Ben Bates	70	74	76	75	295	3,600
Nolan Henke	72	69	76	80	297	3,564
Mark Carnevale	72	72	79	76	299	3,528

GTE Byron Nelson Classic

TPC at Las Colinas: Par 35-35–70; 6,899 yards — May 14-17
Cottonwood Valley Course: Par 34-36–70; 6,846 yards — purse, $2,500,000
Irving, Texas

	SCORES				TOTAL	MONEY
John Cook	66	68	66	65	265	$450,000
Fred Couples	66	67	63	72	268	186,666.67
Hal Sutton	66	65	68	69	268	186,666.67
Harrison Frazar	64	68	66	70	268	186,666.66
Steve Stricker	67	72	65	65	269	100,000
Bob Friend	63	70	68	69	270	83,750
Scott McCarron	66	72	68	64	270	83,750
Phil Mickelson	66	68	69	67	270	83,750
Jim Carter	68	68	66	69	271	67,500
Clark Dennis	67	72	63	69	271	67,500
Tim Herron	69	69	67	66	271	67,500
Bob Estes	66	68	70	68	272	52,500
Jeff Sluman	67	67	69	69	272	52,500
Tiger Woods	65	71	69	67	272	52,500
Phil Blackmar	69	69	69	66	273	41,250
Jim Furyk	66	70	68	69	273	41,250
Mark O'Meara	67	69	69	68	273	41,250
Kirk Triplett	69	70	67	67	273	41,250
Jay Don Blake	67	68	69	70	274	29,250
Peter Jacobsen	70	68	67	69	274	29,250
Payne Stewart	68	67	68	71	274	29,250
Phil Tataurangi	70	68	68	68	274	29,250
Ted Tryba	66	68	70	70	274	29,250
Bob Tway	70	66	69	69	274	29,250
Tommy Armour III	67	72	66	70	275	17,512.50
Russ Cochran	68	67	70	70	275	17,512.50
Glen Day	68	70	67	70	275	17,512.50
Brad Fabel	70	69	68	68	275	17,512.50
Steve Flesch	71	66	69	69	275	17,512.50
Dan Forsman	67	71	69	68	275	17,512.50
Gabriel Hjertstedt	70	66	70	69	275	17,512.50
Steve Jones	69	70	69	67	275	17,512.50
Tom Kite	69	70	66	70	275	17,512.50
Corey Pavin	70	67	69	69	275	17,512.50
Donnie Hammond	66	70	70	70	276	11,546.88
Mike Heinen	70	69	70	67	276	11,546.88
Len Mattiace	71	66	70	69	276	11,546.88
Blaine McCallister	65	72	69	70	276	11,546.88
Robert Damron	68	65	72	71	276	11,546.87
Chris DiMarco	67	71	68	70	276	11,546.87
Justin Leonard	68	69	69	70	276	11,546.87

	SCORES				TOTAL	MONEY
Esteban Toledo	72	67	66	71	276	11,546.87
Ben Crenshaw	70	69	70	68	277	7,612.50
Trevor Dodds	68	71	65	73	277	7,612.50
R.W. Eaks	66	73	69	69	277	7,612.50
Scott Gump	65	70	69	73	277	7,612.50
Guy Hill	70	69	71	67	277	7,612.50
Doug Martin	69	68	70	70	277	7,612.50
Larry Mize	69	69	70	69	277	7,612.50
Tom Watson	64	70	72	71	277	7,612.50
Tom Byrum	68	71	70	69	278	5,883.34
Vance Veazey	69	70	69	70	278	5,883.34
Ronnie Black	73	66	66	73	278	5,883.33
Rocco Mediate	67	70	70	71	278	5,883.33
Craig Stadler	71	67	69	71	278	5,883.33
Willie Wood	69	68	70	71	278	5,883.33
Mike Hulbert	71	68	69	71	279	5,525
Jeff Maggert	69	70	71	69	279	5,525
Chris Perry	67	70	73	69	279	5,525
Kenny Perry	67	72	66	74	279	5,525
Don Pooley	67	71	70	71	279	5,525
Lee Rinker	69	68	69	73	279	5,525
Fulton Allem	69	70	69	72	280	5,225
Craig Barlow	69	68	72	71	280	5,225
Ben Bates	65	74	70	71	280	5,225
Ernie Els	69	69	71	71	280	5,225
Paul Goydos	72	66	69	73	280	5,225
Frank Lickliter	65	72	72	71	280	5,225
Nolan Henke	75	64	70	72	281	5,050
Glen Hnatiuk	68	69	72	73	282	4,925
Jim McGovern	71	67	71	73	282	4,925
Tom Pernice, Jr.	73	66	71	72	282	4,925
Mike Springer	71	68	71	72	282	4,925
Richard Coughlan	70	68	74	73	285	4,750
David Frost	68	71	74	72	285	4,750
David Ogrin	67	72	72	74	285	4,750
John Daly	67	71	70	79	287	4,625
Omar Uresti	69	68	79	71	287	4,625
Jeff Gallagher	69	69	74	76	288	4,550

MasterCard Colonial

Colonial Country Club, Ft. Worth, Texas — May 21-24
Par 35-35–70; 7,010 yards — purse, $2,300,000

	SCORES				TOTAL	MONEY
Tom Watson	68	66	65	66	265	$414,000
Jim Furyk	66	67	66	68	267	248,400
Jeff Sluman	67	67	66	69	269	156,400
Harrison Frazar	64	67	68	71	270	110,400
John Cook	68	66	69	68	271	92,000
Jim Gallagher, Jr.	69	69	68	66	272	79,925
Kenny Perry	68	65	69	70	272	79,925
Brian Henninger	70	66	68	69	273	69,000
Justin Leonard	70	70	67	66	273	69,000
Stuart Appleby	68	69	69	68	274	55,200
Steve Flesch	68	66	72	68	274	55,200
Dan Forsman	69	67	71	67	274	55,200

	SCORES				TOTAL	MONEY
Craig Parry	68	69	69	68	274	55,200
Mike Brisky	70	70	66	69	275	40,250
Clark Dennis	68	68	68	71	275	40,250
David Duval	66	70	68	71	275	40,250
David Frost	68	69	69	69	275	40,250
Fred Couples	72	69	67	68	276	24,484.55
Skip Kendall	68	71	69	68	276	24,484.55
Jeff Maggert	69	72	67	68	276	24,484.55
Doug Martin	67	69	70	70	276	24,484.55
Payne Stewart	68	72	66	70	276	24,484.55
Lanny Wadkins	66	71	70	69	276	24,484.55
Scott Hoch	67	73	66	70	276	24,484.54
John Huston	70	69	66	71	276	24,484.54
Scott McCarron	70	67	67	72	276	24,484.54
Rocco Mediate	67	68	67	74	276	24,484.54
Kirk Triplett	69	68	68	71	276	24,484.54
Tommy Armour III	70	65	72	70	277	15,295
Nick Faldo	72	69	70	66	277	15,295
Fred Funk	75	65	68	69	277	15,295
Bruce Lietzke	67	69	67	74	277	15,295
Jerry Kelly	67	69	71	71	278	13,282.50
Frank Nobilo	69	68	73	68	278	13,282.50
Phil Blackmar	66	68	72	73	279	11,097.50
Steve Jones	69	69	72	69	279	11,097.50
Len Mattiace	71	69	70	69	279	11,097.50
Nick Price	71	69	68	71	279	11,097.50
Bob Tway	67	71	72	69	279	11,097.50
Scott Verplank	70	69	71	69	279	11,097.50
Stewart Cink	68	72	67	73	280	7,625.78
Glen Day	72	66	71	71	280	7,625.78
David Edwards	72	69	68	71	280	7,625.78
David Ogrin	71	64	71	74	280	7,625.78
Corey Pavin	73	66	69	72	280	7,625.78
Joey Sindelar	69	70	74	67	280	7,625.78
Mark Wiebe	71	70	71	68	280	7,625.78
Mark Calcavecchia	68	65	70	77	280	7,625.77
Brent Geiberger	70	69	67	74	280	7,625.77
Rick Fehr	70	69	70	72	281	5,658
Dudley Hart	68	72	69	72	281	5,658
Peter Jacobsen	69	70	71	71	281	5,658
Dan Pohl	70	66	77	69	282	5,156.19
Kevin Sutherland	69	71	73	69	282	5,156.19
Fulton Allem	69	69	72	72	282	5,156.18
Jay Don Blake	72	68	72	70	282	5,156.18
Guy Boros	68	73	71	70	282	5,156.18
Mark Brooks	71	70	70	71	282	5,156.18
Brandel Chamblee	68	69	75	70	282	5,156.18
Brad Fabel	67	68	71	76	282	5,156.18
Gabriel Hjertstedt	70	69	73	70	282	5,156.18
Blaine McCallister	69	71	71	71	282	5,156.18
Lee Rinker	69	68	74	71	282	5,156.18
Jim Carter	67	72	71	73	283	4,830
Tom Kite	69	70	74	70	283	4,830
Grant Waite	69	72	69	73	283	4,830
Dave Stockton, Jr.	71	69	75	69	284	4,738
R.W. Eaks	67	73	74	71	285	4,692
Robert Damron	74	66	70	76	286	4,600
Steve Lowery	70	69	75	72	286	4,600
Craig Stadler	71	70	71	74	286	4,600
David Toms	71	69	76	71	287	4,508

	SCORES				TOTAL	MONEY
Billy Andrade	71	69	77	71	288	4,439
Neal Lancaster	69	71	73	75	288	4,439

Memorial Tournament

Muirfield Village Golf Club, Dublin, Ohio — May 28-31
Par 36-36–72; 7,163 yards — purse, $2,200,000

	SCORES				TOTAL	MONEY
Fred Couples	68	67	67	69	271	$396,000
Andrew Magee	67	71	68	69	275	237,600
David Duval	74	66	67	69	276	149,600
Jim Furyk	74	68	67	68	277	105,600
Brandel Chamblee	71	72	66	69	278	83,600
Davis Love III	66	73	66	73	278	83,600
Mark Calcavecchia	68	69	72	70	279	66,275
Ernie Els	67	72	67	73	279	66,275
Tim Herron	72	72	67	68	279	66,275
Ted Tryba	67	71	68	73	279	66,275
Robert Damron	70	70	69	71	280	46,640
Glen Day	73	71	65	71	280	46,640
Tom Lehman	68	70	70	72	280	46,640
Jesper Parnevik	73	71	66	70	280	46,640
Craig Stadler	67	73	70	70	280	46,640
Neal Lancaster	73	69	68	71	281	30,862.86
Justin Leonard	69	70	71	71	281	30,862.86
Frank Nobilo	71	72	69	69	281	30,862.86
Kirk Triplett	67	71	70	73	281	30,862.86
Bob Tway	70	73	68	70	281	30,862.86
Chris Perry	71	69	68	73	281	30,862.85
Bobby Wadkins	71	72	65	73	281	30,862.85
Dan Forsman	69	75	68	70	282	19,580
Jay Haas	69	76	67	70	282	19,580
Steve Lowery	73	71	71	67	282	19,580
Brett Quigley	69	69	70	74	282	19,580
Mark Wiebe	72	70	68	72	282	19,580
Brad Fabel	71	71	70	71	283	15,620
Steve Jones	68	71	72	72	283	15,620
Larry Mize	72	70	66	75	283	15,620
Lee Janzen	68	74	70	72	284	12,477.15
Billy Mayfair	72	73	68	71	284	12,477.15
John Cook	74	68	68	74	284	12,477.14
Nick Faldo	71	70	69	74	284	12,477.14
John Huston	69	75	65	75	284	12,477.14
Len Mattiace	68	67	73	76	284	12,477.14
Steve Stricker	71	72	68	73	284	12,477.14
Stewart Cink	75	69	70	71	285	9,240
Trevor Dodds	66	72	72	75	285	9,240
Harrison Frazar	68	69	75	73	285	9,240
Edward Fryatt	73	70	69	73	285	9,240
Fred Funk	75	69	70	71	285	9,240
Scott Verplank	72	70	71	72	285	9,240
Bob Estes	72	68	74	72	286	7,040
Greg Kraft	67	74	76	69	286	7,040
Kenny Perry	71	69	76	70	286	7,040
Joey Sindelar	66	72	73	75	286	7,040
Mark Brooks	68	75	72	72	287	5,764

	SCORES				TOTAL	MONEY
Brad Elder	70	72	70	75	287	5,764
Brent Geiberger	69	70	76	72	287	5,764
Phil Blackmar	73	69	71	75	288	5,148
Brad Faxon	74	71	69	74	288	5,148
Jeff Gallagher	71	74	68	75	288	5,148
Don Pooley	71	73	73	71	288	5,148
Doug Tewell	73	67	74	74	288	5,148
David Toms	72	73	70	73	288	5,148
Tiger Woods	70	74	71	73	288	5,148
Jim Carter	74	71	69	75	289	4,884
Naomichi Ozaki	75	70	72	72	289	4,884
Esteban Toledo	73	70	73	73	289	4,884
Gabriel Hjertstedt	69	75	70	76	290	4,752
Mike Hulbert	70	75	70	75	290	4,752
Frank Lickliter	72	70	69	79	290	4,752
David Edwards	74	69	72	76	291	4,620
Jeff Maggert	75	69	74	73	291	4,620
Kevin Sutherland	70	73	70	78	291	4,620
Steve Pate	66	74	73	79	292	4,532
David Ogrin	74	70	70	79	293	4,466
Vijay Singh	73	70	76	74	293	4,466
Jeff Sluman	73	70	75	77	295	4,400
Payne Stewart	67	72	74	83	296	4,356

Kemper Open

TPC at Avenel, Potomac, Maryland
Par 36-35–71; 7,005 yards

June 4-7
purse, $2,000,000

	SCORES				TOTAL	MONEY
Stuart Appleby	70	63	69	72	274	$360,000
Scott Hoch	69	68	68	70	275	216,000
Clark Dennis	70	65	70	73	278	90,200
Brad Fabel	69	66	70	73	278	90,200
Fred Funk	64	66	71	77	278	90,200
Mark O'Meara	68	70	71	69	278	90,200
Tommy Tolles	70	68	66	74	278	90,200
Craig Parry	67	66	76	70	279	58,000
Steve Stricker	70	69	71	69	279	58,000
Hal Sutton	69	69	69	72	279	58,000
Steve Flesch	69	68	74	69	280	48,000
Blaine McCallister	70	71	70	69	280	48,000
Dudley Hart	69	71	71	70	281	42,000
John Adams	71	69	72	70	282	32,000
Craig Barlow	71	71	73	67	282	32,000
Ronnie Black	68	68	72	74	282	32,000
Chris DiMarco	68	65	70	79	282	32,000
Larry Mize	75	67	72	68	282	32,000
Kenny Perry	70	68	74	70	282	32,000
Willie Wood	73	66	70	73	282	32,000
Jay Don Blake	68	70	70	75	283	21,600
Joe Durant	69	66	74	74	283	21,600
Lee Janzen	71	64	79	69	283	21,600
Loren Roberts	71	69	70	73	283	21,600
Jim McGovern	70	70	73	71	284	13,718.19
Lee Porter	72	68	76	68	284	13,718.19
Barry Cheesman	72	70	70	72	284	13,718.18

	SCORES				TOTAL	MONEY
Dan Forsman	68	69	70	77	284	13,718.18
Jerry Kelly	69	72	72	71	284	13,718.18
Justin Leonard	68	67	76	73	284	13,718.18
Sandy Lyle	70	68	70	76	284	13,718.18
Naomichi Ozaki	71	68	70	75	284	13,718.18
Chris Perry	65	74	70	75	284	13,718.18
Scott Simpson	71	68	70	75	284	13,718.18
Esteban Toledo	69	69	71	75	284	13,718.18
Tommy Armour III	67	70	76	72	285	9,216.67
Bruce Fleisher	72	70	74	69	285	9,216.67
J.L. Lewis	67	74	73	71	285	9,216.67
Mike Springer	71	70	75	69	285	9,216.67
Trevor Dodds	69	70	74	72	285	9,216.66
Brent Geiberger	69	69	73	74	285	9,216.66
Jay Haas	69	72	73	72	286	5,913.34
Franklin Langham	74	68	72	72	286	5,913.34
Lee Rinker	71	71	74	70	286	5,913.34
Vijay Singh	70	72	75	69	286	5,913.34
Brad Elder	71	63	78	74	286	5,913.33
Glen Hnatiuk	74	67	72	73	286	5,913.33
P.H. Horgan III	74	68	72	72	286	5,913.33
Jonathan Kaye	70	71	72	73	286	5,913.33
Michael Muehr	70	69	70	77	286	5,913.33
Tom Pernice, Jr.	69	70	68	79	286	5,913.33
Joey Sindelar	71	71	71	73	286	5,913.33
Mike Weir	67	69	73	77	286	5,913.33
Woody Austin	68	69	73	77	287	4,600
Donnie Hammond	70	69	74	74	287	4,600
Brett Quigley	68	69	73	77	287	4,600
Dave Barr	70	68	77	73	288	4,460
Billy Ray Brown	69	73	76	70	288	4,460
Kelly Gibson	71	68	70	79	288	4,460
Jimmy Johnston	68	70	76	74	288	4,460
Doug Barron	70	72	69	78	289	4,280
Tom Byrum	71	70	74	74	289	4,280
Jesper Parnevik	69	71	75	74	289	4,280
Mike Small	68	71	74	76	289	4,280
Joe Daley	72	70	72	75	289	4,280
Scott Gump	73	69	71	77	290	4,120
Brian Kamm	69	66	78	77	290	4,120
Tom Lehman	71	66	77	76	290	4,120
Hugh Royer III	71	70	76	74	291	4,040
David Edwards	70	68	75	79	292	3,980
Bobby Wadkins	73	69	74	76	292	3,980
Olin Browne	69	73	73	78	293	3,900
Pete Jordan	70	70	72	81	293	3,900
Mike Reid	71	70	78	75	294	3,840
Greg Kraft	72	66	74	83	295	3,800
Wayne Grady	69	72	81	75	297	3,760

Buick Classic

Westchester Country Club, Rye, New York — June 11-14
Par 36-35–71; 6,722 yards — purse, $1,800,000
(Fourth round cancelled — rain.)

	SCORES			TOTAL	MONEY
J.P. Hayes	66	67	68	201	$324,000
Jim Furyk	70	63	68	201	194,400
(Hayes defeated Furyk on first extra hole.)					
Tom Lehman	67	72	65	204	122,400
Bruce Fleisher	68	68	69	205	86,400
Tom Byrum	69	71	66	206	68,400
Jeff Maggert	68	71	67	206	68,400
Kevin Sutherland	64	70	73	207	58,050
Bob Tway	66	70	71	207	58,050
Steve Lowery	66	72	70	208	52,200
Jesper Parnevik	69	67	73	209	46,800
Chris Perry	72	69	68	209	46,800
Brad Faxon	72	69	69	210	35,280
Greg Kraft	69	73	68	210	35,280
Naomichi Ozaki	70	70	70	210	35,280
Hugh Royer III	68	72	70	210	35,280
Craig Stadler	72	70	68	210	35,280
Lee Rinker	73	69	69	211	23,554.29
Joey Sindelar	74	71	66	211	23,554.29
Mike Standly	69	75	67	211	23,554.29
Omar Uresti	72	71	68	211	23,554.29
Mark Calcavecchia	67	71	73	211	23,554.28
Davis Love III	73	68	70	211	23,554.28
Mark Wurtz	68	73	70	211	23,554.28
Paul Azinger	72	73	67	212	13,927.50
Brian Claar	71	75	66	212	13,927.50
Darren Clarke	73	71	68	212	13,927.50
Keith Fergus	68	73	71	212	13,927.50
Steve Jones	70	73	69	212	13,927.50
Brian Kamm	71	70	71	212	13,927.50
Jose Maria Olazabal	73	72	67	212	13,927.50
Vijay Singh	71	70	71	212	13,927.50
Ben Bates	72	70	71	213	9,340
Mark Brooks	72	68	73	213	9,340
Steve Elkington	72	73	68	213	9,340
Bob Friend	72	70	71	213	9,340
Jim Gallagher, Jr.	71	72	70	213	9,340
Lee Porter	68	72	73	213	9,340
David Sutherland	68	75	70	213	9,340
Ted Tryba	74	72	67	213	9,340
Willie Wood	71	73	69	213	9,340
Billy Andrade	74	66	74	214	6,480
Robert Damron	69	71	74	214	6,480
Scott Gump	73	71	70	214	6,480
Guy Hill	73	69	72	214	6,480
Frank Nobilo	74	69	71	214	6,480
Craig Parry	74	72	68	214	6,480
Stewart Cink	74	69	72	215	4,623.43
Nick Faldo	74	70	71	215	4,623.43
Paul Goydos	66	74	75	215	4,623.43
Darrell Kestner	74	71	70	215	4,623.43
John Riegger	72	73	70	215	4,623.43
Lee Westwood	68	74	73	215	4,623.43

	SCORES			TOTAL	MONEY
Steve Jurgensen	70	76	69	215	4,623.42
Olin Browne	73	73	70	216	4,032
Wayne Grady	71	72	73	216	4,032
Kent Jones	74	72	70	216	4,032
Jonathan Kaye	75	70	71	216	4,032
Tim Loustalot	73	70	73	216	4,032
Blaine McCallister	70	73	73	216	4,032
Scott Simpson	73	70	73	216	4,032
Mike Sullivan	72	71	73	216	4,032
Phil Tataurangi	72	72	72	216	4,032
Mark Carnevale	72	73	72	217	3,780
Ben Crenshaw	72	69	76	217	3,780
Joe Durant	74	71	72	217	3,780
Gary Hallberg	75	69	73	217	3,780
Nolan Henke	75	71	71	217	3,780
Bob Gilder	71	75	72	218	3,618
Donnie Hammond	72	73	73	218	3,618
Brett Quigley	72	73	73	218	3,618
Chris Smith	77	69	72	218	3,618
Jim Estes	69	75	75	219	3,474
Bobby Gage	73	73	73	219	3,474
Jeff Gallagher	73	73	73	219	3,474
Franklin Langham	71	75	73	219	3,474
Glen Hnatiuk	73	72	75	220	3,366
Len Mattiace	71	74	75	220	3,366
Frank Lickliter	75	70	76	221	3,312
Tim Conley	73	73	76	222	3,276
Gabriel Hjertstedt	70	76	77	223	3,240
Mike Brisky	73	73	81	227	3,204

U.S. Open Championship

The Olympic Club, Lake Course, San Francisco, California — June 18-21
Par 35-35–70; 6,797 yards — purse, $3,000,000

	SCORES				TOTAL	MONEY
Lee Janzen	73	66	73	68	280	$535,000
Payne Stewart	66	71	70	74	281	315,000
Bob Tway	68	70	73	73	284	201,730
Nick Price	73	68	71	73	285	140,597
Tom Lehman	68	75	68	75	286	107,392
Steve Stricker	73	71	69	73	286	107,392
David Duval	75	68	75	69	287	83,794
Jeff Maggert	69	69	75	74	287	83,794
Lee Westwood	72	74	70	71	287	83,794
Stuart Appleby	73	74	70	71	288	64,490
Stewart Cink	73	68	73	74	288	64,490
Phil Mickelson	71	73	74	70	288	64,490
Jeff Sluman	72	74	74	68	288	64,490
Paul Azinger	75	72	77	65	289	52,214
Jim Furyk	74	73	68	74	289	52,214
Jesper Parnevik	69	74	76	70	289	52,214
*Matt Kuchar	70	69	76	74	289	
Frank Lickliter	73	71	72	74	290	41,833
Colin Montgomerie	70	74	77	69	290	41,833
Jose Maria Olazabal	68	77	71	74	290	41,833
Loren Roberts	71	76	71	72	290	41,833

	SCORES				TOTAL	MONEY
Tiger Woods	74	72	71	73	290	41,833
Glen Day	73	72	71	75	291	34,043
Casey Martin	74	71	74	72	291	34,043
Thomas Bjorn	72	75	70	75	292	25,640
Mark Carnevale	67	73	74	78	292	25,640
Per-Ulrik Johansson	71	75	73	73	292	25,640
Chris Perry	74	71	72	75	292	25,640
Eduardo Romero	72	70	76	74	292	25,640
Vijay Singh	73	72	73	74	292	25,640
D.A. Weibring	72	72	75	73	292	25,640
Chris DiMarco	71	71	74	77	293	18,372
Joe Durant	68	73	76	76	293	18,372
Padraig Harrington	73	72	76	72	293	18,372
John Huston	73	72	72	76	293	18,372
Mark O'Meara	70	76	78	69	293	18,372
Steve Pate	72	75	73	73	293	18,372
Lee Porter	72	67	76	78	293	18,372
Bruce Zabriski	74	71	74	74	293	18,372
Justin Leonard	71	75	77	71	294	15,155
Scott McCarron	72	73	77	72	294	15,155
Frank Nobilo	76	67	76	75	294	15,155
Joe Acosta, Jr.	73	72	76	74	295	12,537
Olin Browne	73	70	77	75	295	12,537
Darren Clarke	74	72	77	72	295	12,537
Tom Kite	70	75	76	74	295	12,537
Jack Nicklaus	73	74	73	75	295	12,537
Joey Sindelar	71	75	75	74	295	12,537
Ernie Els	75	70	75	76	296	9,711
Brad Faxon	73	68	76	79	296	9,711
Michael Reid	76	70	73	77	296	9,711
Scott Verplank	74	72	73	77	296	9,711
Fred Couples	72	75	79	71	297	8,531
John Daly	69	75	75	78	297	8,531
Tim Herron	75	72	77	73	297	8,531
James Johnson	74	73	79	71	297	8,531
Mark Brooks	75	71	76	76	298	8,030
Scott Simpson	72	71	78	79	300	7,844
Rocky Walcher	77	70	77	79	303	7,669
Tom Sipula	75	71	78	81	305	7,549

Out of Final 36 Holes

			TOTAL
Billy Andrade	74	74	148
John Cook	75	73	148
Brad Fabel	75	73	148
Gene Fieger	76	72	148
Brent Geiberger	71	77	148
Derek Gilchrist	74	74	148
Retief Goosen	74	74	148
Jay Haas	76	72	148
Hale Irwin	80	68	148
Patrick Lee	72	76	148
Andrew Magee	70	78	148
Corey Pavin	76	72	148
*Paul Simson	76	72	148
Grant Waite	77	71	148
Tom Watson	73	75	148
Briny Baird	75	74	149
*David Eger	78	71	149
Nick Faldo	77	72	149

	SCORES		TOTAL
Edward Fryatt	73	76	149
Gary Hallberg	77	72	149
Scott Hoch	74	75	149
Steve Jones	72	77	149
Chris Kaufman	77	72	149
Doug Martin	74	75	149
Masashi Ozaki	78	71	149
Paul Stankowski	76	73	149
Omar Uresti	78	71	149
Kevin Wentworth	76	73	149
Mark Calcavecchia	74	76	150
Christian Chernock	73	77	150
Trevor Dodds	74	76	150
Steve Elkington	77	73	150
Jimmy Green	76	74	150
David Kirkpatrick	78	72	150
David Ogrin	70	80	150
Sam Randolph	80	70	150
Clarence Rose	75	75	150
Phil Tataurangi	77	73	150
Mark Wilson	74	76	150
Willie Wood	74	76	150
Grant Clough	78	73	151
Don Pooley	74	77	151
Ian Woosnam	72	79	151
Fuzzy Zoeller	75	76	151
Robert Deruntz	75	77	152
Graham Marsh	75	77	152
Dick Mast	76	76	152
Tim Straub	74	78	152
Tom Sutter	79	73	152
Kirk Triplett	73	79	152
*Vaughn Taylor	76	76	152
Mike Brisky	74	79	153
Brandel Chamblee	76	77	153
Jason Gore	77	76	153
Pete Jordan	81	72	153
Bernhard Langer	75	78	153
Davis Love III	78	75	153
Mike Small	76	77	153
Kevin Sutherland	77	76	153
Garrett Willis	83	70	153
Jason Allen	76	78	154
Shane Bertsch	77	77	154
Jim Estes	77	77	154
Ignacio Garrido	76	78	154
Robert Karlsson	78	76	154
Martin Lonardi	76	78	154
Perry Moss	76	78	154
Perry Parker	75	79	154
Costantino Rocca	71	83	154
Chip Beck	78	77	155
Rick Gehr	73	82	155
Ted Oh	74	81	155
*Ryan Palmer	82	73	155
Curtis Strange	77	78	155
Wes Weston	79	76	155
Guy Boros	77	79	156
Chris Tidland	76	80	156
Rick Todd	80	76	156

	SCORES		TOTAL
Mike Burke, Jr.	81	76	157
Gary March	76	81	157
*Joel Kribel	83	75	158
Jeff Thorsen	77	81	158
Brett Wetterich	78	80	158
Garrett Larson	80	79	159
Ken Peyre-Ferry	80	79	159
Ben Crenshaw	82	78	160
Howard Twitty	79	81	160
Jimmy Johnston	84	78	162
Alan Morin	80	82	162
Rene Rangel	82	80	162
Jeff McMillian	82	81	163
Tom Anderson	84	80	164
Adrian Stills	85	81	166
Richard Ames	86	81	167
Dudley Hart	78		WD
Tommy Tolles			WD

(Professionals who did not complete 72 holes received $5,000.)

Motorola Western Open

Cog Hill Golf & Country Club, Lemont, Illinois — June 25-28
Par 36-36–72; 7,037 yards — purse, $2,200,000

	SCORES				TOTAL	MONEY
Joe Durant	68	67	70	66	271	$396,000
Vijay Singh	68	68	65	72	273	237,600
Dudley Hart	74	70	70	63	277	127,600
Lee Janzen	68	69	69	71	277	127,600
Greg Kraft	67	70	66	75	278	83,600
Steve Stricker	71	69	67	71	278	83,600
Jim Furyk	72	71	68	68	279	70,950
Scott Hoch	71	67	70	71	279	70,950
Stuart Appleby	73	71	68	69	281	49,225
Clark Dennis	71	69	73	68	281	49,225
Dan Forsman	74	71	68	68	281	49,225
Harrison Frazar	74	70	69	68	281	49,225
Justin Leonard	72	72	69	68	281	49,225
Naomichi Ozaki	71	69	68	73	281	49,225
Scott Verplank	75	71	68	67	281	49,225
Tiger Woods	76	67	69	69	281	49,225
Tommy Armour III	72	69	69	72	282	33,000
Skip Kendall	70	69	74	69	282	33,000
Frank Lickliter	75	68	72	67	282	33,000
Robert Damron	74	71	68	70	283	27,500
Duffy Waldorf	74	70	71	68	283	27,500
Tom Byrum	70	71	75	68	284	18,822.23
Nick Price	72	74	69	69	284	18,822.23
Tim Conley	71	70	69	74	284	18,822.22
Steve Flesch	69	70	70	75	284	18,822.22
Scott Gump	71	72	71	70	284	18,822.22
Chris Perry	73	69	69	73	284	18,822.22
Loren Roberts	72	73	68	71	284	18,822.22
Hal Sutton	76	69	69	70	284	18,822.22
Mark Wiebe	74	70	67	73	284	18,822.22
J.P. Hayes	72	72	73	68	285	13,337.50

	SCORES				TOTAL	MONEY
Tim Herron	70	70	74	71	285	13,337.50
Clarence Rose	74	66	72	73	285	13,337.50
Ted Tryba	70	72	70	73	285	13,337.50
Brandel Chamblee	76	70	72	68	286	10,387.15
Jeff Sluman	74	66	76	70	286	10,387.15
Trevor Dodds	75	69	72	70	286	10,387.14
R.W. Eaks	73	73	69	71	286	10,387.14
David Frost	72	69	74	71	286	10,387.14
Phil Mickelson	77	69	69	71	286	10,387.14
Joey Sindelar	73	72	68	73	286	10,387.14
Scott Simpson	75	71	71	70	287	7,920
Kevin Sutherland	73	73	71	70	287	7,920
Tommy Tolles	73	70	74	70	287	7,920
Bob Tway	73	69	72	73	287	7,920
John Huston	74	69	71	74	288	6,600
Larry Rinker	73	69	73	73	288	6,600
Donnie Hammond	72	74	72	71	289	5,596.80
Neal Lancaster	72	71	73	73	289	5,596.80
Doug Martin	77	68	72	72	289	5,596.80
David Toms	72	74	69	74	289	5,596.80
Bobby Wadkins	72	69	72	76	289	5,596.80
Brian Kamm	72	72	73	73	290	5,093
J.L. Lewis	74	70	75	71	290	5,093
Larry Mize	74	71	70	75	290	5,093
Chris Smith	75	71	74	70	290	5,093
Jay Delsing	73	72	71	75	291	4,840
Bruce Fleisher	75	67	76	73	291	4,840
Franklin Langham	74	70	72	75	291	4,840
Jim McGovern	69	72	73	77	291	4,840
Mike Reid	74	69	74	74	291	4,840
Hugh Royer III	72	74	75	70	291	4,840
Payne Stewart	72	74	69	76	291	4,840
*Danny Green	75	70	75	71	291	
Doug Barron	74	71	79	69	293	4,554
Bob Estes	72	73	74	74	293	4,554
Nolan Henke	72	73	71	77	293	4,554
Len Mattiace	73	72	74	74	293	4,554
Billy Mayfair	71	74	74	74	293	4,554
David Ogrin	73	69	78	73	293	4,554
Jim Carter	75	71	74	74	294	4,356
Brad Fabel	74	70	76	74	294	4,356
Tom Pernice, Jr.	73	69	79	73	294	4,356
Wayne Grady	78	68	77	73	296	4,202
Rocco Mediate	72	74	74	76	296	4,202
John Morse	73	69	76	78	296	4,202
Dave Rummells	76	68	77	75	296	4,202
Guy Hill	72	72	73	82	299	4,092

Canon Greater Hartford Open

TPC at River Highlands, Cromwell, Connecticut — July 2-5
Par 35-35–70; 6,820 yards — purse, $2,000,000

	SCORES				TOTAL	MONEY
Olin Browne	67	66	66	67	266	$360,000
Stewart Cink	67	65	67	67	266	176,000
Larry Mize	68	63	66	69	266	176,000

(Browne defeated Cink and Mize on first extra hole.)

	SCORES				TOTAL	MONEY
Fred Funk	70	66	65	66	267	82,666.67
Duffy Waldorf	70	67	64	66	267	82,666.67
Doug Tewell	66	66	68	67	267	82,666.66
David Duval	68	65	66	69	268	64,500
Scott Hoch	65	68	64	71	268	64,500
Len Mattiace	67	69	66	67	269	54,000
Kenny Perry	65	69	67	68	269	54,000
Joey Sindelar	69	66	69	65	269	54,000
Mark Brooks	69	65	67	69	270	44,000
Vijay Singh	68	67	73	62	270	44,000
Billy Andrade	68	69	66	68	271	37,000
Mike Springer	71	67	68	65	271	37,000
Mark Calcavecchia	70	69	64	69	272	31,000
Joe Durant	70	68	69	65	272	31,000
Grant Waite	68	64	65	75	272	31,000
Willie Wood	70	66	64	72	272	31,000
Jim Carter	68	71	67	67	273	22,480
Neal Lancaster	71	63	69	70	273	22,480
John Riegger	67	70	67	69	273	22,480
Gene Sauers	71	65	68	69	273	22,480
David Toms	72	66	70	65	273	22,480
Ben Bates	69	68	67	70	274	15,266.67
Steve Flesch	71	66	67	70	274	15,266.67
Donnie Hammond	67	70	67	70	274	15,266.67
Fuzzy Zoeller	69	68	68	69	274	15,266.67
Chris DiMarco	70	64	68	72	274	15,266.66
Kevin Sutherland	66	67	69	72	274	15,266.66
Keith Fergus	69	68	68	70	275	11,860
Justin Leonard	70	68	66	71	275	11,860
Spike McRoy	66	72	69	68	275	11,860
Lee Porter	69	70	66	70	275	11,860
Kirk Triplett	72	67	67	69	275	11,860
Glen Hnatiuk	70	68	70	68	276	8,209.10
Jeff Gallagher	68	67	72	69	276	8,209.09
Scott Gump	68	62	72	74	276	8,209.09
Jay Haas	71	66	67	72	276	8,209.09
Brian Henninger	68	69	70	69	276	8,209.09
Tim Herron	67	70	67	72	276	8,209.09
Greg Kraft	69	67	67	73	276	8,209.09
J.L. Lewis	69	67	69	71	276	8,209.09
Andrew Magee	71	65	67	73	276	8,209.09
Vance Veazey	74	65	68	69	276	8,209.09
Bobby Wadkins	73	65	67	71	276	8,209.09
Bruce Fleisher	69	70	68	70	277	5,022.23
Dave Stockton, Jr.	68	69	70	70	277	5,022.23
Paul Azinger	66	72	68	71	277	5,022.22
Mark Carnevale	69	70	67	71	277	5,022.22
Nolan Henke	69	69	68	71	277	5,022.22
Jonathan Kaye	67	66	73	71	277	5,022.22
Chris Smith	68	68	70	71	277	5,022.22
Omar Uresti	67	64	72	74	277	5,022.22
Pete Morgan	64	71	69	73	277	5,022.22
Guy Boros	70	68	70	70	278	4,460
Jim Estes	67	70	69	72	278	4,460
Brad Faxon	68	70	74	66	278	4,460
Harrison Frazar	66	67	73	72	278	4,460
Jimmy Johnston	67	70	71	70	278	4,460
Doug Martin	69	68	69	72	278	4,460
*J.J. Henry	68	71	69	70	278	
Lennie Clements	74	65	69	71	279	4,300

	SCORES				TOTAL	MONEY
Esteban Toledo	69	68	71	71	279	4,300
Craig Barlow	72	67	70	71	280	4,160
Joe Daley	70	69	67	74	280	4,160
Bobby Gage	72	66	70	72	280	4,160
Brent Geiberger	67	71	68	74	280	4,160
Kent Jones	72	67	70	71	280	4,160
Richard Coughlan	69	70	69	73	281	4,020
Frank Lickliter	69	69	74	69	281	4,020
Gary Hallberg	72	67	72	71	282	3,920
Blaine McCallister	73	66	69	74	282	3,920
Ted Tryba	68	70	70	74	282	3,920
Kevin Wentworth	69	70	72	72	283	3,840
John Daly	71	68	70	76	285	3,800

Quad City Classic

Oakwood Country Club, Coal Valley, Illinois — July 9-12
Par 35-35–70; 6,796 yards — purse, $1,550,000

	SCORES				TOTAL	MONEY
Steve Jones	64	65	68	66	263	$279,000
Scott Gump	65	67	64	68	264	167,400
Kenny Perry	65	65	67	68	265	105,400
David Toms	65	65	65	71	266	74,400
Brad Fabel	68	66	65	68	267	54,443.75
Fred Funk	66	70	65	66	267	54,443.75
Scott McCarron	67	66	66	68	267	54,443.75
D.A. Weibring	64	68	65	70	267	54,443.75
Russ Cochran	65	66	70	67	268	40,300
Dave Stockton, Jr.	64	71	68	65	268	40,300
Hal Sutton	64	68	71	65	268	40,300
Scott Verplank	67	66	71	64	268	40,300
Jim Carter	67	67	68	67	269	29,062.50
Paul Goydos	67	68	66	68	269	29,062.50
Frank Lickliter	65	64	68	72	269	29,062.50
Tom Pernice, Jr.	67	71	68	63	269	29,062.50
Ben Bates	71	67	66	66	270	17,192.09
Curt Byrum	63	69	72	66	270	17,192.09
John Morse	66	66	72	66	270	17,192.09
Brett Quigley	68	68	69	65	270	17,192.09
Doug Barron	65	72	66	67	270	17,192.08
Andy Bean	66	68	68	68	270	17,192.08
Mark Carnevale	67	67	66	70	270	17,192.08
Brian Claar	70	66	64	70	270	17,192.08
Dan Forsman	67	69	66	68	270	17,192.08
Nolan Henke	65	67	67	71	270	17,192.08
Mike Springer	66	67	68	69	270	17,192.08
Stan Utley	67	67	68	68	270	17,192.08
Lennie Clements	65	71	70	65	271	9,855.50
Robin Freeman	69	67	71	64	271	9,855.50
P.H. Horgan III	65	66	71	69	271	9,855.50
David Sutherland	66	67	69	69	271	9,855.50
Omar Uresti	65	70	68	68	271	9,855.50
Mark Wiebe	70	65	67	69	271	9,855.50
Richard Coughlan	65	71	72	64	272	7,478.67
Mike Hulbert	70	68	70	64	272	7,478.67
Mike Small	66	70	69	67	272	7,478.67

	SCORES				TOTAL	MONEY
Mike Weir	69	68	69	66	272	7,478.67
Jeff Sluman	70	68	65	69	272	7,478.66
Doug Tewell	65	71	67	69	272	7,478.66
Guy Boros	68	68	70	67	273	4,719.16
Greg Kraft	67	71	68	67	273	4,719.16
Jim McGovern	68	70	69	66	273	4,719.16
Gene Sauers	66	70	71	66	273	4,719.16
Kevin Wentworth	69	69	68	67	273	4,719.16
Barry Cheesman	68	66	67	72	273	4,719.15
Keith Clearwater	66	69	69	69	273	4,719.15
Tim Conley	72	63	68	70	273	4,719.15
Bruce Fleisher	70	67	67	69	273	4,719.15
Steve Flesch	66	69	70	68	273	4,719.15
Bobby Gage	65	69	71	68	273	4,719.15
John Riegger	65	68	72	68	273	4,719.15
Hugh Royer III	66	69	69	69	273	4,719.15
Dave Barr	66	66	70	72	274	3,487.50
Bobby Clampett	66	70	68	70	274	3,487.50
Jim Estes	69	64	69	72	274	3,487.50
Kelly Gibson	67	68	72	67	274	3,487.50
Peter Jacobsen	70	66	69	69	274	3,487.50
Skip Kendall	69	66	68	71	274	3,487.50
Doug Martin	71	66	63	74	274	3,487.50
Chris Perry	66	70	66	72	274	3,487.50
Mike Brisky	70	67	69	69	275	3,301.50
Joe Daley	68	66	71	70	275	3,301.50
Franklin Langham	69	68	68	70	275	3,301.50
Shaun Micheel	70	68	68	69	275	3,301.50
Glen Hnatiuk	65	67	72	72	276	3,177.50
Tim Loustalot	69	69	68	70	276	3,177.50
Casey Martin	66	68	73	69	276	3,177.50
Chris Smith	68	70	70	68	276	3,177.50
Olin Browne	69	69	72	67	277	3,022.50
Jay Delsing	66	71	71	69	277	3,022.50
Keith Fergus	67	68	69	73	277	3,022.50
Brian Henninger	66	69	70	72	277	3,022.50
David Ogrin	67	68	69	73	277	3,022.50
Phil Tataurangi	72	66	69	70	277	3,022.50
David Edwards	67	68	71	72	278	2,883
Barry Jaeckel	69	68	72	69	278	2,883
Tony Sills	67	71	71	69	278	2,883
Wayne Grady	69	67	72	71	279	2,805.50
Mike Smith	69	68	73	69	279	2,805.50
David Peoples	66	72	72	71	281	2,743.50
Willie Wood	69	67	74	71	281	2,743.50
Jack Renner	72	66	75	71	284	2,697

Deposit Guaranty Golf Classic

Annandale Golf Club, Madison, Mississippi — July 16-19
Par 36-36–72; 7,157 yards — purse, $1,200,000

	SCORES				TOTAL	MONEY
Fred Funk	69	64	69	68	270	$216,000
Paul Goydos	66	66	72	68	272	89,600
Franklin Langham	67	67	70	68	272	89,600
Tim Loustalot	69	69	68	66	272	89,600

	SCORES				TOTAL	MONEY
P.H. Horgan III	76	66	66	65	273	45,600
John Maginnes	70	71	66	66	273	45,600
Allan Doyle	67	69	69	69	274	36,150
Jerry Kelly	70	66	70	68	274	36,150
Chris Smith	66	68	71	69	274	36,150
Kirk Triplett	68	72	68	66	274	36,150
Ben Bates	69	70	70	66	275	27,600
Jay Delsing	67	73	69	66	275	27,600
Grant Waite	68	70	67	70	275	27,600
Mike Brisky	68	68	66	74	276	21,000
Tim Conley	69	69	67	71	276	21,000
Hal Sutton	69	71	66	70	276	21,000
Doug Tewell	66	66	72	72	276	21,000
Brian Henninger	66	70	69	72	277	16,800
Jonathan Kaye	67	70	72	68	277	16,800
Paul Stankowski	74	67	67	69	277	16,800
Richard Coughlan	74	69	67	68	278	12,000
Keith Fergus	69	68	69	72	278	12,000
Robin Freeman	73	67	70	68	278	12,000
David Ogrin	75	68	66	69	278	12,000
Esteban Toledo	71	66	72	69	278	12,000
Kevin Wentworth	74	65	71	68	278	12,000
Billy Ray Brown	70	72	66	71	279	7,987.50
Mark Carnevale	70	67	72	70	279	7,987.50
Mike Heinen	69	70	68	72	279	7,987.50
Steve Lowery	71	68	71	69	279	7,987.50
Steve Pate	71	66	71	71	279	7,987.50
Sam Randolph	74	66	72	67	279	7,987.50
Sonny Skinner	72	67	71	69	279	7,987.50
Dave Stockton, Jr.	72	70	66	71	279	7,987.50
Chris DiMarco	70	69	69	72	280	6,045
Doug Dunakey	72	68	70	70	280	6,045
John Riegger	72	65	71	72	280	6,045
Mike Weir	68	74	73	65	280	6,045
Guy Boros	68	70	74	69	281	4,560
Brian Claar	69	69	74	69	281	4,560
Mike Donald	70	72	71	68	281	4,560
Brad Fabel	68	71	75	67	281	4,560
Kelly Gibson	75	66	66	74	281	4,560
Neal Lancaster	72	71	72	66	281	4,560
Lee Porter	69	73	71	68	281	4,560
Richard Zokol	68	72	73	68	281	4,560
*Rett Crowder	69	74	68	70	281	
John Adams	71	68	68	75	282	3,172.80
Marco Dawson	72	70	70	70	282	3,172.80
Lan Gooch	71	70	69	72	282	3,172.80
Dick Mast	74	68	73	67	282	3,172.80
Spike McRoy	70	69	72	71	282	3,172.80
Curt Byrum	65	73	71	74	283	2,832
Greg Kraft	71	70	70	72	283	2,832
Willie Wood	71	72	70	70	283	2,832
Bradley Hughes	70	70	70	74	284	2,724
J.L. Lewis	71	70	69	74	284	2,724
Mike Springer	70	72	68	74	284	2,724
David Toms	74	69	74	67	284	2,724
Craig Barlow	71	71	71	72	285	2,652
Gene Sauers	71	70	71	73	285	2,652
Jack O'Keefe	73	70	75	68	286	2,592
Tony Sills	69	73	75	69	286	2,592
Tray Tyner	71	72	72	71	286	2,592

	SCORES				TOTAL	MONEY
Kent Jones	70	73	71	73	287	2,508
Bob Lohr	69	72	75	71	287	2,508
Blaine McCallister	72	70	71	74	287	2,508
Greg Powers	69	67	77	74	287	2,508
Dan Halldorson	73	69	75	71	288	2,436
Hugh Royer III	68	74	73	73	288	2,436
Taylor Smith	73	70	76	71	290	2,400
Bunky Henry	73	70	79	79	301	2,376

CVS Charity Classic

Pleasant Valley Country Club, Sutton, Massachusetts — July 23-26
Par 36-35–71; 7,110 yards — purse, $1,500,000

	SCORES				TOTAL	MONEY
Steve Pate	70	65	67	67	269	$270,000
Scott Hoch	68	68	69	65	270	132,000
Bradley Hughes	68	69	67	66	270	132,000
Mike Heinen	74	65	65	67	271	62,000
Nolan Henke	69	65	70	67	271	62,000
Willie Wood	64	69	68	70	271	62,000
Bill Glasson	69	68	67	68	272	43,650
Loren Roberts	71	70	65	66	272	43,650
Dave Stockton, Jr.	67	68	66	71	272	43,650
Esteban Toledo	69	71	68	64	272	43,650
Mark Wiebe	69	67	68	68	272	43,650
Paul Azinger	68	65	71	69	273	31,500
Steve Flesch	66	70	67	70	273	31,500
Larry Rinker	67	69	71	66	273	31,500
Olin Browne	70	68	65	71	274	24,750
John Cook	70	66	69	69	274	24,750
Kelly Gibson	71	68	67	68	274	24,750
Frank Lickliter	71	69	64	70	274	24,750
Scott Gump	73	68	66	68	275	18,825
Brian Henninger	71	66	69	69	275	18,825
Steve Lowery	69	67	68	71	275	18,825
Omar Uresti	67	72	66	70	275	18,825
Craig Parry	69	71	68	68	276	15,000
Mike Springer	65	67	72	72	276	15,000
Fred Funk	70	66	70	71	277	11,962.50
P.H. Horgan III	64	72	67	74	277	11,962.50
Jim McGovern	70	70	67	70	277	11,962.50
Chris Perry	68	71	69	69	277	11,962.50
Keith Fergus	67	70	70	71	278	9,750
Gary Hallberg	69	69	71	69	278	9,750
John Maginnes	67	69	69	73	278	9,750
Blaine McCallister	71	69	67	71	278	9,750
Lee Rinker	67	67	73	71	278	9,750
Guy Boros	67	70	72	70	279	7,414.29
Chris Smith	71	70	70	68	279	7,414.29
Phil Tataurangi	71	66	72	70	279	7,414.29
Fuzzy Zoeller	68	65	74	72	279	7,414.29
Brad Faxon	68	67	69	75	279	7,414.28
Robin Freeman	70	71	66	72	279	7,414.28
D.A. Weibring	67	71	69	72	279	7,414.28
Brian Claar	69	69	70	72	280	5,107.50
Lennie Clements	73	68	70	69	280	5,107.50

	SCORES				TOTAL	MONEY
Niclas Fasth	69	71	69	71	280	5,107.50
Pete Jordan	70	71	70	69	280	5,107.50
Brian Kamm	69	71	66	74	280	5,107.50
Doug Martin	68	69	71	72	280	5,107.50
Dicky Pride	71	67	71	71	280	5,107.50
Brett Quigley	71	69	69	71	280	5,107.50
Chris DiMarco	71	70	70	70	281	3,790
Greg Kraft	70	70	68	73	281	3,790
Rocco Mediate	69	72	73	67	281	3,790
Ronnie Black	71	70	73	68	282	3,462.86
Curt Byrum	71	69	70	72	282	3,462.86
Joe Durant	69	71	71	71	282	3,462.86
Pete Morgan	70	71	71	70	282	3,462.86
Jeff Sluman	67	72	71	72	282	3,462.86
Fran Quinn	70	71	69	72	282	3,462.85
Iain Steel	68	72	70	72	282	3,462.85
Dick Mast	72	69	69	73	283	3,285
Sonny Skinner	70	70	74	69	283	3,285
Grant Waite	72	69	69	73	283	3,285
Richard Zokol	68	70	76	69	283	3,285
Andy Bean	70	67	71	76	284	3,165
Allen Doyle	70	69	73	72	284	3,165
Wayne Grady	72	66	76	70	284	3,165
Kevin Sutherland	71	70	70	73	284	3,165
Peter Jacobsen	69	69	72	75	285	3,090
Mike Donald	67	74	75	70	286	3,030
Joey Sindelar	72	69	75	70	286	3,030
Lance Ten Broeck	67	69	75	75	286	3,030
Bruce Fleisher	69	72	69	77	287	2,940
Jeff Gallagher	69	71	73	74	287	2,940
Mark Pfeil	69	70	77	71	287	2,940
Dave Rummells	73	68	73	74	288	2,880
*James Driscoll	70	70	72	76	288	
Don Pooley	71	69	73	76	289	2,850
Steve Jurgensen	72	69	69	80	290	2,820
Gene Sauers	71	70	72	78	291	2,790
Lon Hinkle	74	66	77	75	292	2,760

FedEx St. Jude Classic

TPC at Southwind, Memphis, Tennessee
Par 36-35–71; 7,006 yards

July 30-August 2
purse, $1,800,000

	SCORES				TOTAL	MONEY
Nick Price	65	67	70	66	268	$324,000
Jeff Sluman	70	67	66	65	268	194,400
(Price defeated Sluman on second extra hole.)						
Glen Day	69	64	72	65	270	122,400
Bob Estes	68	67	67	69	271	86,400
Tim Conley	68	68	67	69	272	72,000
Paul Goydos	72	66	69	67	274	72,000
Paul Azinger	65	69	69	72	275	54,225
Robert Damron	68	74	66	67	275	54,225
Jay Haas	70	67	70	68	275	54,225
Kirk Triplett	68	70	69	68	275	54,225
Scott Hoch	66	68	74	68	276	45,000
Michael Bradley	70	69	71	67	277	32,175

	SCORES				TOTAL	MONEY
Barry Cheesman	73	65	72	67	277	32,175
Joe Durant	71	67	67	72	277	32,175
Tim Herron	72	66	71	68	277	32,175
Neal Lancaster	67	65	77	68	277	32,175
Lee Porter	73	69	69	66	277	32,175
Scott Verplank	69	70	67	71	277	32,175
Kevin Wentworth	67	70	67	73	277	32,175
Mike Hulbert	70	70	69	69	278	19,500
Rocco Mediate	69	72	67	70	278	19,500
David Ogrin	74	67	70	67	278	19,500
Larry Rinker	67	69	71	71	278	19,500
Kevin Sutherland	67	70	70	71	278	19,500
Omar Uresti	69	68	72	69	278	19,500
Brandel Chamblee	67	72	74	66	279	13,050
Chris DiMarco	72	70	68	69	279	13,050
Lee Janzen	69	73	70	67	279	13,050
John Riegger	69	68	76	66	279	13,050
Esteban Toledo	69	70	73	67	279	13,050
Mark Wiebe	70	69	69	71	279	13,050
Mark Carnevale	66	71	76	67	280	10,188
Russ Cochran	65	70	75	70	280	10,188
Bruce Fleisher	74	66	71	69	280	10,188
Blaine McCallister	70	71	68	71	280	10,188
Hal Sutton	69	70	68	73	280	10,188
Ben Bates	73	65	71	72	281	7,920
Jay Delsing	72	70	69	70	281	7,920
Bob Friend	69	70	71	71	281	7,920
Clarence Rose	73	66	72	70	281	7,920
Chris Smith	70	70	74	67	281	7,920
Mike Weir	69	71	70	71	281	7,920
Dudley Hart	67	74	68	73	282	5,616
P.H. Horgan III	67	70	75	70	282	5,616
Bradley Hughes	68	71	72	71	282	5,616
Skip Kendall	71	69	67	75	282	5,616
Jim McGovern	70	72	70	70	282	5,616
Shaun Micheel	69	71	71	71	282	5,616
Dicky Pride	74	68	68	72	282	5,616
Billy Andrade	71	70	69	73	283	4,308
Ronnie Black	70	69	76	68	283	4,308
Donnie Hammond	66	69	79	69	283	4,308
Mike Small	72	67	72	72	283	4,308
Paul Stankowski	73	69	69	72	283	4,308
Ted Tryba	73	67	73	70	283	4,308
Jay Don Blake	69	69	71	75	284	4,014
Brian Henninger	71	70	74	69	284	4,014
Jonathan Kaye	71	70	76	67	284	4,014
Brett Quigley	72	69	72	71	284	4,014
Lee Rinker	72	69	71	72	284	4,014
Loren Roberts	68	73	72	71	284	4,014
Guy Boros	72	70	71	72	285	3,798
Keith Clearwater	68	73	73	71	285	3,798
Mike Reid	70	72	75	68	285	3,798
David Sutherland	75	67	69	74	285	3,798
Bob Tway	69	69	71	76	285	3,798
Willie Wood	73	69	72	71	285	3,798
Clark Dennis	71	69	75	71	286	3,636
J.P. Hayes	74	68	70	74	286	3,636
Jimmy Johnston	71	70	72	73	286	3,636
Jerry Kelly	71	69	75	72	287	3,564
*David Gossett	66	70	74	77	287	

	SCORES				TOTAL	MONEY
Doug Martin	74	68	72	74	288	3,528
Richard Coughlan	73	68	75	73	289	3,456
Larry Mize	71	71	75	72	289	3,456
David Toms	72	69	76	72	289	3,456
Mike Standly	71	71	74	77	293	3,384
Michael Christie	70	69	82	76	297	3,348

Buick Open

Warwick Hills Golf & Country Club,
Grand Blanc, Michigan
Par 36-36–72; 7,105 yards

August 6-9
purse, $1,800,000

	SCORES				TOTAL	MONEY
Billy Mayfair	70	69	65	67	271	$324,000
Scott Verplank	71	67	71	64	273	194,400
Andrew Magee	69	71	70	64	274	122,400
Eric Booker	71	68	70	66	275	79,200
Tiger Woods	71	67	69	68	275	79,200
Joey Sindelar	69	71	72	64	276	62,550
Steve Stricker	69	67	68	72	276	62,550
Phil Blackmar	67	68	70	72	277	50,400
Brandel Chamblee	65	68	72	72	277	50,400
Jeff Gallagher	70	70	71	66	277	50,400
Vijay Singh	66	70	69	72	277	50,400
Dudley Hart	66	69	75	68	278	37,800
Kent Jones	67	67	73	71	278	37,800
Hal Sutton	70	67	70	71	278	37,800
Stewart Cink	70	70	71	68	279	26,145
Fred Funk	70	69	68	72	279	26,145
Paul Goydos	68	73	68	70	279	26,145
Gary Hallberg	66	73	70	70	279	26,145
Scott McCarron	67	71	70	71	279	26,145
David Ogrin	70	70	67	72	279	26,145
Jeff Sluman	68	69	72	70	279	26,145
Bob Tway	67	73	69	70	279	26,145
John Cook	69	70	70	71	280	15,570
J.L. Lewis	65	76	72	67	280	15,570
Doug Martin	69	72	69	70	280	15,570
Chris Perry	67	72	72	69	280	15,570
John Riegger	68	74	70	68	280	15,570
Clarence Rose	67	73	70	70	280	15,570
Jim Carter	74	66	72	69	281	11,198.58
Woody Austin	69	69	69	74	281	11,198.57
Brent Geiberger	68	70	69	74	281	11,198.57
Donnie Hammond	71	71	67	72	281	11,198.57
Bradley Hughes	69	73	65	74	281	11,198.57
Jonathan Kaye	70	71	66	74	281	11,198.57
Rocco Mediate	68	70	73	70	281	11,198.57
Doug Barron	72	69	74	67	282	8,850
Skip Kendall	70	72	71	69	282	8,850
Jim McGovern	69	73	71	69	282	8,850
David Berganio, Jr.	69	71	71	72	283	6,487.20
Glen Day	69	72	70	72	283	6,487.20
Jay Delsing	73	68	70	72	283	6,487.20
Chris DiMarco	67	73	69	74	283	6,487.20
Franklin Langham	71	70	70	72	283	6,487.20
Blaine McCallister	70	70	72	71	283	6,487.20

	SCORES				TOTAL	MONEY
Paul Stankowski	68	73	72	70	283	6,487.20
Curtis Strange	71	71	70	71	283	6,487.20
Ted Tryba	69	71	71	72	283	6,487.20
Duffy Waldorf	72	70	73	68	283	6,487.20
Steve Elkington	70	72	73	69	284	4,361.15
Pete Jordan	72	69	75	68	284	4,361.15
Joe Acosta, Jr.	68	73	71	72	284	4,361.14
J.P. Hayes	67	72	73	72	284	4,361.14
Len Mattiace	72	70	68	74	284	4,361.14
Lee Porter	70	72	72	70	284	4,361.14
Phil Tataurangi	74	68	70	72	284	4,361.14
Jay Don Blake	72	68	72	73	285	3,960
Bruce Fleisher	71	71	69	74	285	3,960
Scott Hebert	73	69	73	70	285	3,960
Naomichi Ozaki	70	70	74	71	285	3,960
Don Pooley	71	70	72	72	285	3,960
Jeff Roth	73	69	71	72	285	3,960
Hugh Royer III	72	69	72	72	285	3,960
Mike Standly	69	70	73	73	285	3,960
D.A. Weibring	70	72	74	69	285	3,960
Craig Barlow	68	71	74	73	286	3,708
Andy Bean	72	70	72	72	286	3,708
David Edwards	72	69	75	70	286	3,708
Harrison Frazar	71	71	71	73	286	3,708
Lee Rinker	70	70	76	70	286	3,708
Billy Ray Brown	75	67	71	74	287	3,582
Nolan Henke	69	72	74	72	287	3,582
Tommy Armour III	70	71	76	71	288	3,510
Jimmy Johnston	69	72	72	75	288	3,510
Mark Brooks	70	71	77	71	289	3,456
Fuzzy Zoeller	73	67	77	77	294	3,420

PGA Championship

Sahalee Country Club, Redmond, Washington — August 13-16
Par 35-35–70; 6,906 yards — purse, $3,000,000

	SCORES				TOTAL	MONEY
Vijay Singh	70	66	67	68	271	$540,000
Steve Stricker	69	68	66	70	273	324,000
Steve Elkington	69	69	69	67	274	204,000
Nick Price	70	73	68	65	276	118,000
Mark O'Meara	69	70	69	68	276	118,000
Frank Lickliter	68	71	69	68	276	118,000
Billy Mayfair	73	67	67	70	277	89,500
Davis Love III	70	68	69	70	277	89,500
John Cook	71	68	70	69	278	80,000
Kenny Perry	69	72	70	68	279	69,000
Tiger Woods	66	72	70	71	279	69,000
Skip Kendall	72	68	68	71	279	69,000
Brad Faxon	70	68	74	68	280	46,000
Fred Couples	74	71	67	68	280	46,000
Bob Tway	69	76	67	68	280	46,000
Paul Azinger	68	73	70	69	280	46,000
Bill Glasson	68	74	69	69	280	46,000
Steve Flesch	75	69	67	69	280	46,000
John Huston	70	71	68	71	280	46,000
Robert Allenby	72	68	69	71	280	46,000

	SCORES				TOTAL	MONEY
Ernie Els	72	72	71	66	281	32,000
Andrew Magee	70	68	72	71	281	32,000
Per-Ulrik Johansson	69	74	71	68	282	26,000
Fred Funk	70	71	71	70	282	26,000
Scott Gump	68	69	72	73	282	26,000
Greg Kraft	71	73	65	73	282	26,000
Jeff Sluman	71	73	70	69	283	20,500
Hal Sutton	72	68	72	71	283	20,500
Glen Day	68	71	75	70	284	17,100
Tom Lehman	71	71	70	72	284	17,100
Ian Woosnam	70	75	67	72	284	17,100
Lee Rinker	70	70	71	73	284	17,100
Scott Hoch	72	69	70	73	284	17,100
Phil Mickelson	70	70	78	67	285	14,250
Bob Estes	68	76	69	72	285	14,250
Paul Goydos	70	70	72	73	285	14,250
Russ Cochran	69	71	70	75	285	14,250
Craig Stadler	69	74	71	72	286	12,750
Duffy Waldorf	74	70	70	72	286	12,750
Joey Sindelar	71	71	75	70	287	11,250
Jay Haas	72	73	73	69	287	11,250
Joe Durant	75	68	74	70	287	11,250
Carlos Franco	71	70	73	73	287	11,250
Naomichi Ozaki	73	71	75	69	288	7,990
Jeff Maggert	71	73	73	71	288	7,990
Steve Lowery	76	69	72	71	288	7,990
David Ogrin	73	72	71	72	288	7,990
Kevin Sutherland	74	71	71	72	288	7,990
Colin Montgomerie	70	67	77	74	288	7,990
P.H. Horgan III	71	71	72	74	288	7,990
Mark Calcavecchia	70	73	71	74	288	7,990
Dudley Hart	70	75	69	74	288	7,990
Billy Andrade	68	77	68	75	288	7,990
Nick Faldo	73	71	72	73	289	6,500
Scott Verplank	71	71	71	76	289	6,500
Ted Tryba	70	74	76	70	290	6,175
Mark Brooks	72	73	72	73	290	6,175
Brian Watts	72	73	72	73	290	6,175
Jim Carter	71	73	72	74	290	6,175
David Frost	70	69	76	75	290	6,175
Jay Don Blake	70	72	73	75	290	6,175
Trevor Dodds	69	75	75	72	291	5,900
Tom Byrum	72	71	74	74	291	5,900
Olin Browne	73	71	71	76	291	5,900
Robert Karlsson	71	73	75	73	292	5,750
Shigeki Maruyama	68	77	73	74	292	5,750
Loren Roberts	72	71	74	75	292	5,750
Stephen Leaney	72	70	72	79	293	5,650
Andrew Coltart	70	75	75	74	294	5,600
David Sutherland	77	68	77	73	295	5,550
Brent Geiberger	73	70	79	74	296	5,450
Craig Parry	70	75	74	77	296	5,450
Brad Fabel	73	72	73	78	296	5,450
Chris Perry	73	71	75	78	297	5,350
Tim Herron	73	70	79	76	298	5,300

Out of Final 36 Holes

			TOTAL
Robert Thompson	73	73	146
Larry Mize	75	71	146

	SCORES		TOTAL
Paul Stankowski	72	74	146
Jesper Parnevik	70	76	146
Len Mattiace	71	75	146
Ben Crenshaw	70	76	146
Jim Furyk	72	74	146
Rocco Mediate	75	72	147
Costantino Rocca	73	74	147
Gene Fieger	74	73	147
Tommy Armour III	78	69	147
Stewart Cink	73	74	147
Justin Leonard	70	77	147
Mark Wiebe	75	72	147
Scott McCarron	69	78	147
Retief Goosen	73	74	147
Harrison Frazar	69	78	147
Scott Simpson	70	78	148
Eduardo Romero	70	78	148
Greg Chalmers	75	73	148
Masashi Ozaki	74	74	148
Thomas Bjorn	75	73	148
Brandt Jobe	70	78	148
Ignacio Garrido	73	75	148
Mark Mielke	74	74	148
Eddie Terasa	72	76	148
Michael Burke, Jr.	75	73	148
David Toms	72	76	148
Tom Watson	72	76	148
Lee Janzen	76	72	148
Clark Dennis	73	75	148
Stephen Keppler	73	76	149
Jay Overton	77	72	149
Jose Maria Olazabal	75	74	149
Bob Gaus	72	77	149
Lee Westwood	74	76	150
Tom Kite	73	77	150
Stuart Appleby	77	73	150
Kent Stauffer	74	76	150
Jim Schuman	71	79	150
J.P. Hayes	74	76	150
Neal Lancaster	75	75	150
Payne Stewart	76	74	150
Corey Pavin	71	79	150
Kirk Triplett	73	77	150
Bob Boyd	77	74	151
Ronald McDougal	77	74	151
Steve Pate	72	79	151
Bob Ford	72	79	151
John Daly	80	72	152
Robert Damron	74	78	152
Tommy Tolles	80	72	152
Greg Turner	72	80	152
Scott Williams	78	74	152
Frank Nobilo	75	78	153
Bruce Zabriski	79	74	153
Peter Lonard	72	81	153
Patrik Sjoland	74	79	153
Jeff Thomsen	78	76	154
Phil Blackmar	79	75	154
Todd Smith	77	77	154
David Duval	76	78	154

	SCORES		TOTAL
Gabriel Hjertstedt	76	78	154
Karl Kimball	80	75	155
Chris Tucker	78	78	156
Al Geiberger	81	77	158
Wayne Grady	76	82	158
Bob Groff	84	74	158
Will Frantz	81	77	158
Grant Waite	79	79	158
Ron Stelten	78	81	159
Ken Schall	79	80	159
Jeffrey Lankford	78	81	159
Paul Earnest	85	82	167

(Professionals who did not complete 72 holes received $1,500.)

Sprint International

Castle Pines Golf Club, Castle Rock, Colorado — August 20-23
Par 36-36–72; 7,559 yards — purse, $2,000,000

	POINTS				TOTAL	MONEY
Vijay Singh	15	12	6	14	47	$360,000
Phil Mickelson	8	5	16	12	41	176,000
Willie Wood	9	8	15	9	41	176,000
Tiger Woods	14	3	14	7	38	96,000
Rocco Mediate	7	9	14	7	37	80,000
Brad Faxon	3	9	11	13	36	64,750
Steve Flesch	12	11	5	8	36	64,750
Brandt Jobe	13	9	5	9	36	64,750
Bob Tway	4	9	7	16	36	64,750
Steve Elkington	9	8	8	10	35	54,000
David Toms	7	4	7	16	34	50,000
Brandel Chamblee	6	11	2	14	33	46,000
Peter Jacobsen	2	12	11	7	32	40,000
Jesper Parnevik	5	16	3	8	32	40,000
Andrew Magee	10	6	2	13	31	35,000
Kirk Triplett	11	0	14	6	31	35,000
Tom Pernice, Jr.	4	10	6	10	30	32,000
David Sutherland	13	9	1	6	29	30,000
Chris Perry	8	3	7	10	28	28,000
Steve Jones	10	-2	11	8	27	26,000
Stewart Cink	6	8	7	5	26	20,800
Davis Love III	13	7	5	1	26	20,800
Billy Mayfair	5	3	14	4	26	20,800
Larry Rinker	4	10	5	7	26	20,800
Mike Weir	12	-3	9	8	26	20,800
Jim Carter	15	4	1	5	25	15,400
Jay Haas	2	6	14	3	25	15,400
Greg Turner	4	5	12	4	25	15,400
Stuart Appleby	3	11	8	1	23	13,600
John Riegger	11	1	7	4	23	13,600
Mike Reid	9	1	8	5	23	13,600
Olin Browne	4	4	13	1	22	11,833.33
Kent Jones	7	7	6	2	22	11,833.33
Esteban Toledo	-2	14	7	3	22	11,833.33
Dudley Hart	4	9	5	2	20	10,550
Joey Sindelar	9	6	4	1	20	10,550

	POINTS				TOTAL	MONEY
Robert Allenby	0	12	10	-3	19	9,600
Mark Brooks	9	4	13	7	19	9,600
Andy Bean	-3	12	11	-2	18	9,000
Clark Dennis	3	11	5	-3	16	8,600
Neal Lancaster	2	7	9	-5	13	8,200

IN THE MONEY

				TOTAL	MONEY
Craig Barlow	8	7	2	17	6,435
Jay Don Blake	8	1	8	17	6,435
Ernie Els	6	9	2	17	6,435
Bob Gilder	8	4	5	17	6,435
Steve Pate	7	3	7	17	6,435
Corey Pavin	13	1	3	17	6,435
Mike Springer	8	5	4	17	6,435
Bobby Wadkins	6	7	4	17	6,435
Trevor Dodds	12	1	3	16	4,920
Scott Gump	8	2	6	16	4,920
Glen Hnatiuk	3	8	5	16	4,920
Ben Bates	4	8	3	15	4,653.34
Brian Henninger	10	9	-4	15	4,653.33
Craig Stadler	9	-1	7	15	4,653.33
Robert Damron	4	8	2	14	4,520
Kenny Perry	5	4	5	14	4,520
Kevin Wentworth	5	3	6	14	4,520
Jim Furyk	9	4	0	13	4,400
Craig Parry	7	2	4	13	4,400
Scott Verplank	12	1	0	13	4,400
Tim Loustalot	1	8	3	12	4,320
Lee Janzen	5	3	3	11	4,220
Brian Kamm	5	5	1	11	4,220
Clarence Rose	2	6	3	11	4,220
Paul Stankowski	9	3	-1	11	4,220
Rick Fehr	5	5	0	10	4,100
Frank Nobilo	5	3	2	10	4,100
Tom Kite	4	5	0	9	4,000
Jim McGovern	12	-3	0	9	4,000
Kevin Sutherland	8	6	-5	9	4,000
Nick Price	4	4	0	8	3,920
Phil Tataurangi	6	3	-2	7	3,880
Tim Herron	9	2	-5	6	3,840

NEC World Series of Golf

Firestone Country Club, South Course, Akron, Ohio — August 27-30
Par 35-35–70; 7,189 yards — purse, $2,250,000

	SCORES				TOTAL	MONEY
David Duval	69	66	66	68	269	$405,000
Phil Mickelson	66	71	66	68	271	243,000
Davis Love III	71	69	67	65	272	153,000
John Cook	71	69	62	71	273	108,000
Loren Roberts	72	67	69	67	275	85,500
Tiger Woods	67	68	70	70	275	85,500
Joe Durant	73	67	70	66	276	72,562.50
Mark O'Meara	72	67	65	72	276	72,562.50
Scott Hoch	70	69	71	69	279	63,000

	SCORES				TOTAL	MONEY
Craig Parry	67	68	72	72	279	63,000
Bill Glasson	71	71	68	70	280	51,750
Shigeki Maruyama	75	68	65	72	280	51,750
Jesper Parnevik	71	70	66	73	280	51,750
Mark Calcavecchia	70	70	69	72	281	38,250
Brandt Jobe	70	71	67	73	281	38,250
Steve Pate	72	71	69	69	281	38,250
Vijay Singh	71	68	71	71	281	38,250
Shinichi Yokota	68	72	69	72	281	38,250
Ernie Els	69	74	72	67	282	31,500
Billy Mayfair	72	74	68	69	283	29,250
Stuart Appleby	73	71	72	68	284	25,800
Steve Jones	73	69	73	69	284	25,800
Nick Price	76	70	68	70	284	25,800
Olin Browne	73	68	72	72	285	21,900
Fred Couples	72	73	65	75	285	21,900
Tim Herron	68	76	71	70	285	21,900
John Huston	70	71	70	74	285	21,900
Greg Turner	68	77	71	70	286	20,300
Brian Watts	68	72	70	76	286	20,300
Andrew Coltart	70	73	69	75	287	19,900
Justin Leonard	68	71	74	74	287	19,900
Per-Ulrik Johansson	73	69	75	72	289	19,600
Fred Funk	70	71	71	79	291	19,400
Bradley Hughes	72	71	72	77	292	19,300
David Carter	77	73	72	74	296	19,050
Trevor Dodds	72	74	73	77	296	19,050
Gabriel Hjertstedt	77	74	73	72	296	19,050
Mitsutaka Kusakabe	75	68	77	76	296	19,050
Michael Bradley	75	75	75	72	297	18,800
J.P. Hayes	77	70	81	72	300	18,725
Scott Simpson	76	75	78	73	302	18,650
Tony Johnstone	79	76	73	75	303	18,575
Bruce Zabriski	77	75	79	73	304	18,500

Greater Vancouver Open

Northview Golf & Country Club, Ridge Course, August 27-30
Surrey, British Columbia, Canada purse, $2,200,000
Par 36-35–71; 6,789 yards

	SCORES				TOTAL	MONEY
Brandel Chamblee	67	64	68	66	265	$360,000
Payne Stewart	64	69	65	70	268	216,000
Lee Porter	67	67	71	66	271	136,000
Brian Claar	68	68	69	67	272	96,000
Russ Cochran	71	67	66	69	273	65,500
Bob Estes	67	70	67	69	273	65,500
Jeff Maggert	68	67	70	68	273	65,500
Hugh Royer III	67	68	70	68	273	65,500
Omar Uresti	71	68	68	66	273	65,500
Mike Weir	70	66	68	69	273	65,500
Bob Friend	69	68	69	68	274	44,000
Brent Geiberger	71	66	66	71	274	44,000
Tom Pernice, Jr.	70	66	67	71	274	44,000
Paul Stankowski	67	73	65	69	274	44,000
Kelly Gibson	68	72	67	68	275	32,000

	SCORES				TOTAL	MONEY
John Maginnes	66	71	68	70	275	32,000
Hal Sutton	71	68	65	71	275	32,000
Esteban Toledo	69	71	67	68	275	32,000
Ted Tryba	68	69	71	67	275	32,000
Craig Barlow	68	70	69	69	276	20,175
Tom Byrum	68	68	68	72	276	20,175
Jim Carter	68	71	69	68	276	20,175
Mike Springer	68	71	68	69	276	20,175
Dave Stockton, Jr.	72	69	68	67	276	20,175
Kevin Sutherland	71	69	69	67	276	20,175
Kevin Wentworth	69	68	68	71	276	20,175
Fuzzy Zoeller	70	69	69	68	276	20,175
Robert Allenby	71	66	68	72	277	12,200
Glen Day	67	70	69	71	277	12,200
Chris DiMarco	68	63	72	74	277	12,200
Jim Estes	67	70	71	69	277	12,200
Harrison Frazar	68	66	69	74	277	12,200
Mike Hulbert	69	70	68	70	277	12,200
Peter Jacobsen	70	67	70	70	277	12,200
John Riegger	71	66	71	69	277	12,200
Larry Rinker	68	66	69	74	277	12,200
Richard Zokol	69	69	71	68	277	12,200
Doug Martin	67	68	73	70	278	9,200
David Ogrin	70	69	69	70	278	9,200
Barry Cheesman	72	66	68	73	279	8,000
Steve Flesch	69	69	70	71	279	8,000
Gary Hallberg	71	69	72	67	279	8,000
Chris Smith	72	65	70	72	279	8,000
Mark Carnevale	71	67	69	73	280	6,400
Jeff Gallagher	73	67	69	71	280	6,400
Greg Kraft	67	70	74	69	280	6,400
Mark Wiebe	70	67	71	72	280	6,400
Eric Booker	69	72	71	69	281	5,088
Paul Devenport	73	66	69	73	281	5,088
David Edwards	71	69	68	73	281	5,088
Peter O'Malley	72	68	66	75	281	5,088
Phil Tataurangi	71	66	69	75	281	5,088
Franklin Langham	67	70	71	74	282	4,653.34
Ken Green	71	70	68	73	282	4,653.33
Philip Jonas	70	71	72	69	282	4,653.33
Guy Boros	67	67	72	77	283	4,420
Stewart Cink	71	69	74	69	283	4,420
Richard Coughlan	69	66	73	75	283	4,420
David Frost	71	67	71	74	283	4,420
Scott Gump	70	71	70	72	283	4,420
Ian Leggatt	70	70	71	72	283	4,420
Danny Mijovic	69	71	74	69	283	4,420
Sonny Skinner	69	68	70	76	283	4,420
Ben Bates	68	73	75	68	284	4,140
Ronnie Black	70	70	69	75	284	4,140
Tim Conley	70	69	70	75	284	4,140
Tim Loustalot	69	72	73	70	284	4,140
Mike Reid	70	67	72	75	284	4,140
David Sutherland	70	69	71	74	284	4,140
John Adams	71	70	71	74	286	3,980
Jim Thorpe	69	72	73	72	286	3,980
Andrew Magee	67	71	75	74	287	3,900
Frank Nobilo	68	71	72	76	287	3,900
Jay Hobby	67	67	75	79	288	3,800

	SCORES				TOTAL	MONEY
P.H. Horgan III	70	67	74	77	288	3,800
Steve Jurgensen	68	73	74	73	288	3,800
Ray Stewart	70	71	72	76	289	3,700
Doug Tewell	71	70	71	77	289	3,700
Keith Clearwater	69	71	73	79	292	3,640

Greater Milwaukee Open

Brown Deer Park Golf Course, Milwaukee, Wisconsin — September 3-6
Par 35-36–71; 6,739 yards — purse, $1,800,000

	SCORES				TOTAL	MONEY
Jeff Sluman	68	66	63	68	265	$324,000
Steve Stricker	68	63	67	68	266	194,400
Mark Calcavecchia	66	64	69	69	268	93,600
Nolan Henke	70	62	67	69	268	93,600
Chris Perry	68	62	67	71	268	93,600
Doug Barron	67	67	68	67	269	64,800
Mark Carnevale	66	66	69	69	270	58,050
Fred Funk	68	70	65	67	270	58,050
Billy Andrade	74	64	65	68	271	46,800
Tom Byrum	67	68	69	67	271	46,800
Gabriel Hjertstedt	66	67	69	69	271	46,800
Kevin Wentworth	68	65	68	70	271	46,800
Brian Kamm	70	66	67	69	272	37,800
Tommy Armour III	68	68	66	71	273	31,500
Woody Austin	68	68	69	68	273	31,500
Kevin Sutherland	69	66	69	69	273	31,500
David Ogrin	69	64	68	72	273	31,500
John Cook	67	71	69	67	274	23,472
David Edwards	67	69	70	68	274	23,472
J.P. Hayes	68	70	68	68	274	23,472
John Maginnes	67	65	68	74	274	23,472
Tom Pernice, Jr.	68	67	73	66	274	23,472
Brian Claar	66	70	69	70	275	14,805
Jay Delsing	68	68	70	69	275	14,805
Skip Kendall	68	71	71	65	275	14,805
Lee Porter	66	68	71	70	275	14,805
Sonny Skinner	71	66	67	71	275	14,805
David Sutherland	71	68	70	66	275	14,805
David Toms	67	69	71	68	275	14,805
Duffy Waldorf	68	67	70	70	275	14,805
Chris DiMarco	67	69	70	70	276	10,912.50
Kelly Gibson	71	65	70	70	276	10,912.50
Mike Hulbert	67	69	69	71	276	10,912.50
Kent Jones	69	69	70	68	276	10,912.50
Mike Reid	69	70	68	70	277	8,498.58
Andy Bean	69	68	70	70	277	8,498.57
Ken Green	71	68	66	72	277	8,498.57
Bradley Hughes	71	66	70	70	277	8,498.57
J.L. Lewis	74	63	64	76	277	8,498.57
Loren Roberts	62	70	72	73	277	8,498.57
Mike Springer	66	72	69	70	277	8,498.57
Chip Beck	69	68	73	68	278	6,300
Mike Brisky	68	68	71	71	278	6,300
Pete Jordan	71	67	73	67	278	6,300
Blaine McCallister	72	65	70	71	278	6,300

	SCORES				TOTAL	MONEY
Vijay Singh	67	70	71	70	278	6,300
Ben Bates	72	67	66	74	279	4,759.20
Jay Don Blake	65	71	72	71	279	4,759.20
Scott Hoch	70	67	69	73	279	4,759.20
Jim McGovern	67	67	72	73	279	4,759.20
Willie Wood	70	65	74	70	279	4,759.20
Barry Cheesman	67	69	72	72	280	4,197.60
Paul Goydos	69	69	70	72	280	4,197.60
Dan Halldorson	68	68	69	75	280	4,197.60
Glen Hnatiuk	74	65	70	71	280	4,197.60
Larry Rinker	72	67	71	70	280	4,197.60
Keith Fergus	68	69	71	73	281	3,978
Bruce Fleisher	70	69	72	70	281	3,978
Robert Gamez	67	71	74	69	281	3,978
Bill Glasson	67	70	71	73	281	3,978
Jimmy Johnston	70	68	72	71	281	3,978
Jerry Kelly	72	67	71	71	281	3,978
Bob Gilder	70	65	74	73	282	3,834
Bobby Wadkins	70	68	73	71	282	3,834
Joe Durant	71	68	70	74	283	3,744
Jim Estes	71	66	72	74	283	3,744
Clarence Rose	70	69	71	73	283	3,744
Joe Daley	70	69	75	72	286	3,654
Omar Uresti	70	67	72	77	286	3,654
Iain Steel	70	67	79	72	288	3,600

Bell Canadian Open

Glen Abbey Golf Club, Oakville, Ontario, Canada — September 10-13
Par 36-36–72; 7,112 yards — purse, $2,200,000

	SCORES				TOTAL	MONEY
Billy Andrade	68	69	69	69	275	$396,000
Bob Friend	69	67	68	71	275	237,600
(Andrade defeated Friend on first extra hole.)						
Mike Hulbert	72	70	66	68	276	149,600
Bradley Hughes	73	72	69	66	280	90,933.34
Glen Day	74	71	64	71	280	90,933.33
Hal Sutton	71	69	67	73	280	90,933.33
Sandy Lyle	75	70	66	70	281	70,950
Mike Standly	72	71	71	67	281	70,950
Jay Delsing	76	68	68	70	282	57,200
Chris DiMarco	73	65	71	73	282	57,200
Mike Small	68	71	71	72	282	57,200
Scott Verplank	68	71	71	72	282	57,200
Mark Calcavecchia	73	69	72	69	283	35,444.45
Richard Coughlan	70	75	70	68	283	35,444.45
Tim Loustalot	73	70	72	68	283	35,444.45
Andrew Magee	73	70	70	70	283	35,444.45
Stephen Ames	71	73	68	71	283	35,444.44
Ashley Chinner	76	70	66	71	283	35,444.44
Steve Jones	74	69	69	71	283	35,444.44
Joey Sindelar	71	73	65	74	283	35,444.44
Fuzzy Zoeller	69	76	67	71	283	35,444.44
Brad Faxon	74	68	72	70	284	22,880
Jim Furyk	71	72	69	72	284	22,880
Vijay Singh	74	70	69	71	284	22,880

	SCORES				TOTAL	MONEY
Tim Herron	68	75	71	71	285	15,742.23
Doug Martin	74	69	71	71	285	15,742.23
Michael Bradley	75	70	68	72	285	15,742.22
Robert Damron	71	67	75	72	285	15,742.22
Trevor Dodds	72	69	72	72	285	15,742.22
David Edwards	69	71	72	73	285	15,742.22
Keith Fergus	71	72	70	72	285	15,742.22
Peter Jacobsen	73	68	71	73	285	15,742.22
Bob Tway	72	69	72	72	285	15,742.22
Franklin Langham	72	74	67	73	286	12,155
Spike McRoy	72	72	67	75	286	12,155
Tommy Armour III	70	75	70	72	287	9,915.72
Bob Gilder	70	71	72	74	287	9,915.72
Glen Hnatiuk	70	74	71	72	287	9,915.72
Kelly Gibson	68	72	71	76	287	9,915.71
Len Mattiace	70	73	69	75	287	9,915.71
Chris Smith	66	77	70	74	287	9,915.71
Kevin Sutherland	71	71	71	74	287	9,915.71
Dudley Hart	68	74	72	74	288	7,480
P.H. Horgan III	71	72	73	72	288	7,480
Neal Lancaster	75	71	70	72	288	7,480
Jeff Sluman	69	77	72	70	288	7,480
Phil Blackmar	69	71	76	73	289	5,918
Brad Fabel	72	74	68	75	289	5,918
Tom Pernice, Jr.	72	73	70	74	289	5,918
Tommy Tolles	72	71	70	76	289	5,918
Paul Azinger	72	70	76	72	290	5,209.60
Brian Henninger	70	70	76	74	290	5,209.60
Kent Jones	75	71	70	74	290	5,209.60
David McKenzie	74	69	72	75	290	5,209.60
Frank Nobilo	72	74	71	73	290	5,209.60
Doug Barron	72	71	74	74	291	4,972
Tim Conley	72	71	73	75	291	4,972
Bruce Fleisher	74	70	74	73	291	4,972
Craig Barlow	71	72	69	80	292	4,774
Tom Byrum	75	71	69	77	292	4,774
Scott McCarron	75	70	74	73	292	4,774
Larry Rinker	71	71	73	77	292	4,774
Phil Tataurangi	69	75	74	74	292	4,774
Mark Wiebe	72	71	74	75	292	4,774
Dave Barr	71	75	70	77	293	4,598
J.L. Lewis	72	70	69	82	293	4,598
Danny Edwards	74	71	72	77	294	4,422
Dan Halldorson	75	71	69	79	294	4,422
Philip Jonas	76	70	72	76	294	4,422
Steve Lowery	76	69	75	74	294	4,422
Tom Purtzer	70	75	75	74	294	4,422
Grant Waite	75	71	68	80	294	4,422
Paul Devenport	75	71	71	79	296	4,246
Guy Hill	70	76	72	78	296	4,246
Iain Steel	73	72	72	80	297	4,180

B.C. Open

En-Joie Golf Club, Endicott, New York
Par 37-35–72; 6,994 yards

September 17-20
purse, $1,500,000

	SCORES				TOTAL	MONEY
Chris Perry	67	70	69	67	273	$270,000
Peter Jacobsen	68	70	71	67	276	162,000
Nolan Henke	69	69	67	72	277	102,000
Robert Allenby	69	70	71	68	278	62,000
Curt Byrum	71	73	69	65	278	62,000
Ted Tryba	72	69	67	70	278	62,000
Doug Barron	67	71	70	71	279	48,375
Mike Weir	71	68	69	71	279	48,375
Chris DiMarco	66	70	72	72	280	34,714.29
Brian Henninger	69	69	70	72	280	34,714.29
Skip Kendall	71	69	70	70	280	34,714.29
Brett Quigley	72	71	69	68	280	34,714.29
Richard Coughlan	69	71	67	73	280	34,714.28
R.W. Eaks	73	65	69	73	280	34,714.28
Bruce Fleisher	69	72	63	76	280	34,714.28
Billy Andrade	70	70	73	68	281	23,250
Fred Funk	71	67	71	72	281	23,250
Clarence Rose	71	68	70	72	281	23,250
Fred Wadsworth	72	71	69	69	281	23,250
Dave Barr	70	65	73	74	282	16,860
Gary Hallberg	74	68	70	70	282	16,860
Sonny Skinner	69	74	67	72	282	16,860
Mike Springer	71	71	67	73	282	16,860
Phil Tataurangi	68	70	73	71	282	16,860
Mark Carnevale	72	70	70	71	283	10,968.75
Jim Furyk	70	72	69	72	283	10,968.75
Franklin Langham	72	71	68	72	283	10,968.75
Sandy Lyle	68	72	69	74	283	10,968.75
Steve Pate	70	71	73	69	283	10,968.75
Lee Rinker	72	69	70	72	283	10,968.75
Mike Small	71	70	70	72	283	10,968.75
Duffy Waldorf	72	71	69	71	283	10,968.75
Barry Cheesman	70	73	71	70	284	7,757.15
Mike Standly	72	71	74	67	284	7,757.15
Mike Heinen	72	70	72	70	284	7,757.14
Eduardo Herrera	70	71	71	72	284	7,757.14
P.H. Horgan III	73	70	70	71	284	7,757.14
Mike Hulbert	69	73	68	74	284	7,757.14
Tim Loustalot	69	73	69	73	284	7,757.14
Phil Blackmar	75	69	71	70	285	5,550
Jim Carter	73	69	71	72	285	5,550
Trevor Dodds	72	71	73	69	285	5,550
Gabriel Hjertstedt	73	70	66	76	285	5,550
Blaine McCallister	72	71	70	72	285	5,550
Greg Twiggs	73	70	72	70	285	5,550
Grant Waite	69	75	72	69	285	5,550
Donnie Hammond	69	73	72	72	286	4,035
Jim McGovern	75	65	72	74	286	4,035
Hugh Royer III	73	71	74	68	286	4,035
Iain Steel	72	71	68	75	286	4,035
Jonathan Kaye	71	73	71	72	287	3,610
John Maginnes	74	70	69	74	287	3,610
Stan Utley	70	73	71	73	287	3,610
Kelly Gibson	72	72	74	70	288	3,435

	SCORES				TOTAL	MONEY
Steve Lowery	71	71	73	73	288	3,435
Dick Mast	73	70	68	77	288	3,435
Shannon Sykora	74	69	73	72	288	3,435
Stephen Ames	72	71	77	69	289	3,285
Ronnie Black	75	69	69	76	289	3,285
Bob Friend	72	71	74	72	289	3,285
Brian Kamm	67	73	79	70	289	3,285
Corey Pavin	71	70	73	75	289	3,285
Mark Pfeil	69	72	75	73	289	3,285
Brad Elder	75	68	73	74	290	3,165
J.J. Henry	71	70	72	77	290	3,165
Dan Pohl	71	73	76	71	291	3,120
Keith Fergus	71	73	74	74	292	3,075
Tommy Tolles	69	74	80	69	292	3,075
Doug Martin	70	74	74	75	293	3,015
John Riegger	71	72	74	76	293	3,015
Bobby Cole	71	71	74	78	294	2,970

Westin Texas Open

LaCantera Golf Club, San Antonio, Texas — September 24-27
Par 36-36–72; 7,001 yards — purse, $1,700,000

	SCORES				TOTAL	MONEY
Hal Sutton	67	68	67	68	270	$306,000
Jay Haas	70	69	64	68	271	149,600
Justin Leonard	67	67	69	68	271	149,600
Steve Lowery	70	70	69	64	273	66,937.50
Andrew Magee	68	72	67	66	273	66,937.50
Mike Reid	70	69	72	62	273	66,937.50
Loren Roberts	67	68	71	67	273	66,937.50
Scott Gump	68	70	65	71	274	51,000
Jeff Maggert	71	68	69	66	274	51,000
Corey Pavin	71	68	67	69	275	45,900
Steve Jones	68	71	70	67	276	31,733.34
Mike Springer	70	71	71	64	276	31,733.34
Ted Tryba	71	68	70	67	276	31,733.34
Tommy Armour III	69	67	71	69	276	31,733.33
Jim Carter	73	67	69	67	276	31,733.33
Stewart Cink	67	70	69	70	276	31,733.33
Clark Dennis	71	69	67	69	276	31,733.33
Bob Estes	68	67	73	68	276	31,733.33
Bill Glasson	68	70	69	69	276	31,733.33
Fred Funk	73	69	67	68	277	19,108
Gary Hallberg	71	68	68	70	277	19,108
J.L. Lewis	69	69	73	66	277	19,108
Frank Lickliter	72	68	66	71	277	19,108
John Riegger	70	69	68	70	277	19,108
Ronnie Black	68	70	68	72	278	12,976.67
Dan Forsman	68	72	70	68	278	12,976.67
Bradley Hughes	73	67	71	67	278	12,976.67
John Maginnes	67	67	73	71	278	12,976.67
Brad Fabel	71	64	70	73	278	12,976.66
Mike Small	67	70	68	73	278	12,976.66
Jay Delsing	70	68	69	72	279	9,860
Jim Estes	72	70	68	69	279	9,860
Blaine McCallister	67	70	71	71	279	9,860
Larry Rinker	71	69	71	68	279	9,860

	SCORES				TOTAL	MONEY
Lee Rinker	70	71	69	69	279	9,860
Richard Zokol	69	70	69	71	279	9,860
Robert Allenby	70	71	72	67	280	7,140
Brandel Chamblee	67	72	72	69	280	7,140
David Frost	72	64	70	74	280	7,140
John Huston	73	69	69	69	280	7,140
David Ogrin	72	65	70	73	280	7,140
Pete Jordan	69	72	66	73	280	7,140
Esteban Toledo	69	72	70	69	280	7,140
Mike Weir	70	70	70	70	280	7,140
Tom Byrum	72	68	70	71	281	4,679.25
Mark Carnevale	73	68	68	72	281	4,679.25
Steve Flesch	72	69	69	71	281	4,679.25
Tim Loustalot	71	70	70	70	281	4,679.25
Len Mattiace	71	71	71	68	281	4,679.25
Jim McGovern	66	73	73	69	281	4,679.25
Doug Tewell	73	69	71	68	281	4,679.25
D.A. Weibring	65	74	74	68	281	4,679.25
Jim Gallagher, Jr.	69	71	73	69	282	3,898.67
Bob Tway	71	70	72	69	282	3,898.67
Vance Veazey	73	69	70	70	282	3,898.67
Mark Wurtz	69	69	73	71	282	3,898.67
Donnie Hammond	71	71	69	71	282	3,898.66
Duffy Waldorf	70	69	70	73	282	3,898.66
Ben Bates	73	68	74	68	283	3,706
Ken Green	68	71	73	71	283	3,706
J.J. Henry	71	71	74	67	283	3,706
Doug Martin	69	72	71	71	283	3,706
Bobby Wadkins	73	69	69	72	283	3,706
Craig Barlow	67	71	72	74	284	3,553
J.P. Hayes	67	75	73	69	284	3,553
Clarence Rose	71	71	74	68	284	3,553
Chris Smith	69	72	74	69	284	3,553
Barry Cheesman	72	70	74	69	285	3,400
Greg Gregory	69	73	72	71	285	3,400
Kent Jones	70	69	71	75	285	3,400
Steve Jurgensen	72	70	67	76	285	3,400
Greg Kraft	70	72	69	74	285	3,400
Curt Byrum	70	71	70	75	286	3,247
Harrison Frazar	78	64	75	69	286	3,247
Dan Pohl	72	69	74	71	286	3,247
Brett Quigley	68	70	73	75	286	3,247
Mike Brisky	68	74	72	73	287	3,128
P.H. Horgan III	70	71	71	75	287	3,128
Larry Mize	73	68	72	74	287	3,128
Dave Rummells	70	71	73	75	289	3,060

Buick Challenge

Callaway Gardens Resort, Mountain View Course, Pine Mountain, Georgia
Par 36-36–72; 7,057 yards

October 1-4
purse, $1,500,000

	SCORES				TOTAL	MONEY
Steve Elkington	66	70	66	65	267	$270,000
Fred Funk	63	67	68	69	267	162,000

(Elkington defeated Funk on first extra hole.)

	SCORES				TOTAL	MONEY
Bill Glasson	69	65	65	69	268	102,000
J.L. Lewis	66	69	66	68	269	72,000
Skip Kendall	71	70	67	63	271	60,000
David Duval	66	68	70	69	273	52,125
Steve Flesch	67	66	69	71	273	52,125
Ben Bates	71	69	67	67	274	39,000
Jim Carter	63	71	69	71	274	39,000
Neal Lancaster	70	67	66	71	274	39,000
Jeff Maggert	69	69	69	67	274	39,000
Chris Perry	70	68	69	67	274	39,000
Hal Sutton	72	66	67	69	274	39,000
Billy Andrade	71	67	67	70	275	24,750
Tim Herron	66	74	68	67	275	24,750
Davis Love III	69	70	70	66	275	24,750
Larry Mize	70	71	67	67	275	24,750
Payne Stewart	70	67	71	67	275	24,750
Kevin Wentworth	68	71	68	68	275	24,750
J.P. Hayes	68	70	67	71	276	17,475
Frank Lickliter	66	71	69	70	276	17,475
David Peoples	71	68	68	69	276	17,475
Bob Tway	71	67	69	69	276	17,475
Stephen Ames	68	68	70	71	277	13,200
Brandel Chamblee	67	68	73	69	277	13,200
Justin Leonard	67	73	71	66	277	13,200
Michael Bradley	70	69	71	68	278	11,100
Bob Gilder	71	67	69	71	278	11,100
D.A. Weibring	68	65	71	74	278	11,100
Brent Geiberger	68	69	72	70	279	8,533.34
David Ogrin	70	67	71	71	279	8,533.34
Clarence Rose	70	71	68	70	279	8,533.34
Mike Brisky	72	69	67	71	279	8,533.33
Glen Day	71	70	65	73	279	8,533.33
Billy Mayfair	69	71	68	71	279	8,533.33
Mike Reid	71	69	68	71	279	8,533.33
Mike Small	70	69	71	69	279	8,533.33
Kirk Triplett	70	68	73	68	279	8,533.33
Rick Fehr	68	68	72	72	280	6,150
Glen Hnatiuk	69	70	73	68	280	6,150
Brett Quigley	69	68	71	72	280	6,150
Curtis Strange	70	70	68	72	280	6,150
Grant Waite	69	69	70	72	280	6,150
Gary Hallberg	71	70	73	67	281	4,800
Corey Pavin	68	71	71	71	281	4,800
David Sutherland	68	72	72	69	281	4,800
Omar Uresti	69	70	72	70	281	4,800
Tom Byrum	65	73	75	69	282	3,636
Russ Cochran	64	71	73	74	282	3,636
Clark Dennis	69	70	74	69	282	3,636
Robert Gamez	72	69	71	70	282	3,636
Scott Gump	70	71	72	69	282	3,636
Franklin Langham	66	72	72	72	282	3,636
Scott McCarron	70	71	69	72	282	3,636
Dicky Pride	71	68	73	70	282	3,636
Loren Roberts	69	71	69	73	282	3,636
Jeff Sluman	71	70	74	67	282	3,636
Mark Brooks	70	71	70	72	283	3,315
Harrison Frazar	69	72	72	70	283	3,315
Jim McGovern	69	71	72	71	283	3,315
Vijay Singh	69	70	70	74	283	3,315
*Matt Kuchar	72	67	73	71	283	

	SCORES				TOTAL	MONEY
Scott Hoch	70	70	72	72	284	3,210
Don Pooley	71	69	71	73	284	3,210
Mike Springer	69	69	73	73	284	3,210
Mark Calcavecchia	68	73	74	70	285	3,150
Dan Forsman	71	70	72	73	286	3,105
Tommy Tolles	67	74	73	72	286	3,105
Phil Tataurangi	72	69	75	71	287	3,060
Guy Boros	72	68	78	72	290	3,030
Iain Steel	73	68	81	77	299	3,000

Michelob Championship

Kingsmill Golf Club, Williamsburg, Virginia — October 8-11
Par 36-35–71; 6,797 yards — purse, $1,800,000

	SCORES				TOTAL	MONEY
David Duval	65	67	68	68	268	$342,000
Phil Tataurangi	65	68	69	69	271	205,200
Barry Cheesman	69	68	69	66	272	129,200
Bradley Hughes	68	67	69	69	273	83,600
Payne Stewart	70	67	67	69	273	83,600
Gary Hallberg	68	67	66	74	275	61,512.50
John Huston	69	70	68	68	275	61,512.50
Frank Lickliter	66	67	70	72	275	61,512.50
Billy Mayfair	67	70	70	68	275	61,512.50
Tommy Armour III	70	71	70	66	277	47,500
Corey Pavin	67	70	70	70	277	47,500
Jeff Sluman	68	72	71	66	277	47,500
Ben Bates	67	70	73	68	278	35,625
J.L. Lewis	69	67	70	72	278	35,625
Loren Roberts	69	69	68	72	278	35,625
Kevin Wentworth	67	70	69	72	278	35,625
Robert Allenby	69	70	70	70	279	26,600
Mark Brooks	68	71	69	71	279	26,600
Bruce Fleisher	69	70	70	70	279	26,600
Steve Pate	66	69	72	72	279	26,600
Joey Sindelar	68	69	70	72	279	26,600
Bob Gilder	72	68	68	72	280	19,760
Scott Hoch	69	69	70	72	280	19,760
Kent Jones	70	71	71	68	280	19,760
Ronnie Black	70	70	70	71	281	13,893.75
Jay Don Blake	72	68	70	71	281	13,893.75
Guy Boros	69	67	71	74	281	13,893.75
Stewart Cink	71	71	67	72	281	13,893.75
Tom Lehman	71	67	70	73	281	13,893.75
Justin Leonard	68	69	73	71	281	13,893.75
John Maginnes	70	70	71	70	281	13,893.75
Scott Verplank	71	71	70	69	281	13,893.75
Larry Mize	71	71	68	72	282	10,038.34
Vance Veazey	70	68	73	71	282	10,038.34
Billy Andrade	67	70	75	70	282	10,038.33
Brian Claar	67	68	80	67	282	10,038.33
Lee Porter	70	72	71	69	282	10,038.33
Larry Rinker	70	69	69	74	282	10,038.33
Richard Coughlan	70	72	70	71	283	7,790
Jim Furyk	70	71	72	70	283	7,790
Jonathan Kaye	69	68	72	74	283	7,790

	SCORES				TOTAL	MONEY
Chris Perry	69	71	72	71	283	7,790
Kevin Sutherland	73	68	72	70	283	7,790
Fred Funk	73	68	73	70	284	6,080
Neal Lancaster	71	69	73	71	284	6,080
Brett Quigley	73	69	71	71	284	6,080
Duffy Waldorf	70	72	69	73	284	6,080
Lennie Clements	71	71	70	73	285	4,775.34
Mike Springer	69	71	72	73	285	4,775.34
Glen Hnatiuk	73	65	70	77	285	4,775.33
Skip Kendall	69	72	73	71	285	4,775.33
John Morse	69	72	72	72	285	4,775.33
David Peoples	68	72	77	68	285	4,775.33
Tom Byrum	69	72	72	73	286	4,332
Chad Campbell	71	69	71	75	286	4,332
Harrison Frazar	68	68	73	77	286	4,332
Paul Goydos	72	70	72	72	286	4,332
Lee Janzen	71	70	73	72	286	4,332
Tommy Tolles	72	67	68	80	287	4,218
Phil Blackmar	69	70	72	77	288	4,142
Michael Bradley	71	69	77	71	288	4,142
Chris Smith	70	71	75	72	288	4,142
Bob Estes	69	73	74	73	289	3,971
Steve Hart	69	72	77	71	289	3,971
Franklin Langham	71	70	76	72	289	3,971
John Riegger	73	67	74	75	289	3,971
Kirk Triplett	67	68	74	80	289	3,971
Lanny Wadkins	73	69	76	71	289	3,971
Grant Waite	69	68	78	75	290	3,819
Mike Weir	67	73	74	76	290	3,819
Keith Fergus	73	67	72	79	291	3,743
Curtis Strange	66	74	77	74	291	3,743
Guy Hill	68	74	74	76	292	3,686
Dave Stockton, Jr.	69	72	73	81	295	3,648
Sonny Skinner	71	70	76	82	299	3,610

Las Vegas Invitational

Las Vegas, Nevada — October 14-18
TPC at Summerlin: Par 36-36–72; 7,234 yards — purse, $2,000,000
Desert Inn Country Club: Par 36-36–72; 7,111 yards
Las Vegas Country Club: Par 36-36–72; 7,164 yards

	SCORES					TOTAL	MONEY
Jim Furyk	67	68	69	63	68	335	$360,000
Mark Calcavecchia	65	71	69	65	66	336	216,000
Scott Verplank	67	68	69	67	67	338	136,000
Bob Tway	68	65	69	72	65	339	96,000
Davis Love III	70	66	68	70	66	340	80,000
Justin Leonard	70	66	71	66	68	341	69,500
Paul Stankowski	67	71	68	70	65	341	69,500
Rick Fehr	69	65	71	69	68	342	60,000
Kirk Triplett	70	65	72	66	69	342	60,000
Brandel Chamblee	69	68	70	68	68	343	52,000
Kevin Wentworth	71	70	68	67	67	343	52,000
Tom Byrum	67	70	70	70	67	344	42,000
Robert Damron	65	68	72	72	67	344	42,000
Steve Pate	70	72	68	66	68	344	42,000

	SCORES					TOTAL	MONEY
Tom Pernice, Jr.	66	75	70	66	68	345	36,000
Stewart Cink	72	65	74	71	64	346	31,000
Bob May	69	65	72	67	73	346	31,000
Lee Porter	69	65	71	70	71	346	31,000
D.A. Weibring	69	69	72	67	69	346	31,000
Paul Azinger	66	68	79	68	66	347	25,000
Rocco Mediate	68	69	74	68	68	347	25,000
Fred Couples	71	70	73	66	68	348	19,200
Brent Geiberger	67	70	72	68	71	348	19,200
Andrew Magee	68	71	73	72	64	348	19,200
Joey Sindelar	69	71	71	68	69	348	19,200
Mike Springer	71	68	71	68	70	348	19,200
Kelly Gibson	72	65	75	66	71	349	14,200
Paul Goydos	70	69	72	67	71	349	14,200
Lee Janzen	67	71	74	66	71	349	14,200
Steve Jones	68	69	72	72	68	349	14,200
Craig Stadler	68	71	72	67	71	349	14,200
Bob Estes	68	70	73	68	71	350	11,575
Nolan Henke	69	67	71	69	74	350	11,575
Blaine McCallister	72	69	69	71	69	350	11,575
Chris Perry	68	69	72	72	69	350	11,575
Skip Kendall	70	70	71	73	67	351	8,611.12
John Cook	69	69	70	71	72	351	8,611.11
R.W. Eaks	67	72	70	72	70	351	8,611.11
Jim Gallagher, Jr.	69	69	72	70	71	351	8,611.11
Bob Gilder	72	68	71	72	68	351	8,611.11
Bill Glasson	69	65	76	69	72	351	8,611.11
David Ogrin	67	66	71	76	71	351	8,611.11
Kenny Perry	72	70	69	69	71	351	8,611.11
Larry Rinker	68	72	71	73	67	351	8,611.11
Doug Barron	66	71	74	71	70	352	5,720
Ben Bates	73	65	75	66	73	352	5,720
Donnie Hammond	68	71	71	70	72	352	5,720
Spike McRoy	68	68	73	74	69	352	5,720
Mike Standly	70	69	73	70	70	352	5,720
Kevin Sutherland	72	70	71	65	74	352	5,720
Jay Don Blake	71	69	71	70	72	353	4,860
Mark Brooks	73	68	73	69	70	353	4,860
Chip Beck	67	68	78	69	72	354	4,565.72
Jeff Gallagher	74	69	71	68	72	354	4,565.72
Tom Lehman	69	72	72	68	73	354	4,565.72
Mark Carnevale	71	69	70	70	74	354	4,565.71
John Daly	68	70	72	67	77	354	4,565.71
Dudley Hart	66	72	70	73	73	354	4,565.71
Don Pooley	67	70	74	70	73	354	4,565.71
David Sutherland	67	71	76	72	69	355	4,400
J.L. Lewis	68	74	71	71	72	356	4,340
Tim Loustalot	73	69	72	68	74	356	4,340
Dave Barr	69	70	74	73	71	357	4,240
Brian Henninger	66	72	75	73	71	357	4,240
Corey Pavin	69	70	75	69	74	357	4,240
Tim Conley	68	69	75	71	75	358	4,120
Richard Coughlan	68	70	75	71	74	358	4,120
Duffy Waldorf	66	70	76	73	73	358	4,120
Esteban Toledo	68	70	71	78	72	359	4,040
Jerry Kelly	71	72	70	70	77	360	4,000
Billy Andrade	68	69	76	76	72	361	3,940
Grant Waite	67	70	77	73	74	361	3,940
Kent Jones	71	68	73	74	77	363	3,880
Mike Hulbert	69	70	75	73	78	365	3,840

National Car Rental Classic

Lake Buena Vista, Florida — October 21-25
Magnolia Course: Par 36-36–72; 7,190 yards — purse, $2,000,000
Palm Course: Par 36-36–72; 6,957 yards

	SCORES				TOTAL	MONEY
John Huston	67	70	69	66	272	$360,000
Davis Love III	73	64	65	71	273	216,000
Brent Geiberger	72	70	68	65	275	136,000
Rocco Mediate	67	70	71	68	276	82,666.67
Tom Purtzer	69	68	72	67	276	82,666.67
Jesper Parnevik	66	72	69	69	276	82,666.66
Fred Funk	72	67	68	70	277	60,250
Nolan Henke	69	70	72	66	277	60,250
Doug Martin	69	68	68	72	277	60,250
Tiger Woods	66	73	68	70	277	60,250
Glen Day	70	67	68	73	278	50,000
Pete Jordan	70	72	68	69	279	42,000
Larry Rinker	69	75	67	68	279	42,000
Vijay Singh	69	71	69	70	279	42,000
Tom Lehman	72	72	66	70	280	33,000
J.L. Lewis	69	72	68	71	280	33,000
Tommy Tolles	71	70	68	71	280	33,000
Ted Tryba	72	72	67	69	280	33,000
Doug Barron	69	71	71	70	281	21,750
Mark Brooks	69	69	70	73	281	21,750
Brandel Chamblee	68	71	72	70	281	21,750
John Cook	70	73	69	69	281	21,750
Richard Coughlan	73	68	70	70	281	21,750
Glen Hnatiuk	68	72	70	71	281	21,750
Tom Pernice, Jr.	70	70	70	71	281	21,750
Joey Sindelar	71	72	70	68	281	21,750
Billy Andrade	71	69	70	72	282	11,275
Ben Bates	72	71	69	70	282	11,275
Mike Brisky	69	72	70	71	282	11,275
Jim Carter	70	72	67	73	282	11,275
Robert Damron	72	71	68	71	282	11,275
Rick Fehr	72	69	71	70	282	11,275
Robert Gamez	70	69	73	70	282	11,275
Brian Henninger	70	73	68	71	282	11,275
P.H. Horgan III	73	71	69	69	282	11,275
Franklin Langham	70	74	71	67	282	11,275
Len Mattiace	66	72	70	74	282	11,275
David Ogrin	71	70	69	72	282	11,275
Brett Quigley	72	69	71	70	282	11,275
John Riegger	69	69	71	73	282	11,275
Clarence Rose	69	69	70	74	282	11,275
Esteban Toledo	71	73	67	71	282	11,275
Trevor Dodds	71	70	71	71	283	6,090
David Duval	68	72	68	75	283	6,090
Bob Friend	72	71	73	67	283	6,090
Paul Goydos	68	71	71	73	283	6,090
Skip Kendall	69	69	71	74	283	6,090
Blaine McCallister	71	73	73	66	283	6,090
Larry Nelson	67	76	66	74	283	6,090
Bob Tway	71	67	73	72	283	6,090
Jay Haas	68	72	72	72	284	4,813.34
Stewart Cink	70	70	68	76	284	4,813.33
Steve Flesch	70	72	71	71	284	4,813.33
Spike McRoy	69	74	69	73	285	4,600
Jeff Sluman	70	72	71	72	285	4,600

	SCORES				TOTAL	MONEY
David Sutherland	73	71	68	73	285	4,600
Jeff Gallagher	71	73	70	72	286	4,480
Bill Glasson	74	69	72	71	286	4,480
Loren Roberts	71	70	75	70	286	4,480
Clark Dennis	69	71	72	75	287	4,340
Chris Smith	71	70	73	73	287	4,340
Kirk Triplett	71	73	70	73	287	4,340
Mark Wiebe	70	74	71	72	287	4,340
Phil Blackmar	69	72	72	75	288	4,140
Frank Nobilo	73	71	75	69	288	4,140
Mark O'Meara	71	71	75	71	288	4,140
Omar Uresti	71	70	75	72	288	4,140
Duffy Waldorf	63	78	73	74	288	4,140
Mike Weir	72	71	71	74	288	4,140
Mark Carnevale	72	72	70	75	289	3,940
Tim Conley	73	69	72	75	289	3,940
Joe Durant	71	71	72	75	289	3,940
Sandy Lyle	71	72	70	76	289	3,940
Barry Cheesman	73	71	73	73	290	3,840
Kelly Gibson	69	72	74	76	291	3,800
Brad Faxon	76	67	71	79	293	3,760
Fulton Allem	71	72	74	78	295	3,720

Tour Championship

East Lake Golf Club, Atlanta, Georgia
Par 35-35–70; 6,980 yards

October 29-November 1
purse, $4,000,000

	SCORES				TOTAL	MONEY
Hal Sutton	69	67	68	70	274	$720,000
Vijay Singh	63	70	70	71	274	432,000
(Sutton defeated Singh on first extra hole.)						
Jim Furyk	67	68	69	71	275	234,000
Jesper Parnevik	70	70	67	68	275	234,000
Steve Stricker	69	71	71	69	280	146,666.67
Scott Verplank	70	70	71	69	280	146,666.67
Justin Leonard	68	72	68	72	280	146,666.66
David Duval	75	69	69	68	281	120,533.34
Davis Love III	70	71	70	70	281	120,533.33
Bob Tway	71	70	70	70	281	120,533.33
John Huston	72	72	70	68	282	105,200
Jeff Sluman	68	72	71	71	282	105,200
Billy Mayfair	66	77	71	69	283	95,200
Mark O'Meara	71	70	71	71	283	95,200
Tom Lehman	67	70	75	72	284	88,000
Jeff Maggert	73	70	71	71	285	84,800
Phil Mickelson	73	74	69	70	286	81,600
Glen Day	73	70	69	75	287	79,200
Tom Watson	73	71	69	74	287	79,200
Tiger Woods	75	76	69	69	289	76,800
John Cook	73	75	71	71	290	73,600
Scott Hoch	73	71	74	72	290	73,600
Andrew Magee	73	73	75	69	290	73,600
Fred Couples	73	67	75	76	291	68,200
Fred Funk	73	68	74	76	291	68,200
Lee Janzen	77	72	71	71	291	68,200
Payne Stewart	69	72	76	74	291	68,200
Bob Estes	71	76	74	71	292	65,600
Mark Calcavecchia	73	73	73	75	294	64,800
Nick Price	74	76	72	75	297	64,000

Special Events

Panama Open Panasonic

Coronado Golf Course, Coronado, Republic of Panama — January 7-10
Par 36-36–72; 6,983 yards — purse, $175,000

	SCORES				TOTAL	MONEY
Bob Friend	68	74	69	70	281	$30,000
Rick Todd	71	71	69	70	281	17,500
(Friend defeated Todd on first extra hole.)						
Roger Rowland	70	68	69	75	282	9,750
Esteban Toledo	67	72	74	69	282	9,750
Brian Kontak	73	66	72	72	283	7,000
Joe Durant	70	72	69	73	284	5,750
Stan Utley	70	72	70	72	284	5,750
Rigoberto Velasquez	72	71	71	71	285	5,000
Billy Bulmer	71	74	67	74	286	4,500
Sonny Skinner	75	70	70	71	286	4,500
Damon Green	76	71	71	68	286	4,500
Brian Claar	71	71	68	77	287	3,850
Marion Dantzler	70	69	74	74	287	3,850
Alan Bratton	71	67	72	78	288	3,100
Greg Towne	69	71	76	72	288	3,100
Jaxon Brigman	72	72	72	72	288	3,100
Jaime Gomez	70	76	66	77	289	2,400
Briny Baird	76	76	67	70	289	2,400
Carlos Espinosa	74	73	73	69	289	2,400
Bob Menne	70	72	74	74	290	1,900
Bobby Gage	73	72	73	72	290	1,900
Rex Caldwell	77	74	69	70	290	1,900
Shane Bertsch	75	73	68	75	291	1,650
Brian Gay	72	74	72	73	291	1,650
Steve Waggoner	71	73	71	77	292	1,350
Tim Straub	73	72	74	73	292	1,350
Cliff Kresge	73	73	75	71	292	1,350
Chad Magee	75	76	72	69	292	1,350
Sam Scheibel	72	69	74	78	293	1,000
Rafael Alarcon	75	72	69	77	293	1,000
Derek Gilchrist	74	74	71	74	293	1,000

Fred Meyer Challenge

Reserve Vineyards and Golf Club, Aloha, Oregon — August 24-25
Par 36-36–72; 7,099 yards — purse, $925,000

	SCORES		TOTAL	MONEY (Team)
David Duval/Jim Furyk	65	61	126	$150,000
Steve Elkington/Craig Stadler	63	67	130	92,500
Scott McCarron/Paul Stankowski	66	64	130	92,500
Stewart Cink/Steve Jones	64	67	131	71,333.33
Billy Andrade/Brad Faxon	65	66	131	71,333.33
John Daly/Fuzzy Zoeller	66	65	131	71,333.33

	SCORES		TOTAL	MONEY (Team)
Jay Haas/Phil Mickelson	67	65	132	66,000
Tom Lehman/Lee Janzen	66	67	133	63,500
Bob Gilder/Brian Henninger	67	66	133	63,500
John Cook/Mark O'Meara	67	67	134	62,000
Peter Jacobsen/Arnold Palmer	67	68	135	60,500
Mark Calcavecchia/Billy Mayfair	69	66	135	60,500

Subaru Sarazen World Open

The Legends at Chateau Elan, Braselton, Georgia — November 5-8
Par 36-36–72; 6,955 yards — purse, $2,000,000

	SCORES				TOTAL	MONEY
Dudley Hart	72	69	62	69	272	$360,000
Bob Tway	66	70	66	74	276	210,000
Bernhard Langer	68	72	69	68	277	124,000
John Huston	70	71	72	65	278	80,000
Miguel Angel Jimenez	72	69	67	71	279	67,500
Andrew Coltart	69	68	73	69	279	67,500
Ricardo Gonzalez	69	68	70	73	280	60,000
Peter O'Malley	73	67	72	69	281	55,000
Greg Turner	68	72	68	75	283	47,500
Bob Friend	74	66	69	74	283	47,500
Mark McNulty	69	72	73	70	284	38,500
Peter Mitchell	72	71	72	69	284	38,500
Padraig Harrington	70	73	67	75	285	32,500
Brad Faxon	69	76	69	71	285	32,500
Stephen Leaney	72	72	70	72	286	26,333.34
David Carter	73	72	69	72	286	26,333.33
Garrett Willis	73	67	75	71	286	26,333.33
Trevor Dodds	71	70	72	74	287	24,000
Adam Mednick	73	71	70	74	288	23,000
Craig Stadler	70	71	72	76	289	20,000
Michael Long	72	68	75	74	289	20,000
Stewart Cink	72	68	75	74	289	20,000
Philip Jonas	76	70	71	72	289	20,000
Gordon Sherry	71	72	75	71	289	20,000
Edward Fryatt	67	67	83	73	290	17,000
Paul McGinley	73	68	73	77	291	15,500
Christian Chernock	69	71	74	77	291	15,500
Mark Calcavecchia	72	74	70	76	292	13,166.67
Sven Struver	73	75	71	73	292	13,166.67
Johan Rystrom	76	72	72	72	292	13,166.66
Desvonde Botes	72	72	72	77	293	11,000
Kevin Wentworth	71	73	73	76	293	11,000
Scott Verplank	75	71	71	76	293	11,000
Retief Goosen	72	73	74	74	293	11,000
John Mellor	75	69	76	73	293	11,000
Tim Conley	72	74	76	71	293	11,000
Joakim Rask	74	70	75	75	294	9,750
Payne Stewart	71	75	74	74	294	9,750
Jonathan Lomas	72	72	77	73	294	9,750
Clinton Whitelaw	73	72	75	75	295	9,250
Pedro Martinez	75	71	72	78	296	8,825
Patrik Sjoland	75	71	74	76	296	8,825
Kevin Stone	74	73	74	75	296	8,825
Gustavo Mendoza	76	71	77	72	296	8,825

	SCORES				TOTAL	MONEY
Tripp Isenhour	77	71	71	78	297	7,750
Billy Andrade	74	73	75	75	297	7,750
Gustavo Rojas	75	73	74	75	297	7,750
Stephen Allan	78	68	74	78	298	6,983.34
Bradley Dredge	74	74	73	77	298	6,983.33
Rodrigo Cuello	75	72	77	74	298	6,983.33
Jorge Berendt	73	75	74	78	300	6,600
Lars Tingvall	69	78	81	73	301	6,400
Kim Jong-duk	74	73	75	80	302	6,150
Kevin Carissimi	73	74	83	73	303	6,100
Taimur Hussain	72	74	81	77	304	6,050
Frank Nobilo	76	72	78	81	307	6,000

General Motors Mexican Open

Golf Club of Mexico, Mexico City, Mexico — November 12-15
Par 36-36–72; 7,333 yards — purse, $275,000

	SCORES				TOTAL	MONEY
Eduardo Romero	67	63	69	70	269	$54,486
Larry Mize	67	74	68	67	276	34,507
Emlyn Aubrey	68	69	69	71	277	18,943
Sean Murphy	60	70	66	71	277	18,943
Harrison Frazar	71	69	67	70	277	18,943
Nick Price	70	70	69	68	277	18,943
Tommy Armour III	70	68	72	71	281	11,351
Joe Ogilvie	71	72	70	70	283	10,443
Allan Bratten	69	70	72	73	284	7,912
Grant Masson	69	73	68	73	284	7,912
Esteban Toledo	68	71	73	72	284	7,912
*Sergio Garcia	70	73	74	67	284	7,912
Marco Gortana	72	76	69	67	284	7,912
Octavio Gonzalez	72	71	72	70	285	5,721
Robin Freeman	75	74	66	70	285	5,721
Chris Zambri	68	70	73	75	286	4,540
Tim Conley	74	69	75	68	286	4,540
Jorge Perez Leon	72	74	70	71	287	3,314
Cesar Perez	76	69	72	70	287	3,314
Brian Gay	71	75	71	70	287	3,314
Rafael Alarcon	69	74	75	69	287	3,314
Carlos Pelaez	66	73	77	72	288	2,610
Jaime Gomez	75	71	72	70	288	2,610
Rene Rangel	73	75	69	72	289	2,255
Matt Gogel	76	71	72	70	289	2,255
Alejandro Quiroz	76	74	69	70	289	2,255
Alejandro Munoz	75	68	72	75	290	1,399
Angel Romero	78	67	71	74	290	1,399
Mario Navarro	76	69	72	73	290	1,399
Eric Booker	70	75	72	73	290	1,399
Steve Flesch	73	71	74	72	290	1,399
Danny Ellis	71	73	76	70	290	1,399

Franklin Templeton Shark Shootout

Sherwood Country Club, Thousand Oaks, California — November 13-15
Par 36-36–72; 7,025 yards — purse, $1,100,000

	SCORES			TOTAL	MONEY (Team)
Steve Elkington/Greg Norman	67	64	58	189	$320,000
Peter Jacobsen/John Cook	68	66	55	189	180,000
(Elkington/Norman defeated Jacobsen/Cook on third extra hole.)					
Costantino Rocca/Scott Hoch	66	65	60	191	122,000
Davis Love III/Brad Faxon	68	62	62	192	89,333
Tom Kite/Billy Mayfair	69	62	61	192	89,333
John Daly/Fuzzy Zoeller	65	66	61	192	89,333
Fred Couples/Justin Leonard	69	65	59	193	79,000
Bruce Lietzke/Scott McCarron	72	62	61	195	71,500
Ben Crenshaw/Craig Stadler	70	66	59	195	71,500
Hal Sutton/Glen Day	68	68	60	196	65,000
Billy Andrade/Jay Haas	68	63	66	197	63,000
Mark Calcavecchia/Andrew Magee	73	65	60	198	60,000

PGA Grand Slam

Poipu Bay Resort, Kauai, Hawaii — November 17-18
Par 36-36–72; 6,957 yards — purse, $1,000,000

FIRST-ROUND MATCHES

Vijay Singh defeated Mark O'Meara, 2 up
Tiger Woods defeated Lee Janzen, 3 and 2

CHAMPIONSHIP MATCH

Woods defeated Singh, 2 up
(Woods received $400,000; Singh received $250,000.)

THIRD-PLACE MATCH

Janzen defeated O'Meara, 1 up
(Janzen received $200,000; O'Meara received $150,000.)

World Cup of Golf

Gulf Harbor Country Club, Whangaparaoa, New Zealand — November 19-22
Par 36-36–72; 6,850 yards — purse, US$1,500,000

	INDIVIDUAL SCORES				TOTAL
ENGLAND (568)—$400,000					
David Carter	73	71	76	68	288
Nick Faldo	68	70	73	69	280
ITALY (570)—$200,000					
Costantino Rocca	65	74	71	70	280
Massimo Florioli	74	77	71	68	290
UNITED STATES (571)—$101,667					
John Daly	70	77	77	68	292
Scott Verplank	70	72	74	63	279

	INDIVIDUAL SCORES				TOTAL
SCOTLAND (571)—$101,667					
Colin Montgomerie	72	69	75	68	284
Andrew Coltart	70	74	77	66	287
ARGENTINA (571)—$101,667					
Angel Cabrera	69	71	71	73	284
Ricardo Gonzalez	73	74	72	68	287
IRELAND (572)—$60,000					
Padraig Harrington	72	72	72	71	287
Paul McGinley	67	76	73	69	285
ZIMBABWE (573)—$38,500					
Mark McNulty	67	78	73	67	285
Tony Johnstone	72	73	73	70	288
NEW ZEALAND (573)—$38,500					
Frank Nobilo	72	76	73	70	291
Greg Turner	73	71	70	68	282
AUSTRALIA (574)—$28,000					
Peter O'Malley	69	73	74	67	283
Richard Green	69	73	77	72	291
SPAIN (579)—$24,000					
Santiago Luna	71	74	77	68	290
Miguel Angel Martin	76	70	74	69	289
SWEDEN (580)—$18,500					
Patrik Sjoland	68	77	74	63	282
Mathias Gronberg	70	80	77	71	298
JAPAN (580)—$18,500					
Mitsutaka Kusakabe	70	80	80	69	299
Yasuharu Imano	64	75	75	67	281
COLOMBIA (581)—$14,000					
Rigoberto Velasquez	72	77	73	74	296
Gustavo Mendoza	70	76	74	65	285
CANADA (581)—$14,000					
Ian Leggatt	69	70	76	69	284
Rick Gibson	71	76	77	73	297
FRANCE (583)—$11,000					
Jean Van de Velde	72	75	72	70	289
Thomas Levet	69	76	75	74	294
CHILE (589)—$9,500					
Roy MacKenzie	68	78	76	74	296
Guillermo Encina	72	73	77	71	293
SOUTH AFRICA (589)—$9,500					
David Frost	66	74	75	71	286
Nic Henning	71	73	80	79	303
WALES (590)—$8,800					
Ian Woosnam	70	74	81	71	296
Phillip Price	72	79	72	71	294

	INDIVIDUAL SCORES				TOTAL
GERMANY (592)—$8,600					
Thomas Gogele	73	79	78	73	303
Sven Struver	69	74	76	70	289
PARAGUAY (593)—$8,300					
Felix Ramon Franco	71	78	76	73	298
Pedro Martinez	75	71	76	73	295
SWITZERLAND (593)—$8,300					
Paolo Quirici	75	74	70	72	291
Christopher Bovet	73	79	74	76	302
DENMARK (599)—$8,000					
Soren Hansen	74	76	78	74	302
Soren Kjeldsen	75	76	75	71	297
NORWAY (602)—$7,700					
Per Haugsrud	74	81	76	76	307
Oyvind Rojahn	72	75	75	73	295
KOREA (602)—$7,700					
Kwon Young-suk	74	77	76	77	304
Choi Kwang-soo	77	69	77	75	298
MEXICO (603)—$7,400					
Esteban Toledo	72	72	76	70	290
Cesar Perez	80	78	81	74	313
MALAYSIA (604)—$7,200					
Periasamy Gunasegaran	71	74	82	74	301
Ali Kadir	71	79	75	78	303
AUSTRIA (607)—$7,000					
Claude Grenier	72	73	81	70	296
Karl Ableidinger	74	80	80	77	311
BRAZIL (613)—$6,800					
Acacio Jorge	73	78	75	71	297
Ruberlei Felizardo	75	80	85	76	316
VENEZUELA (614)—$6,600					
Damaso Galban	77	80	81	78	316
Miguel Martinez	75	74	78	71	298
JAMAICA (626)—$6,400					
Seymour Rose	80	84	80	80	324
Delroy Cambridge	72	79	80	71	302
HOLLAND (643)—$6,200					
Ruben Wechgelaer	90	81	89	81	341
Hayo Bensdorp	73	80	76	73	302
LUXEMBOURG (647)—$6,000					
John Penning	75	80	84	76	315
John Pickford	84	83	86	79	332

INTERNATIONAL TROPHY

WINNER: Verplank - 279 - $100,000. RUNNERS-UP: Faldo, Rocca - 280 - $37,500 each. ORDER OF FINISH: Imano -281 - $15,000; Turner, Sjoland - 282 - $5,000 each.

Callaway Golf Pebble Beach Invitational

Pebble Beach Golf Links, Pebble Beach, California
Par 36-36–72; 6,799 yards

November 19-22
purse, $300,000

	SCORES				TOTAL	MONEY
Tom Lehman	66	70	69	68	273	$60,000
Rocco Mediate	69	69	66	71	275	24,450
Kirk Triplett	71	69	68	67	275	24,450
Jim Carter	70	71	66	71	278	10,600
Bruce Fleisher	68	71	69	71	279	9,000
Gary Hallberg	76	70	65	69	280	8,000
David Graham	79	72	67	72	281	7,000
Loren Roberts	73	67	76	66	282	6,250
Kris Tschetter	74	67	70	71	282	6,250
Johnny Miller	71	69	69	74	283	5,350
David Peoples	72	70	70	71	283	5,350
Kevin Sutherland	76	66	70	72	284	4,900
Bob Friend	73	73	69	70	285	4,450
Keith Fergus	70	72	71	72	285	4,450
Bob Murphy	69	73	72	72	286	3,850
David Toms	73	71	68	74	286	3,850
Brian Henninger	75	70	71	71	287	3,300
Bob Ford	74	70	72	71	287	3,300
Brian Mogg	76	71	68	72	287	3,300
Walter Morgan	68	76	70	74	288	2,800
Terry Dill	74	69	73	72	288	2,800
Frank Conner	76	69	71	72	288	2,800
Mike Reid	71	73	74	71	289	2,600
Mark Pfeil	77	69	68	76	290	2,500
Cindy Figg-Currier	72	69	72	78	291	2,350
Todd Fischer	74	75	72	70	291	2,350
Frank Lickliter	73	73	71	75	292	2,200
Mark Wiebe	72	70	76	74	292	2,200
Darrell Kestner	69	79	71	73	292	2,200
Barry Jaeckel	76	73	70	74	293	2,100
Jeff McMillian	73	75	70	76	294	2,040
Roger Maltbie	74	75	74	71	294	2,040
Cindy Flom	74	74	75	71	294	2,040
Todd Southard	73	71	75	75	294	2,040
Glen Stubblefield	75	76	70	73	294	2,040
Don Pooley	74	74	74	73	295	1,940
Robert Irving	75	73	74	73	295	1,940
Mike Soll	76	75	70	74	295	1,940
Chuck Milne	77	72	70	76	295	1,940
Greg Powers	75	76	71	74	296	1,870
Janice Moodie	75	76	71	74	296	1,870
Dan Forsman	75	71	75	75	296	1,870
Al Geiberger	78	75	71	73	297	1,830
Laird Small	74	68	76	79	297	1,830
Jane Geddes	74	73	77	74	298	1,790
Marion Dantzler	75	74	73	76	298	1,790
Tommy Masters	76	72	76	75	299	1,740
David Eichelberger	70	77	72	80	299	1,740
Joan Pitcock	75	76	69	79	299	1,740
Bud Allin	71	73	77	78	299	1,740
Rob Bold	76	71	74	78	299	1,740
Jimmy Powell	73	76	79		WD	

JCPenney Classic

Westin Innisbrook Resort, Copperhead Course, Palm Harbor, Florida
Par 36-35–71; 7,054 yards (men), 6,330 yards (women)

December 3-6
purse, $1,750,000

	SCORES				TOTAL	MONEY (Each)
Meg Mallon/Steve Pate	61	66	66	62	255	$218,750
Rachel Hetherington/Rocco Mediate	63	65	62	69	259	100,000
Catrin Nilsmark/Chris Perry	63	65	66	68	262	70,000
Dottie Pepper/Jeff Sluman	67	65	65	66	263	43,000
Helen Alfredsson/Billy Andrade	65	67	64	67	263	43,000
Dale Eggeling/Fuzzy Zoeller	64	66	64	69	263	43,000
Melissa McNamara/Glen Day	69	68	65	62	264	20,600
Pat Hurst/Scott McCarron	66	68	64	66	264	20,600
Kris Tschetter/Steve Jones	64	63	68	69	264	20,600
Chris Johnson/Steve Lowery	64	63	65	72	264	20,600
Michele Redman/Skip Kendall	66	67	62	69	264	20,600
Dawn Coe-Jones/Dudley Hart	66	66	68	65	265	10,600
Se Ri Pak/David Frost	66	67	65	67	265	10,600
Vickie Odegard/Jim Carter	62	69	67	67	265	10,600
Tracy Hanson/Doug Barron	62	70	64	69	265	10,600
Catriona Matthew/Dan Forsman	63	68	65	69	265	10,600
Pearl Sinn/Eric Booker	67	66	66	67	266	8,500
Dina Ammaccapane/Omar Uresti	65	69	65	67	266	8,500
Kristi Albers/J.P. Hayes	66	69	63	68	266	8,500
Rosie Jones/Robert Gamez	67	69	65	66	267	7,250
Cindy Figg-Currier/Mark Brooks	69	67	68	63	267	7,250
Tina Barrett/Fred Funk	66	69	66	67	268	6,500
Maria Hjorth/Scott Gump	67	69	65	67	268	6,500
Cindy McCurdy/Russ Cochran	61	72	67	68	268	6,500
Colleen Walker/Michael Bradley	68	67	68	65	268	6,500
Beth Daniel/Doug Martin	63	67	66	72	268	6,500
Michelle Estill/Tom Pernice, Jr.	67	67	67	68	269	6,050
Lorie Kane/Mike Weir	69	68	64	68	269	6,050
Dana Dormann/Paul Stankowski	66	67	66	70	269	6,050
Donna Andrews/Mike Hulbert	68	66	65	70	269	6,050
Charlotta Sorenstam/Mathias Gronberg	66	67	68	69	270	5,700
Laura Davies/John Daly	64	71	65	70	270	5,700
Helen Dobson/Tim Herron	67	69	68	66	270	5,700
Amy Fruhwirth/Clarence Rose	65	68	71	67	271	5,450
Juli Inkster/Tom Purtzer	66	69	68	68	271	5,450
Emilee Klein/Stewart Cink	69	69	62	72	272	5,250
Marta Figueras-Dotti/Brad Bryant	65	70	67	70	272	5,250
Jenny Lidback/Emlyn Aubrey	65	71	65	72	273	4,900
Jackie Gallagher-Smith/David Toms	69	70	64	70	273	4,900
Wendy Ward/David Ogrin	66	73	64	70	273	4,900
Hollis Stacy/Bob Friend	66	71	70	66	273	4,900
Lisa Hackney/David Gilford	69	69	69	66	273	4,900
Janice Moodie/Steve Flesch	65	72	66	71	274	4,500
Susie Redman/Ted Tryba	63	72	69	70	274	4,500
Joan Pitcock/Bill Glasson	69	68	66	71	274	4,500
Cathy Johnston-Forbes/Willie Wood	68	69	69	69	275	4,300
Kim Saiki/Dennis Paulson	67	71	66	72	276	4,200
Michelle McGann/Len Mattiace	65	72	72	68	277	4,100
Jan Stephenson/Frank Lickliter	67	69	71	71	278	4,000
Annika Sorenstam/David Esch	70	71	69	69	279	3,900
Amy Alcott/Tommy Armour III	70	71	71	68	280	3,800
Pat Bradley/Mark Bradley	71	72	71	71	285	3,750

Office Depot Father-Son Challenge

Windsor Club, Vero Beach, Florida — December 5-6
Par 36-36–72; 6,709 yards — purse, $860,000

	SCORES		TOTAL	MONEY (Won by professional)
Bob Charles/David Charles	57	62	119	$150,000
Craig Stadler/Kevin Stadler	63	60	123	100,000
Hale Irwin/Steve Irwin	59	65	124	80,000
Raymond Floyd/Robert Floyd	61	64	125	48,833.34
Larry Nelson/Josh Nelson	62	63	125	48,833.34
Johnny Miller/John Miller	64	61	125	48,833.33
Jerry Pate/Wesley Pate	63	62	125	48,833.33
Dave Stockton/Ron Stockton	64	61	125	48,833.33
Lee Trevino/Rick Trevino	62	63	125	48,833.33
Billy Casper/Bobby Casper	64	63	127	37,000
Charles Coody/Kyle Coody	62	66	128	35,500
Tom Weiskopf/Eric Weiskopf	64	64	128	35,500
David Graham/Andrew Graham	65	64	129	34,000
Al Geiberger/John Geiberger	65	67	132	32,500
Tony Jacklin/Warren Jacklin	67	65	132	32,500
Hubert Green/Myatt Green	66	67	133	30,000

Presidents Cup

Royal Melbourne Golf Club, Melbourne, Australia — December 11-13
Par 36-36–72; 6,981 yards

FIRST DAY
Foursomes

Frank Nobilo and Greg Turner (Int.) defeated Mark O'Meara and David Duval, 1 up.
Greg Norman and Steve Elkington (Int.) defeated Jim Furyk and John Huston, 2 up.
Shigeki Maruyama and Craig Parry (Int.) defeated Lee Janzen and Scott Hoch, 3 and 2.
Tiger Woods and Fred Couples (US) defeated Ernie Els and Vijay Singh, 5 and 4.
Stuart Appleby and Nick Price (Int.) halved with Davis Love III and Justin Leonard.

Fourballs

Norman and Elkington (Int.) defeated O'Meara and Furyk, 2 and 1.
Maruyama and Naomichi Ozaki (Int.) defeated Mark Calcavecchia and Huston, 4 and 3.
Duval and Phil Mickelson (US) halved with Els and Price.
Couples and Love (US) defeated Parry and Carlos Franco, 1 up.
Appleby and Singh (Int.) defeated Leonard and Woods, 2 and 1.

POINTS: International 7, United States 3

SECOND DAY
Foursomes

Nobilo and Turner (Int.) defeated Love and Leonard, 2 up.
Norman and Elkington (Int.) halved with Janzen and Calcavecchia.
Maruyama and Parry (Int.) defeated Woods and Couples, 1 up.
Appleby and Price (Int.) defeated Duval and Mickelson, 1 up.
Els and Singh (Int.) defeated Hoch and Furyk, 6 and 4.

Fourballs

O'Meara and Hoch (US) defeated Nobilo and Turner, 1 up.
Els and Singh (Int.) defeated Woods and Huston, 1 up.
Maruyama and Ozaki (Int.) defeated Duval and Mickelson, 3 and 2.
Janzen and Calcavecchia (US) defeated Price and Franco, 3 and 2.
Norman and Elkington (Int.) defeated Couples and Love, 2 and 1.

POINTS: International 7½, United States 2½

THIRD DAY
Singles

Parry (Int.) defeated Leonard, 5 and 3.
Price (Int.) defeated Duval, 2 and 1.
Furyk (US) defeated Nobilo, 4 and 2.
Mickelson (US) halved with Franco.
Maruyama (Int.) defeated Huston, 3 and 2.
Hoch (US) defeated Ozaki, 4 and 3.
Calcavecchia (US) halved with Turner.
Janzen (US) halved with Elkington.
Els (Int.) defeated Love, 1 up.
Couples (US) halved with Singh.
Woods (US) defeated Norman, 1 up.
O'Meara (US) defeated Appleby, 1 up.

POINTS: International 6, United States 6

TOTAL POINTS: International 20½, United States 11½

Lexus Challenge

La Quinta Resort & Club, La Quinta, California — December 19-20
Par 36-36–72; 6,825 yards — purse, $1,000,000

	SCORES		TOTAL	MONEY (Won by professional)
Jim Colbert/Kevin Costner	58	62	120	$180,000
Hubert Green/Matt Lauer	65	56	121	120,000
Larry Nelson/Sean Connery	61	65	126	105,000
Raymond Floyd/William Devane	65	62	127	95,000
Bob Murphy/Ken Griffey, Jr.	62	66	128	80,000
Jay Sigel/Randy Quaid	62	66	128	80,000
Hale Irwin/Michael Jordan	67	67	134	58,000
Johnny Miller/Glenn Frey	67	67	134	58,000
Dave Stockton/Craig T. Nelson	71	63	134	58,000
Arnold Palmer/Joe Pesci	70	64	134	58,000
Lee Trevino/Alberto Tomba	71	63	134	58,000
Gary Player/Roger Clemens	69	67	136	50,000

Nike Tour

Lakeland Classic

Grasslands Golf & Country Club, Lakeland, Florida — January 8-11
Par 36-36–72; 7,040 yards — purse, $225,000

	SCORES				TOTAL	MONEY
Casey Martin	66	69	65	69	269	$40,500
Steve Lamontagne	69	69	65	67	270	25,537.50
Jeff Julian	69	69	65	69	272	18,562.50
Pete Jordan	69	70	65	69	273	12,000
Gary Koch	68	67	69	69	273	12,000
Tom Scherrer	68	71	69	65	273	12,000
Marco Gortana	69	69	67	69	274	7,875
Charlie Rymer	68	70	71	65	274	7,875
Mike Small	70	67	66	71	274	7,875
Keith Fergus	69	67	70	69	275	5,062.50
Dave Schreyer	70	66	67	72	275	5,062.50
Woody Austin	69	66	67	74	276	3,408.75
Mike Brisky	69	71	65	71	276	3,408.75
Joey Gullion	70	69	69	68	276	3,408.75
Ryan Howison	68	70	71	67	276	3,408.75
Greg Lesher	66	71	70	69	276	3,408.75
Bob Sowards	70	70	68	68	276	3,408.75
Don Walsworth	71	68	68	70	277	2,812.50
Ben Bates	71	67	73	67	278	2,362.50
Curt Byrum	70	70	69	69	278	2,362.50
Paul Claxton	71	69	73	65	278	2,362.50
Chris Couch	67	68	75	68	278	2,362.50
Tim Loustalot	67	69	73	69	278	2,362.50
Tom R. Shaw	66	73	68	71	278	2,362.50
Michael Walton	69	70	70	69	278	2,362.50
Brian Bateman	71	68	71	69	279	1,642.50
Jeff Brehaut	68	67	73	71	279	1,642.50
Michael Clark	68	67	70	74	279	1,642.50
Joe Daley	70	70	66	73	279	1,642.50
Steve Hart	72	67	73	67	279	1,642.50
Sean Murphy	66	74	71	68	279	1,642.50

South Florida Classic

Palm-Aire Country Club, Pompano Beach, Florida — January 15-18
Par 36-36–72; 6,932 yards — purse, $225,000

	SCORES				TOTAL	MONEY
Eric Johnson	66	71	63	67	267	$40,500
Chris Riley	67	65	68	69	269	25,538
Woody Austin	66	67	69	68	270	14,813
Tommy Armour	69	67	66	68	270	14,813
Don Reese	67	66	66	71	270	14,813
Deane Pappas	70	69	68	64	271	9,000

	SCORES				TOTAL	MONEY
Sean Murphy	70	66	68	67	271	9,000
Jim Thorpe	68	67	68	68	271	9,000
Brian Tennyson	68	69	68	67	272	6,750
Joe Daley	67	71	69	66	273	3,947
Greg Kraft	71	65	69	68	273	3,947
Ivan Smith	69	71	65	68	273	3,947
Dennis Paulson	71	67	66	69	273	3,947
Jim Estes	69	67	67	70	273	3,947
Ben Bates	68	68	65	72	273	3,947
Gary Rusnak	67	67	67	72	273	3,947
Chris Stutts	70	68	70	66	274	2,762
Perry Moss	69	71	69	65	274	2,762
Gary Nicklaus	67	69	69	69	274	2,762
Dave Schreyer	70	69	71	64	274	2,762
John Kernohan	68	69	68	70	275	2,475
David Peoples	68	69	70	69	276	1,863
Bobby Wadkins	75	64	68	69	276	1,863
Tim Loustalot	70	69	68	69	276	1,863
Fred Wadsworth	72	67	67	70	276	1,863
Robert Floyd	68	68	70	70	276	1,863
Greg Lesher	68	72	65	71	276	1,863
Gene Fieger	70	69	66	71	276	1,863
Danny Briggs	69	69	67	71	276	1,863
Patrick Lee	68	67	68	73	276	1,863
Rocky Walcher	67	70	67	72	276	1,863

Greater Austin Open

The Hills Country Club, Austin, Texas — March 5-8
Par 36-36–72; 6,954 yards — purse, $225,000

	SCORES				TOTAL	MONEY
Michael Allen	66	72	66	76	280	$40,500
Chris Zambri	68	67	70	77	282	22,050
Gene Sauers	70	69	65	78	282	22,050
Darrett Brinker	68	71	69	75	283	14,063
Don Walsworth	67	71	70	76	284	10,969
Keith Fergus	68	68	69	79	284	10,969
Jay Williamson	72	68	71	74	285	8,438
Paul Claxton	71	70	67	77	285	8,438
Jeff Julian	68	69	74	75	286	4,905
Greg Lesher	71	71	68	76	286	4,905
Denis Watson	72	67	71	76	286	4,905
Curt Byrum	73	67	70	76	286	4,905
Michael Muehr	68	72	70	76	286	4,905
*Brad Elder	70	65	71	81	287	
Charlie Rymer	71	65	68	83	287	3,488
Bud Still	73	68	71	76	288	3,032
Carl Paulson	70	73	68	77	288	3,032
Mark Hensby	69	72	70	77	288	3,032
Casey Martin	69	69	72	78	288	3,032
Michael Flynn	68	72	72	77	289	2,419
Ryan Howison	75	68	70	76	289	2,419
Pat Bates	69	72	70	78	289	2,419
Dave Stockton, Jr.	73	68	74	74	289	2,419
Dennis Zinkon	72	67	71	79	289	2,419
Robin Freeman	71	70	66	82	289	2,419

	SCORES				TOTAL	MONEY
David Berganio, Jr.	71	70	70	79	290	1,913
David Peoples	69	74	67	80	290	1,913
Terry Dill	71	70	75	74	290	1,913
Sean Murphy	68	74	72	77	291	1,499
Steve Haskins	67	73	74	77	291	1,499
Steve Hart	68	73	74	76	291	1,499
Chris Riley	74	68	73	76	291	1,499
Dan Bateman	73	70	74	74	291	1,499

Monterrey Open

Club Campestre, Monterrey, Mexico — March 19-22
Par 36-36–72; 6,945 yards — purse, $300,000

	SCORES				TOTAL	MONEY
Joe Ogilvie	70	68	70	66	274	$45,000
Jaxon Brigman	70	70	71	65	276	16,500
Perry Moss	68	70	71	67	276	16,500
Chris Riley	65	71	72	68	276	16,500
John Wilson	66	74	68	68	276	16,500
Robin Freeman	65	69	73	69	276	16,500
John Elliott	69	68	68	71	276	16,500
Deane Pappas	71	71	67	68	277	6,375
Emlyn Aubrey	71	68	69	69	277	6,375
Charles Raulerson	68	70	68	71	277	6,375
Craig Perks	69	69	69	70	277	6,375
Oscar Serna	69	67	68	73	277	6,375
Casey Martin	69	71	70	68	278	3,875
Michael Walton	68	69	72	69	278	3,875
David Seawell	70	71	67	70	278	3,875
Greg Lesher	70	73	68	68	279	3,283
Patrick Lee	72	70	69	68	279	3,283
Geoffrey Sisk	71	68	70	70	279	3,283
Jeff Gove	70	71	71	68	280	2,938
Keith Fergus	69	73	70	68	280	2,938
*Sergio Garcia	66	67	75	72	280	
Kevin Riley	64	75	71	71	281	2,688
Joey Snyder	68	68	72	73	281	2,688
Mark Wurtz	69	72	70	71	282	2,313
Pat Bates	69	71	71	71	282	2,313
Bob Sowards	67	73	70	72	282	2,313
Robert Floyd	67	68	74	73	282	2,313
Jay Williamson	73	68	72	70	283	1,875
Dave Stockton, Jr.	72	69	71	71	283	1,875
Jeff Brehaut	68	74	70	71	283	1,875

Louisiana Open

Le Triomphe Country Club, Broussard, Louisiana — March 26-29
Par 36-36–72; 6,954 yards — purse, $300,000

	SCORES				TOTAL	MONEY
John Wilson	73	65	67	69	274	$54,000
Steve Flesch	71	71	70	67	279	34,050
Doug Dunakey	69	74	71	68	282	24,750

	SCORES				TOTAL	MONEY
Esteban Toledo	74	74	71	64	283	18,750
David Berganio, Jr.	71	72	73	68	284	10,607.15
Charlie Rymer	75	74	68	67	284	10,607.15
Emlyn Aubrey	71	70	72	71	284	10,607.14
Woody Austin	68	75	72	69	284	10,607.14
Eric Booker	75	70	68	71	284	10,607.14
Deane Pappas	72	72	66	74	284	10,607.14
Joey Snyder	71	78	67	68	284	10,607.14
Danny Briggs	73	71	69	72	285	5,250
Pat Bates	73	71	72	70	286	4,650
Kevin Johnson	76	73	69	68	286	4,650
Sean Murphy	72	72	72	70	286	4,650
Chris Couch	70	80	69	68	287	4,035
Fran Quinn	75	71	73	68	287	4,035
Kawika Cotner	75	71	74	68	288	3,525
P.J. Cowan	72	76	71	69	288	3,525
Jeff Julian	76	74	72	66	288	3,525
Geoffrey Sisk	72	74	70	72	288	3,525
Brian Bateman	70	73	71	75	289	2,700
Curt Byrum	78	72	68	71	289	2,700
Keith Fergus	70	73	72	74	289	2,700
Mike Heinen	74	72	71	72	289	2,700
Bradley Hughes	77	73	68	71	289	2,700
Steve Schneiter	73	73	67	76	289	2,700
Chris Zambri	70	74	71	74	289	2,700
Michael Clark	69	80	70	71	290	1,860
Scott Dunlap	77	71	71	71	290	1,860
Mark Hensby	77	72	69	72	290	1,860
Mike Sposa	73	73	73	71	290	1,860
Adam Spring	76	72	73	69	290	1,860
Michael Walton	73	73	71	73	290	1,860

Shreveport Open

Southern Trace Country Club, Shreveport, Louisiana — April 9-12
Par 36-36–72; 6,916 yards — purse, $225,000

	SCORES				TOTAL	MONEY
Vance Veazey	76	70	65	69	280	40,500
John Wilson	72	69	71	68	280	25,537.50
(Veazey defeated Wilson on first extra hole.)						
Brian Kamm	68	73	69	71	281	16,312.50
Deane Pappas	72	68	66	75	281	16,312.50
Doug Tewell	76	69	68	70	283	10,968.75
Dennis Paulson	74	69	69	71	283	10,968.75
Craig Spence	70	74	72	68	284	8,437.50
Jimmy Green	73	69	68	74	284	8,437.50
Mike Sposa	74	73	67	71	285	4,905
Mark Hensby	67	74	71	73	285	4,905
Ron Philo	74	70	67	74	285	4,905
Charlie Rymer	66	73	72	74	285	4,905
Eric Booker	70	67	69	79	285	4,905
Tim Conley	78	69	68	71	286	3,123
Chris Zambri	70	75	69	72	286	3,123
Jaxon Brigman	71	71	70	74	286	3,123
Steve Hart	72	71	69	74	286	3,123
Keith Fergus	72	70	68	76	286	3,123

	SCORES				TOTAL	MONEY
Michael Muehr	72	72	74	69	287	2,418.75
Craig Perks	72	73	72	70	287	2,418.75
Michael Walton	73	70	72	72	287	2,418.75
Michael Clark	72	70	71	74	287	2,418.75
Jimmy Johnston	72	72	69	74	287	2,418.75
Tripp Isenhour	70	69	73	75	287	2,418.75
Jeff Gove	70	72	76	70	288	1,747.50
Marco Gortana	74	73	71	70	288	1,747.50
Dicky Pride	71	76	70	71	288	1,747.50
Craig Bowden	73	71	70	74	288	1,747.50
Craig Barlow	73	69	72	74	288	1,747.50
Clark Dennis	71	73	70	74	288	1,747.50

Upstate Classic

Verdae Greens Golf Club, Greenville, South Carolina — April 16-19
Par 36-36–72; 6,773 yards — purse, $225,000
(Fourth round cancelled — rain.)

	SCORES			TOTAL	MONEY
Tom Scherrer	67	67	66	200	$40,500
J.L. Lewis	67	69	65	201	25,538
Mike Sullivan	71	68	66	205	18,563
Jay Williamson	70	67	69	206	12,938
Eric Booker	73	70	63	206	12,938
Don Walsworth	73	69	65	207	8,438
Deane Pappas	68	71	68	207	8,438
Eric Johnson	69	69	69	207	8,438
John Kernohan	70	68	69	207	8,438
Jeff Gove	71	71	66	208	4,444
Danny Briggs	69	70	69	208	4,444
Scott Dunlap	70	69	69	208	4,444
Dennis Paulson	74	65	69	208	4,444
Craig Spence	69	72	68	209	2,860
Robin Freeman	72	70	67	209	2,860
Franklin Langham	75	67	67	209	2,860
Paul Gow	71	70	68	209	2,860
Joe Ogilvie	73	68	68	209	2,860
Kevin Johnson	70	69	70	209	2,860
Brian Tennyson	67	71	71	209	2,860
Woody Austin	69	68	72	209	2,860
Don Reese	65	71	73	209	2,860
Fran Quinn	71	69	70	210	2,194
Dick Mast	70	70	70	210	2,194
Tripp Isenhour	74	68	69	211	1,800
Tom R. Shaw	69	71	71	211	1,800
John Maginnes	72	68	71	211	1,800
Chris Anderson	72	71	68	211	1,800
Chris Zambri	71	67	73	211	1,800
Marco Gortana	70	71	71	212	1,311
John Wilson	72	69	71	212	1,311
Michael Clark	70	71	71	212	1,311
Jay Delsing	70	69	73	212	1,311
Tony Sills	67	71	74	212	1,311
Rocky Walcher	70	73	69	212	1,311
Denis Watson	72	71	69	212	1,311

Huntsville Open

Hampton Grove Golf Club, Highlands Course, Owens Cross Roads, Alabama
Par 36-36–72; 7,200 yards

April 23-26
purse, $225,000

	SCORES				TOTAL	MONEY
Dennis Paulson	68	68	72	71	279	$40,500
Brent Schwarzrock	68	73	70	68	279	25,537.50
(Paulson defeated Schwarzrock on first extra hole.)						
Perry Moss	69	70	68	73	280	18,562.50
Pat Bates	69	69	75	68	281	12,937.50
Jeff Brehaut	73	70	69	69	281	12,937.50
John Elliott	72	67	72	71	282	9,562.50
Mike Sullivan	71	69	71	71	282	9,562.50
Eric Booker	71	70	71	71	283	7,875
Emlyn Aubrey	71	73	70	70	284	4,905
Scott Johnson	73	66	70	75	284	4,905
Deane Pappas	71	68	71	74	284	4,905
Geoffrey Sisk	68	71	73	72	284	4,905
Chris Stutts	72	67	69	76	284	4,905
Mark Hensby	73	71	68	73	285	3,285
Kevin Johnson	72	69	73	71	285	3,285
Craig Kanada	73	70	70	72	285	3,285
Rod Butcher	67	70	75	74	286	2,820
Curt Byrum	74	69	70	73	286	2,820
Jeff Gove	73	71	70	72	286	2,820
Michael Clark	71	72	70	74	287	2,362.50
Jimmy Green	73	70	69	75	287	2,362.50
Casey Martin	75	68	70	74	287	2,362.50
Mike Sposa	71	71	74	71	287	2,362.50
Karl Zoller	70	71	68	78	287	2,362.50
Bob Burns	74	68	76	70	288	1,579.50
Chris Couch	70	70	71	77	288	1,579.50
Joey Gullion	71	71	73	73	288	1,579.50
Tripp Isenhour	70	73	74	71	288	1,579.50
John Kernohan	72	70	73	73	288	1,579.50
Greg Lesher	68	74	72	74	288	1,579.50
Craig Perks	73	71	71	73	288	1,579.50
Don Reese	71	70	73	74	288	1,579.50
Tom Scherrer	71	71	71	75	288	1,579.50
Tom R. Shaw	70	72	73	73	288	1,579.50

South Carolina Classic

Country Club of South Carolina, Florence, South Carolina
Par 36-36–72; 7,150 yards

April 30-May 3
purse, $225,000

	SCORES				TOTAL	MONEY
Gene Sauers	70	69	72	69	280	$40,500
Craig Kanada	70	70	70	71	281	22,050
Sean Murphy	70	71	70	70	281	22,050
Rob McKelvey	70	69	73	70	282	12,937.50
Sam Randolph	72	69	70	71	282	12,937.50
Ty Armstrong	76	68	71	68	283	6,830.36
Pat Bates	70	71	72	70	283	6,830.36
Jeff Gove	75	69	71	68	283	6,830.36
Steve Lamontagne	76	67	71	69	283	6,830.36

	SCORES				TOTAL	MONEY
Don Reese	68	70	74	71	283	6,830.36
Woody Austin	75	68	69	71	283	6,830.35
John Kernohan	71	67	72	73	283	6,830.35
Paul Claxton	72	66	72	74	284	3,391.88
Fred Wadsworth	71	69	71	73	284	3,391.88
Jimmy Green	69	69	71	75	284	3,391.87
Chris Wollmann	71	68	71	74	284	3,391.87
Jay Davis	73	70	71	71	285	2,590.72
Casey Martin	72	68	75	70	285	2,590.72
Charlie Rymer	70	69	74	72	285	2,590.72
Robert Floyd	73	69	71	72	285	2,590.71
Michael Muehr	71	66	72	76	285	2,590.71
Deane Pappas	73	67	73	72	285	2,590.71
Gary Rusnak	73	66	70	76	285	2,590.71
Steve Hart	70	70	75	71	286	1,968.75
Eric Johnson	69	75	72	70	286	1,968.75
Joe Walsh	73	69	74	70	286	1,968.75
Garrett Willis	73	69	71	73	286	1,968.75
Bob Burns	74	69	71	73	287	1,498.50
Jerry Foltz	72	71	74	70	287	1,498.50
Vance Heafner	72	70	74	71	287	1,498.50
Bill McDonald	71	73	74	69	287	1,498.50
Adam Spring	71	68	73	75	287	1,498.50

Carolina Classic

Prestonwood Country Club, Cary, North Carolina — May 7-10
Par 36-36–72; 7,271 yards — purse, $225,000

	SCORES				TOTAL	MONEY
Brian Bateman	68	66	67	65	266	$40,500
Jimmy Green	60	68	69	70	267	25,537.50
Jeff Julian	65	71	65	68	269	16,312.50
Joey Snyder	67	68	66	68	269	16,312.50
Jason Gore	68	67	66	69	270	9,112.50
Kevin Johnson	65	70	66	69	270	9,112.50
Chris Riley	66	68	66	70	270	9,112.50
Dave Schreyer	69	65	69	67	270	9,112.50
Michael Walton	67	64	70	69	270	9,112.50
Emlyn Aubrey	70	66	67	68	271	4,443.75
Allen Doyle	68	65	68	70	271	4,443.75
Brian Gay	69	69	67	66	271	4,443.75
Garrett Willis	69	68	69	65	271	4,443.75
Matt Gogel	62	72	70	68	272	3,200.63
Tom Scherrer	68	69	68	67	272	3,200.63
Steve Haskins	67	66	68	71	272	3,200.62
Rob McKelvey	68	64	72	68	272	3,200.62
Danny Briggs	71	67	72	63	273	2,812.50
Jerry Foltz	70	69	65	70	274	2,643.75
Adam Spring	70	68	65	71	274	2,643.75
Scott Dunlap	69	68	68	70	275	2,418.75
Bob Sowards	67	69	67	72	275	2,418.75
Robert Floyd	70	65	69	72	276	2,137.50
Steve Hart	66	68	74	68	276	2,137.50
Barry Jaeckel	67	69	66	74	276	2,137.50
Mark Hensby	71	68	71	67	277	1,642.50
Craig Kanada	70	69	71	67	277	1,642.50

	SCORES				TOTAL	MONEY
John Kernohan	67	71	69	70	277	1,642.50
Carl Paulson	68	70	70	69	277	1,642.50
Charles Raulerson	67	69	71	70	277	1,642.50
Chris Stutts	67	72	69	69	277	1,642.50

Dominion Open

The Dominion Club, Richmond, Virginia — May 14-17
Par 36-36–72; 7,020 yards — purse, $225,000

	SCORES				TOTAL	MONEY
Bob Burns	71	65	66	72	274	$40,500
Pat Bates	70	69	66	71	276	17,493.75
Eric Johnson	70	71	66	69	276	17,493.75
Perry Moss	73	65	70	68	276	17,493.75
Mike Sullivan	67	68	67	74	276	17,493.75
Emlyn Aubrey	71	69	67	70	277	8,437.50
Notah Begay III	70	59	74	74	277	8,437.50
Doug Dunakey	70	68	66	73	277	8,437.50
John Maginnes	73	66	68	70	277	8,437.50
Brian Bateman	66	69	71	72	278	4,252.50
Greg Lesher	68	69	71	70	278	4,252.50
Mike Sposa	70	70	66	72	278	4,252.50
Shane Tait	67	71	72	68	278	4,252.50
Michael Walton	69	71	68	70	278	4,252.50
P.J. Cowan	69	70	70	70	279	3,031.88
Tom R. Shaw	73	67	68	71	279	3,031.88
Steve Haskins	66	67	73	73	279	3,031.87
John Kernohan	70	69	69	71	279	3,031.87
Chris Anderson	73	68	69	70	280	2,083.13
Billy Downes	68	69	72	71	280	2,083.13
Jim Estes	72	65	72	71	280	2,083.13
Jason Gore	69	68	73	70	280	2,083.13
Cliff Kresge	70	71	68	71	280	2,083.13
Dave Schreyer	71	68	70	71	280	2,083.13
Keith Fergus	70	68	70	72	280	2,083.12
Tom Scherrer	73	67	66	74	280	2,083.12
Fred Wadsworth	67	69	67	77	280	2,083.12
Don Walsworth	70	71	66	73	280	2,083.12
Garrett Willis	71	66	69	74	280	2,083.12
Karl Zoller	70	66	69	75	280	2,083.12

Knoxville Open

Three Ridges Golf Club, Knoxville, Tennessee — May 28-31
Par 36-36–72; 7,035 yards — purse, $225,000

	SCORES				TOTAL	MONEY
Robin Freeman	68	66	66	70	270	$40,500
Ryan Howison	68	66	67	69	270	25,537.50
(Freeman defeated Howison on third extra hole.)						
Jimmy Green	65	70	66	70	271	16,312.50
Dick Mast	68	71	65	67	271	16,312.50
Joe Ogilvie	67	71	67	67	272	9,703.13
Charles Raulerson	70	68	68	66	272	9,703.13

	SCORES				TOTAL	MONEY
Craig Kanada	63	68	71	70	272	9,703.12
Gene Sauers	67	73	63	69	272	9,703.12
Greg Lesher	71	68	66	68	273	6,750
Michael Allen	68	67	68	71	274	5,625
Joe Cioe	72	68	64	71	275	4,500
Sam Randolph	67	71	71	67	276	3,712.50
Tim Straub	67	66	75	68	276	3,712.50
Garrett Willis	74	67	68	67	276	3,712.50
Notah Begay III	66	70	74	67	277	2,902.50
Bob Burns	71	67	70	69	277	2,902.50
Doug Dunakey	69	72	69	67	277	2,902.50
Dennis Paulson	72	69	68	68	277	2,902.50
Charlie Rymer	67	73	70	67	277	2,902.50
Chris Zambri	71	70	65	71	277	2,902.50
Danny Briggs	73	67	70	68	278	2,193.75
Allen Doyle	70	68	70	70	278	2,193.75
Danny Edwards	65	71	70	72	278	2,193.75
Deane Pappas	70	64	76	68	278	2,193.75
Tom Scherrer	71	69	69	69	278	2,193.75
Greg Twiggs	67	70	72	69	278	2,193.75
JC Anderson	69	69	71	70	279	1,687.50
Craig Bowden	68	71	69	71	279	1,687.50
Fran Quinn	70	68	68	73	279	1,687.50
Tim Loustalot	68	68	73	71	280	1,288.13
John Maginnes	71	70	68	71	280	1,288.13
Mike Sullivan	69	68	72	71	280	1,288.13
Rocky Walcher	68	70	70	72	280	1,288.13
Matthew Lane	70	70	67	73	280	1,288.12
Adam Spring	67	73	67	73	280	1,288.12
Iain Steel	68	70	69	73	280	1,288.12
Fred Wadsworth	69	72	66	73	280	1,288.12

Miami Valley Open

Heatherwoode Golf Club, Springboro, Ohio — June 4-7
Par 36-35–71; 6,730 yards — purse, $225,000

	SCORES				TOTAL	MONEY
Craig Bowden	65	64	68	67	264	$40,500
Doug Dunakey	69	59	67	71	266	22,050
Ryan Howison	64	68	66	68	266	22,050
Michael Clark	67	71	66	65	269	14,062.50
Greg Lesher	68	68	62	72	270	11,812.50
JC Anderson	66	68	71	66	271	9,562.50
Charles Raulerson	67	66	71	67	271	9,562.50
James Gilleon	70	68	66	68	272	5,126.79
Dennis Paulson	66	70	68	68	272	5,126.79
Craig Perks	68	72	68	64	272	5,126.79
Chris Zambri	66	68	69	69	272	5,126.79
Patrick Lee	68	61	69	74	272	5,126.78
Casey Martin	67	72	64	69	272	5,126.78
Sam Randolph	67	64	71	70	272	5,126.78
Charlie Rymer	66	68	70	69	273	3,262.50
Joey Gullion	67	66	72	69	274	2,830.50
Gene Sauers	65	73	70	66	274	2,830.50
Mike Sposa	69	71	66	68	274	2,830.50
Chris Stutts	74	63	66	71	274	2,830.50

	SCORES				TOTAL	MONEY
Don Walsworth	67	72	71	64	274	2,830.50
Trey Coker	69	67	70	69	275	2,306.25
Steve Hart	66	68	71	70	275	2,306.25
Steve Lamontagne	69	69	70	67	275	2,306.25
Perry Moss	68	70	66	71	275	2,306.25
Brian Fogt	70	69	68	69	276	1,968.75
Jimmy Green	69	65	71	71	276	1,968.75
David Berganio, Jr.	68	68	67	74	277	1,588.50
David Branshaw	67	73	71	66	277	1,588.50
Gary Rusnak	66	71	66	74	277	1,588.50
Michael Walton	67	69	68	73	277	1,588.50
Garrett Willis	66	70	75	66	277	1,588.50

Cleveland Open

Quail Hollow Resort, Devlin Course, Concord, Ohio — June 11-14
Par 36-36–72; 6,712 yards — purse, $225,000

	SCORES				TOTAL	MONEY
Doug Dunakey	68	72	65	65	270	$40,500
Dennis Paulson	70	69	64	68	271	25,537.50
Woody Austin	70	66	70	66	272	18,562.50
Emlyn Aubrey	66	69	72	67	274	12,937.50
John Maginnes	66	68	72	68	274	12,937.50
Craig Kanada	68	70	70	67	275	9,562.50
Sam Randolph	68	70	70	67	275	9,562.50
Ty Armstrong	67	70	73	66	276	6,187.50
Danny Briggs	67	70	71	68	276	6,187.50
Paul Claxton	69	69	68	70	276	6,187.50
Carl Paulson	67	71	68	70	276	6,187.50
Deane Pappas	72	67	75	63	277	3,825
Chris Zambri	67	70	68	72	277	3,825
Allen Doyle	71	67	70	70	278	3,375
Ivan Smith	70	70	70	68	278	3,375
Bob Burns	71	70	69	69	279	2,771.25
Lon Hinkle	68	67	70	74	279	2,771.25
Matthew Lane	69	70	71	69	279	2,771.25
Patrick Lee	70	70	71	68	279	2,771.25
Tom R. Shaw	67	71	68	73	279	2,771.25
Joey Snyder	68	73	69	69	279	2,771.25
Michael Allen	71	70	70	69	280	1,968.75
Pat Bates	71	64	74	71	280	1,968.75
Joel Edwards	72	69	72	67	280	1,968.75
Jeff Julian	70	69	70	71	280	1,968.75
Steve Lamontagne	67	71	72	70	280	1,968.75
Kevin Riley	74	67	68	71	280	1,968.75
Gary Rusnak	71	70	71	68	280	1,968.75
Tom Scherrer	68	70	73	69	280	1,968.75
Scott Dunlap	70	70	74	67	281	1,288.13
James Gilleon	71	70	71	69	281	1,288.13
Jimmy Green	66	75	72	68	281	1,288.13
Joey Gullion	71	68	73	69	281	1,288.13
Notah Begay III	70	70	68	73	281	1,288.12
Paul Gow	69	69	69	74	281	1,288.12
Bob Sowards	70	69	70	72	281	1,288.12
Mike Sposa	69	71	69	72	281	1,288.12

Lehigh Valley Open

Center Valley Club, Center Valley, Pennsylvania — June 18-21
Par 36-36–72; 6,904 yards — purse, $225,000

	SCORES				TOTAL	MONEY
Eric Booker	67	67	72	65	271	$40,500
Notah Begay III	70	66	64	71	271	25,537.50
(Booker defeated Begay on ninth extra hole.)						
Robin Freeman	70	70	65	67	272	18,562.50
Joe Ogilvie	67	65	72	69	273	14,062.50
Jeff Brehaut	68	68	68	71	275	10,968.75
Jay Williamson	70	67	72	66	275	10,968.75
Chris Anderson	67	66	71	72	276	6,281.25
Emlyn Aubrey	70	69	70	67	276	6,281.25
Robert Floyd	69	67	68	72	276	6,281.25
J.L. Lewis	68	70	68	70	276	6,281.25
Rob McKelvey	67	69	71	69	276	6,281.25
Brian Tennyson	70	66	68	72	276	6,281.25
Don Walsworth	72	69	70	66	277	3,712.50
Bob Burns	67	70	68	73	278	2,860
Doug Dunakey	66	72	69	71	278	2,860
Marco Gortana	73	66	70	69	278	2,860
Jeff Gove	68	72	70	68	278	2,860
Matthew Lane	71	70	72	65	278	2,860
John Maginnes	70	66	71	71	278	2,860
Sean Murphy	65	75	68	70	278	2,860
David Seawell	73	66	70	69	278	2,860
Roger Tambellini	68	66	70	74	278	2,860
Craig Bowden	69	66	71	73	279	2,025
Paul Claxton	71	70	69	69	279	2,025
Greg Lesher	71	68	67	73	279	2,025
Michael Muehr	71	67	71	70	279	2,025
Geoffrey Sisk	69	67	75	68	279	2,025
Tim Loustalot	71	69	72	68	280	1,535.63
Charlie Wi	69	67	74	70	280	1,535.63
Ryan Howison	70	69	66	75	280	1,535.62
Dennis Paulson	71	69	69	71	280	1,535.62

Greensboro Open

Sedgefield Country Club, Greensboro, North Carolina — June 25-28
Par 35-35–70; 6,737 yards — purse, $225,000

	SCORES				TOTAL	MONEY
Joe Ogilvie	65	69	66	66	266	$40,500
Chris Zambri	63	67	69	71	270	25,537.50
Bob Burns	69	65	72	66	272	13,640.63
John Maginnes	70	66	71	65	272	13,640.63
Emlyn Aubrey	68	67	69	68	272	13,640.62
Joey Snyder	65	66	71	70	272	13,640.62
*Sergio Garcia	72	67	65	68	272	
Greg Lesher	64	72	70	67	273	7,312.50
Charles Raulerson	70	68	69	66	273	7,312.50
Charles Warren	70	67	69	67	273	7,312.50
Jay Williamson	70	66	66	71	273	7,312.50
Pat Bates	69	67	69	69	274	4,050
Brian Tennyson	66	70	70	68	274	4,050

	SCORES				TOTAL	MONEY
Don Walsworth	67	68	70	69	274	4,050
Woody Austin	69	64	72	70	275	3,285
Jeff Gove	67	67	71	70	275	3,285
Tim Straub	69	69	69	68	275	3,285
Chris Anderson	69	67	73	67	276	2,647.50
Jeff Brehaut	68	66	77	65	276	2,647.50
Matthew Lane	69	60	75	72	276	2,647.50
Michael Muehr	70	68	68	70	276	2,647.50
Geoffrey Sisk	68	69	69	70	276	2,647.50
Rocky Walcher	71	68	67	70	276	2,647.50
Scott Dunlap	67	67	73	70	277	1,968.75
Tim Dunlavey	69	65	75	68	277	1,968.75
Steve Hart	71	67	69	70	277	1,968.75
Kevin Johnson	68	70	70	69	277	1,968.75
Steve Lamontagne	71	68	68	70	277	1,968.75
Bud Still	69	69	68	71	277	1,968.75
Jay Davis	69	69	72	68	278	1,395
Steve Haskins	68	70	67	73	278	1,395
Patrick Lee	67	70	68	73	278	1,395
Michael Walton	67	71	69	71	278	1,395
Dave Wedzik	68	69	71	70	278	1,395
Greg Whisman	69	70	66	73	278	1,395

Hershey Open

Country Club of Hershey, East Course, July 2-5
Hershey, Pennsylvania purse, $225,000
Par 36-35–71; 7,081 yards

	SCORES				TOTAL	MONEY
Michael Clark	66	68	66	73	273	$40,500
Bob Burns	69	71	64	71	275	25,537.50
Mike Sposa	68	69	69	70	276	18,562.50
Chris Zambri	67	71	67	73	278	14,062.50
Paul Gow	72	69	69	69	279	11,812.50
Charlie Wi	74	68	70	68	280	10,125
Jeff Brehaut	68	72	69	72	281	7,875
Tom Scherrer	72	69	70	70	281	7,875
Geoffrey Sisk	74	67	68	72	281	7,875
John Kernohan	73	66	72	71	282	5,062.50
Tim Straub	72	71	66	73	282	5,062.50
John Elliott	74	70	71	68	283	3,712.50
Rocky Walcher	68	72	69	74	283	3,712.50
Greg Whisman	71	70	70	72	283	3,712.50
Craig Bowden	71	73	69	71	284	3,031.88
Charles Warren	72	72	70	70	284	3,031.88
Patrick Burke	73	69	68	74	284	3,031.87
Kevin Johnson	71	72	68	73	284	3,031.87
Steve Lamontagne	68	74	70	73	285	2,587.50
Michael Muehr	73	68	72	72	285	2,587.50
Jack O'Keefe	73	71	73	68	285	2,587.50
Robin Freeman	72	67	71	77	287	2,081.25
Cliff Kresge	73	71	71	72	287	2,081.25
Carl Paulson	72	69	69	77	287	2,081.25
Charles Raulerson	68	72	75	72	287	2,081.25
Wes Short	72	72	69	74	287	2,081.25
Chris Starkjohann	73	69	71	74	287	2,081.25

	SCORES				TOTAL	MONEY
Jeff Barlow	73	69	69	77	288	1,498.50
Jaxon Brigman	70	75	74	69	288	1,498.50
John Maginnes	73	65	76	74	288	1,498.50
Bob Sowards	71	71	72	74	288	1,498.50
Jay Williamson	72	71	69	76	288	1,498.50

St. Louis Golf Classic

Missouri Bluffs Golf Club, St. Charles, Missouri — July 16-19
Par 36-35–71; 7,047 yards — purse, $225,000

	SCORES				TOTAL	MONEY
Chris Starkjohann	69	67	64	63	263	$40,500
Notah Begay III	68	65	64	67	264	25,537.50
Greg Lesher	69	63	67	67	266	14,812.50
Joe Ogilvie	68	68	65	65	266	14,812.50
Ron Whittaker	67	67	65	67	266	14,812.50
David Berganio, Jr.	67	69	64	67	267	9,000
Jay Davis	68	63	68	68	267	9,000
Carl Paulson	67	70	66	64	267	9,000
Woody Austin	69	66	66	67	268	5,625
Sean Murphy	71	65	64	68	268	5,625
Mike Sposa	68	70	64	66	268	5,625
Michael Clark	70	66	69	64	269	3,600
Craig Kanada	68	67	68	66	269	3,600
Rocky Walcher	66	69	67	67	269	3,600
Chris Zambri	67	65	69	68	269	3,600
Pat Bates	72	64	68	66	270	2,955
Craig Bowden	66	66	70	68	270	2,955
Paul Gow	69	67	68	66	270	2,955
Marco Gortana	69	66	68	68	271	2,587.50
Arden Knoll	70	67	67	67	271	2,587.50
Karl Zoller	66	67	68	70	271	2,587.50
Bob Gaus	67	70	67	68	272	2,025
Deane Pappas	67	65	72	68	272	2,025
John Restino	66	67	68	71	272	2,025
Jason Schultz	65	69	68	70	272	2,025
Geoffrey Sisk	66	69	67	70	272	2,025
Joey Snyder	67	70	68	67	272	2,025
Brian Tennyson	68	70	65	69	272	2,025
Eric Booker	71	66	69	67	273	1,485
David McCampbell	68	68	65	72	273	1,485
Michael Walton	67	71	66	69	273	1,485

Wichita Open

Willowbend Golf Club, Wichita, Kansas — July 23-26
Par 36-36–72; 7,000 yards — purse, $225,000

	SCORES				TOTAL	MONEY
Emlyn Aubrey	66	61	71	67	265	$40,500
Carl Paulson	65	67	68	66	266	22,050
Anthony Rodriguez	68	66	64	68	266	22,050
Geoffrey Sisk	65	68	69	65	267	12,937.50
Charlie Wi	69	66	66	66	267	12,937.50

	SCORES				TOTAL	MONEY
Jaime Gomez	68	70	67	63	268	10,125
Paul Gow	65	68	65	71	269	8,437.50
Adam Spring	68	65	71	65	269	8,437.50
Woody Austin	67	68	66	69	270	6,187.50
Steve Lamontagne	67	69	69	65	270	6,187.50
Jaxon Brigman	67	70	68	66	271	4,218.75
Greg Lesher	70	68	68	65	271	4,218.75
Brian Bateman	65	74	67	66	272	3,600
Eric Booker	69	65	70	68	272	3,600
Doug Dunakey	66	71	69	67	273	3,031.88
Karl Zoller	69	71	66	67	273	3,031.88
Notah Begay III	73	62	70	68	273	3,031.87
Jeff Gove	65	69	69	70	273	3,031.87
Brian Gay	69	67	69	69	274	2,531.25
Dennis Paulson	70	69	70	65	274	2,531.25
Brian Tennyson	68	68	68	70	274	2,531.25
Bruce Vaughan	70	69	67	68	274	2,531.25
Bob Burns	68	69	69	69	275	2,025
Keoke Cotner	69	70	70	66	275	2,025
David McCampbell	68	70	66	71	275	2,025
Pat McTigue	66	68	68	73	275	2,025
Charles Raulerson	65	70	69	71	275	2,025
Eric Bogar	71	69	67	69	276	1,498.50
Michael Clark	68	70	69	69	276	1,498.50
Roger Dibble	70	67	70	69	276	1,498.50
Steve Gotsche	70	68	70	68	276	1,498.50
Arden Knoll	72	66	66	72	276	1,498.50

Dakota Dunes Open

Dakota Dunes Country Club, Dakota Dunes, South Dakota — July 30-August 2
Par 36-36–72; 7,165 yards — purse, $325,000

	SCORES				TOTAL	MONEY
John Maginnes	62	68	73	71	274	$58,500
Ryan Howison	67	68	70	69	274	31,850
Sean Murphy	69	67	69	69	274	31,850
(Maginnes defeated Howison and Murphy on second extra hole.)						
Eric Booker	68	65	72	70	275	18,687.50
Don Walsworth	66	70	70	69	275	18,687.50
David Berganio, Jr.	69	70	68	69	276	14,625
Robin Freeman	66	69	71	72	278	11,375
Mark Hensby	71	69	69	69	278	11,375
Jeff Julian	68	71	70	69	278	11,375
Marco Gortana	69	67	73	70	279	6,770.84
Scott Dunlap	71	67	69	72	279	6,770.83
Mike Sullivan	70	68	68	73	279	6,770.83
David Kirkpatrick	67	69	74	71	281	4,899.38
Tom R. Shaw	72	67	72	70	281	4,899.38
Jeff Gove	68	68	73	72	281	4,899.37
Garrett Willis	66	69	73	73	281	4,899.37
Woody Austin	67	67	76	72	282	3,989.38
Jimmy Green	67	72	76	67	282	3,989.38
Brian Bateman	68	71	71	72	282	3,989.37
Craig Spence	69	69	70	74	282	3,989.37
Ahmad Bateman	68	67	76	72	283	3,087.50
Pat Bates	67	70	74	72	283	3,087.50

	SCORES				TOTAL	MONEY
Bob Burns	65	73	74	71	283	3,087.50
Matt Gogel	69	68	74	72	283	3,087.50
Matt Peterson	71	67	71	74	283	3,087.50
Charles Raulerson	71	67	76	69	283	3,087.50
Charles Warren	72	68	70	73	283	3,087.50
Craig Bowden	69	68	75	72	284	2,075.36
John Kernohan	67	72	72	73	284	2,075.36
Adam Spring	66	66	79	73	284	2,075.36
Brian Tennyson	69	69	75	71	284	2,075.36
Chris Zambri	67	71	73	73	284	2,075.36
Craig Kanada	67	73	71	73	284	2,075.35
Shane Tait	71	68	66	79	284	2,075.35

Omaha Classic

The Champions Club, Omaha, Nebraska — August 6-9
Par 36-36–72; 7,034 yards — purse, $250,000

	SCORES				TOTAL	MONEY
Matt Gogel	66	69	69	67	271	$45,000
Jay Williamson	64	67	69	71	271	28,375
(Gogel defeated Williamson on fourth extra hole.)						
Eric Johnson	69	70	67	66	272	14,125
John Maginnes	69	71	68	64	272	14,125
Chris Riley	70	66	66	70	272	14,125
Gene Sauers	63	69	69	71	272	14,125
Don Walsworth	61	68	71	72	272	14,125
Craig Bowden	72	66	68	67	273	8,125
Marco Gortana	67	62	74	70	273	8,125
Scott Dunlap	73	69	67	65	274	5,625
Patrick Lee	71	69	69	65	274	5,625
Charles Raulerson	72	70	64	69	275	4,375
Jimmy Green	64	72	68	72	276	3,875
Casey Martin	70	72	69	65	276	3,875
Adam Spring	75	65	71	65	276	3,875
Jeff Thorsen	69	70	70	68	277	3,283.34
Craig Kanada	69	70	69	69	277	3,283.33
Bruce Vaughan	66	70	69	72	277	3,283.33
Jeff Barlow	67	68	74	69	278	2,812.50
Jeff Brehaut	72	67	72	67	278	2,812.50
Steve Hart	71	68	70	69	278	2,812.50
Taylor Smith	73	69	65	71	278	2,812.50
JC Anderson	67	69	71	72	279	2,125
John Elliott	74	67	72	66	279	2,125
Tripp Isenhour	68	69	70	72	279	2,125
Greg Lesher	69	71	71	68	279	2,125
Dave Schreyer	72	68	71	68	279	2,125
Geoffrey Sisk	71	67	70	71	279	2,125
John Wilson	71	68	73	67	279	2,125
Chris Couch	67	75	69	69	280	1,431.25
Jay Davis	69	72	67	72	280	1,431.25
Jerry Foltz	69	71	68	72	280	1,431.25
Rick Heath	67	70	66	77	280	1,431.25
Cliff Kresge	73	67	71	69	280	1,431.25
Sam Randolph	71	70	70	69	280	1,431.25
Tom R. Shaw	73	67	73	67	280	1,431.25
Chris Stutts	69	72	66	73	280	1,431.25

Ozarks Open

Highland Springs Country Club, Springfield, Missouri — August 13-16
Par 36-36–72; 7,058 yards — purse, $225,000

	SCORES				TOTAL	MONEY
Anthony Painter	67	63	68	69	267	$40,500
Scott Dunlap	72	67	62	67	268	25,537.50
Marco Gortana	66	67	67	70	270	18,562.50
Matt Gogel	68	63	71	70	272	11,250
Jimmy Green	69	66	71	66	272	11,250
Casey Martin	69	69	66	68	272	11,250
Mike Sposa	67	72	68	65	272	11,250
Jason Gore	66	68	69	70	273	7,875
Brian Bateman	71	68	68	67	274	5,625
Danny Briggs	69	67	73	65	274	5,625
Charles Raulerson	68	70	68	68	274	5,625
Woody Austin	73	66	68	68	275	3,825
Paul Claxton	70	68	71	66	275	3,825
Bruce Vaughan	68	73	69	66	276	2,986.08
David Kirkpatrick	69	70	65	72	276	2,986.07
John Maginnes	66	69	70	71	276	2,986.07
Rob McKelvey	67	73	67	69	276	2,986.07
Joey Snyder III	73	67	68	68	276	2,986.07
John Wilson	71	69	69	67	276	2,986.07
Dennis Zinkon	67	68	68	73	276	2,986.07
Michael Allen	71	70	67	69	277	2,081.25
Craig Bowden	70	71	70	66	277	2,081.25
Bob Burns	68	70	70	69	277	2,081.25
Brian Gay	69	70	67	71	277	2,081.25
Sean Murphy	67	70	68	72	277	2,081.25
Dennis Paulson	72	69	67	69	277	2,081.25
Gary Rusnak	71	67	68	71	277	2,081.25
Geoffrey Sisk	70	71	67	69	277	2,081.25
Tom Scherrer	69	70	72	67	278	1,530
Brian Tennyson	66	68	70	74	278	1,530

Fort Smith Classic

Hardscrabble Country Club, Fort Smith, Arkansas — August 20-23
Par 36-36–72; 6,620 yards — purse, $225,000

	SCORES				TOTAL	MONEY
Mark Hensby	65	68	62	65	260	$40,500
Woody Austin	64	68	64	66	262	25,537.50
John Kernohan	69	66	62	66	263	18,562.50
David Berganio, Jr.	65	67	64	68	264	14,062.50
Eric Booker	70	67	64	66	267	11,812.50
Jeff Barlow	66	71	65	66	268	8,437.50
Craig Perks	67	64	73	64	268	8,437.50
Craig Spence	66	67	69	66	268	8,437.50
Bruce Vaughan	68	66	63	71	268	8,437.50
Craig Bowden	67	69	65	68	269	5,062.50
David McCampbell	64	66	70	69	269	5,062.50
Sean McCarty	73	64	65	68	270	3,600
Rob McKelvey	66	67	69	68	270	3,600
Anthony Painter	69	66	68	67	270	3,600
Kevin Riley	67	67	68	68	270	3,600

	SCORES				TOTAL	MONEY
Jeff Gove	70	66	69	66	271	2,712.86
Joe Ogilvie	66	72	65	68	271	2,712.86
Dave Rummells	68	67	68	68	271	2,712.86
Gene Sauers	68	69	65	69	271	2,712.86
Bob Sowards	65	71	67	68	271	2,712.86
Brian Bateman	68	66	66	71	271	2,712.85
Chris Couch	67	67	67	70	271	2,712.85
Jaime Gomez	64	69	68	71	272	2,081.25
Nick O'Hern	71	66	67	68	272	2,081.25
Carl Paulson	69	68	69	66	272	2,081.25
Dennis Paulson	66	69	73	64	272	2,081.25
Scott Dunlap	68	69	72	64	273	1,636.88
Stiles Mitchell	71	67	68	67	273	1,636.88
Paul Claxton	69	68	67	69	273	1,636.87
Tag Ridings	70	66	68	69	273	1,636.87

Permian Basin Open

The Club at Mission Dorado, Odessa, Texas — August 27-30
Par 36-36–72; 7,135 yards — purse, $225,000

	SCORES				TOTAL	MONEY
Stiles Mitchell	69	69	67	71	276	$40,500
Woody Austin	71	68	69	68	276	22,050
Jeff Barlow	72	67	68	69	276	22,050
(Mitchell defeated Austin and Barlow on first extra hole.)						
Robin Freeman	72	68	70	67	277	14,062.50
Brian Bateman	75	67	67	69	278	9,112.50
Notah Begay III	71	71	66	70	278	9,112.50
Carl Paulson	75	66	69	68	278	9,112.50
Rocky Walcher	67	72	68	71	278	9,112.50
David Wedzik	72	66	69	71	278	9,112.50
David Berganio, Jr.	66	70	71	72	279	4,443.75
Marco Gortana	69	66	70	74	279	4,443.75
Mark Hensby	73	70	67	69	279	4,443.75
Ted Oh	73	67	68	71	279	4,443.75
Bob Burns	72	68	73	67	280	3,123
Rick Cramer	73	69	66	72	280	3,123
John Kernohan	68	71	73	68	280	3,123
Nick O'Hern	73	70	67	70	280	3,123
Jay Williamson	71	71	70	68	280	3,123
Rod Butcher	68	73	68	72	281	2,193.75
Jaime Gomez	73	67	64	77	281	2,193.75
Jeff Gove	70	73	71	67	281	2,193.75
Brian Hull	71	71	64	75	281	2,193.75
Steve Lamontagne	72	67	69	73	281	2,193.75
Jon Levitt	74	66	71	70	281	2,193.75
Sam Randolph	70	70	70	71	281	2,193.75
Charles Raulerson	74	68	69	70	281	2,193.75
Gene Sauers	73	69	68	71	281	2,193.75
Greg Towne	75	68	66	72	281	2,193.75
Chad Campbell	74	67	68	73	282	1,451.25
Michael Clark	69	70	71	72	282	1,451.25
Jimmy Green	73	70	70	69	282	1,451.25
Matthew Lane	69	71	71	71	282	1,451.25

Tri-Cities Open

Meadow Springs Country Club, Richland, Washington — September 10-13
Par 36-36–72; 6,926 yards — purse, $225,000

	SCORES				TOTAL	MONEY
Matt Gogel	70	73	68	65	276	$40,500
Brian Bateman	66	69	69	72	276	25,537.50
(Gogel defeated Bateman on third extra hole.)						
Andrew McLardy	73	69	69	66	277	14,812.50
Deane Pappas	67	72	67	71	277	14,812.50
Kevin Riley	71	67	69	70	277	14,812.50
Ty Armstrong	70	69	70	70	279	8,437.50
Robin Freeman	72	70	68	69	279	8,437.50
Jimmy Green	72	67	70	70	279	8,437.50
Rob McKelvey	71	68	71	69	279	8,437.50
Michael Allen	70	71	69	70	280	4,443.75
John Kernohan	69	69	71	71	280	4,443.75
Mike Sullivan	70	67	71	72	280	4,443.75
Garrett Willis	67	70	70	73	280	4,443.75
Notah Begay III	72	71	71	67	281	2,986.08
Emlyn Aubrey	71	74	69	67	281	2,986.07
Rod Butcher	68	70	73	70	281	2,986.07
Scott Dunlap	73	69	65	74	281	2,986.07
Jason Gore	70	72	68	71	281	2,986.07
Marco Gortana	72	69	71	69	281	2,986.07
Bill Porter	72	71	67	71	281	2,986.07
David Berganio, Jr.	70	68	74	70	282	2,250
Casey Martin	67	73	70	72	282	2,250
Don Reese	69	72	72	69	282	2,250
Geoffrey Sisk	68	74	69	71	282	2,250
Bruce Vaughan	73	70	69	70	282	2,250
Craig Bowden	72	71	69	71	283	1,692
Jeff Brehaut	71	68	72	72	283	1,692
David Kirkpatrick	70	69	67	77	283	1,692
Mike Sposa	70	74	70	69	283	1,692
Bud Still	76	68	74	65	283	1,692

Boise Open

Hillcrest Country Club, Boise, Idaho — September 17-20
Par 36-35–71; 6,885 yards — purse, $300,000

	SCORES				TOTAL	MONEY
Mike Sposa	63	71	66	65	265	$54,000
Notah Begay III	66	68	68	65	267	29,400
Dennis Paulson	67	64	69	67	267	29,400
Pat Bates	67	70	66	66	269	17,250
Eric Booker	69	64	67	69	269	17,250
John Elliott	70	66	68	66	270	13,500
Joey Gullion	67	66	69	69	271	10,500
Joe Ogilvie	70	68	67	66	271	10,500
Geoffrey Sisk	70	69	64	68	271	10,500
Jimmy Green	68	69	66	69	272	6,750
Tom Scherrer	67	68	71	66	272	6,750
Billy Downes	67	67	71	68	273	4,800
Gary Rusnak	69	68	70	66	273	4,800
Mike Sullivan	69	68	69	67	273	4,800

	SCORES				TOTAL	MONEY
Jay Williamson	71	69	64	69	273	4,800
Paul Claxton	68	70	66	70	274	4,035
Jeff Julian	69	69	69	67	274	4,035
Chris Anderson	69	69	69	68	275	3,675
Steve Haskins	69	71	68	67	275	3,675
Jim Benepe	66	75	67	68	276	3,075
Bob Burns	69	71	69	67	276	3,075
Deane Pappas	69	68	70	69	276	3,075
Tom Silva	69	67	69	71	276	3,075
Taylor Smith	69	72	68	67	276	3,075
Rocky Walcher	66	68	70	72	276	3,075
James Blair	69	67	71	70	277	2,085
Robin Freeman	72	69	69	67	277	2,085
Brian Gay	67	71	71	68	277	2,085
Matt Gogel	64	68	72	73	277	2,085
Jeff Gove	69	67	72	69	277	2,085
Craig Kanada	69	69	70	69	277	2,085
Greg Lesher	70	67	73	67	277	2,085
Don Reese	69	71	69	68	277	2,085

Oregon Classic

Shadow Hills Country Club, Junction City, Oregon — September 24-27
Par 36-36–72; 7,007 yards — purse, $225,000

	SCORES				TOTAL	MONEY
Charles Raulerson	68	69	65	70	272	$40,500
Notah Begay III	67	69	72	69	277	19,387.50
John Elliott	70	66	69	72	277	19,387.50
Tom Scherrer	70	72	65	70	277	19,387.50
Eric Booker	68	67	69	74	278	10,312.50
Chris Couch	70	67	71	70	278	10,312.50
Joey Gullion	69	70	71	68	278	10,312.50
Craig Bowden	67	73	71	68	279	6,750
Kevin Johnson	73	68	69	69	279	6,750
Joe Ogilvie	65	74	70	70	279	6,750
Brian Gay	71	69	71	69	280	4,500
Bob Burns	71	70	69	71	281	3,712.50
Don Reese	66	72	70	73	281	3,712.50
Bud Still	71	70	70	70	281	3,712.50
Danny Briggs	74	68	72	68	282	3,183.75
Matthew Lane	71	73	71	67	282	3,183.75
Dennis Zinkon	73	69	69	72	283	2,947.50
Brian Bateman	72	71	71	70	284	2,643.75
Ted Oh	74	69	69	72	284	2,643.75
Brent Schwarzrock	71	69	74	70	284	2,643.75
Mike Sposa	67	70	74	73	284	2,643.75
Billy Downes	73	70	70	72	285	2,081.25
Robin Freeman	71	71	72	71	285	2,081.25
Steve Lamontagne	70	67	73	75	285	2,081.25
Rob McKelvey	72	70	71	72	285	2,081.25
Michael Muehr	71	71	72	71	285	2,081.25
Bruce Vaughan	74	68	71	72	285	2,081.25
Scott Dunlap	70	71	73	72	286	1,498.50
Todd Fischer	72	71	71	72	286	1,498.50
Casey Martin	75	69	70	72	286	1,498.50
Sam Randolph	73	71	68	74	286	1,498.50
John Wilson	71	73	69	73	286	1,498.50

San Jose Open

Almaden Country Club, San Jose, California — October 1-4
Par 37-35–72; 6,960 yards — purse, $225,000

	SCORES				TOTAL	MONEY
Robin Freeman	66	71	69	66	272	$40,500
Sean Murphy	66	68	70	68	272	22,050
Tom Scherrer	64	69	71	68	272	22,050
(Freeman defeated Murphy on first and Scherrer on fourth extra hole.)						
Doug Dunakey	69	66	70	68	273	12,937.50
Brian Tennyson	67	68	70	68	273	12,937.50
Don Reese	69	71	69	65	274	9,562.50
Chris Zambri	66	71	67	70	274	9,562.50
Michael Allen	68	68	66	73	275	6,750
Woody Austin	68	69	70	68	275	6,750
Gene Sauers	70	61	71	73	275	6,750
Danny Briggs	67	70	68	71	276	4,218.75
John Maginnes	70	70	71	65	276	4,218.75
Bob Burns	66	72	67	72	277	3,712.50
Michael Clark	70	69	70	69	278	3,375
Mike Sposa	67	67	77	67	278	3,375
Notah Begay III	69	68	67	75	279	3,026.25
Eric Booker	67	67	72	73	279	3,026.25
Paul Claxton	69	68	71	72	280	2,587.50
Matt Gogel	68	70	73	69	280	2,587.50
Gary Rusnak	69	68	72	71	280	2,587.50
Joey Snyder III	69	71	69	71	280	2,587.50
Dennis Zinkon	73	67	71	69	280	2,587.50
Chris Anderson	70	69	72	70	281	1,968.75
Pat Bates	71	69	72	69	281	1,968.75
Jeff Gove	69	70	71	71	281	1,968.75
Joe Ogilvie	69	69	74	69	281	1,968.75
Deane Pappas	72	67	74	68	281	1,968.75
Karl Zoller	70	67	73	71	281	1,968.75
Timothy Bogue	72	67	74	69	282	1,320
Joey Gullion	71	69	70	72	282	1,320
Chris Hunsucker	71	69	68	74	282	1,320
Robert Huxtable	68	69	72	73	282	1,320
Eric Johnson	68	72	71	71	282	1,320
Kevin Johnson	70	68	73	71	282	1,320
Kevin Riley	68	69	74	71	282	1,320
Brent Schwarzrock	70	69	71	72	282	1,320
Charlie Wi	68	66	77	71	282	1,320

Inland Empire Open

Moreno Valley Ranch Golf Club, Moreno Valley, California — October 8-11
Par 36-36–72; 6,880 yards — purse, $225,000

	SCORES				TOTAL	MONEY
Charles Raulerson	66	70	66	66	268	$40,500
Jay Williamson	66	66	71	68	271	25,537.50
Anthony Painter	68	73	66	67	274	16,312.50
Mike Sposa	67	70	70	67	274	16,312.50
David Berganio, Jr.	66	69	71	69	275	10,312.50
Jeff Gove	70	66	69	70	275	10,312.50
Geoffrey Sisk	68	68	70	69	275	10,312.50

	SCORES				TOTAL	MONEY
Rick Cramer	68	68	70	70	276	6,750
Matt Gogel	65	70	71	70	276	6,750
Karl Zoller	68	71	66	71	276	6,750
Jimmy Green	70	67	70	70	277	4,500
Pat Bates	71	68	72	67	278	3,501
Michael Clark	68	71	66	73	278	3,501
John Kernohan	75	66	65	72	278	3,501
Dick Mast	69	72	71	66	278	3,501
Bruce Vaughan	70	71	64	73	278	3,501
Perry Moss	70	71	69	69	279	2,590.72
Sean Murphy	70	72	69	68	279	2,590.72
Chris Zambri	68	74	67	70	279	2,590.72
Michael Allen	70	69	68	72	279	2,590.71
Jeff Hart	71	65	73	70	279	2,590.71
Greg Lesher	69	67	71	72	279	2,590.71
Carl Paulson	68	72	69	70	279	2,590.71
Danny Briggs	69	69	74	68	280	1,856.25
Jason Gore	70	71	69	70	280	1,856.25
Craig Kanada	68	74	69	69	280	1,856.25
Deane Pappas	67	73	68	72	280	1,856.25
Dennis Paulson	70	71	68	71	280	1,856.25
Don Walsworth	66	72	70	72	280	1,856.25
Joey Gullion	73	68	69	71	281	1,410
Sam Randolph	68	71	70	72	281	1,410
Brian Tennyson	71	67	71	72	281	1,410

Nike Tour Championship

Magnolia Grove, Crossings Course, Semmes, Alabama — October 22-25
Par 36-36–72; 7,043 yards — purse, $300,000

	SCORES				TOTAL	MONEY
Bob Burns	73	69	67	74	283	$63,000
Jeff Gove	75	71	71	69	286	39,725
Jimmy Green	69	73	72	73	287	29,750
Michael Clark	72	78	65	73	288	19,250
John Maginnes	72	78	69	69	288	19,250
Sean Murphy	73	76	68	71	288	19,250
Emlyn Aubrey	72	72	69	76	289	13,125
Jeff Julian	77	72	71	69	289	13,125
Ryan Howison	71	77	72	71	291	7,735
Perry Moss	66	77	73	75	291	7,735
Dennis Paulson	74	78	67	72	291	7,735
Don Reese	70	76	72	73	291	7,735
Mike Sposa	77	71	74	69	291	7,735
Woody Austin	74	74	71	73	292	4,858
Eric Booker	73	75	72	72	292	4,858
Robin Freeman	75	74	72	71	292	4,858
Tom Scherrer	71	74	70	77	292	4,858
Chris Zambri	72	79	67	74	292	4,858
David Berganio, Jr.	77	75	67	74	293	4,200
Doug Dunakey	73	75	71	75	294	3,850
Scott Dunlap	77	77	74	66	294	3,850
Steve Lamontagne	75	76	71	72	294	3,850
Notah Begay III	73	76	70	76	295	3,325
Carl Paulson	70	75	74	76	295	3,325
Chris Riley	72	75	73	75	295	3,325

	SCORES				TOTAL	MONEY
Joe Ogilvie	71	75	76	74	296	2,887.50
Anthony Painter	73	78	73	72	296	2,887.50
Charles Raulerson	71	77	72	77	297	2,660
Pat Bates	76	76	73	73	298	2,327.50
Marco Gortana	73	81	71	73	298	2,327.50
Greg Lesher	77	79	71	71	298	2,327.50
Don Walsworth	70	80	76	72	298	2,327.50

Canadian Tour

Payless Open

Cordova Bay Golf Course, Victoria, British Columbia — May 28-31
Par 36-36–72; 6,668 yards — purse, C$125,000

	SCORES				TOTAL	MONEY
Jay Hobby	70	65	72	68	275	C$22,500
Ian Leggatt	70	64	71	70	275	12,500
(Hobby defeated Leggatt on first extra hole.)						
Jim Rutledge	72	68	71	65	276	6,750
Tyler Shelton	69	68	70	69	276	6,750
Philip Jonas	73	70	68	66	277	4,625
Arden Knoll	69	70	69	69	277	4,625
Marty Schiene	71	71	68	67	277	4,625
Paul Devenport	69	72	68	69	278	2,922
Rich Massey	73	67	67	71	278	2,922
Perry Parker	72	69	70	67	278	2,922
Chris Tidland	69	64	71	74	278	2,922
Greg Bruckner	74	68	67	70	279	2,188
Cam Emerson	72	68	69	70	279	2,188
Dennis Harrington	70	71	73	65	279	2,188
Brad Sutterfield	74	69	69	67	279	2,188
Jeff Bloom	72	70	68	70	280	1,781
Tim Hegna	68	72	73	67	280	1,781
Bobby Kalinowski	75	69	69	67	280	1,781
Stuart Wallace	73	71	66	70	280	1,781
Tony Carolan	70	68	71	72	281	1,563
Ted Purdy	67	65	74	75	281	1,563
John Robertson	73	71	71	66	281	1,563
John Bizik	71	72	68	71	282	1,277
Marcus Cain	69	73	69	71	282	1,277
Mike Fergin	71	72	71	68	282	1,277
Davidson Matyczuk	73	68	70	71	282	1,277
Daniel Pelczarski	70	73	70	69	282	1,277
Scott Petersen	69	75	70	68	282	1,277
Frank Schiro	75	68	71	68	282	1,277
Richard Zokol	69	70	71	72	282	1,277

BC Tel Open

Mayfair Lakes Golf & Country Club, June 4-7
Richmond, British Columbia purse, C$150,000
Par 36-35–71; 6,641 yards

	SCORES				TOTAL	MONEY
Ian Hutchings	66	69	68	68	271	C$27,000
John Bizik	65	66	70	71	272	10,400
Carlos Espinosa	66	71	67	68	272	10,400
Steve Woods	63	67	68	74	272	10,400
Stephen Woodard	68	69	66	70	273	6,300
Kris Cox	70	71	65	69	275	4,275
Neil Homann	71	66	66	72	275	4,275
Chris Jorgensen	69	66	71	69	275	4,275
Tyler Shelton	71	65	71	68	275	4,275
Jerry Smith	69	69	69	68	275	4,275
Tim Balmer	73	68	69	66	276	2,400
Tony Carolan	73	67	67	69	276	2,400
Rick Dalpos	69	69	69	69	276	2,400
Bryan DeCorso	69	67	73	67	276	2,400
Paul Devenport	71	68	70	67	276	2,400
Ken Duke	67	72	65	72	276	2,400
Davidson Matyczuk	67	67	71	71	276	2,400
David McKenzie	73	69	71	63	276	2,400
Jim Rutledge	69	71	71	65	276	2,400
Shane Supple	73	67	67	69	276	2,400
Mike Grob	69	68	69	72	278	1,762.50
Allan MacDonald	70	69	67	72	278	1,762.50
Danny Mijovic	71	69	70	68	278	1,762.50
Grant Moorhead	75	67	72	64	278	1,762.50
Perry Parker	69	70	67	73	279	1,537.50
Scott Rowe	68	73	65	73	279	1,537.50
Rick Todd	71	70	70	68	279	1,537.50
Todd Fanning	68	74	70	68	280	1,312.50
Ray Freeman	71	68	68	73	280	1,312.50
Darren Griff	70	67	68	75	280	1,312.50
Arden Knoll	69	70	70	71	280	1,312.50
Grant Masson	70	72	65	73	280	1,312.50
Scott Petersen	70	72	68	70	280	1,312.50
Stuart Thompson	73	66	68	73	280	1,312.50
Chris Tidland	67	71	71	71	280	1,312.50
Richard Zokol	72	70	67	71	280	1,312.50

Telus Calgary Open

Heritage Pointe Golf and Country Club, Calgary, Alberta June 11-14
Par 36-36–72; 7,119 yards purse, C$150,000

	SCORES				TOTAL	MONEY
Scott Wearne	68	65	65	68	266	C$27,000
Derek Gilchrist	64	72	64	69	269	15,000
Paul Devenport	68	69	67	66	270	8,100
Philip Jonas	66	67	69	68	270	8,100
Ben Walter	64	66	71	70	271	5,925
Zhang Lian-wei	69	68	65	69	271	5,925
David McKenzie	70	68	70	64	272	4,425
David Morland	67	70	68	67	272	4,425

	SCORES				TOTAL	MONEY
Mike Grob	67	71	65	70	273	3,675
Shane Supple	69	68	67	70	274	3,300
Davidson Matyczuk	68	67	72	68	275	2,850
Scott Petersen	67	71	69	68	275	2,850
Chris Tidland	71	69	67	68	275	2,850
Jason Bohn	65	69	69	73	276	2,475
Conrad Ray	70	67	72	67	276	2,475
Ben Ferguson	70	70	69	68	277	2,137.50
Kari Kekki	66	68	74	69	277	2,137.50
Ian Leggatt	70	65	72	70	277	2,137.50
Alan McLean	69	68	71	69	277	2,137.50
Todd Pence	70	66	69	73	278	1,950
Brian Kontak	70	69	71	69	279	1,725
Grant Masson	69	69	70	71	279	1,725
Blair Philip	69	68	74	68	279	1,725
John Robertson	67	69	70	73	279	1,725
Steve Woods	69	69	69	72	279	1,725
Darren Eckhardt	71	70	72	67	280	1,500
Tom Stankowski	66	68	71	75	280	1,500
Brad Wilson	66	75	68	71	280	1,500
Bobby Kalinowski	72	66	72	71	281	1,331.25
Brennan Little	70	69	73	69	281	1,331.25
Blair Piercy	72	69	72	68	281	1,331.25
Warren Schutte	71	68	71	71	281	1,331.25
Andrew Smeeth	71	70	69	71	281	1,331.25
J.J. West	71	68	71	71	281	1,331.25

Dundee Realty International Team Matches

Willows Golf and Country Club, Saskatoon, Saskatchewan — June 17-18
Par 36-36–72; 7,119 yards — purse, C$50,000

FIRST DAY
Alternate Shot

Steve Woods and Paul Devenport (International) defeated Arden Knoll and Philip Jonas, 3 and 2.
Ian Leggatt and Ashley Chinner (Canada) defeated Scott Petersen and Mike Grob, 2 up.
John Robertson and Kari Kekki (Canada) defeated John Bizik and Tyler Shelton, 3 and 1.
Stuart Hendley and David Morland (Canada) defeated Ken Druce and Scott Wearne, 1 up.
Dave Pashko and Davidson Matyczuk (Canada) defeated Manny Zerman and Ken Duke, 1 up.
Ian Hutchings and Ray Freeman (International) defeated Brennan Little and Todd Fanning, 3 and 2.

POINTS: Canada 4, International Team 2

Best Ball

Grob and Petersen (International) defeated Jonas and Little, 1 up.
Zerman and Duke (International) defeated Knoll and Hendley, 4 and 3.
Woods and Devenport (International) defeated Morland and Fanning, 3 and 2.
Robertson and Kekki (Canada) defeated Druce and Wearne, 1 up.
Pashko, and Matyczuk (Canada) defeated Bizik and Shelton, 4 and 3.
Leggatt and Chinner (Canada) defeated Hutchings and Freeman, 1 up.

POINTS: Canada 3, International Team 3

SECOND DAY
Individual Matchplay

Jonas (Canada) halved with Grob.
Pashko (Canada) defeated Shelton, 4 and 3.
Robertson (Canada) defeated Druce, 3 and 1.
Wearne (International) defeated Kekki, 1 up.
Chinner (Canada) defeated Zerman, 4 and 3.
Bizik (International) defeated Little, 2 and 1.
Woods (International) defeated Fanning, 3 and 2.
Petersen (International) defeated Morland, 4 and 3.
Leggatt (Canada) defeated Duke, 2 and 1.
Knoll (Canada) halved with Hutchings.
Devenport (International) defeated Matyczuk, 2 and 1.
Hendley (Canada) defeated Freeman, 3 and 1.

POINTS: Canada 6, International 6

TOTAL POINTS: Canada 13, International 11

(Each member of Canada team received C$2,666; each member of International team received C$1,500.)

Telus Edmonton Open

Glendale Golf and Country Club, Edmonton, Alberta — June 25-28
Par 36-36–72; 6,858 yards — purse, C$150,000
(Fourth round cancelled — rain.)

	SCORES			TOTAL	MONEY
Brian Kontak	68	69	71	208	C$27,000
Bryan DeCorso	70	66	72	208	15,000
(Kontak defeated DeCorso on first extra hole.)					
Greg Cuthill	70	67	72	209	7,012.50
Paul Devenport	68	72	69	209	7,012.50
Ian Hutchings	67	73	69	209	7,012.50
Ben Walter	71	70	68	209	7,012.50
Mike Grob	70	69	71	210	4,175
Stephane Talbot	73	69	68	210	4,175
Rick Todd	70	71	69	210	4,175
Ian Leggatt	68	73	70	211	2,800
Marcus Meloan	70	70	71	211	2,800
Scott Rowe	68	71	72	211	2,800
Jim Rutledge	74	70	67	211	2,800
Brad Sutterfield	68	71	72	211	2,800
Chris Tidland	71	72	68	211	2,800
Kris Cox	72	71	69	212	2,137.50
Norm Jarvis	71	71	70	212	2,137.50
Grant Moorhead	69	72	71	212	2,137.50
David Morland	70	71	71	212	2,137.50
Duane Bock	71	70	72	213	1,800
Greg Bruckner	75	69	69	213	1,800
Philip Jonas	73	73	67	213	1,800
Kari Kekki	73	72	68	213	1,800
Neale Smith	70	74	69	213	1,800
Ken Druce	74	70	70	214	1,575
Danny Mijovic	74	68	73	215	1,500
Tyler Shelton	70	73	72	215	1,500
Jerry Springer	71	72	72	215	1,500

	SCORES			TOTAL	MONEY
John Bizik	68	77	71	216	1,331.25
Stuart Bouvier	69	73	74	216	1,331.25
Tony Carolan	75	69	72	216	1,331.25
Todd Pence	71	72	73	216	1,331.25

Henry Singer Alberta Open

Wolf Creek Golf Resort, Ponoka, Alberta — July 2-5
Par 35-35–70; 6,516 yards — purse, C$150,000

	SCORES				TOTAL	MONEY
Brian Kontak	68	64	65	63	260	C$27,000
David Morland	65	66	67	65	263	15,000
Scott Petersen	68	70	62	67	267	9,000
Todd Fanning	66	68	66	68	268	6,350
Jay Hobby	67	70	66	65	268	6,350
Ian Leggatt	66	70	66	66	268	6,350
Stephane Talbot	67	66	67	69	269	4,800
David McKenzie	69	64	70	68	271	3,863
Rick Todd	71	69	70	61	271	3,863
Jason Bohn	73	67	69	63	272	2,880
Grant Masson	64	71	69	68	272	2,880
Alan McLean	68	69	70	65	272	2,880
Scott Rowe	67	71	66	68	272	2,880
Ray Stewart	67	69	69	67	272	2,880
Ashley Chinner	64	69	69	71	273	2,072
Paul Devenport	68	67	69	69	273	2,072
Cam Emerson	66	71	69	67	273	2,072
Jim Rutledge	72	65	70	66	273	2,072
Warren Schutte	68	68	68	69	273	2,072
Scott Wearne	71	67	71	64	273	2,072
J.J. West	69	70	68	66	273	2,072
Zhang Lian-wei	71	68	65	69	273	2,072
Brad Sutterfield	71	67	68	68	274	1,725
Derek Gilchrist	71	69	67	68	275	1,545
Rich Massey	64	70	69	72	275	1,545
Danny Mijovic	70	68	65	72	275	1,545
Kenneth Staton	70	68	67	70	275	1,545
Keith Whitecotton	68	66	69	72	275	1,545
Ken Druce	69	71	66	70	276	1,425
Dirk Ayers	68	71	67	71	277	1,313
Kris Cox	64	69	70	74	277	1,313
Mike Grob	69	70	69	69	277	1,313
Dan Halldorson	71	67	69	70	277	1,313
Bobby Kalinowski	68	71	67	71	277	1,313

MTS Classic

Elmhurst Golf and Country Club, Winnipeg, Manitoba — July 9-12
Par 35-36–71; 6,690 yards — purse, C$125,000

	SCORES				TOTAL	MONEY
Perry Parker	70	66	72	69	277	C$22,500
Don Fardon	69	68	69	72	278	12,500
Tim Balmer	68	70	70	71	279	7,500

	SCORES				TOTAL	MONEY
Greg Bruckner	73	71	64	72	280	4,385.42
Marcus Cain	69	69	70	72	280	4,385.42
Keith Whitecotton	70	69	69	72	280	4,385.42
Kent Wiese	69	72	71	68	280	4,385.42
Steve Woods	67	74	69	70	280	4,385.42
Chad Wright	70	67	74	69	280	4,385.42
Ben Ferguson	71	68	70	72	281	2,267.86
Nasho Kamungeremu	71	70	70	70	281	2,267.86
Scott Petersen	73	70	70	68	281	2,267.86
Conrad Ray	70	71	71	69	281	2,267.86
Jerry Springer	71	69	72	69	281	2,267.86
Kenneth Staton	71	72	69	69	281	2,267.86
Shane Supple	71	73	70	67	281	2,267.86
*Garth Collings	69	75	67	71	282	
Brian Kontak	66	74	77	65	282	1,781.25
Davidson Matyczuk	71	69	72	70	282	1,781.25
Brian Mogg	65	70	70	78	283	1,656.25
Grant Moorhead	72	68	75	68	283	1,656.25
John Connelly	73	70	75	66	284	1,468.75
Bruce Heuchan	70	71	70	73	284	1,468.75
John Robertson	73	69	73	69	284	1,468.75
Warren Schutte	71	69	73	71	284	1,468.75
John Curley	67	74	74	70	285	1,265.63
Paul Devenport	70	73	70	72	285	1,265.63
*Doug Labelle	72	73	71	69	285	
Alan McLean	69	73	68	75	285	1,265.63
Marty Scoles	72	71	71	71	285	1,265.63

Infiniti Championship

Diamond Back Golf Club, Richmond Hill, Ontario — July 16-19
Par 36-36–72; 7,087 yards — purse, C$125,000

	SCORES				TOTAL	MONEY
Brian Kontak	66	66	68	71	271	C$22,500
Ian Leggatt	64	71	70	66	271	12,500
(Kontak defeated Leggatt on first extra hole.)						
Roy MacKenzie	69	70	69	68	276	6,750
Jim Rutledge	68	71	71	66	276	6,750
Mike Grob	73	67	66	71	277	5,250
Alan McLean	70	67	72	69	278	4,625
Paul Devenport	70	69	68	72	279	3,479.17
Todd Fanning	68	72	72	67	279	3,479.17
Brad Sutterfield	71	70	68	70	279	3,479.17
Greg Bruckner	69	71	70	70	280	2,267.86
Ken Druce	70	73	69	68	280	2,267.86
Craig Marseilles	71	72	67	70	280	2,267.86
Davidson Matyczuk	71	70	69	70	280	2,267.86
Scott Rowe	70	72	71	67	280	2,267.86
Ray Stewart	68	73	72	67	280	2,267.86
Keith Whitecotton	69	71	70	70	280	2,267.86
Greg Cuthill	66	71	71	73	281	1,750
Tom Stankowski	68	71	72	70	281	1,750
Rick Todd	67	71	72	71	281	1,750
Tony Carolan	72	73	69	68	282	1,441.96
John Curley	67	69	74	72	282	1,441.96
Derek Gilchrist	67	71	73	71	282	1,441.96

	SCORES				TOTAL	MONEY
Bruce Heuchan	71	72	71	68	282	1,441.96
Warren Schutte	70	66	75	71	282	1,441.96
Stephane Talbot	70	71	71	70	282	1,441.96
Steve Woods	72	70	71	69	282	1,441.96
Stuart Bouvier	68	75	66	74	283	1,171.88
Marcus Cain	72	70	74	67	283	1,171.88
Nasho Kamungeremu	73	70	73	67	283	1,171.88
Grant Masson	69	71	70	73	283	1,171.88
Ben Walter	73	68	69	73	283	1,171.88
Manny Zerman	73	70	65	75	283	1,171.88

Canadian Masters

Heron Point Golf Links, Ancaster, Ontario — July 23-26
Par 35-36–71; 6,841 yards — purse, C$200,000

	SCORES				TOTAL	MONEY
Mike Grob	69	70	65	64	268	C$36,000
Ben Walter	65	69	65	71	270	20,000
Paul Devenport	69	71	66	67	273	12,000
Derek Gilchrist	70	74	66	64	274	9,000
Warren Schutte	65	70	70	69	274	9,000
Shane Supple	68	69	71	67	275	7,400
Ian Leggatt	68	68	70	70	276	5,900
David McKenzie	65	71	71	69	276	5,900
Dirk Ayers	72	69	71	65	277	4,140
Tony Carolan	73	69	68	67	277	4,140
Martin Price	66	71	70	70	277	4,140
Neale Smith	67	65	75	70	277	4,140
Ray Stewart	72	67	70	68	277	4,140
Roy MacKenzie	69	73	67	69	278	3,125
Wes Martin	76	68	65	69	278	3,125
Conrad Ray	75	69	69	65	278	3,125
Steve Woods	71	69	69	69	278	3,125
*Jon Drewery	74	71	70	64	279	
Todd Fanning	74	70	66	69	279	2,600
David Morland	70	70	69	70	279	2,600
Brad Sutterfield	69	71	72	67	279	2,600
Keith Whitecotton	68	71	72	68	279	2,600
Kent Wiese	70	72	70	67	279	2,600
Jason Bohn	72	69	66	73	280	2,100
Greg Bruckner	71	65	72	72	280	2,100
Ben Ferguson	70	73	70	67	280	2,100
Danny Mijovic	70	75	66	69	280	2,100
Dave Pashko	68	72	68	72	280	2,100
Jason Samuelian	71	69	69	71	280	2,100
Kris Cox	67	73	72	69	281	1,775
Ken Duke	71	72	71	67	281	1,775
Carlos Espinosa	69	72	69	71	281	1,775
Mike Fergin	68	73	67	73	281	1,775
Frank Schiro	73	71	69	68	281	1,775
Todd Spain	76	68	67	70	281	1,775

Eagle Creek Classic

Eagle Creek Golf Club, Ottawa, Ontario — July 30-August 2
Par 36-36–72; 7,067 yards — purse, C$125,000

	SCORES				TOTAL	MONEY
Perry Parker	67	73	68	68	276	C$22,500
Todd Fanning	70	71	68	68	277	7,812.50
Mike Grob	69	70	71	67	277	7,812.50
Ian Leggatt	67	66	70	74	277	7,812.50
Dave Pashko	68	67	73	69	277	7,812.50
Norm Jarvis	71	71	68	69	279	4,000
Alan McLean	71	73	70	65	279	4,000
Kenneth Staton	72	71	68	68	279	4,000
Ken Druce	70	70	70	70	280	2,906.25
Danny Mijovic	67	69	71	73	280	2,906.25
Jeff Bloom	69	68	73	71	281	2,437.50
Ian Hutchings	70	71	69	71	281	2,437.50
Kip Byrne	73	69	72	68	282	2,125
Rich Massey	69	73	67	73	282	2,125
Rick Todd	69	73	71	69	282	2,125
Derek Gilchrist	72	69	70	72	283	1,781.25
Grant Masson	71	70	72	70	283	1,781.25
Blair Piercy	70	71	71	71	283	1,781.25
Tom Stankowski	68	67	72	76	283	1,781.25
Conrad Ray	70	71	71	72	284	1,593.75
Todd Spain	70	66	74	74	284	1,593.75
Tim Clark	71	72	70	72	285	1,437.50
David McKenzie	69	73	72	71	285	1,437.50
Chris Tidland	72	71	73	69	285	1,437.50
Kevin Altenhof	68	75	75	68	286	1,265.63
Bob Conrad	70	74	69	73	286	1,265.63
Kris Cox	72	73	71	70	286	1,265.63
Greg Cuthill	69	71	72	74	286	1,265.63
Ashley Chinner	72	71	70	74	287	1,109.38
Simon Cooke	68	74	78	67	287	1,109.38
Ben Ferguson	68	72	73	74	287	1,109.38
David Kureluk	70	75	70	72	287	1,109.38
Darron Stiles	69	76	69	73	287	1,109.38
Stephen Woodard	70	72	71	74	287	1,109.38

American Express - Shell Cup

Club de Golf Le Blainvillier, Blainville, Quebec — August 6-9
Par 71; 6,950 yards — purse, C$125,000

FOURTH ROUND

Rob McMillan defeated Ken Staton, 19th hole
David McKenzie defeated Ken Duke, 2 and 1
Scott Ford defeated David Morland, 2 and 1
Wes Martin defeated Manny Zerman, 3 and 2
Scott Petersen defeated Alan McLean, 19th hole
Ian Hutchings defeated Derek Gilchrist, 19th hole
Paul Devenport defeated Norm Jarvis, 2 up
Ian Leggatt defeated Stephane Talbot, 5 and 4

FIFTH ROUND

Martin defeated McMillan, 3 and 2
McKenzie defeated Petersen, 1 up
Hutchings defeated Ford, 4 and 2
Davenport defeated Leggatt, 3 and 1

CONSOLATION ROUND

Gilchrist defeated Morland, 4 and 3
Staton defeated Zerman, 3 and 2
Duke defeated McLean, 1 up
Talbot defeated Jarvis, 5 and 3
(Losers received C$2,325.)

CONSOLATION ROUND SEMI-FINAL

Talbot defeated Duke, 3 and 2
Staton defeated Gilchrist, 19th hole
(Losers received C$2,700.)

CONSOLATION ROUND FINAL

Staton defeated Talbot, 4 and 3
(Staton received C$4,000; Talbot received C$3,300.)

SEMI-FINAL

Martin defeated Hutchings, 4 and 3
Devenport defeated McKenzie, 19th hole
(Losers received C$7,500.)

FINAL

Devenport defeated Martin, 6 and 5
(Devenport received C$30,000; Martin received C$18,000.)

New Brunswick Open

Memramcook Golf Club, Moncton, New Brunswick — August 13-16
Par 36-36–72; 6,036 yards — purse, C$125,000

	SCORES				TOTAL	MONEY
Tim Clark	63	67	67	64	261	C$22,500
David McKenzie	66	64	68	64	262	12,500
Paul Devenport	67	70	66	60	263	7,500
Danny Mijovic	67	68	68	61	264	5,625
Warren Schutte	63	69	66	66	264	5,625
Ken Duke	71	64	67	63	265	4,625
Cam Emerson	68	64	69	65	266	4,000
Shane Supple	72	69	65	62	268	3,375
Dennis Harrington	66	67	68	68	269	2,906.25
Kari Kekki	63	67	70	69	269	2,906.25
Mike Grob	67	66	71	66	270	2,250
Roy Mackenzie	68	65	66	71	270	2,250
Grant Masson	71	65	70	64	270	2,250
Alan McLean	72	69	64	65	270	2,250
Martin Price	67	67	69	67	270	2,250
Ian Hutchings	70	67	70	64	271	1,781.25

	SCORES				TOTAL	MONEY
David Kureluk	68	70	72	61	271	1,781.25
Chris Tidland	69	68	68	66	271	1,781.25
Brad Wilson	66	67	69	69	271	1,781.25
John Bizik	67	68	71	66	272	1,593.75
Philip Jonas	69	68	70	65	272	1,593.75
Grant Moorhead	71	65	69	68	273	1,359.38
Stuart Musgrave	71	67	72	63	273	1,359.38
Dean North	68	70	70	65	273	1,359.38
Blair Piercy	72	69	69	63	273	1,359.38
Jason Samuelian	70	70	69	64	273	1,359.38
Kenneth Staton	71	64	65	73	273	1,359.38
Bryan DeCorso	74	67	66	67	274	1,156.25
Ben Ferguson	72	68	70	64	274	1,156.25
Craig Marseilles	70	70	68	66	274	1,156.25
Rob McMillan	68	70	66	70	274	1,156.25
Steve Woods	73	68	66	67	274	1,156.25

Samsung Canadian PGA Championship

Forest City National Golf Club, London, Ontario — August 20-23
Par 36-36–72; 6,850 yards — purse, C$125,000

	SCORES				TOTAL	MONEY
Tim Clark	71	70	62	69	272	C$22,500
Chris Tidland	69	64	68	71	272	12,500
(Clark defeated Tidland on first extra hole.)						
Ian Leggatt	70	68	70	68	276	6,750
Neale Smith	71	70	67	68	276	6,750
Todd Fanning	69	68	71	69	277	4,938
Shane Supple	77	66	66	68	277	4,938
Philip Jonas	69	68	67	74	278	4,000
Ian Hutchings	72	65	69	73	279	3,375
Greg Bruckner	70	70	71	69	280	2,906
Derek Gilchrist	71	67	70	72	280	2,906
Ashley Chinner	70	68	72	71	281	2,188
Dan Halldorson	74	67	72	68	281	2,188
Danny Mijovic	70	70	68	73	281	2,188
David Morland	70	69	68	74	281	2,188
Conrad Ray	72	66	71	72	281	2,188
Tom Stankowski	74	65	67	75	281	2,188
Duane Bock	75	65	69	73	282	1,781
Scott Petersen	71	71	70	70	282	1,781
Paul Devenport	69	68	73	73	283	1,625
Ben Ferguson	73	70	68	72	283	1,625
Warren Schutte	71	71	65	76	283	1,625
Kris Cox	73	71	70	70	284	1,359
Don Martone	74	68	68	74	284	1,359
Pete McCutcheon	69	71	72	72	284	1,359
Grant Moorhead	70	67	73	74	284	1,359
Blair Piercy	70	70	74	70	284	1,359
Martin Price	71	68	72	73	284	1,359
John Curley	73	68	70	74	285	1,156
Joe Lloyd	67	73	76	69	285	1,156
Stuart Wallace	71	71	72	71	285	1,156
Keith Whitecotton	76	67	73	69	285	1,156
Zhang Lian-wei	72	70	71	72	285	1,156

NewTel Atlantic Cup International Team Matches

Admiral's Green Golf Club, St. John's, Newfoundland — August 25-26
Par 71; 6,532 yards — purse, C$50,000

FIRST DAY
Alternate Shot

Brad Sutterfield and Greg Bruckner (International) defeated Norm Jarvis and Stuart Hendley, 4 and 2.
David McKenzie and Derek Gilchrist (International) defeated Greg Cuthill and Keith Whitecotton, 2 up.
Manny Zerman and Scott Petersen (International) defeated Dave Pashko and Davidson Matyczuk, 1 up.
Cam Emerson and Scott Rowe (Canada) defeated Ken Duke and Ray Freeman, 2 and 1.
Todd Fanning and Wes Martin (Canada) defeated Ken Staton and Steve Woods, 4 and 2.
Kari Kekki and Martin Price (Canada) halved with Alan McLean and Tyler Shelton.

POINTS: International Team 3½, Canada 2½

SECOND DAY
Best Ball

Staton and Zerman (International) defeated Hendley and Whitecotton, 2 and 1.
Kekki and Price (Canada) defeated Petersen and Duke, 2 and 1.
Jarvis and Cuthill (Canada) halved with Freeman and Woods.
Fanning and Martin (Canada) defeated McLean and Shelton, 3 and 2.
Sutterfield and Bruckner (International) defeated Emerson and Rowe, 2 and 1.
McKenzie and Gilchrist (International) defeated Pashko and Matyczuk, 1 up.

POINTS: International Team 3½, Canada 2½

Singles

McLean (International) defeated Cuthill, 2 and 1.
Whitecotton (Canada) halved with Duke.
Staton (International) defeated Fanning, 3 and 1.
Petersen (International) defeated Jarvis, 1 up.
Shelton (International) defeated Rowe, 1 up.
Hendley (Canada) defeated Freeman, 2 and 1.
Price (Canada) defeated Zerman, 1 up.
Emerson (Canada) defeated Bruckner, 1 up.
Pashko (Canada) halved with Sutterfield.
Gilchrist (International) defeated Kekki, 2 and 1.
McKenzie (International) defeated Matyczuk, 3 and 2.
Martin (Canada) halved with Woods.

POINTS: International Team 7½, Canada 4½

TOTAL POINTS: International Team 14½, Canada 9½

(Each member of International team received C$2,666; each member of Canada team received C$1,500.)

Bell Bay International Team Matches

Bell Bay Golf Club, Baddeck, Nova Scotia
Par 36-36–72; 7,037 yards

August 28-29
purse, C$50,000

FIRST DAY
Alternate Shot

Brad Sutterfield and Greg Bruckner (International) defeated Todd Fanning and Wes Martin, 2 and 1.
Stuart Hendley and Dave Pashko (Canada) defeated Alan McLean and Ken Staton, 1 up.
Norm Jarvis and Scott Rowe (Canada) defeated David McKenzie and Derek Gilchrist, 2 up.
Tyler Shelton and Steve Woods (International) defeated Greg Cuthill and Keith Whitecotton, 1 up.
Cam Emerson and Davidson Matyczuk (Canada) defeated Manny Zerman and Scott Petersen, 2 and 1.
Ken Duke and Ray Freeman (International) defeated Kari Kekki and Martin Price, 2 and 1.

POINTS: International Team 3, Canada 3

SECOND DAY
Best Ball

Cuthill and Jarvis (Canada) defeated Duke and Freeman, 3 and 2.
Price and Kekki (Canada) defeated McLean and Shelton, 2 and 1.
McKenzie and Gilchrist (International) defeated Emerson and Rowe, 3 and 2.
Staton and Zerman (International) defeated Whitecotton and Hendley, 1 up.
Sutterfield and Bruckner (International) defeated Pashko and Matyczuk, 2 and 1.
Fanning and Martin (Canada) halved with Petersen and Woods.

POINTS: International Team 3½, Canada 2½

Singles

Zerman (International) defeated Emerson, 3 and 2.
Whitecotton (Canada) defeated Staton, 5 and 4.
McKenzie (International) defeated Matyczuk, 3 and 2.
Rowe (Canada) defeated Duke, 1 up.
Bruckner (International) defeated Jarvis, 3 and 2.
Gilchrist (International) defeated Cuthill, 4 and 2.
Petersen (International) defeated Pashko, 5 and 4.
Woods (International) defeated Price, 7 and 6.
Fanning (Canada) defeated Sutterfield, 1 up.
Freeman (International) defeated Hendley, 1 up.
Martin (Canada) halved with McLean.
Shelton (International) defeated Kekki, 4 and 3.

POINTS: International Team 8½, Canada 3½

TOTAL POINTS: International Team 15, Canada 9

(Each member of International team received C$2,666; each member of Canada team received C$1,500.)

Bayer Championship

Huron Oaks Recreation Centre, Sarnia, Ontario — September 17-20
Par 36-36–72; 6,163 yards — purse, C$125,000

	SCORES				TOTAL	MONEY
Chris Tidland	67	66	65	65	263	C$22,500
Ashley Chinner	65	67	68	66	266	7,812.50
Ken Duke	66	70	62	68	266	7,812.50
Todd Fanning	67	64	68	67	266	7,812.50
Mike Grob	62	65	70	69	266	7,812.50
Paul Devenport	69	68	64	67	268	4,000
Danny Mijovic	69	69	61	69	268	4,000
Keith Whitecotton	68	63	66	71	268	4,000
Bob Conrad	67	69	65	68	269	2,671.88
Chris Greenwood	72	63	65	69	269	2,671.88
David Kureluk	69	67	69	64	269	2,671.88
Mark Maue	67	68	68	66	269	2,671.88
Duane Bock	66	67	70	67	270	2,012.50
Jason Bohn	67	68	67	68	270	2,012.50
Derek Gilchrist	63	71	68	68	270	2,012.50
Warren Schutte	69	70	67	64	270	2,012.50
Shane Supple	67	68	68	67	270	2,012.50
Scott Ford	68	67	70	66	271	1,687.50
Brian Kontak	66	69	68	68	271	1,687.50
James Wingerter	67	71	65	68	271	1,687.50
Bryan DeCorso	68	68	71	65	272	1,411.46
Darren Griff	71	68	63	70	272	1,411.46
Norm Jarvis	70	68	66	68	272	1,411.46
David Morland	66	68	70	68	272	1,411.46
Jerry Springer	69	68	67	68	272	1,411.46
J.J. West	63	66	71	72	272	1,411.46
David McKenzie	69	68	67	69	273	1,234.38
Jordan Young	70	68	66	69	273	1,234.38
Todd Doohan	71	69	64	70	274	1,125
Perry Parker	65	67	76	66	274	1,125
Martin Price	69	69	68	68	274	1,125
Conrad Ray	65	70	68	71	274	1,125
Bruce Rogerson	70	70	69	65	274	1,125

South American Tour

TPG Open

Guataparo Country Club, Valencia, Venezuela — October 22-25
Par 35-35–70; 6,400 yards — purse, US$120,000

	SCORES				TOTAL	MONEY
Claudio Muskus	73	68	63	68	272	US$21,600
Miguel Martinez	68	70	67	68	273	13,680
David Morland	74	66	66	69	275	8,640
Esteban Isasi	76	69	61	69	275	8,640
Raul Fretes	72	67	71	66	276	4,680
Frederick Manson	70	69	69	68	276	4,680
Pedro Martinez	70	68	70	68	276	4,680
Ron Wuensche	73	67	68	68	276	4,680
Angel Romero	70	71	69	67	277	3,000
Angel Franco	71	66	72	68	277	2,000
Damaso Galban	72	72	67	67	278	2,640
Stuart Hendley	72	71	69	67	279	2,160
Roy Mackenzie	69	71	69	70	279	2,160
Victor Leoni	69	69	71	70	279	2,160
Adam Armagost	68	69	70	72	279	2,160
Federico Sauce	71	72	64	72	279	2,160
Gustavo Mendoza	73	71	67	69	280	1,740
Eduardo Pesenti	69	69	72	70	280	1,740
Christian Mattfolk	71	72	73	65	281	1,339.20
Rob Moss	72	71	71	67	281	1,339.20
Jesus Amaya	72	70	70	69	281	1,339.20
Steve Shriver	69	69	72	71	281	1,339.20
Bryan De Corso	71	66	69	75	281	1,339.20
Jonas Torines	71	75	68	68	282	1,080
Bruce Heuchan	70	71	65	76	282	1,080
Marc Amort	72	72	72	67	283	912
Jeffrey Schmid	71	70	73	69	283	912
Rigoberto Velasquez	73	67	73	70	283	912
Hiroshi Matsuo	71	71	70	71	283	912
Ramon Franco	71	71	70	71	283	912
Ricardo Lyon	75	67	68	73	283	912

Peru Open

Los Inkas Country Club, Lima, Peru — October 29-November 1
Par 36-36–72; 7,070 yards — purse, US$120,000

	SCORES				TOTAL	MONEY
Scott Dunlap	64	74	69	68	275	US$20,900
Angel Franco	72	67	69	69	277	13,237
Mauricio Molina	71	68	67	75	281	9,289
Stuart Hendley	69	75	68	70	282	6,115
Gary Gilchrist	72	71	69	70	282	6,115
Jeffrey Schmidt	70	70	71	71	282	6,115

	SCORES				TOTAL	MONEY
Raul Fretes	72	71	71	69	283	3,112
Sandy Morrison	70	66	78	69	283	3,112
Omar Solis	75	67	71	70	283	3,112
Angel Romero	67	73	73	70	283	3,112
Ruben Alvarez	74	71	67	71	283	3,112
Rodolfo Rodriguez	69	74	73	68	284	2,264
Pedro Martinez	69	70	69	76	284	2,264
Ramon Franco	72	71	73	70	286	1,915
Todd Mahovlich	68	72	74	72	286	1,915
Christian Mattfolk	74	70	67	75	286	1,915
Marc Amort	69	70	71	76	286	1,915
Gustavo Acosta	71	73	74	69	287	1,567
Rigoberto Velasquez	72	72	71	72	287	1,567
Miguel Fernandez	72	70	73	73	288	1,285
Fabian Montovia	70	72	72	74	288	1,285
*Roberto Coceres	68	71	74	75	288	
Jose Cantero	72	73	73	71	289	1,068
Niceforo Quispe	69	72	73	75	289	1,068
Eduardo Pesenti	68	75	70	76	289	1,068
Bruce Heuchan	75	70	75	70	290	856
Shawn Savage	72	72	75	71	290	856
Marco Ruiz	78	67	73	72	290	856
Peter Bolle	72	73	73	72	290	856
Ron Wuensche	72	73	72	73	290	856
Hampus Von Post	69	75	73	73	290	856
Brad Wilson	74	74	68	74	290	856
Diego Ferrari	77	69	70	74	290	856

City of La Plata Open

La Plata Golf Course, La Plata, Argentina — November 5-8
Par 71; 6,164 yards — purse, US$50,000

	SCORES			TOTAL	MONEY
Roberto Coceres	70	67	68	205	US$8,100
Peter Bolle	70	66	69	205	4,050
Claudio Machado	69	68	68	205	4,050
(Coceres defeated Machado on second and Bolle on fifth extra hole.)					
Jeffrey Schmidt	71	69	68	208	3,150
Omar Solis	67	71	71	209	2,700
Rodolfo Gonzalez	72	69	69	210	1,654
Ruben Alvarez	68	73	69	210	1,654
Christian Mattfolk	73	66	71	210	1,654
Gustavo Acosta	71	68	71	210	1,654
Angel Rodriguez	69	70	72	211	1,088
Ron Wuensche	68	71	72	211	1,088
Miguel Guzman	73	69	70	212	835
Hiroshi Matsuo	73	69	70	212	835
Jonas Torines	71	71	70	212	835
Stuart Hendley	72	69	71	212	835
Walter Ramos	74	73	66	213	720
Glenn Preciado	69	76	68	213	720
Antonio Ortiz	68	75	70	213	720
Shawn Savage	76	71	67	214	663
Alfonso Barrera	70	70	74	214	663
Ariel Canete	73	74	69	216	595
Bjorn Bach	73	73	70	216	595

	SCORES			TOTAL	MONEY
Bruce Heuchan	69	74	73	216	595
Pablo Leguizamon	71	71	74	216	595
Carlos Sequera	73	74	70	217	501
Mauricio Molina	76	70	71	217	501
Robert Tracy	75	71	71	217	501
Omar Peralta	72	74	71	217	501
Hugo Vizzone	72	74	72	218	393
Eduardo Argiro	71	75	72	218	393
Hampus Von Post	71	74	73	218	393
Andres Romero	68	74	76	218	393

Litoral Open

Rosario Golf Club, Rosario, Argentina — November 12-15
Par 36-36–72; 6,422 yards — purse, US$120,000

	SCORES				TOTAL	MONEY
Tim Hegna	68	69	64	71	272	US$21,600
Armando Saavedra	70	71	63	69	273	13,680
Jorge Berendt	65	73	69	68	275	7,840
Roberto Coceres	73	66	67	69	275	7,840
Rodolfo Gonzalez	72	64	69	70	275	7,840
David Morland	69	75	65	68	277	4,160
Jeffrey Schmidt	66	67	75	69	277	4,160
Gustavo Acosta	72	70	62	73	277	4,160
Sebastian Fernandez	70	71	66	71	278	3,000
Philip Jonas	68	69	68	73	278	3,000
Miguel Fernandez	71	69	73	66	279	2,304
Omar Peralta	70	70	71	68	279	2,304
Juan Abbate	68	70	71	70	279	2,304
Esteban Isasi	69	70	69	71	279	2,304
Bruce Heuchan	65	71	66	77	279	2,304
Greg Petersen	74	68	66	72	280	1,740
Eduardo Argiro	72	67	69	72	280	1,740
Rafael Gomez	70	68	70	72	280	1,740
Rob Moss	66	70	70	74	280	1,740
Miguel Guzman	69	75	70	67	281	1,216
Stuart Hendley	75	70	68	68	281	1,216
Victor Leoni	69	69	74	69	281	1,216
Ricardo Montenegro	67	69	72	73	281	1,216
Ariel Canete	68	75	64	74	281	1,216
Martin Lonardi	68	69	70	74	281	1,216
Rafael Chavez Barcellos	70	73	69	70	282	926
Erik Anderson	70	72	70	70	282	926
Marco Ruiz	66	71	75	70	282	926
Jose Cantero	70	73	68	71	282	926
Alan McDonald	68	67	71	76	282	926

Argentina Masters

Olivos Golf Club, Buenos Aires, Argentina — November 19-22
Par 36-36–72; 6,705 yards — purse, US$180,000

	SCORES				TOTAL	MONEY
Raul Fretes	68	66	70	67	271	US$30,600
Eduardo Romero	66	68	68	72	274	19,380
Blaine McCallister	72	71	65	71	279	13,600
Roberto Coceres	68	71	71	70	280	10,880
Shawn Savage	71	69	69	72	281	7,990
Bernhard Langer	72	74	68	67	281	7,990
Jose Cantero	71	69	71	71	282	5,170
Ron Wuensche	76	69	69	68	282	5,170
Philip Jonas	72	70	68	73	283	4,250
Rodolfo Gonzalez	70	69	74	70	283	4,250
Martin Lonardi	71	71	70	73	285	3,740
Jorge Berendt	71	71	71	73	286	3,060
Stuart Hendley	72	71	71	72	286	3,060
Ricardo Montenegro	72	71	72	71	286	3,060
Mauricio Molina	76	62	78	70	286	3,060
Miguel Guzman	73	70	74	69	286	3,060
Horacio Carbonetti	71	72	72	72	287	2,131
Jeffrey Schmidt	70	72	73	72	287	2,131
Tim Straub	73	69	74	71	287	2,131
Fernando Amico	72	73	72	70	287	2,131
Jose Coceres	71	72	74	70	287	2,131
Sebastian Fernandez	69	74	74	70	287	2,131
Brad Wilson	72	71	69	76	288	1,530
Juan Abbate	73	71	69	75	288	1,530
John Moscrip	72	73	72	71	288	1,530
Greg Green	73	69	76	70	288	1,530
Marco Ruiz	74	72	70	73	289	1,284
Ken Duke	71	72	73	73	289	1,284
Peter Bolle	69	72	76	72	289	1,284
Alan McDonald	72	71	75	71	289	1,284

JPGA Argentina

Circuito Metropolitan, Buenos Aires, Argentina — November 26-29
Par 70

	SCORES				TOTAL	MONEY
Jeffrey Schmidt	70	67	69	64	270	US$10,000
Ricardo Montenegro	66	68	65	71	270	5,490
(Schmidt defeated Montenegro on first extra hole.)						
Sebastian Fernandez	71	68	68	66	273	4,320
Martin Lonardi	66	68	74	66	274	3,240
Miguel Guzman	69	70	68	67	274	3,240
Roberto Coceres	69	69	66	70	274	3,240
Ruben Felizardo	70	70	69	66	275	2,160
Ian Leggatt	64	68	74	70	276	1,755
Rafael Gomez	70	68	67	71	276	1,755
Cesar Monasterio	70	65	76	66	277	1,296
Ruben Alvarez	69	70	71	67	277	1,296
Juan Abbate	70	70	70	67	277	1,296
Gustavo Rojas	70	69	68	70	277	1,296
Miguel Suarez	70	68	70	70	278	985

	SCORES				TOTAL	MONEY
Henrik Stenson	70	68	69	71	278	985
Marcelo Isla	69	71	72	67	279	877
Stuart Hendley	69	68	73	69	279	877
Greg Green	69	67	73	70	279	877
Miguel Fernandez	67	70	72	70	279	877
Alan McDonald	70	66	72	72	280	797
Fabian Montovia	68	70	69	73	280	797
Sergio Acevedo	73	67	71	70	281	756
Brad Wilson	68	71	74	70	283	661
Omar Solis	70	68	74	71	283	661
Omar Peralta	67	73	71	72	283	661
Peter Hansson	73	67	71	72	283	661
Shawn Savage	68	68	73	74	283	661
Erik Anderson	67	73	69	74	283	661
Juan Coceres	70	69	72	74	285	553
Raul Perez	71	69	70	75	285	553

Las Delicias Open

Las Delicias Golf Club, Cordoba, Argentina — December 3-6
Par 35-35–70; 6,798 yards — purse, US$100,000

	SCORES				TOTAL	MONEY
Sebastian Fernandez	68	71	69	66	274	US$18,000
Gustavo Rojas	68	68	69	69	274	11,400
(Fernandez defeated Rojas on second extra hole.)						
Angel Cabrera	67	67	74	67	275	8,000
Shawn Savage	72	67	67	70	276	6,400
Angel Franco	72	68	69	68	277	5,200
Henrik Stenson	69	71	68	71	279	4,200
Ian Leggatt	74	69	69	69	281	3,400
Cesar Monasterio	65	71	75	71	282	2,800
Ricardo Gonzalez	73	67	72	71	283	2,500
Alan McDonald	68	68	75	72	283	2,500
Rafael Gomez	76	67	73	68	284	1,920
Adam Armagost	71	69	72	72	284	1,920
Miguel Fernandez	71	70	70	73	284	1,920
Raul Fretes	68	69	73	74	284	1,920
Hampus Von Post	71	67	71	75	284	1,920
Ariel Canete	71	67	76	71	285	1,450
Pedro Martinez	67	73	73	72	285	1,450
Eduardo Romero	71	69	73	72	285	1,450
Marco Ruiz	72	69	71	73	285	1,450
Tim Hegna	71	73	72	70	286	1,150
Scott Dunlap	72	64	76	74	286	1,150
Ken Duke	70	71	76	70	287	924
Jorge Berendt	68	74	74	71	287	924
Rigoberto Velasquez	70	73	73	71	287	924
Peter Hansson	69	74	71	73	287	924
Jeffrey Schmidt	72	71	69	75	287	924
Philip Jonas	73	70	76	69	288	733
Armandro Saavedra	72	71	74	71	288	733
Roberto Coceres	72	69	74	73	288	733
Gustavo Mendoza	77	67	71	73	288	733
Danny Mijovic	73	67	71	77	288	733
Fabian Montovia	68	72	71	77	288	733

Argentina Open

Jockey Club, Buenos Aires, Argentina — December 10-13
Par 35-35–70; 6,668 yards — purse, US$350,000

	SCORES				TOTAL	MONEY
Raul Fretes	68	67	69	67	271	US$60,000
Angel Cabrera	69	70	72	65	276	31,250
Gustavo Mendoza	68	68	71	69	276	31,250
*Sergio Garcia	67	77	66	66	276	
Scott Dunlap	75	68	66	68	277	12,284
David Frost	71	70	68	68	277	12,284
Dudley Hart	72	64	71	70	277	12,284
Gustavo Rojas	70	67	75	65	277	12,284
Eduardo Romero	72	67	72	66	277	12,284
Craig Stadler	70	69	69	69	277	12,284
Mathias Gronberg	70	71	69	68	278	7,200
Pedro Martinez	70	69	70	70	279	6,300
Henrik Stenson	72	71	70	66	279	6,300
Angel Franco	68	74	71	67	280	5,350
Rob Moss	69	71	73	67	280	5,350
David Morland	71	69	74	67	281	5,000
Miguel Guzman	73	67	73	69	282	4,800
Roberto Coceres	75	70	71	67	283	4,300
Ricardo Gonzalez	72	70	73	68	283	4,300
Philip Jonas	70	72	72	69	283	4,300
Christian Mattfolk	69	73	75	66	283	4,300
Greg Petersen	70	76	69	68	283	4,300
Diego Ferrari	69	73	72	70	284	3,800
Ian Leggatt	72	70	74	68	284	3,800
Ricardo Montenegro	71	70	72	71	284	3,800
Bruce Heuchan	71	71	73	70	285	3,400
Danny Mijovic	70	71	75	69	285	3,400
Jeffrey Schmidt	69	72	72	72	285	3,400
Marcelo Soria	76	67	69	73	285	3,400
Stuart Wallace	70	74	70	71	285	3,400
Stuart Hendley	70	71	73	72	286	2,950
Carlos Larrain	72	67	79	68	286	2,950
Shawn Savage	72	70	79	65	286	2,950
Erik Anderson	72	72	70	72	286	2,950

European Tours

Johnnie Walker Classic

See Australasian Tour chapter.

Heineken Classic

See Australasian Tour chapter.

South African Open

See African Tours chapter.

Alfred Dunhill South African PGA

See African Tours chapter.

Dubai Desert Classic

Emirates Golf Club, Dubai, United Arab Emirates — February 26-March 1
Par 35-37–72; 7,079 yards — purse, £770,000

	SCORES				TOTAL	MONEY
Jose Maria Olazabal	69	67	65	68	269	£130,000
Stephen Allan	67	70	67	68	272	85,000
Robert Karlsson	66	65	67	75	273	43,500
Ernie Els	71	63	67	72	273	43,500
Ian Woosnam	68	69	65	73	275	33,000
Ignacio Garrido	67	67	66	76	276	23,000
Lee Westwood	69	69	68	70	276	23,000
Greg Norman	67	68	68	73	276	23,000
Alex Cejka	75	67	66	69	277	17,000
Andrew Oldcorn	71	66	68	73	278	14,226.67
Seve Ballesteros	68	68	69	73	278	14,226.67
Colin Montgomerie	70	69	70	69	278	14,226.67
David Carter	72	70	67	70	279	11,550
Darren Clarke	68	68	70	73	279	11,550
Mats Hallberg	71	69	69	70	279	11,550
Jose Coceres	71	67	67	74	279	11,550
Roger Wessels	68	69	70	73	280	10,050
David Gilford	72	71	73	64	280	10,050
Clinton Whitelaw	70	71	67	72	280	10,050
Paul Affleck	72	68	70	71	281	8,383.33
Phillip Price	68	71	73	69	281	8,383.33
Mark James	71	70	72	68	281	8,383.33
Peter Baker	69	70	72	70	281	8,383.33
Bob May	73	68	67	73	281	8,383.33
Andrew Coltart	67	75	69	70	281	8,383.33
Robert Coles	73	70	65	73	281	8,383.33
Gary Orr	71	71	66	73	281	8,383.33
Fredrik Jacobson	71	69	67	74	281	8,383.33
Eduardo Romero	72	67	73	70	282	6,950
Gary Evans	72	66	72	72	282	6,950
Per-Ulrik Johansson	69	67	71	75	282	6,950
Jim Payne	73	70	68	71	282	6,950

	SCORES				TOTAL	MONEY
Des Smyth	71	71	68	73	283	5,850
Paul McGinley	72	68	64	79	283	5,850
Jarmo Sandelin	73	68	66	76	283	5,850
Jonathan Lomas	72	70	68	73	283	5,850
Michael Jonzon	71	71	70	71	283	5,850
Adam Hunter	69	69	71	74	283	5,850
Anders Forsbrand	69	70	71	73	283	5,850
Jon Robson	72	71	70	71	284	4,675
Angel Cabrera	70	68	68	78	284	4,675
Paul Broadhurst	72	70	72	70	284	4,675
Michele Reale	69	71	73	71	284	4,675
Miguel Angel Martin	68	71	71	74	284	4,675
Steen Tinning	74	67	73	70	284	4,675
Van Phillips	69	73	66	77	285	3,700
Richard Boxall	71	71	70	73	285	3,700
Steven Richardson	73	69	66	77	285	3,700
Retief Goosen	75	68	66	76	285	3,700
Sven Struver	70	72	76	67	285	3,700
Pierre Fulke	70	73	68	74	285	3,700
Mark Mouland	69	67	74	75	285	3,700
Peter Hedblom	69	68	73	76	286	2,844
Per Haugsrud	70	72	67	77	286	2,844
Dean Robertson	70	73	68	75	286	2,844
Mark Davis	70	72	70	74	286	2,844
Peter Mitchell	73	70	68	75	286	2,844
Jay Townsend	73	70	69	75	287	2,280
Miles Tunnicliff	71	72	66	78	287	2,280
Prayad Marksaeng	73	70	70	74	287	2,280
Sam Torrance	71	72	67	77	287	2,280
Rolf Muntz	69	70	72	76	287	2,280
Andrew Sherborne	73	69	70	75	287	2,280
Raymond Burns	71	71	67	79	288	1,352.50
Craig Hainline	73	70	71	74	288	1,352.50
Zhang Lian-wei	71	72	75	70	288	1,352.50
Padraig Harrington	72	69	68	79	288	1,352.50
Anthony Wall	71	68	70	79	288	1,352.50
Paul Eales	71	71	68	78	288	1,352.50
Chang Tse-peng	70	73	66	79	288	1,352.50
Thomas Gogele	73	68	72	75	288	1,352.50
Steven Bottomley	70	72	77	70	289	1,139
Rodrigo Cuello	73	70	71	75	289	1,139
Gordon Brand, Jr.	70	72	73	74	289	1,139
Patrik Sjoland	70	70	69	80	289	1,139
Ian Garbutt	71	70	79	69	289	1,139
Nicolas Joakimides	71	72	72	75	290	1,133
David Tapping	69	71	70	82	292	1,129
Paolo Quirici	71	69	67	85	292	1,129
Thammanoon Sriroj	68	70	73	81	292	1,129
Ross McFarlane	71	72	73	77	293	1,125
Olle Karlsson	72	71	71	81	295	1,123
Wayne Riley	72	71	66	87	296	1,121

Qatar Masters

Doha Golf Club, Doha, Qatar — March 5-8
Par 36-36–72; 7,273 yards — purse, £606,060

	SCORES				TOTAL	MONEY
Andrew Coltart	68	70	65	67	270	£101,006.06
Patrik Sjoland	70	66	67	69	272	52,636.36
Andrew Sherborne	69	64	68	71	272	52,636.36
Van Phillips	70	71	66	66	273	30,303.03
Rolf Muntz	72	68	66	68	274	21,696.97
Retief Goosen	70	72	66	66	274	21,696.97
David Carter	69	75	64	66	274	21,696.97
Paolo Quirici	69	66	71	70	276	15,151.52
Darren Clarke	73	67	69	68	277	11,796.97
Ian Woosnam	72	65	69	71	277	11,796.97
Per-Ulrik Johansson	72	70	67	68	277	11,796.97
Roger Wessels	69	70	70	68	277	11,796.97
Miguel Angel Jimenez	72	67	69	70	278	9,118.18
Sven Struver	72	68	68	70	278	9,118.18
Jay Townsend	69	68	74	67	278	9,118.18
Anders Forsbrand	67	69	72	70	278	9,118.18
Jose Maria Olazabal	71	69	69	70	279	7,696.97
Padraig Harrington	74	70	67	68	279	7,696.97
Ross Drummond	69	70	68	72	279	7,696.97
Angel Cabrera	71	70	69	69	279	7,696.97
Ian Garbutt	69	71	69	71	280	6,636.36
Paul McGinley	70	69	68	73	280	6,636.36
Lee Westwood	73	70	66	71	280	6,636.36
Alex Cejka	72	71	69	68	280	6,636.36
Mark Roe	70	73	68	69	280	6,636.36
David Howell	73	65	69	73	280	6,636.36
Peter Mitchell	72	72	68	69	281	5,386.36
Fernando Roca	71	72	69	69	281	5,386.36
Paul Eales	71	71	68	71	281	5,386.36
Jean Van de Velde	73	70	66	72	281	5,386.36
Mark Davis	75	69	67	70	281	5,386.36
Dean Robertson	73	71	70	67	281	5,386.36
Paul Broadhurst	73	67	69	72	281	5,386.36
Michele Reale	69	69	72	71	281	5,386.36
Miles Tunnicliff	69	69	73	71	282	4,484.85
Clinton Whitelaw	71	70	71	70	282	4,484.85
Heinz P. Thul	70	70	72	70	282	4,484.85
Seve Ballesteros	72	70	68	72	282	4,484.85
David Gilford	69	71	67	75	282	4,484.85
Steen Tinning	70	68	72	73	283	3,696.97
Miguel Angel Martin	70	70	71	72	283	3,696.97
Ignacio Garrido	72	71	70	70	283	3,696.97
Joakim Haeggman	71	71	71	70	283	3,696.97
Philip Walton	71	67	73	72	283	3,696.97
Derrick Cooper	69	71	70	73	283	3,696.97
Robert Karlsson	74	69	70	70	283	3,696.97
Michael Jonzon	74	67	68	74	283	3,696.97
Paul Lawrie	71	72	70	71	284	2,787.88
Daniel Chopra	71	68	72	73	284	2,787.88
Kang Wook-soon	72	71	69	72	284	2,787.88
Tony Johnstone	73	71	70	70	284	2,787.88
Sam Torrance	72	71	68	73	284	2,787.88
Fredrik Jacobson	73	70	68	73	284	2,787.88
David Thomson	72	72	66	74	284	2,787.88

	SCORES				TOTAL	MONEY
Eduardo Romero	72	72	71	70	285	2,072.73
Phillip Price	71	72	73	69	285	2,072.73
Gary Orr	76	67	70	72	285	2,072.73
Klas Eriksson	72	72	72	69	285	2,072.73
Jeev Milkha Singh	74	70	68	73	285	2,072.73
Knud Storgaard	72	71	73	70	286	1,727.27
Costantino Rocca	75	68	73	70	286	1,727.27
Soren Kjeldsen	75	67	74	70	286	1,727.27
Steve Webster	74	70	68	74	286	1,727.27
Des Smyth	75	69	73	70	287	1,226.73
Roger Chapman	72	72	73	70	287	1,226.73
Bob May	73	69	71	74	287	1,226.73
Stuart Cage	72	72	69	74	287	1,226.73
Russell Claydon	73	71	73	71	288	905
Jarmo Sandelin	72	68	72	77	289	903
Mats Hallberg	69	75	71	76	291	901
Jim Payne	74	70	75	73	292	899
Mark Mouland	76	68	78	73	295	897

Moroccan Open

Royal Golf D'Agadir, Agadir, Morocco
Par 36-36–72; 6,657 yards

March 12-15
purse, £350,000

	SCORES				TOTAL	MONEY
Stephen Leaney	68	67	69	67	271	£58,330
Robert Karlsson	70	71	67	71	279	38,880
Mathias Gronberg	67	74	67	74	282	21,910
Miguel Angel Martin	69	78	68	69	284	16,165
Mark Davis	71	65	72	76	284	16,165
Tom Gillis	79	64	73	69	285	10,500
Olle Karlsson	72	69	70	74	285	10,500
Tony Johnstone	72	68	73	72	285	10,500
Roger Chapman	72	71	69	74	286	7,410
Wayne Riley	73	69	71	73	286	7,410
Heinz P. Thul	77	70	70	70	287	6,030
Daniel Chopra	70	71	74	72	287	6,030
Bob May	69	70	76	72	287	6,030
Miguel Angel Jimenez	82	68	69	69	288	5,036.25
Pedro Linhart	67	74	75	72	288	5,036.25
Thomas Gogele	70	67	74	77	288	5,036.25
Des Smyth	64	72	77	75	288	5,036.25
Jose Coceres	69	74	76	70	289	4,515
Fabrice Tarnaud	79	71	70	70	290	4,102
Paul Broadhurst	71	79	70	70	290	4,102
Raphael Jacquelin	74	67	74	75	290	4,102
Diego Borrego	69	72	75	74	290	4,102
Alex Cejka	68	70	74	78	290	4,102
Mathew Goggin	77	71	70	73	291	3,675
John Bickerton	76	68	74	73	291	3,675
Anders Forsbrand	72	71	71	77	291	3,675
Ola Eliasson	75	72	71	74	292	3,202.50
Stephane Talbot	74	74	72	72	292	3,202.50
Angel Cabrera	71	75	74	72	292	3,202.50
Scott Henderson	78	68	74	72	292	3,202.50
Michele Reale	70	75	73	74	292	3,202.50
Phil Golding	71	73	75	73	292	3,202.50

	SCORES				TOTAL	MONEY
Greg Chalmers	75	75	70	73	293	2,835
Clinton Whitelaw	73	71	72	77	293	2,835
Silvio Grappasonni	71	75	78	70	294	2,555
Dennis Edlund	73	74	68	79	294	2,555
Raymond Burns	68	79	73	74	294	2,555
Thomas Bjorn	70	76	76	72	294	2,555
Jesus Maria Arruti	72	73	69	80	294	2,555
Eduardo Romero	71	73	75	75	294	2,555
Nic Henning	76	71	70	78	295	2,205
Darren Cole	76	71	73	75	295	2,205
Emanuele Canonica	71	76	74	74	295	2,205
Peter Mitchell	73	71	74	77	295	2,205
Steve Alker	74	72	74	76	296	1,960
Greg Owen	74	75	74	73	296	1,960
Ross Drummond	79	71	71	75	296	1,960
Adam Hunter	76	71	71	79	297	1,715
Francisco Cea	76	71	74	76	297	1,715
Raymond Russell	74	75	74	74	297	1,715
Jeff Hawkes	74	76	72	75	297	1,715
Sven Struver	81	69	77	71	298	1,505
Olivier Edmond	75	70	76	77	298	1,505
Henrik Nystrom	77	73	74	75	299	1,365
David A. Russell	75	69	76	79	299	1,365
Marten Olander	70	76	84	70	300	1,163.75
Craig Hainline	75	73	71	81	300	1,163.75
Andrew Beal	79	70	80	71	300	1,163.75
Francis Howley	75	70	77	78	300	1,163.75
Fredrik Henge	83	67	72	79	301	1,050
Tjaart van der Walt	77	69	76	80	302	997.50
Stephen Bennett	75	75	77	75	302	997.50
Carl Suneson	78	71	78	76	303	945
Greig Hutcheon	72	76	80	76	304	910
Gordon J. Brand	77	73	74	82	306	700
Daren Lee	70	80	75	81	306	700
Marc Farry	75	73	83	77	308	523
Birgir Hafthorsson	74	73	85	79	311	521

Portuguese Open

Le Meridien Penina, Algarve, Portugal — March 19-22
Par 35-38–73; 6,903 yards — purse, £350,000

	SCORES				TOTAL	MONEY
Peter Mitchell	67	70	67	70	274	£58,330
Jarmo Sandelin	73	71	64	67	275	30,395
David Gilford	70	67	70	68	275	30,395
Eduardo Romero	68	75	68	65	276	14,860
Sam Torrance	74	66	70	66	276	14,860
Jonathan Lomas	71	69	69	67	276	14,860
Peter Baker	72	70	67	68	277	9,625
Wayne Riley	68	66	74	69	277	9,625
Darren Clarke	66	74	69	69	278	7,820
Tony Johnstone	68	73	70	68	279	6,720
David Carter	73	66	71	69	279	6,720
Raphael Jacquelin	76	67	70	67	280	5,535
Francisco Cea	71	72	69	68	280	5,535
Jeev Milkha Singh	69	73	68	70	280	5,535
Alex Cejka	72	72	66	70	280	5,535

	SCORES				TOTAL	MONEY
David Howell	71	72	71	67	281	4,723.33
John Bickerton	73	71	70	67	281	4,723.33
Ian Garbutt	72	68	71	70	281	4,723.33
Van Phillips	70	74	73	65	282	4,211.67
Fredrik Henge	71	71	71	69	282	4,211.67
Miguel Angel Martin	70	72	69	71	282	4,211.67
Thomas Gogele	73	73	68	69	283	3,780
Henrik Nystrom	72	68	73	70	283	3,780
Domingo Hospital	68	75	70	70	283	3,780
Angel Cabrera	75	68	67	73	283	3,780
Santiago Luna	71	67	71	74	283	3,780
Peter Hedblom	72	67	75	70	284	3,412.50
Tom Gillis	71	74	69	70	284	3,412.50
Stephen Leaney	76	70	71	68	285	3,052
Adam Hunter	72	72	73	68	285	3,052
Mark James	71	71	72	71	285	3,052
Steve Alker	74	69	70	72	285	3,052
Raymond Burns	76	69	68	72	285	3,052
Darren Cole	71	74	71	70	286	2,625
Michele Reale	74	69	72	71	286	2,625
Daniel Chopra	74	69	71	72	286	2,625
Jose Rivero	73	70	71	72	286	2,625
Malcolm Mackenzie	74	70	70	72	286	2,625
Patrik Sjoland	72	72	69	73	286	2,625
Des Smyth	71	68	74	72	287	2,170
Jeff Remesy	70	68	77	72	287	2,170
Cameron Clark	74	71	72	70	287	2,170
Derrick Cooper	73	71	73	70	287	2,170
Steen Tinning	72	71	74	70	287	2,170
Paul Eales	75	71	72	69	287	2,170
Paul Lawrie	72	64	69	82	287	2,170
Jean Van de Velde	68	73	74	73	288	1,785
Iain Pyman	73	71	72	72	288	1,785
Gary Evans	74	71	72	71	288	1,785
Craig Hainline	77	68	72	71	288	1,785
Stephen Bennett	74	68	74	73	289	1,505
Johan Rystrom	73	71	74	71	289	1,505
Fredrik Jacobson	72	70	76	71	289	1,505
Greg Owen	72	70	76	71	289	1,505
Richard Boxall	71	72	72	75	290	1,172.50
Jamie Spence	74	72	72	72	290	1,172.50
Howard Clark	77	67	74	72	290	1,172.50
Miguel Angel Jimenez	75	71	73	71	290	1,172.50
Fabrice Tarnaud	75	69	70	76	290	1,172.50
Seve Ballesteros	72	73	69	76	290	1,172.50
Andrew Oldcorn	71	71	74	75	291	962.50
Jim Payne	74	72	71	74	291	962.50
John Hawksworth	75	71	73	72	291	962.50
Russell Claydon	75	71	74	71	291	962.50
Joakim Rask	74	71	72	75	292	611
David Thomson	76	67	74	75	292	611
Dean Robertson	73	73	73	73	292	611
Roger Chapman	72	74	79	67	292	611
Maarten Lafeber	73	73	74	73	293	519
Ola Eliasson	73	71	74	76	294	516
Jose Coceres	69	71	74	80	294	516
Antonio Garrido	72	73	71	79	295	513
Mark Davis	75	71	74	76	296	511
David Lynn	71	73	74	79	297	509
Stuart Cage	73	70	81	74	298	507

Cannes Open

Royal Mougins Golf Club, Cannes, France — April 16-19
Par 35-36–71; 6,594 yards — purse, £300,000

	SCORES				TOTAL	MONEY
Thomas Levet	69	71	65	73	278	£50,000
Greg Turner	70	73	67	69	279	22,370
Phillip Price	74	66	72	67	279	22,370
Sven Struver	69	72	69	69	279	22,370
Steve Webster	70	71	70	69	280	11,600
Clinton Whitelaw	72	71	72	65	280	11,600
Ross McFarlane	76	68	70	67	281	9,000
Mark Davis	69	69	73	71	282	6,730
Peter Lonard	68	71	70	73	282	6,730
Andrew Sherborne	73	68	68	73	282	6,730
Mark Roe	70	75	70	68	283	4,902
Joakim Haeggman	70	73	68	72	283	4,902
Alex Cejka	72	73	68	70	283	4,902
Jeff Remesy	67	74	69	73	283	4,902
Paul Lawrie	74	71	67	71	283	4,902
Mark Mouland	71	71	71	71	284	3,561.82
Ian Garbutt	74	71	74	65	284	3,561.82
Miguel Angel Martin	69	74	76	65	284	3,561.82
Michael Long	69	72	70	73	284	3,561.82
Michael Campbell	70	75	72	67	284	3,561.82
Eamonn Darcy	71	72	66	75	284	3,561.82
Andrew Oldcorn	72	72	70	70	284	3,561.82
David Howell	73	70	72	69	284	3,561.82
Pierre Fulke	73	65	71	75	284	3,561.82
Steen Tinning	70	74	69	71	284	3,561.82
David Higgins	69	69	75	71	284	3,561.82
Christy O'Connor, Jr.	72	64	75	74	285	2,790
Raphael Jacquelin	69	73	70	73	285	2,790
Craig Hainline	71	72	71	71	285	2,790
Miguel Angel Jimenez	75	69	66	75	285	2,790
Bob May	74	71	71	69	285	2,790
Mathias Gronberg	73	71	68	74	286	2,400
Steve Alker	73	71	71	71	286	2,400
Santiago Luna	69	68	77	72	286	2,400
Olivier Edmond	72	71	74	69	286	2,400
Gordon Brand, Jr.	75	69	71	71	286	2,400
David Lynn	67	75	76	69	287	2,070
Andrew Clapp	73	72	71	71	287	2,070
Christophe Pottier	74	71	72	70	287	2,070
Jean Van de Velde	73	72	72	70	287	2,070
Peter Mitchell	71	74	70	71	287	2,070
Pedro Linhart	72	71	69	75	287	2,070
David Gilford	70	74	74	70	288	1,710
Jay Townsend	70	72	72	74	288	1,710
Philip Walton	72	71	73	72	288	1,710
Fabrice Tarnaud	70	74	71	73	288	1,710
Jonathan Lomas	71	70	76	71	288	1,710
Tom Gillis	73	67	73	75	288	1,710
Patrik Sjoland	72	69	72	76	289	1,470
Andrew Sandywell	69	74	72	74	289	1,470
*David Montesi	70	73	75	71	289	
Robert Allenby	67	75	73	75	290	1,350
Chris Van der Velde	71	72	72	75	290	1,350
Dean Robertson	73	70	76	72	291	1,200

	SCORES				TOTAL	MONEY
Stephen Bennett	72	73	73	73	291	1,200
Stephen Allan	71	67	72	81	291	1,200
Wayne Westner	68	77	76	71	292	997.50
Marc Farry	70	73	71	78	292	997.50
Jeev Milkha Singh	67	74	79	72	292	997.50
Stephane Lahary	72	71	77	72	292	997.50
Alberto Binaghi	71	74	74	74	293	885
Jon Robson	71	74	76	72	293	885
David Tapping	75	70	76	73	294	825
Pascal Edmond	76	69	72	77	294	825
Daniel Chopra	69	73	77	76	295	780
Rolf Muntz	74	69	76	79	298	750

Peugeot Open de Espana

El Brat, Barcelona, Spain — April 23-26
Par 35-37–72; 6,639 yards — purse, £550,000

	SCORES				TOTAL	MONEY
Thomas Bjorn	68	67	66	66	267	£91,660
Greg Chalmers	64	66	69	69	268	47,765
Jose Maria Olazabal	66	71	64	67	268	47,765
Eduardo Romero	66	67	70	67	270	25,400
Mark James	68	66	70	66	270	25,400
Roger Wessels	71	69	66	65	271	19,250
Stephen Allan	66	72	69	65	272	14,176.67
Mathias Gronberg	69	67	71	65	272	14,176.67
Katsuyoshi Tomori	67	67	66	72	272	14,176.67
Phillip Price	67	66	71	69	273	11,000
David Howell	65	68	67	74	274	8,223.33
Olle Karlsson	70	70	67	67	274	8,223.33
Angel Cabrera	67	70	69	68	274	8,223.33
Gordon Brand, Jr.	67	66	73	68	274	8,223.33
Roger Chapman	68	71	66	69	274	8,223.33
Andrew Coltart	69	70	68	67	274	8,223.33
Miguel Angel Martin	69	70	70	65	274	8,223.33
Eamonn Darcy	68	71	65	70	274	8,223.33
Robert Allenby	66	64	70	74	274	8,223.33
Miles Tunnicliff	67	69	69	70	275	6,187.50
Daniel Chopra	66	72	70	67	275	6,187.50
Sam Torrance	70	69	65	71	275	6,187.50
Ivo Giner	67	70	67	71	275	6,187.50
Paul Lawrie	68	66	73	68	275	6,187.50
Jay Townsend	64	69	70	72	275	6,187.50
David Carter	68	69	66	73	276	5,039.38
Malcolm Mackenzie	69	67	74	66	276	5,039.38
Domingo Hospital	67	68	72	69	276	5,039.38
Robert Karlsson	72	67	73	64	276	5,039.38
Peter Hedblom	69	67	74	66	276	5,039.38
Patrik Sjoland	66	71	69	70	276	5,039.38
Miguel Angel Jimenez	67	67	69	73	276	5,039.38
Craig Hainline	68	71	67	70	276	5,039.38
Wayne Riley	73	67	70	67	277	4,180
Ian Woosnam	69	70	72	66	277	4,180
Peter Mitchell	69	71	71	66	277	4,180
Paul Eales	68	72	71	66	277	4,180
Mark Roe	69	67	68	73	277	4,180

	SCORES				TOTAL	MONEY
*Sergio Garcia	66	70	70	71	277	
Klas Eriksson	69	71	66	72	278	3,630
Ignacio Garrido	70	66	72	70	278	3,630
Iain Pyman	71	68	72	67	278	3,630
Santiago Luna	68	67	71	72	278	3,630
Jose Rivero	71	69	69	69	278	3,630
Marc Farry	69	68	69	73	279	2,970
Paul Broadhurst	72	67	70	70	279	2,970
Joakim Haeggman	69	70	70	70	279	2,970
Jose Coceres	70	68	69	72	279	2,970
Thomas Levet	68	71	69	71	279	2,970
Stephen Leaney	70	69	71	69	279	2,970
Van Phillips	69	71	69	70	279	2,970
Jeff Remesy	68	69	73	70	280	2,010
Dennis Edlund	69	70	70	71	280	2,010
Silvio Grappasonni	70	66	72	72	280	2,010
Mark Mouland	72	65	71	72	280	2,010
Jose Manuel Lara	69	71	67	73	280	2,010
Kalle Brink	67	73	71	69	280	2,010
Seve Ballesteros	69	71	71	69	280	2,010
Ian Garbutt	67	71	71	71	280	2,010
Ruben Gonzalez	71	68	69	72	280	2,010
Francisco Cea	70	69	69	72	280	2,010
Jose Manuel Carriles	64	70	74	72	280	2,010
Bradley Dredge	69	68	76	68	281	1,512.50
Jean Van de Velde	65	69	72	75	281	1,512.50
Jarmo Sandelin	68	71	67	76	282	1,210
Jonathan Lomas	68	70	70	74	282	1,210
Clinton Whitelaw	68	68	71	75	282	1,210
Des Smyth	69	69	72	73	283	823
Gary Orr	71	69	73	71	284	821
Brian Davis	69	71	74	71	285	817
Peter Baker	69	71	70	75	285	817
Jim Payne	70	69	72	74	285	817
Fernando Roca	71	68	69	80	288	813
*Alejandro Larrazabal	66	72	79	75	292	

Italian Open

Castelconturbia, Milan, Italy — April 30-May 3
Par 37-35–72; 6,820 yards — purse, £491,139
(Fourth round cancelled — rain.)

	SCORES			TOTAL	MONEY
Patrik Sjoland	64	65	66	195	£81,853.82
Jose Maria Olazabal	68	65	65	198	42,655.73
Joakim Haeggman	67	68	63	198	42,655.73
Thomas Bjorn	66	66	68	200	24,557.13
Peter Baker	67	67	67	201	20,824.44
Steen Tinning	68	65	69	202	13,788.83
Lee Westwood	68	67	67	202	13,788.83
Sven Struver	67	69	66	202	13,788.83
Bob May	69	68	65	202	13,788.83
Mark James	65	69	69	203	9,095.96
David Lynn	71	65	67	203	9,095.96
Jean Van de Velde	67	70	66	203	9,095.96
Phillip Price	68	67	69	204	7,237.47

	SCORES			TOTAL	MONEY
Paul McGinley	63	72	69	204	7,237.47
Retief Goosen	70	67	67	204	7,237.47
Greg Turner	66	71	67	204	7,237.47
Jarmo Sandelin	68	70	66	204	7,237.47
Gordon Brand, Jr.	70	66	69	205	5,932.33
Paul Broadhurst	68	68	69	205	5,932.33
Jay Townsend	71	66	68	205	5,932.33
Robert Karlsson	67	70	68	205	5,932.33
Andrew Clapp	72	67	66	205	5,932.33
Silvio Grappasonni	68	68	70	206	4,935.98
Emauele Canonica	69	67	70	206	4,935.98
Massimo Florioli	67	70	69	206	4,935.98
Michael Campbell	68	69	69	206	4,935.98
Andrew Coltart	70	68	68	206	4,935.98
Thomas Levet	69	69	68	206	4,935.98
Robert Allenby	68	71	67	206	4,935.98
Roger Chapman	68	70	67	206	4,935.98
Marc Farry	68	67	72	207	3,687.66
Klas Eriksson	66	70	71	207	3,687.66
Pierre Fulke	67	70	70	207	3,687.66
Wayne Westner	69	68	70	207	3,687.66
Fredrik Henge	68	69	70	207	3,687.66
Costantino Rocca	69	69	69	207	3,687.66
Ignacio Garrido	69	69	69	207	3,687.66
Steve Webster	72	66	69	207	3,687.66
Stephen Leaney	68	71	68	207	3,687.66
Miguel Angel Martin	72	68	67	207	3,687.66
Paolo Quirici	74	66	67	207	3,687.66
Rolf Muntz	69	71	67	207	3,687.66
Mathias Gronberg	70	67	71	208	2,897.74
Padraig Harrington	70	69	69	208	2,897.74
Nicolas Vanhootegem	71	68	69	208	2,897.74
Michael Jonzon	74	66	68	208	2,897.74
Robert Coles	71	65	73	209	2,504.83
Eamonn Darcy	68	70	71	209	2,504.83
Gary Evans	69	71	69	209	2,504.83
Anssi Kankkonen	70	70	69	209	2,504.83
Darren Clarke	65	71	74	210	1,871.80
Martin Gates	70	68	72	210	1,871.80
David Carter	68	70	72	210	1,871.80
Chris Van der Velde	73	66	71	210	1,871.80
Eduardo Romero	72	67	71	210	1,871.80
Rodger Davis	70	70	70	210	1,871.80
Dennis Edlund	70	70	70	210	1,871.80
Michael Long	70	70	70	210	1,871.80
Dean Robertson	70	70	70	210	1,871.80
David Gilford	69	68	74	211	1,375.20
Stephen Allan	69	70	72	211	1,375.20
Angel Cabrera	73	67	71	211	1,375.20
Steven Richardson	72	68	71	211	1,375.20
Jamie Spence	68	72	71	211	1,375.20
Thomas Gogele	71	67	74	212	1,227.86
Raymond Burns	71	66	76	213	735
Van Phillips	70	69	74	213	735
Raphael Jacquelin	72	67	72	213	735
Ronan Rafferty	67	72	76	215	729
Federico Bisazza	71	69	75	215	729
Malcolm Mackenzie	73	67	75	215	729
Scott Henderson	69	69	78	216	725

Turespana Masters Open Baleares

Santa Ponsa I, Mallorca, Spain — May 7-10
Par 36-36–72; 7,155 yards — purse, £350,000

	SCORES				TOTAL	MONEY
Miguel Angel Jimenez	69	68	70	72	279	£58,330
Miguel Angel Martin	67	72	70	72	281	38,880
Paul McGinley	71	73	67	71	282	19,705
Katsuyoshi Tomori	74	67	73	68	282	19,705
Van Phillips	75	69	67	73	284	14,830
Michael Long	71	71	72	71	285	11,375
Santiago Luna	67	70	72	76	285	11,375
Paul Broadhurst	71	72	69	76	288	7,502.50
Massimo Florioli	72	70	72	74	288	7,502.50
Angel Cabrera	71	69	73	75	288	7,502.50
Michele Reale	68	72	70	78	288	7,502.50
Andrew Beal	72	73	70	74	289	5,666.67
Andrew Sandywell	70	74	73	72	289	5,666.67
Richard Johnson	71	72	72	74	289	5,666.67
Alberto Binaghi	72	76	68	74	290	4,827.50
Greig Hutcheon	70	76	70	74	290	4,827.50
David Howell	72	72	72	74	290	4,827.50
Diego Borrego	70	73	74	73	290	4,827.50
Francisco Cea	73	75	66	77	291	4,156.25
Michael Campbell	74	72	73	72	291	4,156.25
Malcolm Mackenzie	72	71	73	75	291	4,156.25
John Bickerton	70	72	73	76	291	4,156.25
Roger Wessels	73	75	77	67	292	3,727.50
Peter Mitchell	72	74	72	74	292	3,727.50
Anders Hansen	73	71	73	75	292	3,727.50
Anthony Wall	70	72	76	74	292	3,727.50
John Mellor	72	75	72	74	293	3,155
Raphael Jacquelin	71	75	74	73	293	3,155
Pedro Linhart	72	73	73	75	293	3,155
Daren Lee	70	75	73	75	293	3,155
Stephen Bennett	70	74	75	74	293	3,155
Andrew Clapp	72	71	74	76	293	3,155
Jose Rivero	69	70	78	76	293	3,155
*Sergio Garcia	70	75	76	72	293	
Robert Lee	71	75	76	72	294	2,520
Mathew Goggin	73	73	77	71	294	2,520
Anders Forsbrand	72	74	72	76	294	2,520
Tom Gillis	76	72	74	72	294	2,520
Greg Owen	77	71	72	74	294	2,520
Ross Drummond	75	73	71	75	294	2,520
Marc Pendaries	72	74	74	74	294	2,520
John Hawksworth	68	78	76	72	294	2,520
Bernhard Langer	72	73	74	75	294	2,520
Heinz P. Thul	73	73	71	78	295	2,100
Jeev Milkha Singh	72	75	74	74	295	2,100
Emanuele Canonica	77	70	72	76	295	2,100
Marco Gortana	74	72	74	76	296	1,750
Francisco Valera	75	72	75	74	296	1,750
Stuart Cage	73	74	75	74	296	1,750
Domingo Hospital	72	75	74	75	296	1,750
Matthew Blackey	76	72	74	74	296	1,750
Paul Curry	74	74	72	76	296	1,750
John Wade	68	75	73	80	296	1,750
Ivo Giner	69	77	77	74	297	1,295

	SCORES				TOTAL	MONEY
Fernando Roca	72	75	75	75	297	1,295
Birgir Hafthorsson	72	75	71	79	297	1,295
Robert Jan Derksen	72	76	72	77	297	1,295
Brian Davis	71	75	75	76	297	1,295
Yago Beamonte	74	72	77	74	297	1,295
Neal Briggs	74	74	76	74	298	1,085
Stephen Scahill	73	74	75	77	299	980
Ola Eliasson	72	75	78	74	299	980
Alvaro Salto	73	74	73	79	299	980
Olivier Edmond	74	74	70	81	299	980
Andrew McKenna	68	78	72	81	299	980
*Raul Quiros	69	76	77	77	299	
Gary Nicklaus	76	71	76	77	300	611
Dennis Edlund	74	74	74	78	300	611
Soren Kjeldsen	73	75	76	76	300	611
Bernardo Solanes	75	73	77	75	300	611
Jon Robson	72	75	77	77	301	517
Francisco de Pablo	75	72	76	78	301	517
Daniel Westermark	73	75	79	74	301	517
Paul Streeter	73	74	79	76	302	512
Ruben Gonzalez	75	73	78	76	302	512
Mark Davis	73	75	82	73	303	509
Steven Richardson	74	74	76	81	305	507
Mark Mouland	74	71	77	85	307	505

Benson and Hedges International

The Oxfordshire Golf Club, Thame, Oxon, England — May 14-17
Par 36-36–72; 7,205 yards — purse, £750,000

	SCORES				TOTAL	MONEY
Darren Clarke	70	69	67	67	273	£125,000
Santiago Luna	69	71	69	67	276	83,320
Thomas Bjorn	68	74	68	67	277	42,220
Massimo Florioli	68	67	71	71	277	42,220
Retief Goosen	71	68	71	68	278	29,010
Colin Montgomerie	69	68	69	72	278	29,010
Rodger Davis	70	70	70	69	279	18,247.50
Mark Mouland	70	70	70	69	279	18,247.50
Greg Turner	72	67	69	71	279	18,247.50
Patrik Sjoland	67	72	68	72	279	18,247.50
Jose Maria Olazabal	72	70	70	68	280	12,560
Paul Lawrie	67	73	70	70	280	12,560
Brian Davis	69	70	72	69	280	12,560
Gary Evans	67	71	69	73	280	12,560
Bob May	71	67	71	72	281	10,571.67
Per Haugsrud	69	68	71	73	281	10,571.67
Phillip Price	69	67	73	72	281	10,571.67
Peter Mitchell	74	68	69	71	282	8,937.50
Russell Claydon	69	73	67	73	282	8,937.50
Andrew Sherborne	69	75	70	68	282	8,937.50
Ian Woosnam	71	70	70	71	282	8,937.50
Stuart Cage	69	71	71	71	282	8,937.50
Barry Lane	69	66	75	72	282	8,937.50
Paul McGinley	69	73	73	68	283	7,200
David Carter	69	73	68	73	283	7,200
Pierre Fulke	71	72	70	70	283	7,200

	SCORES				TOTAL	MONEY
Gordon Brand, Jr.	70	71	69	73	283	7,200
Soren Kjeldsen	70	71	71	71	283	7,200
Paul Affleck	68	73	71	71	283	7,200
Robert Allenby	71	69	69	74	283	7,200
Scott Henderson	69	71	70	73	283	7,200
Peter Baker	73	66	73	71	283	7,200
Carl Suneson	69	73	72	70	284	5,850
Paul Curry	69	73	68	74	284	5,850
Katsuyoshi Tomori	72	70	72	70	284	5,850
Greg Owen	73	71	72	68	284	5,850
Jamie Spence	70	69	70	75	284	5,850
Jim Payne	73	69	70	73	285	5,025
Jonathan Lomas	70	72	71	72	285	5,025
Peter O'Malley	69	73	73	70	285	5,025
Fabrice Tarnaud	71	72	69	73	285	5,025
Mathias Gronberg	70	74	71	70	285	5,025
Bradley Dredge	68	72	76	69	285	5,025
Dean Robertson	67	74	71	74	286	4,275
Stephen Leaney	70	71	71	74	286	4,275
Andrew Coltart	72	69	71	74	286	4,275
Sven Struver	70	71	72	73	286	4,275
*Justin Rose	72	68	72	74	286	
Wayne Westner	70	72	74	71	287	3,675
David Lynn	69	74	71	73	287	3,675
Greg Chalmers	71	73	70	73	287	3,675
Dennis Edlund	74	67	76	70	287	3,675
David Howell	71	71	70	76	288	2,850
Des Smyth	69	74	73	72	288	2,850
Gary Orr	69	74	73	72	288	2,850
Michael Campbell	72	71	71	74	288	2,850
Mats Hallberg	69	72	71	76	288	2,850
Stephen Bennett	73	68	75	72	288	2,850
Robert Jan Derksen	71	69	74	74	288	2,850
Padraig Harrington	70	72	74	73	289	2,325
Eamonn Darcy	74	70	70	76	290	2,250
Chris Van der Velde	70	74	75	72	291	2,137.50
Thomas Gogele	73	71	70	77	291	2,137.50
Carl Watts	69	74	76	73	292	1,987.50
Adam Hunter	72	72	73	75	292	1,987.50
Carl Mason	73	70	73	77	293	1,500
Lee Westwood	71	69	77	76	293	1,500
Miles Tunnicliff	71	73	74	78	296	1,123
Wayne Riley	71	72	78	76	297	1,121
Anders Forsbrand	76	68	78	85	307	1,119

Volvo PGA Championship

Wentworth Club, West Course, Surrey, England — May 22-25
Par 35-37–72; 7,006 yards — purse, £1,200,000

	SCORES				TOTAL	MONEY
Colin Montgomerie	70	70	65	69	274	£200,000
Patrik Sjoland	72	71	66	66	275	89,433.33
Ernie Els	69	69	69	68	275	89,433.33
Gary Orr	70	69	68	68	275	89,433.33
Dean Robertson	70	69	67	70	276	37,160
Peter Lonard	72	65	71	68	276	37,160

	SCORES				TOTAL	MONEY
Andrew Coltart	72	66	70	68	276	37,160
Thomas Bjorn	70	69	69	68	276	37,160
Mats Hallberg	68	69	69	70	276	37,160
Paul McGinley	72	69	68	68	277	24,000
Phillip Price	71	72	68	67	278	20,100
Gordon Brand, Jr.	71	69	72	66	278	20,100
David Gilford	70	69	68	71	278	20,100
Padraig Harrington	70	69	69	70	278	20,100
Costantino Rocca	71	70	70	68	279	17,600
Lee Westwood	71	71	69	69	280	15,564
Sam Torrance	70	71	71	68	280	15,564
Stephen Leaney	69	73	71	67	280	15,564
Jose Maria Olazabal	72	71	70	67	280	15,564
Jean Van de Velde	71	71	69	69	280	15,564
Seve Ballesteros	72	71	65	73	281	12,780
Robert Karlsson	71	71	71	68	281	12,780
Massimo Florioli	75	68	67	71	281	12,780
David Howell	68	71	71	71	281	12,780
Wayne Westner	73	69	68	71	281	12,780
Per-Ulrik Johansson	70	71	72	68	281	12,780
Rodger Davis	73	69	69	70	281	12,780
Van Phillips	70	73	68	70	281	12,780
Jose Coceres	73	69	68	72	282	10,620
Darren Clarke	71	68	75	68	282	10,620
Bernhard Langer	69	70	72	71	282	10,620
Domingo Hospital	69	69	74	70	282	10,620
Fabrice Tarnaud	73	69	72	69	283	9,480
Greg Turner	70	68	70	75	283	9,480
Michael Jonzon	66	70	72	75	283	9,480
Roger Wessels	71	71	71	70	283	9,480
Mark McNulty	69	72	72	71	284	8,520
Peter Senior	72	70	69	73	284	8,520
Mark Roe	71	71	69	73	284	8,520
Tony Johnstone	69	73	73	69	284	8,520
Clinton Whitelaw	69	74	72	70	285	6,960
Peter Baker	74	69	73	69	285	6,960
Russell Claydon	71	72	70	72	285	6,960
Katsuyoshi Tomori	70	70	72	73	285	6,960
Malcolm Mackenzie	68	71	74	72	285	6,960
Jonathan Lomas	71	71	71	72	285	6,960
Santiago Luna	71	71	73	70	285	6,960
Thomas Gogele	71	71	72	71	285	6,960
Dennis Edlund	71	71	74	69	285	6,960
Mark James	69	73	69	75	286	5,400
Brian Davis	67	75	72	72	286	5,400
Rolf Muntz	72	71	71	72	286	5,400
Andrew Sherborne	71	70	74	71	286	5,400
Ian Woosnam	73	70	74	70	287	4,320
Sven Struver	73	69	75	70	287	4,320
Eduardo Romero	70	72	70	75	287	4,320
Sandy Lyle	69	74	72	72	287	4,320
Peter Hedblom	70	70	75	72	287	4,320
Carl Watts	71	69	71	77	288	3,660
Chris Van der Velde	68	75	76	69	288	3,660
Raymond Burns	70	72	74	73	289	3,480
Howard Clark	70	73	74	73	290	3,360
Diego Borrego	71	72	74	76	293	3,240
Steven Richardson	70	73	74	78	295	3,060
David Tapping	69	74	78	74	295	3,060

Deutsche Bank–SAP Open TPC of Europe

Gut Kaden, Hamburg, Germany
Par 36-36–72; 7,029 yards

May 29-June 1
purse, £1,100,000

	SCORES				TOTAL	MONEY
Lee Westwood	69	69	61	66	265	£183,340
Darren Clarke	67	66	65	68	266	122,210
Mark O'Meara	67	69	63	70	269	68,860
Philip Walton	69	70	65	67	271	46,713.33
Bernhard Langer	67	66	70	68	271	46,713.33
Peter Senior	69	67	64	71	271	46,713.33
David Howell	69	68	66	69	272	28,343.33
Miguel Angel Jimenez	69	69	65	69	272	28,343.33
Jim Payne	70	68	69	65	272	28,343.33
Paul Lawrie	68	72	66	67	273	20,370
Bob May	67	68	68	70	273	20,370
Colin Montgomerie	67	67	72	67	273	20,370
Paul Broadhurst	68	65	65	76	274	16,547.50
Peter Mitchell	66	70	67	71	274	16,547.50
Thomas Bjorn	69	68	71	66	274	16,547.50
Joakim Haeggman	69	70	63	72	274	16,547.50
Costantino Rocca	70	71	66	68	275	13,750
Ian Woosnam	69	71	64	71	275	13,750
Gary Orr	71	68	69	67	275	13,750
Paolo Quirici	68	70	67	70	275	13,750
Jean Van der Velde	67	67	67	74	275	13,750
Jeev Milkha Singh	69	70	67	70	276	11,880
Retief Goosen	68	68	69	71	276	11,880
Paul McGinley	65	74	66	71	276	11,880
Nick Price	70	68	68	70	276	11,880
Ian Garbutt	70	68	67	71	276	11,880
Greg Chalmers	67	71	69	70	277	9,915.71
Emanuele Canonica	67	71	68	71	277	9,915.71
Scott Henderson	70	66	66	75	277	9,915.71
Marc Farry	72	66	68	71	277	9,915.71
Alex Cejka	68	70	70	69	277	9,915.71
Jose Maria Olazabal	69	71	67	70	277	9,915.71
Jarmo Sandelin	69	70	71	67	277	9,915.71
Phillip Price	70	71	68	69	278	8,360
Sam Torrance	68	69	69	72	278	8,360
Pierre Fulke	72	67	69	70	278	8,360
Brian Davis	69	68	70	71	278	8,360
Katsuyoshi Tomori	68	69	70	71	278	8,360
Wayne Westner	70	66	70	73	279	7,040
Per Haugsrud	71	66	67	75	279	7,040
Mark James	67	68	72	72	279	7,040
Mats Hallberg	70	70	67	72	279	7,040
Eamonn Darcy	72	69	67	71	279	7,040
Mark Roe	68	70	70	71	279	7,040
Peter O'Malley	67	70	71	71	279	7,040
Wayne Riley	72	69	67	72	280	5,390
Jose Coceres	70	69	72	69	280	5,390
Jamie Spence	67	73	72	68	280	5,390
Domingo Hospital	72	69	69	70	280	5,390
David Gilford	70	71	69	70	280	5,390
Miles Tunnicliff	70	69	69	72	280	5,390
Carl Watts	73	67	69	71	280	5,390
Mark Mouland	70	69	69	72	280	5,390
Russell Claydon	71	67	72	71	281	3,868.33

	SCORES				TOTAL	MONEY
David Carter	70	71	69	71	281	3,868.33
Steve Webster	72	69	66	74	281	3,868.33
Kalle Brink	71	68	72	70	281	3,868.33
Peter Hedblom	73	68	68	71	281	3,868.33
Derrick Cooper	72	69	70	70	281	3,868.33
Padraig Harrington	69	72	72	69	282	3,190
Andrew Coltart	68	68	74	72	282	3,190
Thomas Gogele	70	68	70	74	282	3,190
Thomas Hennig	73	68	71	71	283	2,557.50
Dennis Edlund	67	72	71	73	283	2,557.50
Santiago Luna	72	69	72	70	283	2,557.50
Paul Eales	68	70	73	72	283	2,557.50
Dean Robertson	73	68	70	73	284	1,644
Adam Hunter	70	69	72	73	284	1,644
Roger Chapman	71	69	71	73	284	1,644
Daniel Chopra	72	67	72	73	284	1,644
Raymond Russell	69	69	72	74	284	1,644
Craig Hainline	73	68	72	72	285	1,635
Malcolm Mackenzie	71	68	74	72	285	1,635
Andrew Oldcorn	70	71	69	75	285	1,635
Per-Ulrik Johansson	70	71	72	72	285	1,635
Stephen Allan	67	74	67	78	286	1,627
Mark Davis	70	70	70	76	286	1,627
Raymond Burns	70	70	73	73	286	1,627
Gary Evans	73	68	72	73	286	1,627
Anthony Wall	71	70	70	76	287	1,621
Yusuf Kaya	72	69	72	74	287	1,621
Richard Boxall	71	70	72	75	288	1,618

National Car Rental English Open

Marriott Hanbury Manor, Ware, England — June 4-7
Par 36-36–72; 7,016 yards — purse, £650,000

	SCORES				TOTAL	MONEY
Lee Westwood	68	68	67	68	271	£108,330
Greg Chalmers	70	73	61	69	273	56,450
Olle Karlsson	70	70	67	66	273	56,450
Colin Montgomerie	64	72	69	69	274	32,500
Patrik Sjoland	68	67	70	70	275	27,530
Phillip Price	73	71	67	65	276	22,750
Robert Allenby	67	71	70	69	277	19,500
Roger Wessels	68	69	70	71	278	15,380
Jeev Milkha Singh	71	69	67	71	278	15,380
Christy O'Connor, Jr.	71	70	68	71	280	11,650
Mark McNulty	73	68	66	73	280	11,650
Stephen Leaney	66	69	70	75	280	11,650
Knud Storgaard	71	70	72	67	280	11,650
Gary Evans	70	73	68	70	281	8,978.33
Paul Eales	69	72	70	70	281	8,978.33
Andrew Coltart	67	72	67	75	281	8,978.33
Van Phillips	69	72	71	69	281	8,978.33
Michael Campbell	71	72	71	67	281	8,978.33
Bob May	71	69	69	72	281	8,978.33
Nicolas Vanhootegem	66	72	72	72	282	7,410
Jon Robson	66	73	73	70	282	7,410
Russell Claydon	71	70	72	69	282	7,410

	SCORES				TOTAL	MONEY
Peter Baker	69	72	70	71	282	7,410
Thomas Gogele	70	73	70	69	282	7,410
Derrick Cooper	68	76	68	71	283	6,240
Ian Garbutt	70	72	70	71	283	6,240
Steve Webster	72	68	70	73	283	6,240
Philip Walton	74	69	70	70	283	6,240
Padraig Harrington	74	69	70	70	283	6,240
Michael Jonzon	72	68	72	71	283	6,240
Nicolas Joakimides	65	74	72	72	283	6,240
Jose Rivero	69	73	69	73	284	5,265
Mats Hallberg	72	72	66	74	284	5,265
Pierre Fulke	72	70	69	73	284	5,265
Gary Orr	75	69	68	72	284	5,265
Mark Mouland	72	72	72	69	285	4,680
Dean Robertson	68	73	71	73	285	4,680
Eamonn Darcy	71	72	71	71	285	4,680
Paul Affleck	74	65	74	72	285	4,680
Anthony Wall	75	68	68	74	285	4,680
Mathias Gronberg	73	70	72	71	286	3,835
Fabrice Tarnaud	70	66	75	75	286	3,835
Miguel Angel Jimenez	68	72	70	76	286	3,835
Jeff Remesy	70	71	71	74	286	3,835
David Howell	74	69	70	73	286	3,835
Ronan Rafferty	69	72	72	73	286	3,835
Thomas Bjorn	73	70	70	73	286	3,835
Raphael Jacquelin	69	71	73	73	286	3,835
Greg Owen	72	72	71	72	287	2,795
Michael Long	71	70	72	74	287	2,795
Peter Mitchell	70	73	73	71	287	2,795
Paul Broadhurst	75	69	70	73	287	2,795
Steve Alker	70	71	73	73	287	2,795
Ignacio Garrido	70	74	71	72	287	2,795
Darren Clarke	72	72	75	68	287	2,795
Michele Reale	71	71	72	73	287	2,795
Craig Hainline	71	69	75	73	288	2,063.75
Steen Tinning	74	70	71	73	288	2,063.75
David Gilford	72	71	76	69	288	2,063.75
Rolf Muntz	69	72	76	71	288	2,063.75
Steven Richardson	70	71	74	74	289	1,787.50
Andrew Sandywell	74	70	68	77	289	1,787.50
Massimo Florioli	72	68	74	75	289	1,787.50
Tom Gillis	71	73	71	74	289	1,787.50
Ivo Giner	75	68	73	74	290	1,080
Andrew Sherborne	72	70	70	78	290	1,080
Wayne Riley	68	73	76	73	290	1,080
Paul Curry	73	71	68	78	290	1,080
Jay Townsend	70	73	75	72	290	1,080
Stephen Allan	73	70	73	74	290	1,080
Roger Chapman	71	72	73	76	292	963
Carl Watts	68	75	74	75	292	963
John Bickerton	74	70	72	76	292	963
Howard Clark	71	72	74	79	296	959
Rodger Davis	73	71	79	77	300	957

Madeira Island Open

Santo da Serra Golf Club, Madeira, Portugal
Par 36-36–72; 6,606 yards

June 18-21
purse, £300,000

	SCORES				TOTAL	MONEY
Mats Lanner	70	66	68	73	277	£50,000
Stephen Scahill	72	61	69	76	278	33,330
Andrew Beal	71	68	67	73	279	18,780
Thomas Gogele	68	68	73	73	282	13,850
Francisco Cea	69	69	71	73	282	13,850
Carl Suneson	70	72	69	72	283	9,750
Rudi Sailer	70	68	70	75	283	9,750
John Mellor	69	70	73	72	284	7,095
Christian Cevaer	70	71	69	74	284	7,095
Katsuyoshi Tomori	70	72	68	76	286	5,377.50
Ivo Giner	72	67	70	77	286	5,377.50
Tom Gillis	70	69	69	78	286	5,377.50
Fredrik Jacobson	71	71	65	79	286	5,377.50
John Bickerton	73	69	74	71	287	4,230
Maarten Lafeber	76	68	71	72	287	4,230
Adam Hunter	71	72	71	73	287	4,230
Ross Drummond	71	71	70	75	287	4,230
Roger Winchester	68	73	69	77	287	4,230
Mathew Goggin	73	73	69	73	288	3,242.73
Stephen Ames	68	78	69	73	288	3,242.73
Paul Affleck	76	68	72	72	288	3,242.73
John Wade	76	70	70	72	288	3,242.73
Robert Lee	73	71	70	74	288	3,242.73
Pedro Linhart	70	69	74	75	288	3,242.73
Marten Olander	72	68	73	75	288	3,242.73
Steve Alker	71	74	68	75	288	3,242.73
Joakim Rask	71	69	72	76	288	3,242.73
Greig Hutcheon	71	69	71	77	288	3,242.73
Michael Campbell	71	67	70	80	288	3,242.73
Stephen Bennett	72	72	72	73	289	2,572.50
Andrew Sherborne	74	69	73	73	289	2,572.50
David Tapping	66	73	73	77	289	2,572.50
Andre Stolz	72	69	70	78	289	2,572.50
John Hawksworth	73	72	72	74	291	2,220
Scott Watson	74	71	72	74	291	2,220
Gordon J. Brand	71	69	73	78	291	2,220
Gary Nicklaus	72	71	70	78	291	2,220
Greg Owen	73	72	68	78	291	2,220
Daniel Chopra	73	72	67	79	291	2,220
Santiago Luna	68	71	72	80	291	2,220
Olivier Edmond	73	70	72	77	292	1,890
Brian Nelson	69	76	72	75	292	1,890
Soren Kjeldsen	73	73	71	75	292	1,890
Jeev Milkha Singh	75	72	74	71	292	1,890
Jeff Remesy	71	76	68	78	293	1,650
Jean Louis Guepy	70	76	73	74	293	1,650
Robert Moss	71	73	76	73	293	1,650
Gary Emerson	72	71	66	84	293	1,650
Robert Wragg	72	72	73	77	294	1,470
Ged Furey	71	74	69	80	294	1,470
Paul Streeter	75	69	74	77	295	1,260
Steven Bottomley	69	75	74	77	295	1,260
David Higgins	73	71	74	77	295	1,260
Ola Eliasson	77	69	74	75	295	1,260

	SCORES				TOTAL	MONEY
Daren Lee	72	71	71	81	295	1,260
Craig Hainline	72	72	75	77	296	960
Michele Reale	72	75	72	77	296	960
Stephen Hamill	73	74	72	77	296	960
Stephen Dodd	76	71	72	77	296	960
Mauricio Molina	72	73	76	75	296	960
Henrik Nystrom	73	73	77	73	296	960
Antonio Sobrinho	73	74	71	79	297	840
David Lynn	74	69	75	80	298	697.50
Darren Cole	71	72	75	80	298	697.50
Phil Golding	70	73	79	76	298	697.50
Johan Rystrom	74	70	71	83	298	697.50
Brian Davis	73	72	76	79	300	448
*Stephane Ferriera	74	73	73	80	300	
Anthony Wall	72	74	74	81	301	445
Daniel Silva	71	75	77	78	301	445
Francis Howley	73	74	77	80	304	442

Peugeot Open de France

Le Golf National, Paris, France
Par 36-36–72; 7,122 yards

June 25-28
purse, £500,000

	SCORES				TOTAL	MONEY
Sam Torrance	64	70	72	70	276	£83,330
Massimo Florioli	69	67	75	67	278	33,262.50
Olivier Edmond	70	70	71	67	278	33,262.50
Bernhard Langer	71	70	68	69	278	33,262.50
Mathew Goggin	69	70	69	70	278	33,262.50
Marc Farry	70	67	73	69	279	16,250
Pedro Linhart	66	73	70	70	279	16,250
Russell Claydon	69	70	70	71	280	11,216.67
David Howell	70	69	69	72	280	11,216.67
Santiago Luna	75	68	67	70	280	11,216.67
Soren Kjeldsen	70	72	75	64	281	8,164
Philip Walton	72	73	69	67	281	8,164
Jarmo Sandelin	74	69	71	67	281	8,164
Alex Cejka	70	69	73	69	281	8,164
Michael Campbell	70	67	69	75	281	8,164
Nicolas Joakimides	72	68	73	69	282	6,285.71
Ian Garbutt	73	68	72	69	282	6,285.71
Retief Goosen	70	70	70	72	282	6,285.71
Jean Van de Velde	67	71	73	71	282	6,285.71
Paul McGinley	71	72	72	67	282	6,285.71
Paul Broadhurst	73	70	68	71	282	6,285.71
Tom Gillis	72	71	66	73	282	6,285.71
Francisco Cea	75	68	71	69	283	5,175
Miguel Angel Jimenez	72	73	68	70	283	5,175
Andrew Clapp	72	71	70	70	283	5,175
Colin Montgomerie	74	68	73	68	283	5,175
Eduardo Romero	66	75	72	70	283	5,175
Alexandre Balicki	72	73	72	66	283	5,175
Klas Eriksson	68	71	74	71	284	4,133.33
Ross Drummond	70	71	75	68	284	4,133.33
Stephen Scahill	73	71	68	72	284	4,133.33
Gordon J. Brand	70	73	71	70	284	4,133.33
Van Phillips	71	72	69	72	284	4,133.33

U.S. Tour

Allsport/Andy Lyons

David Duval won four PGA Tour events and led the money list.

Allsport/Matthew Stockmam

Vijay Singh had consecutive wins.

Allsport/Jon Ferrey

Jim Furyk took third on the money list.

Tiger Woods won in Atlanta.

Hal Sutton was the Tour champion.

Fred Couples had two wins.

Phil Mickelson took the Mercedes trophy.

Allsport/Craig Jones

John Huston triumphed in Hawaii.

Allsport/Craig Jones

Davis Love III enjoyed the spoils of victory.

Allsport/Andy Lyons

Justin Leonard finished eighth.

Allsport/Harry How

Steve Stricker won over $1.3 million.

Allsport/Craig Jones

Mark Calcavecchia's moment of triumph.

Allsport/Craig Jones

Jesper Parnevik had a victory cigar.

Allsport/David Cannon

Greg Norman was injured and content to watch his son, Gregory.

Allsport/Stephen Munday

Glen Day climbed into the top 20.

Allsport/Rusty Jarrett

Stuart Appleby won the Kemper Open.

Allsport/Andrew Redington

Ernie Els was the Bay Hill champion.

Allsport/Matthew Stockmam

Billy Mayfair claimed two titles.

Allsport/Harry How

Tom Watson was the Colonial winner.

Allsport/Harry How

Byron Nelson congratulated John Cook.

Allsport/Jamie Squire

Steve Elkington was a Buick champion.

Allsport/Erik Perel

Nick Price won the FedEx prize.

European Tour

Michael Cohen

For the sixth consecutive year, Colin Montgomerie led the PGA European Tour.

Allsport/David Cannon

Darren Clarke won the Volvo Masters.

Allsport/Paul Severn

Lee Westwood had seven worldwide wins.

Allsport/Paul Severn

Miguel Angel Jimenez won in Spain.

Allsport/Andrew Redington

Patrik Sjoland took the Italian title.

Allsport/Andrew Redington

Thomas Bjorn collected two titles.

Allsport/Andrew Redington

It was an oyster for Andrew Coltart.

Allsport/David Cannon

Jose Maria Olazabal won in Dubai.

Allsport/Andrew Redington

Mathias Gronberg won the European Open.

Allsport/Tim Matthews

Stephen Leaney took two cups in Morocco.

Allsport/Andrew Redington

Peter Baker was 12th on the money list.

Allsport/Paul Severn

Sam Torrance enjoyed his French win.

Allsport/David Cannon

At majestic Crans-sur-Sierre, Sven Struver triumphed in the Canon European Masters.

Allsport/David Cannon

Ian Woosnam fell to 20th on the money list.

Allsport/Andrew Redington

Bernhard Langer was winless.

Allsport/Paul Severn

Jesper Parnevik won at home in Sweden.

Allsport/Andrew Redington

Nick Faldo struggled in Europe.

Japan/Asia/Australia

Allsport/Ezra O. Shaw

Masashi (Jumbo) Ozaki again led the Japan PGA Tour.

Michael Cohen

Hidemichi Tanaka won three times.

Allsport/Craig Jones

Shigeki Maruyama had global success.

Michael Cohen

American Brandt Jobe had three victories.

Michael Cohen

Carlos Franco had two early wins.

Tiger Woods triumphed in Thailand.

Shaun Micheel was among the Omega leaders.

Edward Fryatt had two victories.

Bradley Hughes won the Masters title.

Frankie Minoza won four times.

Senior Tours

Allsport/Scott Halleran

Hale Irwin had another fantastic year.

Allsport/Andy Lyons

Gil Morgan took six official titles.

Allsport/Andy Lyons

Larry Nelson won three times.

Allsport/Vincent Laforet

Jay Sigel had two victories.

Allsport/Andy Lyons

Isao Aoki was the BellSouth winner.

Allsport/David Cannon

Hugh Baiocchi won back-to-back.

Allsport/Mike Cooper

Tommy Horton led in Europe.

Allsport/Mike Cooper

Brian Huggett won the British title.

Women's Tours

Allsport/Craig Jones

Annika Sorenstam led the LPGA money list and had five worldwide victories.

Allsport/Craig Jones

Se Ri Pak claimed two major titles.

Allsport/Harry How

Donna Andrews was third on the money list.

Allsport/Jon Ferrey

Karrie Webb won the Australian Masters.

Michael Cohen

Liselotte Neumann had two early wins.

Allsport/Craig Jones

Pat Hurst took the Dinah Shore title.

Allsport/Craig Jones

Juli Inkster was World champion.

Allsport/Andy Lyons

Helen Alfredsson posted three wins.

Allsport/Craig Jones

Kelly Robbins was a double winner.

Allsport/Jamie Squire

Brandie Burton took the du Maurier.

Allsport/Harry How

Danielle Ammaccapane won twice.

Allsport/David Cannon

Sherri Steinhauer won in Britain.

	SCORES				TOTAL	MONEY
Gary Nicklaus	69	75	71	69	284	4,133.33
Peter Mitchell	71	74	68	71	284	4,133.33
Thomas Gogele	74	68	69	73	284	4,133.33
Raphael Jacquelin	73	70	73	68	284	4,133.33
Gary Orr	74	70	73	68	285	3,450
Wayne Riley	70	68	76	71	285	3,450
Jean Louis Guepy	75	70	70	70	285	3,450
Craig Hainline	71	71	73	70	285	3,450
Andre Stolz	74	70	73	69	286	3,050
Adam Hunter	71	74	68	73	286	3,050
Jamie Spence	72	70	69	75	286	3,050
Francis Howley	70	72	73	71	286	3,050
Dean Robertson	68	75	74	70	287	2,650
Heinz P. Thul	69	74	74	70	287	2,650
Mark Roe	74	68	70	75	287	2,650
John Wade	74	71	71	71	287	2,650
Robert Lee	73	71	74	70	288	2,350
Sven Struver	72	73	73	70	288	2,350
Darren Cole	70	74	72	73	289	2,000
Steve Webster	70	73	73	73	289	2,000
Katsuyoshi Tomori	68	73	75	73	289	2,000
Greg Turner	72	73	72	72	289	2,000
Diego Borrego	72	72	69	76	289	2,000
Gary Evans	72	71	76	72	291	1,560
Steve Alker	74	71	77	69	291	1,560
Steven Bottomley	70	73	72	76	291	1,560
Marten Olander	74	71	73	73	291	1,560
Richard Boxall	69	72	73	77	291	1,560
Stephen Field	70	74	78	70	292	1,325
John Hawksworth	71	72	72	77	292	1,325
Ola Eliasson	71	72	78	71	292	1,325
Phil Golding	72	73	72	75	292	1,325
John Bickerton	67	77	77	72	293	749
Johan Rystrom	72	73	70	78	293	749
Des Smyth	69	72	77	76	294	745
Robert Allenby	70	70	75	79	294	745
*Olivier David	74	71	77	79	301	

Murphy's Irish Open

Druids Glen Golf Club, Dublin, Ireland — July 2-5
Par 35-36–71; 7,012 yards — purse, £1,000,000

	SCORES				TOTAL	MONEY
David Carter	68	72	67	71	278	£159,991.65
Colin Montgomerie	65	74	71	68	278	106,631.89
(Carter defeated Montgomerie at first extra hole.)						
Peter Baker	69	75	66	70	280	53,996.25
John McHenry	70	68	70	72	280	53,996.25
Craig Hainline	70	68	72	71	281	40,797.16
Jose Coceres	75	67	70	70	282	31,197.83
Gary Orr	70	69	72	71	282	31,197.83
Peter Lonard	69	74	70	70	283	23,998.33
Ian Garbutt	73	69	71	71	284	17,490.96
Ian Woosnam	73	74	65	72	284	17,490.96
Russell Claydon	71	71	73	69	284	17,490.96
Derrick Cooper	73	70	72	69	284	17,490.96

	SCORES				TOTAL	MONEY
Jose Maria Olazabal	73	72	71	68	284	17,490.96
Steve Webster	71	70	70	73	284	17,490.96
Lee Westwood	70	73	73	69	285	14,085.98
Peter O'Malley	74	70	69	73	286	11,716.29
Jim Payne	71	71	71	73	286	11,716.29
Steven Richardson	68	71	74	73	286	11,716.29
Paolo Quirici	72	75	70	69	286	11,716.29
Klas Eriksson	71	74	72	69	286	11,716.29
Miguel Angel Jimenez	71	71	72	72	286	11,716.29
Paul Broadhurst	70	71	72	73	286	11,716.29
Barry Lane	70	75	62	79	286	11,716.29
Brian Davis	71	71	73	71	286	11,716.29
Mark Davis	68	75	72	72	287	9,935.31
Eamonn Darcy	74	72	69	72	287	9,935.31
Nick Faldo	75	72	67	74	288	8,297.38
Tony Johnstone	71	67	77	73	288	8,297.38
Eduardo Romero	74	71	71	72	288	8,297.38
David Lynn	68	76	70	74	288	8,297.38
Anssi Kankkonen	74	71	73	70	288	8,297.38
Stephen Allan	69	71	78	71	289	8,063.44
Ernie Els	71	71	70	78	290	7,775.46
Peter Senior	75	71	73	71	290	7,775.46
Van Phillips	71	72	71	77	291	7,199.50
Jose Rivero	69	75	74	73	291	7,199.50
Domingo Hospital	74	72	74	71	291	7,199.50
Greg Chalmers	69	75	72	75	291	7,199.50
Keith Nolan	71	74	71	76	292	6,143.57
Jamie Spence	72	74	74	72	292	6,143.57
David Gilford	73	71	72	76	292	6,143.57
Jarmo Sandelin	69	75	76	72	292	6,143.57
Mark McNulty	71	74	74	73	292	6,143.57
Michael Jonzon	75	70	72	75	292	6,143.57
Steen Tinning	75	71	71	75	292	6,143.57
Niclas Fasth	73	69	75	76	293	4,991.65
Mark Roe	74	71	73	75	293	4,991.65
Ignacio Garrido	74	69	78	72	293	4,991.65
Richard Green	71	73	75	74	293	4,991.65
Sven Struver	72	74	75	72	293	4,991.65
Paul Affleck	70	77	72	75	294	4,319.70
Carl Suneson	72	75	74	73	294	4,319.70
Carl Watts	72	72	77	74	295	3,647.75
Dean Robertson	74	72	74	75	295	3,647.75
David Higgins	75	69	72	79	295	3,647.75
Roger Chapman	73	72	73	77	295	3,647.75
Katsuyoshi Tomori	70	73	72	80	295	3,647.75
Raymond Burns	74	71	73	78	296	3,023.79
Robert Allenby	73	73	77	73	296	3,023.79
Alex Cejka	72	70	77	78	297	2,831.81
Fabrice Tarnaud	69	74	72	82	297	2,831.81
*Sergio Garcia	68	73	75	81	297	
Fredrik Jacobson	73	70	81	74	298	2,639.82
Olivier Edmond	71	71	79	77	298	2,639.82
Sam Torrance	71	76	76	76	299	2,495.83
Stephen Ames	68	78	78	76	300	1,919.92
Phillip Price	70	72	81	77	300	1,919.92
Nicolas Joakimides	75	72	77	77	301	1,438
Jonathan Lomas	75	72	74	81	302	1,436
Angel Cabrera	75	72	77	79	303	1,434
Andrew Oldcorn	74	72	80	81	307	1,432

Standard Life Loch Lomond

Loch Lomond Golf Club, Glasgow, Scotland — July 8-11
Par 36-35–71; 7,050 yards — purse, £850,000

	SCORES				TOTAL	MONEY
Lee Westwood	69	69	68	70	276	£141,660
Ian Woosnam	67	73	74	66	280	51,180
Eduardo Romero	71	70	71	68	280	51,180
Robert Allenby	72	72	68	68	280	51,180
David Howell	68	71	70	71	280	51,180
Dennis Edlund	70	69	67	74	280	51,180
Colin Montgomerie	72	71	68	70	281	23,375
Gary Orr	68	72	71	70	281	23,375
Tom Lehman	73	68	69	72	282	17,985
Paul Broadhurst	69	71	71	71	282	17,985
Clark Dennis	74	68	71	70	283	15,130
Derrick Cooper	75	68	67	73	283	15,130
Dean Robertson	72	72	71	69	284	12,017.14
Stewart Cink	70	74	71	69	284	12,017.14
Klas Eriksson	73	72	65	74	284	12,017.14
Stephen Allan	70	68	72	74	284	12,017.14
Craig Hainline	75	66	71	72	284	12,017.14
Massimo Florioli	73	71	69	71	284	12,017.14
Sam Torrance	73	70	72	69	284	12,017.14
Jamie Spence	70	71	72	72	285	9,817.50
Alex Cejka	71	71	69	74	285	9,817.50
Jarmo Sandelin	75	71	72	67	285	9,817.50
Patrik Sjoland	74	73	68	70	285	9,817.50
Ian Garbutt	73	69	72	73	287	8,287.50
Stuart Appleby	73	68	74	72	287	8,287.50
Stephen Ames	75	71	70	71	287	8,287.50
Jean Van de Velde	71	72	73	71	287	8,287.50
Miguel Angel Jimenez	71	70	74	72	287	8,287.50
Peter Baker	73	69	73	72	287	8,287.50
Thomas Gogele	76	69	70	72	287	8,287.50
Pierre Fulke	75	69	72	71	287	8,287.50
Jim Payne	74	70	73	71	288	6,885
Jose Maria Olazabal	72	71	69	76	288	6,885
Thomas Bjorn	73	72	70	73	288	6,885
Paul McGinley	72	69	72	75	288	6,885
Ross Drummond	71	66	72	80	289	6,205
Carl Watts	74	73	73	69	289	6,205
Jesper Parnevik	71	73	72	73	289	6,205
Stephen Field	75	70	70	74	289	6,205
Padraig Harrington	74	69	77	70	290	5,270
Olle Karlsson	74	72	69	75	290	5,270
Robert Damron	70	76	73	71	290	5,270
David Gilford	74	72	71	73	290	5,270
Russell Claydon	74	66	75	75	290	5,270
Thomas Levet	74	71	74	71	290	5,270
Glen Day	75	71	72	72	290	5,270
Greg Turner	73	74	73	71	291	4,250
David Carter	72	75	72	72	291	4,250
Joakim Haeggman	73	71	69	78	291	4,250
John McHenry	73	71	75	72	291	4,250
Costantino Rocca	68	74	77	72	291	4,250
Mats Lanner	72	72	74	74	292	3,740
Carlos Franco	75	72	73	73	293	3,315
Domingo Hospital	74	73	73	73	293	3,315

	SCORES				TOTAL	MONEY
Roger Chapman	76	70	75	72	293	3,315
Paul Eales	76	70	73	74	293	3,315
Stuart Cage	72	75	73	74	294	2,748.33
Sven Struver	74	72	77	71	294	2,748.33
Andrew Coltart	71	69	73	81	294	2,748.33
*Sergio Garcia	71	71	76	76	294	
Silvio Grappasonni	76	69	76	74	295	2,507.50
Angel Cabrera	72	71	76	76	295	2,507.50
Ignacio Garrido	72	73	71	81	297	2,057
Stephen Leaney	75	70	75	77	297	2,057
Brian Davis	73	74	72	78	297	2,057
Ross McFarlane	76	69	75	77	297	2,057
Mathias Gronberg	75	70	76	76	297	2,057
Gary Evans	78	68	73	79	298	1,273
Andrew Oldcorn	71	75	76	77	299	1,269
Jose Coceres	75	72	75	77	299	1,269
Santiago Luna	74	73	77	75	299	1,269

British Open Championship

Royal Birkdale Golf Club, Southport, England — July 16-19
Par 34-36–70; 7,018 yards — purse, £1,750,000

	SCORES				TOTAL	MONEY
Mark O'Meara	72	68	72	68	280	£300,000
Brian Watts	68	69	73	70	280	188,000
(O'Meara defeated Watts in four-hole playoff, 17 to 19.)						
Tiger Woods	65	73	77	66	281	135,000
Jim Furyk	70	70	72	70	282	76,666.67
Jesper Parnevik	68	72	72	70	282	76,666.67
Raymond Russell	68	73	75	66	282	76,666.67
*Justin Rose	72	66	75	69	282	
Davis Love III	67	73	77	68	285	49,500
Thomas Bjorn	68	71	76	71	286	40,850
Costantino Rocca	72	74	70	70	286	40,850
John Huston	65	77	73	72	287	33,333.33
Brad Faxon	67	74	74	72	287	33,333.33
David Duval	70	71	75	71	287	33,333.33
Gordon Brand, Jr.	71	70	76	71	288	29,000
Peter Baker	69	72	77	71	289	23,650
Greg Turner	68	75	75	71	289	23,650
Jose Maria Olazabal	73	72	75	69	289	23,650
Des Smyth	74	69	75	71	289	23,650
Curtis Strange	73	73	74	70	290	17,220
Vijay Singh	67	74	78	71	290	17,220
Sandy Lyle	71	72	75	72	290	17,220
Robert Allenby	67	76	78	69	290	17,220
Mark James	71	74	74	71	290	17,220
Sam Torrance	69	77	75	70	291	12,480
Bob Estes	72	70	76	73	291	12,480
Stephen Ames	68	72	79	72	291	12,480
Peter O'Malley	71	71	78	71	291	12,480
Lee Janzen	72	69	80	70	291	12,480
Scott Dunlap	72	69	80	71	292	10,030
Nick Price	66	72	82	72	292	10,030
Shigeki Maruyama	70	73	75	74	292	10,030
Loren Roberts	66	76	76	74	292	10,030

	SCORES				TOTAL	MONEY
Ernie Els	72	74	74	72	292	10,030
*Sergio Garcia	69	75	76	72	292	
Mark Calcavecchia	69	77	73	74	293	8,900
Santiago Luna	70	72	80	71	293	8,900
Sven Struver	75	70	80	68	293	8,900
Patrik Sjoland	72	72	77	73	294	8,350
Joakim Haeggman	71	74	78	71	294	8,350
Philip Walton	68	76	74	76	294	8,350
Naomichi Ozaki	72	73	76	73	294	8,350
Tom Kite	72	69	79	74	294	8,350
Steen Tinning	69	76	77	72	294	8,350
Katsuyoshi Tomori	75	71	70	79	295	7,581.25
David Howell	68	77	79	71	295	7,581.25
David Frost	72	73	78	72	295	7,581.25
Rodger Davis	76	70	78	71	295	7,581.25
David Carter	71	75	76	73	295	7,581.25
Nick Faldo	72	73	75	75	295	7,581.25
Payne Stewart	71	71	78	75	295	7,581.25
Andrew Coltart	68	77	75	75	295	7,581.25
Steve Stricker	70	72	80	74	296	6,860
Billy Mayfair	72	73	77	74	296	6,860
Brandt Jobe	70	73	82	71	296	6,860
Larry Mize	70	75	79	72	296	6,860
Frankie Minoza	69	75	76	76	296	6,860
Trevor Dodds	73	71	81	72	297	6,264.29
Eduardo Romero	71	70	79	77	297	6,264.29
Steve Jones	73	72	79	73	297	6,264.29
Justin Leonard	73	73	82	69	297	6,264.29
Ignacio Garrido	71	74	80	72	297	6,264.29
Ian Woosnam	72	74	76	75	297	6,264.29
Greg Chalmers	71	75	77	74	297	6,264.29
Lee Westwood	71	71	78	78	298	5,975
Carlos Franco	71	73	76	78	298	5,975
Stewart Cink	71	73	83	72	299	5,800
Mark Brooks	71	73	75	80	299	5,800
Michael Campbell	73	73	80	73	299	5,800
Fred Couples	66	74	78	81	299	5,800
Michael Long	70	74	78	77	299	5,800
*Didier De Vooght	70	76	80	73	299	
Andrew Clapp	72	74	81	73	300	5,650
Gary Evans	69	74	84	74	301	5,600
Bob May	70	73	85	75	303	5,550
Andrew McLardy	72	74	80	78	304	5,500
Fredrik Jacobson	67	78	81	79	305	5,450
Kazuhiro Hosokawa	72	73	81	80	306	5,400
Robert Giles	72	74	83	78	307	5,350
Phil Mickelson	71	74	85	78	308	5,300
Andrew Oldcorn	75	71	84	79	309	5,250
Dudley Hart	73	72	85	80	310	5,200

Out of Final 36 Holes

			TOTAL	MONEY
Barry Lane	72	75	147	1,000
Keiichiro Fukabori	70	77	147	1,000
Colin Montgomerie	73	74	147	1,000
Bob Tway	68	79	147	1,000
Tony Johnstone	73	74	147	1,000
Paul McGinley	72	75	147	1,000
Carl Suneson	77	70	147	1,000
Thomas Levet	72	75	147	1,000

	SCORES		TOTAL	MONEY
Brian Davis	72	75	147	1,000
Jeff Maggert	73	74	147	1,000
Phillip Price	72	75	147	1,000
Craig Parry	73	74	147	1,000
Seve Ballesteros	73	75	148	800
Toru Taniguchi	71	77	148	800
Darren Clarke	73	75	148	800
Peter Mitchell	76	72	148	800
Joe Durant	74	74	148	800
Yoshinori Mizumaki	71	77	148	800
Glen Day	75	73	148	800
Peter Senior	71	77	148	800
*Simon McCarthy	73	75	148	
Tom Watson	73	76	149	800
J.P. Hayes	70	79	149	800
Paul Azinger	76	73	149	800
Padraig Harrington	73	76	149	800
Gary Brown	74	75	149	800
Grant Dodd	70	79	149	800
Bernhard Langer	74	75	149	800
Derrick Cooper	72	77	149	800
Paul Lawrie	73	76	149	800
Richard Bland	71	78	149	800
Jean Louis Guepy	74	76	150	800
Scott Hoch	73	77	150	800
Corey Pavin	74	76	150	800
Per-Ulrik Johansson	74	76	150	800
Choi Kyung-ju	70	80	150	800
Lee Jones	77	73	150	800
Retief Goosen	74	76	150	800
Tom Lehman	71	79	150	800
David Shacklady	76	74	150	800
John Lovell	72	78	150	800
*Matt Kuchar	75	75	150	
Mark McNulty	73	78	151	700
Fredrik Henge	75	76	151	700
Skip Kendall	74	77	151	700
Stephen Leaney	75	76	151	700
John Daly	73	78	151	700
Gary Player	77	74	151	700
Matthew McGuire	74	77	151	700
Stephen Allan	72	80	152	700
Ross Drummond	74	78	152	700
Steven Young	74	78	152	700
Howard Clark	73	79	152	700
Andrew Magee	75	78	153	700
Russell Claydon	74	79	153	700
Frank Nobilo	76	77	153	700
Robert Karlsson	72	82	154	700
Ben Crenshaw	76	78	154	700
Graham Spring	74	80	154	700
Steve Alker	73	81	154	700
Mats Hallberg	77	77	154	700
Daren Lee	76	78	154	700
Steven Armstrong	76	78	154	700
Toru Suzuki	78	77	155	650
Mark Litton	75	80	155	650
Stuart Appleby	76	80	156	650
Greig Hutcheon	73	83	156	650
Gary Orr	78	78	156	650

	SCORES		TOTAL	MONEY
Bradley Dredge	78	78	156	650
Scott Henderson	77	80	157	650
Peter Hedblom	76	82	158	650
Jeff Remesy	77	82	159	650
Miguel Angel Jimenez	73		DQ	
Steve Elkington	75		WD	
Francis Howley	78		WD	

TNT Dutch Open

Hilversumsche Golf Club, Hilversum, Netherlands — July 23-26
Par 36-35–71; 6,636 yards — purse, £800,000

	SCORES				TOTAL	MONEY
Stephen Leaney	66	63	70	67	266	£133,330
Darren Clarke	68	69	67	63	267	88,880
Lee Westwood	63	66	72	67	268	45,035
Nick Price	68	65	69	66	268	45,035
Costantino Rocca	71	65	69	65	270	33,880
Peter Baker	70	68	68	65	271	28,000
Iain Pyman	73	66	66	68	273	22,000
Ian Garbutt	68	69	67	69	273	22,000
Patrik Sjoland	67	70	66	71	274	16,920
Mark James	70	69	67	68	274	16,920
Raphael Jacquelin	68	68	70	69	275	12,773.33
John Huston	67	69	70	69	275	12,773.33
Jonathan Lomas	65	69	71	70	275	12,773.33
Brian Davis	66	72	69	68	275	12,773.33
Philip Walton	68	67	70	70	275	12,773.33
Steen Tinning	70	67	69	69	275	12,773.33
Peter Lonard	68	67	72	69	276	10,160
Gordon Brand, Jr.	69	70	68	69	276	10,160
Andrew Coltart	71	68	68	69	276	10,160
David Gilford	71	67	68	70	276	10,160
Per Haugsrud	65	71	71	70	277	8,760
Mark Mouland	70	67	70	70	277	8,760
Michael Long	70	70	67	70	277	8,760
Miguel Angel Jimenez	69	66	69	73	277	8,760
Andrew Oldcorn	69	70	72	66	277	8,760
Paul Lawrie	67	72	67	71	277	8,760
Jean Van de Velde	69	69	73	67	278	7,680
Michael Campbell	73	65	70	70	278	7,680
Bernhard Langer	70	65	72	71	278	7,680
Marco Gortana	67	70	71	71	279	6,180
Pierre Fulke	71	66	73	69	279	6,180
Mats Lanner	69	72	72	66	279	6,180
Robert Jan Derksen	70	70	71	68	279	6,180
David Howell	71	69	68	71	279	6,180
Greg Turner	71	69	68	71	279	6,180
Paul McGinley	66	71	71	71	279	6,180
Kalle Brink	69	70	69	71	279	6,180
Peter Mitchell	68	71	71	69	279	6,180
Stephen McAllister	68	68	72	71	279	6,180
Jeff Remesy	68	70	71	70	279	6,180
Tom Gillis	71	70	67	71	279	6,180
Sven Struver	65	70	71	74	280	4,960
Phillip Price	69	72	69	70	280	4,960

	SCORES				TOTAL	MONEY
Richard Boxall	70	69	69	72	280	4,960
Scott Henderson	71	70	68	72	281	4,480
Peter O'Malley	70	71	67	73	281	4,480
Mark Roe	71	68	70	72	281	4,480
Jamie Spence	70	70	72	70	282	4,000
Joakim Haeggman	70	68	72	72	282	4,000
Michele Reale	72	69	71	70	282	4,000
Padraig Harrington	69	72	67	75	283	3,520
Katsuyoshi Tomori	71	69	71	72	283	3,520
Francisco Cea	70	71	72	70	283	3,520
Andrew Sandywell	72	68	72	72	284	3,120
Mathias Gronberg	70	70	66	78	284	3,120
Gary Evans	70	70	71	74	285	2,800
Soren Kjeldsen	72	69	71	73	285	2,800
Seve Ballesteros	68	73	71	74	286	2,320
Fredrik Henge	70	69	74	73	286	2,320
Wayne Riley	71	70	72	73	286	2,320
Dean Robertson	72	65	73	76	286	2,320
Massimo Florioli	74	67	70	75	286	2,320
David Lynn	72	69	74	71	286	2,320
Roger Wessels	71	69	75	71	286	2,320
John Bickerton	69	71	74	73	287	1,600
Marc Farry	69	67	77	74	287	1,600
John Hawksworth	70	70	72	76	288	1,198
Ross McFarlane	69	72	76	72	289	1,196

Volvo Scandinavian Masters

Kungsangen Golf Club, Stockholm, Sweden — July 30-August 2
Par 36-35–71; 6,791 yards — purse, £800,000

	SCORES				TOTAL	MONEY
Jesper Parnevik	67	65	71	70	273	£133,330
Darren Clarke	67	70	68	71	276	88,880
Stephen Field	70	68	70	69	277	50,070
Jean Van de Velde	72	67	70	69	278	36,940
Michael Jonzon	69	65	72	72	278	36,940
Jose Rivero	71	73	66	69	279	28,000
Paolo Quirici	72	70	66	72	280	19,460
Per-Ulrik Johansson	69	69	72	70	280	19,460
Mats Lanner	69	69	69	73	280	19,460
Mathias Gronberg	68	69	72	71	280	19,460
Andrew Coltart	72	70	68	71	281	13,072
Katsuyoshi Tomori	69	72	68	72	281	13,072
Mark Davis	72	66	72	71	281	13,072
Paul Broadhurst	69	68	71	73	281	13,072
Brian Davis	65	72	73	71	281	13,072
Van Phillips	73	70	69	70	282	9,768.89
Paul McGinley	73	71	71	67	282	9,768.89
Colin Montgomerie	70	74	69	69	282	9,768.89
Greg Turner	71	73	65	73	282	9,768.89
Greg Chalmers	74	70	67	71	282	9,768.89
Thomas Levet	71	71	69	71	282	9,768.89
Pierre Fulke	73	68	73	68	282	9,768.89
Craig Hainline	68	72	68	74	282	9,768.89
Mats Hallberg	70	67	73	72	282	9,768.89
Scott Henderson	70	73	69	71	283	7,680

	SCORES				TOTAL	MONEY
Sam Torrance	72	71	70	70	283	7,680
Des Smyth	71	73	69	70	283	7,680
Henrik Nystrom	72	70	71	70	283	7,680
Rolf Muntz	71	70	71	71	283	7,680
Stephen Leaney	70	71	68	74	283	7,680
Jarmo Sandelin	68	70	74	71	283	7,680
Jeff Remesy	72	70	71	71	284	6,640
Ed Fryatt	70	69	71	74	284	6,640
David Lynn	74	71	71	69	285	6,080
Paul Affleck	69	72	74	70	285	6,080
Richard Boxall	69	72	71	73	285	6,080
Costantino Rocca	70	71	70	74	285	6,080
David Howell	67	74	69	75	285	6,080
Olle Karlsson	71	72	69	74	286	5,360
Soren Kjeldsen	73	71	73	69	286	5,360
Kalle Brink	69	76	66	75	286	5,360
Raphael Jacquelin	71	69	72	74	286	5,360
Steve Alker	73	70	71	73	287	4,480
Retief Goosen	69	75	72	71	287	4,480
Sven Struver	72	72	71	72	287	4,480
Ignacio Garrido	70	75	70	72	287	4,480
Eamonn Darcy	70	75	71	71	287	4,480
Anssi Kankkonen	75	70	73	69	287	4,480
Paul Eales	71	74	73	69	287	4,480
Max Anglert	74	70	71	73	288	3,520
Santiago Luna	74	71	70	73	288	3,520
Marten Olander	70	75	73	70	288	3,520
Dennis Edlund	71	74	74	69	288	3,520
Thomas Gogele	72	69	72	75	288	3,520
Silvio Grappasonni	69	74	74	72	289	2,800
Mark Roe	75	69	74	71	289	2,800
Michele Reale	73	72	72	72	289	2,800
Thomas Bjorn	76	66	71	76	289	2,800
Domingo Hospital	69	74	73	74	290	2,360
Sandy Lyle	73	72	71	74	290	2,360
Michael Long	74	71	71	74	290	2,360
Peter Lonard	73	69	73	75	290	2,360
*Anders Hultman	65	76	77	72	290	
Christopher Hanell	68	74	78	71	291	1,575.43
Ola Eliasson	71	73	73	74	291	1,575.43
David Carter	69	75	74	73	291	1,575.43
Bradley Dredge	73	71	71	76	291	1,575.43
Padraig Harrington	72	70	74	75	291	1,575.43
Michael Campbell	69	73	78	71	291	1,575.43
Zhang Lian-wei	68	72	72	79	291	1,575.43
Anthony Wall	72	71	76	73	292	
David Tapping	72	73	73	74	292	1,191
Tom Gillis	73	69	74	77	293	1,188
Jim Payne	73	72	73	76	294	1,185
Patrik Sjoland	70	70	72	82	294	1,185
Fabrice Tarnaud	70	74	76	75	295	1,182

German Open

Sporting Club Berlin, Berlin, Germany
Par 36-36–72; 7,082 yards

August 6-9
purse, £700,000

	SCORES				TOTAL	MONEY
Stephen Allan	72	71	68	69	280	£116,660
Steve Webster	69	73	69	70	281	46,557.50
Mark Roe	71	70	69	71	281	46,557.50
Ignacio Garrido	67	72	68	74	281	46,557.50
Padraig Harrington	73	69	70	69	281	46,557.50
Scott Henderson	72	67	73	71	283	24,500
Paul Lawrie	67	73	72	72	284	15,505
Michael Campbell	67	70	73	74	284	15,505
Katsuyoshi Tomori	72	68	72	72	284	15,505
John Wade	73	70	70	71	284	15,505
Malcolm Mackenzie	71	75	66	72	284	15,505
Daniel Chopra	75	71	67	71	284	15,505
Miles Tunnicliff	73	71	70	71	285	9,900
Jonathan Lomas	72	73	69	71	285	9,900
Mathew Goggin	71	72	70	72	285	9,900
Bernhard Langer	74	71	67	73	285	9,900
Van Phillips	71	68	74	72	285	9,900
Dennis Edlund	71	74	69	71	285	9,900
Olivier Edmond	67	73	70	75	285	9,900
Sandy Lyle	73	72	71	70	286	8,295
Eamonn Darcy	77	69	68	72	286	8,295
Sven Struver	71	73	70	73	287	7,875
Jeev Milkha Singh	75	68	67	77	287	7,875
Silvio Grappasonni	70	74	72	72	288	6,622
Olle Karlsson	70	75	69	74	288	6,622
Paul Broadhurst	72	75	72	69	288	6,622
Paul McGinley	73	73	72	70	288	6,622
Robert Karlsson	73	72	73	70	288	6,622
Gordon Brand, Jr.	71	70	75	72	288	6,622
Iain Pyman	73	69	72	74	288	6,622
Derrick Cooper	72	73	69	74	288	6,622
Jamie Spence	71	72	75	70	288	6,622
Paul Affleck	70	71	71	76	288	6,622
*Tobias Dier	72	69	75	72	288	
Craig Hainline	72	74	70	73	289	5,250
Andrew Beal	69	72	69	79	289	5,250
Mats Hallberg	72	73	73	71	289	5,250
Ross McFarlane	73	70	73	73	289	5,250
Richard Johnson	70	72	74	73	289	5,250
Martin Gates	73	74	70	72	289	5,250
Paolo Quirici	74	71	72	73	290	4,410
Tom Gillis	72	70	73	75	290	4,410
Russell Claydon	68	73	73	76	290	4,410
Daren Lee	70	73	72	75	290	4,410
Andrew Sandywell	69	76	76	69	290	4,410
Anthony Wall	74	73	69	74	290	4,410
Rodger Davis	73	74	69	75	291	3,710
Gordon J. Brand	75	71	72	73	291	3,710
Ian Garbutt	72	73	71	75	291	3,710
Wayne Riley	76	71	73	71	291	3,710
Raphael Jacquelin	76	70	72	74	292	3,150
John McHenry	70	75	71	76	292	3,150
Gary Emerson	70	73	74	75	292	3,150
Anssi Kankkonen	71	75	73	73	292	3,150

	SCORES				TOTAL	MONEY
Sam Torrance	75	71	73	74	293	2,362.50
Michael Jonzon	71	73	73	76	293	2,362.50
Michele Reale	74	71	74	74	293	2,362.50
Andrew Oldcorn	74	71	75	73	293	2,362.50
Jarmo Sandelin	72	71	74	76	293	2,362.50
Barry Lane	71	73	72	77	293	2,362.50
Desvonde Botes	70	74	69	80	293	2,362.50
Adam Hunter	73	74	69	77	293	2,362.50
Jeff Remesy	76	71	70	77	294	1,855
Andrew Clapp	72	73	74	75	294	1,855
Brian Davis	75	72	71	76	294	1,855
Heinz P. Thul	75	70	72	77	294	1,855
Pedro Linhart	71	72	73	79	295	1,045
Nic Henning	74	73	73	75	295	1,045
Greg Owen	71	74	73	77	295	1,045
David Higgins	77	70	70	78	295	1,045
Emanuele Canonica	74	73	76	72	295	1,045
Domingo Hospital	73	72	74	76	295	1,045
John Hawksworth	73	73	75	75	296	1,037
Greig Hutcheon	74	73	71	78	296	1,037
Marc Farry	74	73	72	78	297	1,032
Bradley Dredge	72	75	74	76	297	1,032
Kalle Brink	72	74	75	76	297	1,032
Jean Van de Velde	71	76	73	78	298	1,028
Patrick Platz	73	74	73	80	300	1,026

Smurfit European Open

The K Club, Dublin, Ireland — August 20-23
Par 36-36–72; 7,159 yards — purse, £1,250,000

	SCORES				TOTAL	MONEY
Mathias Gronberg	68	71	67	69	275	£208,300
Miguel Angel Jimenez	73	72	71	69	285	108,562.50
Phillip Price	72	74	68	71	285	108,562.50
Darren Clarke	69	74	70	73	286	62,500
Angel Cabrera	72	73	75	67	287	48,375
Craig Hainline	71	69	69	78	287	48,375
Jean Van de Velde	78	69	69	72	288	32,216.67
Paul Broadhurst	72	73	71	72	288	32,216.67
Bernhard Langer	73	65	75	75	288	32,216.67
Paul Lawrie	72	72	72	73	289	21,187.50
Jose Rivero	72	66	75	76	289	21,187.50
David Gilford	75	74	68	72	289	21,187.50
Barry Lane	75	69	72	73	289	21,187.50
Costantino Rocca	72	73	72	72	289	21,187.50
Sam Torrance	71	76	70	72	289	21,187.50
Peter Baker	72	76	70	72	290	16,512.50
Eduardo Romero	74	73	76	67	290	16,512.50
Per Haugsrud	72	73	73	72	290	16,512.50
Santiago Luna	72	73	76	69	290	16,512.50
Roger Wessels	71	71	73	76	291	14,625
Jose Coceres	74	75	69	73	291	14,625
Paul McGinley	72	72	71	76	291	14,625
Fabrice Tarnaud	73	74	74	71	292	13,125
John Wade	76	69	76	71	292	13,125
Thomas Bjorn	76	70	69	77	292	13,125

	SCORES				TOTAL	MONEY
Jarmo Sandelin	72	77	73	70	292	13,125
Padraig Harrington	71	74	74	73	292	13,125
Pierre Fulke	78	71	70	74	293	11,437.50
Greg Owen	72	75	73	73	293	11,437.50
Peter Hedblom	76	72	72	73	293	11,437.50
Miles Tunnicliff	74	74	72	73	293	11,437.50
Francisco Cea	71	75	72	76	294	10,000
Scott Henderson	75	73	73	73	294	10,000
Mark James	75	71	73	75	294	10,000
Stephen Leaney	77	70	72	75	294	10,000
Steen Tinning	73	75	73	73	294	10,000
Ian Garbutt	74	75	73	73	295	8,500
Richard Boxall	77	72	73	73	295	8,500
Ian Woosnam	73	70	72	80	295	8,500
Ignacio Garrido	77	71	72	75	295	8,500
Silvio Grappasonni	74	75	74	72	295	8,500
Gary Nicklaus	74	66	77	78	295	8,500
Jose Maria Olazabal	75	73	75	72	295	8,500
Mark Davis	73	74	74	75	296	7,000
Jim Payne	73	72	75	76	296	7,000
Thomas Levet	73	76	72	75	296	7,000
Paul Affleck	77	72	74	73	296	7,000
Wayne Westner	75	73	74	74	296	7,000
Jamie Spence	75	71	75	76	297	6,125
Paul Eales	74	75	76	72	297	6,125
Sven Struver	77	71	75	75	298	5,625
Stephen Ames	73	76	76	73	298	5,625
Dennis Edlund	76	73	75	75	299	4,875
Kalle Brink	75	74	75	75	299	4,875
Andrew Beal	78	70	75	76	299	4,875
Malcolm Mackenzie	71	77	74	77	299	4,875
Philip Walton	76	71	75	78	300	3,968.75
David Carter	74	75	77	74	300	3,968.75
Raphael Jacquelin	76	73	76	75	300	3,968.75
Damian McGrane	74	74	76	76	300	3,968.75
Roger Chapman	75	71	77	79	302	3,500
David Lynn	76	73	78	75	302	3,500
Des Smyth	73	75	79	75	302	3,500
Peter Senior	76	73	75	82	306	3,187.50
Dean Robertson	74	73	77	82	306	3,187.50
Soren Kjeldsen	75	74	75	83	307	1,875

BMW International Open

Golfclub Munchen Nord-Eichenreid, Munich, Germany
Par 36-36–72; 6,914 yards

August 27-30
purse, £850,000

	SCORES				TOTAL	MONEY
Russell Claydon	66	72	64	68	270	£141,660
Jamie Spence	68	71	66	66	271	94,440
Thomas Gogele	65	71	67	69	272	53,210
Bernhard Langer	68	67	67	71	273	39,250
Angel Cabrera	69	72	65	67	273	39,250
Andrew Beal	68	71	66	69	274	22,494
Miguel Angel Jimenez	69	71	67	67	274	22,494
Thomas Bjorn	64	67	72	71	274	22,494
Derrick Cooper	71	66	69	68	274	22,494

	SCORES				TOTAL	MONEY
Katsuyoshi Tomori	67	70	73	64	274	22,494
Pierre Fulke	72	68	70	65	275	15,640
Domingo Hospital	70	70	68	68	276	14,620
Paul Eales	68	69	72	68	277	13,053.33
Peter Senior	70	71	71	65	277	13,053.33
Darren Clarke	68	70	67	72	277	13,053.33
Mats Lanner	70	68	72	68	278	11,727.50
Sam Torrance	69	70	72	67	278	11,727.50
Steve Webster	69	69	72	70	280	10,129.17
Jean Van de Velde	69	69	68	74	280	10,129.17
Costantino Rocca	70	71	71	68	280	10,129.17
Jose Maria Olazabal	70	66	73	71	280	10,129.17
Greg Chalmers	70	71	66	73	280	10,129.17
Soren Kjeldsen	68	73	71	68	280	10,129.17
Santiago Luna	70	71	69	71	281	9,052.50
Sven Struver	65	69	74	73	281	9,052.50
Olle Karlsson	72	69	74	67	282	7,573.50
Raphael Jacquelin	73	69	70	70	282	7,573.50
Roger Chapman	69	72	69	72	282	7,573.50
Mark Roe	70	70	70	72	282	7,573.50
Eamonn Darcy	68	71	70	73	282	7,573.50
Ian Garbutt	68	73	72	69	282	7,573.50
Paul Lawrie	70	69	72	71	282	7,573.50
Mark Mouland	69	68	72	73	282	7,573.50
Bob May	72	70	69	71	282	7,573.50
Mats Hallberg	70	71	70	71	282	7,573.50
Brian Davis	71	71	70	71	283	6,460
Gary Nicklaus	69	71	68	76	284	5,865
David Howell	69	72	72	71	284	5,865
Fredrik Jacobson	68	72	73	71	284	5,865
Peter Fowler	68	74	72	70	284	5,865
Olivier Edmond	72	70	69	73	284	5,865
Andrew Clapp	68	72	69	75	284	5,865
Francisco Cea	70	72	77	66	285	4,930
Paul Broadhurst	70	69	69	77	285	4,930
Robert Karlsson	72	68	69	76	285	4,930
Eduardo Romero	72	68	73	72	285	4,930
Steen Tinning	69	72	70	74	285	4,930
John Bickerton	70	70	74	72	286	4,250
Andrew Oldcorn	70	67	72	77	286	4,250
Michele Reale	67	75	71	73	286	4,250
Michael Jonzon	68	74	71	74	287	3,655
Fabrice Tarnaud	73	68	74	72	287	3,655
David Lynn	69	72	71	75	287	3,655
Miles Tunnicliff	71	70	70	76	287	3,655
Diego Borrego	68	69	75	76	288	2,975
Peter Baker	69	73	73	73	288	2,975
Greg Owen	69	70	76	73	288	2,975
Michael Long	70	72	73	73	288	2,975
Seve Ballesteros	72	66	74	77	289	2,592.50
Jim Payne	69	73	73	74	289	2,592.50
Scott Henderson	68	73	77	72	290	2,380
David Gilford	70	71	74	75	290	2,380
Martin Gates	73	69	69	79	290	2,380
Michael Campbell	71	70	76	74	291	2,167.50
Richard Boxall	72	67	77	75	291	2,167.50
Stephen Field	68	74	77	73	292	1,275
David Tapping	68	73	78	78	297	1,273

Canon European Masters

Crans-sur-Sierre Golf Club, Crans-sur-Sierre, Switzerland — September 3-6
Par 36-35–71; 6,642 yards — purse, £800,000

	SCORES				TOTAL	MONEY
Sven Struver	69	63	65	66	263	£133,330
Patrik Sjoland	65	66	62	70	263	88,880
(Struver defeated Sjoland on first extra hole.)						
Darren Clarke	64	68	66	67	265	50,070
Costantino Rocca	67	66	67	68	268	40,000
Alex Cejka	70	66	67	66	269	30,940
Gordon Brand, Jr.	68	68	66	67	269	30,940
Jean Van de Velde	67	66	72	65	270	19,460
Miguel Angel Jimenez	67	69	70	64	270	19,460
Mathias Gronberg	69	68	64	69	270	19,460
Robert Karlsson	69	69	66	66	270	19,460
Scott Henderson	68	66	68	69	271	14,720
Lee Westwood	70	68	66	68	272	12,960
Colin Montgomerie	70	66	69	67	272	12,960
Sam Torrance	67	68	70	67	272	12,960
David Gilford	73	66	67	67	273	11,280
Raphael Jacquelin	70	67	68	68	273	11,280
Peter Lonard	70	66	67	70	273	11,280
Christophe Bovet	68	64	70	72	274	10,120
Silvio Grappasonni	68	71	65	70	274	10,120
Eduardo Romero	66	71	70	68	275	9,000
Michele Reale	71	69	70	65	275	9,000
Retief Goosen	69	70	67	69	275	9,000
Santiago Luna	69	67	69	70	275	9,000
Pierre Fulke	69	71	67	68	275	9,000
Mats Lanner	70	67	70	68	275	9,000
Paul Eales	69	67	72	68	276	7,800
Roger Chapman	72	68	69	67	276	7,800
Mats Hallberg	68	71	70	67	276	7,800
Mark Roe	67	70	67	72	276	7,800
Fabrice Tarnaud	71	66	68	72	277	6,594.29
Gary Orr	68	70	68	71	277	6,594.29
Padraig Harrington	70	69	65	73	277	6,594.29
Thomas Bjorn	69	70	68	70	277	6,594.29
Seve Ballesteros	70	70	70	67	277	6,594.29
Jose Rivero	68	68	73	68	277	6,594.29
Jarmo Sandelin	68	72	66	71	277	6,594.29
Angel Cabrera	71	68	70	69	278	5,680
Marc Farry	72	67	69	70	278	5,680
Richard Boxall	70	69	66	73	278	5,680
Ivo Giner	71	69	68	70	278	5,680
Zhang Lian-wei	69	70	68	72	279	4,880
Malcolm Mackenzie	70	69	69	71	279	4,880
Robert Coles	68	71	73	67	279	4,880
Peter Senior	72	68	68	71	279	4,880
Francisco Cea	68	72	69	70	279	4,880
Per Haugsrud	66	71	70	72	279	4,880
Gary Nicklaus	70	69	73	68	280	4,000
Phillip Price	68	70	71	71	280	4,000
Greg Owen	70	68	69	73	280	4,000
Jim Payne	69	71	71	69	280	4,000
Andrew Sherborne	67	69	72	72	280	4,000
Andrew Beal	69	70	75	67	281	3,120
Jose Maria Olazabal	70	70	69	72	281	3,120

	SCORES				TOTAL	MONEY
Jamie Spence	70	69	70	72	281	3,120
Stephen Leaney	74	66	72	69	281	3,120
Stephen Scahill	71	68	71	71	281	3,120
Jonathan Lomas	69	71	71	70	281	3,120
Howard Clark	70	69	71	72	282	2,560
Bradley Dredge	71	67	72	73	283	2,440
Roger Wessels	68	72	70	73	283	2,440
Katsuyoshi Tomori	69	68	73	74	284	2,200
Gary Evans	70	69	70	75	284	2,200
Mark Mouland	70	70	75	69	284	2,200
Mike Cunning	71	66	73	74	284	2,200
Andrew Clapp	73	67	73	72	285	2,000
Jeev Milkha Singh	71	69	75	73	288	1,199
Barry Lane	72	68	74	74	288	1,199
Anthony Wall	71	68	72	82	293	1,196

One 2 One British Masters

Marriott Forest of Arden Hotel & Country Club, Coventry, England
Par 36-36–72; 7,106 yards

September 10-13
purse, £750,000

	SCORES				TOTAL	MONEY
Colin Montgomerie	70	72	70	69	281	£125,000
Pierre Fulke	71	72	72	67	282	65,130
Eduardo Romero	70	69	75	68	282	65,130
Ignacio Garrido	70	73	71	69	283	31,840
Andrew Oldcorn	71	73	71	68	283	31,840
Paolo Quirici	68	73	70	72	283	31,840
Greg Owen	70	71	73	70	284	22,500
Russell Claydon	72	73	68	72	285	16,072.50
John Bickerton	70	75	73	67	285	16,072.50
Sam Torrance	69	72	71	73	285	16,072.50
Daniel Chopra	71	72	69	73	285	16,072.50
Anssi Kankkonen	71	69	76	70	286	11,118.57
Marc Farry	73	72	67	74	286	11,118.57
Mark Roe	72	69	71	74	286	11,118.57
Soren Kjeldsen	72	71	72	71	286	11,118.57
Lee Westwood	73	70	73	70	286	11,118.57
Ian Woosnam	75	66	73	72	286	11,118.57
Greg Chalmers	72	73	74	67	286	11,118.57
*Sergio Garcia	71	73	69	73	286	
Mats Lanner	71	73	73	70	287	8,220
Craig Hainline	72	71	70	74	287	8,220
Carl Suneson	69	69	75	74	287	8,220
Michael Campbell	71	69	76	71	287	8,220
Darren Clarke	67	71	74	75	287	8,220
Miguel Angel Jimenez	70	75	72	70	287	8,220
Peter O'Malley	73	71	72	71	287	8,220
Paul Broadhurst	79	65	74	69	287	8,220
Costantino Rocca	71	72	71	73	287	8,220
Olle Karlsson	75	67	71	74	287	8,220
Robert Coles	73	72	76	67	288	6,450
Santiago Luna	70	73	73	72	288	6,450
Robert Lee	69	74	73	72	288	6,450
Peter Mitchell	75	70	73	70	288	6,450
Ross Drummond	72	72	69	75	288	6,450

	SCORES				TOTAL	MONEY
Michael Long	75	69	73	71	288	6,450
Carl Mason	72	73	68	76	289	5,625
Greig Hutcheon	72	70	71	76	289	5,625
Mathias Gronberg	75	70	75	69	289	5,625
Knud Storgaard	75	69	75	70	289	5,625
Jonathan Lomas	72	72	74	72	290	5,025
Per Haugsrud	72	72	72	74	290	5,025
Diego Borrego	72	70	73	75	290	5,025
Jose Coceres	74	70	71	75	290	5,025
*Trevor Immelman	71	71	76	72	290	
Mark Mouland	72	71	72	76	291	4,350
Andrew Beal	71	71	74	75	291	4,350
Richard Boxall	73	70	71	77	291	4,350
Andrew Coltart	72	70	72	77	291	4,350
Roger Chapman	76	69	71	75	291	4,350
Angel Cabrera	73	69	71	79	292	3,450
Roger Wessels	72	70	73	77	292	3,450
Thomas Levet	76	69	73	74	292	3,450
Gary Orr	71	73	73	75	292	3,450
Massimo Florioli	75	70	75	72	292	3,450
Van Phillips	73	72	73	74	292	3,450
Iain Pyman	76	69	76	71	292	3,450
Steven Richardson	74	70	73	76	293	2,512.50
Stephen Allan	71	72	80	70	293	2,512.50
Gary Evans	74	71	75	73	293	2,512.50
Tony Johnstone	73	72	76	72	293	2,512.50
Stephen Leaney	74	69	74	76	293	2,512.50
Peter Baker	72	73	71	77	293	2,512.50
David Howell	72	73	73	76	294	2,025
Sven Struver	71	73	76	74	294	2,025
Per-Ulrik Johansson	72	71	74	77	294	2,025
Silvio Grappasonni	71	72	77	74	294	2,025
Carl Watts	71	74	71	78	294	2,025
Jim Payne	74	71	73	77	295	1,124
Peter Senior	71	74	74	76	295	1,124
Barry Lane	73	72	77	74	296	1,121
Jarmo Sandelin	70	69	76	82	297	1,119
Stuart Cage	75	68	83	73	299	1,117

Trophee Lancome

Saint-Nom-La-Breteche, Paris, France — September 17-20
Par 36-35–71; 6,903 yards — purse, £800,000

	SCORES				TOTAL	MONEY
Miguel Angel Jimenez	67	70	67	69	273	£133,330
Greg Turner	67	71	68	69	275	53,207.50
Jarmo Sandelin	68	74	70	63	275	53,207.50
Mark O'Meara	70	67	69	69	275	53,207.50
David Duval	69	72	67	67	275	53,207.50
Nick Faldo	70	71	70	65	276	28,000
Anthony Wall	71	70	67	69	277	22,000
Peter O'Malley	68	72	68	69	277	22,000
Fred Couples	70	68	70	70	278	16,920
Per-Ulrik Johansson	74	68	68	68	278	16,920
Sam Torrance	70	73	72	64	279	13,400
Gordon Brand, Jr.	68	72	69	70	279	13,400

	SCORES				TOTAL	MONEY
Alex Cejka	69	69	74	67	279	13,400
Colin Montgomerie	69	68	69	73	279	13,400
Roger Wessels	73	70	68	69	280	11,280
Peter Lonard	71	70	68	71	280	11,280
Silvio Grappasonni	74	69	69	68	280	11,280
Fredrik Jacobson	72	70	72	67	281	9,280
Mats Hallberg	70	70	73	68	281	9,280
Greg Chalmers	72	70	68	71	281	9,280
Jose Coceres	70	70	71	70	281	9,280
Thomas Levet	72	69	69	71	281	9,280
Thomas Bjorn	74	69	67	71	281	9,280
Barry Lane	73	69	70	69	281	9,280
Paul Broadhurst	69	71	69	72	281	9,280
*Sergio Garcia	69	68	73	71	281	
Olivier Edmond	74	69	71	68	282	7,680
David Gilford	72	69	74	67	282	7,680
Peter Mitchell	69	69	72	72	282	7,680
Paul McGinley	71	69	70	72	282	7,680
Marc Pendaries	72	69	70	71	282	7,680
Greg Owen	74	70	70	69	283	6,840
Katsuyoshi Tomori	69	70	71	73	283	6,840
Bob May	69	75	69	71	284	6,080
Patrik Sjoland	71	71	72	70	284	6,080
Nicolas Vanhootegem	70	72	70	72	284	6,080
Brad Faxon	73	69	73	69	284	6,080
Olle Karlsson	73	71	68	72	284	6,080
Stephen Allan	67	73	71	73	284	6,080
Philip Walton	73	71	73	67	284	6,080
Howard Clark	71	72	72	70	285	4,960
Gary Evans	71	69	77	68	285	4,960
Michael Campbell	69	72	76	68	285	4,960
Carl Suneson	72	72	70	71	285	4,960
Mark James	70	68	76	71	285	4,960
Steven Richardson	70	70	71	74	285	4,960
Gary Orr	72	69	68	76	285	4,960
Iain Pyman	72	69	70	75	286	4,080
Jesper Parnevik	73	70	70	73	286	4,080
Derrick Cooper	67	72	72	75	286	4,080
Paolo Quirici	73	71	70	72	286	4,080
Eamonn Darcy	67	71	74	75	287	3,440
Michael Long	75	63	78	71	287	3,440
Jose Rivero	69	73	71	74	287	3,440
Angel Cabrera	70	69	72	76	287	3,440
Mark Mouland	71	71	74	72	288	2,960
Fabrice Tarnaud	73	71	71	73	288	2,960
Rolf Muntz	73	70	71	75	289	2,216
Andrew Coltart	71	69	73	76	289	2,216
Retief Goosen	70	73	73	73	289	2,216
Ivo Giner	74	69	77	69	289	2,216
Paul Lawrie	72	72	72	73	289	2,216
Mathias Gronberg	69	72	76	72	289	2,216
Marc Farry	68	74	72	75	289	2,216
Brian Davis	70	73	77	69	289	2,216
Robert Coles	72	71	74	72	289	2,216
Rodger Davis	72	70	76	71	289	2,216
Raymond Russell	71	72	73	74	290	1,196
Mats Lanner	71	73	78	68	290	1,196
Jim Payne	71	69	76	74	290	1,196
Andrew Sherborne	76	68	74	73	291	1,192
Lee Westwood	70	72	73	77	292	1,188

	SCORES				TOTAL	MONEY
Seve Ballesteros	69	73	75	75	292	1,188
Michael Jonzon	73	70	78	71	292	1,188
Ian Woosnam	68	67	77		WD	

Linde German Masters

Gut Larchenhof, Cologne, Germany
Par 36-36–72; 7,014 yards

September 24-27
purse, £1,000,000

	SCORES				TOTAL	MONEY
Colin Montgomerie	65	68	66	67	266	£166,660
Robert Karlsson	68	65	69	65	267	86,850
Vijay Singh	65	67	69	66	267	86,850
Steve Webster	68	65	68	67	268	50,000
Per-Ulrik Johansson	68	67	67	67	269	42,400
Lee Westwood	66	67	72	66	271	32,500
Paul McGinley	69	68	67	67	271	32,500
Jarmo Sandelin	66	67	74	65	272	22,433.33
Jean Van de Velde	67	67	70	68	272	22,433.33
Padraig Harrington	69	64	67	72	272	22,433.33
Gary Nicklaus	70	71	67	65	273	16,735
Raymond Russell	67	68	68	70	273	16,735
Marc Farry	68	68	67	70	273	16,735
Retief Goosen	68	67	67	71	273	16,735
Gordon Brand, Jr.	67	70	72	65	274	13,266.67
Klas Eriksson	69	71	67	67	274	13,266.67
Bernhard Langer	69	69	68	68	274	13,266.67
Michael Long	71	65	68	70	274	13,266.67
Peter O'Malley	68	69	65	72	274	13,266.67
Rodger Davis	70	69	63	72	274	13,266.67
Peter Mitchell	70	68	70	67	275	10,800
Miles Tunnicliff	68	67	73	67	275	10,800
Jim Payne	69	66	71	69	275	10,800
Darren Clarke	69	70	67	69	275	10,800
Greg Turner	68	71	67	69	275	10,800
Jose Maria Olazabal	69	66	70	70	275	10,800
Iain Pyman	68	67	69	71	275	10,800
Stephen Allan	70	68	69	69	276	8,511.11
Scott Henderson	71	71	65	69	276	8,511.11
Fabrice Tarnaud	72	70	67	67	276	8,511.11
Steven Richardson	69	72	69	66	276	8,511.11
Brad Faxon	68	72	68	68	276	8,511.11
Anthony Wall	70	68	70	68	276	8,511.11
Ignacio Garrido	69	70	70	67	276	8,511.11
Santiago Luna	68	66	71	71	276	8,511.11
Costantino Rocca	70	68	66	72	276	8,511.11
Clinton Whitelaw	68	70	70	69	277	7,100
Ian Garbutt	66	71	69	71	277	7,100
Richard Boxall	66	70	69	72	277	7,100
Sven Struver	66	70	68	73	277	7,100
Richard Green	74	68	67	69	278	6,200
Nick Faldo	71	69	70	68	278	6,200
Paul Broadhurst	68	71	71	68	278	6,200
Mark James	69	68	70	71	278	6,200
Per Haugsrud	67	70	69	72	278	6,200
Thomas Gogele	70	68	71	70	279	5,500
Van Phillips	65	70	70	74	279	5,500
Paul Eales	69	70	70	71	280	4,600

	SCORES				TOTAL	MONEY
David Carter	68	70	71	71	280	4,600
David Gilford	73	68	69	70	280	4,600
Seve Ballesteros	72	69	69	70	280	4,600
Miguel Angel Jimenez	72	68	72	68	280	4,600
Mathias Gronberg	71	68	68	73	280	4,600
Carl Suneson	68	67	71	74	280	4,600
Domingo Hospital	71	71	70	69	281	3,350
Heinz P. Thul	71	71	68	71	281	3,350
Silvio Grappasonni	68	71	71	71	281	3,350
Derrick Cooper	71	70	70	70	281	3,350
Jose Rivero	69	73	70	69	281	3,350
Gary Evans	70	67	71	73	281	3,350
Sam Torrance	71	71	69	72	283	2,750
Russell Claydon	74	68	70	71	283	2,750
Michael Jonzon	73	68	71	71	283	2,750
Patrik Sjoland	73	68	73	69	283	2,750
Daniel Chopra	67	72	71	74	284	1,832.67
Roger Chapman	68	74	71	71	284	1,832.67
Phillip Price	69	73	73	69	284	1,832.67
Felix Lubenau	75	67	72	71	285	1,496
Peter Baker	70	72	71	73	286	1,494
Fredrik Jacobson	72	70	69	76	287	1,491
Dennis Edlund	72	69	71	75	287	1,491
Dean Robertson	73	67	73	75	288	1,488
Jamie Spence	71	70	77	71	289	1,486

Belgacom Open

Royal Zoute, Belgium — October 1-4
Par 34-37–71; 6,907 yards — purse, £400,000

	SCORES				TOTAL	MONEY
Lee Westwood	67	68	67	66	268	£66,660
Fredrik Jacobson	65	67	69	67	268	44,440
(Westwood defeated Jacobson on first extra hole.)						
Robert Karlsson	64	72	68	66	270	22,520
Greg Turner	64	70	67	69	270	22,520
Jarmo Sandelin	70	67	66	69	272	15,470
Peter Mitchell	70	68	66	68	272	15,470
Alex Cejka	69	71	67	66	273	10,306.67
Michael Jonzon	70	67	69	67	273	10,306.67
Mark Mouland	71	71	67	64	273	10,306.67
Paul Affleck	70	70	69	65	274	6,617.14
Peter O'Malley	69	67	69	69	274	6,617.14
Joakim Haeggman	70	68	69	67	274	6,617.14
Paolo Quirici	67	71	66	70	274	6,617.14
Anthony Wall	69	68	67	70	274	6,617.14
Rolf Muntz	66	67	73	68	274	6,617.14
Gordon Brand, Jr.	71	68	68	67	274	6,617.14
Dean Robertson	71	68	69	67	275	5,080
Mark James	68	72	67	68	275	5,080
Jean Van de Velde	69	72	67	67	275	5,080
Jose Rivero	67	71	70	67	275	5,080
Padraig Harrington	74	68	67	67	276	4,320
Sven Struver	67	69	67	73	276	4,320
Raymond Russell	70	69	69	68	276	4,320
Per-Ulrik Johansson	69	67	71	69	276	4,320
Greg Owen	74	62	71	69	276	4,320

	SCORES				TOTAL	MONEY
Gary Evans	71	69	68	68	276	4,320
Robert Jan Derksen	68	70	69	69	276	4,320
Olle Karlsson	70	69	72	66	277	3,780
Adam Hunter	69	70	70	68	277	3,780
Nick Faldo	65	72	72	69	278	3,430
Daniel Chopra	71	69	70	68	278	3,430
Van Phillips	64	72	70	72	278	3,430
Andrew Beal	66	71	72	69	278	3,430
Peter Baker	68	70	69	72	279	3,040
Jose Maria Olazabal	68	71	74	66	279	3,040
Carl Suneson	69	70	72	68	279	3,040
Ross Drummond	68	71	70	70	279	3,040
Stephen Bennett	68	71	71	69	279	3,040
Tom Gillis	67	74	67	72	280	2,720
Howard Clark	71	71	69	69	280	2,720
Pedro Linhart	71	70	71	68	280	2,720
Wayne Riley	68	70	69	74	281	2,480
David Howell	71	69	74	67	281	2,480
Philip Walton	73	69	68	71	281	2,480
Fredrik Henge	69	73	69	71	282	2,120
Richard Boxall	68	74	69	71	282	2,120
Roger Chapman	70	68	73	71	282	2,120
Chris Van der Velde	70	71	69	72	282	2,120
Steve Alker	70	72	71	69	282	2,120
Marc Farry	72	70	70	70	282	2,120
Andrew Sherborne	66	71	73	73	283	1,720
Ivo Giner	70	70	73	70	283	1,720
Ignacio Garrido	73	67	71	72	283	1,720
Olivier Edmond	68	72	75	68	283	1,720
Nicolas Vanhootegem	71	70	70	73	284	1,400
Derrick Cooper	72	70	71	71	284	1,400
Brian Davis	70	71	72	71	284	1,400
Klas Eriksson	73	69	74	68	284	1,400
Francisco Cea	69	72	78	66	285	1,180
Rodger Davis	70	72	71	72	285	1,180
Sam Torrance	70	71	70	74	285	1,180
Stephen Scahill	71	70	71	73	285	1,180
Malcolm Mackenzie	69	71	72	74	286	1,060
Jim Payne	69	73	72	72	286	1,060
Didier De Vooght	70	72	74	72	288	1,000
Phil Golding	72	70	73	74	289	600
Joakim Rask	70	70	73	77	290	598

Alfred Dunhill Cup

Old Course, St. Andrews, Scotland — October 8-11
Par 36-36–72; 7,094 yards — purse, £1,000,000

FIRST ROUND

SWEDEN DEFEATED JAPAN, 3-0
Patrik Sjoland (Swe) defeated Hiroyuki Fujita, 69-77; Mathias Gronberg (Swe) defeated Nobuo Serizawa, 78-79; Per-Ulrik Johansson (Swe) defeated Katsuma Miyamoto, 71-76.

UNITED STATES DEFEATED ENGLAND, 3-0
John Daly (US) defeated Lee Westwood, 70-73; Tiger Woods (US) defeated David Carter, 66-74; Mark O'Meara (US) defeated Peter Baker, 67-74.

SCOTLAND DEFEATED CHINA, 2-1
Gary Orr (Sco) defeated Wu Xiang-bing, 75-76; Andrew Coltart (Sco) defeated Cheng Jun, 73-78; Zhang Lian-wei (C) defeated Colin Montgomerie, 72-73.

SPAIN DEFEATED IRELAND, 2-1
Darren Clarke (I) tied Santiago Luna, 71-71, Clarke won at fourth extra hole; Miguel Angel Jimenez (Sp) defeated Paul McGinley, 70-72; Jose Maria Olazabal (Sp) defeated Padraig Harrington, 73-75.

KOREA DEFEATED NEW ZEALAND, 2-1
Shin Yong-jin (K) defeated Michael Long, 75-76; Kang Wook-soon (K) defeated Frank Nobilo 71-75; Greg Turner (NZ) defeated Kim Jong-duk, 70-73.

AUSTRALIA DEFEATED ARGENTINA, 3-0
Stuart Appleby (Aus) defeated Jose Coceres, 66-77; Craig Parry (Aus) defeated Angel Cabrera, 70-75; Steve Elkington (Aus) tied Eduardo Romero, 70-70, Elkington won at first extra hole.

SOUTH AFRICA DEFEATED FRANCE, 3-0
Retief Goosen (SA) defeated Olivier Edmond, 72-73; David Frost (SA) defeated Thomas Levet, 70-75; Ernie Els (SA) defeated Jean Van de Velde, 69-72.

ZIMBABWE DEFEATED GERMANY, 3-0
Tony Johnstone (Z) defeated Sven Struver, 69-76; Nick Price (Z) defeated Thomas Gogele, 72-73; Mark McNulty (Z) defeated Alex Cejka, 73-75.

SECOND ROUND

UNITED STATES DEFEATED JAPAN, 3-0
John Daly (US) defeated Nobuo Serizawa, 77-80; Tiger Woods (US) defeated Katsumasa Miyamoto, 70-77; Mark O'Meara (US) defeated Hiroyuki Fujita, 70-75.

SWEDEN DEFEATED ENGLAND, 3-0
Mathias Gronberg (Swe) tied Lee Westwood, 72-72, Gronberg won at first extra hole; Per-Ulrik Johansson (Swe) defeated David Carter, 70-73; Patrik Sjoland (Swe) defeated Peter Baker, 70-73.

SPAIN DEFEATED CHINA, 2-1
Wu Xiang-bing (C) defeated Jose Maria Olazabal, 77-78; Miguel Angel Jimenez (Sp) defeated Zhang Lian-wei, 76-83; Santiago Luna (Sp) defeated Cheng Jun, 80-81.

SCOTLAND DEFEATED IRELAND, 2-1
Darren Clarke (I) defeated Andrew Coltart, 73-75; Gary Orr (Sco) defeated Padraig Harrington, 77-78; Colin Montgomerie (Sco) defeated Paul McGinley, 72-78.

NEW ZEALAND DEFEATED ARGENTINA, 2-1
Greg Turner (NZ) defeated Eduardo Romero, 75-DQ; Frank Nobilo (NZ) defeated Angel Cabrera, 71-77; Jose Coceres (Arg) defeated Michael Long, 75-81.

AUSTRALIA DEFEATED KOREA, 3-0
Craig Parry (Aus) tied Shin Yong-jin, 75-75, Parry won at first extra hole; Stuart Appleby (Aus) defeated Kang Wook-soon, 73-77; Steve Elkington (Aus) defeated Kim Jong-duk, 72-77.

FRANCE DEFEATED ZIMBABWE, 2-1
Jean Van de Velde (F) defeated Mark McNulty, 71-81; Thomas Levet (F) defeated Tony Johnstone, 77-79; Nick Price (Z) defeated Olivier Edmond, 70-78.

GERMANY DEFEATED SOUTH AFRICA, 2-1
Thomas Gogele (G) tied David Frost, 78-78, Gogele won at second extra hole; Retief Goosen (SA) defeated Alex Cejka, 76-77; Sven Struver (G) tied Ernie Els, 76-76, Struver won at first extra hole.

THIRD ROUND

UNITED STATES DEFEATED SWEDEN, 2-0
John Daly (US) defeated Per-Ulrik Johansson, 71-72; Tiger Woods (US) defeated Mathias Gronberg, 66-73; Mark O'Meara (US) tied Patrik Sjoland, 68-68.

ENGLAND DEFEATED JAPAN, 3-0
Lee Westwood (E) defeated Katsuma Miyamoto, 70-71; Peter Baker (E) defeated Hiroyuki Fujita, 71-73; David Carter (E) defeated Nobuo Serizawa, 69-75.

SPAIN DEFEATED SCOTLAND, 2-1
Jose Maria Olazabal (Sp) defeated Gary Orr, 68-71; Miguel Angel Jimenez (Sp) tied Colin Montgomerie, 70-70, Jimenez won at first extra hole; Andrew Coltart (Sco) defeated Santiago Luna, 73-74.

IRELAND DEFEATED CHINA, 3-0
Darren Clarke (I) defeated Zhang Lian-wei, 71-73; Paul McGinley (I) defeated Cheng Jun, 74-78; Padraig Harrington (I) defeated Wu Xiang-bing, 71-74.

ARGENTINA DEFEATED KOREA, 2-1
Shin Yong-jin (K) tied Eduardo Romero, 72-72, Shin won at first extra hole; Angel Cabrera (Arg) defeated Kim Jong-duk, 72-73; Jose Coceres (Arg) defeated Kang Wook-soon, 71-72.

NEW ZEALAND DEFEATED AUSTRALIA, 2-1
Craig Parry (Aus) defeated Michael Long, 70-71; Greg Turner (NZ) defeated Stuart Appleby, 72-73; Frank Nobilo (NZ) defeated Steve Elkington, 72-74.

GERMANY DEFEATED FRANCE, 2-1
Thomas Gogele (G) defeated Thomas Levet, 69-72; Jean Van de Velde (F) defeated Alex Cejka, 72-75; Sven Struver (G) defeated Olivier Edmond, 68-70.

SOUTH AFRICA DEFEATED ZIMBABWE, 2-1
Ernie Els (SA) defeated Tony Johnstone, 71-77; Nick Price (Z) defeated David Frost, 69-71; Retief Goosen (SA) defeated Mark McNulty, 71-76.

SEMI-FINALS

SPAIN DEFEATED UNITED STATES, 2-1
John Daly (US) defeated Miguel Angel Jimenez, 73-75; Santiago Luna (Sp) defeated Tiger Woods, 71-72; Jose Maria Olazabal (Sp) defeated Mark O'Meara, 72-76.

SOUTH AFRICA DEFEATED AUSTRALIA, 2-1
David Frost (SA) defeated Craig Parry, 72-78; Retief Goosen (SA) defeated Stuart Appleby, 71-74; Steve Elkington (Aus) defeated Ernie Els, 72-73.

FINAL

SOUTH AFRICA DEFEATED SPAIN, 3-0
Retief Goosen (SA) defeated Santiago Luna, 72-73; David Frost (SA) defeated Miguel Angel Jimenez, 76-78; Ernie Els (SA) defeated Jose Maria Olazabal, 75-77.

	MATCHES WON	INDIVIDUAL GAMES WON (After Round 3)	PRIZE MONEY TEAM	PLAYER
GROUP 1				
United States	3	8	£95,000	£31,666
Sweden	2	6	45,000	15,000
England	1	3	25,500	8,500
Japan	0	0	19,500	6,500
GROUP 2				
Spain	3	6	150,000	50,000
Scotland	2	5	45,000	15,000
Ireland	1	5	25,500	8,500
China	0	2	19,500	6,500
GROUP 3				
Australia	2	7	95,000	31,666
New Zealand	2	5	45,000	15,000
Argentina	1	3	25,500	8,500
Korea	1	3	19,500	6,500
GROUP 4				
South Africa	2	6	300,000	100,000
Germany	2	4	45,000	15,000
Zimbabwe	1	5	25,500	8,500
France	1	3	19,500	6,500

Cisco World Match Play

Wentworth Club, West Course, Surrey, England — October 15-18
Par 434 534 444–35; 345 434 455–37–72; 7,006 yards — purse, £640,000

FIRST ROUND

Patrik Sjoland defeated Steve Stricker, 1 up

Stricker	4 3 4	5 4 4	3 4 4	35	3 4 5	4 3 4	4 6 4	37	72
Sjoland	5 4 4	4 3 4	4 4 4	36	3 4 4	4 3 5	4 5 4	36	72
Match all-square									
Stricker	5 2 5	5 3 4	4 4 4	36	3 5 4	4 3 4	5 4 5	37	73
Sjoland	4 4 4	4 3 5	5 4 5	38	3 4 4	4 3 4	4 6 4	36	74

Colin Montgomerie defeated Thomas Bjorn, 4 and 3

Montgomerie	5 3 3	5 2 4	5 4 5	36	3 4 4	4 2 4	4 6 5	36	72
Bjorn	5 3 3	4 3 4	3 4 4	33	3 4 5	5 3 5	4 5 5	39	72
Montgomerie leads, 1 up									
Montgomerie	4 3 5	5 3 3	3 3 4	33	4 4 5	3 3 4			
Bjorn	4 3 3	4 4 4	4 4 4	34	3 4 6	4 3 4			

Lee Westwood defeated Stuart Appleby, 8 and 7

Westwood	4 3 4	4 3 3	4 3 3	31	2 3 4	4 3 4	4 5 4	33	64
Appleby	4 3 5	5 3 4	3 4 4	35	3 3 5	3 3 4	3 4 4	32	67
Westwood leads, 3 up									
Westwood	4 2 4	5 2 4	4 3 5	33	2 3				
Appleby	4 3 4	5 3 5	4 3 5	36	3 4				

Ian Woosnam defeated Darren Clarke, 4 and 3

Clarke	5 4 4	4 2 4	4 4 5	36	4 4 4	4 3 6	3 4 5	37	73
Woosnam	4 3 4	4 3 3	5 4 5	35	3 4 4	4 3 4	5 4 5	36	71
Woosnam leads, 2 up									
Clarke	4 2 4	4 4 4	4 4 3	33	3 4 4	4 3 4			
Woosnam	4 4 4	4 3 3	3 4 4	33	2 4 5	4 3 3			

SECOND ROUND

Vijay Singh defeated Patrik Sjoland, 7 and 6

Singh	3 3 4	3 2 3	4 3 4	29	2 4 4	4 3 4	4 4 4	33	62
Sjoland	4 3 5	4 3 4	5 5 4	37	3 4 4	5 3 4	4 4 4	35	72
Singh leads, 9 up									
Singh	4 3 3	4 3 3	4 4 5	33	3 4 4				
Sjoland	5 3 4	4 2 4	4 3 4	33	2 3 4				

Mark O'Meara defeated Colin Montgomerie, 5 and 4

O'Meara	5 2 4	4 4 3	4 5 4	35	3 4 4	4 3 5	4 4 3	34	69
Montgomerie	4 2 4	3 4 4	4 4 5	34	2 5 4	3 3 4	4 5 4	34	68
Montgomerie leads, 1 up									
O'Meara	4 3 3	4 3 3	4 3 3	30	3 4 4	5 3			
Montgomerie	4 3 5	5 4 4	4 4 4	37	4 4 4	3 3			

Lee Westwood defeated Ernie Els, 2 and 1

Els	4 3 4	4 3 4	4 4 4	34	3 4 4	3 3 4	4 5 4	34	68
Westwood	4 3 4	4 3 4	4 4 4	34	3 3 4	3 3 4	3 4 4	31	65
Westwood leads, 3 up									
Els	4 2 4	4 3 4	4 4 4	33	3 5 5	5 3 4	4 5		
Westwood	5 3 5	5 3 4	5 4 4	38	3 4 3	3 3 4	3 W		

Tiger Woods defeated Ian Woosnam, 37th hole

Woods	4 3 3	5 3 5	4 5 4	36	3 4 4	4 3 4	4 4 4	34	70
Woosnam	4 2 4	4 3 4	4 4 4	33	4 4 5	4 3 4	4 4 4	36	69
Woosnam leads, 1 up									
Woods	4 3 5	3 3 4	4 4 6	36	3 5 5	4 3 4	4 4 4	36	72
Woosnam	4 3 6	4 3 4	4 5 4	37	3 4 3	4 3 3	5 4 5	34	71
Match all-square									
Woods	4								
Woosnam	5								

SEMI-FINALS

Mark O'Meara defeated Vijay Singh, 11 and 10

Singh	4 3 5	5 3 4	4 3 4	35	3 5 4	4 4 4	5 C 4	X	X
O'Meara	4 2 4	4 2 3	3 3 6	31	2 4 5	3 3 4	4 W 4	X	X
O'Meara leads, 10 up									
Singh	4 4 5	4 3 4	4 4						
O'Meara	4 3 4	5 3 4	4 4						

Tiger Woods defeated Lee Westwood, 5 and 4

Westwood	4 3 4	4 3 5	3 4 4	34	4 4 5	4 3 4	4 5 5	38	72
Woods	5 3 5	4 3 5	4 4 4	37	3 4 5	3 3 4	3 5 4	34	71
Woods leads, 1 up									
Westwood	5 3 4	4 3 4	4 4 4	35	3 4 5	4 4			
Woods	4 3 5	4 3 4	3 3 4	33	2 4 4	5 2			

FINAL

Mark O'Meara defeated Tiger Woods, 1 up

O'Meara	5 3 4	4 3 4	4 4 4	35	3 3 4	4 3 4	4 W 4	X	X
Woods	4 2 3	4 3 3	4 4 4	31	3 4 4	4 3 4	3 C 4	X	X
Woods leads, 3 up									
O'Meara	3 3 4	4 3 3	3 4 4	31	3 4 3	4 2 5	4 4 4	33	64
Woods	4 3 5	4 3 4	4 4 3	34	2 4 4	4 3 3	5 4 4	33	67

PRIZE MONEY: O'Meara £170,000; Woods £90,000; Singh, Westwood £50,000 each; Sjoland, Montgomerie, Els, Woosnam £40,000 each; Stricker, Bjorn, Appleby, Clarke £30,000 each.

LEGEND: C—conceded hole to opponent; W—won hole by concession without holing out; X—no total score.

Open Novotel Perrier

Golf du Medoc, Bordeaux, France — October 15-18
Par 35-36–71; 6,909 yards — purse, £350,000

	SCORES				TOTAL	MONEY (Each)
Jarmo Sandelin/Olle Karlsson	62	68	63	136	329	£35,000
Richard Boxall/Derrick Cooper	65	69	65	133	332	25,000
Seve Ballesteros/Miguel Angel Jimenez	64	69	67	134	334	17,500
Jeff Remesy/Raphael Jacquelin	61	68	68	138	335	12,500
Jonathan Lomas/Steven Bottomley	66	67	71	133	337	7,750
Peter Baker/Paul Broadhurst	67	68	64	138	337	7,750
Mats Lanner/Peter Hedblom	65	70	70	133	338	5,500
*Sergio Garcia/*Trevor Immelman	64	70	66	138	338	
Jose Rivero/Santiago Luna	60	66	71	142	339	4,750
Peter Mitchell/Jamie Spence	67	71	66	137	341	4,375
Ross McFarlane/David J. Russell	63	67	70	141	341	4,375
Dennis Edlund/Klas Eriksson	61	72	73	136	342	4,000
*Oliver David/*David Montesi	62	70	68	143	343	
Jim Payne/Phillip Price	69	73	64	138	344	3,375
Pascal Edmond/Olivier Edmond	65	72	69	138	344	3,375
Ignacio Garrido/Carl Suneson	62	69	72	141	344	3,375
Malcolm Mackenzie/Andrew Sherborne	64	71	68	141	344	3,375
Gary Orr/Adam Hunter	62	70	69	144	345	2,900
Thomas Levet/Benoit Telleria	68	70	67	141	346	2,750
Jon Robson/Fredrik Jacobson	64	72	72	138	346	2,750
Christophe Pottier/Marc Pendaries	67	74	68	138	347	2,550
Roger Chapman/Mark Mouland	66	69	69	143	347	2,550
Paul Lawrie/Scott Henderson	69	72	69	138	348	2,400
David Howell/Wayne Riley	66	74	67	142	349	2,200
David Carter/Iain Pyman	63	74	71	141	349	2,200
Nicolas Joakimides/Christian Cevaer	60	73	65	151	349	2,200
Brian Davis/Van Phillips	67	74	73	137	351	2,000
Diego Borrego/Felix Ortiz	66	68	72	147	353	1,900
Jose Maria Olazabal/Domingo Hospital	67	71	73	143	354	1,800
Michael Jonzon/Anders Forsbrand	67	75	69	144	355	1,650
Stuart Cage/Raymond Russell	66	74	71	144	355	1,650
*Christophe Ravetto/*Gregory Havret	69	73	72	144	358	
*Sebastian Branger/*Nicolas Blactot	64	77	72	155	368	
Mark Roe/Marc Farry	66	71			WD	1,500

Volvo Masters

Montecastillo Hotel & Golf Resort, Jerez, Spain — October 29-November 1
Par 36-36–72; 7,058 yards — purse, £1,000,000

	SCORES				TOTAL	MONEY
Darren Clarke	67	73	68	63	271	£166,000
Andrew Coltart	69	73	65	66	273	110,000
Colin Montgomerie	70	67	69	68	274	63,000
Peter O'Malley	67	71	67	70	275	46,500
Peter Baker	69	72	67	67	275	46,500
Bernhard Langer	72	69	67	68	276	35,500
Jose Maria Olazabal	68	70	70	70	278	30,000
Craig Hainline	73	70	67	69	279	21,125
Robert Allenby	69	73	70	67	279	21,125
Sam Torrance	72	69	69	69	279	21,125

	SCORES				TOTAL	MONEY
Ernie Els	70	71	68	70	279	21,125
Alex Cejka	67	73	69	71	280	15,575
Stephen Leaney	71	70	68	71	280	15,575
Lee Westwood	70	68	67	75	280	15,575
Peter Lonard	68	66	75	71	280	15,575
Padraig Harrington	70	69	70	72	281	13,900
Mathias Gronberg	73	67	68	73	281	13,900
Miguel Angel Jimenez	71	72	69	69	281	13,900
Paul McGinley	68	72	69	73	282	12,500
Greg Chalmers	67	75	70	70	282	12,500
Katsuyoshi Tomori	72	71	70	69	282	12,500
Gordon Brand, Jr.	67	74	68	73	282	12,500
Jarmo Sandelin	67	71	73	72	283	11,500
Jean Van de Velde	75	69	68	72	284	10,950
Santiago Luna	69	72	72	71	284	10,950
Angel Cabrera	70	69	74	72	285	10,200
Greg Turner	73	72	68	72	285	10,200
Robert Karlsson	72	77	68	68	285	10,200
Steve Webster	70	75	67	74	286	9,000
Van Phillips	73	71	71	71	286	9,000
Peter Mitchell	72	70	68	76	286	9,000
Eduardo Romero	75	73	69	69	286	9,000
Roger Wessels	71	71	72	72	286	9,000
Massimo Florioli	74	73	69	71	287	8,100
Paolo Quirici	72	74	73	69	288	7,800
Mark Roe	73	69	75	72	289	6,900
Jamie Spence	69	74	72	74	289	6,900
Mark McNulty	73	70	74	72	289	6,900
Costantino Rocca	71	75	72	71	289	6,900
Nick Faldo	71	73	70	75	289	6,900
Ian Garbutt	72	73	68	77	290	5,300
David Gilford	69	73	75	73	290	5,300
Phillip Price	71	72	74	73	290	5,300
Ian Woosnam	74	71	74	71	290	5,300
Stephen Allan	74	72	73	71	290	5,300
Russell Claydon	72	71	75	72	290	5,300
Seve Ballesteros	72	72	71	75	290	5,300
Thomas Bjorn	72	67	75	76	290	5,300
Gary Orr	69	75	72	75	291	4,120
Per-Ulrik Johansson	71	75	73	72	291	4,120
Retief Goosen	75	68	79	69	291	4,120
Patrik Sjoland	72	72	73	74	291	4,120
David Howell	72	71	72	76	291	4,120
Paul Broadhurst	72	75	71	74	292	3,750
Sven Struver	72	71	71	78	292	3,750
Mats Hallberg	73	72	73	76	294	3,500
Thomas Gogele	72	74	69	79	294	3,500
Mats Lanner	77	72	69	76	294	3,500
Olle Karlsson	75	75	74	71	295	3,300
Pierre Fulke	69	74	75	78	296	3,200
Mike Harwood	74	74	73	77	298	3,050
Tony Johnstone	72	72	74	80	298	3,050
Ignacio Garrido	72	76	73	78	299	2,900
David Carter	77	76	69	78	300	2,800
Cheng Jun	73	70	84	85	312	2,700
Mark James	73	75	69		WD	2,600

Challenge Tour

Ivory Coast Open

Ivoire Golf Club, Abidjan, Ivory Coast
Par 36-36–72; 7,241 yards

March 5-8
purse, £70,000

	SCORES				TOTAL	MONEY
John Mellor	72	71	72	66	281	£11,370.45
Jose Sota	71	69	74	70	284	5,924.10
Fredrik Lindgren	70	70	71	73	284	5,924.10
Jeremy Robinson	72	71	72	72	287	3,412.50
Neal Briggs	75	68	72	73	288	2,774.37
Robert Wragg	76	69	75	68	288	2,774.37
Francois Lamare	72	71	72	74	289	2,443.35
David R. Jones	71	70	76	73	290	2,079.35
Soren Hansen	76	74	67	73	290	2,079.35
Warren Bennett	69	72	77	72	290	2,079.35
Marcel Soumahoro	69	75	74	73	291	1,612.98
Roger Winchester	71	79	72	69	291	1,612.98
Gregory Garbero	76	73	72	70	291	1,612.98
Marc Pendaries	73	72	73	74	292	1,046.50
Thomas Nielsen	70	75	74	73	292	1,046.50
Benoit Telleria	73	76	73	70	292	1,046.50
Morten Backhausen	71	74	75	72	292	1,046.50
Jorge Berendt	77	71	73	71	292	1,046.50
Christopher Hanell	73	72	75	72	292	1,046.50
Leif Westerberg	72	70	77	74	293	708.95
Duncan Muscroft	73	73	72	75	293	708.95
David Park	73	77	73	70	293	708.95
Richard Johnson	74	74	74	71	293	708.95
Andrew Crerar	76	72	71	74	293	708.95
Antony Manasson	70	79	74	70	293	708.95
Matthew Blackey	72	74	74	73	293	708.95
Gordon Sherry	78	71	72	72	293	708.95
Erik Andersson	76	72	75	71	294	578.42
Siaka Kone	74	76	70	74	294	578.42
Per Nyman	71	77	73	73	294	578.42
Mikael Lundberg	74	74	75	71	294	578.42

Tusker Kenya Open

Muthaiga Golf Club, Nairobi, Kenya
Par 35-36–71; 6,836 yards

March 12-15
purse, £65,000

	SCORES				TOTAL	MONEY
Ricardo Gonzalez	69	65	69	69	272	£10,558.28
Jacob Okello	70	67	66	69	272	7,034.63
(Gonzalez defeated Okello on third extra hole.)						
Mark Litton	67	70	65	73	275	3,568.02
Warren Bennett	69	68	70	68	275	3,568.02
Fredrik Lindgren	68	67	72	69	276	2,576.02

	SCORES				TOTAL	MONEY
Sammy Daniels	70	70	67	69	276	2,576.02
Christopher Hanell	68	69	70	70	277	2,180.11
Hennie Otto	67	69	72	69	277	2,180.11
Pauli Hughes	69	73	70	66	278	1,778.73
David R. Jones	70	69	69	70	278	1,778.73
Morten Backhausen	72	69	69	68	278	1,778.73
Duncan Muscroft	72	70	67	70	279	1,429.11
David Park	68	72	71	68	279	1,429.11
Thomas Nielsen	68	72	68	72	280	1,109.06
Max Anglert	67	71	74	68	280	1,109.06
Antoine Lebouc	71	68	71	70	280	1,109.06
Jose Sota	70	67	75	69	281	887.25
Bryan Ingleby	70	72	71	69	282	725.19
Mikko Rantanen	70	66	73	73	282	725.19
Gordon Sherry	68	67	74	73	282	725.19
Euan Little	73	70	71	68	282	725.19
Craig Maltman	73	68	72	69	282	725.19
Anders Hansen	73	71	68	70	282	725.19
Jorge Berendt	72	71	70	69	282	725.19
Antony Manasson	67	72	70	74	283	556.91
John Mellor	70	68	68	77	283	556.91
Peter Njiru	69	73	70	71	283	556.91
Gary Clark	71	73	67	72	283	556.91
Marc Pendaries	74	67	71	71	283	556.91
Jeremy Robinson	69	74	67	73	283	556.91
Scott Watson	73	71	71	68	283	556.91
Michael Welch	74	69	70	70	283	556.91

Is Molas Challenge

Is Molas Golf Club, Sardinia, Italy
Par 36-36–72; 6,980 yards

April 2-5
purse, £40,000

	SCORES				TOTAL	MONEY
Magnus Persson	69	71	69	74	283	£6,497.40
Thomas Levet	72	72	71	70	285	3,385.20
Christophe Pottier	73	68	71	73	285	3,385.20
Erik Andersson	73	73	71	70	287	1,629.23
Stephane Talbot	72	75	68	72	287	1,629.23
Marcello Santi	75	73	72	67	287	1,629.23
Per Nyman	67	72	74	74	287	1,629.23
Pauli Hughes	72	66	69	81	288	1,098.24
Morten Backhausen	74	66	73	75	288	1,098.24
David Park	76	68	71	73	288	1,098.24
Benoit Telleria	73	70	76	69	288	1,098.24
Dominique Nouailhac	72	73	72	71	288	1,098.24
Peter Sefton	75	70	73	71	289	721.50
Mats Lanner	74	73	69	73	289	721.50
David R. Jones	71	72	72	74	289	721.50
Stuart Andrew	72	72	69	76	289	721.50
Massimo Scarpa	67	74	75	74	290	488.28
Federico Bisazza	71	69	73	77	290	488.28
Bryan Ingleby	73	72	71	74	290	488.28
John Bickerton	68	70	80	72	290	488.28
Andrew Butterfield	74	71	73	72	290	488.28
Marco Soffietti	72	73	73	73	291	390
Thomas Nielsen	69	68	78	76	291	390

	SCORES				TOTAL	MONEY
Oyvind Rojahn	71	75	72	73	291	390
Johan Axgren	73	69	76	73	291	390
Alessandro Tadini	76	67	75	73	291	390
Neal Briggs	72	72	74	73	291	390
Stuart McGregor	74	74	72	72	292	330.53
Henrik Nystrom	73	73	74	72	292	330.53
Euan Little	75	73	72	72	292	330.53
Joost Steenkamer	79	69	72	72	292	330.53

Rimini International Open

Rimini Golf Club, Rimini, Italy
Par 36-36–72; 6,760 yards

April 22-25
purse, £67,932

	SCORES				TOTAL	MONEY
Massimo Scarpa	69	73	68	68	278	£11,146.95
Gordon J. Brand	68	72	69	71	280	4,986.91
John Bickerton	70	67	75	68	280	4,986.91
Roger Winchester	71	70	70	69	280	4,986.91
David R. Jones	72	70	70	70	282	2,611.66
Warren Bennett	67	72	73	70	282	2,611.66
Jeremy Robinson	72	70	67	73	282	2,611.66
Markus Brier	70	71	74	68	283	1,884.14
Ben Tinning	69	69	72	73	283	1,884.14
Antony Manasson	71	71	71	70	283	1,884.14
Max Anglert	72	72	72	67	283	1,884.14
Marco Soffietti	67	72	72	72	283	1,884.14
Pauli Hughes	68	77	69	70	284	1,438.53
Frederic Cupillard	69	69	74	73	285	1,237.81
Gary Murphy	70	74	71	70	285	1,237.81
Birgir Hafthorsson	69	74	68	75	286	870.92
Stephen Scahill	72	73	74	67	286	870.92
Daren Lee	70	76	69	71	286	870.92
Peter Sefton	70	76	72	68	286	870.92
Eric Carlberg	71	72	73	70	286	870.92
Paul Streeter	74	72	70	70	286	870.92
Per Nyman	70	71	72	74	287	690.83
Oyvind Rojahn	72	67	75	73	287	690.83
Gary Emerson	72	67	75	73	287	690.83
Mikael Lundberg	75	69	73	70	287	690.83
Ross Drummond	69	75	69	75	288	605.52
Patrik Gottfridsson	68	73	73	74	288	605.52
Erik Andersson	74	71	67	76	288	605.52
Matthew Blackey	73	69	73	73	288	605.52
Greig Hutcheon	72	70	74	73	289	515.20
Benoit Telleria	67	76	74	72	289	515.20
Roberto Zappa	76	69	73	71	289	515.20
Dominique Nouailhac	74	67	77	71	289	515.20
Raphael Eyraud	73	72	72	72	289	515.20
John Mellor	71	72	74	72	289	515.20
Mats Lanner	74	70	73	72	289	515.20
*Stefano Maio	76	68	78	67	289	

Albarella International Open

Albarella, Venice, Italy
Par 36-36–72; 6,085 yards

May 13-16
purse, £40,000

	SCORES				TOTAL	MONEY
Fredrik Lindgren	69	66	66	66	267	£6,497.40
Ricardo Gonzalez	65	74	63	68	270	3,385.20
Mathew Goggin	65	71	67	67	270	3,385.20
Paul Nilbrink	66	65	70	70	271	1,706.90
Per Nyman	64	69	68	70	271	1,706.90
Gary Clark	66	67	69	69	271	1,706.90
Massimo Scarpa	68	69	68	68	273	1,289.60
Andrea Canessa	67	68	72	66	273	1,289.60
David A. Russell	70	69	66	68	273	1,289.60
Gordon Sherry	70	65	71	68	274	1,049.10
Marc Pendaries	67	65	70	72	274	1,049.10
Erol Simsek	65	67	70	73	275	839.80
Dominique Nouailhac	67	72	66	70	275	839.80
Martin Erlandsson	69	66	65	75	275	839.80
Patrik Gottfridsson	70	66	72	68	276	611
Mike Miller	72	67	69	68	276	611
John Wade	66	71	70	69	276	611
Henrik Nystrom	67	69	71	70	277	497.25
Kalle Vainola	71	67	66	73	277	497.25
Gary Murphy	67	69	70	72	278	433.88
Francesco Guermani	67	69	69	73	278	433.88
Christopher Hanell	70	68	66	74	278	433.88
Warren Bennett	69	68	70	71	278	433.88
Pauli Hughes	69	71	68	71	279	388.05
John Mellor	67	68	73	71	279	388.05
Andrea Calcari	69	71	66	74	280	341.90
Andrew Crerar	69	70	70	71	280	341.90
Roger Winchester	66	73	69	72	280	341.90
Kevin Carissimi	68	71	69	72	280	341.90
Johan Axgren	68	71	69	72	280	341.90
Mikael Lundberg	68	69	70	73	280	341.90

Modena Classic

Modena Golf & Country Club, Modena, Italy
Par 36-36–72; 7,024 yards

May 21-24
purse, £40,000

	SCORES				TOTAL	MONEY
Marc Pendaries	64	66	69	71	270	£6,497.40
Pauli Hughes	69	67	68	67	271	4,329
Gianluca Baruffaldi	70	71	66	67	274	2,441.40
Leif Westerberg	66	68	69	72	275	1,801.80
Roger Winchester	66	69	70	70	275	1,801.80
Benoit Telleria	70	71	65	70	276	1,400.10
Mikko Rantanen	70	73	66	67	276	1,400.10
Marten Olander	69	69	67	71	276	1,400.10
Scott Watson	69	70	70	68	277	1,185.60
Max Anglert	69	71	67	71	278	1,049.10
Steve Alker	72	68	70	68	278	1,049.10
Jorge Berendt	68	69	67	75	279	839.80
Mathew Goggin	69	74	66	70	279	839.80
Antoine Lebouc	69	68	70	72	279	839.80

	SCORES				TOTAL	MONEY
Marcello Santi	68	74	69	69	280	585.98
Massimo Scarpa	65	68	76	71	280	585.98
Warren Bennett	74	66	69	71	280	585.98
Stephen Gallacher	71	68	69	72	280	585.98
Kevin Carissimi	72	70	70	69	281	471.90
Emmanuele Lattanzi	68	71	69	73	281	471.90
Martin Erlandsson	69	70	72	71	282	397.24
Hennie Otto	74	68	69	71	282	397.24
Emanuele Canonica	70	70	71	71	282	397.24
Jesus Maria Arruti	71	72	70	69	282	397.24
Paul Nilbrink	69	70	71	72	282	397.24
Raimo Sjoberg	71	72	69	70	282	397.24
Mats Lanner	70	71	69	72	282	397.24
Anders Hansen	71	69	69	74	283	335.40
Juan Ciola	69	74	69	71	283	335.40
Daren Lee	69	73	67	74	283	335.40

Challenge de France

Sable Solesmes, Le Mans, France — May 28-31
Par 36-36–72; 6,787 yards — purse, £50,000

	SCORES				TOTAL	MONEY
Warren Bennett	69	70	65	68	272	£8,121.75
Scott Watson	70	68	64	70	272	5,411.25
(Bennett defeated Watson on second extra hole.)						
Marten Olander	65	69	69	70	273	3,051.75
Thomas Nielsen	68	70	68	70	276	2,133.63
Olivier Edmond	70	67	68	71	276	2,133.63
Alexandre Balicki	67	68	70	71	276	2,133.63
Mike Miller	71	68	69	69	277	1,677
Massimo Scarpa	70	70	69	68	277	1,677
David Higgins	69	67	67	75	278	1,313.81
Daren Lee	67	70	72	69	278	1,313.81
Ricardo Gonzalez	69	67	72	70	278	1,313.81
Arnaud Langenaeken	66	70	72	70	278	1,313.81
Henrik Nystrom	69	69	69	72	279	763.55
John Mellor	72	67	71	69	279	763.55
Marcello Santi	69	71	66	73	279	763.55
Nicolas Kalouguine	70	70	68	71	279	763.55
Stephen Scahill	71	69	71	68	279	763.55
Marc Pendaries	70	71	70	68	279	763.55
Max Anglert	69	71	70	69	279	763.55
Mathew Goggin	68	74	69	68	279	763.55
Jean Pierre Sallat	68	71	70	71	280	550.88
Stephen Gallacher	72	70	69	70	281	531.38
Quentin Dabson	68	72	69	73	282	471.25
Robert Wragg	69	73	75	65	282	471.25
Morten Backhausen	71	71	68	72	282	471.25
Ignacio Feliu	69	70	68	75	282	471.25
Lionel Alexandre	66	69	75	72	282	471.25
Jeremy Robinson	70	70	71	71	282	471.25
Bruno Petit	70	71	69	73	283	411.94
Jorge Berendt	69	71	74	69	283	411.94

KB Golf Challenge

Praha Karlstein, Prague, Czech Republic — June 4-7
Par 35-36–71; 6,803 yards — purse, £40,446

	SCORES				TOTAL	MONEY
Stephen Gallacher	63	71	69	67	270	£6,574.10
Erol Simsek	67	66	71	68	272	4,380.10
Ricardo Gonzalez	68	71	67	67	273	2,221.62
Marten Olander	68	64	68	73	273	2,221.62
Francis Howley	67	68	70	69	274	1,604.06
Antoine Lebouc	69	71	67	67	274	1,604.06
Andreas Lindberg	66	71	68	70	275	1,357.44
David Park	71	68	68	68	275	1,357.44
Olivier Edmond	70	65	74	68	277	1,152.25
Fredrik Lindgren	71	67	70	69	277	1,152.25
Johan Rystrom	68	71	72	67	278	932.58
Johan Skold	70	70	72	66	278	932.58
Per Nyman	69	69	69	71	278	932.58
David A. Russell	71	69	68	71	279	690.56
Jorge Berendt	71	72	69	67	279	690.56
Martin Erlandsson	72	70	70	67	279	690.56
Rudi Sailer	69	67	71	73	280	494.04
Per Jacobson	68	74	72	66	280	494.04
Jeremy Robinson	71	69	68	72	280	494.04
Stephen Scahill	67	73	73	67	280	494.04
Paul Nilbrink	70	72	69	69	280	494.04
Elliot Boult	70	72	72	67	281	388.40
Marcello Santi	69	71	71	70	281	388.40
Gordon Sherry	70	71	70	70	281	388.40
Fredrick Mansson	69	70	71	71	281	388.40
Johan Selberg	70	72	70	69	281	388.40
John Wade	69	73	69	70	281	388.40
Peter Sefton	74	67	73	67	281	388.40
Mauricio Molina	70	72	70	70	282	328.84
Raphael Eyraud	73	70	68	71	282	328.84
Federico Bisazza	69	70	70	73	282	328.84

Diners Club Austrian Open

Milstatter See Golf Club, Austria — June 11-14
Par 35-35–70; 6,380 yards — purse, £55,000

	SCORES				TOTAL	MONEY
Kevin Carissimi	69	67	67	66	269	£8,936.05
Markus Brier	68	72	63	68	271	3,997.80
Per Jacobson	65	69	68	69	271	3,997.80
David R. Jones	66	67	68	70	271	3,997.80
Stephen Scahill	67	71	69	66	273	2,180.38
John Mellor	70	67	69	67	273	2,180.38
Federico Bisazza	69	72	69	64	274	1,705.68
Marc Pendaries	68	70	67	69	274	1,705.68
Jorge Berendt	66	70	70	68	274	1,705.68
Jeremy Robinson	68	67	69	70	274	1,705.68
Christian Cevaer	68	72	69	67	276	1,212.21
Matthew Hazelden	67	72	64	73	276	1,212.21
Mike Miller	68	70	72	66	276	1,212.21
Stephen McAllister	68	69	70	69	276	1,212.21

	SCORES				TOTAL	MONEY
Alberto Binaghi	72	69	71	65	277	805.91
Neal Briggs	72	70	70	65	277	805.91
Ricardo Gonzalez	68	71	72	66	277	805.91
Chuck Johnson	68	69	66	74	277	805.91
Marcus Wheelhouse	70	71	69	68	278	634.72
Stewart Cronin	69	73	68	68	278	634.72
Peter Sefton	70	70	69	69	278	634.72
Dominique Nouailhac	67	73	67	72	279	563.20
Andrew Crerar	66	75	70	68	279	563.20
Robert Lee	68	72	71	68	279	563.20
Roger Winchester	67	73	70	70	280	501.52
Gianluca Baruffaldi	72	69	69	70	280	501.52
Jesus Maria Arruti	69	73	68	70	280	501.52
Christophe Pottier	69	69	68	74	280	501.52
Stephen Gallacher	71	71	72	67	281	453.24
Arnaud Langenaeken	68	71	70	72	281	453.24

NCC Open

Soderasens Golf Club, Stockholm, Sweden — June 11-14
Par 71; 6,616 yards — purse, £40,000

	SCORES				TOTAL	MONEY
Johan Rystrom	66	69	69	72	276	£6,497.40
Fredrik Larsson	65	75	69	68	277	4,329
Charles Challen	68	72	71	68	279	2,195.70
Mikael Lundberg	71	67	72	69	279	2,195.70
Erik Andersson	70	68	71	71	280	1,522.30
Soren Hansen	68	72	71	69	280	1,522.30
Eric Carlberg	69	68	75	68	280	1,522.30
Anders Gillner	70	71	70	70	281	1,236.30
Christopher Hanell	69	73	71	68	281	1,236.30
Raimo Sjoberg	70	69	69	74	282	1,006.20
Mattias Nilsson	68	73	71	70	282	1,006.20
Mattias Eliasson	71	70	72	69	282	1,006.20
Ulrik Gustafsson	70	71	74	68	283	838.50
Mikael Piltz	69	73	67	75	284	721.50
Thomas Nielsen	73	70	74	67	284	721.50
Niclas Bjornsson	72	69	73	71	285	507.65
Daniel Olsson	70	73	71	71	285	507.65
Niclas Johnsson	70	73	69	73	285	507.65
Lars Tingvall	71	69	75	70	285	507.65
Max Anglert	70	75	73	67	285	507.65
Morten Backhausen	71	67	79	68	285	507.65
Martin Erlandsson	70	71	74	71	286	396.24
Morten Hagen	67	71	74	74	286	396.24
Adam Mednick	72	70	75	69	286	396.24
Robert Jonsson	70	71	78	67	286	396.24
Mikael Krantz	70	74	73	69	286	396.24
Leif Westerberg	71	70	75	71	287	341.25
Joakim Rask	72	72	74	69	287	341.25
Mats Johansson	75	67	74	71	287	341.25
Per Nyman	76	68	74	69	287	341.25

Fontana Open

Fontana Golf Club, Austria — June 18-21
Par 36-36–72; 7,105 yards — purse, AS500,000

	SCORES				TOTAL
Uli Weinhandl	76	70	71	71	288
Claude Grenier	75	72	74	70	291
Gordon Manson	76	70	70	78	294
Markus Brier	71	74	70	79	294
Chuck Johnson	75	73	71	76	295
*Clemens Conrad-Prader	72	82	72	71	297
*Nikolaus Zitny	78	78	71	73	300
Donald Stirling	76	76	72	77	301
Ulf Wendling	80	69	77	75	301
Karl Ableidinger	77	72	75	77	301

Lancia Golf Pokal

Ritter Gut, Lancia, Germany — June 19-21
Par 37-36–73; 6,961 yards — purse, DM120,000

	SCORES			TOTAL
Alex Cejka	68	66	68	202
Heinz P. Thul	70	67	70	207
Erol Simsek	71	70	71	212
Mark Mattheis	76	67	73	216
Ulrich Eckhardt	74	73	70	217
Torsten Giedeon	74	72	71	217
Thomas Hennig	72	75	70	217
Patrick Platz	74	72	72	218
Christophe Gunther	72	76	72	220
Nicola Sebastian Marz	72	77	72	221

Championnat de France Professionnel

Arras Golf Club, St. Omer, France — June 18-21
Par 36-36–72; 6,689 yards — purse, FF420,000

	SCORES				TOTAL	MONEY
Jean Van de Velde	68	68	65	66	267	FF69,972
Renaud Guillard	69	67	67	71	274	46,620
Lionel Alexandre	68	70	67	70	275	23,646
Stephane Lahary	72	73	64	66	275	23,646
Benoit Telleria	73	66	69	69	277	17,073
Michel Besanceney	68	73	65	71	277	17,073
Tim Planchin	71	70	69	68	278	15,036
Jean-Pierre Cixous	70	67	76	68	281	13,860
Christophe de Aizpurua	70	72	69	72	283	12,264
Jean Philippe Rochet	71	69	67	76	283	12,264

Omnium National Championship Lloyd Italico

Padua Golf Club, Padua, Italy — June 18-21
Par 36-36–72; 6,619 yards — purse, lire 130,000,000

	SCORES				TOTAL	MONEY
Massimo Scarpa	67	67	63	73	270	lire21,660,000
Stefano Soffietti	71	68	71	68	278	14,430,000
Francesco Guermani	71	70	68	71	280	8,135,000
Gianluca Baruffaldi	71	74	70	66	281	6,005,000
Marco Soffietti	70	73	67	71	281	6,005,000
Giuseppe Cali	68	74	69	71	282	5,060,000
Gianluca Pietrobono	67	71	75	70	283	4,300,000
Mario Tadini	73	71	68	71	283	4,300,000
Andrea Canessa	71	71	70	71	283	4,300,000
*Roberto Paolillo	71	68	71	73	283	

Osmanli Bankasi Klassis Turkish Open

Klassis Golf & Country Club, Klassis, Turkey — June 24-27
Par 36-35–71; 6,574 yards — purse, £60,000

	SCORES				TOTAL	MONEY
Thomas Nielsen	68	70	66	69	273	£9,746.10
Francisco Valera	67	68	73	66	274	6,893.50
David R. Jones	69	68	70	68	275	3,022.50
Jeremy Robinson	67	69	71	68	275	3,022.50
Brian Nelson	71	70	69	65	275	3,022.50
Jesus Maria Arruti	71	67	68	71	277	2,019.71
Steven Young	70	70	67	70	277	2,019.71
Soren Hansen	67	68	70	72	277	2,019.71
Roger Winchester	69	66	69	73	277	2,019.71
Jean-Pierre Cixous	69	70	70	69	278	1,446.41
Nils Rorbaek	67	67	74	70	278	1,446.41
Fredrik Lindgren	70	70	70	68	278	1,446.41
Anders Hansen	70	69	70	69	278	1,446.41
Stuart Andrew	73	69	65	72	279	897
Henrik Bjornstadt	66	70	71	72	279	897
Benoit Telleria	72	64	75	68	279	897
Erol Simsek	74	67	69	69	279	897
Inigo Moral	70	67	72	70	279	897
Marcus Wheelhouse	73	69	66	71	279	897
Robert Wragg	73	68	68	71	280	650.81
Stephen McAllister	65	69	73	73	280	650.81
Leif Westerberg	70	70	71	69	280	650.81
Franck Aumonier	72	65	75	68	280	650.81
Andrew Butterfield	65	69	73	74	281	555.75
Mike Miller	70	70	70	71	281	555.75
Neal Briggs	66	72	71	72	281	555.75
Ben Tinning	75	67	69	70	281	555.75
Martin Pettigrew	68	70	71	72	281	555.75
Euan Little	71	71	67	73	282	468.98
Mark Litton	69	67	76	70	282	468.98
Arnaud Langenaeken	69	70	70	73	282	468.98
Erik Andersson	70	67	76	69	282	468.98
John Mellor	68	71	74	69	282	468.98
Pauli Hughes	73	63	71	75	282	468.98

Open dei Tessali

Riva dei Tessali, Tessali, Italy — June 25-28
Par 35-36–71; 6,503 yards — purse, £40,000

	SCORES				TOTAL	MONEY
Pehr Magnebrant	71	69	65	71	276	£6,497.40
John Senden	71	68	69	68	276	4,329
(Magnebrant defeated Senden on first extra hole.)						
Francesco Guermani	73	67	75	66	281	2,441.40
Patrik Gottfridsson	74	73	67	68	282	1,801.80
Andrea Canessa	73	71	69	69	282	1,801.80
Mattias Nilsson	73	69	76	65	283	1,517.10
Marcello Santi	75	71	70	68	284	1,289.60
Raimo Sjoberg	64	74	74	72	284	1,289.60
Gianluca Pietrobono	67	71	74	72	284	1,289.60
Frederik Andersson	73	70	74	68	285	1,006.20
Gianluca Baruffaldi	72	73	72	68	285	1,006.20
Federico Bisazza	68	74	69	74	285	1,006.20
Mario Tadini	73	72	73	68	286	760.50
Massimo Scarpa	74	73	69	70	286	760.50
Gary Marks	70	75	69	72	286	760.50
Niclas Johnsson	73	72	69	73	287	604.50
Ruben Gonzalez	70	75	75	68	288	488.28
Stefano Soffietti	73	73	73	69	288	488.28
Ulrik Marcher	76	72	71	69	288	488.28
Michiel Janbroers	73	74	71	70	288	488.28
Frederik Orest	70	77	71	70	288	488.28
Emanuele Bolognesi	72	74	74	69	289	409.50
Paolo Terreni	74	70	73	72	289	409.50
Alessandro Tadini	70	73	71	75	289	409.50
Alessio Cocchi	71	71	78	70	290	352.95
Marco Soffietti	74	74	71	71	290	352.95
Marco Durante	72	74	73	71	290	352.95
Andrea Calcari	74	71	72	73	290	352.95
Giovanni Magni	72	72	73	73	290	352.95
Alessandro Napoleoni	72	75	70	73	290	352.95

MasterCard Challenge

Prince's, Kent, England — June 30-July 3
Par 36-36–72; 6,947 yards — purse, £40,000

	SCORES				TOTAL	MONEY
Robert Lee	74	69	68	66	277	£6,497.40
Richard Bland	68	69	72	71	280	4,329
Daren Lee	72	72	70	68	282	2,195.70
Richard Johnson	71	66	70	75	282	2,195.70
Steven Young	71	70	73	69	283	1,653.60
Andrew Barnett	69	72	72	71	284	1,456.65
Brian Nelson	68	74	70	72	284	1,456.65
Simon Wilkinson	72	67	73	73	285	1,188.20
Neal Briggs	74	70	70	71	285	1,188.20
Lee Jones	72	72	69	72	285	1,188.20
Stuart Andrew	69	70	74	73	286	881.40
David A. Russell	70	72	72	72	286	881.40
David Park	71	68	72	75	286	881.40
Pascal Edmond	73	71	72	70	286	881.40

	SCORES				TOTAL	MONEY
Andrew Clapp	69	73	73	72	287	682.50
Roger Winchester	71	72	69	76	288	575.25
Gordon Sherry	70	71	73	74	288	575.25
Simon Hurd	73	72	75	69	289	510.90
Ian Harrison	74	71	71	74	290	443.82
Leon Stanford	71	72	74	73	290	443.82
Ian Spencer	70	75	73	72	290	443.82
Craig Hislop	71	75	71	73	290	443.82
Euan Little	73	70	74	73	290	443.82
Richard Tinworth	73	70	74	74	291	376.35
Simon Griffiths	67	77	75	72	291	376.35
Adam Tillman	70	72	70	79	291	376.35
Shaun Webster	71	72	73	75	291	376.35
Jonathan Langmead	73	72	77	70	292	321.75
Darren Parris	73	73	74	72	292	321.75
Liam Bond	70	75	73	74	292	321.75
Peter Sefton	73	70	76	73	292	321.75
Michael Welch	72	73	73	74	292	321.75
Gary Emerson	74	72	76	70	292	321.75

Audi Quattro Trophy

Bad Abbach, Munich, Germany — July 2-5

Par 36-36–72; 6,725 yards — purse, £56,000

	SCORES				TOTAL	MONEY
Marcello Santi	65	70	68	66	269	£9,094.17
Stephen Gallacher	68	66	67	68	269	6,059.14
(Santi defeated Gallacher on fourth extra hole.)						
John Bickerton	66	68	69	67	270	3,417.14
Marten Olander	68	66	67	70	271	2,729.34
Mikael Lundberg	69	66	69	68	272	2,314.48
Alvaro Salto	68	71	68	67	274	2,123.43
Warren Bennett	69	67	66	73	275	1,805.01
Thomas Nielsen	66	67	71	71	275	1,805.01
Stephane Lahary	66	72	68	69	275	1,805.01
Johan Rystrom	71	67	67	71	276	1,468.38
John Senden	67	71	70	68	276	1,468.38
Kevin Carissimi	67	73	69	68	277	1,015.31
Jesus Maria Arruti	67	68	70	72	277	1,015.31
Markus Brier	70	68	71	68	277	1,015.31
Henrik Bjornstadt	69	72	67	69	277	1,015.31
Nils Rorbaek	72	66	73	66	277	1,015.31
Simon Wakefield	73	67	69	68	277	1,015.31
Darren Cole	68	68	71	71	278	715.09
Massimo Scarpa	68	68	72	71	279	676.88
Henrik Nystrom	68	71	70	71	280	596.09
Per Nyman	67	69	71	73	280	596.09
Max Anglert	73	66	70	71	280	596.09
Felix Lubenau	71	70	67	72	280	596.09
Simon Brown	69	72	69	70	280	596.09
*Stephan Wittkop	69	72	67	72	280	
Christopher Hanell	72	69	71	69	281	526.77
Raphael Eyraud	66	70	74	71	281	526.77
Joost Steenkamer	72	66	73	71	282	502.20
Fredrik Lindgren	69	70	73	71	283	462.62
Martin Erlandsson	69	69	72	73	283	462.62

	SCORES				TOTAL	MONEY
Raimo Sjoberg	69	72	70	72	283	462.62
Arnaud Langenaeken	70	71	72	70	283	462.62

BTC Slovenian Open

Bled Golf & Country Club, Bled, Slovenia — July 9-12
Par 36-37–73; 6,914 yards — purse, £45,000

	SCORES				TOTAL	MONEY
Warren Bennett	65	66	69	70	270	£7,309.58
Marc Pendaries	69	66	68	70	273	3,808.36
Mikael Lundberg	65	69	70	69	273	3,808.36
Gianluca Baruffaldi	67	70	71	66	274	2,193.75
Uli Weinhandl	66	67	72	71	276	1,860.30
Jose Manuel Lara	69	73	64	71	277	1,638.74
Franck Aumonier	67	71	68	71	277	1,638.74
Andrea Canessa	66	71	70	72	279	1,336.73
Frederik Andersson	71	69	68	71	279	1,336.73
Jesus Maria Arruti	74	70	65	70	279	1,336.73
Marco Soffietti	73	72	68	67	280	1,036.91
Marcello Santi	71	73	67	69	280	1,036.91
Neal Briggs	69	73	69	69	280	1,036.91
Jerome Challen	72	72	69	68	281	811.68
Stephen Gallacher	67	72	73	69	281	811.68
Younes El Hassani	71	68	72	71	282	571.11
Steve Rey	73	68	72	69	282	571.11
Massimo Scarpa	69	69	73	71	282	571.11
Christoph Bausek	72	71	70	69	282	571.11
Kevin Carissimi	72	70	67	73	282	571.11
Rudi Sailer	70	70	72	70	282	571.11
Dominique Nouailhac	68	69	76	70	283	453.01
Gary Marks	69	72	71	71	283	453.01
Inigo Moral	73	72	66	72	283	453.01
Christian Arenz	73	72	68	70	283	453.01
Carlos Duran	70	68	73	73	284	403.65
Alvaro Salto	72	70	72	70	284	403.65
Johan Moller	76	68	70	70	284	403.65
Ignacio Feliu	70	69	71	75	285	370.75
Gianluca Pietrobono	69	74	68	74	285	370.75

Volvo Finnish Open

Espoo Golf Club, Espoo, Finland — July 9-12
Par 36-36–72; 6,731 yards — purse, £40,000

	SCORES				TOTAL	MONEY
Christian Cevaer	67	67	71	75	280	£6,497.40
Daniel Westermark	67	70	72	72	281	3,385.20
Fredrik Larsson	68	71	70	72	281	3,385.20
Raimo Sjoberg	68	71	69	74	282	1,706.90
Niclas Johnsson	72	71	66	73	282	1,706.90
Anders Hansen	68	71	73	70	282	1,706.90
Paul Nilbrink	70	72	68	73	283	1,341.60
Johan Edfors	68	71	74	70	283	1,341.60
Robert Jonsson	69	72	68	75	284	1,094.60

	SCORES				TOTAL	MONEY
Per Nyman	72	71	67	74	284	1,094.60
Johan Annerfelt	69	76	72	67	284	1,094.60
Anders Gillner	70	73	73	69	285	645.23
Peter Bolle	73	71	68	73	285	645.23
Niclas Bjornsson	76	70	72	67	285	645.23
Max Anglert	75	70	66	74	285	645.23
Per Jacobson	72	74	66	73	285	645.23
Fredrik Lindgren	72	72	71	70	285	645.23
Marcus Dahlberg	66	75	69	75	285	645.23
Morten Haeraas	72	71	71	71	285	645.23
Jens Nilsson	78	67	69	71	285	645.23
Oyvind Rojahn	72	73	68	73	286	390.98
Morten Hagen	74	72	68	72	286	390.98
Janne Martikainen	68	77	72	69	286	390.98
Per Nyman	73	70	70	73	286	390.98
Mats Johansson	72	72	69	73	286	390.98
Ville Lemon	70	75	70	71	286	390.98
Pasi Purhonen	72	73	69	72	286	390.98
Claes Hovstadius	77	67	68	74	286	390.98
Pehr Magnebrant	71	73	73	70	287	304.69
Emil Madsen	75	71	67	74	287	304.69
Adam Mednick	72	74	67	74	287	304.69
Leif Westerberg	72	74	70	71	287	304.69
Martin Erlandsson	74	69	70	74	287	304.69
Ulrik Marcher	72	72	71	72	287	304.69
Mikael Piltz	72	68	70	77	287	304.69
Erik Andersson	75	70	70	72	287	304.69

Open des Volcans

Golf des Volcans, Volcans d'Auvergne National Park, France — July 16-19
Par 36-36–72; 6,874 yards — purse, £50,403

	SCORES				TOTAL	MONEY
Warren Bennett	69	65	70	73	277	£8,397.18
Euan Little	70	68	71	71	280	4,375
Robert Jan Derksen	68	73	71	68	280	4,375
*Gregory Havret	70	71	71	68	280	
Brian Nelson	73	68	75	65	281	2,520.16
Raphael Eyraud	74	74	68	66	282	2,048.89
Jose Carriles	75	72	68	67	282	2,048.89
Rudi Sailer	72	75	71	65	283	1,804.44
Gary Marks	72	72	72	68	284	1,309.04
Andrew Butterfield	73	73	70	68	284	1,309.04
Inigo Moral	73	75	69	67	284	1,309.04
Stephan Rulton	67	75	72	70	284	1,309.04
Giuseppe Cali	70	73	71	70	284	1,309.04
Robert Lee	68	73	72	71	284	1,309.04
Nicholas Ludwell	74	71	68	71	284	1,309.04
Roberto Coceres	69	73	76	67	285	688.36
Stephane Lahary	73	71	71	70	285	688.36
Frederic Regard	69	74	70	72	285	688.36
Massimo Scarpa	73	68	74	70	285	688.36
Benoit Telleria	73	71	71	70	285	688.36
Roger Sabarros	71	67	73	74	285	688.36
Frederic Cupillard	73	76	68	68	285	688.36
Christophe De Aizpurua	70	73	74	69	286	529.23

	SCORES				TOTAL	MONEY
Franck Aumonier	73	72	72	69	286	529.23
Sean Quinlivan	74	70	73	69	286	529.23
Daniel Silva	75	70	71	71	287	486.39
Jean-Pierre Cixous	69	78	66	74	287	486.39
Neil Cheetham	71	74	69	74	288	456.15
Richard Hussey	77	70	71	70	288	456.15
Marcus Wheelhouse	69	73	75	72	289	420.03
Laurent Lassalle	70	72	72	75	289	420.03
Antony Manasson	74	72	74	69	289	420.03

Rolex Trophy

Golf Club de Geneve, Geneva, Switzerland — July 16-19
Par 36-36–72; 6,877 yards — purse, £50,000

	SCORES				TOTAL	MONEY
David Park	69	65	74	68	276	£6,224.06
Per Nyman	71	67	69	69	276	3,941.90
(Park defeated Nyman on first extra hole.)						
Jorge Berendt	67	71	71	69	278	3,070.54
Francisco Valera	72	70	66	71	279	2,344.40
Christopher Hanell	70	71	66	72	279	2,344.40
Marcello Santi	68	74	70	69	281	1,742.74
John Bickerton	70	70	70	71	281	1,742.74
Roger Winchester	70	68	73	71	282	1,452.28
Matthew Blackey	69	74	73	67	283	1,327.80
Marten Olander	67	77	69	70	283	1,327.80
Christophe Pottier	69	73	72	71	285	1,203.32
Magnus Persson	69	69	76	72	286	1,078.84
Scott Watson	69	71	69	77	286	1,078.84
Peter Sefton	71	74	71	72	288	933.61
Charles Challen	74	69	73	72	288	933.61
Marco Soffietti	73	69	73	74	289	871.37
Federico Bisazza	68	72	76	75	291	829.88
Francesco Guermani	73	70	73	76	292	788.38

Interlaken Open

Golf Club Interlaken, Unterseen, Switzerland — July 23-26
Par 36-36–72; 6,841 yards — purse, £75,000

	SCORES				TOTAL	MONEY
John Senden	67	69	65	62	263	£12,182.63
Stephen Gallacher	65	66	65	69	265	6,347.26
Warren Bennett	69	65	67	64	265	6,347.26
Mikael Lundberg	68	66	69	63	266	3,656.25
Paolo Quirici	67	68	66	67	268	2,854.31
Max Anglert	69	66	65	68	268	2,854.31
Massimo Scarpa	69	67	66	66	268	2,854.31
Christopher Hanell	69	67	65	69	270	2,318.07
Brian Nelson	70	68	65	67	270	2,318.07
Matthew Blackey	70	64	67	70	271	1,731.60
John Mellor	68	71	63	69	271	1,731.60
Robert Lee	68	71	67	65	271	1,731.60
Stephen Scahill	70	66	68	67	271	1,731.60

	SCORES				TOTAL	MONEY
Per Nyman	70	63	70	68	271	1,731.60
Jorge Berendt	67	69	71	65	272	1,145.63
Andrew Butterfield	69	67	68	68	272	1,145.63
Gordon Sherry	70	69	63	70	272	1,145.63
Gary Murphy	69	65	68	71	273	888.47
Kevin Carissimi	68	67	71	67	273	888.47
Roger Winchester	69	68	65	71	273	888.47
Henrik Nystrom	70	68	64	71	273	888.47
Nils Rorbaek	67	72	70	65	274	731.25
Daniel Westermark	70	68	67	69	274	731.25
Marten Olander	70	68	71	65	274	731.25
Scott Watson	67	69	67	71	274	731.25
Jose Carriles	69	68	70	67	274	731.25
Francisco Valera	71	68	67	68	274	731.25
Kalle Vainola	72	64	67	72	275	603.28
Hayo Bensdorp	65	69	71	70	275	603.28
Frederik Andersson	69	70	65	71	275	603.28
Pauli Hughes	68	67	71	69	275	603.28
Eric Carlberg	66	68	73	68	275	603.28
Daren Lee	67	71	63	74	275	603.28

Challenge Tour Championship

East Sussex National, Uckfield, England — July 30-August 2
Par 36-36–72; 7,138 yards — purse, £80,000

	SCORES				TOTAL	MONEY
Warren Bennett	67	70	71	68	276	£12,994.80
John Bickerton	74	71	68	65	278	8,658
Mathew Goggin	73	68	69	69	279	4,882.80
Paul Curry	72	69	72	68	281	3,413.80
Stephen Dodd	71	71	68	71	281	3,413.80
John Mellor	76	68	69	68	281	3,413.80
Daren Lee	73	71	70	68	282	2,683.20
Jeremy Robinson	75	70	66	71	282	2,683.20
Ross Drummond	73	72	67	71	283	2,189.20
Stephen Gallacher	77	63	74	69	283	2,189.20
Kevin Carissimi	73	71	70	69	283	2,189.20
Antoine Lebouc	75	70	70	69	284	1,679.60
Ricardo Gonzalez	75	70	68	71	284	1,679.60
Francisco Valera	74	68	70	72	284	1,679.60
John Wade	72	70	73	70	285	1,131
Robert Lee	72	74	69	70	285	1,131
Andrew Butterfield	76	67	69	73	285	1,131
Jorge Berendt	75	67	71	72	285	1,131
Paul Way	74	72	72	67	285	1,131
Elliot Boult	70	73	75	68	286	851.76
Stephen McAllister	70	71	74	71	286	851.76
Pauli Hughes	76	67	74	69	286	851.76
Richard Bland	72	74	71	69	286	851.76
Andrew Barnett	72	69	76	69	286	851.76
Simon Wakefield	72	71	73	71	287	717.60
Philip Archer	74	72	70	71	287	717.60
Larry Batchelor	72	71	72	72	287	717.60
Andrew Marshall	72	67	72	76	287	717.60
Jesus Maria Arruti	71	75	70	71	287	717.60
Scott Watson	73	69	71	75	288	624

	SCORES				TOTAL	MONEY
Scott Downton	75	71	70	72	288	624
David R. Jones	73	71	72	72	288	624
Ben Tinning	74	69	71	74	288	624

Finnish Masters

Masters Golf Club, Espoo, Finland — August 6-9
Par 36-36–72; 6,640 yards — purse, £80,000

	SCORES				TOTAL	MONEY
Massimo Scarpa	69	70	63	69	271	£12,994.80
Christopher Hanell	67	67	67	71	272	8,658
John Bickerton	72	69	66	69	276	4,391.40
Per Nyman	67	71	68	70	276	4,391.40
Ricardo Gonzalez	68	69	71	69	277	3,307.20
Adam Mednick	67	71	70	70	278	2,913.30
Marten Olander	69	71	68	70	278	2,913.30
John Mellor	69	70	74	66	279	2,376.40
Henrik Bjornstad	70	73	69	67	279	2,376.40
Mikael Lundberg	71	70	69	69	279	2,376.40
Antoine Lebouc	71	72	71	66	280	1,926.60
Jesus Maria Arruti	70	71	70	69	280	1,926.60
John Senden	70	72	72	67	281	1,150.50
Frederic Cupillard	70	74	68	69	281	1,150.50
Soren Hansen	70	73	69	69	281	1,150.50
Christian Cevaer	68	73	70	70	281	1,150.50
Marcello Santi	72	70	69	70	281	1,150.50
Magnus Persson	70	70	70	71	281	1,150.50
Benoit Telleria	74	67	69	71	281	1,150.50
Morten Hagen	72	70	68	71	281	1,150.50
Oyvind Rojahn	70	72	68	71	281	1,150.50
Andreas Lindberg	70	69	70	72	281	1,150.50
Jose Carriles	71	73	70	68	282	790.40
Raphael Eyraud	71	71	69	71	282	790.40
Pehr Magnebrant	70	72	69	71	282	790.40
Jeremy Robinson	72	70	71	70	283	729.30
Robert Jan Derksen	73	69	69	72	283	729.30
*Panu Kylliainen	70	70	75	68	283	
Leif Westerberg	71	72	71	70	284	682.50
Martin Erlandsson	71	71	70	72	284	682.50
Hans Karlsson	74	68	72	71	285	631.80
Marc Pendaries	72	71	72	70	285	631.80
Daniel Westermark	71	72	67	75	285	631.80

Moscow Country Club Russian Open

Moscow Country Club, Moscow, Russia — August 13-16
Par 36-36–72; 7,105 yards — purse, £90,000

	SCORES				TOTAL	MONEY
Warren Bennett	68	71	67	64	270	£14,619.15
Ricardo Gonzalez	65	71	73	68	277	7,616.70
Max Anglert	68	67	73	69	277	7,616.70
Frederic Cupillard	69	72	71	66	278	4,054.05
Jose Manuel Lara	71	64	73	70	278	4,054.05

	SCORES				TOTAL	MONEY
Anders Hansen	71	71	70	68	280	2,806.54
Marcus Wheelhouse	73	70	70	67	280	2,806.54
Fredrik Larsson	77	66	68	69	280	2,806.54
Scott Watson	73	68	70	69	280	2,806.54
John Bickerton	71	69	71	69	280	2,806.54
Tony Edlund	71	68	73	68	280	2,806.54
Soren Hansen	73	66	70	72	281	2,070.90
John Wade	66	73	73	70	282	1,886.63
Kalle Vainola	69	73	74	67	283	1,535.63
Benoit Telleria	71	72	70	70	283	1,535.63
Christopher Hanell	73	66	76	68	283	1,535.63
Johan Skold	72	71	73	68	284	1,098.63
Mark Litton	73	70	70	71	284	1,098.63
John Mellor	71	70	69	74	284	1,098.63
Matthew Hazelden	72	67	73	72	284	1,098.63
Roger Winchester	71	68	71	74	284	1,098.63
Jose Carriles	72	70	72	71	285	906.02
Jorge Berendt	67	75	73	70	285	906.02
Martin Erlandsson	68	73	72	72	285	906.02
Rudi Sailer	71	69	74	71	285	906.02
Marcello Santi	71	71	72	72	286	758.41
Leon Stanford	70	72	74	70	286	758.41
Daren Lee	73	70	75	68	286	758.41
Robert Jan Derksen	68	73	72	73	286	758.41
Henrik Bjornstad	71	70	72	73	286	758.41
Francis Howley	72	68	72	74	286	758.41
Dominique Nouailhac	70	69	72	75	286	758.41

Denmark Closed Event

Esbjerg Golf Club, Esbjerg, Denmark
Par 36-35–71; 6,876 yards

August 14-16
purse, DKK200,000

	SCORES			TOTAL	MONEY
Ben Tinning	67	71	74	212	DKK40,000
Jesper Kjaerbye	71	72	71	214	26,000
Soren Kjeldsen	69	72	73	214	26,000
Niels Rorbaek	73	75	72	220	18,000
Lars Logstrup	73	74	76	223	12,500
Danny Jorgensen	73	73	77	223	12,500
Rene Michelsen	77	75	72	224	10,000
Ole Eskildsen	70	82	73	225	9,000
Ulrik Marcher	75	77	74	226	7,500
Soren Rolner	73	78	75	226	7,500
Christian Post	74	79	75	228	5,500
Arrild Townhill	72	79	77	228	5,500
Jacob Borregaard	75	76	78	229	4,500
Per Moller	74	80	77	231	3,750
Morton Larsen	76	77	78	231	3,750
Nigel Willet	77	77	78	232	3,000
David Philp	77	76	80	233	2,750
Vicente Danielsen	76	78	85	239	2,750

Netcom Norwegian Open

Borre Golf Club, Borre, Norway — August 20-23
Par 73; 6,702 yards — purse, £80,000

	SCORES				TOTAL	MONEY
Gary Emerson	74	63	68	70	275	£12,994.80
Max Anglert	71	70	68	67	276	8,658
Per Nyman	71	72	69	65	277	4,391.40
Soren Hansen	69	69	69	70	277	4,391.40
Fredrik Lindgren	69	70	70	69	278	2,926.95
Francis Howley	72	71	65	70	278	2,926.95
Roger Winchester	72	68	69	69	278	2,926.95
Leif Westerberg	72	71	68	67	278	2,926.95
Daren Lee	66	73	71	69	279	1,934.40
Scott Watson	72	68	72	67	279	1,934.40
Raimo Sjoberg	69	67	72	71	279	1,934.40
Paul Curry	72	65	73	69	279	1,934.40
Christopher Hanell	72	71	67	69	279	1,934.40
Tony Edlund	67	71	66	75	279	1,934.40
Warren Bennett	72	69	68	72	281	1,095.90
Elliot Boult	73	69	70	69	281	1,095.90
Stephen McAllister	71	71	68	71	281	1,095.90
Johan Rystrom	73	69	68	71	281	1,095.90
Frederik Andersson	71	69	70	71	281	1,095.90
John Mellor	69	74	69	69	281	1,095.90
Marcus Wheelhouse	72	69	72	69	282	794.49
Birgir Hafthorsson	73	71	70	68	282	794.49
Jose Carriles	74	69	72	67	282	794.49
John Senden	70	73	70	69	282	794.49
Henrik Nystrom	74	70	69	69	282	794.49
Jose Manuel Lara	70	70	72	70	282	794.49
Simon Wakefield	75	68	71	68	282	794.49
Fredrik Henge	70	71	71	71	283	670.80
Adam Mednick	69	71	71	72	283	670.80
Steven Bottomley	71	72	71	69	283	670.80

Navision Open

Himmerland Golf Club, Himmerland, Denmark — August 28-30
Par 36-36–72; 6,837 yards — purse, £40,000

	SCORES			TOTAL	MONEY
Soren Hansen	71	69	66	206	£6,497.40
Euan Little	70	67	69	206	3,385.20
Rene Budde	68	68	70	206	3,385.20
(Hansen defeated Little and Budde on first extra hole.)					
Per Nyman	72	68	67	207	1,801.80
Jose Manuel Lara	69	69	69	207	1,801.80
Jens Nilsson	73	72	65	210	1,400.10
Fredrik Widmark	72	66	72	210	1,400.10
Fredrik Larsson	69	68	73	210	1,400.10
Simon Wakefield	73	71	68	212	1,051.05
Marcello Santi	72	72	68	212	1,051.05
Charles Challen	69	70	73	212	1,051.05
Alexandre Balicki	68	71	73	212	1,051.05
David Lindqvist	70	71	72	213	838.50
David Park	73	72	69	214	648.38

	SCORES			TOTAL	MONEY
Henrik Nystrom	72	74	68	214	648.38
Morten Backhausen	71	71	72	214	648.38
Fredrik Wickman	70	68	76	214	648.38
Raimo Sjoberg	76	68	71	215	438.26
Lars Tingvall	75	71	69	215	438.26
Martin Erlandsson	74	72	69	215	438.26
Janne Martikainen	74	70	71	215	438.26
Soren Rolner	74	70	71	215	438.26
Sean Quinlivan	73	71	71	215	438.26
Alessandro Napoleoni	72	71	72	215	438.26
Ben Tinning	72	70	73	215	438.26
David A. Russell	73	71	72	216	352.95
Jorgen Aker	73	69	74	216	352.95
Richard Johnson	72	73	71	216	352.95
Bjorn Back	68	75	73	216	352.95
Arild Townhill	74	71	72	217	315.90
Daren Lee	74	71	72	217	315.90
Adam Mednick	73	69	75	217	315.90

Ohrlings Swedish Match Play

Varbergs Golf Club, Varbergs, Sweden — September 3-6
Par 36-36–72; 6,435 yards — purse, £40,000

FINAL

Kevin Carissimi defeated Mattias Eliasson, 2 and 1.

(Carissimi received £6,497.)

Open de Strasbourg - La Wantzenau

La Wantzenau, Strasbourg, France — September 3-6
Par 36-36–72; 6,852 yards — purse, £45,000

	SCORES				TOTAL	MONEY
John Senden	71	70	67	68	276	£7,309.58
Daren Lee	73	65	68	70	276	4,870.13
(Senden defeated Lee on first extra hole.)						
Robert Lee	72	66	70	70	278	2,746.58
John Mellor	72	73	71	63	279	2,027.03
David A. Russell	69	71	69	70	279	2,027.03
Uli Weinhandl	67	71	68	75	281	1,575.12
Roger Winchester	73	67	70	71	281	1,575.12
Renaud Guillard	71	69	68	73	281	1,575.12
Markus Brier	70	71	68	73	282	1,182.43
Marc Pendaries	69	71	71	71	282	1,182.43
Henrik Bjornstad	72	68	70	72	282	1,182.43
Robert Jan Derksen	72	68	71	71	282	1,182.43
Fredrik Lindgren	78	68	64	73	283	739.29
Jose Carriles	72	71	71	69	283	739.29
Richard Bland	71	73	71	68	283	739.29
Christophe De Aizpurua	74	71	69	69	283	739.29
David Park	69	71	69	74	283	739.29
Euan Little	72	70	68	73	283	739.29
Eric Giraud	72	73	71	68	284	544.05

	SCORES				TOTAL	MONEY
Jose Manuel Lara	71	71	69	74	285	497.25
Warren Bennett	70	74	70	71	285	497.25
Warren Bladon	71	70	73	71	285	497.25
Emmanuel Dussart	71	67	75	73	286	437.66
Felix Lubenau	72	71	71	72	286	437.66
Morten Backhausen	70	72	72	72	286	437.66
Benoit Telleria	74	68	72	72	286	437.66
*Julien Van Hauwe	73	72	70	71	286	
Bruno Petit	72	72	70	73	287	397.07
Didier De Vooght	67	72	72	76	287	397.07
Jeremy Robinson	74	70	71	73	288	347.24
Claes Hovstadius	76	69	74	69	288	347.24
Christian Cevaer	74	72	72	70	288	347.24
Michel Besanceney	72	71	74	71	288	347.24
Antony Manasson	70	73	68	77	288	347.24
Janeirik Dahlstrom	71	72	78	67	288	347.24
Alexandre Balicki	74	72	74	68	288	347.24

Warsaw Golf Open

Warsaw Golf Club, Warsaw, Poland — September 10-13
Par 36-35–71; 6,600 yards — purse, £54,256

	SCORES				TOTAL	MONEY
Jose Manuel Lara	69	70	66	68	273	£8,860.09
Raimo Sjoberg	67	68	70	70	275	5,903.18
Eric Carlberg	70	71	70	65	276	2,994.14
Scott Watson	71	71	65	69	276	2,994.14
Jose Carriles	69	66	67	75	277	2,254.91
Stephen Scahill	67	69	74	68	278	1,986.35
Rudi Sailer	70	66	71	71	278	1,986.35
Euan Little	67	70	68	74	279	1,755
Alberto Binaghi	70	70	71	69	280	1,616.73
Magnus Persson	73	66	71	71	281	1,204.57
Gordon Sherry	68	69	73	71	281	1,204.57
Soren Hansen	73	68	69	71	281	1,204.57
Gary Emerson	72	70	68	71	281	1,204.57
Jeremy Robinson	72	68	71	70	281	1,204.57
Scott Downton	70	71	70	70	281	1,204.57
Richard Bland	68	68	74	72	282	755.18
David A. Russell	70	71	69	72	282	755.18
Stuart Andrew	69	68	76	69	282	755.18
Matthew Blackey	70	70	71	72	283	593.87
Jesus Maria Arruti	70	75	68	70	283	593.87
Benoit Telleria	69	68	74	72	283	593.87
Per Nyman	71	72	69	71	283	593.87
Erik Andersson	74	67	68	74	283	593.87
Bruno Petit	68	72	72	71	283	593.87
Mikko Rantanen	70	71	70	73	284	505.23
Daren Lee	75	70	71	68	284	505.23
Leif Westerberg	73	71	71	69	284	505.23
Mike Miller	71	71	73	70	285	457.36
John Mellor	70	71	67	77	285	457.36
Simon Wakefield	69	68	75	73	285	457.36

Eulen Open Galea

Neguri, Bilbao, Spain
Par 36-36–72; 6,868 yards

September 24-27
purse, £59,716

	SCORES				TOTAL	MONEY
Alvaro Salto	67	68	77	68	280	£9,699.93
Daren Lee	67	74	72	68	281	6,462.74
Roger Winchester	67	70	71	74	282	3,008.18
Thomas Nielsen	68	67	71	75	282	3,008.18
Marc Pendaries	68	72	73	69	282	3,008.18
Jose Carriles	66	74	71	72	283	2,174.62
Mike Miller	70	72	68	73	283	2,174.62
Fernando Roca	71	67	76	70	284	1,921.35
Marten Olander	71	73	70	72	286	1,443.93
Fredrik Larsson	70	70	74	72	286	1,443.93
Gary Murphy	69	75	71	71	286	1,443.93
Ricardo Gonzalez	69	72	74	71	286	1,443.93
Ben Tinning	72	68	77	69	286	1,443.93
Henrik Bjornstadt	74	70	71	71	286	1,443.93
Kevin Carissimi	70	72	76	69	287	874.80
Neal Briggs	71	69	73	74	287	874.80
Richard Bland	72	70	74	71	287	874.80
Francisco Valera	70	70	76	71	287	874.80
Eric Carlberg	71	72	72	73	288	704.50
Christopher Hanell	73	70	74	71	288	704.50
David Park	69	73	72	75	289	622.99
Jose Manuel Lara	69	71	75	74	289	622.99
Jeremy Robinson	72	72	71	74	289	622.99
Jean Quiros	69	72	73	75	289	622.99
John Bickerton	72	71	73	74	290	535.65
Frederic Cupillard	72	69	75	74	290	535.65
Fredrik Lindgren	71	72	76	71	290	535.65
Henrik Nystrom	72	71	77	70	290	535.65
Alberto Binaghi	72	71	76	71	290	535.65
Scott Downton	67	73	76	75	291	422.95
Jorge Berendt	73	71	71	76	291	422.95
Christian Cevaer	70	74	74	73	291	422.95
Soren Hansen	68	74	73	76	291	422.95
Matthew Blackey	70	72	74	75	291	422.95
Stephen Scahill	71	72	75	73	291	422.95
Gary Emerson	70	74	75	72	291	422.95
Elliot Boult	71	73	75	72	291	422.95

Telia Grand Prix

Ljunghusens Golf Club, Malmo, Sweden
Par 71; 6,616 yards

October 1-4
purse, £84,422

	SCORES				TOTAL	MONEY
Mats Lanner	71	70	74	69	284	£13,550.73
Morten Backhausen	69	78	66	71	284	7,060.04
Per Nyman	72	73	72	67	284	7,060.04
(Lanner defeated Backhausen and Nyman on first extra hole.)						
*Henrik Stenson	73	67	74	71	285	
Soren Hansen	74	73	66	72	285	4,066.84
Antoine Lebouc	69	70	78	69	286	3,174.85
Elliot Boult	73	71	73	69	286	3,174.85

	SCORES				TOTAL	MONEY
Anders Hansen	72	74	71	69	286	3,174.85
Fredrik Lindgren	72	73	72	70	287	2,200.16
Stephen Gallacher	68	73	73	73	287	2,200.16
Peter Malmgren	67	72	73	75	287	2,200.16
Daren Lee	74	71	70	72	287	2,200.16
Henrik Bjornstad	78	67	72	70	287	2,200.16
Anders Gillner	76	70	74	67	287	2,200.16
Hans Karlsson	75	73	71	69	288	1,586.07
Raimo Sjoberg	74	73	69	73	289	1,110.83
Adam Mednick	72	76	70	71	289	1,110.83
Jose Carriles	72	71	77	69	289	1,110.83
Christian Cevaer	72	71	75	71	289	1,110.83
Gary Murphy	72	75	70	72	289	1,110.83
Ulrik Gustafsson	75	70	73	71	289	1,110.83
Johan Annerfelt	69	72	76	72	289	1,110.83
Gary Emerson	71	74	76	69	290	870.30
Roger Winchester	71	73	71	75	290	870.30
Martin Erlandsson	76	72	67	76	291	760.50
Kenny Cross	70	71	73	77	291	760.50
Mark Litton	76	72	68	75	291	760.50
Max Anglert	76	70	71	74	291	760.50
Marc Pendaries	73	74	71	73	291	760.50
Richard Johnson	75	72	74	70	291	760.50
Matthew Blackey	72	70	76	74	292	634.43
Per Nyberg	77	69	73	73	292	634.43
Nils Rorbaek	73	71	73	75	292	634.43
Mike Miller	74	74	71	73	292	634.43
Jose Manuel Lara	73	75	72	72	292	634.43
John Bickerton	71	73	76	72	292	634.43

San Paolo Vita Open

Margara Golf Club, Margara, Italy — October 7-10
Par 36-36–72; 6,778 yards — purse, £47,000

	SCORES				TOTAL	MONEY
Roger Winchester	70	69	68	65	272	£7,636.67
Emanuele Canonica	64	73	65	71	273	5,087.39
Scott Watson	71	67	68	68	274	2,869.11
Warren Bennett	68	68	69	70	275	2,291.62
Christopher Hanell	69	74	66	67	276	1,719.86
Jorge Berendt	69	69	70	68	276	1,719.86
Markus Brier	68	67	72	69	276	1,719.86
Robert Lee	71	69	67	69	276	1,719.86
Dominique Nouailhac	69	69	72	67	277	1,136.64
Raimo Sjoberg	67	71	71	68	277	1,136.64
David Park	72	68	69	68	277	1,136.64
David R. Jones	69	68	69	71	277	1,136.64
Jeremy Robinson	69	67	70	71	277	1,136.64
John Bickerton	64	70	71	72	277	1,136.64
Michele Reale	71	67	70	70	278	688.63
Jose Manuel Lara	70	69	69	70	278	688.63
Elliot Boult	69	70	67	72	278	688.63
Gary Emerson	70	69	67	72	278	688.63
Daren Lee	70	69	72	68	279	554.57
Francesco Guermani	73	67	70	69	279	554.57
Max Anglert	75	68	69	68	280	517.91

	SCORES				TOTAL	MONEY
Erik Andersson	72	69	70	70	281	458.32
Massimo Scarpa	71	64	76	70	281	458.32
Jose Carriles	72	69	71	69	281	458.32
Gianluca Baruffaldi	71	72	70	68	281	458.32
Anders Hansen	70	71	69	71	281	458.32
Fredrik Lindgren	72	69	69	71	281	458.32
Gordon Sherry	70	72	71	69	282	394.16
Marc Pendaries	69	72	70	71	282	394.16
John Mellor	70	71	70	71	282	394.16

AXA Grand Final

Clube de Golfe de Belas, Lisbon, Portugal — October 21-24
Par 36-36–72; 6,977 yards — purse, £75,000

	SCORES				TOTAL	MONEY
Jorge Berendt	69	67	71	68	275	£12,310
Warren Bennett	67	69	71	68	275	8,200
(Berendt defeated Bennett on fourth extra hole.)						
Per Nyman	75	68	65	68	276	4,400
Markus Brier	70	69	69	70	278	3,300
Fredrik Lindgren	73	68	70	67	278	3,300
Kevin Carissimi	74	67	70	69	280	2,100
Scott Watson	70	67	71	72	280	2,100
Jose Manuel Lara	69	66	72	73	280	2,100
Elliot Boult	68	67	73	73	281	1,575
Jesus Maria Arruti	74	67	70	70	281	1,575
Henrik Bjornstad	72	69	72	69	282	1,385
Francisco Valera	68	72	70	72	282	1,385
Christian Cevaer	73	70	70	69	282	1,385
Jeremy Robinson	74	69	73	66	282	1,385
Mikael Lundberg	72	72	66	72	282	1,385
Roger Winchester	70	71	69	72	282	1,385
Frederic Cupillard	74	73	67	69	283	1,180
Anders Hansen	74	69	71	69	283	1,180
John Bickerton	75	70	65	73	283	1,180
Soren Hansen	74	68	71	70	283	1,180
Marcello Santi	71	73	71	69	284	1,000
Raimo Sjoberg	72	72	72	68	284	1,000
Gary Emerson	71	74	68	71	284	1,000
Massimo Scarpa	70	73	73	68	284	1,000
John Senden	72	69	73	70	284	1,000
Mike Miller	76	68	70	71	285	880
Erik Andersson	73	72	69	72	286	787.50
Marten Olander	75	73	71	67	286	787.50
David R. Jones	76	68	73	69	286	787.50
Johan Rystrom	75	71	68	72	286	787.50

Asia/Japan Tours

Asian Tour

Ericsson Philippine Masters

Villamor Golf Club, Pasay City, Manila, Philippines — February 12-15
Par 36-36–72; 7,056 yards — purse, US$100,000

	SCORES				TOTAL	MONEY
Frankie Minoza	69	67	70	71	277	US$16,667
Rodrigo Cuello	68	69	69	72	278	11,000
Gary Murphy	78	70	71	66	285	5,133.33
Mars Pucay	72	72	68	73	285	5,133.33
Brad Wilson	70	67	75	73	285	5,133.33
Jim Rutledge	74	71	70	71	286	2,610
Felix Casas	68	74	72	72	286	2,610
Danny Mijovic	70	71	73	72	286	2,610
Choi Gwang-soo	70	68	76	72	286	2,610
Grant Masson	74	71	72	70	287	1,733.33
Brian Quinn	75	70	71	71	287	1,733.33
Scott Rowe	78	69	68	72	287	1,733.33
Rodolfo Cuello, Jr.	71	73	75	69	288	1,580
Hiroshi Ueda	72	70	76	70	288	1,580
Christian Chernock	71	74	71	73	289	1,480
Ernie Rellon	71	73	72	73	289	1,480
Benjamin Magada	71	72	73	73	289	1,480
Roger Antonio	71	73	73	73	290	1,340
Danny Zarate	73	70	72	75	290	1,340
David Morland	74	68	73	75	290	1,340
Edgar Ababa	70	70	74	76	290	1,340
Eric Epperson	74	74	75	66	291	1,180
Mike Tschetter	74	74	73	70	291	1,180
Rob Moss	77	71	71	72	291	1,180
David Hutchens	74	73	72	72	291	1,180
Bobby Kalinowski	71	76	71	74	292	1,080
*Juami Rocha	75	72	74	71	292	
Melvin Eso	73	75	72	73	293	960
Andrew Raitt	72	75	72	74	293	960
Dan Cruz	73	74	71	75	293	960
Tsai Chi-huang	75	69	74	75	293	960
Chris Tidland	70	73	75	75	293	980
*Gerald Rosales	73	70	75	75	293	

Benson and Hedges Malaysian Open

Saujana Golf & Country Club, Subang, Malaysia — February 19-22
Par 36-36–72; 7,233 yards — purse, US$300,000

	SCORES				TOTAL	MONEY
Edward Fryatt	70	69	70	69	278	US$50,010
Lee Westwood	70	72	67	69	278	33,000

(Fryatt defeated Westwood on second extra hole.)

	SCORES				TOTAL	MONEY
Kang Wook-soon	72	73	66	68	279	16,800
Christian Chernock	68	71	71	69	279	16,800
Paul McGinley	70	69	71	70	280	12,600
Felix Casas	71	69	75	67	282	8,460
Rodrigo Cuello	69	71	73	69	282	8,460
Frankie Minoza	71	66	74	71	282	8,460
Mike Cunning	73	69	74	67	283	5,520
Marty Schiene	72	71	69	71	283	5,520
Philip Jonas	68	69	73	73	283	5,520
Park Nam-sin	77	69	69	69	284	4,820
Bobby Elliot	70	72	71	71	284	4,820
Thomas Kalinowski	68	70	71	75	284	4,820
Choi Kyung-ju	72	72	70	71	285	4,320
Thomas Bjorn	70	73	71	71	285	4,320
Jerry Smith	71	69	72	73	285	4,320
Choi Sang-ho	65	75	72	73	285	4,320
David Morland	69	70	71	75	285	4,320
Bobby Kalinowski	73	69	75	69	286	3,660
Brian Guetz	72	72	70	72	286	3,660
Chang Tse-peng	68	71	75	72	286	3,660
Gerry Norquist	71	71	71	73	286	3,660
Randy Wylie	70	71	72	73	286	3,660
Yasuharu Imano	70	72	68	76	286	3,660
Mike Tschetter	71	75	72	69	287	3,180
Scott Rowe	68	72	72	75	287	3,180
Danny Mijovic	74	73	74	67	288	2,648.57
Hajime Tanaka	74	73	72	69	288	2,648.57
Nam Young-woo	72	71	73	72	288	2,648.57
Stuart Holmes	73	68	75	72	288	2,648.57
Ian Garbutt	70	73	71	74	288	2,648.57
Rick Todd	72	69	73	74	288	2,648.57
Raul Fretes	69	69	72	78	288	2,648.57

Rolex Masters

Singapore Island Country Club, Bukit Course, Singapore — February 26-March 1
Par 35-36–71; 6,788 yards — purse, US$300,000

	SCORES				TOTAL	MONEY
Frankie Minoza	68	69	67	69	273	US$50,010
Jim Rutledge	69	71	70	64	274	33,000
Mike Tschetter	70	68	69	68	275	18,600
Juan Nutt	70	69	69	68	276	12,600
Gavin Vearing	69	69	70	68	276	12,600
Ian Leggatt	68	69	70	69	276	12,600
Kyi Hla Han	67	66	72	72	277	7,590
Park Nam-sin	68	69	67	73	277	7,590
Jerry Smith	68	74	68	68	278	5,385
Jerry Wood	68	67	71	72	278	5,385
Rick Todd	69	69	67	73	278	5,385
Rob Moss	67	70	66	75	278	5,385
Raul Fretes	68	71	71	69	279	4,620
Danny Zarate	71	68	70	70	279	4,620
Gerry Norquist	68	70	70	71	279	4,620
Scott Rowe	66	66	73	74	279	4,620
Dominique Boulet	70	72	69	69	280	4,320
Tim Straub	70	67	76	68	281	3,900

	SCORES				TOTAL	MONEY
Lin Keng-chi	68	74	69	70	281	3,900
Hidezumi Shirakata	70	68	73	70	281	3,900
Lin Chien-bing	71	69	69	72	281	3,900
Dean Wilson	70	70	69	72	281	3,900
Tim Balmer	70	68	70	73	281	3,900
Randy Wylie	71	72	72	67	282	3,240
Andrew Raitt	71	70	74	67	282	3,240
Gary Rusnak	71	69	73	69	282	3,240
Eric Epperson	66	74	70	72	282	3,240
Chen Tze-chung	70	70	69	73	282	3,240
Edward Fryatt	73	70	73	67	283	2,466.67
Arjun Atwal	67	74	74	68	283	2,466.67
David Morland	73	70	71	69	283	2,466.67
Kim Jong-duk	70	70	74	69	283	2,466.67
Carlos Espinosa	73	68	71	71	283	2,466.67
Aaron Bengoechea	69	72	70	72	283	2,466.67
Brian Wilson	70	72	68	73	283	2,466.67
Hiroshi Ueda	70	69	71	73	283	2,466.67
Periasamy Gunasagaran	70	68	69	76	283	2,466.67

Ericsson Philippine Open

Riviera Golf & Country Club, Fred Couples Course,
Silang, Cavita, Philippines
Par 36-36–72; 7,056 yards

March 19-22
purse, US$250,000

	SCORES				TOTAL	MONEY
Frankie Minoza	66	69	71	72	278	US$41,675
Christian Chernock	67	71	67	75	280	27,500
Jerry Smith	71	71	70	70	282	15,500
Rodrigo Cuello	71	69	69	74	283	12,500
Raul Fretes	69	75	72	68	284	10,500
Jim Rutledge	74	72	71	68	285	7,050
Danny Zarate	67	75	73	70	285	7,050
Philip Jonas	73	68	72	72	285	7,050
Greg Hanrahan	70	67	73	76	286	4,750
Chang Tse-peng	68	67	75	76	286	4,750
*Hong Chia-yuh	73	71	69	73	286	
Carlos Espinosa	73	72	72	70	287	4,150
Rob Moss	73	70	72	72	287	4,150
Scott Rowe	71	70	72	74	287	4,150
Andrew Pitts	73	68	73	74	288	3,750
Rick Todd	74	70	69	75	288	3,750
Rick Gibson	69	74	70	75	288	3,750
Tom Kalinowski	72	73	66	77	288	3,750
David Morland	77	68	73	71	289	3,200
Hans Albertsson	76	69	72	72	289	3,200
Danny Mijovic	68	76	73	72	289	3,200
Ted Gleason	76	70	70	73	289	3,200
Ted Purdy	74	72	68	75	289	3,200
Bobby Elliot	72	72	70	75	289	3,200
Chung Joon	72	68	73	76	289	3,200
Park Unho	75	71	74	70	290	2,550
Stephen Summers	75	72	71	72	290	2,550
John Senden	73	72	71	74	290	2,550
Mo Joong-kyung	75	68	73	74	290	2,550

	SCORES				TOTAL	MONEY
Brian Wilson	74	70	68	78	290	2,550
Willie De Tomas	70	74	68	78	290	2,550

Maekyung LG Fashion Open

Lake Side Country Club, West Course, Seoul, Korea — April 30-May 3
Par 36-36–72; 7,052 yards — purse, US$254,360
(Third round cancelled — rain.)

	SCORES			TOTAL	MONEY
Scott Rowe	67	68	69	204	US$42,401.81
Kwon Young-suk	70	68	70	208	27,979.60
Raul Fretes	67	74	68	209	15,770.32
Choi Kyung-ju	71	70	69	210	12,718.00
Ian Leggatt	72	71	69	212	9,665.68
Park Nam-sin	69	69	74	212	9,665.68
Rodrigo Cuello	70	77	68	215	5,029.06
Kim Jong-duk	71	73	71	215	5,029.06
Chung Joon	74	69	72	215	5,029.06
Carlos Espinosa	72	71	72	215	5,029.06
Gerry Norquist	72	71	72	215	5,029.06
Philip Jonas	71	72	72	215	5,029.06
Choi Gwang-soo	68	74	73	215	5,029.06
Christian Chernock	71	75	70	216	3,917.15
Hideto Shigenobu	71	73	72	216	3,917.15
Tim Straub	73	71	73	217	3,662.78
Lee Joon-suk	71	73	73	217	3,662.78
Mo Joong-kyung	71	72	74	217	3,662.78
David Morland	76	74	68	218	3,357.55
Fredrick Mansson	74	72	72	218	3,357.55
Kim Wan-tae	72	71	75	218	3,357.55
Takeshi Kibamoto	71	79	69	219	3,001.45
Lim Jin-han	73	76	70	219	3,001.45
Rob Moss	74	73	72	219	3,001.45
Nam Young-woo	73	73	73	219	3,001.45
Jim Rutledge	73	77	70	220	2,266.12
Choi Sang-ho	74	75	71	220	2,266.12
Ted Gleason	74	74	72	220	2,266.12
Kang Bum-suk	74	74	72	220	2,266.12
Bradley King	70	78	72	220	2,266.12
Clay Devers	74	73	73	220	2,266.12
Olle Nordberg	73	74	73	220	2,266.12
Moon Sung-wook	73	74	73	220	2,266.12
Kang Wook-soon	72	74	74	220	2,266.12
Rick Todd	75	70	75	220	2,266.12
Ted Purdy	69	71	80	220	2,266.12
*Kim Sung-yoon	76	73	71	220	
*Chung Sung-han	73	73	74	220	

Johnnie Walker Super Tour

Palm Resort, Johor, Malaysia — November 10-15
Par 36-36–72; 6,863 yards — purse, US$350,000

Thai Country Club, Bangkok, Thailand
Par 36-36–72; 6,975 yards

Ta Shee Golf & Country Club, Taipei, Taiwan
Par 36-36–72; 7,004 yards

Mission Hills Golf Club, Shenzhen, China
Par 36-36–72; 6,970 yards

	SCORES				TOTAL	MONEY
Vijay Singh	70	66	71	62	269	US$100,000
Jesper Parnevik	68	70	67	66	271	60,000
Ernie Els	70	68	71	69	278	50,000
Brian Watts	70	69	71	69	279	40,000
Felix Casas	71	71	69	71	282	30,000
Prayad Marksaeng	68	71	72	74	285	25,000
Chang Tse-peng	66	73	71	76	286	20,000
Marimuthu Ramayah	69	71	75	76	291	15,000
Laura Davies	79	78	73	78	308	10,000

Japan PGA Tour

Token Corporation Cup

Kedoin Golf Club, Kagoshima — March 12-15
Par 36-36–72; 7,115 yards — purse, ¥110,000,000

	SCORES				TOTAL	MONEY
Hajime Meshiai	70	71	67	64	272	¥19,800,000
Masashi Ozaki	67	72	65	69	273	9,900,000
Shoichi Kuwabara	72	67	66	70	275	6,732,000
Seiki Okuda	69	69	68	70	276	3,663,000
Shigeki Maruyama	68	70	69	69	276	3,663,000
Frankie Minoza	68	66	71	71	276	3,663,000
Brian Watts	70	68	70	68	276	3,663,000
Carlos Franco	70	71	67	68	276	3,663,000
Ikuo Shirahama	68	70	70	69	277	2,163,150
Tsukasa Watanabe	71	67	69	70	277	2,163,150
Koki Idoki	68	69	68	72	277	2,163,150
Takeshi Sakiyama	70	70	69	68	277	2,163,150
Peter McWhinney	72	67	70	69	278	1,544,400
Todd Hamilton	70	68	67	73	278	1,544,400
Brandt Jobe	71	70	68	69	278	1,544,400
Kaname Yokoo	70	71	68	70	279	1,306,800

	SCORES				TOTAL	MONEY
Hideki Kase	70	69	70	71	280	1,108,800
David Smail	71	71	66	72	280	1,108,800
Takao Nogami	70	69	71	70	280	1,108,800
Tateo Ozaki	71	71	68	71	281	950,400
Hirofumi Miyase	71	72	69	69	281	950,400
Steve Conran	70	70	69	72	281	950,400
Eduardo Herrera	70	68	73	71	282	851,400
Hidemichi Tanaka	65	75	69	73	282	851,400
Keiichiro Fukabori	73	69	67	73	282	851,400
*Hiroshi Kuniyoshi	73	69	68	72	282	
Yukihiro Yamamoto	70	73	70	70	283	792,000
Tsuyoshi Yoneyama	73	69	67	74	283	792,000
Roger Mackay	71	71	72	69	283	792,000
Saburo Fujiki	69	72	69	74	284	732,600
Mitsutaka Kusakabe	71	73	72	68	284	732,600
Kenichi Kuboya	70	70	70	74	284	732,600

Daido Drinko Shizuoka Open

Shizuoka Country Club, Hamaoka Course, Shizuoka — March 19-22
Par 36-36–72; 6,897 yards — purse, ¥75,000,000
(Second round cancelled — high winds.)

	SCORES			TOTAL	MONEY
Eduardo Herrera	66	69	68	203	¥13,500,000
Kaname Yokoo	65	68	71	204	6,750,000
Brian Watts	67	69	69	205	4,590,000
David Smail	67	68	72	207	2,790,000
Roger Mackay	70	70	67	207	2,790,000
Brandt Jobe	71	69	67	207	2,790,000
Yoshinori Kaneko	67	70	72	209	2,058,750
Chen Tze-chung	70	69	70	209	2,058,750
Nobuo Serizawa	69	66	75	210	1,552,500
Katsuyoshi Tomori	72	69	69	210	1,552,500
Peter McWhinney	64	73	73	210	1,552,500
Yoshitaka Yamamoto	70	72	69	211	1,143,000
Stewart Ginn	73	67	71	211	1,143,000
Shinichi Akiba	67	71	73	211	1,143,000
Takaaki Fukuzawa	74	71	67	212	826,200
Tatsuo Takasaki	72	72	68	212	826,200
Anthony Gilligan	68	72	72	212	826,200
Shoichi Kuwabara	69	72	71	212	826,200
Kim Jong-duk	70	66	76	212	826,200
Satoshi Higashi	72	72	69	213	605,571
Kiyoshi Murota	70	73	70	213	605,571
Toru Nakamura	71	68	74	213	605,571
Tsuyoshi Yoneyama	69	66	78	213	605,571
Daisuke Serizawa	70	72	71	213	605,571
Mitsutaka Kusakabe	69	71	73	213	605,571
Toru Taniguchi	73	67	73	213	605,571
Hideki Kase	71	71	72	214	487,800
Tsuneyuki Nakajima	71	70	73	214	487,800
Tsukasa Watanabe	69	71	74	214	487,800
Hirofumi Miyase	72	69	73	214	487,800
Hiroyuki Fujita	72	70	72	214	487,800
Naotoshi Nakamura	72	71	71	214	487,800
Shusaku Sugimoto	73	71	70	214	487,800

	SCORES			TOTAL	MONEY
David Ishii	72	71	71	214	487,800
Carlos Franco	70	72	72	214	487,800

Just System KSB Open

Ayutaki Country Club, Kagawa, Kyodo — March 26-29
Par 35-36–71; 6,718 yards — purse, ¥100,000,000

	SCORES				TOTAL	MONEY
Carlos Franco	70	65	67	65	267	¥18,000,000
Frankie Minoza	70	68	67	66	271	9,000,000
Brandt Jobe	75	70	66	64	275	6,120,000
Yoshinori Kaneko	73	66	69	68	276	3,960,000
Kim Jong-duk	71	72	66	67	276	3,960,000
Toshimitsu Izawa	69	70	68	70	277	2,767,500
Toshiyuki Hiyama	72	68	68	69	277	2,767,500
Rick Gibson	70	71	68	68	277	2,767,500
Brian Watts	70	67	73	67	277	2,767,500
Saburo Fujiki	71	70	69	68	278	1,623,000
Tsukasa Watanabe	72	70	69	67	278	1,623,000
Eduardo Herrera	74	68	67	69	278	1,623,000
Ryoken Kawagishi	72	69	68	69	278	1,623,000
Katsunori Kuwabara	72	71	69	66	278	1,623,000
Roger Mackay	71	68	69	70	278	1,623,000
Satoshi Higashi	73	69	69	68	279	996,000
Toru Suzuki	70	71	68	70	279	996,000
Yoshimitsu Fukuzawa	72	69	66	72	279	996,000
Shoichi Kuwabara	72	71	64	72	279	996,000
Kaname Yokoo	72	71	69	67	279	996,000
Takao Nogami	70	71	69	69	279	996,000
Hideyuki Sato	72	72	66	70	280	768,000
Nobuo Serizawa	72	72	67	69	280	768,000
Tsuneyuki Nakajima	70	72	69	69	280	768,000
Masanobu Kimura	69	74	69	68	280	768,000
Steve Conran	72	73	68	67	280	768,000
Chen Tze-chung	69	74	71	66	280	768,000
Hideki Kase	70	72	67	72	281	626,400
Katsunari Takahashi	70	72	71	68	281	626,400
Hideki Takamiya	74	71	67	69	281	626,400
Kiyoshi Murota	72	71	70	68	281	626,400
Katsuyoshi Tomori	69	72	72	68	281	626,400
Koki Idoki	73	71	68	69	281	626,400
Tsuyoshi Yoneyama	73	71	68	69	281	626,400
Mitsuo Harada	72	73	66	70	281	626,400
Hidemichi Tanaka	70	71	69	71	281	626,400
Kazuhiro Fukunaga	70	72	69	70	281	626,400

Descente Classic Munsingwear Cup

Taiheiyou Club, Ichihara Course, Chiba — April 2-5
Par 36-36–72; 6,796 yards — purse, ¥100,000,000

	SCORES				TOTAL	MONEY
Dinesh Chand	71	66	66	68	271	¥18,000,000
Hidemichi Tanaka	66	71	70	66	273	7,560,000

	SCORES				TOTAL	MONEY
Carlos Franco	73	66	67	67	273	7,560,000
Tatsuo Takasaki	68	70	70	66	274	4,320,000
Katsumasa Miyamoto	68	71	70	66	275	3,600,000
Brandt Jobe	72	68	70	66	276	3,240,000
Hideki Kase	70	67	65	75	277	2,124,000
Saburo Fujiki	71	68	68	70	277	2,124,000
Kiyoshi Murota	72	68	69	68	277	2,124,000
Keiichiro Fukabori	72	68	68	69	277	2,124,000
Shusaku Sugimoto	72	71	64	70	277	2,124,000
Chen Tze-chung	66	68	71	72	277	2,124,000
Kim Jong-duk	72	68	70	67	277	2,124,000
Satoshi Higashi	72	72	68	66	278	1,350,000
Tsuyoshi Yoneyama	71	70	67	70	278	1,350,000
Ryoken Kawagishi	70	66	71	72	279	1,053,000
Takeshi Sakiyama	70	73	68	68	279	1,053,000
Zaw Moe	71	69	69	70	279	1,053,000
Kaname Yokoo	73	69	70	67	279	1,053,000
Tsukasa Watanabe	72	69	67	72	280	846,000
Masahiro Kuramoto	72	68	70	70	280	846,000
Masayuki Kawamura	70	68	70	72	280	846,000
Eduardo Herrera	73	71	68	68	280	846,000
Nobuo Serizawa	69	71	69	72	281	756,000
Toru Suzuki	75	68	70	68	281	756,000
Frankie Minoza	72	70	67	72	281	756,000
Mitsuo Harada	72	73	70	67	282	711,000
Taichi Teshima	72	65	75	70	282	711,000
Hideki Takamiya	73	71	73	66	283	675,000
Stewart Ginn	71	73	70	69	283	675,000

Tsuruya Open

Sports Shinko Country Club, Yamanohara Course,
Kawanishi, Hyogo
Par 36-36–72; 6,827 yards

April 16-19
purse, ¥100,000,000

	SCORES				TOTAL	MONEY
Katsumasa Miyamoto	69	65	69	68	271	¥18,000,000
Peter McWhinney	68	67	67	70	272	9,000,000
Zaw Moe	67	68	67	71	273	6,120,000
Naomichi Ozaki	72	67	66	69	274	3,510,000
Tsuneyuki Nakajima	71	70	67	66	274	3,510,000
Saburo Fujiki	72	64	66	72	274	3,510,000
Kiyoshi Maita	70	68	67	69	274	3,510,000
Hidemichi Tanaka	71	66	70	68	275	2,475,000
Steve Conran	73	64	70	68	275	2,475,000
Katsunari Takahashi	71	72	67	66	276	1,935,000
Seiki Okuda	70	66	70	70	276	1,935,000
Kazuhiro Takami	68	69	71	69	277	1,220,000
Yasunori Ida	69	67	71	70	277	1,220,000
Anthony Gilligan	72	72	68	65	277	1,220,000
Katsunori Kuwabara	68	73	66	70	277	1,220,000
Kazuhiro Fukunaga	73	70	69	65	277	1,220,000
Hiroyuki Fujita	72	70	69	66	277	1,220,000
Kazuhiko Hosokawa	69	69	72	67	277	1,220,000
Yeh Chang-ting	74	67	66	70	277	1,220,000
David Smail	70	71	68	68	277	1,220,000
Hideyuki Sato	69	66	71	72	278	802,800

	SCORES				TOTAL	MONEY
Ikuo Shirahama	71	71	67	69	278	802,800
Koki Idoki	70	72	67	69	278	802,800
Ryoken Kawagishi	71	71	65	71	278	802,800
Taichi Teshima	68	66	70	74	278	802,800
Yoshinori Kaneko	71	68	70	70	279	702,000
Mitsuo Harada	74	69	69	67	279	702,000
Shoichi Kuwabara	72	69	67	71	279	702,000
Shinichi Yokota	72	67	66	74	279	702,000
Todd Hamilton	70	72	65	72	279	702,000

Kirin Open

Ibaragi Golf Club, East Course, Ina, Ibaragi — April 23-26
Par 35-36–71; 7,078 yards — purse, ¥100,000,000

	SCORES				TOTAL	MONEY
Frankie Minoza	71	66	69	73	279	¥18,000,000
Tsukasa Watanabe	70	69	69	72	280	7,300,000
Hidemichi Tanaka	75	66	69	70	280	7,300,000
Brian Watts	75	69	68	68	280	7,300,000
Masashi Ozaki	72	70	68	72	282	3,800,000
Kazuhiro Takami	70	68	73	71	282	3,800,000
Shoichi Kuwabara	71	71	71	70	283	2,534,000
Katsumasa Miyamoto	76	69	68	70	283	2,534,000
Carlos Franco	70	67	75	71	283	2,534,000
Ian Leggatt	71	67	69	76	283	2,534,000
Matthew Goggin	72	68	74	69	283	2,534,000
Shigeki Maruyama	71	66	73	74	284	1,600,000
Zaw Moe	73	70	70	71	284	1,600,000
Roger Mackay	74	71	68	71	284	1,600,000
Edward Fryatt	72	67	75	70	284	1,600,000
Masanobu Kimura	74	69	69	73	285	1,230,000
Peter Senior	73	72	69	71	285	1,230,000
Hajime Meshiai	75	69	71	71	286	1,090,000
Yeh Chang-ting	75	67	71	74	287	973,000
Felix Casas	76	71	66	74	287	973,000
Tim Straub	75	71	72	69	287	973,000
Katsunori Kuwabara	76	68	72	72	288	879,000
David Ishii	75	70	71	72	288	879,000
Satoshi Higashi	74	73	74	68	289	779,000
Takaaki Fukuzawa	76	70	71	72	289	779,000
Yoshinori Mizumaki	75	72	68	74	289	779,000
Hiroyuki Fujita	73	73	71	72	289	779,000
Mike Cunning	76	72	69	72	289	779,000
Mike Tschetter	77	67	73	72	289	779,000
Scott Rowe	77	68	71	73	289	779,000

Chunichi Crowns

Nagoya Golf Club, Wago Course, Togo, Aichi — April 30-May 3
Par 35-35–70; 6,502 yards — purse, ¥120,000,000

	SCORES				TOTAL	MONEY
Davis Love III	64	71	67	67	269	¥21,600,000
Masanobu Kimura	69	68	71	69	277	7,776,000

	SCORES				TOTAL	MONEY
Rick Gibson	66	70	71	70	277	7,776,000
Brian Watts	72	68	67	70	277	7,776,000
Masashi Ozaki	73	69	65	71	278	4,104,000
Tsuneyuki Nakajima	67	73	71	67	278	4,104,000
Tsuyoshi Yoneyama	72	68	71	69	280	3,294,000
Zaw Moe	68	72	70	70	280	3,294,000
Tateo Ozaki	70	71	72	68	281	2,646,000
Kaname Yokoo	69	73	72	67	281	2,646,000
Hideki Kase	70	73	71	68	282	1,771,200
Nobuo Serizawa	71	72	70	69	282	1,771,200
Tsukasa Watanabe	72	72	70	68	282	1,771,200
Ryoken Kawagishi	69	70	70	73	282	1,771,200
David Smail	73	70	69	70	282	1,771,200
Frankie Minoza	68	74	74	66	282	1,771,200
Seiichi Kanai	71	72	72	68	283	1,123,200
Satoshi Higashi	71	72	69	71	283	1,123,200
Seiki Okuda	67	73	70	73	283	1,123,200
Mitsuo Harada	72	71	69	71	283	1,123,200
Toru Suzuki	72	69	71	71	283	1,123,200
Takao Nogami	71	70	70	72	283	1,123,200
Kiyoshi Maita	72	72	70	70	284	939,600
Justin Leonard	69	71	73	71	284	939,600
Kiyoshi Murota	71	70	73	72	286	842,400
Haruo Yasuda	73	72	77	64	286	842,400
Yoshitaka Yamamoto	69	74	72	71	286	842,400
Koki Idoki	69	69	72	76	286	842,400
Shoichi Kuwabara	71	74	69	72	286	842,400
Kazuhiko Hosokawa	72	75	72	67	286	842,400
Yeh Chang-ting	69	74	72	71	286	842,400

Fuji Sankei Classic

Kawana Hotel Golf Club, Ito, Shizuoka — May 7-10
Par 35-36–71; 6,694 yards — purse, ¥120,000,000

	SCORES				TOTAL	MONEY
Carlos Franco	69	70	67	69	275	¥21,600,000
Chen Tze-chung	70	69	70	67	276	10,800,000
Steve Conran	68	76	67	66	277	7,344,000
Frankie Minoza	71	70	69	68	278	4,752,000
Brandt Jobe	70	72	72	64	278	4,752,000
Tateo Ozaki	69	71	69	70	279	3,888,000
Tsuneyuki Nakajima	69	74	68	69	280	2,970,000
Masayuki Kawamura	70	72	68	70	280	2,970,000
Shoichi Kuwabara	69	71	71	69	280	2,970,000
Shigemasa Higaki	69	72	72	67	280	2,970,000
Eduardo Herrera	71	75	68	67	281	2,160,000
Hideki Kase	70	72	72	68	282	1,760,400
Saburo Fujiki	73	69	69	71	282	1,760,400
Shoichi Yamamoto	69	71	69	73	282	1,760,400
Todd Hamilton	68	72	68	74	282	1,760,400
Yoshinori Kaneko	68	69	71	75	283	1,139,400
Hiroshi Ueda	72	71	73	67	283	1,139,400
Satoshi Higashi	70	71	72	70	283	1,139,400
Seiki Okuda	71	71	73	68	283	1,139,400
Tatsuo Takasaki	70	69	75	69	283	1,139,400
Mitsuo Harada	73	70	68	72	283	1,139,400

	SCORES				TOTAL	MONEY
Hirofumi Miyase	72	71	70	70	283	1,139,400
Mitsutaka Kusakabe	64	76	69	74	283	1,139,400
Shinichi Yokota	67	72	74	71	284	928,800
Nobuo Serizawa	75	67	74	69	285	874,800
Katsunari Takahashi	71	69	74	71	285	874,800
Akihito Yokoyama	70	70	71	74	285	874,800
Toru Suzuki	71	70	74	70	285	874,800
Hajime Meshiai	74	69	72	71	286	820,800
Masanobu Kimura	74	72	69	72	287	758,592
Koki Idoki	73	69	76	69	287	758,592
Toshimitsu Izawa	73	69	72	73	287	758,592
Keiichiro Fukabori	71	71	72	73	287	758,592
Shusaku Sugimoto	72	70	72	73	287	758,592

Japan PGA Championship

Grandage Golf Club, Yoshino, Nara — May 14-17
Par 36-36–72; 7,082 yards — purse, ¥120,000,000

	SCORES				TOTAL	MONEY
Brandt Jobe	70	70	72	68	280	¥21,600,000
Masashi Ozaki	68	72	72	68	280	10,800,000
(Jobe defeated Ozaki on first extra hole.)						
Yasuharu Imano	72	69	72	69	282	6,264,000
David Smail	70	71	71	70	282	6,264,000
Keiichiro Fukabori	69	71	70	73	283	4,320,000
Yeh Chang-ting	67	71	74	72	284	3,888,000
Seiki Okuda	71	68	76	70	285	3,456,000
Toshiaki Odate	65	74	73	75	287	3,132,000
Yoshinori Mizumaki	68	72	75	73	288	2,808,000
Masanobu Kimura	71	70	75	73	289	2,026,080
Mitsuo Harada	68	73	76	72	289	2,026,080
Todd Hamilton	75	68	71	75	289	2,026,080
Brian Watts	67	74	74	74	289	2,026,080
Carlos Franco	70	70	78	71	289	2,026,080
Naomichi Ozaki	71	71	77	71	290	1,246,628
Yoshinori Kaneko	73	70	72	75	290	1,246,628
Masayuki Kawamura	72	71	76	71	290	1,246,628
Toru Suzuki	70	73	77	70	290	1,246,628
Ryoken Kawagishi	73	73	71	73	290	1,246,628
Zaw Moe	76	69	74	71	290	1,246,628
Frankie Minoza	73	70	75	72	290	1,246,628
Satoshi Higashi	74	72	75	70	291	945,000
Yasunori Ida	69	72	79	71	291	945,000
Yoshimitsu Fukuzawa	73	70	74	74	291	945,000
Kaname Yokoo	69	71	77	74	291	945,000
Tatsuo Takasaki	76	69	74	73	292	864,000
Toshimitsu Izawa	68	74	71	79	292	864,000
Stewart Ginn	74	72	74	72	292	864,000
Hideyuki Sato	74	72	73	74	293	799,200
Hidemichi Tanaka	79	68	69	77	293	799,200
Katsumasa Miyamoto	70	73	76	74	293	799,200

Ube Kosan Open

Ube Country Club, Mannenike East Course, Ajisu, Yamaguchi
Par 36-36–72; 6,937 yards

May 21-24
purse, ¥100,000,000

	SCORES				TOTAL	MONEY
Brandt Jobe	69	64	68	70	271	¥18,000,000
Shigeki Maruyama	70	69	68	66	273	9,000,000
Hiroyuki Fujita	68	70	69	67	274	6,120,000
Keiichiro Fukabori	73	66	69	67	275	3,960,000
Kazuhiro Fukunaga	66	71	70	68	275	3,960,000
Kazuhiko Hosokawa	66	69	72	70	277	3,060,000
Yeh Chang-ting	67	67	72	71	277	3,060,000
Haruo Yasuda	70	70	70	68	278	2,095,200
Masayuki Kawamura	68	71	69	70	278	2,095,200
Daisuke Serizawa	72	69	68	69	278	2,095,200
Stewart Ginn	73	68	71	66	278	2,095,200
Roger Mackay	71	71	69	67	278	2,095,200
Nobuo Serizawa	73	62	72	72	279	1,296,000
Mitoshi Tomita	70	69	71	69	279	1,296,000
Yoshitaka Yamamoto	69	68	71	71	279	1,296,000
Anthony Gilligan	71	70	71	67	279	1,296,000
Richard Backwell	69	71	69	70	279	1,296,000
Yoshinori Mizumaki	72	69	69	70	280	927,000
Peter McWhinney	71	71	71	67	280	927,000
Shinichi Yokota	70	70	71	69	280	927,000
Yasuharu Imano	72	69	66	73	280	927,000
Kazuhiro Takami	70	71	68	72	281	777,600
Saburo Fujiki	70	68	71	72	281	777,600
Takenori Hiraishi	70	68	71	72	281	777,600
Toyokazu Hioki	71	69	74	67	281	777,600
Naotoshi Nakamura	69	72	72	68	281	777,600
Hikaru Emoto	68	71	74	69	282	642,600
Kiyoshi Maita	69	71	75	67	282	642,600
Tomohiro Maruyama	74	69	70	69	282	642,600
Yoshikazu Yokoshima	72	70	70	70	282	642,600
Yoshikazu Sakamoto	69	71	72	70	282	642,600
Noboru Fujiike	71	71	69	71	282	642,600
Hidezumi Shirakata	69	69	77	67	282	642,600
Taichi Teshima	71	71	75	65	282	642,600
Katsumasa Kiyamoto	69	70	72	71	282	642,600
Todd Hamilton	72	69	73	68	282	642,600

Mitsubishi Galant

Tosa Country Club, Yasu, Kochi
Par 36-35–71; 6,692 yards

May 28-31
purse, ¥120,000,000

	SCORES				TOTAL	MONEY
Toru Taniguchi	71	65	65	67	268	¥21,600,000
Kazuhiko Hosokawa	69	65	67	68	269	10,800,000
Masashi Ozaki	68	68	67	69	272	7,344,000
Tsuyoshi Yoneyama	69	71	64	70	274	4,752,000
Shigemasa Higaki	68	72	64	70	274	4,752,000
Yoshinori Mizumaki	72	67	67	70	276	3,321,000
Shigeki Maruyama	69	64	70	73	276	3,321,000
Takao Nogami	70	68	69	69	276	3,321,000

	SCORES				TOTAL	MONEY
Roger Mackay	70	69	71	66	276	3,321,000
Masahiro Kuramoto	69	67	71	70	277	2,322,000
Peter Teravainen	66	70	69	72	277	2,322,000
Daisuke Serizawa	66	71	71	70	278	1,900,800
Hidemichi Tanaka	72	68	68	70	278	1,900,800
Nobuo Serizawa	68	69	73	69	279	1,490,400
Keiichiro Fukabori	70	67	71	71	279	1,490,400
Katsunori Kuwabara	66	68	67	78	279	1,490,400
David Smail	68	70	71	70	279	1,490,400
Hideyuki Sato	72	69	69	70	280	1,137,600
Noboru Fujiike	60	71	72	77	280	1,137,600
Toru Suzuki	70	68	71	71	280	1,137,600
Ikuo Shirahama	68	69	73	71	281	914,400
Tommy Nakajima	69	71	68	73	281	914,400
Nobumitsu Yuhara	67	71	70	73	281	914,400
Akihito Yokoyama	70	70	69	72	281	914,400
Seiki Okuda	70	70	67	74	281	914,400
Keiji Teshima	73	69	67	72	281	914,400
Shoichi Kuwabara	68	70	72	71	281	914,400
Stewart Ginn	69	68	72	72	281	914,400
David Ishii	72	70	70	69	281	914,400
Nobuhito Sato	70	68	74	70	282	777,600
Toyokazu Hioki	72	68	69	73	282	777,600
Yasuharu Imano	69	69	68	76	282	777,600

JCB Classic Sendai

Omotezao Kokusai Golf Club, Shibata, Miyagi — June 4-7
Par 36-35–71; 6,651 yards — purse, ¥100,000,000

	SCORES				TOTAL	MONEY
Yoshinori Mizumaki	68	66	68	68	270	¥18,000,000
Shigeki Maruyama	69	70	66	66	271	9,000,000
Hidemichi Tanaka	69	71	67	65	272	5,220,000
Lin Keng-chi	69	69	69	65	272	5,220,000
Koki Idoki	67	68	72	66	273	3,600,000
Masashi Ozaki	69	69	70	66	274	3,060,000
Kim Jong-duk	71	69	69	65	274	3,060,000
Katsunari Takahashi	70	66	73	66	275	2,475,000
Kenichi Kuboya	70	67	72	66	275	2,475,000
Kazuhiko Hosokawa	73	66	69	68	276	1,935,000
Kaname Yokoo	68	69	70	69	276	1,935,000
Shuichi Sano	74	69	64	70	277	1,524,000
Toshimitsu Izawa	71	71	69	66	277	1,524,000
Hsieh Chin-sheng	69	70	69	69	277	1,524,000
Tateo Ozaki	72	71	67	68	278	1,068,000
Nobuo Serizawa	66	70	72	70	278	1,068,000
Satoshi Higashi	72	69	69	68	278	1,068,000
Tatsuo Takasaki	66	71	71	70	278	1,068,000
Shoichi Kuwabara	71	70	70	67	278	1,068,000
Shinichi Yokota	68	70	70	70	278	1,068,000
Takaaki Fukuzawa	67	68	72	72	279	802,800
Tetsu Nishikawa	71	64	72	72	279	802,800
Toshiaki Odate	69	71	73	66	279	802,800
Katsunori Kuwabara	73	69	67	70	279	802,800
Shusaku Sugimoto	68	72	73	66	279	802,800
Saburo Fujiki	71	70	70	69	280	693,000

	SCORES				TOTAL	MONEY
Tomohiro Maruyama	69	67	76	68	280	693,000
Masanobu Kimura	74	68	72	66	280	693,000
Seiki Okuda	72	69	69	70	280	693,000
Mamoru Osanai	70	65	76	69	280	693,000
David Smail	73	70	70	67	280	693,000

Sapporo Tokyu Open

Sapporo Kokusai Country Club, Kitahiroshima, Hokkaido — June 11-14
Par 36-36–72; 6,949 yards — purse, ¥100,000,000

	SCORES				TOTAL	MONEY
Toru Suzuki	65	69	69	69	272	¥18,000,000
David Ishii	70	66	70	68	274	9,000,000
Carlos Franco	65	68	72	70	275	6,120,000
Hajime Meshiai	68	70	70	68	276	3,960,000
Kaname Yokoo	66	70	71	69	276	3,960,000
Masayuki Kawamura	73	69	69	66	277	2,910,000
Tsuyoshi Yoneyama	65	68	72	72	277	2,910,000
Shingo Katayama	68	73	70	66	277	2,910,000
Atsushi Takamatsu	68	71	69	70	278	1,966,500
Yoshimitsu Fukuzawa	67	68	71	72	278	1,966,500
Toru Taniguchi	66	71	69	70	278	1,966,500
Frankie Minoza	66	71	72	69	278	1,966,500
Masayoshi Yamazoe	71	67	70	71	279	1,458,000
Hsieh Chin-sheng	67	75	67	70	279	1,458,000
Katsunari Takahashi	68	68	75	69	280	1,012,500
Kazuhiro Takami	70	72	70	68	280	1,012,500
Satoshi Higashi	70	72	70	68	280	1,012,500
Saburo Fujiki	69	68	70	73	280	1,012,500
Katsunori Kuwabara	70	69	67	74	280	1,012,500
Shinichi Yokota	67	72	70	71	280	1,012,500
Shigemasa Higaki	70	69	71	70	280	1,012,500
David Smail	68	68	74	70	280	1,012,500
Tsukasa Watanabe	69	73	71	68	281	747,000
Masanobu Kimura	69	70	69	73	281	747,000
Shoichi Kuwabara	71	71	68	71	281	747,000
Stewart Ginn	67	69	73	72	281	747,000
Hiroyuki Fujita	72	67	72	70	281	747,000
Nobuhito Sato	70	71	71	69	281	747,000
Hideyuki Sato	69	71	70	72	282	666,000
Mitsutaka Kusakabe	70	68	71	73	282	666,000
Dinesh Chand	71	71	70	70	282	666,000

Yomiuri Open

Yomiuri Country Club, Nishinomiya, Hyogo — June 18-21
Par 36-36–72; 7,035 yards — purse, ¥50,000,000
(Third and fourth rounds cancelled — rain.)

	SCORES		TOTAL	MONEY
Brian Watts	66	68	134	¥9,000,000
Kaname Yokoo	66	69	135	4,500,000
Satoshi Higashi	70	66	136	2,340,000
Shigeki Maruyama	68	68	136	2,340,000

	SCORES		TOTAL	MONEY
Katsumasa Miyamoto	69	67	136	2,340,000
Toru Suzuki	65	72	137	1,620,000
Hideyuki Sato	70	68	138	1,237,500
Yoshinori Mizumaki	68	70	138	1,237,500
Frankie Minoza	68	70	138	1,237,500
Kim Jong-duk	71	67	138	1,237,500
Hsieh Chin-sheng	69	70	139	766,800
Katsunori Kuwabara	71	68	139	766,800
Taichi Teshima	72	67	139	766,800
Kenichi Kuboya	72	67	139	766,800
Mamoru Osanai	73	66	139	766,800
Ikuo Shirahama	74	66	140	486,000
Tsuyoshi Yoneyama	70	70	140	486,000
Shoichi Kuwabara	70	70	140	486,000
Hidezumi Shirakata	70	70	140	486,000
Kazuhiko Hosokawa	68	72	140	486,000
Yasuharu Imano	71	69	140	486,000
David Ishii	70	70	140	486,000
Tateo Ozaki	71	70	141	360,000
Takaaki Fukuzawa	71	70	141	360,000
Kiyoshi Maita	71	70	141	360,000
Masayuki Kawamura	71	70	141	360,000
Tatsuo Takasaki	69	72	141	360,000
Kunihiko Masuda	72	69	141	360,000
Yoshimitsu Fukuzawa	71	70	141	360,000
Takeshi Sakiyama	69	72	141	360,000
Roger Mackay	71	70	141	360,000

Mizuno Open

Setonaikai Golf Club, Kasaoka, Okayama — June 25-28
Par 36-36–72; 7,091 yards — purse, ¥100,000,000

	SCORES				TOTAL	MONEY
Brandt Jobe	67	65	74	69	275	¥18,000,000
Yoshinori Mizumaki	67	68	75	69	279	7,560,000
Toru Suzuki	69	66	74	70	279	7,560,000
Toru Taniguchi	72	67	71	70	280	4,320,000
Saburo Fujiki	69	70	71	71	281	2,790,000
Nobumitsu Yuhara	68	71	71	71	281	2,790,000
Anthony Gilligan	67	70	70	74	281	2,790,000
Keiichiro Fukabori	68	68	70	75	281	2,790,000
Frankie Minoza	67	71	69	74	281	2,790,000
Brian Watts	69	68	68	76	281	2,790,000
Yoshimitsu Fukuzawa	70	71	70	71	282	1,728,000
Katsumasa Miyamoto	67	75	71	69	282	1,728,000
Tsukasa Watanabe	65	71	70	77	283	1,404,000
Takenori Hiraishi	66	71	71	75	283	1,404,000
Kyi Hla Han	71	70	69	73	283	1,404,000
Masanobu Kimura	68	71	71	74	284	1,092,000
Hidezumi Shirakata	71	71	69	73	284	1,092,000
Yasuharu Imano	73	69	67	75	284	1,092,000
Tommy Nakajima	72	70	66	77	285	849,000
Daisuke Serizawa	68	73	70	74	285	849,000
Katsunori Kuwabara	71	70	71	73	285	849,000
Takashi Kanemoto	68	74	66	77	285	849,000
Zaw Moe	69	68	71	77	285	849,000
Harry Taylor	69	71	74	71	285	849,000

	SCORES				TOTAL	MONEY
Kiyoshi Maita	67	72	73	74	286	702,000
Masahiro Kuramoto	67	75	69	75	286	702,000
Yoshikazu Sakamoto	68	73	70	75	286	702,000
Yoshitaka Yamamoto	67	73	72	74	286	702,000
Tsutomu Higa	68	72	75	71	286	702,000
Masayoshi Horikawa	68	74	71	73	286	702,000
Shigeki Maruyama	70	68	77	71	286	702,000
*Hong Chia-yuh	70	72	70	74	286	

PGA Philanthropy

Shiromizu Golf Club, Komachi, Gunma — July 2-5
Par 35-36–71; 7,028 yards — purse, ¥100,000,000

	SCORES				TOTAL	MONEY
Shigeki Maruyama	65	66	64	69	264	¥18,000,000
Satoshi Higashi	65	68	68	64	265	9,000,000
Toru Suzuki	67	67	64	68	266	6,120,000
Saburo Fujiki	65	68	69	67	269	4,320,000
Brian Watts	68	66	69	67	270	3,600,000
Keiichiro Fukabori	67	67	67	70	271	3,060,000
Nobuhito Sato	65	68	69	69	271	3,060,000
Stewart Ginn	67	69	69	67	272	2,475,000
Hidezumi Shirakata	66	70	71	65	272	2,475,000
Hajime Meshiai	73	66	66	68	273	1,560,857
Yasunori Ida	65	69	68	71	273	1,560,857
Hidemichi Tanaka	69	65	67	72	273	1,560,857
Takashi Kanemoto	68	67	70	68	273	1,560,857
Kaname Yokoo	66	69	67	71	273	1,560,857
Steven Conran	68	65	69	71	273	1,560,857
Chen Tze-chung	65	68	73	67	273	1,560,857
Katsumasa Miyamoto	67	69	67	71	274	1,080,000
Kiyoshi Murota	70	69	67	69	275	907,200
Shoichi Kuwabara	68	67	70	70	275	907,200
Kazuhiro Fukunaga	69	69	68	69	275	907,200
Taichi Teshima	66	69	70	70	275	907,200
David Smail	68	68	70	69	275	907,200
Nobumitsu Yuhara	67	69	66	74	276	756,000
Masanobu Kimura	67	67	69	73	276	756,000
Yoshitaka Yamamoto	70	69	68	69	276	756,000
Lin Keng-chi	67	71	66	72	276	756,000
Rick Gibson	68	67	73	68	276	756,000
Yukihiro Yamamoto	65	65	72	75	277	693,000
Tsuyoshi Yoneyama	72	65	72	68	277	693,000
Hideki Kase	66	72	70	70	278	573,230
Tsukasa Watanabe	69	67	72	70	278	573,230
Keiji Teshima	70	67	69	72	278	573,230
Takenori Hiraishi	70	69	70	69	278	573,230
Masayuki Kawamura	69	66	70	73	278	573,230
Eduardo Herrera	66	72	68	72	278	573,230
Mitsuo Harada	69	68	75	66	278	573,230
Yoshimitsu Fukuzawa	67	70	72	69	278	573,230
Katsunori Kuwabara	70	67	70	71	278	573,230
Yeh Chang-ting	67	70	72	69	278	573,230
Masanori Ushiyama	68	68	69	73	278	573,230
Shigemasa Higaki	68	69	74	67	278	573,230
Yasuharu Imano	71	66	71	70	278	573,230

Yonex Open Hiroshima

Hiroshima Country Club, Hiroshima — July 9-12
Par 36-36–72; 6,950 yards — purse, ¥100,000,000

	SCORES				TOTAL	MONEY
Masashi Ozaki	68	70	66	66	270	¥18,000,000
Peter McWhinney	69	65	69	68	271	9,000,000
Akihito Yokoyama	67	70	69	66	272	5,220,000
Shingo Katayama	66	70	70	66	272	5,220,000
Kaname Yokoo	68	70	69	67	274	3,600,000
Seiki Okuda	70	67	71	67	275	3,240,000
Hajime Meshiai	69	69	71	67	276	2,880,000
Toru Suzuki	67	69	70	71	277	2,340,000
Shinichi Yokota	70	66	68	73	277	2,340,000
Go Higaki	68	69	72	68	277	2,340,000
Ikuo Shirahama	70	73	68	67	278	1,656,000
Rick Gibson	70	67	72	69	278	1,656,000
David Ishii	72	66	72	68	278	1,656,000
Hidemichi Tanaka	70	69	72	68	279	1,296,000
Shigemasa Higaki	71	68	69	71	279	1,296,000
Takao Nogami	67	66	74	72	279	1,296,000
*Terry Noe	72	69	72	66	279	
Yoshinori Kaneko	70	69	76	65	280	1,008,000
Satoshi Higashi	72	70	72	66	280	1,008,000
Shoichi Yamamoto	70	70	71	69	280	1,008,000
Katsunori Kuwabara	72	71	70	68	281	864,000
Naotoshi Nakamura	74	69	68	70	281	864,000
Dinesh Chand	68	69	72	72	281	864,000
Hideyuki Sato	71	72	71	68	282	747,000
Nobumitsu Yuhara	72	72	72	66	282	747,000
Masanobu Kimura	71	72	74	65	282	747,000
Masayoshi Yamazoe	73	67	74	68	282	747,000
Mitsutaka Kusakabe	70	72	70	70	282	747,000
Shoichi Kuwabara	72	69	72	69	282	747,000
Kazuhiro Takami	69	74	70	70	283	648,720
Takaaki Fukuzawa	69	75	70	69	283	648,720
Tsukasa Watanabe	73	71	73	66	283	648,720
Daisuke Serizawa	70	68	71	74	283	648,720
Taichi Teshima	71	71	71	70	283	648,720

Aiful Cup

Aomori Country Club, Aomori, Kyodo — July 23-26
Par 35-37–72; 6,941 yards — purse, ¥100,000,000

	SCORES				TOTAL	MONEY
Hidemichi Tanaka	68	70	69	66	273	¥18,000,000
Tatsuo Takasaki	69	70	69	66	274	7,560,000
Toshimitsu Izawa	69	69	66	70	274	7,560,000
Hiroyuki Fujita	71	72	66	66	275	4,320,000
Satoshi Higashi	70	68	70	68	276	2,934,000
Nobumitsu Yuhara	69	68	69	70	276	2,934,000
Kinpachi Yoshimura	70	67	68	71	276	2,934,000
Kazumasa Sakaitani	74	66	67	69	276	2,934,000
Chen Tze-chung	70	68	68	70	276	2,934,000
Seiki Okuda	73	68	70	66	277	1,842,000
Takeshi Sakiyama	71	68	68	70	277	1,842,000

	SCORES				TOTAL	MONEY
Steven Conran	65	71	68	73	277	1,842,000
Gohei Sato	69	72	68	69	278	1,512,000
Masashi Ozaki	71	67	68	73	279	1,195,200
Kosaku Hirano	68	68	75	68	279	1,195,200
Anthony Gilligan	71	68	69	71	279	1,195,200
Hidezumi Shirakata	72	70	71	66	279	1,195,200
Yasuharu Imano	70	71	69	69	279	1,195,200
Kiyoshi Murota	73	67	69	71	280	900,000
Yukihiro Yamamoto	69	73	69	69	280	900,000
Tsuyoshi Yoneyama	73	69	70	68	280	900,000
Ikuo Shirahama	73	67	69	72	281	777,600
Katsunari Takahashi	69	71	72	69	281	777,600
Atsushi Takamatsu	71	72	70	68	281	777,600
Nozomi Kawahara	72	68	72	69	281	777,600
Shinichi Yokota	70	71	71	69	281	777,600
Nobuo Serizawa	74	68	71	69	282	658,350
Kazuhiro Takami	71	71	70	70	282	658,350
Tsukasa Watanabe	68	70	75	69	282	658,350
Masayuki Kawamura	72	66	69	75	282	658,350
Nobuhito Sato	72	71	70	69	282	658,350
Zaw Moe	68	69	72	73	282	658,350
Eiji Yokota	71	68	67	76	282	658,350
Nobuyuki Okuwa	69	74	71	68	282	658,350

NST Niigata Open

Forest Golf Club, Niigata, Toyoura — July 30-August 2
Par 36-36–72; 7,065 yards — purse, ¥60,000,000

	SCORES				TOTAL	MONEY
Masayuki Kawamura	69	69	67	63	268	¥10,800,000
Kiyoshi Murota	69	74	64	69	276	4,536,000
Shingo Katayama	69	70	69	68	276	4,536,000
Daisuke Serizawa	69	69	66	74	278	2,232,000
Nobuhito Sato	71	72	66	69	278	2,232,000
Kim Jong-duk	75	69	69	65	278	2,232,000
Kazuhiko Hosokawa	73	70	67	69	279	1,728,000
Hideki Kase	68	72	69	71	280	1,257,120
Noboru Fujiike	69	71	71	69	280	1,257,120
Atsushi Takamatsu	69	71	69	71	280	1,257,120
Go Higaki	69	70	70	71	280	1,257,120
Rick Gibson	66	71	71	72	280	1,257,120
Nobuo Serizawa	67	69	71	74	281	777,600
Yasunori Ida	68	71	72	70	281	777,600
Toshikazu Sugihara	73	68	67	73	281	777,600
Hsieh Chin-sheng	68	75	70	68	281	777,600
Kaname Yokoo	71	67	71	72	281	777,600
Akihito Yokoyama	71	69	70	72	282	532,800
Tatsuo Takasaki	70	72	68	72	282	532,800
Anthony Gilligan	68	71	70	73	282	532,800
Ryoken Kawagishi	70	70	69	73	282	532,800
Toshiaki Odate	69	72	70	71	282	532,800
Naotoshi Nakamura	72	70	73	67	282	532,800
Hiroya Kamide	69	69	70	75	283	426,600
Kazunari Matsunaga	70	72	74	67	283	426,600
Yoshimitsu Fukuzawa	74	68	70	71	283	426,600
Keiichiro Fukabori	69	74	69	71	283	426,600

	SCORES				TOTAL	MONEY
Peter McWhinney	70	71	72	70	283	426,600
Hiroyuki Fujita	71	68	71	73	283	426,600
Masanori Ushiyama	68	72	72	71	283	426,600
Steven Conran	68	74	74	67	283	426,600

Sanko Grand Summer

Sanko 72 Country Club, Yoshii, Gunma — August 6-9
Par 37-35–72; 7,066 yards — purse, ¥100,000,000

	SCORES				TOTAL	MONEY
Shingo Katayama	67	66	68	73	274	¥18,000,000
Kazuhiko Hosokawa	70	68	67	69	274	9,000,000
(Katayama defeated Hosokawa on third extra hole.)						
Hideki Kase	68	70	70	67	275	6,120,000
Kazuhiro Takami	71	70	66	69	276	3,330,000
Tsukasa Watanabe	69	69	69	69	276	3,330,000
Tatsuo Takasaki	70	68	68	70	276	3,330,000
Katsumasa Miyamoto	67	70	70	69	276	3,330,000
Yasuharu Imano	71	67	69	69	276	3,330,000
Tsuyoshi Yoneyama	72	68	71	66	277	2,205,000
Ryoken Kawagishi	68	71	69	69	277	2,205,000
Kiyoshi Maita	72	65	71	70	278	1,593,000
Toshiaki Odate	71	71	69	67	278	1,593,000
Shoichi Kuwabara	66	72	71	69	278	1,593,000
Shigemasa Higaki	68	69	70	71	278	1,593,000
Tsuneyuki Nakajima	70	72	69	68	279	1,296,000
Masayoshi Yamazoe	68	70	73	69	280	1,053,000
Hsieh Chin-sheng	69	67	72	72	280	1,053,000
Steven Conran	71	69	72	68	280	1,053,000
Kim Jong-duk	67	74	71	68	280	1,053,000
Masayuki Okano	69	74	66	72	281	807,428
Daisuke Serizawa	72	68	68	73	281	807,428
Hirofumi Miyase	67	69	74	72	281	807,428
Takeshi Sakiyama	68	72	74	67	281	807,428
Brad Andrews	71	72	69	69	281	807,428
Akinori Tani	71	71	70	69	281	807,428
Takao Nogami	69	74	67	71	281	807,428
Nobuo Serizawa	67	73	71	71	282	684,000
Saburo Fujiki	69	69	72	72	282	684,000
Kiyoshi Murota	72	70	70	70	282	684,000
Nobumitsu Yuhara	64	73	75	70	282	684,000
David Smail	71	70	70	71	282	684,000

KBC Augusta

Keya Golf Club, Shima, Fukuoka — August 27-30
Par 36-36–72; 7,154 yards — purse, ¥100,000,000

	SCORES				TOTAL	MONEY
Masashi Ozaki	66	72	65	72	275	¥18,000,000
Katsunori Kuwabara	69	67	70	73	279	9,000,000
Kazuhiro Takami	73	70	68	69	280	6,120,000
Ikuo Shirahama	69	69	71	73	282	3,330,000
Nobumitsu Yuhara	69	73	71	69	282	3,330,000

	SCORES				TOTAL	MONEY
Tsukasa Watanabe	71	68	72	71	282	3,330,000
Toshimitsu Izawa	73	67	71	71	282	3,330,000
Katsumasa Miyamoto	71	68	70	73	282	3,330,000
Ryoken Kawagishi	72	69	72	70	283	2,070,000
Atsushi Takamatsu	68	75	70	70	283	2,070,000
Yasuharu Imano	69	72	68	74	283	2,070,000
Shuichi Sano	71	73	67	73	284	1,467,000
Kiyoshi Murota	70	71	71	72	284	1,467,000
Toshiaki Odate	70	75	70	69	284	1,467,000
Taichi Teshima	69	71	70	74	284	1,467,000
Tateo Ozaki	70	74	67	74	285	1,134,000
Lin Keng-chi	70	75	69	71	285	1,134,000
Masanobu Kimura	71	70	70	75	286	907,200
Keiji Teshima	67	71	75	73	286	907,200
Zaw Moe	73	70	70	73	286	907,200
Takashi Umiyama	70	70	76	70	286	907,200
Kim Jong-duk	71	72	69	74	286	907,200
Shigemasa Higaki	74	69	69	75	287	783,000
Mamoru Osanai	71	73	71	72	287	783,000
Hiroshi Makino	71	74	69	74	288	693,000
Hajime Meshiai	69	71	71	77	288	693,000
Yoshikazu Yokoshima	72	70	74	72	288	693,000
Kazuo Kanayama	69	74	70	75	288	693,000
Kinpachi Yoshimura	69	72	73	74	288	693,000
Yasunori Ida	72	67	77	72	288	693,000
Shoichi Kuwabara	70	70	70	78	288	693,000
Shusaku Sugimoto	71	70	72	75	288	693,000

Japan Match Play

Nidom Classic Course, Tomakomai, Hokkaido — September 3-6
Par 36-36–72; 6,941 yards — purse, ¥100,000,000

FIRST ROUND

Shigeki Maruyama defeated Tsuyoshi Yoneyama, 3 and 2.
Toru Taniguchi defeated Kazuhiko Hosokawa, 1 up, 23 holes.
Kaname Yokoo defeated Seiki Okuda, 4 and 3.
Naomichi Ozaki defeated Chen Tze-chung, 4 and 3.
Frankie Minoza defeated Kazuhiro Takami, 3 and 2.
Keiichiro Fukabori defeated Shoichi Kuwabara, 2 and 1.
Peter McWhinney defeated Toru Suzuki, 4 and 3.
Shinichi Yokota defeated Hajime Meshiai, 3 and 2.
Brian Watts defeated Masayuki Kawamura, 1 up, 19 holes.
Katsunori Kuwabara defeated Hiroyuki Fujita, 2 and 1.
Satoshi Higashi defeated Tateo Ozaki, 1 up, 21 holes.
Eduardo Herrera defeated David Ishii, 2 and 1.
Zaw Moe defeated Carlos Franco, 3 and 2
Mitsutaka Kusakabe defeated Katsumasa Miyamoto, 1 up, 21 holes.
Kenichi Kuboya defeated Hidemichi Tanaka, 2 up.
Tsukasa Watanabe defeated Yoshinori Mizumaki, 1 up.

(Each losing player received ¥400,000.)

SECOND ROUND

Maruyama defeated Taniguchi, 5 and 4.
Yokoo defeated Naomichi Ozaki, 4 and 3.

Minoza defeated Fukabori, 3 and 2.
Yokota defeated McWhinney, 5 and 4.
Katsunori Kuwabara defeated Watts, 2 and 1.
Herrera defeated Higashi, 1 up.
Moe defeated Kusakabe, 1 up.
Watanabe defeated Kuboya, 3 and 1.

(Each losing player received ¥800,000.)

QUARTER-FINALS

Maruyama defeated Yokoo, 5 and 4.
Yokota defeated Minoza, 2 and 1.
Kuwabara defeated Herrera, 3 and 2.
Moe defeated Watanabe, 5 and 3.

(Each losing player received ¥1,800,000.)

SEMI-FINALS

Yokota defeated Maruyama, 3 and 2.
Kuwabara defeated Moe, 3 and 2.

THIRD-FOURTH PLACE PLAYOFF

Moe defeated Maruyama, 3 and 2.

(Moe received ¥9,000,000; Maruyama received ¥6,000,000.)

FINAL

Kuwabara defeated Yokota, 1 up, 38 holes.

(Kuwabara received ¥30,000,000; Yokota received ¥16,000,000.)

Suntory Open

Sobu Country Club, Inzai, Chiba — September 10-13
Par 35-36–71; 7,161 yards — purse, ¥100,000,000

	SCORES				TOTAL	MONEY
Mamoru Osanai	71	68	66	69	274	¥18,000,000
Masashi Ozaki	70	69	71	67	277	9,000,000
Hideki Kase	69	69	69	71	278	4,680,000
Nobumitsu Yuhara	73	68	70	67	278	4,680,000
Kazuhiko Hosokawa	70	72	66	70	278	4,680,000
Lee Janzen	69	72	70	68	279	3,240,000
Hajime Meshiai	69	72	70	70	281	2,745,000
Norio Hosoya	69	69	73	70	281	2,745,000
Saburo Fujiki	67	72	72	71	282	2,070,000
Katsunori Kuwabara	71	73	66	72	282	2,070,000
Yeh Chang-ting	71	75	69	67	282	2,070,000
Nobuo Serizawa	73	68	70	72	283	1,524,000
Kiyoshi Murota	74	66	71	72	283	1,524,000
Toshimitsu Izawa	70	73	72	68	283	1,524,000
Hikaru Emoto	73	67	71	73	284	1,068,000
Akihito Yokoyama	69	74	71	70	284	1,068,000
Ryoken Kawagishi	73	72	69	70	284	1,068,000
Keiichiro Fukabori	70	70	71	73	284	1,068,000

	SCORES				TOTAL	MONEY
Yasuharu Imano	73	71	69	71	284	1,068,000
Carlos Franco	69	71	73	71	284	1,068,000
Ikuo Shirahama	72	71	70	72	285	762,000
Koki Idoki	71	71	70	73	285	762,000
Mitsutaka Kusakabe	69	74	70	72	285	762,000
Mitsunori Harakawa	68	77	69	71	285	762,000
Hidezumi Shirakata	71	71	73	70	285	762,000
Toru Taniguchi	74	70	70	71	285	762,000
Kyi Hla Han	73	72	70	70	285	762,000
Shingo Katayama	72	71	71	71	285	762,000
Dinesh Chand	74	71	69	71	285	762,000
Eiichi Itai	76	69	70	71	286	639,900
Hisashi Nakase	70	71	71	74	286	639,900
Steven Conran	73	69	74	70	286	639,900
Frankie Minoza	71	75	71	69	286	639,900

ANA Open

Sapporo Golf Club, Wattsu Course,
Kitahiroshima, Hokkaido
Par 36-36–72; 7,063 yards

September 17-20
purse, ¥100,000,000

	SCORES				TOTAL	MONEY
Keiichiro Fukabori	71	71	68	69	279	¥18,000,000
Katsumasa Miyamoto	71	67	71	72	281	7,560,000
Lee Janzen	72	68	72	69	281	7,560,000
Masashi Ozaki	69	73	72	68	282	4,320,000
Kazuhiro Takami	72	71	70	70	283	3,420,000
Tsuyoshi Yoneyama	74	72	70	67	283	3,420,000
Hajime Meshiai	72	68	73	71	284	2,610,000
Shigeki Maruyama	73	71	68	72	284	2,610,000
Chen Tze-chung	70	73	70	71	284	2,610,000
Nobumitsu Yuhara	72	71	73	69	285	1,688,400
Ryoken Kawagishi	72	70	73	70	285	1,688,400
Stewart Ginn	75	69	70	71	285	1,688,400
Kazuhiko Hosokawa	71	76	70	68	285	1,688,400
Mamoru Osanai	72	71	72	70	285	1,688,400
Naomichi Ozaki	71	70	73	72	286	1,012,500
Hideki Kase	73	74	73	66	286	1,012,500
Toru Suzuki	71	72	73	70	286	1,012,500
Toshiaki Odate	73	71	70	72	286	1,012,500
Kenichi Kuboya	70	73	71	72	286	1,012,500
Rick Gibson	76	69	70	71	286	1,012,500
Stuart Appleby	69	70	72	75	286	1,012,500
Carlos Franco	70	71	73	72	286	1,012,500
Yasunori Ida	71	70	74	72	287	765,000
Tsutomu Higa	75	70	74	68	287	765,000
Nobuhito Sato	73	71	68	75	287	765,000
David Ishii	74	73	70	70	287	765,000
Kiyoshi Maita	72	73	69	74	288	720,000
Masahiro Kuramoto	77	68	72	72	289	693,000
Lin Keng-chi	71	75	70	73	289	693,000
Toru Taniguchi	74	73	72	71	290	648,000
Peter McWhinney	70	76	73	71	290	648,000
Yasuharu Imano	73	75	72	70	290	648,000

Gene Sarazen Jun Classic

Rope Club, Shioya, Tochigi — September 24-27
Par 35-37–72; 7,135 yards — purse, ¥110,000,000

	SCORES				TOTAL	MONEY
Todd Hamilton	71	66	68	65	270	¥19,800,000
Craig Parry	68	68	68	68	272	9,900,000
Ryoken Kawagishi	71	68	68	67	274	5,742,000
Nobuhito Sato	70	73	64	67	274	5,742,000
Hajime Meshiai	67	71	69	68	275	3,762,000
Carlos Franco	69	68	65	73	275	3,762,000
Masashi Ozaki	73	68	70	66	277	2,574,000
Satoshi Higashi	67	73	69	68	277	2,574,000
Eduardo Herrera	66	70	70	71	277	2,574,000
Hidemichi Tanaka	68	72	72	65	277	2,574,000
Kazuhiko Hosokawa	69	72	67	69	277	2,574,000
Naomichi Ozaki	70	73	66	69	278	1,552,320
Kiyoshi Maita	70	72	69	67	278	1,552,320
Mitsuo Harada	74	69	68	67	278	1,552,320
Hiroyuki Fujita	69	73	68	68	278	1,552,320
Dinesh Chand	71	70	70	67	278	1,552,320
Katsunari Takahashi	72	70	67	70	279	1,079,100
Toshimitsu Izawa	68	71	69	71	279	1,079,100
Toru Suzuki	69	71	69	70	279	1,079,100
Shigemasa Higaki	72	72	69	66	279	1,079,100
Kiyoshi Murota	73	70	66	71	280	883,080
Tsukasa Watanabe	72	70	67	71	280	883,080
Keiji Teshima	71	73	65	71	280	883,080
Naotoshi Nakamura	72	71	70	67	280	883,080
Mamoru Osanai	70	73	71	66	280	883,080
Hideyuki Sato	73	68	68	72	281	782,100
Tatsuo Takasaki	71	72	68	70	281	782,100
Peter McWhinney	73	70	70	68	281	782,100
Frankie Minoza	70	72	68	71	281	782,100
Ikuo Shirahama	69	71	70	72	282	703,890
Shigeki Maruyama	69	73	70	70	282	703,890
Kyi Hla Han	73	70	66	73	282	703,890
Kim Jong-duk	73	70	68	71	282	703,890

Japan Open

Oarai Golf Club, Oarai, Ibaraki — October 1-4
Par 36-36–72; 7,160 yards — purse, ¥120,000,000

	SCORES				TOTAL	MONEY
Hidemichi Tanaka	72	70	72	69	283	¥24,000,000
Naomichi Ozaki	71	72	68	73	284	13,200,000
Satoshi Higashi	75	72	70	69	286	9,300,000
Toru Taniguchi	76	68	70	73	287	6,120,000
Keiichiro Fukabori	76	73	68	72	289	5,040,000
Masashi Ozaki	72	72	72	74	290	2,961,000
Kazuhiro Takami	70	76	72	72	290	2,961,000
Seiki Okuda	73	73	73	71	290	2,961,000
Toshiaki Odate	73	71	75	71	290	2,961,000
Peter McWhinney	76	71	69	74	290	2,961,000
Craig Parry	72	72	74	72	290	2,961,000
Hsieh Chin-sheng	72	71	74	74	291	1,720,000

	SCORES				TOTAL	MONEY
Takeshi Sakiyama	74	75	72	70	291	1,720,000
Hiroyuki Fujita	72	72	70	77	291	1,720,000
Tsuneyuki Nakajima	76	72	72	72	292	1,404,000
Nobumitsu Yuhara	72	72	78	70	292	1,404,000
Shusaku Sugimoto	76	70	77	69	292	1,404,000
Shigeki Maruyama	77	72	71	73	293	1,203,000
Kaname Yokoo	76	73	72	72	293	1,203,000
Ryuichi Tayasu	70	76	74	73	293	1,203,000
Chen Tze-chung	72	74	72	75	293	1,203,000
Peter Teravainen	73	71	73	77	294	1,106,000
Saburo Fujiki	80	71	71	73	295	1,005,000
Yoshinori Mizumaki	74	74	71	76	295	1,005,000
Koki Idoki	71	75	77	72	295	1,005,000
Tatsuo Takasaki	73	71	74	77	295	1,005,000
Toshimitsu Izawa	73	70	73	79	295	1,005,000
Nobuhito Sato	77	73	71	74	295	1,005,000
Frankie Minoza	77	72	70	76	295	1,005,000
David Ishii	77	73	74	71	295	1,005,000

Tokai Classic

Miyoshi Country Club, West Course, Miyoshi, Aichi — October 8-11
Par 36-36–72; 7,060 yards — purse, ¥110,000,000

	SCORES				TOTAL	MONEY
Toshimitsu Izawa	73	66	70	68	277	¥19,800,000
Nobumitsu Yuhara	69	73	70	68	280	9,900,000
Toshiaki Odate	72	69	70	72	283	4,752,000
Kaname Yokoo	69	70	72	72	283	4,752,000
Mamoru Osanai	73	67	73	70	283	4,752,000
Mark Calcavecchia	73	70	67	73	283	4,752,000
Koki Idoki	71	74	67	72	284	2,448,600
Tsuyoshi Yoneyama	70	69	71	74	284	2,448,600
Yasunori Ida	71	69	72	72	284	2,448,600
Eiji Mizoguchi	75	72	69	68	284	2,448,600
Yasuharu Imano	72	67	69	76	284	2,448,600
Shusaku Sugimoto	75	69	68	72	284	2,448,600
Hidemichi Tanaka	73	71	70	72	286	1,425,600
Nobuhito Sato	72	68	70	76	286	1,425,600
Taichi Teshima	74	71	72	69	286	1,425,600
Brian Watts	71	72	70	73	286	1,425,600
Costantino Rocca	72	71	68	75	286	1,425,600
Saburo Fujiki	73	73	71	70	287	1,019,700
Masayoshi Yamazoe	73	71	72	71	287	1,019,700
Shigeki Maruyama	70	71	74	72	287	1,019,700
Katsunori Kuwabara	78	70	69	70	287	1,019,700
Noboru Fujiike	73	73	72	70	288	866,250
Toru Suzuki	76	70	73	69	288	866,250
Keiichiro Fukabori	75	72	68	73	288	866,250
David Ishii	74	71	70	73	288	866,250
Hideki Kase	70	72	73	74	289	782,100
Kiyoshi Maita	74	71	73	71	289	782,100
Hirofumi Miyase	73	75	70	71	289	782,100
David Smail	76	72	71	70	289	782,100
Masahiro Kuramoto	77	71	67	75	290	703,890
Tsutomu Higa	74	70	72	74	290	703,890
Stewart Ginn	75	73	71	71	290	703,890
Kyi Hla Han	74	73	70	73	290	703,890

Nikkei Cup

Fuji Golf Club, Dejima Course, Kasumigaura, Ibaraki — October 15-18
Par 36-36–72; 7,072 yards — purse, ¥110,000,000

	SCORES				TOTAL	MONEY
Mitsutaka Kusakabe	75	68	68	69	280	¥19,800,000
Masashi Ozaki	65	70	72	74	281	9,900,000
Brian Watts	73	68	69	72	282	6,732,000
Yasuharu Imano	69	71	68	75	283	4,752,000
Hsieh Chin-sheng	72	71	68	73	284	3,762,000
Brandt Jobe	70	69	73	72	284	3,762,000
Anthony Gilligan	75	68	71	71	285	2,871,000
Lin Keng-chi	73	68	73	71	285	2,871,000
Todd Hamilton	68	72	73	72	285	2,871,000
Seiki Okuda	76	68	72	70	286	2,026,200
Kenichi Kuboya	71	71	70	74	286	2,026,200
Takao Nogami	73	72	69	72	286	2,026,200
Kinpachi Yoshimura	75	67	74	71	287	1,323,771
Toshimitsu Izawa	69	70	71	77	287	1,323,771
Katsunori Kuwabara	68	71	78	70	287	1,323,771
Nobuhito Sato	71	71	70	75	287	1,323,771
Taichi Teshima	70	71	73	73	287	1,323,771
Kaname Yokoo	76	70	69	72	287	1,323,771
Takashi Kamiyama	70	70	74	73	287	1,323,771
Kazuhiro Takami	71	70	73	74	288	950,400
Nobumitsu Yuhara	74	69	70	75	288	950,400
Toru Suzuki	73	70	73	72	288	950,400
Tateo Ozaki	73	68	72	76	289	811,800
Hideyuki Sato	75	70	70	74	289	811,800
Toshiaki Odate	72	73	72	72	289	811,800
Kyi Hla Han	74	71	72	72	289	811,800
Shigemasa Higaki	73	72	74	70	289	811,800
Katsumasa Miyamoto	70	69	78	72	289	811,800
Steven Conran	74	69	73	73	289	811,800
Kiyoshi Maita	71	70	74	75	290	703,890
Yukihiro Yamamoto	72	71	76	71	290	703,890
Kazuhiko Hosokawa	74	67	71	78	290	703,890
Shusaku Sugimoto	74	69	74	73	290	703,890

Bridgestone Open

Sodegaura Country Club, Sodegaura, Chiba — October 22-25
Par 36-36–72; 7,151 yards — purse, ¥120,000,000

	SCORES				TOTAL	MONEY
Nobuhito Sato	69	69	67	70	275	¥21,600,000
Tateo Ozaki	67	69	67	72	275	10,800,000
(Sato defeated Ozaki on first extra hole.)						
Taichi Teshima	70	69	71	67	277	7,344,000
Carlos Franco	74	71	69	66	280	5,184,000
Toru Suzuki	68	72	71	70	281	3,348,000
Shigeki Maruyama	71	67	72	71	281	3,348,000
Shingo Katayama	69	69	73	70	281	3,348,000
Steven Conran	74	65	69	73	281	3,348,000
Frankie Minoza	71	71	67	72	281	3,348,000
Brandt Jobe	69	69	72	71	281	3,348,000
Shuichi Sano	72	69	72	69	282	1,987,200

	SCORES				TOTAL	MONEY
Masahiro Kuramoto	73	72	71	66	282	1,987,200
Dinesh Chand	72	69	72	69	282	1,987,200
Masashi Ozaki	71	72	68	72	283	1,267,200
Yukihiro Yamamoto	72	73	69	69	283	1,267,200
Mitsuo Harada	71	72	73	67	283	1,267,200
Anthony Gilligan	71	72	71	69	283	1,267,200
Yoshimitsu Fukuzawa	70	70	73	70	283	1,267,200
Keiichiro Fukabori	72	70	69	72	283	1,267,200
Kenichi Kuboya	71	70	75	67	283	1,267,200
Mamoru Osanai	74	71	73	65	283	1,267,200
Brian Watts	73	73	70	67	283	1,267,200
Hsieh Chin-sheng	69	72	70	73	284	939,600
David Ishii	72	69	70	73	284	939,600
Hideki Kase	74	72	68	71	285	874,800
Toshimitsu Izawa	70	73	71	71	285	874,800
Gregory Meyer	74	71	73	67	285	874,800
Shusaku Sugimoto	69	72	70	74	285	874,800
Hideyuki Sato	72	73	72	69	286	732,672
Ikuo Shirahama	72	72	73	69	286	732,672
Nobuo Serizawa	71	74	70	71	286	732,672
Kiyoshi Maita	73	71	72	70	286	732,672
Seiki Okuda	71	70	76	69	286	732,672
Stewart Ginn	72	74	68	72	286	732,672
Hidezumi Shirakata	71	73	73	69	286	732,672
Hiroyuki Fujita	73	70	72	71	286	732,672
Naotoshi Nakamura	70	70	74	72	286	732,672
Chen Tze-chung	72	73	70	71	286	732,672

Philip Morris Championship

ABC Golf Club, Tojo, Hyogo
Par 36-36–72; 7,176 yards

October 29-November 1
purse, ¥200,000,000

	SCORES				TOTAL	MONEY
Masashi Ozaki	75	68	68	64	275	¥36,000,000
Mitsuo Harada	72	66	68	70	276	15,120,000
Carlos Franco	68	69	68	71	276	15,120,000
Shusaku Sugimoto	68	68	67	74	277	7,440,000
Frankie Minoza	69	71	71	66	277	7,440,000
Brandt Jobe	70	68	69	70	277	7,440,000
Kazuhiko Hosokawa	69	69	68	72	278	5,490,000
Kaname Yokoo	67	67	72	72	278	5,490,000
Tateo Ozaki	67	68	71	73	279	4,140,000
Nobumitsu Yuhara	70	71	69	69	279	4,140,000
Keiichiro Fukabori	70	68	70	71	279	4,140,000
Toru Suzuki	66	73	72	69	280	2,934,000
Eiji Mizoguchi	70	69	68	73	280	2,934,000
Nobuhito Sato	67	71	71	71	280	2,934,000
David Ishii	67	71	71	71	280	2,934,000
Naomichi Ozaki	74	69	70	68	281	2,044,800
Katsunari Takahashi	68	70	72	71	281	2,044,800
Seiki Okuda	72	68	68	73	281	2,044,800
Koki Idoki	71	68	72	70	281	2,044,800
Taichi Teshima	71	69	73	68	281	2,044,800
Hajime Meshiai	71	73	68	70	282	1,728,000
Masahiro Kuramoto	70	69	72	72	283	1,575,000
Shigeki Maruyama	67	73	73	70	283	1,575,000

	SCORES				TOTAL	MONEY
Katsumasa Miyamoto	70	74	69	70	283	1,575,000
Chen Tze-chung	70	72	71	70	283	1,575,000
Hideki Kase	72	71	72	69	284	1,318,320
Yasunori Ida	71	70	71	72	284	1,318,320
Hirofumi Miyase	70	70	73	71	284	1,318,320
Hidemichi Tanaka	67	70	74	73	284	1,318,320
Toru Taniguchi	69	71	71	73	284	1,318,320
Hiroyuki Fujita	73	72	71	68	284	1,318,320
Zaw Moe	71	73	70	70	284	1,318,320
Mamoru Osanai	69	67	75	73	284	1,318,320
Todd Hamilton	69	73	69	73	284	1,318,320
Brian Watts	72	72	72	68	284	1,318,320

Acom International

Seve Ballesteros Golf Club, Izumi Course, November 5-8
Iwaki, Fukushima purse, ¥120,000,000
Par 36-36–72; 6,948 yards

	POINTS				TOTAL	MONEY
Kaname Yokoo	17	5	14	10	46	¥21,600,000
Katsumasa Miyamoto	4	13	12	14	43	10,800,000
Kinpachi Yoshimura	3	9	15	9	36	6,264,000
Taisuke Kitajima	8	-2	20	10	36	6,264,000
Hirofumi Miyase	8	9	10	7	34	4,104,000
Shusaku Sugimoto	0	18	7	9	34	4,104,000
Yoshinori Kaneko	2	9	13	4	28	2,970,000
Saburo Fujiki	5	8	11	4	28	2,970,000
Toshimitsu Izawa	13	5	2	8	28	2,970,000
Ryoken Kawagishi	4	5	17	2	28	2,970,000
Katsunari Takahashi	-1	5	14	9	27	1,987,200
Kazuo Kanayama	6	9	6	6	27	1,987,200
Katsunori Kuwabara	9	-1	14	5	27	1,987,200
Toru Suzuki	10	6	5	5	26	1,684,800
Kazuhiko Hosokawa	9	0	5	9	23	1,490,400
Mamoru Osanai	0	8	8	7	23	1,490,400
Masahiro Kuramoto	2	9	9	2	22	1,296,000
Tsuneyuki Nakajima	-1	7	11	4	21	1,112,400
Toshiyuki Hiyama	8	5	1	7	21	1,112,400
Kazumasa Sakaitani	2	4	12	3	21	1,112,400
Ivo Giner	-3	8	4	12	21	1,112,400
Tsuyoshi Yoneyama	9	-3	15	-1	20	957,600
Takeshi Sakiyama	5	3	3	9	20	957,600
Shinichi Yokota	1	6	8	5	20	957,600
Kiyoshi Maita	1	7	0	11	19	874,800
Tomohiro Maruyama	5	-2	16	0	19	874,800
Tatsuo Takasaki	0	3	10	6	19	874,800
Tsutomu Higa	-1	4	7	9	19	874,800
Kyi Hla Han	6	8	-1	5	18	810,000
Takao Nogami	5	1	10	2	18	810,000

Sumitomo Visa Taiheiyo Masters

Taiheiyo Club, Gotemba, Shizuoka
Par 36-36–72; 7,072 yards

November 12-15
purse, ¥150,000,000

	SCORES				TOTAL	MONEY
Lee Westwood	72	67	67	69	275	¥27,000,000
Masashi Ozaki	69	72	69	67	277	13,500,000
Eduardo Herrera	65	74	68	71	278	9,180,000
Frankie Minoza	68	70	67	74	279	6,480,000
Tateo Ozaki	68	70	71	71	280	5,130,000
Hiroyuki Fujita	73	70	69	68	280	5,130,000
Hajime Meshiai	71	71	65	74	281	4,117,500
Retief Goosen	70	74	67	70	281	4,117,500
Ryoken Kawagishi	67	72	73	70	282	2,949,750
Stewart Ginn	74	71	66	71	282	2,949,750
Toru Taniguchi	72	69	66	75	282	2,949,750
Shigemasa Higaki	71	70	71	70	282	2,949,750
Naomichi Ozaki	72	73	70	68	283	2,106,000
Eiji Mizoguchi	71	71	73	68	283	2,106,000
Andrew Coltart	69	72	72	70	283	2,106,000
Nobuo Serizawa	67	68	75	74	284	1,494,000
Katsunori Kuwabara	71	70	71	72	284	1,494,000
Taichi Teshima	74	71	68	71	284	1,494,000
Jose Maria Olazabal	72	73	70	69	284	1,494,000
Darren Clarke	71	71	70	72	284	1,494,000
David Howell	70	73	73	68	284	1,494,000
Nobumitsu Yuhara	72	72	72	69	285	1,152,000
Koki Idoki	70	72	72	71	285	1,152,000
Tsuyoshi Yoneyama	73	74	69	69	285	1,152,000
Chen Tze-chung	72	70	73	70	285	1,152,000
David Ishii	69	74	71	71	285	1,152,000
Jeff Sluman	73	69	72	71	285	1,152,000
Katsunari Takahashi	69	71	72	74	286	1,026,000
Tsukasa Watanabe	73	73	67	73	286	1,026,000
Shusaku Sugimoto	71	71	69	75	286	1,026,000

Dunlop Phoenix Tournament

Phoenix Country Club, Miyazaki
Par 36-35–71; 6,846 yards

November 19-22
purse, ¥250,000,000

	SCORES				TOTAL	MONEY
Lee Westwood	68	67	66	70	271	¥45,000,000
Darren Clarke	70	67	66	71	274	22,500,000
Naomichi Ozaki	69	71	64	72	276	15,300,000
Masashi Ozaki	71	70	65	71	277	9,300,000
Shigeki Maruyama	70	69	71	67	277	9,300,000
Jeff Sluman	69	70	66	72	277	9,300,000
Tateo Ozaki	75	69	66	69	279	6,862,500
Fred Funk	69	69	66	75	279	6,862,500
Hidemichi Tanaka	70	73	69	68	280	4,689,000
Peter Senior	70	69	67	74	280	4,689,000
Brian Watts	71	67	70	72	280	4,689,000
Peter Teravainen	69	71	71	69	280	4,689,000
Zhang Lian-wei	70	71	70	69	280	4,689,000
Tsuneyuki Nakajima	68	73	68	72	281	3,240,000
Hajime Meshiai	70	73	67	71	281	3,240,000

	SCORES				TOTAL	MONEY
David Ishii	69	69	70	73	281	3,240,000
Hideki Kase	71	72	71	68	282	2,610,000
Yeh Chang-ting	70	73	68	71	282	2,610,000
Toru Suzuki	74	71	65	73	283	2,250,000
Frankie Minoza	73	71	66	73	283	2,250,000
Miguel Angel Jimenez	72	70	72	69	283	2,250,000
Seiki Okuda	73	71	66	74	284	1,944,000
Hiroyuki Fujita	73	69	69	73	284	1,944,000
Kazuhiko Hosokawa	70	74	71	69	284	1,944,000
Kaname Yokoo	68	69	72	75	284	1,944,000
Jose Maria Olazabal	70	69	69	76	284	1,944,000
Ryoken Kawagishi	66	71	75	73	285	1,755,000
Zaw Moe	74	69	69	73	285	1,755,000
Paul Stankowski	73	73	69	70	285	1,755,000
Kiyoshi Maita	70	70	71	75	286	1,620,000
David Smail	73	71	71	71	286	1,620,000
Andrew Magee	71	69	71	75	286	1,620,000

Casio World Open

Ibusuki Golf Club, Kaimon, Kagoshima — November 26-29
Par 36-36–72; 7,105 yards — purse, ¥150,000,000

	SCORES				TOTAL	MONEY
Brian Watts	69	70	67	68	274	¥27,000,000
Toshimitsu Izawa	69	69	68	68	274	13,500,000
(Watts defeated Izawa on second extra hole.)						
Naomichi Ozaki	67	71	67	71	276	9,180,000
Tsuyoshi Yoneyama	74	67	68	68	277	5,580,000
Shigeki Maruyama	71	70	70	66	277	5,580,000
Paul Stankowski	68	71	71	67	277	5,580,000
Nobumitsu Yuhara	69	70	70	69	278	4,117,500
Hidemichi Tanaka	68	69	72	69	278	4,117,500
Kim Jong-duk	69	74	70	68	281	3,510,000
Eduardo Herrera	71	71	71	69	282	2,763,000
Hirofumi Miyase	73	69	67	73	282	2,763,000
David Ishii	74	71	68	69	282	2,763,000
Yoshinori Kaneko	69	72	71	71	283	2,187,000
Tsuneyuki Nakajima	72	70	71	70	283	2,187,000
Masashi Ozaki	70	73	71	70	284	1,602,000
Katsuyoshi Tomori	71	70	71	72	284	1,602,000
Yasuharu Imano	70	75	68	71	284	1,602,000
Mamoru Osanai	68	72	72	72	284	1,602,000
Brandt Jobe	70	77	69	68	284	1,602,000
Tiger Woods	69	74	71	70	284	1,602,000
Yoshinori Mizumaki	71	74	68	72	285	1,242,000
Masahiro Kuramoto	72	73	73	67	285	1,242,000
Yeh Chang-ting	70	73	71	71	285	1,242,000
Hideki Kase	73	72	72	69	286	1,080,000
Satoshi Higashi	71	73	71	71	286	1,080,000
Mitsutaka Kusakabe	74	72	72	68	286	1,080,000
Toru Taniguchi	75	68	72	71	286	1,080,000
Katsumasa Miyamoto	73	72	69	72	286	1,080,000
Fred Funk	71	76	70	69	286	1,080,000
Zhang Lian-wei	71	72	72	71	286	1,080,000

Japan Series

Tokyo Yomiuri Country Club, Tokyo
Par 35-35–70; 6,960 yards

December 3-6
purse, ¥100,000,000

	SCORES				TOTAL	MONEY
Katsumasa Miyamoto	64	67	75	69	275	¥30,000,000
Masashi Ozaki	68	70	69	68	275	13,000,000
(Miyamoto defeated Ozaki on fourth extra hole.)						
Shingo Katayama	70	67	71	68	276	7,000,000
Eduardo Herrera	71	71	70	67	279	4,675,000
Kazuhiko Hosokawa	72	66	71	70	279	4,675,000
Naomichi Ozaki	72	69	70	69	280	2,996,666
Shigeki Maruyama	74	68	68	70	280	2,996,666
Toru Taniguchi	70	67	74	69	280	2,996,666
Frankie Minoza	69	71	72	69	281	2,100,000
Brian Watts	70	67	69	75	281	2,100,000
Todd Hamilton	74	65	74	69	282	1,730,000
Hajime Meshiai	71	72	70	70	283	1,600,000
Mitsutaka Kusakabe	70	67	71	76	284	1,450,000
Nobuhito Sato	68	68	77	71	284	1,450,000
Katsunori Kuwabara	70	73	71	71	285	1,300,000
Toshimitsu Izawa	69	68	76	74	287	1,082,500
Hidemichi Tanaka	71	69	73	74	287	1,082,500
Kaname Yokoo	71	70	74	72	287	1,082,500
Dinesh Chand	73	70	70	74	287	1,082,500
Yoshinori Mizumaki	73	65	72	78	288	852,500
Keiichiro Fukabori	74	70	72	72	288	852,500
Mamoru Osanai	73	69	74	72	288	852,500
Brandt Jobe	76	71	73	68	288	852,500
Masayuki Kawamura	72	75	71	72	290	745,000
Kenichi Kuboya	70	71	74	75	290	745,000
Toru Suzuki	75	70	77	73	295	700,000

Okinawa Open

Daikyo Country Club, Okinawa
Par 36-35–71; 6,359 yards

December 10-13
purse, ¥80,000,000

	SCORES				TOTAL	MONEY
Hidemichi Tanaka	70	67	69	67	273	¥14,400,000
Akihito Yokoyama	69	67	68	72	276	7,200,000
David Ishii	67	68	72	70	277	4,896,000
Eduardo Herrera	71	69	70	68	278	2,976,000
Toru Suzuki	71	71	67	69	278	2,976,000
Mamoru Osanai	72	72	68	66	278	2,976,000
Nobumitsu Yuhara	68	71	68	72	279	1,980,000
Masayuki Kawamura	67	71	71	70	279	1,980,000
Hsieh Chin-sheng	70	69	70	70	279	1,980,000
Richard Backwell	69	69	72	69	279	1,980,000
Takenori Hiraishi	73	73	67	67	280	1,440,000
Satoshi Higashi	72	72	68	69	281	1,128,960
Mitsuo Harada	70	72	75	64	281	1,128,960
Yoshimitsu Fukuzawa	67	75	70	69	281	1,128,960
Yeh Chang-ting	70	73	67	71	281	1,128,960
Shusaku Sugimoto	72	70	70	69	281	1,128,960
Yoshinori Kaneko	73	73	69	67	282	732,342
Kazuo Kanayama	69	72	72	69	282	732,342

	SCORES				TOTAL	MONEY
Masahiro Kuramoto	67	75	70	70	282	732,342
Katsumi Kubo	71	70	74	67	282	732,342
Yasuharu Imano	72	71	70	69	282	732,342
Chen Tze-chung	71	75	68	68	282	732,342
Frankie Minoza	71	68	71	72	282	732,342
Ikuo Shirahama	71	73	71	68	283	604,800
Kiyoshi Maita	69	72	68	74	283	604,800
Takashi Kanemoto	70	65	73	75	283	604,800
Saburo Fujiki	74	72	70	68	284	540,000
Tsukasa Watanabe	71	71	71	71	284	540,000
Noboru Fujiike	72	74	70	68	284	540,000
Koki Idoki	70	73	70	71	284	540,000
Stewart Ginn	67	75	73	69	284	540,000
Katsunori Kuwabara	73	71	72	68	284	540,000

Omega Tour

London Myanmar Open

Bagan Golf Resort, Bagan, Myanmar — March 5-8
Par 36-36–72; 7,147 yards — purse, US$225,000

	SCORES				TOTAL	MONEY
Taimur Hussain	70	73	68	69	280	US$36,337.50
Zhang Lian-wei	71	70	71	69	281	25,042.50
Ted Purdy	72	70	69	71	282	13,950
Vivek Bhandari	71	68	71	74	284	11,250
Christian Chernock	73	76	68	68	285	8,437.50
Thammanoon Sriroj	70	68	75	72	285	8,437.50
Brad Andrews	72	72	72	70	286	5,797.50
Carlos Espinosa	69	69	76	72	286	5,797.50
Edward Fryatt	73	68	72	73	286	5,797.50
Chen Liang-hsi	71	74	73	69	287	3,910.50
Arjun Singh	71	70	75	71	287	3,910.50
Charlie Wi	72	71	70	74	287	3,910.50
Greg Hanrahan	69	72	72	74	287	3,910.50
Gaurav Ghei	75	68	69	75	287	3,910.50
Periasamy Gunasegaran	70	71	74	73	288	3,240
Boonchu Ruangkit	67	75	72	74	288	3,240
Takeshi Ohyama	71	73	73	72	289	2,857.50
Paul Foley	74	68	73	74	289	2,857.50
Nam Young-woo	75	70	69	75	289	2,857.50
Jyoti Randhawa	70	70	71	78	289	2,857.50
Shaun Micheel	71	73	73	73	290	2,598.75
Aaron Meeks	72	68	75	75	290	2,598.75
Win Naing Tun	72	76	71	72	291	2,328.75
Taku Sugaya	71	71	77	72	291	2,328.75
Thaworn Wiratchant	73	72	72	74	291	2,328.75

	SCORES				TOTAL	MONEY
Kanwar Sekhon	72	75	69	75	291	2,328.75
Gilberto Morales	74	71	71	75	291	2,328.75
Prayad Marksaeng	70	70	71	80	291	2,328.75
V. Supphavarangoon	75	74	71	72	292	1,962
Simon Yates	69	73	76	74	292	1,962
Jerry Smith	70	71	76	75	292	1,962
Craig Kamps	73	73	69	77	292	1,962
Robert Huxtable	67	68	74	83	292	1,962

Classic Indian Open

Royal Calcutta Golf Club, Calcutta, India — March 12-15
Par 36-36–72; 7,165 yards — purse, US$300,000

	SCORES				TOTAL	MONEY
Firoz Ali	69	68	67	70	274	US$50,010
Dean Wilson	71	67	69	72	279	33,000
Choi Kyung-ju	71	69	69	71	280	18,600
Chung Joon	72	72	67	70	281	13,800
Rick Todd	74	72	64	71	281	13,800
Edward Fryatt	71	70	71	70	282	9,300
Scott Rowe	73	68	67	74	282	9,300
Nam Young-woo	69	71	70	73	283	6,360
Philip Jonas	70	70	72	71	283	6,360
Rob Moss	72	69	70	73	284	5,460
Hiroshi Ueda	68	74	68	75	285	5,070
Jim Rutledge	72	73	72	68	285	5,070
Carlos Espinosa	70	73	73	70	286	4,440
Charlie Wi	72	69	74	71	286	4,440
Clay Devers	72	73	69	72	286	4,440
Eric Meeks	73	69	71	73	286	4,440
Jeff Bloom	69	72	73	72	286	4,440
Stephen Lindskog	71	70	73	72	286	4,440
Tim Straub	67	70	74	75	286	4,440
Ian Leggatt	72	70	72	73	287	3,900
Jerry Smith	69	74	69	75	287	3,900
Arjun Atwal	69	71	76	72	288	3,240
Arjun Singh	71	72	72	73	288	3,240
Christian Pena	74	73	71	70	288	3,240
David Morland	72	70	72	74	288	3,240
Gustavo Rojas	70	71	72	75	288	3,240
Juan Nutt	73	70	72	73	288	3,240
Leith Wastle	80	66	69	73	288	3,240
Shaun Micheel	77	68	75	68	288	3,240
Ted Purdy	70	70	74	74	288	3,240

Orient Masters

Orient Golf & Country Club, Xiamen, China — April 2-5
Par 36-36–72; 7,048 yards — purse, US$200,000

	SCORES				TOTAL	MONEY
Chawalit Plaphol	71	71	67	69	278	US$32,300
Boonchu Ruangkit	73	69	70	71	283	22,260
Shaun Micheel	71	71	72	70	284	11,200

	SCORES				TOTAL	MONEY
John Senden	76	70	68	70	284	11,200
Lu Chien-soon	74	72	70	70	286	7,000
Andrew Pitts	73	74	69	70	286	7,000
Kang Wook-soon	74	68	72	72	286	7,000
Satoshi Oide	76	72	73	66	287	4,112.80
Thaworn Wiratchant	74	71	73	69	287	4,112.80
Zhang Lian-wei	74	69	74	70	287	4,112.80
Brian Quinn	70	71	75	71	287	4,112.80
Park No-seok	70	71	71	75	287	4,112.80
Chung Joon	76	74	70	68	288	3,138
Leith Wastle	74	72	72	70	288	3,138
Kim Young-il	77	73	70	69	289	2,653.33
Wang Ter-chang	74	69	75	71	289	2,653.33
Lucas Parsons	76	73	69	71	289	2,653.33
Ramon Brobio	74	71	72	72	289	2,653.33
Yuji Kurita	72	72	72	73	289	2,653.33
Craig Kamps	72	72	69	76	289	2,653.33
Nico van Rensburg	75	73	72	70	290	2,280
Charlie Wi	77	69	69	75	290	2,280
Lin Wen-teng	74	69	70	77	290	2,280
Chang Tse-peng	78	72	71	70	291	2,070
Prayad Marksaeng	72	73	72	74	291	2,070
Danny Zarate	71	71	75	74	291	2,070
Lu Wen-teh	76	69	70	69	291	2,070
Takeshi Kibamoto	75	76	71	70	292	1,860
*Liang Wen-chong	77	69	74	72	292	
Nozomi Kawahara	77	71	71	73	292	1,860
Anthony Kang	71	76	72	73	292	1,860

Trans Strait Invitational

Trans Strait Olympic Golf Club, Fuzhou, China — April 9-12
Par 36-36–72; 7,333 yards

	SCORES		TOTAL
Lin Keng-chi	69	70	139
Zhang Lian-wei	74	73	147
Tsai Chi-huang	75	73	148
Cheng Jun	75	74	149
Chen Yuan-chi	75	74	149

Volvo China Open

Sunisland International Club, Shanghai, China — April 16-19
Par 36-36–72; 6,764 yards — purse, US$400,000

	SCORES				TOTAL	MONEY
Edward Fryatt	69	65	69	66	269	US$72,000
Takeshi Ohyama	67	67	71	66	271	44,520
Aaron Meeks	67	68	67	70	272	24,800
Robin Byrd	72	67	67	67	273	17,000
Nico van Rensburg	66	73	64	70	273	17,000
Eric Meeks	66	70	71	68	275	11,000
John Senden	66	71	69	69	275	11,000
Gerry Norquist	67	70	68	70	275	11,000

	SCORES				TOTAL	MONEY
Chung Joon	72	65	74	65	276	7,486.67
Thammanoon Sriroj	71	69	69	67	276	7,486.67
Justin Cooper	67	72	69	68	276	7,486.67
Shaun Micheel	70	71	70	66	277	6,450
Scott Taylor	69	71	67	70	277	6,450
Scott Laycock	71	71	69	67	278	6,000
Chris Williams	69	69	69	71	278	6,000
Takeshi Kibamoto	71	72	71	65	279	4,618.46
Christian Pena	68	72	73	66	279	4,618.46
Jim Rutledge	67	71	74	67	279	4,618.46
Lucas Parsons	72	71	69	67	279	4,618.46
Choi Kyung-ju	70	72	70	67	279	4,618.46
Gilberto Morales	72	72	67	68	279	4,618.46
Adrian Percey	70	71	69	69	279	4,618.46
Kang Wook-soon	68	72	70	69	279	4,618.46
Nam Young-woo	67	73	69	70	279	4,618.46
Felix Casas	70	71	67	71	279	4,618.46
Eric Rustand	70	70	68	71	279	4,618.46
Tsai Chi-huang	70	72	66	71	279	4,618.46
Leith Wastle	66	71	70	72	279	4,618.46
Grant Dodd	69	69	73	69	280	3,640
Philip Chapman	73	67	71	69	280	3,640
Paul Foley	73	71	66	70	280	3,640
Charlie Wi	68	69	71	72	280	3,640

Macau Open

Macau Golf & Country Club, Macau — April 30-May 3
Par 71; 6,557 yards — purse, US$200,000

	SCORES				TOTAL	MONEY
Satoshi Oide	69	75	72	67	283	US$32,300
Vijay Singh	73	73	72	67	285	17,330
Gilberto Morales	73	69	70	73	285	17,330
Chen Tsang-te	73	70	73	70	286	9,000
Chris Williams	74	73	68	71	286	9,000
Lin Wen-tang	71	74	73	69	287	6,000
Shaun Micheel	76	71	71	69	287	6,000
Zhang Lian-wei	72	69	74	72	287	6,000
Charlie Wi	72	75	72	69	288	3,891
Nico van Rensburg	70	74	74	70	288	3,891
Lin Keng-chi	73	75	70	70	288	3,891
Lu Wen-teh	69	72	72	75	288	3,891
Nick Faldo	72	74	73	71	290	2,947.20
Boonchu Ruangkit	73	74	72	71	290	2,947.20
James Kingston	74	76	68	72	290	2,947.20
Andrew Bonhomme	73	72	70	75	290	2,947.20
Chen Liang-hsi	74	73	67	76	290	2,947.20
Arjun Singh	71	74	74	72	291	2,416
Yeh Wei-tze	73	75	70	73	291	2,416
Eric Rustand	69	73	76	73	291	2,416
Chen Yuan-chi	71	73	73	74	291	2,416
Cheng Jun	71	73	71	76	291	2,416
Ramon Brobio	75	75	69	73	292	2,160
Chawalit Plaphol	74	72	71	75	292	2,160
Hsieh Yu-shu	70	74	72	76	292	2,160
Wang Ter-chang	75	74	73	71	293	2,010

	SCORES				TOTAL	MONEY
Hwang Sung-ha	73	73	71	76	293	2,010
John Senden	75	74	73	72	294	1,860
Thammanoon Sriroj	73	76	73	72	294	1,860
Des Terblanche	72	74	73	75	294	1,860

Guam Open

Leo Palace Resort, Manenggon Hills, Guam — May 14-17
Par 36-36–72; 6,609 yards — purse, US$200,000

	SCORES				TOTAL	MONEY
Jerry Smith	69	67	66	70	272	US$32,300
Arjun Atwal	70	69	67	72	278	17,330
Chris Williams	73	67	64	74	278	17,330
Charlie Wi	74	69	68	69	280	10,000
Katsumune Imai	66	73	71	71	281	7,500
Gerry Norquist	70	68	71	72	281	7,500
Vivek Bhandari	69	73	69	72	283	5,153.33
Leith Wastle	72	68	70	73	283	5,153.33
Chung Joon	67	74	67	75	283	5,153.33
Hsieh Yu-shu	71	67	73	73	284	4,000
Carlos Espinosa	72	73	67	73	285	3,552
Lu Wen-teh	71	71	70	73	285	3,552
Cesar Perez	69	74	71	72	286	3,216
Craig Kamps	77	70	71	69	287	3,060
Justin Cooper	74	72	73	69	288	2,704
Chou Hung-nan	75	72	70	71	288	2,704
Scott Laycock	70	71	73	74	288	2,704
Lin Chih-chen	70	70	73	75	288	2,704
Taku Sugaya	73	69	67	79	288	2,704
Yasuhiro Taguchi	73	73	72	71	289	2,220
Ho Chia-feng	68	76	73	72	289	2,220
Chang Chin-kuo	73	71	72	73	289	2,220
Chen Liang-hsi	69	72	75	73	289	2,220
Arjun Singh	74	72	69	74	289	2,220
Takeshi Ohyama	74	70	71	74	289	2,220
Chen Yuan-chi	74	72	68	75	289	2,220
Robin Byrd	69	76	74	71	290	1,802.86
Greg Hanrahan	72	71	76	71	290	1,802.86
Eric Meeks	71	75	72	72	290	1,802.86
Prayad Marksaeng	72	67	76	75	290	1,802.86
Ariel Canete	73	74	67	76	290	1,802.86
John Senden	72	72	70	76	290	1,802.86
Christian Chernock	73	72	69	76	290	1,802.86

Fila Open

Tae Young Country Club, Seoul, Korea — May 20-23
Par 36-36–72; 6,822 yards — purse, US$150,000

	SCORES				TOTAL	MONEY
Robert Huxtable	69	70	66	71	276	US$24,225
Park Nam-sin	70	71	69	66	276	16,695
(Huxtable defeated Park on second extra hole.)						
Choi Kyung-ju	69	68	68	72	277	9,300

	SCORES				TOTAL	MONEY
Ted Purdy	68	71	71	68	278	6,750
Gilberto Morales	67	70	68	73	278	6,750
Kim Wan-tae	66	68	71	75	280	5,250
Kang Wook-soon	69	69	74	70	282	3,865
Cesar Perez	75	71	66	70	282	3,865
Toru Kinoshita	72	72	68	70	282	3,865
Shaun Micheel	71	71	71	71	284	2,775.67
Kim Seung-il	71	68	73	72	284	2,775.67
Kim Hong-sik	66	70	75	73	284	2,775.67
Masayuki Tomita	71	71	70	73	285	2,353.50
Keiichi Asano	72	67	73	73	285	2,353.50
Nam Young-woo	69	72	75	70	286	2,115
Jee Tae-hwa	70	73	71	72	286	2,115
Choi Gwang-soo	68	72	73	73	286	2,115
Lee Bu-young	74	72	71	70	287	1,812
Simon Yates	71	71	75	70	287	1,812
Nozomi Kawahara	74	73	69	71	287	1,812
Chung Joon	71	70	73	73	287	1,812
Ariel Canete	72	66	71	78	287	1,812
Taimur Hussain	74	69	75	70	288	1,552.50
Park No-seok	72	72	74	70	288	1,552.50
Anthony Kang	72	73	72	71	288	1,552.50
Yang Yong-eun	70	72	74	72	288	1,552.50
Choi Sang-ho	72	74	69	73	288	1,552.50
Cho Chul-sang	74	66	74	74	288	1,552.50
Tsutomu Ide	73	70	72	74	289	1,372.50
Dragon Lee	72	69	74	74	289	1,372.50

Sabah Masters

Shan-Shui Golf & Country Club, Tawau, Sabah, Malaysia — August 6-9
Par 36-36–72; 7,257 yards — purse, US$150,000

	SCORES				TOTAL	MONEY
Simon Yates	67	71	67	73	278	US$24,225
Des Terblanche	70	66	70	73	279	16,695
Arjun Atwal	73	71	66	71	281	9,300
Lu Chien-soon	67	73	73	69	282	7,500
Choi Kyung-ju	70	70	69	74	283	6,000
Scott Taylor	72	72	72	68	284	4,875
Nico van Rensburg	73	69	72	70	284	4,875
Mo Joong-kyung	69	74	73	69	285	3,211.75
Bjorn Flygare	69	72	73	71	285	3,211.75
Prayad Marksaeng	71	78	65	71	285	3,211.75
Chris Williams	69	71	72	73	285	3,211.75
Scott Laycock	76	72	72	66	286	2,427.33
Thammanoon Sriroj	74	71	71	70	286	2,427.33
Grant Dodd	71	74	69	72	286	2,427.33
Mardan Mamat	77	70	68	72	287	2,115
Leith Wastle	73	70	70	74	287	2,115
Andrew Pitts	70	69	73	75	287	2,115
Mike Cunning	76	70	71	71	288	1,897.50
Carlos Espinosa	72	70	74	72	288	1,897.50
Norio Shinozaki	75	74	72	68	289	1,755
Gerry Norquist	68	77	74	70	289	1,755
Jerry Smith	70	74	72	73	289	1,755
Ali Kadir	74	71	77	68	290	1,620

	SCORES				TOTAL	MONEY
Taimur Hussain	73	74	75	68	290	1,620
Eric Meeks	72	71	75	72	290	1,620
Stephen Lindskog	73	73	77	68	291	1,485
Peter Teravainen	70	72	76	73	291	1,485
Gilberto Morales	69	78	71	73	291	1,485
Periasamy Gunasegaran	75	74	75	68	292	1,290
Yasuhiro Taguchi	74	73	74	71	292	1,290
Craig Kamps	74	72	74	72	292	1,290
Peter Fowler	71	72	75	74	292	1,290
Park No-seok	69	71	78	74	292	1,290
Thaworn Wiratchant	71	76	71	74	292	1,290

Volvo Masters of Malaysia

Kota Permai Golf and Country Club, August 13-16
Kuala Lumpur, Malaysia purse, US$200,000
Par 36-36–72; 6,962 yards

	SCORES				TOTAL	MONEY
Chris Williams	71	68	71	69	279	US$32,300
Adrian Percey	68	71	69	71	279	17,330
Zaw Moe	67	67	67	78	279	17,330
(Williams defeated Percey on first and Moe on fourth extra hole.)						
Jim Rutledge	72	68	72	68	280	10,000
Wang Ter-chang	68	70	69	74	281	8,000
Peter Teravainen	72	69	73	68	282	5,021.67
Hsieh Yu-shu	76	68	68	70	282	5,021.67
Chung Joon	65	73	73	71	282	5,021.67
Eric Meeks	71	66	74	71	282	5,021.67
Anthony Kang	71	70	68	73	282	5,021.67
Choi Kyung-ju	68	70	69	75	282	5,021.67
Greg Hanrahan	71	70	70	72	283	3,162.50
Fran Quinn	70	69	72	72	283	3,162.50
Mardan Mamat	69	70	72	72	283	3,162.50
Eric Rustand	71	70	69	73	283	3,162.50
Mo Joong-kyung	72	69	74	69	284	2,700
Felix Casas	68	73	70	73	284	2,700
Nico van Rensburg	70	69	72	73	284	2,700
Lu Wen-teh	73	71	70	71	285	2,313.33
James Kingston	70	71	72	72	285	2,313.33
Prayad Marksaeng	73	71	68	73	285	2,313.33
Grant Dodd	70	72	70	73	285	2,313.33
Gerry Norquist	71	70	71	73	285	2,313.33
Carlos Espinosa	71	68	70	76	285	2,313.33
Simon Yates	72	74	73	67	286	1,890
Ramon Brobio	72	71	74	69	286	1,890
Christian Pena	76	70	71	69	286	1,890
Arjun Singh	70	72	72	72	286	1,890
Lin Chih-chen	74	69	70	73	286	1,890
Craig Kamps	73	71	69	73	286	1,890
Ed Fryatt	72	66	74	74	286	1,890
Des Terblanche	71	68	71	76	286	1,890

Ericsson Singapore Open

SAFRA Resort & Country Club, Singapore
Par 36-36–72; 6,913 yards

August 20-23
purse, US$500,000

	SCORES				TOTAL	MONEY
Shaun Micheel	67	69	67	69	272	US$80,750
Hendrik Buhrmann	69	68	66	71	274	55,650
Brad King	69	70	70	67	276	31,000
Nico van Rensburg	70	69	69	69	277	22,500
Lu Chien-soon	68	66	73	70	277	22,500
Christian Chernock	71	71	70	66	278	13,230
Wayne Bradley	71	68	70	69	278	13,230
Des Terblanche	69	67	73	69	278	13,230
Lu Wen-teh	67	72	69	70	278	13,230
Ed Fryatt	71	67	69	71	278	13,230
Grant Dodd	70	71	69	69	279	8,880
Park No-seok	66	69	74	70	279	8,880
Chris Williams	73	71	68	68	280	7,070
Arjun Singh	71	72	69	68	280	7,070
James Kingston	72	66	74	68	280	7,070
Rodney Pampling	72	67	72	69	280	7,070
Olle Nordberg	66	70	75	69	280	7,070
Andrew Raitt	69	71	70	70	280	7,070
Mike Cunning	71	69	69	71	280	7,070
Chung Joon	70	73	71	67	281	5,700
Dominique Boulet	71	71	70	69	281	5,700
Kenneth Druce	71	69	72	69	281	5,700
Clay Devers	71	71	69	70	281	5,700
Gerry Norquist	70	72	69	70	281	5,700
Jim Rutledge	71	71	72	68	282	5,175
Danny Zarate	68	72	71	71	282	5,175
Simon Yates	71	73	70	69	283	4,575
Wang Ter-chang	73	70	71	69	283	4,575
Fran Quinn	70	73	71	69	283	4,575
Eric Meeks	71	70	71	71	283	4,575
Jerry Smith	68	70	71	74	283	4,575
Shin Yong-jin	69	68	69	77	283	4,575

Kolon Sports Korean Open

Seoul Country Club, Seoul, Korea
Par 36-36–72; 6,995 yards

September 17-20
purse, US$300,000

	SCORES				TOTAL	MONEY
*Kim Dae-sub	76	70	67	65	278	
Choi Sang-ho	69	71	74	69	283	US$36,542.52
Fran Quinn	69	70	70	74	283	36,542.52
Adrian Percey	70	74	71	70	285	14,195.36
*Jung Sung-han	70	72	72	71	285	
Chawalit Plaphol	70	73	70	72	285	14,195.36
Gerry Norquist	72	73	71	70	286	8,186.93
Park No-seok	73	71	70	72	286	8,186.93
Choi Gwang-soo	78	69	67	72	286	8,186.93
Eric Rustand	74	68	70	74	286	8,186.93
Han Young-kun	73	72	72	70	287	4,778.64
Chung Do-man	75	66	75	71	287	4,778.64
Scott Laycock	74	71	70	72	287	4,778.64

	SCORES				TOTAL	MONEY
Craig Kamps	69	70	70	78	287	4,778.64
Robin Byrd	72	74	73	69	288	4,005.62
*Kim Sung-yun	76	69	68	75	288	
Kim Jong-duk	75	73	72	69	289	3,706.96
Jim Rutledge	75	69	74	71	289	3,706.96
Yoo Jong-koo	74	72	75	69	290	3,039.35
Rob Huxtable	74	73	73	70	290	3,039.35
Satoshi Oide	74	72	73	71	290	3,039.35
Yoon Kwang-chun	72	72	74	72	290	3,039.35
Lee Joon-suk	76	70	72	72	290	3,039.35
Christian Pena	71	72	74	73	290	3,039.35
James Kingston	75	67	75	73	290	3,039.35
Lee In-woo	72	70	75	73	290	3,039.35
*Kim Hyung-tae	73	71	72	74	290	
Peter Teravainen	76	73	72	70	291	2,565
Mo Joong-kyung	74	72	73	72	291	2,565
Chung Joon	71	70	77	73	291	2,565
Brad Andrews	76	69	72	74	291	2,565

Kuala Lumpur Open

The Mines Resort City, Kuala Lumpur, Malaysia — October 15-18
Par 35-36–71; 6,794 yards — purse, US$200,000

	SCORES				TOTAL	MONEY
Nico van Rensburg	70	70	69	69	278	US$32,300
Jerry Smith	69	73	66	70	278	22,260
(Van Rensburg defeated Smith on fifth extra hole.)						
Rob Willis	73	69	69	69	280	12,400
Scott Taylor	69	71	71	70	281	10,000
Olle Nordberg	73	67	72	70	282	8,000
Ali Kadir	72	72	65	74	283	7,000
Felix Casas	72	75	71	67	285	4,626
Ted Purdy	74	72	71	68	285	4,626
Prayad Marksaeng	74	73	68	70	285	4,626
Jim Rutledge	70	75	68	72	285	4,626
John Senden	67	71	74	73	285	4,626
Paul Foley	72	70	74	70	286	3,325
Chawalit Plaphol	67	68	72	79	286	3,325
Thaworn Wiratchant	70	75	73	69	287	2,940
Gaurav Ghei	70	72	73	72	287	2,940
Justin Cooper	70	70	69	78	287	2,940
Carlos Espinosa	71	73	73	71	288	2,428.57
Yasunobu Kuramoto	72	73	72	71	288	2,428.57
Kenny Walker	68	75	73	72	288	2,428.57
Dominique Boulet	68	71	76	73	288	2,428.57
Jyoti Randhawa	75	72	66	75	288	2,428.57
Takeshi Ohyama	70	71	70	77	288	2,428.57
Vivek Bhandari	75	63	72	78	288	2,428.57
Brad Andrews	71	71	74	73	289	2,010
Simon Owen	71	76	69	73	289	2,010
Des Terblanche	67	76	73	73	289	2,010
Taimur Hussain	75	69	71	74	289	2,010
Boonchu Ruangkit	73	69	71	76	289	2,010
Toru Kinoshita	69	70	74	76	289	2,010
Yurio Akitomi	71	70	78	71	290	1,670
Craig Kamps	71	74	73	72	290	1,670

	SCORES				TOTAL	MONEY
Kasiadi	75	71	72	72	290	1,670
Leith Wastle	71	67	79	73	290	1,670
Rey Pagunsan	71	75	71	73	290	1,670
Greg Hanrahan	72	70	74	74	290	1,670

FedEx PGA Championship

Raffles Country Club, Singapore — October 22-25
Par 36-36–72; 6,829 yards — purse, US$150,000

	SCORES				TOTAL	MONEY
Chris Williams	70	66	69	72	277	US$24,225
Ted Purdy	68	73	71	66	278	16,695
Vivek Bhandari	73	67	71	69	280	7,600
Peter Teravainen	71	69	71	69	280	7,600
Jeev Milkha Singh	69	66	75	70	280	7,600
Lu Wen-teh	68	74	69	70	281	5,250
Gaurav Ghei	73	68	73	68	282	3,865
Gilberto Morales	72	73	69	68	282	3,865
Craig Kamps	70	71	69	72	282	3,865
Jim Rutledge	70	72	72	69	283	2,876
Kyi Hla Han	73	70	69	71	283	2,876
Thaworn Wiratchant	71	74	71	68	284	2,493.50
Richard Kaplan	71	70	73	70	284	2,493.50
Nobuhiro Masuda	72	75	70	68	285	2,115
Mardan Mamat	73	69	71	72	285	2,115
Carlos Espinosa	68	72	72	73	285	2,115
Paul Foley	71	71	70	73	285	2,115
Takeshi Ohyama	72	69	70	74	285	2,115
Soe Kyaw Naing	73	74	70	69	286	1,758
Jerry Smith	74	70	72	70	286	1,758
Shoichi Kita	73	72	71	70	286	1,758
Gerry Norquist	71	70	73	72	286	1,758
James Kingston	72	70	70	74	286	1,758
Boonchu Ruangkit	72	72	74	69	287	1,507.50
Des Terblanche	74	70	73	70	287	1,507.50
Masashige Shinoda	71	69	76	71	287	1,507.50
Park No-seok	70	74	71	72	287	1,507.50
Simon Yates	72	71	70	74	287	1,507.50
Shin Yong-jin	74	69	70	74	287	1,507.50
Thammanoon Sriroj	71	75	75	67	288	1,236.43
Toru Kinoshita	73	72	73	70	288	1,236.43
Chang Tse-peng	73	73	71	71	288	1,236.43
Scott Rowe	73	71	72	72	288	1,236.43
Aaron Meeks	70	74	71	73	288	1,236.43
Park Unho	72	71	72	73	288	1,236.43
Andy Wada	73	68	71	76	288	1,236.43

Ericsson Classic

Formosa First Country Club, Taipei, Taiwan — October 29-November 1
Par 36-36–72; 6,932 yards — purse, US$200,000

	SCORES				TOTAL	MONEY
Lu Wen-teh	66	72	72	70	280	US$32,300
Carlos Espinosa	68	71	72	69	280	17,330
Felix Casas	70	69	71	70	280	17,330
(Lu defeated Espinosa and Casas on second extra hole.)						
Choi Gwang-soo	74	68	73	71	286	9,000
Boonchu Ruangkit	74	68	71	73	286	9,000
Lin Keng-chi	73	73	72	69	287	6,000
Jim Rutledge	70	72	74	71	287	6,000
Tsai Chi-huang	72	69	71	75	287	6,000
Gerry Norquist	69	71	76	72	288	3,891
Eric Meeks	70	73	73	72	288	3,891
Scott Rowe	74	69	73	72	288	3,891
Nozomi Kawahara	69	72	72	75	288	3,891
Andrew Pitts	72	70	76	71	289	2,947.20
Nico van Rensburg	73	72	72	72	289	2,947.20
Wang Ter-chang	75	70	72	72	289	2,947.20
Yeh Wei-tze	71	74	71	73	289	2,947.20
Chris Williams	73	69	73	74	289	2,947.20
Greg Hanrahan	75	72	71	72	290	2,530
Lin Chie-hsiang	69	75	73	73	290	2,530
Craig Kamps	68	77	75	71	291	2,280
Lee Lien-fu	74	71	74	72	291	2,280
Lin Chih-chen	73	71	73	74	291	2,280
Chung Chun-hsing	72	72	73	74	291	2,280
Taku Sugaya	72	68	75	76	291	2,280
Clay Devers	74	74	73	71	292	1,980
Tseng Wen-chi	69	74	77	72	292	1,980
Hsieh Chin-sheng	68	75	76	73	292	1,980
Thaworn Wiratchant	72	74	72	74	292	1,980
Dominique Boulet	73	71	72	76	292	1,980
Hendrik Buhrmann	74	75	73	71	293	1,740
Wayne Bradley	76	72	73	72	293	1,740
Hsieh Yu-shu	69	71	80	73	293	1,740

Hero Honda Masters

Delhi Golf Club, Delhi, India — November 5-8
Par 36-36–72; 6,888 yards — purse, US$200,000

	SCORES				TOTAL	MONEY
Jyoti Randhawa	69	67	73	66	275	US$32,300
Jeev Milkha Singh	67	71	69	72	279	22,260
Gerry Norquist	65	73	70	73	281	12,400
Rob Huxtable	72	72	73	65	282	8,333.33
Arjun Atwal	71	69	71	71	282	8,333.33
Mike Cunning	68	68	72	74	282	8,333.33
Jim Rutledge	73	72	71	67	283	4,626
Craig Kamps	70	73	72	68	283	4,626
Rafael Ponce	71	71	69	72	283	4,626
Carlos Espinosa	70	72	68	73	283	4,626
Scott Taylor	69	71	70	73	283	4,626
Wayne Bradley	73	71	71	69	284	3,325

	SCORES				TOTAL	MONEY
Daniel Chopra	71	69	72	72	284	3,325
Andrew Pitts	73	72	70	70	285	3,060
Scott Rowe	71	70	74	71	286	2,940
Rafiq Ali	74	74	72	67	287	2,700
Clay Devers	72	73	70	72	287	2,700
Basad Ali	72	72	70	73	287	2,700
Indrajit Bhalotia	70	74	74	70	288	2,375
Ali Sher	73	72	73	70	288	2,375
Vivek Bhandari	71	71	70	76	288	2,375
Mardan Mamat	74	67	71	76	288	2,375
James Kingston	70	76	75	68	289	2,160
Amritinder Singh	71	74	69	75	289	2,160
Justin Cooper	70	72	70	77	289	2,160
Mukesh Kumar	72	71	77	70	290	1,890
Aaron Meeks	74	74	71	71	290	1,890
Shiv Prakash	74	71	72	73	290	1,890
Paul Foley	73	73	71	73	290	1,890
Fran Quinn	68	78	71	73	290	1,890
Grant Dodd	70	71	73	76	290	1,890

Thailand Open

Thana City Golf & Country Club, Bangkok, Thailand — November 12-15
Par 36-36–72; 6,896 yards — purse, US$200,000

	SCORES				TOTAL	MONEY
James Kingston	69	64	69	70	272	US$32,300
Jeev Milkha Singh	69	67	70	66	272	22,260
(Kingston defeated Singh on first extra hole.)						
Craig Kamps	67	71	69	66	273	12,400
Jyoti Randhawa	65	66	73	70	274	9,000
Boonchu Ruangkit	68	67	68	71	274	9,000
*Thongchai Jaidee	67	70	69	69	275	
Simon Yates	69	66	70	70	275	7,000
Arjun Atwal	74	65	70	67	276	6,000
Amritinder Singh	71	68	69	69	277	5,000
Ramon Brobio	69	69	69	71	278	4,460
Dominique Boulet	70	70	72	67	279	3,835
Scott Rowe	68	70	73	68	279	3,835
Tadahisa Inoue	74	72	69	66	281	3,236.67
Taimur Hussain	73	65	74	69	281	3,236.67
Kenny Walker	69	67	72	73	281	3,236.67
Gerry Norquist	70	67	74	71	282	2,820
Mardan Mamat	71	71	69	71	282	2,820
Hsieh Yu-shu	71	65	74	72	282	2,820
Andrew Pitts	66	74	75	68	283	2,383.33
Chen Liang-hsi	72	72	69	70	283	2,383.33
Sanchai Senaprom	73	69	70	71	283	2,383.33
Rob Huxtable	69	71	72	71	283	2,383.33
Lu Wen-teh	70	72	69	72	283	2,383.33
Rey Pagunsan	73	70	67	73	283	2,383.33
Danny Zarate	72	70	73	69	284	2,070
Periasamy Gunasegaran	71	72	71	70	284	2,070
Greg Hanrahan	71	67	72	74	284	2,070
Ali Kadir	69	69	71	75	284	2,070
Scott Taylor	74	72	70	69	285	1,830
Philip Chapman	71	74	70	70	285	1,830

	SCORES				TOTAL	MONEY
Thammanoon Sriroj	73	69	71	72	285	1,830
Olle Nordberg	71	69	73	72	285	1,830

Perrier Hong Kong Open

Hong Kong Golf Club, Fanling, Hong Kong
Par 71; 6,727 yards

November 26-29
purse, US$300,000

	SCORES				TOTAL	MONEY
Kang Wook-soon	69	70	66	67	272	US$50,010
Edward Fryatt	70	68	68	68	274	33,000
Paul Friedlander	70	67	68	70	275	15,400
Mark Brooks	68	68	69	70	275	15,400
Chris Williams	68	69	71	67	275	15,400
Jerry Smith	72	69	65	70	276	7,356
Lu Wen-teh	74	67	66	69	276	7,356
Danny Zarate	71	67	68	70	276	7,356
Hendrik Buhrmann	71	68	68	69	276	7,356
Hsieh Chin-sheng	64	70	69	73	276	7,356
Chen Liang-hsi	70	71	67	69	277	4,836
Wang Ter-chang	66	70	68	73	277	4,836
Brad Schadewitz	66	71	69	71	277	4,836
Kyi Hla Han	69	68	70	70	277	4,836
Fran Quinn	69	73	70	65	277	4,836
Ted Purdy	69	69	68	72	278	4,320
Andrew Pitts	70	68	69	71	278	4,320
Eric Meeks	68	71	69	70	278	4,320
Craig Kamps	71	69	67	72	279	3,780
Park Nam-sin	68	69	69	73	279	3,780
David Frost	70	69	69	71	279	3,780
Gerry Norquist	71	67	70	71	279	3,780
John Daly	66	72	70	71	279	3,780
Derek Fung	68	69	72	70	279	3,780
Roger Winchester	71	71	67	71	280	3,240
Andrew Raitt	71	69	68	72	280	3,240
Robert Huxtable	69	69	72	70	280	3,240
Charlie Wi	71	72	68	70	281	2,760
Jeff Bloom	72	68	69	72	281	2,760
Brian Wilson	72	69	69	71	281	2,760
Madasamy Murugiah	71	73	69	68	281	2,760
Anthony Wall	68	65	77	71	281	2,760

Omega PGA Championship

Clearwater Bay Golf & Country Club,
Sai Kung, Hong Kong
Par 35-35–70; 6,115 yards

December 3-6
purse, US$500,000

	SCORES				TOTAL	MONEY
Kang Wook-soon	66	65	66	66	263	US$80,750
Hsieh Chin-sheng	70	64	67	65	266	55,650
Eric Rustand	70	69	67	62	268	31,000
Boonchu Ruangkit	70	66	66	67	269	25,000
Eric Meeks	71	65	69	65	270	18,750
Zhang Lian-wei	68	66	68	68	270	18,750

	SCORES				TOTAL	MONEY
Lai Hung-lin	73	68	68	62	271	13,750
Carlos Espinosa	68	66	69	68	271	13,750
Shaun Micheel	69	67	71	65	272	10,108.33
Choi Kyung-ju	74	67	65	66	272	10,108.33
Chang Tse-peng	66	71	68	67	272	10,108.33
Dominique Boulet	74	66	70	63	273	7,735
Jerry Smith	67	69	72	65	273	7,735
Derek Fung	73	67	67	66	273	7,735
Toru Kinoshita	71	68	67	67	273	7,735
Zaw Moe	69	68	67	69	273	7,735
Taimur Hussain	68	70	70	66	274	6,466.67
Des Terblanche	72	69	63	70	274	6,466.67
Greg Hanrahan	72	66	66	70	274	6,466.67
Park No-seok	69	66	73	67	275	5,775
James Kingston	73	67	68	67	275	5,775
Leith Wastle	72	66	68	69	275	5,775
Rodrigo Cuello	72	65	67	71	275	5,775
Gerry Norquist	74	68	67	67	276	5,025
Rob Huxtable	71	67	70	68	276	5,025
Chawalit Plaphol	70	71	67	68	276	5,025
Adrian Percey	70	65	72	69	276	5,025
Park Nam-sin	72	71	64	69	276	5,025
Brad Andrews	69	66	68	73	276	5,025
Satoshi Oide	70	70	69	68	277	4,230
Ed Fryatt	71	66	71	69	277	4,230
Clay Devers	71	69	68	69	277	4,230
Jyoti Randhawa	73	68	66	70	277	4,230
Wayne Bradley	74	68	65	70	277	4,230

Volvo Asian Match Play

Mission Hills Golf Club, Shenzhen, China — December 10-13
Par 36-36–72; 6,970 yards — purse, US$265,000

FIRST ROUND

Jim Rutledge defeated Robert Huxtable, 2 and 1.
Eric Meeks defeated Nico van Rensburg, 2 and 1.
Chawalit Plaphol defeated Cheng Jun, 3 and 2.
Carlos Espinosa defeated Taimur Hussain on 19th hole.
Gerry Norquist defeated Lu Wen-teh on 22nd hole.
James Kingston defeated Wu Xiang-bing, 1 up.
Jerry Smith defeated Takeshi Ohyama, 4 and 2.
Choi Kyung-ju defeated Hendrik Buhrmann, 3 and 2.

(Losers received US$2,500 each.)

SECOND ROUND

Des Terblanche defeated Rutledge, 2 up.
Meeks defeated Boonchu Ruangkit, 1 up.
Edward Fryatt defeated Plaphol, 2 and 1.
Zhang Lian-wei defeated Espinosa, 4 and 3.
Norquist defeated Chris Williams on 20th hole.
Shaun Micheel defeated Kingston, 2 up.
Smith defeated Jeev Milkha Singh, 2 and 1.
Kang Wook-soon defeated Choi, 3 and 2.

(Losers received US$4,000 each.)

QUARTER-FINALS

Meeks defeated Terblanche, 3 and 1.
Fryatt defeated Zhang after Zhang disqualified.
Smith defeated Kang, 1 up.
Norquist defeated Micheel on 21st hole.

(Losers received US$8,000 each.)

SEMI-FINALS

Norquist defeated Smith, 6 and 5.
Meeks defeated Fryatt, 2 up.

(Smith and Fryatt received US$13,000 each.)

FINAL

Norquist defeated Meeks, 2 and 1.

(Norquist received US$50,000; Meeks received US$25,000.)

HUGO BOSS FOURSOMES
FINAL

Rutledge and Plaphol defeated Fryatt and Smith on 22nd hole.

(Winners received US$12,500 each; losers received US$7,000 each.)

Australasian Tour

Victorian Open

Victoria Golf Club, Melbourne, Victoria
Par 36-36–72; 6,830 yards

January 8-11
purse, A$200,000

	SCORES				TOTAL	MONEY
Bradley King	68	65	67	72	272	A$37,894
Greg Chalmers	69	71	67	70	277	15,263
Terry Price	67	71	70	69	277	15,263
Daniel Chopra	70	69	71	67	277	15,263
Adam Le Vesconte	70	68	69	71	278	8,422
Scott Laycock	68	70	69	72	279	7,158
Stephen Leaney	71	71	66	71	279	7,158
Robert Allenby	71	69	67	73	280	6,106
Roland Baglin	68	73	73	67	281	4,947
Rodney Pampling	70	74	66	71	281	4,947
Shane Tait	71	70	67	73	281	4,947
Anthony Edwards	69	73	68	71	281	4,947
Tony Carolan	70	72	70	70	282	3,790
Wayne Grady	69	77	71	66	283	3,326
Stephen Scahill	75	71	67	70	283	3,326
Paul Devenport	70	70	72	71	283	3,326
Gavin Vearing	74	70	74	66	284	2,335
*Geoff Ogilvy	72	74	72	66	284	
Adrian Percey	71	72	71	70	284	2,335
Michael Long	70	72	71	71	284	2,335
Lucas Parsons	70	70	72	72	284	2,335
Nigel Lane	71	69	72	72	284	2,335
Craig Jones	72	71	66	75	284	2,335
Danny Vera	71	71	71	71	284	2,335
Darren Cole	73	72	71	69	285	1,958
Marcus Cain	70	69	76	70	285	1,958
David Bransdon	74	70	73	69	286	1,547
David Ecob	72	72	72	70	286	1,547
Tim Elliott	67	76	71	72	286	1,547
Dirk Ayers	68	74	71	73	286	1,547
Wayne Smith	68	72	72	74	286	1,547
Peter Lonard	74	71	67	74	286	1,547

Johnnie Walker Classic

Blue Canyon Country Club, Phuket, Thailand
Par 36-36–72; 7,099 yards

January 22-25
purse, £800,000

	SCORES				TOTAL	MONEY
Tiger Woods	72	71	71	65	279	£133,330
Ernie Els	67	65	74	73	279	88,880
(Woods defeated Els on second extra hole.)						
Retief Goosen	71	71	69	69	280	50,070
Andrew Coltart	71	68	72	70	281	31,470
Lee Westwood	71	66	73	71	281	31,470

	SCORES				TOTAL	MONEY
Alex Cejka	67	68	74	72	281	31,470
Peter O'Malley	69	68	72	72	281	31,470
Stephen Leaney	70	68	72	72	282	17,140
Padraig Harrington	69	67	73	73	282	17,140
Prayad Marksaeng	67	72	69	74	282	17,140
Nick Faldo	71	67	69	75	282	17,140
Peter Lonard	70	71	71	71	283	13,320
Robert Allenby	75	70	66	72	283	13,320
Michael Long	76	71	67	71	285	12,000
Peter Baker	73	69	68	75	285	12,000
Steve Alker	68	71	72	75	286	10,384
Bradley King	71	72	68	75	286	10,384
Jose Maria Olazabal	72	72	70	72	286	10,384
Phillip Price	69	72	71	74	286	10,384
Rodney Pampling	73	72	73	68	286	10,384
Shane Tait	69	75	70	73	287	9,240
Paul McGinley	69	71	76	71	287	9,240
Frankie Minoza	73	70	74	71	288	8,760
Hajime Meshiai	73	71	71	73	288	8,760
Sven Struver	73	70	75	71	289	7,920
Felix Casas	72	72	76	69	289	7,920
Arjun Atwal	70	71	73	75	289	7,920
Greg Turner	73	71	73	72	289	7,920
Ian Garbutt	74	73	68	74	289	7,920
Wayne Smith	69	75	75	71	290	6,594.29
Zhang Lian-wei	70	72	74	74	290	6,594.29
Jim Payne	75	72	74	69	290	6,594.29
Lucas Parsons	68	75	76	71	290	6,594.29
Greg Chalmers	72	68	76	74	290	6,594.29
Fabrice Tarnaud	73	69	77	71	290	6,594.29
Rick Gibson	72	74	69	75	290	6,594.29
Patrik Sjoland	71	75	74	71	291	5,760
Darren Cole	70	75	71	75	291	5,760
Anthony Gilligan	73	73	73	72	291	5,760
Chang Tse-peng	73	72	78	69	292	5,360
Thammanoon Sriroj	70	75	74	73	292	5,360
Zaw Moe	72	75	72	74	293	4,960
Park No-seok	72	72	76	73	293	4,960
Justin Cooper	71	70	71	81	293	4,960
Marcus Wheelhouse	72	74	72	76	294	4,160
Jonathan Lomas	72	74	75	73	294	4,160
Mike Harwood	73	72	73	76	294	4,160
Scott Laycock	76	69	77	72	294	4,160
Van Phillips	78	69	73	74	294	4,160
Roger Chapman	77	70	74	73	294	4,160
Craig Jones	72	75	73	74	294	4,160
Daniel Chopra	68	73	76	78	295	3,440
Stephen Allan	76	69	76	74	295	3,440
Chris Van der Velde	75	72	78	71	296	3,120
Per Haugsrud	74	73	74	75	296	3,120
Park Nam-sin	73	72	74	78	297	2,608
David Howell	74	72	72	79	297	2,608
Mark Allen	68	75	82	72	297	2,608
Gary Orr	73	74	77	73	297	2,608
Jean Louis Guepy	74	71	76	76	297	2,608
Matthew Ecob	75	68	76	79	298	2,280
Don Fardon	73	73	76	76	298	2,280
David Ecob	73	74	77	75	299	2,080
Paul Lawrie	71	75	76	77	299	2,080
Jack O'Keefe	76	70	73	80	299	2,080

	SCORES				TOTAL	MONEY
Leith Wastle	71	75	77	77	300	1,198
Elliot Boult	71	76	76	77	300	1,198
Gary Evans	73	73	75	79	300	1,198
John Senden	75	72	77	78	302	1,194
Martin Gates	75	72	74	84	305	1,192

Heineken Classic

The Vines Resort, Perth, Western Australia
Par 36-36–72; 7,101 yards

January 29-February 1
purse, A$1,400,000

	SCORES				TOTAL	MONEY
Thomas Bjorn	70	68	68	74	280	A$265,258
Ian Woosnam	66	69	70	76	281	150,318
Ernie Els	70	71	70	71	282	70,556.50
Jose Maria Olazabal	67	72	68	75	282	70,556.50
Padraig Harrington	74	71	71	66	282	70,556.50
Peter Baker	73	71	67	71	282	70,556.50
Thomas Gogele	68	73	70	72	283	47,152
David Howell	72	68	69	75	284	39,792.67
Greg Chalmers	73	72	70	69	284	39,792.67
Jarmo Sandelin	77	68	67	72	284	39,792.67
Paul Broadhurst	71	70	71	73	285	28,371
Scott Laycock	69	72	70	74	285	28,371
Grant Dodd	70	71	72	72	285	28,371
Bernhard Langer	69	66	76	74	285	28,371
Terry Price	69	71	72	74	286	19,642
Jay Townsend	73	69	77	67	286	19,642
Andrew Beal	70	70	73	73	286	19,642
Andrew Coltart	68	70	71	77	286	19,642
Jeev Milkha Singh	69	70	75	72	286	19,642
Paul McGinley	69	70	74	74	287	15,036
Robert Karlsson	70	74	72	71	287	15,036
Craig Parry	71	67	70	79	287	15,036
Peter McWhinney	74	70	75	68	287	15,036
Glenn Joyner	71	71	72	73	287	15,036
Gavin Coles	70	74	71	73	288	11,178
Robert Allenby	68	71	75	74	288	11,178
Alex Cejka	71	73	70	74	288	11,178
Elliot Boult	74	71	71	72	288	11,178
David Smail	74	71	71	72	288	11,178
Kenny Druce	70	74	71	73	288	11,178
Peter Lonard	73	68	75	72	288	11,178
Richard Green	72	72	68	77	289	8,848
Ian Garbutt	72	70	71	76	289	8,848
Peter O'Malley	72	68	73	76	289	8,848
Martin Gates	68	75	72	75	290	7,660.80
Greg Turner	71	74	69	76	290	7,660.80
Stephen Scahill	70	69	75	76	290	7,660.80
Jim Payne	73	68	73	76	290	7,660.80
Daniel Chopra	71	73	73	73	290	7,660.80
Gary Evans	73	72	70	76	291	6,041
Michael Long	70	71	77	73	291	6,041
Nick O'Hern	71	71	72	77	291	6,041
Robert Willis	72	73	74	72	291	6,041
Jon Robson	70	71	77	73	291	6,041
Raphael Jacquelin	74	71	72	74	291	6,041

	SCORES				TOTAL	MONEY
Paul Eales	72	72	71	77	292	4,166
Peter Senior	69	73	74	76	292	4,166
Rolf Muntz	70	72	80	70	292	4,166
Rodney Pampling	71	71	72	78	292	4,166
Robin Byrd	73	69	72	78	292	4,166
Steve Conran	74	69	76	73	292	4,166
Rodger Davis	71	70	77	75	293	3,283
J.J. West	69	75	77	72	293	3,283
Craig Jones	69	76	71	78	294	3,138.33
Leith Wastle	71	74	73	76	294	3,138.33
Gary Orr	71	73	70	80	294	3,138.33
Lucas Parsons	73	72	73	76	294	3,138.33
Sven Struver	76	68	75	75	294	3,138.33
Philip Walton	72	73	74	75	294	3,138.33
Phillip Price	72	73	74	76	295	3,038
Brian Davis	71	71	73	81	296	2,982
Jack O'Keefe	71	73	74	78	296	2,982
Doug Dunakey	74	71	77	74	296	2,982
Jeff Wagner	72	72	71	82	297	2,912
Marcus Wheelhouse	72	73	80	76	301	2,884

Greg Norman Holden International

Australian Golf Club, Sydney, New South Wales — February 5-8
Par 36-36–72; 6,983 yards — purse, A$1,000,000

	SCORES				TOTAL	MONEY
Greg Norman	68	73	64	67	272	A$189,470
Jose Maria Olazabal	67	67	70	70	274	107,370
Steve Elkington	70	70	72	64	276	54,563.33
Stuart Appleby	69	72	66	69	276	54,563.33
John Cook	69	66	71	70	276	54,563.33
Peter Lonard	69	70	72	67	278	37,900
Doug Dunakey	70	69	71	69	279	33,680
Bradley Hughes	71	71	69	69	280	28,423.33
Nick Price	68	69	72	71	280	28,423.33
Charlie Rymer	70	71	68	71	280	28,423.33
Scott Laycock	70	70	73	68	281	18,843.33
David Smail	69	74	70	68	281	18,843.33
Paul Gow	69	69	74	69	281	18,843.33
Peter Senior	69	71	72	69	281	18,843.33
Kenny Druce	70	72	69	70	281	18,843.33
Peter O'Malley	69	73	68	71	281	18,843.33
Marc Farry	69	74	70	69	282	13,155
Rodger Davis	70	70	71	71	282	13,155
Matthew Ecob	73	68	73	69	283	11,086
Tony Carolan	69	71	72	71	283	11,086
Raymond Russell	69	70	72	72	283	11,086
Marcus Cain	72	72	67	72	283	11,086
Rick Gibson	68	69	73	73	283	11,086
Craig Spence	72	69	75	68	284	8,250
Terry Price	71	71	73	69	284	8,250
Gary Nicklaus	69	75	70	70	284	8,250
Justin Cooper	66	73	73	72	284	8,250
Stephen Scahill	72	69	70	73	284	8,250
Paul Devenport	68	74	69	73	284	8,250
Jason Dawes	71	72	66	75	284	8,250
Stephen Leaney	70	70	73	71	284	8,250

Ericsson Australian Masters

Huntingdale Golf Club, Melbourne, Victoria — February 12-15
Par 36-37–73; 6,970 yards — purse, A$750,000

	SCORES				TOTAL	MONEY
Bradley Hughes	63	72	66	67	268	A$142,102.50
Mathew Goggin	66	68	68	71	273	80,527.50
Rick Gibson	69	67	71	68	275	45,592.50
Frank Nobilo	70	68	70	67	275	45,592.50
Stuart Appleby	66	68	72	71	277	31,582.50
Mark O'Meara	67	72	68	71	278	28,425
Robert Allenby	68	70	71	71	280	23,157.50
Andrew Coltart	76	66	68	70	280	23,157.50
Mark Brooks	69	72	68	71	280	23,157.50
Peter O'Malley	72	69	69	72	282	17,632.50
John Senden	70	71	69	72	282	17,632.50
Raymond Russell	65	70	75	72	282	17,632.50
Peter Fowler	71	70	72	70	283	12,379.50
Shane Tait	72	69	71	71	283	12,379.50
Anthony Painter	69	73	70	71	283	12,379.50
Peter McWhinney	72	68	70	73	283	12,379.50
Lee Westwood	75	66	67	75	283	12,379.50
Robert Karlsson	70	74	73	67	284	8,960
Peter Lonard	70	70	73	71	284	8,960
Paul Devenport	70	71	72	71	284	8,960
Marcus Cain	69	73	72	71	285	8,055
David Ecob	70	70	70	75	285	8,055
Stephen Leaney	71	71	68	75	285	8,055
Bradley King	73	73	70	70	286	6,888.75
Scott Laycock	70	72	73	71	286	6,888.75
Grant Dodd	72	70	71	73	286	6,888.75
Rodney Pampling	72	69	71	74	286	6,888.75
Steve Conran	73	72	73	69	287	5,368.50
Stephen Allan	72	74	72	69	287	5,368.50
Daniel Chopra	67	72	73	75	287	5,368.50
Tony Carolan	68	72	72	75	287	5,368.50
Richard Backwell	72	71	69	75	287	5,368.50

Canon Challenge

Terrey Hills Golf & Country Club, Sydney, New South Wales — February 19-22
Par 36-36–72; 7,059 yards — purse, A$500,000

	SCORES				TOTAL	MONEY
Peter O'Malley	63	73	64	71	271	A$94,736
Paul Gow	64	72	70	74	280	53,684
Wayne Smith	69	74	69	69	281	27,280
Mathew Goggin	68	68	74	71	281	27,280
Ken Druce	70	73	65	73	281	27,280
Michael Long	70	67	74	71	282	16,315
Scott Laycock	71	71	67	73	282	16,315
Shane Tait	69	68	71	74	282	16,315
Jay Townsend	73	70	67	72	282	16,315
Andrew Coltart	71	69	75	68	283	10,737
Grant Kenny	67	69	76	71	283	10,737
Rodger Davis	70	70	72	71	283	10,737
Peter Senior	72	71	66	74	283	10,737
Todd Demsey	72	69	65	77	283	10,737

	SCORES				TOTAL	MONEY
Lucas Parsons	68	73	69	74	284	8,000
Peter Lonard	70	68	71	75	284	8,000
Steve Conran	72	68	74	71	285	6,190
Robert Willis	70	74	70	71	285	6,190
Anthony Edwards	70	69	73	73	285	6,190
Simon Owen	71	69	70	75	285	6,190
Elliott Boult	68	76	73	69	286	5,291
Andrew Bonhomme	73	71	71	71	286	5,291
Justin Cooper	72	68	70	76	286	5,291
Marcus Cain	75	69	71	71	286	5,291
Peter McWhinney	70	74	74	69	287	4,302
Russell Swanson	72	68	75	72	287	4,302
David Carter	68	75	72	72	287	4,302
Craig Parry	73	71	71	72	287	4,302
Peter Fowler	73	70	73	72	288	3,369
Grant Moorhead	74	69	73	72	288	3,369
David Smail	70	72	73	73	288	3,369
Jeff Wagner	74	70	71	73	288	3,369
Stephen Scahill	70	69	74	75	288	3,369
Grant Dodd	71	71	71	75	288	3,369

Australasian Tour Championship

Royal Canberra Golf Club, Canberra, Australia — March 5-8
Par 36-35–71; 6,940 yards — purse, A$500,000

	SCORES				TOTAL	MONEY
Mathew Goggin	66	68	71	73	278	A$94,735
Bradley King	70	66	69	73	278	53,685
(Goggin defeated King on first extra hole.)						
Peter O'Malley	72	68	70	70	280	27,281
Greg Chalmers	67	69	72	72	280	27,281
Peter Senior	67	70	71	72	280	27,281
Michael Long	71	70	71	69	281	17,895
Steve Alker	68	73	71	69	281	17,895
David Ecob	67	71	74	70	282	14,211
Shane Tait	71	67	71	73	282	14,211
Lucas Parsons	70	69	70	73	282	14,211
Todd Demsey	68	70	75	70	283	10,132
Paul Devenport	73	67	73	70	283	10,132
Nick O'Hern	67	71	73	72	283	10,132
Shane Robinson	70	71	70	72	283	10,132
Jarrod Moseley	69	70	75	70	284	7,015
Stuart Thompson	71	72	71	70	284	7,015
Euan Walters	71	70	71	72	284	7,015
Stephen Leaney	69	74	69	72	284	7,015
Darren Cole	71	66	74	73	284	7,015
Steve Conran	70	72	73	70	285	5,685
Robert Allenby	70	73	74	69	286	5,062
Paul Moloney	74	70	72	70	286	5,062
Adrian Percey	71	69	74	72	286	5,062
Peter Fowler	71	69	71	75	286	5,062
Craig Spence	69	73	69	75	286	5,062
Wayne Smith	65	76	69	76	286	5,062
Martin Pettigrew	72	69	75	71	287	3,828
Simon Owen	69	72	74	72	287	3,828
Jason Dawes	73	70	71	73	287	3,828
Richard Backwell	66	70	76	75	287	3,828

Ford Open Championship

Kooyonga Golf Club, Adelaide, South Australia — October 22-25
Par 37-35–72; 6,648 yards — purse, A$500,000

	SCORES				TOTAL	MONEY
Stuart Bouvier	72	70	70	70	282	A$90,000
Craig Parry	71	71	67	75	284	42,375
Stephen Allan	70	70	73	71	284	42,375
Chris Gray	75	67	76	67	285	17,666.66
Stephen Leaney	68	73	70	74	285	17,666.66
Rodney Pampling	74	69	68	74	285	17,666.66
Stephen Scahill	70	71	72	72	285	17,666.66
Robert Stephens	69	74	68	74	285	17,666.66
*Kim Felton	71	74	69	71	285	
Matthew King	68	71	73	73	285	17,666.66
Justin Cooper	70	79	69	68	286	10,200
Peter Lonard	69	72	71	74	286	10,200
Peter O'Malley	71	75	71	69	286	10,200
Chris Gaunt	74	72	69	71	286	10,200
David McKenzie	74	67	74	71	286	10,200
Lucas Parsons	74	71	73	69	287	7,600
*Aaron Baddeley	76	72	68	71	287	
Robin Byrd	70	71	73	73	287	7,600
Robert Allenby	70	75	69	74	288	5,546.42
Peter McWhinney	74	70	72	72	288	5,546.42
Mike Ferguson	75	72	69	72	288	5,546.42
Marcus Cain	70	72	75	71	288	5,546.42
Jarrod Moseley	66	77	74	71	288	5,546.42
Gary Simpson	74	71	70	73	288	5,546.42
Kyle Woodbine	69	79	67	73	288	5,546.42
Mathew Goggin	69	77	72	71	289	4,650
Gavin Coles	73	72	69	75	289	4,650
Andrew Bonhomme	72	74	71	73	290	3,675
Mike Clayton	74	73	75	68	290	3,675
David Ecob	72	74	71	73	290	3,675
Simon Owen	71	70	77	72	290	3,675
Nick O'Hern	71	72	71	76	290	3,675
Scott Wearne	69	73	74	74	290	3,675

MasterCard PGA Championship

New South Wales Golf Club, Sydney, New South Wales — November 19-22
Par 36-36–72; 6,745 yards — purse, A$600,000

	SCORES				TOTAL	MONEY
David Howell	69	66	72	68	275	A$108,000
Terry Price	69	68	76	69	282	50,850
Stephen Ames	70	71	73	68	282	50,850
Craig Spence	75	73	69	67	284	28,800
Robert Willis	75	69	69	73	286	20,550
Brett Partridge	75	71	72	68	286	20,550
Stephen Allan	73	74	70	69	286	20,550
Anthony Wall	71	72	74	69	286	20,550
Paul Marantz	74	69	78	66	287	16,200
Robert Stephens	74	75	67	72	288	15,000
Gavin Coles	73	78	68	70	289	12,600
Neil Kerry	76	74	72	67	289	12,600

	SCORES				TOTAL	MONEY
Jarrod Moseley	74	75	72	69	290	10,800
Tony Carolan	75	71	76	69	291	8,688
Daniel Chopra	76	70	73	72	291	8,688
Tony Mills	73	72	73	73	291	8,688
Jeff Wagner	76	71	71	73	291	8,688
Rodney Pampling	78	71	69	73	291	8,688
Alastair Sidford	77	73	75	67	292	6,107.14
Paul Foley	74	74	75	69	292	6,107.14
Wayne Smith	74	74	73	71	292	6,107.14
Martin Pettigrew	78	72	71	71	292	6,107.14
Anthony Painter	72	73	74	73	292	6,107.14
Anthony Edwards	75	74	70	73	292	6,107.14
Ricky Schmidt	73	73	72	74	292	6,107.14
Adam Le Vesconte	76	75	72	70	293	4,890
Michael Campbell	74	70	75	74	293	4,890
Doug Dunakey	79	72	73	70	294	4,260
Paul Gow	79	72	72	71	294	4,260
Chris Gaunt	71	76	74	73	294	4,260

Australasian Players Championship

Royal Queensland Golf Club, Brisbane, Queensland — November 26-29
Par 36-37–73; 6,962 yards — purse, A$800,000

	SCORES				TOTAL	MONEY
Stephen Leaney	67	73	67	68	275	A$144,000
Corey Pavin	69	66	71	69	275	81,600
(Leaney defeated Pavin on first extra hole.)						
Peter O'Malley	71	68	69	71	279	41,466.66
Richard Backwell	72	71	69	67	279	41,466.66
David McKenzie	68	70	71	70	279	41,466.66
Michael Long	68	71	73	70	282	27,200
Shane Robinson	72	73	69	68	282	27,200
Todd Demsey	70	68	71	74	283	23,200
Jean Van de Velde	70	71	73	70	284	21,600
Geoff Ogilvy	72	70	71	72	285	20,000
Andrew Bonhomme	74	69	71	72	286	13,240
Justin Cooper	77	69	67	73	286	13,240
Mathew Goggin	72	72	71	71	286	13,240
Lucas Parsons	72	67	73	74	286	13,240
Tony Carolan	71	72	71	72	286	13,240
Nick O'Hern	71	73	71	71	286	13,240
Andre Stolz	72	71	73	70	286	13,240
Bob Estes	73	73	68	72	286	13,240
Jean Louis Guepy	69	74	67	77	287	8,530
Rodney Pampling	68	72	72	75	287	8,530
John Senden	73	72	73	69	287	8,530
Sven Struver	70	73	73	71	287	8,530
Greg Chalmers	73	70	70	75	288	6,620
Kenny Druce	74	72	67	75	288	6,620
Peter Lonard	69	73	77	69	288	6,620
Anthony Painter	73	73	73	69	288	6,620
Peter Senior	75	69	71	73	288	6,620
Wayne Smith	71	73	69	75	288	6,620
Robert Stephens	71	75	71	71	288	6,620
Daniel Chopra	73	74	68	73	288	6,620

Holden Australian Open

Royal Adelaide Golf Club, Adelaide, South Australia — December 3-6
Par 37-35–72; 7,178 yards — purse, A$1,000,000

	SCORES				TOTAL	MONEY
Greg Chalmers	71	73	74	70	288	A$180,000
Stuart Appleby	68	76	72	72	289	84,750
Peter Senior	70	73	76	70	289	84,750
Robert Allenby	72	73	75	71	291	44,000
Nick Faldo	77	69	72	73	291	44,000
Rodney Pampling	71	71	77	73	292	36,000
Peter O'Malley	75	74	72	72	293	30,500
Wayne Riley	73	74	75	71	293	30,500
Rodger Davis	72	73	75	74	294	26,000
Stephen Scahill	70	76	75	73	294	26,000
Wayne Grady	75	75	76	69	295	17,833.33
Bradley King	74	78	72	71	295	17,833.33
Craig Parry	75	73	76	71	295	17,833.33
Phil Tataurangi	75	75	75	70	295	17,833.33
Steve Webster	77	74	71	73	295	17,833.33
Richard Green	73	76	73	73	295	17,833.33
Fred Couples	76	76	75	69	296	11,762.50
Carlos Franco	75	74	76	71	296	11,762.50
Greg Turner	75	73	74	74	296	11,762.50
Anthony Edwards	77	70	76	73	296	11,762.50
*Kim Felton	78	74	72	73	297	
Peter Lonard	72	75	76	74	297	9,840
Andrew Bonhomme	74	75	74	74	297	9,840
Anthony Painter	73	75	75	74	297	9,840
Raymond Russell	74	77	71	75	297	9,840
Mark Allen	73	75	74	75	297	9,840
Tim Elliott	71	74	78	75	298	7,700
Bob Estes	76	74	75	73	298	7,700
Geoff Ogilvy	71	78	77	72	298	7,700
Nick O'Hern	77	74	70	77	298	7,700

New Zealand Open

Formosa Auckland Country Club, Auckland, New Zealand — December 10-13
Par 36-36–72; 6,962 yards — purse, NZ$500,000

	SCORES				TOTAL	MONEY
Matthew Lane	72	69	74	64	279	NZ$90,000
Rodney Pampling	69	71	73	69	282	51,000
Grant Moorhead	76	74	65	68	283	22,875
Phil Tataurangi	68	74	75	66	283	22,875
Elliot Boult	73	70	69	72	284	18,000
Peter Lonard	74	73	68	69	284	18,000
Lucas Parsons	72	75	69	68	284	18,000
Peter O'Malley	76	71	70	68	285	14,000
Nick O'Hern	73	68	72	72	285	14,000
Michael Campbell	70	72	73	71	286	11,750
Tsai Chi-huang	75	69	73	69	286	11,750
Justin Cooper	76	69	71	71	287	9,500
Todd Demsey	74	75	68	70	287	9,500
Mark Sheppard	74	76	71	67	288	8,500
Paul Gow	74	75	72	68	289	7,233.33

	SCORES				TOTAL	MONEY
Billy Mayfair	77	72	70	70	289	7,233.33
Chang Tse-peng	76	74	70	69	289	7,233.33
Bradley King	70	74	77	69	290	5,303.57
Shane Tait	76	73	72	69	290	5,303.57
Tony Carolan	74	73	74	69	290	5,303.57
Jason Dawes	72	73	71	74	290	5,303.57
Brett Partridge	76	74	70	70	290	5,303.57
Russell Swanson	72	76	67	75	290	5,303.57
Nathan Green	76	74	71	69	290	5,303.57
Grant Dodd	79	70	75	67	291	4,375
Chris Gray	74	72	71	74	291	4,375
Kenny Druce	77	71	72	72	292	3,560
Bob Charles	76	74	68	74	292	3,560
Michael Jonzon	76	70	77	69	292	3,560
Jim Benepe	73	76	71	72	292	3,560
John Inman	76	73	73	70	292	3,560

Schweppes Coolum Classic

Hyatt Coolum Resort, Coolum, Queensland — December 17-20
Par 36-36–72; 6,660 yards — purse, A$300,000

	SCORES				TOTAL	MONEY
Stuart Appleby	69	70	63	69	271	A$54,000
Craig Spence	65	67	71	72	275	30,600
Craig Parry	72	68	69	69	278	17,325
Tony Carolan	72	71	70	65	278	17,325
Scott Laycock	71	69	69	70	279	10,800
Peter Senior	73	70	65	71	279	10,800
Marcus Cain	70	71	68	70	279	10,800
Anthony Painter	71	72	66	71	280	8,400
Robert Willis	70	72	67	71	280	8,400
Gavin Coles	70	72	67	73	282	7,500
Steve Conran	73	72	67	71	283	5,580
Kenny Druce	70	73	67	73	283	5,580
Paul Gow	70	70	69	74	283	5,580
Paul Moloney	68	68	75	72	283	5,580
Andre Stolz	72	70	70	71	283	5,580
Justin Cooper	70	72	69	73	284	3,798
Grant Dodd	73	72	66	73	284	3,798
Rodney Pampling	73	67	70	74	284	3,798
Adam Crawford	68	76	72	68	284	3,798
Peter Lonard	71	73	71	70	285	3,060
Peter McWhinney	69	71	73	72	285	3,060
Todd Demsey	72	73	71	69	285	3,060
Jarrod Moseley	73	68	74	70	285	3,060
Nick O'Hern	70	75	69	71	285	3,060
Mike Clayton	75	72	72	67	286	2,330
Jason Dawes	70	73	70	73	286	2,330
Scott Hend	72	75	65	74	286	2,330
David Hill	72	73	71	70	286	2,330
Neale Smith	71	75	68	72	286	2,330
Matt Gogel	70	76	68	72	286	2,330

African Tours

Nashua Wild Coast Sun Challenge

Wild Coast Sun County Club, Port Edward, South Africa — January 29-February 1
Par 35-35–70; 6,291 yards — purse, R500,000

	SCORES				TOTAL	MONEY
Adilson da Silva	67	72	69	66	274	R79,000
Chris Davison	66	74	68	68	276	34,325
Scott Dunlap	68	74	63	71	276	34,325
Marco Gortana	66	76	67	67	276	34,325
Hennie Walters	65	73	68	70	276	34,325
Alan McLean	67	68	68	74	277	14,916.66
Mark McNulty	69	68	70	70	277	14,916.66
Clinton Whitelaw	65	69	69	74	277	14,916.66
Bobby Lincoln	69	73	66	71	279	10,800
Darren Fichardt	67	73	68	72	280	9,375
Ronnie McCann	69	74	69	68	280	9,375
James Kingston	70	72	66	73	281	8,100
Andrew McLardy	67	73	70	71	281	8,100
Deane Pappas	68	72	68	74	282	7,225
Fran Quinn	68	76	68	70	282	7,225
Wayne Bradley	71	72	73	67	283	6,360
Warrick Druian	76	70	69	68	283	6,360
Craig Kamps	71	74	68	70	283	6,360
Roger Wessels	67	77	69	70	283	6,360
Wayne Westner	69	76	68	70	283	6,360
Warren Schutte	71	71	70	72	284	5,550
Des Terblanche	71	71	71	71	284	5,550
Steve van Vuuren	68	75	67	74	284	5,550
Hendrik Buhrmann	68	70	73	74	285	5,025
Andre Cruse	67	77	66	75	285	5,025
Ian Hutchings	69	75	69	72	285	5,025
Chris Williams	69	78	66	72	285	5,025
Nic Henning	67	83	68	68	286	4,380
Justin Hobday	69	78	70	69	286	4,380
Greg Petersen	73	75	66	72	286	4,380
Ashley Roestoff	69	72	73	72	286	4,380
Bradford Vaughan	66	73	74	73	286	4,380

South African Open

Durban Country Club, Durban, South Africa — February 5-8
Par 36-36–72; 6,667 yards — purse, R3,710,855

	SCORES				TOTAL	MONEY
Ernie Els	64	72	68	69	273	R581,835
David Frost	68	66	71	71	276	423,487.50
Patrik Sjoland	69	74	68	69	280	254,829
Marco Gortana	70	71	70	70	281	154,419.50
Nic Henning	69	71	70	71	281	154,419.50
Bernhard Langer	71	68	71	71	281	154,419.50
Ignacio Garrido	66	72	72	72	282	99,611.62

	SCORES				TOTAL	MONEY
Mark McNulty	66	79	67	70	282	99,611.62
Alex Cejka	73	72	70	68	283	61,727.90
Massimo Florioli	72	72	68	71	283	61,727.90
Thomas Gogele	69	69	73	72	283	61,727.90
David Howell	72	72	70	69	283	61,727.90
Richard Kaplan	69	73	72	69	283	61,727.90
James Kingston	74	70	70	69	283	61,727.90
Brett Liddle	71	71	71	70	283	61,727.90
Vijay Singh	71	72	67	73	283	61,727.90
Greg Chalmers	66	71	74	73	284	46,767.75
Anthony Wall	73	72	71	68	284	46,767.75
Chris Williams	70	69	71	74	284	46,767.75
Gary Orr	71	71	76	67	285	42,717
Steve Webster	69	76	68	72	285	42,717
Andre Cruse	69	71	74	72	286	38,113.87
Mark Mouland	72	75	67	72	286	38,113.87
Jeff Remesy	68	73	73	72	286	38,113.87
Knud Storgaard	72	71	73	70	286	38,113.87
Heinz P. Thul	70	74	72	70	286	38,113.87
Roger Wessels	73	71	74	68	286	38,113.87
Adilson da Silva	70	73	69	75	287	31,853.62
Scott Dunlap	73	74	67	73	287	31,853.62
Adam Hunter	69	73	74	71	287	31,853.62
Craig Kamps	72	69	70	76	287	31,853.62
Dean van Staden	74	72	67	74	287	31,853.62
Jean Van de Velde	70	68	73	76	287	31,853.62
Chris Davison	69	72	75	72	288	27,987
Jonathan Lomas	74	68	71	75	288	27,987
Andrew McLardy	69	75	74	70	288	27,987
Deane Pappas	70	75	74	66	288	27,987
*Trevor Immelman	73	70	70	76	289	
Tony Johnstone	70	73	71	75	289	25,409.25
Jamie Spence	72	75	73	69	289	25,409.25
Bruce Vaughan	73	74	71	71	289	25,409.25
Paul Affleck	69	75	75	71	290	22,463.25
Michael Archer	72	71	75	72	290	22,463.25
Jeff Hawkes	70	72	73	75	290	22,463.25
Rolf Muntz	73	74	71	72	290	22,463.25
Frank Nobilo	70	73	72	75	290	22,463.25
Phillip Price	70	69	75	77	291	19,885.50
Sven Struver	72	75	70	74	291	19,885.50
Desvonde Botes	72	73	70	77	292	17,676
Wayne Bradley	72	73	77	70	292	17,676
David Lynn	71	76	74	71	292	17,676
Andrew Pitts	74	72	72	74	292	17,676
Paul Blaikie	72	74	75	72	293	13,993.50
Mats Hallberg	66	72	75	80	293	13,993.50
Van Phillips	73	74	70	76	293	13,993.50
Andrew Sandywell	73	72	72	76	293	13,993.50
Kevin Stone	73	74	76	70	293	13,993.50
Tjaart van der Walt	67	75	73	78	293	13,993.50
*Ulrich van den Berg	70	72	77	74	293	
Warren Abery	73	71	78	72	294	11,231.62
Soren Kjeldsen	72	74	73	75	294	11,231.62
Ian Palmer	69	72	75	78	294	11,231.62
Michael Scholz	72	74	68	80	294	11,231.62
Fredrik Jacobson	76	70	72	77	295	9,942.75
Pelop Panagopoulos	74	70	77	74	295	9,942.75
Steve van Vuuren	74	72	72	77	295	9,942.75
Gary Evans	70	73	73	80	296	9,022.12

	SCORES				TOTAL	MONEY
Costantino Rocca	76	71	71	78	296	9,022.12
*Steven Shearer	74	73	77	72	296	
Malcom Mackenzie	77	70	70	80	297	8,285.62
Wayne Riley	76	68	74	79	297	8,285.62
Anders Forsbrand	74	72	75	77	298	7,733.25
Carl Watts	75	70	78	76	299	7,365
Warren Schutte	73	71	79	77	300	7,365
Hugh Inggs	74	73	78	76	301	7,365
Anssi Kankkonan	71	76	79	75	301	7,365
Hendrik Buhrmann	74	73	81	77	305	7,365

Alfred Dunhill South African PGA

Houghton Golf Club, Johannesburg, South Africa — February 12-16
Par 36-36–72; 7,035 yards — purse, R3,327,705

	SCORES				TOTAL	MONEY
Tony Johnstone	68	64	67	72	271	R516,567.30
Ernie Els	69	69	66	69	273	376,160.26
Retief Goosen	71	70	69	65	275	193,467.84
Nick Price	71	67	69	68	275	193,467.84
Scott Dunlap	69	66	71	70	276	135,182.59
Phillip Price	69	71	66	71	277	115,917.44
Anthony Wall	71	72	67	69	279	96,652.29
Anders Forsbrand	68	70	72	71	281	80,652.42
Mathias Gronberg	73	68	71	70	282	70,856.58
Tom Gillis	69	69	73	72	283	54,149.22
Andrew McLardy	72	71	70	70	283	54,149.22
Mark McNulty	71	74	70	68	283	54,149.22
Rolf Muntz	72	67	72	72	283	54,149.22
Steve van Vuuren	70	72	67	74	283	54,149.22
Bruce Vaughan	75	68	71	69	283	54,149.22
Greg Chalmers	74	70	69	71	284	41,002.58
Andre Cruse	70	72	69	73	284	41,002.58
Bradley Dredge	69	72	72	71	284	41,002.58
Don Gammon	71	72	72	69	284	41,002.58
Nic Henning	72	72	68	72	284	41,002.58
Malcolm Mackenzie	74	68	70	72	284	41,002.58
Paolo Quirici	70	72	70	72	284	41,002.58
Andrew Clapp	74	69	72	70	285	31,999.74
Raphael Jacquelin	72	68	73	72	285	31,999.74
Craig Kamps	74	69	70	72	285	31,999.74
Brett Liddle	71	71	70	73	285	31,999.74
Greg Owen	70	73	70	72	285	31,999.74
Greg Petersen	71	71	71	72	285	31,999.74
Sven Struver	69	70	76	70	285	31,999.74
Roger Wessels	68	74	70	73	285	31,999.74
Mark Wiltshire	69	70	72	74	285	31,999.74
Marco Gortana	73	72	70	71	286	26,775.29
John Hawksworth	71	71	76	68	286	26,775.29
James Kingston	69	74	69	74	286	26,775.29
Steve Webster	71	69	73	73	286	26,775.29
Michael Archer	71	74	75	67	287	23,183.48
Wayne Bradley	71	74	75	67	287	23,183.48
Ian Hutchings	71	69	69	78	287	23,183.48
Greig Hutcheon	70	73	72	72	287	23,183.48
Costantino Rocca	68	76	73	70	287	23,183.48
Ashley Roestoff	71	74	74	68	287	23,183.48

	SCORES				TOTAL	MONEY
Jeev Milkha Singh	69	75	71	72	287	23,183.48
Mark Mouland	70	73	69	76	288	19,265.15
Heinz P. Thul	71	73	73	71	288	19,265.15
Nico van Rensburg	74	68	73	73	288	19,265.15
Carl Watts	72	73	74	69	288	19,265.15
Clinton Whitelaw	71	72	72	73	288	19,265.15
Paul Affleck	67	76	70	76	289	15,346.81
Alex Cejka	74	69	73	73	289	15,346.81
Gavin Levenson	72	73	70	74	289	15,346.81
Bobby Lincoln	74	68	74	73	289	15,346.81
Michele Reale	70	73	76	70	289	15,346.81
Jeff Remesy	72	73	72	72	289	15,346.81
Jarmo Sandelin	71	68	80	70	289	15,346.81
Chris Davison	72	69	75	74	290	11,493.78
Olivier Edmond	69	73	78	70	290	11,493.78
Massimo Florioli	73	71	72	74	290	11,493.78
Deane Pappas	73	70	73	74	290	11,493.78
Zhang Lian-wei	72	73	75	70	290	11,493.78
Bobby Collins	73	69	71	78	291	9,632.57
Warrick Druian	72	73	72	74	291	9,632.57
John Mashego	74	69	74	74	291	9,632.57
Mark Murless	74	71	72	74	291	9,632.57
Hendrik Buhrmann	75	69	74	74	292	5,947.94
Raymond Burns	74	68	73	77	292	5,947.94
Adilson da Silva	70	74	76	72	292	5,947.94
Ivo Giner	72	73	74	73	292	5,947.94
Mats Hallberg	78	67	78	69	292	5,947.94
Fran Quinn	72	72	72	76	292	5,947.94
Tjaart van der Walt	70	75	75	72	292	5,947.94
Dennis Edlund	76	68	74	75	293	4,809.92
Jean Van de Velde	73	70	73	77	293	4,809.92
Soren Kjeldsen	71	72	75	76	294	4,777.92
Alan McLean	69	74	75	76	294	4,777.92
Phil Golding	73	70	75	77	295	4,753.92
Eamonn Darcy	77	68	74	80	299	4,737.92
Maarten Lafeber	72	73	77	78	300	4,721.92

Dimension Data Pro-Am

Gary Player Country Club, Sun City, South Africa — February 19-22
Par 36-36–72; 7,526 yards — purse, R2,000,000

	SCORES				TOTAL	MONEY
Nick Price	69	67	68	72	276	R300,200
Mark McNulty	73	66	69	73	281	218,500
Tjaart van der Walt	69	74	70	70	283	131,480
Bobby Lincoln	73	70	67	75	285	79,673.33
Ronnie McCann	73	71	71	70	285	79,673.33
Clinton Whitelaw	72	68	72	73	285	79,673.33
Wallie Coetsee	72	71	73	70	286	51,395
Nico van Rensburg	72	72	73	69	286	51,395
Marco Gortana	69	72	72	74	287	37,430
Fran Quinn	75	72	71	69	287	37,430
Roger Wessels	73	69	69	76	287	37,430
Jannie le Grange	72	75	68	73	288	31,730
Michael Archer	73	68	75	73	289	25,792.50
Paul Blaikie	75	70	73	71	289	25,792.50
Paul Friedlander	77	69	70	73	289	25,792.50

	SCORES				TOTAL	MONEY
Craig Kamps	70	69	76	74	289	25,792.50
Warren Schutte	72	72	72	73	289	25,792.50
Schalk van der Merwe	74	72	72	71	289	25,792.50
Bradford Vaughan	73	71	72	73	289	25,792.50
Hennie Walters	69	75	72	73	289	25,792.50
Don Gammon	74	70	70	76	290	20,520
James Kingston	74	70	74	72	290	20,520
Ashley Roestoff	74	72	66	78	290	20,520
Kevin Stone	77	71	69	73	290	20,520
Dean van Staden	72	74	72	72	290	20,520
Chris Davison	78	68	72	73	291	17,416.66
Scott Dunlap	72	73	71	75	291	17,416.66
David Frost	73	70	78	70	291	17,416.66
Jeff Hawkes	73	73	74	71	291	17,416.66
Nic Henning	73	73	72	73	291	17,416.66
Peter Wilson	72	74	70	75	291	17,416.66

Stenham Royal Swazi Sun Open

Royal Swazi Sun Golf Club, Mbabane, Swaziland — February 26-March 1
Par 36-36–72; 6,680 yards — purse, R500,000
(Third round cancelled — lightning.)

	SCORES			TOTAL	MONEY
Paul Friedlander	65	69	67	201	R79,000
Scott Dunlap	65	72	64	201	57,500
(Friedlander defeated Dunlap on second extra hole.)					
Bobby Lincoln	71	66	66	203	29,575
Bruce Vaughan	65	68	70	203	29,575
Andrew Pitts	68	68	69	205	19,175
Tjaart van der Walt	70	65	70	205	19,175
Des Terblanche	67	70	69	206	13,525
Nico van Rensburg	74	67	65	206	13,525
Nic Henning	73	67	67	207	9,850
James Kingston	71	70	66	207	9,850
Chris Williams	70	70	67	207	9,850
Wimpie Botha	70	68	70	208	7,500
Paul Cuningham	70	69	69	208	7,500
Chris Davison	69	72	67	208	7,500
Ashley Roestoff	71	70	67	208	7,500
Dean van Staden	69	67	72	208	7,500
Paul Blaikie	72	69	68	209	6,237.50
Marco Gortana	71	68	70	209	6,237.50
Brad Ott	69	69	71	209	6,237.50
Sean Pappas	72	69	68	209	6,237.50
Michiel Bothma	66	75	69	210	5,325
Justin Hobday	70	70	70	210	5,325
Ian Hutchings	73	68	69	210	5,325
Sean Ludgater	68	75	67	210	5,325
Brenden Pappas	70	68	72	210	5,325
Bryan Prytz	72	70	68	210	5,325
Adilson da Silva	70	70	71	211	4,450
John Mashego	71	67	73	211	4,450
Lyall McNeill	70	71	70	211	4,450
Grant Muller	72	66	73	211	4,450
Steve van Vuuren	69	70	72	211	4,450
Bradford Vaughan	72	69	70	211	4,450

Vodacom Players Championship

Killarney Golf Club, Johannesburg, South Africa — March 5-8
Par 35-35–70; 6,938 yards — purse, R1,000,000

	SCORES				TOTAL	MONEY
Mark McNulty	67	69	68	71	275	R158,000
Warren Abery	71	69	71	67	278	92,100
Scott Dunlap	74	65	71	68	278	92,100
Michael Archer	68	69	72	70	279	29,875
Marco Gortana	72	72	68	67	279	29,875
Nic Henning	69	71	72	67	279	29,875
James Kingston	73	69	70	67	279	29,875
Brett Liddle	72	72	67	68	279	29,875
Brenden Pappas	72	68	71	68	279	29,875
Andrew Pitts	73	69	69	68	279	29,875
Bradford Vaughan	73	67	71	68	279	29,875
Ashley Roestoff	75	68	68	69	280	16,700
Andre Cruse	67	70	75	69	281	14,866.66
Andrew McLardy	69	71	70	71	281	14,866.66
Hennie Otto	72	66	72	71	281	14,866.66
Ian Hutchings	67	70	76	69	282	13,050
Mark Murless	74	67	74	67	282	13,050
Fran Quinn	65	74	71	72	282	13,050
Des Terblanche	73	75	69	65	282	13,050
Paul Blaikie	70	73	70	70	283	11,433.33
Justin Hobday	71	70	71	71	283	11,433.33
Richard Kaplan	68	70	73	72	283	11,433.33
Chris Davison	67	73	72	72	284	10,500
Jeff Hawkes	73	71	72	68	284	10,500
Hennie Walters	69	75	70	70	284	10,500
Alan McLean	70	76	74	65	285	9,600
Brad Ott	76	70	70	69	285	9,600
Warren Schutte	75	72	72	66	285	9,600
Dion Fourie	72	70	71	73	286	8,733.33
Grant Muller	73	71	71	71	286	8,733.33
Bruce Vaughan	71	72	69	74	286	8,733.33

Vodacom Series: Western Cape

Rondebosch Golf Club, Cape Town, South Africa — April 16-18
Par 36-36–72; 6,633 yards — purse, R165,000

	SCORES			TOTAL	MONEY
Alan McLean	63	67	71	201	R25,905
James Loughnane	68	71	67	206	16,087.50
Sean Ludgater	69	68	69	206	16,087.50
Titch Moore	72	65	70	207	10,395
Robbie Stewart	70	69	69	208	7,012.50
Bradford Vaughan	70	70	68	208	7,012.50
Desvonde Botes	72	67	70	209	4,592.50
Andrew McLardy	69	69	71	209	4,592.50
Ian Palmer	70	66	73	209	4,592.50
Nic Henning	70	70	70	210	3,588.75
Hennie Walters	72	67	71	210	3,588.75
Wimpie Botha	72	69	70	211	2,852.14
Sammy Daniels	71	69	71	211	2,852.14
Neil Homann	72	69	70	211	2,852.14

	SCORES			TOTAL	MONEY
Bobby Lincoln	73	68	70	211	2,852.14
John Nelson	70	73	68	211	2,852.14
Brenden Pappas	73	68	70	211	2,852.14
Tjaart van der Walt	73	70	68	211	2,852.14
Chris Davison	74	69	69	212	2,252.25
Ben Fouchee	74	70	68	212	2,252.25
Justin Hobday	74	68	70	212	2,252.25
Schalk van der Merwe	67	71	74	212	2,252.25
Brett Liddle	74	68	71	213	1,969
Des Terblanche	72	71	70	213	1,969
Steve van Vuuren	67	69	77	213	1,969
Warren Abery	74	66	74	214	1,765.50
Michael Green	72	70	72	214	1,765.50
Jason Lipshitz	70	72	72	214	1,765.50
Colin Sanderson	72	71	72	215	1,633.50
Andre Cruse	73	72	71	216	1,534.50
Grant Muller	76	68	72	216	1,534.50
Phillip Sanderson	71	74	71	216	1,534.50

Kalahari Classic

Sishen Golf Club, Kathu, South Africa — April 23-25
Par 36-36–72; 6,988 yards — purse, R75,000

	SCORES			TOTAL	MONEY
Andrew McLardy	66	66	73	205	R11,625
Ryan Dreyer	69	68	71	208	8,625
Callie Swart	67	70	72	209	6,000
Des Terblanche	70	69	71	210	5,250
Ashley Roestoff	70	72	69	211	4,500
Richard Fulford	69	68	75	212	3,600
Noel Maart	74	67	71	212	3,600
Sammy Daniels	70	72	71	213	2,625
Ben Fouchee	71	69	73	213	2,625
Wayne de Haas	66	74	75	215	1,800
Alan McLean	74	71	70	215	1,800
Justin Hobday	72	70	75	217	1,425
Schalk van der Merwe	69	71	77	217	1,425
Chris Davison	73	75	70	218	1,130
Mark Murless	72	74	72	218	1,130
Colin Sorour	74	69	75	218	1,130
Michael Green	68	70	81	219	939
Gregory Jacobs	70	74	75	219	939
Titch Moore	68	74	77	219	939
David Owen	76	71	72	219	939
Sean Pappas	72	74	73	219	939
Paul Cuningham	72	73	75	220	783
Michael du Toit	70	79	71	220	783
Sean Farrell	73	76	71	220	783
John Mashego	73	72	75	220	783
Brenden Pappas	72	77	71	220	783
Philip van den Berg	73	72	76	221	712.50
Darran Warner	73	74	74	221	712.50
John Bele	71	78	74	223	675
Bafana Hlophe	71	77	75	223	675
John Nelson	72	76	75	223	675

Pietersburg Classic

Pietersburg Golf Club, Phalaborwa, South Africa — April 30-May 2
Par 36-36–72; 7,025 yards — purse, R100,000

	SCORES			TOTAL	MONEY
Desvonde Botes	62	67	68	197	R15,700
Sammy Daniels	64	70	68	202	11,500
Sean Farrell	68	67	68	203	8,000
Brenden Pappas	65	70	69	204	6,300
Brett Liddle	71	65	70	206	3,883.33
Mark Murless	69	67	70	206	3,883.33
Hennie Otto	73	67	66	206	3,883.33
Andrew McLardy	68	70	69	207	2,750
Chris Davison	70	67	71	208	2,083.33
Dion Fourie	68	69	71	208	2,083.33
Alan McLean	64	69	75	208	2,083.33
Ashley Roestoff	69	70	69	208	2,083.33
Schalk van der Merwe	72	69	67	208	2,083.33
Rudy Whitfield	68	69	71	208	2,083.33
Ryan Dreyer	72	68	69	209	1,600
Richard Fulford	68	70	71	209	1,600
Lyall McNeill	66	72	71	209	1,600
Steve van Vuuren	70	71	68	209	1,600
Andre van Staden	70	70	70	210	1,440
Bradley Davison	69	74	68	211	1,340
Darren Fichardt	69	73	69	211	1,340
Bradford Vaughan	72	71	68	211	1,340
Wayne de Haas	72	69	71	212	1,240
Paul Cuningham	72	68	73	213	1,130
Nic Henning	72	71	70	213	1,130
Richard Kaplan	68	73	72	213	1,130
Sean Pappas	69	70	74	213	1,130
Michael du Toit	71	72	71	214	977.50
Greg Fox	72	71	71	214	977.50
Mark Johnson	71	73	70	214	977.50
Callie Swart	71	69	74	214	977.50

Vodacom Series: Eastern Cape

Humewood Golf Club, Port Elizabeth, South Africa — May 14-16
Par 36-36–72; 6,732 yards — purse, R165,000

	SCORES			TOTAL	MONEY
Sammy Daniels	70	68	69	207	R25,905
Ian Palmer	68	70	69	207	18,975
(Daniels defeated Palmer on third extra hole.)					
Darren Fichardt	69	69	70	208	13,200
Richard Kaplan	69	68	72	209	9,075
Des Terblanche	69	66	74	209	9,075
Jason Lipshitz	68	71	72	211	5,733.75
Ashley Roestoff	69	72	70	211	5,733.75
Wayne de Haas	72	68	72	212	3,811.50
Ian Hutchings	71	71	70	212	3,811.50
Noel Maart	71	68	73	212	3,811.50
Kevin Stone	70	72	70	212	3,811.50
Stephen Wilson	71	66	75	212	3,811.50
Justin Hobday	72	69	72	213	3,052.50

	SCORES			TOTAL	MONEY
Hennie Walters	68	75	70	213	3,052.50
Schalk van der Merwe	74	67	73	214	2,755.50
Steve van Vuuren	71	70	73	214	2,755.50
Andre Cruse	69	76	70	215	2,300.57
Chris Davison	69	72	74	215	2,300.57
Michael du Toit	72	67	76	215	2,300.57
Brett Liddle	73	71	71	215	2,300.57
Gary Matthews	71	74	70	215	2,300.57
Alan McLean	71	70	74	215	2,300.57
Titch Moore	73	70	72	215	2,300.57
Robbie Stewart	72	70	74	216	1,963.50
Bradley Davison	72	73	72	217	1,864.50
Keith Horne	73	70	74	217	1,864.50
Paul Cuningham	72	73	73	218	1,643.40
Richard Fulford	73	68	77	218	1,643.40
Mark Johnson	72	74	72	218	1,643.40
Grant Muller	73	74	71	218	1,643.40
Colin Sanderson	72	72	74	218	1,643.40

Vodacom Series: Kwazulu-Natal

Prince's Grant Golf Club, Durban, South Africa — May 29-31
Par 36-36–72; 6,782 yards — purse, R165,000

	SCORES			TOTAL	MONEY
Keith Horne	68	68	68	204	R25,905
Chris Williams	71	68	68	207	18,975
Andre Cruse	68	70	70	208	13,200
Mark Cayeux	75	70	67	212	6,366.25
Paul Cuningham	72	71	69	212	6,366.25
Sammy Daniels	77	67	68	212	6,366.25
Chris Davison	73	68	71	212	6,366.25
Brett Liddle	75	68	69	212	6,366.25
Trevor Sidley	71	73	68	212	6,366.25
James Loughnane	69	72	72	213	3,403.12
Mark Murless	68	70	75	213	3,403.12
Kevin Stone	74	71	68	213	3,403.12
Hennie Walters	76	69	68	213	3,403.12
Richard Fulford	68	72	74	214	2,895.75
Craig Kamps	74	71	69	214	2,895.75
Adilson da Silva	71	71	73	215	2,528.62
Darren Fichardt	69	74	72	215	2,528.62
Justin Hobday	71	75	69	215	2,528.62
Ian Palmer	70	75	70	215	2,528.62
Michael du Toit	74	72	70	216	2,169.75
Mellette Hendrikse	74	72	70	216	2,169.75
Bobby Lincoln	72	75	69	216	2,169.75
Sean Pappas	73	69	74	216	2,169.75
Wayne Bradley	75	69	73	217	1,831.50
John Mashego	77	71	69	217	1,831.50
Gary Matthews	72	74	71	217	1,831.50
Steve van Vuuren	74	71	72	217	1,831.50
Nico van Rensburg	76	72	69	217	1,831.50
Bradley Davison	71	71	76	218	1,584
John Dickson	70	77	71	218	1,584
Pelop Panagopoulos	71	76	71	218	1,584

Vodacom Series: Mpumalanga

White River Country Club, Mpumalanga, South Africa — July 10-12
Par 71; 6,514 yards — purse, R165,000

	SCORES			TOTAL	MONEY
Callie Swart	66	67	69	202	R25,905
Ashley Roestoff	66	69	68	203	18,975
Brenden Pappas	70	66	68	204	13,200
Robbie Stewart	70	66	70	206	9,075
Darran Warner	69	68	69	206	9,075
Gavin Levenson	70	70	68	208	5,733.75
Noel Maart	68	73	67	208	5,733.75
Andre Cruse	72	68	69	209	3,939.37
Justin Hobday	69	70	70	209	3,939.37
Brett Liddle	74	65	70	209	3,939.37
John Mashego	69	72	68	209	3,939.37
Phillip Sanderson	67	73	70	210	3,300
Desvonde Botes	74	68	69	211	2,720.14
Paul Cuningham	73	69	69	211	2,720.14
Gregory Jacobs	68	74	69	211	2,720.14
Bobby Lincoln	71	68	72	211	2,720.14
Bryan Prytz	66	70	75	211	2,720.14
Colin Sorour	70	71	70	211	2,720.14
Bradford Vaughan	71	72	68	211	2,720.14
Paul Friedlander	68	70	74	212	2,211
Richard Kaplan	72	70	70	212	2,211
Mark Murless	71	71	70	212	2,211
Sammy Daniels	71	70	72	213	1,969
Michael du Toit	70	72	71	213	1,969
Schalk van der Merwe	69	74	70	213	1,969
Michiel Bothma	73	69	72	214	1,702.80
Marc Cayeux	70	73	71	214	1,702.80
Mark Matthews	68	73	73	214	1,702.80
Trevor Sidley	68	69	77	214	1,702.80
Steve van Vuuren	71	68	75	214	1,702.80

Fish River Sun Pro-Am

Fish River Sun Country Club, Swaziland — August 6-8
Par 36-36–72; 6,871 yards — purse, R200,000

	SCORES			TOTAL	MONEY
Ashley Roestoff	75	70	68	213	R31,400
Colin Sorour	70	73	74	217	23,000
Andre Cruse	73	76	70	219	12,266.66
Hennie Otto	78	69	72	219	12,266.66
Stephen Wilson	74	71	74	219	12,266.66
Sammy Daniels	79	71	70	220	6,500
Alan Michell	75	72	73	220	6,500
Vaughn Groenewald	81	72	68	221	4,666.66
Gavin Levenson	72	79	70	221	4,666.66
Titch Moore	75	71	75	221	4,666.66
Justin Hobday	82	71	69	222	3,840
Neil Homann	77	72	73	222	3,840
Sean Farrell	72	76	75	223	3,560
Ian Palmer	77	71	76	224	3,400
Brenden Pappas	78	77	70	225	3,200

	SCORES			TOTAL	MONEY
Phillip Sanderson	77	75	73	225	3,200
Bradley Davison	84	71	71	226	2,906.66
Grant Muller	79	75	72	226	2,906.66
James Loughnane	81	72	73	226	2,906.66
John Bele	79	78	70	227	2,504
Wimpie Botha	80	76	71	227	2,504
Sean Pappas	83	70	74	227	2,504
John Mashego	78	74	75	227	2,504
Ben Fouchee	79	70	78	227	2,504
Darren Fichardt	80	78	70	228	2,160
Callie Swart	82	75	71	228	2,160
Richard Fulford	77	75	76	228	2,160
Marc Cayeux	79	77	73	229	1,910
Keith Horne	79	74	76	229	1,910
Paul Cuningham	81	72	76	229	1,910
Bradford Vaughan	80	69	80	229	1,910

Royal Swazi Sun Classic

Royal Swazi Sun Golf Club, Mbabane, Swaziland — August 13-15
Par 36-36–72; 6,680 yards — purse, R150,000

	SCORES			TOTAL	MONEY
Justin Hobday	70	68	69	207	R23,550
Titch Moore	71	73	66	210	17,250
Bradley Davison	68	72	71	211	10,725
Grant Muller	70	70	71	211	10,725
Paul Cuningham	67	74	71	212	7,050
Bradford Vaughan	69	74	70	213	5,700
Neil Homann	72	74	68	214	3,975
Chris Davison	69	75	70	214	3,975
Alan Michell	70	72	72	214	3,975
John Mashego	67	74	73	214	3,975
Bobby Lincoln	73	68	74	215	3,000
Steve van Vuuren	71	70	74	215	3,000
Sean Pappas	69	70	76	215	3,000
Robbie Stewart	71	75	70	216	2,570
Ivano Ficalbi	69	75	72	216	2,570
Ryan Dreyer	66	72	78	216	2,570
Desvonde Botes	74	73	70	217	2,208.75
Brett Liddle	70	76	71	217	2,208.75
Ashley Roestoff	70	76	71	217	2,208.75
Bafana Hlophe	71	71	75	217	2,208.75
Keith Horne	74	73	71	218	1,863
Vaughn Groenewald	73	74	71	218	1,863
Hennie Otto	71	75	72	218	1,863
Brenden Pappas	72	73	73	218	1,863
Paul Marks	69	75	74	218	1,863
Andre Cruse	73	73	73	219	1,605
Nic Henning	74	71	74	219	1,605
Sean Ludgater	67	78	74	219	1,605
Wallie Coetsee	73	73	74	220	1,440
John Nelson	73	72	75	220	1,440
Noel Maart	71	73	76	220	1,440

ABSA Corporate Bank Challenge

Roodepoort Country Club, Johannesburg, South Africa — September 2-4
Par 36-36–72; 7,228 yards — purse, R150,000

	SCORES			TOTAL	MONEY
Warren Abery	67	67	72	206	R23,550
Pelop Panagopoulos	67	73	69	209	12,900
Brett Liddle	71	67	71	209	12,900
Bryan Prytz	68	68	73	209	12,900
Wayne Bradley	72	68	70	210	5,400
Ashley Roestoff	70	69	71	210	5,400
Wallie Coetsee	70	66	74	210	5,400
Chris Williams	69	66	75	210	5,400
Paul Friedlander	69	69	73	211	3,400
Titch Moore	69	69	73	211	3,400
Andre van Staden	67	69	75	211	3,400
Darren Fichardt	72	74	67	213	2,850
Callie Swart	68	73	72	213	2,850
Ian Palmer	65	73	75	213	2,850
Paul Cuningham	71	75	68	214	2,352
Mark Murless	69	76	69	214	2,352
James Kingston	74	68	72	214	2,352
Nico van Rensburg	71	70	73	214	2,352
Rudy Whitfield	69	71	74	214	2,352
Dean van Staden	74	68	73	215	2,010
Sammy Daniels	66	75	74	215	2,010
Craig Kamps	68	69	78	215	2,010
Alan McLean	71	74	71	216	1,638.75
Ryan Dreyer	71	74	71	216	1,638.75
Hennie Walters	75	70	71	216	1,638.75
Bobby Lincoln	74	71	71	216	1,638.75
John Mashego	67	77	72	216	1,638.75
Gavin Drummond	66	78	72	216	1,638.75
Richard Kaplan	72	71	73	216	1,638.75
Phillip Sanderson	70	71	75	216	1,638.75

Bearing Man Highveld Classic

Witbank Golf Club, Witbank, South Africa — September 11-13
Par 36-36–72; 6,764 yards — purse, R100,000

	SCORES			TOTAL	MONEY
Wayne Bradley	68	67	67	202	R15,700
Sammy Daniels	67	70	67	204	11,500
Robbie Stewart	72	69	66	207	3,944.44
Callie Swart	73	67	67	207	3,944.44
Marc Cayeux	70	69	68	207	3,944.44
Gavin Levenson	68	70	69	207	3,944.44
Gregory Jacobs	71	67	69	207	3,944.44
Justin Hobday	68	69	70	207	3,944.44
Titch Moore	68	69	70	207	3,944.44
Chris Davison	66	70	71	207	3,944.44
Richard Fulford	66	69	72	207	3,944.44
Michael Green	69	74	65	208	1,900
Vaughn Groenewald	70	67	71	208	1,900
Noel Maart	68	68	72	208	1,900
Glenn Cayeux	71	68	70	209	1,633.33

	SCORES			TOTAL	MONEY
Brett Liddle	67	72	70	209	1,633.33
Phil Simmons	70	68	71	209	1,633.33
Alan Michell	73	68	69	210	1,366.66
John Mashego	73	68	69	210	1,366.66
Gary Matthews	71	69	70	210	1,366.66
Dean van Staden	70	69	71	210	1,366.66
Sean Ludgater	71	67	72	210	1,366.66
Desvonde Botes	70	68	72	210	1,366.66
Mark Murless	73	69	69	211	1,130
Wallie Coetsee	72	68	71	211	1,130
Bradford Vaughan	70	70	71	211	1,130
Leonard Loxton	71	66	74	211	1,130
Michiel Bothma	74	67	71	212	1,030
Ashley Roestoff	72	71	70	213	915
Ryan Dreyer	72	71	70	213	915
John Bele	72	69	72	213	915
Mellette Hendrikse	69	72	72	213	915
Phillip Sanderson	67	74	72	213	915
Dion Fourie	68	72	73	213	915

Vodacom Series: Free State

Schoeman Park Golf Club, Bloemfontein, South Africa — September 17-19
Par 36-36–72; 7,086 yards — purse, R165,000

	SCORES			TOTAL	MONEY
Gary Matthews	68	67	70	205	R25,905
Justin Hobday	70	66	70	206	16,087.50
Alan Michell	69	66	71	206	16,087.50
Dean van Staden	69	69	69	207	9,075
Wallie Coetsee	66	69	72	207	9,075
Bryan Prytz	67	71	70	208	6,270
Sammy Daniels	68	73	69	210	4,867.50
Bradford Vaughan	68	69	73	210	4,867.50
Michael Green	71	68	72	211	4,042.50
Gavin Levenson	72	70	70	212	3,316.50
Michael du Toit	71	70	71	212	3,316.50
Nic Henning	70	71	71	212	3,316.50
Ashley Roestoff	68	70	74	212	3,316.50
Leonard Loxton	68	68	76	212	3,316.50
Marc Cayeux	73	72	68	213	2,640
Phillip Sanderson	71	69	73	213	2,640
Ryan Dreyer	70	70	73	213	2,640
Hennie Otto	69	70	74	213	2,640
Glenn Cayeux	72	72	70	214	2,293.50
Sean Ludgater	72	71	71	214	2,293.50
Grant Muller	69	71	74	214	2,293.50
Schalk van der Merwe	73	72	70	215	1,973.40
Andre van Staden	74	69	72	215	1,973.40
Stephen Wilson	74	69	72	215	1,973.40
Richard Kaplan	71	71	73	215	1,973.40
John Bele	71	70	74	215	1,973.40
Bradley Davison	73	71	72	216	1,617
Robbie Stewart	74	70	72	216	1,617
Neil Homann	70	73	73	216	1,617
Vaughn Groenewald	75	67	74	216	1,617
John Nelson	74	68	74	216	1,617
Colin Sorour	70	70	76	216	1,617

FNB Botswana Open

Gaborone Golf Club, Gaborone, Botswana — September 25-27
Par 36-35–71; 6,750 yards — purse, R150,000

	SCORES			TOTAL	MONEY
Justin Hobday	66	67	68	201	R23,550
Richard Kaplan	71	62	68	201	17,250
(Hobday defeated Kaplan on first extra hole.)					
Dean van Staden	64	70	68	202	12,000
Warren Abery	70	66	67	203	7,400
Steve van Vuuren	68	67	68	203	7,400
Keith Horne	68	65	70	203	7,400
Alan McLean	68	70	69	207	4,425
Bobby Lincoln	71	64	72	207	4,425
Sean Ludgater	71	70	67	208	3,525
Wayne de Haas	65	69	74	208	3,525
Sammy Daniels	66	71	72	209	3,150
Dion Fourie	69	70	71	210	2,712
Bryan Prytz	68	70	72	210	2,712
Grant Muller	66	72	72	210	2,712
Gregory Jacobs	68	69	73	210	2,712
Darren Fichardt	69	67	74	210	2,712
Adilson da Silva	70	71	70	211	2,250
Wayne Bradley	70	70	71	211	2,250
David Havens	67	70	74	211	2,250
Noel Maart	72	67	73	212	1,935
Ashley Roestoff	68	71	73	212	1,935
Hennie Otto	71	68	73	212	1,935
Michael Green	69	69	74	212	1,935
Colin Sorour	66	72	74	212	1,935
Mellette Hendrikse	72	69	72	213	1,695
John Bele	70	70	73	213	1,695
Nic Henning	71	69	74	214	1,518.75
Nasho Kamungeremu	73	67	74	214	1,518.75
Andre van Staden	71	69	74	214	1,518.75
Richard Fulford	65	74	75	214	1,518.75

Phalaborwa Mafunyane Trophy

Hans Merensky Country Club, Phalaborwa, South Africa — October 2-4
Par 36-36–72; 6,637 yards — purse, R150,000

	SCORES			TOTAL	MONEY
Sammy Daniels	67	67	65	199	R23,550
Hendrik Buhrmann	67	69	68	204	17,250
Des Terblanche	70	70	66	206	12,000
Wayne Bradley	71	69	68	208	6,731.25
Chris Davison	71	69	68	208	6,731.25
Michiel Bothma	71	68	69	208	6,731.25
Bobby Lincoln	67	71	70	208	6,731.25
Titch Moore	69	71	69	209	3,581.25
Wallie Coetsee	68	70	71	209	3,581.25
Neil Homann	70	67	72	209	3,581.25
Marc Cayeux	67	69	73	209	3,581.25
Brenden Pappas	70	71	69	210	2,925
David Havens	69	72	69	210	2,925
Darren Fichardt	73	70	68	211	2,570

	SCORES			TOTAL	MONEY
Nic Henning	70	73	68	211	2,570
Schalk van der Merwe	71	71	69	211	2,570
Wayne de Haas	73	69	70	212	2,250
Sean Ludgater	73	67	72	212	2,250
Ian Hutchings	68	71	73	212	2,250
Richard Michelmore	73	70	70	213	1,935
Lyall McNeill	72	71	70	213	1,935
Mark Murless	72	69	72	213	1,935
Nasho Kamungeremu	69	71	73	213	1,935
Robbie Stewart	68	71	74	213	1,935
Ryan Dreyer	73	70	71	214	1,665
Paul Cuningham	68	74	72	214	1,665
James Loughnane	67	74	73	214	1,665
Andrew Richter	72	72	71	215	1,466.25
Warren Abery	72	72	71	215	1,466.25
Andre Cruse	72	71	72	215	1,466.25
Callie Swart	68	70	77	215	1,466.25

Vodacom Series: Gauteng

Royal Johannesburg Golf Club, Johannesburg, South Africa — October 14-16
Par 71; 7,394 yards — purse, R165,000

	SCORES			TOTAL	MONEY
Brenden Pappas	67	66	69	202	R25,905
John Dickson	69	62	72	203	18,975
Chris Davison	67	67	70	204	13,200
Ashley Roestoff	71	66	68	205	8,140
Darren Fichardt	68	67	70	205	8,140
Ryan Dreyer	70	62	73	205	8,140
Richard Fulford	69	72	65	206	4,042.50
Adilson da Silva	68	69	69	206	4,042.50
Nic Henning	74	63	69	206	4,042.50
Roger Wessels	70	66	70	206	4,042.50
Pelop Panagopoulos	70	65	71	206	4,042.50
Marc Cayeux	67	67	72	206	4,042.50
Rudy Whitfield	70	67	70	207	3,052.50
David Havens	67	67	73	207	3,052.50
Andre van Staden	71	69	68	208	2,755.50
Steve van Vuuren	71	67	70	208	2,755.50
Stephen Wilson	70	72	67	209	2,429.62
Brett Liddle	71	68	70	209	2,429.62
Schalk van der Merwe	70	69	70	209	2,429.62
Ian Hutchings	69	68	72	209	2,429.62
Sammy Daniels	70	70	70	210	1,977.64
Grant Muller	71	69	70	210	1,977.64
Michael Green	72	68	70	210	1,977.64
Robbie Stewart	69	70	71	210	1,977.64
Gregory Jacobs	69	70	71	210	1,977.64
Trevor Sidley	70	66	74	210	1,977.64
Bobby Lincoln	68	67	75	210	1,977.64
Alan McLean	70	70	71	211	1,666.50
Phil Simmons	71	68	72	211	1,666.50
Desvonde Botes	73	69	70	212	1,509.75
Bryan Prytz	72	68	72	212	1,509.75
Bobby Verwey, Jr.	70	70	72	212	1,509.75
Callie Swart	69	70	73	212	1,509.75

FNB Namibia Open

Windhoek Country Club, Windhoek, Namibia — October 23-25
Par 36-35–71; 6,726 yards — purse, R150,000

	SCORES			TOTAL	MONEY
Ashley Roestoff	69	68	66	203	R23,550
Bobby Lincoln	68	70	68	206	14,625
Sammy Daniels	65	73	68	206	14,625
Glenn Cayeux	70	67	71	208	9,450
John Nelson	72	70	68	210	7,050
Marc Cayeux	71	71	69	211	5,212.50
Alan Michell	72	69	70	211	5,212.50
Michiel Bothma	73	70	69	212	3,900
Bradford Vaughan	70	71	71	212	3,900
Gregory Jacobs	72	73	68	213	2,940
Colin Sorour	70	74	69	213	2,940
Grant Muller	71	73	69	213	2,940
Callie Swart	72	71	70	213	2,940
Andre Cruse	73	68	72	213	2,940
Brett Liddle	68	71	74	213	2,940
Alan McLean	67	76	71	214	2,215
Richard Fulford	68	75	71	214	2,215
Ryan Dreyer	70	73	71	214	2,215
Adriaan van Pletzen	68	73	73	214	2,215
Sean Ludgater	69	70	75	214	2,215
Werner Lassen	70	68	76	214	2,215
John Mashego	70	76	69	215	1,762.50
Hugh Bain	72	74	69	215	1,762.50
Dion Fourie	71	75	69	215	1,762.50
Stephen Wilson	71	72	72	215	1,762.50
Wallie Coetsee	71	71	73	215	1,762.50
Paul Cuningham	73	69	73	215	1,762.50
Andre van Staden	76	70	70	216	1,466.25
Rudy Whitfield	71	74	71	216	1,466.25
John Dickson	69	72	75	216	1,466.25
Phillip Sanderson	72	66	78	216	1,466.25

Hassan II Trophy

Royal Golf Dar-es-Salam, Red Course, Rabat, Morocco — November 5-8
Par 36-37–73; 7,362 yards — purse, US$415,000

	SCORES				TOTAL	MONEY
Santiago Luna	71	67	70	69	277	US$100,000
Tom Pernice, Jr.	72	69	69	67	277	50,000
(Luna defeated Pernice on first extra hole.)						
Steve Jones	71	68	70	69	278	27,000
Stephen Ames	71	71	66	70	278	27,000
P.H. Horgan III	71	70	67	71	279	18,500
Spike McRoy	71	68	69	71	279	18,500
Henrik Nystrom	68	71	65	66	280	14,000
Joe Ogilvie	73	69	69	69	280	14,000
Mark Roe	71	69	70	72	282	11,500
Greg Chalmers	67	75	72	68	282	11,500
Raymond Russell	68	70	75	70	283	9,500
Olivier Edmond	74	66	75	68	283	9,500
Clark Dennis	75	69	68	74	286	8,300

	SCORES				TOTAL	MONEY
Anthony Wall	71	73	72	73	289	7,400
Thomas Levet	75	70	74	70	289	7,400
Roger Chapman	70	76	74	70	290	6,400
Pierre Fulke	72	74	70	74	290	6,400
Grant Waite	74	71	74	72	291	5,800
Antoinc Lcbouc	76	71	74	70	291	5,800
John Wilson	71	74	78	69	292	5,450
Younes El Hassani	72	78	73	69	292	5,450
A. Joudar	74	73	74	72	293	5,200
Bobby Casper	76	74	73	74	297	5,100
Derrick Cooper	75	71	80	73	299	5,000
Larry Laoretti	71	78	74	77	300	5,000
Mark Mouland	72	77	73	78	300	5,000
Carlo Blanchard	83	72	75	71	301	5,000
Billy Casper	78	80	74	73	305	5,000
Mohamed Makroune	74	81	75	76	306	5,000
Anders Forsbrand	71	80	79	89	319	5,000

Platinum Classic

Mooi Nooi Golf Club, Windhoek, Namibia — November 6-8
Par 36-36–72; 6,735 yards — purse, R250,000

	SCORES			TOTAL	MONEY
Bobby Lincoln	68	68	66	202	R39,250
Ashley Roestoff	68	70	67	205	28,750
Dean van Staden	69	68	69	206	20,000
Marc Cayeux	68	68	72	208	13,000
Andre Cruse	68	68	72	208	13,000
John Mashego	72	65	72	209	8,125
Roger Wessels	65	72	72	209	8,125
Justin Hobday	70	67	73	210	6,125
Andrew McLardy	70	67	73	210	6,125
Neil Homann	71	72	68	211	4,710
Hennie Walters	73	69	69	211	4,710
Sammy Daniels	69	72	70	211	4,710
Nic Henning	68	73	70	211	4,710
Jeff Hawkes	69	70	72	211	4,710
Brenden Pappas	70	72	70	212	3,850
Brett Liddle	71	71	70	212	3,850
Wimpie Botha	71	71	70	212	3,850
Grant Muller	71	67	74	212	3,850
Glenn Cayeux	73	71	69	213	3,437.50
Alan McLean	72	68	73	213	3,437.50
Darren Fichardt	76	70	68	214	3,125
Doug McGuigan	71	72	71	214	3,125
Richard Kaplan	71	69	74	214	3,125
Schalk van der Merwe	69	74	72	215	2,850
Robbie Stewart	68	75	72	215	2,850
Ian Hutchings	73	74	69	216	2,435.71
Mark Murless	72	74	70	216	2,435.71
Callie Swart	70	74	72	216	2,435.71
Michael du Toit	71	73	72	216	2,435.71
Adilson da Silva	69	74	73	216	2,435.71
Bradford Vaughan	72	69	75	216	2,435.71
Mellette Hendrikse	70	70	76	216	2,435.71

Zambia Open

Lusaka Golf Club, Lusaka, Zambia
Par 37-36–73; 7,159 yards

November 19-22
purse, R300,000

	SCORES				TOTAL	MONEY
Marc Cayeux	68	70	67	68	273	R63,200
Chris Davison	70	72	67	65	274	36,840
Hennie Otto	63	69	72	70	274	36,840
Mark Murless	65	72	74	66	277	16,773.33
Sean Farrell	71	72	65	69	277	16,773.33
Tjaart van der Walt	73	66	67	71	277	16,773.33
Phillip Sanderson	69	71	74	64	278	9,530
Ashley Roestoff	73	68	70	67	278	9,530
Andre van Staden	71	66	72	69	278	9,530
Grant Muller	69	66	73	70	278	9,530
Michael du Toit	71	74	71	64	280	6,920
James Loughnane	70	71	70	69	280	6,920
Darren Fichardt	71	71	70	69	281	6,280
Warren Abery	72	73	71	66	282	5,780
Alan Michell	69	66	76	71	282	5,780
Desvonde Botes	75	67	74	67	283	5,480
Paul Cuningham	71	73	72	68	284	4,904
Bobby Lincoln	74	73	68	69	284	4,904
Justin Hobday	71	73	70	70	284	4,904
Dion Fourie	70	69	71	74	284	4,904
Bradford Vaughan	75	67	68	74	284	4,904
*Madalitso Muthiya	72	72	72	69	285	
John Bele	73	68	73	71	285	4,380
Richard Fulford	71	71	71	72	285	4,380
Nasho Kamungeremu	74	70	72	70	286	4,080
Neil Homann	69	71	74	72	286	4,080
Wimpie Botha	71	70	71	74	286	4,080
Philip van den Berg	73	73	72	69	287	3,560
Werner Lassen	71	71	75	70	287	3,560
Michiel Bothma	70	73	74	70	287	3,560
Bradley Davison	70	70	75	72	287	3,560
Wallie Coetsee	73	70	71	73	287	3,560
Lyall McNeill	67	73	67	80	287	3,560

Zimbabwe Open

Chapman Golf Club, Harare, Zimbabwe
Par 36-36–72; 7,064 yards

November 26-29
purse, R450,000

	SCORES				TOTAL	MONEY
Nick Price	69	68	71	63	271	R71,100
Tjaart van der Walt	66	71	71	66	276	51,750
Hennie Walters	71	69	67	71	278	31,140
Desvonde Botes	73	68	71	67	279	20,340
Darren Fichardt	71	68	69	71	279	20,340
Andrew McLardy	73	71	66	70	280	15,930
Brett Liddle	70	74	68	69	281	10,721.25
Mark McNulty	74	70	68	69	281	10,721.25
Warren Abery	69	68	74	70	281	10,721.25
Hennie Otto	70	71	70	70	281	10,721.25
Adilson da Silva	74	67	70	71	282	8,055
Wallie Coetsee	73	70	71	69	283	7,065

	SCORES				TOTAL	MONEY
Alan McLean	68	75	69	71	283	7,065
Tony Johnstone	72	68	71	72	283	7,065
*Mike Lamb	72	69	75	68	284	
Robbie Stewart	73	72	71	68	284	6,086.25
Justin Hobday	74	71	71	68	284	6,086.25
Andre Cruse	68	73	74	69	284	6,086.25
Marc Cayeux	77	68	67	72	284	6,086.25
Peter Wilson	70	73	74	68	285	5,535
Jacob Okello	73	75	72	66	286	4,866.42
Sean Farrell	76	70	72	68	286	4,866.42
James Loughnane	73	75	70	68	286	4,866.42
Sean Pappas	70	75	71	70	286	4,866.42
Bobby Lincoln	78	68	70	70	286	4,866.42
Hugh Bain	71	70	74	71	286	4,866.42
Richard Fulford	77	70	66	73	286	4,866.42
Sammy Daniels	75	73	70	69	287	4,252.50
Nasho Kamungeremu	75	71	71	70	287	4,252.50
S. Katembenuka	74	74	73	67	288	3,741.42
John Mashego	74	71	74	69	288	3,741.42
Stephen Wilson	74	70	73	71	288	3,741.42
Ashley Roestoff	79	69	68	72	288	3,741.42
Lyall McNeill	71	74	70	73	288	3,741.42
Mark Ireland	72	68	73	75	288	3,741.42
Doug McGuigan	72	74	66	76	288	3,741.42

Nedbank Million Dollar Challenge

Gary Player Country Club, Sun City, South Africa — December 3-6
Par 36-36–72; 7,597 yards — purse, US$2,460,000

	SCORES				TOTAL	MONEY
Nick Price	67	68	72	66	273	$1,000,000
Tiger Woods	72	68	67	66	273	250,000
(Nick Price won on fifth extra hole.)						
Justin Leonard	69	68	68	69	274	200,000
Lee Westwood	72	65	66	73	276	150,000
Mark O'Meara	69	67	72	68	276	150,000
Ernie Els	70	69	70	71	280	105,000
Bernhard Langer	69	70	74	67	280	105,000
Jesper Parnevik	74	70	71	66	281	100,000
Jim Furyk	75	71	72	64	282	100,000
Colin Montgomerie	71	74	70	69	284	100,000
David Duval	72	73	71	68	284	100,000
Tom Watson	72	70	73	70	285	100,000

Senior Tours

MasterCard Championship

Hualalai Golf Club, Kailua-Kona, Hawaii — January 16-18
Par 36-36–72; 7,053 yards — purse, $1,000,000

	SCORES			TOTAL	MONEY
Gil Morgan	65	66	64	195	$200,000
Hale Irwin	69	68	64	201	107,250
Gibby Gilbert	65	68	68	201	107,250
Dave Stockton	67	67	68	202	66,333.34
David Graham	70	66	66	202	66,333.33
Vicente Fernandez	66	68	68	202	66,333.33
Jay Sigel	70	69	65	204	48,000
Bob Eastwood	71	67	67	205	43,000
Hugh Baiocchi	66	74	67	207	38,000
Dave Eichelberger	71	70	68	209	35,000
Dana Quigley	69	70	71	210	30,750
Jim Dent	70	73	67	210	30,750
Isao Aoki	70	72	69	211	26,250
Graham Marsh	68	73	70	211	26,250
Bob Murphy	68	74	70	212	24,000
Bruce Summerhays	72	72	69	213	22,500
Jack Kiefer	69	73	72	214	21,000
Bud Allin	71	75	68	214	21,000
Bruce Crampton	76	79	72	227	20,000

Royal Caribbean Classic

Crandon Park Golf Club, Key Biscayne, Florida — January 30-February 1
Par 35-36–71; 6,744 yards — purse, $850,000

	SCORES			TOTAL	MONEY
David Graham	67	68	67	202	$127,500
Dave Stockton	64	67	71	202	74,800
(Graham defeated Stockton on 10th extra hole.)					
Lee Trevino	67	65	72	204	61,200
Bob Murphy	68	68	69	205	51,000
Larry Nelson	71	67	68	206	40,800
Raymond Floyd	70	68	69	207	34,000
Dana Quigley	69	69	70	208	30,600
Larry Laoretti	69	67	73	209	25,500
Gil Morgan	71	69	69	209	25,500
Hubert Green	71	67	72	210	22,100
Hugh Baiocchi	73	69	69	211	18,700
Jose Maria Canizares	71	70	70	211	18,700
Fred Gibson	72	68	71	211	18,700
John Bland	69	66	77	212	14,450
Bob Dickson	73	70	69	212	14,450
Terry Dill	70	68	74	212	14,450
Al Geiberger	70	71	71	212	14,450
Bruce Summerhays	72	70	70	212	14,450
Bob Duval	68	75	70	213	11,248.34

	SCORES			TOTAL	MONEY
Charles Coody	73	69	71	213	11,248.33
Simon Hobday	72	69	72	213	11,248.33
George Archer	71	70	73	214	8,178.89
Jim Dent	74	68	72	214	8,178.89
Tom Jenkins	72	71	71	214	8,178.89
Jack Kiefer	76	68	70	214	8,178.89
Graham Marsh	70	71	73	214	8,178.89
Jerry McGee	73	72	69	214	8,178.89
J.C. Snead	72	70	72	214	8,178.89
Tom Wargo	71	73	70	214	8,178.89
Leonard Thompson	71	69	74	214	8,178.88
Bob Eastwood	69	68	78	215	5,610
Vicente Fernandez	74	69	72	215	5,610
Gibby Gilbert	77	67	71	215	5,610
John Jacobs	74	72	69	215	5,610
David Lundstrom	73	71	71	215	5,610
Walter Morgan	73	69	73	215	5,610
Jay Sigel	72	71	72	215	5,610
Jim Colbert	73	71	72	216	4,165
Mike Hill	71	72	73	216	4,165
Mike McCullough	70	69	77	216	4,165
Chi Chi Rodriguez	69	73	74	216	4,165
Buzz Thomas	71	73	72	216	4,165
DeWitt Weaver	73	71	72	216	4,165
Larry Ziegler	72	72	72	216	4,165

LG Championship

Bay Colony Golf Club, Naples, Florida
Par 36-36–72; 6,860 yards

February 6-8
purse, $1,200,000

	SCORES			TOTAL	MONEY
Gil Morgan	69	73	68	210	$180,000
Dale Douglass	73	70	69	212	96,000
Raymond Floyd	72	69	71	212	96,000
Jim Colbert	71	74	68	213	64,800
Hale Irwin	70	75	68	213	64,800
Jim Albus	67	70	77	214	40,800
Bob Eastwood	70	77	67	214	40,800
Graham Marsh	71	75	68	214	40,800
Tom Wargo	70	75	69	214	40,800
George Archer	71	72	72	215	26,640
Simon Hobday	76	71	68	215	26,640
David Lundstrom	68	76	71	215	26,640
Dana Quigley	75	69	71	215	26,640
J.C. Snead	72	72	71	215	26,640
Bob Duval	72	72	72	216	19,224
Dave Eichelberger	71	72	73	216	19,224
Jack Kiefer	72	71	73	216	19,224
Gary Player	73	73	70	216	19,224
Bruce Summerhays	75	68	73	216	19,224
Jose Maria Canizares	72	76	69	217	15,360
Calvin Peete	73	74	70	217	15,360
Vicente Fernandez	75	74	69	218	12,068.58
Hugh Baiocchi	73	70	75	218	12,068.57
Al Geiberger	70	77	71	218	12,068.57
David Graham	75	73	70	218	12,068.57

	SCORES			TOTAL	MONEY
Mike McCullough	71	75	72	218	12,068.57
Jay Sigel	75	71	72	218	12,068.57
Leonard Thompson	80	70	68	218	12,068.57
Bob Charles	71	75	73	219	9,072
Bob Dickson	73	73	73	219	9,072
Terry Dill	73	70	76	219	9,072
Fred Gibson	74	74	71	219	9,072
Dave Stockton	74	71	74	219	9,072
Charles Coody	73	77	70	220	7,380
Hubert Green	71	73	76	220	7,380
Jerry McGee	75	73	72	220	7,380
Buzz Thomas	73	77	70	220	7,380
Butch Baird	76	70	75	221	6,240
John Bland	73	80	68	221	6,240
Walter Morgan	74	75	72	221	6,240
Roy Vucinich	74	74	73	221	6,240

GTE Classic

TPC of Tampa Bay, Lutz, Florida
Par 35-36–71; 6,638 yards

February 13-15
purse, $1,100,000

	SCORES			TOTAL	MONEY
Jim Albus	68	69	70	207	$165,000
Simon Hobday	68	70	70	208	80,666.67
Kermit Zarley	74	66	68	208	80,666.67
Jose Maria Canizares	70	67	71	208	80,666.66
Hugh Baiocchi	68	71	70	209	42,900
Vicente Fernandez	70	66	73	209	42,900
Raymond Floyd	67	70	72	209	42,900
Larry Nelson	71	70	68	209	42,900
Brian Barnes	63	72	75	210	28,600
Bob Duval	66	71	73	210	28,600
Dan Wood	71	72	67	210	28,600
John Bland	70	71	70	211	21,725
Dave Eichelberger	72	68	71	211	21,725
David Graham	69	72	70	211	21,725
Jay Sigel	72	66	73	211	21,725
Bud Allin	70	71	71	212	17,077.50
Jim Colbert	66	71	75	212	17,077.50
Mike Hill	72	68	72	212	17,077.50
Tom Jenkins	68	69	75	212	17,077.50
Jim Dent	71	71	71	213	13,640
Gary Player	70	72	71	213	13,640
Dave Stockton	68	72	73	213	13,640
Bob Charles	72	70	72	214	10,780
Bob Dickson	67	73	74	214	10,780
John Jacobs	70	73	71	214	10,780
Dana Quigley	69	71	74	214	10,780
Leonard Thompson	70	69	75	214	10,780
Tom Wargo	71	67	76	214	10,780
George Archer	72	67	76	215	7,796.25
Charles Coody	70	72	73	215	7,796.25
Bruce Crampton	73	72	70	215	7,796.25
Terry Dill	74	71	70	215	7,796.25
Joe Inman	70	70	75	215	7,796.25
John Schroeder	69	74	72	215	7,796.25

	SCORES			TOTAL	MONEY
Bruce Summerhays	69	73	73	215	7,796.25
Buzz Thomas	72	69	74	215	7,796.25
Jim Ferree	70	72	74	216	5,940
Mike McCullough	68	73	75	216	5,940
Bob Murphy	75	71	70	216	5,940
Lee Trevino	75	76	65	216	5,940

American Express Invitational

TPC at Prestancia, Sarasota, Florida
Par 36-36–72; 6,876 yards

February 20-22
purse, $1,200,000

	SCORES			TOTAL	MONEY
Larry Nelson	63	69	71	203	$180,000
Dave Stockton	68	67	72	207	105,600
George Archer	70	68	70	208	79,200
Vicente Fernandez	69	66	73	208	79,200
Hale Irwin	70	66	73	209	49,600
John Jacobs	68	69	72	209	49,600
Gary Player	67	71	71	209	49,600
John Bland	69	71	70	210	34,400
Jim Dent	66	69	75	210	34,400
J.C. Snead	65	69	76	210	34,400
Jose Maria Canizares	67	72	72	211	24,000
Terry Dill	71	71	69	211	24,000
Bob Duval	68	71	72	211	24,000
Dave Eichelberger	67	73	71	211	24,000
Bob Murphy	67	71	73	211	24,000
Jay Sigel	68	70	73	211	24,000
Al Geiberger	71	68	73	212	17,490
Jack Kiefer	71	72	69	212	17,490
Bruce Summerhays	74	67	71	212	17,490
Lee Trevino	68	72	72	212	17,490
Mike Hill	71	69	73	213	13,650
Gil Morgan	67	74	72	213	13,650
Chi Chi Rodriguez	68	71	74	213	13,650
DeWitt Weaver	66	73	74	213	13,650
Brian Barnes	73	72	69	214	10,013.34
Kurt Cox	77	69	68	214	10,013.34
Don January	68	76	70	214	10,013.34
Jim Colbert	68	67	79	214	10,013.33
Bob Eastwood	72	70	72	214	10,013.33
Larry Laoretti	70	72	72	214	10,013.33
Mike McCullough	69	73	72	214	10,013.33
Jerry McGee	70	70	74	214	10,013.33
Leonard Thompson	71	70	73	214	10,013.33
Bob Charles	75	71	69	215	6,942.86
Bruce Crampton	71	73	71	215	6,942.86
Gibby Gilbert	73	73	69	215	6,942.86
Jack Nicklaus	72	70	73	215	6,942.86
Rocky Thompson	71	70	74	215	6,942.86
Fred Gibson	69	69	77	215	6,942.85
David Graham	69	71	75	215	6,942.85

Senior Slam

Cabo del Sol, Ocean Course, Cabo San Lucas, Mexico — March 9-10
Par 36-36–72; 6,841 yards — purse, $600,000

	SCORES		TOTAL	MONEY
Gil Morgan	66	68	134	$300,000
Hale Irwin	71	69	140	150,000
Isao Aoki	73	73	146	90,000
Graham Marsh	80	72	152	60,000

Toshiba Senior Classic

Newport Beach Country Club,
Newport Beach, California — March 13-15
Par 35-36–71; 6,598 yards — purse, $1,100,000

	SCORES			TOTAL	MONEY
Hale Irwin	70	68	62	200	$165,000
Hubert Green	67	66	68	201	96,800
Jay Sigel	68	69	67	204	72,600
Mike McCullough	66	70	68	204	72,600
Larry Nelson	71	70	65	206	40,480
Dave Eichelberger	69	71	66	206	40,480
David Graham	67	71	68	206	40,480
J.C. Snead	66	71	69	206	40,480
Gil Morgan	68	69	69	206	40,480
Butch Baird	70	68	69	207	25,300
Dana Quigley	67	70	70	207	25,300
Bob Eastwood	70	67	70	207	25,300
Jim Albus	69	65	73	207	25,300
Lee Trevino	70	68	70	208	19,800
John Schroeder	72	66	70	208	19,800
Jose Maria Canizares	67	70	71	208	19,800
Graham Marsh	73	66	70	209	17,600
Bud Allin	71	73	66	210	14,586
John Jacobs	72	69	69	210	14,586
Jim Colbert	71	67	72	210	14,586
Buzz Thomas	66	71	73	210	14,586
Bob Duval	70	67	73	210	14,586
Bruce Crampton	73	70	68	211	11,022
Gary Player	72	69	70	211	11,022
Harry Toscano	71	69	71	211	11,022
Jimmy Powell	71	68	72	211	11,022
Leonard Thompson	71	69	71	211	11,022
Bob Dickson	71	73	68	212	8,344
Tom Wargo	74	69	69	212	8,344
Dave Stockton	70	72	70	212	8,344
Joe Inman	70	72	70	212	8,344
Rocky Thompson	72	69	71	212	8,344
Dale Douglass	75	66	71	212	8,344
Jerry McGee	71	69	72	212	8,344
Charles Coody	73	70	70	213	6,765
Walter Zembriski	72	67	74	213	6,765
Don Bies	74	71	69	214	5,830
Al Geiberger	72	71	71	214	5,830
Bruce Devlin	71	71	72	214	5,830
David Lundstrom	66	74	74	214	5,830
Larry Ziegler	71	69	74	214	5,830

Liberty Mutual Legends of Golf

Golf Club of Amelia Island at Summer Beach, Amelia Island, Florida
Par 36-36–72; 6,681 yards

March 20-22
purse, $1,500,000

	SCORES			TOTAL	MONEY (Each)
Charles Coody/Dale Douglass	62	66	64	192	$150,000
Hugh Baiocchi/David Graham	63	64	65	192	85,000
(Coody/Douglass defeated Baiocchi/Graham on second extra hole.)					
Larry Nelson/Dave Stockton	64	64	65	193	60,000
Simon Hobday/George Archer	64	67	64	195	45,000
Bob Eastwood/Bob Duval	65	65	67	197	32,500
John Bland/Graham Marsh	68	64	66	198	25,000
Jim Colbert/Bob Murphy	67	67	65	199	20,500
Chi Chi Rodriguez/Harold Henning	66	71	62	200	17,000
Calvin Peete/Jim Dent	65	65	70	200	17,000
Hubert Green/Gil Morgan	67	70	64	201	15,000
Tom Shaw/Tom Wargo	68	68	67	203	13,500
Lee Trevino/Mike Hill	65	70	68	203	13,500
Miller Barber/Jim Ferree	71	66	67	204	12,000
Bud Allin/Jerry Heard	68	69	68	205	11,000
Gibby Gilbert/J.C. Snead	66	71	69	206	10,000
Don Bies/Bruce Devlin	67	70	70	207	8,500
Orville Moody/Jimmy Powell	70	67	70	207	8,500
Jim Albus/Larry Laoretti	67	69	71	207	8,500
Dave Hill/Bobby Nichols	67	69	71	207	8,500
Homero Blancas/Butch Baird	68	67	72	207	8,500
Tommy Jacobs/Bob Toski	70	68	71	209	7,000
Don January/Gene Littler	71	67	72	210	6,500
Tommy Aaron/Doug Sanders	72	70	69	211	6,000
Billy Casper/Gay Brewer	69	69	74	212	5,250
Lou Graham/Don Massengale	70	71	71	212	5,250
Billy Maxwell/Larry Mowry	68	70	75	213	5,000
Tony Jacklin/Bob Lunn	68	71	75	214	4,500
Lee Elder/Ken Still	70	71	75	216	4,500
Johnny Pott/Mason Rudolph	74	71	77	222	4,000
Dow Finsterwald/Bob Goalby	77	74	74	225	4,000

Southwestern Bell Dominion

Dominion Country Club, San Antonio, Texas
Par 36-36–72; 6,835 yards

March 27-29
purse, $1,000,000

	SCORES			TOTAL	MONEY
Lee Trevino	69	69	67	205	$150,000
Mike McCullough	67	73	67	207	88,000
Dave Eichelberger	68	74	67	209	60,000
Jay Sigel	70	71	68	209	60,000
Dave Stockton	71	67	71	209	60,000
Jim Colbert	69	71	70	210	40,000
Jose Maria Canizares	73	71	67	211	32,000
David Lundstrom	69	70	72	211	32,000
Dana Quigley	74	67	70	211	32,000
Raymond Floyd	72	68	72	212	25,000
Leonard Thompson	73	70	69	212	25,000
Terry Dill	70	73	70	213	17,144.45

	SCORES			TOTAL	MONEY
Larry Laoretti	76	67	70	213	17,144.45
John Schroeder	68	75	70	213	17,144.45
Buzz Thomas	75	68	70	213	17,144.45
Jim Albus	73	68	72	213	17,144.44
George Archer	70	69	74	213	17,144.44
Bob Dickson	70	67	76	213	17,144.44
John Jacobs	70	71	72	213	17,144.44
Tom Wargo	72	68	73	213	17,144.44
Jim Barker	68	70	76	214	11,375
Frank Conner	68	74	72	214	11,375
Bob Eastwood	73	70	71	214	11,375
Tom Shaw	74	68	72	214	11,375
Bruce Crampton	74	68	73	215	9,120
Vicente Fernandez	75	72	68	215	9,120
Simon Hobday	73	69	73	215	9,120
Joe Inman	72	71	72	215	9,120
Walter Morgan	73	73	69	215	9,120
John Bland	73	70	73	216	7,220
John Paul Cain	68	73	75	216	7,220
Walter Hall	71	71	74	216	7,220
Jerry McGee	72	71	73	216	7,220
Bobby Stroble	72	72	72	216	7,220
Gay Brewer	74	68	75	217	6,150
Charles Coody	73	74	70	217	6,150
Bud Allin	75	72	71	218	5,200
Don Bies	72	74	72	218	5,200
Al Geiberger	76	70	72	218	5,200
Tom Jenkins	73	73	72	218	5,200
Jack Kiefer	76	71	71	218	5,200
John Morgan	73	73	72	218	5,200

The Tradition

Desert Mountain Golf Club, Cochise Course, April 2-5
Scottsdale, Arizona purse, $1,400,000
Par 36-36–72; 6,954 yards

	SCORES				TOTAL	MONEY
Gil Morgan	71	66	69	70	276	$210,000
Tom Wargo	68	67	69	74	278	123,200
Vicente Fernandez	71	70	69	69	279	100,800
Hale Irwin	69	69	74	68	280	84,000
Raymond Floyd	73	68	69	72	282	67,200
John Jacobs	71	72	70	70	283	50,400
Mike McCullough	73	69	70	71	283	50,400
Dave Stockton	73	70	73	67	283	50,400
Bruce Summerhays	73	71	66	74	284	39,200
John Morgan	70	71	69	75	285	36,400
Jim Colbert	70	72	75	69	286	32,200
Bob Dickson	71	68	74	73	286	32,200
Isao Aoki	72	75	66	74	287	25,900
George Archer	71	71	71	74	287	25,900
Graham Marsh	72	73	71	71	287	25,900
Jimmy Powell	70	72	71	74	287	25,900
Terry Dill	71	72	72	73	288	21,047
Gary Player	76	72	71	69	288	21,047
Bob Murphy	77	68	67	76	288	21,047

	SCORES				TOTAL	MONEY
Bob Eastwood	73	73	73	70	289	17,360
Mike Hill	73	75	69	72	289	17,360
Jack Kiefer	73	74	71	71	289	17,360
Al Geiberger	73	70	74	73	290	15,050
David Lundstrom	75	72	70	73	290	15,050
Hugh Baiocchi	74	69	76	72	291	12,768
John Bland	70	72	78	71	291	12,768
Jose Maria Canizares	69	74	73	75	291	12,768
Jack Nicklaus	72	70	74	75	291	12,768
J.C. Snead	73	73	73	72	291	12,768
Brian Barnes	75	70	75	72	292	11,060
Bob Charles	77	73	70	73	293	9,870
Bob Duval	75	72	75	71	293	9,870
Jerry McGee	73	78	71	71	293	9,870
Dana Quigley	77	75	69	72	293	9,870
Frank Conner	74	75	73	72	294	8,225
Walter Hall	77	74	72	71	294	8,225
Dick Hendrickson	70	72	79	73	294	8,225
Kermit Zarley	72	74	74	74	294	8,225
Simon Hobday	71	78	74	72	295	7,140
Larry Laoretti	74	74	72	75	295	7,140
Rocky Thompson	74	77	69	75	295	7,140

PGA Seniors' Championship

PGA National Golf Club, Champion Course, April 16-19
Palm Beach Gardens, Florida purse, $1,500,000
Par 36-36–72; 6,869 yards

	SCORES				TOTAL	MONEY
Hale Irwin	68	68	69	70	275	$270,000
Larry Nelson	69	71	70	72	282	162,000
Gil Morgan	69	72	70	72	283	102,000
Dave Stockton	73	73	73	68	287	63,500
Dale Douglass	71	72	71	73	287	63,500
Jay Sigel	72	75	71	71	289	43,000
Jack Nicklaus	68	74	75	72	289	43,000
Walter Morgan	76	76	66	71	289	43,000
Vicente Fernandez	75	72	70	72	289	43,000
Dana Quigley	71	72	71	75	289	43,000
George Archer	73	73	72	72	290	33,750
Tom Wargo	71	71	74	74	290	33,750
Mike McCullough	71	77	71	72	291	28,750
John Jacobs	74	72	73	72	291	28,750
Raymond Floyd	76	69	71	76	292	25,000
David Lundstrom	73	73	75	72	293	21,750
Jack Lewis	76	74	71	72	293	21,750
Bob Dickson	74	75	75	70	294	18,500
Bill Kennedy	73	75	76	70	294	18,500
Graham Marsh	73	76	73	72	294	18,500
Bud Allin	74	76	70	74	294	18,500
Bob Duval	72	75	76	72	295	13,000
Simon Hobday	72	74	78	71	295	13,000
Bob E. Smith	77	73	73	72	295	13,000
Jim Dent	74	75	71	75	295	13,000
Bob Murphy	73	72	75	75	295	13,000
Jose Maria Canizares	75	69	75	76	295	13,000

	SCORES				TOTAL	MONEY
Leonard Thompson	71	72	75	77	295	13,000
Larry Laoretti	78	74	72	72	296	8,257
John Bland	73	73	78	72	296	8,257
Terry Dill	72	77	72	75	296	8,257
Buddy Whitten	73	78	71	74	296	8,257
David Oakley	74	76	75	71	296	8,257
Bob Charles	73	72	74	77	296	8,257
Jack Kiefer	76	75	67	78	296	8,257
John Schroeder	75	77	72	73	297	6,617
J.C. Snead	75	76	73	73	297	6,617
Hugh Baiocchi	77	74	73	73	297	6,617
Rocky Thompson	76	74	74	74	298	5,600
Bruce Crampton	76	73	74	75	298	5,600
Gary Player	73	78	74	73	298	5,600
Jim Albus	75	70	83	70	298	5,600
Kermit Zarley	73	75	69	81	298	5,600

Las Vegas Senior Classic

Las Vegas, Nevada — April 23-26
TPC at Summerlin: Par 36-36–72; 6,963 yards — purse, $1,400,000
TPC at The Canyons: Par 36-35–71; 6,839 yards

	SCORES				TOTAL	MONEY
Hale Irwin	69	67	70	75	281	$210,000
Vicente Fernandez	69	72	73	68	282	123,200
Jose Maria Canizares	71	68	73	74	286	92,400
Dale Douglass	66	72	74	74	286	92,400
Walter Morgan	72	71	75	70	287	67,200
Graham Marsh	72	69	76	72	289	56,000
Jim Colbert	72	65	78	75	290	47,600
David Graham	78	69	69	74	290	47,600
Hugh Baiocchi	68	71	77	75	291	37,800
Leonard Thompson	75	68	75	73	291	37,800
Jim Dent	72	68	74	78	292	32,200
Larry Nelson	73	70	74	75	292	32,200
Terry Dill	72	72	74	75	293	25,900
Hubert Green	77	67	76	73	293	25,900
Dave Hill	73	69	80	71	293	25,900
Buzz Thomas	71	66	78	78	293	25,900
Bob Eastwood	69	73	76	76	294	20,405
Dana Quigley	79	67	73	75	294	20,405
Tom Wargo	73	73	74	74	294	20,405
Jim Wilkinson	75	68	76	75	294	20,405
Isao Aoki	81	69	74	71	295	15,166.67
George Archer	70	75	78	72	295	15,166.67
John Bland	70	70	80	75	295	15,166.67
Gil Morgan	75	72	76	72	295	15,166.67
Dave Eichelberger	78	66	75	76	295	15,166.66
Mike Hill	70	75	77	73	295	15,166.66
Butch Baird	73	70	76	77	296	12,180
Bob Duval	76	69	78	73	296	12,180
Dave Stockton	76	70	74	76	296	12,180
Miller Barber	75	72	78	72	297	11,060
Bruce Summerhays	74	69	79	76	298	10,500
Jay Sigel	78	69	79	73	299	9,870
J.C. Snead	78	70	77	74	299	9,870

	SCORES				TOTAL	MONEY
Harold Henning	77	74	75	74	300	9,030
Mike McCullough	75	74	77	74	300	9,030
Joe Inman	75	71	83	72	301	8,026.67
John Jacobs	78	70	79	74	301	8,026.67
Chi Chi Rodriguez	76	73	77	75	301	8,026.66
Bob Dickson	71	70	82	80	303	7,420
Bob Charles	77	72	76	79	304	6,300
Frank Conner	83	71	73	77	304	6,300
Gibby Gilbert	77	75	77	75	304	6,300
Dick Hendrickson	74	77	74	79	304	6,300
Jimmy Powell	76	71	77	80	304	6,300
Tom Shaw	74	73	80	77	304	6,300
Rocky Thompson	73	67	83	71	304	6,300

Bruno's Memorial Classic

Greystone Country Club, Hoover, Alabama — May 1-3
Par 36-36–72; 6,967 yards — purse, $1,150,000

	SCORES			TOTAL	MONEY
Hubert Green	70	69	64	203	$172,500
Hale Irwin	69	70	65	204	101,200
Jim Colbert	72	67	67	206	75,900
Terry Dill	63	72	71	206	75,900
Graham Marsh	69	69	69	207	55,200
Hugh Baiocchi	67	70	71	208	41,400
Jose Maria Canizares	68	73	67	208	41,400
Mike Hill	71	68	69	208	41,400
John Bland	66	71	72	209	31,050
J.C. Snead	69	70	70	209	31,050
Gil Morgan	70	66	74	210	25,300
Larry Nelson	68	75	67	210	25,300
Jimmy Powell	70	69	71	210	25,300
Tommy Aaron	77	69	65	211	17,925.63
Vicente Fernandez	68	73	70	211	17,925.63
Harold Henning	71	69	71	211	17,925.63
Dave Stockton	72	69	70	211	17,925.63
Bob Dickson	69	70	72	211	17,925.62
Dale Douglass	70	69	72	211	17,925.62
Dave Eichelberger	72	68	71	211	17,925.62
David Lundstrom	69	70	72	211	17,925.62
George Archer	70	68	74	212	12,098
Bob Charles	69	71	72	212	12,098
Frank Conner	68	69	75	212	12,098
Walter Morgan	71	71	70	212	12,098
Leonard Thompson	75	69	68	212	12,098
Bud Allin	69	74	70	213	9,545
Jim Dent	74	69	70	213	9,545
Dave Hill	70	73	70	213	9,545
Joe Inman	72	70	71	213	9,545
Chi Chi Rodriguez	71	72	70	213	9,545
Bob Duval	76	68	70	214	7,935
Buzz Thomas	72	71	71	214	7,935
Rocky Thompson	73	71	70	214	7,935
Brian Barnes	74	71	70	215	6,374.29
David Graham	71	74	70	215	6,374.29
Bob Murphy	74	75	66	215	6,374.29

	SCORES			TOTAL	MONEY
Tom Wargo	73	73	69	215	6,374.29
Jerry McGee	72	71	72	215	6,374.28
Dana Quigley	72	72	71	215	6,374.28
Bruce Summerhays	68	70	77	215	6,374.28

Home Depot Invitational

TPC at Piper Glen, Charlotte, North Carolina — May 8-10
Par 36-36–72; 6,774 yards — purse, $1,100,000

	SCORES			TOTAL	MONEY
Jim Dent	67	68	72	207	$165,000
Bob Charles	71	69	67	207	96,800
(Dent defeated Charles on second extra hole.)					
Jay Sigel	69	69	70	208	79,200
Graham Marsh	68	69	72	209	54,266.67
DeWitt Weaver	67	75	67	209	54,266.67
John Morgan	68	67	74	209	54,266.66
Isao Aoki	77	68	65	210	37,400
Leonard Thompson	71	68	71	210	37,400
Frank Conner	70	67	74	211	27,500
Raymond Floyd	70	73	68	211	27,500
Walter Morgan	73	66	72	211	27,500
Tom Wargo	67	72	72	211	27,500
George Archer	75	67	70	212	19,250
Bob Duval	69	71	72	212	19,250
Fred Gibson	72	69	71	212	19,250
Mike Hill	70	70	72	212	19,250
Larry Nelson	68	71	73	212	19,250
John Schroeder	70	70	72	212	19,250
Jose Maria Canizares	73	71	69	213	13,706
Vicente Fernandez	76	72	65	213	13,706
Mike McCullough	72	71	70	213	13,706
Bobby Stroble	73	68	72	213	13,706
Kermit Zarley	74	70	69	213	13,706
Terry Dill	73	73	68	214	10,752.50
Dick Hendrickson	71	73	70	214	10,752.50
J.C. Snead	77	70	67	214	10,752.50
Bruce Summerhays	74	70	70	214	10,752.50
Jim Albus	73	71	71	215	7,993.34
Simon Hobday	74	73	68	215	7,993.34
John Jacobs	74	71	70	215	7,993.34
Hugh Baiocchi	71	71	73	215	7,993.33
Dale Douglass	71	72	72	215	7,993.33
Walter Hall	72	71	72	215	7,993.33
Dana Quigley	72	69	74	215	7,993.33
Dave Stockton	69	70	76	215	7,993.33
Walter Zembriski	75	68	72	215	7,993.33
Tommy Aaron	73	72	71	216	5,720
Charles Coody	72	71	73	216	5,720
David Graham	75	72	69	216	5,720
Hubert Green	73	72	71	216	5,720
Tom Shaw	71	73	72	216	5,720
Dan Wood	76	65	75	216	5,720

Saint Luke's Classic

Loch Lloyd Country Club, Belton, Missouri — May 15-17
Par 35-35–70; 6,539 yards — purse, $1,000,000

	SCORES			TOTAL	MONEY
Larry Ziegler	69	67	72	208	$150,000
Tom Shaw	73	66	70	209	88,000
Isao Aoki	70	73	68	211	60,000
Hugh Baiocchi	75	65	71	211	60,000
Walter Morgan	75	65	71	211	60,000
Bob Murphy	72	69	71	212	38,000
Bruce Summerhays	68	70	74	212	38,000
Bob Duval	71	71	71	213	27,500
Rik Massengale	73	72	68	213	27,500
Jesse Patino	76	69	68	213	27,500
Tom Wargo	71	68	74	213	27,500
Jim Dent	75	68	71	214	19,750
Fred Gibson	65	74	75	214	19,750
Jerry McGee	73	70	71	214	19,750
Dana Quigley	72	72	70	214	19,750
Frank Conner	79	65	71	215	16,000
David Graham	74	68	73	215	16,000
Mike McCullough	72	70	73	215	16,000
Don January	74	71	71	216	11,828.58
Jim Colbert	72	72	72	216	11,828.57
Ed Dougherty	78	67	71	216	11,828.57
Dave Eichelberger	73	71	72	216	11,828.57
Walter Hall	78	68	70	216	11,828.57
Joe Inman	76	68	72	216	11,828.57
Lee Trevino	74	69	73	216	11,828.57
Harold Henning	76	70	71	217	8,700
Tom Jenkins	73	70	74	217	8,700
John Mahaffey	76	66	75	217	8,700
Bob E. Smith	71	72	74	217	8,700
Dave Stockton	78	71	68	217	8,700
Don Bies	76	69	73	218	6,462.50
John Paul Cain	76	71	71	218	6,462.50
Charles Coody	71	73	74	218	6,462.50
Bruce Crampton	75	67	76	218	6,462.50
John Schroeder	76	68	74	218	6,462.50
Bobby Stroble	72	71	75	218	6,462.50
Buzz Thomas	76	73	69	218	6,462.50
Leonard Thompson	76	69	73	218	6,462.50
Ray Arinno	74	74	71	219	4,900
John Jacobs	77	70	72	219	4,900
Don Klenk	71	71	77	219	4,900
Ed Sneed	71	75	73	219	4,900
Kermit Zarley	74	69	76	219	4,900

Bell Atlantic Classic

Hartefeld National, Avondale, Pennsylvania — May 22-24
Par 36-36–72; 6,969 yards — purse, $1,100,000

	SCORES			TOTAL	MONEY
Jay Sigel	74	62	69	205	$165,000
Jose Maria Canizares	69	71	65	205	96,800

(Sigel defeated Canizares on third extra hole.)

	SCORES			TOTAL	MONEY
Ed Dougherty	70	74	64	208	66,000
Dale Douglass	68	71	69	208	66,000
Bob Duval	71	70	67	208	66,000
Raymond Floyd	69	71	69	209	41,800
Tom Shaw	72	68	69	209	41,800
Jack Nicklaus	70	72	68	210	35,200
John Bland	73	67	71	211	28,600
Frank Conner	72	70	69	211	28,600
Bruce Summerhays	69	73	69	211	28,600
John Jacobs	71	70	71	212	23,100
John Schroeder	74	69	69	212	23,100
Kurt Cox	70	70	73	213	19,250
John Mahaffey	70	74	69	213	19,250
Bob Murphy	72	74	67	213	19,250
Walter Zembriski	74	70	69	213	19,250
Hubert Green	73	72	69	214	13,114.45
John Morgan	75	68	71	214	13,114.45
Gary Player	71	74	69	214	13,114.45
Lee Trevino	76	71	67	214	13,114.45
Hugh Baiocchi	74	69	71	214	13,114.44
Bruce Crampton	69	70	75	214	13,114.44
Tom Jenkins	72	70	72	214	13,114.44
Mike McCullough	70	71	73	214	13,114.44
Larry Ziegler	68	73	73	214	13,114.44
John Paul Cain	74	69	72	215	9,570
Jim Colbert	74	70	71	215	9,570
Walter Hall	75	72	68	215	9,570
George Archer	72	70	74	216	8,470
Don Bies	74	72	70	216	8,470
Ray Carrasco	70	78	69	217	7,095
Dave Eichelberger	73	74	70	217	7,095
Dick Hendrickson	74	69	74	217	7,095
Walter Morgan	73	71	73	217	7,095
Calvin Peete	77	70	70	217	7,095
Bobby Stroble	71	74	72	217	7,095
Charles Coody	78	69	71	218	5,720
Harold Henning	77	73	68	218	5,720
Joe Inman	75	74	69	218	5,720
Buzz Thomas	74	72	72	218	5,720

Pittsburgh Senior Classic

Sewickley Heights Golf Club, Pittsburgh, Pennsylvania — May 29-31
Par 36-36–72; 6,781 yards — purse, $1,100,000

	SCORES			TOTAL	MONEY
Larry Nelson	65	65	74	204	$165,000
Bob Duval	72	69	68	209	96,800
Jay Sigel	72	66	72	210	79,200
Al Geiberger	67	72	72	211	66,000
Ed Dougherty	71	70	71	212	36,771.43
Raymond Floyd	71	69	72	212	36,771.43
Hubert Green	72	72	68	212	36,771.43
Gil Morgan	73	67	72	212	36,771.43
Gary Player	72	69	71	212	36,771.43
Bobby Stroble	70	73	69	212	36,771.43
John Bland	72	66	74	212	36,771.42

	SCORES			TOTAL	MONEY
Fred Gibson	73	71	69	213	21,725
Joe Inman	68	72	73	213	21,725
Walter Morgan	67	72	74	213	21,725
J.C. Snead	70	75	68	213	21,725
Jose Maria Canizares	73	72	69	214	17,077.50
Frank Conner	72	68	74	214	17,077.50
Bob Eastwood	70	73	71	214	17,077.50
David Graham	70	72	72	214	17,077.50
Rocky Thompson	72	73	71	216	14,520
Dana Quigley	69	71	77	217	13,640
Tommy Aaron	71	72	75	218	11,572
George Archer	71	71	76	218	11,572
Dale Douglass	71	72	75	218	11,572
John Jacobs	77	71	70	218	11,572
Lee Trevino	74	70	74	218	11,572
Bruce Crampton	73	74	72	219	8,928.34
Bob Murphy	75	74	70	219	8,928.34
Jim Colbert	74	72	73	219	8,928.33
Bob Dickson	73	70	76	219	8,928.33
Mike Hill	71	70	78	219	8,928.33
Tom Wargo	70	76	73	219	8,928.33
Dave Eichelberger	77	70	73	220	6,930
Dick Hendrickson	73	75	72	220	6,930
John Mahaffey	72	73	75	220	6,930
Jerry McGee	75	72	73	220	6,930
Leonard Thompson	70	75	75	220	6,930
Hugh Baiocchi	74	73	74	221	5,610
Bruce Lehnhard	75	67	79	221	5,610
Mike McCullough	71	72	78	221	5,610
John Morgan	72	76	73	221	5,610
John Schroeder	70	73	78	221	5,610

Nationwide Championship

Golf Club of Georgia, Lakeside Course, Alpharetta, Georgia — June 5-7
Par 36-36–72; 6,777 yards — purse, $1,350,000

	SCORES			TOTAL	MONEY
John Jacobs	72	67	67	206	$202,500
Hale Irwin	70	70	67	207	118,800
Gil Morgan	67	69	72	208	89,100
Leonard Thompson	72	67	69	208	89,100
Jose Maria Canizares	68	69	73	210	55,800
Bob Dickson	73	66	71	210	55,800
Bob Eastwood	68	68	74	210	55,800
Gibby Gilbert	71	70	70	211	43,200
Brian Barnes	72	72	68	212	29,362.50
John Bland	71	71	70	212	29,362.50
Bob Charles	70	72	70	212	29,362.50
Frank Conner	71	71	70	212	29,362.50
Dave Eichelberger	74	68	70	212	29,362.50
David Graham	72	73	67	212	29,362.50
Gary Player	67	72	73	212	29,362.50
Dana Quigley	70	75	67	212	29,362.50
Isao Aoki	72	70	71	213	20,295
Jim Colbert	74	70	69	213	20,295
Jay Sigel	71	72	70	213	20,295

	SCORES			TOTAL	MONEY
Jim Dent	71	71	72	214	15,457.50
Raymond Floyd	69	72	73	214	15,457.50
John Mahaffey	73	70	71	214	15,457.50
Graham Marsh	72	74	68	214	15,457.50
Walter Morgan	72	69	73	214	15,457.50
Larry Nelson	72	72	70	214	15,457.50
Jim Albus	74	69	72	215	12,555
J.C. Snead	71	69	75	215	12,555
Kurt Cox	68	75	73	216	11,205
Mike McCullough	71	76	69	216	11,205
Bob Murphy	73	71	72	216	11,205
Terry Dill	74	72	71	217	8,550
Al Geiberger	73	71	73	217	8,550
Simon Hobday	71	74	72	217	8,550
Joe Inman	72	71	74	217	8,550
David Lundstrom	74	73	70	217	8,550
Tom Shaw	69	72	76	217	8,550
Rocky Thompson	72	70	75	217	8,550
Lee Trevino	71	72	74	217	8,550
Larry Ziegler	74	67	76	217	8,550
Fred Gibson	73	73	72	218	6,345
Billy King	74	71	73	218	6,345
Dwight Nevil	69	71	78	218	6,345
Chi Chi Rodriguez	76	73	69	218	6,345
Bruce Summerhays	74	76	68	218	6,345

BellSouth Senior Classic

Springhouse Golf Club, Nashville, Tennessee — June 12-14
Par 36-36–72; 6,783 yards — purse, $1,300,000

	SCORES			TOTAL	MONEY
Isao Aoki	62	66	70	198	$195,000
Larry Nelson	68	68	64	200	114,400
Hale Irwin	66	70	65	201	93,600
John Jacobs	65	71	69	205	78,000
Gil Morgan	64	73	69	206	57,200
Dave Stockton	70	68	68	206	57,200
Tom Jenkins	66	71	70	207	41,600
David Lundstrom	68	71	68	207	41,600
Walter Morgan	72	68	67	207	41,600
Jim Albus	69	72	67	208	27,950
Bud Allin	70	70	68	208	27,950
Fred Gibson	69	70	69	208	27,950
David Graham	71	68	69	208	27,950
Graham Marsh	70	68	70	208	27,950
Dana Quigley	70	69	69	208	27,950
Gibby Gilbert	68	71	70	209	20,800
Gary Player	71	69	69	209	20,800
Jay Sigel	70	71	68	209	20,800
Hugh Baiocchi	70	70	70	210	17,745
Mike McCullough	68	75	67	210	17,745
Jose Maria Canizares	70	72	69	211	14,083.34
Jesse Patino	69	73	69	211	14,083.34
Frank Conner	70	71	70	211	14,083.33
John Schroeder	71	68	72	211	14,083.33
Rocky Thompson	68	72	71	211	14,083.33

	SCORES			TOTAL	MONEY
Kermit Zarley	69	71	71	211	14,083.33
George Archer	71	72	69	212	11,050
Bob Duval	68	74	70	212	11,050
Walter Hall	74	70	68	212	11,050
Leonard Thompson	72	71	69	212	11,050
Brian Barnes	70	74	69	213	9,555
DeWitt Weaver	71	69	73	213	9,555
Tommy Aaron	72	71	71	214	8,385
John Bland	72	71	71	214	8,385
John Morgan	70	73	71	214	8,385
J.C. Snead	76	69	69	214	8,385
Ed Dougherty	74	74	67	215	7,150
Bob Eastwood	74	73	68	215	7,150
Bobby Nichols	71	71	73	215	7,150
Al Geiberger	72	73	71	216	6,370
Simon Hobday	71	74	71	216	6,370
John Mahaffey	72	73	71	216	6,370

AT&T Canada Senior Open

Glencoe Golf & Country Club, Calgary, Alberta, Canada — June 18-21
Par 36-36–72; 6,686 yards — purse, $1,100,000

	SCORES				TOTAL	MONEY
Brian Barnes	69	67	73	68	277	$165,000
Dana Quigley	71	71	69	68	279	80,666.67
Bruce Summerhays	65	73	71	70	279	80,666.67
Tom Jenkins	65	71	73	70	279	80,666.66
Walter Hall	69	68	69	74	280	52,800
Hank Cooper	71	70	72	69	282	41,800
Mike McCullough	70	75	73	64	282	41,800
Bud Allin	72	71	76	65	284	30,250
Ed Dougherty	69	76	69	70	284	30,250
Jesse Patino	70	70	73	71	284	30,250
Dave Stockton	72	70	73	69	284	30,250
Jim Albus	71	73	71	70	285	21,120
John Bland	70	72	71	72	285	21,120
Frank Conner	70	73	71	71	285	21,120
John Morgan	70	73	71	71	285	21,120
Bobby Stroble	66	73	71	75	285	21,120
Jim Colbert	73	75	71	67	286	16,536.67
J.C. Snead	70	72	73	71	286	16,536.67
Jimmy Adams	71	70	73	72	286	16,536.66
John Jacobs	74	76	71	66	287	14,080
Tom Wargo	71	73	74	69	287	14,080
Bob Dickson	70	72	72	74	288	11,852.50
Joe Inman	73	69	73	73	288	11,852.50
Walter Morgan	73	69	75	71	288	11,852.50
Gary Player	71	71	72	74	288	11,852.50
Larry Laoretti	73	66	73	77	289	10,010
Bob Murphy	73	70	70	76	289	10,010
Jimmy Powell	70	77	69	73	289	10,010
Bob Panasik	72	75	72	71	290	8,910
Buzz Thomas	77	71	73	69	290	8,910
Terry Dill	70	76	74	71	291	7,108.75
Gibby Gilbert	72	77	72	70	291	7,108.75
Dick Hendrickson	70	75	74	72	291	7,108.75

	SCORES				TOTAL	MONEY
David Lundstrom	70	76	70	75	291	7,108.75
John Mahaffey	74	77	66	74	291	7,108.75
David Ojala	75	72	71	73	291	7,108.75
Ed Sneed	74	70	76	71	291	7,108.75
DeWitt Weaver	73	75	73	70	291	7,108.75
Bruce Lehnhard	75	74	73	70	292	5,720
Leonard Thompson	75	73	70	74	292	5,720

Cadillac NFL Classic

Upper Montclair Country Club, Clifton, New Jersey — June 26-28
Par 36-36–72; 6,816 yards — purse, $1,100,000

	SCORES			TOTAL	MONEY
Bob Dickson	68	69	70	207	$165,000
Jim Colbert	68	68	71	207	88,000
Larry Nelson	70	66	71	207	88,000
(Dickson defeated Colbert and Nelson on first extra hole.)					
Bruce Crampton	67	70	71	208	50,600
Dana Quigley	68	72	68	208	50,600
J.C. Snead	71	69	68	208	50,600
Dave Stockton	67	70	71	208	50,600
Jim Dent	68	70	71	209	30,250
Tom Jenkins	71	69	69	209	30,250
Bruce Summerhays	68	68	73	209	30,250
Lee Trevino	70	71	68	209	30,250
Frank Conner	69	71	70	210	22,366.67
Tom Wargo	70	72	68	210	22,366.67
Simon Hobday	71	69	70	210	22,366.66
Homero Blancas	69	71	71	211	16,610
Terry Dill	68	74	69	211	16,610
Ed Dougherty	71	70	70	211	16,610
Bruce Lehnhard	70	71	70	211	16,610
Graham Marsh	70	69	72	211	16,610
Mike McCullough	69	65	77	211	16,610
Jay Sigel	71	64	76	211	16,610
Hugh Baiocchi	74	65	73	212	12,430
Joe Inman	69	73	70	212	12,430
Isao Aoki	72	72	69	213	10,057.15
Walter Morgan	72	73	68	213	10,057.15
Bob Eastwood	72	70	71	213	10,057.14
Lee Elder	73	69	71	213	10,057.14
Raymond Floyd	71	72	70	213	10,057.14
Hubert Green	73	68	72	213	10,057.14
Walter Hall	70	73	70	213	10,057.14
Bob Duval	71	69	74	214	7,425
Tony Jacklin	76	66	72	214	7,425
Larry Laoretti	72	74	68	214	7,425
Bob Murphy	70	68	76	214	7,425
Bobby Stroble	71	71	72	214	7,425
Leonard Thompson	71	72	71	214	7,425
Bob Charles	72	70	73	215	5,940
David Lundstrom	72	74	69	215	5,940
Jerry McGee	70	73	72	215	5,940
Walter Zembriski	69	74	72	215	5,940

State Farm Senior Classic

Hobbit's Glen Golf Club, Columbia, Maryland — July 3-5
Par 36-36–72; 6,983 yards — purse, $1,250,000

	SCORES			TOTAL	MONEY
Bruce Summerhays	69	68	69	206	$187,500
Walter Hall	68	70	69	207	100,000
Hale Irwin	69	69	69	207	100,000
Jim Albus	68	72	68	208	48,214.29
Bob Duval	69	68	71	208	48,214.29
Hubert Green	70	70	68	208	48,214.29
Leonard Thompson	72	66	70	208	48,214.29
Terry Dill	67	68	73	208	48,214.28
David Graham	69	65	74	208	48,214.28
Dave Stockton	67	69	72	208	48,214.28
Graham Marsh	66	70	73	209	28,750
J.C. Snead	70	68	71	209	28,750
Jerry McGee	71	69	70	210	23,125
Larry Nelson	69	70	71	210	23,125
Tom Shaw	67	72	71	210	23,125
Bobby Stroble	70	69	71	210	23,125
Bud Allin	69	70	72	211	18,218.75
Vicente Fernandez	69	70	72	211	18,218.75
Tom Wargo	73	69	69	211	18,218.75
Fred Gibson	69	67	75	211	18,218.75
Bob Eastwood	75	70	67	212	14,583.34
Ed Dougherty	73	68	71	212	14,583.33
John Morgan	71	68	73	212	14,583.33
Tom Jenkins	65	69	79	213	13,125
Hugh Baiocchi	74	69	71	214	10,656.25
Kurt Cox	68	75	71	214	10,656.25
Bob Dickson	70	72	72	214	10,656.25
Dale Douglass	71	71	72	214	10,656.25
Walter Morgan	72	69	73	214	10,656.25
Jimmy Powell	73	69	72	214	10,656.25
Dana Quigley	70	71	73	214	10,656.25
Kermit Zarley	72	72	70	214	10,656.25
Jose Maria Canizares	70	71	74	215	7,875
Frank Conner	76	65	74	215	7,875
Charles Coody	71	71	73	215	7,875
Jay Sigel	70	74	71	215	7,875
Lee Trevino	68	74	73	215	7,875
Tommy Aaron	71	72	73	216	6,375
Jim Colbert	70	71	75	216	6,375
John Mahaffey	73	70	73	216	6,375
David Oakley	72	68	76	216	6,375
Chuck Thorpe	71	75	70	216	6,375

Ford Senior Players Championship

TPC of Michigan, Dearborn, Michigan — July 9-12
Par 36-36–72; 6,676 yards — purse, $2,000,000

	SCORES				TOTAL	MONEY
Gil Morgan	69	64	68	66	267	$300,000
Hale Irwin	66	69	67	68	270	176,000
Isao Aoki	71	69	66	69	275	144,000

	SCORES				TOTAL	MONEY
Jim Colbert	69	71	66	72	278	108,000
Bob Murphy	67	72	64	75	278	108,000
Jack Nicklaus	67	70	72	70	279	80,000
Jose Maria Canizares	68	72	71	69	280	72,000
Lee Trevino	69	69	73	70	281	64,000
Mike McCullough	70	69	71	72	282	52,000
J.C. Snead	72	66	69	75	282	52,000
Kermit Zarley	71	71	69	71	282	52,000
Bob Duval	68	73	74	68	283	40,666.67
Jay Sigel	72	66	76	69	283	40,666.67
Mike Hill	71	72	70	70	283	40,666.66
Hugh Baiocchi	71	70	71	72	284	35,000
Terry Dill	67	73	70	74	284	35,000
Simon Hobday	70	72	75	68	285	31,000
Bobby Stroble	74	74	67	70	285	31,000
Bob Charles	74	69	72	71	286	24,920
Raymond Floyd	72	74	70	70	286	24,920
Gibby Gilbert	70	74	66	76	286	24,920
Jimmy Powell	70	71	73	72	286	24,920
Bruce Summerhays	75	71	73	67	286	24,920
Jim Albus	68	69	78	72	287	18,700
Al Geiberger	74	67	73	73	287	18,700
John Jacobs	66	76	72	73	287	18,700
Larry Nelson	69	76	72	70	287	18,700
Dave Stockton	69	69	78	71	287	18,700
Buzz Thomas	70	71	76	70	287	18,700
Dave Eichelberger	76	67	77	68	288	13,244.45
Vicente Fernandez	71	68	79	70	288	13,244.45
John Morgan	71	70	74	73	288	13,244.45
Dan Wood	76	70	71	71	288	13,244.45
Dale Douglass	70	69	71	78	288	13,244.44
Hubert Green	73	71	69	75	288	13,244.44
Walter Hall	70	70	73	75	288	13,244.44
Walter Morgan	71	72	71	74	288	13,244.44
John Schroeder	75	65	70	78	288	13,244.44
Brian Barnes	74	72	72	71	289	10,400
Bob Eastwood	71	71	73	74	289	10,400

Ameritech Senior Open

Kemper Lakes Golf Course, Long Grove, Illinois — July 17-19
Par 36-36–72; 6,951 yards — purse, $1,300,000

	SCORES			TOTAL	MONEY
Hale Irwin	62	66	73	201	$195,000
Larry Nelson	69	67	68	204	114,400
Hugh Baiocchi	66	71	72	209	85,800
David Graham	69	72	68	209	85,800
Walter Hall	70	71	70	211	57,200
Leonard Thompson	69	68	74	211	57,200
Terry Dill	70	71	71	212	37,960
Mike McCullough	68	74	70	212	37,960
Bob Murphy	71	71	70	212	37,960
J.C. Snead	71	68	73	212	37,960
Bruce Summerhays	68	68	76	212	37,960
Frank Conner	70	71	72	213	25,675
Vicente Fernandez	70	70	73	213	25,675

	SCORES			TOTAL	MONEY
Jerry McGee	70	71	72	213	25,675
Gil Morgan	69	73	71	213	25,675
Raymond Floyd	71	66	77	214	21,450
Walter Morgan	72	68	74	214	21,450
Jim Albus	69	69	77	215	17,238
Bob Duval	73	69	73	215	17,238
John Mahaffey	72	73	70	215	17,238
Graham Marsh	76	70	69	215	17,238
Larry Ziegler	72	72	71	215	17,238
George Archer	73	67	76	216	12,740
Al Geiberger	68	74	74	216	12,740
Simon Hobday	75	71	70	216	12,740
Larry Laoretti	75	69	72	216	12,740
Jimmy Powell	76	71	69	216	12,740
Kermit Zarley	72	71	73	216	12,740
Kurt Cox	71	75	71	217	10,270
Joe Inman	65	73	79	217	10,270
Dana Quigley	74	73	70	217	10,270
John Bland	76	69	73	218	8,970
Billy King	73	75	70	218	8,970
John Morgan	74	70	74	218	8,970
Jose Maria Canizares	73	75	71	219	7,637.50
Bob Charles	75	71	73	219	7,637.50
Bob Dickson	71	70	78	219	7,637.50
Tom Shaw	72	72	75	219	7,637.50
Brian Barnes	70	76	74	220	6,760
Jim Dent	73	72	75	220	6,760

U.S. Senior Open

Riviera Country Club, Pacific Palisades, California — July 23-26
Par 35-36–71; 6,906 yards — purse, $1,500,000

	SCORES				TOTAL	MONEY
Hale Irwin	77	68	71	69	285	$267,500
Vicente Fernandez	73	71	74	68	286	157,500
Raymond Floyd	70	70	73	74	287	101,537
Isao Aoki	72	71	73	72	288	64,040
Brian Barnes	72	72	75	69	288	64,040
Dave Stockton	73	70	73	73	289	50,796
Hugh Baiocchi	71	73	73	73	290	39,122
Jose Maria Canizares	73	72	74	71	290	39,122
Ed Dougherty	72	76	70	72	290	39,122
Gil Morgan	73	72	73	72	290	39,122
Dan Wood	75	73	72	70	290	39,122
John Mahaffey	76	70	74	71	291	31,247
Tom Jenkins	73	73	71	75	292	27,812
Mike McCullough	74	77	71	70	292	27,812
Jack Nicklaus	74	72	79	67	292	27,812
Jim Colbert	76	72	71	74	293	23,546
Billy King	72	75	73	73	293	23,546
Dana Quigley	77	74	73	69	293	23,546
David Graham	78	74	72	70	294	20,990
Simon Hobday	75	72	78	70	295	19,240
Bruce Summerhays	71	71	77	76	295	19,240
Bob Duval	79	74	75	68	296	16,122
Tom Shaw	72	75	72	77	296	16,122

	SCORES				TOTAL	MONEY
J.C. Snead	75	74	74	73	296	16,122
Roy Vucinich	71	71	75	79	296	16,122
Frank Conner	76	76	68	77	297	13,286
Charles Coody	75	75	73	74	297	13,286
Dale Douglass	77	75	73	73	298	10,758
Bob Eastwood	76	72	75	75	298	10,758
Al Geiberger	77	73	75	73	298	10,758
Bob Murphy	71	74	76	77	298	10,758
Jay Sigel	71	78	75	74	298	10,758
Bob Charles	77	74	73	75	299	9,245
Bobby Cole	75	78	74	72	299	9,245
Gibby Gilbert	72	72	77	78	299	9,245
Gary McCord	74	74	73	78	299	9,245
DeWitt Weaver	76	77	74	73	300	8,507
John Grace	72	74	77	79	302	7,627
Walter Morgan	73	75	77	77	302	7,627
Bobby Stroble	75	74	80	73	302	7,627
Leonard Thompson	76	75	78	73	302	7,627
Kermit Zarley	77	74	77	74	302	7,627

Utah Showdown

Park Meadows Country Club, Park City, Utah — July 31-August 2
Par 36-36–72; 7,169 yards — purse, $1,000,000

	SCORES			TOTAL	MONEY
Gil Morgan	66	67	67	200	$150,000
Isao Aoki	70	68	66	204	80,000
John Mahaffey	70	66	68	204	80,000
Hugh Baiocchi	71	69	66	206	60,000
Bob Duval	66	71	70	207	36,800
Vicente Fernandez	70	68	69	207	36,800
David Graham	70	69	68	207	36,800
Joe Inman	70	68	69	207	36,800
John Schroeder	72	67	68	207	36,800
John Jacobs	68	72	68	208	24,000
Jay Sigel	71	69	68	208	24,000
Dave Stockton	70	67	71	208	24,000
Bob Eastwood	73	70	66	209	17,500
Gibby Gilbert	72	68	69	209	17,500
Mike McCullough	69	70	70	209	17,500
J.C. Snead	70	70	69	209	17,500
Tom Wargo	69	70	70	209	17,500
Kermit Zarley	70	71	68	209	17,500
Tom Shaw	72	73	65	210	13,233.34
Bruce Lehnhard	71	71	68	210	13,233.33
Lee Trevino	71	68	71	210	13,233.33
David Lundstrom	72	71	68	211	11,033.34
Hank Cooper	71	67	73	211	11,033.33
Larry Ziegler	73	69	69	211	11,033.33
Dana Quigley	73	69	70	212	10,000
Walter Hall	76	67	70	213	9,300
Jerry McGee	68	71	74	213	9,300
Bruce Crampton	70	72	72	214	8,500
Walter Morgan	73	72	69	214	8,500
Kurt Cox	73	75	67	215	6,622.23
Dave Eichelberger	76	73	66	215	6,622.23

	SCORES			TOTAL	MONEY
Ray Arinno	70	73	72	215	6,622.22
Terry Dill	69	71	75	215	6,622.22
Fred Gibson	74	72	69	215	6,622.22
Simon Hobday	71	71	73	215	6,622.22
Tom Jenkins	74	71	70	215	6,622.22
Billy King	71	72	72	215	6,622.22
Bob Wynn	73	70	72	215	6,622.22
Jim Albus	70	72	74	216	4,800
Miller Barber	73	71	72	216	4,800
Bob Dickson	72	69	75	216	4,800
Graham Marsh	72	72	72	216	4,800
Bob Murphy	72	70	74	216	4,800
Bob E. Smith	74	72	70	216	4,800

Coldwell Banker Burnet Classic

Bunker Hills Golf Club, Coon Rapids, Minnesota — August 7-9
Par 36-36–72; 6,909 yards — purse, $1,500,000
(First round cancelled — rain.)

	SCORES		TOTAL	MONEY
Leonard Thompson	68	66	134	$225,000
Isao Aoki	66	68	134	132,000
(Thompson defeated Aoki on second extra hole.)				
Hale Irwin	65	70	135	99,000
Dave Stockton	68	67	135	99,000
Butch Baird	68	69	137	52,500
Jim Colbert	69	68	137	52,500
Hubert Green	69	68	137	52,500
John Mahaffey	69	68	137	52,500
Dana Quigley	68	69	137	52,500
Jay Sigel	67	70	137	52,500
Bruce Crampton	69	69	138	27,516.67
Bob Dickson	71	67	138	27,516.67
Ed Dougherty	70	68	138	27,516.67
Gil Morgan	69	69	138	27,516.67
Bob Murphy	70	68	138	27,516.67
Bruce Summerhays	70	68	138	27,516.67
Vicente Fernandez	67	71	138	27,516.66
Tom Jenkins	65	73	138	27,516.66
Graham Marsh	68	70	138	27,516.66
Larry Laoretti	72	67	139	16,757.15
Tom Wargo	70	69	139	16,757.15
Bob Eastwood	69	70	139	16,757.14
David Graham	69	70	139	16,757.14
Simon Hobday	68	71	139	16,757.14
Joe Inman	69	70	139	16,757.14
Jerry McGee	68	71	139	16,757.14
Jose Maria Canizares	72	68	140	13,050
Frank Conner	69	71	140	13,050
Walter Hall	69	71	140	13,050
Tommy Aaron	69	72	141	10,600
George Archer	68	73	141	10,600
Jim Ferree	71	70	141	10,600
David Ojala	72	69	141	10,600
Bobby Stroble	70	71	141	10,600
Bob Wynn	70	71	141	10,600

	SCORES		TOTAL	MONEY
Bud Allin	70	72	142	7,363.64
Hugh Baiocchi	72	70	142	7,363.64
Bob Duval	72	70	142	7,363.64
Gibby Gilbert	73	69	142	7,363.64
Jack Lewis	71	71	142	7,363.64
Walter Morgan	71	71	142	7,363.64
Lee Trevino	73	69	142	7,363.64
Terry Dill	69	73	142	7,363.63
John Jacobs	69	73	142	7,363.63
Mike McCullough	69	73	142	7,363.63
Buzz Thomas	68	74	142	7,363.63

First of America Classic

Egypt Valley Country Club, Ada, Michigan
Par 36-36–72; 6,909 yards

August 14-16
purse, $1,000,000

	SCORES			TOTAL	MONEY
George Archer	68	67	64	199	$150,000
Jim Dent	70	66	68	204	88,000
Jose Maria Canizares	67	69	69	205	60,000
Gil Morgan	72	65	68	205	60,000
Bruce Summerhays	68	65	72	205	60,000
Jim Colbert	70	68	69	207	40,000
Dave Stockton	67	72	69	208	36,000
Dana Quigley	68	73	69	210	30,000
Bobby Stroble	74	66	70	210	30,000
Larry Laoretti	73	68	71	212	26,000
Frank Conner	78	67	68	213	19,428.58
Bud Allin	74	67	72	213	19,428.57
Hugh Baiocchi	71	72	70	213	19,428.57
Bob Dickson	72	71	70	213	19,428.57
Tom Jenkins	71	72	70	213	19,428.57
Mike McCullough	69	72	72	213	19,428.57
Tom Wargo	71	71	71	213	19,428.57
Ed Dougherty	71	70	73	214	14,100
Bruce Lehnhard	72	72	70	214	14,100
John Mahaffey	70	71	73	214	14,100
Dave Eichelberger	74	71	70	215	11,666.67
Tom Shaw	69	71	75	215	11,666.67
Walter Hall	72	67	76	215	11,666.66
Bruce Crampton	74	73	69	216	10,500
Butch Baird	74	71	72	217	8,714.29
Bob Duval	73	72	72	217	8,714.29
Babe Hiskey	70	75	72	217	8,714.29
Dan Wood	76	70	71	217	8,714.29
John Jacobs	71	73	73	217	8,714.28
Billy King	71	72	74	217	8,714.28
Gary Player	72	72	73	217	8,714.28
Bobby Cole	77	68	73	218	7,050
Will Sowles	73	71	74	218	7,050
Dave Hill	73	71	75	219	6,450
Mike Hill	75	72	72	219	6,450
Bruce Devlin	77	71	72	220	5,520
Fred Gibson	74	68	78	220	5,520
Orville Moody	74	73	73	220	5,520
Jimmy Powell	78	72	70	220	5,520
Kermit Zarley	72	71	77	220	5,520

Northville Long Island Classic

Meadow Brook Club, Jericho, New York — August 21-23
Par 36-36–72; 6,842 yards — purse, $1,000,000

	SCORES			TOTAL	MONEY
Gary Player	68	68	68	204	$150,000
Walter Hall	65	69	71	205	80,000
J.C. Snead	68	70	67	205	80,000
John Schroeder	72	65	69	206	54,000
Lee Trevino	68	69	69	206	54,000
Terry Dill	74	66	67	207	38,000
Tom Shaw	68	66	73	207	38,000
Jose Maria Canizares	68	68	72	208	32,000
Jim Colbert	70	72	67	209	26,000
Ed Dougherty	68	70	71	209	26,000
Leonard Thompson	71	67	71	209	26,000
Ray Arinno	74	71	65	210	18,142.86
Fred Gibson	69	71	70	210	18,142.86
Gibby Gilbert	70	70	70	210	18,142.86
David Graham	70	72	68	210	18,142.86
Jay Sigel	73	70	67	210	18,142.86
Dana Quigley	73	68	69	210	18,142.85
Bruce Summerhays	69	69	72	210	18,142.85
Al Geiberger	73	71	67	211	12,133.34
Mike McCullough	71	71	69	211	12,133.34
Jim Albus	70	71	70	211	12,133.33
Joe Inman	69	70	72	211	12,133.33
Billy King	73	65	73	211	12,133.33
Buzz Thomas	73	67	71	211	12,133.33
Tommy Aaron	72	74	66	212	9,120
Frank Conner	69	73	70	212	9,120
Dale Douglass	69	74	69	212	9,120
Mike Hill	71	72	69	212	9,120
Bobby Stroble	72	70	70	212	9,120
Tom Jenkins	71	69	73	213	7,700
Tom Wargo	69	73	71	213	7,700
Bud Allin	70	74	70	214	6,600
Hugh Baiocchi	75	68	71	214	6,600
Bob Charles	71	72	71	214	6,600
Raymond Floyd	69	77	68	214	6,600
Jerry McGee	74	68	72	214	6,600
Charles Coody	76	68	71	215	5,100
Jim Ferree	72	70	73	215	5,100
Hubert Green	72	73	70	215	5,100
John Morgan	71	72	72	215	5,100
Walter Morgan	75	74	66	215	5,100
Chuck Thorpe	75	70	70	215	5,100
DeWitt Weaver	72	72	71	215	5,100

BankBoston Classic

Nashawtuc Country Club, Concord, Massachusetts — August 28-30
Par 36-36–72; 6,797 yards — purse, $1,000,000

	SCORES			TOTAL	MONEY
Hale Irwin	69	64	68	201	$150,000
Jay Sigel	68	69	66	203	88,000

	SCORES			TOTAL	MONEY
David Graham	68	68	68	204	66,000
Joe Inman	67	66	71	204	66,000
Allen Doyle	70	66	69	205	44,000
Al Geiberger	67	67	71	205	44,000
Gibby Gilbert	67	69	71	207	36,000
George Archer	66	72	70	208	27,500
Bobby Stroble	64	73	71	208	27,500
Rocky Thompson	72	69	67	208	27,500
Tom Wargo	69	71	68	208	27,500
Frank Conner	65	71	73	209	19,200
Hubert Green	70	71	68	209	19,200
Walter Hall	67	73	69	209	19,200
Mike Hill	71	70	68	209	19,200
Tom Jenkins	70	70	69	209	19,200
Jose Maria Canizares	72	70	68	210	14,575
Kurt Cox	71	66	73	210	14,575
Bob Duval	74	70	66	210	14,575
Leonard Thompson	71	69	70	210	14,575
Jim Albus	70	69	72	211	11,100
Ed Dougherty	67	69	75	211	11,100
Dave Eichelberger	71	70	70	211	11,100
John Morgan	69	70	72	211	11,100
Dan Wood	70	69	72	211	11,100
Bud Allin	69	72	71	212	8,700
Brian Barnes	75	67	70	212	8,700
Bob Dickson	70	70	72	212	8,700
Dale Douglass	67	71	74	212	8,700
Tom Shaw	68	72	72	212	8,700
Bob Eastwood	69	70	74	213	6,900
Mike McCullough	69	70	74	213	6,900
John Schroeder	72	74	67	213	6,900
Bob E. Smith	70	74	69	213	6,900
Bruce Summerhays	71	72	70	213	6,900
Tommy Aaron	75	71	68	214	5,212.50
Bob Charles	72	70	72	214	5,212.50
John Jacobs	76	72	66	214	5,212.50
David Lundstrom	72	71	71	214	5,212.50
Bob Murphy	73	69	72	214	5,212.50
Dana Quigley	73	70	71	214	5,212.50
DeWitt Weaver	74	68	72	214	5,212.50
Kermit Zarley	71	73	70	214	5,212.50

Emerald Coast Classic

The Moors Golf Club, Milton, Florida — September 4-6
Par 35-35–70; 6,719 yards — purse, $1,100,000

	SCORES			TOTAL	MONEY
Dana Quigley	69	66	65	200	$165,000
Jim Colbert	69	66	66	201	96,800
Leonard Thompson	66	67	69	202	79,200
Isao Aoki	65	66	72	203	50,600
Bob Duval	67	69	67	203	50,600
Hale Irwin	67	67	69	203	50,600
David Lundstrom	63	71	69	203	50,600
Frank Conner	69	70	65	204	35,200
Walter Hall	69	67	69	205	28,600

	SCORES			TOTAL	MONEY
Gil Morgan	67	72	66	205	28,600
Bobby Stroble	71	66	68	205	28,600
Bobby Cole	69	69	68	206	23,100
Jay Sigel	69	70	67	206	23,100
Gibby Gilbert	68	71	68	207	18,168.34
Babe Hiskey	67	73	67	207	18,168.34
Ed Dougherty	67	68	72	207	18,168.33
Tom Jenkins	70	68	69	207	18,168.33
Mike McCullough	69	67	71	207	18,168.33
Dan Wood	70	66	71	207	18,168.33
Allen Doyle	68	69	71	208	14,080
John Mahaffey	73	70	65	208	14,080
Ray Arinno	73	66	70	209	11,311.67
Vicente Fernandez	70	72	67	209	11,311.67
Fred Gibson	69	72	68	209	11,311.67
Buzz Thomas	69	69	71	209	11,311.67
Dale Douglass	68	68	73	209	11,311.66
J.C. Snead	72	66	71	209	11,311.66
Horacio Carbonetti	71	71	68	210	9,350
Jim Dent	67	68	75	210	9,350
Rocky Thompson	70	72	69	211	7,773.34
DeWitt Weaver	70	72	69	211	7,773.34
Billy King	69	72	70	211	7,773.33
Jerry McGee	70	66	75	211	7,773.33
John Morgan	73	69	69	211	7,773.33
Tom Shaw	71	71	69	211	7,773.33
Hugh Baiocchi	73	69	70	212	6,187.50
Brian Barnes	70	75	67	212	6,187.50
Hank Cooper	68	74	70	212	6,187.50
Bruce Summerhays	67	73	72	212	6,187.50
Homero Blancas	75	69	69	213	4,950
Bob Dickson	72	73	68	213	4,950
Bob Eastwood	72	73	68	213	4,950
Bob Murphy	69	71	73	213	4,950
Lee Trevino	74	69	70	213	4,950
Kermit Zarley	71	73	69	213	4,950
Larry Ziegler	69	73	71	213	4,950

Comfort Classic

Brickyard Crossing, Indianapolis, Indiana — September 11-13
Par 36-36–72; 6,678 yards — purse, $1,150,000

	SCORES			TOTAL	MONEY
Hugh Baiocchi	66	63	67	196	$172,500
Bruce Summerhays	64	66	68	198	101,200
Bud Allin	68	66	68	202	75,900
Isao Aoki	68	66	68	202	75,900
Terry Dill	65	68	70	203	42,320
Ed Dougherty	67	70	66	203	42,320
Hale Irwin	66	69	68	203	42,320
Chi Chi Rodriguez	70	66	67	203	42,320
Steve Veriato	69	64	70	203	42,320
George Archer	65	68	71	204	27,600
Bob Duval	68	67	69	204	27,600
Simon Hobday	65	67	72	204	27,600
Brian Barnes	68	70	67	205	20,700

	SCORES			TOTAL	MONEY
Jim Colbert	67	67	71	205	20,700
Gibby Gilbert	71	64	70	205	20,700
Hubert Green	66	69	70	205	20,700
John Mahaffey	67	65	73	205	20,700
Vicente Fernandez	70	72	64	206	16,215
Gil Morgan	67	71	68	206	16,215
Bobby Stroble	65	68	73	206	16,215
John Jacobs	68	71	68	207	13,416.67
Tom Shaw	73	70	64	207	13,416.67
Mike Hill	69	68	70	207	13,416.66
Homero Blancas	70	71	67	208	10,514.29
Bob Eastwood	69	68	71	208	10,514.29
Tom Jenkins	71	70	67	208	10,514.29
Larry Laoretti	70	70	68	208	10,514.29
John Morgan	69	68	71	208	10,514.28
Jimmy Powell	67	67	74	208	10,514.28
Kermit Zarley	69	66	73	208	10,514.28
Fred Gibson	66	71	72	209	7,935
Walter Hall	71	68	70	209	7,935
Joe Inman	70	68	71	209	7,935
Jerry McGee	70	70	69	209	7,935
Leonard Thompson	73	67	69	209	7,935
Graham Marsh	73	69	68	210	6,229.17
Mike McCullough	72	71	67	210	6,229.17
Lee Trevino	70	72	68	210	6,229.17
Tom Wargo	74	70	66	210	6,229.17
Ray Arinno	73	67	70	210	6,229.16
J.C. Snead	72	69	69	210	6,229.16

Kroger Senior Classic

Golf Center at Kings Island, Grizzly Course, Mason, Ohio — September 18-20
Par 36-35–71; 6,673 yards — purse, $1,100,000
(Third round cancelled — rain.)

	SCORES		TOTAL	MONEY
Hugh Baiocchi	67	66	133	$165,000
Bob Charles	69	64	133	73,700
Frank Conner	69	64	133	73,700
Larry Nelson	67	66	133	73,700
Bruce Summerhays	64	69	133	73,700
(Baiocchi won on second extra hole.)				
Hubert Green	68	66	134	35,640
Harold Henning	67	67	134	35,640
John Jacobs	67	67	134	35,640
Graham Marsh	66	68	134	35,640
Kermit Zarley	68	66	134	35,640
Terry Dill	69	66	135	24,200
Bob Eastwood	68	67	135	24,200
Vicente Fernandez	70	65	135	24,200
Kurt Cox	70	66	136	17,647.15
Leonard Thompson	69	67	136	17,647.15
Al Geiberger	69	67	136	17,647.14
John Mahaffey	67	69	136	17,647.14
Dana Quigley	67	69	136	17,647.14
Jay Sigel	69	67	136	17,647.14
Walter Zembriski	68	68	136	17,647.14

	SCORES		TOTAL	MONEY
Brian Barnes	67	70	137	11,385
Jim Dent	71	66	137	11,385
Bob Duval	71	66	137	11,385
Mike Hill	66	71	137	11,385
Tom Jenkins	69	68	137	11,385
David Lundstrom	70	67	137	11,385
J.C. Snead	70	67	137	11,385
Bobby Stroble	71	66	137	11,385
Jim Albus	66	72	138	8,316
Bud Allin	68	70	138	8,316
Gibby Gilbert	68	70	138	8,316
Buzz Thomas	71	67	138	8,316
Tom Wargo	70	68	138	8,316
Dale Douglass	71	68	139	6,765
Simon Hobday	70	69	139	6,765
Bobby Nichols	70	69	139	6,765
Larry Ziegler	68	71	139	6,765
Dave Eichelberger	71	69	140	5,610
Joe Inman	68	72	140	5,610
Mike McCullough	72	68	140	5,610
Walter Morgan	70	70	140	5,610
John Schroeder	72	68	140	5,610

Boone Valley Classic

Boone Valley Golf Club, Augusta, Missouri — September 25-27
Par 36-36–72; 6,731 yards — purse, $1,300,000

	SCORES			TOTAL	MONEY
Larry Nelson	70	65	65	200	$195,000
Graham Marsh	67	67	68	202	114,400
Walter Hall	70	66	71	207	93,600
Jose Maria Canizares	66	72	72	210	59,800
Mike McCullough	67	73	70	210	59,800
John Morgan	70	73	67	210	59,800
Bruce Summerhays	66	72	72	210	59,800
Bud Allin	68	74	69	211	39,000
George Archer	68	71	72	211	39,000
Simon Hobday	70	70	72	212	31,200
Gil Morgan	69	69	74	212	31,200
Gary Player	70	71	71	212	31,200
Kurt Cox	69	71	73	213	22,750
Mike Hill	74	64	75	213	22,750
Jim Holtgrieve	69	71	73	213	22,750
Hale Irwin	69	73	71	213	22,750
Gary McCord	65	78	70	213	22,750
Dan Wood	71	67	75	213	22,750
Hugh Baiocchi	72	72	70	214	17,203.34
Terry Dill	73	69	72	214	17,203.33
Jay Sigel	71	70	73	214	17,203.33
Dale Douglass	72	72	71	215	14,343.34
Joe Inman	71	67	77	215	14,343.33
Jerry McGee	68	73	74	215	14,343.33
Bob Charles	69	72	75	216	10,847.78
Vicente Fernandez	72	73	71	216	10,847.78
Al Geiberger	69	72	75	216	10,847.78
Walter Morgan	71	76	69	216	10,847.78

	SCORES			TOTAL	MONEY
Bob Murphy	68	75	73	216	10,847.78
Dana Quigley	71	71	74	216	10,847.78
Bob E. Smith	74	70	72	216	10,847.78
Billy King	68	71	77	216	10,847.77
Bobby Stroble	68	71	77	216	10,847.77
Isao Aoki	70	72	75	217	7,670
Jim Colbert	73	68	76	217	7,670
Ed Dougherty	70	66	81	217	7,670
Gibby Gilbert	72	73	72	217	7,670
Tom Jenkins	72	72	73	217	7,670
Larry Ziegler	74	71	72	217	7,670
Bob Duval	71	74	73	218	6,630

Vantage Championship

Tanglewood Park, Championship Course,
Clemmons, North Carolina
Par 35-36–71; 6,680 yards

October 2-4
purse, $1,500,000

	SCORES			TOTAL	MONEY
Gil Morgan	66	67	65	198	$225,000
Hale Irwin	67	65	67	199	132,000
Jerry McGee	66	63	71	200	99,000
Tom Wargo	69	67	64	200	99,000
John Jacobs	68	68	65	201	66,000
Lee Trevino	66	68	67	201	66,000
Terry Dill	68	72	62	202	43,800
Walter Hall	68	68	66	202	43,800
Joe Inman	66	66	70	202	43,800
Dana Quigley	68	67	67	202	43,800
Jay Sigel	65	69	68	202	43,800
Brian Barnes	64	71	68	203	28,000
Ed Dougherty	68	68	67	203	28,000
Allen Doyle	68	65	70	203	28,000
Raymond Floyd	64	69	70	203	28,000
David Lundstrom	68	70	65	203	28,000
Larry Nelson	65	71	67	203	28,000
Bud Allin	64	75	65	204	18,337.50
Hugh Baiocchi	71	69	64	204	18,337.50
Jose Maria Canizares	72	65	67	204	18,337.50
Frank Conner	67	71	66	204	18,337.50
Bob Duval	70	68	66	204	18,337.50
Bob Murphy	69	71	64	204	18,337.50
Dave Stockton	70	65	69	204	18,337.50
Dan Wood	70	66	68	204	18,337.50
Isao Aoki	69	67	69	205	13,650
Vicente Fernandez	69	71	65	205	13,650
Bob E. Smith	65	72	68	205	13,650
Dave Eichelberger	68	71	68	207	11,587.50
Tom Jenkins	76	66	65	207	11,587.50
Graham Marsh	66	73	68	207	11,587.50
John Schroeder	72	69	66	207	11,587.50
Gibby Gilbert	70	67	71	208	9,675
Simon Hobday	70	70	68	208	9,675
Larry Laoretti	70	66	72	208	9,675
Gary Player	69	70	69	208	9,675
George Archer	71	71	67	209	8,250

	SCORES			TOTAL	MONEY
Dale Douglass	70	72	67	209	8,250
John Mahaffey	69	70	70	209	8,250
Ray Arinno	76	67	67	210	6,750
Jim Colbert	70	70	70	210	6,750
David Graham	72	67	71	210	6,750
Mike Hill	71	68	71	210	6,750
Leonard Thompson	69	73	68	210	6,750
Rocky Thompson	73	70	67	210	6,750
Kermit Zarley	66	73	71	210	6,750

The Transamerica

Silverado Country Club, South Course, Napa, California — October 9-11
Par 35-37–72; 6,632 yards — purse, $1,000,000

	SCORES			TOTAL	MONEY
Jim Colbert	70	68	67	205	$150,000
David Lundstrom	69	68	69	206	88,000
Jose Maria Canizares	71	68	68	207	55,000
Jay Sigel	70	67	70	207	55,000
Bruce Summerhays	76	67	64	207	55,000
Leonard Thompson	68	71	68	207	55,000
John Morgan	67	74	67	208	36,000
Isao Aoki	72	68	69	209	32,000
Dana Quigley	76	68	67	211	28,000
Raymond Floyd	70	70	72	212	23,000
Tom Wargo	70	73	69	212	23,000
Dan Wood	70	71	71	212	23,000
Kermit Zarley	69	73	70	212	23,000
Kurt Cox	72	73	68	213	16,516.67
Joe Inman	72	70	71	213	16,516.67
Tom Jenkins	73	74	66	213	16,516.67
Dick McClean	68	75	70	213	16,516.67
Hugh Baiocchi	70	67	76	213	16,516.66
Bobby Stroble	70	72	71	213	16,516.66
Ray Carrasco	68	76	70	214	10,666.67
Fred Gibson	73	71	70	214	10,666.67
Hubert Green	70	75	69	214	10,666.67
Bob Murphy	70	73	71	214	10,666.67
John Schroeder	68	76	70	214	10,666.67
J.C. Snead	72	73	69	214	10,666.67
John Bland	68	70	76	214	10,666.66
Jim Ferree	68	73	73	214	10,666.66
John Jacobs	70	71	73	214	10,666.66
Charles Coody	71	70	74	215	7,725
Harold Henning	70	71	74	215	7,725
Larry Laoretti	71	73	71	215	7,725
Tom Shaw	73	73	69	215	7,725
Miller Barber	79	70	67	216	5,925
Bob Duval	76	70	70	216	5,925
Walter Hall	75	68	73	216	5,925
Graham Marsh	71	74	71	216	5,925
Gary McCord	68	75	73	216	5,925
Dave Stockton	72	74	70	216	5,925
Rocky Thompson	76	69	71	216	5,925
Steven Veriato	68	72	76	216	5,925

Raley's Gold Rush Classic

Serrano Country Club, El Dorado Hills, California — October 16-18
Par 36-36–72; 6,772 yards — purse, $1,000,000

	SCORES			TOTAL	MONEY
Dana Quigley	71	68	64	203	$150,000
John Morgan	73	63	70	206	88,000
David Graham	71	69	67	207	72,000
Dale Douglass	71	68	69	208	54,000
Allen Doyle	72	68	68	208	54,000
Jim Colbert	72	67	70	209	38,000
Gary McCord	71	68	70	209	38,000
Jim Albus	69	71	70	210	27,500
Bob Eastwood	73	72	65	210	27,500
Dave Stockton	72	72	66	210	27,500
Buzz Thomas	73	67	70	210	27,500
George Archer	74	67	70	211	19,200
John Bland	72	68	71	211	19,200
Jose Maria Canizares	76	67	68	211	19,200
Bob Charles	74	72	65	211	19,200
Bobby Stroble	72	70	69	211	19,200
Al Geiberger	74	70	68	212	14,575
Mike McCullough	73	70	69	212	14,575
Bruce Summerhays	71	69	72	212	14,575
Leonard Thompson	71	70	71	212	14,575
David Lundstrom	71	72	70	213	10,833.34
Walter Morgan	75	70	68	213	10,833.34
Brian Barnes	72	70	71	213	10,833.33
Terry Dill	70	70	73	213	10,833.33
Joe Inman	71	70	72	213	10,833.33
Gary Player	73	70	70	213	10,833.33
Ray Arinno	71	69	74	214	8,300
Hugh Baiocchi	72	70	72	214	8,300
Kurt Cox	69	72	73	214	8,300
John Schroeder	69	76	69	214	8,300
Tom Wargo	75	69	70	214	8,300
Jim Dent	74	71	70	215	6,314.29
Dave Eichelberger	76	70	69	215	6,314.29
Raymond Floyd	73	71	71	215	6,314.29
Larry Ziegler	77	69	69	215	6,314.29
Frank Conner	73	70	72	215	6,314.28
Charles Coody	72	68	75	215	6,314.28
Bob Murphy	73	71	71	215	6,314.28
Bob Duval	71	75	70	216	4,500
Jim Ferree	73	72	71	216	4,500
Fred Gibson	70	75	71	216	4,500
Walter Hall	74	71	71	216	4,500
John Mahaffey	77	69	70	216	4,500
Orville Moody	73	72	71	216	4,500
Jay Sigel	72	73	71	216	4,500
J.C. Snead	72	72	72	216	4,500
Kermit Zarley	74	69	73	216	4,500

EMC² Kaanapali Classic

Kaanapali Golf Club, North Course,
Kaanapali, Maui, Hawaii
Par 35-36–71; 6,590 yards

October 23-25
purse, $1,000,000

	SCORES			TOTAL	MONEY
Jay Sigel	61	72	68	201	$150,000
Hugh Baiocchi	65	71	67	203	80,000
Larry Laoretti	66	68	69	203	80,000
Terry Dill	68	66	70	204	60,000
Bob Murphy	69	67	69	205	44,000
Steven Veriato	68	68	69	205	44,000
Bob Charles	69	67	70	206	32,000
Fred Gibson	68	68	70	206	32,000
Tom Jenkins	69	70	67	206	32,000
Jim Colbert	68	69	70	207	21,500
Walter Hall	65	71	71	207	21,500
John Jacobs	72	64	71	207	21,500
Bob E. Smith	67	71	69	207	21,500
Bobby Stroble	71	68	68	207	21,500
Buzz Thomas	69	67	71	207	21,500
Gibby Gilbert	67	74	67	208	15,525
Hale Irwin	73	70	65	208	15,525
John Mahaffey	69	70	69	208	15,525
Tom Shaw	67	72	69	208	15,525
Jim Albus	73	67	69	209	12,050
Bob Eastwood	64	77	68	209	12,050
David Lundstrom	71	68	70	209	12,050
Rocky Thompson	70	66	73	209	12,050
Isao Aoki	70	70	70	210	9,350
Brian Barnes	68	71	71	210	9,350
Dick McClean	66	71	73	210	9,350
Gary Player	69	70	71	210	9,350
J.C. Snead	70	67	73	210	9,350
Kermit Zarley	70	66	74	210	9,350
Leonard Thompson	73	69	69	211	7,533.34
Bob Duval	73	74	64	211	7,533.33
Jerry McGee	67	69	75	211	7,533.33
Jose Maria Canizares	72	71	69	212	6,300
Hubert Green	71	69	72	212	6,300
Walter Morgan	73	70	69	212	6,300
Dana Quigley	69	70	73	212	6,300
John Schroeder	69	70	73	212	6,300
Frank Conner	68	72	73	213	5,400
Mike McCullough	69	71	73	213	5,400
Joe Inman	72	71	71	214	4,900
Bruce Summerhays	68	73	73	214	4,900
Bob Wynn	70	72	72	214	4,900

Pacific Bell Senior Classic

Wilshire Country Club, Los Angeles, California
Par 35-36–71; 6,575 yards

October 30-November 1
purse, $1,100,000

	SCORES			TOTAL	MONEY
Joe Inman	66	68	68	202	$165,000
Lee Trevino	67	71	65	203	96,800
Brian Barnes	68	70	66	204	72,600

	SCORES			TOTAL	MONEY
Gil Morgan	66	68	70	204	72,600
Hubert Green	72	65	69	206	52,800
Bobby Stroble	70	68	69	207	44,000
Jim Albus	74	67	67	208	33,550
Hugh Baiocchi	71	69	68	208	33,550
Terry Dill	71	70	67	208	33,550
Gary McCord	73	69	66	208	33,550
George Archer	70	66	73	209	25,300
Dave Eichelberger	70	70	69	209	25,300
Jose Maria Canizares	75	66	69	210	20,900
Allen Doyle	69	69	72	210	20,900
Walter Morgan	72	67	71	210	20,900
Larry Nelson	69	72	70	211	16,078.34
Bruce Summerhays	72	70	69	211	16,078.34
Bruce Crampton	71	68	72	211	16,078.33
Bob Dickson	70	70	71	211	16,078.33
Raymond Floyd	68	71	72	211	16,078.33
David Graham	71	68	72	211	16,078.33
Isao Aoki	73	70	69	212	12,136.67
Dana Quigley	70	72	70	212	12,136.67
Buzz Thomas	68	73	71	212	12,136.66
Bobby Cole	72	71	70	213	9,178.89
Jim Dent	73	69	71	213	9,178.89
Dale Douglass	71	72	70	213	9,178.89
John Jacobs	73	71	69	213	9,178.89
David Lundstrom	71	72	70	213	9,178.89
Graham Marsh	75	69	69	213	9,178.89
Dave Stockton	71	70	72	213	9,178.89
Rocky Thompson	72	69	72	213	9,178.89
Ed Dougherty	66	71	76	213	9,178.89
Bud Allin	76	68	70	214	6,622
Jim Colbert	72	71	71	214	6,622
Al Geiberger	74	67	73	214	6,622
Walter Hall	69	75	70	214	6,622
Leonard Thompson	72	70	72	214	6,622
Don Bies	73	69	73	215	5,390
Charles Coody	76	72	67	215	5,390
John Morgan	72	74	69	215	5,390
Bob Murphy	73	69	73	215	5,390
John Schroeder	71	74	70	215	5,390

Energizer Senior Tour Championship

Dunes Golf & Beach Club, Myrtle Beach, South Carolina — November 5-8
Par 36-36–72; 6,815 yards — purse, $2,000,000

	SCORES				TOTAL	MONEY
Hale Irwin	66	73	70	65	274	$347,000
Gil Morgan	70	70	68	71	279	203,000
Jay Sigel	73	71	66	70	280	166,000
Vicente Fernandez	74	73	66	69	282	125,000
David Graham	76	73	67	66	282	125,000
Jim Albus	71	68	70	74	283	87,500
Joe Inman	71	73	72	67	283	87,500
Hugh Baiocchi	71	73	71	69	284	66,333.34
Jim Dent	72	71	70	71	284	66,333.33
Dave Stockton	71	72	71	70	284	66,333.33
Jose Maria Canizares	72	72	71	70	285	49,250

	SCORES				TOTAL	MONEY
Jim Colbert	75	71	70	69	285	49,250
Raymond Floyd	69	68	72	76	285	49,250
Lee Trevino	73	72	71	69	285	49,250
Bob Duval	68	76	73	69	286	41,000
George Archer	76	68	74	71	289	37,000
Larry Nelson	70	76	75	68	289	37,000
Bruce Summerhays	69	77	73	70	289	37,000
Terry Dill	74	76	70	70	290	32,000
Leonard Thompson	73	74	73	70	290	32,000
Tom Wargo	71	72	71	77	291	29,000
John Jacobs	71	72	72	77	292	27,000
J.C. Snead	74	73	76	70	293	25,500
Graham Marsh	74	75	70	75	294	24,000
Dana Quigley	73	74	72	76	295	23,000
Isao Aoki	74	73	74	75	296	21,000
Walter Hall	77	73	73	73	296	21,000
Bob Murphy	71	75	77	73	296	21,000
Dale Douglass	74	74	73	77	298	19,000
Mike McCullough	76	71	75	77	299	18,500
Hubert Green	73	78	73	76	300	18,000

Senior Match Play Challenge

Bighorn Golf Club, Palm Desert, California — November 13-15
Par 36-36–72; 6,871 yards — purse, $720,000

FIRST ROUND

Bruce Summerhays defeated Dave Stockton, 1 up.
Dana Quigley defeated Jose Maria Canizares, 1 up.
Jim Colbert defeated Vicente Fernandez, 2 and 1.
David Graham defeated Hugh Baiocchi, 5 and 3.
Jay Sigel defeated George Archer, 6 and 4.
Bob Charles defeated Larry Nelson, 2 and 1.
Gil Morgan defeated Bob Murphy, 2 and 1.
Hale Irwin defeated Gary Player, 3 and 2.

(Each losing player received $15,000.)

SECOND ROUND

Irwin defeated Summerhays, 2 and 1.
Morgan defeated Quigley, 3 and 2.
Charles defeated Colbert, 2 and 1.
Graham defeated Sigel, 2 and 1.

(Each losing player received $30,000.)

SEMI-FINALS

Irwin defeated Graham, 6 and 5.
Morgan defeated Charles, 7 and 5.

(Graham and Charles received $60,000 each.)

FINALS

Irwin defeated Morgan, 6 and 4.

(Irwin received $240,000; Morgan received $120,000.)

European Seniors Tour

El Bosque Seniors Open

El Bosque Golf Club, Valencia, Spain — May 1-3
Par 36-36–72; 6,668 yards — purse, £100,000

	SCORES			TOTAL	MONEY
Tommy Horton	66	67	68	201	£16,660
Noel Ratcliffe	71	68	71	210	11,100
Bernard Hunt	70	71	71	212	4,847.50
Brian Huggett	71	71	70	212	4,847.50
Craig Defoy	73	69	70	212	4,847.50
Bob Lendzion	69	72	71	212	4,847.50
Norman Wood	72	72	69	213	3,440
Malcolm Gregson	69	72	72	213	3,440
Renato Campagnoli	73	72	69	214	2,920
Roger Fidler	74	68	72	214	2,920
Terry Gale	71	74	70	215	2,363.33
David Jones	70	67	78	215	2,363.33
Eddie Polland	73	75	67	215	2,363.33
John Morgan	74	69	73	216	1,850
Brian Waites	70	71	75	216	1,850
Ossie Gartenmaier	69	77	71	217	1,375
Antonio Garrido	70	74	73	217	1,375
Jose Maria Roca	74	73	70	217	1,375
Joe McDermott	74	72	71	217	1,375
Denis O'Sullivan	74	69	75	218	1,112.50
DeRay Simon	72	77	69	218	1,112.50
David Creamer	72	73	73	218	1,112.50
Maurice Bembridge	74	72	72	218	1,112.50
Jim Rhodes	72	69	78	219	935
Roger Stern	74	72	73	219	935
Peter Townsend	76	73	70	219	935
Bob Menne	76	72	71	219	935
Neil Coles	74	72	73	219	935
David Huish	71	75	73	219	935
Jose Cabo	72	75	73	220	780
Arthur Spring	74	73	73	220	780
Alberto Croce	73	72	75	220	780
Jose Luis Mangas Espuche	72	69	79	220	780
Jan Bjornsson	72	75	73	220	780
Snell Lancaster	76	71	73	220	780

Beko Classic

Gloria Golf Resort, Antalya, Turkey — May 8-10
Par 36-36–72; 6,288 yards — purse, £150,000

	SCORES			TOTAL	MONEY
Bob Lendzion	71	71	69	211	£25,000
Bobby Verwey	70	71	70	211	12,995
Antonio Garrido	70	73	68	211	12,995

(Lendzion defeated Verwey and Garrido on first extra hole.)

	SCORES			TOTAL	MONEY
Jim Rhodes	72	70	71	213	6,345
David Jones	74	68	71	213	6,345
John Garner	73	72	68	213	6,345
Tommy Horton	70	75	68	213	6,345
Geoff Parslow	68	71	76	215	5,120
Brian Waites	72	70	74	216	3,571.43
Malcolm Gregson	71	72	73	216	3,571.43
Noel Ratcliffe	72	71	73	216	3,571.43
Bill Lockie	71	73	72	216	3,571.43
John Fourie	71	73	72	216	3,571.43
Bill Brask	72	75	69	216	3,571.43
Jay Dolan III	70	77	69	216	3,571.43
Alberto Croce	72	70	75	217	1,857.50
Guy Hunt	73	71	73	217	1,857.50
Michael Slater	73	72	72	217	1,857.50
Terry Gale	74	72	71	217	1,857.50
David Huish	73	73	71	217	1,857.50
Craig Defoy	73	74	70	217	1,857.50
Brian Huggett	77	70	70	217	1,857.50
Bob Menne	76	72	69	217	1,857.50
David Oakley	70	75	73	218	1,420
Andrew Brooks	76	71	71	218	1,420
Denis O'Sullivan	72	75	71	218	1,420
Renato Campagnoli	75	69	75	219	1,224
Stewart Adwick	71	75	73	219	1,224
Harry Flatman	74	72	73	219	1,224
Joe McDermott	70	77	72	219	1,224
Paul Leonard	70	79	70	219	1,224

AIB Irish Seniors Open

Woodbrook Golf Club, Dublin, Ireland — May 15-17
Par 36-36–72; 6,500 yards — purse, £87,305

	SCORES			TOTAL	MONEY
Joe McDermott	70	72	76	208	£14,445.50
Noel Ratcliffe	68	69	71	208	7,526.23
Terry Gale	71	68	69	208	7,526.23
(McDermott defeated Ratcliffe on first and Gale on fifth extra hole.)					
Brian Waites	68	70	72	210	4,335.39
Tommy Horton	72	67	72	211	3,676.41
Doug Dalziel	72	69	72	213	3,238.54
Michael Slater	72	74	67	213	3,238.54
Antonio Garrido	72	66	76	214	2,441.69
Brian Barnes	74	71	69	214	2,441.69
J.R. Delich	71	71	72	214	2,441.69
Bob Lendzion	69	70	75	214	2,441.69
Ian Richardson	70	72	72	214	2,441.69
Jose Cabo	72	71	72	215	1,777.51
Renato Campagnoli	73	71	71	215	1,777.51
Barry Sandry	69	72	75	216	1,302.78
Tony Jacklin	68	73	75	216	1,302.78
Eddie Polland	71	74	71	216	1,302.78
Norman Wood	75	72	69	216	1,302.78
Brian Huggett	69	74	74	217	1,005.81
Liam Higgins	74	72	71	217	1,005.81
Malcolm Gregson	73	73	71	217	1,005.81
Bill Hardwick	71	76	70	217	1,005.81

	SCORES			TOTAL	MONEY
Roger Stern	73	75	70	218	838.18
Bobby Verwey	73	74	71	218	838.18
David Oakley	71	74	73	218	838.18
Tienie Britz	74	73	71	218	838.18
David Huish	73	75	70	218	838.18
David Creamer	70	73	75	218	838.18
David Jones	71	72	76	219	704.07
Craig Defoy	72	74	73	219	704.07
Denis O'Sullivan	75	72	72	219	704.07
Stewart Adwick	71	76	72	219	704.07
Don McCart	70	75	74	219	704.07

Philips PFA Golf Classic

Marriott Meon Valley Hotel & Country Club,
Southampton, England
Par 36-36–72; 6,441 yards

May 29-31
purse, £100,000

	SCORES			TOTAL	MONEY
Neil Coles	67	69	67	203	£15,700
David Jones	70	65	68	203	10,500
(Coles defeated Jones on first extra hole.)					
David Oakley	70	70	66	206	5,970
Joe McDermott	67	70	70	207	4,900
Barry Sandry	71	68	70	209	4,150
John Garner	73	70	66	209	4,150
David Creamer	67	70	73	210	3,550
Tommy Horton	71	68	72	211	3,200
John Fourie	70	71	71	212	2,440
Jim Rhodes	71	70	71	212	2,440
Joe Carr	69	72	71	212	2,440
Paul Leonard	70	70	72	212	2,440
Liam Higgins	70	69	73	212	2,440
Michael Slater	66	73	74	213	1,675
Craig Defoy	76	65	72	213	1,675
Jay Dolan III	75	70	69	214	1,312.50
David Snell	73	71	70	214	1,312.50
J.R. Delich	69	70	75	214	1,312.50
Randall Vines	72	70	72	214	1,312.50
Eddie Polland	72	70	73	215	1,150
Lloyd Monroe	73	73	70	216	1,050
Alberto Croce	73	72	71	216	1,050
Gordon Parkhill	75	71	70	216	1,050
Geoff Parslow	77	69	71	217	847.14
Brian Huggett	74	71	72	217	847.14
Peter Butler	73	73	71	217	847.14
Antonio Garrido	70	74	73	217	847.14
Bob Lendzion	72	70	75	217	847.14
Malcolm Gregson	70	73	74	217	847.14
Chick Evans	73	72	72	217	847.14

Jersey Seniors Open

La Moye Golf Club, Jersey — June 5-7
Par 36-36–72; 6,581 yards — purse, £70,000

	SCORES			TOTAL	MONEY
Bob Shearer	71	73	67	211	£10,000
Tony Jacklin	72	71	70	213	6,600
Brian Waites	68	71	75	214	3,465
Michael Slater	69	67	78	214	3,465
Bob Menne	72	70	73	215	2,800
Craig Defoy	72	67	77	216	2,400
David Creamer	70	69	77	216	2,400
Paul Leonard	71	71	75	217	1,812.50
John Fourie	70	72	75	217	1,812.50
Antonio Garrido	69	73	75	217	1,812.50
Eddie Polland	73	71	73	217	1,812.50
Gordon Parkhill	74	69	75	218	1,168
Alberto Croce	72	72	74	218	1,168
Noel Ratcliffe	73	73	72	218	1,168
Liam Higgins	75	69	74	218	1,168
Peter Butler	74	71	73	218	1,168
Denis O'Sullivan	75	73	71	219	741.25
Ian Richardson	72	74	73	219	741.25
Geoff Parslow	73	75	71	219	741.25
Norman Wood	74	68	77	219	741.25
David Jones	71	74	74	219	741.25
Hugh Inggs	77	69	73	219	741.25
Malcolm Gregson	73	73	73	219	741.25
Tommy Horton	78	71	70	219	741.25
DeRay Simon	72	75	73	220	590
Barry Sandry	75	75	71	221	553.33
John Hudson	75	72	74	221	553.33
Jay Dolan III	74	71	76	221	553.33
Harry Flatman	76	73	73	222	510
Snell Lancaster	77	72	73	222	510
Jim Rhodes	73	73	76	222	510
Kenny Stevenson	74	71	77	222	510
John Garner	78	70	74	222	510

De Vere Hotels Seniors Classic

Belton Woods Golf Club, Grantham, England — June 12-14
Par 36-36–72; 6,564 yards — purse, £90,000

	SCORES			TOTAL	MONEY
Tommy Horton	68	76	67	211	£15,000
Ian Richardson	70	67	75	212	10,000
Barry Sandry	68	74	71	213	5,690
David Jones	68	71	75	214	4,450
Tony Jacklin	70	71	74	215	3,850
Denis O'Sullivan	72	69	74	215	3,850
Malcolm Gregson	71	72	73	216	3,400
John Fourie	72	74	71	217	2,950
Steve Wild	70	72	75	217	2,950
Michael Slater	73	74	71	218	2,104
Jose Cabo	69	75	74	218	2,104
Jim Rhodes	73	74	71	218	2,104

	SCORES			TOTAL	MONEY
Joe McDermott	71	74	73	218	2,104
John Garner	69	75	74	218	2,104
Doug Dalziel	71	76	72	219	1,486.67
Eddie Polland	72	74	73	219	1,486.67
David Creamer	73	74	72	219	1,486.67
Bill Brask	74	71	75	220	1,056.67
Brian Waites	68	75	77	220	1,056.67
Noel Ratcliffe	72	72	76	220	1,056.67
Bob Shearer	72	75	73	220	1,056.67
Peter Townsend	72	72	76	220	1,056.67
Norman Wood	67	74	79	220	1,056.67
Iain Clark	72	74	75	221	800
Maurice Bembridge	72	78	71	221	800
Joe Carr	73	75	73	221	800
Francisco Abreu	79	71	72	222	730
Hugh Inggs	76	72	74	222	730
T.R. Jones	72	79	72	223	672.50
Gordon Parkhill	74	72	77	223	672.50
Geoff Parslow	73	75	75	223	672.50
Renato Campagnoli	77	75	71	223	672.50

Ryder Seniors Classic

Welcombe Hotel, Stratford upon Avon, England — June 19-21
Par 35-35–70; 6,229 yards — purse, £100,000

	SCORES			TOTAL	MONEY
Bill Hardwick	70	69	63	202	£16,660
Renato Campagnoli	68	68	68	204	8,680
David Creamer	66	69	69	204	8,680
Bill Brask	68	70	68	206	4,376.67
Maurice Bembridge	67	70	69	206	4,376.67
Jim Rhodes	66	69	71	206	4,376.67
Joe McDermott	68	72	67	207	3,180
Barry Sandry	71	64	72	207	3,180
Eddie Polland	68	71	68	207	3,180
Iain Clark	69	68	70	207	3,180
Snell Lancaster	69	71	69	209	2,056.67
Bob Shearer	69	68	72	209	2,056.67
Roger Stern	69	69	71	209	2,056.67
Brian Waites	75	69	65	209	2,056.67
Bill Lockie	66	73	70	209	2,056.67
Jose Cabo	69	68	72	209	2,056.67
Neil Coles	70	69	71	210	1,282.50
Denis O'Sullivan	72	69	69	210	1,282.50
Michael Slater	71	69	70	210	1,282.50
Arnold O'Connor	72	67	71	210	1,282.50
Alberto Croce	70	70	71	211	1,052
David Oakley	69	71	71	211	1,052
John Garner	72	71	68	211	1,052
Hugh Inggs	70	71	70	211	1,052
John Fourie	72	67	72	211	1,052
Tony Jacklin	69	68	75	212	890
Ian Richardson	73	67	72	212	890
Steve Wild	72	72	68	212	890
Bob Menne	69	73	70	212	890
Tommy Horton	68	71	73	212	890

Swedish Seniors

Fagelbro Golf Club, Stockholm, Sweden — June 25-27
Par 36-35–71; 6,456 yards — purse, £80,000

	SCORES			TOTAL	MONEY
Maurice Bembridge	70	67	72	209	£13,000
Jim Rhodes	70	69	70	209	8,460
(Bembridge defeated Rhodes on first extra hole.)					
Alberto Croce	73	71	66	210	4,940
J.R. Delich	71	73	67	211	3,860
Noel Ratcliffe	74	71	67	212	3,190
John Hudson	71	71	70	212	3,190
Eddie Polland	74	71	68	213	2,546.67
DeRay Simon	71	70	72	213	2,546.67
Tommy Horton	74	71	68	213	2,546.67
Renato Campagnoli	71	73	70	214	2,065
Bill Hardwick	71	73	70	214	2,065
Norman Wood	70	73	72	215	1,686.50
Brian Waites	74	70	71	215	1,686.50
David Jones	72	73	70	215	1,686.50
Ian Richardson	71	72	72	215	1,686.50
Terry Gale	74	73	69	216	1,285
Chick Evans	72	73	71	216	1,285
Liam Higgins	71	71	74	216	1,285
Tienie Britz	80	68	68	216	1,285
Antonio Garrido	74	71	71	216	1,285
David Creamer	75	74	67	216	1,285
Bobby Verwey	73	69	75	217	1,040
David Snell	73	73	71	217	1,040
T.R. Jones	75	74	69	218	867.50
Hugh Inggs	76	70	72	218	867.50
Peter Townsend	75	74	69	218	867.50
Malcolm Gregson	71	75	72	218	867.50
Joe McDermott	72	77	70	219	752
Harry Flatman	74	73	72	219	752
Craig Defoy	71	72	77	220	724
John Fourie	75	71	74	220	724

Lawrence Batley Seniors

Huddersfield Golf Club, West Yorkshire, England — July 2-4
Par 35-36–71; 6,463 yards — purse, £90,000

	SCORES			TOTAL	MONEY
Bobby Verwey	66	75	69	210	£14,550
Antonio Garrido	74	66	70	210	9,500
(Verwey defeated Garrido on first extra hole.)					
Brian Waites	67	73	71	211	4,900
Hugh Inggs	70	68	73	211	4,900
Brian Huggett	72	72	69	213	3,225
Paul Leonard	72	68	73	213	3,225
Noel Ratcliffe	68	73	72	213	3,225
J.R. Delich	69	69	75	213	3,225
David Snell	69	73	72	214	2,550
Ian Richardson	70	73	72	215	2,200
David Creamer	72	72	71	215	2,200
Joe McDermott	73	73	69	215	2,200

	SCORES			TOTAL	MONEY
Malcolm Gregson	70	73	73	216	1,850
Maurice Bembridge	69	71	76	216	1,850
Jim Rhodes	68	73	76	217	1,655
Guy Hunt	72	73	72	217	1,655
DeRay Simon	77	71	70	218	1,355
Liam Higgins	73	73	72	218	1,355
John Fourie	75	73	70	218	1,355
David Talbot	75	72	71	218	1,355
T.R. Jones	67	75	76	218	1,355
Bob Shearer	77	68	73	218	1,355
Norman Wood	72	76	71	219	1,005
Terry Kendall	73	72	74	219	1,005
David Jones	68	75	76	219	1,005
Bill Hardwick	69	74	76	219	1,005
Steve Wild	72	74	74	220	843.33
Alberto Croce	70	75	75	220	843.33
Terry Gale	68	73	79	220	843.33
John Hudson	74	73	74	221	805
Eddie Polland	74	74	73	221	805

Credit Suisse Private Banking Seniors Open

Bad Ragaz Golf Club, Zurich, Switzerland — July 24-26
Par 35-35–70; 6,288 yards — purse, £100,000

	SCORES			TOTAL	MONEY
Bobby Verwey	66	66	68	200	£16,660
Maurice Bembridge	67	68	67	202	8,680
Tommy Horton	72	66	64	202	8,680
Bill Brask	69	65	69	203	5,000
Jim Rhodes	68	67	69	204	4,065
Malcolm Gregson	65	70	69	204	4,065
Alberto Croce	68	66	71	205	3,180
Neil Coles	69	66	70	205	3,180
Jose Cabo	70	68	67	205	3,180
Liam Higgins	70	72	63	205	3,180
Hugh Inggs	70	65	71	206	2,260
Michael Slater	71	68	67	206	2,260
John Fourie	66	70	70	206	2,260
Brian Waites	70	72	64	206	2,260
Norman Wood	72	67	68	207	1,405
Eddie Polland	71	68	68	207	1,405
Harry Flatman	69	68	70	207	1,405
Renato Campagnoli	69	68	70	207	1,405
Terry Gale	67	72	68	207	1,405
Glenn MacDonald	70	67	70	207	1,405
Stewart Adwick	69	68	71	208	1,090
Hiro Tahara	68	71	69	208	1,090
Antonio Garrido	70	71	67	208	1,090
Tienie Britz	69	74	66	209	965
Bob Lendzion	68	71	70	209	965
Paul Leonard	69	70	70	209	965
Bill Hardwick	72	68	69	209	965
Sukree Onchum	71	70	69	210	875
Craig Defoy	69	73	68	210	875
Jan Bjornsson	72	72	67	211	780
Denis O'Sullivan	74	69	68	211	780

	SCORES			TOTAL	MONEY
Noel Ratcliffe	73	66	72	211	780
Chick Evans	75	69	67	211	780
Francisco Abreu	66	74	71	211	780
Barry Sandry	70	70	71	211	780

Schroder Senior Masters

Wentworth Club, Edinburgh Course, Surrey, England — July 31-August 2
Par 36-36–72; 6,598 yards — purse, £150,000

	SCORES			TOTAL	MONEY
Brian Huggett	72	71	66	209	£25,000
Neil Coles	73	68	68	209	12,995
Eddie Polland	71	68	70	209	12,995
(Huggett defeated Coles and Polland on first extra hole.)					
Barry Sandry	66	75	71	212	6,910
Tommy Horton	72	71	69	212	6,910
Terry Gale	74	72	67	213	5,340
Doug Dalziel	72	71	70	213	5,340
John Morgan	72	70	71	213	5,340
Bobby Verwey	74	68	71	213	5,340
Renato Campagnoli	71	73	70	214	4,060
Gordon Parkhill	72	71	71	214	4,060
Gary Player	69	73	73	215	3,520
Agim Bardha	68	76	72	216	2,893.33
Bill Brask	70	72	74	216	2,893.33
Jim Rhodes	74	68	74	216	2,893.33
Alberto Croce	75	70	72	217	2,012
David Jones	72	73	72	217	2,012
Jose Cabo	73	71	73	217	2,012
Guy Hunt	74	72	71	217	2,012
Noel Ratcliffe	73	72	72	217	2,012
John Hudson	71	75	72	218	1,600
Paul Leonard	69	74	75	218	1,600
Bob Shearer	73	73	72	218	1,600
John Garner	77	71	71	219	1,390
Brian Waites	72	71	76	219	1,390
Bernard Hunt	76	72	71	219	1,390
Maurice Bembridge	74	70	75	219	1,390
Francisco Abreu	78	67	75	220	1,192
Antonio Garrido	73	73	74	220	1,192
David Creamer	76	73	71	220	1,192
Bob Menne	75	73	72	220	1,192
Denis O'Sullivan	77	71	72	220	1,192

Senior British Open

Royal Portrush Golf Club, Portrush, Northern Ireland — August 6-9
Par 36-36–72; 6,692 yards — purse, £375,000

	SCORES				TOTAL	MONEY
Brian Huggett	71	70	71	71	283	£60,000
Eddie Polland	71	71	71	70	283	38,000
(Huggett defeated Polland on first extra hole.)						
Brian Barnes	70	73	68	73	284	22,000

	SCORES				TOTAL	MONEY
Noel Ratcliffe	74	71	71	69	285	18,000
Terry Gale	70	70	75	71	286	12,975
Tommy Horton	72	68	69	77	286	12,975
Malcolm Gregson	76	71	72	67	286	12,975
Denis O'Sullivan	71	73	71	71	286	12,975
David Jones	69	77	71	74	291	9,700
Bob Charles	75	73	73	70	291	9,700
Paul Leonard	72	74	70	75	291	9,700
John Morgan	77	72	72	71	292	5,771.43
Gary Player	70	75	72	75	292	5,771.43
Norman Wood	72	73	73	74	292	5,771.43
Jay Dolan III	74	77	67	74	292	5,771.43
Brian Waites	75	72	72	73	292	5,771.43
Bob Shearer	72	76	72	72	292	5,771.43
Antonio Garrido	71	75	71	75	292	5,771.43
Jim Rhodes	68	77	74	74	293	4,000
Dale Douglass	73	76	72	72	293	4,000
Iain Clark	69	76	74	75	294	3,533.33
Neil Coles	74	74	73	73	294	3,533.33
Bill Brask	72	76	70	76	294	3,533.33
Chuck Milne	76	76	74	69	295	3,250
David Creamer	71	77	76	71	295	3,250
Michael Slater	75	77	71	73	296	2,930
Bill Hardwick	74	73	71	78	296	2,930
Bob Lendzion	79	69	70	78	296	2,930
Geoff Parslow	73	71	76	76	296	2,930
Jerry Bruner	71	79	73	73	296	2,930

West of Ireland Seniors Championship

East Clare Golf Club, Bodyke, Ireland
Par 36-36–72; 6,482 yards

August 14-16
purse, £90,000

	SCORES			TOTAL	MONEY
John Morgan	67	66	72	205	£12,945.54
Denis O'Sullivan	72	67	67	206	8,630.36
David Jones	68	66	73	207	4,910.68
Bill Brask	68	69	71	208	3,646.33
Terry Gale	67	70	71	208	3,646.33
Bill Hardwick	69	67	73	209	3,063.78
Neil Coles	70	70	69	209	3,063.78
Michael Slater	70	69	71	210	2,416.50
Liam Higgins	70	71	69	210	2,416.50
David Creamer	70	68	72	210	2,416.50
J.R. Delich	69	74	68	211	1,984.98
Bob Lendzion	72	68	72	212	1,812.38
Bob Menne	74	70	69	213	1,445.59
Ian Richardson	71	72	70	213	1,445.59
Andrew Brooks	70	68	75	213	1,445.59
Jim Rhodes	70	71	72	213	1,445.59
Jay Dolan III	69	77	68	214	1,021.84
Tommy Horton	73	69	72	214	1,021.84
Agim Bardha	72	71	71	214	1,021.84
John Hudson	72	74	68	214	1,021.84
David Huish	70	73	71	214	1,021.84
John Garner	73	71	71	215	759.47
Geoff Parslow	69	72	74	215	759.47

	SCORES			TOTAL	MONEY
Paul Leonard	70	70	75	215	759.47
Noel Ratcliffe	73	72	71	216	690.43
Gordon Gray	72	74	72	218	592.62
Hugh Inggs	72	74	72	218	592.62
Norman Wood	72	71	75	218	592.62
Bob Shearer	74	73	71	218	592.62
Joe McDermott	75	71	72	218	592.62
Glenn MacDonald	73	72	73	218	592.62
Skip Pratt	74	70	74	218	592.62
Lloyd Monroe	77	69	72	218	592.62
Chick Evans	68	77	73	218	592.62

The Belfry PGA Seniors Championship

PGA National, The Belfry, Birmingham, England — August 28-31
Par 36-36–72; 6,626 yards — purse, £175,000

	SCORES				TOTAL	MONEY
Tommy Horton	69	71	66	71	277	£29,000
Renato Campagnoli	72	66	72	69	279	14,750
Jim Rhodes	73	66	71	69	279	14,750
John Fourie	71	68	70	71	280	8,600
Bill Hardwick	71	69	73	68	281	7,300
Eddie Polland	69	69	73	70	281	7,300
Bill Brask	69	71	70	73	283	5,200
Tony Jacklin	71	70	70	72	283	5,200
Norman Wood	72	70	68	73	283	5,200
Snell Lancaster	71	70	69	73	283	5,200
Peter Townsend	69	69	74	71	283	5,200
Arnold O'Connor	72	69	67	75	283	5,200
Maurice Bembridge	70	70	72	73	285	3,187.50
Christy O'Connor, Jr.	71	72	69	73	285	3,187.50
David Huish	70	72	70	73	285	3,187.50
Neil Coles	69	71	75	70	285	3,187.50
Craig Defoy	69	71	71	75	286	2,426.67
Denis O'Sullivan	72	73	69	72	286	2,426.67
David Jones	69	68	76	73	286	2,426.67
Barry Sandry	73	68	72	74	287	2,110
Noel Ratcliffe	72	70	75	70	287	2,110
Brian Huggett	73	70	76	68	287	2,110
Bob Lendzion	71	72	72	73	288	1,885
David Creamer	70	66	79	73	288	1,885
John Garner	74	72	69	74	289	1,725
David Oakley	74	68	75	72	289	1,725
Alberto Croce	74	73	70	73	290	1,620
Graham Burroughs	73	70	73	75	291	1,480
T.R. Jones	74	69	70	78	291	1,480
Hugh Inggs	69	72	74	76	291	1,480

Golden Charter PGA Scottish Seniors Open

Marriott Dalmahoy Hotel & Country Club, Edinburgh, Scotland
Par 36-36–72; 6,511 yards

September 3-6
purse, £150,000

	SCORES				TOTAL	MONEY
David Huish	70	65	70	68	273	£25,000
David Jones	66	70	70	67	273	16,640
(Huish defeated Jones on second extra hole.)						
David Oakley	72	70	66	66	274	9,350
Bill Brask	74	66	68	68	276	6,910
Christy O'Connor, Jr.	69	71	71	65	276	6,910
Antonio Garrido	70	67	72	68	277	6,000
John Garner	71	71	72	66	280	5,120
Iain Clark	74	69	66	71	280	5,120
Norman Wood	70	73	69	68	280	5,120
John Fourie	72	69	72	68	281	3,100
Tommy Horton	70	72	68	71	281	3,100
David Creamer	73	69	72	67	281	3,100
Joe Carr	73	66	70	72	281	3,100
Terry Gale	72	66	72	71	281	3,100
Neil Coles	73	73	66	69	281	3,100
Noel Ratcliffe	69	74	70	68	281	3,100
Agim Bardha	74	69	70	68	281	3,100
Bob Lendzion	73	70	70	69	282	2,000
Ian Richardson	67	72	73	71	283	1,710
Michael Slater	72	68	72	71	283	1,710
Arnold O'Connor	72	70	71	70	283	1,710
Malcolm Gregson	75	69	66	73	283	1,710
Guy Hunt	73	72	69	70	284	1,480
Jim Rhodes	74	69	67	74	284	1,480
Barry Sandry	72	69	74	69	284	1,480
Bill Hardwick	75	72	69	69	285	1,285
Denis O'Sullivan	74	71	68	72	285	1,285
T.R. Jones	74	71	70	70	285	1,285
Hugh Inggs	75	71	70	69	285	1,285
Liam Higgins	75	71	72	68	286	1,150
Bobby Verwey	71	74	67	74	286	1,150
Maurice Bembridge	72	74	69	71	286	1,150
Gordon Parkhill	72	73	72	69	286	1,150

Efteling European Trophy

Efteling Golf Park, Holland
Par 36-36–72; 6,501 yards

September 18-20
purse, £100,000

	SCORES			TOTAL	MONEY
Paul Leonard	68	66	70	204	£16,600
Denis O'Sullivan	68	73	70	211	6,322.50
Maurice Bembridge	74	66	71	211	6,322.50
Neil Coles	71	71	69	211	6,322.50
Liam Higgins	71	71	69	211	6,322.50
Craig Defoy	70	73	69	212	3,250
Noel Ratcliffe	68	72	72	212	3,250
Snell Lancaster	72	70	70	212	3,250
Tommy Horton	68	74	70	212	3,250
Jim Rhodes	69	73	71	213	2,300
Eddie Polland	72	68	73	213	2,300

	SCORES			TOTAL	MONEY
Arnold O'Connor	70	73	70	213	2,300
Tony Jacklin	76	69	69	214	1,740
John Fourie	69	71	74	214	1,740
Michael Slater	72	73	69	214	1,740
Bobby Verwey	72	72	71	215	1,330
David Huish	73	73	69	215	1,330
Antonio Garrido	69	74	72	215	1,330
Gordon Gray	74	67	74	215	1,330
Geoff Parslow	75	68	73	216	1,080
Jan Bjornsson	72	74	71	217	910
David Jones	75	71	71	217	910
John Garner	74	71	72	217	910
Bob Lendzion	70	73	74	217	910
Norman Wood	74	72	72	218	800
Hugh Jackson	76	68	75	219	750
Barry Sandry	73	74	72	219	750
Joe McDermott	73	74	72	219	750
Lloyd Monroe	75	73	71	219	750
Hugh Inggs	75	73	72	220	690
Glenn MacDonald	76	69	75	220	690
Kenneth Magnusson	74	72	74	220	690

Elf Seniors Open

Pau Golf Club, Pau, France
Par 35-34–69; 5,804 yards

September 24-26
purse, £90,000

	SCORES			TOTAL	MONEY
Brian Waites	66	66	63	195	£15,739.77
Denis O'Sullivan	68	64	67	199	10,493.18
John Fourie	68	68	65	201	5,970.62
Maurice Bembridge	68	67	67	202	4,433.37
Noel Ratcliffe	70	68	64	202	4,433.37
Arnold O'Connor	68	65	70	203	3,725.08
Lloyd Monroe	66	69	68	203	3,725.08
Jay Dolan III	71	67	66	204	2,686.25
Neil Coles	68	68	68	204	2,686.25
Antonio Garrido	70	69	65	204	2,686.25
Peter Townsend	69	67	68	204	2,686.25
Bobby Verwey	67	69	68	204	2,686.25
David Jones	69	67	69	205	1,899.27
Barry Sandry	72	69	64	205	1,899.27
Tommy Horton	69	71	66	206	1,559.99
Harry Flatman	70	67	69	206	1,559.99
Snell Lancaster	68	69	69	206	1,559.99
Bill Hardwick	64	73	70	207	1,238.20
Eddie Polland	71	69	67	207	1,238.20
Jose Cabo	69	70	68	207	1,238.20
Hugh Inggs	71	69	68	208	979.36
David Huish	71	67	70	208	979.36
Jim Rhodes	67	72	69	208	979.36
Dr. Arthur Spring	74	68	67	209	823.72
Steve Wild	70	70	69	209	823.72
T.R. Jones	70	70	69	209	823.72
Norman Wood	75	66	68	209	823.72
David Creamer	75	69	66	210	755.51
Paul Leonard	71	71	69	211	734.52
Liam Higgins	72	70	70	212	713.54

Is Molas Seniors Open

Is Molas Golf Club, Sardinia
Par 36-36–72; 6,586 yards

October 15-17
purse, £90,000

	SCORES			TOTAL	MONEY
Malcolm Gregson	67	73	69	209	£14,500
Tommy Horton	75	70	66	211	9,300
David Jones	72	70	70	212	4,540
Michael Slater	71	69	72	212	4,540
Bob Lendzion	71	71	70	212	4,540
Jay Dolan III	71	72	70	213	3,500
Craig Defoy	68	76	70	214	2,775
Jose Cabo	71	69	74	214	2,775
David Huish	74	69	71	214	2,775
Peter Townsend	73	70	71	214	2,775
John Fourie	75	69	71	215	2,000
Noel Ratcliffe	72	72	71	215	2,000
Eddie Polland	72	72	71	215	2,000
Jim Rhodes	67	76	73	216	1,433.33
Brian Waites	68	74	74	216	1,433.33
Bill Brask	75	71	70	216	1,433.33
T.R. Jones	70	73	74	217	1,180
Geoff Parslow	71	74	72	217	1,180
Brian Huggett	72	74	72	218	1,055
Paul Leonard	75	74	69	218	1,055
Snell Lancaster	72	73	74	219	910
Bill Hardwick	71	74	74	219	910
Alberto Croce	71	71	77	219	910
David Creamer	70	76	73	219	910
Harry Flatman	76	69	75	220	820
J.R. Delich	73	76	72	221	730
Antonio Garrido	75	75	71	221	730
Joe Carr	75	75	71	221	730
John Hudson	75	74	72	221	730
DeRay Simon	72	72	77	221	730
John Garner	74	76	71	221	730
Chick Evans	74	70	77	221	730

Senior Tournament of Champions

Buckinghamshire Golf Club, Denham, England
Par 36-36–72; 6,664 yards
(Third round cancelled — rain.)

October 23-25
purse, £120,000

	SCORES		TOTAL	MONEY
John Garner	69	70	139	£20,000
Liam Higgins	69	71	140	10,400
Eddie Polland	69	71	140	10,400
Bill Brask	68	73	141	6,000
Alberto Croce	69	74	143	4,700
Barry Sandry	71	72	143	4,700
Malcolm Gregson	73	70	143	4,700
Bob Lendzion	71	72	143	4,700
Ian Richardson	70	74	144	3,750
David Huish	72	72	144	3,750
Jim Rhodes	70	75	145	3,300
David Jones	72	73	145	3,300

	SCORES		TOTAL	MONEY
Paul Leonard	75	71	146	2,800
Antonio Garrido	74	72	146	2,800
Tommy Horton	74	72	146	2,800
Michael Slater	72	75	147	2,187.50
Bill Hardwick	71	76	147	2,187.50
Christy O'Connor, Jr.	69	78	147	2,187.50
Neil Coles	71	76	147	2,187.50
Peter Townsend	76	72	148	1,800
Craig Defoy	69	79	148	1,800
Noel Ratcliffe	72	76	148	1,800
Jay Dolan III	71	78	149	1,517.50
David Oakley	71	78	149	1,517.50
Maurice Bembridge	71	78	149	1,517.50
Brian Waites	71	78	149	1,517.50
Joe McDermott	73	77	150	1,295
Terry Gale	73	77	150	1,295
Denis O'Sullivan	71	79	150	1,295
Brian Huggett	74	76	150	1,295

Praia D'El Rey European Cup

See European LPGA Tour section.

Japan Senior Tour

Komatsu Nagoya TV Open

Hananoki Golf Club, Aichi
Par 36-36–72; 6,771 yards

May 29-31
purse, ¥50,000,000

	SCORES			TOTAL	MONEY
Hisao Inoue	67	67	69	203	¥7,500,000
Tadao Nakamura	71	69	69	209	2,750,000
Haruo Yasuda	68	69	72	209	2,750,000
Hiroshi Ishii	69	70	70	209	2,750,000
Fujio Kobayashi	68	70	72	210	1,750,000
Wataru Horiguchi	71	70	70	211	1,375,000
Ichiro Teramoto	67	72	72	211	1,375,000
Seiichi Kanai	73	70	69	212	1,100,000
Toru Nakayama	73	71	69	213	1,000,000
Masaru Amano	70	71	73	214	870,000
Koichi Uehara	74	71	69	214	870,000
Sadao Ogawa	70	73	72	215	786,666
Toshiki Matsui	74	70	71	215	786,666
Terry Gale	71	69	75	215	786,666
Hsieh Min-nan	76	69	71	216	742,500
Koji Nakajima	74	72	70	216	742,500
Hisashi Iwamoto	72	72	73	217	690,000
Katsuji Hasegawa	72	76	69	217	690,000

	SCORES			TOTAL	MONEY
Eitaro Deguchi	74	70	73	217	690,000
Norihiko Matsumoto	73	72	72	217	690,000
Kenichi Tsurumoto	75	73	69	217	690,000
Fumio Tanaka	73	71	74	218	645,000
Shoji Kikuchi	72	74	73	219	622,500
Hideo Hashimoto	72	75	72	219	622,500
Tooru Kurihara	72	72	76	220	580,000
Hiro Sakai	73	71	76	220	580,000
Hiroshi Kazami	74	72	74	220	580,000
Kazuaki Yamamoto	75	68	77	220	580,000
Shigeru Uchida	72	73	75	220	580,000
Hisao Kinoshita	74	71	76	221	535,000
Mitoshi Tomita	73	72	76	221	535,000
Mitsuo Hirukawa	73	72	76	221	535,000
Kuo Chie-hsiung	72	77	72	221	535,000
*Nagahide Tsushima	74	74	73	221	

TPC Starts

Narita Golf Club, Ibaragi
Par 36-36–72; 6,884 yards

June 4-7
purse, ¥50,000,000

	SCORES				TOTAL	MONEY
Toru Nakayama	67	68	73	74	282	¥7,500,000
Seiichi Kanai	68	73	73	68	282	3,500,000
(Nakayama defeated Kanai on third extra hole.)						
Haruo Yasuda	71	68	73	72	284	2,750,000
Joji Yokoi	68	67	78	72	285	2,000,000
Masaru Amano	69	71	71	76	287	1,587,500
Fujio Kobayashi	67	73	76	71	287	1,587,500
Kikuo Arai	66	73	75	74	288	1,016,666
Masaji Kusakabe	70	73	74	71	288	1,016,666
Terry Gale	71	72	71	74	288	1,016,666
Koji Nakajima	71	70	74	74	289	800,000
Shoji Kikuchi	73	72	74	71	290	775,000
Eitaro Deguchi	71	72	72	75	290	775,000
Akira Kawamata	73	72	75	72	292	725,000
Hisao Inoue	69	77	73	73	292	725,000
Yutaka Suzuki	74	71	76	72	293	700,000
Seiji Ogawa	73	75	74	72	294	662,500
Teruo Sugihara	71	72	78	73	294	662,500
Toshiharu Horimoto	72	72	77	73	294	662,500
Mitsuo Iwata	72	72	77	73	294	662,500
Koichi Uehara	74	73	75	73	295	595,000
Kesakiho Uchida	73	71	72	79	295	595,000
Takashi Kurihara	71	74	75	75	295	595,000
Tetsuhiro Ueda	75	70	73	77	295	595,000
Koshirou Kubo	72	74	77	72	295	595,000
Tooru Kurihara	70	73	76	77	296	540,000
Akira Yatabe	74	71	74	77	296	540,000
Hiroshi Ishii	71	69	77	79	296	540,000
Takaaki Komo	74	75	72	76	297	495,000
Hideyo Sugimoto	73	71	76	77	297	495,000
Teruo Suzumura	74	70	78	75	297	495,000
Hideo Hashimoto	75	73	74	75	297	495,000
Toshiki Matsui	73	75	76	73	297	495,000
Tadao Furuichi	73	73	75	76	297	495,000

Castle Hill Open

Castle Hill County Club, Hoi-gun, Aichi — June 12-14
Par 36-36–72; 6,703 yards — purse, ¥30,000,000
(Third round cancelled — rain.)

	SCORES		TOTAL	MONEY
Koichi Uehara	64	71	135	¥4,500,000
Akira Kawamata	71	67	138	1,875,000
Hisao Inoue	69	69	138	1,875,000
Hiroshi Kazami	72	68	140	1,125,000
Terry Gale	69	71	140	1,125,000
Sadao Ogawa	72	69	141	900,000
Toshiki Matsui	68	74	142	750,000
Masaji Kusakabe	70	73	143	576,000
Tooru Kurihara	71	72	143	576,000
Fumio Tanaka	73	70	143	576,000
Katsumi Hara	70	73	143	576,000
Seiji Ogawa	72	72	144	466,500
Yoshiharu Nakase	72	72	144	466,500
Teruo Suzumura	72	72	144	466,500
Ichiro Teramoto	71	73	144	466,500
Tamotsu Ito	72	73	145	418,500
Fujio Kobayashi	69	76	145	418,500
Katsuji Hasegawa	71	74	145	418,500
Eitaro Deguchi	72	73	145	418,500
Norihiko Matsumoto	73	72	145	418,500
Kuo Chie-hsiung	73	72	145	418,500
Koji Nakajima	70	76	146	373,500
Toru Nakayama	70	76	146	373,500
Mitsuhiro Kitta	73	73	146	373,500
Mitoshi Tomita	72	74	146	373,500
Seiichi Kanai	74	73	147	333,000
Shoichi Sato	70	77	147	333,000
Kanae Nobechi	74	73	147	333,000
Isao Matsui	73	74	147	333,000
Syunji Kanazawa	75	72	147	333,000
Akio Toyoda	70	77	147	333,000
Mitsuo Hirukawa	72	75	147	333,000
Mitsuo Iwata	75	72	147	333,000

Old Man Par Senior Open

Ohara Onjuku Golf Club, Isumi-gun, Chiba — August 28-29
Par 36-36–72; 6,777 yards — purse, ¥5,840,000

	SCORES		TOTAL	MONEY
Toru Nakayama	69	68	137	¥1,200,000
Hiroshi Kazami	68	70	138	600,000
Seiji Ogawa	71	70	141	287,500
Koji Nakajima	68	73	141	287,500
Hisao Inoue	72	69	141	287,500
Mitoshi Tomita	69	72	141	287,500
Fujio Kobayashi	70	72	142	155,000
Katsuji Hasegawa	73	70	143	147,500
Toshiki Matsui	66	77	143	147,500
Ichiro Ino	73	72	145	133,750
Masaji Kusakabe	71	74	145	133,750

	SCORES		TOTAL	MONEY
Tooru Kurihara	74	71	145	133,750
Minoru Nakamura	69	76	145	133,750
Norihiko Matsumoto	73	72	145	133,750
Kenichi Tsurumoto	72	73	145	133,750
Ichio Sato	74	72	146	125,000
Kiyokuni Kimoto	75	72	147	118,750
Hideo Jibiki	74	73	147	118,750
Teruo Suzumura	73	74	147	118,750
Yoshihiro Takata	74	73	147	118,750
Yuji Ogawa	74	74	148	111,250
Hisao Kinoshita	72	76	148	111,250
Isao Matsui	73	76	149	107,500
Masao Kikuchi	75	76	151	103,750
Ryosuke Ota	74	77	151	103,750
Masaharu Ohshima	75	77	152	100,000
Hiroshi Kaimata	72	81	153	100,000
Yasushi Katayama	75	78	153	100,000
*Haruo Hashimoto	80	73	153	
Syuushin Yamagishi	78	76	154	100,000
*Nakakita Shouji	77	77	154	

HTB Senior Classic

Mitsui Kanko Iris Golf Club, Hokkaido
Par 36-36–72; 6,442 yards

September 12-13
purse, ¥8,000,000

	SCORES		TOTAL	MONEY
Hsieh Min-nan	67	71	138	¥2,000,000
Koichi Uehara	69	73	142	750,000
Fujio Kobayashi	68	74	142	750,000
Hisao Inoue	69	74	143	400,000
Fumio Tanaka	69	75	144	250,000
Kenichi Tsurumoto	71	74	145	190,000
Seiji Ogawa	75	71	146	170,000
Shigeru Uchida	73	73	146	170,000
Ichiro Togawa	72	74	146	170,000
Masaru Amano	69	78	147	160,000
Masaji Kusakabe	73	75	148	158,500
Toru Nakayama	72	76	148	158,500
Seiichi Kanai	71	79	150	156,500
Teruo Suzumura	71	79	150	156,500
Kikuo Arai	73	78	151	154,000
Toshiyuki Tsucheyama	77	74	151	154,000
Kanae Nobechi	73	78	151	154,000
Hideyo Sugimoto	74	78	152	151,500
Hiroshi Tahara	74	78	152	151,500
*Hisao Saito	71	81	152	
Ichiro Ino	73	80	153	148,500
Joji Yokoi	74	79	153	148,500
Hiroshi Ishii	73	80	153	148,500
Shozo Miyamoto	74	79	153	148,500
*Katsuyuki Sakura	75	78	153	
*Kuniaki Kikawa	71	82	153	
Yoshiro Takeda	75	79	154	146,000
*Minoru Saito	77	77	154	
*Hideshi Doi	78	77	155	
*Takayuki Fudo	79	76	155	

Japan PGA Senior Championship

Shimoakima Country Club, Annaka, Gunma — October 8-10
Par 36-36–72; 6,749 yards — purse, ¥50,000,000

	SCORES				TOTAL	MONEY
Seiichi Kanai	74	72	70	71	287	¥7,500,000
Koji Nakajima	74	69	70	65	288	3,500,000
Kikuo Arai	76	72	70	71	289	2,166,666
Teruo Sugihara	70	72	76	71	289	2,166,666
Kuo Chie-hsiung	72	71	73	73	289	2,166,666
Haruo Yasuda	72	70	71	77	290	1,425,000
Katsuji Hasegawa	77	75	72	69	293	1,150,000
Akira Kawamata	71	70	76	77	294	900,000
Fumio Tanaka	76	74	72	72	294	900,000
Toru Nakayama	75	73	70	76	294	900,000
Hsieh Min-nan	72	76	73	74	295	740,000
Teruo Suzumura	77	70	74	74	295	740,000
Ichiro Teramoto	74	69	77	75	295	740,000
Kenichi Tsurumoto	77	71	73	74	295	740,000
Toshikazu Izumi	75	71	76	73	295	740,000
Koichi Uehara	73	77	74	73	297	670,000
Fujio Kobayashi	71	77	71	78	297	670,000
Koshirou Kubo	75	75	71	76	297	670,000
Masaru Amano	75	77	74	72	298	640,000
Hiroshi Kazami	73	76	75	75	299	610,000
Wataru Horiguchi	73	74	76	76	299	610,000
Mitoshi Tomita	76	71	75	77	299	610,000
Yoshiharu Nakase	74	74	76	76	300	572,500
Mitsuo Iwata	78	75	72	75	300	572,500
Tamotsu Ito	77	72	77	75	301	540,000
Shoji Kikuchi	74	73	77	77	301	540,000
Minoru Nakamura	73	74	78	76	301	540,000
Sadao Ogawa	76	75	72	79	302	500,000
Akira Yatabe	76	72	80	74	302	500,000
Osamu Watanabe	75	78	74	75	302	500,000
Kiyotaka Mochida	79	72	78	73	302	500,000
Terry Gale	75	73	77	77	302	500,000

Japan Senior Open

Ube County Club, Sadohara — November 26-29
Par 36-36–72; 6,764 yards — purse, ¥50,000,000

	SCORES				TOTAL	MONEY
Graham Marsh	65	70	69	70	274	¥7,500,000
Toru Nakayama	71	71	68	68	278	3,500,000
Isao Aoki	65	74	70	70	279	2,750,000
Hsieh Min-nan	69	73	69	70	281	1,875,000
Teruo Suzumura	71	71	69	70	281	1,875,000
Mitsuo Iwata	71	72	71	70	284	1,425,000
Fumio Tanaka	68	76	70	71	285	1,150,000
Seiichi Kanai	71	73	70	72	286	950,000
Terry Gale	74	73	71	68	286	950,000
Hiroshi Kazami	78	69	69	71	287	800,000
Fujio Kobayashi	73	73	69	73	288	775,000
Yoshiharu Nakase	72	73	70	73	288	775,000
Wataru Horiguchi	72	70	75	73	290	735,000

	SCORES				TOTAL	MONEY
Seiji Ogawa	74	71	75	71	291	685,000
Katsuji Hasegawa	74	73	70	74	291	685,000
Haruo Yasuda	78	72	70	71	291	685,000
Hiroshi Ishii	72	72	72	75	291	685,000
Hisao Inoue	72	69	75	75	291	685,000
Norihiko Matsumoto	76	72	70	74	292	632,500
Kenichi Tsurumoto	75	75	69	73	292	632,500
Masaru Amano	71	74	73	75	293	580,000
Koichi Uehara	74	77	73	69	293	580,000
Takashi Kurihara	75	72	71	75	293	580,000
Eitaro Deguchi	76	73	75	69	293	580,000
Mitoshi Tomita	72	73	77	71	293	580,000
*Masanori Yoshimizu	73	72	73	75	293	
Hiro Sakai	73	73	72	76	294	535,000
Yasuo Tanabe	71	75	73	75	294	535,000
Tamotsu Ito	76	72	72	76	296	505,000
Ichiro Ino	72	75	74	75	296	505,000
Tadao Nakamura	71	72	79	74	296	505,000
Hisashi Suzumura	74	78	74	70	296	505,000

South Africa Senior Tour

Vodacom Senior Series: Pretoria

Silver Lakes Golf Club, Pretoria, South Africa — July 15-17
Par 36-36–72; 7,111 yards — purse, R100,000

	SCORES			TOTAL	MONEY
Gabriel Putsoe	68	70	73	211	R15,700
Allan Henning	65	73	80	218	11,500
John Fourie	72	75	72	219	7,150
John Howie	73	71	75	219	7,150
Bobby Verwey	71	84	70	225	4,700
Daddy Naidoo	73	80	73	226	3,800
Vincent Tshabalala	70	78	79	227	3,150
David Burd	81	75	74	230	2,387.50
Joe Dlamini	80	75	75	230	2,387.50
Emmanuel Maabane	77	78	75	230	2,387.50
Solly Sepeng	77	76	77	230	2,387.50
Peter Mkata	74	79	79	232	2,000
Obed Matlou	77	77	80	234	1,850
Shadrack Molefe	76	80	78	234	1,850
Graham Henning	73	77	85	235	1,710
Buster Masango	80	73	83	236	1,563.33
Zach Mavundla	80	76	80	236	1,563.33
Godfrey Zwane	76	78	82	236	1,563.33
Brian Ferreira	82	79	76	237	1,440
Bobby Jones	74	77	87	238	1,390
Israel Khunou	80	90	69	239	1,290
John Mabe	77	82	80	239	1,290

	SCORES			TOTAL	MONEY
Mike Mbele	80	80	79	239	1,290
Tony Finlayson	78	80	82	240	1,170
Patrick Madiba	77	81	82	240	1,170
Chris Van Wyk	80	76	85	241	1,110
Thomas Ntebele	75	84	87	246	1,050
Bob Vosloo	81	83	82	246	1,050
Mike Burraston	79	77	91	247	990
Tony Rice	81	83	84	248	960

Vodacom Senior Series: Wild Coast

Wild Coast Sun Country Club, Port Edward, South Africa — August 5-7
Par 35-35–70; 6,291 yards — purse, R100,000

	SCORES			TOTAL	MONEY
Tertius Claassens	70	72	76	218	R15,700
Gabriel Putsoe	77	73	71	221	9,750
Allan Henning	74	74	73	221	9,750
Joe Dlamini	73	73	76	222	6,300
Peter Mkata	73	74	76	223	4,700
Shadrack Molefe	74	76	77	227	3,475
Muss Gammon	75	73	79	227	3,475
Tony Finlayson	75	75	78	228	2,750
Terry Westbrook	78	74	81	233	2,450
Vincent Tshabalala	78	76	80	234	2,250
Gert van Biljon	77	80	78	235	2,100
John Mabe	77	83	76	236	1,852.50
Graham Henning	81	76	79	236	1,852.50
Solly Sepeng	79	78	79	236	1,852.50
Ranjith Singh	73	77	86	236	1,852.50
Brian Ferreira	86	76	78	240	1,595
Daddy Naidoo	80	79	81	240	1,595
Trevor Wilkes	78	78	85	241	1,500
David Masilo	80	80	82	242	1,440
Zach Mavundla	81	78	84	243	1,365
Don Knight	80	77	86	243	1,365
Patrick Madiba	81	81	82	244	1,290
John Howie	92	75	78	245	1,215
Buster Masango	89	75	81	245	1,215
Absolom Nkosi	87	77	82	246	1,150
Thomas Ntebele	80	84	83	247	1,090
Daniel Pitso	80	82	85	247	1,090
Bobby Jones	88	78	82	248	1,010
Bernard Kgantsi	80	83	85	248	1,010
Mike Mbele	85	84	80	249	930
Joseph Ntuli	85	83	81	249	930
Emmanuel Maabane	80	85	84	249	930

Vodacom Senior Series: Mmabatho

Leopard Park Golf Club, Johannesburg, South Africa — September 18-20
Par 36-36–72; 7,280 yards — purse, R100,000

	SCORES			TOTAL	MONEY
Tertius Claassens	71	67	70	208	R15,700
Allan Henning	67	72	71	210	9,750
Gabriel Putsoe	68	70	72	210	9,750
John Howie	76	70	70	216	5,500
John Mabe	70	75	71	216	5,500
Solly Sepeng	78	71	70	219	3,475
David Burd	76	70	73	219	3,475
Joe Dlamini	74	71	75	220	2,750
Freddie Mkwanazi	72	76	73	221	2,450
Shadrack Molefe	68	77	77	222	2,250
Peter Mkata	75	74	74	223	2,100
Coen Dreyer	79	74	72	225	2,000
Patrick Madiba	76	78	72	226	1,720
Gert van Biljon	77	76	73	226	1,720
Tony Finlayson	78	73	75	226	1,720
Graham Henning	72	76	78	226	1,720
Zach Mavundla	73	74	79	226	1,720
Ranjith Singh	72	76	79	227	1,500
Brian Ferreira	77	77	74	228	1,440
Obed Matlou	78	76	76	230	1,365
Chris Van Wyk	72	75	83	230	1,365
Bob Vosloo	77	80	74	231	1,265
Daddy Naidoo	79	77	75	231	1,265
David Masilo	78	78	76	232	1,190
Absolom Nkosi	78	77	78	233	1,110
Mike Mbele	77	78	78	233	1,110
Daniel Pitso	75	79	79	233	1,110
Thomas Ntebele	78	79	77	234	1,010
Mike Burraston	77	77	80	234	1,010
Israel Khunou	79	78	78	235	945
Tony Rice	80	76	79	235	945

Vodacom Senior Series: Welkom

Oppenheimer Park Golf Club, Welkom, Free State, South Africa — October 18-20
Par 36-36–72; 7,036 yards — purse, R100,000

	SCORES			TOTAL	MONEY
Allan Henning	67	72	70	209	R15,700
Gabriel Putsoe	72	69	69	210	11,500
Solly Sepeng	71	72	72	215	8,000
Hugh Inggs	73	72	74	219	6,300
Vincent Tshabalala	76	76	68	220	4,250
Ranjith Singh	75	75	70	220	4,250
Rinus van Niekerk	73	77	74	224	2,950
Peter Mkata	75	75	74	224	2,950
Peter Loeb	72	81	72	225	2,266.66
John Howie	78	75	72	225	2,266.66
Ian Smith	72	80	73	225	2,266.66
Daddy Naidoo	73	79	74	226	1,950
Joe Dlamini	76	73	77	226	1,950

	SCORES			TOTAL	MONEY
David Burd	79	75	73	227	1,713.33
Richard Lyon	74	78	75	227	1,713.33
John Mabe	75	76	76	227	1,713.33
Chris Van Wyk	76	78	74	228	1,420
Gert van Biljon	80	73	75	228	1,420
Tony Rice	75	77	76	228	1,420
Graham Henning	74	76	78	228	1,420
Bob Vosloo	75	75	78	228	1,420
David Masilo	77	69	82	228	1,420
Mike Mbele	73	80	77	230	1,240
Shadrack Molefe	79	79	73	231	1,170
Godfrey Zwane	75	78	78	231	1,170
Freddie Mkwanazi	78	75	79	232	1,090
Peter Shibambo	75	77	80	232	1,090
Bobby Jones	79	80	74	233	1,030
Roy Van Wezel	77	81	76	234	960
Ronnie Nair	77	78	79	234	960
Absolom Nkosi	83	71	80	234	960

Franklin Templeton Senior South African Open

Kensington Golf Club, Johannesburg, South Africa — November 13-15
Par 36-36–72; 7,245 yards — purse, R200,000

	SCORES			TOTAL	MONEY
John Bland	69	68	68	205	R31,400
Simon Hobday	74	72	65	211	16,933.33
Allan Henning	72	72	67	211	16,933.33
John Fourie	68	71	72	211	16,933.33
Gabriel Putsoe	73	71	68	212	9,000
John Howie	72	71	70	213	6,500
Theo Manyama	71	71	71	213	6,500
Richard Lyon	70	73	72	215	5,200
Solly Sepeng	71	76	69	216	4,600
Daddy Naidoo	75	71	71	217	4,200
*Errol Mills	74	73	71	218	
Tertius Claassens	69	78	72	219	3,840
Denis Hutchinson	73	73	73	219	3,840
Harold Henning	75	75	70	220	3,480
Rinus van Niekerk	75	70	75	220	3,480
Joe Dlamini	74	73	74	221	3,260
Bobby Jones	74	74	75	223	3,140
Absolom Nkosi	76	74	74	224	2,960
*Duncan Lindsay-Smith	76	73	75	224	
Terry Westbrook	73	75	76	224	2,960
Muss Gammon	73	80	73	226	2,650
Colin Luckhoff	80	71	75	226	2,650
Peter Mkata	76	74	76	226	2,650
Hugh Inggs	75	73	78	226	2,650
Alex Manikum	77	79	71	227	2,360
Peter Loeb	77	77	73	227	2,360
Abel Khame	77	75	76	228	2,240
Vincent Tshabalala	78	76	75	229	2,045
Ian Smith	77	77	75	229	2,045
Geoffrey King	77	74	78	229	2,045
Shadrack Molefe	76	73	80	229	2,045

Vodacom Senior Classic

Dainfern Country Club, Johannesburg, South Africa — November 20-22
Par 36-36–72; 7,200 yards — purse, R450,000

	SCORES			TOTAL	MONEY
Solly Sepeng	69	64	68	201	R70,650
Simon Hobday	67	68	68	203	51,750
John Bland	69	67	68	204	36,000
Allan Henning	70	69	70	209	24,750
John Fourie	67	74	69	210	16,110
Tertius Claassens	71	68	71	210	16,110
Gary Player	68	70	72	210	16,110
John Howie	69	66	76	211	11,790
Gabriel Putsoe	71	71	71	213	9,990
Vincent Tshabalala	72	69	72	213	9,990
Richard Lyon	71	71	73	215	8,820
Daddy Naidoo	68	76	72	216	7,920
Harold Henning	76	68	72	216	7,920
John Mabe	73	74	70	217	6,975
Joe Dlamini	72	72	73	217	6,975
Bobby Verwey	72	75	71	218	6,412.50
Geoffrey King	75	71	72	218	6,412.50
Rinus van Niekerk	70	78	71	219	5,865
David Burd	70	74	75	219	5,865
Graham Henning	71	71	77	219	5,865
Lee Trevino	73	74	73	220	5,490
Ian Smith	75	71	75	221	5,220
Hugh Inggs	76	70	75	221	5,220
Emmanuel Maabane	76	73	74	223	4,950
Peter Mkata	77	75	72	224	4,680
Terry Westbrook	74	75	75	224	4,680
Pheyane Selepe	74	70	80	224	4,680
Gert van Biljon	74	74	77	225	4,410
Bobby Jones	74	76	76	226	4,275
Brian Ferreira	77	75	75	227	4,140

John Bland Invitational

Randpark Golf Club, Johannesburg, South Africa — November 25-27
Par 36-36–72; 7,373 yards — purse, R100,000

	SCORES			TOTAL	MONEY
Allan Henning	68	69	68	205	R15,700
John Fourie	70	65	70	205	11,500
(Henning defeated Fourie on first extra hole.)					
John Bland	68	67	72	207	8,000
Joe Dlamini	66	72	70	208	6,300
Simon Hobday	68	70	73	211	4,700
Harold Henning	69	74	70	213	3,800
Solly Sepeng	75	72	68	215	2,950
Bobby Verwey	73	68	74	215	2,950
Peter Mkata	71	75	70	216	2,350
Gabriel Putsoe	72	72	72	216	2,350
Tertius Claassens	73	71	73	217	2,050
Bobby Jones	73	71	73	217	2,050
Ian Smith	76	71	71	218	1,900
John Howie	73	72	75	220	1,713.33

	SCORES			TOTAL	MONEY
Obed Matlou	70	79	71	220	1,713.33
Vincent Tshabalala	74	75	71	220	1,713.33
John Mabe	71	76	74	221	1,500
Rinus van Niekerk	75	74	72	221	1,500
Chris Van Wyk	71	79	71	221	1,500
Pheyane Selepe	74	71	79	224	1,340
Muss Gammon	73	74	77	224	1,340
Patrick Madiba	79	75	70	224	1,340
David Burd	76	72	77	225	1,215
Thomas Ntebele	78	75	72	225	1,215
Richard Lyon	73	75	78	226	1,110
Mike Burraston	73	76	77	226	1,110
Daddy Naidoo	74	78	74	226	1,110
Terry Bloom	76	77	75	228	1,010
Graham Henning	74	81	73	228	1,010
Gert van Biljon	77	72	80	229	930
Shadrack Molefe	75	74	80	229	930
Alex Manikum	78	75	76	229	930

Women's Tours

HealthSouth Inaugural

Grand Cypress Resort, Orlando, Florida
Par 36-36–72; 6,220 yards

January 16-18
purse, $600,000

	SCORES			TOTAL	MONEY
Kelly Robbins	76	67	66	209	$90,000
Meg Mallon	71	71	69	211	55,855
Patty Sheehan	71	72	69	212	40,759
Dana Dormann	74	70	69	213	26,166
Jane Crafter	70	72	71	213	26,166
Juli Inkster	73	66	74	213	26,166
Michelle McGann	76	69	70	215	15,901
Donna Andrews	75	70	70	215	15,901
Jenny Lidback	69	73	73	215	15,901
Brandie Burton	73	74	69	216	11,573
Susie Redman	76	69	71	216	11,573
Kris Tschetter	74	67	75	216	11,573
Moira Dunn	77	73	67	217	8,815
Nancy Lopez	76	72	69	217	8,815
Amy Benz	73	74	70	217	8,815
Helen Alfredsson	76	70	71	217	8,815
Se Ri Pak	72	73	72	217	8,815
Lorie Kane	74	74	70	218	7,548
Pat Bradley	80	71	68	219	6,648
Alicia Dibos	75	74	70	219	6,648
Tina Barrett	75	73	71	219	6,648
Catriona Matthew	75	73	71	219	6,648
Jenny Jooeun Lee	72	75	72	219	6,648
Wendy Ward	76	76	68	220	5,494
Judy Dickinson	79	70	71	220	5,494
Nanci Bowen	76	73	71	220	5,494
Kristi Albers	78	69	73	220	5,494
Jill Briles-Hinton	72	73	75	220	5,494
Hollis Stacy	78	75	68	221	4,373
Cindy McCurdy	75	78	68	221	4,373
Barb Mucha	80	72	69	221	4,373
Liselotte Neumann	75	76	70	221	4,373
Jackie Gallagher-Smith	81	69	71	221	4,373
Kate Golden	76	73	72	221	4,373
Terry-Jo Myers	74	75	72	221	4,373
Becky Iverson	77	71	73	221	4,373

Office Depot

Ibis Golf & Country Club, West Palm Beach, Florida
Par 36-36–72; 6,323 yards

January 21-24
purse, $600,000

	SCORES				TOTAL	MONEY
Helen Alfredsson	68	71	67	71	277	$90,000
Liselotte Neumann	70	70	71	68	279	55,855
Kelly Robbins	72	70	73	67	282	27,414

	SCORES				TOTAL	MONEY
Michelle McGann	72	68	75	67	282	27,414
Tracy Hanson	70	73	69	70	282	27,414
Pat Hurst	67	75	67	73	282	27,414
Wendy Ward	69	68	71	74	282	27,414
Kris Monaghan	72	69	69	73	283	15,700
Mayumi Hirase	72	75	68	69	284	12,227
Cindy Rarick	70	73	72	69	284	12,227
Betsy King	72	71	71	70	284	12,227
Tammie Green	72	70	68	74	284	12,227
Donna Andrews	71	72	71	71	285	9,057
Lisa Hackney	71	71	72	71	285	9,057
Tina Barrett	70	69	74	72	285	9,057
Maggie Halpin	69	72	69	75	285	9,057
Lorie Kane	72	74	71	69	286	7,698
Laura Davies	71	70	69	76	286	7,698
Dawn Coe-Jones	73	73	66	75	287	7,246
Alicia Dibos	68	76	76	68	288	6,145
Barb Mucha	74	72	72	70	288	6,145
Rosie Jones	74	74	69	71	288	6,145
Jane Crafter	74	74	68	72	288	6,145
Cindy Figg-Currier	76	71	69	72	288	6,145
Charlotta Sorenstam	73	73	69	73	288	6,145
Meg Mallon	67	74	73	74	288	6,145
Kathryn Marshall	74	74	70	71	289	5,222
Gail Graham	74	74	65	76	289	5,222
Jane Geddes	75	72	69	74	290	4,951
Karen Weiss	71	79	71	70	291	4,291
Penny Hammel	72	74	74	71	291	4,291
Trish Johnson	72	72	76	71	291	4,291
Dale Eggeling	70	73	76	72	291	4,291
Chris Johnson	72	72	74	73	291	4,291
Marianne Morris	70	73	74	74	291	4,291
Emilee Klein	73	74	68	76	291	4,291

Los Angeles Women's Championship

Oakmont Country Club, Glendale, California — February 13-15
Par 36-36–72; 6,276 yards — purse, $650,000
(Third round cancelled — rain.)

	SCORES		TOTAL	MONEY
Dale Eggeling	72	69	141	$97,500
Hiromi Kobayashi	67	74	141	60,510
(Eggeling defeated Kobayashi on first extra hole.)				
Cindy McCurdy	72	70	142	35,433
Karrie Webb	72	70	142	35,433
Elaine Crosby	70	72	142	35,433
Cindy Figg-Currier	74	69	143	16,043
Shelley Hamlin	72	71	143	16,043
Vicki Fergon	72	71	143	16,043
Laura Davies	72	71	143	16,043
Pat Hurst	72	71	143	16,043
Nancy Lopez	71	72	143	16,043
Annika Sorenstam	71	72	143	16,043
Dottie Pepper	71	73	144	10,198
Helen Alfredsson	71	73	144	10,198
Janice Moodie	70	74	144	10,198
Colleen Walker	74	71	145	7,908

	SCORES		TOTAL	MONEY
Tammie Green	74	71	145	7,908
Joan Pitcock	73	72	145	7,908
Tracy Hanson	73	72	145	7,908
Michelle Estill	72	73	145	7,908
Leigh Ann Mills	72	73	145	7,908
Karen Weiss	70	75	145	7,908
Trish Johnson	74	72	146	6,016
Lorie Kane	74	72	146	6,016
Rachel Hetherington	74	72	146	6,016
Laurie Brower	73	73	146	6,016
Danielle Ammaccapane	72	74	146	6,016
Charlotta Sorenstam	72	74	146	6,016
Wendy Ward	71	75	146	6,016
Patty Sheehan	76	71	147	4,873
Akiko Fukushima	75	72	147	4,873
Kristi Albers	74	73	147	4,873
Eva Dahllof	74	73	147	4,873
Julie Piers	72	75	147	4,873

Cup Noodles Hawaiian Ladies Open

Kapolei Golf Course, Kapolei, Oahu, Hawaii — February 19-21
Par 36-36–72; 6,100 yards — purse, $650,000

	SCORES			TOTAL	MONEY
Wendy Ward	65	69	70	204	$97,500
Dana Dormann	66	66	72	204	60,510
(Ward defeated Dormann on first extra hole.)					
Laura Davies	68	68	69	205	44,156
Kristi Albers	68	69	69	206	28,346
Annika Sorenstam	69	67	70	206	28,346
Brandie Burton	67	69	70	206	28,346
Meg Mallon	69	67	71	207	19,297
Wendy Doolan	71	68	69	208	16,190
Karen Weiss	70	69	69	208	16,190
Chris Johnson	68	72	69	209	12,145
Jane Geddes	69	70	70	209	12,145
Lisa Hackney	69	67	73	209	12,145
Dale Eggeling	68	67	74	209	12,145
Tina Barrett	69	72	69	210	9,086
Jenn Kangas	68	71	71	210	9,086
Donna Andrews	72	66	72	210	9,086
Cindy Rarick	68	70	72	210	9,086
Hiromi Kobayashi	68	69	73	210	9,086
Liselotte Neumann	72	68	71	211	7,418
Natsuko Noro	73	66	72	211	7,418
Eva Dahllof	71	68	72	211	7,418
Tracy Hanson	69	67	75	211	7,418
Rachel Hetherington	69	70	73	212	6,518
Jackie Gallagher-Smith	69	70	73	212	6,518
Kelly Robbins	73	71	69	213	5,619
Lora Fairclough	73	70	70	213	5,619
Mayumi Hirase	71	72	70	213	5,619
Catrin Nilsmark	70	72	71	213	5,619
Maggie Halpin	71	70	72	213	5,619
Michelle Dobek	70	70	73	213	5,619
Amy Benz	70	70	73	213	5,619

Welch's/Circle K Championship

Randolf North Golf Course, Tucson, Arizona — March 12-15
Par 35-37–72; 6,222 yards — purse, $500,000

	SCORES				TOTAL	MONEY
Helen Alfredsson	68	64	70	72	274	$75,000
Liselotte Neumann	71	69	67	68	275	40,256
Dana Dormann	70	68	68	69	275	40,256
Dottie Pepper	70	67	69	70	276	23,902
Chris Johnson	69	67	67	73	276	23,902
Donna Andrews	71	71	68	67	277	12,915
Cindy Figg-Currier	70	70	70	67	277	12,915
Amy Fruhwirth	73	69	67	68	277	12,915
Rosie Jones	71	68	69	69	277	12,915
Lorie Kane	70	68	69	70	277	12,915
Charlotta Sorenstam	69	67	71	70	277	12,915
Susie Redman	73	68	70	67	278	7,072
Hollis Stacy	69	72	68	69	278	7,072
Kim Bauer	70	69	70	69	278	7,072
Smriti Mehra	67	72	70	69	278	7,072
Karrie Webb	67	70	72	69	278	7,072
Tammie Green	73	67	68	70	278	7,072
Nancy Lopez	72	68	68	70	278	7,072
Moira Dunn	71	67	69	71	278	7,072
Brandie Burton	70	68	69	71	278	7,072
Cathy Johnston-Forbes	70	72	73	64	279	5,097
Carin Koch	67	72	72	68	279	5,097
Hiromi Kobayashi	71	70	69	69	279	5,097
Kristi Albers	75	62	71	71	279	5,097
Juli Inkster	72	65	71	71	279	5,097
Wendy Ward	73	68	71	68	280	3,924
Marianne Morris	71	70	71	68	280	3,924
Lisa Hackney	70	68	74	68	280	3,924
Janice Moodie	69	68	75	68	280	3,924
Cindy Rarick	71	69	71	69	280	3,924
Patty Sheehan	70	70	70	70	280	3,924
Pat Hurst	71	68	71	70	280	3,924
Maggie Halpin	69	73	67	71	280	3,924
Luciana Bemvenuti	72	67	68	73	280	3,924
Tina Barrett	67	69	70	74	280	3,924

Standard Register Ping

Moon Valley Country Club, Phoenix, Arizona — March 19-22
Par 36-37–73; 6,435 yards — purse, $850,000

	SCORES				TOTAL	MONEY
Liselotte Neumann	69	67	69	74	279	$127,500
Rosie Jones	70	72	67	70	279	79,129
(Neumann defeated Jones on third extra hole.)						
Cathy Johnston-Forbes	71	71	69	69	280	57,743
Lorie Kane	71	72	71	67	281	37,069
Donna Andrews	74	71	67	69	281	37,069
Annika Sorenstam	72	68	72	69	281	37,069
Jackie Gallagher-Smith	69	72	70	71	282	23,738
Helen Alfredsson	69	70	72	71	282	23,738
Jane Crafter	72	68	73	70	283	17,329

	SCORES				TOTAL	MONEY
Michelle McGann	71	69	71	72	283	17,329
Cindy Figg-Currier	67	72	71	73	283	17,329
Juli Inkster	74	64	72	73	283	17,329
Charlotta Sorenstam	75	71	71	67	284	13,273
Wendy Ward	73	68	72	71	284	13,273
Meg Mallon	70	69	73	72	284	13,273
Laura Davies	70	77	69	69	285	10,492
Sherri Steinhauer	73	74	68	70	285	10,492
Vickie Odegard	72	68	75	70	285	10,492
Deb Richard	72	71	71	71	285	10,492
Penny Hammel	70	70	73	72	285	10,492
Chris Johnson	74	70	67	74	285	10,492
Jane Geddes	69	75	73	69	286	8,638
Catrin Nilsmark	74	68	73	71	286	8,638
Tammie Green	73	70	70	73	286	8,638
Amy Fruhwirth	74	73	70	70	287	7,541
Pat Hurst	73	71	73	70	287	7,541
Brandie Burton	72	73	71	71	287	7,541
Diane Barnard	70	73	71	73	287	7,541
Tina Barrett	69	72	73	73	287	7,541
Kelly Robbins	71	75	71	71	288	6,201
Danielle Ammaccapane	74	73	69	72	288	6,201
Betsy King	72	72	72	72	288	6,201
Emilee Klein	70	73	72	73	288	6,201
Tracy Hanson	73	65	76	74	288	6,201
Dottie Pepper	71	71	71	75	288	6,201

Nabisco Dinah Shore

Mission Hills Country Club, Rancho Mirage, California — March 26-29
Par 36-36–72; 6,460 yards — purse, $1,000,000

	SCORES				TOTAL	MONEY
Pat Hurst	68	72	70	71	281	$150,000
Helen Dobson	70	74	71	67	282	93,093
Laura Davies	75	70	70	68	283	60,385
Helen Alfredsson	70	73	70	70	283	60,385
Donna Andrews	71	72	71	70	284	38,998
Liselotte Neumann	69	71	71	73	284	38,998
Annika Sorenstam	76	71	69	70	286	27,928
Karrie Webb	71	72	70	73	286	27,928
Dottie Pepper	73	72	74	68	287	22,393
Sherri Steinhauer	69	76	71	71	287	22,393
Amy Fruhwirth	73	71	73	71	288	18,438
Dawn Coe-Jones	70	72	74	72	288	18,438
Catriona Matthew	75	74	70	70	289	15,670
Penny Hammel	73	72	71	73	289	15,670
Nancy Lopez	71	71	73	74	289	15,670
Meg Mallon	75	69	76	70	290	13,658
*Beth Bauer	76	70	72	72	290	
Lorie Kane	76	71	74	70	291	12,147
Rosie Jones	75	66	78	72	291	12,147
JoAnne Carner	73	72	73	73	291	12,147
Muffin Spencer-Devlin	72	70	76	73	291	12,147
Lisa Hackney	71	71	73	76	291	12,147
*Grace Park	77	73	71	71	292	
Emilee Klein	76	74	73	70	293	9,256

	SCORES				TOTAL	MONEY
Juli Inkster	74	75	74	70	293	9,256
Cindy Figg-Currier	74	72	77	70	293	9,256
Becky Iverson	74	72	77	70	293	9,256
Barb Mucha	72	75	74	72	293	9,256
Tammie Green	72	72	76	73	293	9,256
Danielle Ammaccapane	75	73	71	74	293	9,256
Michelle McGann	74	71	72	76	293	9,256
Mayumi Hirase	73	69	73	78	293	9,256

Longs Drugs Challenge

Twelve Bridges Golf Club, Lincoln, California — April 2-5
Par 36-36–72; 6,412 yards — purse, $600,000

	SCORES				TOTAL	MONEY
Donna Andrews	70	69	70	69	278	$90,000
Carin Koch	66	70	73	70	279	55,855
Annika Sorenstam	73	73	66	70	282	40,759
Luciana Bemvenuti	73	72	71	67	283	28,682
Barb Mucha	74	65	71	73	283	28,682
Brandie Burton	70	73	74	68	285	17,209
Tracy Hanson	73	72	71	69	285	17,209
Chris Johnson	75	70	72	68	285	17,209
Mayumi Hirase	72	71	70	72	285	17,209
Cindy McCurdy	70	70	75	71	286	12,681
Se Ri Pak	74	75	72	66	287	11,504
Alicia Dibos	75	69	71	73	288	9,138
Alison Nicholas	71	74	74	69	288	9,138
Lorie Kane	73	70	74	71	288	9,138
Dana Dormann	75	70	74	69	288	9,138
Stefania Croce	75	71	70	72	288	9,138
Hiromi Kobayashi	73	71	74	70	288	9,138
Amy Benz	72	74	69	74	289	7,126
Charlotta Sorenstam	72	74	71	72	289	7,126
Dottie Pepper	75	73	71	70	289	7,126
Pat Bradley	71	74	73	71	289	7,126
Cindy Figg-Currier	73	72	75	70	290	5,822
Jan Stephenson	70	73	76	71	290	5,822
Caroline Blaylock	72	74	71	73	290	5,822
Sherri Steinhauer	73	72	72	73	290	5,822
Patty Sheehan	75	74	71	70	290	5,822
Rosie Jones	72	71	74	73	290	5,822
Kim Saiki	75	75	74	67	291	4,567
Mhairi McKay	76	73	73	69	291	4,567
Marta Figueras-Dotti	76	74	72	69	291	4,567
Cindy Rarick	74	72	75	70	291	4,567
Katie Peterson	75	72	73	71	291	4,567
Nancy Scranton	72	74	72	73	291	4,567
Catriona Matthew	74	71	76	70	291	4,567
Janice Moodie	76	72	69	74	291	4,567

City of Hope Myrtle Beach Classic

Wachesaw East Golf Club, Myrtle Beach, South Carolina — April 16-19
Par 36-36–72; 6,231 yards — purse, $600,000

	SCORES				TOTAL	MONEY
Karrie Webb	68	66	68	67	269	$90,000
Meg Mallon	62	73	68	69	272	55,855
Dottie Pepper	73	68	68	64	273	40,759
Liselotte Neumann	70	74	63	67	274	28,682
Janice Moodie	69	69	67	69	274	28,682
Kelly Robbins	70	70	71	64	275	17,209
Lorie Kane	72	68	70	65	275	17,209
Catrin Nilsmark	66	68	73	68	275	17,209
Tina Barrett	70	69	66	70	275	17,209
Dina Ammaccapane	69	70	68	70	277	12,082
Jane Crafter	68	69	70	70	277	12,082
Hollis Stacy	67	73	72	66	278	9,671
Emilee Klein	70	70	68	70	278	9,671
Helen Alfredsson	69	70	69	70	278	9,671
Cindy McCurdy	65	71	70	72	278	9,671
Luciana Bemvenuti	68	71	68	72	279	8,162
Dawn Coe-Jones	73	69	70	68	280	7,708
Sherri Steinhauer	69	68	72	71	280	7,708
Kristi Albers	73	72	68	68	281	6,658
Vickie Odegard	70	71	70	70	281	6,658
Jan Stephenson	71	69	71	70	281	6,658
Danielle Ammaccapane	70	70	68	73	281	6,658
Pat Hurst	67	70	71	73	281	6,658
Joanne Morley	72	70	70	70	282	5,595
Lisa Hackney	71	68	73	70	282	5,595
Joan Pitcock	72	70	67	73	282	5,595
Terry-Jo Myers	71	68	67	76	282	5,595
Laura Davies	70	72	73	68	283	4,704
Julie Piers	75	68	70	70	283	4,704
Angie Ridgeway	69	73	70	71	283	4,704
Elaine Crosby	70	70	72	71	283	4,704
Alicia Dibos	75	67	69	72	283	4,704
Deb Richard	76	66	68	73	283	4,704

Chick-fil-A Charity Championship

Eagle's Landing Country Club, Stockbridge, Georgia — April 24-26
Par 36-36–72; 6,187 yards — purse, $700,000

	SCORES			TOTAL	MONEY
Liselotte Neumann	67	65	70	202	$105,000
Lorie Kane	70	68	67	205	56,359
Dottie Pepper	68	68	69	205	56,359
Barb Mucha	70	68	68	206	33,462
Vickie Odegard	70	67	69	206	33,462
Nancy Ramsbottom	66	72	69	207	24,656
Alison Nicholas	69	70	69	208	19,549
Pat Hurst	65	70	73	208	19,549
Rosie Jones	72	69	68	209	15,674
Dawn Coe-Jones	72	68	69	209	15,674
Chris Johnson	72	67	71	210	12,880
Michelle Estill	68	67	75	210	12,880

	SCORES			TOTAL	MONEY
Betsy King	69	74	68	211	11,295
Dale Eggeling	69	72	70	211	11,295
Barb Whitehead	72	71	69	212	8,880
Helen Alfredsson	70	72	70	212	8,880
Val Skinner	74	67	71	212	8,880
Karrie Webb	73	68	71	212	8,880
Donna Andrews	69	72	71	212	8,880
Caroline McMillan	70	70	72	212	8,880
Charlotta Sorenstam	69	71	72	212	8,880
Cindy McCurdy	73	71	69	213	6,779
Catriona Matthew	71	72	70	213	6,779
Se Ri Pak	70	72	71	213	6,779
Jenn Kangas	69	73	71	213	6,779
Danielle Ammaccapane	72	68	73	213	6,779
Hiromi Kobayashi	71	69	73	213	6,779
Laurie Rinker-Graham	73	69	72	214	5,799
Brandie Burton	73	69	72	214	5,799
Meg Mallon	70	70	74	214	5,799

Mercury Titleholders Championship

LPGA International, Daytona Beach, Florida — April 30-May 3
Par 36-36–72; 6,393 yards — purse, $1,000,000

	SCORES				TOTAL	MONEY
Danielle Ammaccapane	70	68	67	71	276	$150,000
Michelle Estill	68	71	69	69	277	93,093
Annika Sorenstam	67	69	69	73	278	67,933
Carin Koch	69	68	68	74	279	52,837
Chris Johnson	68	68	73	71	280	42,772
Catrin Nilsmark	69	68	74	70	281	27,173
Dawn Coe-Jones	65	70	74	72	281	27,173
Eva Dahllof	66	71	71	73	281	27,173
Lorie Kane	71	68	67	75	281	27,173
Donna Andrews	70	68	68	75	281	27,173
Charlotta Sorenstam	70	73	68	71	282	19,174
Gail Graham	70	73	71	69	283	15,651
Kristi Albers	71	70	73	69	283	15,651
Jenny Lidback	71	70	70	72	283	15,651
Dana Dormann	67	72	71	73	283	15,651
Mayumi Hirase	67	72	69	75	283	15,651
Julie Piers	72	69	75	68	284	11,404
Nancy Scranton	69	73	73	69	284	11,404
Suzanne Strudwick	70	71	73	70	284	11,404
Penny Hammel	74	68	71	71	284	11,404
Stefania Croce	70	72	71	71	284	11,404
Missie McGeorge	67	75	71	71	284	11,404
Hollis Stacy	70	70	72	72	284	11,404
Kris Monaghan	67	69	71	77	284	11,404
Sherri Steinhauer	71	68	79	67	285	8,320
Leslie Spalding	72	71	71	71	285	8,320
Stephanie Lowe	71	72	71	71	285	8,320
Pat Hurst	65	74	74	72	285	8,320
Cindy Figg-Currier	72	70	70	73	285	8,320
Kim Saiki	69	71	72	73	285	8,320
Kelli Kuehne	70	69	73	73	285	8,320
Amy Alcott	71	69	71	74	285	8,320
Lisa Walters	71	69	70	75	285	8,320

Sara Lee Classic

Hermitage Golf Course, Old Hickory, Tennessee — May 8-10
Par 36-36–72; 6,290 yards — purse, $750,000

	SCORES			TOTAL	MONEY
Barb Mucha	67	69	69	205	$112,500
Donna Andrews	65	73	67	205	53,465
Nancy Lopez	66	71	68	205	53,465
Jenny Lidback	72	63	70	205	53,465
(Mucha won on second extra hole.)					
Meg Mallon	69	70	67	206	23,625
Jennifer Feldott	69	70	67	206	23,625
Pat Hurst	70	68	68	206	23,625
Cindy Figg-Currier	69	69	68	206	23,625
Rachel Hetherington	67	68	71	206	23,625
Annika Sorenstam	73	68	66	207	13,963
Dale Eggeling	71	69	67	207	13,963
Juli Inkster	70	69	68	207	13,963
Marianne Morris	69	67	71	207	13,963
Kris Monaghan	72	68	68	208	9,765
Lisa Kiggens	72	68	68	208	9,765
Cathy Johnston-Forbes	70	70	68	208	9,765
Vickie Odegard	69	71	68	208	9,765
Catriona Matthew	69	71	68	208	9,765
Carin Koch	69	70	69	208	9,765
Becky Iverson	72	66	70	208	9,765
Dottie Pepper	72	64	72	208	9,765
Susie Redman	73	68	68	209	7,358
Suzanne Strudwick	71	67	71	209	7,358
Lora Fairclough	71	67	71	209	7,358
Amy Read	70	68	71	209	7,358
Kate Golden	70	68	71	209	7,358
Colleen Walker	72	67	71	210	6,189
Corinne Dibnah	72	67	71	210	6,189
Chris Johnson	70	69	71	210	6,189
Moira Dunn	69	70	71	210	6,189
Missie Berteotti	72	66	72	210	6,189

McDonald's LPGA Championship

DuPont Country Club, Wilmington, Delaware — May 14-17
Par 35-36–71; 6,386 yards — purse, $1,300,000

	SCORES				TOTAL	MONEY
Se Ri Pak	65	68	72	68	273	$195,000
Donna Andrews	71	67	69	69	276	104,666
Lisa Hackney	70	66	69	71	276	104,666
Karrie Webb	71	73	67	66	277	62,145
Wendy Ward	71	67	69	70	277	62,145
Meg Mallon	71	69	68	70	278	39,467
Chris Johnson	69	71	67	71	278	39,467
Emilee Klein	72	67	68	71	278	39,467
Catrin Nilsmark	69	73	70	67	279	29,110
Kelly Robbins	69	71	68	71	279	29,110
Joan Pitcock	69	75	70	66	280	23,180
Annette DeLuca	70	70	71	69	280	23,180
Jane Geddes	69	69	70	72	280	23,180

	SCORES				TOTAL	MONEY
Tammie Green	72	68	70	71	281	19,691
Lisa Walters	66	69	73	73	281	19,691
Maria Hjorth	71	70	73	68	282	17,402
Juli Inkster	70	71	69	72	282	17,402
Michele Redman	70	71	74	68	283	15,767
Carin Koch	71	73	69	70	283	15,767
Cathy Johnston-Forbes	71	70	70	72	283	15,767
Janice Moodie	75	69	73	67	284	13,558
Helen Dobson	76	70	70	68	284	13,558
Pat Hurst	71	73	68	72	284	13,558
Jenny Lidback	70	73	68	73	284	13,558
Dana Dormann	71	74	74	66	285	11,579
Michelle McGann	68	74	73	70	285	11,579
Nancy Scranton	73	73	67	72	285	11,579
Susie Redman	68	76	69	72	285	11,579
Dale Eggeling	68	69	74	74	285	11,579
Wendy Doolan	73	72	71	70	286	9,365
Vickie Odegard	69	74	73	70	286	9,365
Annika Sorenstam	73	71	71	71	286	9,365
Rachel Hetherington	71	71	72	72	286	9,365
Lorie Kane	72	73	68	73	286	9,365
Kris Tschetter	71	71	71	73	286	9,365
Joanne Morley	73	69	69	75	286	9,365

Corning Classic

Corning Country Club, Corning, New York — May 21-24
Par 36-36–72; 6,062 yards — purse, $700,000

	SCORES				TOTAL	MONEY
Tammie Green	67	70	66	65	268	$105,000
Emilee Klein	71	69	68	67	275	56,359
Brandie Burton	68	66	71	70	275	56,359
Penny Hammel	70	70	71	67	278	36,985
Sherri Steinhauer	74	69	69	67	279	22,049
Gail Graham	71	71	68	69	279	22,049
Mardi Lunn	72	70	67	70	279	22,049
Dottie Pepper	70	68	71	70	279	22,049
Helen Alfredsson	69	70	68	72	279	22,049
Suzanne Strudwick	73	70	70	67	280	13,080
Hollis Stacy	69	73	71	67	280	13,080
Maria Hjorth	71	71	68	70	280	13,080
Rosie Jones	73	66	71	70	280	13,080
Val Skinner	74	71	70	66	281	10,278
Jan Stephenson	70	72	69	70	281	10,278
Caroline McMillan	73	67	71	70	281	10,278
Nanci Bowen	72	71	69	70	282	8,693
Jane Geddes	69	72	70	71	282	8,693
Kathryn Marshall	71	67	73	71	282	8,693
Stephanie Lowe	68	69	72	73	282	8,693
Alicia Dibos	72	71	72	68	283	6,848
Pat Bradley	72	71	70	70	283	6,848
Melissa McNamara	70	69	74	70	283	6,848
Amy Benz	72	68	71	72	283	6,848
Catrin Nilsmark	70	68	73	72	283	6,848
Janice Moodie	73	72	65	73	283	6,848
Cristie Kerr	70	69	71	73	283	6,848

	SCORES				TOTAL	MONEY
Susan Florin	71	70	68	74	283	6,848
Karen Lunn	73	71	72	68	284	4,898
Cindy McCurdy	73	71	71	69	284	4,898
Kristi Albers	69	72	74	69	284	4,898
Kate Golden	73	67	75	69	284	4,898
Kris Monaghan	71	73	70	70	284	4,898
Carolyn Hill	74	71	68	71	284	4,898
Corinne Dibnah	71	68	74	71	284	4,898
Mayumi Hirase	75	67	69	73	284	4,898
Vickie Odegard	69	72	70	73	284	4,898
Susie Redman	69	71	70	74	284	4,898
Nancy Harvey	72	67	69	76	284	4,898

Wegmans Rochester International

Locust Hill Country Club, Pittsford, New York — May 28-31
Par 35-37–72; 6,162 yards — purse, $700,000

	SCORES				TOTAL	MONEY
Rosie Jones	74	69	64	72	279	$105,000
Juli Inkster	71	68	74	68	281	65,165
Hollis Stacy	74	67	71	70	282	47,553
Meg Mallon	71	73	72	67	283	30,527
Moira Dunn	67	72	73	71	283	30,527
Sherri Steinhauer	74	71	66	72	283	30,527
Alicia Dibos	71	74	68	71	284	20,782
Lisa Walters	71	70	72	72	285	18,316
Nancy Ramsbottom	73	74	71	68	286	14,271
Lorie Kane	73	71	71	71	286	14,271
Dottie Pepper	73	71	69	73	286	14,271
Jenny Lidback	71	71	70	74	286	14,271
Missie McGeorge	74	69	71	73	287	11,283
Dale Eggeling	72	71	69	75	287	11,283
Amy Read	75	73	71	69	288	9,639
Nancy Lopez	76	70	71	71	288	9,639
Eva Dahllof	71	69	74	74	288	9,639
Cristie Kerr	73	75	70	71	289	7,942
Betsy King	71	77	70	71	289	7,942
Rachel Hetherington	76	71	70	72	289	7,942
Beth Daniel	72	71	74	72	289	7,942
Shelley Hamlin	71	71	72	75	289	7,942
Joan Pitcock	67	72	75	75	289	7,942
Sally Little	74	71	72	73	290	6,633
Nancy Scranton	72	72	71	75	290	6,633
Dawn Coe-Jones	68	73	74	75	290	6,633
Cindy Figg-Currier	73	73	73	72	291	5,893
Janice Gibson	70	76	72	73	291	5,893
Caroline McMillan	76	69	73	73	291	5,893
Brandie Burton	68	71	78	74	291	5,893

Michelob Light Classic

Forest Hills Country Club, St. Louis, Missouri — June 5-7
Par 36-36–72; 6,337 yards — purse, $600,000

	SCORES			TOTAL	MONEY
Annika Sorenstam	67	73	68	208	$90,000
Donna Andrews	72	66	70	208	55,855
(Sorenstam defeated Andrews on second extra hole.)					
Sara Hallock	74	68	69	211	40,759
Lorie Kane	71	76	67	214	28,682
Pat Hurst	75	70	69	214	28,682
Jackie Gallagher-Smith	71	72	72	215	21,134
Muffin Spencer-Devlin	73	76	67	216	12,718
Allison Finney	73	72	71	216	12,718
Caroline Keggi	72	72	72	216	12,718
Stephanie Lowe	70	74	72	216	12,718
Karrie Webb	74	69	73	216	12,718
Cindy McCurdy	71	72	73	216	12,718
Lori West	71	71	74	216	12,718
Caroline McMillan	68	73	75	216	12,718
Julie Piers	74	74	69	217	8,076
Juli Inkster	73	74	70	217	8,076
Caroline Blaylock	72	73	72	217	8,076
Cindy Figg-Currier	71	70	76	217	8,076
*Marisa Baena	69	73	75	217	
Nanci Bowen	76	72	70	218	6,516
Barb Mucha	76	71	71	218	6,516
Vicki Fergon	76	70	72	218	6,516
Chris Johnson	71	75	72	218	6,516
Kate Golden	71	75	72	218	6,516
Kelly Robbins	76	69	73	218	6,516
Meg Mallon	73	75	71	219	5,403
Cindy Mueller	75	71	73	219	5,403
Se Ri Pak	72	74	73	219	5,403
Laurie Rinker-Graham	70	73	76	219	5,403
Emilee Klein	76	74	70	220	4,528
Kristi Albers	73	77	70	220	4,528
Pearl Sinn	78	70	72	220	4,528
Dale Eggeling	73	72	75	220	4,528
Dana Dormann	73	72	75	220	4,528
Jean Bartholomew	71	72	77	220	4,528

Oldsmobile Classic

Walnut Hills Country Club, East Lansing, Michigan — June 11-14
Par 36-36–72; 6,191 yards — purse, $650,000

	SCORES				TOTAL	MONEY
Lisa Walters	67	67	65	66	265	$97,500
Donna Andrews	64	68	72	67	271	60,510
Karrie Webb	66	70	69	67	272	44,156
Lisa Hackney	68	73	69	68	278	31,072
Emilee Klein	69	68	71	70	278	31,072
Dottie Pepper	67	73	72	67	279	18,643
Pat Hurst	68	72	71	68	279	18,643
Karen Weiss	70	66	73	70	279	18,643
Meg Mallon	69	66	74	70	279	18,643

	SCORES				TOTAL	MONEY
Vicki Fergon	77	69	69	65	280	13,083
Cindy Figg-Currier	69	70	69	72	280	13,083
Liselotte Neumann	71	72	73	65	281	9,194
Dina Ammaccapane	67	74	74	66	281	9,194
Liz Earley	71	73	69	68	281	9,194
Janice Moodie	71	69	73	68	281	9,194
Dana Dormann	74	69	69	69	281	9,194
Jenny Lidback	67	73	72	69	281	9,194
Wendy Ward	67	72	73	69	281	9,194
Val Skinner	66	72	73	70	281	9,194
Becky Iverson	68	74	68	71	281	9,194
Kelly Robbins	73	72	70	67	282	6,514
Hiromi Kobayashi	73	73	68	68	282	6,514
Barb Mucha	73	69	72	68	282	6,514
Julie Piers	68	68	76	70	282	6,514
Karen Noble	70	72	69	71	282	6,514
Muffin Spencer-Devlin	70	67	71	74	282	6,514
Erika Wicoff	72	71	75	65	283	5,658
Susie Redman	71	72	72	68	283	5,658
Dale Eggeling	70	76	69	69	284	5,167
Mary Beth Zimmerman	67	77	71	69	284	5,167
Jane Geddes	68	74	70	72	284	5,167

Friendly's Classic

Crestview Country Club, Agawam, Massachusetts — June 18-21
Par 36-36–72; 6,381 yards — purse, $600,000

	SCORES				TOTAL	MONEY
Amy Fruhwirth	69	71	68	72	280	$90,000
Charlotta Sorenstam	69	70	73	70	282	48,307
Kim Saiki	72	71	68	71	282	48,307
Pamela Kometani	73	68	70	72	283	31,702
Nancy Scranton	72	73	70	69	284	17,863
Sherri Steinhauer	76	67	72	69	284	17,863
Maria Hjorth	70	75	69	70	284	17,863
Rosie Jones	72	71	70	71	284	17,863
Lisa Kiggens	72	72	68	72	284	17,863
Heather Daly-Donofrio	67	71	73	73	284	17,863
Karen Noble	72	75	68	70	285	10,340
Corinne Dibnah	71	73	71	70	285	10,340
Danielle Ammaccapane	71	70	71	73	285	10,340
Chris Johnson	73	68	70	74	285	10,340
Catrin Nilsmark	72	74	70	70	286	8,076
Christy Erb	69	69	77	71	286	8,076
Ji Hyun Suh	69	72	72	73	286	8,076
Brandie Burton	72	72	67	75	286	8,076
Erika Wicoff	73	73	72	69	287	6,283
Missie Berteotti	75	67	75	70	287	6,283
Catriona Matthew	72	74	69	72	287	6,283
Mitzi Edge	74	72	68	73	287	6,283
Lisa Walters	71	72	71	73	287	6,283
Janice Moodie	72	71	70	74	287	6,283
Leigh Ann Mills	71	71	70	75	287	6,283
Marilyn Lovander	69	68	74	76	287	6,283
*Grace Park	75	69	71	72	287	
Cindy McCurdy	71	72	75	70	288	5,132

	SCORES				TOTAL	MONEY
Joanne Morley	74	73	69	72	288	5,132
Leslie Spalding	71	72	73	72	288	5,132

ShopRite Classic

Marriott Seaview Resort, Bay Course, Atlantic City, New Jersey
Par 36-35–71; 6,024 yards

June 26-28
purse, $1,000,000

	SCORES			TOTAL	MONEY
Annika Sorenstam	66	65	65	196	$150,000
Juli Inkster	67	66	67	200	93,093
Lorie Kane	69	67	67	203	67,933
Helen Dobson	71	68	65	204	52,837
Lisa Walters	70	67	68	205	33,463
Kelly Robbins	69	67	69	205	33,463
Donna Andrews	68	68	69	205	33,463
Tina Barrett	66	69	70	205	33,463
Dina Ammaccapane	70	69	67	206	22,393
Rosie Jones	67	69	70	206	22,393
Karrie Webb	72	71	64	207	17,286
Anna Acker-Macosko	69	71	67	207	17,286
Luciana Bemvenuti	67	71	69	207	17,286
Alicia Dibos	66	72	69	207	17,286
Nanci Bowen	70	70	68	208	13,512
Barb Mucha	68	71	69	208	13,512
Becky Iverson	70	68	70	208	13,512
Dawn Coe-Jones	71	65	72	208	13,512
Tammie Green	67	73	69	209	10,912
Suzanne Strudwick	70	69	70	209	10,912
Beth Daniel	68	71	70	209	10,912
Wendy Ward	68	71	70	209	10,912
Vickie Odegard	70	67	72	209	10,912
Caroline McMillan	66	71	72	209	10,912
Jackie Gallagher-Smith	72	71	67	210	8,047
Nancy Scranton	72	70	68	210	8,047
Kim Saiki	71	70	69	210	8,047
Wendy Doolan	71	70	69	210	8,047
Liselotte Neumann	68	73	69	210	8,047
Marianne Morris	68	73	69	210	8,047
Amy Alcott	70	70	70	210	8,047
Emilee Klein	70	70	70	210	8,047
Kristi Coats	69	71	70	210	8,047
Helen Alfredsson	70	68	72	210	8,047
Moira Dunn	66	71	73	210	8,047

U.S. Women's Open

Blackwolf Run Golf Course, Kohler, Wisconsin
Par 35-36–71; 6,412 yards

July 2-5
purse, $1,500,000

	SCORES				TOTAL	MONEY
Se Ri Pak	69	70	75	76	290	$267,500
*Jenny Chuasiriporn	72	71	75	72	290	

(Pak defeated Chuasiriporn on 20th hole of Monday playoff.)

	SCORES				TOTAL	MONEY
Liselotte Neumann	70	70	75	76	291	157,500
Danielle Ammaccapane	76	71	74	71	292	77,351
Pat Hurst	69	75	75	73	292	77,351
Chris Johnson	72	70	76	74	292	77,351
Stefania Croce	74	71	76	72	293	46,736
Tammie Green	73	71	76	73	293	46,736
Mhairi McKay	72	70	73	78	293	46,736
Trish Johnson	73	71	77	73	294	39,015
Laura Davies	68	75	78	74	295	34,929
Dottie Pepper	71	71	78	75	295	34,929
Helen Alfredsson	75	75	73	73	296	30,684
Carin Koch	72	74	77	73	296	30,684
Hollis Stacy	76	68	82	71	297	25,871
Anna Acker-Macosko	74	74	76	73	297	25,871
Brandie Burton	74	72	77	74	297	25,871
Dina Ammaccapane	75	70	78	74	297	25,871
Lorie Kane	74	72	82	70	298	18,998
Jenny Lidback	71	73	79	75	298	18,998
Rosie Jones	74	74	74	76	298	18,998
Akiko Fukushima	72	71	79	76	298	18,998
Lisa Walters	76	70	74	78	298	18,998
Wendy Ward	76	69	75	78	298	18,998
Donna Andrews	70	75	75	78	298	18,998
Dana Dormann	72	76	79	72	299	12,972
Nancy Scranton	76	72	78	73	299	12,972
Michelle Estill	75	74	76	74	299	12,972
Laurie Rinker-Graham	75	71	77	76	299	12,972
Helen Dobson	71	75	77	76	299	12,972

Jamie Farr Kroger Classic

Highland Meadows Golf Club, Sylvania, Ohio — July 9-12
Par 34-37–71; 6,319 yards — purse, $800,000

	SCORES				TOTAL	MONEY
Se Ri Pak	71	61	63	66	261	$120,000
Lisa Hackney	69	68	68	65	270	74,474
Karrie Webb	67	70	67	67	271	54,346
Pat Hurst	68	69	69	67	273	34,888
Charlotta Sorenstam	67	68	71	67	273	34,888
Cindy Figg-Currier	68	69	68	68	273	34,888
Juli Inkster	68	71	69	66	274	20,128
Amy Alcott	69	68	71	66	274	20,128
Brandie Burton	66	74	66	68	274	20,128
Lorie Kane	68	69	68	69	274	20,128
Helen Alfredsson	68	69	71	67	275	13,437
Rosie Jones	67	70	70	68	275	13,437
Jenny Lidback	68	68	70	69	275	13,437
Meg Mallon	66	71	68	70	275	13,437
Dana Dormann	64	70	71	70	275	13,437
Dottie Pepper	71	71	68	66	276	10,740
Vickie Odegard	64	70	71	71	276	10,740
Janice Moodie	68	73	70	66	277	9,331
Denise Killeen	69	69	70	69	277	9,331
Marta Figueras-Dotti	69	69	68	71	277	9,331
Maria Hjorth	67	71	68	71	277	9,331
Betsy King	67	67	72	71	277	9,331

	SCORES				TOTAL	MONEY
Lisa Kiggens	70	71	71	66	278	7,526
Emilee Klein	68	69	74	67	278	7,526
Jane Geddes	70	71	68	69	278	7,526
Liz Earley	68	72	69	69	278	7,526
Beth Daniel	68	71	70	69	278	7,526
Luciana Bemvenuti	71	68	68	71	278	7,526
Nanci Bowen	70	71	70	68	279	6,111
Anna Acker-Macosko	69	72	70	68	279	6,111
Christy Erb	71	70	69	69	279	6,111
Cindy Flom	71	71	66	71	279	6,111
Patti Rizzo	70	70	68	71	279	6,111
Cindy McCurdy	68	72	67	72	279	6,111

JAL Big Apple Classic

Wykagyl Country Club, New Rochelle, New York — July 16-19
Par 35-36–71; 6,161 yards — purse, $775,000

	SCORES				TOTAL	MONEY
Annika Sorenstam	67	66	65	67	265	$116,250
Joan Pitcock	70	67	70	66	273	72,147
Michelle Estill	71	68	65	71	275	52,648
Betsy King	72	67	70	67	276	40,948
Janice Moodie	69	70	69	69	277	30,233
Tina Barrett	67	70	70	70	277	30,233
Anna Acker-Macosko	71	70	70	67	278	21,643
Meg Mallon	68	66	74	70	278	21,643
Sherri Steinhauer	71	68	71	69	279	15,794
Lisa Hackney	68	70	71	70	279	15,794
Kim Saiki	68	69	72	70	279	15,794
Penny Hammel	64	71	70	74	279	15,794
Jenny Lidback	68	68	69	75	280	12,869
Emilee Klein	69	72	68	72	281	11,699
Juli Inkster	67	70	70	74	281	11,699
Maria Hjorth	69	70	72	71	282	9,944
Nanci Bowen	71	67	70	74	282	9,944
Barb Mucha	71	68	67	76	282	9,944
Chris Johnson	68	68	69	77	282	9,944
Beth Daniel	69	71	72	71	283	8,394
Pearl Sinn	72	68	67	76	283	8,394
Mardi Lunn	67	71	68	77	283	8,394
Leslie Spalding	68	69	69	77	283	8,394
Lorie Kane	73	70	75	66	284	6,980
Cathy Johnston-Forbes	72	70	72	70	284	6,980
Vickie Odegard	74	69	70	71	284	6,980
Robin Walton	68	72	72	72	284	6,980
Danielle Ammaccapane	69	68	74	73	284	6,980
Leta Lindley	71	68	70	75	284	6,980
Michelle McGann	72	74	72	67	285	5,543
Kristi Albers	75	68	74	68	285	5,543
Shani Waugh	69	72	75	69	288	5,543
Angie Ridgeway	74	67	73	71	285	5,543
Hiromi Kobayashi	74	71	68	72	285	5,543
Cindy Figg-Currier	71	69	72	73	285	5,543
Michele Redman	72	69	69	75	285	5,543

Giant Eagle Classic

Avalon Lakes Golf Course, Warren, Ohio — July 24-26
Par 36-36–72; 6,308 yards — purse, $800,000

	SCORES			TOTAL	MONEY
Se Ri Pak	65	69	67	201	$120,000
Dottie Pepper	67	64	71	202	74,474
Robin Walton	69	70	64	203	54,346
Kelly Robbins	71	68	65	204	34,888
Leta Lindley	67	70	67	204	34,888
Pearl Sinn	69	65	70	204	34,888
Karrie Webb	72	68	65	205	22,342
Kate Golden	68	65	72	205	22,342
Sara Hallock	72	67	67	206	17,060
Dawn Coe-Jones	69	70	67	206	17,060
Annika Sorenstam	70	66	70	206	17,060
Michele Redman	67	70	70	207	13,341
Maria Hjorth	69	67	71	207	13,341
Wendy Ward	68	67	72	207	13,341
Ji Hyun Suh	71	67	70	208	10,602
Liselotte Neumann	70	68	70	208	10,602
Anna Acker-Macosko	72	65	71	208	10,602
Dale Reid	70	66	72	208	10,602
Becky Iverson	65	71	72	208	10,602
Val Skinner	72	68	69	209	8,720
Charlotta Sorenstam	72	68	69	209	8,720
Kim Saiki	70	70	69	209	8,720
Amy Fruhwirth	72	66	71	209	8,720
Joanne Morley	74	67	69	210	7,140
Cindy Flom	73	68	69	210	7,140
Nancy Harvey	72	68	70	210	7,140
Barb Whitehead	69	70	71	210	7,140
Sally Little	70	67	73	210	7,140
Alicia Dibos	65	72	73	210	7,140
Tammie Green	65	71	74	210	7,140

du Maurier Classic

Essex Golf & Country Club, Windsor, Ontario, Canada — July 30-August 2
Par 36-36–72; 6,359 yards — purse, $1,200,000

	SCORES				TOTAL	MONEY
Brandie Burton	68	64	66	72	270	$180,000
Annika Sorenstam	68	66	67	70	271	111,711
Betsy King	64	69	70	72	275	81,519
Gail Graham	70	70	68	68	276	44,804
Dawn Coe-Jones	67	70	69	70	276	44,804
Deb Richard	67	69	70	70	276	44,804
Michelle Estill	69	69	66	72	276	44,804
Meg Mallon	65	69	67	75	276	44,804
Sherri Steinhauer	70	71	69	67	277	26,871
Hiromi Kobayashi	68	70	66	73	277	26,871
Tammie Green	66	69	74	69	278	21,335
Alicia Dibos	68	68	69	73	278	21,335
Pat Hurst	67	65	71	75	278	21,335
Juli Inkster	74	68	68	69	279	15,624
Catriona Matthew	68	68	74	69	279	15,624

	SCORES				TOTAL	MONEY
Michele Redman	70	70	69	70	279	15,624
Charlotta Sorenstam	69	69	71	70	279	15,624
Karrie Webb	69	69	69	72	279	15,624
Allison Finney	70	67	70	72	279	15,624
Dottie Pepper	66	70	71	72	279	15,624
Dana Dormann	68	68	70	73	279	15,624
Penny Hammel	73	68	69	70	280	11,774
Sally Little	67	74	69	70	280	11,774
Donna Andrews	70	70	68	72	280	11,774
Rosie Jones	67	73	66	74	280	11,774
Laura Davies	69	67	70	74	280	11,774
Nancy Lopez	69	72	72	68	281	9,566
Hollis Stacy	71	69	72	69	281	9,566
Lisa Kiggens	71	71	68	71	281	9,566
Smriti Mehra	68	69	72	72	281	9,566
Marta Figueras-Dotti	68	71	68	74	281	9,566
Chris Johnson	66	72	69	74	281	9,566
Mardi Lunn	68	68	70	75	281	9,566

Star Bank Classic

Country Club of the North, Beavercreek, Ohio — August 7-9
Par 36-36–72; 6,331 yards — purse, $600,000

	SCORES			TOTAL	MONEY
Meg Mallon	64	67	68	199	$90,000
Dottie Pepper	63	70	66	199	55,855
(Mallon defeated Pepper on first extra hole.)					
Donna Andrews	67	65	68	200	40,759
Juli Inkster	67	69	65	201	31,702
Patty Sheehan	67	69	67	203	25,663
Lisa Walters	68	68	68	204	19,473
Tammie Green	67	67	70	204	19,473
Michelle McGann	74	67	64	205	13,511
Pat Hurst	69	69	67	205	13,511
Tina Barrett	69	67	69	205	13,511
Pearl Sinn	65	70	70	205	13,511
Muffin Spencer-Devlin	68	72	66	206	9,107
Sally Little	68	71	67	206	9,107
Emilee Klein	67	72	67	206	9,107
Penny Hammel	70	68	68	206	9,107
Chris Johnson	69	69	68	206	9,107
Hiromi Kobayashi	67	69	70	206	9,107
Sara Hallock	72	68	67	207	6,798
Dana Dormann	71	68	68	207	6,798
Mitzi Edge	68	69	70	207	6,798
Brandie Burton	68	68	71	207	6,798
Lisa Kiggens	68	67	72	207	6,798
Beth Daniel	66	67	74	207	6,798
Kelli Kuehne	69	71	68	208	5,585
Colleen Walker	70	69	69	208	5,585
Jackie Gallagher-Smith	68	70	70	208	5,585
Terry-Jo Myers	67	69	72	208	5,585
Erika Wicoff	73	69	67	209	4,536
Karen Weiss	70	72	67	209	4,536
Laurie Rinker-Graham	70	70	69	209	4,536
Eva Dahllof	72	67	70	209	4,536

	SCORES			TOTAL	MONEY
Lori Atsedes	69	70	70	209	4,536
Judy Dickinson	66	71	72	209	4,536
Amy Alcott	67	69	73	209	4,536
Nancy Scranton	69	66	74	209	4,536

Weetabix Women's British Open

See European LPGA Tour section.

Rainbow Foods Classic

Rush Creek Golf Club, Maple Grove, Minnesota — August 21-23
Par 36-36–72; 6,370 yards — purse, $600,000

	SCORES			TOTAL	MONEY
Hiromi Kobayashi	69	68	69	206	$90,000
Tracy Hanson	67	70	69	206	55,855
(Kobayashi defeated Hanson on first extra hole.)					
Meg Mallon	71	69	67	207	36,230
Michelle Estill	65	71	71	207	36,230
Leta Lindley	71	69	68	208	21,536
Lisa Walters	71	69	68	208	21,536
Wendy Doolan	69	71	68	208	21,536
Jill McGill	71	70	68	209	12,944
Lisa Kiggens	71	68	70	209	12,944
Liz Earley	68	71	70	209	12,944
Rachel Hetherington	70	68	71	209	12,944
Wendy Ward	69	67	73	209	12,944
Jenny Lidback	73	69	68	210	8,465
Michelle McGann	71	70	69	210	8,465
Cristie Kerr	70	71	69	210	8,465
Marnie McGuire	69	71	70	210	8,465
Marianne Morris	68	72	70	210	8,465
Anna Acker-Macosko	70	68	72	210	8,465
Laura Philo	70	67	73	210	8,465
Barb Mucha	70	74	67	211	6,425
Sherri Steinhauer	68	72	71	211	6,425
Vicki Fergon	71	68	72	211	6,425
Alicia Dibos	71	68	72	211	6,425
Vickie Odegard	70	68	73	211	6,425
Danielle Ammaccapane	73	70	69	212	5,100
Karen Noble	71	72	69	212	5,100
Lori West	75	67	70	212	5,100
Suzanne Strudwick	70	71	71	212	5,100
Annette DeLuca	68	73	71	212	5,100
Patti Rizzo	71	69	72	212	5,100
Dana Dormann	70	69	73	212	5,100
Nancy Harvey	66	72	74	212	5,100

State Farm Rail Classic

Rail Golf Club, Springfield, Illinois — August 28-30
Par 36-36–72; 6,403 yards — purse, $700,000

	SCORES			TOTAL	MONEY
Pearl Sinn	69	66	65	200	$105,000
Michele Redman	70	63	68	201	65,165
Tammie Green	66	67	69	202	47,553
Michelle Estill	71	68	64	203	24,539
Betsy King	68	70	65	203	24,539
Danielle Ammaccapane	71	66	66	203	24,539
Susie Redman	68	68	67	203	24,539
Dottie Pepper	63	72	68	203	24,539
Cristie Kerr	69	65	69	203	24,539
Nancy Harvey	71	67	66	204	11,491
Se Ri Pak	70	68	66	204	11,491
Dana Dormann	70	67	67	204	11,491
Meg Mallon	68	69	67	204	11,491
Tina Barrett	69	67	68	204	11,491
Emilee Klein	67	67	70	204	11,491
Cindy McCurdy	67	66	71	204	11,491
Vickie Odegard	65	68	71	204	11,491
Denise Killeen	70	68	67	205	7,773
Cindy Figg-Currier	69	69	67	205	7,773
Mitzi Edge	68	70	67	205	7,773
Dina Ammaccapane	66	71	68	205	7,773
Eva Dahllof	69	67	69	205	7,773
Janice Moodie	67	67	71	205	7,773
Martha Nause	67	66	72	205	7,773
Michelle McGann	71	67	68	206	6,199
Beth Daniel	68	70	68	206	6,199
Leta Lindley	70	67	69	206	6,199
Dale Eggeling	69	68	69	206	6,199
Lorie Kane	69	68	69	206	6,199
Sherri Steinhauer	72	69	66	207	5,006
Suzanne Strudwick	70	69	68	207	5,006
Pamela Wright	68	71	68	207	5,006
Jane Crafter	67	70	70	207	5,006
Smriti Mehra	67	69	71	207	5,006
Barb Mucha	66	69	72	207	5,006
Penny Hammel	66	69	72	207	5,006

Safeway Championship

Columbia Edgewater Country Club, Portland, Oregon — September 4-6
Par 36-36–72; 6,307 yards — purse, $600,000

	SCORES			TOTAL	MONEY
Danielle Ammaccapane	65	67	72	204	$90,000
Emilee Klein	68	67	70	205	55,855
Dina Ammaccapane	71	70	66	207	40,759
Kris Tschetter	71	72	65	208	28,682
Erika Wicoff	70	68	70	208	28,682
Kim Saiki	72	70	67	209	21,134
Donna Andrews	72	67	71	210	15,901
Juli Inkster	70	68	72	210	15,901
Tina Barrett	69	69	72	210	15,901

	SCORES			TOTAL	MONEY
Lorie Kane	73	71	68	212	9,594
Mardi Lunn	70	73	69	212	9,594
Penny Hammel	69	74	69	212	9,594
Deb Richard	73	69	70	212	9,594
Kristi Albers	71	71	70	212	9,594
Se Ri Pak	72	69	71	212	9,594
Sherri Turner	70	69	73	212	9,594
Maria Hjorth	70	69	73	212	9,594
Charlotta Sorenstam	69	69	74	212	9,594
Karrie Webb	71	71	71	213	7,246
Catriona Matthew	76	70	68	214	6,145
Barb Mucha	73	72	69	214	6,145
Lisa Walters	74	70	70	214	6,145
Luciana Bemvenuti	74	70	70	214	6,145
Becky Iverson	72	71	71	214	6,145
Dale Eggeling	68	75	71	214	6,145
Pat Hurst	68	73	73	214	6,145
Carin Koch	75	71	69	215	4,865
Michelle Estill	72	73	70	215	4,865
Janice Moodie	72	73	70	215	4,865
Dawn Coe-Jones	75	69	71	215	4,865
Vickie Odegard	72	72	71	215	4,865
Stefania Croce	72	72	71	215	4,865

Safeco Classic

Meridian Valley Country Club, Kent, Washington — September 10-13
Par 36-36–72; 6,241 yards — purse, $600,000

	SCORES				TOTAL	MONEY
Annika Sorenstam	68	70	67	68	273	$90,000
Laura Davies	69	71	70	68	278	48,307
Patty Sheehan	71	66	67	74	278	48,307
Danielle Ammaccapane	70	75	70	64	279	31,702
Deb Richard	71	69	72	68	280	23,398
Brandie Burton	72	67	72	69	280	23,398
Jan Stephenson	70	70	74	67	281	15,096
Dale Eggeling	73	69	71	68	281	15,096
Michelle McGann	69	71	73	68	281	15,096
Juli Inkster	73	69	67	72	281	15,096
Rachel Hetherington	72	74	70	66	282	10,340
Wendy Doolan	69	74	70	69	282	10,340
Sherri Steinhauer	65	71	75	71	282	10,340
Rosie Jones	70	69	71	72	282	10,340
Helen Dobson	72	72	72	67	283	7,749
Lisa Kiggens	74	69	73	67	283	7,749
Catriona Matthew	71	75	69	68	283	7,749
Pat Hurst	68	73	72	70	283	7,749
Charlotta Sorenstam	72	70	69	72	283	7,749
Karrie Webb	71	70	69	73	283	7,749
Dawn Coe-Jones	70	78	73	63	284	5,624
Maria Hjorth	75	72	71	66	284	5,624
Tina Barrett	74	71	70	69	284	5,624
Joan Pitcock	73	71	70	70	284	5,624
Meg Mallon	74	69	71	70	284	5,624
Donna Andrews	72	70	72	70	284	5,624
Cindy Flom	70	72	72	70	284	5,624

	SCORES				TOTAL	MONEY
Robin Walton	71	72	69	72	284	5,624
Beth Daniel	72	66	74	72	284	5,624
Se Ri Pak	67	68	74	75	284	5,624

Solheim Cup

Muirfield Village Golf Club, Dublin, Ohio September 18-20
Par 36-36–72; 6,428 yards

FIRST ROUND
Foursomes

Dottie Pepper and Juli Inkster (US) defeated Laura Davies and Trish Johnson, 3 and 1.
Meg Mallon and Brandie Burton (US) defeated Helen Alfredsson and Alison Nicholas, 3 and 1.
Kelly Robbins and Pat Hurst (US) defeated Lisa Hackney and Liselotte Neumann, 1 up.
Annika Sorenstam and Catriona Matthew (Europe) defeated Donna Andrews and Tammie Green, 3 and 2.

POINTS: United States 3, Europe 1

Four-Ball

Betsy King and Chris Johnson (US) halved with Laura Davies and Charlotta Sorenstam.
Pat Hurst and Rosie Jones (US) defeated Lisa Hackney and Sophie Gustafson, 7 and 5.
Helen Alfredsson and Marie-Laure de Lorenzi (Europe) defeated Kelly Robbins and Sherri Steinhauer, 2 and 1.
Dottie Pepper and Brandie Burton (US) defeated Annika Sorenstam and Catrin Nilsmark, 2 up.

POINTS: United States 2½, Europe 1½

SECOND ROUND
Foursomes

Andrews and Steinhauer (US) defeated Annika Sorenstam and Matthew, 3 and 2.
Davies and Charlotta Sorenstam (Europe) defeated Mallon and Burton, 3 and 2.
Pepper and Inkster (US) defeated Alfredsson and de Lorenzi, 1 up.
Robbins and Hurst (US) defeated Neumann and Nilsmark, 1 up.

POINTS: United States 3, Europe 1

Four-Ball

Annika Sorenstam and Nilsmark (Europe) defeated King and Jones, 5 and 3.
Davies and Hackney (Europe) defeated Chris Johnson and Green, 2 up.
Andrews and Steinhauer (US) defeated de Lorenzi and Alfredsson, 4 and 3.
Mallon and Inkster (US) defeated Neumann and Charlotta Sorenstam, 2 and 1.

POINTS: United States 2, Europe 2

FINAL ROUND
Singles

Davies (Europe) defeated Hurst, 1 up.
Alfredsson (Europe) defeated Inkster, 2 and 1.

Annika Sorenstam (Europe) defeated Andrews, 2 and 1.
Neumann (Europe) defeated Burton, 1 up.
Pepper (US) defeated Trish Johnson, 3 and 2.
Robbins (US) defeated Charlotta Sorenstam, 2 and 1.
De Lorenzi (Europe) defeated Chris Johnson, 1 up.
Jones (US) defeated Nilsmark, 6 and 4.
Green (US) defeated Nicholas, 1 up.
Steinhauer (US) defeated Matthew, 3 and 2.
Hackney (Europe) defeated King, 6 and 5.
Mallon (US) halved with Gustafson.

POINTS: United States 5½, Europe 6½

TOTAL POINTS: United States 16, Europe 12

First Union Betsy King Classic

Berkleigh Country Club, Kutztown, Pennsylvania — September 24-27
Par 35-37–72; 6,075 yards — purse, $650,000

	SCORES				TOTAL	MONEY
Rachel Hetherington	69	66	70	69	274	$97,500
Annika Sorenstam	71	69	68	66	274	60,510
(Hetherington defeated Sorenstam on first extra hole.)						
Beth Daniel	67	69	70	71	277	44,156
Meg Mallon	70	73	68	68	279	26,084
Hiromi Kobayashi	70	71	68	70	279	26,084
Laura Davies	68	72	68	71	279	26,084
Se Ri Pak	68	71	69	71	279	26,084
Charlotta Sorenstam	69	70	70	72	281	17,008
Nancy Scranton	73	69	69	71	282	14,555
Shani Waugh	71	70	70	71	282	14,555
Barb Mucha	75	69	68	71	283	10,869
Eva Dahllof	73	70	69	71	283	10,869
Deb Richard	67	74	71	71	283	10,869
Cathy Johnston-Forbes	68	70	74	71	283	10,869
Muffin Spencer-Devlin	68	74	69	72	283	10,869
Stefania Croce	75	70	72	67	284	8,351
Moira Dunn	75	67	74	68	284	8,351
Trish Johnson	70	72	73	69	284	8,351
Wendy Doolan	72	71	71	70	284	8,351
Lisa Hackney	71	71	73	70	285	6,129
Dana Dormann	73	72	69	71	285	6,129
Betsy King	73	69	72	71	285	6,129
Caroline McMillan	72	70	72	71	285	6,129
Michele Redman	71	70	73	71	285	6,129
Helen Alfredsson	73	70	69	73	285	6,129
Marianne Morris	71	70	71	73	285	6,129
Chris Johnson	75	69	67	74	285	6,129
Jill McGill	73	70	68	74	285	6,129
Kelli Kuehne	71	70	70	74	285	6,129
Karrie Webb	71	68	70	76	285	6,129
Juli Inkster	69	69	70	77	285	6,129

AFLAC Tournament of Champions

Grand National, Opelika/Auburn, Alabama — October 8-11
Par 36-36–72; 6,300 yards — purse, $750,000

	SCORES				TOTAL	MONEY
Kelly Robbins	66	73	67	70	276	$122,000
Juli Inkster	67	73	71	69	280	75,500
Sherri Steinhauer	70	70	70	71	281	54,250
Annika Sorenstam	69	70	74	70	283	42,300
Cindy Figg-Currier	71	74	70	69	284	34,050
Chris Johnson	70	70	75	70	285	25,875
Alison Nicholas	70	73	68	74	285	25,875
Hiromi Kobayashi	73	73	70	70	286	19,925
Brandie Burton	75	71	69	71	286	19,925
Michelle McGann	75	75	71	67	288	15,111
Karrie Webb	72	73	73	70	288	15,111
Se Ri Pak	68	69	79	72	288	15,111
Meg Mallon	73	69	73	73	288	15,111
Nancy Lopez	75	73	73	68	289	11,433
Mayumi Hirase	73	74	74	68	289	11,433
Barb Mucha	73	73	72	71	289	11,433
Dottie Pepper	69	74	74	72	289	11,433
Rosie Jones	71	72	72	74	289	11,433
Gail Graham	72	73	76	69	290	9,818
Pat Hurst	68	73	76	73	290	9,818
Betsy King	76	77	69	69	291	9,006
Helen Alfredsson	69	70	76	76	291	9,006
Penny Hammel	77	70	75	70	292	8,207
Dale Eggeling	72	74	75	71	292	8,207
Michele Redman	72	74	71	75	292	8,207
Rachel Hetherington	79	74	71	69	293	7,721
Pearl Sinn	70	76	78	70	294	7,143
Donna Andrews	72	74	77	71	294	7,143
Lisa Walters	74	70	78	72	294	7,143
Danielle Ammaccapane	78	72	70	74	294	7,143

Samsung World Championship

Tierra del Sol Golf Course, The Villages, Florida — October 22-25
Par 36-36–72; 6,326 yards — purse, $550,000

	SCORES				TOTAL	MONEY
Juli Inkster	70	73	66	66	275	$137,000
Annika Sorenstam	69	73	66	70	278	78,500
Brandie Burton	70	72	71	69	282	44,750
Dottie Pepper	69	70	71	72	282	44,750
Donna Andrews	75	71	70	69	285	28,500
Liselotte Neumann	75	67	74	70	286	25,275
*Grace Park	73	74	73	66	286	
Karrie Webb	71	73	73	70	287	22,775
Hiromi Kobayashi	75	73	70	71	289	19,775
Helen Alfredsson	72	72	72	73	289	19,775
Laura Davies	74	76	71	70	291	16,525
Lorie Kane	74	76	70	71	291	16,525
Danielle Ammaccapane	77	73	71	71	292	15,275
Se Ri Pak	72	75	73	72	292	15,275
Pat Hurst	76	70	72	74	292	15,275
Meg Mallon	78	75	70	72	295	14,275

Nichirei International

See Japan LPGA Tour section.

LPGA Japan Classic

See Japan LPGA Tour section.

PageNet Tour Championship

Desert Inn Golf Club, Las Vegas, Nevada — November 19-22
Par 36-36–72; 6,373 yards — purse, $1,000,000

	SCORES				TOTAL	MONEY
Laura Davies	66	67	75	69	277	$215,000
Brandie Burton	69	74	71	67	281	86,000
Karrie Webb	70	69	74	68	281	86,000
Pat Hurst	74	69	68	70	281	86,000
Kelly Robbins	70	73	69	70	282	46,500
Juli Inkster	68	72	71	71	282	46,500
Dale Eggeling	72	71	73	67	283	33,000
Lorie Kane	74	71	68	70	283	33,000
Dottie Pepper	69	71	72	72	284	26,500
Meg Mallon	72	71	67	75	285	24,000
Helen Alfredsson	70	73	72	71	286	21,250
Donna Andrews	71	72	72	72	287	18,250
Tina Barrett	71	66	74	76	287	18,250
Annika Sorenstam	74	71	71	72	288	15,250
Chris Johnson	70	74	71	73	288	15,250
Wendy Ward	71	71	70	76	288	15,250
Betsy King	77	69	76	67	289	12,916
Liselotte Neumann	71	72	74	72	289	12,916
Sherri Steinhauer	72	71	73	73	289	12,916
Rosie Jones	72	72	74	74	292	11,500
Lisa Walters	70	73	76	74	293	11,250
Michelle Estill	74	73	75	73	295	10,650
Dana Dormann	72	77	72	74	295	10,650
Charlotta Sorenstam	74	69	74	78	295	10,650
Se Ri Pak	72	77	72	75	296	10,000
Danielle Ammaccapane	75	76	74	72	297	9,700
Lisa Hackney	76	74	75	73	298	9,300
Hiromi Kobayashi	73	77	77	72	299	9,000
Emilee Klein	79	75	73	73	300	8,850
Barb Mucha	78	74	76	78	306	8,700

European LPGA Tour

Evian Masters

Royal Golf Club Evian, Evians-les-Bains, France — June 3-6
Par 36-36–72; 5,958 yards — purse, £500,000

	SCORES				TOTAL	MONEY
Helen Alfredsson	70	69	73	65	277	£75,000
Maria Hjorth	69	70	72	70	281	50,625
Trish Johnson	70	70	69	73	282	30,950
Alison Nicholas	70	70	71	71	282	30,950
Shani Waugh	69	72	68	74	283	17,875
Helen Dobson	71	70	72	70	283	17,875
Hiromi Kobayashi	70	70	73	70	283	17,875
Karen Pearce	73	71	73	67	283	11,832.50
Laura Philo	73	71	69	71	283	11,832.50
Catriona Matthew	70	71	73	71	285	10,000
Diane Barnard	68	72	73	73	286	9,185
Laura Davies	68	73	74	72	287	7,925
Corinne Dibnah	73	69	73	72	287	7,925
Laurette Maritz	72	69	70	76	287	7,925
Estefania Knuth	73	74	66	74	287	7,925
Lora Fairclough	73	71	72	71	287	7,925
Carin Koch	67	74	70	77	288	7,100
Fiona Pike	73	69	74	72	288	7,100
Katharina Poppmeier	73	71	73	71	288	7,100
Catrin Nilsmark	75	72	70	72	289	6,365
Charlotta Sorenstam	76	73	68	72	289	6,365
Asa Gottmo	76	70	70	73	289	6,365
Patricia Meunier Lebouc	73	68	73	75	289	6,365
Jane Leary	68	74	76	71	289	6,365
Stefania Croce	70	74	73	73	290	5,487.50
Sophie Gustafson	72	76	69	73	290	5,487.50
Joanne Morley	74	71	74	71	290	5,487.50
Sandrine Mendiburu	72	75	73	70	290	5,487.50
Anne-Marie Knight	69	74	74	73	290	5,487.50
Regine Lautens	75	69	76	71	291	4,812.50
Wendy Dicks	74	74	72	71	291	4,812.50
Tina Fischer	74	74	71	72	291	4,812.50
*Connie Wei	74	73	74	70	291	

Ladies' Austrian Open

Steiermarkischer Golf Club Murhof, Frohnleiten, Austria — July 16-18
Par 36-36–72; 6,148 yards — purse, £80,000

	SCORES			TOTAL	MONEY
Lynnette Brooky	64	70	69	203	£12,000
Trish Johnson	70	66	68	204	8,120
Federica Dassu	69	69	67	205	4,028
Laura Davies	68	66	71	205	4,028

	SCORES			TOTAL	MONEY
Estefania Knuth	70	66	69	205	4,028
Laura Philo	67	69	69	205	4,028
Samantha Head	64	74	69	207	2,400
Claire Duffy	67	70	71	208	1,896
Raquel Carriedo	73	67	68	208	1,896
Marie-Laure de Lorenzi	71	69	69	209	1,482.66
Kathryn Marshall	68	72	69	209	1,482.66
Pernilla Sterner	73	68	68	209	1,482.66
Patricia Meunier Lebouc	73	67	70	210	1,242.66
Anne-Marie Knight	72	70	68	210	1,242.66
Mhairi McKay	73	72	65	210	1,242.66
Helen Wadsworth	73	72	66	211	1,136
Marlene Hedblom	70	69	72	211	1,136
Ana Belen Sanchez Torreblanca	69	70	72	211	1,136
Karen Pearce	70	70	72	212	1,017.60
Mette Hageman	70	69	73	212	1,017.60
Amaia Arruti	73	71	68	212	1,017.60
Ludivine Kreutz	71	70	71	212	1,017.60
Lotte Greve	70	68	74	212	1,017.60
Barbara Pestana	74	69	70	213	848
Marie-Therese Pistolet-Boselli	71	73	69	213	848
Loraine Lambert	73	72	68	213	848
Joanne Mills	71	66	76	213	848
Julie Forbes	67	75	71	213	848
Iben Tinning	76	69	68	213	848
Joanne Oliver	74	71	68	213	848
Silvia Cavalleri	71	71	71	213	848
Elisabeth Esterl	71	72	70	213	848

Chrysler Open

Sjogarde Golf Club, Frillcsas, Swcden — July 23-26
Par 36-37–73; 6,242 yards — purse, £125,000

	SCORES				TOTAL	MONEY
Laura Davies	72	71	71	70	284	£18,750
Trish Johnson	73	76	71	70	290	10,718.75
Raquel Carriedo	71	74	72	73	290	10,718.75
Alison Nicholas	73	73	72	73	291	6,750
Pernilla Sterner	72	73	71	76	292	5,300
Sophie Gustafson	75	74	71	74	294	4,375
Karen Lunn	71	73	74	77	295	3,750
Julie Forbes	75	74	74	73	296	2,962.50
Lora Fairclough	75	76	72	73	296	2,962.50
Caroline Hall	73	77	75	72	297	2,400
Helen Alfredsson	75	78	72	72	297	2,400
Marie-Laure de Lorenzi	73	75	75	75	298	2,081.25
Malin Burstrom	74	72	77	75	298	2,081.25
Catrin Nilsmark	74	78	74	73	299	1,879.16
Carin Koch	69	75	78	77	299	1,879.16
Susan Farron	73	74	73	79	299	1,879.16
Federica Dassu	74	77	76	73	300	1,656.25
Sofie Eriksson	71	78	75	76	300	1,656.25
Joanne Mills	70	78	79	73	300	1,656.25
Kathryn Marshall	73	76	73	78	300	1,656.25
Iben Tinning	73	74	76	77	300	1,656.25
Lisa Educate	74	75	75	76	300	1,656.25

	SCORES				TOTAL	MONEY
Sally Prosser	75	74	78	74	301	1,493.75
Anne-Marie Knight	72	75	73	81	301	1,493.75
Xonia Wunsch-Ruiz	78	75	74	75	302	1,381.25
Caryn Louw	75	75	80	72	302	1,381.25
Stephanie Dallongeville	73	76	77	76	302	1,381.25
Mhairi McKay	75	74	79	74	302	1,381.25
Regine Lautens	71	74	79	79	303	1,231.25
Barbara Pestana	74	77	76	76	303	1,231.25
Anna Berg	77	75	75	76	303	1,231.25
Marina Arruti	71	80	72	80	303	1,231.25

Ladies' German Open

Marriott Hotel Treudelberg Golf & Country Club, Hamburg, Germany
Par 36-37–73; 6,221 yards

July 30-August 2
purse, £100,000

	SCORES				TOTAL	MONEY
Lora Fairclough	67	71	70	74	282	£15,000
Stephanie Dallongeville	71	73	68	73	285	8,575
Joanne Morley	74	70	71	70	285	8,575
Iben Tinning	70	73	70	73	286	5,400
Sophie Gustafson	72	68	72	75	287	4,240
Trish Johnson	71	69	72	76	288	3,000
Wendy Dicks	74	71	71	72	288	3,000
Raquel Carriedo	70	73	74	71	288	3,000
Loraine Lambert	73	72	73	71	289	2,240
Sally Prosser	74	75	69	72	290	1,853.33
Pernilla Sterner	74	72	71	73	290	1,853.33
Ana Belen Sanchez Torreblanca	75	68	73	74	290	1,853.33
Asa Gottmo	75	74	70	72	291	1,553.33
Tina Fischer	72	75	68	76	291	1,553.33
Laura Philo	72	74	73	72	291	1,553.33
Tracy Eakin	71	76	72	73	292	1,400
Nicola Moult	76	72	72	72	292	1,400
Jane Leary	74	74	71	73	292	1,400
Anne-Marie Knight	70	76	73	73	292	1,400
Anna Berg	77	73	73	70	293	1,300
Marie-Laure de Lorenzi	74	71	77	72	294	1,240
Mia Lojdahl	77	75	71	71	294	1,240
Lynnette Brooky	72	72	75	75	294	1,240
Martina Koch	71	75	76	73	295	1,150
Lisa Educate	77	72	74	72	295	1,150
Ana Larraneta	77	72	75	71	295	1,150
Kathryn Marshall	72	75	74	75	296	1,045
Sandrine Mendiburu	70	77	74	75	296	1,045
Valerie Van Ryckeghem	75	73	74	74	296	1,045
Lisa Dermott	75	73	71	77	296	1,045

McDonald's WPGA Championship of Europe

The Gleneagles Hotel, King's Course, Perthshire, Scotland
Par 37-35–72; 6,048 yards

August 6-9
purse, £300,000

	SCORES				TOTAL	MONEY
Catriona Matthew	71	69	67	69	276	£45,000
Helen Alfredsson	72	68	70	71	281	25,725
Laura Davies	72	69	68	72	281	25,725
Mhairi McKay	74	70	69	69	282	14,460
Karen Pearce	73	71	67	71	282	14,460
Maria Hjorth	73	69	73	69	284	9,750
Catrin Nilsmark	77	70	68	69	284	9,750
Laura Philo	76	71	67	71	285	7,110
Diane Barnard	73	71	69	72	285	7,110
Sophie Gustafson	72	75	68	71	286	5,760
Marie-Laure de Lorenzi	71	70	72	73	286	5,760
Charlotta Sorenstam	76	68	68	75	287	5,160
Trish Johnson	71	75	72	70	288	4,660
Caroline Hall	73	72	72	71	288	4,660
Myra Murray	72	74	68	74	288	4,660
Anne-Marie Knight	76	72	72	69	289	4,320
Janice Moodie	73	70	73	73	289	4,320
Stefania Croce	71	75	74	70	290	4,020
Kirsty Taylor	73	74	71	72	290	4,020
Dale Reid	75	69	73	73	290	4,020
Sally Prosser	72	74	75	70	291	3,630
Wendy Dicks	74	72	74	71	291	3,630
Pamela Wright	76	71	72	72	291	3,630
Claire Duffy	74	70	74	73	291	3,630
Catherine Schmitt	75	71	71	74	291	3,630
Ludivine Kreutz	78	69	75	70	292	3,270
Joanne Morley	77	69	73	73	292	3,270
Pernilla Sterner	71	75	72	74	292	3,270
Helen Wadsworth	77	72	73	71	293	3,000
Loraine Lambert	77	73	69	74	293	3,000
Corinne Dibnah	76	71	71	75	293	3,000

Weetabix Women's British Open

Royal Lytham & St. Anne's Golf Club, Lancashire, England
Par 35-37–72; 6,355 yards

August 13-16
purse, £575,000

	SCORES				TOTAL	MONEY
Sherri Steinhauer	81	72	70	69	292	£100,000
Sophie Gustafson	78	71	74	70	293	50,000
Brandie Burton	71	74	77	71	293	50,000
Janice Moodie	75	72	72	75	294	30,000
Karrie Webb	76	76	71	73	296	25,000
Leslie Spalding	76	70	75	76	297	17,000
Wendy Ward	76	71	74	76	297	17,000
Smriti Mehra	73	77	71	76	297	17,000
Betsy King	71	77	72	77	297	17,000
Catrin Nilsmark	77	77	69	75	298	12,000
Trish Johnson	72	77	77	73	299	9,687.50
Juli Inkster	75	75	76	73	299	9,687.50
Annika Sorenstam	75	73	77	74	299	9,687.50
Marie-Laure de Lorenzi	79	70	76	74	299	9,687.50

	SCORES				TOTAL	MONEY
Mhairi McKay	75	74	75	76	300	8,000
Myra Murray	81	76	69	75	301	7,300
Dale Reid	73	79	73	76	301	7,300
Helen Wadsworth	79	74	72	76	301	7,300
Hiromi Kobayashi	77	74	75	76	302	6,800
Maria Hjorth	82	73	76	72	303	6,300
Kris Tschetter	79	75	73	76	303	6,300
Jackie Gallagher-Smith	76	74	74	79	303	6,300
Kathryn Marshall	79	74	71	79	303	6,300
Donna Andrews	81	72	76	75	304	5,600
Joanne Morley	79	74	74	77	304	5,600
Pat Hurst	76	77	70	81	304	5,600
Cathy Johnston-Forbes	78	76	79	72	305	5,100
Suzanne Strudwick	75	72	75	83	305	5,100
Carin Koch	79	74	76	77	306	4,700
Kim Saiki	80	76	73	77	306	4,700

Compaq Open

Barseback Golf & Country Club, Malmo, Sweden — August 20-23
Par 36-36–72; 6,193 yards — purse, £300,000

	SCORES				TOTAL	MONEY
Annika Sorenstam	70	71	71	67	279	£45,000
Catrin Nilsmark	72	73	72	72	289	22,550
Johanna Head	71	70	74	74	289	22,550
Helen Alfredsson	75	69	70	75	289	22,550
Lisa Hackney	79	68	72	71	290	11,610
Laura Davies	74	71	71	74	290	11,610
Carin Koch	74	73	75	69	291	9,000
Elisabeth Esterl	70	74	74	74	292	7,500
Kelly Robbins	75	67	77	75	294	6,360
Sophie Gustafson	70	74	75	75	294	6,360
Shani Waugh	71	74	77	73	295	5,170
Karrie Webb	72	75	73	75	295	5,170
Charlotta Sorenstam	72	72	75	76	295	5,170
Liselotte Neumann	75	75	74	72	296	4,447.50
Marie-Laure de Lorenzi	74	75	74	73	296	4,447.50
Catriona Matthew	77	73	73	73	296	4,447.50
Lora Fairclough	75	69	76	76	296	4,447.50
Karen Lunn	75	74	76	72	297	4,080
Alison Nicholas	75	73	75	74	297	4,080
Karen Pearce	76	76	73	73	298	3,720
Joanne Mills	76	71	77	74	298	3,720
Asa Gottmo	76	74	74	74	298	3,720
Maria Hjorth	78	74	72	74	298	3,720
Sofia Gronberg	72	76	75	75	298	3,720
Kirsty Taylor	76	74	77	72	299	3,360
Joanne Morley	79	74	73	73	299	3,360
Caroline Hall	73	76	76	74	299	3,360
Iben Tinning	74	73	78	75	300	3,090
Kathryn Marshall	75	76	74	75	300	3,090
Natascha Fink	77	74	73	76	300	3,090

Donegal Irish Ladies' Open

Ballyliffin Golf Club, Donegal, Ireland
Par 35-37–72; 6,267 yards
(Fourth round cancelled — high winds.)

September 3-6
purse, £100,000

	SCORES			TOTAL	MONEY
Sophie Gustafson	68	78	68	214	£12,900
Iben Tinning	73	73	68	214	8,729
(Gustafson defeated Tinning on first extra hole.)					
Asa Gottmo	70	78	70	218	6,020
Aideen Rogers	73	76	71	220	4,644
Julie Forbes	78	74	69	221	3,646.40
Laura Davies	77	75	70	222	2,580
Marie-Therese Pistolet-Boselli	75	76	71	222	2,580
Raquel Carriedo	71	76	75	222	2,580
Mette Hageman	75	74	74	223	1,926.40
Lotte Greve	75	77	72	224	1,499.84
Johanna Head	72	79	73	224	1,499.84
Katharina Larsson	76	74	74	224	1,499.84
Anne-Marie Knight	73	76	75	224	1,499.84
Ana Larraneta	73	75	76	224	1,499.84
Barbara Pestana	76	76	73	225	1,255.60
Riikka Hakkarainen	76	76	73	225	1,255.60
Sara Forster	74	76	75	225	1,255.60
Elisabeth Esterl	72	82	72	226	1,169.60
Kirsty Taylor	75	78	73	226	1,169.60
Valerie Michaud	77	72	78	227	1,079.30
Vibeke Stensrud	80	74	73	227	1,079.30
Karen Lunn	76	78	73	227	1,079.30
Tina Poulton	74	76	77	227	1,079.30
Sandrine Mendiburu	74	77	77	228	1,014.80
Tracey Craik	75	79	75	229	963.20
Lynnette Brooky	76	75	78	229	963.20
Karolina Andersson	73	76	80	229	963.20
Sally Prosser	77	80	73	230	872.90
Myra Murray	77	78	75	230	872.90
Anna Berg	74	79	77	230	872.90
Claire Duffy	76	77	77	230	872.90

Air France Madame Open

New Golf de Deauville, Deauville, France
Par 35-36–71; 5,970 yards

October 15-17
purse, £63,000

	SCORES			TOTAL	MONEY
Patricia Meunier Lebouc	69	67	72	208	£9,450
Maria Hjorth	71	68	70	209	6,394.50
Diane Barnard	74	68	69	211	4,410
Nicola Moult	70	71	71	212	3,402
Laurette Maritz	73	67	73	213	2,671.20
Sophie Gustafson	76	72	66	214	2,047.50
Stephanie Dallongeville	71	71	72	214	2,047.50
Shani Waugh	74	70	71	215	1,415.40
Alison Nicholas	71	72	72	215	1,415.40
Corinne Dibnah	69	70	76	215	1,415.40
Catherine Schmitt	69	78	69	216	1,058.40
Natascha Fink	72	71	73	216	1,058.40

	SCORES			TOTAL	MONEY
Mette Hageman	68	74	74	216	1,058.40
Valerie Michaud	69	72	75	216	1,058.40
Anna Berg	74	74	69	217	894.60
Caroline Hall	72	74	71	217	894.60
Lora Fairclough	72	73	72	217	894.60
Pernilla Sterner	69	75	73	217	894.60
Mhairi McKay	73	70	74	217	894.60
Jane Leary	76	71	71	218	790.65
Sandrine Mendiburu	73	72	73	218	790.65
Mia Lojdahl	71	73	74	218	790.65
Iben Tinning	72	72	74	218	790.65
Joanne Mills	73	73	73	219	715.05
Marie-Laure de Lorenzi	68	77	74	219	715.05
Raquel Carriedo	74	75	70	219	715.05
Elisabeth Aron-Quelhas	72	73	74	219	715.05
Anna Radford	71	72	77	220	667.80
Tina Fischer	71	76	74	221	620.55
Wendy Dicks	73	75	73	221	620.55
Barbara Pestana	74	72	75	221	620.55
Laura Navarro	71	71	79	221	620.55

Marrakesh Palmeraie Open

Palmeraie Golf Palace, Marrakesh, Morocco
Par 36-36–72; 6,237 yards

October 22-24
purse, £80,000

	SCORES			TOTAL	MONEY
Sophie Gustafson	66	67	68	201	£12,000
Marie-Laure de Lorenzi	69	68	72	209	8,120
Wendy Dicks	67	74	69	210	5,600
Trish Johnson	70	72	69	211	3,504
Loraine Lambert	70	70	71	211	3,504
Sandrine Mendiburu	69	71	71	211	3,504
Ana Belen Sanchez Torreblanca	68	71	73	212	2,400
Anna Berg	71	74	68	213	1,797.33
Iben Tinning	73	71	69	213	1,797.33
Sofia Gronberg	71	71	71	213	1,797.33
Karen Lunn	67	79	68	214	1,378.66
Caroline Hall	72	72	70	214	1,378.66
Silvia Cavalleri	74	69	71	214	1,378.66
Elisabeth Esterl	75	69	71	215	1,153.33
Johanna Head	71	73	71	215	1,153.33
Xonia Wunsch-Ruiz	72	72	71	215	1,153.33
Marina Arruti	70	74	71	215	1,153.33
Helen Wadsworth	72	71	72	215	1,153.33
Shani Waugh	71	71	73	215	1,153.33
Ludivine Kreutz	73	73	70	216	1,028
Joanne Mills	70	73	73	216	1,028
Mia Lojdahl	75	70	72	217	944
Jane Leary	71	74	72	217	944
Joanne Morley	74	70	73	217	944
Maria Hjorth	72	71	74	217	944
Lora Fairclough	73	69	75	217	944
Lara Tadiotto	74	73	71	218	836
Catherine Schmitt	76	70	72	218	836
Alison Munt	73	70	75	218	836
Mette Hageman	73	70	75	218	836

Princess Lalla Meriem Cup

Royal Golf Dar-es-Salam, Red Course, Rabat, Morocco — November 5-8
Par 73; 6,400 yards — purse, US$70,000

	SCORES			TOTAL	MONEY
Sophie Gustafson	69	68	69	206	US$13,000
Patricia Meunier Lebouc	72	69	70	211	9,000
Federica Dassu	70	70	72	212	5,500
Sandrine Mendiburu	74	69	71	214	4,500
Joanne Morley	71	71	73	215	3,500
Xonia Wunsch-Ruiz	74	71	74	219	2,900
Johanna Head	71	74	74	219	2,900
Helen Wadsworth	74	73	74	221	2,650
Regine Lautens	75	74	72	221	2,650
Valerie Michaud	76	72	74	222	2,600
Sofia Gronberg	68	78	77	223	2,600
Kristel Mourgue d'Algue	67	80	77	224	2,600
Anne Marie Palli	73	76	76	225	2,600
Samantha Head	72	84	75	231	2,600
Amaia Arruti	76	77	78	231	2,600
Veronique Palli	76	80	81	237	2,600
Mounia Amalou	80	87	84	251	2,600
Diane Barnard	74	77		WD	

Praia D'El Rey European Cup

Praia D'El Rey Golf & Country Club, Obidos, Portugal — November 13-15
Par 36-36–72; 6,094 yards — purse, £150,000

FIRST DAY
Foursomes

Eddie Polland and Christy O'Connor, Jr. defeated Trish Johnson and Karen Lunn, 3 and 2.
Bobby Verwey and Denis O'Sullivan defeated Alison Nicholas and Marie-Laure de Lorenzi, 3 and 2.
Maria Hjorth and Lora Fairclough defeated Brian Waites and Brian Huggett, 1 up.
Catriona Matthew and Mhairi McKay defeated David Jones and Jim Rhodes, 2 and 1.
Sophie Gustafson and Catrin Nilsmark defeated Neil Coles and Tommy Horton, 1 up.

POINTS: European LPGA 3, European Seniors 2

SECOND DAY
Fourball

Polland and Jones defeated Gustafson and Nilsmark, 1 up.
O'Sullivan and Verwey halved with Lunn and Johnson.
Coles and Rhodes defeated Fairclough and Hjorth, 4 and 3.
Waites and Huggett defeated de Lorenzi and Nicholas, 1 up.
O'Connor and Horton defeated Matthew and McKay, 4 and 3.

POINTS: European Seniors 6½, European LPGA 3½

THIRD DAY
Singles

Gustafson defeated O'Sullivan, 4 and 3.
Johnson defeated Waites, 2 and 1.
Matthew defeated Verwey, 4 and 2.
Lunn defeated Rhodes, 3 and 2.
Huggett halved with Nilsmark.
Coles defeated Nicholas, 2 and 1.
Jones defeated Fairclough, 2 and 1.
Hjorth defeated Polland, 5 and 4.
O'Connor defeated McKay, 5 and 4.
De Lorenzi defeated Horton, 4 and 2.

TOTAL POINTS: European Seniors 10, European LPGA 10

(Each member of European Seniors team received £7,500; each member of European LPGA team received £7,500.)

Japan LPGA Tour

Daikin Orchid Ladies

Ryukyu Golf Club, Okinawa — March 6-8
Par 36-36–72; 6,260 yards — purse, ¥60,000,000

	SCORES			TOTAL	MONEY
Ae-Sook Kim	68	72	71	211	¥10,800,000
Mayumi Murai	71	69	71	211	4,740,000
Hisako Ohgane	69	71	71	211	4,740,000
(Kim defeated Murai and Ohgane on first extra hole.)					
Ok-Hee Ku	69	71	72	212	3,600,000
Bie-Shyun Huang	71	74	68	213	2,325,000
Kaori Higo	71	71	71	213	2,325,000
Michiko Hattori	74	68	71	213	2,325,000
Megumi Matsuo	68	71	74	213	2,325,000
Woo-Soon Ko	72	71	71	214	1,264,000
Kasumi Fujii	69	73	72	214	1,264,000
Ayako Okamoto	67	71	76	214	1,264,000
Tomoko Ueda	72	72	71	215	942,000
Mariko Watanabe	71	72	72	215	942,000
Akiko Fukushima	70	73	72	215	942,000
Takayo Bandoh	72	69	74	215	942,000
Ai-Yu Tu	71	74	71	216	672,000
Junko Yasui	74	72	70	216	672,000
Yu-Chuan Tai	73	71	72	216	672,000
Nayoko Yoshikawa	73	73	70	216	672,000
Ikuyo Shiotani	74	70	72	216	672,000
Fuki Kido	77	68	72	217	498,000
Jae-Sook Won	70	75	72	217	498,000

	SCORES			TOTAL	MONEY
Yuri Kawanami	74	72	71	217	498,000
Hiromi Takamura	72	72	73	217	498,000
Lee Oh-Soon	73	71	73	217	498,000
Wen-Lin Li	77	69	71	217	498,000
Chie Yoshida	75	72	70	217	498,000
Fusako Nagata	71	69	77	217	498,000
Chieko Nishida	73	72	73	218	408,000
Yukiko Ishiguro	73	71	74	218	408,000
Mikino Kubo	76	70	72	218	408,000
Nobuko Kizawa	74	69	75	218	408,000
Kayoko Motoki	75	68	75	218	408,000
Ayumi Sobue	68	74	76	218	408,000
Sachiko Ohshima	77	70	71	218	408,000

Saishunkan Ladies

Kumamoto Kuukou Country Club, Kumamoto — March 20-22
Par 36-36–72; 6,470 yards — purse, ¥60,000,000

	SCORES			TOTAL	MONEY
Michiko Hattori	68	75	72	215	¥10,800,000
Ok-Hee Ku	73	72	70	215	5,280,000
(Hattori defeated Ku on third extra hole.)					
Chie Yoshida	70	73	76	219	4,200,000
Hisako Ohgane	74	75	71	220	3,000,000
Tomiko Ikebuchi	71	73	76	220	3,000,000
Mieko Nomura	71	70	79	220	3,000,000
Kaori Higo	74	74	74	222	2,100,000
Lee Oh-Soon	75	73	75	223	1,800,000
Man-Soo Kim	74	76	74	224	1,218,000
Yuri Fudoh	73	75	76	224	1,218,000
Yuri Kawanami	75	73	76	224	1,218,000
Mayumi Murai	74	72	78	224	1,218,000
*Miho Koga	74	76	75	225	
Maki Sasayama	76	75	74	225	761,333
Kayo Yamada	78	73	74	225	761,333
Aki Takamura	79	71	75	225	761,333
Nayoko Yoshikawa	76	74	75	225	761,333
Mariko Watanabe	79	70	76	225	761,333
Akemi Yamaoka	74	75	76	225	761,333
Takayo Bandoh	74	72	79	225	761,333
Yuko Motoyama	78	70	77	225	761,333
Aki Nakano	72	72	81	225	761,333
Ai-Yu Tu	74	76	76	226	528,000
Toshiko Fujisaki	75	75	76	226	528,000
Hisako Takeda	73	76	77	226	528,000
Junko Yasui	77	72	77	226	528,000
Tomoko Ueda	75	74	77	226	528,000
Marnie McGuire	77	75	75	227	474,000
Woo-Soon Ko	75	77	75	227	474,000
Kaori Harada	76	77	74	227	474,000
Megumi Matsuo	78	75	74	227	474,000

Yellow Hat Tokyo Ladies Open

Wakasu Golf Links, Tokyo — March 27-29
Par 36-36–72; 6,355 yards — purse, ¥50,000,000

	SCORES			TOTAL	MONEY
Akemi Yamaoka	69	69	74	212	¥9,000,000
Nayoko Yoshikawa	71	67	75	213	3,950,000
Kaori Harada	69	71	73	213	3,950,000
Kozue Azuma	73	72	69	214	3,000,000
Junko Yasui	74	72	69	215	2,250,000
Fuki Kido	73	72	70	215	2,250,000
Aiko Takasu	72	75	69	216	1,375,000
Young-Me Lee	73	68	75	216	1,375,000
Man-Soo Kim	74	70	72	216	1,375,000
Ok-Hee Ku	74	70	72	216	1,375,000
Ai-Yu Tu	76	69	72	217	915,000
Michiko Hattori	76	69	72	217	915,000
Aki Nakano	74	74	70	218	815,000
Kaori Higo	74	71	73	218	815,000
Jean Bartholomew	77	73	69	219	690,000
Mineko Nasu	76	73	70	219	690,000
Ae-Sook Kim	74	71	74	219	690,000
Megumi Higuchi	79	70	71	220	490,000
Fumiko Muraguchi	73	75	72	220	490,000
Aki Takamura	75	72	73	220	490,000
Kayo Yamada	74	73	73	220	490,000
Marnie McGuire	71	75	74	220	490,000
Toshimi Kimura	77	69	74	220	490,000
Natsuko Noro	76	69	75	220	490,000
Akane Ohshiro	73	71	76	220	490,000
Hisako Takeda	75	75	71	221	395,000
Hsiu-Feng Tseng	77	73	71	221	395,000
Yukiyo Haga	77	72	72	221	395,000
Huang Yu-Chen	75	74	72	221	395,000
Hiromi Takamura	73	75	73	221	395,000
Mayumi Murai	75	73	73	221	395,000
Kikuko Shibata	76	72	73	221	395,000
Woo-Soon Ko	74	72	75	221	395,000

Kenshoen Ladies

Dohgo Golf Club, Matsuyama, Ehime — April 10-12
Par 36-36–72; 6,271 yards — purse, ¥50,000,000

	SCORES			TOTAL	MONEY
Chihiro Furukawa	68	69	70	207	¥9,000,000
Natsuko Noro	68	67	73	208	4,400,000
Kaori Harada	75	70	65	210	3,500,000
Keiko Arai	70	72	69	211	2,500,000
Aiko Takasu	70	70	71	211	2,500,000
Lee Oh-Soon	71	70	70	211	2,500,000
Akane Ohshiro	68	71	74	213	1,750,000
Man-Soo Kim	72	70	72	214	1,500,000
Takayo Bandoh	75	69	71	215	1,250,000
Akemi Yamaoka	74	73	69	216	898,750
Yueh-Chyn Huang	72	73	71	216	898,750
Rie Fujiwara	69	75	72	216	898,750

	SCORES			TOTAL	MONEY
Akiko Fukushima	72	71	73	216	898,750
Mitsuko Hamada	73	73	71	217	665,000
Yuri Kawanami	70	75	72	217	665,000
Fuki Kido	73	75	69	217	665,000
Mineko Nasu	72	72	73	217	665,000
Fumiko Muraguchi	69	73	75	217	665,000
Hisako Takeda	70	76	72	218	434,000
Kayo Yamada	69	77	72	218	434,000
Mikako Kanamori	73	73	72	218	434,000
Kaori Higo	74	72	72	218	434,000
Megumi Higuchi	74	72	72	218	434,000
Hiromi Takamura	72	75	71	218	434,000
Ok-Hee Ku	72	76	70	218	434,000
Kozue Azuma	72	76	70	218	434,000
Yukiyo Haga	73	72	73	218	434,000
Ikuyo Shiotani	71	70	77	218	434,000
Michie Ohba	73	73	73	219	340,000
Yuri Fudoh	75	72	72	219	340,000
Tomiko Ikebuchi	74	72	73	219	340,000
Yuka Irie	73	74	72	219	340,000
Hiroko Tanabe	72	75	72	219	340,000
Nayoko Yoshikawa	74	72	73	219	340,000
Yuka Shiroto	65	78	76	219	340,000
Toshiko Fujisaki	73	71	75	219	340,000

Glory Queen's Cup

Shishido Country Club, Omiya, Ibaraki
Par 36-36–72; 6,358 yards

April 17-19
purse, ¥50,000,000

	SCORES			TOTAL	MONEY
Kaori Harada	73	70	72	215	¥9,000,000
Michiko Hattori	70	73	73	216	3,950,000
Yuko Motoyama	74	68	74	216	3,950,000
Aki Takamura	70	77	70	217	2,312,500
Akane Ohshiro	72	73	72	217	2,312,500
Huang Yu-Chen	72	72	73	217	2,312,500
Akemi Yamaoka	71	71	75	217	2,312,500
Akiko Fukushima	72	76	70	218	1,173,750
Hsiu-Feng Tseng	76	72	70	218	1,173,750
Nayoko Yoshikawa	72	72	74	218	1,173,750
Ae-Sook Kim	73	71	74	218	1,173,750
Man-Soo Kim	71	76	72	219	845,000
Chieko Nishida	74	71	74	219	845,000
Marnie McGuire	74	70	75	219	845,000
Takayo Bandoh	76	73	71	220	645,000
Hisako Ohgane	76	72	72	220	645,000
Keiko Arai	76	72	72	220	645,000
Kaori Higo	75	71	74	220	645,000
Junko Yasui	70	75	75	220	645,000
Mayumi Murai	75	75	71	221	465,000
Shin Sora	75	74	72	221	465,000
Fuki Kido	71	77	73	221	465,000
Harumi Sakagami	71	77	73	221	465,000
Tomiko Ikebuchi	75	73	73	221	465,000
Yuri Kawanami	74	71	76	221	465,000
Tomoko Ueda	73	72	76	221	465,000
Megumi Matsuo	76	75	71	222	410,000

	SCORES			TOTAL	MONEY
Young-Me Lee	76	74	72	222	410,000
Jae-Sook Won	79	69	74	222	410,000
Kozue Azuma	70	75	77	222	410,000

Nasu Ogawa Ladies

Nasu Ogawa Golf Club, Ogawa, Tochigi — April 24-26
Par 36-36–72; 6,163 yards — purse, ¥50,000,000

	SCORES			TOTAL	MONEY
Michiko Hattori	69	71	76	216	¥9,000,000
Chieko Nishida	70	73	73	216	4,400,000
(Hattori defeated Nishida on first extra hole.)					
Ai-Yu Tu	76	71	70	217	2,750,000
Yukiyo Haga	74	72	71	217	2,750,000
Hsiu-Feng Tseng	71	73	73	217	2,750,000
Yu-Chuan Tai	73	71	73	217	2,750,000
Yuri Kawanami	72	73	73	218	1,375,000
Takayo Bandoh	73	71	74	218	1,375,000
Mikino Kubo	71	72	75	218	1,375,000
Mayumi Ishii	74	69	75	218	1,375,000
Michie Ohba	73	71	75	219	885,000
Natsuko Noro	73	71	75	219	885,000
Kasumi Fujii	76	72	72	220	614,444
Aki Nakano	74	75	71	220	614,444
Kaori Higo	78	71	71	220	614,444
Ok-Hee Ku	77	70	73	220	614,444
Yuko Moriguchi	74	73	73	220	614,444
Woo-Soon Ko	71	74	75	220	614,444
Fumiko Muraguchi	72	73	75	220	614,444
Hiromi Takamura	72	73	75	220	614,444
Suzuko Maeda	72	73	75	220	614,444
Megumi Matsuo	78	70	73	221	430,000
Misayo Fujisawa	71	77	73	221	430,000
Marnie McGuire	71	75	75	221	430,000
Huang Yu-Chen	75	74	73	222	395,000
Junko Yasui	75	75	72	222	395,000
Kumiko Fuchi	78	72	72	222	395,000
Mineko Nasu	76	75	71	222	395,000
Yoko Inoue	75	73	75	223	335,000
Toshimi Kimura	76	72	75	223	335,000
Ikuyo Shiotani	73	76	74	223	335,000
Nobuko Kizawa	72	74	77	223	335,000
Man-Soo Kim	75	71	77	223	335,000
Kaori Harada	74	71	78	223	335,000
Akane Ohshiro	79	72	72	223	335,000
Hiroe Tani	71	70	82	223	335,000

Katokichi Queens

Sakaide Country Club, Sakaide, Kagawa — May 1-3
Par 36-36–72; 6,290 yards — purse, ¥50,000,000

	SCORES			TOTAL	MONEY
Tamayo Ueda	71	71	74	216	¥9,000,000
Mieko Nomura	73	73	71	217	3,350,000

	SCORES			TOTAL	MONEY
Mikino Kubo	76	69	72	217	3,350,000
Yueh-Chyn Huang	73	72	72	217	3,350,000
Hiromi Takamura	72	71	74	217	3,350,000
Yuri Kawanami	70	79	69	218	1,750,000
Ae-Sook Kim	73	73	72	218	1,750,000
Chihiro Furukawa	69	76	73	218	1,750,000
Kaori Higo	71	78	70	219	987,000
Ayako Okamoto	76	72	71	219	987,000
Fumiko Muraguchi	73	74	72	219	987,000
Yuko Motoyama	76	71	72	219	987,000
Mariko Watanabe	74	70	75	219	987,000
Natsuko Noro	79	71	70	220	695,000
Junko Yoshida	77	71	72	220	695,000
Junko Yasui	73	75	72	220	695,000
Michie Ohba	72	75	73	220	695,000
Kumiko Hiyoshi	75	73	72	220	695,000
Yu-Chuan Tai	73	75	73	221	508,333
Kaori Harada	74	72	75	221	508,333
Yoshiko Masuda	74	69	78	221	508,333
Misako Toba	77	74	71	222	470,000
Wen-Lin Li	74	74	74	222	470,000
Yuka Shiroto	76	75	72	223	440,000
Chieko Amanuma	74	75	74	223	440,000
Lee Oh-Soon	73	74	76	223	440,000
Hiromi Hirakata	74	72	77	223	440,000
Mineko Nasu	74	77	73	224	385,000
Keiko Suzuki	76	75	73	224	385,000
Syoko Asano	72	77	75	224	385,000
Harumi Hyodoh	73	75	76	224	385,000
Huang Yu-Chen	75	74	75	224	385,000
Megumi Matsuo	75	73	76	224	385,000
Kayo Yamada	72	73	79	224	385,000

Gunze Cup World Ladies

Yomiuri Golf Club, Inagi, Tokyo — May 7-10
Par 36-36–72; 6,411 yards — purse, ¥60,000,000

	SCORES				TOTAL	MONEY
Liselotte Neumann	75	70	65	72	282	¥10,800,000
Woo-Soon Ko	67	70	73	72	282	4,740,000
Young-Me Lee	68	75	70	69	282	4,740,000
(Neumann defeated Lee and Ko on third extra hole.)						
Hiromi Takamura	71	75	70	67	283	3,600,000
Hisako Ohgane	74	76	69	65	284	3,000,000
Man-Soo Kim	72	73	70	70	285	2,250,000
Yueh-Chyn Huang	71	70	74	70	285	2,250,000
Karrie Webb	74	72	72	69	287	1,800,000
Akane Ohshiro	72	74	73	69	288	1,266,000
Fuki Kido	71	76	71	70	288	1,266,000
Natsuko Noro	71	73	73	71	288	1,266,000
Fumiko Muraguchi	73	75	71	70	289	1,008,000
Yuko Moriguchi	69	74	73	73	289	1,008,000
Tomoko Ueda	71	75	78	68	292	738,000
Chieko Nishida	78	74	70	70	292	738,000
Patricia Meunier Lebouc	77	74	70	71	292	738,000
Kaori Higo	73	75	73	71	292	738,000
Kiyoe Yamazaki	71	75	74	72	292	738,000

	SCORES				TOTAL	MONEY
Yuka Shiroto	75	75	69	73	292	738,000
Yuri Kawanami	72	73	72	75	292	738,000
Laura Davies	74	76	73	71	294	510,000
Lee Oh-Soon	74	77	73	70	294	510,000
Kumiko Hiyoshi	77	74	71	72	294	510,000
Aki Nakano	74	75	72	73	294	510,000
Yuri Fudoh	75	73	72	74	294	510,000
Nayoko Yoshikawa	73	73	73	75	294	510,000
Toshimi Kimura	70	75	73	76	294	510,000
Ok-Hee Ku	76	74	73	72	295	456,000
Aiko Hashimoto	72	76	72	75	295	456,000
Chie Yoshida	76	76	71	73	296	420,000
Ae-Sook Kim	71	78	73	74	296	420,000
Yukiyo Haga	74	77	70	75	296	420,000
Aiko Takasu	72	80	76	68	296	420,000

Yakult Ladies

Kokusai Country Club, Munakata, Fukuoka — May 15-17
Par 36-36–72; 6,279 yards — purse, ¥60,000,000

	SCORES			TOTAL	MONEY
Aiko Takasu	71	70	72	213	¥10,800,000
Kayo Yamada	71	73	69	213	4,740,000
Fumiko Muraguchi	73	71	69	213	4,740,000
(Takasu defeated Yamada on first and Muraguchi at second extra hole.)					
Toshiko Fujisaki	72	71	71	214	3,300,000
Hisako Takeda	71	69	74	214	3,300,000
Akemi Yamaoka	75	69	71	215	2,250,000
Michie Ohba	72	71	72	215	2,250,000
Hsiu-Feng Tseng	74	73	69	216	1,399,500
Aki Nakano	72	74	70	216	1,399,500
Fuki Kido	72	72	72	216	1,399,500
Hiromi Takamura	71	72	73	216	1,399,500
Kaori Higo	74	75	68	217	888,000
Yuko Moriguchi	72	75	70	217	888,000
Yuri Fudoh	73	74	70	217	888,000
Nayoko Yoshikawa	75	71	71	217	888,000
Aki Takamura	74	71	72	217	888,000
Kumiko Fuchi	72	72	73	217	888,000
Tatsuko Morimoto	72	76	70	218	576,000
Mariko Watanabe	72	74	72	218	576,000
Tomiko Ikebuchi	76	70	72	218	576,000
Chihiro Furukawa	75	71	72	218	576,000
Hisako Ohgane	71	73	74	218	576,000
Ae-Sook Kim	70	72	76	218	576,000
Kotomi Akiyama	76	73	70	219	450,000
Shin Sora	74	75	70	219	450,000
Nahoko Hirao	72	76	71	219	450,000
Megumi Matsuo	73	75	71	219	450,000
Huang Yu-Chen	74	74	71	219	450,000
Keiko Arai	76	71	72	219	450,000
Natsuko Noro	73	73	73	219	450,000
Yuka Shiroto	73	72	74	219	450,000
Jae-Sook Won	71	73	75	219	450,000
Kasumi Fujii	72	72	75	219	450,000
Woo-Soon Ko	71	72	76	219	450,000

Chukyo TV Bridgestone Ladies

Kasugai Country Club, Aichi — May 22-24
Par 36-36–72; 6,261 yards — purse, ¥50,000,000

	SCORES			TOTAL	MONEY
Ok-Hee Ku	70	68	75	213	¥9,000,000
Miyuki Shimabukuro	69	69	75	213	4,400,000
(Ku defeated Shimabukuro on first extra hole.)					
Nayoko Yoshikawa	70	75	69	214	2,550,000
Chieko Nishida	72	71	71	214	2,550,000
Fuki Kido	73	69	72	214	2,550,000
Kris Tschetter	69	72	73	214	2,550,000
Ae-Sook Kim	70	70	74	214	2,550,000
Michie Ohba	70	75	70	215	1,157,500
Junko Yasui	74	70	71	215	1,157,500
Hsiu-Feng Tseng	70	70	75	215	1,157,500
Fumiko Muraguchi	75	66	74	215	1,157,500
Man-Soo Kim	73	70	74	217	830,000
Aiko Takasu	72	75	71	218	680,000
Wen-Lin Li	72	73	73	218	680,000
Yu-Chuan Tai	69	75	74	218	680,000
Aki Takamura	69	74	75	218	680,000
Mieko Nomura	73	70	75	218	680,000
Mariko Watanabe	75	72	72	219	465,000
Hisako Takeda	75	72	72	219	465,000
Yoko Inoue	71	74	74	219	465,000
Natsuko Noro	76	69	74	219	465,000
Tomiko Ikebuchi	77	67	76	220	410,000
Fusako Nagata	72	78	71	221	385,000
Akemi Yamaoka	72	74	75	221	385,000
Megumi Matsuo	71	74	76	221	385,000
Ai-Yu Tu	71	72	78	221	385,000
Kotomi Akiyama	73	77	72	222	340,000
Yuri Fudoh	73	75	74	222	340,000
Kiyoe Yamazaki	75	72	75	222	340,000
Takayo Bandoh	75	72	75	222	340,000
Mineko Nasu	72	73	77	222	340,000

Toto Motors Ladies

Toto Hannoh Country Club, Saitama — May 29-31
Par 36-36–72; 6,205 yards — purse, ¥50,000,000

	SCORES			TOTAL	MONEY
Young-Me Lee	71	68	69	208	¥9,000,000
Kaori Harada	70	69	70	209	4,400,000
Fusako Nagata	73	66	72	211	3,500,000
Ok-Hee Ku	72	71	70	213	2,500,000
Akiko Fukushima	70	72	71	213	2,500,000
Aiko Takasu	74	69	70	213	2,500,000
Kayo Fukumoto	69	71	74	214	1,625,000
Woo-Soon Ko	71	70	73	214	1,625,000
Yu-Chuan Tai	75	70	70	215	1,061,666
Maki Sasayama	74	70	71	215	1,061,666
Wen-Lin Li	72	71	72	215	1,061,666
Takayo Bandoh	74	71	71	216	860,000
Megumi Matsuo	73	69	74	216	860,000

	SCORES			TOTAL	MONEY
Tomiko Ikebuchi	70	73	74	217	735,000
Tomoko Ueda	70	72	75	217	735,000
Mayumi Murai	70	72	75	217	735,000
Chihiro Furukawa	74	72	72	218	585,000
Shin Sora	73	71	74	218	585,000
Fumiko Muraguchi	72	70	76	218	585,000
Michie Ohba	74	71	74	219	465,000
Yuko Motoyama	71	73	75	219	465,000
Hiromi Takamura	73	71	75	219	465,000
Huang Yu-Chen	72	71	76	219	465,000
Hiromi Hirakata	74	68	77	219	465,000
Yumiko Akagi	74	71	75	220	390,000
Fuki Kido	76	70	74	220	390,000
Toshiko Fujisaki	74	72	74	220	390,000
Ai-Yu Tu	74	71	75	220	390,000
Lee Jui-Hui	74	71	75	220	390,000
Junko Yoshida	74	71	75	220	390,000
Harumi Sakagami	73	73	74	220	390,000
Akemi Yamaoka	76	71	73	220	390,000
Kasumi Fujii	73	74	73	220	390,000
Yueh-Chyn Huang	73	74	73	220	390,000

Resort Trust Ladies

Maple Point Golf Club, Uenohara, Yamanashi — June 5-7
Par 36-36–72; 6,433 yards — purse, ¥50,000,000

	SCORES			TOTAL	MONEY
Kaori Harada	69	68	70	207	¥9,000,000
Natsuko Noro	68	71	70	209	4,400,000
Yuri Fudoh	72	70	68	210	3,250,000
Hsiu-Feng Tseng	69	70	71	210	3,250,000
Fumiko Muraguchi	71	71	69	211	2,250,000
Akiko Fukushima	70	67	74	211	2,250,000
Kasumi Fujii	70	73	69	212	1,500,000
Keiko Suzuki	72	70	70	212	1,500,000
Man-Soo Kim	70	71	71	212	1,500,000
Kaori Higo	72	71	70	213	943,333
Ok-Hee Ku	70	72	71	213	943,333
Yuka Shiroto	69	71	73	213	943,333
Kozue Azuma	75	68	71	214	840,000
Ae-Sook Kim	73	72	70	215	715,000
Kotomi Akiyama	70	73	72	215	715,000
Nayoko Yoshikawa	70	72	73	215	715,000
Aki Nakano	67	71	77	215	715,000
Huang Yu-Chen	70	73	73	216	565,000
Chie Yoshida	73	70	73	216	565,000
Young-Me Lee	73	74	70	217	450,000
Bie-Shyun Huang	74	72	71	217	450,000
Akane Ohshiro	73	72	72	217	450,000
Yuko Motoyama	71	73	73	217	450,000
Miyuki Shimabukuro	71	72	74	217	450,000
Masako Ishihara	68	74	75	217	450,000
Michiko Okada	72	70	75	217	450,000
Woo-Soon Ko	73	68	76	217	450,000
Lee Oh-Soon	73	69	75	217	450,000
Toshiko Fujisaki	72	75	71	218	380,000
Yumi Kubota	70	76	72	218	380,000

	SCORES			TOTAL	MONEY
Chikayo Yamazaki	76	69	73	218	380,000
Yu-Chuan Tai	72	72	74	218	380,000
Yuko Moriguchi	71	71	76	218	380,000

Suntory Ladies Open

Arima Royal Golf Club, Kobe — June 11-14
Par 36-36–72; 6,346 yards — purse, ¥50,000,000

	SCORES				TOTAL	MONEY
Marnie McGuire	68	71	72	72	283	¥9,000,000
Yuri Kawanami	74	69	74	69	286	4,400,000
Kaori Harada	74	71	74	69	288	3,250,000
Aki Nakano	71	72	72	73	288	3,250,000
Yuko Moriguchi	74	70	76	70	290	2,250,000
Natsuko Noro	75	69	75	71	290	2,250,000
Kotomi Akiyama	72	73	75	71	291	1,750,000
Mikiyo Nishizuka	72	74	75	71	292	1,250,000
Akemi Yamaoka	75	72	74	71	292	1,250,000
Kaori Higo	73	71	74	74	292	1,250,000
Nayoko Yoshikawa	69	73	76	75	293	845,000
Fuki Kido	76	69	70	78	293	845,000
Suzuko Maeda	75	70	77	72	294	695,000
Hiromi Takamura	73	68	79	74	294	695,000
Michiko Hattori	73	73	74	74	294	695,000
Kiyo Yamamura	75	71	74	74	294	695,000
Kasumi Fujii	73	69	80	73	295	436,666
Chieko Nishida	73	75	75	72	295	436,666
Kozue Azuma	72	72	78	73	295	436,666
Keiko Arai	75	73	73	74	295	436,666
Young-Me Lee	71	71	79	74	295	436,666
Hisako Takeda	73	69	78	75	295	436,666
Yukiyo Haga	71	77	72	75	295	436,666
Ayako Shibata	70	76	74	75	295	436,666
Ae-Sook Kim	71	71	74	79	295	436,666
Huang Yu-Chen	73	71	79	73	296	330,000
Sachiko Ohshima	73	73	78	72	296	330,000
Yu-Chuan Tai	75	73	77	71	296	330,000
Aiko Takasu	74	70	77	75	296	330,000
Reiko Kashiwado	73	73	79	71	296	330,000
Mei-Chi Cheng	75	69	76	76	296	330,000
Yoko Inoue	72	70	77	77	296	330,000

Dunlop Ladies Open

Cypress Golf Club, Hikami, Hyogo — June 19-21
Par 36-36–72; 6,378 yards — purse, ¥50,000,000

	SCORES			TOTAL	MONEY
Huang Yu-Chen	72	68	73	213	¥9,000,000
Akiko Fukushima	74	74	69	217	3,350,000
Mayumi Inoue	72	73	72	217	3,350,000
Man-Soo Kim	72	72	73	217	3,350,000
Chieko Nishida	71	71	75	217	3,350,000
Fumiko Muraguchi	75	68	75	218	2,000,000

	SCORES			TOTAL	MONEY
Lee Oh-Soon	73	74	72	219	1,625,000
Shin Sora	76	68	75	219	1,625,000
Aiko Takasu	76	70	74	220	1,250,000
Fuki Kido	80	69	72	221	960,000
Yuri Fudoh	70	74	77	221	960,000
Chie Yoshida	77	75	70	222	695,000
Tomoko Ueda	77	72	73	222	695,000
Harumi Sakagami	74	74	74	222	695,000
Yoko Inoue	75	73	74	222	695,000
Kasumi Fujii	75	73	74	222	695,000
Natsuko Noro	79	67	76	222	695,000
Ae-Sook Kim	73	72	77	222	695,000
Toshimi Kimura	72	73	77	222	695,000
Ok-Hee Ku	74	76	73	223	440,000
Yuka Shiroto	74	76	73	223	440,000
Ayako Shibata	77	72	74	223	440,000
Junko Yasui	77	72	74	223	440,000
Yuko Motoyama	74	74	75	223	440,000
Fusako Nagata	74	73	76	223	440,000
Michiko Hattori	75	70	78	223	440,000
Junko Omote	79	72	73	224	390,000
Tomiko Ikebuchi	75	75	74	224	390,000
Ai-Yu Tu	79	68	77	224	390,000
Akane Ohshiro	80	72	73	225	340,000
Chikako Matsuzawa	76	76	73	225	340,000
Yukiyo Haga	78	73	74	225	340,000
Mayumi Murai	78	71	76	225	340,000
Megumi Matsuo	74	72	79	225	340,000
Kyoko Ono	75	71	79	225	340,000
Hisako Takeda	76	69	80	225	340,000

Japan Women's Open

Miyosi Country Club, Miyoshi, Aichi — June 25-28
Par 36-36–72; 6,320 yards — purse, ¥70,000,000

	SCORES				TOTAL	MONEY
Natsuko Noro	68	75	71	72	286	¥14,000,000
Huang Yu-Chen	68	74	73	73	288	7,700,000
Shin Sora	71	71	76	73	291	3,978,333
Ok-Hee Ku	72	75	71	73	291	3,978,333
Akiko Fukushima	77	71	68	75	291	3,978,333
Yuri Fudoh	73	73	75	71	292	2,096,000
Akemi Yamaoka	70	74	73	75	292	2,096,000
Marnie McGuire	74	69	72	77	292	2,096,000
Nayoko Yoshikawa	77	75	71	70	293	1,450,666
Rie Mitsuhashi	73	72	77	71	293	1,450,666
*Yun-Jye Wei	73	75	71	74	293	
Michiko Okada	70	73	75	75	293	1,450,666
Kumiko Hiyoshi	74	76	76	68	294	1,154,000
Tomiko Ikebuchi	72	75	74	74	295	964,000
Kayo Yamada	71	74	74	76	295	964,000
Megumi Matsuo	74	72	72	77	295	964,000
Mutsuko Maekawa	74	74	75	73	296	777,333
Yuko Motoyama	73	75	73	75	296	777,333
Wen-Lin Li	72	78	68	78	296	777,333
Aki Takamura	71	76	77	73	297	649,200

	SCORES				TOTAL	MONEY
Fuki Kido	77	73	74	73	297	649,200
Hiromi Takamura	75	71	76	75	297	649,200
Harumi Sakagami	76	72	73	76	297	649,200
Yukiyo Haga	73	71	75	78	297	649,200
Yuri Kawanami	73	75	77	73	298	574,500
Ae-Sook Kim	73	78	74	73	298	574,500
Mayumi Murai	70	79	75	74	298	574,500
Michie Ohba	72	79	72	75	298	574,500
Syoko Asano	73	73	81	72	299	498,500
*Ayaka Shigaki	78	73	76	72	299	
Yueh-Chyn Huang	75	77	75	72	299	498,500
Kaori Harada	73	78	75	73	299	498,500
Rie Fujiwara	72	78	74	75	299	498,500
Yoko Inoue	72	80	71	76	299	498,500
Mayumi Inoue	75	73	73	78	299	498,500
Young-Me Lee	75	73	71	80	299	498,500
Mei-Chi Cheng	74	74	70	81	299	498,500

Toyo Suisan Ladies

Kosaido Sapporo Country Club, Hokkaido — July 10-12
Par 36-36–72; 6,412 yards — purse, ¥50,000,000

	SCORES			TOTAL	MONEY
Michie Ohba	69	75	66	210	¥9,000,000
Woo-Soon Ko	66	70	75	211	4,400,000
Kumiko Hiyoshi	67	74	71	212	3,500,000
Nayoko Yoshikawa	69	70	74	213	2,750,000
Yuri Fudoh	70	69	74	213	2,750,000
Yuko Moriguchi	72	71	72	214	1,875,000
Akemi Yamaoka	71	70	73	214	1,875,000
Ok-Hee Ku	74	73	68	215	1,250,000
Jae-Sook Won	74	69	72	215	1,250,000
Kayo Yamada	69	72	74	215	1,250,000
Misayo Fujisawa	71	74	71	216	850,000
Kasumi Fujii	73	72	71	216	850,000
Kaori Higo	71	72	73	216	850,000
Aki Takamura	72	71	73	216	850,000
Yuri Kawanami	74	69	73	216	850,000
Junko Ishii	72	74	71	217	625,000
Natsuko Noro	72	73	72	217	625,000
Yumiko Akagi	73	72	72	217	625,000
Bie-Shyun Huang	70	72	75	217	625,000
Ai-Yu Tu	73	74	71	218	465,000
Yukiyo Haga	75	72	71	218	465,000
Fuki Kido	74	72	72	218	465,000
Fumiko Muraguchi	74	70	74	218	465,000
Chie Yoshida	71	73	74	218	465,000
Sachiko Ohshima	71	72	75	218	465,000
Toshimi Kimura	73	70	75	218	465,000
Tomiko Ikebuchi	71	68	79	218	465,000
Chieko Nishida	76	71	72	219	400,000
Kozue Azuma	75	72	72	219	400,000
Junko Omote	70	74	75	219	400,000
Michiko Okada	70	74	75	219	400,000
Aki Nakano	73	70	76	219	400,000

Sumitomo Visa Taiheiyo Ladies

Taiheiyo Golf Gotenba, West Course, Shi — July 24-26
Par 36-36–72; 6,177 yards — purse, ¥60,000,000

	SCORES			TOTAL	MONEY
Aki Nakano	70	71	67	208	¥10,800,000
Yuri Fudoh	71	73	67	211	5,280,000
Pat Hurst	70	68	74	212	4,200,000
Mieko Nomura	71	73	70	214	3,600,000
Kayo Yamada	72	71	72	215	3,000,000
Man-Soo Kim	72	73	71	216	2,100,000
Kaori Higo	75	69	72	216	2,100,000
Yu-Chuan Tai	74	70	72	216	2,100,000
Yoko Inoue	74	76	67	217	1,166,400
Yuka Shiroto	74	74	69	217	1,166,400
Megumi Higuchi	72	75	70	217	1,166,400
Akemi Yamaoka	77	70	70	217	1,166,400
Mayumi Murai	73	69	75	217	1,166,400
Chihiro Furukawa	75	73	70	218	804,000
Chieko Amanuma	72	73	73	218	804,000
Michiko Hattori	71	74	73	218	804,000
Natsuko Noro	70	72	76	218	804,000
Megumi Matsuo	72	71	75	218	804,000
Mitsuyo Hirata	74	75	70	219	561,600
Syoko Asano	75	73	71	219	561,600
Huang Yu-Chen	73	73	73	219	561,600
Akane Ohshiro	72	72	75	219	561,600
Tomoko Ueda	72	72	75	219	561,600
Toshimi Kimura	70	79	71	220	492,000
Chieko Nishida	76	71	73	220	492,000
Ok-Hee Ku	74	73	73	220	492,000
Kaori Harada	77	69	74	220	492,000
Janice Moodie	74	71	75	220	492,000
Tamayo Ueda	78	73	70	221	426,000
Hsiu-Feng Tseng	74	75	72	221	426,000
Hisako Ohgane	75	74	72	221	426,000
Aiko Takasu	73	75	73	221	426,000
Fuki Kido	74	72	75	221	426,000
Yumiko Akagi	72	74	75	221	426,000

Golf 5 Ladies

Mizunami Country Club, Gifu — July 31-August 2
Par 36-36–72; 6,449 yards — purse, ¥50,000,000

	SCORES			TOTAL	MONEY
Akiko Fukushima	69	70	69	208	¥9,000,000
Ok-Hee Ku	69	71	69	209	4,400,000
Marnie McGuire	69	69	72	210	3,500,000
Takayo Bandoh	71	69	72	212	3,000,000
Yoko Inoue	72	71	71	214	2,250,000
Kozue Azuma	70	72	72	214	2,250,000
Huang Yu-Chen	77	69	69	215	1,750,000
Miyuki Shimabukuro	74	71	71	216	1,375,000
Kaori Higo	73	68	75	216	1,375,000
Tomiko Ikebuchi	72	72	73	217	926,666
Yukiko Ishiguro	68	74	75	217	926,666

	SCORES			TOTAL	MONEY
Michiko Hattori	71	70	76	217	926,666
Chihiro Furukawa	70	76	72	218	640,000
Masako Ishihara	75	71	72	218	640,000
Natsuko Noro	74	72	72	218	640,000
Hiromi Takamura	71	74	73	218	640,000
Junko Yasui	72	72	74	218	640,000
Aki Nakano	73	75	70	218	640,000
Ai-Yu Tu	73	71	74	218	640,000
Yuri Kawanami	72	71	75	218	640,000
Nayoko Yoshikawa	73	73	73	219	440,000
Suzuko Maeda	74	72	73	219	440,000
Mieko Nomura	74	74	71	219	440,000
Fuki Kido	70	75	74	219	440,000
Mayumi Inoue	72	74	74	220	380,000
Yuko Motoyama	75	72	73	220	380,000
Young-Me Lee	73	74	73	220	380,000
Ae-Sook Kim	76	72	72	220	380,000
Lee Oh-Soon	74	71	75	220	380,000
Mei-Chi Cheng	69	72	79	220	380,000
Syoko Asano	73	76	71	220	380,000
Mitsuyo Hirata	77	72	71	220	380,000

Mizuno Ladies

Asahikokusai Tojo Country Club, Tojo, Hyogo — August 6-9
Par 36-36–72; 6,480 yards — purse, ¥60,000,000

	SCORES				TOTAL	MONEY
Fuki Kido	72	70	69	70	281	¥10,800,000
Young-Me Lee	75	72	69	71	287	4,740,000
Yuka Irie	69	74	71	73	287	4,740,000
Akiko Fukushima	74	74	73	67	288	2,775,000
Yuko Motoyama	70	75	74	69	288	2,775,000
Hisako Ohgane	71	73	74	70	288	2,775,000
Ae-Sook Kim	73	72	71	72	288	2,775,000
Huang Yu-Chen	77	72	67	73	289	1,800,000
Shin Sora	75	73	73	69	290	1,184,400
Kaori Harada	73	70	76	71	290	1,184,400
Kyoko Ono	70	77	72	71	290	1,184,400
Kaori Higo	73	73	73	71	290	1,184,400
Natsuko Noro	75	73	71	71	290	1,184,400
Junko Ishii	76	69	73	73	291	924,000
Aki Nakano	70	72	72	77	291	924,000
Akane Ohshiro	76	70	74	72	292	804,000
Suzuko Maeda	73	72	71	76	292	804,000
Chihiro Furukawa	75	72	74	72	293	622,800
Tomoko Ueda	71	74	76	72	293	622,800
Toshimi Kimura	72	74	74	73	293	622,800
Yukiyo Haga	74	71	74	74	293	622,800
Kozue Azuma	69	74	72	78	293	622,800
Michiko Hattori	76	70	75	73	294	540,000
Chikayo Yamazaki	73	76	75	70	294	540,000
Fumiko Muraguchi	75	73	72	74	294	540,000
Chieko Amanuma	70	74	73	77	294	540,000
Chikako Matsuzawa	69	75	77	74	295	510,000
Yueh-Chyn Huang	72	77	74	73	296	486,000
Yu-Chuan Tai	72	76	75	73	296	486,000
Mieko Nomura	72	73	74	77	296	486,000

NEC Karuizawa 72

Karuizawa 72 Golf Club, Karuizawa, Nagano — August 14-16
Par 36-36–72; 6,483 yards — purse, ¥60,000,000

	SCORES			TOTAL	MONEY
Yuka Irie	67	67	70	204	¥10,800,000
Kaori Harada	66	74	68	208	4,360,000
Akiko Fukushima	70	69	69	208	4,360,000
Michiko Hattori	69	71	68	208	4,360,000
Mikino Kubo	67	74	68	209	3,000,000
Kyoko Ono	66	76	69	211	2,100,000
Misayo Fujisawa	73	69	69	211	2,100,000
Aki Nakano	71	70	70	211	2,100,000
Harumi Sakagami	68	75	70	213	1,280,000
Yoko Inoue	71	71	71	213	1,280,000
Young-Me Lee	72	69	72	213	1,280,000
Kasumi Fujii	71	71	73	215	1,050,000
Yuri Fudoh	69	73	73	215	1,050,000
Nayoko Yoshikawa	71	73	72	216	870,000
Wen-Lin Li	70	73	73	216	870,000
Chikayo Yamazaki	70	72	74	216	870,000
Ok-Hee Ku	70	71	75	216	870,000
Mina Nishikawa	72	72	73	217	660,000
Yuri Kawanami	72	72	73	217	660,000
Akane Ohshiro	72	70	75	217	660,000
Masako Ishihara	71	76	71	218	552,000
Megumi Matsuo	71	76	71	218	552,000
Rie Fujiwara	71	74	73	218	552,000
Mayumi Murai	71	74	73	218	552,000
Chikako Matsuzawa	72	72	74	218	552,000
Jae-Sook Won	72	72	74	218	552,000
Kotomi Akiyama	70	71	77	218	552,000
Momoyo Kawakubo	69	77	73	219	486,000
Mitsuyo Hirata	71	74	74	219	486,000
Junko Yasui	70	75	74	219	486,000
Shin Sora	71	73	75	219	486,000

New Caterpillar Mitsubishi Ladies

Daihakone Country Club, Hakone, Kanagawa — August 21-23
Par 36-37–73; 6,662 yards — purse, ¥60,000,000

	SCORES			TOTAL	MONEY
Kyoko Ono	74	70	72	216	¥10,800,000
Yuri Fudoh	73	73	72	218	4,740,000
Fuki Kido	71	70	77	218	4,740,000
Ok-Hee Ku	72	76	71	219	2,775,000
Harumi Sakagami	73	74	72	219	2,775,000
Hiromi Takamura	70	77	72	219	2,775,000
Chikayo Yamazaki	69	73	77	219	2,775,000
Yuko Motoyama	76	71	73	220	1,650,000
Akane Ohshiro	73	73	74	220	1,650,000
Michie Ohba	72	76	73	221	1,137,000
Aki Takamura	70	75	76	221	1,137,000
Aiko Takasu	72	78	72	222	924,000
Kasumi Fujii	76	74	72	222	924,000
Kayo Yamada	78	72	72	222	924,000

	SCORES			TOTAL	MONEY
Aki Nakano	74	73	75	222	924,000
Kiyoe Yamazaki	76	75	72	223	684,000
Natsuko Noro	73	76	74	223	684,000
Yuko Moriguchi	74	74	75	223	684,000
Yoko Inoue	70	76	77	223	684,000
Huang Yu-Chen	75	78	71	224	504,000
Fumiko Muraguchi	75	77	72	224	504,000
Chihiro Furukawa	71	79	74	224	504,000
Woo-Soon Ko	73	77	74	224	504,000
Nayoko Yoshikawa	75	73	76	224	504,000
Junko Ishii	73	74	77	224	504,000
Ae-Sook Kim	73	79	73	225	432,000
Yukiko Ishiguro	72	79	74	225	432,000
Yueh-Chyn Huang	73	76	76	225	432,000
Kaori Harada	75	75	75	225	432,000
Hisako Takeda	74	75	76	225	432,000
Mikiyo Nishizuka	73	75	77	225	432,000

Goyo Kensetsu Ladies

Nobozaki Golf Club, Nobosaki, Nagasaki — August 28-30
Par 36-36–72; 6,307 yards — purse, ¥60,000,000

	SCORES			TOTAL	MONEY
Harumi Sakagami	73	69	67	209	¥10,800,000
Atsuko Hikage	69	72	68	209	4,740,000
Kaori Higo	73	69	67	209	4,740,000
(Sakagami defeated Higo on second and Hikage on fourth extra hole.)					
Fuki Kido	68	71	71	210	3,000,000
Fusako Nagata	70	68	72	210	3,000,000
Aiko Hashimoto	67	71	72	210	3,000,000
Chie Yoshida	68	70	73	211	1,950,000
Mayumi Murai	71	67	73	211	1,950,000
Yumiko Akagi	72	72	68	212	1,350,000
Jae-Sook Won	73	69	70	212	1,350,000
Yuri Kawanami	69	76	68	213	900,000
Hisako Takeda	71	72	70	213	900,000
Miki Furuya	70	73	70	213	900,000
Takayo Bandoh	73	70	70	213	900,000
Man-Soo Kim	72	71	70	213	900,000
Natsuko Noro	70	72	71	213	900,000
Kasumi Fujii	75	67	71	213	900,000
Huang Yu-Chen	73	69	71	213	900,000
Chieko Nishida	70	70	73	213	900,000
Woo-Soon Ko	69	75	70	214	576,000
Hiroe Tani	70	72	72	214	576,000
Chikako Matsuzawa	70	72	72	214	576,000
Kayo Yamada	70	71	73	214	576,000
Toshimi Kimura	71	69	74	214	576,000
Yuri Fudoh	70	73	72	215	528,000
Michiko Okada	70	73	72	215	528,000
Mayumi Inoue	71	72	72	215	528,000
Miho Takayama	74	71	71	216	462,000
Yuko Ogura	75	69	72	216	462,000
Nayoko Yoshikawa	71	73	72	216	462,000
Mika Tajiri	69	74	73	216	462,000
Megumi Higuchi	74	69	73	216	462,000

	SCORES			TOTAL	MONEY
Junko Yasui	72	71	73	216	462,000
Mikino Kubo	72	71	73	216	462,000
Megumi Matsuo	71	71	74	216	462,000

Fuji Sankei Ladies Classic

Fujizakura Country Club, Kawaguchiko, Yamanashi — September 4-6
Par 35-36–71; 6,291 yards — purse, ¥60,000,000

	SCORES			TOTAL	MONEY
Masako Ishihara	72	70	71	213	¥10,800,000
Akiko Fukushima	70	75	68	213	4,740,000
Shin Sora	69	72	72	213	4,740,000
(Ishihara defeated Fukushima on first and Sora on second extra hole.)					
Yumiko Akagi	71	71	72	214	3,000,000
Kumiko Hiyoshi	72	70	72	214	3,000,000
Hsiu-Feng Tseng	68	70	76	214	3,000,000
Kaori Harada	72	72	71	215	1,800,000
Kaori Higo	69	73	73	215	1,800,000
Mayumi Murai	72	71	72	215	1,800,000
Yuri Fudoh	72	71	73	216	1,200,000
Ok-Hee Ku	71	72	74	217	1,044,000
*Mayumi Nakajima	75	72	70	217	
Kyoko Ono	73	69	75	217	1,044,000
Syoko Asano	72	73	72	217	1,044,000
Chieko Nishida	67	73	77	217	1,044,000
Ayumi Sobue	73	75	70	218	864,000
Mikino Kubo	71	75	72	218	864,000
Kasumi Fujii	71	73	75	219	663,600
Yukiko Ishiguro	71	76	72	219	663,600
Kiyoe Yamazaki	75	73	71	219	663,600
Asayo Itoh	78	70	71	219	663,600
Keiko Arai	72	76	71	219	663,600
Suzuko Maeda	71	72	77	220	546,000
Takayo Bandoh	73	75	72	220	546,000
Tomiko Ikebuchi	72	74	74	220	546,000
Man-Soo Kim	74	75	71	220	546,000
Jae-Sook Won	76	72	72	220	546,000
Aki Takamura	72	77	72	221	474,000
Toshimi Kimura	74	74	73	221	474,000
Ae-Sook Kim	76	73	72	221	474,000
Kayoko Motoki	73	72	76	221	474,000
Yuka Irie	75	73	73	221	474,000
Akane Ohshiro	73	75	73	221	474,000
Mitsuyo Hirata	74	74	73	221	474,000

Japan LPGA Championship

Miho Golf Club, Miho, Ibaraki — September 10-13
Par 36-36–72; 6,550 yards — purse, ¥70,000,000

	SCORES				TOTAL	MONEY
Michiko Hattori	72	73	69	76	290	¥12,600,000
Yuri Kawanami	74	72	74	73	293	6,160,000
Yuri Fudoh	76	72	70	76	294	4,900,000

	SCORES				TOTAL	MONEY
Woo-Soon Ko	73	77	73	72	295	3,237,500
Huang Yu-Chen	76	77	70	72	295	3,237,500
Lee Oh-Soon	73	70	77	75	295	3,237,500
Hiromi Kobayashi	75	75	71	74	295	3,237,500
Akiko Fukushima	76	73	69	78	296	2,100,000
Yuko Moriguchi	70	77	75	76	298	1,750,000
Michie Ohba	77	78	73	71	299	1,159,200
Aki Nakano	77	74	75	73	299	1,159,200
Yumiko Akagi	71	77	76	75	299	1,159,200
Fuki Kido	76	70	77	76	299	1,159,200
Kyoko Ono	74	78	71	76	299	1,159,200
Hisako Takeda	75	74	78	73	300	819,000
Mayumi Inoue	76	75	75	74	300	819,000
Ok-Hee Ku	80	72	74	74	300	819,000
Marnie McGuire	76	77	73	74	300	819,000
Kaori Higo	70	79	83	69	301	571,200
Tomoko Ueda	77	78	72	74	301	571,200
Ayako Shibata	72	80	74	75	301	571,200
Toshimi Kimura	76	73	76	76	301	571,200
Mei-Chi Cheng	78	72	74	77	301	571,200
Kumiko Hiyoshi	76	78	76	72	302	504,000
Yukiko Ishiguro	73	82	72	75	302	504,000
Hiromi Takamura	77	76	71	78	302	504,000
Mika Tajiri	77	78	76	72	303	435,000
Jae-Sook Won	76	76	76	75	303	435,000
Aiko Takasu	77	79	73	74	303	435,000
Kotomi Akiyama	77	77	74	75	303	435,000
Aki Takamura	75	77	76	75	303	435,000
Suzuko Maeda	75	75	77	76	303	435,000
Mieko Takano	76	74	77	76	303	435,000

Yukijirushi Ladies Tokai Classic

Ryosen Golf Club, Inabe, Mie — September 18-20
Par 36-36–72; 6,351 yards — purse, ¥60,000,000

	SCORES			TOTAL	MONEY
Kaori Higo	67	73	67	207	¥10,800,000
Yuri Kawanami	70	73	68	211	4,740,000
Michiko Hattori	72	69	70	211	4,740,000
Fuki Kido	75	70	68	213	2,775,000
Kaori Harada	72	71	70	213	2,775,000
Akane Ohshiro	69	74	70	213	2,775,000
Ok-Hee Ku	69	73	71	213	2,775,000
Nayoko Yoshikawa	74	72	68	214	1,260,000
Kyoko Ono	74	70	70	214	1,260,000
Akiko Fukushima	74	68	72	214	1,260,000
Hsiu-Feng Tseng	71	71	72	214	1,260,000
Hee-Won Han	70	72	72	214	1,260,000
Aiko Takasu	73	68	73	214	1,260,000
Yuko Motoyama	74	74	68	216	720,000
Chieko Nishida	74	73	69	216	720,000
Kotomi Akiyama	70	77	69	216	720,000
Chihiro Furukawa	74	73	69	216	720,000
Michie Ohba	75	72	69	216	720,000
Marnie McGuire	73	72	71	216	720,000
Young-Me Lee	73	72	71	216	720,000
Kayoko Motoki	72	76	69	217	492,000

	SCORES			TOTAL	MONEY
Mei-Chi Cheng	75	73	69	217	492,000
Tomiko Ikebuchi	71	75	71	217	492,000
Kayo Yamada	71	74	72	217	492,000
Yuko Moriguchi	73	72	72	217	492,000
Chikayo Yamazaki	74	71	72	217	492,000
Mikino Kubo	72	71	74	217	492,000
Hiromi Takamura	73	73	72	218	432,000
Maki Sasayama	72	72	74	218	432,000
Chikako Matsuzawa	73	71	74	218	432,000

Miyagi TV Cup Dunlop Ladies Open

Rainbow Hills Golf Club, Tomiya, Miyagi — September 25-27
Par 36-36–72; 6,467 yards — purse, ¥60,000,000

	SCORES			TOTAL	MONEY
Akiko Fukushima	69	68	71	208	¥10,800,000
Hee-Won Han	71	72	69	212	4,740,000
Ok-Hee Ku	68	69	75	212	4,740,000
Kaori Harada	70	72	71	213	3,600,000
Natsuko Noro	76	71	67	214	2,160,000
Kaori Higo	74	70	70	214	2,160,000
Aki Takamura	73	70	71	214	2,160,000
Megumi Matsuo	72	71	71	214	2,160,000
Fumiko Omata	71	69	74	214	2,160,000
Masako Ishihara	72	73	70	215	1,124,000
Wen-Lin Li	71	72	72	215	1,124,000
Hisako Takeda	69	74	72	215	1,124,000
Hiromi Takamura	72	72	72	216	996,000
Yuko Moriguchi	74	74	69	217	846,000
Mikino Kubo	77	71	69	217	846,000
Toshimi Kimura	73	72	72	217	846,000
Akane Ohshiro	72	72	73	217	846,000
Aiko Takasu	71	77	70	218	604,800
Harumi Sakagami	76	71	71	218	604,800
Man-Soo Kim	71	74	73	218	604,800
Kayo Yamada	70	74	74	218	604,800
Fumiko Muraguchi	72	72	74	218	604,800
Shin Sora	74	75	70	219	498,000
Young-Me Lee	72	75	72	219	498,000
Fuki Kido	69	77	73	219	498,000
Kotomi Akiyama	72	74	73	219	498,000
Chieko Nishida	70	76	73	219	498,000
Jae-Sook Won	71	75	73	219	498,000
Sachiko Ohshima	71	74	74	219	498,000
Mayumi Murai	70	75	74	219	498,000

Kosaido Ladies Golf Cup

Chiba Kosaido Country Club, Ichihara, Chiba — October 2-4
Par 36-36–72; 6,257 yards — purse, ¥60,000,000

	SCORES			TOTAL	MONEY
Mayumi Murai	69	73	71	213	¥10,800,000
Huang Yu-Chen	72	73	69	214	5,280,000

	SCORES			TOTAL	MONEY
Nayoko Yoshikawa	70	74	71	215	3,900,000
Ok-Hee Ku	70	72	73	215	3,900,000
Mei-Chi Cheng	74	73	69	216	3,000,000
Young-Me Lee	74	75	69	218	2,250,000
Chikayo Yamazaki	73	73	72	218	2,250,000
Woo-Soon Ko	72	75	72	219	1,407,000
Kaori Harada	72	74	73	219	1,407,000
Akane Ohshiro	75	72	72	219	1,407,000
Kiyoe Yamazaki	71	73	75	219	1,407,000
Natsuko Noro	73	76	71	220	858,000
Nahoko Hirao	75	74	71	220	858,000
Lee Oh-Soon	71	76	73	220	858,000
Junko Yasui	73	74	73	220	858,000
Yukiyo Haga	75	72	73	220	858,000
Hiromi Takamura	76	71	73	220	858,000
Shin Sora	73	73	74	220	858,000
Aki Takamura	74	69	77	220	858,000
Kayo Yamada	72	77	72	221	582,000
Kasumi Adachi	76	72	73	221	582,000
Hee-Won Han	71	80	71	222	528,000
Toshimi Kimura	82	69	71	222	528,000
Kyoko Ono	74	76	72	222	528,000
Ae-Sook Kim	73	76	73	222	528,000
Yuri Fudoh	73	76	73	222	528,000
Jae-Sook Won	74	73	75	222	528,000
Tomiko Ikebuchi	74	72	76	222	528,000
Yumiko Fukuda	78	74	71	223	456,000
Yukiko Ishiguro	75	74	74	223	456,000
Megumi Matsuo	73	75	75	223	456,000
Tomoko Ueda	71	76	76	223	456,000
Yuka Shiroto	74	73	76	223	456,000

TaKaRa World Invitational

Caledonian Golf Club, Yokoshiba, Chiba — October 8-11
Par 36-36–72; 6,226 yards — purse, ¥80,000,000

	SCORES				TOTAL	MONEY
Aki Takamura	72	74	69	73	288	¥14,400,000
Hiromi Takamura	72	72	71	74	289	7,040,000
Natsuko Noro	77	75	69	72	293	5,600,000
Hee-Won Han	77	74	71	72	294	4,800,000
Nayoko Yoshikawa	75	76	65	79	295	4,000,000
Woo-Soon Ko	77	73	71	76	297	3,000,000
Mei-Chi Cheng	71	75	70	81	297	3,000,000
Mikino Kubo	73	78	71	76	298	2,400,000
Miyuki Shimabukuro	76	76	75	72	299	1,706,666
Ae-Sook Kim	75	75	75	74	299	1,706,666
Yuri Fudoh	71	78	74	76	299	1,706,666
Toshimi Kimura	69	78	82	71	300	1,280,000
Bie-Shyun Huang	75	77	75	73	300	1,280,000
Chieko Nishida	79	74	73	74	300	1,280,000
Kaori Higo	76	75	74	75	300	1,280,000
Huang Yu-Chen	73	79	72	76	300	1,280,000
Yoko Kobayashi	80	70	79	72	301	892,800
Junko Ishii	77	76	74	74	301	892,800
Harumi Sakagami	78	74	72	77	301	892,800

	SCORES				TOTAL	MONEY
Michiko Hattori	72	75	74	80	301	892,800
Ok-Hee Ku	71	74	75	81	301	892,800
Lee Oh-Soon	75	77	75	75	302	752,000
Fumiko Muraguchi	74	77	73	78	302	752,000
Hisako Takeda	75	77	72	78	302	752,000
Kyoko Ono	78	73	77	75	303	704,000
Ai-Yu Tu	77	76	73	77	303	704,000
Man-Soo Kim	73	75	78	77	303	704,000
Fuki Kido	70	78	82	74	304	648,000
Junko Yasui	75	72	80	77	304	648,000
Mitsuyo Hirata	76	72	78	78	304	648,000
Michie Ohba	75	73	74	82	304	648,000

Fujitsu Ladies

Tokyu Seven Hundred Club, Chiba — October 16-18
Par 36-36–72; 6,483 yards — purse, ¥60,000,000

	SCORES			TOTAL	MONEY
Kaori Higo	69	72	70	211	¥10,800,000
Kumiko Hiyoshi	68	73	71	212	5,280,000
Nahoko Hirao	67	70	76	213	4,200,000
Hiromi Takamura	68	77	69	214	3,000,000
Marnie McGuire	71	72	71	214	3,000,000
Man-Soo Kim	73	68	73	214	3,000,000
Miyuki Shimabukuro	69	71	75	215	2,100,000
Yoko Inoue	70	75	71	216	1,500,000
Kyoko Ono	71	72	73	216	1,500,000
Mei-Chi Cheng	73	68	75	216	1,500,000
Mayumi Murai	73	73	71	217	1,038,000
Mayumi Hirase	70	75	72	217	1,038,000
Takayo Bandoh	71	72	74	217	1,038,000
Chieko Nishida	68	74	75	217	1,038,000
Young-Me Lee	69	76	73	218	714,857
Aki Nakano	72	73	73	218	714,857
Yuko Motoyama	71	73	74	218	714,857
Michiko Hattori	70	73	75	218	714,857
Kotomi Akiyama	71	72	75	218	714,857
Yuri Fudoh	68	73	77	218	714,857
Aki Takamura	70	72	76	218	714,857
Aiko Takasu	74	72	73	219	552,000
Michie Ohba	71	74	74	219	552,000
Yueh-Chyn Huang	70	74	75	219	552,000
Hisako Takeda	72	75	73	220	504,000
Masako Ishihara	74	73	73	220	504,000
Yuri Kawanami	76	70	74	220	504,000
Lee Oh-Soon	71	74	75	220	504,000
Toshimi Kimura	66	78	76	220	504,000
Fukumi Tani	71	76	74	221	468,000

Hisako Higuchi Kibun Classic

The Greenbrier West Village, Nishigo, Fukushima — October 23-25
Par 36-36–72; 6,290 yards — purse, ¥70,000,000

	SCORES			TOTAL	MONEY
Michiko Hattori	68	73	71	212	¥12,600,000
Kaori Harada	77	70	67	214	5,530,000
Hee-Won Han	73	68	73	214	5,530,000
Man-Soo Kim	72	69	74	215	4,200,000
Yoko Inoue	74	70	72	216	3,500,000
Marnie McGuire	73	73	71	217	2,625,000
Huang Yu-Chen	69	75	73	217	2,625,000
Mayumi Murai	74	74	70	218	1,925,000
Chihiro Furukawa	70	71	77	218	1,925,000
Ayako Shibata	73	74	72	219	1,358,000
Ok-Hee Ku	74	69	76	219	1,358,000
Miyuki Shimabukuro	75	73	72	220	1,141,000
Kayoko Motoki	72	74	74	220	1,141,000
Woo-Soon Ko	75	70	75	220	1,141,000
Fuki Kido	71	72	77	220	1,141,000
Chikayo Yamazaki	74	74	74	222	763,000
Mikino Kubo	71	76	75	222	763,000
Mayumi Hirase	76	72	74	222	763,000
Yukiyo Haga	74	76	72	222	763,000
Hsiu-Feng Tseng	73	74	75	222	763,000
Toshimi Kimura	73	74	75	222	763,000
Aki Nakano	71	75	76	222	763,000
Kumiko Hiyoshi	74	72	76	222	763,000
Mika Adaniya	76	73	74	223	616,000
Akiko Fukushima	72	75	76	223	616,000
Natsuko Noro	75	72	76	223	616,000
Michie Ohba	75	73	76	224	581,000
Akemi Kuwashima	76	71	77	224	581,000
Fumiko Muraguchi	76	74	75	225	546,000
Bie-Shyun Huang	73	77	75	225	546,000
Jae-Sook Won	75	76	74	225	546,000

Nichirei International

Tsukuba Country Club, Ina, Ibaraki — October 30-November 1
Par 36-36–72; 6,294 yards — purse, US$702,000

FIRST DAY
Better Ball

Pat Hurst and Hiromi Kobayashi (USA) defeated Fuki Kido and Mayumi Murai, 62-67.
Hiromi Takamura and Aiko Takasu (Japan) defeated Lorie Kane and Lisa Walters, 65-68.
Chris Johnson and Betsy King (USA) defeated Kaori Higo and Yuri Kawanami, 64-66.
Michiko Hattori and Kaori Harada (Japan) defeated Dana Dormann and Dale Eggeling, 64-66.
Akiko Fukushima and Huang Yu-Chen (Japan) defeated Barb Mucha and Wendy Ward, 65-69.
Young-Me Lee and Aki Nakano (Japan) defeated Danielle Ammaccapane and Michelle Estill, 69-71.
Rosie Jones and Sherri Steinhauer (USA) defeated Yuri Fudoh and Nayoko Yoshikawa, 64-68.

Emilee Klein and Janice Moodie (USA) defeated Ae-Sook Kim and Aki Takamura, 65-67.
Lisa Hackney and Charlotta Sorenstam (USA) defeated Ok-Hee Ku and Natsuko Noro, 66-69.

POINTS: United States 5, Japan 4

SECOND DAY
Better Ball

Hurst and Kobayashi (USA) defeated Takamura and Takasu, 58-67.
Kido and Murai (Japan) defeated Kane and Walters, 64-66.
Johnson and King (USA) halved with Higo and Kawanami, 62-62.
Dormann and Eggeling (USA) defeated Hattori and Harada, 67-68.
Mucha and Ward (USA) defeated Lee and Nakano, 66-69.
Fukushima and Huang (Japan) defeated Ammaccapane and Estill, 67-69.
Hackney and Sorenstam (USA) defeated Yoshikawa and Fudoh, 64-68.
Jones and Steinhauer (USA) defeated Kim and Takamura, 67-71.
Moodie and Klein (USA) defeated Ku and Noro, 70-71.

POINTS: United States 6½, Japan 2½

THIRD DAY
Singles

Hurst (USA) defeated Kido, 65-72.
King (USA) defeated Murai, 69-74.
Takamura (Japan) defeated Kobayashi, 69-72.
Dormann (USA) defeated Takasu, 71-74.
Kane (USA) defeated Higo, 70-71.
Eggeling (USA) defeated Kawanami, 73-75.
Hattori (Japan) defeated Hackney, 64-67.
Sorenstam (USA) defeated Harada, 69-70.
Huang (Japan) defeated Ward, 69-70.
Fukushima (Japan) defeated Estill, 70-76.
Ammaccapane (USA) defeated Nakano, 72-74.
Lee (Japan) defeated Walters, 73-75.
Ku (Japan) halved with Moodie, 70-70.
Mucha (USA) defeated Noro, 70-71.
Klein (USA) defeated Takamura, 68-75.
Johnson (USA) defeated Kim, 71-74.
Steinhauer (USA) defeated Fudoh, 71-72.
Jones (USA) defeated Yoshikawa, 70-75.

POINTS: United States 12½, Japan 5½

TOTAL POINTS: United States 24, Japan 12

(Each member of USA team received US$25,000; each member of Japanese team received US$14,000.)

LPGA Japan Classic

Musashigaoka Golf Club, Hannoh, Saitama — November 6-8
Par 36-36–72; 6,338 yards — purse, ¥95,440,000

	SCORES			TOTAL	MONEY
Hiromi Kobayashi	68	68	69	205	¥14,316,000
Tina Barrett	65	74	66	205	8,884,748
(Kobayashi defeated Barrett on third extra hole.)					
Lorie Kane	70	64	73	207	6,483,478
Helen Alfredsson	71	67	71	209	4,162,138
Betsy King	72	67	70	209	4,162,138
Huang Yu-Chen	67	68	74	209	4,162,138
Lisa Walters	71	67	72	210	2,833,494
Rosie Jones	73	70	68	211	2,056,016
Chris Johnson	74	68	69	211	2,056,016
Gail Graham	70	71	70	211	2,056,016
Kris Tschetter	70	69	72	211	2,056,016
Megumi Matsuo	70	69	72	211	2,056,016
Luciana Bemvenuti	72	72	68	212	1,442,218
Jenny Lidback	67	74	71	212	1,442,218
Woo-Soon Ko	70	71	71	212	1,442,218
Ae-Sook Kim	70	70	72	212	1,442,218
Dale Eggeling	72	71	70	213	1,202,067
Kristi Albers	73	74	66	213	1,202,067
Lee Oh-Soon	72	68	73	213	1,202,067
Cindy McCurdy	70	74	70	214	1,035,166
Susie Redman	75	70	69	214	1,035,166
Liselotte Neumann	72	72	70	214	1,035,166
Charlotta Sorenstam	73	70	71	214	1,035,166
Pearl Sinn	69	75	71	215	846,672
Ok-Hee Ku	72	72	71	215	846,672
Dana Dormann	72	71	72	215	846,672
Shin Sora	71	71	73	215	846,672
Aki Takamura	69	73	73	215	846,672
Yuri Fudoh	71	71	73	215	846,672
Hollis Stacy	69	71	75	215	846,672

Itoen Ladies

Great Island Club, Chonan, Chiba — November 13-15
Par 36-36–72; 6,364 yards — purse, ¥60,000,000

	SCORES			TOTAL	MONEY
Michiko Hattori	65	66	66	197	¥10,800,000
Ok-Hee Ku	71	63	74	208	4,740,000
Kaori Higo	71	67	70	208	4,740,000
Kaori Harada	72	68	70	210	2,775,000
Hee-Won Han	69	72	69	210	2,775,000
Fumiko Muraguchi	69	69	72	210	2,775,000
Yuri Fudoh	72	67	71	210	2,775,000
Takayo Bandoh	69	70	72	211	1,800,000
Akiko Fukushima	70	68	74	212	1,500,000
Yoko Inoue	74	72	68	214	1,132,000
Helen Alfredsson	69	74	71	214	1,132,000
Ae-Sook Kim	75	67	72	214	1,132,000
Kayo Yamada	74	71	70	215	978,000
Aki Nakano	73	70	72	215	978,000

	SCORES			TOTAL	MONEY
Masako Ishihara	73	73	70	216	858,000
Fuki Kido	73	73	70	216	858,000
Akemi Yamaoka	71	76	70	217	642,000
Yuko Motoyama	71	74	72	217	642,000
Woo-Soon Ko	72	73	72	217	642,000
Chieko Nishida	75	70	72	217	642,000
Young-Me Lee	73	72	72	217	642,000
Natsuko Noro	73	69	75	217	642,000
Mei-Chi Cheng	71	75	72	218	534,000
Megumi Matsuo	69	75	74	218	534,000
Hsiu-Feng Tseng	70	74	74	218	534,000
Yoko Kobayashi	73	70	75	218	534,000
Yumiko Akagi	73	74	72	219	474,000
Kikuko Shibata	74	73	72	219	474,000
Chikayo Yamazaki	76	69	74	219	474,000
Kiyoe Yamazaki	73	72	74	219	474,000
Aiko Takasu	71	73	75	219	474,000
Chie Yoshida	74	69	76	219	474,000

Daio Seishi Elleair Ladies Open

Elleair Golf Club, Matsuyama, Ehime — November 20-22
Par 36-36–72; 6,352 yards — purse, ¥65,000,000

	SCORES			TOTAL	MONEY
Chikayo Yamazaki	67	72	71	210	¥11,700,000
Jae-Sook Won	70	71	71	212	4,723,333
Ok-Hee Ku	74	68	70	212	4,723,333
Aki Takamura	69	71	72	212	4,723,333
Kaori Higo	72	70	71	213	3,250,000
Akiko Fukushima	72	73	70	215	2,275,000
Miyuki Shimabukuro	73	70	72	215	2,275,000
Wen-Lin Li	72	69	74	215	2,275,000
Hsiu-Feng Tseng	72	75	69	216	1,375,833
Nahoko Hirao	69	76	71	216	1,375,833
Mieko Nomura	74	71	71	216	1,375,833
Nayoko Yoshikawa	73	73	71	217	910,000
Mayumi Murai	74	72	71	217	910,000
Kiyoe Yamazaki	73	73	71	217	910,000
Yuka Irie	73	74	70	217	910,000
Kaori Harada	70	74	73	217	910,000
Michiko Hattori	71	72	74	217	910,000
Kumiko Hiyoshi	71	73	73	217	910,000
Woo-Soon Ko	72	71	74	217	910,000
Fumiko Muraguchi	76	70	72	218	578,500
Tomiko Ikebuchi	76	71	71	218	578,500
Takayo Bandoh	68	77	73	218	578,500
Aiko Takasu	71	73	74	218	578,500
Natsuko Noro	74	69	75	218	578,500
Mitsuko Hamada	71	71	76	218	578,500
Norimi Terasawa	70	72	76	218	578,500
Kyoko Ono	75	73	71	219	520,000
Masako Ishihara	71	74	74	219	520,000
Mikino Kubo	73	73	74	220	487,500
Lee Oh-Soon	73	74	73	220	487,500
Young-Me Lee	70	72	78	220	487,500

JLPGA Meiji Nyugyo Cup

Hibiscus Golf Club, Miyazaki — November 26-29
Par 36-36–72; 6,379 yards — purse, ¥60,000,000

	SCORES				TOTAL	MONEY
Young-Me Lee	69	67	70	68	274	¥10,800,000
Kaori Harada	69	65	72	70	276	5,400,000
Fumiko Muraguchi	69	71	71	68	279	3,600,000
Michie Ohba	68	71	73	68	280	2,550,000
Tomiko Ikebuchi	73	66	72	69	280	2,550,000
Michiko Hattori	70	71	69	71	281	1,980,000
Hsiu-Feng Tseng	68	72	71	71	282	1,860,000
Miyuki Shimabukuro	71	74	69	69	283	1,620,000
Kaori Higo	68	73	71	71	283	1,620,000
Hisako Takeda	67	73	68	75	283	1,620,000
Kyoko Ono	71	69	72	72	284	1,380,000
Aiko Takasu	68	76	68	72	284	1,380,000
Lee Oh-Soon	68	69	73	74	284	1,380,000
Yuri Fudoh	70	73	72	70	285	1,053,750
Chihiro Furukawa	71	71	73	70	285	1,053,750
Megumi Matsuo	72	73	70	70	285	1,053,750
Woo-Soon Ko	68	70	76	71	285	1,053,750
Yuri Kawanami	70	71	73	71	285	1,053,750
Akiko Fukushima	74	70	70	71	285	1,053,750
Yueh-Chyn Huang	70	74	69	72	285	1,053,750
Chieko Nishida	71	68	72	74	285	1,053,750
Mieko Nomura	69	71	75	71	286	810,000
Hiromi Takamura	69	73	72	72	286	810,000
Kayo Yamada	72	72	70	72	286	810,000
Fuki Kido	74	69	73	71	287	750,000
Tamayo Ueda	71	75	72	70	288	649,200
Harumi Sakagami	70	73	72	73	288	649,200
Marnie McGuire	74	70	71	73	288	649,200
Nayoko Yoshikawa	70	70	74	74	288	649,200
Mei-Chi Cheng	69	71	74	74	288	649,200

Women's Australasian Tours

Republic of China Open

Formosa First Country Club, Taipei, Taiwan — January 22-24
Par 36-36–72; 6,198 yards — purse, US$112,170
(First round cancelled — rain.)

	SCORES		TOTAL	MONEY
Helen Wadsworth	78	70	148	US$16,500
Laura Philo	78	72	150	11,000
Huang Yu-Chen	78	73	151	6,490
Mei-Chi Cheng	77	74	151	6,490
Nicola Moult	74	77	151	6,490
Aideen Rogers	80	72	152	3,410
Yueh-Chyn Huang	76	76	152	3,410
Mary Grace Estuesta	75	77	152	3,410
Lara Tadiotto	81	72	153	2,410
Mitsuyo Hirata	78	75	153	2,410
Chen Li-Ying	76	77	153	2,410
Loraine Lambert	81	73	154	1,950
Sophie Gustafson	78	76	154	1,950
Hsiu-Feng Tseng	78	76	154	1,950
Sarah Bennett	79	76	155	1,750
Mitsuko Kawasaki	79	76	155	1,750
Ai-Yu Tu	78	77	155	1,750
Yu-Chuan Tai	77	78	155	1,750
Lo Shu-Chen	81	75	156	1,480
Anna Berg	79	77	156	1,480
Bie-Shyun Huang	79	77	156	1,480
Hisako Ohgane	78	78	156	1,480
Kristel Mourgue d'Algue	77	79	156	1,480
Hitomi Notsu	75	81	156	1,480
Tai Yu-Hsia	82	75	157	1,230
Anna Radford	81	76	157	1,230
Karen Lunn	81	76	157	1,230
Valerie Michaud	81	77	158	1,040
Wendy Dicks	80	78	158	1,040
Junko Ishii	79	79	158	1,040
Wu Ying-Yi	75	83	158	1,040

Toyota Philippine Open

Sta. Elena Golf Club, Manila, Philippines — January 29-31
Par 36-36–72; 5,984 yards — purse, US$98,001

	SCORES			TOTAL	MONEY
Kristel Mourgue d'Algue	73	71	75	219	US$15,000
Il Mi Chung	72	73	74	219	10,000
(Mourgue d'Algue defeated Chung on second extra hole.)					
Loraine Lambert	75	75	70	220	5,275
Lara Tadiotto	74	75	71	220	5,275

	SCORES			TOTAL	MONEY
Karen Lunn	76	71	73	220	5,275
Helen Wadsworth	71	75	74	220	5,275
Laura Philo	77	74	70	221	2,950
Sophie Gustafson	76	72	73	221	2,950
Sara Melin	80	71	71	222	2,032
Wendy Dicks	74	76	72	222	2,032
Tina Fischer	77	73	72	222	2,032
Ludivine Kreutz	75	73	74	222	2,032
Mary Grace Estuesta	75	72	75	222	2,032
Camie Hoshino	74	78	71	223	1,720
Masako Ishihara	77	75	72	224	1,595
Joanne Mills	77	75	72	224	1,595
Lee Jui-Hui	76	75	73	224	1,595
Seung Ja Park	73	77	74	224	1,595
Heather Bowie	75	74	76	225	1,470
Dodie Mazzuca	79	73	74	226	1,320
Anna Berg	78	73	75	226	1,320
Erin O'Neil	81	70	75	226	1,320
Jenny Park	81	72	73	226	1,320
Chen Yueh-Shuang	76	74	76	226	1,320
Sarah Bennett	79	73	75	227	1,120
Anna-Carin Jonasson	78	75	74	227	1,120
Mette Hageman	76	78	73	227	1,120
Fumi Doi	79	75	74	228	1,020
Nicola Moult	74	78	77	229	824
Yumi Kokubo	76	76	77	229	824
Stephanie Dallongeville	73	79	77	229	824
Karolina Andersson	81	72	76	229	824
Valerie Michaud	78	75	76	229	824
Diane Irvin	82	72	75	229	824
Mitsuko Kawasaki	79	75	75	229	824
Mika Ishijima	78	76	75	229	824
Sara Eklund	81	74	74	229	824

Thailand Open

Panya Park Golf Course, Thailand — February 5-7
Par 36-36–72; 6,172 yards — purse, US$89,541

	SCORES			TOTAL	MONEY
*Connie Wei	74	72	70	216	
Il Mi Chung	71	71	75	217	US$13,500
Valerie Michaud	74	72	73	219	9,000
Sophie Gustafson	70	71	79	220	6,750
Nicola Moult	71	74	76	221	4,590
Wendy Dick	71	77	73	221	4,590
Shelley Sanders	73	77	72	222	2,655
Pernilla Sterner	76	75	71	222	2,655
Seung Ja Park	71	78	73	222	2,655
Anne-Marie Knight	72	76	74	222	2,655
Karolina Andersson	75	75	73	223	1,723
Joanne Mills	73	74	76	223	1,723
Sandrine Mendiburu	76	71	76	223	1,723
Loraine Lambert	72	74	77	223	1,723
Sara Melin	72	78	74	224	1,413
Helen Wadsworth	75	74	75	224	1,413
Kristel Mourgue d'Algue	75	74	75	224	1,413

	SCORES			TOTAL	MONEY
Liz Earley	76	72	76	224	1,413
Katharina Poppmeier	70	76	78	224	1,413
Michelle Bell	72	74	78	224	1,413
Megumi Higuchi	73	73	78	224	1,413
Christine Miller	75	75	75	225	1,143
Yukari Tsuboyama	77	75	73	225	1,143
Lara Tadiotto	73	76	76	225	1,143
Hitomi Notsu	75	73	77	225	1,143
Kozue Azuma	78	75	72	225	1,143
Kiyoe Yamazaki	72	77	77	226	963
Kristen Putman	74	75	77	226	963
Shelly Stouffer	78	69	79	226	963
Karen Lunn	76	74	77	227	814
Asa Gottmo	77	73	77	227	814
Tina Fischer	76	77	74	227	814
Diane Irvin	76	77	74	227	814

Malaysian Open

Glenmarie Golf & Country Club, Subang, Malaysia — February 12-14
Par 36-36–72; 6,062 yards — purse, US$84,997

	SCORES			TOTAL	MONEY
Sandrine Mendiburu	71	66	74	211	US$12,750
Loraine Lambert	73	71	68	212	8,500
Jenny Park	74	71	68	213	5,737
Il Mi Chung	69	73	71	213	5,737
Irene Yeoh	70	76	69	215	3,570
Lim Siew Ai	71	74	71	216	2,890
Sara Eklund	75	73	69	217	2,507
Joanne Mills	76	67	74	217	2,507
Stephanie Dallongeville	76	73	69	218	1,997
Mary Grace Estuesta	73	71	74	218	1,997
Mette Hageman	73	72	74	219	1,568
Martina Koch	71	72	76	219	1,568
Laura Philo	72	73	75	220	1,483
Heather Bowie	73	72	75	220	1,483
Lara Tadiotto	77	73	71	221	1,334
Malin Burstrom	75	74	72	221	1,334
Sofie Eriksson	78	71	72	221	1,334
Lee Jui-Hui	77	71	73	221	1,334
Helen Wadsworth	74	73	74	221	1,334
Ji Hyun Suh	75	75	72	222	1,121
Abby Pearson	74	76	72	222	1,121
Sarah Bennett	74	73	75	222	1,121
Laree Sugg	75	70	77	222	1,121
Mie Hasegawa	72	72	78	222	1,121
Anne-Marie Knight	73	76	74	223	888
Caroline Hall	74	75	74	223	888
Yuka Arita	72	76	75	223	888
Karen Lunn	77	75	71	223	888
Wendy Dicks	77	75	71	223	888
Seung Ja Park	72	71	80	223	888

Indonesian Open

Paitai Indah Kapuku Course, Jakarta, Indonesia — February 18-20
Par 36-36–72; 6,150 yards — purse, US$99,398

	SCORES			TOTAL	MONEY
Tina Fischer	68	72	72	212	US$15,000
Loraine Lambert	71	70	78	219	10,000
Pernilla Sterner	75	74	71	220	5,900
Johanna Head	74	73	73	220	5,900
Silvia Torres	72	69	79	220	5,900
Lee Chiou-Yann	75	75	71	221	2,527
Stephanie Dallongeville	74	76	71	221	2,527
Kristel Mourgue d'Algue	73	73	75	221	2,527
Mary Grace Estuesta	75	70	76	221	2,527
Masako Ishihara	72	73	76	221	2,527
Wen-Lin Li	77	67	77	221	2,527
Martina Koch	72	72	77	221	2,527
Caroline Hall	76	73	73	222	1,745
Seung Ja Park	75	72	75	222	1,745
Helen Wadsworth	80	70	73	223	1,670
Sally Dee	75	72	77	224	1,595
Anna Radford	75	72	77	224	1,595
Ludivine Kreutz	78	73	74	225	1,420
Cindy Wulf	75	73	77	225	1,420
Samantha Head	74	74	77	225	1,420
Diane Irvin	74	71	80	225	1,420
Rei Ito	77	76	72	225	1,420
Mitsuko Kawasaki	75	75	76	226	1,095
Mayumi Morioka	74	76	76	226	1,095
Fiona Pike	79	70	77	226	1,095
Yukari Tsuboyama	74	75	77	226	1,095
Jane Shearwood	73	76	77	226	1,095
Kozue Azuma	75	73	78	226	1,095
Yuka Arita	74	77	75	226	1,095
Valerie Michaud	78	75	73	226	1,095

Australian Ladies Masters

Royal Pines Resort, Ashmore, — February 26-March 1
Gold Coast, Queensland — purse, US$700,000
Par 37-35–72; 6,250 yards

	SCORES				TOTAL	MONEY
Karrie Webb	69	69	64	70	272	US$105,000
Hyun Soon Park	70	68	71	68	277	56,359
Annika Sorenstam	69	68	70	70	277	56,359
Smriti Mehra	74	69	68	67	278	36,985
Kim Saiki	68	70	70	71	279	29,940
Laurie Brower	70	70	73	67	280	21,251
Jackie Gallagher-Smith	69	71	70	70	280	21,251
Cindy McCurdy	70	66	72	72	280	21,251
Charlotta Sorenstam	75	68	68	70	281	15,674
Julie Piers	69	69	71	72	281	15,674
Pernilla Sterner	73	73	72	64	282	11,694
Laura Davies	79	65	71	67	282	11,694
Liselotte Neumann	72	72	71	67	282	11,694
Kristel Mourge d'Algue	70	69	73	70	282	11,694

	SCORES				TOTAL	MONEY
Cindy Rarick	65	73	73	71	282	11,694
Cristie Kerr	71	74	69	69	283	9,158
Maria Hjorth	71	70	72	70	283	9,158
Mi Hyun Kim	69	68	70	76	283	9,158
Sherri Steinhauer	71	70	76	67	284	7,461
Jane Crafter	72	73	71	68	284	7,461
Alison Munt	68	73	75	68	284	7,461
Tina Barrett	72	72	70	70	284	7,461
Jane Leary	71	70	73	70	284	7,461
Karen Pearce	72	70	71	71	284	7,461
Catriona Matthew	69	69	72	74	284	7,461
Shani Waugh	75	69	72	69	285	6,093
Vicki Goetze-Ackerman	70	72	74	69	285	6,093
Joanne Morley	71	70	69	75	285	6,093
Lorie Kane	70	70	69	76	285	6,093
Penny Hammel	72	70	74	70	286	5,184
Jenny Lidback	73	71	70	72	286	5,184
Loraine Lambert	73	69	72	72	286	5,184
Kelly Robbins	69	72	71	74	286	5,184
Stephanie Lowe	72	67	71	76	286	5,184

AAMI Women's Australian Open

Yarra Yarra Golf Club, Melbourne, Victoria — November 12-15
Par 37-36–73; 5,959 yards — purse, A$350,000

	SCORES				TOTAL	MONEY
Marnie McGuire	72	72	69	67	280	A$52,500
Kelly Robbins	75	74	65	70	284	35,000
Jane Crafter	79	71	70	67	287	21,000
Karrie Webb	78	70	70	71	289	17,500
Liselotte Neumann	73	74	69	74	290	14,000
Laura Philo	75	74	75	68	292	11,900
Mardi Lunn	76	73	70	73	292	11,900
Jan Stephenson	74	72	72	74	292	11,900
Tina Fischer	79	71	73	71	294	9,450
Cristie Kerr	74	78	77	66	295	8,050
Karen Pearce	76	76	71	73	296	6,825
Jane Leary	78	76	69	73	296	6,825
Alison Munt	78	72	70	77	297	5,401.66
Corinne Dibnah	74	72	73	78	297	5,401.66
Lynnette Brooky	75	73	70	79	297	5,401.66
Anne-Marie Knight	74	79	74	71	298	4,480
Claire Duffy	79	71	75	73	298	4,480
Kang Soo-yun	78	79	67	74	298	4,480
Marie-Josee Rouleau	75	73	74	76	298	4,480
Nicole Lowien	81	75	71	72	299	3,955
Rachel Hetherington	77	75	71	76	299	3,955
Ji Hyun Suh	76	77	74	73	300	3,675
Kim Young	84	74	68	74	300	3,675
Carmen Hajjar	76	80	73	72	301	3,465
Gloria Hee Jung Park	79	77	72	74	302	3,325
Mi Hyun Kim	79	78	76	70	303	3,045
Fiona Pike	77	78	76	72	303	3,045
*Lindsey Wright	80	75	75	73	303	
Rachel Kirkwood	74	78	74	77	303	3,045
*Sandy Grimshaw	74	78	81	71	304	

	SCORES				TOTAL	MONEY
*Nadina Taylor	80	75	78	71	304	
Joanne Mills	80	74	76	74	304	2,695
Lim Siew Ai	72	81	75	76	304	2,695

Women's African Tour

Vodacom Ladies South African Open

Kensington Golf Club, Johannesburg, South Africa — April 2-5
Par 37-36–73; 5,993 yards — purse, R125,000

	SCORES			TOTAL	MONEY
Barbara Pestana	70	71	68	209	R18,000
Nicola Moult	76	69	72	217	13,000
*Sanet Marais	70	73	76	219	
*Vannessa Smith	75	70	74	219	
Helen Wadsworth	72	74	73	219	8,900
Federica Dassu	71	73	76	220	5,450
Claire Duffy	72	72	76	220	5,450
Laurette Maritz	75	71	74	220	5,450
*Cherry Moulder	75	72	73	220	
Kirsty Taylor	72	73	75	220	5,450
Janet Soulsby	77	75	71	223	3,900
Johanna Head	77	75	72	224	3,700
Lesley Copeman	77	75	74	226	3,580
Mandy Adamson	77	75	76	228	3,430
Debbie Dowling	75	78	75	228	3,430
Michelle de Vries	74	76	80	230	3,225
Morag Wright	80	74	76	230	3,225
Caryn Louw	77	77	77	231	3,050
*Joanne Norton	76	77	78	231	
*Lindsay Cummings	80	76	76	232	
*Wendy Appelbaum	77	81	81	239	
Brenda Lunsford	76	84	79	239	2,950
Alison Sheard	72	86	84	242	2,900
*Loma Steynberg	81	80	81	242	
Colleen Eaton	80	80	83	243	2,830
*Marietta Language	80	79	84	243	
*Cas Bridge	80	83	81	244	
Lisle Nel	80	79	85	244	2,715
Karen Pringle	78	84	82	244	2,715
*Nadine Johnston	84	83	78	245	

Vodacom South African Ladies Masters

Kensington Golf Club, Johannesburg, South Africa — October 29-November 1
Par 37-36–73; 5,993 yards — purse, R125,000

	SCORES			TOTAL	MONEY
Laurette Maritz	74	67	66	207	R18,150
Barbara Pestana	70	72	66	208	13,150
Joanne Mills	70	70	73	213	9,050
Zoe Grimbeek	75	71	71	217	7,150
Rae Hast	74	73	71	218	5,950
Caryn Louw	73	78	68	219	4,456.66
Sarah Bennett	80	71	68	219	4,456.66
Claire Duffy	75	75	69	219	4,456.66
Cherry Moulder	74	74	72	220	3,870
Mandy Adamson	77	70	74	221	3,750
Lesley Copeman	75	72	75	222	3,600
Charlaine Coetzee-Hirst	80	71	71	222	3,600
Brenda Lunsford	77	74	73	224	3,450
*Vannessa Smith	79	75	72	226	
*Annarie Wessels	78	71	77	226	
*Sanet Marais	78	75	75	228	
*Lindsay Cummings	80	76	74	230	
Karen Pringle	78	79	74	231	3,340
*Nadine Johnston	77	76	78	231	
*Alison Rademaker	78	75	78	231	
Michelle De Vries	83	74	75	232	3,102.50
Brenda Campbell-Harris	79	77	76	232	3,102.50
Sonia van Wyk	77	76	79	232	3,102.50
Alison Sheard	74	77	81	232	3,102.50
Elmi duToit	79	76	78	233	2,920
*Claudette Beukes	76	78	79	233	
Tania Fourie	81	76	78	235	2,850
*Marietta Language	81	80	76	237	
*Joanne Norton	75	82	80	237	
Elsabe Hefer	77	80	80	237	2,780